INTRODUCTION *to* BUSINESS

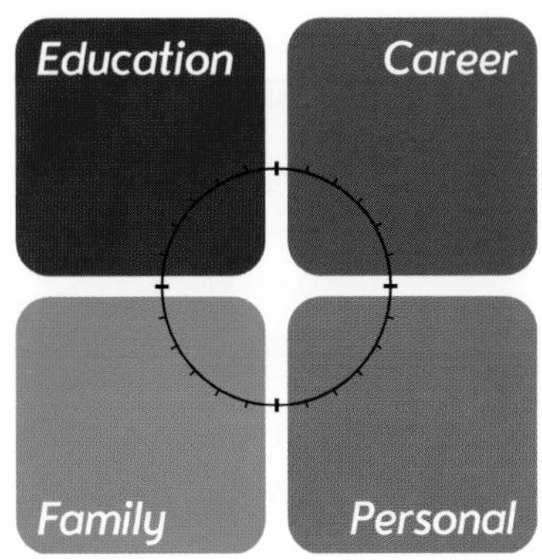

CUSTOM EDITION

Taken from:
Business, Seventh Edition
by Ricky W. Griffin and Ronald J. Ebert

Taken from:

Business, Seventh Edition
by Ricky W. Griffin and Ronald J. Ebert

Published by Prentice-Hall, Inc.
Upper Saddle River, New Jersey 07458

This special edition published in cooperation with Pearson Custom Publishing.

Printed in the United States of America

10 9 8 7 6 5 4 3 2 1

ISBN 0-536-81409-0

BA 999248

SS

Please visit our web site at *www.pearsoncustom.com*

PEARSON CUSTOM PUBLISHING
75 Arlington Street, Suite 300, Boston, MA 02116
A Pearson Education Company

Overview

Contents

From the Authors Ricky Griffin and Ron Ebert

At about the time we sat down to assemble this preface, we both kept seeing a TV ad promoting "Financial Knowledge for the New Economy" as the number-one ingredient for business success. Generally speaking, you can't argue with the premise, but we feel that, especially for introductory business students, "knowledge for the new economy" has to go beyond the "financials." Students need to know something about every aspect of business and the environment in which business prospers. And make no mistake about it: We have prosperity because-or maybe despite the fact that-the rules of the game are constantly changing throughout the business environment and across the entire range of business practices. There are new forces at work. Nowadays, companies come together on short notice for collaborative projects and then, just as quickly, return to their original shapes as separate (and often competing) entities. Employees and companies share new ideas about work-about when and where it takes place, about how it gets done, about who determines roles and activities in the workplace. With communications technologies having shattered the barriers of physical distance, tight-knit teams with members positioned around the world share information just as effectively as groups huddled together in the same room.

In nearly every aspect of business today, from relationships with customers and suppliers to employees and stockholders, there are new ways of doing things, and a lot of them are surpassing traditional business practices, with surprising speed and often with better competitive results. Along with new ways come a host of unique legal and ethical (and financial) issues to challenge the creativity and judgment of people who do business. For all of these reasons we, as authors and teachers, felt a certain urgency when it became obvious that, in revising Business for its seventh edition, we had to capture the flavor and convey the excitement of the new economy in all of its rapidly evolving practices.

Ricky Griffin
Ron Ebert

Doing the Basics BEST—Learn. Evaluate. Apply.

While always remembering the principle that guided the book's creation—"**Doing the Basics Best**"— Business, 7/e by Ricky Griffin and Ronald Ebert continues its tradition of introducing cutting edge firsts with the most up-to-date issues shaping business today and creative, pedagogy by focusing on three simple rules:

1. ***Learn***
2. ***Evaluate***
3. ***Apply***

SEE WHAT'S NEW!

NEW! CHAPTER 2: UNDERSTANDING THE ENVIRONMENTS OF BUSINESS

NEW CHAPTER

This brand-new chapter puts business operations in a contemporary context, explaining the idea of *organizational boundaries* and describing the ways in which elements from *multiple environments* cross those boundaries and shape organizational activities. It also sets the stage as an introduction to some of the most important topics covered in the rest of the book, for example:

- ***Economics*** (including the role of aggregate output, standard of living, GDP, and productivity in determining *economic growth*; methods of measuring inflation and unemployment and their effects *on economic stability*; the role of fiscal and monetary policies on *stabilization policy*; surveys of the major forces and projected trends in the *global economy of the 21st century).*
- ***Technology*** (with special attention to new tools for competiveness in both goods and services and *business process technologies*, including *enterprise resource planning*).
- ***Ethics*** (focusing not only on what happened at Enron and Arthur Andersen but why).
- ***The General Business Environment*** (featuring sections on such emerging areas of interest as *outsourcing, viral marketing*, and *business process management*).
- ***The Aftermath of 9/11*** Not only what these events did to the U.S. economy, but what, because of its flexibility and strength, they did not do.

NEW FEATURE

SAY WHAT YOU MEAN

This new feature emphasizes what students need to communicate effectively using verbal and written skills across cultures. These new boxes will make students more sensitive to cultural differences and help prepare them to address the needs of others with numerous country-specific examples.

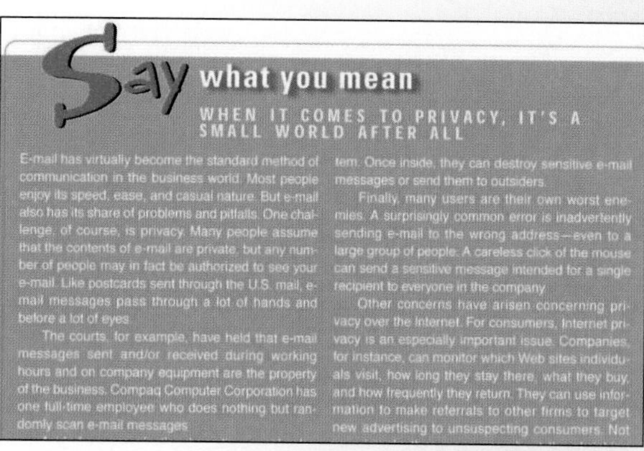

Say what you mean

WHEN IT COMES TO PRIVACY, IT'S A SMALL WORLD AFTER ALL

E-mail has virtually become the standard method of communication in the business world. Most people enjoy its speed, ease, and casual nature. But e-mail also has its share of problems and pitfalls. One challenge, of course, is privacy. Many people assume that the contents of e-mail are private, but any number of people may in fact be authorized to see your e-mail. Like postcards sent through the U.S. mail, e-mail messages pass through a lot of hands and before a lot of eyes.

The courts, for example, have held that e-mail messages sent and/or received during working hours and on company equipment are the property of the business. Compaq Computer Corporation has one full-time employee who does nothing but randomly scan e-mail messages.

tem. Once inside, they can destroy sensitive e-mail messages or send them to outsiders.

Finally, many users are their own worst enemies. A surprisingly common error is inadvertently sending e-mail to the wrong address—even to a large group of people. A careless click of the mouse can send a sensitive message intended for a single recipient to everyone in the company.

Other concerns have arisen concerning privacy over the Internet. For consumers, Internet privacy is an especially important issue. Companies, for instance, can monitor which Web sites individuals visit, how long they stay there, what they buy, and how frequently they return. They can use information to make referrals to other firms to target new advertising to unsuspecting consumers. Not

Self-Check Questions 1–3

*You should now be able to answer Self-Check Questions 1–3**

1. MULTIPLE CHOICE Marketers know that consumers buy products which offer the best *value*. Which of the following **is not** true regarding value for the buyer? [select one] **(a)** It is related to the buyer's wants and needs. **(b)** It compares a product's benefits with its costs. **(c)** **(d)** It depends on product price. **(e)** Market strategies focus on increasing it.

2. MULTIPLE CHOICE A program in which a bank offers free services to long-standing customers is an example of which of the following? [select one] **(a)** industrial marketing; **(b)** services marketing; **(c)** brand competition; **(d)** product differentiation; **(e)** relationship marketing.

3. MULTIPLE CHOICE All of the following are elements in the *marketing mix* (the "Four Ps" of marketing) **except** [select one]: **(a)** product differentiation; **(b)** place (or distribution); **(c)** promotion; **(d)** product; **(e)** pricing.

*ANSWERS TO SELF-CHECK QUESTIONS 1–3 CAN BE FOUND ON P. XXX.

NEW FEATURE

SELF-CHECK EXERCISES

Special self-check assessment exercises are introduced at three points in the chapter allowing students to review their understanding of the core concepts presented in the chapter.

Doing the Basics BEST—Learn. Evaluate. Apply.

NEW FEATURE

INTERNET FIELD TRIPS

These two-part Internet activities take students inside real world companies to explore how these companies conduct business. Starting in the middle of the chapter, after students have become acquainted with the fundamentals, students begin a focused, hands-on exploration of a real world organization. The second part of the exercise continues online with more detailed questions. Plus, students can check their final answers online at **http://www.prenhall.com/griffin.**

Mid-Chapter Internet Field Trip

"welcome to marriott.com"

In the first part of this chapter, we discussed the concept of marketing products to meet the needs and wants of customers in both consumer and industrial markets. We also saw how relationship marketing promotes customer loyalty and found that a sound marketing strategy involves the entire marketing mix—product, pricing, place (distribution), and promotion.

Let's look further into these marketing practices by exploring the Web site of a successful international company—Marriott International Inc., at <www.marriott.com>. The home page has five sections that we will use for exploring the marketing function at Marriott:

- **View Our 13 Lodging Brands** (see selection box at top of the page)
- **Explore & Plan** (box at middle of the page)
- **Marriott Rewards** (box at middle of the page)
- **Events & Meetings** (small box at bottom of the page)
- **Vacation Ownership** (small box at bottom of the page)

Begin by clicking on each of the following—**View Our 13 Lodging Brands, Events & Meetings,** and **Explore & Plan**—and examine their contents:

- What types of products does Marriott offer in its marketing mix?

On the home page, go to **View Our 13 Lodging Brands** and select **Marriott Hotels, Resorts & Suites.** Then drop down to the bottom of the page and click on **For Getaways.** Finally, click on **Marriott Resorts** and examine the information on that page:

- Which type of customer—consumer or industrial—is the target for information on this page?

At the home page, go to **View Our 13 Lodging Brands** and select **ExecuStay.** On the **Marriott ExecuStay** screen, go to the left side and click on **About ExecuStay.** Examine the information on that page:

- What product features on this page indicate the type of customer—consumer or industrial—that Marriott is targeting for this product?

On the home page, click on **Marriott Rewards.** After examining the contents of this page, go to the left side of the screen, click on **Elite Membership,** and read its contents:

- Is the Marriott Rewards program an example of relationship marketing? Give examples of incentives that Marriott uses to build relationships with its clients.

Briefly review the material at the Web pages entitled **Marriott Resorts** and **Executstay:**

- Which segmentation variables—demographic, geographic, psychographic, or behavioral—has Marriott used for differentiating its Marriott Resorts and ExecuStay products?

For the second leg of this Internet Field Trip, go to www. prenhall.com/griffin

NEW FEATURE

KEY TERMS

To help students review the major topics in each chapter, a new section at the end of each chapter collects all the boldfaced key terms and refers readers to the pages on which they appear. As always, we also provide marginal definitions of all key terms and collect them in an alphabetized glossary at the end of the book.

KEY TERMS

marketing (p. 000)
value (p. 000)
utility (p. 000)
consumer goods (p. 000)
industrial goods (p. 000)
services (p. 000)
relationship marketing (p. 000)
external environment (p. 000)
substitute product (p. 000)
brand competition (p. 000)
international competition (p. 000)
marketing manager (p. 000)
marketing plan (p. 000)
marketing mix (p. 000)
product (p. 000)
product differentiation (p. 000)
distribution (p. 000)
target market (p. 000)
market segmentation (p. 000)
geographic variables (p. 000)
demographic variables (p. 000)
psychographic variables (p. 000)
behavioral variables (p. 000)
marketing research (p. 000)
secondary data (p. 000)
primary data (p. 000)
observation (p. 000)
survey (p. 000)
focus group (p. 000)
experimentation (p. 000)
data warehousing (p. 000)
data mining (p. 000)
consumer behavior (p. 000)
brand loyalty (p. 000)
rational motives (p. 000)
emotional motives (p. 000)
industrial market (p. 000)
reseller market (p. 000)
institutional market (p. 000)

NEW FEATURE

EXERCISING YOUR ETHICS

To bring ethics to the forefront, new end-of-chapter exercises ask students to resolve an ethical situation. Each dilemma includes a description of the situation and concludes with questions that focus on how to approach and resolve these ethical challenges.

Exercising Your Ethics

DRIVING A LEGITIMATE BARGAIN

The Situation

A firm's marketing methods are sometimes at odds with the consumer's buying process. This exercise illustrates how ethical issues can become entwined with personal selling activities, product pricing, and customer relations.

The Dilemma

In buying his first-ever new car, Matt visited showrooms and Web sites for every make of SUV. After weeks of reading and test-driving, he settled on a well-known Japanese-made vehicle with a manufacturer's suggested retail price of $34,500 for the 2002 model. The price included accessories and options that Matt considered essential. Because he planned to own the car for at least five years, he was willing to wait for just the right package rather than accept a lesser-equipped car already on the lot. Negotiations with Gary, the sales representative, continued for two weeks. Finally, a sales contract was signed for $30,600, with delivery due no more than two or three months later if the vehicle had to be special-ordered from the factory, earlier if Gary found the exact car when he searched other dealers around the country. On April 30, to close the deal, Matt had to write a check for $1,000.

Matt received a call on June 14 from Angela, Gary's sales manager: "We cannot get your car before October," she reported, "so it will have to be a 2003 model. You will have to pay the 2003 price." Matt replied that the agreement called for a stated price and delivery deadline for 2002, pointing out that money had exchanged hands for the contract. When asked what the 2003 price would be, Angela responded that it had not yet been announced. Angrily, Matt replied that he would be foolish to agree now on some unknown future price. Moreover, he didn't like the way the dealership was treating him. He told Angela to send back to him everything he had signed; the deal was off.

Questions for Discussion

1. Given the factors involved in the consumer buying process, how would you characterize the particular ethical issues in this situation?
2. From an ethical standpoint, what are the obligations of the sales rep and the sales manager regarding the pricing of the product in this situation?
3. If you were responsible for maintaining good customer relations at the dealership, how would you handle this matter?

■ ALL NEW!!!!

"ON LOCATION" VIDEOS & EXERCISES

NEW FEATURE

Twenty new, custom videos are linked to the end-of-chapter exercises to help students see how real-life businesses and the people who run them apply fundamental business principles on a daily basis. The format for each video is the same: 1) a moderator sets the scene; 2) concepts unfold; 3) the moderator recaps core issues as the video can be paused for additional in-class discussion; 4) the video concludes with answers to the in-class discussion questions. The unique structure and format of these videos not only brings the concepts to life, but also provides an interactive environment to stimulate critical thinking and discussion in your course.

Chapter		Company / Agency
1	Helping Businesses Do Business	*U.S. Department of Commerce*
2	Viewing the Environment	*MTV Europe*
3	Doing Business Privately	*Amy's Ice Cream*
4	Globalizing the Long Arm of the Law	*Printrak*
5	Doing the Right Thing	*American Red Cross*
6	Imaginative Management	*Creative Age Publications*
7	Juicing Up the Organization	*Nantucket Nectars*
8	Managing the Human Side of Business	*Park Place Entertainment*
9	Computing Family Values	*Kingston Technology*
10	In Consumers' Shoes	*Sketchers USA*
11	Sending Products into Space	*MCCI*
12	Through the Grapevine	*Clos du Bois Winery*
13	Revving Up Promotion	*BMW Motorcycles*
14	Managing Global Production	*Body Glove*
15	Glowing with Quality	*Liquid Lab*
16	Space Age Information Systems	*Boeing Satellite Systems*
17	Accounting for Billions of Burgers	*McDonald's*
18	Funding the Business World	*Coast Business Credit*
19	Information Pays Off	*Motley Fool*
20	Nailing Down Financial Management	*Seche International*

SUPER COMPANION WEBSITE

The Prentice Hall Companion Website offers the following features for students and instructors:

- ***Powerful Homepage:*** Students and faculty can unite all their texts on one personal homepage.
- ***Study Guide***: Test your knowledge with this interactive study guide that offers a wide variety of self-assessment questions for each chapter. Results from the automatically graded questions provide immediate feedback and can serve as practice or can be e-mailed to the instructor for extra credit.
- **NEW!** ***Interactive Summaries:*** A complete version of each end-of-chapter summary has been prepared with blanks to be filled in for the key terms of the chapter. Students merely have to supply terms as they study and click to find out how well they've retained the most important content of each chapter.
- ***Study Hall:*** Includes information on personal finance, time management, study skills, and academic majors. Get career information, view sample resumes, and even apply for jobs online.
- ***Current Events:*** Check out links to articles in today's business news.
- ***Financial Times Week Ahead.*** Andrew Hill, U.S. business editor for the *Financial Times,* previews top stories weekend that are sure to be in the business news.
- ***Downloadable supplements for Faculty:*** In this password-protected area, faculty have access to all the student resources, plus instructor support material such as Instructor's Manuals, Test Item Files, PowerPoints, and the answers to all student study materials.
- ***Communication Tools for Faculty:***
  - ***Messages:*** Faculty can post messages that appear on every one of their student's homepages
  - ***Bulletins:*** Faculty can send bulletins that go out to every one of their student's email addresses
  - ***Discussions:*** Faculty can initiate threaded discussions for each of their courses on MyCompanion Website
- ***Smart Calendar:*** Helps students and faculty keep track of all class events and due dates. One online calendar can be used to organize important dates from multiple courses.
- ***Syllabus Editor:*** Follow the easy to follow steps for creating and revising an online syllabus where changes you make are immediately available to your students on the Smart Calendar. Faculty can also upload their own documents, coordinate discussions, link to Prentice Hall online educational resources, and input links to any other site on the web.
- ***Research Links:*** Links to a wide variety of online research tools.

HALLMARK STRENGTHS UPDATED!

LEARN. What better way to learn about business than by getting down to business. The following features engage students and bring the business concepts to life.

■ ***Wraparound Vignettes*** Each chapter opens with a different two-part case study centering on a real-life business situation and closes by revisiting and posing follow-up questions for discussion.

Xbox Spots the Market

Once the domain of teenage boys, interactive games now lure a much broader audience, including younger kids and adults. It's easy to become addicted: With cinematically realistic graphics and challenging action sequences, games require split-second timing and rapid-fire reactions

players with the most advanced hardware and hottest graphics in the industry. Microsoft intends for the site to become *the* gathering place for players and to promote enthusiasm among gamers everywhere. Thus far, Xbox.com has succeeded both in establishing relationships among gamers and in forming new bonds between gamers and the Xbox brand. Microsoft wants gamers to become loyal members of an Xbox community.

But industry experts know that it takes more than relationship building and nifty hardware to succeed in this market. Success depends on a steady flow of exciting ... capture players' imagina... ware, reports Phaedra ... omengamers.com, "far out... on for speed and memory," ... re's a serious problem with ... so far." The initial launch ... es, most of them action and

Continued from page 000

Microsoft's Great Xpectations

Xbox is Microsoft's first venture into game consoles, and the company's marketing strategy differs from that of competitors, especially Nintendo, which targets the younger end of the market. Xbox, says product-team leader Robbie Rash, targets a different audience. "Let's face it," he says, "Nintendo's system is for kids. We're for sophisticated gamers. I don't know any 30-year-olds who want a GameCube [by Nintendo]." Both Xbox and PlayStation 2 (by Sony) are aimed at the 16-

that Microsoft will have more than 200 Xbox games with a total of 300 titles in development by the next holiday season. For international appeal, Sega's participation also gives Xbox an important boost: Many Japanese gamers doubted Xbox's credibility until they learned of Microsoft's alliance with Sega's respected game publishers.

The Xbox product itself is also different from competing products. Sony's PS2 plays music CDs and DVD movies right out of the box. Xbox can also play music and movies—in fact, it delivers

High-Tech Hits the Highway

Nicole Gunther's four-year-old daughter is happy in the back seat of the family's Honda minivan. There are no more whining cries of "When are we going to get there?" With the rear-seat DVD player delivering Disney films, Nicole is absorbed in entertainment that lets Mom concentrate on after-school traffic. Other services, such as a satellite-controlled navigation system, keep drivers from getting lost and alert them to road or traffic conditions. Competitors are also getting in on the act. Cadillac's OnStar navigation service offers satellite radio services in more than 30 GM car and truck models, and satellite feeds are linked into dozens of Ford, GM, and DaimlerChrysler models.

Telematics, automobile versions of the electronic entertainment systems that have become staples in many homes, were packaged in about 2 percent of new vehicles sold in 2002, but the industry is on the verge of a boom: Wireless communications for the highway had total sales of $1.6 billion in 2001 but will reach $20 billion annually in 2006.

Industry demographics are changing, too. Currently, buyers consist mostly of middle- to upper-class drivers who can

suburban lifestyles in which many parents find themselves staffing dawn-to-dusk transportation services.

Launched in Cadillacs during the 1999 to 2001 model years, the first in-car communications systems offered on-road monitoring of performance and location and traffic-guidance advisories for high-income drivers. But that target audience, say industry experts, will change by 2007, when 80 percent of all new cars will contain factory-installed telematics. For model years 2002–2004, the target is active families in midrange- and higher-income groups who have young children and who use in-car technology for safety and entertainment. Even midrange, lower-priced cars will be equipped with a variety of wireless appliances—hands-free cell phones, monitoring systems for roadside assistance, and satellite radios. Satellite subscription fees, currently ranging from $200 to $400 per year for GM's OnStar, will permit technology-oriented drivers to receive music and movies from home and elsewhere.

Still another target group for 2003–2006 is high-income professionals who use in-car communications technolo-

■ ***"It's a Wired World" Boxes*** These unique boxes offer brief real-world examples of the steps that new and established companies are taking to keep pace with competition in the e-business environment.

EVALUATE. To ensure students have ample opportunity to master key concepts, *Business, 7/e* introduces some new features to help them evaluate their own progress.

■ ***Self-Check Exercises*** Special self-check assessment exercises are introduced at three points in the chapter allowing students to review their understanding of the core concepts presented in the chapter. All answers are presented in the back of the book with a specific page reference for reviewing those areas where students need additional practice.

■ ***Online Summaries***

■ ***Key Terms***

Self-Check Questions 7–9

*You should now be able to answer Self-Check Questions 7–9**

7. MULTIPLE CHOICE The following is **not** a stage in the *consumer buying process* [select one]: **(a)** substitution purchase; **(b)** evaluation of alternatives; **(c)** postpurchase evaluation; **(d)** information seeking; **(e)** problem/need recognition.

8. TRUE/FALSE In terms of market size, *organizational buying* in the United States is economically much more significant than *consumer buying*.

9. MULTIPLE CHOICE Which of the following is **not** true of the *international marketing mix* [select one]: **(a)** Products that sell for a given price in the United States may sell at a different price in another country. **(b)** The International Standards Act ensures the existence of uniform advertising practices in most countries. **(c)** A company can speed up its international distribution activities by buying an existing business in another country. **(d)** Some products can be sold abroad with virtually no changes. **(e)** Cultural differences can cause negative reactions to products that are advertised improperly.

*Answers to Self-Check Questions 7–9 can be found on p. xxx.

Doing the Basics BEST—Learn. Evaluate. Apply.

APPLY. The following end-of-chapter exercises prepare students to apply both critical- and creative-thinking skills to solve real-world problems.

Building Your Business Skills

DEALING WITH VARIABLES

This exercise enhances the following SCANS workplace competencies: demonstrating basic skills, demonstrating thinking skills, exhibiting interpersonal skills, and working with information.

Goal

To encourage students to analyze the ways in which various market segmentation variables affect business success.

The Situation

You and four partners are thinking of purchasing a heating and air conditioning (H/AC) dealership that specializes in residential applications priced between $2,000 and $40,000. You are now in the process of deciding where that dealership should be located. You are considering four locations: Miami, Florida; Westport, Connecticut; Dallas, Texas; and Spokane, Washington.

Method

Step 1

Working with your partnership group, do library research to learn how H/AC makers market residential products. Check for articles in the *Wall Street Journal*, *Business Week*, *Fortune*, and other business publications.

Step 2

Continue your research. This time, focus on the specific marketing variables that define each prospective location. Check Census Bureau and Department of Labor data at your library and on the Internet and contact local chambers of commerce (by phone and via the Internet) to learn about the following factors for each location:

■ ***Building Your Business Skills*** Created to address SCANS requirements, these exercises allow students to apply both their knowledge and critical-thinking skills to extended problems drawn from realistic business situations. Each exercise begins with a list of goals, a description of the situation, a step-by-step methodology for proceeding, and follow-up questions to help students focus their responses to the challenge.

■ ***Mastering Business Essentials CD-ROM Activities*** This innovative, cross-functional CD revolves around an e-business called CanGo. Twelve interactive episodes are linked to the appropriate end-of-chapter material in *Business, 7/e*. The format for each episode includes: 1) unique video scenarios; 2) informative and stimulating interactive exercises with follow-up video clips; and 3) additional case and discussion questions. This can be value-packed for **FREE** with the text. To order, use ISBN 0-13-141898-X.

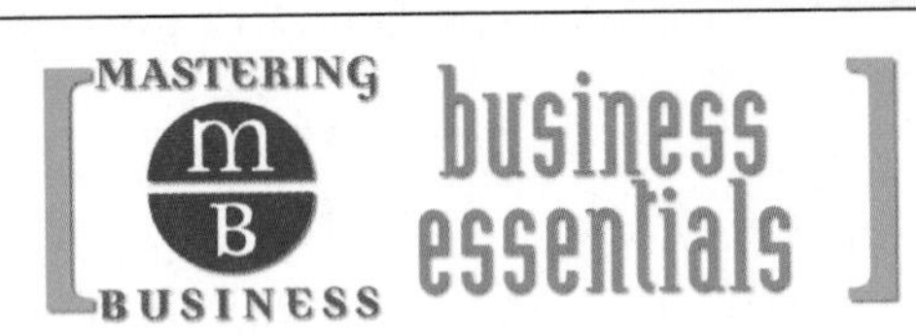

■ ***Crafting Your Business Plan Exercises*** Chapter-ending exercises apply text material to the task of developing a business plan. The educational version of the best-selling *Business Plan Pro* Software can be packaged with the text for $10. ***The new version of this software allows users to create plans with greater ease and speed.*** Based on responses to a series of "yes / no" questions, the EasyPlan Wizard automatically selects the plan outline, reports, charts, and tables. This feature simplifies the plan-creation process and is unique to this business planning software. In addition, *Business Plan Pro* provides numerous sample plans and provides step-by-step examples and instructions for making and assessing plans.

Business PlanPro

SUPPLEMENTS

Study Guide

A *Study Guide for Business, 7th edition* by Ray Polchow at Ohio University, is designed to increase your students' comprehension of the concepts presented in this text. The guide provides chapter-by-chapter explanations and exercises designed to reinforce comprehension of key terms and concepts to promote concept-application skills.

Instructor's Resource Manual

Written by Sal Veas of Santa Monica College, each chapter of the Instructor's Resource Manual includes:

- A chapter overview
- Description of the changes between the 6th and 7th edition within the chapter
- Brief chapter outline
- Learning Objectives
- An opening class exercise, and a chapter closing project
- Detailed lecture outlines customized for both PowerPoint users and acetate users, featuring traditional lecture notes, as well as discussion points
- Answers to all end-of-chapter questions, problems, and assignments
- A detailed video guide with answers to video exercise questions
- Supplemental cases
- Sample syllabi
- Recommended web sites/additional resources for professors

ALL NEW???? Test Item File

An all-new *Test Item File* contains 20 chapters of approximately 200 questions per chapter, all of which have been carefully checked for accuracy and quality. This comprehensive set, written by M. Kathryn Demarest, Carroll Community College, consists of multiple-choice, true/false, short answer, and essay questions. Each test question is ranked based on Bloom's Taxonomy and by level of difficulty (easy, moderate, or difficult) and contains page references to allow the instructor a quick and easy way to balance the level of exams or quizzes. One Quick Quiz (a short 10 question quiz for in-class use to test basic chapter concepts) and One Prepared Exam are also included for each chapter of the test item file.

Prentice Hall's Computerized Test Manager

Our user-friendly software allows you to generate error-free tests quickly and easily by previewing questions individually on the screen and then selecting randomly, by query, or by number. The Computerized Test Manager allows you to generate random tests with our extensive bank of questions. You can create an exam, administer it traditionally or online, and analyze your success with a simple click of a mouse.

Telephone Test Preparation

For those instructors who prefer not to use the Computerized Test Item File, Prentice Hall also provides a special 800 call-in service for ease of use. All you need to do is call the Testing Help Desk at 1-800- 550-1701 to have a customized test created. This test can then be delivered by e-mail, U.S. mail, or overnight carrier.

PowerPoint Slides

Created by Martha Laham of Diablo Valley College, this edition's PowerPoint presentation contains more than 500 text-specific slides highlighting fundamental concepts by integrating key graphs, figures, and illustrations from the text. PowerPoint slides come complete with lecture notes, which are available in the Instructor's Resource Manual, or on the Instructor's Resource CD-ROM. Free to adopters, PowerPoints are available on the Instructor's Resource CD-ROM, or can be downloaded from the Faculty Resource web site at **www.prenhall.com/griffin.**

Overhead Transparencies

This extensive set of over 300 full-color overhead transparencies focus on the main points of the chapter and include illustrations and figures from the text. Overhead transparencies come complete with lecture notes, available either in the Instructor's Resource Manual, or on the Instructor's Resource CD-ROM.

Custom Video Library—as described in the previous section!

Instructor's Resource CD-ROM

This all-in-one multimedia product is an invaluable asset for professors who prefer to work with electronic files rather than traditional print supplements. This CD-ROM contains the Instructor's Resource Manual, PowerPoints, Test Item File, and Prentice Hall Test Manager.

Business Plan Pro Software

Business Plan Pro (BPP) provides students with a step-by-step approach to creating a comprehensive business plan. The software is designed to stimulate student thinking about the many tasks and decisions that go into planning and running a business. Preformatted report templates, charts, and tables do the mechanics so that students can focus on the thinking. Planners can also publish to a protected Internet site, where readers can access all or part of posted plans. *Business Plan Pro* can be packaged with the textbook for a nominal fee of $10.

NEW! Business Plan Supplement

This comprehensive saleable supplement, written by David Tooch, The University of New Hampshire's Thompson School, provides step-by-step lessons with actual case studies to guide the student's preparation of a winning business plan. Upon completion of all the cumulative lessons, each student will have created a polished and professional business plan, whether they choose to do it by hand or with Palo Alto's Business Plan Pro software.

NEW! Career Portfolio Supplement

This unique saleable supplement, written by James O'Rourke, The University of Notre Dame, takes students through the process of building their individualized career portfolio. Students walk through the process of self-assessment, matching career opportunities, initiating the job search using the latest internet-based search vehicles, preparing all job search related documents, and following up. Upon completion of the supplement, students will have a career portfolio they can use and build on as their career progresses.

NEW! Business Ethics in Uncertain Times: A Special Supplement

This special supplement covers key issues in contemporary business ethics, including

- Management's responsibility for accountability; conflicts of interest, protection of employees, protection of stockholders, and compliance with legal and regulatory standards
- Corporate governance, including how and why it's supposed to work, outside directors versus insiders with conflicts of interest, and audit committees.
- Accounting practices, including why and how public corporations hide debt and mischaracterize expenses, how previously accepted accounting practices are now being questioned, the role of CPA firms in auditing statements, and ways to manage conflicts of interest with consulting clients.
- Stakeholder relations, including the importance of honest and complete financial statements to inform current and potential shareholders, and ways to maintain employee trust, and relations with unions.
- Ethical decisions and behavior, including what can be done to encourage and support ethical actions, such as codes of conduct, ethical training, whistleblower and ombudsman structures, legal and regulatory oversight of auditors and managers, separation of consulting and auditing, and director accountability.
- Dedicated sections on analyzing ethics at Enron, Arthur Andersen, and at WorldCom. Chapter-ending pedagogy includes: Questions for Review, Questions for Discussion and Analysis, For Further Research, and Ethics Resources Online. This new supplement can be packaged with the text for free. To order, use ISBN 0-13-141899-8.

Self-Assessment Library

Organized according to individual, group, and organizational needs, the Self-Assessment Library features self-assessment tools designed to give students insights into their skills, abilities, and interests.

New York Times Offer

Prentice Hall is pleased to offer students a discounted 10-week subscription to the *New York Times* for $20 packaged with the text. This saves students over 50% off the regular student subscription rate! In addition, instructors ordering this subscription package receive a complementary one-semester subscription.

expect the world®
The New York Times
nytimes.com

Financial Times Offer

You can receive a 15-week print subscription to the Financial Times for $10 with this text. The Prentice Hall textbook + subscription package will contain a 16-page, full-color *Financial Times* Student Guide, shrink-wrapped with the textbook. Bound inside the Student Guide will be a postcard that entitles the student to claim a prepaid 15-week subscription. After the student mails in the reply card, the subscription should begin in 5 to 7 business days.

FINANCIAL TIMES
World business newspaper.

OFFERING YOUR INTRODUCTION TO BUSINESS COURSE ONLINE?

WE HAVE WHAT YOU NEED!

Now you have the freedom to personalize your own online course materials! Prentice Hall Business Publishing provides content and support to create and manage your own online course materials in WebCT, Blackboard, and CourseCompass.

WebCT

Blackboard

CourseCompass

Standard content, which is free to adopters, consists of test questions from the Test Item File and the ability to link from our Companion Websites to access student quizzes. You are free to integrate your course materials to create a customized course. All pre-loaded content can be edited.

Prentice Hall provides **premium content**, which is available for $12.00 when packaged with the text, and $24.00 stand-alone. In addition to the resources available with the standard course, critical content from each chapter is presented by section, and each section contains assessment and applications designed to compliment and enhance students' reading and classroom experience. Each section features a pre-assessment quiz, a learning activity and learning application, and a post-assessment quiz. Please contact your local representative for details.

Acknowledgments

Although only two names appear on the cover of this book, we could never have completed *Business, 7/e* without the assistance of many fine individuals. Everyone who worked on the book was committed to making it the best that it could be. Quality and closeness to the customer are things that we read a lot about today. Both we and the people who worked with us took these concepts to heart in this book and made quality our watchword by listening to our users and trying to provide what they want.

First, we would like to thank all the professionals who took time from their busy schedules to review materials for Business:

Ed Blevins
DeVry Institute of Technology

Mary Jo Boehms
Jackson State Community College

Karen Collins
Lehigh University

Dr. Shiv Gupta
University of Findlay

James H. Kennedy
Angelina College

Robert Markus
Babson College

Bronna McNeeley
Midwestern State University

William Morrison
San Jose State

Christopher Rogers
Miami-Dade Community College

Phyllis T. Shafer
Brookdale Community College

Lynne Spellman White
Trinity Christian College

JoAnn Wiggins
Walla Walla College

A number of other professionals also made substantive contributions to the text, ranging from draft material on specialized topics to suggested resource materials to proposals for cases and examples. In particular, we are greatly indebted to Elisa Adams and Judy Block for their inventive and indefatigable contributions in their capacity as professional writers and researchers.

The supplements package for *Business, 7/e* also benefited from the able contributions of several individuals. We would like to thank these people for developing the finest set of instructional and learning materials for this field.

Meanwhile, a superb team of professionals at Prentice Hall made this book a pleasure to write. Authors often get the credit when a book is successful, but the success of this book must be shared with an outstanding group of people in New Jersey. Our development editor, Ron Librach, has been a true product champion and has improved both the book and the package in more ways than we can list. Marcy Maslanczuk, the production editor, also made many truly outstanding contributions to the project.

We also want to acknowledge the contributions of the entire team at Prentice Hall Business Publishing, including Jeff Shelstad, editor in chief; Jennifer Glennon, senior managing editor; Annie Todd, director of marketing; Steve Deitmer, director of development; Debbie Clare, executive marketing manager; Kelly Wendrychowicz, editorial assistant; Melanie Olsen, assistant editor; Judy Leale, managing editor; Arnold Vila, production manager; Maria Lange, design manager; Melinda Alexander, photo researcher; Beth Brenzel, image permission supervisor; and Michelina Viscusi, image coordinator.

Our colleagues at Texas A&M University and the University of Missouri–Columbia also deserve recognition. Each of us has the good fortune to be a part of a community of scholars who enrich our lives and challenge our ideas. Without their intellectual stimulation and support, our work would suffer greatly. Phyllis Wasburn, Dr. Griffin's staff assistant, deserves special mention of the myriad contributions she has made to this project as well.

Finally, our families. We take pride in the accomplishments of our wives, Glenda and Mary, and draw strength from the knowledge that they are there for us to lean on. And we take joy from our children, Ashley, Dustin, Matt, and Kristen. Sometimes in the late hours when we're ready for sleep but have to get one or two more pages written, looking at your pictures keeps us going. Thanks to all of you for making us what we are.

—Ricky W. Griffin

—Ronald J. Ebert

BUSINESS

SEVENTH EDITION

PART I

Understanding the Contemporary Business Environment

CHAPTER 1

Understanding the U.S. Business System

After reading this chapter, you should be able to:

1. Define the nature of U.S. *business* and identify its main goals and functions.
2. Describe the different types of global *economic systems* according to the means by which they control the *factors of production* through *input and output markets.*
3. Show how *demand* and *supply* affect resource distribution in the United States.
4. Identify the elements of *private enterprise* and explain the various degrees of *competition* in the U.S. economic system.
5. Trace the history of business in the United States.

Megawatt Laundering and Other Bright Business Ideas

The final chapters haven't been written yet, but the Enron saga has already become a part of American business lore. As just about everybody knows by now, Enron Corp. < www.enron.com> (yes, there is still a Web site) is the largest U.S. company ever to fail (also managing to bring down its lead auditor, Arthur Andersen, in the process). Enron is no doubt destined to figure in dozens of case studies on such themes as fraudulent financial practices, corrupt corporate strategy, and lawless leadership.

The Enron story also throws light on some of the basics of the capitalistic free-enterprise system—namely, supply, demand, and freedom of choice. As we will see, Enron managers exploited the relationships between supply and demand to an almost unprecedented degree in their quest for riches beyond legitimate profit.

This chapter of the Enron story opens in California. Like most states, California had long regulated public utility companies. A state agency dictated how much energy was produced and the prices at which it was sold. In the process, the profits of utility companies were indirectly controlled as well. Regulation also meant that supply and demand were closely aligned. Utilities produced just as much energy as customers needed. After all, there was no reason to produce more than they could sell, and the state wouldn't let them produce any less. State rules also required each customer to buy energy from a single local provider authorized to conduct business in a specified geographic area.

But in the late 1990s, California adopted a new hands-off policy regarding supply and demand in the utilities business. This shift in thinking resulted from a massive lobbying effort by major utilities interests, as representatives from Enron and other big energy companies persuaded the state to loosen its grip on the production and delivery of electricity. They argued that increased competition among producers and suppliers would make them deliver energy more efficiently while allowing consumers to choose their own providers.

Under the new system, responsibility for matching supply and demand fell to an Independent System Operator (ISO). This intermediary agent (or wholesaler) bought electricity from unregulated providers such as Enron, Dynergy, and Calpine and then sold it to local energy retailers such as Pacific Gas & Electric. The ISO paid providers to sell excess electricity out of state if supplies grew too large. Consumers, meanwhile, could choose to buy electricity from different retailers, making decisions based on price, service, and so forth.

The integrity of the system required the big companies involved to operate with a sense of social responsibility and fair play. Says David Freeman, top energy adviser to California governor Gray Davis; "It never occurred to us in our innocence that something so vital to society would be treated like a casino. We thought that somehow the [invisible] hand of Adam Smith would be benign."

Another flaw in the system was the fact that the state hadn't really created a free market for electricity. It had merely laid down a new and more bewildering array of rules and regulations. In some cases, regulations actually masked incentives for companies to misuse the system. With or without such incentives, however, Enron—and other energy providers—seized every opportunity they could to exploit the system by ducking through highly profitable loopholes.

Two of Enron's most notorious plans were code-named *Death Star* and *Ricochet*. With *Death Star*, Enron took advantage of the payouts through which the state managed its power grid. Essentially,

"It never occurred to us that something so vital to society would be treated like a casino."

~David Freeman

CALIFORNIA ENERGY OFFICIAL ON THE TACTICS OF POWER COMPANIES IN THE STATE'S POWER SHORTAGE

California paid as much as $750 per megawatt hour to persuade providers not to ship power on overburdened power lines, especially those running north to south. To create the illusion of congestion on these lines, Enron began overbooking shipments and scheduling power transmissions that it had no intention of making. In each case, it then collected money from the state for changing plans that it never meant to carry out.

Ricochet was a scheme known as "megawatt laundering." To protect consumers from price gouging by unregulated suppliers, California had set price caps for electrical power. Those caps, however, applied only to electricity that was bought and transmitted within the state. Enron began buying electricity in California, which it then transmitted across state lines over a regional power grid. It then turned around and transmitted the same electricity back to California. Naturally, it looked as if it were coming from out of state. Because California price caps didn't apply, Enron was free to sell the rerouted power at much higher prices.

Our opening story is continued on page 21

The Concept of Business and the Concept of Profit

What do you think of when you hear the word *business*? Does it conjure up images of successful corporations, such as General Motors and IBM? Or of less successful operations, such as Enron and Kmart? Are you reminded of smaller firms, such as your local supermarket or car-repair shop? Or do you think of even smaller one-person operations, such as the dry cleaner around the corner or your neighborhood pizzeria?

business

An organization that provides goods or services to earn profits

profits

The difference between a business's revenues and its expenses

All of these organizations are **businesses**—organizations that provide goods or services to earn profits. Indeed, the prospect of earning **profits**—the difference between a business's revenues and expenses—is what encourages people to open and expand businesses. After all, profits reward owners for risking their money and time. The legitimate right to pursue profits distinguishes a business from those organizations, such as most universities, hospitals, and government agenices, which run in much the same way but which generally don't seek profits.[1]

In a capitalistic system, then, businesses exist in order to earn profits for owners who are free to set them up. But consumers also have freedom of choice. In choosing how to pursue profits, businesses must take into account what consumers want and/or need. No matter how efficient a business is, it won't survive if there is no demand for its goods or services. Neither a snow-blower shop in Florida nor a beach-umbrella store in Alaska is likely to do very well.

But if enterprising businesspeople can identify either unmet consumer needs or better ways of satisfying consumer needs, they can be successful. In other words, someone who can spot a promising opportunity and then develop a good plan for capitalizing on it can succeed. The opportunity always involves goods or services that consumers need and/or want—especially if no one else is supplying them or if existing businesses are doing so inefficiently or incompletely.

Businesses produce most of the goods and services we consume and employ most working people. They create most new innovations and provide a vast range of opportunities for new businesses, which serve as their suppliers. A healthy business climate also contributes directly to quality of life and standard of living. New forms of technology, service businesses, and international opportunities promise to keep production, consumption, and employment growing indefinitely. Business profits enhance the personal incomes of millions of owners and stockholders, and business taxes help to support governments at all levels. Many businesses support charities and provide community leadership.

In this chapter, we begin our introduction to business by examining economic systems around the world. Once you understand the differences among them, you will better appreciate the workings of the U.S. system. We also investigate the concepts of demand and supply and their role in private enterprise. Finally, we briefly trace the history of U.S. business.

Economic Systems Around the World

A U.S. business operates differently from a business in, say, France or the People's Republic of China, and businesses in these countries differ from those in Japan or Brazil. A key factor in these differences is the economic system of a firm's *home country*—the nation in which it does most of its business. An **economic system** is a nation's system for allocating its resources among its citizens, both individuals and organizations. In this section, we show how economic systems differ according to the ownership or control of these resources, which are often called *factors of production*. We will also describe the economic systems of a few other countries.[2]

economic system
A nation's system for allocating its resources among its citizens

Factors of Production

A basic difference between economic systems is the way in which a system manages its **factors of production**—the resources that a country's businesses use to produce goods and services.[3] Economists have long focused on four factors of production: labor, capital, entrepreneurs, and physical resources. Newer perspectives, however, broaden the idea of natural resources to include all physical resources. In addition to the classic four, information resources are now often considered as well.[4] (The concept of factors of production can also be applied to the resources that an organization manages in order to produce goods and services.)

factors of production
Resources used in the production of goods and services—labor, capital, entrepreneurs, physical resources, and information resources

Labor People who work for businesses provide labor. Sometimes called **human resources, labor** includes the physical and intellectual contributions people make while engaged in economic production. AOL Time Warner <www.aoltimewarner.com>, for example, employs 88,000 people. Such large operations require widely skilled workforces, ranging from software engineers and media experts to financial analysts.

labor (or **human resources**)
The physical and mental capabilities of people as they contribute to economic production

Capital Obtaining and using labor and other resources requires **capital**—the financial resources needed to operate an enterprise. You need capital to start a new business and then to keep it running and growing. AOL Time Warner needs millions of dollars in cash (and millions more in equipment and other assets) to run its operations. A major source of capital for small businesses is personal investment by owners. Investments can come from individual entrepreneurs, from partners who start businesses together, and/or from investors who buy stock. Revenue from the sale of products is a key and ongoing source of capital once a business has opened its doors.[5]

capital
The funds needed to create and operate a business enterprise

Capital can also include the market value of corporate stock. When America Online acquired Time Warner for $106 billion in 2001, the deal involved very little actual cash. Most of it was handled through transfers of stock. Bank lines of credit and the market value of *liquid assets* (those that can be quickly and easily sold for cash) are also forms of capital.

Entrepreneurs An **entrepreneur** is an individual who accepts the risks and opportunities entailed by creating and operating a new business. AOL was started by James Kimsey, who had the technical skills to understand how the Internet works, the conceptual skills to see its huge future potential, and the risk-taking acumen to bet his own career and capital on the idea of AOL. Both Time Inc. and Warner Brothers Studios, two older companies that later merged into Time Warner, were also started (both in 1922) by entrepreneurs who risked personal fortunes on the success of their new ventures.

entrepreneur
An individual who accepts the risks and opportunities involved in creating and operating a new business venture

In 2001, the entrepreneurial vision of leaders at both AOL and Time Warner saw the potential benefits of merging the two firms. Most economic systems encourage entrepreneurs, both to start new businesses and to make the decisions that turn small businesses into larger ones big enough to move into new markets.

Some sectors of the economy tend to get a lift even when the overall economy slips. Entrepreneur Jonathan Fields found out that physical and spiritual therapy is one of them when he opened his Sonic Yoga NYC <http://sonicyoga.com> *in Manhattan one month after 9/11. Within thirty days, he had three times as many clients as he had projected, and the business continues to flourish. "So far, so good," says Fields, a one-time lawyer with the Securities and Exchange Commission.*

physical resources
Tangible things organizations use in the conduct of their business

Physical Resources **Physical resources** are the tangible things that organizations use to conduct their business. They include natural resources and raw materials, offices, storage, production facilities, parts and supplies, computers and peripherals, and a variety of other equipment. AOL Time Warner, for example, needs land, buildings, and computers. The CDs on which it distributes its software and music and the videotapes and DVDs on which it distributes movies are supplied by other manufacturers; forest products are used for packaging.

information resources
Data and other information used by business

Information Resources The production of tangible goods once dominated most economic systems, but today **information resources** play a major role. Businesses rely on market forecasts, on the specialized knowledge of people, and on economic data for much of their work. In turn, much of what they do results either in the creation of new information or the repackaging of existing information for new users.

AOL Time Warner produces few tangible products. Instead, America Online provides online services for millions of subscribers who pay monthly access fees. Time Warner Entertainment produces movies and television programming. A subsidiary, Turner Broadcasting System, gathers information about world events and then transmits it to consumers over its Cable News Network (CNN). Essentially, then, AOL Time Warner is in the information business.[6]

Types of Economic Systems

Different types of economic systems manage these factors of production differently. In some systems, all ownership is private; in others, all factors of production are owned or controlled by the government. Most systems fall between these extremes.

planned economy
Economy that relies on a centralized government to control all or most factors of production and to make all or most production and allocation decisions

Economic systems also differ in the ways decisions are made about production and allocation. A **planned economy** relies on a centralized government to control all or most factors of production and to make all or most production and allocation decisions. In a **market economy,** individual producers and consumers control production and allocation by creating combinations of supply and demand. We will describe each of these types of economic systems and then discuss mixed market economies.

market economy
Economy in which individuals control production and allocation decisions through supply and demand

Planned Economies There are two basic forms of planned economies: *communism* (discussed here) and *socialism* (discussed as a mixed market economy). As envisioned by nineteenth-century German economist Karl Marx, communism is a system in which the government owns and operates all factors of production. Marx proposed an economy in which individuals would contribute according to their abilities and receive benefits according to their needs. He also expected government ownership of production factors to be temporary: Once society had matured, government would wither away and workers would take direct ownership of the factors of production.[7]

The Soviet Union and many Eastern European countries embraced communism until the end of the twentieth century. In the early 1990s, one country after another renounced communism as both an economic and a political system. Today, Cuba, North Korea, Vietnam, and the People's Republic of China are among the few nations with openly communist systems. Even in these countries, however, planned economic systems are making room for features of the free enterprise system.

Market Economies A **market** is a mechanism for exchange between the buyers and sellers of a particular good or service. (Like *capital,* the term *market* can have multiple meanings.) Market economies rely on capitalism and free enterprise to create an environment in which producers and consumers are free to sell and buy what they choose (within certain limits). As a result, items produced and prices paid are largely determined by supply and demand.

market
Mechanism for exchange between buyers and sellers of a particular good or service

To understand how a market economy works, consider what happens when you go to a fruit market to buy apples. While one vendor is selling apples for $1 per pound, another is charging $1.50. Both vendors are free to charge what they want, and you are free to buy what you choose. If both vendors' apples are of the same quality, you will buy the cheaper ones. If the $1.50 apples are fresher, you may buy them instead. In short, both buyers and sellers enjoy freedom of choice.

The "Wired World" box in this chapter discusses a much more complicated and technologically sophisticated market that has been created to bring buyers and sellers together through the Internet. This market is an outgrowth of a trend in information technology called "business-to-business," or "B2B." Whereas most early commercial Internet applications were directed toward consumers, B2B is a more recent development. Some experts think that it will be handling trillions of dollars annually in just a few years. As the term suggests, B2B involves electronic transactions between two or more businesses.

+ mixed economy

Input and Output Markets Figure 1.1, on page 9, shows a more complete model for better understanding how factors of production work in a pure market economy. According to this view, businesses and households interact in two different market relationships.[8] In the **input market,** firms buy resources from households, which are thus resource suppliers. In the **output market,** firms supply goods and services in response to household demand. (We provide a more detailed discussion of supply and demand later in this chapter.)

input market
Market in which firms buy resources from supplier households

As you can see, the activities of these two markets create a circular flow. Ford Motor Co., for example, relies on various kinds of inputs. It buys labor directly from households, which may also supply capital by using their savings to buy Ford stock. Consumer buying patterns furnish information when Ford must decide which models to produce and which to discontinue. In turn, Ford uses

output market
Market in which firms supply goods and services in response to demand on the part of households

Electronic B2B in the Auto Industry

In earlier times, markets were physical locations where buyers and sellers gathered to conduct transactions. We still use such venues for selling fish, fruits and vegetables, and antiques and collectibles, but most markets today differ in a fundamental respect: Buyers and sellers do not actually meet at some place, but rather they arrange exchanges via mail, telephone, fax machine, and so forth. The growth of the Internet makes it even easier for buyers and sellers to do business at great distances in what might be called *virtual markets* (the best known of which is perhaps eBay).

A good example of this trend is a partnership formed by some of the world's largest carmakers. It started when individual automakers began creating global purchasing Web sites. Ford Motor Co. <www.ford.com>, for instance, planned a site dubbed AutoXchange. The company intended to post all of its global procurement needs here, while requesting that suppliers post information on availability and prices.

When it became apparent that other automakers were planning to do the same thing, major suppliers to the auto industry realized that they might soon be facing an unwieldy array of separate Web sites—a situation that would potentially drive up rather than reduce their costs. A group of large suppliers approached Ford and GM with an alternative: Why not team up and create one site that both automakers and suppliers could use?

Ford and GM executives quickly saw the wisdom of the idea and then convinced DaimlerChrysler to join them. They announced plans to establish a single Web site as a marketplace for all automobile manufacturers, suppliers, and dealers—essentially, a global virtual market consisting of every firm in the industry. France's Renault and Japan's Nissan signed up almost immediately, along with Oracle (which would handle the software) and banker Commerce One (to provide the financing). France's PSA Peugeot Citroen joined in late 2001.

As things began to take shape, the partners realized that their venture could be a stand-alone business. They named it Covisint <www.covisint.com>, and by 2002, the new venture had offices in Southfield, Michigan, Amsterdam, and Tokyo. The impact of Covisint has already been profound. Before Covisint, it cost GM <www.gm.com> about $100 in ordering costs to buy parts or supplies the traditional way—on paper or over the telephone. Now, however, GM reports that the same costs have dipped under $10. Clearly, automakers are realizing substantial savings, and experts say that suppliers will also benefit. Besides getting access to more information about the needs of their customers, they can now buy and sell among themselves.

inputs to become a supplier to households, designing and building automobiles, trucks, and sports utility vehicles and offering them for sale to consumers.

Capitalism Individuals, meanwhile, are free to work for Ford or anyone else, and they are free to invest in Ford stock or to put their money elsewhere, whether saving it or spending it on products they need or want. Likewise, Ford can create the vehicles it chooses and sell them at the prices it chooses. Consumers, of course, are free to buy their next car from Ford or Toyota or BMW. This process contrasts markedly with that of a planned economy, in which individuals may be told where they can and cannot work, companies may be told what they can and cannot make, and consumers may have little or no choice in what they purchase or how much they pay. The political basis of market processes is called **capitalism,** which sanctions the private ownership of the factors of production and encourages entrepreneurship by offering profits as an incentive. The economic basis of market processes is the operation of demand and supply, which we discuss in the next section.

capitalism

Market economy that provides for private ownership of production and encourages entrepreneurship by offering profits as an incentive

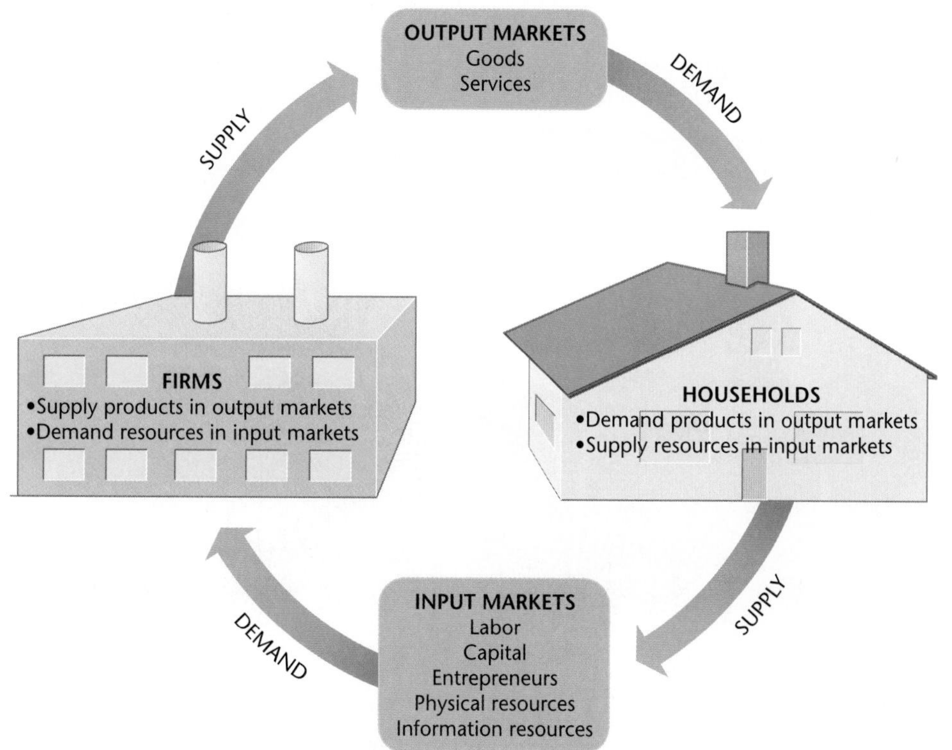

FIGURE 1.1
Circular Flow in a Market Economy

Mixed Market Economies There is no such thing as "pure" planned or "pure" market economies. Most countries rely on some form of **mixed market economy** that features characteristics of both planned and market economies. Even a market economy that strives to be as free and open as possible, such as the U.S. economy, restricts certain activities. Some products can't be sold legally, others can be sold only to people of a certain age, advertising must be truthful, and so forth.

mixed market economy
Economic system featuring characteristics of both planned and market economies

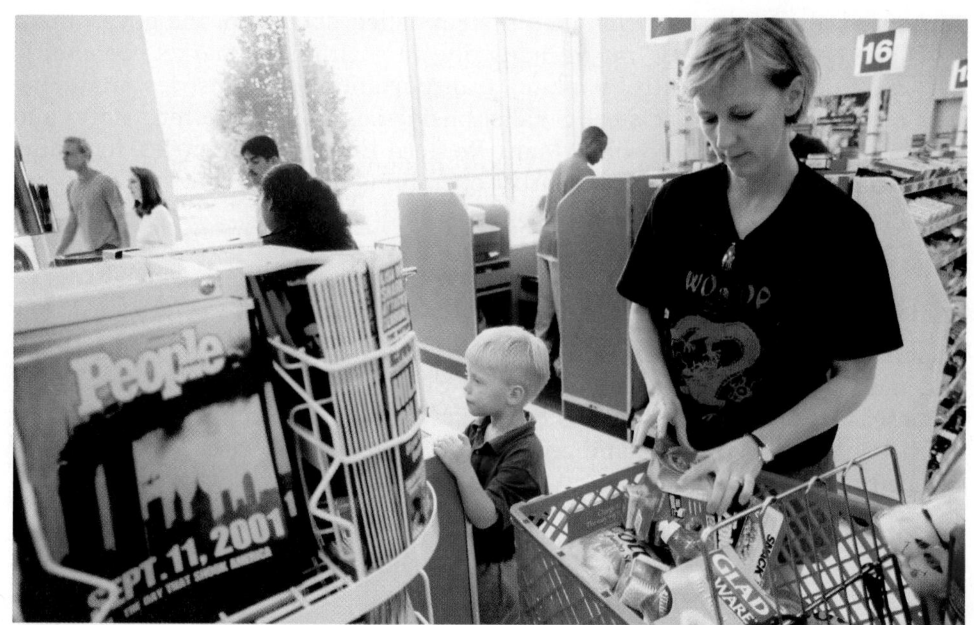

According to the model of circular flow in a market economy, this shopper at an Atlanta Target store plays a role in the output market: she demands goods that are supplied by a firm in the retailing business. Think of the employees who work for the firms from which Target <www.target.com> *buys its products as households that supply the input market with labor, time, and skills.*

"Your Honor, my client pleads guilty to an overzealous but well-intentioned pursuit of the profit motive."

privatization
Process of converting government enterprises into privately owned companies

Many former Eastern bloc countries have adopted market mechanisms through **privatization**—the process of converting government enterprises into privately owned companies. In recent years, the practice has spread to many other countries as well. For example, the postal system in many countries is government-owned and government-managed. The Netherlands, however, recently began privatizing its TNT Post Group N.V., already among the world's most efficient post-office operations. Canada has privatized its air traffic control system. In each case, the new enterprise reduced its payroll, boosted efficiency and productivity, and quickly became profitable.

socialism
Planned economic system in which the government owns and operates only selected major sources of production

Socialism In the partially planned system called **socialism,** the government owns and operates *selected* major industries. In such mixed market economies, the government may control banking, transportation, or industries producing such basic goods as oil and steel. Smaller businesses, such as clothing stores and restaurants, are privately owned. Many Western European countries, including England and France, allow free market operations in most economic areas but keep government control of others, such as health care.

The Economics of a Market System

Understanding the complex nature of the U.S. economic system is essential to understanding the environment in which U.S. businesses operate. In this section, we describe the workings of the U.S. market economy. Specifically, we examine markets, the nature of demand and supply, private enterprise, and degrees of competition.

Demand and Supply in a Market Economy

A market economy consists of many different markets. We have already described input and output markets, but we need to remember that the inputs

Self-Check Questions 1–3

*You should now be able to answer Self Check Questions 1–3**

1. MULTIPLE CHOICE Which of the following is **not** considered a basic *factor of production?* [select one] **(a)** labor; **(b)** buildings and equipment; **(c)** capital; **(d)** entrepreneurs; **(e)** physical resources.

2. MULTIPLE CHOICE If you buy stock in Newell Rubbermaid Corp., you have entered which of the following markets? [select one] **(a)** over-the-counter; **(b)** reseller; **(c)** labor; **(d)** output; **(e)** input.

3. TRUE/FALSE If 18 percent of its total production and 16 percent of its employment are created by its government, which also collects 30 percent of its total income in taxes, a nation does not really have a *free market economy.*

*ANSWERS TO SELF-CHECK QUESTIONS 1–3 CAN BE FOUND ON P. AN-1.

used by business and the products created by business have their own markets. In each of these markets, businesses decide what inputs to buy, what to make and in what quantities, and what prices to charge. Likewise, customers decide what to buy and how much they want to pay. Literally billions of such exchanges take place every day between businesses and individuals; between businesses; and among individuals, businesses, and governments. Moreover, exchanges conducted in one area often affect exchanges elsewhere.

Since 2000, for example, several factors have influenced computer purchases. In the late 1990s, for instance, many companies increased computer budgets in anticipation of Y2K problems but then cut them once the scare was over. Some companies began to reallocate outlays for technology, spending less on desktop computers and more on back-office equipment for e-business.

In addition, some firms simply started to slow down their upgrade cycles because brand-new computers were not sufficiently superior to those they had purchased just a few years earlier. Rather than upgrade every two or three years, as they had in the 1990s, many firms now upgrade every three or four years. As U.S. demand dropped, firms like Dell and IBM cut prices to keep sales from slumping too far, and lower prices mean lower profits per unit. At the same time, however, demand in other parts of the world, notably in China and India, has continued to rise, though not enough to offset domestic declines. Finally, lower profit expectations induced investors to pay less for the stocks of some computer firms, causing those prices to fall as well.[9]

The Laws of Demand and Supply On all economic levels, decisions about what to buy and what to sell are determined primarily by the forces of demand and supply.[10] **Demand** is the willingness and ability of buyers to purchase a product (a good or a service). **Supply** is the willingness and ability of producers to offer a good or service for sale. Generally speaking, demand and supply follow basic laws:

- The **law of demand:** Buyers will purchase (*demand*) more of a product as its price drops and less as its price increases.

demand
The willingness and ability of buyers to purchase a good or service

supply
The willingness and ability of producers to offer a good or service for sale

law of demand
Principle that buyers will purchase (demand) more of a product as its price drops and less as its price increases

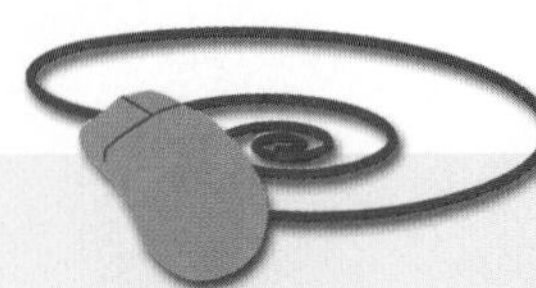

Mid-Chapter Internet Field Trip

"Easy as Dell"

In the first part of this chapter, we defined a *business* as an organization that provides goods and services to earn profits. What's the difference between a *good* and a *service*? To fit our definition, must a business offer *both* goods and services? Or do some businesses offer just goods and some just services?

Let's look further into these questions by exploring the Web site of a successful American company—Dell Computer Corp., at <www.dell.com>. The home page shows that the site is divided into five major areas:

- Servers & Storage
- Notebooks & Desktops
- Networking
- Software & Peripherals
- Services

Click on **Notebooks & Desktops:**

❶ What general product categories are promoted on this page?

Now click on **Desktops:**

❷ What general product categories are promoted on this page? Are these products primarily goods or services?

❸ What is the first service that Dell offers on this page?

Now go back to the home page at <www.dell.com>. Click on **Services:**

❹ How does Dell classify its service products?

On the **Services** page, scroll up the menu and click on **Case Studies.** Now scroll down to the heading **Rapid Deployment (Installation and Dell Custom Factory Integration Services).** Scroll down the list and click on **Fleming:**

❺ What did Dell do for Fleming?

To continue your Internet Field Trip, click on www.prenhall.com/griffin

law of supply
Principle that producers will offer (supply) more of a product for sale as its price rises and less as its price drops

demand and supply schedule
Assessment of the relationships among different levels of demand and supply at different price levels

demand curve
Graph showing how many units of a product will be demanded (bought) at different prices

supply curve
Graph showing how many units of a product will be supplied (offered for sale) at different prices

market price (or equilibrium price)
Profit-maximizing price at which the quantity of goods demanded and the quantity of goods supplied are equal

- The **law of supply:** Producers will offer (*supply*) more of a product for sale as its price rises and less as its price drops.[11]

The Demand and Supply Schedule To appreciate these laws in action, consider the market for pizza in your town (or neighborhood). If everyone is willing to pay $25 for a pizza (a relatively high price), the town's only pizzeria will produce a large supply. But if everyone is willing to pay only $5 (a relatively low price), it will make fewer pizzas. Through careful analysis, we can determine how many pizzas will be sold at different prices. These results, called a **demand and supply schedule,** are obtained from marketing research, historical data, and other studies of the market. Properly applied, they reveal the relationships among different levels of demand and supply at different price levels.

Demand and Supply Curves The demand and supply schedule can be used to construct demand and supply curves for pizza in your town. A **demand curve** shows how many products—in this case, pizzas—will be demanded (bought) at different prices. A **supply curve** shows how many pizzas will be supplied (baked or offered for sale) at different prices.

Figure 1.2 shows demand and supply curves for pizzas. As you can see, demand increases as price decreases; supply increases as price increases. When demand and supply curves are plotted on the same graph, the point at which they intersect is the **market price** or **equilibrium price**—the price at which the quantity of goods demanded and the quantity of goods supplied are equal. In Figure 1.2, the equilibrium price for pizzas in our example is $10. At this point, the quantity of pizzas demanded and the quantity of pizzas supplied are the same: 1,000 pizzas per week.

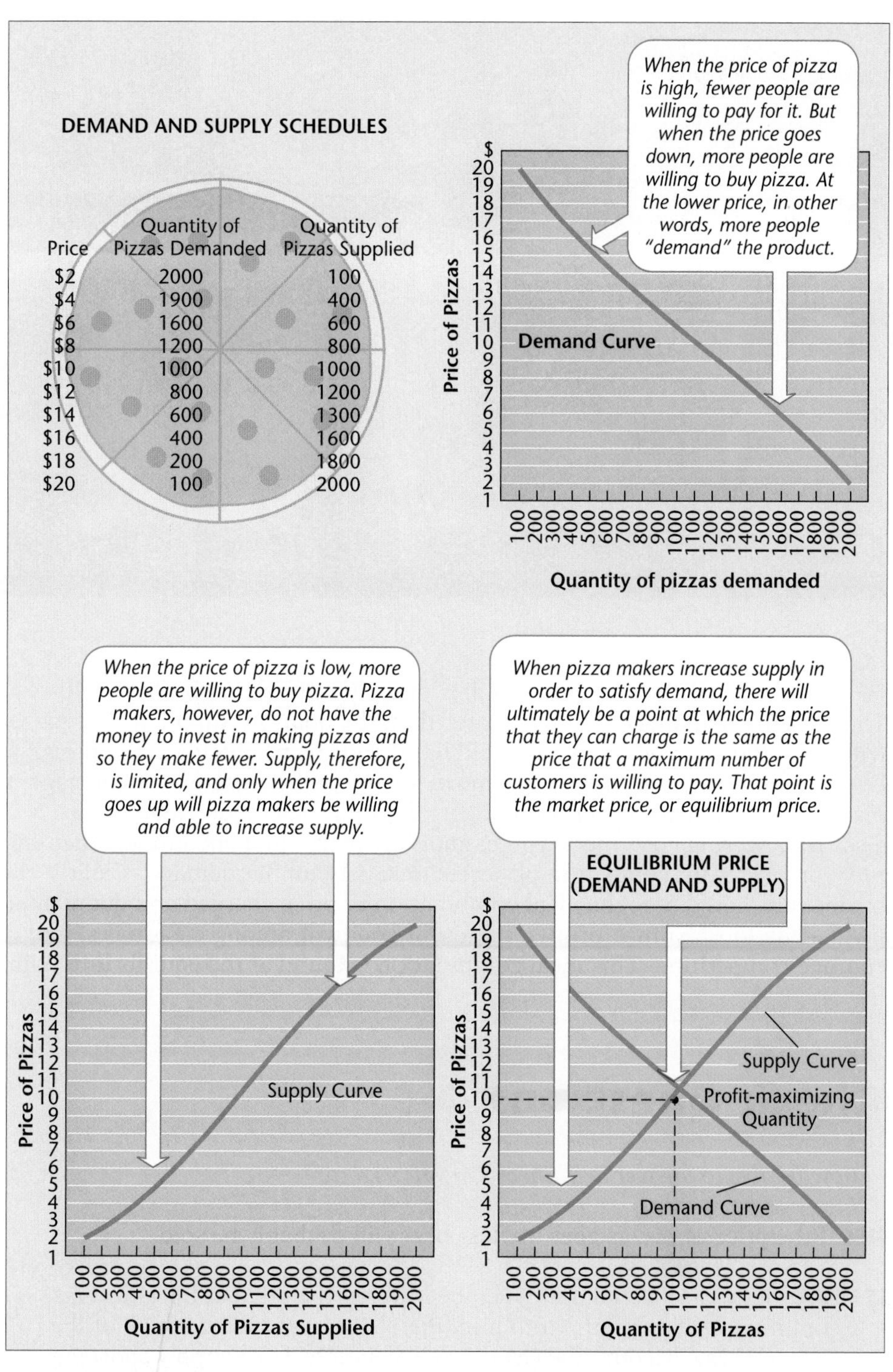

DEMAND AND SUPPLY SCHEDULES
Price
Quantity of Pizzas Demanded
Quantity of Pizzas Supplied
$2 2000 100
$4 1900 400
$6 1600 600
$8 1200 800
$10 1000 1000
$12 800 1200
$14 600 1300
$16 400 1600
$18 200 1800
$20 100 2000
When the price of pizza is high, fewer people are willing to pay for it. But when the price goes down, more people are willing to buy pizza. At the lower price, in other words, more people "demand" the product.
Demand Curve
Price of Pizzas
Quantity of pizzas demanded
When the price of pizza is low, more people are willing to buy pizza. Pizza makers, however, do not have the money to invest in making pizzas and so they make fewer. Supply, therefore, is limited, and only when the price goes up will pizza makers be willing and able to increase supply.
Supply Curve
Quantity of Pizzas Supplied
When pizza makers increase supply in order to satisfy demand, there will ultimately be a point at which the price that they can charge is the same as the price that a maximum number of customers is willing to pay. That point is the market price, or equilibrium price.
EQUILIBRIUM PRICE (DEMAND AND SUPPLY)
Supply Curve
Profit-maximizing Quantity
Demand Curve
Quantity of Pizzas

FIGURE 1.2
Demand and Supply

Surpluses and Shortages What if the pizzeria decides to make some other number of pizzas? For example, what would happen if the owner tried to increase profits by making *more* pizzas to sell? Or what if the owner wanted to lower overhead, cut back on store hours, and *reduce* the number of pizzas offered for sale? In either case, the result would be an inefficient use of resources and lower profits. For instance, if the pizzeria supplies 1,200 pizzas and tries to sell them for $10 each, 200 pizzas will not be bought. Our demand schedule shows that only 1,000 pizzas will be demanded at this price. The pizzeria will therefore have a **surplus**—a situation in which the quantity supplied exceeds the quantity demanded. It will lose the money that it spent making those extra 200 pizzas.

surplus
Situation in which quantity supplied exceeds quantity demanded

Economically speaking, surfing's up, but demand for surfware is riding an even higher crest—about 20 percent higher than a year ago. Surfware covers a lot of products—from wet suits to bikinis and boardshorts—and the demand comes from free-spending though notoriously fickle teenagers. Suppliers have to work hard not merely to meet demand, but to figure out what it's going to be hot from one week to the next. "I hang out at high schools and shopping malls," admits one designer. "I try to be a sponge and see what they want."

shortage
Situation in which quantity demanded exceeds quantity supplied

Conversely, if the pizzeria supplies only 800 pizzas, a **shortage** will result. The quantity demanded will be greater than the quantity supplied. The pizzeria will "lose" the extra profit that it could have made by producing 200 more pizzas. Even though consumers may pay more for pizzas because of the shortage, the pizzeria will still earn lower total profits than if it had made 1,000 pizzas. It will also risk angering customers who cannot buy pizzas and encourage other entrepreneurs to set up competing pizzerias to satisfy unmet demand. Clearly, then, businesses should seek the ideal combination of price charged and quantity supplied so as to maximize profits, maintain goodwill among customers, and discourage competition. This ideal combination is found at the equilibrium point.

Self-Check Questions 4–6

*You should now be able to answer Self-Check Questions 4–6**

4. TRUE/FALSE If the price of pizzas goes up, less beer will probably be sold.

5. MULTIPLE CHOICE Pierre discovered that when he lowered the price of his paintings, more people commissioned portraits from him. Pierre is experiencing which of the following? [select one] **(a)** discounting; **(b)** the law of supply; **(c)** a supply shortage; **(d)** the law of demand; **(e)** economic justice.

6. MULTIPLE CHOICE According to the principle of *demand and supply,* which of the following should happen if the price of eggs goes up? [select one] **(a)** Egg importers will try to persuade egg exporters to produce more eggs. **(b)** Producers will produce fewer eggs. **(c)** Shoppers will buy fewer eggs. **(d)** Shoppers will buy more eggs. **(e)** All of the above.

*Answers to Self-Check Questions 4–6 can be found on p. AN-1.

Our example involves only one company, one product, and a few buyers. Obviously, the U.S. economy is far more complex. Thousands of companies sell hundreds of thousands of products to millions of buyers every day. In the end, however, the result is much the same: Companies try to supply the quantity and selection of goods that will earn them the largest profits.

Private Enterprise and Competition in a Market Economy

Market economies rely on a **private enterprise** system—one that allows individuals to pursue their own interests with minimal government restriction. In turn, private enterprise requires the presence of four elements: private property rights, freedom of choice, profits, and competition.

private enterprise
Economic system that allows individuals to pursue their own interests without undue governmental restriction

- *Private property.* Ownership of the resources used to create wealth is in the hands of individuals.[12]
- *Freedom of choice.* You can sell your labor to any employer you choose. You can also choose which products to buy, and producers can usually choose whom to hire and what to produce.
- *Profits.* The lure of profits (and freedom) leads some people to abandon the security of working for someone else and to assume the risks of entrepreneurship. Anticipated profits also influence individuals' choices of which goods or services to produce.
- *Competition.* If profits motivate individuals to start businesses, competition motivates them to operate those businesses efficiently. **Competition** occurs when two or more businesses vie for the same resources or customers. To gain an advantage over competitors, a business must produce its goods or services efficiently and be able to sell at a reasonable profit. To achieve these goals, it must convince customers that its products are either better or less expensive than those of its competitors. Competition, therefore, forces all businesses to make products better or cheaper. A company that produces inferior, expensive products is likely to fail. We discuss competition more fully in the next section.

competition
Vying among businesses for the same resources or customers

Degrees of Competition Even in a free enterprise system, not all industries are equally competitive. Economists have identified four degrees of competition in a private enterprise system: *perfect competition, monopolistic competition, oligopoly,* and *monopoly.* Table 1.1 summarizes the features of these four degrees.

Characteristic	Perfect Competition	Monopolistic Competition	Oligopoly	Monopoly
Example	Local farmer	Stationery store	Steel industry	Public utility
Number of competitors	Many	Many, but fewer than in pure competition	Few	None
Ease of entry into industry	Relatively easy	Fairly easy	Difficult	Regulated by government
Similarity of goods or services offered by competing firms	Identical	Similar	Can be similar or different	No directly competing goods or services
Level of control over price by individual firms	None	Some	Some	Considerable

TABLE 1.1
Degrees of Competition

perfect competition
Market or industry characterized by numerous small firms producing an identical product

Perfect Competition For **perfect competition** to exist, two conditions must prevail: (1) all firms in an industry must be small and (2) the number of firms in the industry must be large. Under these conditions, no single firm is powerful enough to influence the price of its product. Prices are therefore determined by such market forces as supply and demand.

In addition, these two conditions also reflect four principles:

1. The products of each firm are so similar that buyers view them as identical to those of other firms.
2. Both buyers and sellers know the prices that others are paying and receiving in the marketplace.
3. Because each firm is small, it is easy for firms to enter or leave the market.
4. Going prices are set exclusively by supply and demand and accepted by both sellers and buyers.

U.S. agriculture is a good example of perfect competition. The wheat produced on one farm is the same as that from another. Both producers and buyers are aware of prevailing market prices. It is relatively easy to start producing wheat and relatively easy to stop when it's no longer profitable.

monopolistic competition
Market or industry characterized by numerous buyers and relatively numerous sellers trying to differentiate their products from those of competitors

Monopolistic Competition Fewer sellers are involved in **monopolistic competition** than in pure competition, but because there are still many buyers, sellers try to make products at least *seem* to differ from those of competitors. Differentiating strategies include brand names (Tide and Cheer), design or styling (Polo and Tommy Hilfiger jeans), and advertising (Coke and Pepsi). For example, in an effort to attract health-conscious consumers, the Kraft Foods division of Philip Morris <www.kraftfoods.com/index.cgi> promotes such differentiated products as low-fat Cool Whip, low-calorie Jell-O, and sugar-free Kool-Aid.

Monopolistically competitive businesses may be large or small, but they can still enter or leave the market easily. For example, many small clothing stores compete successfully with large apparel retailers such as Liz Claiborne <www.lizclaiborne.com> and Limited Brands <www.limited.com>. bebe stores <www.bebe.com> is a good case in point. The small clothing chain controls its own manufacturing facilities and can respond just as quickly as firms like Gap Inc. <www.gap.com> to changes in fashion tastes.[13] Many single-store clothing businesses in college towns compete by developing their own T-shirt and cap designs with copyrighted slogans and logos.

Product differentiation also gives sellers some control over prices. For instance, even though Sears shirts may have similar styling and other features, Ralph Lauren Polo shirts can be priced with little regard for lower Sears prices. But the large number of buyers relative to sellers applies potential limits to prices: Although Polo might be able to sell shirts for, say, \$20 more than a comparable Sears shirt, it could not sell as many shirts if they were priced at \$200 more.

oligopoly
Market or industry characterized by a handful of (generally large) sellers with the power to influence the prices of their products

Oligopoly When an industry has only a handful of sellers, an **oligopoly** exists. As a general rule, these sellers are quite large. The entry of new competitors is hard because large capital investment is needed. Thus oligopolistic industries (the automobile, airline, and steel industries) tend to stay that way.[14] Only two companies make large commercial aircraft: Boeing (a U.S. company) and Airbus (a European consortium). Furthermore, as the trend toward globalization continues, most experts believe that, as one forecaster puts it, "global oligopolies are as inevitable as the sunrise."[15]

Oligopolists have more control over their strategies than monopolistically competitive firms, but the actions of one firm can significantly affect the sales of every other firm in the industry. For example, when one firm cuts prices or offers incentives to increase sales, the others usually protect sales by doing the same. Likewise, when one firm raises prices, others generally follow suit. Therefore, the prices of comparable products are usually similar. When an airline announces new fare discounts, others adopt the same strategy almost immediately. Just as quickly, when discounts end for one airline, they usually end for everyone else.

"Global oligopolies are as inevitable as the sunrise."
~Louis Galambos
BUSINESS HISTORIAN

Monopoly A **monopoly** exists when an industry or market has only one producer. Obviously, a sole supplier enjoys complete control over the prices of its products. Its only constraint is a decrease in consumer demand due to increased prices.[16] In the United States, laws such as the Sherman Antitrust Act (1890) and the Clayton Act (1914) forbid many monopolies and regulate prices charged by **natural monopolies**—industries in which one company can most efficiently supply all needed goods or services.[17] Many electric companies are natural monopolies because they can supply all the power needed in a local area. Duplicate facilities—such as two power plants and two sets of power lines—would be wasteful. In addition, the Enron debacle (as chronicled in our chapter-opening story) shows what kinds of things can happen if utilities are carelessly deregulated.

monopoly
Market or industry in which there is only one producer, which can therefore set the prices of its products

natural monopoly
Industry in which one company can most efficiently supply all needed goods or services

A Short History of Business in the United States

The landscape of U.S. business has evolved over the course of many decades. Specifically, a look at the history of U.S. business shows a steady development from sole proprietorships to today's intricate corporate structures. We can gain a more detailed understanding of this development by tracing its history.

The Factory System and the Industrial Revolution

With the coming of the **Industrial Revolution** in the middle of the eighteenth century, a manufacturing revolution was made possible by advances in technology and by the development of the factory system. Replacing hundreds of cottage workers who had turned out one item at a time, the factory system brought together in one place the materials and workers required to produce items in large quantities and the new machines needed for mass production.

Industrial Revolution
Major mid-eighteenth century change in production characterized by a shift to the factory system, mass production, and the specialization of labor

In turn, mass production reduced duplication of equipment and allowed firms to buy raw materials at better prices by buying in large lots. Even more important, it encouraged specialization of labor. Mass production replaced a system of highly skilled craftspeople who performed all the different tasks required to make a single item. Instead, a series of semiskilled workers, each trained to perform only one task and aided by specialized equipment, greatly increased output.

Laissez-Faire and the Entrepreneurial Era

Despite problems during the nineteenth century, the U.S. banking system began freeing businesses from European capital markets. In addition, improvements in transportation—steamboat navigation on major rivers and the development of railroads—soon made it economical to move products to distant markets.

Another key feature of the times was the rise of the entrepreneur on a grand scale. Like businesses in many other nations, U.S. business embraced the philosophy of *laissez-faire*—the idea that the government should not interfere in the economy. Rather, it should let business run without regulation and according to its own "natural" laws.[18]

Risk taking and entrepreneurship became hallmarks of aggressive practices that created some of the biggest companies in the country and, ultimately, the world. During the last half of the 1800s, for instance, Andrew Carnegie founded U.S. Steel and Andrew Mellon created the Aluminum Company of America (Alcoa). J. P. Morgan's Morgan Guarantee and Trust came to dominate the U.S. financial system, and John D. Rockefeller's Standard Oil controlled—in fact, monopolized—the petroleum industry.

The rise of such enterprises increased the national standard of living and made the United States a world power. But the economic power of such firms made it hard, if not impossible, for competitors to enter their markets. Complete market control became a watchword in many industries, with major corporations opting to collude rather than compete. Price fixing and other forms of market manipulation became business as usual, with captains of industry often behaving as robber barons. Reacting against unethical practices and the unregulated struggle for dominance, critics called for corrective action and, ultimately, for antitrust laws and the breakup of monopolies.

Among other important laws, the Sherman Antitrust Act of 1890 and the Clayton Act of 1914 were passed specifically to limit the control that a single business could gain over a market. Other laws sought to regulate a variety of employment and advertising practices, and still others regulated the ways in which businesses could handle their financial affairs. This antitrust legislation was the basis for the U.S. government's 1998 lawsuit against Microsoft Corp.[19] (The appendix to this book gives more information about the legal environment of U.S. business, much of which is rooted in this era.)

The Production Era

The concepts of specialization and mass production were further refined in the early twentieth century, when many analysts sought to focus management's attention on the production process. As a result of the work of the theorists of so-called scientific management, increased efficiency through the "one best way" to accomplish production tasks became a major goal of management. Developed during the early 1900s, scientific management focused on maximizing output by developing the most efficient and productive ways for workers to perform carefully designed tasks.

Scientific management was given further impetus when, in 1913, Henry Ford introduced the moving assembly line and ushered in the **production era.** Ford's focus was on manufacturing efficiency: By adopting fixed workstations, increasing task specialization, and moving the work to the worker, Ford increased productivity and lowered prices. In so doing, he made the automobile affordable for the average person.

production era

Period during the early twentieth century in which U.S. business focused primarily on improving productivity and manufacturing efficiency

The Concept of Countervailing Powers Both the growth of corporations and improved assembly-line output came at the expense of worker freedom. The dominance of big firms made it harder for individuals to go into business for themselves, and in some cases, employer-run company towns gave people little freedom of choice, either in selecting an employer or in choosing what products to buy. If balance were to be restored to the system, two elements had to grow in power: government and organized labor. Thus, the production era witnessed the rise of labor unions and the advent of collective bargaining (see Chapter 9).

In addition, the Great Depression of the 1930s and World War II prompted the government to intervene in the economic system on an unprecedented scale. Today, economists and politicians often refer to business, government, and labor as the three countervailing powers in American society. Although all are big and all are strong, none completely dominates the others.

The Marketing Era

After World War II, the demand for consumer goods that had been frustrated by wartime shortages fueled the U.S. economy for some time. Despite brief recessions, the 1950s and 1960s were prosperous. Production continued to increase, technology to advance, and the standard of living to rise. During this era, a new philosophy of business came of age—the marketing concept. Previously, businesses had been production and sales oriented. They tended to produce what other businesses produced, what they thought customers wanted, or simply what owners wanted to produce. Henry Ford, for example, is supposed to have said that his customers could buy his cars in whatever color they wanted—as long as it was black.

According to the **marketing concept,** however, business starts with the customer. Producers start by determining what customers want and then provide it. Successful practitioners of the marketing concept include such companies as Procter & Gamble (P&G) and Anheuser-Busch. Such firms let consumers choose what best suits their needs by offering an array of products within a given market (toothpaste or beer, for example).

marketing concept
Idea that a business must focus on identifying and satisfying consumer wants in order to be profitable

The Global Era

The 1980s saw the continuation of technological advances in production, computer technology, information systems, and communications capabilities. They also witnessed the emergence of a truly global economy. American consumers now drive cars made in Japan, wear sweaters made in Italy, and listen to CD players made in Taiwan. Elsewhere around the world, people drive Fords, drink Pepsi, wear Levi's, use IBMs, and watch Disney movies and television shows.

As we will see in Chapter 3, globalization is a fact of life for most businesses today. Improved communication and transportation, in addition to more efficient international methods for financing, producing, distributing, and marketing products and services, have combined to open distant marketplaces to businesses as never before.[20]

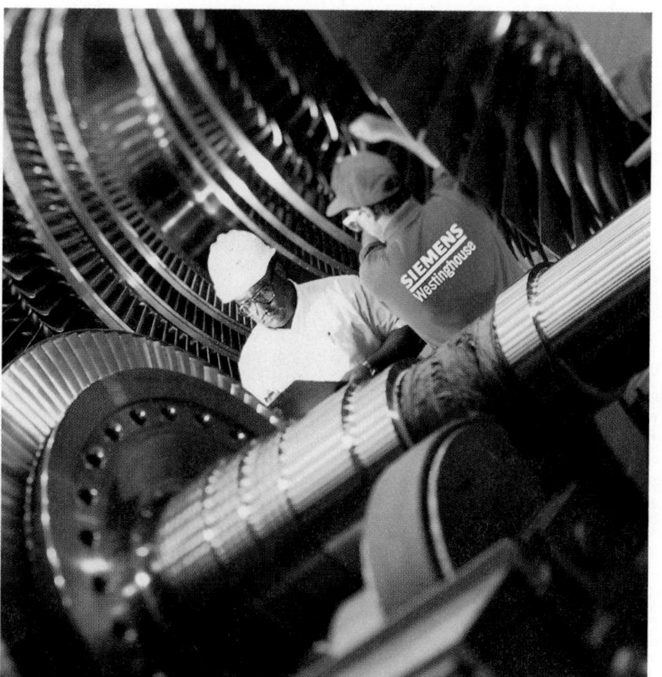

Globalization is a fact of contemporary business life, and even the powerhouse U.S. conglomerate General Electric has an international archrival. Based in Germany, Siemens A.G. <www.siemens.com> *(which, like GE, makes everything from high-tech medical equipment to light bulbs) spent $6 billion in the last three years to buy American companies like this plant in Charlotte, North Carolina, which makes turbine-engine components. Last year, Siemens piled up $16.2 billion in U.S. sales, and it expects to do $25 billion by 2004.*

Admittedly, many U.S. businesses have been hurt by foreign competition. Many others, however, have profited from new foreign markets. International competition has also forced many U.S. businesses to work harder to cut costs, increase efficiency, and improve quality. We explore a variety of important trends, opportunities, and challenges in the new global era throughout this book.

The Internet Era

The turn of the century has been accompanied by what many experts are calling the Internet era. Internet usage in North America grew from about 100 users per 1,000 people in 1995 to over 450 users per 1,000 in 2000. Projections call for this figure to grow to nearly 750 users per 1,000 by 2005. The growth rate in Western Europe, however, is expected to be even faster and, by 2005, will become significant in the Asia Pacific region as well.

How does the growth of the Internet affect business? In at least three ways:

1. ***The Internet will give a dramatic boost to trade in all sectors of the economy, especially services.*** If the Internet makes it easier for all trade to grow, this is particularly true for trade in services on an international scale.
2. ***The Internet will help to level the playing field, at least to some extent, between larger and smaller enterprises regardless of their products.*** In the past, a substantial investment was needed in order to enter some industries and to expand into foreign markets. Now, however, a small business in central Missouri, southern Italy, eastern Malaysia, or northern Brazil can set up a Web site and compete with much larger businesses located around the world.
3. ***The Internet holds considerable potential as an effective and efficient networking mechanism.*** So-called business-to-business networks (discussed earlier in this chapter) can link firms with suppliers, customers, and strategic partners in ways that make it faster and easier for everyone to do business.[21]

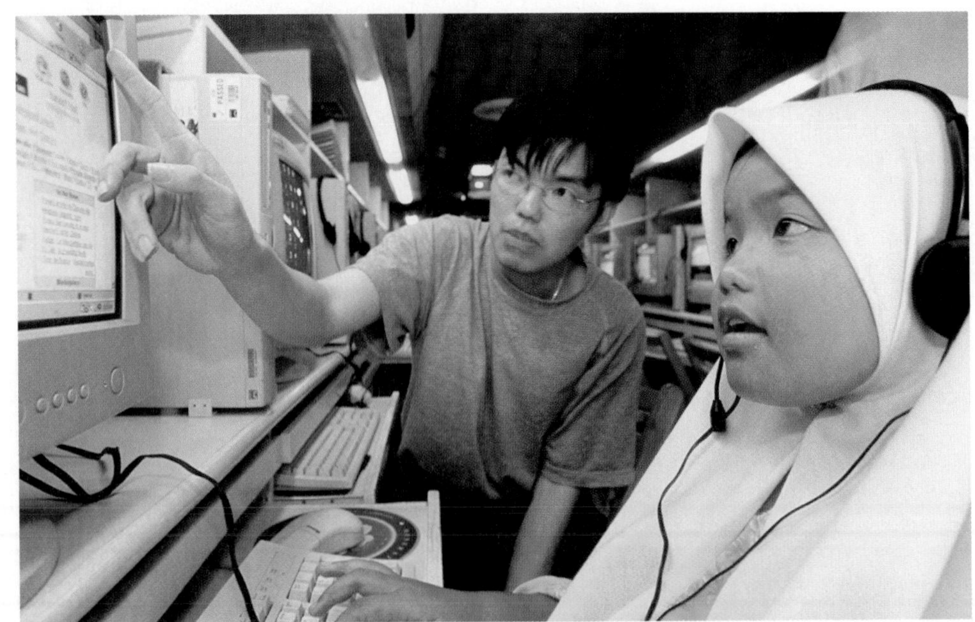

The Mobile Internet Unit is a sort of digital bookmobile for students at the poorest, most remote schools in Malaysia. Developed in conjunction with the United Nations, the program introduces students to PCs and provides teachers to help them learn how to navigate the Internet and send e-mail. Converted buses also leave behind PCs, modems, and Internet account numbers so that students can practice and teachers can build computer skills into their curricula.

Self-Check Questions 7–9

*You should now be able to answer Self-Check Questions 7–9.**

7. MULTIPLE CHOICE In addition to competition, which of the following is a required element in *private enterprise?* [select one] **(a)** adequate representation in government; **(b)** freedom from foreign competition; **(c)** natural resources; **(d)** freedom of choice; **(e)** all of the above.

8. TRUE/FALSE If you have to buy a newspaper from a store in a town that has only one newspaper publisher, then your local newspaper has a *monopoly.*

9. MULTIPLE CHOICE Which of the following is the most likely pricing approach to be taken by a monopoly [select one] **(a)** charging customers whatever it pleases; **(b)** giving customers a real bargain on price; **(c)** charging a price that will not depress consumer demand; **(d)** undercutting the prices of the competition; **(e)** concentrating on quality and service rather than price.

*ANSWERS TO SELF-CHECK QUESTIONS 1–3 CAN BE FOUND ON P. AN-1.

Continued from page 4

Blackouts and Other Dark Forces

The energy situation in California became dire in late 2000. Weakened by complicated market patterns and the schemes of Enron and other energy providers, the state's ISO could no longer monitor everything, and control of the process was essentially abandoned. An early cold spell in Oregon and Washington forced those states to keep all their surplus energy, thus reducing the supply of power available for sale to California. Meanwhile, Enron and other suppliers had managed to manufacture their own power shortage in California by sending much of their electricity to other markets with higher prices. Blackouts became more common because the electricity supply could not meet consumer demand.

In response, California lifted its price caps, raising the price of a megawatt hour from $43.80 at the beginning of 2000 to $292.10 at the beginning of 2001. Although the supply of power increased immediately, consumer electric bills shot up by 67 percent, causing a statewide uproar. Price caps were reinstated in June 2001, but only as a temporary measure. Shortly thereafter, Enron began to collapse like a house of cards, and California seems to have been spared future shenanigans. Critics of current measures, however, worry that if price caps are permanently lifted, other companies can step in and do the same sort of things that Enron did.

Although Adam Smith lived in simpler times, it's amazing how well his theories of free enterprise hold up today. But in our complex business world, it is also clear that in the process of amassing profits, businesses which focus exclusively on profits can do a great deal of harm. Enron is today's standard for abuse of the free-enterprise system, but other examples will no doubt emerge in years to come. On the other hand, we shouldn't forget that there are literally thousands of businesses that routinely rely on supply and demand and freedom of choice while applying ethical and socially responsible principles, appropriate corporate strategies, and effective leadership in their pursuit of legitimate goals.

Questions for Discussion

1. What were the basic factors of production used by Enron?
2. Describe the concepts of input and output markets as they apply to Enron's operations.
3. Explain how the concepts of demand and supply affected both Enron's successes and failures.
4. Does the Enron case increase or decrease your confidence in a capitalistic system based on private enterprise?
5. What degree of competition exists in a regulated utility environment? What kind of competition did California attempt to create?

Summary of Learning Objectives

1. ***Define the nature of U.S.* business *and identify its main goals and functions.***

A **business** is an organization that provides goods or services to earn profits. The prospect of earning **profits**—the difference between a business's revenues and expenses—encourages people to open and expand businesses. Profits reward owners for taking the risks involved in investing their money and time.

Businesses produce most of the goods and services that Americans consume and employ most working people. New forms of technology, service businesses, and international opportunities promise to keep production, consumption, and employment growing indefinitely. Business profits go to millions of owners and stockholders, and business taxes help support governments. Finally, many businesses support charitable causes and provide community leadership.

2. ***Describe the different types of global* economic systems *according to the means by which they control the* factors of production *through* input and output markets.**

An **economic system** is a nation's system for allocating its resources among its citizens, both individuals and organizations. Economic systems differ in the ways in which they manage the five **factors of production**—the basic resources that a country's businesses use to produce goods and services: (1) The people who work for businesses provide **labor,** or **human resources,** which includes both the physical and mental contributions that people make during economic production. (2) Obtaining and using material resources and labor requires **capital**—the funds needed to start a business and to keep it operating and growing. *Capital* may also include nonfinancial resources.

(3) **Entrepreneurs** embrace the opportunities and accept the risks inherent in starting new businesses and expanding small businesses. (4) **Physical resources** are the tangible things (including natural resources, facilities, parts and supplies, and other equipment) with which organizations conduct business. (5) Much business activity consists of **information resources**—in either creating new information or repackaging existing information for new users.

Different types of economic systems also differ in the ways decisions are made about production and allocation. A **planned economy** relies on a centralized government to control factors of production and make decisions. Under *communism,* the government owns and operates all sources of production. In a **market economy,** individuals—producers and consumers—control production and allocation decisions through supply and demand. A **market** is a mechanism for exchange between the buyers and sellers of a particular product or service. Sellers can charge what they want, and customers can buy what they choose.

In a market economy, businesses and households interact in two different relationships. In the **input market,** firms buy resources from households, which are thus suppliers. In the **output market,** firms supply goods and services in response to demand on the part of households. The political basis of market processes is **capitalism,** which fosters private ownership of the factors of production and encourages entrepreneurship by offering profits as an incentive.

There is no such thing as a "pure" planned or a "pure" market economy. In reality, most countries rely on some form of **mixed market economy**—a system featuring characteristics of both planned and market economies. Many countries that once had planned economies are now adopting market mechanisms through **privatization**—the process of converting government enterprises into privately owned companies. Under **socialism,** the government owns and operates selected major industries while smaller businesses are privately owned.

3. ***Show how* demand *and* supply *affect resource distribution in the United States.***

A market economy consists of many different markets. On all economic levels, decisions about what to buy and what to sell are determined by the forces of demand and supply. **Demand** is the willingness and ability of buyers to purchase a product or service. **Supply** is the willingness and ability of producers to offer a product or service for sale. The **law of demand** holds that buyers will purchase (*demand*) more of a product as its price drops and less as its price increases. The **law of supply** holds that producers will offer (*supply*) more of a product for sale as its price rises and less as its price drops.

A **demand and supply schedule,** which is obtained from marketing research and other studies of the market, reveals the relationships among different levels of demand and supply at different price levels. It can be used to construct both demand and supply curves. A **demand curve** shows how many products will be demanded (bought) at different prices. A **supply curve** shows how many products will be supplied (offered for sale) at different prices. When both curves are plotted on the same graph, the point at which they intersect is the **market price** or **equilibrium price**—the price at which the quantity of goods demanded and the quantity of goods supplied are equal. A **surplus** occurs when the quantity supplied exceeds the quantity demanded. A **shortage** results when the quantity demanded is greater than the quantity supplied. To maximize profits, all businesses must constantly seek the right combination of price charged and quantity supplied—the *equilibrium point.*

4. *Identify the elements of* private enterprise *and explain the various degrees of* competition *in the U.S. economic system.*

Market economies reflect the operation of a **private enterprise** system—a system that allows individuals to pursue their own interests without government restriction. Private enterprise requires and works according to four principles: (1) *Private property rights:* Ownership of the resources used to create wealth is in the hands of individuals. (2) *Freedom of choice:* Individuals can sell their labor to any employer they choose and choose which products to buy; producers can choose whom to hire and what to produce. (3) *Profits:* The lure of profits leads some people to assume the risks of entrepreneurship, and anticipated profits play a part in the choice of products sold. (4) *Competition:* **Competition** occurs when two or more businesses vie for the same resources or customers. To gain an advantage over its competitors, a business must produce products efficiently and sell them at a reasonable profit. To achieve these goals, it must convince customers that its products are better or less expensive than those of its competitors. Competition, therefore, forces all businesses to make products better or cheaper.

Economists have identified four degrees of competition in a private enterprise system. (1) For **perfect competition** to exist, no single firm can be powerful enough to influence the prices of its products, which are determined by such market forces as demand and supply. Every firm's products are so similar that buyers regard them as identical to those of all competitors. (2) Fewer sellers are involved in **monopolistic competition,** but because there are still many buyers, sellers try to make products *seem* different from those of competitors. Product differentiation gives sellers some control over prices. Differentiating strategies include brand names, design or styling, and advertising.

(3) When an industry has only a handful of sellers, an **oligopoly** exists. Oligopolists have more control over strategies than monopolistically competitive firms, but the actions of one firm can affect the sales of every other firm. Thus the prices of comparable products are usually similar. (4) A **monopoly** exists when an industry or market has only one producer, which enjoys complete control over prices. Its only constraint is a decrease in consumer demand due to increased prices. U.S. law regulates the prices charged by **natural monopolies**—industries in which one company can most efficiently supply all needed goods or services.

5. *Trace the history of business in the United States.*

The landscape of U.S. business has evolved over the course of many decades. This history can be broken down into six stages or eras.

(1) *The Factory System and the Industrial Revolution.* With the coming of the **Industrial Revolution** in the middle of the eighteenth century, the factory system brought together in one place the materials and workers required to produce items in large quantities and the new machines needed for mass production. Mass production reduced duplication of equipment and allowed firms to purchase raw materials at better prices by buying in large lots. Even more important, it encouraged specialization of labor.

(2) *Laissez-Faire and the Entrepreneurial Era.* The nineteenth century witnessed the rise of the entrepreneur on a grand scale, and U.S. business embraced the philosophy of *laissez-faire*—the principle that the government should not interfere in the economy but should let business function without regulation. Risk taking and entrepreneurship created some of the biggest companies in the world, increased the national standard of living, and made the United States a world power. Unfortunately, price fixing and other forms of market manipulation became common practices. Critics called for corrective action, and laws were passed to limit the control that a business could gain in any market.

(3) *The Production Era.* The concepts of specialization and mass production were refined in the early twentieth century, as many experts focused on the production process. *Scientific management* stressed maximizing output by developing the most efficient and productive ways for workers to perform tasks. In 1913, Henry Ford introduced the moving assembly line, concentrated on manufacturing efficiency, and ushered in the **production era.** Both the growth of corporations and improved assembly-line output came at the expense of worker freedom. Thus, the production era saw the rise of labor unions and the government protected practice of collective bargaining. Today, business, government, and labor are often referred to as the three *countervailing powers* in society.

(4) *The Marketing Era.* The 1950s and 1960s were generally prosperous, and a new philosophy of business came of age. According to the **marketing concept,** producers of goods and services begin by determining what customers want and then provide it.

(5) *The Global Era.* The 1980s saw further technological advances and the emergence of a global economy. Improved communication and transportation, in addition to more efficient international methods for financing, producing, distributing, and marketing products and services, have combined to open distant marketplaces to businesses. Although many U.S. businesses have been hurt by foreign competition, many others have profited from new foreign markets. International competition also has forced many U.S. businesses to cut costs, increase efficiency, and improve quality.

(6) *The Internet Era.* Internet usage should give a boost to trade in all sectors of the economy, especially services. It should also help to level the playing field between larger and smaller enterprises regardless of their products. Finally, the Net is promising as a networking mechanism among businesses.

KEY TERMS

business (p. 4)
profits (p. 4)
economic system (p. 5)
factors of production (p. 5)
labor (or ***human resources***) (p. 5)
capital (p. 5)
entrepreneur (p. 5)
physical resources (p. 6)
information resources (p. 6)
planned economy (p. 6)
market economy (p. 7)
market (p. 7)
input market (p. 7)
output market (p. 7)
capitalism (p. 8)
mixed market economy (p. 9)
privatization (p. 10)
socialism (p. 10)
demand (p. 12)
supply (p. 12)
law of demand (p. 12)
law of supply (p. 12)
demand and supply schedule (p. 12)
demand curve (p. 12)
supply curve (p. 12)
market price (or ***equilibrium price***) (p. 12)
surplus (p. 13)
shortage (p. 14)
private enterprise (p. 15)
competition (p. 15)
perfect competition (p. 16)
monopolistic competition (p. 16)
oligopoly (p. 16)
monopoly (p. 17)
natural monopoly (p. 17)
Industrial Revolution (p. 17)
production era (p. 18)
marketing concept (p. 19)

QUESTIONS AND EXERCISES

Questions for Review

1. What are the factors of production? Is one factor more important than the others? If so, which one? Why?
2. What are input and output markets? How are they related?
3. What is a demand curve? A supply curve? What is the term for the point at which they intersect?
4. Explain the differences between the four degrees of competition and give an example of each one. (Do not use the examples given in the text.)

Questions for Analysis

5. In recent years, many countries have moved from planned economies to market economies. Why do you think this has occurred? Can you envision a situation that would cause a resurgence of planned economies?
6. Cite an instance in which a surplus of a product led to decreased prices. Cite an instance in which a shortage led to increased prices. What eventually happened in each case? Why?
7. In your opinion, what industries in the United States should be regulated by the government? Why?

Application Exercises

8. Choose a locally owned business. Interview the owner to find out how it uses the factors of production and have him or her describe its means of acquiring them.
9. Visit a local shopping mall or shopping area. List each store that you see and determine what degree of competition it faces in its immediate environment. For example, if there is only one store in the mall that sells shoes, that store represents a monopoly. Note those businesses with direct competitors (two jewelry stores) and show how they compete with one another.
10. Go to the library or log onto the Internet and research 10 different industries. Classify each according to degree of competition.

Building Your Business Skills

PAYING THE PRICE OF DOING E-BUSINESS

This exercise enhances the following SCANS workplace competencies: demonstrating basic skills, demonstrating thinking skills, exhibiting interpersonal skills, and working with information.

Goal

To encourage students to understand how the competitive environment affects a product's price.

The Situation

Assume that you own a local business that provides Internet access to individuals and businesses. Yours is one of four such businesses in the local market. Each one charges the same price: $12 per month for unlimited dial-up service. You also provide e-mail service, as do two of your competitors. Two competitors give users free personal Web pages. One competitor just dropped its price to $10 per month, and the other two have announced that they'll follow suit. Your breakeven price is $7 per customer—that is, you must charge $7 for your service package in order to cover your costs. You are concerned about getting into a price war that may destroy your business.

Method

Divide into groups of four or five people. Each group should develop a general strategy for responding to competitors' price changes. Be sure to consider the following factors:

1. How demand for your product is affected by price changes
2. The number of competitors selling the same or a similar product
3. The methods you can use—other than price—to attract new customers and retain current customers

Analysis

Develop specific pricing strategies based on each of the following situations:

- A month after dropping the price to $10, one of your competitors raises it back to $12.
- Two of your competitors drop their prices even further—to $8 a month. As a result, your business falls off by 25 percent.
- One of the competitors who offers free Web pages announces that the service will become optional for an extra $2 a month.
- Two competitors announce that they will charge individual users $8 a month but will charge a higher price (not yet announced) for businesses.
- All four providers (including you) are charging $8 a month. One goes out of business, and you know that another is in poor financial health.

Follow-Up Questions

1. Discuss the role that various inducements other than price might play in affecting demand and supply in this market.
2. Is it always in a company's best interest to feature the lowest prices?
3. Eventually, what form of competition is likely to characterize this market?

Exercising Your Ethics

PRESCRIBING A DOSE OF COMPETITIVE MEDICINE

The Purpose of the Assignment

Demand and supply are key elements of the U.S. economic system. So, too, is competition. This exercise will challenge you to better understand the ethical dimensions of a system that relies on demand, supply, and competition.

The Situation

You are a businessperson in a small town, where you run one of two local pharmacies. The population and economic base are fairly stable. Each pharmacy controls about 50 percent of the market. Each is reasonably profitable, generating solid if unspectacular revenues.

The Dilemma

You have just been approached by the owner of the other pharmacy. He has indicated an interest either in buying your pharmacy or in selling his to you. He argues that neither of you can substantially increase your profits and complains that if one pharmacy raises its prices, customers will simply go to the other one. He tells you outright that if you sell to him, he plans to raise prices by 10 percent. He believes that the local market will have to accept the increase for two reasons: (1) The town is too small to attract national competitors, such as Walgreens, and (2) local customers can't go elsewhere to shop because the nearest town with a pharmacy is 40 miles away.

Questions for Discussion

1. What are the roles of supply, demand, and competition in this scenario?
2. What are the underlying ethical issues?
3. What would you do if you were actually faced with this situation?

Mastering Business Essentials

EPISODE 2 reminds us that although we live in a world of limited resources, our wants and needs remain unlimited. It thus encourages students to think about such phenomena as scarcity and such principles as opportunity costs. *This episode focuses on the chapter discussion of factors of production by raising issues about the use and availability of resources among modern organizations.*

Crafting Your Business Plan

MAKING SCENTS OF COMPETITION

The Purpose of the Assignment

1. To acquaint you with the process of navigating the *Business PlanPro (BPP)* software package.
2. To stimulate your thinking about how two chapter topics—forms of competition and factors of production—can be integrated as components in the *BPP* planning environment.

Assignment

After reading Chapter 1 in the textbook, open the BPP *software and look around for information about types of competition and factors of production as they apply to a sample firm:* Fantastic Florals Inc. *To find* Fantastic Florals, *do the following:*

Open the *Business PlanPro.* If it asks if you want to "create a new business plan" or "open an existing plan," select "create a new business plan" (even though you're not going to create a plan at this time). You will then be taken to the *Business PlanPro EasyPlan Wizard.* Click on the option entitled **Research It.** You will then be presented a new list of options, including **Sample Plan Browser.** After clicking on the **Sample Plan Browser,** go down the alphabetical list of sample plans and double-click on **Import—Artificial Flowers,** which is the location for *Fantastic Florals Inc.* The screen you are looking at is the introduction page for *Fantastic Florals'* business plan. Next, scroll down until you reach the **Table of Contents** for the company's business plan.

Now respond to the following items:

1. The Table of Contents page contains an outline of the company's business plan. After scanning the outline, click on **1.0 Executive Summary.** Explore the information on the screen to see what an Executive Summary looks like in BPP. As you will see, the length of the Executive Summary will vary for different companies' plans, with some containing longer summaries.
2. After returning to the Table of Contents page, scroll down the outline to review the categories within the business plan. Then click on some of the lines that you think might contain information about two of the chapter topics—forms of competition and factors of production. For example, **3.2 Competitive Comparison** may be one of the likely places to find information on forms of competition. As you explore, see how many of this company's factors of production (labor, capital, entrepreneurs, physical resources, information resources) you can find. Try to identify at least one example of each factor in *Fantastic Florals'* business plan.
3. After finishing with one sample company, you can get to other companies in various industries by returning to the **Sample Plan Browser,** entering the selection box containing the list of sample plans, and double-clicking on the plan for another firm of your choice. Choose at least one other plan, open it, and scan its contents.

When you are finished, you can close the **Sample Plan Browser** page by going to the top of the screen and clicking on **File** (on the bar menu). Then select **exit.** You can then exit from the *BPP* program by going to the top of the screen and clicking on **File** (on the bar menu) and selecting **exit.**

Video Exercise

HELPING BUSINESSES DO BUSINESS: U.S. DEPARTMENT OF COMMERCE

Learning Objectives

The purpose of this video is to help you:

1. Understand world economic systems and their effect on competition.
2. Identify the factors of production.
3. Discuss ways in which supply and demand affect a product's price.

Synopsis

The U.S. Department of Commerce (DOC) <www.doc.gov> seeks to support U.S. economic stability and help U.S.-based companies do business in other countries. In contrast to the planned economy of the People's Republic of China, the United States features a market economy in which firms are free to set their own missions and transact business with any other company or individual. They do, however, face some constraints. U.S. firms must comply with governmental regulations that set such standards as minimum safety requirements. When doing business in other countries, they must consider tariffs and other restrictions that govern imports to those markets. In addition, supply and demand affect a company's ability to set prices and generate profits.

Discussion Questions

1. *For analysis:* If a U.S. company must pay more for factors of production such as human resources, what is the likely effect on its competitiveness in world markets?

Online Exploration

Visit the U.S. Department of Commerce Web site <www.commerce.gov> and follow various links from the home page to examine some of the agency's resources for businesses. Also follow the link to the DOC's history. What assistance can a U.S. business expect from this agency? How have the agency's offerings evolved over the years to meet the changing needs and demands of business?

CHAPTER 2

Understanding the Environments of Business

After reading this chapter, you should be able to:

1. Explain the concepts of *organizational boundaries* and *multiple organizational environments*.
2. Explain the importance of the *economic environment* to business and identify the factors used to evaluate the performance of an economic system.
3. Discuss the current economic picture in the United States and summarize expert predictions about its future.
4. Describe the *technological environment* and its role in business.
5. Describe the *political-legal environment* and its role in business.
6. Describe the *sociocultural environment* and its role in business.
7. Identify emerging challenges and opportunities in the *business environment*.

Making the Grade

At first blush, it seems almost laughable these days to talk about businesses that are admired. The woes of Enron, Arthur Andersen, Worldcom, Kmart, Global Crossing, Warnaco, and Tyco—just to name a few—have made these businesses and their CEOs fodder for late-night comedians and *Dilbert* comics strips. A casual observer might conclude that the term *admirable* no longer applies to the institution of business. Fortunately, our casual observer would be wrong.

For the last twenty years, *Fortune* magazine has compiled an annual list of the most admired companies in the United States. A careful review of the list (and its criteria) provides some reassuring testimony on the vitality—and values—of many businesses and the manner in which they conduct their operations as well as some insights into how companies must perform in order to gain the kind of stellar reputation necessary to get on the list.

Fortune uses eight criteria in determining its most admired companies:

- Innovation
- Financial soundness
- Employee talent
- Use of corporate assets
- Long-term investment value
- Social responsibility
- Quality of management
- Quality of products/services

Evaluations are based on data collected from 10,000 executives, directors, and securities analysts. Respondents are asked to rate companies both within their own industries and on an overall basis.

These eight criteria all have one underlying theme: They reflect in one way or another the extent to which an organization and its managers effectively meet or exceed the needs and expectations of their external constituents. For example, hiring and developing the brightest and most motivated people from the labor market results in high levels of employee talent. Likewise, respecting the needs of shareholders and other investors affects several criteria, including financial soundness, use of corporate assets, and long-term investment value. Says one expert, "We admire companies that cater to their constituents."

So what firms make the grade? Interestingly, over the 20 years that the list has been compiled, only five different firms have held the number-one spot: IBM (1983–86), Merck (1987–93), Rubbermaid (1994–95), Coca-Cola (1996–97), and General Electric (1998–2002). Furthermore, each of these firms has been in the top 10 at least five times, as have 13 others: 3M, Procter & Gamble, Wal-Mart, Johnson & Johnson, Microsoft, Intel, Boeing, Berkshire Hathaway, Hewlett-Packard, Dow Jones, Home Depot, J.P. Morgan, and Southwest Airlines.

Reigning champion GE has an enviable record among its peers. For one thing, it's known as a major training ground for corporate executives. Rubbermaid made the top 10 under CEO Stanley Gault, a former GE executive. Under recently retired CEO Jack Welch, GE managed to achieve smooth and steady earnings growth quarter after quarter. It's also America's number-one wealth creator, and current CEO Jeff Immelt has already announced that one of his goals is to be on top of the *Fortune* list again next year!

After GE, the remainder of the 2002 list includes (in order) Southwest Airlines, Wal-Mart, Microsoft,

"We admire companies that cater to their constituents."

~Paul Argent,
PROFESSOR OF MANAGEMENT, DARTMOUTH

Berkshire Hathaway, Home Depot, Johnson & Johnson, FedEx, Citigroup, and Intel. *Fortune* has also begun to compile a list of the most admired global companies. Interestingly, the top 23 businesses are American firms. (The top-10 non-U.S. companies include Nokia, Toyota, Sony, Nestlé, Honda, BP, Singapore Airlines, L'Oréal, Royal Dutch/Shell, and Canon.)

Our opening story continues on page 55.

Organizational Boundaries and Environments

external environment

Everything outside an organization's boundaries that might affect it

All businesses, regardless of their size, location, or mission, operate within a larger external environment. This **external environment** consists of everything outside an organization's boundaries that might affect it. Not surprisingly, the external environment plays a major role in determining the success or failure of any organization. Managers must therefore have a complete and accurate understanding of their environment and then strive to operate and compete within it. Of course, businesses can also influence their environments. To better explain the environment of business, we begin by discussing *organizational boundaries,* and then we introduce the concept of *multiple organizational environments.*

Organizational Boundaries

organizational boundary

That which separates the organization from its environment

Quite simply, an **organizational boundary** is that which separates the organization from its environment. But whereas boundaries were once relatively easy to identify, they are becoming increasingly complicated and hard to pin down. Consider the simple case of a small neighborhood grocery that includes a retail customer area, a storage room, and an owner/manager's office. In many ways, the store's boundary coincides with its physical structure: When you walk through the door, you're crossing the boundary into the business, and when you go back onto the sidewalk, you cross the boundary back into the environment.

But even this simple example isn't as simple as it seems. During the course of the business day, distributors of soft drinks, beer, snack foods, ice, and bread products may enter the store, inventory the products that they distribute, and automatically refill coolers and shelves just as if they were employees. Although these distributors are normally considered part of the environment rather than the organization, during the time that they're inside the store, they are essentially part of the business. Assuming that they're store employees, customers may ask them questions as they restock shelves. The bread distributor may even offer someone a fresh loaf instead of the one that he or she has taken from the shelf.

Now consider the case of a large domestic business (such as Carnation) that is owned by an even larger international corporation (such as Nestlé S.A.). The domestic business itself has a complex network of relationships with other businesses. Carnation, for example, deals with milk suppliers, metal can manufacturers, advertising agencies, distributors, large grocery chains, and so forth. But Carnation also functions within the boundaries of its international parent, Swiss-owned Nestlé S.A. <www.nestle.com>, which has its own network of business relationships, some overlapping and some distinct from Carnation's network.

We can also examine similar complexities from the customer's perspective. McDonald's, for example, has a contract with Coca-Cola, stipulating that it will sell only Coke soft-drink products. McDonald's also has partnerships with Wal-Mart and Disney that allow it to open stores inside those firms' facilities. So when you buy a Coca-Cola soft drink from a McDonald's restaurant located inside a Wal-Mart store or Disney theme park, you are essentially affecting, and being affected by, multiple businesses. As you can see, the boundaries of any spe-

Before September 11, 2001, the computer consulting firm of Kasadel <www.kasadel.com> *was located on the 15th floor of the World Trade Center's south tower. Now the firm and its employees work out of a friend's donated basement in Queens, N.Y. An estimated 700 companies and organizations that called the Trade Center home had to relocate after the towers fell. Most stayed in New York City. A handful moved to surrounding states. Kasadel was one of 30 that moved to private homes.*

cific business are becoming increasingly difficult to define and more complicated to manage.

Multiple Organizational Environments

Although we tend to speak of "the external environment" as if it were a single entity, organizations actually have multiple environments. Some of them are relatively general. Prevailing economic conditions, for instance, will affect the performance of almost every business. But other dimensions are much more precise. Our neighborhood grocery will be influenced not only by an increase in unemployment in the area, but also by the pricing and other marketing policies of its nearest competitor.

Figure 2.1 shows the major dimensions and elements of the external environment as it affects most businesses. As you can see, these include economic conditions, technology, political-legal considerations, social issues, the global environment, issues of ethical and social responsibility, the business environment itself, and numerous other emerging challenges and opportunities. Because this book devotes detailed coverage of global and ethical issues in Chapters 4 and 5, respectively, we will introduce them here only as they relate directly to the other areas in this chapter.

The Economic Environment

The **economic environment** refers to the conditions of the economic system in which an organization operates.[1] McDonald's U.S. operations, for example, are (as of this writing) functioning in an economic environment characterized by weak growth, moderate unemployment, and low inflation. Such economic factors often affect business in multiple ways. Moderate unemployment means that most people can afford to eat out, but it also means that McDonald's must pay higher wages to attract employees. Low inflation means that McDonald's pays relatively constant prices for its supplies, but it also means that McDonald's is constrained from increasing the prices it charges consumers.

economic environment
Conditions of the economic system in which an organization operates

Economic conditions are also important to nonbusiness organizations. When the economy is weak, funding for state universities may drop, and charitable organizations like the Salvation Army are asked to provide greater assistance

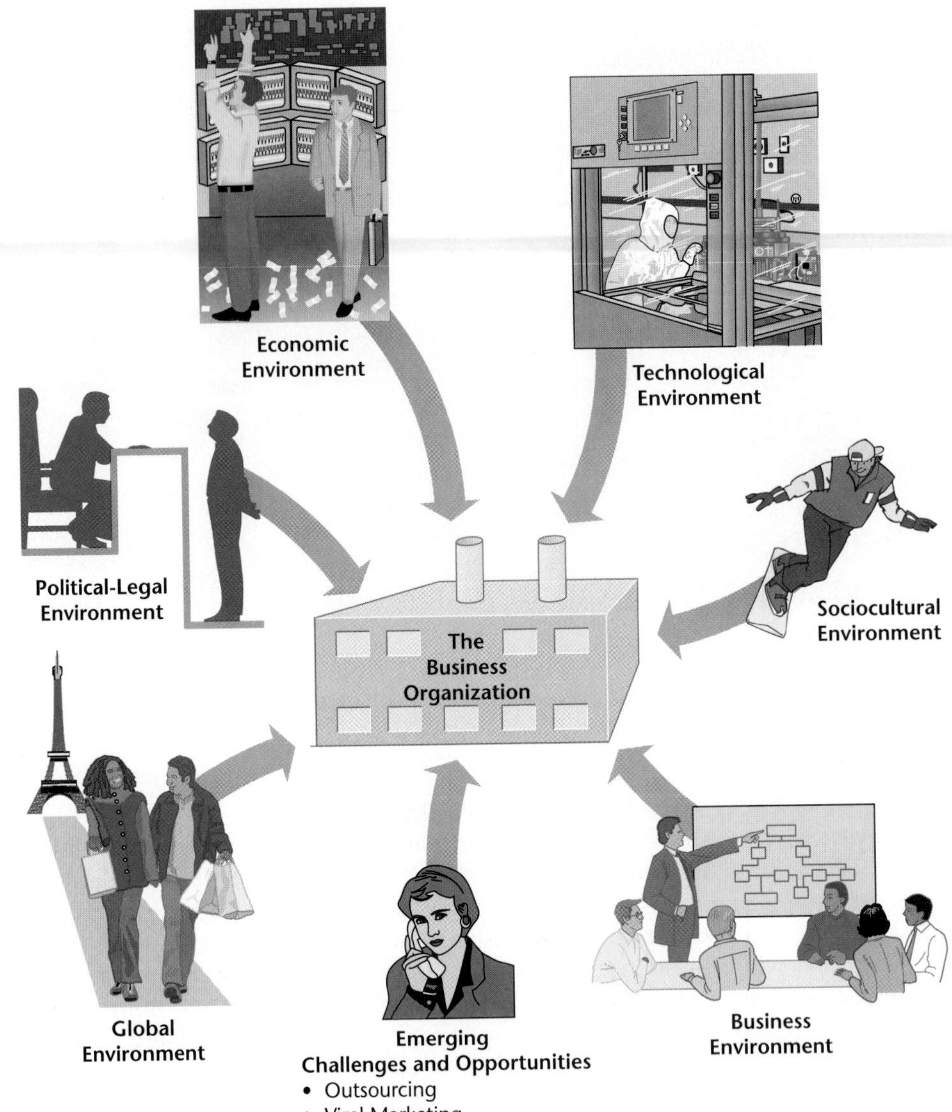

FIGURE 2.1
Dimensions of the External Environment

at the same time that their own incoming contributions are down. Hospitals are affected by the availability of government grants and the number of low-income patients they must treat for free.

Given the importance of the economic environment, we will closely examine the two key goals of the U.S. economic system: *economic growth* and *economic stability*. We begin by focusing on the tools with which we measure economic growth, including *aggregate output, standard of living, gross domestic product,* and *productivity*. We then discuss the main threats to economic stability—namely, *inflation* and *unemployment*. We conclude this section by discussing government attempts to manage the U.S. economy in the interest of meeting national economic goals.

Economic Growth

At one time, about half the population of this country was involved in producing the food that we needed. Today, less than 2.5 percent of the U.S. population works in agriculture. Agricultural efficiency has improved because we devised

■ TABLE 2.1
U.S. GDP and GDP per Capita

Gross Domestic Product (GDP) ($ Billion)	GDP: Real Growth Rate (%)	GDP Per Capita: Purchasing Power Parity
9,255.00	4.1	$33,900

better ways of producing products and invented better technology for getting the job done. We can therefore say that agricultural production has *grown* because we have been able to increase total output in the agricultural sector.

Aggregate Output and Standard of Living We can apply the same concepts to a nation's economic system, but the computations are vastly more complex. A fundamental question, then, is how we know whether or not an economic system is growing. Experts call the pattern of short-term ups and downs (or, better, expansions and contractions) in an economy the **business cycle.** The main measure of *growth* in the business cycle is **aggregate output:** the total quantity of goods and services produced by an economic system during a given period.[2]

business cycle
Pattern of short-term ups and downs (expansions and contractions) in an economy

aggregate output
Total quantity of goods and services produced by an economic system during a given period

To put it simply, an increase in aggregate output is growth (or economic growth).[3] When output grows more quickly than the population, two things usually follow: Output per capita—the quantity of goods and services per person—goes up and the system provides relatively more of the goods and services that people want.[4] And when these two things occur, people living in an economic system benefit from a higher **standard of living,** which refers to the total quantity and quality of goods and services that they can purchase with the currency used in their economic system.

standard of living
Total quantity and quality of goods and services that a country's citizens can purchase with the currency used in their economic system

Among other things, then, growth makes possible higher standards of living. Thus, in order to know how much your standard of living is improving, you need to know how much your nation's economic system is growing. Let's start to address this question by considering the data in Table 2.1.

Gross Domestic Product The first number, **GDP,** or **gross domestic product,** refers to the total value of all goods and services produced within a given period by a national economy through domestic factors of production. Obviously, GDP is a measure of aggregate output. Generally speaking, if GDP is going up, aggregate output is going up; if aggregate output is going up, the nation is experiencing *economic growth.*

gross domestic product (GDP)
Total value of all goods and services produced within a given period by a national economy through domestic factors of production

Sometimes, economists also use the term **gross national product (GNP),** which refers to the total value of all goods and services produced by a national economy within a given period regardless of where the factors of production are located. What, precisely, is the difference between GDP and GNP? Consider an American-owned automobile plant in Brazil. The profits earned by the factory are included in U.S. GNP—but not in GDP—because its output is not produced domestically (that is, in the United States). Conversely, those profits are included in Brazil's GDP—but not GNP—because they are produced domestically (that is, in Brazil). Calculations quickly become complex because of different factors of production. The labor, for example, will be mostly Brazilian but the capital mostly American. Thus, wages paid to Brazilian workers are part of Brazil's GNP even though profits are not.

gross national product (GNP)
Total value of all goods and services produced by a national economy within a given period regardless of where the factors of production are located

Real Growth Rate GDP and GNP usually differ by less than 1 percent, but GDP is the preferred method of calculating national income and output. With that in mind, let's look at the middle column in Table 2.1. Here we find that the *real growth rate of U.S. GDP*—the growth rate of GDP *adjusted for inflation and changes in the value of the country's currency*—is 4.1 percent. How good is that rate? Remember that *growth depends on output increasing at a faster rate than population.* The U.S. population is growing at a rate of 0.91 percent. The *real*

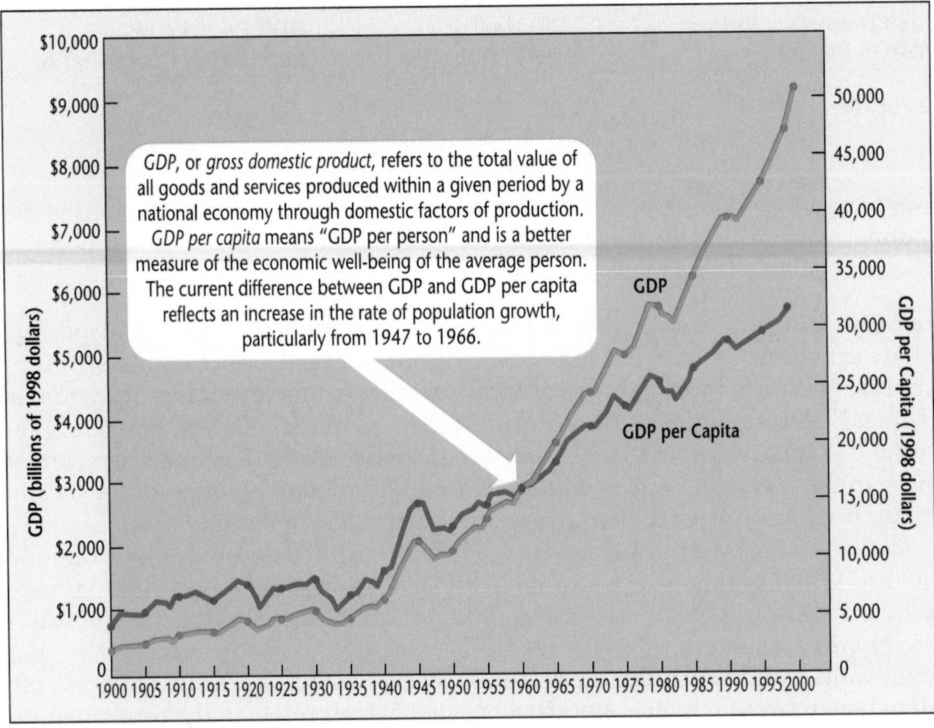

FIGURE 2.2
GDP and GDP per Capita.

growth rate of the U.S. economic system, therefore, seems quite healthy, and our standard of living should be improving.

GDP per Capita The number in the third column of Table 2.1 is, in fact, a reflection of standard of living: *GDP per capita* means GDP per person. We get this figure by dividing total GDP ($9.255 trillion) by total population, which happens to be about 275.5 million. In a given period (usually calculated on an annual basis), the United States produces goods and services equal in value to $33,900 for every person in the country.[5] Figure 2.2 shows both GDP and GDP per capita in the United States between 1900 and 2000. GDP per capita is a better measure than GDP itself of the economic well-being of the average person.

Real GDP "Real GDP" means that GDP has been adjusted. To understand why adjustments are necessary, assume that pizza is the only product in a hypothetical economy. In 2001, a pizza cost $10; the next year, a pizza cost $11. In both years, exactly 1,000 pizzas were produced. In 2001, the local GDP was $10,000 ($10 × 1,000); in 2002, the local "GDP" was $11,000 ($11 × 1,000). Has the economy grown? No. Because 1,000 pizzas were produced in both years, *aggregate output* remained the same. The point is to not be misled into believing that an economy is doing better than it is. If it is *not* adjusted, local GDP for 2002 is **nominal GDP:** GDP measured in current dollars or with all components valued at current prices.[6]

nominal GDP
GDP measured in current dollars or with all components valued at current prices

real GDP
GDP calculated to account for changes in currency values and price changes

purchasing power parity
Principle that exchange rates are set so that the prices of similar products in different countries are about the same

Purchasing Power Parity In our example, *current prices* would be 2003 prices. On the other hand, we calculate **real GDP** when we calculate GDP to account for *changes in currency values and price changes.* When we make this adjustment, we account for both GDP and **purchasing power parity**—the principle that exchange rates are set so that the prices of similar products in different countries are about the same. Purchasing power parity gives us a much better idea of *what people can actually buy with the financial resources allocated to them by their respective economic systems.* In other words, it gives us a better sense of standards of living across the globe.

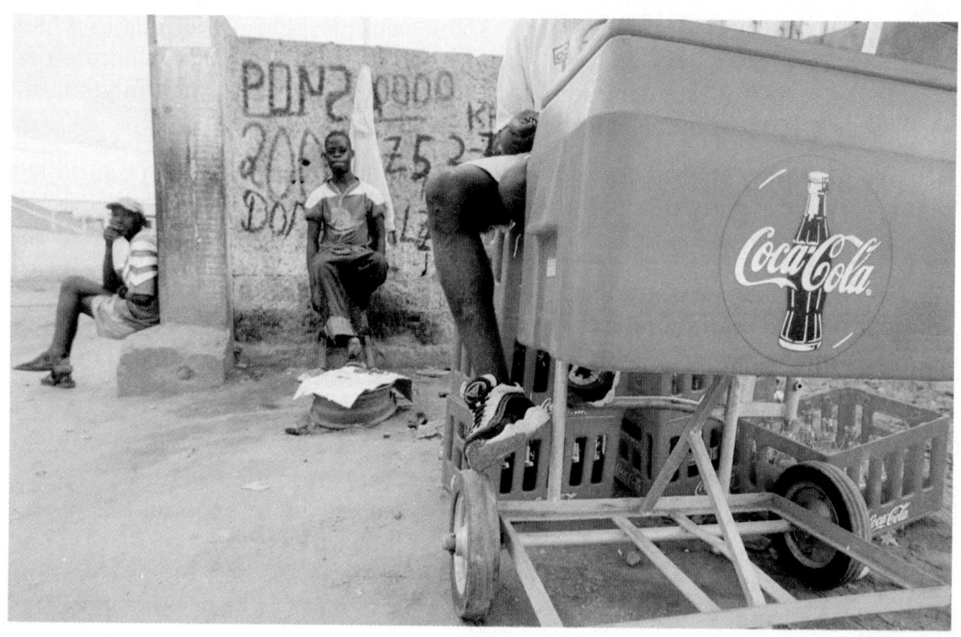
Coca-Cola

The GDP of the African nation of Angola is $11.6 billion. Adjusted to calculate purchasing power parity, GDP per capita is $1,000. Angolans can buy a 12-ounce bottle of Coke for 8 new kwanza (the country's currency), or about 40 cents. Thus, although the country is extremely poor, Coke is not prohibitively expensive: Working from about 8 A.M. to 7 P.M., street vendors like this one in the capital of Luanda can sell 5 cases and take home $8 per day. If he works 6 days a week, he makes more than enough to pay the rent.

Productivity A major factor in the growth of an economic system is **productivity,** which is a measure of economic growth that compares how much a system produces with the resources needed to produce it. Let's say, for instance, that it takes 1 U.S. worker and 1 U.S. dollar to make 10 soccer balls in an 8-hour workday. Let's also say that it takes 1.2 Saudi workers and the equivalent of $1.2 (in riyals, the currency of Saudi Arabia) to make 10 soccer balls in the same 8-hour workday. We can say, then, that the U.S. soccer-ball industry is more *productive* than the Saudi soccer-ball industry. The two factors of production in this extremely simple case are labor and capital.

productivity
Measure of economic growth that compares how much a system produces with the resources needed to produce it

Now let's look at productivity from a different perspective. If more products are being produced with fewer factors of production, what happens to the prices of these products? They go down. As a consumer, therefore, you would need less of your currency to purchase the same quantity of these products. In short, your standard of living—at least with regard to these products—has improved. If your entire economic system increases its productivity, then your overall standard of living improves. In fact, *standard of living improves only through increases in productivity.*[7] Real growth in GDP reflects growth in productivity.

U.S. workers are among the most productive in the world. Figure 2.3 gives us just one way of measuring improved productivity. It shows the relationship between increases in output per hour and hourly compensation in the U.S. manufacturing sector between 1993 and 1999 as compared with year 1992. You can read the graph this way: While the increase in output was 33.3 percent, the increase in the cost of one factor of production (labor) was only 25.3 percent. In this respect, therefore, productivity improved.[8]

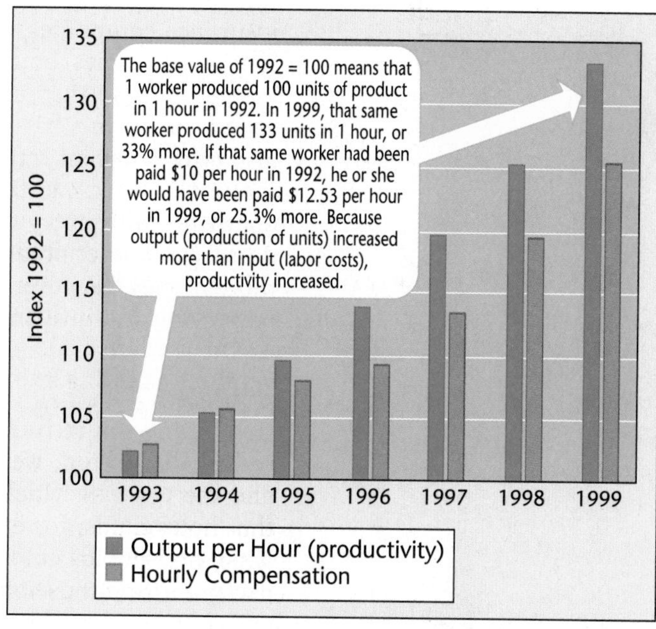
135
130
125
120
115
110
105
100
Index 1992 = 100
The base value of 1992 = 100 means that 1 worker produced 100 units of product in 1 hour in 1992. In 1999, that same worker produced 133 units in 1 hour, or 33% more. If that same worker had been paid $10 per hour in 1992, he or she would have been paid $12.53 per hour in 1999, or 25.3% more. Because output (production of units) increased more than input (labor costs), productivity increased.
1993 1994 1995 1996 1997 1998 1999
Output per Hour (productivity)
Hourly Compensation

FIGURE 2.3
Productivity and Labor Compensation in U.S. Manufacturing

Productivity in the United States, then, is increasing, and as a result, so are GDP and GDP per capita. Ultimately, increases in these measures of growth mean an improvement in the standard of living. But obviously, things don't always proceed so smoothly. Figure 2.3, for example, reveals periods in which productivity growth was considerably less than in others. What factors can inhibit the growth of an economic system? There are several such factors, but we'll focus on two of them: *balance of trade* and the *national debt.*

Balance of Trade Its *balance of trade* is the economic value of all the products that a country *exports* minus the economic value of its *imported* products. The principle here is quite simple:

- A *positive* balance of trade results when a country exports (sells to other countries) more than it imports (buys from other countries).
- A *negative* balance of trade results when a country imports more than it exports.

A negative balance of trade is commonly called a *trade deficit.* In 2001, the United States compiled a deficit (as it has every year since the mid-1970s), spending nearly $360 billion more on imports than it received for exports. The United States is thus a *debtor nation* rather than a *creditor nation.*

How does a trade deficit affect economic growth? The deficit exists because the amount of money spent on foreign products has not been paid in full. In effect, therefore, it is borrowed money, and borrowed money costs more money in the form of interest. The money that flows out of the country to pay off the deficit can't be used to invest in productive enterprises, either at home or overseas.

national debt

Amount of money that a government owes its creditors

National Debt Its **national debt** is the amount of money that the government owes its creditors. As of this writing, the U.S. national debt is over $5.9 *trillion.* (You can find out the national debt on any given day by going to any one of several Internet sources, including the U.S. National Debt Clock at <www.brillig.com/debt_clock>.)

How does the national debt affect economic growth? While taxes are the most obvious way the government raises money, it also sells *bonds*—securities through which it promises to pay buyers certain amounts of money by specified future dates. The government sells bonds to individuals, households, banks, insurance companies, industrial corporations, nonprofit organizations, and government agencies, both at home and overseas.[9] These bonds are attractive investments because they are extremely safe: The U.S. government is not going to *default* on them (that is, fail to make payments when due). Even so, they must also offer a decent return on the buyer's investment, and they do this by paying interest at a competitive rate. By selling bonds, therefore, the U.S. government competes with every other potential borrower—individuals, households, businesses, and other organizations—for the available supply of loanable money. The more money the government borrows, the less money is available for the private borrowing and investment that increases productivity.

Economic Stability

Combining the introductory economics material from Chapter 1 with the preceding discussion, we have now learned a great deal about economic systems and the ways in which they allocate resources among their citizens. We know that households, for example, receive capital in return for labor. We know that when households enter consumer markets to purchase goods and services, their decisions (and those of the firms trying to sell them goods and services) are influenced by the laws of demand and supply. We know that the laws of demand and supply result in equilibrium prices when the quantity of goods demanded and the quantity of goods supplied are equal. We know that households enjoy higher standards of living when there is balanced growth in the quantity of goods demanded and the quantity of goods supplied. We know that we can measure growth and productivity in terms of gross domestic product and standard of living in terms of the purchasing power parity of a system's currency: Living standards are stable when purchasing power parity remains stable.[10]

We may thus conclude that a chief goal of an economic system is **stability:** a condition in which the amount of money available in an economic system and the quantity of goods and services produced in it are growing at about the same rate. Now we can focus on certain factors that threaten stability—namely, *inflation* and *unemployment.*

stability
Condition in an economic system in which the amount of money available and the quantity of goods and services produced are growing at about the same rate

Inflation **Inflation** occurs when there are widespread price increases throughout an economic system. How does it threaten stability? Inflation occurs when the amount of money injected into an economy outstrips the increase in actual output. When this happens, people will have more money to spend, but there will still be the same quantity of products available for them to buy. As they compete with one another to buy available products, prices go up. Before long, high prices will erase the increase in the amount of money injected into the economy. Purchasing power, therefore, declines.

inflation
Occurrence of widespread price increases throughout an economic system

Obviously, then, inflation can also hurt you as a consumer because your primary concern when deciding whether to purchase a product is often price. In other words, you will probably decide to make a purchase if the value of the product justifies the price that you'll have to pay. Now look at Table 2.2, which reduces a hypothetical purchase decision to three bare essentials:

1. Your household income over a three-year period
2. The price of a hamburger over a three-year period
3. The rates of increase for both over a three-year period

In which year did the cost of a hamburger go up? At first glance, you might say in both YR2 and YR3 (to $4 and to $7.50). In YR2, your income kept pace: Although a hamburger cost twice as much, you had twice as much money to spend. In effect, the price to you was actually the same. In YR3, however, your income increased by 250 percent while the price of a hamburger increased by 275 percent. In YR3, therefore, you got hit by inflation (how hard, of course, depends on your fondness for hamburgers). This ratio—the comparison of your increased income to the increased price of a hamburger—is all that counts if you want to consider inflation when you're making a buying decision. Inflation, therefore, can be harmful to you as a consumer because *inflation decreases the purchasing power of your money.*

Measuring Inflation: The CPI What is a good way to measure inflation? Remember our definition of inflation as the occurrence of widespread price increases throughout an economic system. It stands to reason, therefore, that we can measure inflation by measuring price increases. To do this, we can turn to such price indexes as the **consumer price index (CPI):** a measure of the prices of typical products purchased by consumers living in urban areas.[11]

consumer price index (CPI)
Measure of the prices of typical products purchased by consumers living in urban areas

YR1 Income	YR2 Income	YR2 % Increase Over YR1 Base	YR3 Income	YR3 % Increase Over YR1 Base
$5,000	$10,000	100	$17,500	250
YR1 Hamburger Price	**YR2 Hamburger Price**	**YR2 % Increase Over YR1 Base**	**YR3 Hamburger Price**	**YR3 % Increase Over YR1 Base**
$2	$4	100	$7.50	275

TABLE 2.2
When Did the Cost of a Hamburger Go Up?

Year	CPI
1951	26.0
1961	29.9
1971	40.6
1981	90.9
1989	124.0
1990	130.7
1991	136.2
1992	140.3
1993	144.5
1994	148.2
1995	152.4
1996	156.9
1997	160.5
1998	163.0

TABLE 2.3
Selected CPI Values

Here's how the CPI works. First we need a *base period*—an arbitrarily selected time period against which other time periods are compared. The CPI base period is 1982–84, which has been given an average value of 100. Table 2.3 gives CPI values computed for selected years. The CPI value for 1951, for instance, is 26. This means that 1 dollar's worth of typical purchases in 1982–84 would have cost 26 cents in 1951. Conversely, you would have needed $1.63 to purchase the same 1 dollar's worth of typical goods in 1998. The difference registers the effect of inflation. In fact, that's what an *inflation rate* is—*the percentage change in a price index.*

We can thus calculate the *CPI rate of inflation* by using the data in Table 2.3. To find the inflation rate between 1997 and 1998, you need to know the *change* from one year to the next. To find this change, simply subtract the value of 1997 from the value of 1998: 163.0 − 160.5 = 2.5

Now apply the following formula:

$$\text{Inflation rate} = \frac{\text{Change in price index}}{\text{Initial price index}} \times 100$$

or

$$\frac{2.5}{160.5} \times 100 = 1.6\%$$

unemployment
Level of joblessness among people actively seeking work in an economic system

Unemployment Finally, we need to consider the effect of unemployment on economic stability. **Unemployment** is the level of joblessness among people actively seeking work in an economic system. When unemployment is low, there is a shortage of labor available for businesses to hire. As they compete with one another for the available supply of labor, businesses raise the wages that they are willing to pay. Then because higher labor costs eat into profit margins, they raise the prices of their products. Thus, although consumers have more money to inject into the economy, this increase is soon erased by higher prices. Purchasing power declines.

There are at least two related problems. If wage rates get too high, businesses will respond by hiring fewer workers and unemployment will, therefore, go up. Businesses could, of course, raise prices to counter increased labor costs, but if they charge higher prices, they won't be able to sell as much of their products. Because of reduced sales, they will cut back on hiring and, once again, unemployment will go up. What if the government tries to correct this situation by injecting more money into the economic system—say, by cutting taxes or spending more money? Prices in general may go up because of increased consumer demand. Again, purchasing power declines and, indeed, inflation may set in.[12]

Recessions and Depressions Finally, unemployment is sometimes a symptom of a system-wide disorder in the economy. During a downturn in the business cycle, people in numerous different sectors may lose their jobs at the same time. As a result, overall income and spending may drop. Feeling the pinch of reduced revenues, businesses may cut spending on the factors of production—including labor. Yet more people will be put out of work and unemployment will only increase further. Unemployment that results from this vicious cycle is called *cyclical unemployment.*[13]

In examining the relationship between unemployment and economic stability, we are thus reminded that when prices get high enough, consumer demand for goods and services goes down. We are also reminded that when demand for products goes down, producers cut back on hiring and, not surprisingly, eventu-

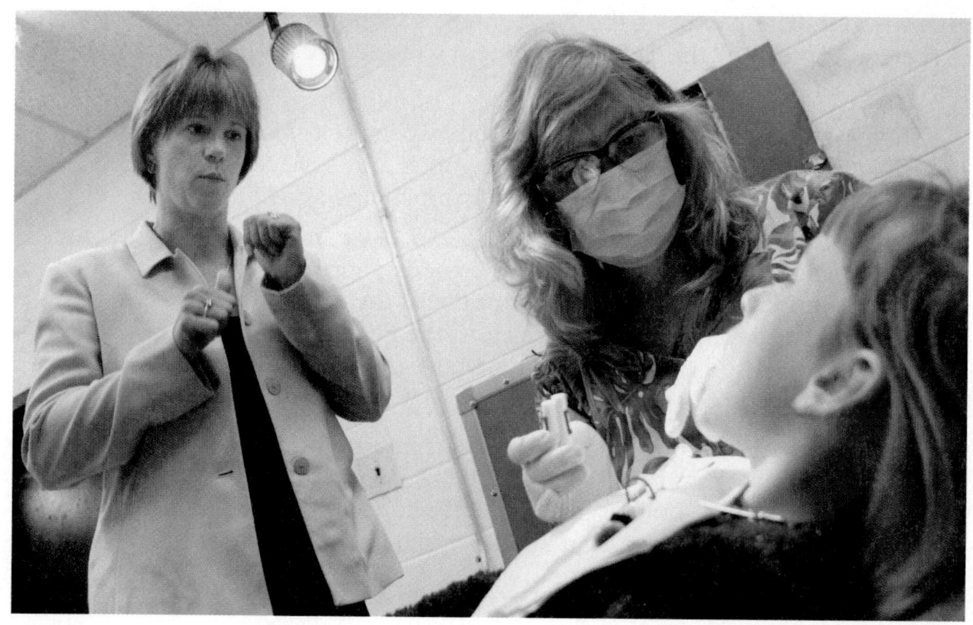

Accountancy, dentistry, and medical technology might not have been the professions of choice during the dot-com boom years of the late 1990s, but they offered steady employment during the recession that followed. Donna Beacham (left) works at Health Promotion Specialists, a South Carolina dentistry company founded in 2000 by Tammi Byrd, a hygienist who responded to the promise of steady employment by opening offices in areas where dental services were scarce. The Department of Commerce predicts that nationwide demand for hygienists will increase 36 percent by 2008.

ally start producing less. Consequently, of course, aggregate output decreases. When we go through a period during which aggregate output declines, we have a *recession.* During a recession, producers need fewer employees—less labor—to produce products. Unemployment, therefore, goes up.

How do we know whether or not we're in a recession? Clearly, we must start by measuring aggregate output. Recall that this is the function of real GDP, which we find by making necessary adjustments to the total value of all goods and services produced within a given period by a national economy through domestic factors of production. A **recession,** therefore, is more precisely defined as a period during which aggregate output, as measured by real GDP, declines. A prolonged and deep recession is a **depression.**[14]

recession
Period during which aggregate output, as measured by real GDP, declines

depression
Particularly severe and long-lasting recession

Managing the U.S. Economy

The government acts to manage the U.S. economic system through two sets of policies: fiscal and monetary. It manages the collection and spending of its revenues through **fiscal policies.** Tax increases can function as fiscal policies, not only to increase revenues but to manage the economy as well. Thus, in January 2001, President George W. Bush proposed a tax cut of $1.6 trillion. Said the president: "A warning light is flashing on the dashboard of the economy. We just can't drive on and hope for the best." Bush was referring to evidence that the economy was slowing—or, more accurately, that its growth rate was decreasing—and was arguing that his tax cut would stimulate renewed economic growth. The administration was calling for government action to bring stability to the economic system.

fiscal policies
Government economic policies that determine how the government collects and spends its revenues

Monetary policies focus on controlling the size of the nation's money supply. Working primarily through the Federal Reserve System (the nation's central bank), the government can influence the ability and willingness of banks throughout the country to lend money. It can also influence the supply of money by prompting interest rates to go up or down.

monetary policies
Government economic policies that determine the size of a nation's monetary supply

In the year preceding President Bush's call for a tax cut, the Federal Reserve Bank (the Fed) had cut interest rates six times. Why? Because it saw signs of an economy threatened by both inflation (rising prices) and recession (a slowing growth rate). The power of the Fed to makes changes in the supply of money is the centerpiece of the U.S. government's monetary policy. The principle is fairly simple:

- Higher interest rates make money more expensive to borrow and thereby reduce spending by those who produce goods and services; when the Fed restricts the money supply, we say that it is practicing a *tight monetary policy.*
- Lower interest rates make money less expensive to borrow and thereby increase spending by those who produce goods and services; when the Fed loosens the money supply—and thus stimulates the economy—we say that it is practicing an *easy monetary policy.* Thus, the Fed cut interest rates several times in late 2001 to help the economy recover from the terrorist attacks in the United States on September 11.

In short, the Fed can influence the aggregate market for products by influencing the supply of money. Taken together, fiscal policy and monetary policy make up **stabilization policy:** government economic policy whose goal is to smooth out fluctuations in output and unemployment and to stabilize prices.

stabilization policy

Government policy, embracing both fiscal and monetary policies, whose goal is to smooth out fluctuations in output and unemployment and to stabilize prices

The Global Economy in the Twenty-First Century

Let's end our discussion of the economic environment of business with a brief look back and a more detailed look ahead. The decade of the 1990s saw a sustained period of expansion and growth that served to increase business profits, boost individual wealth, and fuel optimism. During the latter part of 2001 and into 2002, however, economic growth began to stall. Business profits started to taper off, stock portfolios declined in value, and optimism waned. But experts themselves disagreed as to whether the slowdown was temporary or represented a major shift in the U.S. economy that might last for years.[15]

Three Major Forces So, what does the economic future hold? First of all, most experts see three major forces driving the economy for at least the next decade:

1. The information revolution will continue to enhance productivity across all sectors of the economy, most notably in such information-dependent industries as finance, media, and wholesale and retail trade.[16]
2. New technological breakthroughs in areas such as biotechnology will create entirely new industries.
3. Increasing globalization will create much larger markets while also fostering tougher competition among global businesses; as a result, companies will need to focus even more on innovation and cost cutting.[17]

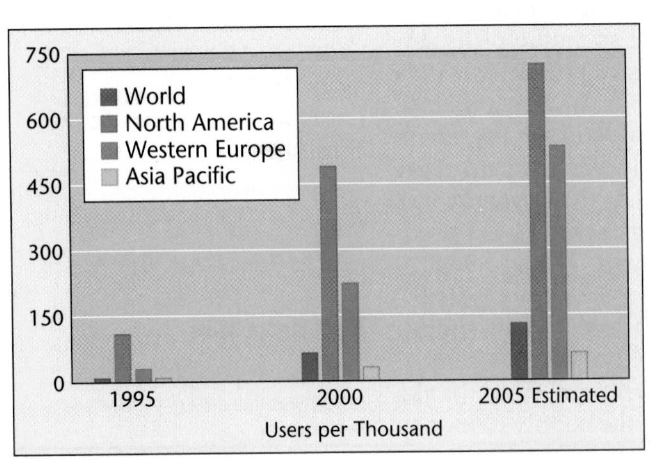

FIGURE 2.4

Internet Users per 1,000 People

Figures 2.4 through 2.6 clearly illustrate the significance of these forces. Figure 2.4 highlights the increased use of the Internet per 1,000 people for the entire world and for North America, Western Europe, and the Asia Pacific region for 1995 and 2000. As you can see, it also provides an estimate for 2005. The trends are clear and unambiguous: More and more people are using the Internet, and although the United States still leads the way, Western Europe is catching up and the Asia Pacific region is growing rapidly as well. Figure 2.5 amplifies these trends by isolating information-technology spending as a proportion of gross domestic product for numerous countries. Again, while the United States continues to lead the way, other countries are clearly catching up.[18]

Finally, Figure 2.6 underscores the fact that world exports are growing. Exports grew rapidly from the late 1980s through 1997 but then flattened and subsequently declined for two years. This downward trend was primarily attributable to the currency crisis and resultant economic downturn in Asia. Between 1999 and 2000, however, exports again began increasing and are projected to continue to rise at least through 2002.[19] Taken together, then, these data clearly reinforce the significance of information, technology, and globalization as the economic forces to be reckoned with in the twenty-first century.

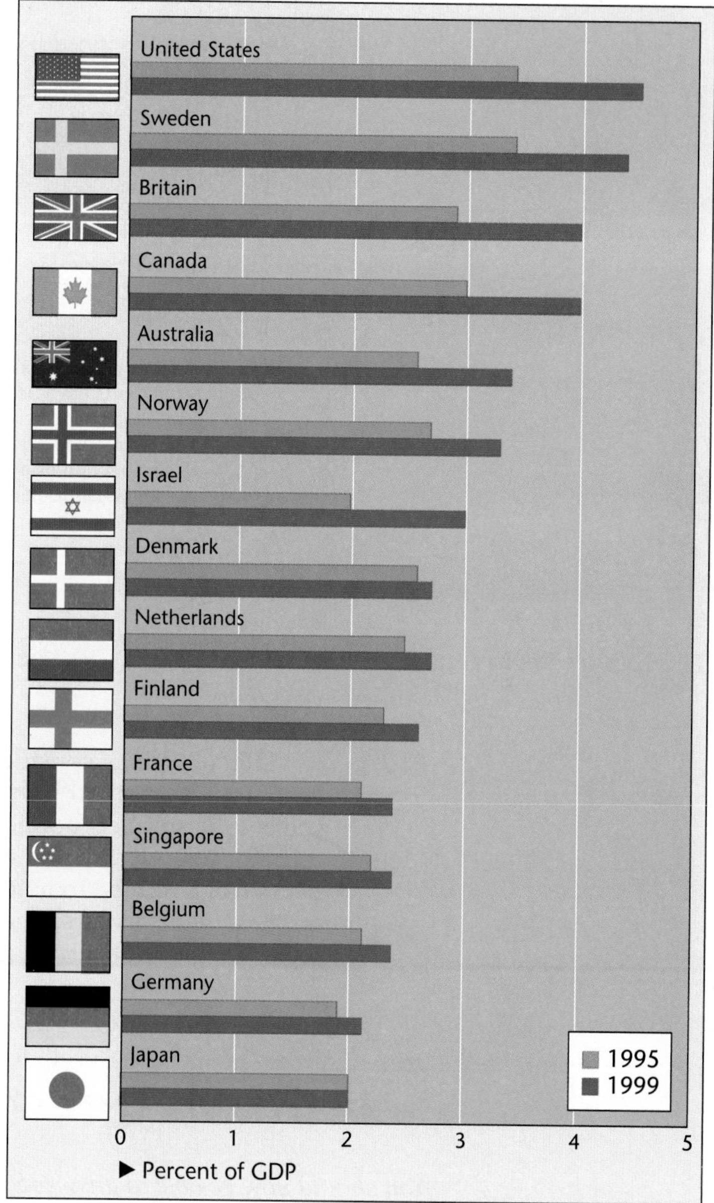

FIGURE 2.5
Information-Technology Spending

Projected Trends and Patterns As a result of these forces, economists also predict certain trends and patterns in economic indicators and competitive dynamics for at least the rest of this decade. Projected trends and patterns include the following:

- Some experts now foresee the current economic slowdown ending quickly, while others predict that the economy will remain stalled for several years.
- Inflationary surges and large budget deficits will likely be avoided.
- Countries that encourage free trade, innovation, and open financial systems will bounce back first and will prosper in the long-term.
- The most successful businesses will be those that are able most effectively to master new technologies and keep abreast of their competitors.[20]

Unfortunately, it is also important to note the following statistics as sobering reminders that the U.S. economy faces several problems:

- Because we import more than we export, the U.S. trade deficit continues to grow, making the United States a debtor nation.
- Income inequality in the United States continues to be a problem. Although the median household income is around $40,000 a year, the bottom fifth of U.S. households receive less than four percent of the national income. The top fifth, on the other hand, receive almost 50 percent of the national income.
- Consumer debt is steadily increasing. Nonbusiness bankruptcies increased over 60 percent between 1991 and 2001, and many people are not saving enough to ensure themselves a comfortable retirement.
- Even those individuals who have been diligently investing for their retirement have seen their savings eroded by recent declines in the stock market.
- About 44 million Americans lack health insurance.[21]

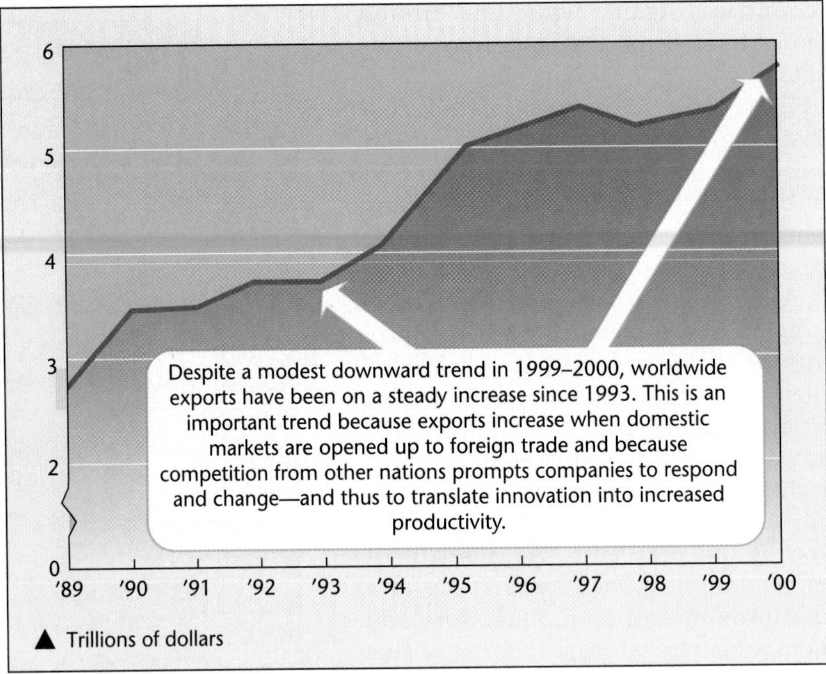

FIGURE 2.6
The Export Resurgence

Still, all things considered, both the U.S. domestic economy and the global economy are in good shape in most respects. Although leading indicators have stalled, the solid economic foundation built in the 1990s should serve as a platform for new growth and expansion in the near future. Businesses and entrepreneurs will continue to enjoy opportunities for growth and expansion for at least the next several years, and managers astute enough to navigate economic currents will probably arrive at greater prosperity.

Self-Check Questions 1–3

*You should now be able to answer Self-Check Questions 1–3**

1. TRUE/FALSE The boundary between an organization and its environment is clearly and easily identified.

2. MULTIPLE CHOICE Which of the following is **not** generally used as a measure of *economic growth?* [select one] **(a)** standard of living; **(b)** inflation; **(c)** aggregate output; **(d)** productivity; **(e)** gross domestic product.

3. MULTIPLE CHOICE Which of the following statements about *gross domestic product* and *gross national product* is **true**? [select one] **(a)** They mean the same thing. **(b)** They mean different things and are usually very different from one another. **(c)** They mean different things but are usually very similar. **(d)** They lead directly to inflation. **(e)** They are added together to determine purchasing power parity.

*ANSWERS TO SELF-CHECK QUESTIONS 1–3 CAN BE FOUND ON P. AN-1.

The Technological Environment

technology

All the ways by which firms create value for their constituents

Technology has a variety of meanings, but as applied to the environment of business, it generally includes all the ways by which firms create value for their constituents. Technology includes human knowledge, work methods, physical equipment, electronics and telecommunications, and various processing systems that are used to perform business activities. Although technology is applied within the organization, the forms and availability of that technology come from the general environment. Boeing, for example, uses computer-assisted manufacturing and design techniques developed by external vendors to simulate the four miles of hydraulic tubing that run through a 777. The advantages include decreased warehouse needs, higher quality tube fittings, and overall lower costs.

Product and Service Technologies

Product and service technologies are the technologies employed for creating products—both physical goods and services—for customers. Although many people associate technology with manufacturing, it is also a significant force in the service sector. Just as an automobile is built as it follows a predetermined pathway along an assembly line, a hamburger at McDonald's is cooked, assembled, and wrapped and bagged as it moves along a predefined path. The rapid advancement of the Internet into all areas of business is also a reflection of the technological environment. Indeed, new technologies continue to revolutionize nearly every aspect of business, ranging from the ways that customers and companies interact to where, when, and how employees perform their work.

Technology is the basis of competition for some firms, especially those whose goals include being the technology leaders in their industries. A company, for example, might focus its efforts on being the low-cost producer or always having the most technologically advanced products on the market. But because of the rapid pace of new developments, keeping a leadership position based on technology is increasingly challenging. Another challenge is meeting constant demands to decrease *cycle time*—the time from beginning to end that it takes a firm to accomplish some recurring activity or function.

Businesses have increasingly found that they can be more competitive if they can systematically decrease cycle times. Many companies, therefore, now focus on decreasing cycle times in areas ranging from developing products to making deliveries and collecting credit payments. Twenty years ago, it took a carmaker about five years from the decision to launch a new product until it was available in dealer showrooms. Now most companies can complete the cycle in less than two years. The speedier process allows them to respond more quickly to changing economic conditions, consumer preferences, and new competitive products while recouping their product-development costs more quickly.

Some firms compete directly on how quickly they can get things done for consumers. In the early days of personal computers, for instance, getting a made-to-order system took six to eight weeks. Today, firms like Dell can usually ship exactly what the customer wants in a matter of days.

Intel exemplifies the challenge and the risks of adopting a strategic dependence on technological leadership. Before cofounding Intel with Bob Noyce in 1968, Gordon Moore made a prediction about microprocessors (the processing components of microcomputers) that eventually became know as Moore's Law: The number of transistors in a microprocessor would double every 18 months. In effect, this rate would entail a twofold increase in processing power every 18 months—a seemingly impossible pace. Intel <www.intel.com>, however, has adopted Moore's Law as a performance requirement for each new generation of processor since 1970, up though the Pentium 4.

Granted, the company has struggled to sustain the pace. Even though spending $7.5 billion in 2001 alone for research and development, the firm is straining resources in search of ways to cram twice as many transistors into a space that already holds millions. Such a task will require a revolution in technology that, as yet, Intel hasn't found. Without a technological breakthrough, Moore's Law—and Intel's technological leadership position—may not be sustainable. The financial stakes, of course, are high. If Intel can't meet industry-wide goals, it faces threats from new competitors, such as Advanced Micro Devices (AMD) <www.amd.com>, whose microprocessor market share recently grew from 13 percent to 18 percent in just one year.

Business Process Technologies

Business process technologies are used not so much to create products as to improve a firm's performance of internal operations (such as accounting, managing information flows, creating activity reports, and so forth). They also help create better relationships with external constituents, such as suppliers and customers.

Enterprise Resource Planning One recent business technology innovation worthy of special attention is **enterprise resource planning,** or **ERP:** a large-scale information system for organizing and managing a firm's processes across product lines, departments, and geographic locations. Companywide processes—such as materials management, production planning, order management, and financial reporting—can all be managed by ERP. Figure 2.7 shows some of the

enterprise resource planning (ERP)
Large-scale information system for organizing and managing a firm's processes across product lines, departments, and geographic locations

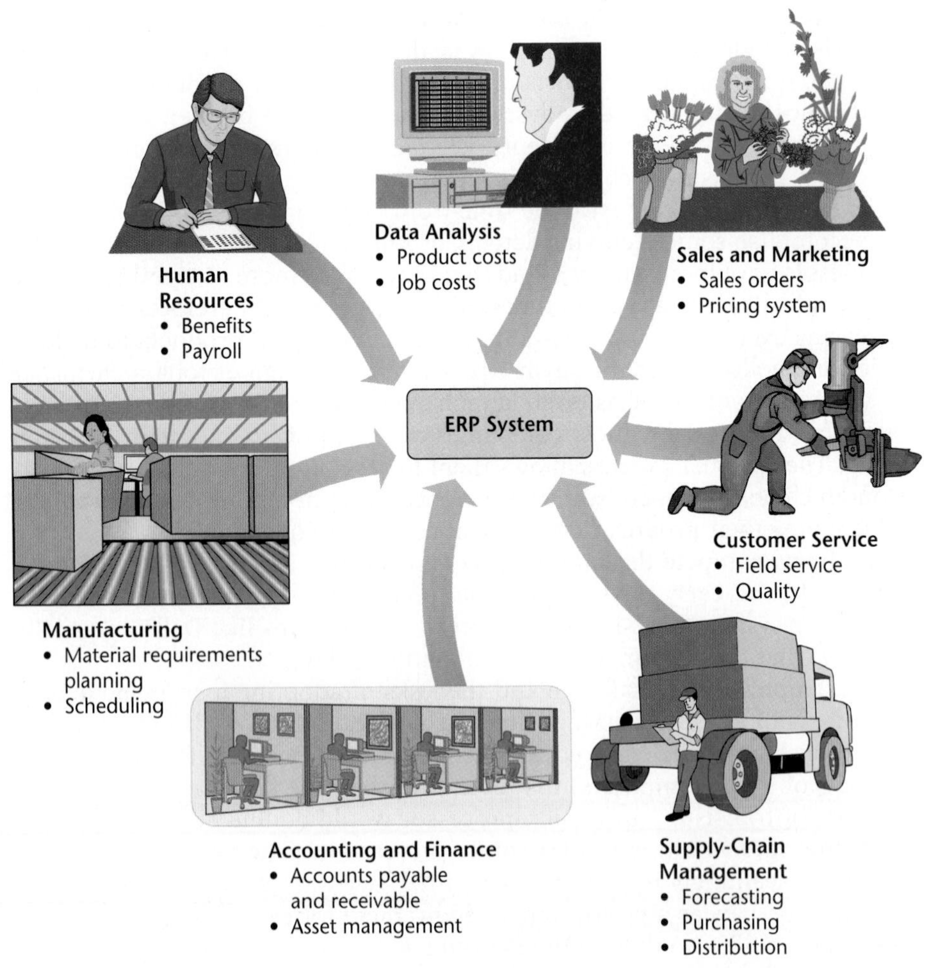

FIGURE 2.7
ERP Applications

areas in which ERP can be applied, including some of the common processes performed in each area.[22]

In developing the ERP system, the firm starts by identifying the processes that need critical attention, such as supplier relationships, materials flows, or customer order fulfillment. The resulting system would thus integrate the sales process with production planning and then both of these operations into the financial accounting system. Let's say that a customer in Rome orders a product to be manufactured in Ireland. The ERP-integrated seller can schedule the order shipment via air cargo to Rome, where it can be picked it up by a truck at the airport and delivered to the customer's warehouse by a specified date. All of these activities are synchronized in one massive database.

The ERP also stores updated real-time information on activities, reports recent and upcoming transactions, and posts electronic notices that certain action is required if certain schedules are to be met. It coordinates internal operations with activities by outside suppliers and notifies customers of current order status and upcoming deliveries and billings. It can integrate financial flows among the firm, its suppliers, customers, and banks and generate up-to-the-minute financial reports at a moment's notice (reduced from the traditional one-month time span).

The Political-Legal Environment

The **political-legal environment** reflects the relationship between business and government, usually in the form of government regulation of business. It is important for several reasons. First, the legal system defines in part what an organization can and can't do. Although the United States is basically a free market economy, it still has major regulation of business activity. McDonald's, for example, is subject to a

political-legal environment
Conditions reflecting the relationship between business and government, usually in the form of government regulation

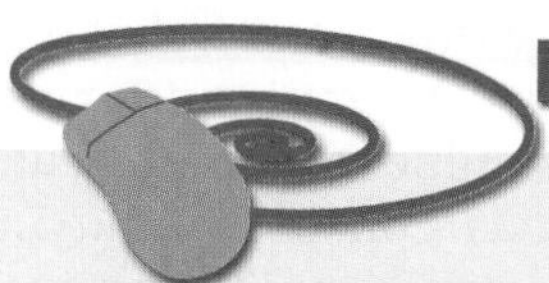

Mid-Chapter Internet Field Trip

"The Cisco Connection"

This chapter introduces the many environments of business, including the economic and technological, in which firms must operate. We've seen that these external environments—and the ability of managers to understand and respond to them—can play a major role in a firm's success or failure.

Cisco Systems Inc., the worldwide leader in networking for the Internet, both operates in and contributes to the technological environment of business. We can begin to understand Cisco's complex relationship to the technological environment by exploring its Web site at <www.cisco.com>. Scroll down to the bottom of the homepage and click on **About Cisco Systems.** You'll find menus for several different kinds of information, including:

- Corporate information.
- Vision and leadership.
- Corporate programs.
- Culture.

Select **Culture** and, on the scroll-down menu, click on **Technology:**

❶ What are some of the technology areas in which Cisco operates?

Next, click on **e-learning:**

❷ Who are some of the customers for Cisco's e-learning products?

Use your *Back* button to return to **About Cisco Systems.** Scroll down to **Vision and Leadership,** and from the menu, click on the biography of CEO John Chambers. On the left side of the page, select **Vision:**

❸ In what ways does Cisco think the Internet will change the way we live?

❹ How has technology already changed the way Cisco operates?

Again, use your *Back* button to return to **About Cisco Systems.** Select **Corporate Information,** and from the scroll-down menu, click on **Fact Sheet:**

❺ In how many different international markets does Cisco operate?

To continue your Internet field trip, click on www.prenhall.com/griffin

As one of the most recognized brands in the world, and with restaurants in more than 120 countries, McDonald's <www.mcdonalds.com> *is often a target of people who see the company as an icon of American imperialism. McDonald's, however, maintains that it's highly sensitive to local cultures, even encouraging foreign franchisers to run outlets. "We're a confederation of very local companies," says a McDonald's spokesman. This local McDonald's in Istanbul, Turkey, was the target of a small explosive in September 2001.*

variety of political and legal forces, including food-preparation standards and local zoning requirements. Likewise, various government agencies regulate important areas such as advertising practices, safety and health considerations, and acceptable standards of business conduct.

Pro- or antibusiness sentiment in government can further influence business activity. During periods of probusiness sentiment, firms find it easier to compete and have fewer concerns about antitrust issues. On the other hand, during a period of antibusiness sentiment, firms may find their competitive activities more restricted. There may, for example, be fewer opportunities for mergers and acquisitions because of antitrust concerns. Nestlé has considered buying Hershey for some time, but the Swiss-owned company worries that the acquisition would be blocked because the two firms, if combined, would dominate the U.S. confectionery market at a level unacceptable to the U.S. government.

Political stability is also an important consideration, especially for international firms. No business wants to set up shop in another country unless trade relationships with that country are relatively well defined and stable. Thus, U.S. firms are more likely to do business with England, Mexico, and Canada than with Haiti and Afghanistan. Similar issues also pertain to assessments of local and state governments. A new mayor or governor can affect many organizations, especially small firms that do business in a single location and are thus susceptible to zoning restrictions, property and school taxes, and the like.

The Sociocultural Environment

sociocultural environment
Conditions including the customs, mores, values, and demographic characteristics of the society in which an organization functions

The **sociocultural environment** includes the customs, mores, values, and demographic characteristics of the society in which an organization functions. Sociocultural processes determine the goods and services as well as the standards of business conduct that a society is likely to value and accept.

Customer Preferences and Tastes

Customer preferences and tastes vary both across and within national boundaries. In some countries, consumers are willing and able to pay premium prices for

Self-Check Questions 4–6

*You should now be able to answer Self-Check Questions 4–6**

4. TRUE/FALSE *Technology* includes all the ways by which firms create value for their constituents.

5. MULTIPLE CHOICE Which of the following refers to a large-scale information system used to integrate and synchronize business activities? [select one] **(a)** management information system; **(b)** decision support system; **(c)** expert system; **(d)** enterprise resource planning; **(d)** all of the these.

6. MULTIPLE CHOICE Which of the following would be **least** likely to happen during a period of antibusiness sentiment by the U.S. government? [select one] **(a)** A merger between two industry leaders would be quickly approved. **(b)** Business taxes might be increased. **(c)** Business regulation might increase. **(d)** Business leaders would have a greater voice in Washington; D.C. **(e)** Business taxes might be decreased.

*Answers to Self-check Questions 4–6 can be found on p. AN-2.

designer clothes with labels such as Armani or Calvin Klein. But the same clothes have virtually no market in other countries. Product usage also varies between nations. In China, bicycles are primarily seen as a mode of transportation, but in the United States, they are marketed primarily for recreational purposes.

Similarly, consumer preferences can also vary widely within the same country. For example, prepackaged chili is more popular in the southwest states than in the northeast. Meanwhile, northeasterners buy more clam chowder than do consumers in the northwest. McDonald's is a company clearly affected by sociocultural factors. In response to concerns about nutrition and health, McDonald's has added salads to its menus and experimented with other low-fat foods. It was the first fast-food chain to provide customers with information about the ingredients in its products, and it attracted national media attention in late 2002 when it announced that it would reduce the fat content in its popular French fries.

Consumer preferences and tastes also change over time. Preferences for color, style, taste, and so forth change from season to season. In some years, brightly colored clothes sell best, while in other years, people want more subdued colors. Soft drinks, of course, usually sell better during hot summer months than in cold winter months. Drinking whiskey, vodka, and gin and smoking cigarettes are less common in the United States today than they were just a few years ago. These and many other related issues regarding businesses and their customers are explored more fully in Part III of this book, which deals with the principles of marketing products.

Finally, sociocultural factors influence the way workers in a society feel about their jobs and organizations. In some cultures, work carries meaningful social significance, with certain employers and job titles being highly desired by workers. But in other cultures, because work is simply a means to an end, people are concerned only with pay and job security. McDonald's has occasionally struggled with its operations in the Middle East because many people there are unwilling to work in food-service operations.

Ethical Compliance and Responsible Business Behavior

An especially critical element of the sociocultural environment is the practice of ethical conduct and social responsibility. While we cover these areas in detail in

Chapter 5, they are sufficiently important to justify a preview of current issues here. The central issue today revolves around the fact that rapid changes in business relationships, organizational structures, and financial flows pose unsurpassed difficulties in keeping accurate track of a company's financial position. The public—current and potential investors—often get blurred pictures of a firm's competitive health. Stakeholders, however—employees, stockholders, consumers, unions, creditors, and government—are entitled to a fair accounting so they can make enlightened personal and business decisions. Even the American Institute for Certified Public Accountants (AICPA) admits that keeping up with today's increasingly fast-paced business activities is putting a strain on the accounting profession's traditional methods for auditing, financial reporting, and time-honored standards for professional ethics.

The Enron scandal, for example, involved extended enterprises using fast-moving financial transactions among layers of subsidiary firms, some domestic and many offshore, with large-scale borrowing from some of the world's largest financial institutions. The flood of electronic transactions that drove financial flows through a vast network of quickly formed and rapidly dissolved partnerships among energy brokers and buyers was so byzantine complex that Enron's accounting reports failed completely to reflect the firm's disastrous financial and managerial condition. In a blatant display of social irresponsibility, Enron's public reports concealed many of its partnerships (and obligations) with other companies, thus hiding its true operating condition.

Furthermore, why did Arthur Andersen, the accounting firm that audited Enron's finances, not catch its client's distorted reports? Auditors are supposed to provide an objective and independent assessment of the accuracy of financial information reported by corporations to key stakeholders, such as investors and governmental agencies. Indeed, publicly traded corporations are legally required to use an external auditor for just this purpose.

The answer to this question reveals a further illustration of the hazards faced by today's extended firm. Andersen, like other major accounting firms, had expanded from auditing into more lucrative nonaccounting areas such as management consulting. Reports suggest that Andersen's desire for future high-revenue consulting services with Enron may have motivated the CPA's auditors to turn a blind eye on questionable practices that eventually turned up during audits of Enron's finances.

Arthur Andersen LLP was one of the premier CPA firms in the United States. But its unethical and illegal practices—including obstruction of justice for shredding and doctoring documents related to Enron audits—destroyed the public's trust. Recognizing the futility of trying to revive its ruined reputation, Andersen, after 89 years in business, notified the Securities and Exchange Commission in September 2002 that it was giving up its licenses to audit public companies in the United States. None of the firm's 1,200 corporate clients remain, nearly all of its 28,000 employees are gone, and the last of the firm's office supplies have been donated to charity. "It's like a family member who has terminal cancer," said Gary Brentlinger, an Andersen human resource director. "We're watching the firm die."[23]

"It's like a family member who has terminal cancer."

~Gary Brentlinger
ONE OF THE LAST OF ARTHUR ANDERSEN'S 28,000 EMPLOYEES

As we've seen, Andersen's downfall can be attributed, at least in part, to its expansion into new lines of business and the accompanying client relationships that created conflicts of interest. Potential conflicts of interest pose serious ethical questions for surviving CPA firms, the CPA profession itself, and their clients. Accountants themselves have identified many of the reasons for these new complications. These include corporate globalization and collaboration, the growth in outsourcing, fragmented employee–employer relationships, and the electronic mobility of capital. The accounting profession has also mapped out a plan for meeting the challenges in AICPA's "CPA Vision Project" that we discuss in Chapter 17.

Don't blame these workers for dismantling Arthur Andersen. The international accounting firm did a nice job of self-destructing. Andersen was the auditor behind some of the biggest corporate accounting scandals in history—Enron, WorldCom, and Sunbeam were among the firm's high-profile clients—and was successfully prosecuted by the federal government for obstruction of justice in June 2002.

Finally, appropriate standards of business conduct also vary across cultures. In the United States, accepting bribes in return for political favors is unethical. In other countries, however, payments to local politicians are expected in return for favorable responses to such common business transactions as zoning and operating permits. The shape of the market, the ethics of political influence, and the attitudes of its workforce are only a few of the many ways in which culture can affect an organization.

The Business Environment

There is no doubt that business today is faster paced, more complex, and more demanding than ever before. In less than a decade, the hunt for new goods and services has been accelerated by product life cycles measured in weeks or months rather than years. Individual consumers and business customers want high-quality goods and services—often customized and with lower prices and immediate delivery. Sales offices, service providers, and production facilities are shifting geographically as new markets and resources emerge in other countries. Employees want flexible working hours and opportunities to work at home. Stockholder expectations also add pressure for productivity increases, growth in market share, and larger profits. At the same time, however, a more vocal public issues greater demands for honesty, fair competition, and respect for the environment.

Redrawing Corporate Boundaries

Successful companies are responding to these challenges in new, often unprecedented ways. To stay competitive, they are redrawing traditional organizational boundaries. Today, firms join together with other companies, even with competitors, to develop new goods and services. Some of these relationships are permanent, but others are temporary alliances formed on short notice so that, working together, partners can produce and deliver products with shorter lead times than either firm could manage alone.

Increasingly, the most successful firms are getting leaner by focusing on their **core competencies**—the skills and resources with which they compete best and create the most value for owners. They *outsource* noncore business processes, paying suppliers and distributors to perform them and thereby increasing their reliance on suppliers. These new business models call for

core competency
Skills and resources with which an organization competes best and creates the most value for owners

"Can anyone remember what our core business is?"

unprecedented coordination—not only among internal activities, but also among customers, suppliers, and strategic partners—and they often involve globally dispersed processes and supply chains. The key to coordinating all these elements is new networking and communications technologies. Interestingly, the same technologies can be instrumental in meeting a firm's social-responsibility requirements as well as improving its operations. The "Wired World" box in this chapter highlights another new method, called *disruption management,* by which some organizations are responding to crises in their environments.

Emerging Challenges and Opportunities in the Environment of Business

In addition to the general dimensions of the external environment that we've just discussed, there are numerous emerging challenges and opportunities in today's business environment. In this section, we'll discuss some of the most important innovations in the way that companies respond to them, including *outsourcing, viral marketing,* and *business process management.*

outsourcing
Strategy of paying suppliers and distributors to perform certain business processes or to provide needed materials or resources

Outsourcing **Outsourcing** is the strategy of paying suppliers and distributors to perform certain business processes or to provide needed materials or services. It is an increasingly popular strategy because it helps firms focus on their core activities and avoid getting sidetracked onto secondary activities.[24]

The cafeteria at a large bank may be important to employees and some customers, but running it is not the bank's main line of business and expertise. Bankers need to focus on money management and financial services, not food-service operations. That's why most banks outsource cafeteria operations to food-service management companies whose main line of business includes cafeterias. The result, ideally, is more attention to banking by bankers, better food service for cafeteria customers, and formation of a new supplier–client

Replanning for Disruption Management

Remarkable, even violent, disruptions to business activities seem to have become the rule rather than the exception in recent years. Most memorable, of course, are the confusion, grief, and discontinuity in every walk of life wrought by the 9/11 terrorism attacks on the United States. But additional disruptions are arising more frequently than ever before from various sources. Financial fortunes are recast in a matter of mere minutes by sudden and steep changes on the stock market. Trusted suppliers, long relied upon for dependable goods or services, suddenly fail and shut down. Widespread product failures, such as fatally defective tires, leave companies facing consumer distrust. Products and business processes are suddenly revolutionized as new technologies require rapid redirection and changeovers to new ways of doing things. Business, of course, has always been threatened by disruption, but a number of factors make the threat today more frequent and severe. Moreover, when problems do arise, organizations are faced with the need for fast—nearly instantaneous—reaction if they want to minimize negative, even disastrous, consequences.

In response to the growing need to reduce adverse effects, a new technology called *disruption management (DM)* has emerged. DM is unlike traditional emergency-management procedures, which typically call for special organizations to respond to disaster by assisting victims in cleanup, treatment, and recovery on an as-needed basis. Instead of outside assistance, DM stresses internal self-reliance in planning for and preparing responses to disruptions in an organization's external environment. It calls for a firm to adapt its organizational structure, technology, and policies so that it will be better prepared to continue operations during and after major disruptions. In short, the firm becomes "disruption sensitive" in order to anticipate environmental disruptions and adapt rapidly when disaster strikes.

DM is a decision support system that's been under development for more than two years by researchers at the Technical University of Denmark's Department of Informatics and Mathematical Modeling. The core technology consists of computer-based models to simulate different possible responses to various disruptions. Developers use mathematical models to represent cause-and-effect relationships among real-world variables. Then they test each model to evaluate its effectiveness in guiding management response to disruption. With the right model, managers can replan activities instantaneously in light of a disruption to ordinary activities. They can even make alternative plans in case of potential future problems.

DM replanning considers a complex set of variables, the ways they interact, and the consequences for the firm and its customers. The objective is to identify a recovery solution that minimizes negative effects—that is, minimizes costs and maximizes revenues—by considering two aspects of response for each replanning option: immediate (or short-term) consequences and strategic (long-term) analysis.

Consider a hypothetical shutdown at Chicago's O'Hare Airport. An airline's least costly solution would be to cancel all incoming flights immediately. But although cancellation cuts the airline's operating costs, it is a terrible option for passengers who can't get where they're going. Replanning models consider alternatives to cancellation, such as rescheduling flights into neighboring airports and providing ground transportation into Chicago. Of course, pilots and aircraft must also be rescheduled from diverted to new destinations. A DM model would quickly simulate the costs and benefits of these (and other) options in order to facilitate an effective decision.

In developing DM, researchers have experimented with various kinds of disruptions. A telecommunications system is disconnected, causing a communications blackout that deprives users of point-to-point connections. Airports are shut down due to weather conditions or terrorism, preventing scheduled flights from arriving or departing. Manufacturing firms are deprived of needed assembly components when suppliers are shut down by strike or flood. For every application, digital communications are the key to success in using DM. The simulator relies on information both from the organization's internal communications networks and from external sources (such as suppliers, customers, and news agencies) via the Internet. Once replanning decisions have been made, directions can be sent instantaneously to facilities and customers throughout the firm.

Say
what you mean
COMMUNICATING THE CORPORATE MESSAGE

The business environment is in a constant state of change, sometimes providing a company with major opportunities, sometimes presenting it with serious challenges, sometimes both at once. The most successful companies take change for granted, continually adapting to ensure the best possible business outcomes. Being adaptable means communicating effectively not only with stakeholders, but with the public at large.

Corporate communications—the means by which a company communicates to its stakeholders—is an increasingly important business activity. In fact, many major companies now maintain corporate communications teams whose members are skilled in the art of public relations, who understand the media, and who can communicate a company's mission. They're also responsible for dealing with problems that may affect the relationship between the company and the larger environment in which it operates.

In recent years, the pace of corporate change has been unprecedented: mergers, acquisitions, corporate failures, and the emergence of new names and brands—all have caused profound shifts in the business landscape. In addition, one of the biggest ongoing challenges to any company is effectively communicating what it does and where it stands on the major issues in the public mind, including social responsibility, the environment, human rights, and diversity, to name just a few.

The most successful companies control their communications activities by making clear mission statements, remaining open about both internal policies and external relationships, and making sure that the public knows that they are ready to respond to environmental change. The process, of course, varies from company to company. In some instances, top managers become spokespeople, attracting media attention and providing the organization with a face. In other cases, communications teams interact on a daily basis with the media, interest groups, politicians, and the general public to project a company's image and respond to concerns.

One thing's certain: The ever-increasing pace of change makes it harder for companies to stay ahead of the curve. They can't afford to be perceived as outdated and unresponsive and must project images of dynamic, up-to-date organizations that know how to get engaged with the larger community.

relationship (food-service company/bank). Firms today outsource numerous activities, including payroll, employee training, and research and development.

vertical integration

Strategy of owning the means by which an organization produces goods or services

Outsourcing Versus Vertical Integration Outsourcing is also why **vertical integration** is no longer as popular as it once was. Many firms that once owned their own raw-materials supply lines have changed their thinking and outsource instead. Although owning a supplier assures a steady supply of incoming materials, ownership also means learning to manage the supplier's business—which is usually quite different from the owner's. Too often, the owner ends up devoting too many resources to the supply business and too few to its core competencies.

Consider a company that cuts and packages paper for photocopiers and computer printers. It can reduce the risk of paper shortages by buying a mill that makes paper from wood pulp. But in reducing the risk of paper shortages, the company increases the risk of losing focus on its main line of business—cutting and packaging paper. Moreover, in trading one risk for another, managers with no expertise in running a paper mill will find themselves competing against firms that are. Facing keen competition in both industries, they may well end up by failing to compete in either.

A basic rule of thumb is that the advantages of vertical integration are the disadvantages of outsourcing, and vice versa. In many cases, however, outsourcing often saves time and money, increases effectiveness in a firm's core business, and results in more value for customers and owners.[25] "Vertical integration," observes one expert, "makes sense only when a company can't be sure of getting the supplies or distribution channels it needs—as in the former Soviet Union. . . . If you have functioning markets, you don't need it."

"If you have functioning markets, you don't need vertical integration."

~F.M. Sherer, JOHN F. KENNEDY SCHOOL OF GOVERNMENT

Disadvantages of Outsourcing Not everyone, however, agrees. A Dun & Bradstreet study found that one-quarter of all outsourcing relationships fail within two years and one-half within five. In addition, many executives told researchers that suppliers too often don't understand what they are supposed to do, charge too much, and provide poor service. Moreover, when disruptions occur in the supply chain, the costs to both parties can be high. For one thing, replacing failed outsourced operations can be very expensive, especially if the firm wants to return to the outsourced activity. Another risk in outsourcing is loss of control over both operations and information.

Viral Marketing Combining technology with marketing methods usually results in new ways to attract customers. **Viral marketing,** so called because it uses word of mouth that spreads information like a virus from customer to customer, relies on the vast reaches of the Internet to supplant face-to-face communications. Messages about new cars, sports events, and numerous other goods and services flow via the Internet among potential customers who pass the information on to others. Using various formats—games, contests, chat rooms, and bulletin boards—marketers encourage potential customers to try out products and tell other people about them.[26]

viral marketing
Strategy of using the Internet and word-of-mouth marketing to spread product information

Viral marketing can lead to consumer awareness faster and with wider reach than traditional media messages—and at a lower cost. It works for two reasons. First, people rely on the Internet for information that they used to get from newspapers, magazines, and television. Equally important, however, is the interactive element: The customer becomes a participant in the process of spreading the word by forwarding information to other Internet users.

Business Process Management Every company performs numerous processes that provide the goods or services, whether for customers or for other departments within the firm. Human resource departments perform interviewing and hiring processes; payroll departments perform the employee-payment process; the purchasing department performs the process of ordering materials; accounting performs the financial reporting process; marketing performs the process of taking orders from customers. A **process,** in short, is any activity that adds value to some input, transforming it into an output for a customer (whether external or internal).[27]

process
Any activity that adds value to some input by transforming it into an output for a customer (whether internal or external)

In today's business environment, many firms are moving away from the department-oriented organization—one that is organized around departments grouped according to processes or functions. Firms are moving toward process-oriented team structures that cut across old departmental boundaries. This approach is called **business process management.** Often, they begin by asking, "What must we do well to stay in business and win new orders?" Next, they identify the major processes that must be performed well to satisfy these general goals. Then they organize resources and skills around those essential processes. By organizing according to processes rather than functional departments, they gain a number of benefits. Decision making is faster and more customer-oriented, materials and operations are coordinated, and products get to customers more rapidly.[28]

business process management
Approach by which firms move away from department-oriented organization and toward process-oriented team structures that cut across old departmental boundaries

The Aftermath of 9/11

At this point, it seems almost trite to say that the events of September 11, 2001, changed things. But there is value in revisiting the tragic events of that day and in examining the ways in which they continue to affect the U.S. economy. In many ways, September 11 demonstrated dramatically that the U.S. business system works. In other ways, the events of that day did indeed change profoundly the way business operates in the United States.[29]

In some ways, the year after September 11, 2001, demonstrated conclusively the resilience of U.S. institutions. The 12 months following the terrorist attacks witnessed a declining stock market, a significant drop in personal wealth, widespread corporate corruption, and as much uncertainty as the nation has faced since the attack on Pearl Harbor in 1941. In the wake of these events, some skeptics—admittedly, those of the gloomiest faction—predicted that the United States was doomed to become a terrorist-racked, depression-ridden nation spiraling out of control.

In reality, the flexibility and strength inherent in the U.S. political and economic systems became just as obvious as their flaws. Most people kept their jobs, and most businesses kept going. Even as some economic sectors declined, others continued to expand. Exports continue to flow into other countries, as did foreign direct investment.

On the other hand, American business now faces major changes. For the last 20 years or so, the government has maintained a fairly low profile in business-related matters. Since President Ronald Reagan proclaimed in his first inaugural address in 1981 that "government is not the solution to our problems, government is the problem," free markets, deregulation, and private enterprise have carried the day. But history since September 11 promises to change all that. Government is already beginning to resume its traditional role as provider of homeland security. In the wake of September 11 and the rash of scandals in corporate governance that dominated the news in 2002, we will probably see more market controls and hear more calls for regulation.

A more specific effect that businesses themselves are already addressing involves workplace security. Gated entrances, restricted access to sensitive areas, and the requirement that visitors sign in and wear badges are long-time practices at many firms. But the events of September 11 have further heightened security

Monitoring the capital's major buildings is just one task in safeguarding American lives and property. The federal Office of Homeland Security <www.whitehouse.gov/deptofhomeland/> *is responsible for developing programs and standards to protect against, and minimize damage from, terrorist attacks. Standard & Poor's* <www.standardandpoors.com> *estimates that Corporate America spent $135 billion to comply with new security standards in 2002: $35 billion on insurance, $20 billion in workplace security upgrades, and $15 billion in information systems backups.*

Self-Check Questions 7–9

*You should now be able to answer Self-Check Questions 7–9**

7. MULTIPLE CHOICE The *sociocultural environment* is influenced by all of the following **except** [select one] **(a)** consumer tastes; **(b)** customs; **(c)** mores; **(d)** values; **(e)** demographic characteristics.

8. TRUE/FALSE The fact that accounting firms have ventured into the consulting business is an asset to the industry because it allows firms to achieve synergies and increase profits without generating conflicts of interest.

9. MULTIPLE CHOICE Which of the following activities is **least** likely to be *outsourced* by an automobile manufacturer? [select one] **(a)** maintaining the lawns and landscaping in front of the factory; **(b)** operating the company cafeteria; **(c)** managing employee payroll; **(d)** repainting the stripes on the parking lot; **(e)** attaching seat assemblies to the interior of new cars on the assembly line.

*Answers to Self-check Questions 7–9 can be found on p. AN-2.

concerns in many firms, and many firms have bolstered existing measures. Some are conducting more extensive background checks when hiring new employees. Others have not only beefed up security, both for physical work sites and information networks, but also developed elaborate crisis plans.

Continued from page 30

Firms That Flunked

We've seen how *Fortune* identifies the *most* admired businesses in the United States, and we identified several of the prominent firms that regularly make the list. But whenever such a ranking is compiled, it's instructive to look not just at the top of the list, but also at the bottom. Just exactly who are the *least* admired companies in the United States?

Actually, *Fortune*'s current list doesn't say, at least not in so many words. But it does name some of the firms ranked at the bottom on each of its eight criteria. Polaroid, for example, had the third-lowest ranking on financial soundness and the second-lowest ranking on employee talent and use of corporate assets. Perhaps worst of all, however, was the Warnaco Group—dead last in financial soundness, employee talent, use of corporate assets, long-term investment value, social responsibility, and quality of management. LTV and America West Holdings were also among the lowest-ranked firms on at least two different criteria.

We also noted earlier that many firms have been highly ranked on the *Fortune* list for several years. But other firms seem to burst onto the scene from practically nowhere, only to fade into the background almost as quickly. Enron is the classic case. Enron was ranked first in its industry (though not in the top ten overall) in the 2001 list and last in the 2002 list. Likewise, Vivendi Universal, a media and entertainment company, was unranked on the 2001 list but entered the 2002 list at number four. The firm's recent financial crisis promises to drop it far back down the list in 2003.

Questions for Discussion

1. What is your opinion of the value of the *Fortune* rankings?
2. Do you think the criteria used by *Fortune* are appropriate? Can you suggest others?
3. Is the ranking something that investors should rely on in buying stock?
4. If you were a top manager and wanted your firm to move up in the rankings, how would you proceed?
5. On the 2002 list, Wal-Mart and FedEx made the top 10 overall list of most admired firms. Each, however, finished second in its industry group (behind Target and UPS, respectively). How might this apparent contradiction be explained?

Summary of Learning Objectives

1. ***Explain the concepts of* organizational boundaries *and* multiple organizational environments.**

All businesses operate within a larger **external environment** consisting of everything outside an organization's boundaries that might affect it. Because the external environment plays a major role in determining success or failure, managers must have a complete understanding of their environments so that they can operate and compete within it.

An **organizational boundary** is that which separates the organization from its environment. But while they were once relatively easy to identify, they are becoming harder to pin down. For one thing, organizations have multiple environments. Some environments are relatively general, such as prevailing economic conditions. Others are much more precise, such as the pricing policies of competitors.

A full picture of a company's organizational environments would include the following elements: economic conditions, technology, political-legal considerations, social issues, the global environment, issues of ethical and social responsibility, the business environment itself, and numerous other emerging challenges and opportunities.

2. ***Explain the importance of the* economic environment *to business and identify the factors used to evaluate the performance of an economic system.***

The overall health of the **economic environment**—the economic system in which they operate—affects organizations. The two key goals of the U.S. system are *economic growth* and *economic stability.*

(1) *Economic growth*: The pattern of short-term ups and downs in an economy constitute its **business cycle.** The main measure of *growth* in this cycle is **aggregate output:** the total quantity of goods and services produced by a system in a given period. An increase in aggregate output is growth.

In a growing economy, two things happen: (i) *Output per capita*—the quantity of goods and services provided by the system per person—goes up. (ii) People then benefit from a higher **standard of living:** They can buy more goods and services with their currency. To know how much standard of living is improving, we consider the following factors: (i) **Gross national product (GNP)**—the total value of all goods and services produced by a national economy within a given period *regardless of where the factors of production are located.* (ii) **Gross domestic product (GDP)**—the total value of all goods and services produced within a given period by a national economy *through domestic factors of production.* If GDP is going up, so is aggregate output; if aggregate output is going up, we have *economic growth.*

GDP is preferred for calculating national income and output. The *real growth rate* of a system is the growth rate of GDP adjusted for inflation and changes in the value of the country's currency. *GDP per capita* means GDP per person and is a better measure than GDP itself of the average person's economic well-being. **Nominal GDP** means GDP measured in current dollars, but we calculate **real GDP** when we calculate GDP to account for *changes in currency values and price changes.* This adjustment accounts for **purchasing power parity**—the principle that exchange rates are set so that the prices of similar products in different countries are about the same. Purchasing power parity gives us a much better idea of *what people can actually buy with the financial resources allocated to them by their respective economic systems.* In other words, it gives us a better sense of standards of living across the globe.

Productivity compares how much a system produces with the resources needed to produce it. Standard of living improves only through increases in productivity, and real growth in GDP reflects growth in productivity. Among the factors that can inhibit growth, two of the most important are *balance of trade* and the *national debt.* (i) *Balance of trade* is the value of all products *exported* minus the value of *imported* products. A *positive* balance results when a country exports (sells to other countries) more than it imports (buys from other countries). A *negative* balance means that a country imports more than it exports. A negative balance is a *trade deficit.* (ii) **National debt** is the amount of money that a government owes its creditors.

(2) *Economic stability*: **Stability** means that the amount of money available in an economic system and the quantity

of goods and services produced in it are growing at about the same rate. There are two key threats to stability: *inflation* and *unemployment.* (i) **Inflation** occurs when there are widespread price increases throughout an economic system. When the amount of money injected into an economy outstrips the increase in actual output, people have more money but no more products to buy. As they compete to buy available products, prices go up until they erase the increase in the amount of money injected into the economy. Purchasing power, therefore, declines. We measure inflation by measuring price increases through such indexes as the **consumer price index (CPI)**—the prices of typical products purchased by consumers living in urban areas.

(ii) **Unemployment** is the level of joblessness among people actively seeking work. When it's low, there's a shortage of labor available. As they compete for the available labor supply, businesses raise wages. Then because higher labor costs eat into profit margins, they raise product prices. Consumers have more money to spend, but this increase is soon erased by higher prices. Again, purchasing power declines.

If people in different sectors lose their jobs at the same time, overall income and spending drop and businesses cut spending further—including spending on labor. Unemployment goes up further. This kind of unemployment is called *cyclical unemployment.* Meanwhile, producers also start producing less because they can't sell as much. Aggregate output then decreases and we have a **recession**—a period during which aggregate output, as measured by real GDP, declines. A prolonged and deep recession is a **depression.**

The government manages the economy through two sets of policies. (1) It manages the collection and spending of its revenues through **fiscal policies** (such as tax increases). (2) **Monetary policies** focus on controlling the size of the nation's money supply. Through the Federal Reserve System, the government can influence the ability and willingness of banks throughout the country to lend money. It can also influence the supply of money by prompting interest rates to go up or down. (i) Higher interest rates make money more expensive to borrow; when the Fed restricts the money supply, it's practicing a *tight monetary policy.* (ii) Lower interest rates make money less expensive to borrow; when the Fed loosens the money supply, it's practicing an *easy monetary policy.* Together, fiscal policy and monetary policy make up **stabilization policy:** government economic policy whose goal is to smooth out fluctuations in output and unemployment and to stabilize prices.

3. *Discuss the current economic picture in the United States and summarize expert predictions about its future.*

Most experts see three major forces driving the economy for the next decade: (1) The information revolution will continue to enhance productivity. (2) New technological breakthroughs will create new industries. (3) Increasing globalization will create larger markets while also fostering tougher global competition.

As a result of these forces, economists also predict certain economic trends: (1) We'll avoid inflationary surges and large budget deficits. (2) Countries that encourage free trade and open financial systems will prosper. (3) Successful businesses will master new technologies.

There are also factors that may limit future U.S. economic growth: (1) Because we import more than we export, the trade deficit will grow, making us a debtor nation. (2) Income inequality in the United States is a problem. (3) Consumer debt is steadily increasing, and many people are not saving enough for retirement. (4) Even those individuals who are for saving for retirement are being hurt by declines in the stock market. (5) Too many Americans lack health insurance.

4. *Describe the* technological environment *and its role in business.*

Technology refers to all the ways by which firms create value for their constituents, including human knowledge, work methods, physical equipment, electronics and telecommunications, and various processing systems. It's applied within the organization but comes from the general environment. There are two general categories of business-related technologies: *product and service technologies* and *business process technologies.*

(1) *Product and service technologies* create products—both physical goods and services—for customers, and although we associate technology with manufacturing, it's also important in the service sector. New technologies, including the Internet, are revolutionizing nearly every aspect of business—from the ways that customers and companies interact to where, when, and how employees do their work. Technology is the basis of competition for some firms, especially those whose goals include being the technology leaders in their industries. Other firms compete directly on how quickly they can get things done for consumers.

(2) *Business process technologies* are used to improve a firm's performance of internal operations (such as accounting) and to help to create better relationships with external constituents, such as suppliers and customers. **Enterprise resource planning (ERP)** is a large-scale information system for organizing and managing a firm's processes across product lines, departments, and geographic locations. The ERP stores information on activities, coordinates internal operations with activities by outside suppliers and customers, and generates up-to-the-minute financial reports.

5. *Describe the* political-legal environment *and its role in business.*

The **political-legal environment** reflects the relationship between business and government, usually in the form of government regulation. The legal system defines in part what an organization can and can't do. Various government agencies regulate important areas such as advertising practices, safety and health considerations, and acceptable standards of business conduct.

Pro- or antibusiness sentiment in government can further influence business activity. During periods of probusiness sentiment, firms find it easier to compete and have fewer concerns about antitrust issues. During periods of antibusiness sentiment, firms may find their competitive activities more restricted. Political stability is an important consideration for international firms: No business wants to set up shop in another country unless trade relationships with that country are stable.

6. ***Describe the* sociocultural environment *and its role in business.***

The **sociocultural environment** includes the customs, mores, values, and demographic characteristics of the society in which an organization functions. Sociocultural processes determine the goods and services as well as the standards of business conduct that a society values and accepts.

(1) *Customer preferences and tastes*: Customer preferences and tastes vary both across and within national boundaries. In fact, they can vary widely within the same country, and they can change over time (the way preferences for color, style, taste, and so forth change from season to season). Sociocultural factors also influence the way workers feel about their jobs and organizations. In some cultures, work carries meaningful social significance; in others, it's simply a means to an end and people are concerned only with pay and job security.

(2) *Ethical compliance and responsible business behavior*: An especially critical element of the sociocultural environment is the practice of ethical conduct and social responsibility. The central issue today revolves around the fact that rapid changes in business relationships, organizational structures, and financial flows pose difficulties in keeping track of a company's financial position. Stakeholders—employees, stockholders, consumers, unions, creditors, and government—are entitled to a fair accounting so they can make enlightened personal and business decisions, but the public often gets blurred pictures of a firm's competitive health.

Appropriate standards of conduct also vary across cultures. The shape of the market, the ethics of political influence, and the attitudes of its workforce are only a few of the many ways in which culture can affect an organization.

7. ***Identify emerging challenges and opportunities in the* business environment.**

Business today is more complex and demanding than ever before. The hunt for new products has accelerated, customers want higher-quality goods and services, new markets are emerging in other countries, employees want flexible working conditions, stockholders expect larger profits, and the public demands honesty and respect for the environment.

Successful companies are responding to these challenges in new ways. They are redrawing traditional boundaries, joining together to develop new goods and services. They are focusing on their **core competencies**—the skills and resources with which they compete best and create the most value for owners. They *outsource* noncore business processes, paying suppliers and distributors to perform them but also increasing reliance on suppliers. These new business models call for unprecedented coordination and often involve globally dispersed processes and supply chains. The key to coordinating all these elements is new networking and communications technologies.

The innovative ways in which companies respond to emerging challenges and opportunities include *outsourcing, viral marketing,* and *business process management.* (1) **Outsourcing** is the strategy of paying suppliers and distributors to perform certain business processes or to provide needed materials or services. It has decreased reliance on **vertical integration:** Many firms that once owned their raw-materials supply lines now outsource instead because it saves time and money and improves the firm's core business. But there are disadvantages: (i) Suppliers don't always understand what they are supposed to do, charge too much, and provide poor service. (ii) Supply-chain disruptions are expensive. (iii) The firm risks loss of control over operations and information.

(2) Combining technology with marketing methods, **viral marketing** relies on the Internet to supplant face-to-face communications. Messages about products flow via the Internet among potential customers who pass the information on to others. Viral marketing leads to consumer awareness faster and with wider reach than traditional media messages—and at lower cost.

(3) *Business process management*: A **process** is any activity that adds value to some input by transforming it into an output for a customer (whether external or internal). Many firms are moving away from the department-oriented organization and toward process-oriented team structures that cut across old departmental boundaries—an approach called **business process management.** They identify the processes that they must perform well and then organize their resources around those essential processes. Decision making is faster and more customer-oriented, materials and operations are coordinated, and products get to customers more rapidly.

KEY TERMS

external environment (p. 30)
organizational boundary (p. 30)
economic environment (p. 31)
business cycle (p. 33)
aggregate output (p. 33)
standard of living (p. 33)
gross domestic product (GDP) (p. 33)
gross national product (GNP) (p. 33)
nominal GDP (p. 34)
real GDP (p. 34)
purchasing power parity (p. 34)
productivity (p. 35)
national debt (p. 36)
stability (p. 37)
inflation (p. 37)
consumer price index (p. 37)
unemployment (p. 38)
recession (p. 39)
depression (p. 39)
fiscal policies (p. 39)
monetary policies (p. 39)
stabilization policy (p. 40)
technology (p. 43)
enterprise resource planning (ERP) (p. 44)
political-legal environment (p. 45)
sociocultural environment (p. 46)

core competency (p. 49)
outsourcing (p. 50)
vertical integration (p. 52)
viral marketing (p. 53)
process (p. 53)
business process management (p. 53)

QUESTIONS AND EXERCISES

Questions for Review

1. What is GDP? Real GDP? What does each measure?
2. Why is inflation both good and bad? How does the government try to control it?
3. What is technology? How does it affect organizations?
4. What is outsourcing? What are its benefits and risks?

Questions for Analysis

5. Why is it important for managers to understand the environment in which their businesses operate?
6. Explain how current economic indicators such as inflation and unemployment affect you personally. Explain how they will affect you as a manager.
7. At first glance, it might seem as though the goals of economic growth and stability are inconsistent with one another. How can you reconcile this apparent inconsistency?
8. What is the current climate regarding the regulation of business? How might it affect you if you were a manager today?

Application Exercises

9. Select two businesses with which you have some familiarity. Identify the major elements of their environments that are most likely to affect them in important and meaningful ways.
10. Using the Internet, identify the major suppliers of software for enterprise resource planning. Try to locate information about their primary customers.
11. Interview a business owner or senior manager. Ask this individual to describe for you the following things: (1) what business functions, if any, he or she outsources; (2) whether or not he or she is focusing more attention on business process management; and (3) how the events of September 11, 2001, have affected his or her work (not so much how it has affected him or her as a human being, but how it has affected the jobs, the organization, and so forth).

Building Your Business Skills

THE LETDOWN FROM ENVIRONMENTAL UPHEAVAL

This exercise enhances the following SCANS workplace competencies: demonstrating basic skills, demonstrating thinking skills, exhibiting interpersonal skills, and working with information.

Goal

To encourage students to understand how local events can affect other businesses in a number of ways

The Situation

The collapse of Enron affected literally hundreds of other businesses. While attention has been directed primarily at the demise of Arthur Andersen, many other businesses suffered as well. For example, Enron's headquarters was located in a large office building on the edge of Houston's downtown business district. A new office tower for the firm was also under construction on an adjacent property. Because of both Enron's rapid growth and the prosperity of its employees, numerous other service providers had set up shop nearby—a shoeshine stand, a coffee shop, a bank branch, a dry cleaner, and two restaurants. When Enron collapsed, the construction on the new building was also halted.

Larger businesses were also caught up in the ripple effect. Enron, for example, had bought the rights to name the new home of baseball's Houston Astros Enron Field. The Astros were forced to remove all Enron signage and seek a new sponsor. Continental Airlines dominates the air traffic market out of Houston, and Enron was one of Continental's largest corporate clients. Combined with the events of September 11, 2001, and major staff reductions at Compaq Computer, another big Continental client, the end of business travel by Enron managers cost the airline considerable revenue.

Assignment

Divide up into groups of four or five students. Each group should begin by doing the following:

Step 1

Identify five kinds of small businesses likely to have been affected by Enron's collapse. You can include some of those identified above, but try to identify at least two others.

Step 2

Identify five kinds of large businesses likely to have been affected by Enron's collapse. Again, you can use some of those identified above, but try to identify at least two others.

Step 3

As a group, develop answers to each of the following:

1. For each company that you identify, both small and large, describe the precise effects of the Enron collapse on its business.
2. Describe the most logical organizational response of each company to these effects.
3. What kinds of plans, if any, should each organization develop in the event of similar future events?
4. Identify businesses that might have benefited economically from the collapse of Enron.

Alternative Assignment

Select a different high-profile environmental upheaval, such as the destruction of the World Trade Center, or another major business closure, and substitute it for your choice of Enron. Then proceed with Steps 1–3 above.

Follow-Up Questions

1. What does this exercise demonstrate about the pitfalls of relying too heavily on one business?
2. Could any of these businesses have been better prepared for the Enron collapse?
3. Managers are advised to be on the alert to environmental change. Is it possible for a manager to spend too much time trying to anticipate future events? Why or why not?

Exercising Your Ethics

ASSESSING THE ETHICS OF TRADE-OFFS

The Purpose of the Assignment

Managers must often make choices among options that are presented by environmental circumstances. This exercise will help you better appreciate the nature and complexity of the kinds of tradeoffs that often result.

The Situation

Let's say that you are owner and manager of a medium-sized nonunionized manufacturing company located in a town of about 4,000 people. The nearest major city is about 100 miles away. With about 500 workers, you are one of the five largest employers in town. A regional recession has caused two of the other largest employers to close down (one went out of business and the other relocated to another area). A new foreign competitor has set up shop in the area, but local unemployment has still risen sharply. All in all, the regional economic climate and the new competitor are hurting your business. Your sales have dropped 20 percent this year, and you forecast another drop next year before things begin to turn around.

The Dilemma

You face two unpleasant choices. *Choice 1*: You can tell your employees that you need them to take cuts in pay and benefits. You know that because of the local unemployment rate, you can easily replace anyone who refuses. Unfortunately, you may need your employees to take another cut next year if your forecasts hold true. At the same time, you do have reason to believe that when the economy rebounds (in about two years, according to your forecasts), you can begin restoring pay cuts. Here are the advantages of this choice: You can probably (1) preserve all 500 jobs, (2) maintain your own income, (3) restore pay cuts in the future, and (4) keep the business open indefinitely. And the disadvantages: Pay cuts will (1) pose economic hardships for your employees and (2) create hard feelings and undercut morale.

Choice 2: You can maintain the status quo as far as your employees are concerned, but in that case, you'll be facing two problems: (1) You'll have to cut your own salary. While you can certainly afford to live on less income, doing so would be a blow to your personal finances. (2) If economic conditions get worse and/or last longer than forecast, you may have to close down altogether. The firm has a cash surplus, but because you'll have to dip into these funds to maintain stable wages, they'll soon run out. The advantages of this option: You can (1) avoid economic hardship for your workers and (2) maintain good employee relations. The downside: You will reduce your own standard of living and may eventually cost everyone his or her job.

Questions for Discussion

1. What are the basic ethical issues in this situation?
2. Can you identify any other options?
3. Of the two options posed in the situation as presented, which would you choose? Why?

Crafting Your Business Plan

WASTE NOT, WANT NOT

The Purpose of the Assignment

1. To determine where, in the framework of the *Business PlanPro (BPP)* software package, external environment issues for a business might appropriately be presented in developing a sample business plan.
2. To familiarize students with some of the planning issues faced by a firm as it considers how it fits into and interacts with the external environment.

Assignment

After reading Chapter 2 in the textbook, open the BPP *software and search for information about the types of external environ-*

ment considerations that would be of concern to a sample firm: Good Earth Resources Inc. *To find* Good Earth Resources, *do the following:*

Open the *Business PlanPro*. If it asks if you want to "create a new business plan" or "open an existing plan," select "create a new business plan" (even though you are not going to create a plan at this time). You will then be taken to the *Business PlanPro EasyPlan Wizard*. Click on the option entitled **Research It.** You will then be presented with a new list of options, including **Sample Plan Browser.** After clicking on the **Sample Plan Browser,** go down the alphabetical list of sample plans and double-click on **Recycling—Energy Conversion,** which is the location of *Good Earth Resources Inc.* The screen you are looking at is the introduction page for the *Good Earth* business plan. Next, scroll down until you reach the **Table of Contents** for the company's business plan. Read section **1.0 Executive Summary** to gain an understanding of *Good Earth*'s business concept.

Now respond to the following items:

1. Consider today's economic environment as it relates to Good Earth's business plan. Is the present economic climate suitable for starting such a business? Discuss why or why not. [Sites to see in *BPP* (for this item): On the Table of Contents page, click on each of the following in turn: **1.1 Objectives, 2.2 Start-up Summary, 2.0 Company Summary, 3.2 Competitive Comparison, 4.1 Market Trends,** and **7.1 Important Assumptions.**]
2. Consider the technological environment for Good Earth's line of business. What role, if any, does technology play in Good Earth's business plan? Do you find any evidence that this industry might benefit from new technologies? Explain. [Sites to see in *BPP*: From the Table of Contents page, click on each of the following in turn: **1.1 Objectives, 1.3 Keys to Success, 2.0 Company Summary, 3.0 Operations,** and **3.4 Technology.**]
3. Do you believe that today's political and legal environments would be receptive to Good Earth's business concept? Where in Good Earth's business plan should these issues be presented? Explain. [Sites to see in *BPP*: On the Table of Contents page, click on each of the following in turn: **2.3 Adjacent Property Option** and **3.5.1 New York City Waste System.**]
4. Consider outsourcing as it might apply at Good Earth. Which of Good Earth's business activities, if any, might be outsourced? What advantages and drawbacks would result from outsourcing? Where, in the firm's business plan, do you suggest that outsourcing be discussed? [Sites to see in *BPP*: On the Table of Contents page, click on **2.2 Start-up Summary** and then on **3.0 Operations.** Next, click on **4.2.1 Customers.**]

Video Exercise

VIEWING THE ENVIRONMENT: MTV EUROPE

Learning Objectives

The purpose of this video is to help you

1. Understand how the external environment affects a company's ability to enter and compete in different markets.
2. Explain why a company must analyze the economic, technological, political-legal, and sociocultural environments of the countries in which it operates.
3. Understand how a company relies on its core competencies to compete in the global marketplace.

Synopsis

MTV had built a large and loyal following in the United States long before it thought about expanding into Europe. When the time came, one of the key issues that management had to address was the technological development of targeted countries—in particular, how many people had televisions. MTV also had to assess the economic development of each country and evaluate sociocultural trends, such as the direction of local music and the attitudes and interests of the local youth market. Finally, it had to consider such political-legal issues as the dominance of state-operated television stations. Today, MTV's pan-European approach combines a mix of popular American and British music that's broadcast to the entire region, plus special programs customized for northern, central, and southern European markets.

Discussion Questions

1. *For analysis*: Why would MTV be interested in the ownership structure of television stations in Europe?
2. *For analysis*: What are MTV Europe's core competencies and how do they help the company compete?
3. *For application*: In planning future expansion, what elements might MTV Europe weigh most heavily when analyzing a country's economic status?
4. *For application*: What elements of the sociocultural environment should MTV Europe's management follow especially closely?
5. *For debate*: Should MTV Europe do more to customize programming for the sociocultural environment in different countries? Support your position.

Online Exploration

Browse the MTV Europe Web site at <www.mtveurope.com> and review the regional links that appear on the home page. Also follow the links to see upcoming special events being promoted by MTV Europe and to read more about the company and its activities. Finally, choose and follow one country-specific link. How does MTV Europe give its Web site an international flavor in keeping with its overall image? Why would the company provide links for different countries and languages? How has MTV applied its core competencies on this Web site?

CHAPTER

Understanding Entrepreneurship and Business Ownership

After reading this chapter, you should be able to:

1. Define *small business,* discuss its importance to the U.S. economy, and explain which *types of small business* are most likely to succeed.
2. Explain *entrepreneurship* and describe some key characteristics of entrepreneurial personalities and activities.
3. Describe the *business plan* and the *start-up decisions* made by small businesses and identify sources of *financial aid* available to such enterprises.
4. Explain the main reasons why new business start-ups are increasing and identify the main reasons for success and failure in small businesses.
5. Explain *sole proprietorships* and *partnerships* and discuss the advantages and disadvantages of each.
6. Describe *corporations,* discuss their advantages and disadvantages, and identify different kinds of corporations.
7. Explain the basic issues involved in creating and managing a corporation and identify recent trends and issues in corporate ownership.

The Big Cheese in Vermont

People familiar with the business landscape in Vermont point with justifiable pride to Ben Cohen and Jerry Greenfield, founders of Ben and Jerry's Homemade Holdings Inc., as the state's foremost entrepreneurs. But the ice cream boys are getting some competition these days from another pair of entrepreneurs who are making a popular line of cheese products the cream of local business.

The story starts in 1919, when 94 Vermont dairy farmers banded together to create a cooperative—a form of business enterprise owned by its members—to make and market cheese. The initial membership fee was $5.00 per cow and a cord of wood to fuel the boiler. Cabot Creamery <www.cabotcheese.com> is now a multimillion-dollar dairy-products company with a membership of 1,500 farm families. Its cheeses have won numerous awards, including Best Cheddar in the World at the World Cheese Championship in Green Bay, Wisconsin.

Cabot has always built its brand on quality. Whereas many companies use enzymes to speed up the cheese-making process, Cabot uses only natural methods. Naturally processing high-quality cheese means that a 640-pound block of cheddar might have to sit in a warehouse for a year before it gets its rich, full-bodied flavor. At any time, therefore, Cabot might have 25 million pounds of cheese in the warehouse. And because costs are pegged to the price of milk *when the cheese is first manufactured,* profit margins are hard to predict. Managers have to forecast both the price of milk and the demand for cheese as much as a year in advance. Furthermore, the price of milk fluctuates just as much as the price of crude oil. "There's a pretty good temptation to play around with enzymes," admits Cabot CEO Richard Stammer. "If you can put out an extra-sharp cheddar in 5 months instead of 12, you're less likely to get stung by a spread in the price of milk."

In the early 1990s, Cabot was in danger of going under. Even with revenues of $35 million a year, annual profits were less than $1 million. Members were getting restless, and there was talk of abandoning Cabot and launching a new cooperative. But because a new venture would have been a big risk, members decided on another approach: In 1992, Cabot agreed to be taken over by Agri-Mark Inc., a dairy co-op based in Methuen, Massachusetts. Agri-Mark <www.agri-mark.net> was the fourteenth largest dairy co-op in the United States and wanted to expand. Given the obvious fit between a dairy co-op and a cheese maker, the move seemed like a good one.

Our opening story continues on page 86.

"There's a pretty good temptation to play around with enzymes."

~Richard Stammer
CABOT CHEESE CEO

What Is a "Small" Business?

The term *small business* defies easy definition. Locally owned and operated restaurants and hair salons are small businesses, and giant corporations such as Sony, Caterpillar, and Eastman Kodak are big businesses. Between these two extremes fall thousands of companies that cannot be easily categorized.

Small Business Administration (SBA)
Federal agency charged with assisting small businesses

The U.S. Department of Commerce <www.osec.doc.gov> considers a business small if it has fewer than 500 employees. The U.S. **Small Business Administration (SBA)** <www.sba.gov>, a government assistance agency, regards some companies with 1,500 employees as small. The SBA relies on two different factors: (1) *number of employees* and (2) *total annual sales.* Manufacturers may be small according to the first criterion, and grocery stores may be small according to the second. Although an independent grocery store with $13 million in sales may sound large, the SBA sees it as small when comparing its revenues to those of truly large food retailers.

small business
Independently owned and managed business that does not dominate its market

Because it's sometimes hard to deal in strictly numerical terms, we define a **small business** as one that is independently owned and managed and does not dominate its market. A small business, then, can't be part of another business and must have relatively little influence in its market. Dell Computer <www.dell.com> was a small business when founded by Michael Dell in 1984, but today it's number one in the personal computer market and is not small in any sense of the term.

The Importance of Small Business in the U.S. Economy

As Figure 3.1 shows, most U.S. businesses employ fewer than 100 people, and most U.S. workers are employed by small firms. Figure 3.1(a) shows that 86.09 percent of all businesses employ 20 or fewer people and another 11 percent between 20 and 99 people. Only about one-tenth of 1 percent employ 1,000 or more. Figure 3.1(b) shows that 25.60 percent of all workers are employed by firms with fewer than 20 people; another 29.10 percent work in firms that employ between 20 and 99. The vast majority of these companies are owner operated.[1] Figure 3.1(b) also shows that only 12.70 percent of workers are employed by firms with 1,000 or more employees.

We can measure the contribution of small business in terms of its impact on key aspects of the U.S. economic system, including *job creation, innovation,* and *importance to big business.*

Job Creation Relative job growth among businesses of different sizes is hard to determine. For one thing, when a successful small business starts adding employees at a rapid clip, it may quickly cease being small. Dell Computer had one employee in 1984 (Michael Dell himself). But the payroll grew to 100 employees in 1986, to 2,000 in 1992, and to 40,000 in 2001. While there was no precise point at which Dell turned from "small" into "large," some of the jobs it created should be counted in the small business sector and some in the large.

Small businesses—especially in certain industries—are an important source of new (and often well-paid) jobs. In recent years, small businesses have accounted for 38 percent of all new jobs in high-technology sectors of the economy.[2] Jobs, of course, are created by companies of all sizes, all of which hire and lay off workers. Although small firms often hire at a faster rate, they are likely to cut jobs at a far higher rate. They are the first to hire in times of economic recovery, but big firms are the last to lay off workers during downswings.

Innovation History reminds us that major innovations are as likely to come from small businesses (or individuals) as from big ones. Small firms and individuals invented the PC and the stainless-steel razor blade, the transistor radio and the photocopier, the jet engine and the self-developing photograph. The device

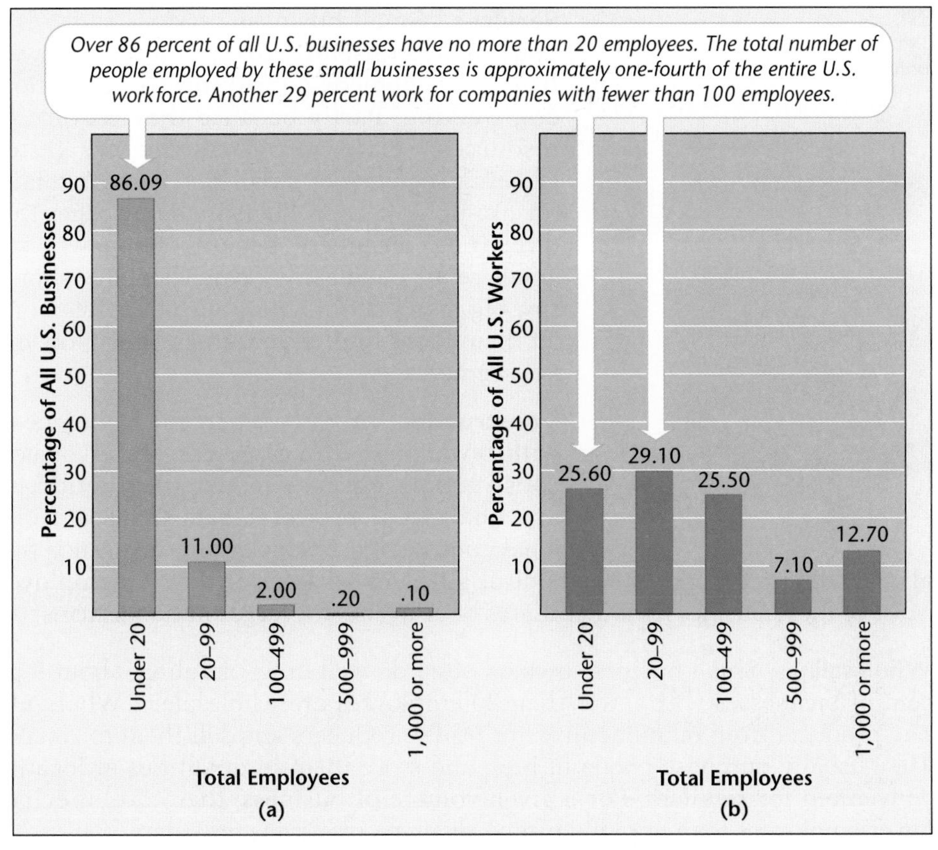

FIGURE 3.1
The Importance of Small Business in the United States

used to repair Vice President Dick Cheney's ailing heart was developed by a small business, as was the new battery-powered one-person vehicle called the Segway Human Transporter.[3]

In addition, innovations are not always new *products*. Michael Dell didn't invent the PC, but he developed an innovative way to build it (buy finished components and then assemble them) and an innovative way to sell it (directly to consumers, first by telephone and now via the Internet). Today, says the SBA, small business supplies 55 percent of all innovations that reach the U.S. marketplace.[4]

Importance to Big Business Most of the products made by big businesses are sold to consumers by small ones. Most dealerships that sell Fords, Toyotas, and Volvos are independently operated. Moreover, small businesses provide big ones with many of their services and raw materials. Microsoft <www.microsoft.com>, for instance, relies on hundreds of small firms for most of its routine code-writing functions.

Popular Areas of Small-Business Enterprise

Not surprisingly, small businesses are more common in some industries than in others. The major small-business industry groups are *services, construction, wholesaling,* and *transportation and manufacturing.* Each industry differs in its needs for employees, money, materials, and machines, but as a general rule, the more resources required, the harder it is to start a business and the less likely an industry is dominated by small firms. Remember, too, that *small* is a relative term. The criteria (number of employees and total annual sales) differ from industry to industry and are often meaningful only when compared with truly large businesses. Figure 3.2 shows the distribution of all U.S. businesses employing fewer than 20 people across industry groups.

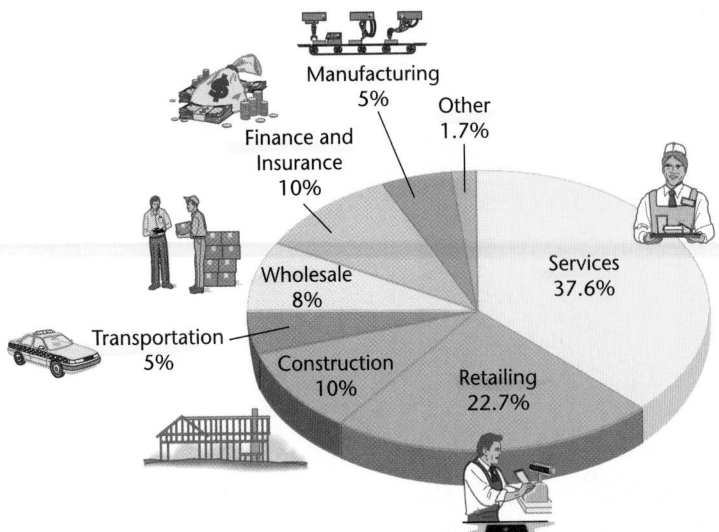

FIGURE 3.2
Small Business by Industry

Services Small-business services range from marriage counseling to computer software, from management consulting to professional dog walking. Partly because they require few resources, service providers are the fastest-growing segment of small business. A retailer, for example, sells products made by other firms directly to consumers. Usually, people who start small retail businesses favor specialty shops—say, big men's clothing or gourmet coffees—that let them focus limited resources on narrow market segments.

Construction About 10 percent of businesses with fewer than 20 employees are involved in construction. Because many construction jobs are small local projects, local firms are often ideal contractors. Financial and insurance firms also account for about 10 percent of all firms with fewer than 20 employees. Most of these businesses are affiliates of or agents for larger national firms.

Wholesaling Small-business owners often do well in wholesaling; about 8 percent of businesses with fewer than 20 employees are wholesalers. Wholesalers buy products from manufacturers or other producers and sell them to retailers. They usually purchase goods in bulk and store them in quantities at locations convenient for retailers. For a given volume of business, therefore, they need fewer employees than manufacturers, retailers, or service providers.

Transportation and Manufacturing Some small firms—about 5 percent of all companies with fewer than 20 employees—do well in transportation and related businesses. These include taxi and limousine companies, charter airplane services, and tour operators. More than any other industry, manufacturing lends itself to big business, but this doesn't mean that there are no small businesses that do well in manufacturing; about 5 percent of firms with fewer than 20 employees are involved in manufacturing. Indeed, small manufacturers some-

Peter and Christina Ruprecht operate a small business in the service sector. Located in Fairfield, New Jersey, Drive-Master Co. Inc. <www.drivemaster.net> *makes driving systems for the physically challenged and adapts vans so that they can be driven by disabled persons from wheelchairs. The company was started by Ruprecht's father, who lost the use of both legs to polio in 1952, and today, it distributes through 400 dealerships nationwide.*

times outperform big ones in such innovation-driven industries as electronics, toys, and computer software.

Entrepreneurship

We noted earlier that Dell Computer started as a one-person operation and grew into a giant corporation. Dell's growth was spurred by the imagination and skill of Michael Dell, the *entrepreneur* who founded the company. Although the concepts of *entrepreneurship* and *small business* are closely related, we begin by discussing some important, though often subtle, differences between them. Then we describe some key characteristics of entrepreneurial personalities and activities.

Distinctions Between Entrepreneurship and Small Business

entrepreneur

Businessperson who accepts both the risks and the opportunities involved in creating and operating a new business venture

Entrepreneurs are people who assume the risk of business ownership with a primary goal of growth and expansion.[5] Many small business owners characterize themselves as entrepreneurs, but a lot of them don't really aspire to expand their business the way the true entrepreneur does. Indeed, a person may be a small-business owner only, an entrepreneur only, or both. Consider Jack Matz, a former corporate executive in Houston who lost his job when his firm was merged. Rather than look for another management position, Matz opened a photocopying business near a local university. His goal is to earn enough money to lead a comfortable life until he retires in 10 years. Matz is a small-business owner, but with no plans to grow and expand, he's not really an entrepreneur.

Conversely, an entrepreneur would open one copy center with the idea of creating a national chain to rival Kinko's. Although this person may begin as a small-business owner, the firm's growth depends on entrepreneurial vision and astute business planning. Thus, the key distinctions between small-business ownership and entrepreneurship are vision, aspiration, and strategy. Whereas the small business owner has no plans for dramatic growth, seeking only a secure and comfortable income, the entrepreneur is motivated to grow, expand, and build—that is, to risk.

Entrepreneurial Characteristics

Many successful entrepreneurs share characteristics that set them apart from most other business owners—for example, resourcefulness and a concern for good, often personal, customer relations. Most of them also have a strong desire to be their own bosses. Many express a need to "gain control over my life" or "build for the family" and believe that building successful businesses will help them do it. They can also deal with uncertainty and risk.

Yesterday's entrepreneur was often stereotyped as "the boss"—self-reliant, male, and able to make quick, firm decisions. Today's entrepreneur is seen more often as an open-minded leader who relies on networks, business plans, and consensus. Although today's entrepreneur may be male, she is just as likely to be female. Past and present entrepreneurs also have different views on such topics as how to succeed, how to automate business, and when to rely on experience in the trade or basic business acumen.[6]

Consider Patrick Byrne. Byrne runs Overstock.com, an e-commerce firm that buys excess inventory from makers of clothing, electronics, and other products, and then offers the merchandise for resale on the Internet at deeply discounted prices. Byrne started out by creating a personal-investment fund called High Plains. After amassing a $100 million portfolio, he bought Overstock.com. Along the way, he earned a Ph.D. in philosophy from Stanford and a black belt in tae

Self-Check Questions 1–3

*You should now be able to answer Self-Check Questions 1–3**

1. MULTIPLE CHOICE Which of the following is the **best** definition of a *small business?* [select one]: **(a)** one that employs fewer than 25 people; **(b)** one that operates out of a single location; **(c)** one with annual revenues of less than $100,000; **(d)** one that does business in a single country; **(e)** one that is independently owned and managed and does not dominate its market

2. MULTIPLE CHOICE Which area of small business is likely to be the most difficult to enter? [select one]: **(a)** services; **(b)** manufacturing; **(c)** construction; **(d)** wholesaling; **(e)** transportation.

3. TRUE/FALSE Small-business owners and entrepreneurs have extremely similar profiles.

*ANSWERS TO SELF-CHECK QUESTIONS 1–3 CAN BE FOUND ON P. AN-2.

kwon do. He bicycled across the United States three times, studied more philosophy at Cambridge, and learned five languages. He discovered Overstock.com when its owners came to High Plains seeking capital. "The financials," admits Byrne, "were a joke. But buried in all that was this billion-dollar idea." And so instead of investing in the business, Byrne bought it. Unlike many Internet ventures, Overstock.com has prospered.[7]

Among other things, Byrne's story illustrates the role of *risk* in entrepreneurship. Assuming risk is almost always a key element in entrepreneurship. Interestingly, most successful entrepreneurs seldom see what they do as risky. Whereas others may focus on possibilities for failure and balk at gambling everything on a new venture, most entrepreneurs are so passionate about their ideas and plans that they see little or no likelihood of failure. Byrne, for example, detected major problems in Overstock.com's financial outlook but believed so strongly in its promise that he took an enormous gamble on the company's prospects for success.[8]

Starting and Operating the Small Business

The Internet has changed the rules for starting and operating a small business. Setting up is easier and faster than ever before, there are more potential opportunities than at any time in history, and the ability to gather and assess information is at an all-time high. Today, for example, many one-person retailers do most of their business—both buying and selling—on Internet auction sites such as eBay.

Even so, would-be entrepreneurs must make the right start-up decisions. They must decide how to get into business—should they buy an existing business or build from the ground up? They must know when to seek expert advice and where to find sources of financing. If, for example, a new firm needs financial backing from investors or a line of credit from vendors or distributors, the entrepreneur should have in place a comprehensive, well-crafted business plan.

Crafting a Business Plan

The starting point for virtually every new business is a **business plan** in which the entrepreneur summarizes business strategy for the new venture and shows how it will be implemented.[9] A real benefit of a business plan is the fact that in the act of preparing it, the would-be entrepreneur must develop the business idea on paper and firm up his or her thinking about how to launch it before investing time and money in it. The idea of the business plan isn't new. What is new is the use of specialized business plans, mostly because creditors and investors demand them as tools for deciding whether to finance or invest.

business plan

Document in which the entrepreneur summarizes her or his business strategy for the proposed new venture and how that strategy will be implemented

Setting Goals and Objectives A business plan describes the match between the entrepreneur's abilities and experiences and the requirements for producing and/or marketing a particular product. It also defines strategies for production and marketing, legal elements and organization, and accounting and finance. In particular, a business plan should answer three questions: (1) What are the entrepreneur's goals and objectives? (2) What strategies will be used to obtain them? (3) How will these strategies be implemented?

Sales Forecasting Business plans should also account for the sequential nature of strategic decision making in new ventures. Entrepreneurs, for example, can't forecast sales revenues without first researching markets. Simply asserting that the new venture will sell 100,000 units per month is not credible. Instead, the entrepreneur must demonstrate an understanding of the current market, of the strengths and weaknesses of existing firms, and of the means by which the new venture will compete. In fact, the *sales forecast* is among the most important elements in the business plan. Without it, no one can estimate the required size of a plant, store, or office or decide how much inventory to carry and how many employees to hire.

Financial Planning *Financial planning* refers to the entrepreneur's plan for turning all other activities into dollars. It generally includes a cash budget, an income statement, balance sheets, and a breakeven chart. Most important is the *cash budget,* which shows how much money you need before you open for business and how much you need to keep the business going before it starts earning a profit.[10]

Starting the Small Business

An old Chinese proverb says that a journey of 1,000 miles begins with a single step. This is also true of a new business. The first step, of course, is the individual's commitment to becoming a business owner. In preparing a business plan, the entrepreneur must choose the industry and market in which he or she plans to compete. This choice means assessing not only industry conditions and trends but also one's own abilities and interests. Like big-business managers, small-business owners must understand the nature of the enterprises in which they are engaged.

Buying an Existing Business Next, the entrepreneur must decide whether to buy an existing business or start from scratch. Many experts recommend the first approach because, quite simply, the odds are better: If it's successful, an existing business has already proven its ability to attract customers and generate profit. It has also established relationships with lenders, suppliers, and other stakeholders. Moreover, an existing track record gives potential buyers a much clearer picture of what to expect than any estimate of a new business's prospects.[11]

Ray Kroc bought McDonald's as an existing business, added entrepreneurial vision and business acumen, and produced a multinational giant. Both Southwest

Airlines and Starbucks were small struggling operations when entrepreneurs took over and made them successful. About 35 percent of all new businesses that were started in the past decade were bought from someone else.

Starting from Scratch Despite the odds, some people seek the satisfaction that comes from planting an idea and growing it into a healthy business. There are also practical reasons to start from scratch. A new business doesn't suffer the ill effects of a prior owner's errors, and the start-up owner is free to choose lenders, equipment, inventories, locations, suppliers, and workers. Of all new businesses begun in the past decade, 64 percent were started from scratch.

But as we have already noted, the risks of starting a business from scratch are greater than those of buying an existing firm. New-business founders can only make projections about their prospects. Success or failure depends on identifying a genuine opportunity, such as a product for which many customers will pay well but which is currently unavailable. To find openings, entrepreneurs must study markets and answer the following questions:

- Who are my customers?
- Where are they?
- At what price will they buy my product?
- In what quantities will they buy?
- Who are my competitors?
- How will my product differ from those of my competitors?

Financing the Small Business

Although the choice of how to start is obviously important, it's meaningless unless you can get the money. Among the more common sources for funding are family and friends, personal savings, lending institutions, investors, and governmental agencies. Lending institutions are more likely to help finance the purchase of an existing business because the risks are better understood. Individuals starting new businesses will probably have to rely on personal resources.

According to the National Federation of Independent Business <www.nfibonline.com>, personal resources, not loans, are the most important source of money. Including money borrowed from friends and relatives, personal resources account for over two-thirds of all money invested in new small businesses and one-half of that is used to purchase existing businesses. Getting money from banks, independent investors, and government loans requires extra effort. At a minimum, banks and private investors will want to review business plans, and government loans have strict eligibility guidelines.

venture capital company
Group of small investors who invest money in companies with rapid growth potential

Other Sources of Investment **Venture capital companies** are groups of small investors seeking to make profits on companies with rapid growth potential. Most of these firms do not lend money. They invest it, supplying capital in return for partial ownership. They may also demand representation on boards of directors. In some cases, managers need approval from the venture capital company before making major decisions. Of all venture capital currently committed in the United States, 29 percent comes from true venture capital firms. The economic downturn that plagued U.S. business in mid-2002, however, sharply reduced new investment by venture capitalists.[12]

small-business investment company (SBIC)
Government-regulated investment company that borrows money from the SBA to invest in or lend to a small business

Small-business investment companies (SBICs) also invest in companies with potential for rapid growth. They are federally licensed to borrow money from the SBA and to invest it in or lend it to small businesses, and they are themselves investments for their shareholders. Past beneficiaries of SBIC capital include

"The lust for entrepreneurship has not changed," says Hans Severiens (left). "And now there are great bargains to be had." Why are there are so many "bargains"—so many good new companies to invest in? For one thing, venture-capital investment is down more than 50 percent. Severiens is a managing director of Band of Angels <www.bandangels.com>, *a club of about 150 private investors, or "angels," who get together once a month to hear pitches from companies looking for seed money. If they like what they hear, interested members may write personal checks (up to about $100,000) for small stakes in bankrolled firms.*

Apple Computer, Intel, and FedEx. The government also sponsors *minority enterprise small-business investment companies (MESBICs).* As the name suggests, MESBICs target minority-owned businesses.

SBA Financial Programs Since its founding in 1953, the SBA has sponsored financing programs for small businesses that meet standards in size and independence. Eligible firms must be unable to get private financing at reasonable terms. Under the SBA's *guaranteed loans program,* for example, small businesses can borrow from commercial lenders. The SBA guarantees to repay 75 to 85 percent of the loan up to $750,000. Through the *immediate participation loans program,* the SBA and a bank each put up shares of a loan. Under the *local development companies (LDCs) program,* the SBA works with a local corporation devoted to boosting the local economy. Spurred in large part by the boom in Internet businesses, both venture capital and loans are becoming easier to get. Most small businesses report that it has generally gotten easier to obtain loans over the last 10 years.

Other SBA Programs Even more important than its financing role is the SBA's role in helping small-business owners improve their management skills. It's easy for entrepreneurs to spend money; SBA programs show them how to spend it wisely. The SBA offers management counseling programs at virtually no cost. For example, a small-business owner who needs help in starting a new business can get it free through the *Service Corps of Retired Executives (SCORE)* <www.score.org>. All SCORE members are retired executives, and all are volunteers.

The newest of the SBA's management counseling projects is its **Small Business Development Center (SBDC)** program <www.sba.gov/sbdc>. Begun in 1976, SBDCs are designed to consolidate information from various disciplines and institutions, including technical and professional schools. Then they make this knowledge available to new and existing small businesses.

Small Business Development Center (SBDC)
SBA program designed to consolidate information from various disciplines and make it available to small businesses

"Eventually I'd like to have a business where the money rolls in and I wouldn't have to be there much."

Franchising

franchise

Arrangement in which a buyer (*franchisee*) purchases the right to sell the good or service of the seller (*franchiser*)

McDonald's, Subway, 7-Eleven, RE/Max, Ramada, and Blockbuster are all franchises operating under licenses issued by parent companies to local owners. A **franchise** permits the *franchisee* (buyer) to sell the product of the *franchiser* (seller, or parent company) and is a well-traveled road to entrepreneurship.[13]

Franchisees benefit from the parent corporation's experience and expertise, and the franchiser may even supply financing. It may pick the store location, negotiate the lease, design the store, and purchase equipment. It may train the first set of employees and managers and issue standard policies and procedures. Once the business is open, the franchiser may offer savings by allowing the franchisee to purchase from a central location. Marketing strategy (especially advertising) may also be handled by the franchiser. In short, franchisees receive—that is, invest in—not only their own ready-made businesses but also expert help in running them.

Advantages and Disadvantages of Franchising

Franchises have advantages for both sellers and buyers. Franchisers can grow rapidly by using the investment money provided by franchisees. The franchisee gets to own a business and has access to big-business management skills. The franchisee does not have to build a business step by step, and because each franchise outlet is probably a carbon copy of every other outlet, failure is less likely.

Mid-Chapter Internet Field Trip

"Counselors to America's Small Business"

So far in this chapter, we've defined *small business* and *entrepreneurship* and explained the typical steps in starting a small business. Once a business owner has launched a firm, where does he or she go for help and advice while the company is still young? We can find some good answers to this question at the Web site of SCORE, the Service Corps of Retired Executives, at <www.score.org>. SCORE is a national, nonprofit association with thousands of volunteer members "dedicated to aiding in the formation, growth, and success of small business nationwide."

On the SCORE home page, you'll find a number of articles and special features that change every month. At the top of the page, however, are six icons that summarize the organization of the site:

- About Counseling
- Get E-mail Counseling
- How-to Articles
- Find SCORE
- Client Successes
- FAQs

First, click on **About Counseling:**

1. What different forms of counseling does SCORE offer the business owner?
2. To whom is the counseling available?

Go back to the home page and click on **E-mail Counseling.** Scroll down and select **Complete Listing of Counselor Skills:**

3. How many skills are currently listed?

Now return to the home page and select **FAQs:**

4. Why is SCORE qualified to offer business advice?

Continue looking through the **FAQs:**

5. How can a business owner be sure that information shared with SCORE will remain confidential?

To continue your Internet Field Trip, click on www.prenhall.com/griffin

Perhaps the most significant disadvantage in owning a franchise is start-up cost. Franchise prices vary widely. The fee for a Fantastic Sam's <www.fantasticsams.com> hair salon is $30,000, but a McDonald's franchise costs $650,000 to $750,000, and a professional sports team can cost several hundred million dollars. Franchisees may also be obligated to contribute percentages of sales to parent corporations.

An unhappy General Nutrition Companies <www.gnc.com> franchisee in West Lafayette, Indiana, Ed Bishop is one of 300 GNC franchise owners who are suing their franchiser. The plaintiffs' main complaint is that the parent company is opening too many stores of its own and, what's worse, supplying them with multivitamins, muscle-building supplements, and herbal remedies. The result, they claim, is a dual pricing structure that works against franchise outlets. "Our worst competition," says a franchiser in Washington state, "is the company."

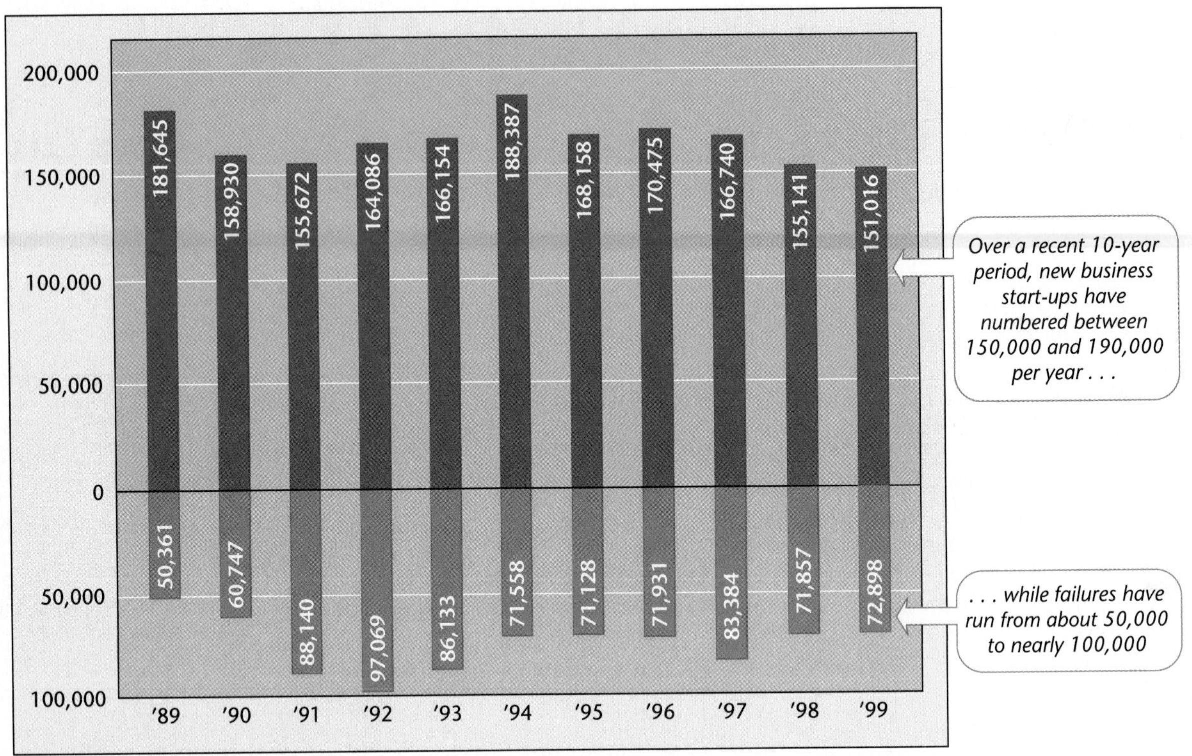

FIGURE 3.3
Start-Ups: Success and Failure

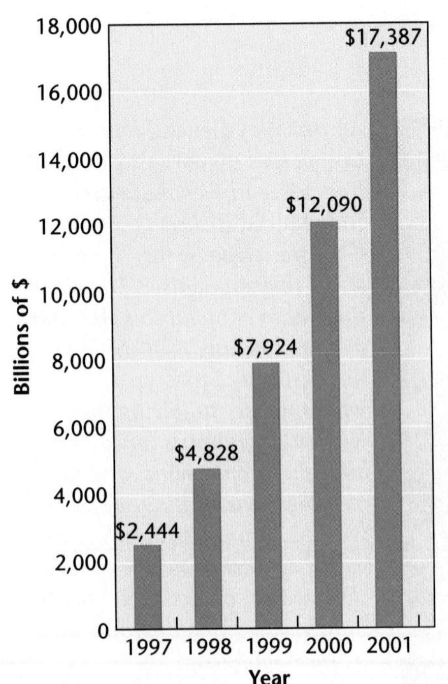

FIGURE 3.4
Growth of Online Commerce

Success and Failure in Small Business

For every Henry Ford, Walt Disney, Mary Kay Ash, or Bill Gates—people who transformed small businesses into big ones—there are many small-business owners who fail. Figure 3.3 illustrates recent trends in new business start-ups and failures. As you can see, over a recent 10-year period, new business start-ups have numbered between 150,000 and 190,000 per year. Failures have run between 50,000 and 100,000, with a high of 97,000. In this section, we look first at a few key trends in small-business start-ups. Then we examine some of the reasons for success and failure in small-business undertakings.[14]

Trends in Small-Business Start-Ups

Thousands of new businesses are started in the United States every year. Several factors account for this trend, and in this section, we focus on five of them.

Emergence of E-Commerce The most significant recent trend is the rapid emergence of electronic commerce. Because the Internet provides fundamentally new ways of doing business, savvy entrepreneurs have created and expanded new businesses faster and easier than ever before.[15] Such leading-edge firms as America Online, Amazon.com, E*Trade™, and eBay owe their very existence to the Internet. Figure 3.4 underscores this point by summarizing the growth in online commerce from 1997 through 2001, and the "Wired World" box in this chapter discusses profitability trends among so-called dot-coms.

What Doth It Profit a Dot-Com?

As we all know, dot-coms don't make money and they're all doomed to failure. The phrase *profitable Internet company* is a contradiction in terms. But is Internet business really *that* bad? During the short-lived glory days of dot-coms, venture capitalists were virtually throwing money at them, and some experts predicted that they would soon take over and make over the business world. But of course big shakeouts in 2000 and 2001 sent most of the upstarts packing.

A closer look reveals, however, that the survivors are holding up pretty well. In fact, many are starting to show nice profits. In the travel sector, Expedia, Hotels.com, and Priceline are making money. No fewer than 10 public finance companies are now profitable, with firms such as E*Trade™ performing quite well. Although hurt by a recent ad slump, some media and advertising businesses are in the black, and several e-tailers, including Amazon.com and Ticketmaster USA, are doing well. In other sectors, successful dot-coms include auctioneer eBay, Intuit and McAfee (software), WebEx Communications (infrastructure), and Razorfish and Inforte (consulting).

But just because some firms seem to have turned the corner doesn't mean that there will be another spurt in Internet start-ups. In fact, just the opposite may be true, because entrepreneurs have come to realize that e-commerce is much more than putting up a Web site. As in most other areas of the business world, firms with strong business plans and well-considered strategies are most likely to survive.

Crossovers from Big Business More businesses are being started by people who have opted to leave big corporations and put their experience to work for themselves. In some cases, they see great new ideas that they want to develop. Others get burned out in the corporate world. Some have lost their jobs, only to discover that working for themselves was a better idea anyway. John Chambers, the CEO of Cisco Systems <www.cisco.com>, is acknowledged as one of the best entrepreneurs around. But he spent several years working at IBM and Wang Laboratories <www.wang.com/GLOBAL> before he set out on his own. Under his leadership, Cisco <www.cisco.com> has become one of the largest and most important technology companies in the world.[16]

Opportunities for Minorities and Women More small businesses are also being started by minorities and women.[17] The number of businesses owned by African Americans increased by 46 percent during the most recent five-year period for which data are available and now totals about 620,000. Hispanic-owned businesses have grown at an even faster rate of 76 percent and now number about 862,000. Ownership among Asians and Pacific Islanders has increased 56 percent, to over 600,000. Although ownership among Native Americans and Alaskan natives is still modest, at slightly over 100,000, the total represents a five-year increase of 93 percent.

Finally, there are now 9.1 million businesses owned by women—38 percent of all businesses in the United States. Combined, they generate nearly $4 trillion in revenue a year—an increase of 132 percent since 1992. Since 1992, the

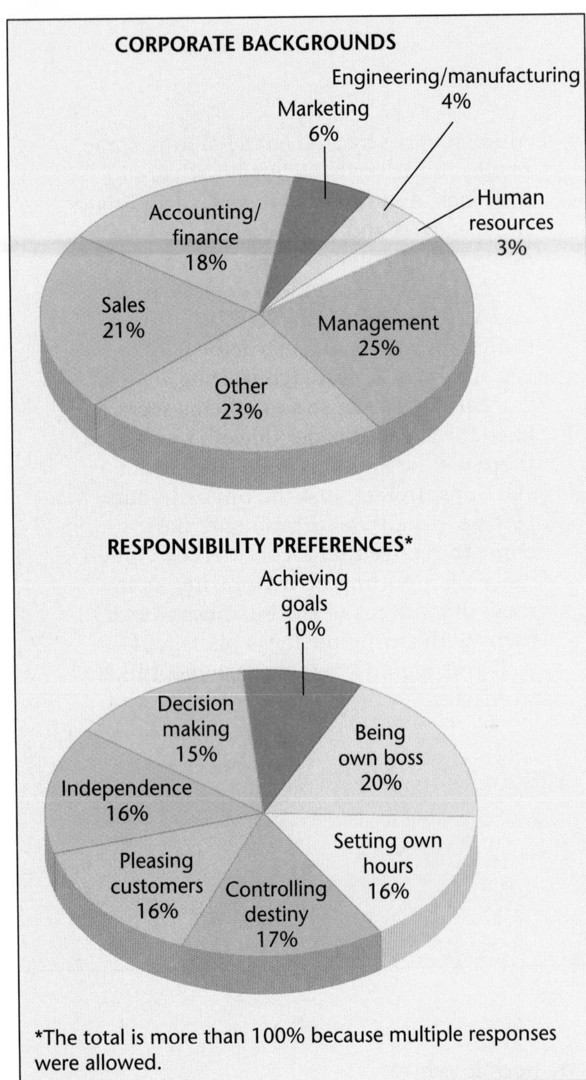

FIGURE 3.5
Profiles of Women Entrepreneurs

number of people that they employ has grown to around 27.5 million—an increase of 108 percent.[18]

Figure 3.5 summarizes the corporate backgrounds of women entrepreneurs and provides some insight into what they like about running their own businesses. Corporate positions in general management (25 percent), sales (21 percent), and accounting and finance (18 percent) account for almost two-thirds of the women who start their own businesses. Once in charge of their own businesses, women also report that they like being their own bosses, setting their own hours, controlling their own destinies, relating to customers, making decisions, and achieving goals. "Women-owned businesses," says Teresa Cavanaugh, director of the Women Entrepreneur's Connection at BankBoston, "are the largest emerging segment of the small-business market. Women-owned businesses are an economic force that no bank can afford to overlook."[19]

Global Opportunities Many entrepreneurs are also finding new opportunities in foreign markets.[20] Doug Mellinger is founder and CEO of PRT Group Inc., a software development company. One of Mellinger's biggest problems was finding trained programmers. There aren't enough American programmers to go around, and foreign-born programmers face strict immigration quotas. So Mellinger set up shop on Barbados, a Caribbean island where the government helps him attract foreign programmers and does everything it can to make things easier. Today, PRT, which is a part of enherent Corp. <www.enherent.com>, has customers and suppliers from dozens of nations.

Better Survival Rates Finally, more people are encouraged to test their skills as entrepreneurs because the small-business failure rate has declined. During the 1960s and 1970s, less than half of all new start-ups survived more than 18 months; only one in five lasted 10 years. Now, however, new businesses have a better chance. Of all those started in the 1980s, over 77 percent remained in operation for at least three years. The SBA now estimates that 40 percent can expect to survive for six years.

"Women-owned businesses are an economic force that no bank can afford to overlook."

~Teresa Cavanaugh, Women Entrepreneur's Connection, BankBoston

Reasons for Failure

Unfortunately, 63 percent of all new businesses will not celebrate a sixth anniversary. Why do some succeed and others fail? Although no set pattern has been established, four general factors contribute to failure:

1. ***Managerial incompetence or inexperience.*** Some entrepreneurs put their faith in commonsense, overestimate their own managerial skills, or believe that hard work alone ensures success. If managers don't know how to make basic business decisions or don't understand basic management principles, they aren't likely to succeed in the long run.
2. ***Neglect.*** Some entrepreneurs try to launch ventures in their spare time, and others devote only limited time to new businesses. But starting a small business demands an overwhelming time commitment. If you aren't willing to put in the time and effort that a business requires, you aren't likely to survive.

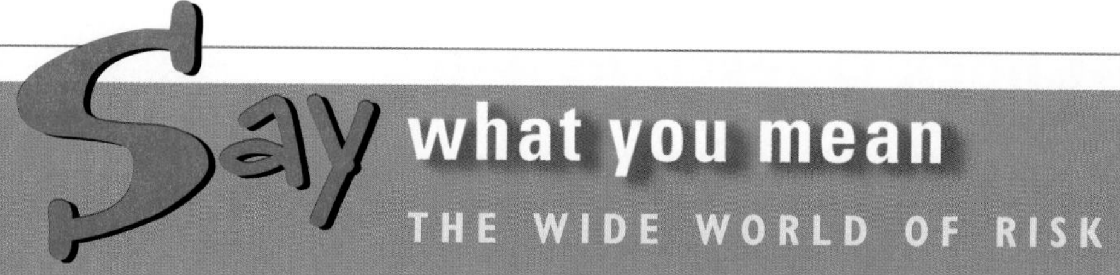

Say what you mean
THE WIDE WORLD OF RISK

One reason why globalization has become such a factor in everyday business life is the expanded reach and power of multinational companies. Many large corporations have actually become engines for innovation as well as growth, adapting to new markets and new economic circumstances. In a highly interconnected world, however, it's often hard to figure out the complex ownership and organizational structures of many global corporations. Sometimes, for example, their branding practices and management structures lead people to think that they're local companies when, in fact, the real source of corporate power may lie thousands of miles away in another country.

One thing's for sure: If you're going to be dealing with a company overseas, you'd better have a good idea of where and how decisions are made and who has the real power to make them.

At the same time, of course, different cultures have different attitudes when it comes to entrepreneurship. In some countries and cultures, like that of the United States, there's a vibrant entrepreneurial spirit. Businesspeople are open to taking risks, and if they fail, they tend to pick themselves up and move on to something else. In Japan, however, the entrepreneurial spirit is often tempered by the need for consensus and getting everyone on board. This approach requires a lot of patience and the ability to compromise. Moreover, when it comes to failure, it's not so easy to brush off past mistakes.

Knowing the cultural forces that shape both a business organization and people's attitudes toward risk, success, and failure is an elementary but important component of international business. In any case, global companies are major players in today's business world, and a lot of people are demanding that they also be good global citizens by respecting human-rights covenants and cultural diversity, being sensitive to the local environment, and giving back to the local communities in which they operate.

3. ***Weak control systems.*** Effective control systems keep a business on track and alert managers to potential trouble. If your control systems don't signal impending problems, you may be in serious trouble before you spot more obvious difficulties.
4. ***Insufficient capital.*** Some entrepreneurs are overly optimistic about how soon they'll start earning profits. In most cases, it takes months or even years. Amazon.com didn't earn a profit for 10 years but obviously still required capital to pay employees and to cover other expenses. Experts say you need enough capital to operate at least six months without earning a profit; some recommend enough to last a year.[21]

Reasons for Success

Four basic factors are also typically cited to explain small-business success:

1. ***Hard work, drive, and dedication.*** Small-business owners must be committed to succeeding and willing to spend the time and effort to make it happen. Gladys Edmunds, a single mother in Pittsburgh, washed laundry, made chicken dinners to sell to cab drivers, and sold fire extinguishers door to door to earn start-up money. Today, Edmunds Travel Consultants employs eight people and earns about $6 million a year.[22]

Self-Check Questions 4–6

*You should now be able to answer Self-Check Questions 4–6**

4. TRUE/FALSE Preparing a *business plan* is usually an optional step for a would-be entrepreneur.

5. MULTIPLE CHOICE Which of the following is usually the most important source of financing for a new business? [select one]: **(a)** banks; **(b)** investors; **(c)** government agencies such as the SBA; **(d)** personal resources; **(e)** lottery winnings.

6. MULTIPLE CHOICE Which of the following is **not** a common cause of business failure? [select one]: **(a)** managerial incompetence and inexperience; **(b)** neglect; **(c)** weak controls; **(d)** employee theft or sabotage; **(e)** insufficient capital.

*ANSWERS TO SELF-CHECK QUESTIONS 4–6 CAN BE FOUND ON P. AN-2.

2. ***Market demand for the products or services being provided.*** Careful analysis of market conditions can help small-business owners assess the probable reception of their products. Attempts to expand restaurants specializing in baked potatoes, muffins, and gelato have largely failed, but hamburger and pizza chains continue to expand.
3. ***Managerial competence.*** Successful owners may acquire competence through training or experience or by drawing on the expertise of others. Few, however, succeed alone or straight out of college. Most spend time in successful companies or partner with others in order to bring expertise to a new business.
4. ***Luck.*** After Alan McKim started Clean Harbors <www.cleanharbors.com>, an environmental cleanup firm in New England, he struggled to keep his business afloat. Then the U.S. government committed $1.6 billion to toxic waste cleanup—McKim's specialty. He landed several large government contracts and put his business on solid financial footing. Had the government fund not been created at just the right time, McKim may well have failed.

Noncorporate Business Ownership

Whether they intend to run small farms, large factories, or online e-tailers, all business operators must decide which form of legal ownership best suits their goals: *sole proprietorship, partnership,* or *corporation.* Because this choice affects a host of managerial and financial issues, few decisions are more critical. Entrepreneurs must consider their own preferences, their immediate and long-range needs, and the advantages and disadvantages of each form. Table 3.1 compares the most important differences among the three major ownership forms.

Business Form	Liability	Continuity	Management	Sources of Investment
Proprietorship	Personal, unlimited	Ends with death or decision of owner	Personal, unrestricted	Personal
General Partnership	Personal, unlimited	Ends with death or decision of any partner	Unrestricted or depends on partnership agreement	Personal by partner(s)
Corporation	Capital invested	As stated in charter, perpetual or for specified period of years	Under control of board of directors, which is selected by stockholders	Purchase of stock

TABLE 3.1
Comparative Summary: Three Forms of Business

Sole Proprietorships

The **sole proprietorship** is owned and usually operated by one person.[23] About 73 percent of all U.S. businesses are sole proprietorships; however, they account for only about 5 percent of total business revenues.[24] Though usually small, they may be as large as steel mills or department stores.

sole proprietorship
Business owned and usually operated by one person who is responsible for all of its debts

Advantages of Sole Proprietorships Freedom may be the most important benefit of sole proprietorships. Because they own their businesses, sole proprietors answer to no one but themselves. Sole proprietorships are also easy to form. Sometimes, you can go into business simply by putting a sign on the door. The simplicity of legal setup procedures makes this form appealing to self-starters and independent spirits, as do low start-up costs.

Another attractive feature is the tax benefits extended to businesses that are likely to suffer losses in their early stages. Tax laws permit owners to treat sales revenues and operating expenses as part of their personal finances. They can thus cut taxes by deducting business losses from income earned from personal sources other than the business.

Disadvantages of Sole Proprietorships A major drawback is **unlimited liability:** A sole proprietor is personally liable for all debts incurred by the business. If it fails to generate enough cash, bills must be paid out of the owner's pocket. Another disadvantage is lack of continuity: A sole proprietorship legally dissolves when the owner dies. Although the business can be reorganized by a successor, executors or heirs must otherwise sell its assets.[25]

unlimited liability
Legal principle holding owners responsible for paying off all debts of a business

Finally, a sole proprietorship depends on the resources of one person whose managerial and financial limitations may constrain the business. Sole proprietors often find it hard to borrow money to start up or expand. Many bankers fear that they won't be able to recover loans if owners become disabled or insolvent.

Partnerships

The partnership is frequently used by professionals.[26] The most common type, the **general partnership,** is a sole proprietorship multiplied by the number of partner-owners. There is no legal limit to the number of parties, but the average is slightly under 10. Partners may invest equal or unequal sums of money and may earn profits that bear no relation to their investments. Thus, a partner with no financial investment in a two-person partnership could receive 50 percent or more of the profits if he or she has made some other contribution—say, a well-known name or special expertise.

general partnership
Business with two or more owners who share in both the operation of the firm and the financial responsibility for its debts

Advantages of Partnerships The most striking advantage of general partnerships is the ability to grow by adding new talent and money. Because banks prefer to make loans to enterprises that are not dependent on single individuals, partnerships find it easier to borrow than sole proprietorships. They can also invite new partners to join by investing money.

Like a sole proprietorship, a partnership can be organized by meeting only a few legal requirements. Even so, all partnerships must begin with an agreement of some kind. In all but two states, the Revised Uniform Limited Partnership Act requires the filing of specific information about the business and its partners. Partners may also agree to bind themselves in ways not specified by law. In any case, an agreement should answer questions such as the following:

- Who invested what sums?
- Who will receive what share of the profits?
- Who does what and who reports to whom?
- How may the partnership be dissolved? In the event of dissolution, how will assets be distributed?
- How will surviving partners be protected from claims made by a deceased partner's heirs?

The partnership agreement is strictly a private document. No laws require partners to file agreements with any government agency. Nor are partnerships regarded as legal entities. In the eyes of the law, a partnership is just two or more people working together. Because partnerships have no independent legal standing, the Internal Revenue Service (IRS) taxes partners as individuals.

Disadvantages of Partnerships For general partnerships as for sole proprietorships, unlimited liability is the greatest drawback. Each partner may be liable for all debts incurred by the partnership. If any partner incurs a business debt (with or without the knowledge of the others), all partners may be liable.

Partnerships also share with sole proprietorships the potential lack of continuity. When one partner dies or leaves, the original partnership dissolves, even if one or more of the other partners want it to continue. But dissolution need not mean a loss of sales revenues. Survivors may form a new partnership to retain the old firm's business. A related disadvantage is difficulty in transferring ownership. No partner may sell out without the consent of the others. A partner who wants to retire or to transfer interest to a son or daughter must have the other partners' consent.

limited partnership
Type of partnership consisting of limited partners and an active or managing partner

limited partner
Partner who does not share in a firm's management and is liable for its debts only to the limits of said partner's investment

general (or **active**) **partner**
Partner who actively manages a firm and who has unlimited liability for its debts

master limited partnership (MLP)
Form of ownership that sells shares to investors who receive profits and who pay taxes on income from profits

Alternatives to General Partnerships Because of these disadvantages, general partnerships are among the least popular forms of business. Roughly 1.86 million U.S. partnerships generate only about 6 percent of total sales revenues.[27] To resolve some of the problems inherent in general partnerships, especially unlimited liability, some partners have tried alternative agreements. The **limited partnership** allows for **limited partners** who invest money, and also are liable for debts only to the extent of their investments. They cannot, however, take active roles in business operations. A limited partnership must have at least one **general** (or **active**) **partner,** mostly for liability purposes. This is usually the person who runs the business and is responsible for its survival and growth.

Under a **master limited partnership (MLP),** an organization sells shares (partnership interests) to investors on public markets such as the New York Stock Exchange <www.nyse.com>. Investors are paid back from profits. The master partner retains at least 50-percent ownership and runs the business, while minority partners have no management voice. (The master partner differs from a general partner, who has no such ownership restriction.) The master partner must regularly provide minority partners with detailed operating and financial reports.

Cooperatives

Sometimes, groups of sole proprietorships or partnerships agree to work together for their common benefit by forming **cooperatives.** Cooperatives combine the freedom of sole proprietorships with the financial power of corporations. They give members greater production power, greater marketing power, or both. On the other hand, they are limited to serving the specific needs of their members. Although cooperatives make up only a minor segment of the U.S. economy, their role is still important in agriculture.

cooperative
Form of ownership in which a group of sole proprietorships and/or partnerships agree to work together for common benefits

Corporations

There are about 4.85 million corporations in the United States. As you can see from Figure 3.6, they account for about 20 percent of all U.S. businesses but generate about 89 percent of all sales revenues.[28] Almost all large businesses use this form, and corporations dominate global business. According to the most recent data, ExxonMobil <www.exxonmobil.com>, the world's largest petroleum and petrochemicals business, posted annual revenue of over $191 billion, with total profits of over $15 billion. Even "smaller" large corporations post huge sales figures. The New York Times Co. <www.newyorktimes.com>, though 500th among U.S. corporations, posted a profit of $445 million on annual sales of $3.04 billion. Given the size and influence of this form of ownership, we will devote a great deal of attention to various aspects of corporations.[29]

The Corporate Entity

When you think of corporations, you probably think of giant operations such as General Motors and IBM. The very word *corporation* inspires images of size and power. In reality, however, your corner newsstand has as much right to incorporate as a giant automaker. Moreover, the newsstand and GM would share the characteristics of all **corporations:** legal status as separate entities, property rights and obligations, and indefinite life spans.[30]

corporation
Business that is legally considered an entity separate from its owners and is liable for its own debts; owners' liability extends to the limits of their investments

In 1819, the U.S. Supreme Court defined a corporation as "an artificial being, invisible, intangible, and existing only in contemplation of the law." The Court

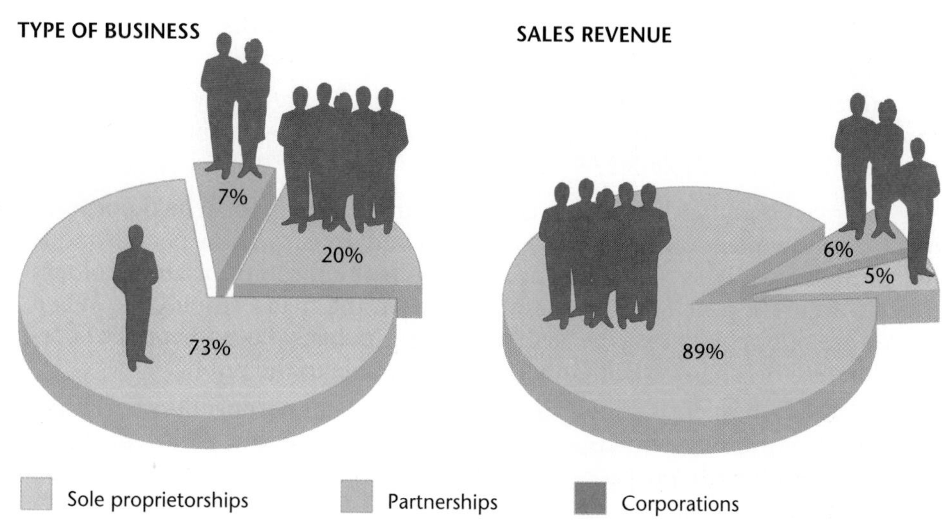

FIGURE 3.6
Proportions of U.S. Firms in Terms of Organization Type and Sales Revenue

thus defined the corporation as a legal person. Corporations may, therefore, perform the following activities:

- Sue and be sued
- Buy, hold, and sell property
- Make and sell products
- Commit crimes and be tried and punished for them

limited liability
Legal principle holding investors liable for a firm's debts only to the limits of their personal investments in it

Advantages of Incorporation The biggest advantage of corporations is **limited liability:** Investor liability is limited to personal investment in the corporation.[31] In the event of failure, the courts may seize and sell a corporation's assets but cannot touch the investors' personal possessions. If, for example, you invest $1,000 in a corporation that goes bankrupt, you may lose your $1,000, but no more. In other words, $1,000 is the extent of your liability.

Another advantage is continuity. Because it has a legal life independent of founders and owners, a corporation can, at least in theory, continue forever. Shares of stock may be sold or passed on to heirs, and most corporations also benefit from the continuity provided by professional management. Finally, corporations have advantages in raising money. By selling stock, they expand the number of investors and the amount of available funds. Continuity and legal status tend to make lenders more willing to grant loans.

tender offer
Offer to buy shares made by a prospective buyer directly to a target corporation's shareholders, who then make individual decisions about whether to sell

Disadvantages of Incorporation Although a chief attraction is ease of transferring ownership, this same feature can create complications. For example, using a legal process called a **tender offer**—an offer to buy shares made by a prospective buyer directly to a corporation's shareholders—a corporation can be taken over against the will of its managers. Another disadvantage is start-up cost. Corporations are heavily regulated, and incorporation entails meeting the complex legal requirements of the state in which the firm is chartered.

double taxation
Situation in which taxes may be payable both by a corporation on its profits and by shareholders on dividend incomes

Double Taxation The biggest disadvantage of incorporation is **double taxation.** First, a corporation pays income taxes on company profits. In addition, stockholders pay taxes on income returned by their investments in the corporation. Thus, the profits earned by corporations are taxed twice—once at the corporate level and again at the ownership level. Because profits are treated as owners' personal income, sole proprietorships and partnerships are taxed only once.

The advantages and disadvantages of corporate ownership have inspired laws establishing different kinds of corporations. Most are intended to help businesses take advantage of the benefits of the corporate model without assuming all of the disadvantages. We discuss these corporate forms next.

Types of Corporations

We can classify corporations as either *public* or *private.* But within these broad categories, we can identify several specific types of corporations, some of which are summarized in Table 3.2.[32]

closely held (or private) corporation
Corporation whose stock is held by only a few people and is not available for sale to the general public

publicly held (or public) corporation
Corporation whose stock is widely held and available for sale to the general public

S corporation
Hybrid of a closely held corporation and a partnership, organized and operated like a corporation but treated as a partnership for tax purposes

- The most common form of U.S. corporation is the **closely held corporation** (or simply **private corporation**). Stock is held by only a few people and is not available for sale to the public. The controlling group of stockholders may be a family, a management group, or even the firm's employees. When shares are publicly issued, the firm becomes a **publicly held** (or **public**) **corporation.** Stock is widely held and available for sale to the public.
- The **S corporation** is a hybrid of a closely a held corporation and partnership. It is organized and operates like a corporation, but it is treated like a partnership for tax purposes. To qualify, firms must meet stringent legal conditions.

Type	Distinguishing Features	Examples
Closely Held	Stock held by only a few people Subject to corporate taxation	Blue Cross/Blue Shield MasterCard Primestar
Publicly Held	Stock widely held among many investors Subject to corporate taxation	Dell Computer Starbucks Texas Instruments
Subchapter S	Organized much like a closely held corporation Subject to additional regulation Subject to partnership taxation	Minglewood Associates Entech Pest Systems Frontier Bank
Limited Liability	Organized much like a publicly held corporation Subject to additional regulation Subject to partnership taxation	Pacific Northwest Associates Global Ground Support Ritz Carlton
Professional	Organized like a partnership Subject to partnership taxation Limited business liability Unlimited professional liability	Norman Hui, DDS & Associates B & H Engineering Anderson, McCoy & Orta
Multinational	Spans national boundaries Subject to regulation in multiple countries	Toyota Nestlé General Electric

TABLE 3.2
Types of Corporations

Another hybrid is the **limited liability corporation,** or **LLC.** Owners are taxed like partners, each paying personal taxes only. However, they also enjoy the benefits of limited liability accorded to publicly held corporations. LLCs have grown in popularity in recent years, partially because of IRS rulings that allow corporations, partnerships, and foreign investors to be partial owners.

Professional corporations are most likely comprised of doctors, lawyers, accountants, or other professionals. They are not immune from unlimited liability. Professional negligence by a member entails personal liability on the individual's part.

As the term implies, the **multinational** or **transnational corporation** spans national boundaries. Stock may be traded on the exchanges of several countries, and managers are likely to be of different nationalities.

limited liability corporation (LLC)
Hybrid of a publicly held corporation and a partnership in which owners are taxed as partners but enjoy the benefits of limited liability

professional corporation
Form of ownership allowing professionals to take advantage of corporate benefits while granting them limited business liability and unlimited professional liability

multinational or **transnational corporation**
Form of corporation spanning national boundaries

Managing a Corporation

Creating any type of corporation can be complicated. In addition, once the corporate entity comes into existence, it must be managed by people who understand the principles of **corporate governance**—the roles of shareholders, directors, and other managers in corporate decision making. In this section, we discuss the principles of *stock ownership* and *stockholders' rights* and describe the role of *boards of directors.* We then examine some important trends in corporate ownership.

corporate governance
Roles of shareholders, directors, and other managers in corporate decision making

Corporate Governance Corporate governance is established by the firm's bylaws and usually involves three distinct bodies. **Stockholders** (or **shareholders**) are the owners of a corporation—investors who buy ownership shares in the form of stock. The *board of directors* is a group elected by stockholders to oversee

stockholder (or **shareholder**)
Owner of shares of stock in a corporation

corporate management. Corporate *officers* are top managers hired by the board to run the corporation on a day-to-day basis.[33]

stock
Share of ownership in a corporation

preferred stock
Stock that offers its holders fixed dividends and priority claims over assets but no corporate voting rights

common stock
Stock that pays dividends and guarantees corporate voting rights but offers last claims over assets

board of directors
Governing body of a corporation that reports to its shareholders and delegates power to run its day-to-day operations while remaining responsible for sustaining its assets

chief executive officer (CEO)
Top manager hired by the board of directors to run a corporation

Stock Ownership and Stockholders' Rights Corporations sell shares, called **stock,** to investors who then become stockholders, or shareholders. Profits are distributed among stockholders in the form of dividends, and corporate managers serve at stockholders' discretion. In a closely held corporation, only a few people own stock. Shares of publicly held corporations are widely held.

Preferred stock pays fixed dividends, much like the interest on savings accounts. Preferred stockholders are so called because they have preference, or priority, over common stockholders when dividends are distributed and, if a business liquidates, when the value of assets is distributed. Preferred stockholders do not vote.

Common stock usually pays dividends only if the company makes a profit, and common stockholders have the last claims to any of a bankrupt company's assets. They do, however, enjoy voting rights, with each share worth one vote. Dividends on all stock are paid on a per-share basis.

Boards of Directors The governing body of a corporation is its **board of directors.** Boards communicate with stockholders and other stakeholders through such channels as the annual report—a summary of the firm's financial health. They also set policy on dividends, major spending, and executive compensation. They are legally responsible for corporate actions and are increasingly being held liable for them.

Officers Although board members oversee operations, most do not participate in day-to-day management. Rather, they hire a team of managers to run the firm. This team, called *officers,* is usually headed by the firm's **chief executive officer,** or **CEO,** who is responsible for overall performance. Other officers typically include a *president,* who is responsible for internal management, and *vice presidents,* who oversee various functional areas such as marketing and operations.

One of the outgrowths of the Enron debacle is heightened criticism of corporate governance in the United States.[34] Many Enron-related lawsuits target the firm's officers and directors. In a classic example of how governing bodies can fail shareholders, Enron's board of directors formally voted in at least one instance to set aside the company's code of ethics because its members wanted to approve an action that violated it. Similar charges have been leveled at the board of WorldCom. Other corporations whose boards have come in for ethical scrutiny, include Bank of America, Eastman Kodak, Lucent, Xerox, and ICN Pharmaceuticals.[35] Of course, many other boards continue to function very effectively, including those at Texas Instruments, Intel, Pfizer, Target, and Coca-Cola.

strategic alliance
Strategy in which two or more organizations collaborate on a project for mutual gain

joint venture
Strategic alliance in which the collaboration involves joint ownership of the new venture

employee stock ownership plan (ESOP)
Arrangement in which a corporation holds its own stock in trust for its employees, who gradually receive ownership of the stock and control its voting rights

Special Issues in Corporate Ownership

In recent years, several issues have grown in importance in the area of corporate ownership, including *joint ventures* and *strategic alliances, employee stock ownership plans,* and *institutional ownership.* Other important issues in contemporary corporate ownership involve *mergers, acquisitions, divestitures,* and *spin-offs.*

Joint Ventures and Strategic Alliances In a **strategic alliance,** two or more organizations collaborate on a project for mutual gain. When partners share ownership of what is essentially a new enterprise, it is called a **joint venture.** The number of strategic alliances has increased rapidly in recent years on both domestic and international fronts.[36]

Employee Stock Ownership Plans An **employee stock ownership plan (ESOP)** allows employees to own a significant share of the corporation through trusts established on their behalf. Current estimates count almost 10,000 ESOPs in the United States. The growth rate in new ESOPs has slowed a bit in recent years, but they still are an important part of corporate ownership patterns in the United States.[37]

"I had no idea the company was in anything but excellent shape," pleads former Enron CEO Jeffrey K. Skilling. Skilling, who quit Enron in August 2001, five months before the company filed for the nation's largest bankruptcy, was CEO for only six months but had been chief operating officer since 1996. He has implied that his gravest sin as chief executive was losing touch with subordinates who turned out to be corrupt.

Institutional Ownership Most individual investors don't own enough stock to exert influence on corporate managers. In recent years, however, more stock has been purchased by **institutional investors.** Because they control enormous resources, these investors—especially mutual and pension funds—can buy huge blocks of stock. The national teachers' retirement system (TIAA-CREF) <www.tiaa-cref.org> has assets of over $255 billion, much of it invested in stocks. Institutional investors own almost 40 percent of all the stock issued in the United States.

institutional investor
Large investor, such as a mutual fund or a pension fund, that purchases large blocks of corporate stock

Mergers, Acquisitions, Divestitures, and Spin-Offs Another important set of issues includes mergers, acquisitions, divestitures, and spin-offs. Mergers and acquisitions involve the legal joining of two or more corporations. A divestiture occurs when a corporation sells a business operation to another corporation; with a spin-off, it creates a new operation.

Mergers and Acquisitions (M&As) A **merger** occurs when two firms combine to create a new company. In an **acquisition,** one firm buys another outright. Many deals that are loosely called mergers are really acquisitions. Why? Because one of the two firms will usually control the newly combined ownership. In general, when the two firms are roughly the same size, the combination is usually called a merger even if one firm is taking control of the other. When the acquiring firm is substantially larger than the acquired firm, the deal is really an acquisition. So-called *M&As* are an important form of corporate strategy. They let firms increase product lines, expand operations, go international, and create new enterprises.

merger
The union of two corporations to form a new corporation

acquisition
The purchase of one company by another

Divestitures and Spin-Offs Sometimes, a corporation decides to sell a part of its existing business operations or set it up as a new and independent corporation. There may be several reasons for such a step. A firm might decide, for example, that it should focus more specifically on its core businesses, and thus it will sell off unrelated and/or underperforming businesses. Such a sale is called a **divestiture.**

When a firm sells part of itself to raise capital, the strategy is known as a **spin-off.** A spin-off may also mean that a firm deems a business unit more valuable as a separate company. The Limited <www.limited.com>, for example, spun off three of its subsidiaries—Victoria's Secret, Bath & Body Works, and White Barn Candle Co.—to create a new firm called Intimate Brands, Inc. <www.intimatebrands.com>, which it then offered through an IPO. The Limited retained 84-percent ownership of Intimate Brands while getting an infusion of new capital.

divestiture
Strategy whereby a firm sells one or more of its business units

spin-off
Strategy of setting up one or more corporate units as new, independent corporations

Self-Check Questions 7–9

*You should now be able to answer Self-Check Questions 7–9**

7. MULTIPLE CHOICE The *sole proprietorship* enjoys which of the following advantages? [select one]: **(a)** freedom; **(b)** simplicity; **(c)** tax benefits; **(d)** all of the above; **(e)** none of the above.

8. TRUE/FALSE Because of their numerous advantages, *general partnerships* are among the most popular forms of business ownership.

9. MULTIPLE CHOICE Which of the following is **not** a kind of corporation? [select one]: **(a)** public corporation; **(b)** private corporation; **(c)** master limited corporation; **(d)** limited liability corporation; **(e)** professional corporation.

*Answers to Self-Check Questions 7–9 can be found on p. AN-2.

Continued from page 63

The Odd Couple of Cheese

After Agri-Mark took control of Cabot in 1992, parent-company president Paul Johnston decided to install a new CEO. He didn't have to look far. His choice was Richard Stammer, Agri-Mark's chief economist. While Johnston was working his way up the ladder at an Agri-Mark milk-producing plant, Stammer had been an economics professor at Rutgers, where he had developed a strong understanding of the dynamics of prices in agricultural markets.

Johnston and Stammer couldn't have been more different, but they worked well together. Johnston is a demanding boss known for his bluntness and, occasionally, lack of tact. Stammer is reserved, polite, and gracious. But the two executives have managed to set aside their differences and focus on a common goal: running an efficient business that earns profits for its owners.

Among the first things they did was improve forecasting methods. The process is never perfect, but Cabot now does a much better job of predicting demand and prices for milk and cheese. They also set about to make Cabot a national brand by concentrating more heavily on product marketing. So far, the plan seems to be paying off: Profits have topped $8 million on annual revenues of $175 million.

Questions for Discussion

1. Why do you think Cabot is organized as a cooperative?
2. What elements of business ownership are illustrated in this case?
3. What role has entrepreneurship played in the history and success of Cabot?
4. Under what circumstances might it make sense for Cabot to reorganize as a corporation?
5. What issues of taxation and legal liability might be especially pertinent for Cabot and Agri-Mark?

Summary of Learning Objectives

1. *Define* small business, *discuss its importance to the U.S. economy, and explain which* types of small business *are most likely to succeed.*

A **small business** is independently owned and managed and does not dominate its market. Thus, it can't be part of another business and must have relatively little influence in its market. Most U.S. businesses employ fewer than 100 people, and most U.S. workers are employed by small firms. The **Small Business Administration (SBA),** a government assistance agency, relies on two different factors in deciding whether a business is small: (1) *number of employees* and (2) *total annual sales.* Manufacturers may be small according to the first criterion and grocery stores may be small according to the second.

The contribution of small business can be measured by its effects on three aspects of the economic system: (1) *Job creation:* Small business is an important source of new (and often well-paid) jobs. (2) *Innovation:* Major innovations are as likely to come from small businesses (or individuals) as from big businesses. (3) *Importance to big business:* Most products made by big manufacturers are sold to consumers by small businesses. Small businesses also provide big businesses with many of their services and raw materials.

The more resources an industry requires, the harder it is to start a business in it and the less likely it is to be dominated by small firms. There are four major small-business industry groups: (1) *Services:* Small-business services range from shoeshine parlors to management consulting, and they are the fastest-growing segment of small business. (2) *Construction:* Because many construction jobs are small local projects, local firms are often ideally suited as contractors. Finance and insurance also comprise about 10 percent of all firms with fewer than 20 employees. In most cases, these businesses are either affiliates or agents of larger national firms. (3) *Wholesaling:* Wholesalers buy goods in bulk and store them in quantities at locations convenient for retailers. For a given volume of business, therefore, they need fewer employees than manufacturers, retailers, or service providers. (4) *Transportation and manufacturing:* Transportation firms include local taxi companies, charter airplane services, and tour operators. Although manufacturing lends itself to big business, small manufacturers often outperform big ones in such innovation-driven industries as electronics, and computer software.

2. *Explain* entrepreneurship *and describe some key characteristics of entrepreneurial personalities and activities.*

Entrepreneurs assume the risk of business ownership with a primary goal of growth and expansion. Many small-business owners like to think of themselves as entrepreneurs, but a person may be a small-business owner only, an entrepreneur only, or both. The basic distinction between small-business ownership and entrepreneurship is aspiration—the entrepreneur's desire to start a business and make it grow.

Most successful entrepreneurs are resourceful and concerned for customer relations. They have a strong desire to be their own bosses and can handle ambiguity and surprises. Today's entrepreneur is often an open-minded leader who relies on networks, business plans, and consensus and is just as likely to be female as male.

Finally, although successful entrepreneurs understand the role of *risk,* they do not necessarily regard what they do as risky. Whereas others may see possibilities for failure and balk at gambling on a new venture, most entrepreneurs feel so strongly about their ideas and plans that they see little or no likelihood of failure.

3. *Describe the* business plan *and the* start-up decisions *made by small businesses and identify sources of* financial aid *available to such enterprises.*

Would-be entrepreneurs must decide how to get into business and know how to find financing. The first step is the commitment to become a business owner. Next, comes choosing the goods or services to be offered—a process that means investigating one's chosen industry and market. Entrepreneurs must assess their own skills as well as industry trends.

The starting point for virtually every new business is a **business plan,** in which the entrepreneur summarizes business strategy for the new venture and shows how it will be implemented. Business plans are increasingly important because creditors and investors demand them as tools for deciding whether to finance or invest.

A business plan defines strategies for production and marketing, legal elements and organization, and accounting and finance. It should answer three questions: (1) What are the entrepreneur's goals and objectives? (2) What strategies will be used to obtain them? (3) How will these strategies be implemented? In their business plans, entrepreneurs must demonstrate an understanding of the current market, of the strengths and weaknesses of existing firms, and of the means by which the new venture will compete. The *sales forecast* is an important element. Without it, no one can estimate the required size of a plant, store, or office or decide how much inventory to carry and how many employees to hire. *Financial planning* refers to the entrepreneur's plan for turning all other activities into dollars. Thus, the business plan generally includes a *cash budget,* which shows how much money one needs before opening for business and how much one needs to keep the business going before it starts earning a profit.

Then entrepreneurs must decide whether to buy an existing business or to start from scratch. The odds are better with the first approach: A successful business has already proved its ability to draw customers at a profit, it has established working relationships with lenders and suppliers, and its track record gives a clearer picture of what to expect than any estimate of a new business's prospects. Conversely, a new business does not suffer the ill effects of the prior owner's decisions. The start-up owner is also free to choose lenders, equipment, inventories, locations, suppliers, and workers. But founders of new businesses can only make predictions and projections about their prospects. Success or failure thus depends heavily on identifying a genuine business opportunity—a product for which many customers will pay well but that is currently unavailable to them. Entrepreneurs must thus study markets and answer such questions as these: Who are my customers? How will my product differ from those of my competitors'?

Common funding sources include family and friends, savings, lenders, investors, and governmental agencies. Lending institutions are more likely to finance an existing business than a new business because the risks are better understood. Individuals starting up new businesses usually have to rely on personal resources.

Banks and private investors usually want to see formal business plans—detailed outlines of proposed businesses and markets, owners' backgrounds, and other sources of funding. Government loans have strict eligibility guidelines. Other sources include **venture capital companies**—groups of small investors seeking to make profits on companies with rapid growth potential. Most of these firms invest in companies, supplying capital in return for stock. Federally licensed to borrow money from the SBA and to invest it in or lend it to small businesses, **small-business investment companies (SBICs)** also seek profits in companies with potential for rapid growth. *Minority enterprise small-business investment companies (MESBICs)* specialize in financing minority-owned and -operated businesses.

Under the SBA's *guaranteed loans program,* small businesses can borrow from commercial lenders, with the SBA guaranteeing most of the loan amount. Through the *immediate participation loans program,* the SBA and a bank each put up a share of the loan amount. Under the *local development companies (LDCs) program,* the SBA works with a corporation founded by citizens who want to boost the local economy. **Small Business Development Centers (SBDC)** are designed to consolidate information from various disciplines and institutions, including technical and professional schools, which they make available to small businesses.

4. *Explain the main reasons why new business start-ups are increasing and identify the main reasons for success and failure in small businesses.*

Five factors account for the fact that thousands of new businesses are started in the United States every year: (1) *The emergence of e-commerce*: Because the Internet provides new ways of doing business, entrepreneurs are creating and expanding new businesses faster than ever before. (2) *Entrepreneurs who cross over from big business*: More businesses are being started by people who have left big corporations and put their experience to work for themselves. (3) *Increased opportunities for minorities and women*: More small businesses are being started by minorities and women. (4) *New opportunities in global enterprise*: Many entrepreneurs are also finding new opportunities in foreign markets. (5) *Improved rates of survival among small businesses*: More people are encouraged to try entrepreneurship because the failure rate among small businesses is going down.

Four factors contribute to small-business failure: (1) *Managerial incompetence or inexperience*: If managers don't know how to make decisions or don't understand the basic principles of management, they aren't likely to succeed. (2) *Neglect*: Some entrepreneurs try to launch ventures in their spare time, others to devote only a limited amount of time to a new business. But starting a small business requires an overwhelming time commitment. (3) *Weak control systems*: If control systems don't signal impending problems, managers may be in serious trouble before more visible difficulties alert them. (4) *Insufficient capital*: Some entrepreneurs are overly optimistic about how soon they'll start earning profits.

Similarly, four basic factors explain most small-business success: (1) *Hard work, drive, and dedication*: Small-business owners must be willing to put in time and effort. (2) *Market demand for the products or services being provided*: Analyzing market conditions can help owners assess the probable reception of their products. (3) *Managerial competence*: Owners may gain competence through training or experience or by using others' expertise. Most spend time working in successful companies or with partners to bring in more expertise. (4) *Luck.*

5. *Explain* sole proprietorships *and* partnerships *and discuss the advantages and disadvantages of each.*

The **sole proprietorship** is owned and usually operated by one person. Though usually small, it may be as large as a steel mill. The ease of setting up a sole proprietorship makes it appealing to self-starters, as do the low start-up costs. There are tax benefits for new businesses that are likely to suffer losses in early stages: Because sole proprietors may treat revenues and expenses as part of their personal finances, they can cut their taxes by deducting business losses from income earned elsewhere.

A major drawback is **unlimited liability.** A sole proprietor is personally liable for all debts incurred by the business. Another disadvantage is lack of continuity: A sole proprietorship dissolves when the owner dies. Finally, a sole proprietorship depends on the resources of a single individual.

The **general partnership** is a sole proprietorship multiplied by the number of partner-owners. The biggest advantage is its ability to grow by adding new talent and money. Because banks prefer to make loans to enterprises that are not dependent on single individuals, it's easier for partnerships to borrow money. They can also invite new partners to join by investing. Although they must meet only a few legal requirements, all partnerships must have an agreement that answers such questions such as these: Who invested what sums of money? Who will receive what share of the profits?

A partnership is not a legal entity. It is just two or more people working together. Partners are taxed as individuals, and unlimited liability is a drawback. Each partner may be liable for all partnership debts. Partnerships may lack continuity, and transferring ownership may be hard. No partner may sell out without the consent of the others.

To resolve some of these problems, other types of agreements have been developed. The **limited partnership** allows for **limited partners,** who are liable only to the extent of their investments. A **general** (or **active**) **partner** runs the business and bears the responsibility for its survival and growth. Under a **master limited partnership (MLP),** an organization sells partnership interests to investors who are paid back from profits. The master partner retains at least 50-percent ownership and runs the business.

Finally, groups of sole proprietorships or partnerships sometimes agree to work together by forming **cooperatives,** which combine the freedom of sole proprietorships with the financial power of corporations. They give members greater production power, greater marketing power, or both.

6. *Describe* corporations, *discuss their advantages and disadvantages, and identify different kinds of corporations.*

All **corporations** share certain characteristics: legal status as separate entities, property rights and obligations, and indefinite life spans. They may sue and be sued; buy, hold, and sell property; make and sell products; commit crimes and be tried and punished for them.

The biggest advantage of incorporation is **limited liability:** Investor liability is limited to one's personal investments in the corporation. If it fails, the courts may sell a corporation's assets but cannot touch the personal possessions of investors. Another advantage is continuity. With a legal life independent of founders and owners, a corporation can continue forever. Shares can be sold or passed on to heirs, and most corporations benefit from the continuity of professional management. Finally, corporations have advantages in raising money. By selling stock, they expand the number of investors and the amount of available funds. Legal protections tend to make lenders more willing to grant loans.

One disadvantage goes hand in hand with ease of transferring ownership. Using a legal process called a **tender offer**—an offer to buy shares made by a prospective buyer directly to a corporation's shareholders—a corporation can be taken over against the will of its managers. Another disadvantage is start-up cost. Corporations are heavily regulated and must meet complex legal requirements in the states in which they're chartered. The greatest potential drawback to incorporation is **double taxation.** A regular corporation pays income taxes on company profits, and its stockholders pay taxes on income returned by their investments. Thus, corporate profits are taxed twice—at the corporate and ownership levels.

Different kinds of corporations help businesses take advantage of incorporation without assuming all of the disadvantages. In a **closely held corporation** (or **private corporation**), the stock is held by a few people and isn't available for public sale. When shares are publicly issued, the firm becomes a **publicly held corporation** (or **public corporation**). Stock is widely held and available for public sale. The **S corporation** is organized and operates like a corporation, but it is treated like a partnership for tax purposes.

Owners of **limited liability corporations,** or **LLCs,** are taxed like partners, each paying personal taxes only, but they also enjoy the benefits of corporate limited liability. **Professional corporations** are usually comprised of doctors, lawyers, accountants, or other professionals and are not immune from unlimited liability. The **multinational** or **transnational corporation** spans national boundaries. Stock may be traded on several international exchanges, and managers are likely to be from different countries.

7. *Explain the basic issues involved in creating and managing a corporation and identify recent trends and issues in corporate ownership.*

The corporate entity is managed by people who understand the principles of **corporate governance**—the roles of shareholders, directors, and other managers in corporate decision making. Corporations sell shares, called **stock,** to investors who then become **stockholders** (or **shareholders**) and the real owners. Profits are distributed among stockholders in the form of dividends, and managers serve at their discretion. **Preferred stock** offers holders fixed dividends. Preferred stockholders have preference, or priority, over common stockholders when dividends are distributed and, if a business fails, when the value of assets is distributed. **Common stock** usually pays dividends only if the corporation makes a profit, and holders have the last claims to any assets. Dividends on both types of stock are paid on a per-share basis. While preferred stockholders have no voting rights, common stockholders always have one vote per share.

The governing body of a corporation is its **board of directors.** Boards communicate with stockholders and other stakeholders through such channels as the annual report—a summary of the company's financial health. They set policy on dividends, major spending, and executive compensation. They are legally responsible for corporate actions and are increasingly being held liable for them. Most board members do not participate in day-to-day management but rather hire a team of managers. This team, called *officers,* is usually headed by a **chief executive officer**, or **CEO,** who is responsible for overall performance. Other officers typically include a *president,* who is responsible for internal management, and *vice presidents,* who oversee various functional areas such as marketing and operations.

In a **strategic alliance,** two or more organizations collaborate on a project for mutual gain. When partners share ownership of a new enterprise, the arrangement is called a **joint venture.** The **employee stock ownership plan (ESOP)** allows employees to own a significant share of the corporation through trusts established on their behalf. More stock is now being purchased by **institutional investors.** Because they control enormous resources, these investors—especially mutual and pension funds—can buy huge blocks of stock and thus exert influence on management.

A **merger** occurs when two firms combine to create a new company. In an **acquisition,** one firm buys another outright. When the two firms are of roughly the same size, the combination is usually called a *merger* even if one firm assumes control over the other. When the acquiring firm is substantially larger than the acquired firm, it is more likely called an *acquisition.* M&As allow firms to increase product lines, expand operations, go international, and create new enterprises. A **divestiture** occurs when a corporation sells a part of its existing business operations or sets it up as a new and independent corporation. When a firm sells part of itself to raise capital, the strategy is known as a **spin-off.**

KEY TERMS

Small Business Administration (SBA) (p. 64)
small business (p. 64)
entrepreneur (p. 67)
business plan (p. 69)
venture capital company (p. 70)
small-business investment company (SBIC) (p. 70)
Small Business Development Center (SBDC) (p. 71)
franchise (p. 72)
sole proprietorship (p. 79)
unlimited liability (p. 79)
general partnership (p. 79)
limited partnership (p. 80)
limited partner (p. 80)
general** (or **active**) **partner (p. 80)
master limited partnership (MLP) (p. 80)
cooperative (p. 81)
corporation (p. 81)
limited liability (p. 82)
tender offer (p. 82)
double taxation (p. 82)
closely held** (or **private**) **corporation (p. 82)
publicly held** (or **public**) **corporation (p. 82)
S corporation (p. 82)
limited liability corporation (LLC) (p. 83)
professional corporation (p. 83)
multinational** or **transnational corporation (p. 83)
corporate governance (p. 83)
***stockholder** (or **shareholder**)* (p. 83)
stock (p. 84)
preferred stock (p. 84)
common stock (p. 84)
board of directors (p. 84)
chief executive officer (CEO) (p. 84)
strategic alliance (p. 84)
joint venture (p. 84)
employee stock ownership plan (ESOP) (p. 84)
institutional investor (p. 85)
merger (p. 85)
acquisition (p. 85)
divestiture (p. 85)
spin-off (p. 85)

QUESTIONS AND EXERCISES

Questions for Review

1. Why are small businesses important to the U.S. economy?
2. What is the basic difference between a small business owner and an entrepreneur?
3. From the standpoint of the franchisee, what are the primary advantages and disadvantages of most franchise arrangements?
4. Which industries are easiest for start-ups to enter? Which are hardest? Why?

Questions for Analysis

5. Why might a closely held corporation choose to remain private? Why might it choose to be publicly traded?
6. If you were going to open a small business, what type would it be? Why?
7. Would you prefer to buy an existing business or start from scratch? Why?
8. Under what circumstances might it be wise for an entrepreneur to reject venture capital? Under what circumstances might it be advisable to take more venture capital than he or she actually needs?

Application Exercises

9. Interview the owner-manager of a sole proprietorship or a general partnership. What characteristics of that business form led the owner to choose it? Does he or she ever contemplate changing the form of the business?
10. Identify two or three of the fastest growing businesses in the United States during the last year. What role has entrepreneurship played in the growth of these firms?

Building Your Business Skills

WORKING THE INTERNET

This exercise enhances the following SCANS workplace competencies: demonstrating basic skills, demonstrating thinking skills, exhibiting interpersonal skills, and working with information.

Goal

To encourage students to define the opportunities and problems for small companies doing business on the Internet

The Situation

Let's say that you and two partners own a company that specializes in special-occasion gift baskets for individual and corporate clients. You're doing well, but you think there may be opportunity for growth through a virtual storefront on the Internet.

Method

Step 1

Join with two other students and assume the role of business partners. Start by researching Internet businesses. Look at books and articles at the library, and contact the following Web sites for help:

- Small Business Administration <www.sba.gov>
- IBM Small Business Center <www.business center.ibm.com>
- Apple Small Business Home Page <www.smallbusiness.apple.com>

These sites may lead you to others, so keep an open mind.

Step 2

Based on your research, determine the importance of the following small-business issues:

- Analyzing changing company finances as a result of expansion onto the Internet
- Analyzing your new competitive marketplace (the world) and how it affects your current marketing approach, which focuses on your local community
- Identifying sources of management advice as expansion proceeds
- The role of technology consultants in launching and maintaining a Web site
- Customer-service policies in a virtual environment

Follow-Up Questions

1. Do you think your business would be successful on the Internet? Why or why not?
2. Based on your analysis, how will Internet expansion affect your current business practices? What specific changes are you likely to make?
3. Do you think that operating a virtual storefront will be harder or easier than doing business in your local community? Explain your answer.

Exercising Your Ethics

BREAKING UP IS HARD TO DO

The Situation

Connie and Mark began a 25-year friendship after finishing college and discovering their mutual interest in owning a business. Established as a general partnership, their home-furnishings center is a successful business sustained for 20 years by a share-and-share-alike relationship. Start-up cash, daily responsibilities, and profits have all been shared equally. The partners both work four days each week except when busy seasons require both of them to be in the store. Shared goals and compatible personalities have led to a solid give-and-take relationship that helps them overcome business problems while maintaining a happy interpersonal relationship.

The division of work is a natural match and successful combination because of the partners' different but complementary interests. Mark buys the merchandise and maintains up-to-date contacts with suppliers; he also handles personnel matters (hiring and training employees). Connie manages the inventory, buys shipping supplies, keeps the books, and manages the finances. Mark does more selling, with Connie helping out only during busy seasons. Both partners share in decisions about advertising and promotions.

The Dilemma

Things began changing two years ago, when Connie became less interested in the business and got more involved in other activities. Whereas Mark's enthusiasm remained high, Connie's time was increasingly consumed by travel, recreation, and community-service activities. At first, she reduced her work commitment from four to three days a week. Then she indicated that she wanted to cut back further, to just two days. "In that case," Mark replied, "we'll have to make some changes."

Mark insisted that profit sharing be adjusted to reflect his larger role in running the business. He proposed that Connie's monthly salary be cut in half (from $4,000 to $2,000). Connie agreed. He recommended that the $2,000 savings be shifted to his salary because of his increased workload, but this time Connie balked, arguing that Mark's current $4,000 salary already compensated him for his contributions. She proposed to split the difference, with Mark getting a $1,000 increase and the other $1,000 going into the firm's cash account. Mark said no and insisted on a full $2,000 raise. To avoid a complete falling out, Connie finally gave in, even though she thought it unfair for Mark's salary to jump from $4,000 per month to $6,000. At that point, she made a promise to herself: "To even things out, I'll find a way to get $2,000 worth of inventory for personal use each month."

Questions for Discussion

1. Identify the ethical issues, if any, regarding Mark's and Connie's respective positions on Mark's proposed $2,000 salary increase.
2. What kind of salary adjustments do you think would be fair in this situation? Explain why.
3. There is, of course, another way for Mark and Connie to solve their differences: Because the terms of participation have changed, it might make sense to dissolve the existing partnership. What do you recommend in this regard?

Crafting Your Business Plan

FITTING IN TO THE ENTREPRENEURIAL MOLD

The Purpose of the Assignment

1. To familiarize students with the ways in which entrepreneurship and small business considerations enter into the business planning framework of the *Business PlanPro (BPP)* software package.
2. To encourage students to think about how to apply their textbook information on entrepreneurship to the preparation of a small business plan using the *BPP* planning environment.

Assignment

After reading Chapter 3 in the textbook, open the BPP *software and look around for information about the types small business and entrepreneurship considerations that would be of concern to a sample firm:* Corporate Fitness. *To find* Corporate Fitness, *do the following:*

Open the *Business PlanPro.* If it asks if you want to "create a new business plan" or "open an existing plan," select "create a new business plan" (even though you are not going to create a plan at this time). You will then be taken to the *Business PlanPro EasyPlan Wizard.* Click on the option entitled **Research It.** You will then be presented with a new list of options, including **Sample Plan Browser.** After clicking on the **Sample Plan Browser,** go down the alphabetical list of sample plans and double-click on **Health Fitness Program,** which is the location for *Corporate Fitness.* The screen you are looking at is the introductory page for the *Corporate Fitness* business plan. Next, scroll down from this page until you reach the **Table of Contents** for the company's business plan.

Now respond to the following items:

1. In the Table of Contents page, click on **1.0 Executive Summary** to familiarize yourself with an overview of this firm. Which industry category for small business—construction, wholesaling, services, transportation, or manufacturing—best describes the *Corporate Fitness* line of business?
2. The textbook identifies several characteristics of successful entrepreneurs. Judging by its business plan, do you think the management team of *Corporate Fitness* has an entrepreneurial orientation? Explain why or why not. [Sites to see in *BPP* for this item: On the Table of Contents page, click on each of the following in turn: **6.0 Management Summary, 6.2 Management Team,** and **6.3 Management Team Gaps.**]
3. The textbook identifies several sources of advice and assistance for starting and running small businesses. Judging from its business plan, do you think that *Corporate Fitness* is planning to seek advice from any of those sources in getting started? Do you think it is a good idea to discuss the planned uses of such sources in the business plan? Explain why or why not. [Sites to see in *BPP:* From the Table of Contents page, explore the *Corporate Fitness* business plan using your judgment as to where you would expect to find information on start-up advice.]
4. What sources of advice and assistance do you recommend for getting Corporate Fitness off to a sound start? In which areas of the business and for which of its business activities will it benefit the most from outside advice and assistance? Where in its business plan do you recommend reporting its planned use of such assistance?

Video Exercise

DOING BUSINESS PRIVATELY: AMY'S ICE CREAM

Learning Objectives

The purpose of this video is to help you:

1. Distinguish among types of corporations.
2. Consider the advantages and disadvantages of incorporation.
3. Understand the role that shareholders play in a privately held corporation.

Synopsis

Amy's Ice Creams, based in Austin, Texas, is a privately held corporation formed in 1984 by Amy Miller and owned by Miller and a small group of family members and friends. At the outset, one of the most important decisions Miller faced was choosing an appropriate legal ownership structure for the new business. Fueled by the founder's dedication to creating happy ice cream memories for customers, Amy's has continued to evolve and grow. The company now operates nine stores and rings up close to $3.5 million in annual sales. Applying for a job is an adventure in creativity, and Miller welcomes employees' suggestions for new flavors and new promotions.

Discussion Questions

1. *For analysis*: How does Amy's Ice Cream differ from a publicly held corporation?
2. *For analysis*: What are some of the particular advantages of corporate ownership for a firm such as Amy's Ice Cream?

3. *For application*: How well do you think Amy's is working to ensure its continued survival and success? Looking ahead to future growth, what marketing, financial, or other suggestions would you make?
4. *For application*: What are some of the issues that Amy Miller may have to confront because her 22 investors are family members and friends?
5. *For debate*: Should Amy's Ice Cream become a publicly held corporation? Support your chosen position.

Online Exploration

Find out what's required to incorporate a business in your state. You might begin by searching the CCH Business Owner's Toolkit site at <www.toolkit.cch.com>. If you were going to start a small business, would you choose incorporation or a different form of legal organization? List the pros and cons that incorporation presents for the type of business that you would consider.

CHAPTER

Understanding the Global Context of Business

After reading this chapter, you should be able to:

1. Discuss the rise of international business and describe the *major world marketplaces.*
2. Explain how differences in *competitive advantage, import-export balances, exchange rates,* and *foreign competition* determine the ways in which countries and businesses respond to the international environment.
3. Discuss the factors involved in deciding to do business internationally and in selecting the appropriate *levels of international involvement* and *international organizational structure.*
4. Describe some of the ways in which *social, cultural, economic, legal,* and *political differences* among nations affect international business.

"We Must Americanize"

Toyota is a giant Japanese car company with a stellar reputation for quality, but today it's also a firm with an apparent identity crisis. Although it's among the world's largest—and most profitable—companies, Toyota seems to be changing its mind about the character of its operations and, indeed, its perception of itself as a global manufacturer.

Toyota <www.toyota.com> was founded in 1930 and first entered the U.S. market in 1957, where, despite a few early missteps, it has enjoyed almost unqualified success. By 1970, Toyota was the world's fourth-largest automaker, and today, it's in third place. Profits in 2001 were $5.5 billion on revenues of $108 billion. The firm employs 215,000 workers worldwide and operates 56 manufacturing facilities in 25 countries. It will open its tenth U.S. assembly plant in Alabama in 2003.

Since it first ventured into foreign markets, however, Toyota has steadfastly remained a Japanese company. It's long been the market leader at home, and new product design has always been handled by Japanese designers from a centralized development center. Company policy has always been to fill top spots in foreign affiliates with senior Japanese executives, and managers at foreign operations have always had to get key decisions reviewed by corporate headquarters in aptly named Toyota City.

In the early 1990s, Toyota also had a clear strategy for growth based on competitive advantages and economic forecasts. The firm intended to grow steadily in its domestic market, make modest gains in the United States, expand significantly in Europe, and make significant gains in Southeast Asia. Formidable domestic competition dampened prospects in the United States, but the Japanese market was booming, and Toyota fully expected to be able to extend its market dominance into neighboring countries. Europe, too, was targeted as an area with growth opportunities.

But even the best plans and forecasts sometimes go awry. Over the course of the 1990s, Toyota's market situation began to change on all fronts. The home market stalled along with the rest of the Japanese economy, and Toyota also began to lose its youngest domestic consumers to Honda and a resurgent Nissan. In addition, a currency crisis in Southeast Asia, coupled with competition from youth-oriented upstarts such as Kia and Hyundai, undermined Toyota's plans in South Korea, Indonesia, and China. Toyota also stalled in Europe, where it faced an economic downturn and renewed competition from Volkswagen and Renault.

Ironically, however, it's in the U.S. market that things have turned out better than Toyota had hoped. In 2001, Toyota sold more vehicles in the United States (1.74 million) than in Japan (1.71 million). Its U.S. factories and dealerships also employ 123,000 Americans—more than Coca-Cola, Microsoft, and Oracle combined. More and more of the firm's top U.S. executives are local hires who have either climbed the ladder or been lured away from domestic firms like Ford and General Motors. Toyota's recent U.S. successes, such as the Tundra pickup and Sequoia sport utility vehicle (SUV), have had significant input from U.S. design teams.

Most of these successes come from changes in Toyota's American operations. "Thirty years ago," says James Press, the COO of Toyota Motor Sales USA, "we were more dependent on Japan, [but now] there's not much Japanese influence on a day-to-day basis." In fact, the influence of U.S. operations is beginning to be felt in Japan, where CEO Fujio Cho has advised his managers that "We must Americanize."

Our opening story continues on page 117

"Now there's not much Japanese influence on a day-to-day basis."

~James Press, COO
TOYOTA MOTOR SALES USA

The Rise of International Business

Total volume of world trade is immense—over $8 trillion in merchandise trade each year. Foreign investment in the United States and U.S. investment abroad have each passed the $1 trillion mark.[1] As more firms engage in international business, the world economy is fast becoming an interdependent system—a process called **globalization.**[2] We often take for granted the diversity of products we can buy as a result of international trade. Your TV set, your shoes, and even your morning coffee are probably **imports**—products made or grown abroad and sold domestically in the United States. At the same time, the success of many U.S. firms depends on **exports**—products made or grown here and shipped for sale abroad.

globalization
Process by which the world economy is becoming a single interdependent system

import
Product made or grown abroad but sold domestically

export
Product made or grown domestically but shipped and sold abroad

The Contemporary Global Economy

International trade is becoming increasingly important to most nations and their largest businesses. Many countries that once followed strict policies to protect domestic business now encourage trade just as aggressively. They are opening borders to foreign business, offering incentives for domestic businesses to expand internationally, and making it easier for foreign firms to partner with local firms. Likewise, as more industries and markets become global, so, too, are the firms that compete in them.

Several forces have combined to spark and sustain globalization. For one thing, governments and businesses are more aware of the benefits of globalization to businesses and shareholders. For another, new technologies have made international travel, communication, and commerce much faster and cheaper. Figure 4.1, for example, shows the decrease in the costs of two international business activities over the last several decades: the cost of a three-minute phone call from New York to London and the cost of transatlantic shipping per ton. Today, too, travelers can easily fly between most major cities in the United States and Europe in less than a day. Finally, there are competitive pressures. Sometimes, a firm must expand into foreign markets simply to keep up with competitors.

Trade Agreements Various legal agreements have also sparked international trade. Indeed, virtually every nation has formal trade treaties with other nations.

Fisherman Ratish Karthikeyan can sometimes double the revenue from a day's take by phoning around to compare prices at markets within reach of his boat. That's one reason why companies like AT&T (United States) and Hutchison Telecom (Hong Kong) are finding India a thriving export market for cellular phones. For another, about half of India's 600,000 rural communities aren't even wired for fixed-line phone service. Between now and 2005, the number of mobile-phone users should jump from 3 million to 30 million.

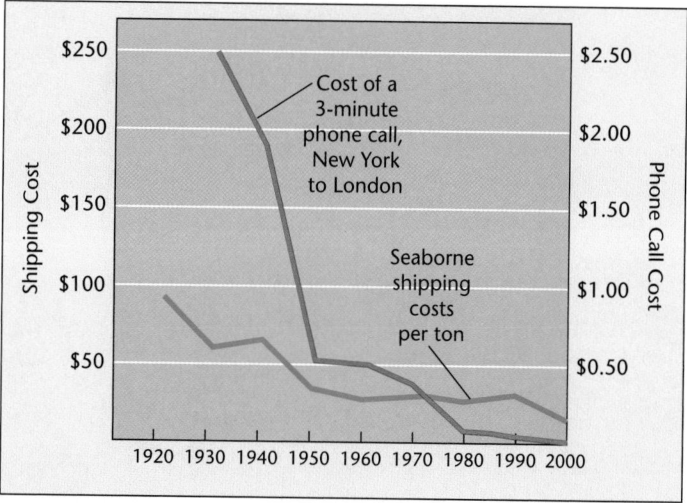

FIGURE 4.1
The Price of Global Communication

Among the most significant multilateral agreements are the General Agreement on Tariffs and Trade and the North American Free Trade Agreement. The European Union and the World Trade Organization, both governed by treaties, are also instrumental in promoting international business activity.

General Agreement on Tariffs and Trade The **General Agreement on Tariffs and Trade (GATT)** was signed after World War II. Its purpose is to reduce or eliminate trade barriers, such as tariffs and quotas. It does so by encouraging nations to protect domestic industries within agreed-upon limits and to engage in multilateral negotiations.

General Agreement on Tariffs and Trade (GATT)
International trade agreement to encourage the multilateral reduction or elimination of trade barriers

A revision of GATT went into effect in 1994, but many issues remain unresolved—for example, the opening of foreign markets to most financial services. Governments may still subsidize builders of civil aircraft, and there is no agreement to limit the distribution of American cultural exports—movies, music, and the like—in Europe. Thanks to those agreements that are in place, however, world commerce may increase another $270 billion by 2002.

North American Free Trade Agreement The **North American Free Trade Agreement (NAFTA)** removes tariffs and other trade barriers among the United States, Canada, and Mexico (Figure 4.2) and includes agreements on environmental issues and labor abuses. Some barriers came down on January 1, 1994, and others will follow at 5-, 10-, or 15-year intervals.

North American Free Trade Agreement (NAFTA)
Agreement to gradually eliminate tariffs and other trade barriers among the United States, Canada, and Mexico

In its first year, observers agreed that NAFTA had achieved its basic purpose—to create a more active North American market. The following were among its first-year results:

- Direct foreign investment increased. With $2.4 billion, U.S. and Canadian firms accounted for 55 percent of all foreign investment in Mexico. Companies from other nations—for instance, Japan's Toyota—also made new investments to take advantage of the freer movement of goods.
- U.S. exports to Mexico increased by about 20 percent. Procter & Gamble, for example, enjoyed an increase of nearly 75 percent, and the giant agribusiness firm Archer Daniels Midland tripled exports to Mexico. Mexico passed Japan as the second-largest buyer of U.S. goods, and trade with Canada rose 10 percent (twice the gain in Europe and Asia).
- U.S. imports from Mexico and Canada rose even faster than rates in the opposite direction, setting records of $48 billion and $120 billion, respectively. In particular, electronics, computers, and communications products

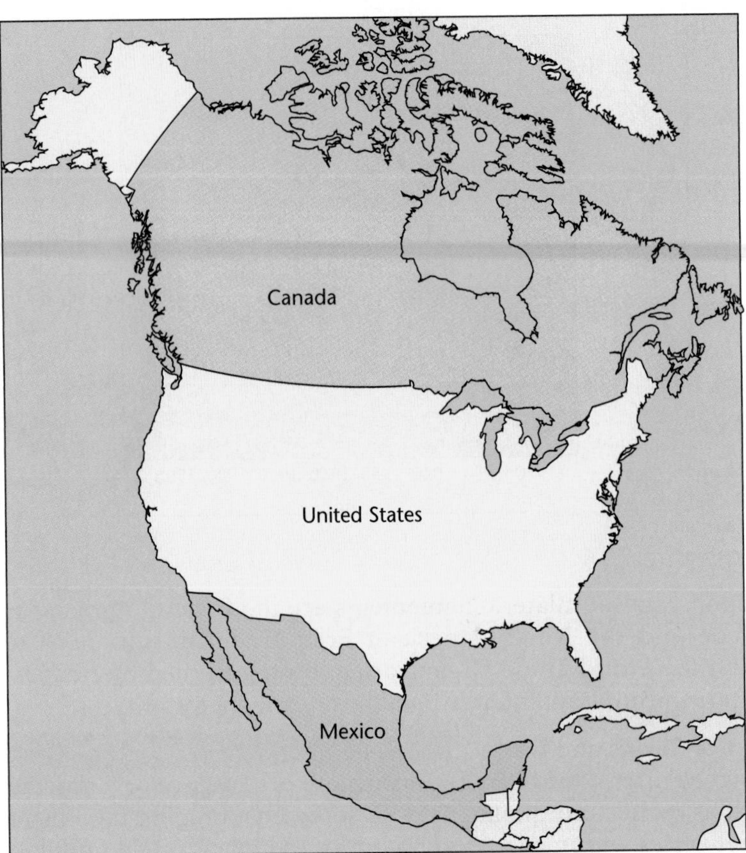

FIGURE 4.2
The North American Marketplace and the Nations of NAFTA

came into the United States twice as fast as they went out. "We pointed out," says one NAFTA opponent, "that there was a fairly sophisticated manufacturing base in Mexico that pays peanuts, and the numbers bear that out."

- NAFTA created fewer jobs than proponents had hoped. Although the U.S. economy added 1.7 million new jobs in 1994, perhaps only 100,000 were NAFTA related. At the same time, however, the flood of U.S. jobs lost to Mexico predicted by NAFTA critics, especially labor unions, did not occur. In fact, Ford Motor Co.'s Mexicican division claims that it has created jobs in both countries. Ford's exports of Mexican-made vehicles to the United States went up 30 percent, but 80 percent of all components in those cars are American-made. Ford also reports that its exports of American-made cars to Mexico rose from 1,200 to 30,000.

European Union (EU)
Agreement among major Western European nations to eliminate or make uniform most trade barriers affecting group members

European Union Originally called the Common Market, the **European Union (EU)** includes the principal Western European nations, who have eliminated most quotas and set uniform tariff levels on products imported and exported within their group. In 1992, virtually all internal trade barriers went down, making the EU the largest free marketplace in the world. We discuss the EU more fully later in the chapter.

World Trade Organization (WTO)
Organization through which member nations negotiate trading agreements and resolve disputes about trade policies and practices

World Trade Organization To further globalization, most of the world's countries joined to create the **World Trade Organization (WTO)** <www.wto.org>, which was born on January 1, 1995. The 140 member countries are required to open markets to international trade, and the WTO is empowered to pursue three goals:

1. Promote trade by encouraging members to adopt fair trade practices.
2. Reduce trade barriers by promoting multilateral negotiations.
3. Establish fair procedures for resolving disputes among members.

In the remainder of this section, we examine some other key factors that shaped—and are still shaping—today's global business environment. First, we identify the *major world marketplaces*. Then we discuss some important factors that determine the ways in which both nations and businesses respond to the international environment: the roles of different forms of *competitive advantage*, *import-export balances*, and *exchange rates*.

The Major World Marketplaces

The world economy revolves around three major marketplaces: North America, Europe, and Asia. These three geographic regions are home to most of the world's largest economies, biggest multinational corporations, most influential financial markets, and highest-income consumers.

The World Bank, an agency of the United Nations <www.worldbank.org>, uses *per capita income*—average income per person—as a measure to divide countries into one of three groups:[3]

- ***High-income countries:*** those with per capita income greater than $9,386. These include the United States, Canada, most of the countries in Europe, Australia, New Zealand, Japan, South Korea, Kuwait, the United Arab Emirates, Israel, Singapore, and Taiwan. Hong Kong, though technically no longer an independent nation, also falls into this category.
- ***Middle-income countries:*** those with per capita income of less than $9,386 but more than $765. This group includes, among others, the Czech Republic, Greece, Hungary, Poland, most of the countries of the former Soviet bloc, Turkey, Mexico, Argentina, and Uruguay. Some of these nations, most notably Poland, Argentina, and Uruguay, are developing economically and will soon move into the high-income category.
- ***Low-income countries,*** also called *developing countries:* those with per capita income of less than $765. Some of these countries, such as China and India, have huge populations and are seen as potentially attractive markets. Due to low literacy rates, weak infrastructures, and unstable governments, other countries in this group are less attractive. For example, the East African nation of Somalia, plagued by drought, starvation, and internal strife and civil war, plays virtually no role in the world economy.

This boy's home country, the arid landlocked African nation of Burkina Faso, is a "low-income" country. That's why he's working on a cocoa plantation in the Ivory Coast, one of the continent's more prosperous nations, for about 50 cents a day. Even at that rate, he's far from the bottom rung on Africa's economic ladder. As for the cocoa farmer who pays him, he's finally been able to buy a tractor after farming 48 acres for 33 years. The cocoa is sold to local buyers and then to exporters who sell it to companies like Nestlé and Hershey.

North America As the world's largest marketplace and most stable economy, the United States dominates the North American market. Canada also plays a major role in the international economy, and the United States and Canada are each other's largest trading partner. Many U.S. firms, such as General Motors <www.gmcanada.com> and Procter & Gamble <www.pg.com/canada>, have maintained successful Canadian operations for years, and many Canadian firms, such as Northern Telecom <www.nt.com> and Alcan Aluminum <www.alcan.com>, are also major international competitors.

Mexico has become a major manufacturing center, especially along the U.S. border, where cheap labor and low transportation costs have encouraged many firms from the United States and other countries to build factories. The auto industry has been especially active, with DaimlerChrysler <www.daimlerchrysler.com>, General Motors <www.gm.com>, Volkswagen <www.vw.com>, Nissan <www.nissandriven.com>, and Ford <www.ford.com> all running large assembly plants in the region. Several major suppliers have also built facilities in the area. From 1993 to 2001, exports of cars and automobile parts from Mexico increased from $7.2 billion to $23.6 billion, and the Mexican auto industry now employs over 400,000 workers. The industry grew by 10 percent in 2001 and is expected to grow even more rapidly in 2002 and 2003.[4]

Europe Europe is often regarded as two regions—Western and Eastern. Western Europe, which is dominated by Germany, the United Kingdom, France, and Italy, has long been a mature but fragmented marketplace. But the transformation of the EU into a unified marketplace in 1992 further increased the region's importance (see Figure 4.3). Major international firms such as Unilever <www.unilver.com>, Renault <www.renault.com>, Royal Dutch/Shell <www.shell.com>, Michelin <www.michelin.com>, Siemens <www.siemens.de>, and Nestlé <www.nestle.com> are all headquartered in Western Europe.

E-commerce and technology have also become increasingly important in this region.[5] There has been a surge in Internet start-ups in southeastern England, the Netherlands, and the Scandinavian countries; and Ireland is now the world's number-two exporter of software (after the United States). Strasbourg, France, is a major center for biotech start-ups. Barcelona, Spain, has many flourishing software and Internet companies, and the Frankfurt region of Germany is dotted with both software and biotech start-ups.[6]

Eastern Europe, once primarily communist, has also gained in importance, both as a marketplace and as a producer. Such multinational corporations as Daewoo <www.daewoo.com>, Nestlé, General Motors, and ABB Asea Brown Boveri <www.abb.com> have all set up operations in Poland. Ford, General Motors, Suzuki <www.suzuki.com>, and Volkswagen have all built new factories in Hungary. On the other hand, governmental instability has hampered development in Russia, Bulgaria, Albania, Romania, and other countries.

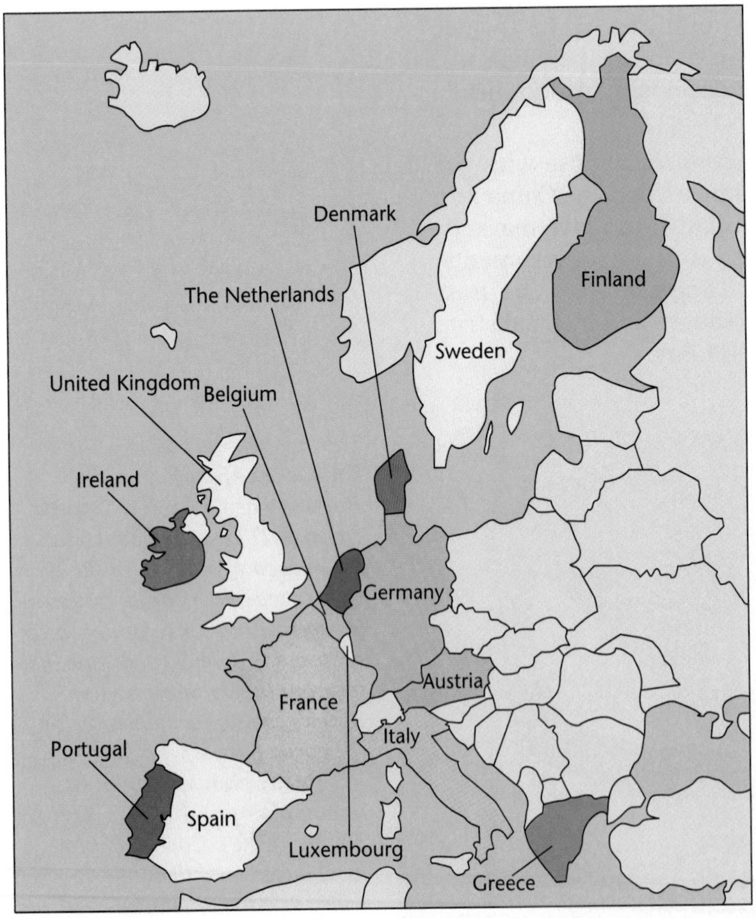

FIGURE 4.3

Europe and the Nations of the European Union

Pacific Asia Pacific Asia consists of Japan, China, Thailand, Malaysia, Singapore, Indonesia, South Korea, Taiwan, the Philippines, and Australia. Some experts still distinguish Hong Kong, though now part of China, as a part of the region, and others include Vietnam. Fueled by strong entries in the automobile, electronics, and banking industries, the economies of these countries grew rapidly in the 1970s and 1980s. Unfortunately, a currency crisis in the late 1990s slowed growth in virtually every country of the region.

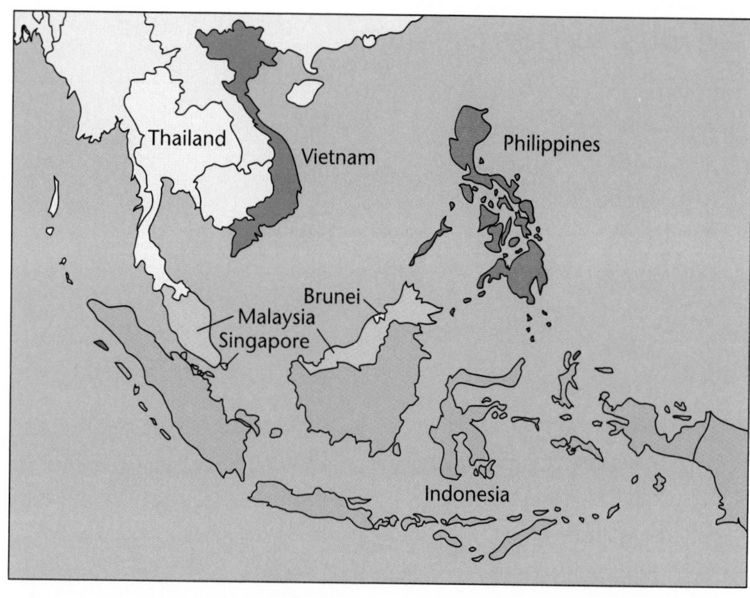

FIGURE 4.4
The Nations of ASEAN

The currency crisis aside, however, Pacific Asia is an important force in the world economy and a major source of competition for North American firms. Led by firms such as Toyota, Toshiba <www.toshiba.com>, and Nippon Steel <www.nsc.co.jp/english>, Japan dominates the region. South Korea (home to such firms as Samsung <www.samsung.com> and Hyundai <www.hyundai.com>), Taiwan (owner of Chinese Petroleum <www.cpc.com.tw/english> and manufacturing home of many foreign firms), and Hong Kong (a major financial center) are also successful players in the international economy. China, the world's most densely populated country, has emerged as an important market and now boasts the world's third-largest economy behind that of the United States and only slightly behind that of Japan.

As in North America and Western Europe, technology promises to play an increasingly important role in the future of this region. In Asia, however, the emergence of technology firms has been hampered by a poorly developed electronic infrastructure, slower adoption of computers and information technology, and a higher percentage of lower-income consumers. Thus, although the future looks promising, technology companies are facing several obstacles as they work to keep pace with foreign competitors.[7]

Figure 4.4 is a map of the Association of Southeast Asian Nations (ASEAN) <www.aseansec.org> countries of Pacific Asia. ASEAN (pronounced *OZZIE-on*) was founded in 1967 as an organization for economic, political, social, and cultural cooperation. In 1995, Vietnam became the group's first communist member. Today, the ASEAN group has a population of over 500 million and a GDP of approximately $800 billion.[8]

Table 4.1 lists the major trading partners of the United States. As we noted earlier, these partners are located all over the world and include high-, middle-, and low-income countries. The left side of the table identifies the 25 countries from which the United States buys the most products. Germany, for example, is our fifth-biggest supplier, Malaysia tenth, and Thailand fifteenth. The right side identifies the 25 largest export markets for U.S. businesses. Germany is our fifth-biggest customer, Singapore tenth, and Australia fifteenth. Note that many countries are on both lists (indeed, Canada is at the top of both).

Forms of Competitive Advantage

Why is there so much international business activity? Because no country can produce everything that it needs, countries tend to export what they can produce better or less expensively than other countries and use the proceeds to import what they can't produce as effectively.

TOP 25 U.S. SUPPLIER COUNTRIES Rank/Country		2000 Imports ($ bil.)	TOP 25 U.S. EXPORT MARKETS Rank/Country		2000 Exports ($ bil.)
1	Canada	230.8	1	Canada	178.9
2	Japan	146.5	2	Mexico	111.3
3	Mexico	135.9	3	Japan	64.9
4	China	100.0	4	United Kingdom	41.6
5	Germany	58.5	5	Germany	29.4
6	United Kingdom	43.3	6	Korea	27.8
7	Taiwan	40.5	7	Taiwan	24.4
8	Korea, South	40.3	8	Netherlands	21.8
9	France	29.8	9	France	20.4
10	Malaysia	25.6	10	Singapore	17.8
11	Italy	25.0	11	China	16.2
12	Singapore	19.2	12	Brazil	15.3
13	Venezuela	18.6	13	Hong Kong	14.6
14	Ireland	16.5	14	Belgium+ Luxembourg	14.3
15	Thailand	16.4	15	Australia	12.5
16	Saudi Arabia	14.4	16	Italy	11.1
17	Philippines	13.9	17	Malaysia	10.9
18	Brazil	13.9	18	Switzerland	10.0
19	Israel	13.0	19	Philippines	8.8
20	Hong Kong	11.4	20	Israel	7.7
21	India	10.7	21	Ireland	7.7
22	Nigeria	10.5	22	Thailand	6.6
23	Indonesia	10.4	23	Spain	6.3
24	Belgium+ Luxembourg	10.3	24	Saudi Arabia	6.2
25	Switzerland	10.2	25	Venezuela	5.6

TABLE 4.1
The Major Trading Partners of the United States

Of course, this principle doesn't fully explain why nations export and import *what* they do. Such decisions hinge partly on the advantages that a particular country enjoys regarding its abilities to create and/or sell certain products and resources.[9] Traditionally, economists focused on *absolute* and *comparative advantage* to explain international trade. But because this approach focuses narrowly on such factors as natural resources and labor costs, the more complex view of *national competitive advantage* has emerged.

absolute advantage
The ability to produce something more efficiently than any other country can

Absolute Advantage An **absolute advantage** exists when a country can produce something cheaper and/or of higher quality than any other country. Saudi oil, Brazilian coffee beans, and Canadian timber come close, but examples of true absolute advantage are rare. In reality, "absolute" advantages are always relative. For example, most experts say that the vineyards of France produce the world's finest wines. But the burgeoning wine business in California demonstrates that producers there can also make very good wine—wines that rival those from France but come in more varieties and at lower prices.

Comparative Advantage A country has a **comparative advantage** in goods that it can produce more efficiently or better than other goods. If businesses in a given country can make computers more efficiently than they can make automobiles, then that nation has a comparative advantage in computer manufacturing. The United States has comparative advantages in the computer industry (because of technological sophistication) and in farming (because of fertile land and a temperate climate). South Korea has a comparative advantage in electronics manufacturing because of efficient operations and cheap labor. As a result, U.S. firms export computers and grain to South Korea and import VCRs and stereos from South Korea. South Korea, of course, can produce food, and the United States can build VCRs, but each nation imports certain products because the other holds a comparative advantage in the relevant industry.[10]

comparative advantage
The ability to produce some products more efficiently or better than other products

National Competitive Advantage In recent years, a theory of national competitive advantage has become a widely accepted model of why nations engage in international trade.[11] **National competitive advantage** derives from four conditions:

national competitive advantage
International competitive advantage stemming from a combination of factor conditions; demand conditions; related and supporting industries; and firm strategies, structures, and rivalries

1. *Factor conditions* are the factors of production that we identified in Chapter 1.
2. *Demand conditions* reflect a large domestic consumer base that promotes strong demand for innovative products.
3. *Related and supporting industries* include strong local or regional suppliers and/or industrial customers.
4. *Strategies, structures, and rivalries* refer to firms and industries that stress cost reduction, product quality, higher productivity, and innovative products.

Figure 4.5 shows why these four attributes are referred to as a national diamond: The interaction of the four elements determines the environment in which a nation's firms compete.

When all attributes exist, a nation is likely to do international business. Japan, for instance, has an abundance of natural resources and strong domestic demand for automobiles. Its carmakers have well-oiled supplier networks, and domestic firms have competed intensely with each other for decades. These circumstances explain why Japanese car companies like Toyota <www.toyota.com>, Honda <www.hondacorporate.com>, Nissan <www.nissandriven.com>, and Mazda <www.mazda.com> are successful in foreign markets.

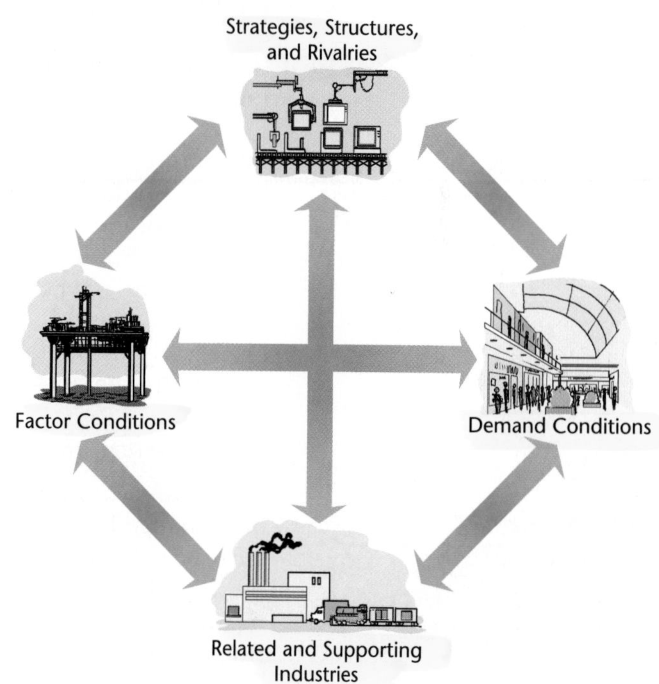

FIGURE 4.5
Attributes of National Competitive Advantage

Import-Export Balances

Although international trade has many advantages, it can pose problems if a country's imports and exports don't strike an acceptable balance. In deciding whether an overall balance exists, economists use two measures: *balance of trade* and *balance of payments.*

Balance of Trade A nation's **balance of trade** is the total economic value of all products that it imports minus the total value of everything it exports. Relatively small trade imbalances are common and are unimportant. Large imbalances, however, are another matter. In 2000, for example, the United States had a negative balance in *merchandise* trade of $466.8 billion and a positive balance in *service* trade of $76.5 billion. The result was an overall negative balance of $390.3 billion—large enough to be a concern for U.S. business and political leaders.[12]

balance of trade
Economic value of all products a country imports minus the economic value of all products it exports

trade deficit
Situation in which a country's imports exceed its exports, creating a negative balance of trade

trade surplus
Situation in which a country's exports exceed its imports, creating a positive balance of trade

Trade Deficits and Surpluses When a country's imports exceed its exports—that is, when it has a negative balance of trade—it suffers a **trade deficit.** In short, more money is flowing out than flowing in. A positive balance occurs when exports exceed imports, and then the nation enjoys a **trade surplus:** More money is flowing in than flowing out. Trade deficits and surpluses are influenced by several factors, such as absolute, comparative, or national competitive advantages, general economic conditions, and the effect of trade agreements. For example, higher domestic costs, greater international competition, and continuing economic problems among some of its regional trading partners have slowed the tremendous growth in exports that Japan once enjoyed. But rising prosperity in China and India has led to strong increases in both exports from and imports to those countries.

In general, the United States suffers from large deficits with Japan ($81.6 billion), China ($83.8 billion), Germany ($29.1 billion), Canada ($51.9 billion), Mexico ($24.6 billion), and Taiwan ($16.1 billion). In any given year, the United States may also have smaller deficits with other countries. Our present deficit with Singapore is only $1.4 billion.

On the other hand, we enjoy healthy surpluses with many countries. The most current figures report a $10.6 billion surplus with the Netherlands, $7.5 billion with Australia, $4 billion with Belgium-Luxembourg, and $2.8 billion with Egypt. More modest surpluses with Jordan and Haiti are about $250 million each.[13]

balance of payments
Flow of all money into or out of a country

Balance of Payments The **balance of payments** refers to the flow of money into or out of a country. The money that a nation pays for imports and receives for exports—its balance of trade—comprises much of its balance of payments. Other financial exchanges are also factors. Money spent by tourists, money spent on foreign-aid programs, and money exchanged by buying and selling currency on international money markets all affect the balance of payments.[14]

For many years, the United States enjoyed a positive balance of payments (more inflows than outflows). Recently, the balance has been negative, but the trend is gradually reversing itself, and many economists soon expect a positive balance. Some U.S. industries have positive balances, and others have negative balances. Such firms as Dow Chemical <www.dow.com> and Monsanto <www.pharmacia.com> are among world leaders in chemical exports. The cigarette, truck, and industrial-equipment industries also have positive balances. Conversely, the metalworking-machinery, airplane-parts, and auto industries suffer negative balances because we import more than we export.

Exchange Rates

exchange rate
Rate at which the currency of one nation can be exchanged for the currency of another country

The balance of imports and exports between two countries is affected by the rate of exchange between their currencies. An **exchange rate** is the rate at which the currency of one nation can be exchanged for that of another.[15] The exchange rate between U.S. dollars and British pounds is about 1.5 dollars to 1 pound. This means that it costs 1 pound to "buy" 1.5 dollars or 1 dollar to "buy" .67 pounds. It also means that 1 pound and 1.5 dollars have the same purchasing power.

At the end of World War II, the major nations agreed to set *fixed exchange rates.* The value of any country's currency relative to that of another would remain constant. Today, however, *floating exchange rates* are the norm, and the value of one country's currency relative to that of another varies with market conditions. For example, when many British citizens want to spend pounds to buy U.S. dollars (or goods), the value of the dollar relative to the pound increases. *Demand* for the dollar is high, and a currency is *strong* when demand for it is high. It's also strong when there's high demand for the goods manufactured at the expense of that currency. Thus, the value of the dollar rises with the demand for U.S. goods. On a daily basis, exchange rates fluctuate very little. Significant variations usually occur over greater time spans.

Exchange rate fluctuation can have an important impact on balance of trade. Suppose you want to buy some English tea for 10 pounds per box. At an exchange rate of 1.5 dollars to the pound, a box will cost you \$15 (10 pounds × 1.5 = 15). But what if the pound is weaker? At an exchange rate of, say, 1.25 dollars to the pound, the same box would cost you only \$12.50 (10 pounds × 1.25 = 12.50).

If the dollar is strong in relation to the pound, the prices of all American-made products will rise in England and the prices of all English-made products will fall in the United States. The English would buy fewer American-made products, and Americans would be prompted to spend more on English-made products. The result will probably be a U.S. trade deficit with England.

One of the most significant developments in foreign exchange has been the introduction of the **euro**—a common currency among most of the members of the European Union (Denmark, Sweden, and the United Kingdom do not to participate). The euro was officially introduced in 2002 and will, for a while, circulate along with currencies of the participating nations. But those currencies will be phased out, and they are to be replaced by the euro as the only accepted currency. The EU anticipates that the euro will become as important as the dollar and the yen in international commerce. Though of course subject to fluctuation, the euro is currently equal to about one dollar.

euro
A common currency shared among most of the members of the European Union (excluding Denmark, Sweden, and the United Kingdom)

Exchange Rates and Competition Companies with international operations must watch exchange-rate fluctuations closely because changes affect overseas demand for their products and can be a major factor in competition. In general, when the value of a country's currency rises—becomes stronger—companies based there find it harder to export products to foreign markets and easier for foreign companies to enter local markets. It also makes it more cost-efficient for domestic companies to move operations to lower-cost foreign sites. When the value of a currency declines—becomes weaker—the opposite occurs. As the value of a country's currency falls, its balance of trade should improve because domestic companies should experience a boost in exports. There should also be less reason for foreign companies to ship products into the domestic market.

A good case in point is the recent decline of the Canadian dollar relative to the U.S. dollar. In the mid-1990s, because the Canadian dollar was relatively strong compared to the U.S. dollar, Canadian consumers shopped for bargains in the United States. But a global currency crisis in 1997 had longer-lasting effects in Canada than in the United States, weakening the Canadian relative to the U.S. dollar. It's now cheaper for U.S. consumers to do what their Canadian counterparts used to do—drive across the border to shop. Table 4.2 illustrates the effects of this trend. The same hamburger costing \$2.39 in Niagara Falls, New York, sells for \$2.18 (in U.S. currency) just across the border in Ontario, Canada. A café latte in Seattle costs \$2.70 but only \$2.29 (again, in U.S. currency) in Vancouver.[16]

Common Product	Niagara Falls, New York	Niagara Falls, Ontario
Saturday stay at Days Inn, with jacuzzi	\$260	\$165
Whopper with cheese at Burger King	\$2.39	\$2.18
	Seattle	**Vancouver, British Columbia**
Lauryn Hill CD	\$17.99	\$12.60
Nintendo 64 game system	\$130	\$119
Grande latte at Starbucks	\$2.70	\$2.29
Levi's 501 jeans at the Original Levi's Store	\$50	\$45

TABLE 4.2
Canadian vs. U.S. Prices

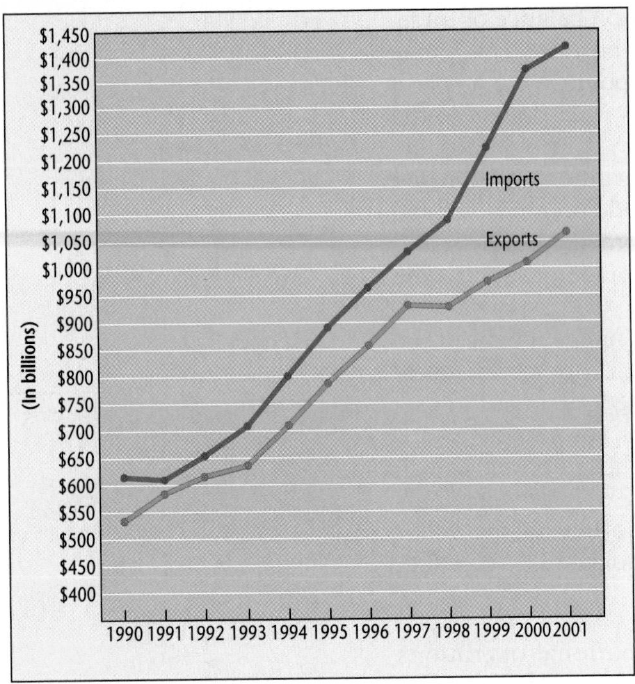

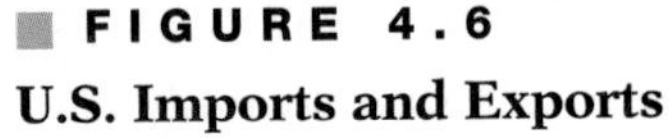

FIGURE 4.6
U.S. Imports and Exports

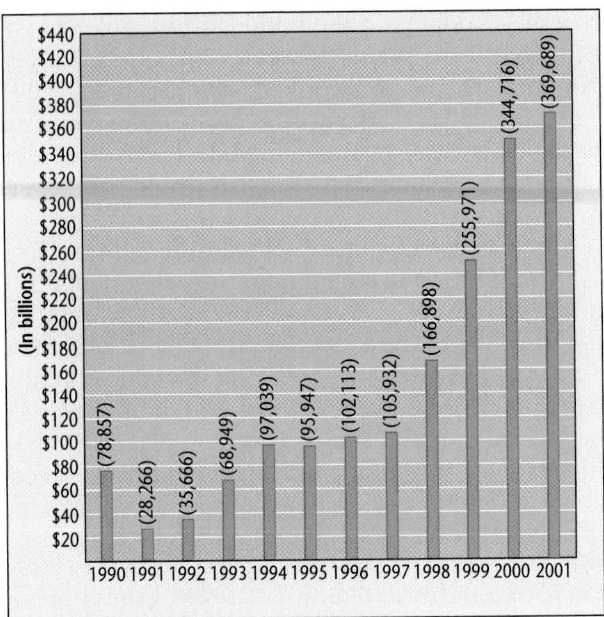

FIGURE 4.7
U.S. Trade Deficit

The U.S. Economy and Foreign Trade Figures 4.6 and 4.7 highlight two series of events: (1) recent trends in U.S. exports and imports and (2) the resulting trade deficit. As Figure 4.6 shows, both imports into the United States and U.S. exports to other countries have increased steadily for 10 years—a trend that's projected to continue.

In 2001, the United States exported $1,068 billion in goods and services. In the same year, the United States imported $1,438 billion in goods and services. Because imports exceeded exports, the United States had a trade deficit of $369 billion (the difference between imports and exports). Trade deficits between 1991 and 2001 are shown in Figure 4.7: There was a *deficit* in each of these years because more money flowed out to pay for foreign imports than flowed in to pay for U.S. exports. Had exports exceeded imports, we would have had a *surplus*.

International Business Management

Wherever a firm is located, its success depends largely on how well it's managed. International business is so challenging because basic management tasks—planning, organizing, directing, and controlling—are much more difficult when a firm operates in markets scattered around the globe.

Managing means making decisions. In this section, we examine the three basic decisions that a company must make when considering globalization. The first decision is whether to go international at all. Once that decision has been made, managers must decide on level of international involvement and on the organizational structure that will best meet the firm's global needs.

Going International

As the world economy becomes globalized, more firms are conducting international operations. Wal-Mart <www.walmart.com>, for example, was once the quintessential U.S. growth company. But as managers saw both fewer expansion

Mid-Chapter Internet Field Trip

"The Best-Known Brand Name in the World"

In this chapter so far, we've looked at the major world marketplaces and seen just a sampling of the ways in which the needs and wants of customers can differ from region to region. How does a truly global company deal with the complexities of a global market? One good example is the Atlanta-based Cola-Cola Co., whose Web site, at <www.coca-cola.com>, offers an interesting glimpse into the consumer markets of nearly 200 different countries.

You'll probably notice that the home page is designed to serve several purposes and cover a wide range of topics, including:

- Consumer Information
- Online Shopping for Coca-Cola Merchandise
- Product Promotions
- Information about Employment Opportunities
- Public Relations Information
- Company Information

Start at the top of the home page by clicking on **Country Sites:**

1. Scan the list of countries. Are there any that surprise you? Now click in turn on the sites for Denmark, Peru, and Turkey. What do they all have in common?

Now return to the home page and click on **Our Company:**

2. When was Cola-Cola founded, how many different beverages did it produce?

On the left-hand side of the screen, click on **Our Brands.** Using the link in the bottom-left corner, examine the complete list of Coca-Cola's beverage brands:

3. How does this list demonstrate a possible competitive advantage for Coca-Cola?

Return to **Our Brands** and click on the **Brand Sampler** arrow at the right. Select **Cappy:**

4. What is this drink like, and where is it popular?

Now try clicking on **Tian Yu Di:**

5. What can you find out about this beverage?

To continue your Internet Field Trip, click on www.prenhall.com/griffin

opportunities inside the United States and stronger competition from domestic competitors, they decided that foreign expansion was the key to future growth.

By aggressively opening new stores and buying existing retail chains in other countries, Wal-Mart more than quintupled foreign sales, to $32 billion, between 1995 and 2001. Because this total still represents only 17 percent of total revenues, Wal-Mart has made international sales growth its primary goal for the future. Today, the firm has stores in the United Kingdom, Mexico, Canada, Germany, Brazil, Argentina, China, and South Korea, and it has ambitious plans for continued international expansion.[17] When asked to explain why his firm set up shop in Germany, one Wal-Mart executive simply noted that "Germany, being the third-largest economy in the world, is very important to us and one obviously that we can't ignore."

"Germany, being the third-largest economy in the world, is obviously one that we can't ignore."

~Ron Tiarks,
WAL-MART EXECUTIVE IN GERMANY

This route, however, isn't appropriate for every company. If you buy and sell fresh fish, you'll find it more profitable to confine your activities to limited geographic areas because storage and transport costs may be too high to make international operations worthwhile. As Figure 4.8 shows, several factors affect the decision to go international. One key factor is the business climate in other nations. Even experienced firms have met cultural, legal, and economic roadblocks (problems that we discuss in more detail later in this chapter).[18]

Gauging International Demand In considering international expansion, a company should also consider at least two other questions:

1. Is there a demand for my products abroad?
2. If so, must I adapt those products for international consumption?

*You should now be able to answer Self-Check Questions 1–3**

1. MULTIPLE CHOICE In general, which of the following has the **least** impact on U.S. business? [select one] **(a)** General Agreement on Tariffs and Trade; **(b)** World Trade Organization; **(c)** Association of South American Agricultural Producers; **(d)** North American Free Trade Association; **(e)** European Union.

2. MULTIPLE CHOICE The United States has a *comparative advantage* in which of the following? [select one] **(a)** consumer electronics products; **(b)** coffee growing; **(c)** athletic shoe production; **(d)** movies and other filmed entertainment; **(e)** fine watches.

3. TRUE/FALSE The World Bank divides countries into five categories based on *per capita income levels*—high income, moderately high income, middle income, moderately low income, and low income.

*ANSWERS TO SELF-CHECK QUESTIONS 1–3 CAN BE FOUND ON P. AN-3.

Products that are successful in one country may be useless in another. Snowmobiles are popular for transportation and recreation in Canada and actually revolutionized reindeer herding in Lapland, but there's no demand for them in Central America. Although this is an extreme example, the point is basic: Foreign demand for a company's product may be greater than, the same as, or weaker than

"Grab some lederhosen, Sutfin. We're about to climb aboard the globalization bandwagon."

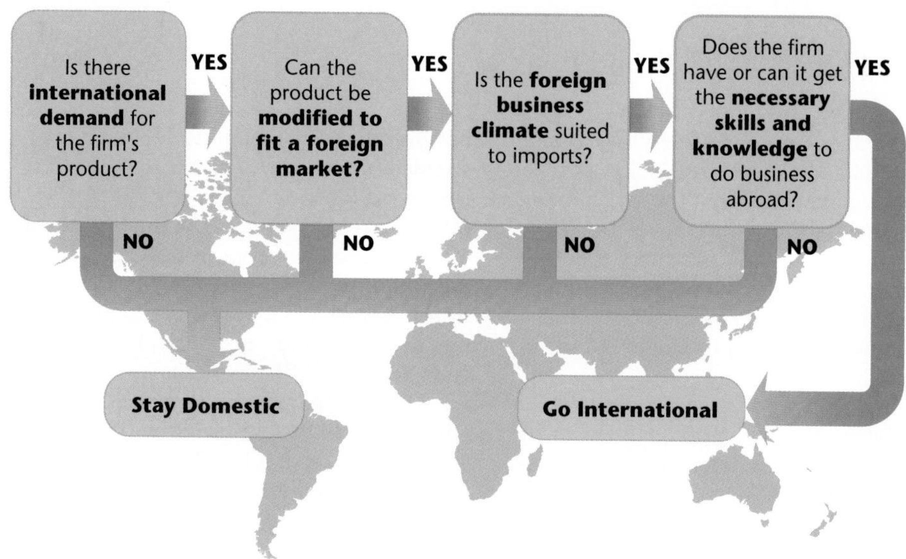

FIGURE 4.8
Going International

domestic demand. Market research and/or the prior market entry of competitors may indicate whether there's an international demand for a firm's products.

One large category of U.S. products that travels well is American popular culture. Many U.S. movies, for example, earn as much or more abroad than they do in domestic release. In its first nine months, *Harry Potter and the Sorcerer's Stone* earned \$317 million in the United States while racking up another \$648 million overseas.[19] Billions of dollars are also involved in popular music, TV shows, books, and even street fashions. Super Mario Brothers is advertised on billboards in Bangkok, Thailand, and Bart Simpson piñatas are sold at Mexico City bazaars. Teenagers in Rome and Beirut sport American baseball caps, and vintage Levi's from the 1950s and 1960s sell for \$3,000 in Finland and Australia.

Adapting to Customer Needs If there is demand for its product, a firm must decide whether and how to adapt it to meet the special demands of foreign customers. To satisfy local tastes, McDonald's sells wine in France, beer in Germany, and meatless sandwiches in India. Fords must have steering wheels mounted on the right if they're to be sold in England and Japan. When Toyota launches upscale cars at home, it keeps the Toyota nameplate. The same cars, however, sell under the Lexus nameplate <www.lexus.com> in the United States because the firm has concluded that Americans won't pay a premium price for a Toyota.

Levels of Involvement

After deciding to go international, a firm must determine the level of its involvement. Several levels are possible: A firm may act as an *exporter* or *importer,* organize as an *international firm,* or (like most of the world's largest industrial firms) operate as a *multinational firm.*

Exporters and Importers An **exporter** makes products in one country to distribute and sell in others. An **importer** buys products in foreign markets and imports them for resale at home. Both conduct most of their business in their home nations. Both kinds of doing business entail the lowest level of involvement in international operations, and both are good ways to learn the fine points of global business. Many large firms entered international business as exporters. IBM <www.ibm/planetwide/europe> and Coke <www.thecocacolacompany.com/world>, among others, exported to Europe for several years before producing there.

exporter
Firm that distributes and sells products to one or more foreign countries

importer
Firm that buys products in foreign markets and then imports them for resale in its home country

Rolling in the Worldwide Dough

Is any business more confined to a local market than a bakery? Breads and pastries get stale quickly, and even the largest operations, such as those that makes buns for McDonald's, only move products over short distances. But a baker in Paris has refused to accept geographic limitations and is now selling his famous bread in global markets.

When Lionel Poilane took over the family business <www.poilane.fr> about 30 years ago, he was determined to return breadmaking to its roots. As a result of studying the craft of breadmaking, Polaine built clay ovens based on sixteenth-century plans and technology. Then he trained his breadmakers in ancient techniques and soon began selling old-style dark bread known for a thick, chewy, fire-tinged flavor. It quickly became a favorite in Parisian bistros, and demand soared.

To help meet demand, Poilane built two more bakeries in Paris, and today he sells 15,000 loaves of bread a day—about 2.5 percent of all the bread sold in Paris. Polaine has opened a bakery in London, but his efforts to expand to Japan were stymied because local ordinances prohibited wood-burning ovens, and Polaine refused to compromise. During this negotiation process, however, he realized that he didn't really *want* to build new bakeries all over the world. "I'm not eager to have a business card that says 'Paris, London, New York' on it," he explains.

Instead, he turned to modern technology to expand his old-fashioned business. The key was the big FedEx hub at Roissy-Charles-de-Gaulle Airport near Polaine's largest Paris bakery. After launching a Web site with minimal marketing support, Polaine started taking international orders. New orders are packaged as the bread cools and then picked up by FedEx. At about four pounds, the basic loaf travels well, and a quick warm-up in the customer's oven gives it the same taste as it had when it came out of Polaine's. Today, a loaf of bread baked in Paris in the morning can easily be reheated for tomorrow night's dinner in more than 20 countries.

"I'm not eager to have a business card that says 'Paris, London, New York' on it."

~French baker Lionel Polaine
ON WHY HE USED THE INTERNET TO GLOBALIZE

Exporting and importing have steadily increased over the last several decades. U.S. exports totaled $344 billion in 1980 and $708 billion in 1990, and they exceeded $1.3 trillion in 2000. Imports into the United States have risen from $335 billion in 1980 to $1 trillion in 1990 and $1.4 trillion in 2000.[20] Although big business was responsible for much of this growth, many smaller firms are successful exporters.[21] San Antonio's Pace Foods <www.pacefoods.com>, a maker of Tex-Mex products, began exporting to Mexico after discovering that Mexican consumers enjoyed its picante sauce as much as U.S. consumers. The "Wired World" box in this chapter shows how the Internet and other advances in technology have made it easier for small firms to compete in global markets.

international firm
Firm that conducts a significant portion of its business in foreign countries

International Firms As exporters and importers gain experience and grow, many move to the next level of involvement. **International firms** conduct a good deal of their business abroad and may even maintain overseas manufacturing facilities. Wal-Mart, for instance, is an international firm: Although most of its stores are in the United States, the company is rapidly expanding into foreign markets.

An international firm may be large, but it's still basically a domestic company with international operations. Its main concern is its domestic market (Wal-Mart gets 83 percent of its revenues from U.S. sales), and product and manufacturing decisions typically reflect this concern. Burlington Industries <www.burlington.com>, Toys "Я" Us <www.toysrus.com>, and BMW <www.bmw.com> are also international firms.

Multinational Firms Most **multinational firms,** such as ExxonMobil, Nestlé, IBM, and Ford, don't think of themselves as having domestic and international divisions. Headquarters locations are almost irrelevant, and planning and decision making are geared to international markets.

multinational firm
Firm that designs, produces, and markets products in many nations

We can't underestimate the economic import of multinationals. Consider just the impact of the 500 largest multinationals. In 2001, these 500 firms generated $14 trillion in revenues and $306 billion in owner profits. They employed almost 48 million people, bought materials and equipment from literally thousands of other firms, and paid billions in taxes. Moreover, their products affected the lives of hundreds of millions of consumers, competitors, investors, and even protestors.[22]

International Organizational Structures

Different levels of international involvement entail different kinds of organizational structure. A structure that would help coordinate an exporter's activities would be inadequate for those of a multinational. In this section, we consider the spectrum of organizational strategies, including *independent agents, licensing arrangements, branch offices, strategic alliances,* and *foreign direct investment.*

Independent Agents An **independent agent** is a foreign individual or organization that represents an exporter in foreign markets. Independent agents often act as sales representatives: They sell the exporter's products, collect payment, and make sure that customers are satisfied. They often represent several firms at once and usually don't specialize in a particular product or market. Levi Strauss <www.levi.com> uses agents to market products in many small countries in Africa, Asia, and South America.

independent agent
Foreign individual or organization that agrees to represent an exporter's interests

Licensing Arrangements Companies seeking more substantial involvement may opt for **licensing arrangements.** Firms give foreign individuals or companies exclusive rights to manufacture or market their products in that market. In return, the exporter receives a fee plus ongoing payments called *royalties* that are calculated as a percentage of the license holder's sales.[23]

licensing arrangement
Arrangement in which firms choose foreign individuals or organizations to manufacture or market their products in another country

Franchising is an increasingly popular form of licensing. McDonald's <www.mcdonalds.com/corporate/franchise/outside> and Pizza Hut <www.pizzahut.com> franchise around the world. Accor SA <www.accor.com/sf>, a French hotel chain, franchises Ibis, Sofitel, and Novotel hotels in the United States.

Branch Offices Instead of developing relationships with foreign agents or companies, a firm may send its own managers to overseas **branch offices,** where it has more direct control than it does over agents or license holders. Branch offices also furnish a more visible public presence in foreign countries, and foreign customers tend to feel more secure when there's a local branch office.

branch office
Foreign office set up by an international or multinational firm

Strategic Alliances In a **strategic alliance,** a company finds a partner in the country in which it wants to do business. Each party agrees to invest resources and capital into a new business or else to cooperate in some mutually beneficial way. This new business—the alliance—is owned by the partners, who divide its profits. Such alliances are sometimes called *joint ventures,* but the term *strategic alliance* has arisen because such partnerships are playing increasingly important roles in the strategies of major companies.[24]

strategic alliance (or **joint venture**)
Arrangement in which a company finds a foreign partner to contribute approximately half of the resources needed to establish and operate a new business in the partner's country

The number of strategic alliances among major companies has increased significantly over the last decade and is likely to grow even more. The new Disney theme park near Hong Kong is a joint venture with local partners, and in many countries, such as Mexico, India, and China, laws make alliances virtually the only way to do international business. Mexico, for example, requires that all foreign firms investing there have local partners.

In addition to easing the way into new markets, alliances give firms greater control over foreign activities than agents and licensees. (Even so, all partners retain some say in an alliance's decisions.) Perhaps most important, alliances allow firms to benefit from the knowledge and expertise of foreign partners. Microsoft, for example, relies heavily on alliances as it expands into international markets. This approach has helped the firm learn the intricacies of doing business in China and India, two of the hardest emerging markets to crack.

foreign direct investment (FDI)
Arrangement in which a firm buys or establishes tangible assets in another country

Foreign Direct Investment **Foreign direct investment (FDI)** involves buying or establishing tangible assets in another country.[25] Dell Computer, for example, has built assembly plants in Europe and China. Disney is building a theme park in Hong Kong, and Volkswagen is building a factory in Brazil. Each of these activities represents FDI by a firm in another country. Ford's purchase of Land Rover from the German firm BMW is an instance of FDI, as the acquisition of both Ben & Jerry's and Slim-Fast by the Dutch company Unilever.[26] FDI in the United States by foreign firms in 1999 totaled $294 billion. U.S. firms invested $980 billion in other countries.[27] "There can be no doubt," says the director-general of the World Trade Organization, "that foreign direct investment has joined international trade as a primary motor of globalization."[28]

Say what you mean
PLAYING BY THE RULES OF ENGAGEMENT

Venturing into the wide world of global business requires not only knowledge about local people and cultures, but sensitivity to their ways of doing things. The sights and sounds of another country will, of course, be new, and more importantly, so will the rules of engagement—what policies govern business activities, how your competition operates, and so forth. When it comes to doing global business, there's a good deal that's going to be beyond your control, but cultivating a little cultural understanding and personal flexibility will take you a long way toward business success.

Despite the effects of globalization, local conditions have a big impact on the way business is conducted around the world. Even the largest multinationals adapt their ways of doing things to the cultural conditions that prevail in host countries. It's a basic fact of business life that local culture is far too important, and far too powerful, to be ignored. If you're going to be a member of the global business community, you're going to need good adaptation skills, and the more readily you accept the need to adapt, the more likely you'll be to thrive in a multicultural world.

We've all been raised with a certain set of cultural values that tell us how to interact with other people—how to work, to think, to negotiate, to learn, to relax. That's how we know the "right" way to act in most situations. In order to adapt to cultural differences, we have to make a conscious effort to remember that our values are not necessarily the ones that should govern our behavior in someone else's culture.

Here are a few key things to bear in mind if you're thinking about doing business on a multicultural scale:

- Despite the impact of globalization, local culture is extremely important when it comes to the way business is conducted in different places.
- We're all raised with a set of cultural values which determine the way we view the world and which we may have to adapt to do business with people who have different values.
- The international businessperson must understand cultural differences and see them not as a challenge but as an opportunity to improve interactions of all kinds, not just business transactions.

Self-Check Questions 4–6

*You should now be able to answer Self-Check Questions 4–6**

4. MULTIPLE CHOICE Which of the following is **not** an immediate consideration when considering the decision to "go international"? [select one] **(a)** international demand; **(b)** exchange rates; **(c)** foreign business climate; **(d)** ease of product modification; **(e)** availability of knowledge and expertise.

5. MULTIPLE CHOICE The most complex form of *international organizational structure* involves which of the following? [select one] **(a)** foreign direct investment; **(b)** independent agents; **(c)** licensing arrangements; **(d)** branch offices; **(e)** an international division.

6. TRUE/FALSE As relatively low levels of *international involvement,* importing and exporting are excellent entry strategies for firms just launching international activities.

*ANSWERS TO SELF-CHECK QUESTIONS 4–6 CAN BE FOUND ON P. AN-3.

Barriers to International Trade

Whether a business is truly multinational or sells to only a few foreign markets, several factors will affect its international operations. Success in foreign markets will largely depend on the ways it responds to *social, economic, legal,* and *political barriers* to international trade.

Social and Cultural Differences

Any firm planning to conduct business abroad must understand the social and cultural differences between host country and home country. Some differences are obvious. You must, for example, consider language factors when adjusting packaging, signs, and logos. Pepsi <www.pepsico.com> is the same product in Seattle and Moscow—except for the lettering on the bottle. Less universal products, however, face several conditions that force them to make adjustments. When Bob's Big Boy <www.bobs.net> launched new restaurants in Thailand, it had to add deep-fried shrimp to the menu. Kentucky Fried Chicken <www.kfc.com> has altered menus, ingredients, and hours of operation to suit Thai culture.

A wide range of subtle value differences can also affect operations. For example, many Europeans shop daily. To U.S. consumers accustomed to weekly supermarket trips, the European pattern may seem like a waste of time. For many Europeans, however, shopping is not just a matter of buying food; it's an outlet for meeting friends and exchanging political views. Consider the implications of this difference for U.S. firms selling food and food-related products in Europe. First, large American supermarkets are not the norm in many parts of Europe. Second, people who shop daily don't need large refrigerators and freezers.

Economic Differences

While cultural differences are often subtle, economic differences can be fairly pronounced. In dealing with mixed economies like those of France and Sweden, firms must know when—and to what extent—the government is involved in a given

On the first Muslim holy day after American warplanes went into Afghanistan, this crowd in Karachi, Pakistan, set fire to a (locally owned) KFC outlet. The immediate problem was a political one: Pakistanis objected to their government's support of the U.S. assault on the Muslim government of neighboring Afghanistan. A deeper problem, however, reflects social and cultural conflict: Muslim societies resent the invasion of foreign influences that often rip holes in the fabric of traditional social life. The red, white, and blue logo of KFC <www.kfc.com>*, which runs 6,000 restaurants abroad, is a conspicuous symbol of those influences.*

industry. The French government, for instance, is heavily involved in all aspects of airplane design and manufacturing. The impact of economic differences can be even greater in planned economies like those of China and Vietnam.[29]

Legal and Political Differences

Governments can affect international business in many ways. They can set conditions for doing business within their borders and even prohibit doing business altogether. They can control the flow of capital and use tax legislation to discourage or encourage activity in a given industry. They can even confiscate the property of foreign-owned companies. In this section, we discuss some of the more common legal and political issues in international business: *quotas, tariffs,* and *subsidies; local content laws;* and *business practice laws.*

Quotas, Tariffs, and Subsidies Even free market economies have some quotas and/or tariffs, both of which affect prices and quantities of foreign-made products. A **quota** restricts the number of products of a certain type that can be imported and, by reducing supply, raises the prices of those imports. That's why Belgian ice-cream makers can't ship any more than 922,315 kilograms to the United States each year. Canada can ship no more than 14.7 billion board feet of softwood timber per year. Quotas are often determined by treaties. Better terms are often given to friendly trading partners, and quotas are typically adjusted to protect domestic producers.

quota
Restriction on the number of products of a certain type that can be imported into a country

The ultimate quota is an **embargo:** a government order forbidding exportation and/or importation of a particular product—or even all products—from a specific country. Many nations control bacteria and disease by banning certain agricultural products. Because the United States has embargoes against Cuba, Iraq, Libya, and Iran, American firms can't invest in these countries, and their products can't legally be sold on American markets.

embargo
Government order banning the exportation and/or importation of a particular product or all products from a particular country

tariff
Tax levied on imported products

Tariffs are taxes on imported products. They raise the prices of imports by making consumers pay not only for the products but also for tariff fees. Tariffs

At a rally in Washington, D.C., steelworkers urge the government to protect the U.S. steel industry from low-priced imports. Three months later, the Bush Administration announced tariffs of 8 percent to 30 percent on certain foreign steel products. In the last few years, 25 old-line U.S. steel companies have filed for bankruptcy, and in two decades, employment in the industry has fallen from 450,000 to 150,000. But even in the United States, so-called mini-mills, which run high-tech, low-cost operations, oppose the protectionist measure as corporate welfare for inefficient competitors.

take two forms. *Revenue tariffs* are imposed to raise money for governments, but most tariffs, called *protectionist tariffs,* are meant to discourage particular imports. Did you know that firms which import ironing-board covers into the United States pay a 7-percent tariff on the price of the product? Firms that import women's athletic shoes pay a flat rate of 90 cents per pair plus 20 percent of the product price. Such figures are determined through a complicated process designed to put foreign and domestic firms on competitive footing.

A **subsidy** is a government payment to help a domestic business compete with foreign firms. They're actually indirect tariffs that lower the prices of domestic goods rather than raise the prices of foreign goods. Many European governments subsidize farmers to help them compete against U.S. grain imports.

subsidy
Government payment to help a domestic business compete with foreign firms

Quotas and tariffs are imposed for numerous reasons. The U.S. government aids domestic automakers by restricting the number of Japanese cars imported into this country. Because of national security concerns, we limit the export of technology (for example, computer and nuclear technology to China). The United States, of course, isn't the only country that uses tariffs and quotas. To protect domestic firms, Italy imposes high tariffs on electronic goods. As a result, a Sony Walkman costs $150 there, and CD players are prohibitively expensive.

The Protectionism Debate In the United States, **protectionism**—the practice of protecting domestic business at the expense of free market competition—is controversial. Supporters argue that tariffs and quotas protect domestic firms and jobs as well as shelter new industries until they're able to compete internationally. They contend that we need such measures to counter steps taken by other nations. Other advocates justify protectionism in the name of national security. A nation, they argue, must be able to produce efficiently the goods needed for survival in case of war. Thus, the U.S. government requires the Air Force to buy planes only from U.S. manufacturers.

protectionism
Practice of protecting domestic business against foreign competition

Critics cite protectionism as a source of friction between nations. They also charge that it drives up prices by reducing competition. They maintain that although jobs in some industries would be lost as a result of free trade, jobs in other industries (for example, electronics and automobiles) would be created if all nations abandoned protectionist tactics.

Protectionism sometimes takes on almost comic proportions. Neither Europe nor the United States grows bananas, but both European and U.S. firms buy and sell bananas in foreign markets. Problems arose when the EU put a quota on bananas imported from Latin America—a market dominated by two U.S. firms, Chiquita <www.chiquita.com> and Dole <www.dole.com>—in order to help firms based in current and former European colonies in the Caribbean. To retaliate, the United States imposed a 100-percent tariff on certain luxury products imported from Europe, including Louis Vuitton handbags <www.vuitton.com>, Scottish cashmere sweaters, and Parma ham.[30]

local content law

Law requiring that products sold in a particular country be at least partly made there

Local Content Laws Many countries, including the United States, have **local content laws**—requirements that products sold in a country be at least partly made there. Firms seeking to do business in a country must either invest there directly or take on a domestic partner. In this way, some of the profits from doing business in a foreign country stay there rather than flowing out to another nation. In some cases, the partnership arrangement is optional but wise. In Mexico, for instance, Radio Shack de Mexico is a joint venture owned by Tandy Corp. <www.radioshackunlimited.com> (49 percent) and Mexico's Grupo Gigante <www.gigante.com.mx> (51 percent). Both China and India currently require that when a foreign firm enters into a joint venture with a local firm, the local partner must have controlling ownership stake.

business practice law

Law or regulation governing business practices in given countries

Business Practice Laws Many businesses entering new markets encounter problems in complying with stringent regulations and bureaucratic obstacles. Such practices are affected by the **business practice laws** by which host countries govern business practices within their jurisdictions. As part of its entry strategy in Germany, Wal-Mart has had to buy existing retailers rather than open brand-new stores. Why? Because the German government is not currently issuing new licenses to sell food products. Wal-Mart also had to stop refunding price differences on items sold for less by other stores because the practice is illegal in Germany. Finally, Wal-Mart must comply with business-hour restrictions: Stores can't open before 7 A.M., must close by 8 P.M. on weeknights and 4 P.M. on Saturday, and must remain closed on Sunday.

cartel

Association of producers whose purpose is to control supply and prices

dumping

Practice of selling a product abroad for less than the cost of production

Cartels and Dumping Sometimes, a legal—even an accepted—practice in one country is illegal in another. In some South American countries, for example, it is sometimes legal to bribe business and government officials. The existence of **cartels**—associations of producers that control supply and prices—gives tremendous power to some nations, such as those belonging to the Organization of Petroleum Exporting Countries (OPEC). United States law forbids both bribery and cartels.

Finally, many (but not all) countries forbid **dumping**—selling a product abroad for less than the cost of production at home.[31] U.S. antidumping legislation sets two conditions for determining whether dumping is being practiced:

1. Products are being priced at "less than fair value."
2. The result unfairly harms domestic industry.

In 1999, the United States charged Japan and Brazil with dumping steel at prices 70 percent below normal value. In order to protect local manufacturers, the government imposed a significant tariff on steel imported from those countries.

Self-Check Questions 7–9

*You should now be able to answer Self-Check Questions 7–9**

7. MULTIPLE CHOICE Which of the following does **not** serve as a *barrier to international trade?* [select one] **(a)** social differences; **(b)** cultural differences; **(c)** economic differences; **(d)** political differences; **(e)** transportation differences.

8. MULTIPLE CHOICE Which of the following is **not** a *legal barrier to international trade?* [select one] **(a)** quotas and tariffs; **(b)** exchange rate parameters; **(c)** local content laws; **(d)** business practice laws; **(e)** subsidies.

9. TRUE/FALSE *Protectionism* refers to the practice of hiring local mobsters to protect a foreign company from local competitors.

*ANSWERS TO SELF-CHECK QUESTIONS 7–9 CAN BE FOUND ON P. AN-3.

Continued from page 97

National Identity Crisis in Toyota City

Toyota has enjoyed increasing success in the United States. But one question facing the Japanese carmaker is how to take the fullest advantage of this situation. In fact, the growing importance of U.S. operations has created some tension between corporate and subsidiary operations. Some top managers at home, for example, don't want Toyota to lose too much of its Japanese heritage. They also remain commited to the practices responsible for the firm's long-term success—consensus-style decision making, merciless cost cutting, and fanatical devotion to quality and customer satisfaction.

To help ensure that these qualities and practices aren't sacrificed, the company recently opened a new training center in Toyota City. Called the Toyota Institute, the center offers management-development courses patterned after M.B.A. courses but largely taught by senior company executives. Of course, compromises are necessary even here. When academic instructors are needed, they'll come from the University of Pennsylvania's Wharton School of Business.

As it moves forward on the international front, Toyota is flexible when it comes to accomodating national identity to global aspirations. One positive result of this stance is a willingness to learn from its foreign subsidiaries. Officials in Japan, for example, long resisted making a full-size pickup truck with a V8 engine because they saw such a vehicle as useful only for commercial purposes. So when U.S. executives invited their Japanese counterparts to a Dallas Cowboys football game in Texas, they had an ulterior motive. As they walked through the parking lot before the game, the visitors were overwhelmed by row upon row of full-size pickups with chrome logos touting horse power and towing capacity. Shortly thereafter, Japanese headquarters okayed the new Tundra pickup truck that has become a top seller almost overnight.

Toyota has been doing well in the United States, but it still faces a few problems down the road. Perhaps the biggest potential concern is the aging of its customer base. The average age of an American Toyota buyer is 45, highest among any Japanese carmaker. To help counter this threat to future market share, the company has begun introducing new models specifically targeted at younger buyers. It also plans to launch an entirely new brand in this country called Scion. Although the new line is aimed at younger buyers, Toyota's marketing strategy is patterned on the strategy by which it has successfully marketed its Lexus luxury line—distancing the new line from the parent brand and sidestepping consumer preconceptions.

Questions for Discussion

1. What are Toyota's primary advantages and disadvantages in its current competitive environment?
2. What are Toyota's biggest challenges in trying to maintain harmony between Japanese and U.S. operations?
3. How important is it for a company to maintain a national identity?
4. What are your own personal impressions of Toyota products?

Summary of Learning Objectives

1. ***Discuss the rise of international business and describe the* major world marketplaces.**

The world economy is becoming a complex interdependent system—a process called **globalization.** Everyday, we use many **imports**—products made or grown abroad and sold in the United States—and the success of many U.S. firms depends on **exports**—products made or grown here and shipped for sale abroad.

International trade is becoming increasingly important to most nations of the world, and as more industries and markets become global, firms that compete in them also become global. Several forces combined to spark and sustain globalization: (1) Governments and businesses are more aware of the benefits of globalization; (2) new technologies make international travel, communication, and commerce faster and cheaper; (3) competitive pressures sometimes force firms to expand into foreign markets just to keep up with competitors.

(4) Treaties and trade agreements also play a major role. The four most important agreements are as follows: (i) The purpose of the **General Agreement on Tariffs and Trade (GATT)** is to reduce or eliminate trade barriers by encouraging nations to protect domestic industries within agreed-upon limits and to engage in multilateral negotiations. (ii) The **North American Free Trade Agreement (NAFTA)** removes trade barriers among the United States, Canada, and Mexico and includes agreements on environmental and labor abuses. NAFTA has achieved its basic purpose—creating a more active North American market. Although NAFTA created fewer jobs than proponents hoped, direct foreign investment and importing and exporting increased. (iii) The **European Union (EU)** includes the principal Western European nations, which have eliminated most quotas and set uniform tariff levels. With virtually all internal trade barriers removed, the EU is the largest free marketplace in the world.

(iv) The **World Trade Organization (WTO),** which requires member countries to open markets to international trade, is empowered to pursue three goals: (a) Promote trade by encouraging members to adopt fair trade policies and practices; (b) reduce trade barriers by promoting multilateral negotiations; and (c) establish fair procedures for resolving disputes.

The World Bank uses *per capita income*—average income per person—as a measure to divide countries into one of three groups: (1) *High-income countries*—those with per capita income greater than $9,386; (2) *middle-income countries*—those with per capita income of less than $9,386 but more than $765; and (3) *low-income countries* (or *developing countries*)—those with per capita income of less than $765.

The contemporary world economy revolves around three major marketplaces. These three geographic regions are home to most of the world's largest economies, biggest multinational corporations, most influential financial markets, and highest-income consumers.

(1) *North America:* The United States is the largest marketplace and has the most stable economy in the world. Canada also plays a major role in the international economy, and the two countries are each other's largest trading partner. Mexico has become a major manufacturing center. (2) *Europe:* Europe is often regarded as two regions—Western and Eastern Europe. Western Europe, which is dominated by Germany, the United Kingdom, France, and Italy, has long been a mature but fragmented marketplace, but the advent of the European Union (EU) substantially increased its importance. Eastern Europe, once primarily communist, has also gained in importance, both as a marketplace and as a producer. (3) *Pacific Asia:* Pacific Asia consists of Japan, China, Thailand, Malaysia, Singapore, Indonesia, South Korea, Taiwan, the Philippines, and Australia. Fueled by strong entries in the automobile, electronics, and banking

industries, it is an important force in the world economy and a major source of competition for North American firms.

2. ***Explain how differences in* competitive advantage, import-export balances, exchange rates, *and* foreign competition *determine the ways in which countries and businesses respond to the international environment.***

Countries export what they can produce better or less expensively than other countries and use the proceeds to import what they can't produce as effectively. Decisions about *why* nations export and import *what* they do hinge partly on the advantages that country has regarding its abilities to create and/or sell various products and resources. Economists once focused on two forms of *advantage* to explain international trade: (1) An **absolute advantage** exists when a country can produce something cheaper and/or of higher quality than any other country. Examples of true absolute advantage are rare, and in reality, "absolute" advantages are always relative. (2) A country has a **comparative advantage** in goods that it can produce more efficiently or better than other goods. If businesses in a country can make computers more efficiently than they can make automobiles, then the nation's firms have a comparative advantage in computer manufacturing.

The new theory of **national competitive advantage** is a widely accepted model of why nations engage in international trade. Such advantage derives from four conditions: (1) *Factor conditions* are factors of production; (2) *demand conditions* reflect a large domestic consumer base that promotes strong demand for innovative products; (3) *related and supporting industries* include strong local or regional suppliers and/or industrial customers; (4) *strategies, structures, and rivalries* refer to firms and industries that stress cost reduction, product quality, higher productivity, and innovative new products. When all of these attributes exist, a nation will engage in international business.

International trading can pose problems if a country's imports and exports do not balance. A nation's **balance of trade** is the total economic value of all products that it imports minus the total economic value of all products that it exports. When a country's imports exceed its exports—when it has a *negative* balance of trade—it suffers a **trade deficit:** More money is flowing out than flowing in. A *positive* balance occurs when exports exceed imports; in that case, a nation has a **trade surplus** in which more money is flowing in than flowing out. Trade deficits and surpluses are influenced by such factors as the absolute, comparative, or national competitive advantages, general economic conditions prevailing in various countries, and the effect of trade agreements. The **balance of payments** refers to the flow of money into or out of a country. The money that a nation pays for imports and receives for exports—its balance of trade—comprises much of its balance of payments. The balance of imports and exports between two countries is affected by the rate of exchange between their currencies.

An **exchange rate** is the rate at which one nation's currency can be exchanged for that of another. If the exchange rate between British pounds and U.S. dollars is 1.5 to 1, it costs 1 dollar to "buy" 1.5 pounds and 1.5 pounds to "buy" one dollar. This also means that 1 dollar and 1.5 pounds have the same purchasing power. A significant development in foreign exchange is the introduction of the **euro**—a common currency among most members of the European Union.

Under today's *floating exchange rates,* the value of one currency relative to that of another varies with market conditions. A currency is *strong* when demand for it is high or there is high demand for the goods manufactured at the expense of that currency. Companies with international operations must monitor exchange-rate fluctuations because such changes affect overseas demand for their products and can be a major factor in international competition. When the value of a country's currency rises—becomes stronger—companies based there find it harder to export products, and it is easier for foreign companies to enter local markets. When the value of its currency declines—becomes weaker—a nation's balance of trade should improve because domestic companies should experience a boost in exports. Foreign companies would also be less apt to ship products into the domestic market.

3. ***Discuss the factors involved in deciding to do business internationally and in selecting the appropriate* levels of international involvement *and* international organizational structure.**

Several factors enter into the decision to go international. One overriding factor is the business climate in other nations. Even experienced firms have encountered cultural, legal, and economic roadblocks. A company should also consider at least two other issues: (1) Is there a demand for my products abroad? (2) If so, must I adapt those products for international consumption? Foreign demand for a product may be greater than, the same as, or weaker than domestic demand. Market research and/or the prior entry of competitors may indicate whether there is international demand for a product. If there is, the firm must decide whether and how to adapt the product to meet the needs of foreign customers.

After deciding to go international, a firm must decide on its level of involvement. Several levels are possible: (1) *Exporters and importers*: An **exporter** makes products in one country for sale in others. An **importer** buys products in foreign markets and imports them for resale at home. Both conduct most of their business in their home nations, and both ways of doing business are good ways to learn global business. (2) *International firms*: An **international firm** maintains facilities and conducts much of its business abroad. But it is basically a domestic firm with international operations and is most concerned with its domestic market. (3) *Multinational firms*: In most **multinational firms,** planning and decision making are geared to international markets, and headquarters locations are almost irrelevant.

Different levels of involvement require different kinds of organizational structure. The spectrum of international organizational strategies includes the following: (1) **Independent agents** are foreign parties that represent an exporter's interests in foreign markets. They sell the exporter's products, collect payment, and make sure that customers are satisfied. (2) Under **licensing arrangements,** firms give foreign individuals or companies exclusive rights to make or market their products in a given market. The exporter receives a fee plus ongoing payments called *royalties. Franchising* is a form of licensing.

(3) A firm may send its own managers to overseas **branch offices** because it has more direct control over branch managers than over agents or license holders. Branch offices also give a company a more visible public presence in foreign countries. (4) In a **strategic alliance (or joint venture),** a company finds a partner in the country in which it wants to conduct business. Each party invests resources and capital into a new business or agrees to cooperate in some mutually beneficial way. The partners own the new business—the alliance—and divide its profits. In addition to easing the way into new markets, alliances give firms greater control over their foreign activities than agents and licensees. (5) **Foreign direct investment (FDI)** means buying or establishing tangible assets in another country.

4. ***Describe some of the ways in which* social, cultural, economic, legal, *and* political differences *among nations affect international business.***

(1) *Social and cultural differences*: Some differences, like language, are obvious, but a wide range of subtle value differences can also affect operations. For example, because many Europeans shop daily, large American supermarkets are not the norm in Europe. In addition, people who shop daily don't need large refrigerators and freezers.

(2) *Economic differences*: Economic differences can be fairly pronounced. In dealing with mixed economies, firms must be aware of when—and to what extent—the government is involved in a given industry. The impact of economic differences can be even greater in planned economies.

(3) *Legal and political differences*: Governments can set conditions for doing business and even prohibit it altogether. They can control the flow of capital and use taxes to influence activity in a given industry. They can even confiscate foreign-owned property. Common legal and political issues in international business include the following: A **quota** restricts the number of products that can be imported and, by reducing supply, raises the prices of imports. The ultimate quota is an **embargo,** a government order forbidding exportation and/or importation of a particular product—or even all products—from a particular country. **Tariffs,** which are taxes on imported products, directly affect prices by raising the price of imports, forcing consumers to pay not only for products but also for tariff fees. Tariffs take two forms: (i) *Revenue tariffs* are imposed to raise money for governments. (ii) The much more common *protectionist tariffs* discourage the import of particular products. A **subsidy** is a government payment to help a domestic business compete with foreign firms. It lowers prices of domestic goods rather than raises prices of foreign goods.

In the United States, supporters of **protectionism**—the practice of protecting domestic business at the expense of free market competition—argue that tariffs and quotas protect domestic firms and jobs and shelter new industries until they can compete internationally. Others contend that the United States needs such measures to counter those imposed by other nations, and some advocates justify protectionism in the name of national security. Critics reply that protectionism causes friction between nations and drives up prices by reducing competition. They maintain that although free trade would cost jobs in some industries, jobs in other industries would be created if all nations abandoned protectionist tactics.

Many countries have **local content laws**—requirements that products sold in a particular country be at least partly made there. Firms seeking to do business in a country must either invest there directly or take on a domestic partner. **Business practice laws** pose problems because they force firms to comply with regulations and bureaucratic obstacles.

Sometimes, a legal—even an accepted—business practice in one country is illegal in another. The formation of **cartels**—associations of producers that control supply and prices—gives tremendous power to some nations, such as those belonging to OPEC. United States law forbids both bribery and cartels, and many (but not all) countries forbid **dumping**—selling a product abroad for less than the cost of production.

KEY TERMS

globalization (p. 96)
import (p. 96)
export (p. 96)
General Agreement on Tariffs and Trade (GATT) (p. 97)
North American Free Trade Agreement (NAFTA) (p. 97)
European Union (EU) (p. 98)
World Trade Organization (WTO) (p. 98)
absolute advantage (p. 102)
comparative advantage (p. 103)
national competitive advantage (p. 103)
balance of trade (p. 103)
trade deficit (p. 104)
trade surplus (p. 104)
balance of payments (p. 104)
exchange rate (p. 104)
euro (p. 105)
exporter (p. 109)
importer (p. 109)
international firm (p. 110)
multinational firm (p. 111)
independent agent (p. 111)
licensing arrangement (p. 111)
branch office (p. 111)
strategic alliances (p. 111)
foreign direct investment (FDI) (p. 112)
quota (p. 115)
embargo (p. 115)
tariff (p. 115)
subsidy (p. 115)
protectionism (p. 115)
local content law (p. 116)
business practice law (p. 116)
cartel (p. 116)
dumping (p. 116)

QUESTIONS AND EXERCISES

Questions for Review

1. How does the balance of trade differ from the balance of payments?
2. What are the three possible levels of involvement in international business? Give examples of each.
3. How does a country's economic system affect the decisions of foreign firms interested in doing business there?
4. What aspects of the culture in your state or region would be of particular interest to a foreign firm thinking about locating there?

Questions for Analysis

5. List all the major items in your bedroom, including furnishings. Try to identify the country in which each item was made. Offer possible reasons why a given nation might have a comparative advantage in producing a given good.
6. Suppose that you're the manager of a small firm seeking to enter the international arena. What basic information would you need about the market that you're thinking of entering?
7. Do you support protectionist tariffs for the United States? If so, in what instances and for what reasons? If not, why not?
8. Do you think that a firm operating internationally is better advised to adopt a single standard of ethical conduct or to adapt to local conditions? Under what kinds of conditions might each approach be preferable?

Application Exercises

9. Interview the manager of a local firm that does at least some business internationally. Why did the company decide to go international? Describe the level of the firm's international involvement and the organizational structure(s) it uses for international operations.
10. Select a product familiar to you. Using library reference works to gain some insight into the culture of India, identify the problems that might arise in trying to market this product to Indian consumers.

Building Your Business Skills

PUTTING YOURSELF IN YOUR PLACE

This exercise enhances the following SCANS workplace competencies: demonstrating basic skills, demonstrating thinking skills, exhibiting interpersonal skills, and working with information.

Goal

To encourage students to apply global business strategies to a small-business situation.

Background

Some people might say that Yolanda Lang is a bit too confident. Others might say that she needs confidence—and more—to succeed in the business she's chosen. But one thing is certain: Lang is determined to grow INDE, her handbag design company, into a global enterprise. At only 28 years of age, she has time on her side—if she makes the right business moves now.

These days, Lang spends most of her time in Milan, Italy. Backed by $50,000 of her parents' personal savings, she is trying to compete with Gucci, Fendi, and other high-end handbag makers. Her target market is American women willing to spend $200 on a purse. Ironically, Lang was forced to set up shop in Italy because of the snobbishness of these customers, who buy high-end bags only if they're European-made. "Strangely enough," she muses, "I need to be in Europe to sell in America."

To succeed, she must first find ways to keep production costs down—a tough task for a woman in a male-dominated business culture. Her fluent Italian is an advantage, but she's often forced to turn down inappropriate dinner invitations. She also has to figure out how to get her 22-bag collection into stores worldwide. Retailers are showing her bags in Italy and Japan, but she's had little luck in the United States. "I intend to be a global company," says Lang. The question is how to succeed first as a small business.

Method

Step 1

Join together with three or four other students to discuss the steps that Lang has taken so far to break into the U.S. retail market. These steps include:

- Buying a mailing list of 5,000 shoppers from high-end department store Neiman Marcus and selling directly to these customers.
- Linking with a manufacturer's representative to sell her line in major U.S. cities while she herself concentrates on Europe.

Step 2

Based on what you learned in this chapter, suggest other strategies that might help Lang grow her business. Working with group members, consider whether the following options would help or hurt Lang's business. Explain why a strategy is likely to work or likely to fail.

- Lang could relocate to the United States and sell abroad through an independent agent.
- Lang could relocate to the United States and set up a branch office in Italy.
- Lang could find a partner in Italy and form a strategic alliance that would allow her to build her business on both continents.

Step 3

Working alone, create a written marketing plan for INDE. What steps would you recommend that Lang take to reach her goal of becoming a global company? Compare your written response with those of other group members.

Follow-Up Questions

1. What are the most promising steps that Lang can take to grow her business? What are the least promising?
2. Lang thinks that her trouble breaking into the U.S. retail market stems from the fact that her company is unknown. How would this circumstance affect the strategies suggested in Steps 1 and 2?
3. When Lang deals with Italian manufacturers, she is a young, attractive woman in a man's world. Often, she must convince men that her purpose is business and nothing else. How should Lang handle personal invitations that get in the way of business? How can she say no while still maintaining business relationships? Why is it often difficult for American women to do business in male-dominated cultures?
4. The American consulate has given Lang little business help because her products are made in Italy. Do you think the consulate's treatment of an American businessperson is fair or unfair? Explain your answer.
5. Do you think Lang's relocation to Italy will pay off? Why or why not?
6. With Lang's goals of creating a global company, can INDE continue to be a one-person operation?

Exercising Your Ethics

PAYING HEED TO FOREIGN PRACTICES

The Purpose of the Assignment

Managers conducting business in other countries must often contend with differences in legal systems, customs, mores, and business practices. This exercise will help you better understand how such differences can affect the success of managers and companies trying to conduct business in foreign markets.

The Situation

Assume that you're an up-and-coming manager in a regional U.S. distribution company. Firms in your industry are just beginning to enter foreign markets, and you've been assigned to head up your company's new operations in a Latin American country. Because at least two of your competitors are also trying to enter this same market, your boss wants you to move as quickly as possible. You also sense that your success in this assignment will likely determine your future with the company.

You have just completed meetings with local government officials, and you're pessimistic about your ability to get things moving quickly. You've learned, for example, that it will take 10 months to get a building permit for a needed facility. Moreover, once the building's up, it will take another six months to get utilities. Finally, the phone company says that it may take up to two years to install the phone-lines that you need for high-speed Internet access.

The Dilemma

Various officials have indicated that time frames could be considerably shortened if you were willing to pay special "expediting" fees. You realize, of course, that these "fees" are bribes, and you're well aware that the practice of paying such "fees" is both unethical and illegal in the United States. In this foreign country, however, it's not illegal and not even considered unethical. Moreover, if you don't pay and one of your competitors does, you'll be at a major competitive disadvantage. In any case, your boss isn't likely to understand the long lead times necessary to get the operation running. Fortunately, you have access to a source of funds that you could spend without the knowledge of anyone in the home office.

Questions for Discussion

1. What are the key ethical issues in this situation?
2. What do you think most managers would do in this situation?
3. What would you do?

Mastering Business Essentials

EPISODE 9 stresses the importance of developing a marketing strategy that identifies and makes the best use of a company's competitive advantage. A firm must not only develop one or more capabilities that are superior to those of competitors, but it must also turn its advantage into an effective marketing strategy and growth plan. *This episode illustrates and enhances the concept of national competitive advantage.*

EPISODE 10 reminds us that there are international variations in the consumer buying process. *This episode shows how personal, psychological, social, and cultural influences on consumer behavior differ across borders.*

Crafting Your Business Plan

CONSIDERING THE WORLD

The Purpose of the Assignment

1. To familiarize students with issues faced by a firm that has decided to go global.
2. To determine where, in the framework of the *BPP* business plan, global issues might appropriately be presented.

Assignment

After reading Chapter 4 in the textbook, open the BPP *software and examine the information dealing with the types of global business considerations that would be of concern to the sample firm of Acme Consulting.*

Now respond to the following items:

1. What products does Acme plan to offer and in which international markets will they be competing? [Sites to see in *BPP* (for this assignment): In the Plan Outline screen, click on **1.0 Executive Summary;** then click on **1.2 Mission** and then **4.0 Market Analysis Summary** and **4.1 Market Segmentation.** Next, while still in the Plan Outline screen, click on **2.0 Company Summary.** Finally, in the Plan Outline screen, click on **5.2 Strategic Alliances.**]
2. In Acme's business plan, see if you can find any discussion of the international organizational structures used by Acme's competitors. Do you think this information is adequate or inadequate? [Sites to see in *BPP* for this item: In the Plan Outline screen, click on **4.3.2 Distribution Service** and **4.3.4 Main Competitors.**]
3. What is the planned organization structure for Acme's international activities? Would you categorize Acme's relationship to its Paris partner as that of a branch office or that of a strategic alliance? [Sites to see in *BPP* for this item: In the Plan Outline screen, click on **6.1 Organization Structure** and then on **6.2 Management Team.**]
4. Chapter 4 states that going international requires "necessary skills and knowledge." Does Acme's business plan indicate that the company possesses the skills and knowledge to succeed internationally? [Sites to see in *BPP* for this item: In the Plan Outline screen, click on **6.0 Management Summary** and then on **6.2 Management Team.** Next, in the Plan Outline screen, click on **3.1 Service Description,** and then click on **3.2 Competitive Comparison.**]

Video Exercise

GLOBALIZING THE LONG ARM OF THE LAW

Learning Objectives

The purpose of this video is to help you

1. Understand how and why a company adapts to the needs of foreign customers.
2. Identify the levels of international involvement that are available to companies.
3. Discuss some of the legal and ethical obstacles to a company's international operations.

Synopsis

Scotland Yard and the Canadian Mounties are only two of the many worldwide organizations that use security technology from Printrak <www.printrakinternational.com>. Originally a computerized fingerprint-management system, Printrak, a Motorola company, has added a number of security and criminal-information products as it's expanded from its California headquarters to serve international customers. In addition to studying each country's legal, political, economic, and cultural characteristics, general manager Darren Reilly and his management team analyze local demand and customer needs. Rather than invest in local plants and equipment, Printrak works through local sales agents to ensure that its products are presented in a culturally savvy way in each market. Despite country-by-country differences in business customs and ethics, the decisions and actions of Printrak employees are guided by parent company Motorola's code of conduct.

Discussion Questions

1. *For analysis:* What are some of the barriers that affect Printrak's ability to do business in foreign markets?
2. *For analysis:* From Printrak's perspective, what are the advantages and disadvantages of hiring and training local sales agents in each foreign market?
3. *For application:* In addition to establishing users committees, what else should Printrak do to track changing customer needs?
4. *For application:* How would you suggest that Printrak build on its relations with "beachhead customers" to expand in particular regions?
5. *For debate:* Printrak employees and managers must comply with Motorola's global ethics policy. Should local sales agents be allowed to take any action they deem necessary to make local sales, regardless of Motorola policy? Support your chosen position.

Online Exploration

Browse Printrak's home page <www.printrakinternational.com>, find out where the company has customers, and read some of the news releases about international operations. Also look at the resource links that Printrak has posted for customers and site visitors. Why would Printrak publicize its customer list in this way? Why would it post a glossary of security-related terms and acronyms? Finally, do you think the company should translate some or all of its Web site to accommodate foreign customers? Explain your response.

CHAPTER

Conducting Business Ethically and Responsibly

After reading this chapter, you should be able to:

1. Explain how individuals develop their personal *codes of ethics* and why ethics are important in the workplace.
2. Distinguish *social responsibility* from *ethics*, identify *organizational stakeholders,* and characterize social consciousness today.
3. Show how the concept of social responsibility applies both to environmental issues and to a firm's relationships with customers, employees, and investors.
4. Identify four general *approaches to social responsibility* and describe the four steps that a firm must take to implement a *social responsibility program.*
5. Explain how issues of social responsibility and ethics affect small business.

The Rules of Tipping

Until recently, ImClone <www.imclone.com> was a darling of biotech. But alleged improprieties have caused the firm to crash and burn, and its CEO has been indicted on criminal charges. The scandal has even rubbed off on popular lifestyle maven Martha Stewart. Much of the problem, as it turns out, all hinges on who said what, when, and to whom.

Dr. Samuel Waksal spent much of his career as a respected immunologist. But in 1984, he decided to leave the research field and launch a biotech business called ImClone. Its mission was to explore new treatment options for serious illnesses such as cancer. Shortly after launching the company, Waksal hired his brother Harlan, also a physician, to help run it. For the next several years, they struggled to keep the enterprise afloat, dividing their time between seeking investment money and trying to develop drugs that would make them rich.

It seemed that they'd found just the ticket in the early 1990s, when a professional acquaintance, research scientist John Mendelsohn, indicated that he'd made a discovery that might eventually be a major breakthrough in the fight against cancer. Based on Mendelsohn's preliminary tests, Erbitux, as the new drug was called, seemed to show significant potential for treating certain forms of cancer. With additional funding, Mendelsohn was confident that he could get federal approval to market the drug. The Warkals convinced Mendelsohn to license Erbitux to ImClone.

For the next few years, as the drug was being further developed and refined, Samuel Waksal devoted much of his time to building enthusiasm for Erbitux. After all, a medical breakthrough on the cancer front would have incredible market value. Waksal's marketing efforts paid off. Investors seemed to be lining up at his door, and ImClone became the talk of New York. Mick Jagger came to Waksal's Christmas party, and the Doobie Brothers entertained at the ImClone party at a major cancer-research meeting. Waksal himself partied with Martha Stewart and dated her daughter.

As Erbitux drew closer to becoming a reality, enthusiasm continued to mount. The American Society of Clinical Oncologists predicted that Erbitux would be for the twenty-first century what polio and smallpox vaccines were for the twentieth. Waksal, meanwhile, began dropping hints that the testing process at the Food and Drug Administration (FDA) was going well and that he anticipated full approval just as soon as FDA evaluations were complete.

In the fall of 2001, Bristol-Myers Squibb <www.bms.com> announced plans to invest $2 billion in ImClone. In return, the giant drugmaker would get a 20-percent stake in ImClone and a share of the U.S. rights to Erbitux. Fueled in part by the Bristol-Myers investment and in part by Waksal's promotional campaign, ImClone stock, already performing impressively, took off, reaching a high of $75.45 a share in early December 2001. But then a giant shoe dropped.

In early December 2001, rumors began to circulate among key Bristol-Myers and ImClone officials that the Erbitux approval was in trouble. Allegedly, Samuel and Harlan Waksal launched furious lobbying efforts with personal contacts at the FDA in order to get the decision delayed or deferred. On December 6, Harlan sold $50 million of his ImClone stock. On December 26, Samuel learned that the FDA had made up its mind: It had denied the Erbitux application and refused to approve commercial production.

That night and early the next morning, Waksal reportedly relayed this information to certain family members and close friends. On December 27, family

"In placing my trade I had no improper information. My transaction was entirely lawful."

~Martha Stewart

ON CHARGES OF INSIDER TRADING OF IMCLONE STOCK

members sold more than $9 million in ImClone stock. Waksal tried to unload $5 million in ImClone stock but was refused by his broker, who had already put a hold on all ImClone transactions. On the same day, good friend Martha Stewart sold 3,928 shares of ImClone. Responding to suggestions that she had acted on the basis of inside information, Stewart stated, "In placing my trade I had no improper information. My transaction was entirely lawful. After directing my broker to sell, I called Dr. Waksal's office to inquire about ImClone. I did not reach Dr. Waksal and he did not return my call."

The official FDA announcement came on December 28. On December 31, the first day of trading after the announcement, the volume of ImClone trading increased 179 percent as its value dropped 15 percent. Throughout the spring of 2002, ImClone stock continued to plummet, and by June 2002, it stood at a measly $7.83 a share. The ImClone board persuaded Samuel Waksal to resign because the Securities and Exchange Commission (SEC) investigation into his actions was hurting the firm's performance.

On June 12, 2002, the FBI arrested Samuel Waksal, charging him with insider trading and obstruction of justice. Although no other formal charges were filed, investigators continued to look into Harlan Waksal's stock sale of December 6 and Stewart's sale of December 27. Things remained quiet for several weeks, but so far, only one shoe had dropped.

Our opening story continues on page 152

Ethics in the Workplace

ethics
Beliefs about what is right and wrong or good and bad in actions that affect others

ethical behavior
Behavior conforming to generally accepted social norms concerning beneficial and harmful actions

unethical behavior
Behavior that does not conform to generally accepted social norms concerning beneficial and harmful actions

business ethics
Ethical or unethical behaviors by a manager or employer of an organization

Just what is ethical behavior? **Ethics** are beliefs about what's right and wrong or good and bad. An individual's values and morals, plus the social context in which his or her behavior occurs, determine whether behavior is regarded as ethical or unethical. In other words, **ethical behavior** conforms to individual beliefs and social norms about what's right and good. **Unethical behavior** is behavior that individual beliefs and social norms that are defined as wrong and bad. **Business ethics** is a term often used to refer to ethical or unethical behaviors by employees of commercial organizations.

Individual Ethics

The Problem of Ambiguity Because ethics are based on both individual beliefs and social concepts, they vary from person to person, from situation to situation, and from culture to culture. Social standards are broad enough to support differences in beliefs. Without violating general standards, therefore, people may develop personal codes of ethics reflecting a wide range of attitudes and beliefs.

Thus ethical and unethical behavior is determined partly by the individual and partly by culture. For instance, virtually everyone would agree that if you see someone drop a $20 bill, it would be ethical to return it to the owner. But there'll be less agreement if you find $20 and don't know who dropped it. Should you turn it in to the lost-and-found department? Or, since the rightful owner isn't likely to claim it, can you just keep it?

Societies generally adopt formal laws that reflect prevailing ethical standards or social norms. For example, because most people regard theft as unethical, we have laws against such behavior and ways of punishing those who steal. We try to make unambiguous laws, but interpreting and applying them can still lead to ethical ambiguities. Real-world situations can often be interpreted in different ways, and it isn't always easy to apply statutory standards to real-life behavior. Samuel Waksal has been charged with insider trading for tipping off certain investors, such as Martha Stewart and members of his own family, about the impending fall of ImClone stock. But what about the behavior of Stewart? She says that she'd already ordered her broker to sell the stock if it slipped below $60. Whether she had or hadn't, she's widely suspected of questionable behavior, and the stock of her own company, Martha Stewart Living Omnimedia, has dropped 60 percent. Meanwhile, Waksal's daughter, who also sold her ImClone stock after getting information from her father, has so far been treated as an "innocent tippee"—someone who got inside information but didn't think that's what it was at the time.[1]

Unfortunately, the epidemic of recent scandals ranging from Enron and Arthur Andersen to Tyco and WorldCom only serves to show how willing people can be to take advantage of potentially ambiguous situations—indeed, to create them. In 1997, a U.S. company named Tyco <www.tyco.com> effectively sold itself in a merger with a firm called ADT Ltd. ADT was smaller than Tyco, but because its new parent company was based in the tax haven of Bermuda, Tyco no longer had to pay U.S. taxes on its non-U.S. income. In 2000 and 2001, Tyco's subsidiaries in such tax-friendly nations doubled from 75 to 150, and the company slashed its 2001 U.S. tax bill by $600 million. "Tyco," complained a U.S. congressman, "has raised tax avoidance to an art," but one tax expert replies that Tyco's schemes "are very consistent with the [U.S.] tax code."[2]

"Tyco has raised tax avoidance to an art."

~Congressman Richard E. Neal

Individual Values and Codes How should we deal with business behavior that we regard as unethical—especially when it's legally ambiguous? No doubt we have to start with the individuals in a business—its managers, employees, agents, and other legal representatives. Each of these people's personal code of ethics is determined by a combination of factors. We start to form ethical standards as children in response to our perceptions of the behavior of parents and other adults. Soon, we enter school, where we're influenced by peers, and as we grow into adulthood, experience shapes our lives and contributes to our ethical beliefs and our behavior. We also develop values and morals that contribute to ethical standards. If you put financial gain at the top of your priority list, you may develop a code of ethics that supports the pursuit of material comfort. If you set family and friends as a priority, you'll no doubt adopt different standards.

Business and Managerial Ethics

Managerial ethics are the standards of behavior that guide individual managers in their work.[3] Although your ethics can affect your work in any number of ways, it's helpful to classify them in terms of three broad categories.

managerial ethics
Standards of behavior that guide individual managers in their work

Behavior Toward Employees This category covers such matters as hiring and firing, wages and working conditions, and privacy and respect. Ethical and legal guidelines suggest that hiring and firing decisions should be based solely on ability to perform a job. A manager who discriminates against African Americans in hiring exhibits both unethical and illegal behavior. But what about the manager who hires a friend or relative when someone else might be more qualified? Such decisions may not be illegal; but they may be objectionable on ethical grounds.

Wages and working conditions, though regulated by law, are also areas for controversy. Consider a manager who pays a worker less than he deserves because the manager knows that the employee can't afford to quit or risk his job by complaining. While some people will see the behavior as unethical, others will see it as smart business. Cases such as these are hard enough to judge, but consider the behavior of Enron management toward company employees. It encouraged employees to invest retirement funds in company stock and then, when financial problems began to surface, refused to permit them to sell the stock (even though top officials were allowed to sell). Ultimately, the firm's demise cost thousands of jobs.

Behavior Toward the Organization Ethical issues also arise from employee behavior toward employers, especially in such areas as conflict of interest, confidentiality, and honesty. A *conflict of interest* occurs when an activity may benefit the individual to the detriment of his or her employer. Most companies have policies that forbid buyers from accepting gifts from suppliers. Businesses in highly

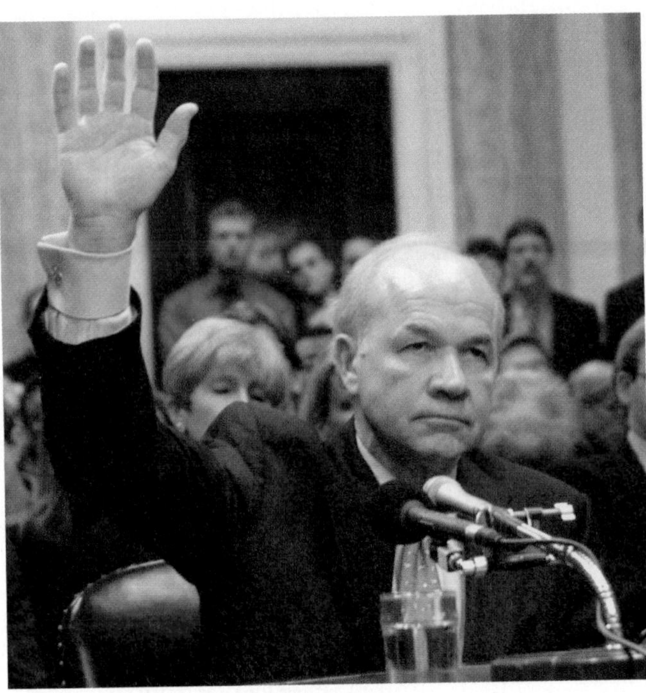

In Houston, former employees protest their treatment by Enron (left), which laid off or suspended 7,500 workers in December 2001. In October and November, Enron had barred employees from selling any company stock in their retirement accounts, and as the value of the stock plummeted, many lost 70–90 percent of their retirement assets. In February 2002, former Enron chairman Kenneth L. Lay (right) told Congress that he felt "a profound sadness about what has happened to . . . current and former employees [and] retirees." During the freeze of employee assets, Lay reportedly sold Enron stock worth $101.3 million.

competitive industries—software and fashion apparel, for example—have safeguards against designers selling company secrets to competitors. Relatively common problems in the general area of honesty include such behavior as stealing supplies, padding expense accounts, and using a business phone to make personal long-distance calls. Most employees are honest, but most organizations are nevertheless vigilant. Again, Enron is a good example of employees' unethical behavior toward an organization. Top managers not only misused corporate assets, but they often committed the company to risky ventures in order to further personal interests.

Behavior Toward Other Economic Agents Ethics also comes into play in the relationship between the firm and its employees with so-called *primary agents of interest*—mainly customers, competitors, stockholders, suppliers, dealers, and unions. In dealing with such agents, there is room for ethical ambiguity in just about every activity—advertising, financial disclosure, ordering and purchasing, bargaining and negotiation, and other business relationships.

For example, businesses in the pharmaceuticals industry are under criticism because of the rising prices of drugs. They argue that high prices cover the costs of research and development programs to develop new drugs. The solution to such problems seems obvious: find the right balance between reasonable pricing and *price gouging* (responding to increased demand with overly steep price increases). But like so many questions involving ethics, there are significant differences of opinion about the proper balance.[4]

Another recent area of concern is financial reporting, especially by high-tech firms like WorldCom. Some of these companies have been very aggressive in presenting their financial positions in a positive light, and in a few cases, they have overstated earnings projections in order to entice more investment.[5] Certainly,

Samuel Waksal's aggressive promotion of ImClone stock fits into this category. And again, there's Enron.

- Senior officials continued to mislead investors into thinking that the firm was solvent long after they knew that it was in serious trouble.
- The company violated numerous state regulations during the California energy crisis, causing thousands of consumers hardships and inconvenience.
- Many of its partnerships with other firms violated terms of full disclosure and honesty, resulting in losses for other firms and their employees.

Another problem is global variations in business practices. In many countries, bribes are a normal part of doing business. U.S. law, however, forbids bribes, even if rivals from other countries are paying them. A U.S. power-generating company recently lost a $320 million contract in the Middle East because it refused to pay bribes that a Japanese firm used to get the job.

Assessing Ethical Behavior

What distinguishes ethical from unethical behavior is often subjective and subject to differences of opinion.[6] So how can we decide whether a particular action or decision is ethical? Figure 5.1 presents a simplified three-step model for applying ethical judgments to situations that may arise during the course of business activities:

1. Gather the relevant factual information.
2. Analyze the facts to determine the most appropriate moral values.
3. Make an ethical judgment based on the rightness or wrongness of the proposed activity or policy.

Unfortunately, the process doesn't always work as smoothly as the scheme in Figure 5.1 suggests. What if the facts aren't clear-cut? What if there are no agreed-upon moral values? Nevertheless, a judgment and a decision must be made. Experts point out that, otherwise, trust is impossible. And trust is indispensable in any business transaction.

In order to assess more fully the ethics of specific behavior, we need a more complex perspective. Consider a common dilemma faced by managers with expense accounts. Companies routinely provide managers with accounts to cover work-related expenses—hotel bills, meals, rental cars, or taxis—when they're traveling on company business or entertaining clients for business purposes. They expect employees to claim only work-related expenses. For example, if a manager takes a client to dinner and spends $100, submitting a $100 reimbursement receipt for that dinner is accurate and appropriate. But suppose that our manager has a $100 dinner the next night with a good friend for purely social purposes. Submitting that receipt for reimbursement would be unethical, but some managers rationalize that it's okay to submit a receipt for dinner with a friend. Perhaps they'll tell themselves that they're underpaid and just "recovering" income due to them.

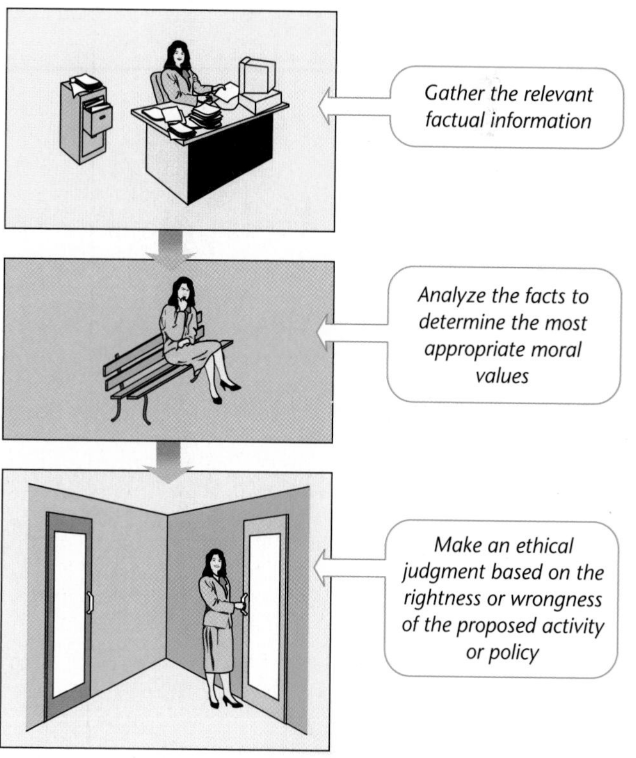
Gather the relevant factual information
Analyze the facts to determine the most appropriate moral values
Make an ethical judgment based on the rightness or wrongness of the proposed activity or policy

FIGURE 5.1
Steps in Making Ethical Judgments

Ethical *norms* also come into play in a case like this. Consider four such norms and the issues they entail:

- *Utility:* Does a particular act optimize the benefits to those who are affected by it?

- *Rights:* Does it respect the rights of the individuals involved?
- *Justice:* Is it consistent with what's fair?
- *Caring:* Is it consistent with people's responsibilities to each other?

Figure 5.2 is an expanded version of Figure 5.1 that incorporates the consideration of these ethical norms.

Now let's return to our case of the inflated expense account. While the utility norm acknowledges that the manager benefits from a padded account, others, such as coworkers and owners, don't. Most experts would also agree that the act doesn't respect the rights of others (such as investors, who have to foot the bill). Moreover, it's clearly unfair and compromises the manager's responsibilities to others. This particular act, then, appears to be clearly unethical.

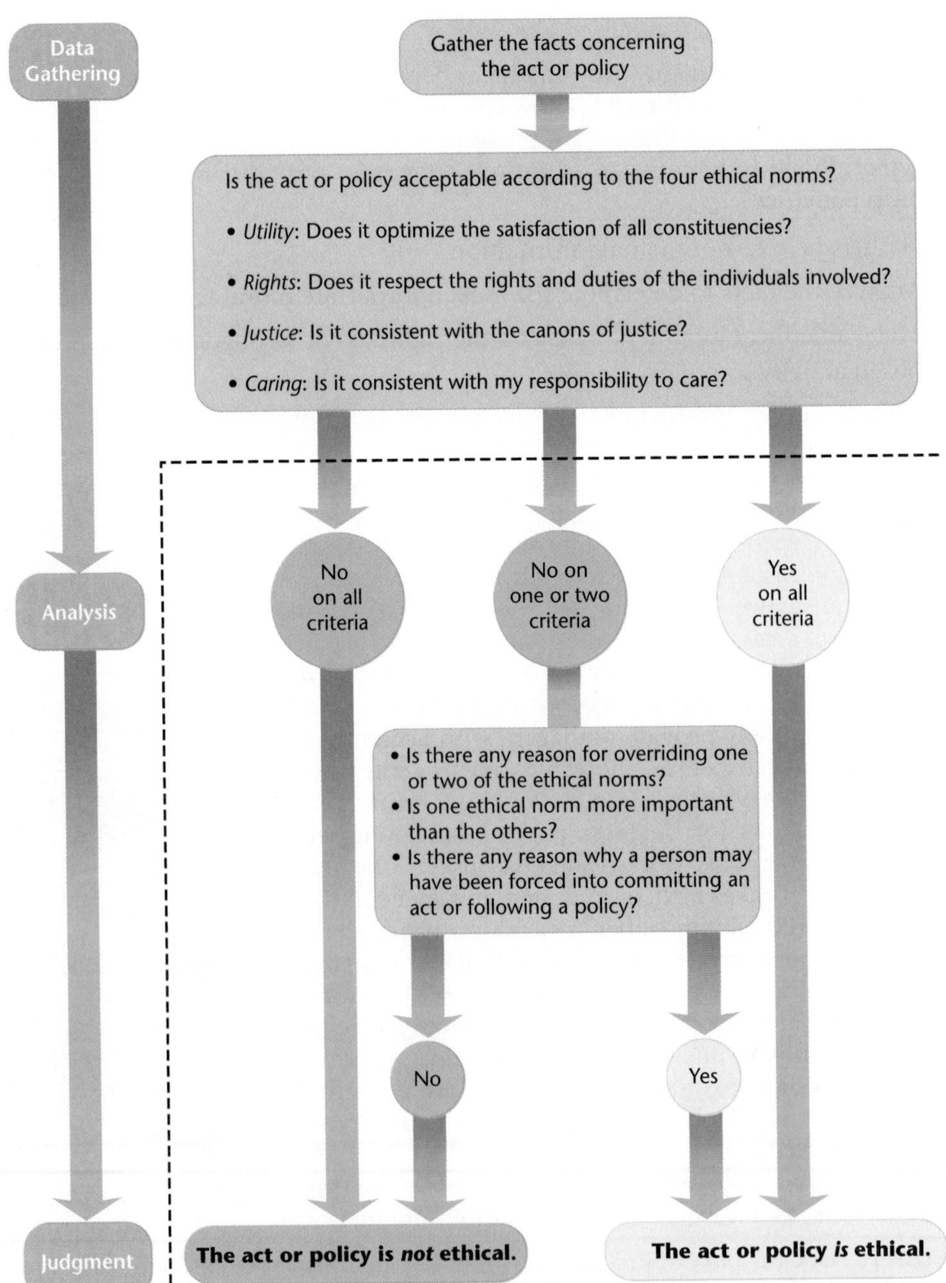

FIGURE 5.2

Expanded Model of Ethical Judgment Making

Figure 5.2, however, also provides mechanisms for dealing with unique circumstances—those that apply only in limited situations. Suppose, for example, that our manager loses the receipt for the legitimate dinner but retains the receipt for the social dinner. Some people will now argue that it's okay to submit the illegitimate receipt because the manager is only doing so to get proper reimbursement. Others, however, will reply that submitting the alternative receipt is wrong under any circumstances. We won't pretend to arbitrate the case, and we will simply make the following point: Changes in most situations can make ethical issues either more or less clear-cut.

Company Practices and Business Ethics

As unethical and even illegal activities by both managers and employees plague more and more companies, many firms have taken additional steps to encourage ethical behavior in the workplace. Many set up codes of conduct and develop clear ethical positions on how the firm and its employees will conduct business. An increasingly controversial area regarding business ethics and company practices involves the privacy of e-mail and other communications that take place inside an organization. The "Wired World" box in this chapter discusses these issues more fully.

Perhaps the single most effective step that a company can take is to demonstrate top management support of ethical standards. This policy contributes to a

"Don't spin anything. Don't try to hide anything."

~Agency.com CEO Kyle Shannon

ON THE IMPORTANCE OF KEEPING EMPLOYEES IN THE LOOP

Online Griping and Other Issues in High-Tech Ethics

Technological developments are creating all sorts of brand-new ethical problems—cloning, satellite reconnaissance, and bioengineered foods, to name just a few. For every innovation that promises convenience or safety, there seems to be a related ethical issue. The Internet and e-mail, for example, are certainly convenient and efficient, but they present businesspeople with a variety of ethics-related problems.

In one set of age-old concerns, electronic communications merely substitute for traditional forms of communication, such as mail or the telephone. By the same token, however, they make it possible to run all the classic swindles, such as Ponzi or pyramid schemes, with greater efficiency than ever before. Federal law enforcement personnel routinely surf the Web looking for illegal or unethical practices, often finding hundreds of questionable sites in a typical sting. Employers are also using e-mail to test employee loyalty, as in the case of the manager who sent false e-mails to his workers, pretending to be a recruiter from a competing firm. Any employees who responded were skipped for promotion.

Sophisticated software is another source of potential abuse. E-mail management software can be legally used to monitor employee e-mail. Critics complain, however, that if monitoring is secret or used inappropriately, employees' privacy rights can be infringed. And, in fact, 46 percent of employers monitor employee e-mail—most of them without employees' knowledge. There's a good reason for the policy, says William Caple, Executive VP of OTG Software, a maker of e-mail management systems: "To help protect their businesses from potential liability or security threats, companies need a . . . monitoring system."

Employees have been known to post opinions about employers on online message boards. For some managers, such as Agency.com CEO Kyle Shannon, the messages can be wake-up calls. When Shannon's company was slammed on Vault.com, Shannon discovered that his employees felt ill-prepared, stressed, and uninformed. He hired a VP of People Management to alleviate the problem. "In this new information environment," he warns, "you've got to assume everyone knows everything. So being straight with employees is important. Don't spin anything. Don't try to hide anything."

"From a purely business viewpoint, taking what doesn't belong to you is usually the cheapest way to go."

corporate culture that values ethical standards and announces that the firm is as concerned with good citizenship as with profits. When United Technologies (UT) <www.utc.com>, a Connecticut-based industrial conglomerate, published its 21-page code of ethics, it also named a VP for business practices to see that UT conducted business ethically and responsibly.[7] With a detailed code of ethics and a senior official to enforce it, the firm sends a signal that it expects ethical conduct from its employees.

Two of the most common approaches to formalizing top management commitment to ethical business practices are *adopting written codes* and *instituting ethics programs.*

Adopting Written Codes Many companies have written codes that formally announce their intent to do business in an ethical manner. The number of such companies has risen dramatically in the last three decades, and today almost all major corporations have written codes of ethics. Even Enron had a code of ethics, but managers must follow the code if it's going to work. On one occasion, Enron's board of directors voted to set aside the code in order to complete a deal that would violated it.

Figure 5.3 illustrates the role that corporate ethics and values should play in corporate policy. You can use it to see how a good ethics statement might be structured. Basically, the figure suggests that although strategies and practices can change frequently and objectives can change occasionally, an organization's core principles and values should remain steadfast. Hewlett-Packard <www.hp.com>, for example, has had the same written code of ethics, called *The HP Way,* since 1957. Its essential elements are as follows:

- We have trust and respect for individuals.
- We focus on a high level of achievement and contribution.
- We conduct our business with uncompromising integrity.
- We achieve our common objectives through teamwork.
- We encourage flexibility and innovation.

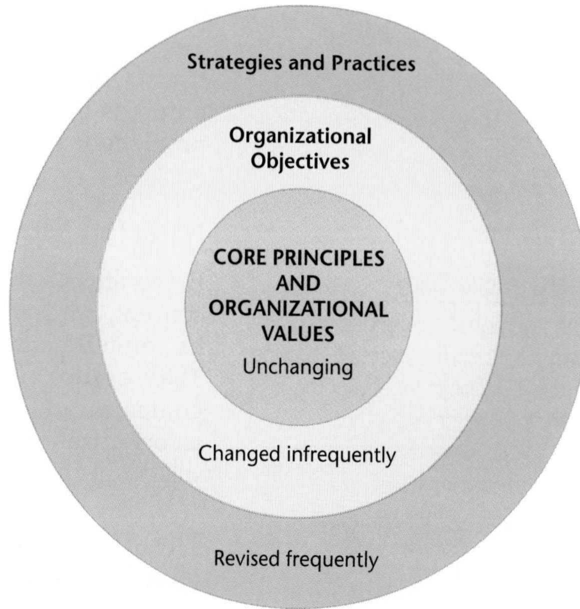

FIGURE 5.3
Core Principles and Organizational Values

Instituting Ethics Programs Many examples suggest that ethical responses can be learned through experience. For instance, in a classic case several years ago, a corporate saboteur poisoned Tylenol capsules, resulting in the deaths of several consumers. Employees at Johnson & Johnson <www.jnj.com>, maker of Tylenol, all knew that without waiting for instructions or a company directive, they should get to retailers' shelves and pull the product as quickly as possible. In retrospect, they reported simply knowing that this was what the company would want to do. But can business ethics be taught, either in the workplace or in schools? Not surprisingly, business schools have become important players in the debate about ethics education. Most analysts agree that even though business schools must address the issue of ethics in the workplace, companies must take the chief responsibility for educating employees. In fact, more and more firms are doing so.

For example, both ExxonMobil <www.exxonmobil.com/overview> and Boeing <www.boeing.com/companyoffices/aboutus/ethics> have major ethics programs. All managers must go through periodic ethics training to remind

Self-Check Questions 1–3

*You should now be able to answer Self-Check Questions 1–3**

1. MULTIPLE CHOICE Suppose a manager cheats on his or her expense account. Into which of the following areas of managerial ethics does this behavior fall? [select one] **(a)** organizational behavior toward other economic agents; **(b)** employee behavior toward the organization ; **(c)** organizational behavior toward the employee; **(d)** individual behavior toward other economic agents; **(e)** behavior of other economic agents toward the organization.

2. MULTIPLE CHOICE Which of the following is **not** one of the norms for assessing ethical behavior discussed in this section? [select one] **(a)** utility; **(b)** rights; **(c)** justice; **(d)** caring; **(e)** regulation.

3. TRUE/FALSE All businesses are legally required to develop and publish a corporate *code of ethics.*

*ANSWERS TO SELF-CHECK QUESTIONS 1–3 CAN BE FOUND ON P. AN-3.

them of the importance of ethical decision making and to update them on the most current laws and regulations that might be particularly relevant to their firms. Others, such as Texas Instruments <www.ti.com>, have ethical hot lines—numbers that an employee can call, either to discuss the ethics of a particular problem or situation or to report unethical behavior or activities by others.

Social Responsibility

social responsibility
The attempt of a business to balance its commitments to groups and individuals in its environment, including customers, other businesses, employees, investors, and local communities

organizational stakeholders
Those groups, individuals, and organizations that are directly affected by the practices of an organization and who therefore have a stake in its performance

Ethics affect individual behavior in the workplace. **Social responsibility** is a related concept, but it refers to the overall way in which a business itself tries to balance its commitments to relevant groups and individuals in its social environment.[8] These groups and individuals are often called **organizational stakeholders**—those groups, individuals, and organizations that are directly affected by the practices of an organization and, therefore, have a stake in its performance.[9] Major corporate stakeholders are identified in Figure 5.4.

The Stakeholder Model of Responsibility

Most companies that strive to be responsible to their stakeholders concentrate first and foremost on five main groups: *customers, employees, investors, suppliers,* and the *local communities* where they do business. They may then select other stakeholders that are particularly relevant or important to the organization and try to address their needs and expectations as well.

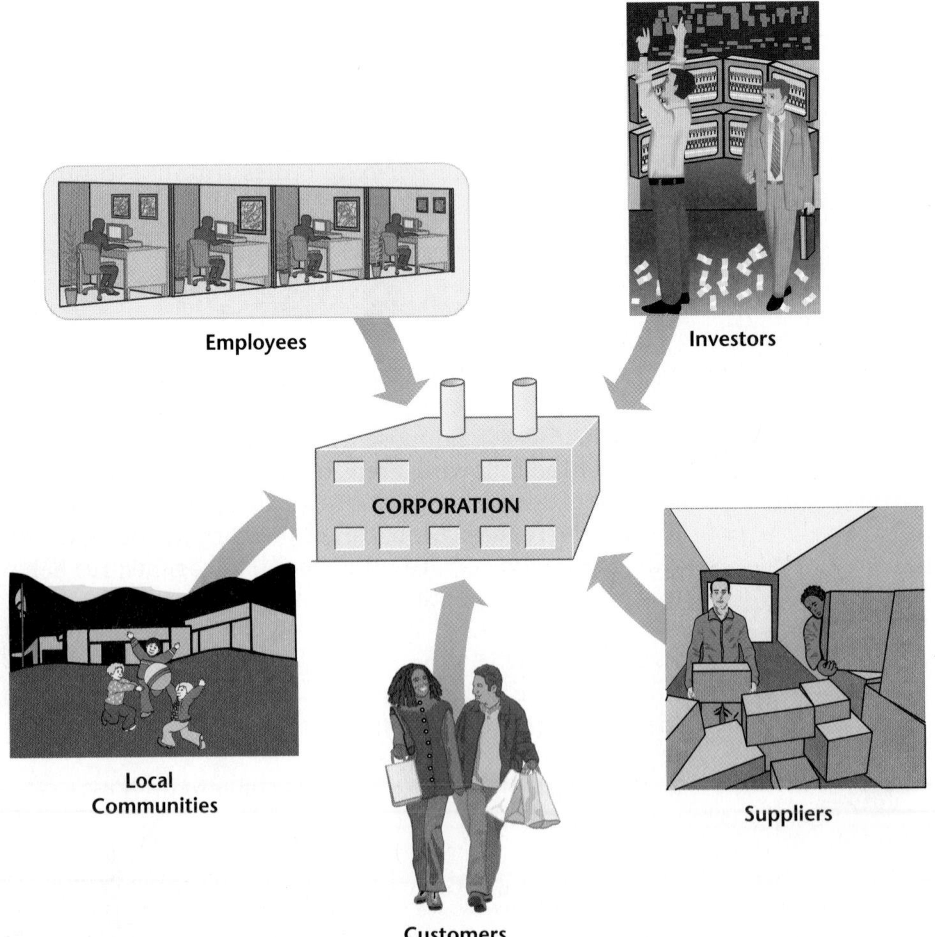

FIGURE 5.4
Major Corporate Stakeholders

Mid-Chapter Internet Field Trip

"Changing the World One Organic Acre at a Time"

Thus far, the chapter has shown us that companies experience a wide variety of opportunities for ethical and socially responsible behavior. Firms that look beyond the bottom line in their dealings with employees and customers, and whose business policies show they are environmentally aware, are often proud of their efforts to foster an ethical corporate culture.

We can take a closer look at one such firm, Horizon Organic, by checking its Web site at <www.horizonorganic.com>. Horizon markets the leading brand of organic foods (milk, dairy products, juice, and eggs) in the United States and is a recent winner of the Colorado Ethics in Business award. The home page has sections devoted to several topics, among them:

- Our Company
- Investor Relations
- Our Products
- Consumer Services
- All about Organic

Start at the home page and click on **Our Company:**

1. What makes Horizon Organic products unique?

Next, go to the left of the screen and click on **Our Products:**

2. How does Horizon work with its suppliers to ensure that it meets its goal of producing only organically grown food?

Now, still in the panel on the left of the screen, click on **Producer Info:**

3. What does Horizon require of its milk and feed suppliers?

On the same page, click on **Organic Planning:**

4. What techniques or processes are not allowed in the production of organic foods?

Now click on **Consumer Services** and select **FAQs:**

5. Browse any one of the FAQ topics. Why do you think Horizon Organic posts so much information about each of its products?

To continue your Internet Field Trip, click on www.prenhall.com/griffin

Customers Businesses that are responsible to their customers strive to treat them fairly and honestly. They also seek to charge fair prices, honor warranties, meet delivery commitments, and stand behind the quality of the products they sell. L.L. Bean <www.llbean.com>, Lands' End <www.landsend.com>, Dell Computer <www.dell.com>, and Johnson & Johnson <www.jmj.com> are among those companies with excellent reputations in this area. In recent years, many small banks have increased their profits by offering much stronger customer service than the large national banks (such as Wells Fargo and Bank of America). For instance, some offer their customers free Starbucks coffee and childcare while they are in the bank conducting business. According to Gordon Goetzmann, a leading financial services executive, "Big banks just don't get it" when it comes to understanding what customers want. As a result, small bank profits have been growing at a rate of 11.8 percent annually, while profits for the larger chain banks have remained around 8.5 percent.[10]

Employees Businesses that are socially responsible in their dealings with employees treat workers fairly, make them a part of the team, and respect their dignity and basic human needs. Organizations such as MBNA <www.mbna.com/about_careers>, Continental Airlines <www.continental.com>, 3M Corporation <www.3m.com>, Hoechst Celanese <www.hoechst.com>, and Southwest Airlines <www.southwest.com> have all established strong reputations in this area. In addition, many of the same firms also go to great lengths to find, hire, train, and promote qualified minorities. Each year, Fortune magazine publishes lists of the Best Companies to Work for in America and the Best

Say what you mean

DOING ETHICAL TAP DANCES

To bribe or not to bribe? That is the question. Well, actually, it's not really a question at all because the textbook answer is a plain and simple no. No matter what business environment you're in, whatever culture or country you're in, the answer is always no.

In reality, of course, it's a little more complicated than that. Business dealings that ignore the strict letter of the law happen all the time—more so in some countries than in others. Not just bribes, but offering or accepting incentives to get things done or extracting a personal favor or two. In reality, we do it all the time in the United States—using the power and influence of people we know to get things done the way we want. Granted, American business practices overseas are subject to certain constraints, such as those embodied in the Foreign Corrupt Practices Act.

Elsewhere, however, the answer is not necessarily no. A hallmark of Brazilian business culture, for example, is a creative approach to problem solving known as *jeitinho*. *Jeitinho* means "to find a way." For Brazilians, there's always another way to get something done. If you need some kind of official document, for instance, you might set out on the straight and narrow path, determined to take all the proper bureaucratic steps to get it. Unfortunately, you may soon find yourself in a maze of rules and regulations from which it's impossible to extricate yourself. That's when you're most likely to resort to *jeitinho*—using personal connections, bending the rules, making a "contribution," or simply approaching the problem from a different angle.

The focus of *jeitinho* appears to be on the goal—in this case, on obtaining a document. For Brazilians, however, it's really on the process of accomplishing it—on being willing and able to find another way no matter what the obstacle. After all, every obstacle forces you in another direction, and during the process of negotiating the maze, you may even be forced to change your original destination. *Jeitinho* almost never involves butting heads with authority. Rather, it's a complex dance that enables individuals to go around problems instead of having to go through them. It's a philosophy in which ends justify a sometimes complicated web of means.

But of course, even if you're operating in a country (like Brazil) in which sidestepping the rules is business as usual, you don't *have* to do ethical tap dances. In fact, many global companies have strict ethical guidelines for doing business, and the steps generally don't change just because you're dancing with a foreign partner. The key is understanding the culture of the host country—observing the way business is conducted and preparing yourself for any challenges—before you get out on the dance floor.

Companies for Minorities. These lists, in turn, attract more individuals who are anxious to work for such highly regarded employers.

Investors To maintain a socially responsible stance toward investors, managers should follow proper accounting procedures, provide appropriate information to shareholders about financial performance, and manage the organization to protect shareholder rights and investments. These managers should be accurate and candid in assessing future growth and profitability, and they should avoid even the appearance of impropriety in such sensitive areas as insider trading, stock-price manipulation, and the withholding of financial data.

In 2002, for example, WorldCom, a giant telecommunications business and owner of MCI, announced that it had overstated previous years' earnings by as much as $6 billion. The SEC also announced that it was investigating the firm's accounting practices, and investors learned that the firm had lent CEO Bernard

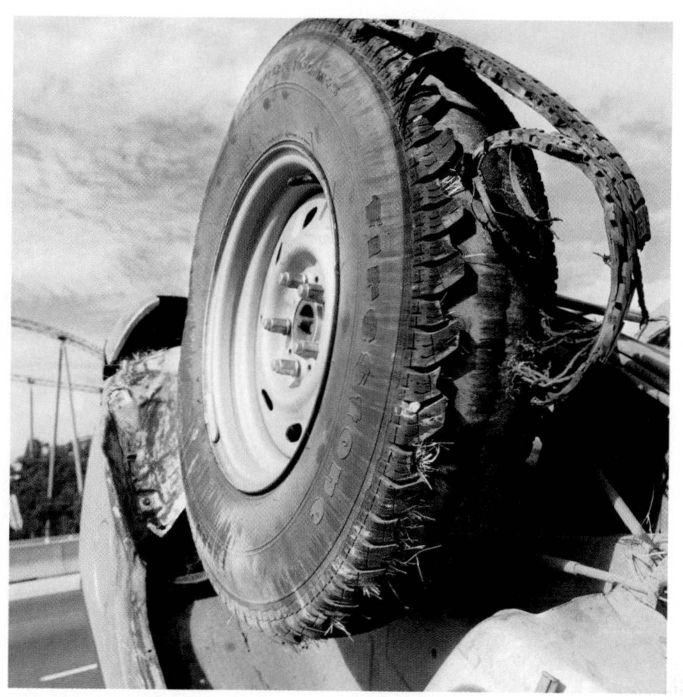

In August 2000, Bridgestone/Firestone Inc. <www.firestone.com> announced a consumer-protection recall of 6.5 million light-truck tires that blew or lost tread and that may have contributed to dozens of fatal accidents. The cost to the tire manufacturer was $350 million. The cost to Ford Motor Co. <www.ford.com>, which had installed—and issued warranties for—most of those 6.5 million tires on its sport-utility vehicles ran to $500 million. The next year, following further consumer-protection measures, Ford took an after-tax charge of $2.1 billion to replace another 13 million Firestone tires.

Ebbers $366 million that he might not be able to repay. On the heels of these problems, WorldCom's stock price dropped by over 43 percent, and the company eventually had to seek bankruptcy protection as it attempted to dig out of the hole it had created for itself.[11]

Suppliers Relations with suppliers should also be managed with care. For example, it might be easy for a large corporation to take advantage of suppliers by imposing unrealistic delivery schedules and reducing profit margins by constantly pushing for lower and lower prices. Many firms now recognize the importance of mutually beneficial partnership arrangements with suppliers. Thus, they keep them informed about future plans, negotiate delivery schedules and prices that are acceptable to both firms, and so forth. Ford <www.ford.com> and Wal-Mart <www.walmart.com> are among the firms acknowledged to have excellent relationships with their suppliers.

Local Communities Finally, most businesses try to be socially responsible to their local communities. They may contribute to local programs like Little League baseball, get actively involved in charitable programs like the United Way, and strive to simply be a good corporate citizen by minimizing their negative impact on the community. Target stores <www.targetcorp.com>, for example, donate a percentage of sales to the local communities where they do business.

The stakeholder model can also provide some helpful insights on the conduct of managers in international business. In particular, to the extent that an organization acknowledges its commitments to its stakeholders, it should also recognize that it has multiple sets of stakeholders in each country where it does business. DaimlerChrysler <www.daimlerchrysler.com>, for example, has investors not only in Germany but also in the United States, Japan, and other countries where its shares are publicly traded. It also has suppliers, employees, and customers in multiple countries, and its actions affect many different communities in dozens of different countries. Similarly, international businesses must also address their responsibilities in areas such as wages, working conditions, and

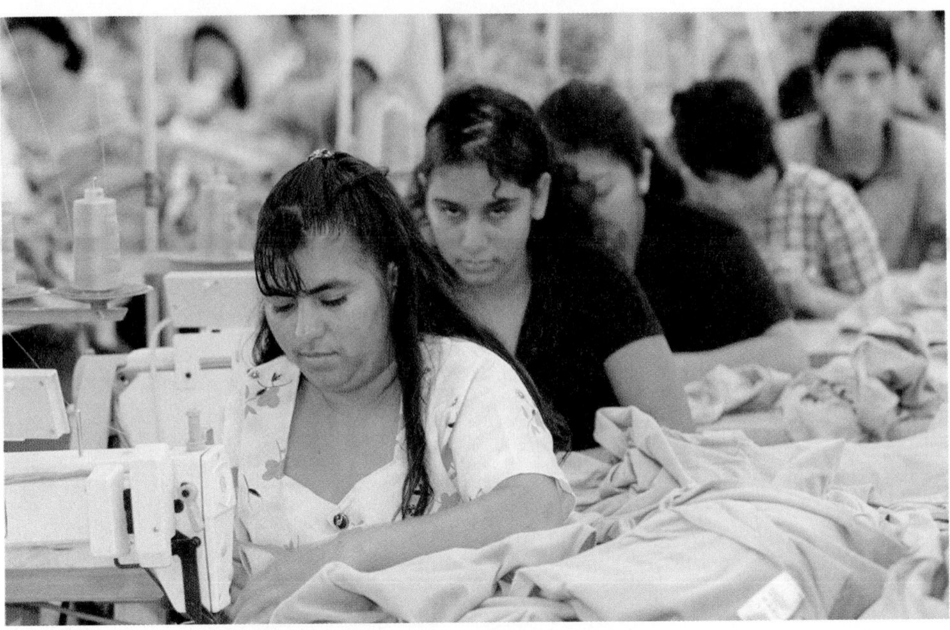

Abigail Martínez used to make 55 cents an hour sewing clothes for 18 hours a day in an El Salvador factory that had neither ventilation nor drinkable water. Then Gap <www.gap.com>*, one of the factory's biggest customers, stepped in to demand improved conditions. The factory is now cooled by breezes, there's an outdoor cafeteria, and managers don't lock the restrooms. Unfortunately, for laborers in El Salvador, the only alternative to subsistence-level work is no work. Besides, the name of the game is still holding down costs, especially labor costs, so Martínez now makes 60 cents an hour.*

environmental protection across different countries that have varying laws and norms regulating such responsibilities.

Contemporary Social Consciousness

Social consciousness and views toward social responsibility continue to evolve. The business practices of such entrepreneurs as John D. Rockefeller, J. P. Morgan, and Cornelius Vanderbilt raised concerns about abuses of power and led to the nation's first laws regulating basic business practices. In the 1930s, many people blamed the Great Depression on a climate of business greed and lack of restraint. Out of this economic turmoil emerged new laws that dictated an expanded role for business in protecting and enhancing the general welfare of society.

In the 1960s and 1970s, business was again characterized as a negative social force. Some critics even charged that defense contractors had helped to promote the Vietnam War to spur their own profits. Eventually, increased social activism prompted increased government regulation in a variety of areas. Health warnings were placed on cigarettes, for instance, and stricter environmental protection laws were enacted.

During the 1980s and 1990s, the general economic prosperity enjoyed in most sectors of the economy led to another period of laissez-faire attitudes toward business. While there was the occasional scandal or major business failure, people for the most part seemed to view business as a positive force in society and one that was generally able to police itself through self-control and free market forces. And many businesses continue to operate in enlightened and socially responsible ways. For example, retailers such as Sears <www.sears.com> and Target have policies against selling handguns and other weapons. Likewise, national toy retailers KayBee and Toys "Я" Us <www.toysrus.com> refuse to sell toy guns that look too realistic. And Anheuser Busch promotes the concept of responsible drinking in some of its advertising.

Firms in numerous other industries have also integrated socially conscious thinking into their production plans and marketing efforts. The production of environmentally safe products has become a potential boom area as many companies introduce products designed to be environmentally friendly. Electrolux, a Swedish appliance maker <www.electrolux.com>, has developed a line of water-efficient washing machines, a solar-powered lawn mower, and ozone-free refrigerators. Ford <www.ford.com> has set up an independent brand called Think to develop and market low-pollution, electric-powered vehicles.[12]

Unfortunately, the spate of corporate scandals and incredible revelations in the last few years may revive negative attitudes and skepticism toward business. As just a single illustration, there was widespread moral outrage when some of the perquisites provided to former Tyco International CEO Dennis Kozlowski were made public in 2002. These perks included such extravagances as a $50 million mansion in Florida and an $18 million apartment in New York, along with $11 million for antiques and furnishings (including a $6,000 shower curtain). The firm even paid for a $2.1 million birthday party for Kozlowski's wife in Italy. It's not as though Kozlowski was a pauper—he earned almost $300 million between 1998 and 2001 in salary, bonuses, and stock proceeds. (Kozlowski is now under investigation for tax evasion.)[13]

In Washington, critics and government officials alike are already calling for tighter standards for business practices and increased control on accounting procedures. And to the extent that society begins to see economic problems as stemming from irresponsible business activities and unethical executive conduct, there may indeed be a return to the mindset of the 1930s. Such a shift could result in business being seen as less capable of controlling itself and thus requiring increased control and constraint by the government.[14]

Areas of Social Responsibility

When defining its sense of social responsibility, a firm typically confronts four areas of concern: responsibilities toward the *environment*, its *customers*, its *employees*, and its *investors*.

Responsibility Toward the Environment

During the first several months of his administration, the harshest criticism directed at President George W. Bush was leveled at his environmental policies. For example, he openly championed proposals for oil exploration in protected

Self-Check Questions 4–6

*You should now be able to answer Self-Check Questions 4–6**

4. TRUE/FALSE Though closely related, *ethics* and *social responsibility* do not mean the same thing.

5. MULTIPLE CHOICE The *stakeholder model of social responsibility* generally includes which of the following? [select one] **(a)** customers; **(b)** employees; **(c)** suppliers; **(d)** investors; **(e)** all of these.

6. MULTIPLE CHOICE Contemporary social consciousness toward business currently reflects which of the following? [select one] **(a)** universal admiration; **(b)** calls for higher taxes; **(c)** universal condemnation; **(d)** growing skepticism and concern regarding responsible corporate governance; **(e)** a *laissez-faire* philosophy.

*ANSWERS TO SELF-CHECK QUESTIONS 4–6 CAN BE FOUND ON P. AN-4.

When President George W. Bush met with leaders of the European Union in Goteborg, Sweden, protestors gathered to pillory his papier-mâché image. The main bone of contention—between Bush and European leaders as well as Bush and European protestors—was what to do about global warming. Although no EU government ever ratified the agreement, the Europeans support the so-called Kyoto Protocol, which calls for industrialized nations to reduce greenhouse-gas emissions below 1990 levels. Bush argues that we can cut global warming and do less damage to the economy by developing new technologies.

areas of Alaska, and he has steadfastly rejected the proposals of the 1997 Kyoto Protocol dealing with global warming. Most of the world's major countries endorsed that agreement, designed to slow global warming, but the United States has been condemned for its refusal to participate. "We know the surface temperature of the earth is rising," admits Bush, but he argues that his policies reflect a sound combination of free-market expansion and exploration balanced against environmental protection and conservation.[15]

Figure 5.5, however, tells a troubling story. The chart shows atmospheric carbon dioxide (CO_2) levels for the period between 1750 and 2000, and it offers three possible scenarios for future levels under different sets of conditions. The three projections—lowest, middle, highest—were developed by the Intergovernmental Panel on Climate Change <www.ipcc.ch>, which calculated likely changes in the atmosphere during this century if no efforts were made to reduce so-called *greenhouse emissions*—waste industrial gases that trap heat in the atmosphere. The criteria for estimating changes are population, economic growth, energy supplies, and technologies: The less pressure exerted by these conditions, the less the increase in CO_2 levels. Energy supplies are measured in *exajoules*—roughly the annual energy consumption of the New York Metropolitan area.

Under the lowest, or best-case, scenario, by 2100 the population would only grow to 6.4 billion people, economic growth would be no more than 1.2 to 2.0 percent a year, and energy supplies would require only 8,000 exajoules of conventional oil. However, under the highest, or worst-case, scenario, the population would increase to 11.3 billion people, annual economic growth would be between 3.0 and 3.5 percent, and energy supplies would require as much as 18,400 exajoules of conventional oil.

The resulting changes in climate would be relatively mild; we would hardly experience any day-to-day changes in the weather. We would, however, increase the likelihood of having troublesome weather around the globe: droughts, hurricanes, winter sieges, and so forth. The charges leveled against greenhouse emissions are disputed, but as one researcher puts it, "The only way to prove them for sure is hang around 10, 20, or 30 more years, when the evidence would be overwhelming. But in the meantime, we're conducting a global experiment. And we're all in the test tube."[16]

"We're conducting a global experiment. And we're all in the test tube."

~Researcher on greenhouse emissions

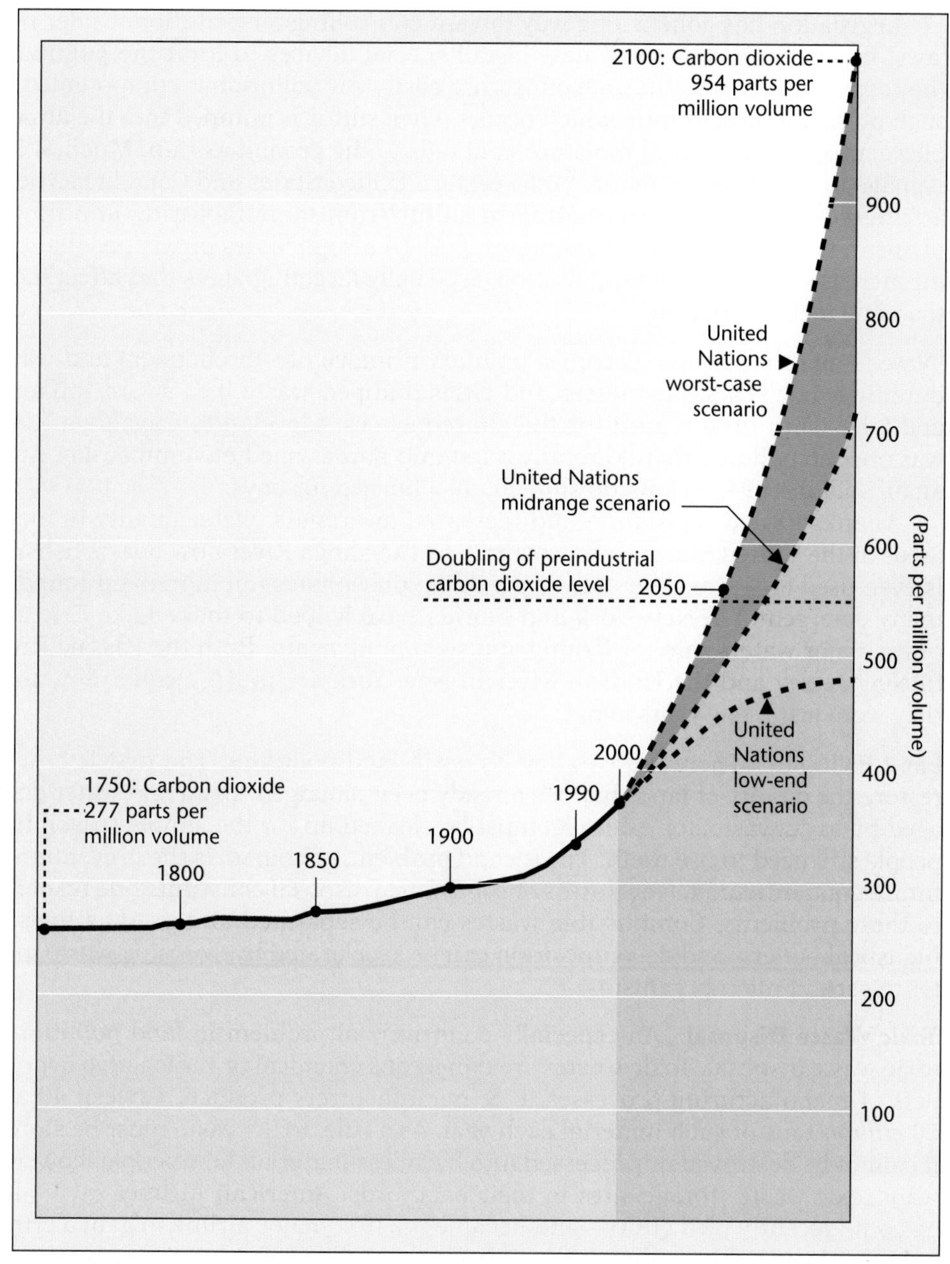

FIGURE 5.5
CO_2 Emissions, Past and Future

Controlling *pollution*—the injection of harmful substances into the environment—is a significant challenge for contemporary business. Although noise pollution is now attracting increased concern, air, water, and land pollution remains the greatest problems in need of solutions from governments and businesses alike. In the following sections, we focus on the nature of the problems in these areas and on some of the current efforts to address them.[17]

Air Pollution Air pollution results when several factors combine to lower air quality. Carbon monoxide emitted by automobiles contributes to air pollution, as do smoke and other chemicals from manufacturing plants. Air quality is usually worst in certain geographic locations, such as the Denver area and the Los Angeles basin, where pollutants tend to get trapped in the atmosphere. For this very reason, the air around Mexico City is generally considered to be the most polluted in the entire world.

Legislation has gone a long way toward controlling air pollution. Under new laws, many companies must now install special devices to limit the pollutants they expel into the air. But such efforts are costly. Air pollution is compounded by such problems as acid rain, which occurs when sulfur is pumped into the atmosphere, mixes with natural moisture, and falls to the ground as rain. Much of the damage to forests and streams in the eastern United States and Canada has been attributed to acid rain originating in sulfur from manufacturing and power plants in the midwestern United States. NAFTA also includes provisions that call for increased controls on air pollution, especially targeting areas that affect more than one member nation.

Water Pollution Water becomes polluted primarily from chemical and waste dumping. For years, businesses and cities dumped waste into rivers, streams, and lakes with little regard for the consequences. Cleveland's Cuyahoga River was once so polluted that it literally burst into flames one hot summer day. After an oil spill in 1994, a Houston ship channel burned for days.

Thanks to new legislation and increased awareness, water quality in many areas of the United States is improving. The Cuyahoga River now boasts fish and is even used for recreation. Laws forbidding phosphates (an ingredient found in many detergents) in New York and Florida have helped to make Lake Erie and other major waters safe for fishing and swimming again. Both the Passaic River in New Jersey and the Hudson River in New York are much cleaner now than they were just a few years ago.

Land Pollution There are two key issues in land pollution. The first is how to restore the quality of land that has already been damaged. Land and water damaged by toxic waste, for example, must be cleaned up for the simple reason that people still need to use them. The second problem, of course, is the prevention of future contamination. New forms of solid-waste disposal constitute one response to these problems. Combustible wastes can be separated and used as fuels in industrial boilers, and decomposition can be accelerated by exposing waste matter to certain microorganisms.

Toxic Waste Disposal An especially controversial problem in land pollution is toxic waste disposal. Toxic wastes are dangerous chemical or radioactive byproducts of manufacturing processes. U.S. manufacturers produce between 40 and 60 *million* tons of such material each year. As a rule, toxic waste must be stored; it cannot be destroyed or processed into harmless material. Few people, however, want toxic waste storage sites in their backyards. American Airlines <www.im.aa.com> recently pled guilty—and became the first major airline to gain a criminal record—to a felony charge that it had mishandled some hazardous materials packed as cargo in passenger airplanes.[18] While fully acknowledging the firm's guilt, Anne McNamara, American's general counsel, argued that "this is an incredibly complicated area with many layers of regulation. It's very easy to inadvertently step over the line."

Recycling Recycling is another controversial area in land pollution. *Recycling*—the reconversion of waste materials into useful products—has become an issue not only for municipal and state governments but also for many companies engaged in high-waste activities. Certain products, such as aluminum beverage cans and glass, can be very efficiently recycled. Others, such as plastics, are more troublesome. For example, brightly colored plastics like detergent and juice bottles must be recycled separately from clear plastics like milk jugs. Most plastic bottle caps, meanwhile, contain a vinyl lining that can spoil a normal recycling batch. Amber plastic beer containers, currently being test-marketed by Philip Morris's Miller Brewing Co. <www.millerbrewing.com>, cannot be mixed for recycling with clear soda bottles.[19] Nevertheless, many local communities actively support various recycling programs, including curbside pickup of aluminum, plastics, glass, and pulp paper. Unfortunately, consumer awareness and interest in this area—and, thus, the policy priorities of business—are more acute at some times than at others.

Responsibility Toward Customers

A company that does not act responsibly toward its customers will ultimately lose their trust—and thus their business. Moreover, the government controls or regulates many aspects of what businesses can and cannot do regarding consumers. The Federal Trade Commission (FTC) <www.ftc.gov> regulates advertising and pricing practices. The Food and Drug Administration (FDA) <www.fda.gov> enforces guidelines for labeling food products.

Unethical and irresponsible business practices toward customers can result in government-imposed penalties and expensive civil litigation. For example, a few years ago, Abbott Laboratories <www.abbott.com> agreed to pay $100 million to settle accusations that the firm failed to meet federal quality standards when it made hundreds of different medical test kits. The FDA indicated that at the time, it was the largest fine the agency had ever levied.[20]

Social responsibility toward customers generally falls into two categories: providing quality products and pricing products fairly. Naturally, firms differ as much in their level of concern about their responsibility toward customers as in their approaches to environmental responsibility. Yet unlike environmental problems, many customer problems do not require expensive solutions. In fact, most problems can be avoided if companies simply adhere to regulated practices and heed laws regarding consumer rights.

Consumer Rights Much of the current interest in business responsibility toward customers can be traced to the rise of **consumerism:** social activism dedicated to protecting the rights of consumers in their dealings with businesses. The first formal declaration of consumer rights protection came in the early 1960s when President John F. Kennedy identified four basic consumer rights. Since that time, general agreement on two additional rights has also emerged; these rights are also backed by numerous federal and state laws:

consumerism
Form of social activism dedicated to protecting the rights of consumers in their dealings with businesses

1. ***Consumers have a right to safe products.*** Businesses can't knowingly sell products that they suspect of being defective. For example, a central legal argument in the recent problems involving Firestone tires was whether or not company officials knew in advance that the firm was selling defective tires.
2. ***Consumers have a right to be informed about all relevant aspects of a product.*** For example, apparel manufacturers are now required to provide full disclosure on all fabrics used (cotton, silk, polyester, and so forth) and instructions for care (dry-clean, machine wash, hand wash).
3. ***Consumers have a right to be heard.*** Labels on most products sold today have either a telephone number or address through which customers can file complaints or make inquiries.
4. ***Consumers have a right to choose what they buy.*** Customers getting auto-repair service are allowed to know and make choices about pricing and warranties on new versus used parts. Similarly, with the consent of their doctors, people have the right to choose between name-brand medications versus generic products that might be cheaper.

5. ***Consumers have a right to be educated about purchases.*** All prescription drugs now come with detailed information regarding dosage, possible side effects, and potential interactions with other medications.
6. ***Consumers have a right to courteous service.*** This right, of course, is hard to legislate. But as consumers become increasingly knowledgeable, they're more willing to complain about bad service. Consumer hotlines can also be used to voice service-related issues.

American Home Products <www.ahp.com> provides an instructive example of what can happen to a firm that violates one or more of these consumer rights. Throughout the early 1990s, the firm aggressively marketed a drug called Pondimin, its brand name for a diet pill containing fenfluramine. In 1996, doctors wrote 18 million prescriptions for Pondimin and other medications containing fenfluramine. In 1997, however, the FDA reported a linkage between the pills and heart-valve disease. A class-action lawsuit against the firm charged that the drug was unsafe and that users had not been provided with complete information about possible side effects. American Home Products eventually agreed to pay $3.75 billion to individuals who had used the drug.[21]

collusion
Illegal agreement between two or more companies to commit a wrongful act

Unfair Pricing Interfering with competition can take the form of illegal pricing practices. **Collusion** occurs when two or more firms agree to collaborate on such wrongful acts as *price fixing*. The U.S. Justice Department <www.usdoj.gov> recently charged three international pharmaceutical firms with illegally controlling worldwide supplies and prices of vitamins. France's Rhone-Poulenc <www.aventis.com> cooperated with the investigation, helped break the case several months earlier than expected, and was not fined. Switzerland's F. Hoffmann-LaRoche <www.laroche-sa/fr> was fined $500 million and one of its senior executives was sentenced to four months in a U.S. prison. Germany's BASF <www.basf.com> was fined $225 million.[22]

Under some circumstances, firms can also come under attack for *price gouging*—responding to increased demand with overly steep (and often unwarranted) price increases. For example, when DaimlerChrysler launched its PT Cruiser in 2000, demand for the vehicles was so strong that some dealers sold them only to

Up until about 1993, London-based Sotheby's <www.sothebys.com> *and New York-based Christie's* <www.christies.com> *competed for 90 percent of the world's art auctions. Then, however, Sotheby CEO A. Alfred Taubman and Christie CEO Sir Anthony Tenant secretly agreed to charge the same rates for all sales. Within a few years, they had collected an extra half billion dollars in commissions paid by sellers. The U.S. Justice Dept.* <www.usdoj.gov> *began investigating in 1999, and in 2002 the two auction houses agreed to split a $537 million settlement with former customers. Sotheby's has to pay an additional fine of $45 million, and Taubman is looking at three years in prison.*

customers willing to pay thousands of dollars over sticker prices. A similar practice was adopted by some Ford dealers when the new Thunderbird was launched in 2002. There were even widespread reports of gasoline retailers doubling or even tripling prices immediately after the events of September 11, 2001. They were apparently counting on consumer panic in response to fear and uncertainty.

Ethics in Advertising In recent years, increased attention has been given to ethics in advertising and product information. Because of controversies surrounding the potential misinterpretation of words and phrases such as *light, reduced calorie, diet,* and *low fat,* food producers are now required to use a standardized format for listing ingredients on product packages. Similarly, controversy arose in 2001 when it was discovered that Sony had literally created a movie critic who happened to be particularly fond of movies released by Sony's Columbia Pictures <www.spe.sony.com> unit. The studio had been routinely using glowing quotes from a fictitious critic in advertising its newest theatrical releases. After *Newsweek* magazine reported what was going on, Sony hastily stopped the practice and apologized.

Another issue concerns advertising that some consumers consider morally objectionable. Examples include advertising for products such as underwear, condoms, alcohol, tobacco products, and firearms. Laws regulate some of this advertising (for instance, tobacco can no longer be promoted in television commercials but can be featured in print ads in magazines), and many advertisers use common sense and discretion in their promotions. But some companies, such as Calvin Klein and Victoria's Secret, have come under fire for being overly explicit in their advertising.

Responsibility Toward Employees

In Chapter 8, we will see how a number of human resource management activities are essential to a smoothly functioning business. These activities—recruiting, hiring, training, promoting, and compensating—are also the basis for social responsibility toward employees.

Legal and Social Commitments Socially responsible behavior toward employees has both legal and social components. By law, businesses cannot practice numerous forms of illegal discrimination against people in any facet of the employment relationship. For example, a company cannot refuse to hire someone because of ethnicity or pay someone a lower salary than someone else on the basis of gender. Such actions must be taken for job-related purposes only. A company that provides its employees with equal opportunities for rewards and advancement without regard to race, sex, or other irrelevant factors is meeting both its legal and its social responsibilities. Firms that ignore these responsibilities run the risk of losing productive, highly motivated employees. They also leave themselves open to lawsuits.

In the opinion of many people, however, social responsibility toward employees goes beyond equal opportunity. According to popular opinion, an organization should strive to ensure that the workplace is physically and socially safe. It should also recognize its obligations to help protect the health of its employees by providing opportunities to balance work and life pressures and preferences. From this point of view, social responsibility toward workers would also include helping them maintain proper job skills and, when terminations or layoffs are necessary, treating them with respect and compassion.

Ethical Commitments: The Special Case of Whistle-Blowers Respecting employees as people also means respecting their behavior as ethically responsible individuals. Suppose, for instance, an employee discovers that a business has been engaging in practices that are illegal, unethical, or socially irresponsible. Ideally, this employee should be able to report the problem to higher level

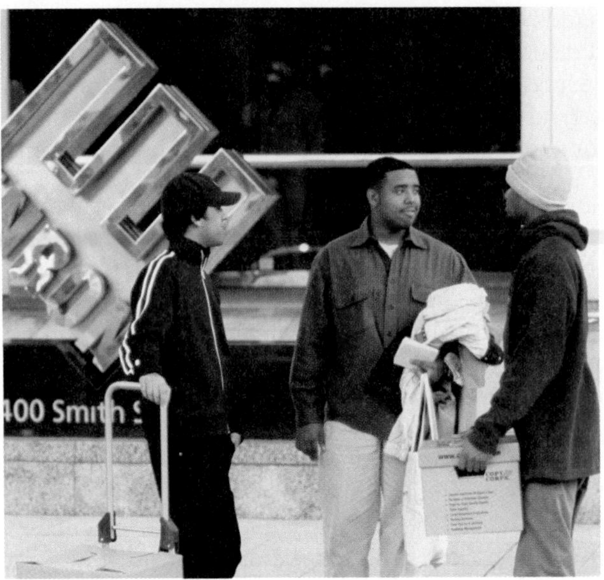

Even before the company collapsed in November 2001, Enron had a so-called "forced ranking" policy by which all employees were periodically rated. Those in the bottom 20 percent were shortly out of jobs. Of those who survived, 4,200 were fired in December 2001. Many expressed complete shock at the sudden demise of a company which, less than a year earlier, had been valued at about $60 billion.

management, confident that managers will stop the questionable practices. Enron's Sherron Watkins reported concerns about the company's accounting practices well before the company's problems were made public, warning top management that Enron would "implode in a wave of accounting scandals." CEO Kenneth Lay commissioned a legal review of the firm's finances but told his investigators not to "second-guess" decisions by Enron's auditor, accounting firm Arthur Andersen.[23]

Too often, people who try to act ethically on the job find themselves in trouble with their employers. If no one in the organization will take action, the employee might elect to drop the matter. Occasionally, however, the individual will inform a regulatory agency or perhaps the media. At this point, he or she becomes a **whistle-blower**—an employee who discovers and tries to put an end to a company's unethical, illegal, or socially irresponsible actions by publicizing them.[24] The 1999 Al Pacino–Russell Crowe movie *The Insider* told the true story of a tobacco-industry whistle-blower named Jeffrey Wigand.

whistle-blower
Employee who detects and tries to put an end to a company's unethical, illegal, or socially irresponsible actions by publicizing them

"I went from making $300,000 a year plus stock options to making $30,000."

~Jeffrey Wigand, Tobacco Industry Whistle-Blower

Unfortunately, whistle-blowers are sometimes demoted—and even fired—when they take their accusations public. Jeffrey Wigand was fired. "I went from making $300,000 a year," he reports, "plus stock options, plus, plus, plus—to making $30,000. Yes, there is a price I've paid."[25] Even if they retain their jobs, they may still be treated as outsiders and suffer resentment or hostility from coworkers. Many coworkers see whistle-blowers as people who simply can't be trusted. One recent study suggests that about half of all whistle-blowers eventually get fired, and about half of those who get fired subsequently lose their homes and/or families.[26]

The law does offer some recourse to employees who take action. The current whistle-blower law stems from the False Claims Act of 1863, which was designed to prevent contractors from selling defective supplies to the Union Army during the Civil War. With 1986 revisions to the law, the government can recover triple damages from fraudulent contractors. If the Justice Department does not intervene, a whistle-blower can proceed with a civil suit. In that case, the whistle-blower receives 25 to 30 percent of any money recovered.[27]

When Phillip Adams worked in the computer industry, he discovered a flaw in the chip-making process that, under certain circumstances, could lead to data being randomly deleted or altered. He reported the flaw to manufacturers, but several years later, he found that one company, Toshiba <www.toshiba.com>, had ignored the problem and continued to make flawed chips for 12 years. He went on to report the problem and became actively involved in a class-action lawsuit based heavily on his research. Toshiba eventually agreed to a $2.1 billion settlement. Adams's share was kept confidential, but he did receive a substantial reward for his efforts.[28] Unfortunately, the prospect of large cash rewards has also generated a spate of false or questionable accusations.

Responsibility Toward Investors

Because shareholders are the owners of a company, it may sound odd to say that a firm can act irresponsibly toward its investors. Managers can abuse their responsibilities to investors in several ways. As a rule, irresponsible behavior toward shareholders means abuse of a firm's financial resources. In such cases, the ultimate losers are indeed the shareholder-owners who do not receive their due earnings or dividends. Companies can also act irresponsibly toward shareholder-owners by misrepresenting company resources.

Improper Financial Management Occasionally, organizations or their officers are guilty of blatant financial mismanagement—offenses that are unethical but not necessarily illegal. Some firms, for example, have been accused of paying excessive salaries to senior managers, of sending them on extravagant "retreats" to exotic and expensive resorts, and of providing frivolous perks, including ready access to corporate jets, lavish expense accounts, and memberships at plush country clubs.

In such situations, creditors can often do little, and stockholders have few options. Trying to force a management changeover is a difficult process that can drive down stock prices—a penalty that shareholders are usually unwilling to impose on themselves.

Check Kiting Certain unethical practices are illegal. **Check kiting,** for instance, involves writing a check against money that has not yet arrived at the bank on which it is drawn. In a typical scheme, managers deposit customer checks totaling, say, $1 million into the company account. Knowing that the bank will not collect all of the total deposit for several days, they proceed to write checks against the total amount deposited, knowing that their account is so important to the bank that the checks will be covered until the full deposits have been collected.

check kiting
Illegal practice of writing checks against money that has not yet been credited at the bank on which the checks are drawn

Insider Trading When someone uses confidential information to gain from the purchase or sale of stocks, that person is practicing *insider trading.* Suppose, for example, that a small firm's stock is currently trading at $50 a share. If a larger firm is going to buy the smaller one, it might have to pay as much as $75 a share for a controlling interest. Individuals who are aware of the impending acquisition before it is publicly announced might, therefore, be able to gain by buying the stock at $50 in anticipation of selling it for $75 after the proposed acquisition is announced.[29] Individuals in a position to take advantage of such a situation generally include managers of the two firms and key individuals at banking firms working on the financial arrangements.

At the other extreme, informed executives can avoid financial loss by selling stock that's about to drop in value. Selling stock, of course, is not illegal, but, legally, you can sell only on the basis of public information that's available to all investors. Potential violations of this regulation are at the heart of investigations into ImClone, Samuel Waksal, and Martha Stewart. Did Waksal warn Stewart that her stock was going to drop in value before the FDA rejected Erbitux? Was prior knowledge the basis of her decision to sell? If the answer is yes, both could be guilty of insider trading. But if Stewart didn't know about the impending news and the timing of her stock sale was purely coincidental, then she did nothing wrong.

Misrepresentation of Finances Certain behaviors regarding financial representation is also illegal. In maintaining and reporting its financial status, every corporation must conform to *generally accepted accounting principles* (*GAAP*) (see Chapter 17). Sometimes, however, unethical managers project profits far in excess of what they actually expect to earn; others go so far as to hide losses and/or expenses in order to boost paper profits. When the truth comes out, however, the damage is often substantial.

Various issues involving the misrepresentation of finances were central in the Enron case. One review, for example, called Enron's accounting practices "creative and aggressive." It seems that CFO Andrew Fastow had set up a complex network of partnerships that were often used to hide losses. Enron, for instance, could report all of the earnings from a partnership as its own while transferring all or most of the costs and losses to the partnership. Inflated profits would then support increased stock prices.[30]

Implementing Social Responsibility Programs

Thus far, we have discussed social responsibility as if there were some agreement on how organizations should behave. In fact, there are dramatic differences of opinion concerning the role of social responsibility as a business goal. Some people oppose any business activity that threatens profits. Others argue that social responsibility must take precedence over profits.

Even businesspeople who agree on the importance of social responsibility will cite different reasons for their views. Some skeptics of business-sponsored social projects fear that if businesses become too active, they will gain too much control over the ways in which those projects are addressed by society as a whole. These critics point to the influence that many businesses have been able to exert on the government agencies that are supposed to regulate their industries. Other critics claim that business organizations lack the expertise needed to address social issues. They argue, for instance, that technical experts, not businesses, should decide how to clean up polluted rivers.

Proponents of socially responsible business believe that corporations are citizens and should, therefore, help to improve the lives of fellow citizens. Still others point to the vast resources controlled by businesses and note that they help to create many of the problems social programs are designed to alleviate.

Approaches to Social Responsibility

Given these differences of opinion, it is little wonder that corporations have adopted a variety of approaches to social responsibility. Not surprisingly, organizations themselves adopt a wide range of positions on social responsibility.[31] As Figure 5.6 illustrates, the four stances that an organization can take concerning its obligations to society fall along a continuum ranging from the lowest to the highest degree of socially responsible practices.

obstructionist stance

Approach to social responsibility that involves doing as little as possible and may involve attempts to deny or cover up violations

Obstructionist Stance The few organizations that take what might be called an **obstructionist stance** to social responsibility usually do as little as possible to solve social or environmental problems. When they cross the ethical or legal line that separates acceptable from unacceptable practices, their typical response is to deny or cover up their actions. Firms that adopt this position have little regard for ethical conduct and will generally go to great lengths to hide wrongdoing. IBP, a leading meat-processing firm, has a long (and undistinguished) record of breaking environmental protection, labor, and food processing laws and then trying to cover up its offenses.

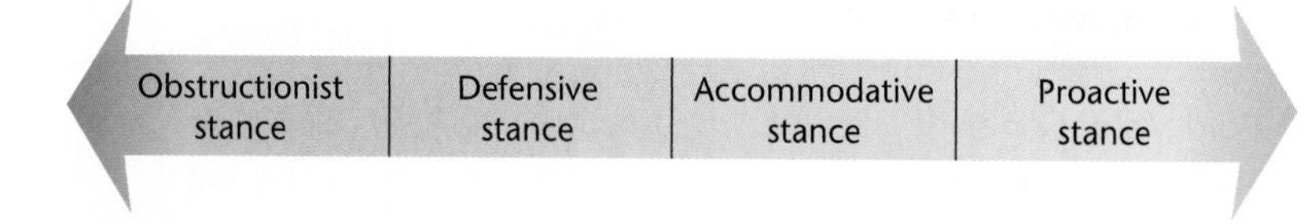

FIGURE 5.6
Spectrum of Approaches to Corporate Social Responsibility

Defensive Stance One step removed from the obstructionist stance is the **defensive stance,** whereby the organization will do everything that is required of it legally but nothing more. This approach is most consistent with arguments against corporate social responsibility. Managers who take a defensive stance insist that their job is to generate profits. Such a firm, for example, would install pollution-control equipment dictated by law but would not install higher quality equipment even though it might further limit pollution.

defensive stance
Approach to social responsibility by which a company meets only minimum legal requirements in its commitments to groups and individuals in its social environment

Tobacco companies generally take this position in their marketing efforts. In the United States, they are legally required to include warnings to smokers on their products and to limit advertising to prescribed media. Domestically, they follow these rules to the letter of the law but use more aggressive marketing methods in countries that have no such rules. In many Asian and African countries, cigarettes are heavily promoted, contain higher levels of tar and nicotine than those sold in the United States, and carry few or no health warning labels. Firms that take this position are also unlikely to cover up wrongdoing, will generally admit to mistakes, and will take appropriate corrective actions.

Accommodative Stance A firm that adopts an **accommodative stance** meets its legal and ethical requirements but will also go further in certain cases. Such firms voluntarily agree to participate in social programs, but solicitors must convince them that given programs are worthy of their support. Both Shell and IBM, for example, will match contributions made by their employees to selected charitable causes. Many organizations respond to requests for donations to Little League, Girl Scouts, youth soccer programs, and so forth. The point, however, is that someone has to knock on the door and ask. Accommodative organizations do not necessarily or proactively seek avenues for contributing.

accommodative stance
Approach to social responsibility by which a company, if specifically asked to do so, exceeds legal minimums in its commitments to groups and individuals in its social environment

Proactive Stance The highest degree of social responsibility that a firm can exhibit is the **proactive stance.** Firms that adopt this approach take to heart the arguments in favor of social responsibility. They view themselves as citizens in a society and proactively seek opportunities to contribute. The most common—and direct—way to implement this stance is by setting up a foundation through which to provide direct financial support for various social programs. Table 5.1 lists the top 15 largest corporate foundations based on total giving to social programs.

proactive stance
Approach to social responsibility by which a company actively seeks opportunities to contribute to the well-being of groups and individuals in its social environment

Unfortunately, recent economic difficulties and the decline of stock prices have caused donors to reduce philanthropic giving or to earmark funds over longer periods of time. Ted Turner, vice chairman of AOL Time Warner, has pledged $250 million to an organization dedicated to reducing the threat of nuclear war. But because of a drop in the value of his stock holdings, he has been forced to fund his commitment over a period of seven years rather than the five that he'd originally intended.[32]

An excellent example of a different kind of proactive stance is the Ronald McDonald House <www.mcdonalds.com> program undertaken by McDonald's Corp. These houses, located close to major medical centers, can be used by families for minimal cost while sick children are receiving medical treatment nearby.

■ TABLE 5.1
Top 15 Corporate Foundations

Foundation	State	Total Giving	Fiscal Data
1. Ford Motor Company Fund	MI	$169,100,475	12/31/00
2. Bank of America Foundation	NC	85,755,841	12/31/00
3. SBC Foundation	TX	68,678,574	12/31/00
4. Wal-Mart Foundation	AR	62,617,641	1/31/00
5. J. P. Morgan Chase Foundation	NY	44,656,806	12/31/00
6. Lucent Technologies Foundation	NJ	43,932,312	9/30/00
7. AT&T Foundation	NY	43,539,963	12/31/00
8. General Motors Foundation	MI	43,280,242	12/31/00
9. Citigroup Foundation	NY	43,068,029	12/31/00
10. ExxonMobil Foundation	TX	42,188,567	12/31/00
11. Aventis Pharmaceuticals Health Care Foundation	NJ	41,558,325	12/31/00
12. Verizon Foundation	NY	41,205,556	12/30/00
13. GE Fund	CT	40,701,047	12/31/00
14. Prudential Foundation	NJ	36,219,045	12/31/00
15. Fannie Mae Foundation	DC	34,835,347	12/31/00

Similarly, some firms, such as UPS <www.ups.com>, Home Depot <www.homedepot.com>, and US West <www.uswest.com>, employ individuals who hope to compete in the Olympics and support them in various ways. UPS, for instance, underwrites the training and travel costs of four employees competing for Olympic berths and allows them to maintain flexible work schedules.[33] These and related programs exceed the accommodative stance—they indicate a sincere commitment to improving the general social welfare and thus represent a proactive stance to social responsibility.

Remember, however, that these categories are not sharply distinct: They merely label stages along a continuum of approaches. Organizations do not always fit neatly into one category or another. The Ronald McDonald House program has been widely applauded, but McDonald's has also come under fire for allegedly misleading consumers about the nutritional value of its food products. Likewise, while UPS has sincere motives for helping Olympic athletes, the company will also benefit by featuring the athletes' photos on its envelopes and otherwise promoting its own benevolence. And even though Enron may have taken an obstructionist stance in the past, many individual employees and managers at the firm no doubt made substantial contributions to society in a number of different ways.

Managing Social Responsibility Programs

Making a company socially responsible in the full sense of the social response approach takes a carefully organized and managed program. In particular, managers must take steps to foster a companywide sense of social responsibility. Figure 5.7 summarizes those steps.[34]

1. ***Social responsibility must start at the top and be considered as a factor in strategic planning.*** Without the support of top management, no program can succeed. Thus, top management must embrace a strong stand on social responsibility and develop a policy statement outlining that commitment.

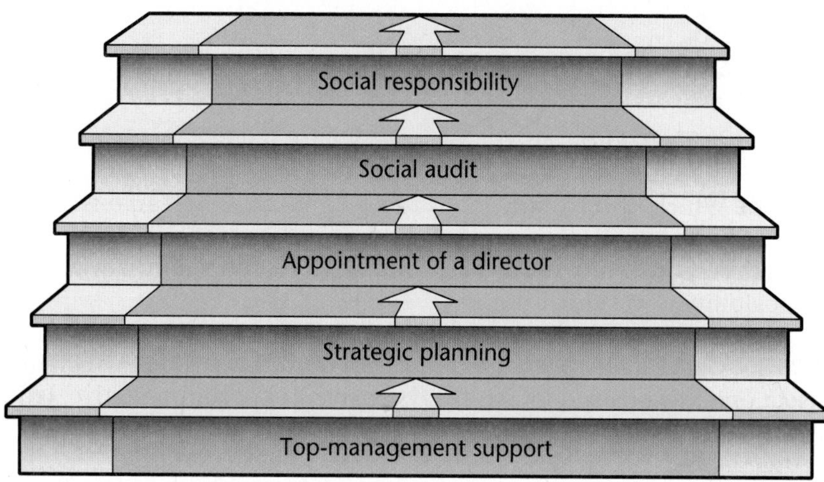

FIGURE 5.7
Establishing a Social Responsibility Program

2. ***A committee of top managers must develop a plan detailing the level of management support.*** Some companies set aside percentages of profits for social programs. Levi Strauss, for example, earmarks 2.4 percent of pretax earnings for worthy projects. Managers must also set specific priorities. For instance, should the firm train the hard-core unemployed or support the arts?
3. ***One executive must be put in charge of the firm's agenda.*** Whether the role is created as a separate job or added to an existing one, the selected individual must monitor the program and ensure that its implementation is consistent with the firm's policy statement and strategic plan.
4. ***The organization must conduct occasional* social audits: *systematic analyses of its success in using funds earmarked for its social responsibility goals.***[35] Consider the case of a company whose strategic plan calls for spending $100,000 to train 200 hard-core unemployed people and to place 180 of them in jobs. If at the end of a year, the firm has spent $98,000, trained 210 people, and filled 175 jobs, a social audit will confirm the program's success. But if the program has cost $150,000, trained only 90 people, and placed only 10 of them, the audit will reveal the program's failure. Such failure should prompt a rethinking of the program's implementation and its priorities.

social audit
Systematic analysis of a firm's success in using funds earmarked for meeting its social responsibility goals

Social Responsibility and the Small Business

As the owner of a garden supply store, how would you respond to a building inspector's suggestion that a cash payment will speed your application for a building permit? As the manager of a liquor store, would you call the police, refuse to sell, or sell to a customer whose identification card looks forged? As the owner of a small laboratory, would you call the state board of health to make sure that it has licensed the company with whom you want to contract to dispose of medical waste? Who will really be harmed if a small firm pads its income statement to help it get a much-needed bank loan?

Many of the examples in this chapter illustrate big-business responses to ethical and social responsibility issues. Such examples, however, show quite clearly that small businesses must answer many of the same questions. Differences are primarily differences of scale.

At the same time, these are largely questions of *individual* ethics. What about questions of *social* responsibility? Can a small business, for example, afford a social agenda? Should it sponsor Little League baseball teams, make donations

Self-Check Questions 7–9

*You should now be able to answer Self-Check Questions 7–9**

7. MULTIPLE CHOICE Which of the following is **not** an area of *social responsibility?* [select one] **(a)** responsibility toward the board of directors; **(b)** responsibility toward the environment; **(c)** responsibility toward customers; **(d)** responsibility toward employees; **(e)** responsibility toward investors.

8. MULTIPLE CHOICE General *approaches to social responsibility* include which of the following? [select one] **(a)** obstructionist; **(b)** defensive; **(c)** accommodative; **(d)** proactive; **(e)** all of these.

9. TRUE/FALSE Because of their size and limited financial resources, small businesses should not be concerned about social responsibility.

*ANSWERS TO SELF-CHECK QUESTIONS 7–9 CAN BE FOUND ON P. AN-4.

to the United Way, and buy light bulbs from the Lion's Club? Do joining the chamber of commerce and supporting the Better Business Bureau cost too much? Clearly, ethics and social responsibility are decisions faced by all managers in all organizations, regardless of rank or size. One key to business success is to decide in advance how to respond to the issues that underlie all questions of ethical and social responsibility.

Continued from page 126

When Does a Stock Warrant Warrant a Warrant for Arrest?

Just when things couldn't seem to get any worse for Samuel Waksal and ImClone, they did. In early August 2002, several new charges were filed against Waksal, including perjury and bank fraud. At the heart of these new charges was an allegation that he had deceived two major financial institutions, Bank of America and Refco Capital Markets.

Authorities claim that in late 1999, Waksal had in his possession a warrant allowing him to buy 350,000 shares of ImClone for $5.50 a share. He used that warrant as collateral in obtaining loans from each lender, neither of which knew that it was being used to get a loan from the other one. In 2000, Waksal cashed in the warrant, rendering it worthless as collateral for either loan.

Later that year, Bank of America requested confirmation from Waksal that he still held the warrant. According to indictments handed down in August 2002, Waksal forged the signature of ImClone's general counsel on a letter dated November 10, 2000, verifying that the warrant was still valid as collateral.

This news, of course, only fueled suspicions about Waksal's other activities. He now faces additional charges, and family members and friends are under growing scrutiny. Two major lenders are looking at major losses from worthless loans. ImClone stock value has plummeted, and Bristol-Myers's investment in the company will almost certainly have to be written off as well. As for all other investors, the best they can do is hope that there are no more shoes to be dropped.

Questions for Discussion

1. What are the major legal issues in this case? What are the major ethical issues?
2. Aside from personal greed, what factors might lead a drug company like ImClone to aggressively promote potential new products before they have been approved?
3. Some observers argue that the FDA should be more open in sharing news of pending product reviews with the public. What are the pros and cons of such an argument?
4. Distinguish between ethical issues and social responsibility issues as they apply to the ImClone case.

Summary of Learning Objectives

1. ***Explain how individuals develop their personal*** **codes of ethics** ***and why ethics are important in the workplace.***

Ethics are beliefs about what's right and wrong or good and bad. Individual values and morals, along with the social context in which it occurs, determine whether a particular behavior is ethical or unethical. Thus, **ethical behavior** conforms to individual beliefs and social norms about what's right and good. **Unethical behavior** is behavior that individual beliefs and social norms define as wrong and bad. **Business ethics** refers to behaviors by managers or employees of organizations.

Managerial ethics are standards of behavior that guide managers. There are three broad categories of ways in which managerial ethics can affect people's work: (1) *Behavior Toward Employees:* This category covers such matters as hiring and firing, wages and working conditions, and privacy and respect. Sometimes, legal decisions in these areas may be objectionable on ethical grounds. (2) *Behavior Toward the Organization:* Ethical issues also arise from employee behavior toward employers, especially in such areas as conflict of interest, confidentiality, and honesty. A *conflict of interest* occurs when an activity may benefit the individual to the detriment of his or her employer. Common problems include such behavior as stealing supplies and padding expense accounts. (3) *Behavior Toward Other Economic Agents:* Ethics affect the relationships between the firm and its employees with so-called *primary agents of interest*—customers, competitors, stockholders, suppliers, dealers, and unions.

A model for applying ethical judgments to business situations recommends the following three steps: (1) Gather relevant factual information; (2) analyze the facts to determine the most appropriate moral values; (3) make an ethical judgment based on the rightness or wrongness of the proposed activity or policy.

Four other principles may affect any situation: (1) *Utility:* Does an act optimize what's best for those who are affected by it? (2) *Rights:* Does it respect the rights of the individuals involved? (3) *Justice:* Is it consistent with what's fair? (4) *Caring:* Is it consistent with people's responsibilities to each other?

To encourage ethical behavior in the workplace, many firms establish codes of conduct and state clear ethical positions for conducting business. Perhaps the single most effective step that a company can take is to demonstrate top management support. In addition to promoting attitudes of honesty and openness, firms can also take specific steps to formalize their commitment: (1) *Adopting written codes:* Such codes formally acknowledge the intent to do business in an ethical manner. (2) *Instituting ethics programs:* In taking responsibility for educating employees, many firms have programs in which managers must go through periodic ethics training. Others have ethical hot lines—numbers that an employee can call to discuss ethical problems or to report unethical activities.

2. ***Distinguish*** **social responsibility** ***from ethics, identify*** **organizational stakeholders,** ***and characterize social consciousness today.***

Ethics affect individuals. **Social responsibility** refers to the way a firm attempts to balance its commitments to **organizational stakeholders**—those groups, individuals, and organizations that are directly affected by the practices of an organization and, therefore, have a stake in its performance.

Many companies concentrate five main groups: (1) *Customers:* Businesses seek to charge fair prices, honor warranties, meet delivery commitments, and stand behind products. (2) *Employees:* Businesses treat workers fairly, make them a part of the team, and respect their dignity and basic human needs. (3) *Investors:* Managers follow proper accounting procedures, provide appropriate information to shareholders, and protect shareholder rights and investments. (4) *Suppliers:* Firms keep suppliers informed about future plans and negotiate acceptable delivery schedules and prices. (5) *Local communities:* Businesses contribute to local programs, get involved in charities, and minimize negative impact on the community.

Attitudes toward social responsibility have changed. The late nineteenth century, though characterized by the entrepreneurial spirit and the *laissez-faire* philosophy, also featured labor strife and predatory business practices. Concern about unbridled business activity was soon translated into laws regulating business practices. In the 1930s, many people blamed the failure of businesses and banks and the widespread loss of jobs on a general climate of business greed and lack of restraint. Out of the economic turmoil of the 1930s, when greed was blamed for business failures and the loss of jobs, came new laws protecting and enhancing social well-being. During the 1960s and 1970s, activism prompted increased government regulation in many areas of business. Today's attitudes stress a greater social role for business. Perhaps globalization and environmentalism have made businesses more sensitive to their social responsibilities. This view, combined with the economic prosperity of the 1980s and 1990s, marked a return to the laissez-faire philosophy, but the recent epidemic of corporate scandals threatens to revive the 1930s call for more regulation and oversight.

3. *Show how the concept of social responsibility applies both to environmental issues and to a firm's relationships with customers, employees, and investors.*

When defining social responsibility, a firm confronts four areas of concern: (1) *Responsibility toward the environment:* Controlling *pollution* is a key challenge to business. Legislation has done a great deal, but such efforts are costly. An especially controversial problem in land pollution is disposal of toxic waste—dangerous chemical or radioactive byproducts of manufacturing processes. Another controversial area pollution is *recycling*—the reconversion of waste materials into useful products.

(2) *Responsibility toward customers:* Social responsibility toward customers means providing quality products and pricing products fairly. Much current interest in responsibility toward customers comes from **consumerism**—social activism dedicated to protecting the rights of consumers in their dealings with businesses. In the early 1960s, President John F. Kennedy identified four consumer rights: (i) The right to safe products; (ii) the right to be informed about a product; (iii) the right to be heard; and (iv) the right to choose what they buy. State and federal law support two additional rights: (i) the right to be educated about purchases and (ii) the right to courteous service. Important issues in this area include *unfair pricing.* **Collusion** occurs when firms agree to collaborate on such wrongful acts as *price fixing.* Increased attention has also been given to *ethics in advertising.*

(3) *Responsibility toward employees:* Businesses can't practice illegal discrimination against people in employment. But social responsibility goes beyond equal opportunity. The workplace should be safe, and businesses should protect employee health by helping them balance work and life pressures and preferences. If a business engages in illegal or unethical activities, an employee who informs a regulatory agency or the media may become a **whistle-blower.**

(4) *Responsibility toward investors:* Organizations and managers may be guilty of *financial mismanagement*—offenses that are unethical but not necessarily illegal. In such situations, creditors can often do little, and stockholders have few options. But certain unethical practices are illegal. **Check kiting** involves writing a check against money that has not yet arrived at the bank on which it is drawn. Using confidential information to gain from a stock transaction is *insider trading.* Certain behavior regarding *financial representation* is also unlawful.

4. *Identify four general* approaches to social responsibility *and describe the four steps that a firm must take to implement a* social responsibility program.

Some people oppose any activity that threatens profits. Others argue that social responsibility must take precedence over profits. Still others point to the vast resources controlled by businesses and charge that they create many of the problems social programs are designed to alleviate. A business can take one of four stances concerning its social obligations to society: (1) Those that take an **obstructionist stance** do as little as possible to solve social or environmental problems. Their typical response is to deny or cover up wrongdoing.

(2) In taking a **defensive stance,** organizations will do everything that they have to do legally but nothing more. But they aren't likely to cover up wrongdoing, will admit to mistakes, and will take corrective action. (3) A firm that adopts an **accommodative stance** meets its legal and ethical requirements but will go further in certain cases. It will participate in social programs if convinced that they're worthy of support. (4) Firms adopting a **proactive stance** agree with arguments in favor of social responsibility. Viewing themselves as citizens of society, they seek opportunities to contribute, often by setting up foundations to channel financial support.

One model suggests a four-step approach to fostering a companywide sense of social responsibility: (1) Social responsibility must start at the top and be included in strategic planning. (2) Top managers must develop a plan detailing the level of management support. (3) One executive must be put in charge of the agenda. (4) The organization must conduct occasional **social audits**—analyses of its success in using funds earmarked for social responsibility goals.

5. *Explain how issues of social responsibility and ethics affect small business.*

For small businesspeople, ethical issues are questions of *individual* ethics. But in questions of *social* responsibility, they must ask themselves if they can afford a social agenda—sponsoring Little League baseball teams or making donations to the United Way? They should also realize that managers in all organizations face issues of ethics and social responsibility.

KEY TERMS

ethics (p. 126)
ethical behavior (p. 126)
unethical behavior (p. 126)
business ethics (p. 126)
managerial ethics (p. 127)
social responsibility (p. 133)
organizational stakeholders (p. 133)
consumerism (p. 143)
collusion (p. 144)

whistle-blower (p. 146)
check kiting (p. 147)
obstructionist stance (p. 148)
defensive stance (p. 149)
accommodative stance (p. 149)
proactive stance (p. 149)
social audit (p. 151)

QUESTIONS AND EXERCISES

Questions for Review

1. What basic factors should be considered in any ethical decision?
2. Who are an organization's stakeholders? Who are the major stakeholders with which most businesses must be concerned?
3. What are the major areas of social responsibility with which businesses should be concerned?
4. What are the four basic approaches to social responsibility?
5. In what ways do you think your personal code of ethics might clash with the operations of some companies? How might you try to resolve these differences?

Questions for Analysis

6. What kind of wrongdoing would most likely prompt you to be a whistle-blower? What kind of wrongdoing would be least likely? Why?
7. In your opinion, which area of social responsibility is most important? Why? Are there areas other than those noted in the chapter that you consider important?
8. Identify some specific ethical or social responsibility issues that might be faced by small-business managers and employees in each of the following areas: environment, customers, employees, and investors.

Application Exercises

9. Develop a list of the major stakeholders of your college or university. As a class, discuss the ways in which you think the school prioritizes these stakeholders. Do you agree or disagree with this prioritization?
10. Using newspapers, magazines, and other business references, identify and describe at least three companies that take a defensive stance to social responsibility, three that take an accommodative stance, and three that take a proactive stance.

Building Your Business Skills

TO LIE OR NOT TO LIE: THAT IS THE QUESTION

This exercise enhances the following SCANS workplace competencies: demonstrating basic skills, demonstrating thinking skills, exhibiting interpersonal skills, and working with information.

Goal

To encourage students to apply general concepts of business ethics to specific situations.

Background

Workplace lying, it seems, has become business as usual. According to one survey, one-quarter of working American adults said that they had been asked to do something illegal or unethical on the job. Four in 10 did what they were told. Another survey of more than 2,000 secretaries showed that many employees face ethical dilemmas in their day-to-day work.

Method

Step 1

- Working with four other students, discuss ways in which you would respond to the following ethical dilemmas. When there is a difference of opinion among group members, try to determine the specific factors that influence different responses.
- Would you lie about your supervisor's whereabouts to someone on the phone?
- Would you lie about who was responsible for a business decision that cost your company thousands of dollars to protect your own or your supervisor's job?
- Would you inflate sales and revenue data on official company accounting statements to increase stock value?
- Would you say that you witnessed a signature when you did not if you were acting in the role of a notary?
- Would you keep silent if you knew that the official minutes of a corporate meeting had been changed?
- Would you destroy or remove information that could hurt your company if it fell into the wrong hands?

Step 2

Research the commitment to business ethics at Johnson & Johnson <www.jnj.com> and Texas Instruments <www.ti.com/corp/docs/ethics/home.htm> by clicking on their respective Web sites. As a group, discuss ways in which these statements are likely to affect the specific behaviors mentioned in Step 1.

Step 3

Working with group members, draft a corporate code of ethics that would discourage the specific behaviors mentioned in

Step 1. Limit your code to a single typewritten page, but make it sufficiently broad to cover different ethical dilemmas.

Follow-Up Questions

1. What personal, social, and cultural factors do you think contribute to lying in the workplace?
2. Do you agree or disagree with the following statement? "The term *business ethics* is an oxymoron." Support your answer with examples from your own work experience or that of a family member.
3. If you were your company's director of human resources, how would you make your code of ethics a "living document"?
4. If you were faced with any of the ethical dilemmas described in Step 1, how would you handle them? How far would you go to maintain your personal ethical standards?

Exercising Your Ethics

TAKING A STANCE

The Situation

A perpetual debate revolves around the roles and activities of business owners in contributing to the greater social good. Promoting the so-called *proactive stance,* some people argue that businesses should be socially responsible by seeking opportunities to benefit the society in which they are permitted to conduct their affairs. Others maintain that because businesses exist to make profits for owners, they have no further obligation to society than that (the *defensive stance*).

The Dilemma

Pair up with one of your classmates. Using a coin toss, each of you should select or be assigned one side of this debate. You and your partner should then enter into a dialogue to formulate the three most convincing arguments possible to support each side. Then select the single strongest argument in support of each position. Each team of two partners should then present to the class its strongest arguments for and against social responsibility on the part of business.

Questions for Discussion

1. Which side of the debate is easier to defend? Why?
2. What is your personal opinion about the appropriate stance that a business should take regarding social responsibility?
3. To what extent is the concept of social responsibility relevant to nonbusiness organizations such as universities, government units, health care organizations, and so forth?

Mastering Business Essentials

■ **EPISODE 3** raises the issue of corporate social responsibility when CanGo management debates the potential effects of violent online games. As team members try to balance the firm's image and needs against the demands of its market, they discuss its social responsibility toward the environment and toward key stakeholders, including customers, employees, and investors. *This episode presents some key problems encountered by managers who want to coordinate company policy and strategy with personal values.*

■ **EPISODE 8** shows what kind of dilemmas can arise in a workplace where different people have different ethical values. *This episode provides a practical illustration of the textbook discussion on the purpose and value of written codes of ethics.*

Crafting Your Business Plan

GOING IN THE ETHICAL DIRECTION

The Purpose of the Assignment

1. To familiarize students with some of the ethical and social responsibility considerations faced by a sample firm in developing its business plan, in the planning framework of the *Business PlanPro (BPP)* software package.
2. To show where ethical and social responsibility considerations can be found in various sections of the *BPP* planning environment.

Assignment

After reading Chapter 5 in the textbook, open the BPP software, and look around for information about the types of ethical considerations and social responsibility factors that would be of concern to the sample firm: Southeast Health Plans Inc. *To find* Southeast Health Plans, *do the following:*

Open the *Business PlanPro.* If it asks if you want to "create a new business plan" or "open an existing plan," select "create a new business plan" (even though you are not going to create a plan at this time). You will then be taken to the *Business PlanPro EasyPlan Wizard.* On the screen, go to the option entitled, "**Research It > >,**" and click on that option. You will then be presented with a new list of options, including **Sample Plan Browser.** After clicking on the **Sample Plan Browser,** go down the alphabetical list of sample plans and double-click on **Plan Administration—Health,** which is the location for *Southeast Health Plans Inc.* The screen you are looking at is the introduction page for *Southeast's* business plan. On this page, scroll down until you reach the **Table of Contents** for the company's business plan.

Now respond to the following questions:

1. Do you think a company in Southeast's line of business should have a code of ethics? Call up Southeast's Table of Contents page. In which sections of the company's business plan would you expect to find its code of ethics? Go into those sections, and identify information pertaining to the firm's code of ethics. What did you find?
2. The textbook states that a firm's social responsibility includes providing quality products for its customers. Explore Southeast's business plan and describe its position on providing quality products. [Sites to see in *BPP* for this item: On the Table of Contents page, click on **1.0 Executive Summary.** Then click on and read each of the following in turn: **1.1 Objectives, 1.2 Mission,** and **1.3 Keys to Success.**]
3. Another dimension of social responsibility is pricing products fairly. Search through Southeast's plan for information about its policies for pricing services. Does Southeast's planned gross margin reflect "fair pricing"? Why or why not? [Sites to see in *BPP:* From the Table of Contents page, click on **3.1 Competitive Comparison** and then on **3.3 Fulfillment.** After returning to the Table of Contents page, click on **5.1.1 Pricing Strategy** and then **1.0 Executive Summary.**]

Video Exercise

DOING THE RIGHT THING: AMERICAN RED CROSS

Learning Objectives

The purpose of this video is to help you:

1. Identify some of the social responsibility and ethics challenges faced by a nonprofit organization.
2. Discuss the purpose of an organizational code of ethics.
3. Understand the potential conflicts that can emerge between an organization and its stakeholders.

Synopsis

Founded in 1881 by Clara Barton, the American Red Cross is a nonprofit organization dedicated to helping victims of war, natural disasters, and other catastrophes. The organization's 1,000 chapters are governed by volunteer boards of directors who oversee local activities and enforce ethical standards in line with community norms and the Red Cross' own code of ethics. Over the years, the Red Cross has been guided in its use of donations by honoring donor intent. This policy helped the organization deal with a major ethical challenge after the terrorist attacks of September 11, 2001. The Red Cross received more than $1 billion in donations and initially diverted some money to ancillary operations, such as creating a strategic blood reserve. After donors objected, however, the organization reversed its decision and—honoring donor intent—used the contributions to directly benefit people affected by the tragedy.

Discussion Questions

1. *For analysis:* What are the social responsibility implications of the decision to avoid accepting donations of goods for many local relief efforts?
2. *For analysis:* What kinds of ethical conflicts might arise because the American Red Cross relies so heavily on volunteers?
3. *For application:* What can the American Red Cross do to ensure that local chapters are properly applying its code of ethics?
4. *For application:* How might a nonprofit such as the American Red Cross gain a better understanding of its stakeholders' needs and preferences?
5. *For debate:* Should the American Red Cross have reversed its initial decision to divert some of the money donated for September 11 relief efforts to pressing but ancillary operations? Support your chosen position.

Online Exploration

Visit the American Red Cross site <www.redcross.org> and scan the headlines referring to the organization's response to recent disasters. Also look at the educational information available through links to news stories, feature articles, and other material. Next, carefully examine the variety of links addressing the needs and involvement of different stakeholder groups. What kinds of stakeholders does the American Red Cross expect to visit its Web site? Why are these stakeholders important to the organization? Do you think the organization should post its code of ethics prominently on this site? Explain your answer.

PART 2

Understanding the Business of Managing

CHAPTER

Managing the Business Enterprise

After reading this chapter, you should be able to:

1. Explain the importance of setting *goals* and formulating *strategies* as the starting points of effective management.
2. Describe the four activities that constitute the *management process*.
3. Identify *types of managers* by level and area.
4. Describe the five basic *management skills*.
5. Describe the development and explain the importance of *corporate culture*.

Yellow Delivers the Goods

Since its founding in 1923, Yellow Corporation <www.yellowcorp.com> has been a leader in the transportation industry, using trucks to haul goods between points in the United States, Canada, and Mexico. For decades, yellow achieved success by concentrating virtually all of its attention on increasing efficiency at every turn. Yellow has long been a master at ensuring that trucks are full before they leave a warehouse, and it has also developed precisely timed delivery schedules.

Ironically, Yellow eventually fell victim to its own success. As operational efficiency increased, customer service received less and less attention, and before long, newer and more responsive companies were luring away the firm's customers. Compounding this problem was the fact that the customers most likely to seek a more service-oriented transportation provider were also the ones willing to pay premium prices for the extra service. As a result, Yellow's financial performance began to decline, slowly at first, but then more dramatically. Naturally, the decline in revenue led to even worse across-the-board service.

To help turn Yellow around, the board of directors offered Bill Zollars the position of chief executive officer (CEO) in 1996. Already a highly respected manager, Zollars was intrigued by the opportunity to revitalize the carrier. "We were a defensive company—a follower, not a leader," recalls James Welch, president and chief operating officer. "We were yearning for leadership. This company was ready for change."

Zollars quickly learned that organizational change at Yellow would have to be profound. Over a period of decades, people throughout the company had come to accept mediocrity and were often willing to do only the minimal amount necessary to get their jobs done. Zollars knew that he had to alter the attitudes, behavior, and performance of 30,000 employees.

He began by improving communication. The CEO spent 18 months traveling to several hundred locations, and at each site, he talked face-to-face with customers and with employees at all levels. He asked for opinions and consistently provided his own message—namely, that enhanced customer service was to become the firm's new calling card.

Zollars' plan consisted of more than promises and motivational speeches. Whereas previous leaders often glossed over problems and refused to divulge information about the firm's performance, Zollars openly acknowledged the company's defect rate—the percentage of shipments that were late, wrong, or damaged. Employees were stunned to find that the rate was a whopping 40 percent, but that knowledge was necessary to enhance motivation and set a benchmark for improvement. Zollars also instituted the company's first ongoing program for surveying customer satisfaction, and the results were reported openly throughout the company. Zollars made a real effort to listen to employees, gave them authority to make decisions, and developed an enviable reputation for honesty and commitment. "If people doing the work don't believe what's coming from the leadership," says Zollars, "it doesn't get implemented. Period."

Our opening story continues on page 181

"We were a defensive company. We were yearning for leadership."

~James Welch
YELLOW CORP. COO

Who Are Managers?

All corporations depend on effective management. Regardless of whether they run a major international shipping business like Yellow or a small local or regional delivery company, they perform many of the same functions, are responsible for many of the same tasks, and have many of the same responsibilities. The work of all managers involves developing strategic and tactical plans. Along with numerous other things, they must analyze their competitive environments and plan, organize, direct, and control day-to-day operations.

Although our focus is on managers in *business* settings, remember that the principles of management apply to all kinds of organizations. Managers work in charities, churches, social organizations, educational institutions, and government agencies. The prime minister of Canada, curators at the Museum of Modern Art, the dean of your college, and the chief administrator of your local hospital are all managers. Remember, too, that managers bring to small organizations much the same kinds of skills—the ability to make decisions and respond to a variety of challenges—that they bring to large ones.

Regardless of the nature and size of an organization, managers are among its most important resources. Consider the profiles of the following three managers:

- Texas native Marjorie Scardino runs Pearson PLC <www.pearson.com>, a huge British media company. When she was named CEO, Pearson was considered a stodgy old-line company that had diversified into too many different areas. Scardino set about systematically pruning unrelated businesses and sharpening the firm's focus into three basic business groups. One group is heavily involved in educational publishing; the second operates the *Financial Times*, a leading business newspaper; and the third consists of the Penguin publishing group. The current economic climate has limited her ability to focus on additional growth and to look for new acquisitions. Instead, she is currently looking for ways to increase efficiency and lower costs. If she is successful, Pearson will be well positioned for new growth when economic conditions improve.[1]
- Kenneth Chenault is considered one of the best young senior managers around. He joined American Express <www.americanexpress.com> in 1981 as a marketing specialist and then systematically worked his way up the corporate ladder until he became president in 1997. During the next two years, Chenault presided over a major overhaul at AmEx as the firm sought to undo an ill-fated diversification strategy undertaken by a previous CEO. So impressive was Chenault's performance that in April 2001, he was named chairman and CEO of the company. Having reorganized a huge number of services into four core businesses—Global Financial Services, U.S. Consumer and Small Business Services, Global Corporate Services, and Global Establishment Services and Travelers Cheque Group—Chenault now has to show that AmEx can profitably service 52 million cardholders and 2.3 million financial services customers.[2]
- Twenty years ago, when he was running PepsiCo <www.pepsico.com>, Andrall Pearson was identified as one of the 10 toughest bosses in America. Much of that reputation was based on his ability to humiliate employees and to lead through fear and intimidation. Although he was credited with increasing the firm's revenues from less than $1 billion to over $8 billion, he was also vilified by almost everyone who worked for him. Today, however, Pearson runs Tricon Global Restaurants <www.triconglobal.com> (owners of KFC, Pizza Hut, and Taco Bell) with a much different approach. He remains demanding and results-oriented, but he has become much more concerned about the personal and professional welfare of his employees. Indeed, colleagues describe his current leadership style in terms of his warmth, energy, and charisma.[3]

Although Marjorie Scardino, Kenneth Chenault, and Andrall Pearson are clearly different people who work in different kinds of organizations and have different approaches to what they do, they also share one fundamental commonality with other high-level managers: responsibility for the performance and effectiveness of business enterprises. Thus, they are accountable to shareholders, employees, customers, and other key constituents. In this chapter, we describe the management process and the skills that managers must develop to perform their functions in organizations. Perhaps you will then have a better feel for the reasons why organizations value good managers so highly.

goal
Objective that a business hopes and plans to achieve

strategy
Broad set of organizational plans for implementing the decisions made for achieving organizational goals

corporate strategy
Strategy for determining the firm's overall attitude toward growth and the way it will manage its businesses or product lines

business (or competitive) strategy
Strategy, at the business-unit or product-line level, focusing on a firm's competitive position

functional strategy
Strategy by which managers in specific areas decide how best to achieve corporate goals through productivity

Setting Goals and Formulating Strategy

The starting point in effective management is setting **goals**—objectives that a business hopes and plans to achieve. Every business needs goals. We begin, therefore, by discussing the basic aspects of organizational goal setting. Remember, however, that deciding what it *intends* to do is only the first step for an organization. Managers must also make decisions about *actions* will and will not achieve company goals. Decisions cannot be made on a problem-by-problem basis or merely to meet needs as they arise. In most companies, a broad program underlies those decisions. That program is called a **strategy,** which is a broad set of organizational plans for implementing the decisions made for achieving organizational goals.

Types of Strategy

Figure 6.1 shows the relationship among the three types of strategy that are usually considered by a company:[4]

- The purpose of **corporate strategy** is to determine the firm's overall attitude toward growth and the way it will manage its businesses or product lines. A company may decide to *grow* by increasing its activities or investment or to *retrench* by reducing them. Under Kenneth Chenault, AmEx corporate strategy calls for strengthening operations through a principle of growth called e-partnering—buying shares of small companies that can provide technology that AmEx itself does not have.
- **Business (or competitive) strategy,** which takes place at the level of the business unit or product line, focuses on improving the company's competitive position. At this level, AmEx makes decisions about how best to compete in an industry that includes Visa, MasterCard, and other credit card companies. In this respect, the company has committed heavily to expanding its product offerings and serving customers through new technology.
- At the level of **functional strategy,** managers in specific areas decide how best to achieve corporate goals by being as productive as possible. At AmEx, each business unit has considerable autonomy in deciding how to use the single Web site at which the company has located its entire range of services.

We will complete this section by detailing the basic steps in strategy formulation.

FIGURE 6.1
Hierarchy of Strategy

Setting Business Goals

Goals are performance targets—the means by which organizations and their managers measure success or failure at every level. For example, Marjorie Scardino's goals at Pearson are currently tied to cost reductions and improved profitability; in the future, she will likely focus more on growth. At AmEx, however, Kenneth Chenault is focusing more on revenue growth and the firm's stock price. Andrall Pearson's goals, meanwhile, focus generally on motivating lower-wage workers in a highly competitive business environment while simultaneously leading a major global expansion.

Purposes of Goal Setting An organization functions systematically because it sets goals and plans accordingly. An organization commits its resources on all levels to achieving its goals. Specifically, we can identify four main purposes in organizational goal setting:

1. ***Goal setting provides direction and guidance for managers at all levels.*** If managers know precisely where the company is headed, there is less potential for error in the different units of the company. Starbucks, for example, has a goal of increasing capital spending by 15 percent, with all additional expenditures devoted to opening new stores. This goal clearly informs everyone in the firm that expansion into new territories is a high priority for the firm.
2. ***Goal setting helps firms allocate resources. Areas that are expected to grow will get first priority.*** The company allocates more resources to new projects with large sales potential than it allocates to mature products with established but stagnant sales potential. Thus, Starbucks is primarily emphasizing new store expansion, while its e-commerce initiatives are currently given a lower priority. "Our management team," says CEO Howard Schultz, "is 100% focused on growing our core business without distraction . . . from any other initiative."
3. ***Goal setting helps to define corporate culture.*** For years, the goal at General Electric <www.ge.com> has been to push each of its divisions to first or second in its industry. The result is a competitive (and often stressful) environment and a culture that rewards success and has little tolerance for failure. At the same time, however, GE's appliance business, television network (NBC), aircraft engine unit, and financial services business are each among the very best in their respective industries. Eventually, former CEO Jack Welch set an even higher companywide standard—to make the firm the most valuable in the world.
4. ***Goal setting helps managers assess performance.*** If a unit sets a goal of increasing sales by 10 percent in a given year, managers in that unit who attain or exceed the goal can be rewarded. Units failing to reach the goal will also be compensated accordingly. GE has a long-standing reputation for stringently evaluating managerial performance, richly rewarding those who excel—and getting rid of those who do not. Each year, the lower 10 percent of GE's managerial force are informed that either they make dramatic improvements in performance or consider alternative directions for their careers.

"Our management team is 100% focused on growing our core business without distraction from any other initiative."

~Howard Schultz, CEO OF STARBUCKS

Kinds of Goals Goals differ from company to company, depending on the firm's purpose and mission. Every enterprise has a *purpose,* or a reason for being. Businesses seek profits, universities seek to discover and transmit new knowledge, and government agencies seek to set and enforce public policy. Many enterprises also have missions and **mission statements**—statements of how they will achieve their purposes in the environments in which they conduct their businesses.

mission statement

Organization's statement of how it will achieve its purpose in the environment in which it conducts its business

A company's mission is usually easy to identify, at least at a basic level. Dell Computer <www.dell.com>, for example, set out to make a profit by selling personal computers directly to consumers. In San Francisco, Platinum Concepts Inc. <www.mousedriver.com> intends to become profitable by developing "unique and innovative products." So far, the company's only product is the MouseDriver, a computer mouse shaped like the head of a golf club, but it expected to sell $1 million worth of MouseDrivers in 2002.[5]

Businesses often have to rethink their missions as the competitive environment changes. In 1999, for example, Starbucks announced that Internet marketing and sales were going to become core business initiatives. Managers subsequently realized, however, that this initiative did not fit the firm as well as they first thought. As a result, they scaled back this effort and, as we noted, made a clear recommitment to their existing retail business. The demands of change force many companies to rethink their missions and thus revise their statements of what they are and what they do. (We discuss more fully the problems in managing change—as well as some solutions—later in this chapter.)

At many companies, top management drafts and circulates detailed mission statements. Because such a statement reflects a company's understanding of its activities as a *marketer,* it is not easily described. Consider the similarities and differences between Timex and Rolex. Although both firms share a common purpose—to sell watches at a profit—they have very different missions. Timex <www.timex.com> sells low-cost, reliable watches in outlets ranging from department stores to corner drugstores. Rolex <www.rolex.com> sells high-quality, high-priced watches through selected jewelry stores.

Regardless of a company's purpose and mission, however, every firm has long-term, intermediate, and short-term goals:

- **Long-term goals** relate to extended periods of time, typically five years or more. For example, American Express might set a long-term goal of doubling the number of participating merchants during the next 10 years. Kodak might adopt a long-term goal of increasing its share of the 35mm film market by 10 percent during the next eight years.

long-term goal
Goal set for an extended time, typically five years or more into the future

- **Intermediate goals** are set for a period of one to five years. Companies usually set intermediate goals in several areas. For example, the marketing department's goal might be to increase sales by 3 percent in two years. The production department might want to reduce expenses by 6 percent in four years. Human resources might seek to cut turnover by 10 percent in two years. Finance might aim for a 3-percent increase in return on investment in three years.

intermediate goal
Goal set for a period of one to five years into the future

- **Short-term goals** are set for perhaps one year and are developed for several different areas. Increasing sales by 2 percent this year, cutting costs by 1 percent next quarter, and reducing turnover by 4 percent over the next six months are examples of short-term goals.

short-term goal
Goal set for the very near future, typically less than one year

Formulating Strategy

Planning is often concerned with the nuts and bolts of setting goals, choosing tactics, and establishing schedules. In contrast, strategy tends to have a wider scope. It is by definition a broad program that describes an organization's intentions. A business strategy outlines how the business intends to meet its goals and includes the organization's responsiveness to new challenges and new needs. Because a well-formulated strategy is so vital to a business's success, most top managers devote substantial attention and creativity to this process. **Strategy formulation** involves the three basic steps summarized in Figure 6.2.[6]

strategy formulation
Creation of a broad program for defining and meeting an organization's goals

It is interesting to note at least one change in contemporary thinking about the role of strategy. Once the responsibility of top management, strategy made its

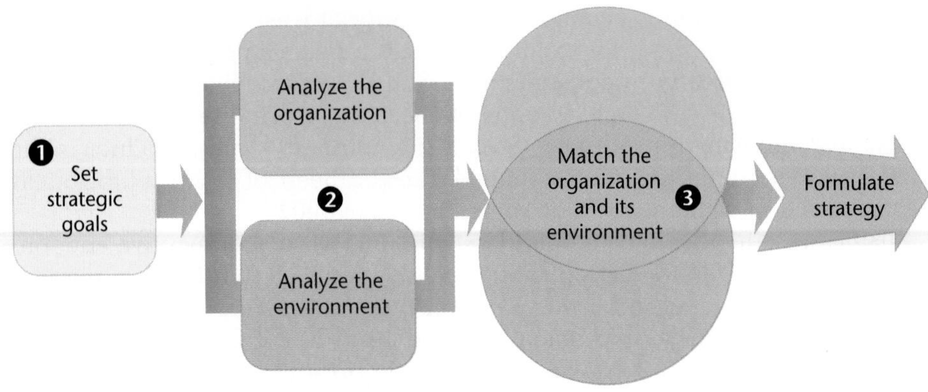

FIGURE 6.2
Strategy Formulation

way into the everyday world of setting and implementing goals (planning) by means of a fairly rigid top-down process. Today, however, strategy formulation in many organizations is often a much more inclusive process involving people from throughout the organization.

strategic goal
Long-term goal derived directly from a firm's mission statement

Setting Strategic Goals Described as long-term goals, **strategic goals** are derived directly from a firm's mission statement. For example, Ferdinand Piëch, CEO of Volkswagen <www.vw.com>, has clear strategic goals for the European carmaker. When he took over in 1993, Volkswagen was only marginally profitable, was regarded as an also-ran in the industry, and was thinking about pulling out of the U.S. market altogether because its sales were so poor. Over the next few years, however, Piëch totally revamped the firm and has it making big profits. Volkswagen is now a much more formidable force in the global automobile industry. It competes with Toyota for the number-three spot in the industry (behind only General Motors and Ford), but Piëch is clearly not finished. "For the moment," he reports, "we are happy with the bronze medal. But we want to step up."[7]

SWOT
Identification and analysis of organizational strengths and weaknesses and environmental opportunities and threats as part of strategy formulation

SWOT Analysis After strategic goals have been established, organizations usually go through a process called a **SWOT** analysis as they continue to formulate their strategy. This process involves assessing organizational strengths and weaknesses (the *S* and *W*) and environmental opportunities and threats (the *O* and *T*). In formulating strategy, they then attempt to capitalize on organizational strengths and take advantage of environmental opportunities. During this same process, they may seek ways to overcome or offset organizational weaknesses and avoid or counter environmental threats.[8]

environmental analysis
Process of scanning the business environment for threats and opportunities

Analyzing the Organization and Its Environment Scanning the environment for threats and opportunities is often called **environmental analysis.** Changing consumer tastes and fighting hostile takeover offers are *threats,* as are new government regulations that will limit a firm's opportunities. Even more important threats come from new products and new competitors. *Opportunities,* meanwhile, are areas in which the firm can potentially expand, grow, or take advantage of existing strengths.

Consider the case of British entrepreneur Sir Richard Branson and his company, Virgin Group Ltd. <www.virgin.com>. Branson started the firm in 1968, when he was 17, naming it in acknowledgment of his own lack of experience in the business world. Over the years, he has built Virgin into one of the world's best-known brands, comprising a conglomeration of over 200 entertainment, media, and travel companies worldwide. Among the best known of his enterprises are Virgin Atlantic (an international airline), Virgin Megastores (retailing), and V2 Music (record labels). Branson sees potential threats in the form of other competitors, such as British Airways and KLM for Virgin Atlantic, Tower Records (retailing), and the EMI Group (recorded music).

He also sees significant opportunities because of his firm's strong brand name (especially in Europe). One of his most recent ventures is a new e-commerce firm. The business is called Virgin Mobile <www.virginmobile.com> and operates like a cellular telephone company. But in addition to providing conventional cellular service, the Virgin telephone permits the user to press a red button to go directly to a Virgin operator who can sell products, make airline and hotel reservations, and provide numerous other services. A companion Web site also complements the cellular service and its related programs. Virgin Mobile signed up more than a million new customers during its first year of operation and is now one of the market leaders in Great Britain.[9]

In addition to performing an environmental analysis, which is an analysis of *external* factors, managers must also examine *internal* factors. The purpose of **organizational analysis** is to better understand a company's strengths and weaknesses. Strengths might include surplus cash, a dedicated workforce, an ample supply of managerial talent, technical expertise, or little competition. A cash shortage, aging factories, a heavily unionized workforce, and a poor public image can all be important weaknesses.

organizational analysis
Process of analyzing a firm's strengths and weaknesses

Branson, for example, started Virgin Mobile in part because he saw so many of his current operations as old-line, traditional businesses that might be at future risk from new forms of business and competition. One strength he employs is the widespread name recognition his businesses enjoy. Another relates to finances. He sold 49 percent of Virgin Atlantic to Singapore Airlines <www.singaporeair.com> for almost $1 billion in cash, retaining ownership control but raising funds he needed to launch his new venture. On the other hand, he also admits that neither he nor many of his senior managers have much experience in or knowledge about e-commerce, which may be a significant weakness.

Matching the Organization and Its Environment The final step in strategy formulation is matching environmental threats and opportunities against corporate strengths and weaknesses. This matching process is at the heart of strategy formulation. More than any other facet of strategy, matching companies with their environments lays the foundation for successfully planning and conducting business.

Over the long term, this process may also determine whether a firm typically takes risks or behaves more conservatively. Either strategy can be successful. Blue Bell <www.bluebell.com>, for example, is one of the most profitable ice-cream makers in the world, even though it sells its products in only about a dozen states. Based in Brenham, Texas, Blue Bell controls more than 50 percent of the market in each state where it does business. The firm, however, has resisted the temptation to expand too quickly. Its success is based on product freshness and frequent deliveries—strengths that may suffer if the company grows too large.

A Hierarchy of Plans Plans can be viewed on three levels: strategic, tactical, and operational. Managerial responsibilities are defined at each level. The levels constitute a hierarchy because implementing plans is practical only when there is a logical flow from one level to the next.

- **Strategic plans** reflect decisions about resource allocations, company priorities, and the steps needed to meet strategic goals. They are usually created by the firm's top management team but, as noted earlier, often rely on input from others in the organization. General Electric's decision that viable businesses must rank first or second within their respective markets is a matter of strategic planning.

strategic plan
Plan reflecting decisions about resource allocations, company priorities, and steps needed to meet strategic goals

tactical plan
Generally short-range plan concerned with implementing specific aspects of a company's strategic plans

operational plan
Plan setting short-term targets for daily, weekly, or monthly performance

- **Tactical plans** are shorter range plans for implementing specific aspects of the company's strategic plans. They typically involve upper and middle management. Coca-Cola's decision to increase sales in Europe by building European bottling facilities is an example of tactical planning.
- **Operational plans,** which are developed by midlevel and lower level managers, set short-term targets for daily, weekly, or monthly performance. McDonald's, for example, establishes operational plans when it explains to franchisees precisely how Big Macs are to be cooked, warmed, and served.

Contingency Planning and Crisis Management

Because business environments are often difficult to predict and because the unexpected can create major problems, most managers recognize that even the best-laid plans sometimes simply do not work out. For instance, when the Walt Disney Co. <www.disney.go.com> announced plans to launch a cruise line replete with familiar Disney characters and themes, managers also began aggressively developing and marketing packages linking three- and four-day cruises with visits to Disney World in Florida. Indeed, the inaugural sailing was sold out more than a year in advance, and the first year was booked solid six months before the ship was launched. Three months before the first sailing, however, the shipyard constructing Disney's first ship (the *Disney Magic*) notified the company that it was behind schedule and that delivery would be several weeks late. When similar problems befall other cruise lines, they can offer to rebook passengers on alternative itineraries. But because Disney had no other ship, it had no choice but to refund the money it had collected as prebooking deposits for its first 15 cruises.

The 20,000 displaced customers were offered big discounts if they rebooked on a later cruise. Many of them, however, could not rearrange their schedules and requested full refunds. Moreover, quite a few blamed Disney for the problem, and a few expressed outrage at what they saw as poor planning by the entertainment giant. Fortunately for Disney, however, the *Disney Magic* was eventually launched and has now become very popular and very profitable.[10]

Because managers know such things can happen, they often develop alternative plans in case things go awry. Two common methods of dealing with the unknown and unforeseen are *contingency planning* and *crisis management.*

contingency planning
Identifying aspects of a business or its environment that might entail changes in strategy

Contingency Planning

Contingency planning recognizes the need to find solutions to specific aspects of a problem. By its very nature, a contingency plan is a hedge against changes that might occur. **Contingency planning,** then, is planning for change: It seeks to identify in advance important aspects of a business or its market that might change. It also identifies the ways in which a company will respond to changes. Today, many companies use computer programs for contingency planning.

Suppose, for example, that a company develops a plan to create a new division. It expects sales to increase at an annual rate of 10 percent for the next five years, and it develops a marketing strategy for maintaining that level. But suppose that sales have increased by only 5 percent by the end of the first year. Does the firm abandon the venture, invest more in advertising, or wait to see what happens in the second year? Any of these alternatives is possible. Regardless of the firm's choice, however, its efforts will be more efficient if managers decide in advance what to do in case sales fall below planned levels. Contingency planning helps them do exactly that. Disney learned from its mistake with its first ship, and when the second (the *Disney Wonder*) was launched a year later, managers did several things differently. For one thing, they allowed for an extra two weeks between when the ship was supposed to be ready for sailing and its first scheduled cruise. They also held open a few cabins on the *Disney Magic* as a backup for any especially disgruntled customers who might need accommodations if there were unexpected delays in the launching of the *Disney Wonder.*

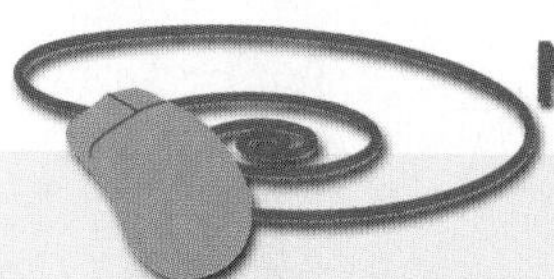

Mid-Chapter Internet Field Trip

"Do You Yahoo?"

So far, this chapter has described some of the challenges of managing a business and highlighted the kinds of skills and strategies that help managers meet those challenges. Goal setting and planning are critical elements at every stage of the business life cycle, as are organizing, directing, and controlling performance.

Let's see at how a highly successful Internet firm, Yahoo!, handles the management process by exploring the portion of its Web site dedicated to company information, at <http://docs.yahoo.com/info/>. Yahoo! was the first online navigational guide to the Web and is now the leader in traffic, advertising, and household and business reach. It's also the most recognized and valuable Internet brand in the world, reaching over 237 million users in 25 countries and 13 languages. You'll notice that Yahoo!'s information home page contains several categories:

- Employment Opportunities
- Press Room
- Speakers' Bureau
- Investor Relations
- Advertising Opportunities
- Business Opportunities
- Privacy Center and Others

Start at the home page (don't confuse this page with the home page for Yahoo!'s popular search engine) and select **Press Room** and then **Company History:**

❶ How old is Yahoo!, and how was it started?

Continue to read the **Company History** page:

❷ Who were among the earliest hires at the fast-growing firm, and what do you think they brought to Yahoo! that founders Filo and Yang found attractive?

Return to the **Press Room** page and select **Management Team:**

❸ Who is the current chief executive officer, and what does he or she do?

Return to the **Press Room** page and select **FAQs:**

❹ How many different types of businesses and services does Yahoo! provide?

Return once more to the **Press Room** page, click on **The World of Yahoo!,** and scroll down to **World Yahoo's!:**

❺ Take a quick look at several of Yahoo!'s international sites (choose any that interest you). What do you notice about the similarities among these sites? What do these similarities suggest about the nature of Yahoo!'s corporate strategy?

To continue your Internet Field Trip, click on www.prenhall.com/griffin

Crisis Management A crisis is an unexpected emergency requiring immediate response. **Crisis management** involves an organization's methods for dealing with emergencies. The tragic events of September 11, 2001, clearly served to underscore the importance of crisis management. In addition to the horrific loss of human life, virtually every business in the United States experienced direct or indirect financial costs. For example, because all U.S. airlines were shut down for several days and air traffic was slow to return, they lost billions of dollars. The ripple effects lasted for months, resulting in, among other things, the bankruptcy of U.S. Airways and major cutbacks at American Airlines in mid-2002.

crisis management
Organization's methods for dealing with emergencies

But other businesses were also affected. Tourist destinations like Disney World and resort hotels lost customers. Because fewer people traveled in the months after September 11, profits also declined at restaurants, car rental agencies, and gasoline retailers. Broadway shows in New York sold fewer tickets, and shaken consumers across the country delayed major purchases and withdrew funds from their banks. Shipping companies like FedEx and UPS found it necessary to subject cargo to more intense (and costly) security screenings. And many people simply stayed home for a few days after that tragic day, resulting in lost work time and a drop in productivity.

As a result of September 11, more firms than ever before have developed crisis management plans. For example, both Reliant Energy <www.reliantenergy.com> and Duke Energy <www.duke-energy.com> rely on computer trading centers where trading managers actively buy and sell energy-related commodities. If a terrorist attack or natural disaster such as a hurricane were to strike their trading

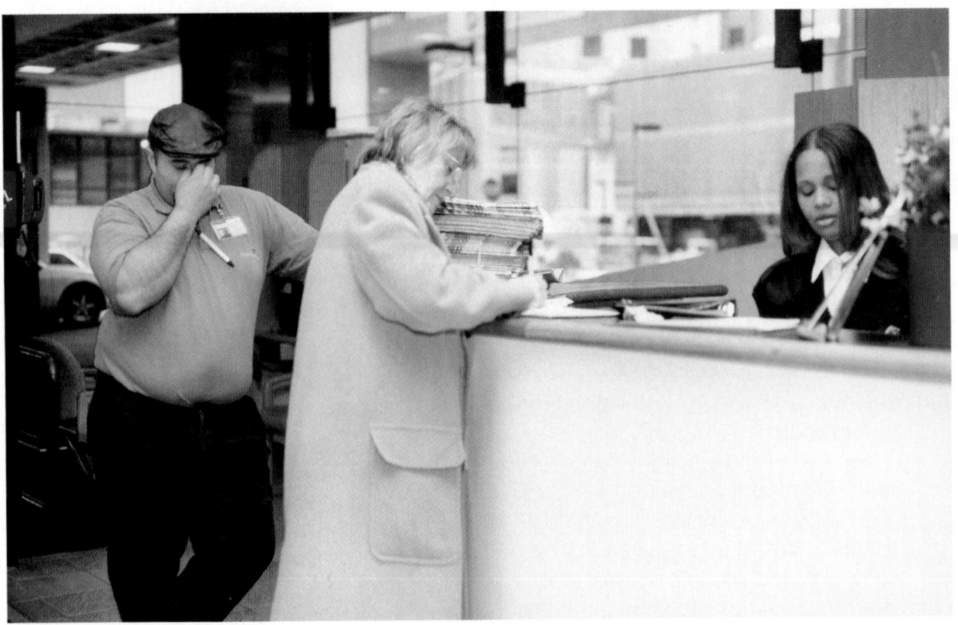

It's a problem that neither Filterfresh <www.filterfresh.com>*, a national coffee distributor, nor delivery man Rusty Pasquale could have predicted. Since 9/11, Pasquale can no longer simply enter clients' buildings and do his job. Security measures have added an hour to Pasquale's route and that of every company driver. Nationwide, reports Filterfresh, the slowdown adds up to 1,250 hours per week that have to be filled by an additional 24 delivery people. "That's a 10-percent increase in our labor costs, just so we can hold our ground," says a company manager.*

centers, they would essentially be out of business. Prior to September 11, each firm had relatively vague and superficial crisis plans. But now they and most other companies have much more detailed and comprehensive plans in the event of another crisis. Both Reliant and Duke, for example, have created secondary trading centers at other locations. In the event of a shutdown at their main trading centers, these firms can quickly transfer virtually all of their core trading activities to their secondary centers within 30 minutes or less. Unfortunately, however, because it is impossible to forecast the future precisely, no organization can ever be perfectly prepared for every eventuality.

Self-Check Questions 1–3

*You should now be able to answer Self-Check Questions 1–3**

1. MULTIPLE CHOICE Which of the following is **not** a basic purpose served by *goal setting*? [select one] **(a)** Goals show the government what the firm hopes to achieve. **(b)** Goals set direction and guidance. **(c)** Goals help direct resource allocation. **(c)** Goals help define corporate culture. **(e)** Goals help managers assess performance.

2. TRUE/FALSE Although organizations need to set *long-term, intermediate,* and *short-term goals,* there is little relationship among these three kinds of goals.

3. MULTIPLE CHOICE Which of the following is a *contingency plan*? [select one] **(a)** scheduling supply orders; **(b)** placing an ad to hire new employees; **(c)** creating a new advertising campaign; **(d)** deciding which division to sell if the firm runs short of cash; **(e)** all of these.

*Answers to Self-Check Questions 1–3 can be found on p. AN-4.

The Management Process

Management is the process of planning, organizing, directing, and controlling an organization's financial, physical, human, and information resources to achieve its goals. Managers oversee the use of all these resources in their respective firms. All aspects of a manager's job are interrelated. In fact, any given manager is likely to be engaged in each of these activities during the course of any given day.

management
Process of planning, organizing, directing, and controlling an organization's resources to achieve its goals

Planning

Determining what the organization needs to do and how best to get it done requires planning. **Planning** has three main components. As we have seen, it begins when managers determine the firm's goals. Next, they develop a comprehensive strategy for achieving those goals. After a strategy is developed, they design tactical and operational plans for implementing the strategy.

planning
Management process of determining what an organization needs to do and how best to get it done

When Yahoo! <www.yahoo.com> was created, for example, the firm's top managers set a strategic goal of becoming a top firm in the then-emerging market for Internet search engines. But then came the hard part—figuring out how to do it. They started by assessing the ways in which people actually use the Web and concluded that users wanted to be able to satisfy a wide array of needs, preferences, and priorities by going to as few sites as possible to find what they were looking for.

Thus, one key component of Yahoo!'s strategy was to foster partnerships and relationships with other companies so that potential Web surfers could draw upon several sources through a single portal—which would be Yahoo!. Thus, the goal of partnering emerged as one set of tactical plans for moving forward. Yahoo! managers then began fashioning alliances with such diverse partners as Reuters <www.reuters.com>, Standard & Poor's <www.standardpoor.com>, and the Associated Press <www.ap.org> (for news coverage), RE/Max <www.remax.com> (for real estate information), and a wide array of information providers specializing in sports, weather, entertainment, shopping, and travel. The creation of individual partnership agreements with each of these partners represents a form of operational planning.

Organizing

Once one of the leading-edge high-tech firms in the world, Hewlett-Packard <www.hewlett-packard.com> began to lose some of its luster a few years ago. Ironically, one of the major reasons for its slide could be traced back to what had once been a major strength. Specifically, HP had long prided itself on being little more than a corporate confederation of individual businesses. Sometimes, these businesses even ended up competing among themselves. This approach had been beneficial for much of the firm's history: It was easier for each business to make its own decisions quickly and efficiently, and the competition kept each unit on its toes. By the late 1990s, however, problems had become apparent, and no one could quite figure out what was going on.

Enter Ann Livermore, then head of the firm's software and services business. Livermore realized that the structure that had served so well in the past was now holding the firm back. To regain its competitive edge, HP needed an integrated, organizationwide Internet strategy. Unfortunately, the company's highly decentralized organization made that impossible. Livermore led the charge to create one organization to drive a single Internet plan. "I felt we could be the most powerful company in the industry," she said, "if we could get our hardware, software, and services aligned." Eventually, a new team of top managers was handed control of the company, and every major component of the firm's structure was reorganized. Today, under the leadership of CEO Carly Fiorina and with its acquisition of Compaq Computer, HP is showing signs of recreating the magic of its early years.[11]

This process—determining the best way to arrange a business's resources and activities into a coherent structure—is called **organizing.** (We explore this topic further in Chapter 7.)

organizing

Management process of determining how best to arrange an organization's resources and activities into a coherent structure

Directing

directing

Management process of guiding and motivating employees to meet an organization's objectives

Managers have the power to give orders and demand results. Directing, however, involves more complex activities. When **directing,** a manager works to guide and motivate employees to meet the firm's objectives. Andrall Pearson, for example, has clearly changed his entire approach to directing employees. Gordon Bethune, CEO of Continental Airlines <www.continental.com>, is an excellent example of a manager who excels at motivating his employees. When he took the helm of the troubled carrier in 1994, morale was dismal, most employees hated their jobs, and the company's performance was among the worst in the industry.

Almost immediately, Bethune started listening to his employees to learn about their problems and to hear how they thought the company could be improved. He also began to reward everyone when things went well and continued communicating with all Continental employees on a regular basis. Today, the firm is ranked among the best in the industry and is regularly identified as one of the best places to work in the United States. In both 2000 and 2001, Continental was named the highest quality airline in the United States, based on the J.D. Powers Survey of Customer Satisfaction.[12]

Controlling

controlling

Management process of monitoring an organization's performance to ensure that it is meeting its goals

Controlling is the process of monitoring a firm's performance to make sure that the firm is meeting its goals. All CEOs must pay close attention to costs and performance. Indeed, skillful controlling, like innovative directing, is one reason that Gordon Bethune has been so successful at Continental. For example, the firm focuses almost relentlessly on numerous indicators of performance that can be constantly measured and adjusted. Everything from on-time arrivals to baggage-handling errors to the number of empty seats on an airplane to surveys of employee and customer satisfaction are regularly and routinely monitored. If on-time arrivals start to slip, Bethune focuses on the problem and gets it fixed. If a manager's subordinates provide less than glowing reviews, that manager loses

As field boss of the New York Yankees < www.yankees.com>, Joe Torre has managed (since 1996) to hold on to a slippery job (the team has had 21 managers in 25 years). Of course, he's won 4 World Series in a 7-year stretch, and by most accounts, Torre's success stems from his ability as a motivator. He prefers one-on-one dealings with "subordinates" (multimillion-dollar baseball players), and he sees no reason to punish failure (which is a routine pitfall of a baseball player's job). Many observers—including Torre's boss, George Steinbrenner—think that his approach would be effective in a business setting.

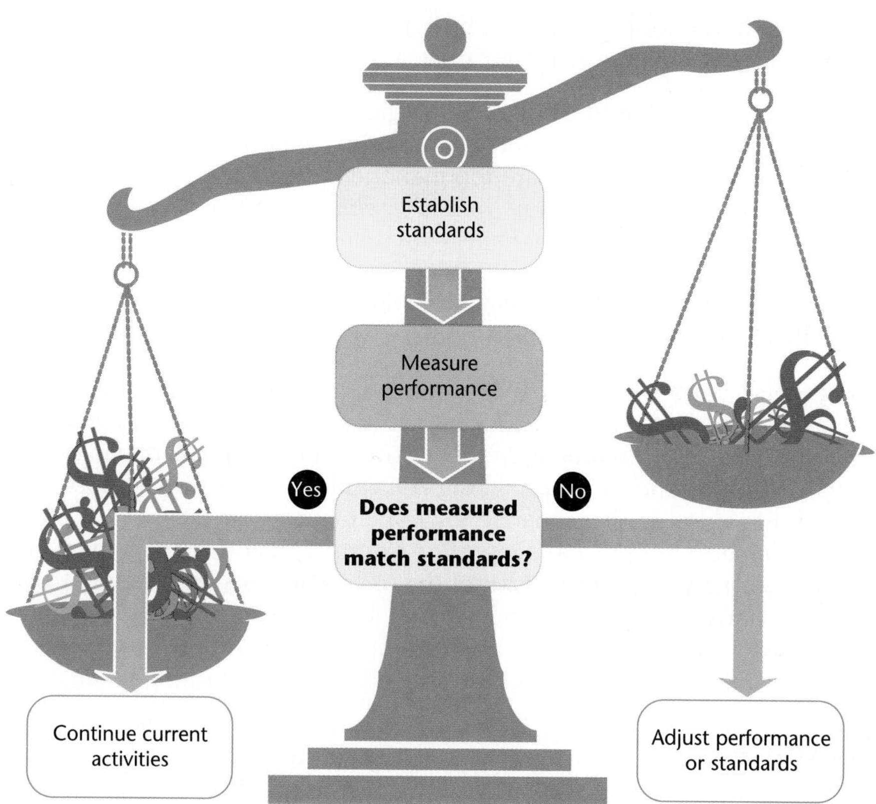

FIGURE 6.3
The Control Process

part of his or her bonus. As a result, no single element of the firm's performance can slip too far before it's noticed and fixed.

Figure 6.3 illustrates the control process that begins when management establishes standards, often for financial performance. If, for example, a company wants to increase sales by 20 percent over the next 10 years, then an appropriate standard might be an increase of about 2 percent a year.

Managers then measure actual performance against standards. If the two amounts agree, the organization continues along its present course. If they vary significantly, however, one or the other needs adjustment. If sales have increased 2.1 percent by the end of the first year, things are probably fine. If sales have dropped 1 percent, some revision in plans may be needed. Perhaps the original goal should be lowered or more money should be spent on advertising.

Control can also show where performance is running better than expected and, thus, can serve as a basis for providing rewards or reducing costs. For example, when Ford recently introduced the new Explorer SportsTrac (an SUV with a pickup bed), initial sales were so strong that the firm was able to delay a major advertising campaign for three months because it was selling all of the vehicles it could make anyway.

Types of Managers

Although all managers plan, organize, direct, and control, not all managers have the same degree of responsibility for these activities. Thus, it is helpful to classify managers according to levels and areas of responsibility.

Levels of Management

The three basic levels of management are *top, middle,* and *first-line management.* Most firms have more middle managers than top managers and more first-line managers than middle managers. Both the power of managers and the complexity of their duties increase as they move up the ladder.

top manager
Manager responsible to the board of directors and stockholders for a firm's overall performance and effectiveness

Top Managers Like Marjorie Scardino, Kenneth Chenault, and Andrall Pearson, the fairly small number of executives who get the chance to guide the fortunes of most companies are **top managers.** Common titles for top managers include *president, vice president, treasurer, chief executive officer* (*CEO*), and *chief financial officer* (*CFO*). Top managers are responsible for the overall performance and effectiveness of the firm. They set general policies, formulate strategies, approve all significant decisions, and represent the company in dealings with other firms and with government bodies.

middle manager
Manager responsible for implementing the strategies, policies, and decisions made by top managers

Middle Managers Just below the ranks of top managers is another group of managers who also occupy positions of considerable autonomy and importance and who are called **middle managers.** Titles such as *plant manager, operations manager,* and *division manager* designate middle-management slots. In general, middle managers are responsible for implementing the strategies, policies, and decisions made by top managers. For example, if top management decides to introduce a new product in 12 months or to cut costs by 5 percent in the next quarter, middle management must decide how to meet these goals. The manager of an American Express service center, a Pearson distribution center, or a regional collection of Tricon restaurants will likely be a middle manager.

first-line manager
Manager responsible for supervising the work of employees

First-Line Managers Those who hold such titles as *supervisor, office manager,* and *group leader* are **first-line managers.** Although they spend most of their time working with and supervising the employees who report to them, first-line managers' activities are not limited to that arena. At a building site, for example, the project manager not only ensures that workers are carrying out construction as specified by the architect, but also interacts extensively with materials suppliers, community officials, and middle- and upper-level managers at the home office. A sales manager for Pearson's Educational Publishing Group and the manager for an individual Taco Bell outlet would also be considered first-line managers.

Areas of Management

In any large company, top, middle, and first-line managers work in a variety of areas, including *human resources, operations, marketing, information,* and *finance.* For the most part, these areas correspond to the types of basic management skills described later in this chapter and to the wide range of business principles and activities discussed in the rest of this book.

Human Resource Managers Most companies have *human resource managers* who hire and train employees, who evaluate performance, and who determine compensation. At large firms, separate departments deal with recruiting and hiring, wage and salary levels, and labor relations. A smaller firm may have a single department—or a single person—responsible for all human resource activities. (We discuss some key issues in human resource management in Chapter 8.)

Operations Managers As we will see in Chapter 14, the term *operations* refers to the systems by which a firm produces goods and services. Among other duties, operations managers are responsible for production, inventory, and quality control. Manufacturing companies such as Texas Instruments, Ford, and Caterpillar have a strong need for operations managers at many levels. Such firms typically have a *vice president for operations* (top), *plant managers* (middle), and *production supervisors* (first-line managers). In recent years, sound operations management practices have become increasingly important to a variety of service organizations.

Marketing Managers As we will see in Chapter 10, marketing encompasses the development, pricing, promotion, and distribution of goods and services. Marketing managers are responsible for getting products from producers to consumers. Marketing is especially important for firms that manufacture consumer products, such as Procter & Gamble, Coca-Cola, and Levi Strauss. Such firms often have large numbers of marketing managers at several levels. For example, a large consumer products firm is likely to have a *vice president for marketing* (top), several *regional marketing managers* (middle), and several *district sales managers* (first-line managers). (The different areas of marketing are discussed in Part 3.)

Information Managers Occupying a fairly new managerial position in many firms, information managers design and implement systems to gather, organize, and distribute information. Huge increases in both the sheer volume of information and the ability to manage it have led to the emergence of this important function.

Although relatively few in number, the ranks of *information managers* are growing at all levels. Some firms have a top-management position called a *chief information officer (CIO)*. Middle managers help design information systems for divisions or plants. Computer systems managers within smaller businesses are usually first-line managers. (Information management is discussed in more detail in Chapter 16.)

Financial Managers Nearly every company has financial managers to plan and oversee its accounting functions and financial resources. Levels of financial management may include *chief financial officer* (*CFO*) or *vice president for finance* (top), a *division controller* (middle), and an *accounting supervisor* (first-line manager). Some institutions—NationsBank <www.nationsbank.com> and Prudential <www.prudential.com>, for example—have even made effective financial management the company's reason for being. (Financial management is treated in more detail in Part 5.)

Other Managers Some firms also employ other specialized managers. Many companies, for example, have public relations managers. Chemical and pharmaceutical companies such as Monsanto <www.pharmacia.com> and Merck <www.merck.com> have research and development managers. The range of possibilities is wide, and the areas of management are limited only by the needs and imagination of the firm.

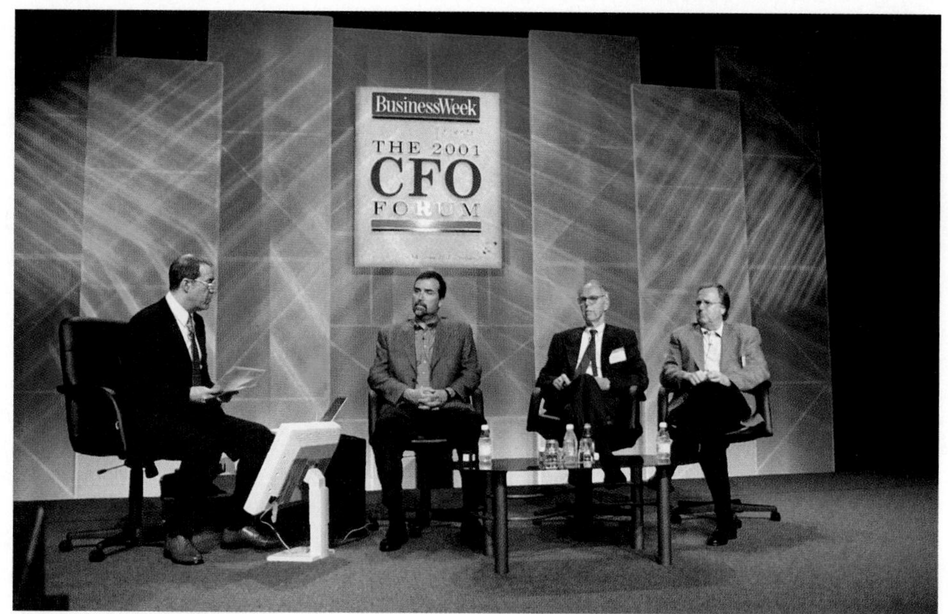

At Business Week's annual CFO Forum, the chief financial officers of such companies as GE Capital, Toysrus.com, and Oracle Corp. stressed the fact that the CFO is no longer just a high-ranking numbers cruncher. In a world that's constantly being changed by technology, today's CFO plays a key role in so-called "e-transformation," especially in evaluating new technologies as investment opportunities and figuring out how to finance new business models.

Self-Check Questions 4–6

*You should now be able to answer Self-Check Questions 4–6**

4. MULTIPLE CHOICE Which of the following activities is **not** part of the *management process*? [select one] **(a)** planning; **(b)** organizing; **(c)** coordinating; **(d)** leading; **(e)** controlling.

5. TRUE/FALSE In general, there are three basic *levels of management* in most organizations.

6. MULTIPLE CHOICE Which of the following is a basic *area of management*? [select one] **(a)** human resources; **(b)** operations; **(c)** marketing; **(d)** finance; **(e)** all of these.

*ANSWERS TO SELF-CHECK QUESTIONS 4–6 CAN BE FOUND ON P. AN-4.

Basic Management Skills

Although the range of managerial positions is almost limitless, the success that people enjoy in those positions is often limited by their skills and abilities. Effective managers must develop *technical, human relations, conceptual, decision-making,* and *time management skills.* Unfortunately, these skills are quite complex, and it is the rare manager who excels in every area.

Technical Skills

technical skills
Skills needed to perform specialized tasks

The skills needed to perform specialized tasks are called **technical skills.** A programmer's ability to write code, an animator's ability to draw, and an accountant's ability to audit a company's records are all examples of technical skills. People develop technical skills through a combination of education and experience. Technical skills are especially important for first-line managers. Many of these managers spend considerable time helping employees solve work-related problems, training them in more efficient procedures, and monitoring performance.

Human Relations Skills

human relations skills
Skills in understanding and getting along with people

Effective managers also generally have good **human relations skills**—specifically, skills that enable them to understand and get along with other people. A manager with poor human relations skills may have trouble getting along with subordinates, cause valuable employees to quit or transfer, and contribute to poor morale. Today, Andrall Pearson works well with people, has fun when he works, and makes everyone feel excited about the work. He also genuinely cares about the welfare of his employees. So, too, does Gordon Bethune, who routinely visits his employees throughout the company. Reports one baggage manager at Continental's Newark, New Jersey, hub: "Anybody who's worked here longer than two months can recognize Gordon."

Although human relations skills are important at all levels, they are probably most important for middle managers, who must often act as bridges between top managers, first-line managers, and managers from other areas of the organiza-

"I like to think of myself as a nice guy. Naturally, sometimes you have to step on a few faces."

tion. Managers should possess good communication skills. Many managers have found that being able both to understand others and to get others to understand them can go a long way toward maintaining good relations in an organization.[13]

"Anybody who's worked here longer than two months can recognize Gordon."

~Baggage manager at Continental's Newark, New Jersey, hub, on the airline's CEO, Gordon Bethune

Conceptual Skills

Conceptual skills refer to a person's ability to think in the abstract, to diagnose and analyze different situations, and to see beyond the present situation. Conceptual skills help managers recognize new market opportunities and threats. They can also help managers analyze the probable outcomes of their decisions. The need for conceptual skills differs at various management levels. Top managers depend most on conceptual skills, first-line managers least. Although the purposes and everyday needs of various jobs differ, conceptual skills are needed in almost any job-related activity.

In many ways, conceptual skills may be the most important ingredient in the success of executives in e-commerce businesses. For example, the ability to foresee how a particular business application will be affected by or can be translated to the Internet is clearly conceptual in nature. The "Wired World" box in this chapter discusses this idea in more detail.

conceptual skills

Abilities to think in the abstract, diagnose and analyze different situations, and see beyond the present situation

Decision-Making Skills

Decision-making skills include the ability to define problems and to select the best course of action. Figure 6.4 illustrates the following basic steps in decision making:

decision-making skills

Skills in defining problems and selecting the best courses of action

1. ***Define the problem, gather facts, and identify alternative solutions.*** Vivendi Universal <www.vivendiuniversal.com>, for example, is a large French entertainment and media company. The firm's top managers recently decided that they needed a stronger presence in the United States if they were to continue their quest to become a global media powerhouse. Thus, they defined their problem as how to best enter the U.S. media market. They subsequently determined that there were two alternatives: starting a new media business from scratch or buying an existing one.

■ FIGURE 6.4
The Decision-Making Process

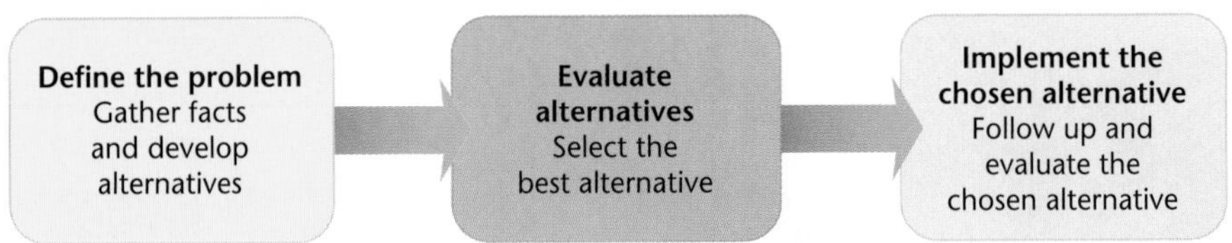

2. ***Evaluate each alternative and select the best one.*** Managers at Vivendi Universal realized that it would take many years and a huge cash investment to launch a new media enterprise from scratch. They also recognized that because there was ongoing consolidation in the U.S. media industry, buying an existing firm might be relatively easy. Further analysis identified Houghton Mifflin, one of the last remaining independent publishers, as an attractive acquisition target.
3. ***Implement the chosen alternative, periodically following up and evaluating the effectiveness of that choice.*** Vivendi Universal executives quietly began negotiating with senior managers at Houghton Mifflin in mid-2001. Within a matter of weeks, the two firms had reached an agreement: Vivendi Universal would acquire 100 percent of Houghton Mifflin, thus providing the French company with exactly what it had been seeking—a viable entry into U.S. markets.[14] Unfortunately, Vivendi subsequently fell on hard times, and on August 14, 2002, it announced that it would attempt to sell Houghton Mifflin in order to raise much-needed cash.

Time Management Skills

time management skills
Skills associated with the productive use of time

Time management skills refer to the productive use that managers make of their time. In 2001, for example, ExxonMobil CEO Lee Raymond was paid $5,200,000 in salary. Assuming that he worked 50 hours a week and took two weeks' vacation, Raymond earned $2,000 an hour—about $33 per minute. Any amount of time that Raymond wastes clearly represents a large cost to ExxonMobil and its stockholders. Most managers, of course, receive much smaller salaries than Raymond. Their time, however, is valuable, and poor use of it still translates into costs and wasted productivity. (Actually, this example underestimates Raymond's earnings; he also received additional deferred compensation such as stock options and retirement benefits.)

To manage time effectively, managers must address four leading causes of wasted time:

1. ***Paperwork.*** Some managers spend too much time deciding what to do with letters and reports. Most documents of this sort are routine and can be handled quickly. Managers must learn to recognize those documents that require more attention.
2. ***Telephone.*** Experts estimate that managers get interrupted by the telephone every five minutes. To manage this time more effectively, they suggest having an assistant screen all calls and setting aside a certain block of time each day to return the important ones. Unfortunately, the explosive use of cell phones seems to be making this problem even worse for many managers.
3. ***Meetings.*** Many managers spend as much as four hours a day in meetings. To help keep this time productive, the person handling the meeting should specify a clear agenda, start on time, keep everyone focused on the agenda, and end on time.

Always in Touch

Once a novelty, cellular telephones are ubiquitous today. Walking through any large airport or business center, you'll see dozens of people sitting in chairs, leaning against walls, or strolling around while conducting business on their cell phones. Other popular communication technologies include personal digital assistants (PDAs), and extra-small "subnotebook" laptop computers. Some devices incorporate all three functions: phone communication, computing, and Internet connectivity. You can get accessories (portable printers, folding keyboards), and if you don't want to learn an array of new technologies, Internet service providers can make voice mail, e-mail, and business information available over the World Wide Web through your conventional PC.

New technologies have made many managers considerably more productive than before. It's easier to supervise workers in remote locations, to stay in touch with clients and customers, and to share information with the home office when they're on the road. At the same time, however, the same devices pose certain problems for many busy executives. Because they're always available, they have less downtime and less opportunity to disconnect from their work.

In the past, managers had free time when they were traveling to and from work or when they were away from their offices at lunch. Now, many are readily accessible during these times. Thus what might have once been a nice hour-long break for lunch in the middle of the day may turn into a work session as conducted over the phone at the corner deli. Even vacations are falling victim to the technology—parents vacationing at Disney World with their children can duck into the resort's Internet café for a few minutes to take online messages from the office.

Fortunately, the astute manager who wants to regain some control over this aspect of his or her life really actually has more control than you might expect. Let's face it—all they have to do is turn everything off. Even so, with the onslaught of more ways to stay connected, it's getting harder for stressed managers to find a few minutes' respite from the ongoing demands of the executive's life.

4. ***E-mail.*** Increasingly, more and more managers are also relying heavily on e-mail and other forms of electronic communication. Like memos and telephone calls, many e-mail messages are not particularly important—some are even trivial. As a result, time is wasted when managers have to sort through a variety of electronic folders, in-baskets, and archives.

Management Skills for the Twenty-First Century

Although the skills discussed in this chapter have long been an important part of every successful manager's career, new skill requirements continue to emerge. As we enter the twenty-first century, most experts point to the growing importance of skills involving *global management* and *technology.*

Global Management Skills Tomorrow's managers must equip themselves with the special tools, techniques, and skills needed to compete in a global environment. They will need to understand foreign markets, cultural differences, and the motives and practices of foreign rivals.

On a more practical level, businesses will need managers who are capable of understanding international operations. In the past, most U.S. businesses hired local managers to run their operations in the various countries in which they operated. More recently, however, the trend has been to transfer U.S. managers to foreign locations. This practice helps firms better transfer their corporate cultures to foreign operations. In addition, foreign assignments help managers become better prepared for international competition as they advance within the

What MTV <www.mtv.com> *needed to run its operations in China was someone who understood both conservative Chinese television regulators and China's young urban elite. The company chose 37-year-old Li Yifei, a former Baylor University political science student, U.N. intern, public relations consultant, and tai chi champion. Li has already brought the Chinese equivalent of the MTV awards to state-owned television, and although the show got only a 7.9-percent rating, she's quick to point out that in China, that's 150 million people (about half the U.S. population).*

organization. General Motors <www.gm.com> now has almost 500 U.S. managers in foreign posts.

Management and Technology Skills Another significant issue facing tomorrow's managers is technology, especially as it relates to communication. Managers have always had to deal with information. In today's world, however, the amount of information has reached staggering proportions. In the United States alone, people exchange hundreds of millions of e-mail messages every day. New forms of technology have added to a manager's ability to process information while simultaneously making it even more important to organize and interpret an ever-increasing wealth of input.

Technology has also begun to change the way the interaction of managers shapes corporate structures. Computer networking, for example, exists because it is no longer too expensive to put a computer on virtually every desk in the company. In turn, this elaborate network controls the flow of the firm's lifeblood—information. This information no longer flows strictly up and down through hierarchies. It now flows to everyone simultaneously. As a result, decisions are made more quickly, and more people are directly involved. With e-mail, teleconferencing, and other forms of communication, neither time nor distance—nor such corporate boundaries as departments and divisions—can prevent people from working more closely together. More than ever, bureaucracies are breaking down, while planning, decision making, and other activities are beginning to benefit from group building and teamwork.

Management and the Corporate Culture

corporate culture
The shared experiences, stories, beliefs, and norms that characterize an organization

Every organization—big or small, more successful or less successful—has an unmistakable "feel" to it. Just as every individual has a unique personality, every company has a unique identity called **corporate culture:** the shared experiences, stories, beliefs, and norms that characterize an organization. This culture helps define the work and business climate that exists in an organization.

A strong corporate culture serves several purposes. For one thing, it directs employees' efforts and helps everyone work toward the same goals. Some cul-

Say what you mean

ARE YOU TALKING TO ME?

Just because we have international communications tools such as the Internet, we can't simply ignore local culture when we're communicating with someone in another country. It's always a good idea to remember who's on the other end of the T-3 line.

Americans are notoriously informal when talking to one another. The same goes for our e-mail communications, and the Internet enables us to spread the message of informality all over the world. Unfortunately, however, being too informal in your e-mail can send the wrong message. In some places, you'll come across as too familiar (or even too aggressive). In some cultures, including the United Kingdom, Germany, and Japan, people like a little formality, even in their e-mail.

For example, be careful about using first names or a casual tone of voice (yes, you do have a tone of voice when you're writing). Pay attention to your grammar: Sloppy language is often a turn-off, and many people automatically regard it as a sign of poor education. Try to organize your message in a logical way. In some cultures, an Internet message is perceived as a letter with a formal structure.

Don't always expect people to reply immediately. Different cultures have different concepts of time, and a person's concept of time plays a big part in his or her sense of when to respond to messages. Demanding an immediate response in Brazil or Mexico is a good way to send your message to the bottom of the electronic pile. Finally, remember that a lot of people are bombarded with e-mail, and many of them regard dealing a constant barrage of communications as a strain on their time. Communicate electronically only when you have something that needs to be said sooner rather than later or when you need a question answered.

As usual, the bottom line in communications is knowing the culture in which your message is going to be received. Find out something about the culture of the person you're dealing with before you engage him or her in electronic conversation.

tures, for example, stress financial success to the extreme, while others focus more on quality of life. In addition, corporate culture helps newcomers learn accepted behaviors. If financial success is the key to a culture, newcomers quickly learn that they are expected to work long, hard hours and that the "winner" is the one who brings in the most revenue. But if quality of life is more fundamental, newcomers learn that it's more acceptable to spend less time at work and that balancing work and nonwork is encouraged.

Where does a business's culture come from? In some cases, it emanates from the days of an organization's founder. Firms such as the Walt Disney Co., Hewlett-Packard, Wal-Mart <www.walmart.com>, and J.C. Penney <www.jcpenney.com>, for example, still bear the imprint of their founders. In other cases, an organization's culture is forged over a long period of time by a constant and focused business strategy. PepsiCo <www.pepsico.com>, for example, has an achievement-oriented culture tied to its long-standing goal of catching its biggest competitor, Coca-Cola <www.cokecce.com>. Similarly, Apple Computer <www.apple.com> has a sort of "counterculture" culture stemming from its self-styled image as the alternative to the staid IBM <www.ibm.com> corporate model for computer makers.

Communicating the Culture and Managing Change

Corporate culture influences management philosophy, style, and behavior. Managers, therefore, must carefully consider the kind of culture they want for their organizations and then work to nourish that culture by communicating with everyone who works there. Wal-Mart, for example, is acutely conscious of

Back when the company was worth $60 billion (or a lot of people thought it was), Enron paid little attention to the cost of trotting elephants into employee meetings. Secretaries Day called for gifts of Waterford Crystal, and on the day Enron stock topped $50, employees found $100 bills on their desks. Laptops and state-of-the-art ergonomic chairs were on the company, and just about everybody traveled first-class and stayed in five-star hotels. Enron's was a risk-taking, full-speed-ahead culture, and experts agree that one of the reasons for its failure was the absence of controls on overly aggressive behavior among managers at all levels.

the need to spread the message of its culture as it opens new stores in new areas. One of the company's methods is to regularly assign veteran managers to lead employees in new territories. Gordon Bethune delivers weekly messages for all Continental employees to update them on what's going on in the firm; the employees can either listen to it on a closed-circuit broadcast or else call an 800 telephone number and hear a recorded version at their own convenience.

Communicating the Culture To use a firm's culture to its advantage, managers must accomplish several tasks, all of which hinge on effective communication. First, managers themselves must have a clear understanding of the culture. Second, they must transmit the culture to others in the organization. Thus, communication is one aim in training and orienting newcomers. A clear and meaningful statement of the organization's mission is also a valuable communication tool. Finally, managers can maintain the culture by rewarding and promoting those who understand it and work toward maintaining it.

Managing Change Organizations must sometimes change their cultures. In such cases, they must also communicate the nature of the change to both employees and customers. According to the CEOs of several companies that have undergone radical change in the last decade or so, the process usually goes through three stages:

1. ***At the highest level, analysis of the company's environment highlights extensive change as the most effective response to its problems.*** This period is typically characterized by conflict and resistance.
2. ***Top management begins to formulate a vision of a new company.*** Whatever that vision, it must include renewed focus on the activities of competitors and the needs of customers.
3. ***The firm sets up new systems for appraising and compensating employees who enforce the firm's new values.*** The purpose is to give the new culture solid shape from within the firm.

While some firms like to build on their legacies, others know better. When Gordon Bethune announced his rebuilding plans at Continental, he dubbed it the

Self-Check Questions 7–9

*You should now be able to answer Self-Check Questions 7–9**

7. MULTIPLE CHOICE The ability to think in the abstract reflects which of the following *managerial skills*? [select one] **(a)** technical skills; **(b)** human relations skills; **(c)** conceptual skills; **(d)** decision-making skills; **(e)** time management skills.

8. MULTIPLE CHOICE Which of the following identifies two emerging skill sets that managers will need to master in the twenty-first century? [select one] **(a)** interpersonal and global; **(b)** global and technology; **(c)** time management and conceptual; **(d)** conceptual and technology; **(e)** technical and human relations.

9. TRUE/FALSE Although every corporate organization has a unique culture, it is for the most part not particularly important.

*ANSWERS TO SELF-CHECK QUESTIONS 7–9 CAN BE FOUND ON P. AN-4.

"Go Forward" program. He stressed that the firm had little to look back on with pride, and he wanted everyone to look only to the future. Likewise, Procter & Gamble <www.pg.com> is in the midst of a major overhaul designed to remake its corporate culture into one more suited to today's competitive global business environment. Because its brands have been dominant for such a long time, managers at P&G have been criticized for having tunnel vision—focusing only on the ways they've done things in the past and then trying to repeat them. Procter & Gamble's popular Tide laundry detergent, for example, has been through more than 60 formula upgrades since it was first introduced. A new top-management team, however, is working to shake things up by advocating new approaches, new ways of thinking, and new models of product development.[15]

Continued from page 159

"Our Business Isn't Really About Moving Freight"

Of course, leadership alone is seldom enough to turn around a major company. Technology has also played a big role in Yellow's recent success. For instance, the firm implemented a variety of automated systems to improve customer service and satisfaction. These systems use the Internet to provide up-to-the-minute information about the progress of shipments, maintain a customer database that enables faster scheduling, and develop the trailer-loading time tables and routes that ensure on-time delivery. Ultimately, the real technology success story at Yellow isn't merely the innovative and efficient use of technology, but rather the savvy application of those systems in support of employees and customers.

Beyond leadership and technology, however, perhaps the most challenging and yet the most important change at Yellow was the revisioning of the company's mission, transforming it from the delivery of freight to a strong and consistent focus on customer service. For instance, when the firm's employees saw their primary goal as the efficient movement of cargo, the firm focused on one set of processes.

But perhaps the most challenging—and most important—change at Yellow was the revisioning of the company's mission. When employees saw their primary goal as the efficient movement of cargo, the firm focused on one set of processes. Today, thanks to the efforts of Zollars and other managers, employees realize that supporting the customer by meeting his or her delivery needs is the paramount task. This shift in perspective now enables the firm to provide better service, to develop innovative new products and services, to improve performance, and ultimately, to compete successfully in an increasingly tough industry. As Bill Zollars says in the firm's 2000 Annual Report, "... [O]ur business really isn't about moving freight. It's about earning the trust of the consumers of our services."

Questions for Discussion

1. Describe the role of goals and strategy at Yellow.
2. What kind of crisis or contingency plans does a firm like Yellow need?
3. Identify examples to illustrate each of the various parts of the management process at Yellow.
4. Identify and briefly describe management titles that Yellow most likely has that reflect both the different levels and the different areas of management.
5. Discuss how Bill Zollars has used various management skills in his turnaround of Yellow.

Summary of Learning Objectives

1. ***Explain the importance of setting goals and formulating strategies as the starting points of effective management.***

Effective management starts with setting **goals**—objectives that a business hopes (and plans) to achieve. In most companies, a broad program underlies decisions. That program is called a **strategy**—a broad set of organizational plans for implementing the decisions made for achieving organizational goals.

Companies usually consider three types of strategy: (1) **Corporate strategy** determines overall attitude toward growth and how the firm will manage its businesses or product lines. (2) **Business (or competitive) strategy,** which takes place at the level of the business unit or product line, focuses on improving competitive position. (3) At the level of **functional strategy,** managers in specific areas decide how best to achieve corporate goals by being as productive as possible.

Goals are performance targets—the means by which organizations measure success or failure. Organizations function systematically because they set goals and plan accordingly. Goal setting has four specific purposes: (1) It provides guidance for managers. If they know where the company is headed, there's less chance of error throughout the company. (2) Goal setting helps allocate resources. If growth is a goal in an area, it will get first priority. (3) Goal setting helps define corporate culture. (4) It helps managers assess performance.

Company goals differ, but every firm has a *purpose* or a reason for being. Many also have missions and **mission statements**—statements of how they will achieve their purposes in the environments in which they do business. Regardless of its purpose and mission, however, every firm sets three types of goals: (1) **Long-term goals** cover extended periods of time (say, five years or more). (2) **Intermediate goals** are set for one to five years and may vary from area to area. (3) **Short-term goals** are set for perhaps one year and are also developed for different areas.

A *strategy* outlines how a business intends to meet its goals and respond to new challenges. **Strategy formulation** involves three steps: (1) *Setting strategic goals*: **Strategic goals** are long-term goals derived directly from the mission statement (say, developing new products). After they've set strategic goals, organizations may conduct a **SWOT analysis.** They assess their strengths and weaknesses (the *S* and *W*) and environmental opportunities and threats (the *O* and *T*) in order to capitalize on strengths, take advantage of opportunities, offset weaknesses, and counter threats. (2) *Analyzing the organization and its environment*: **Environmental analysis** means scanning the environment for *external* factors, including threats (say, new competitors) and opportunities (new growth areas). **Organizational analysis** examines such *internal* factors as a company's strengths (for example, surplus cash) and weaknesses (a lack of managerial talent). (3) *Matching the organization and its environment*: The heart of strategy formulation is matching environmental threats and opportunities against corporate strengths and weaknesses.

Plans takes place on three levels that constitute a hierarchy, because implementing plans is practical only when there is a logical flow from one level to the next: (1) Determined by the board and top management, **strategic plans** reflect decisions about resource allocations, company priorities, and strategic plans. (2) **Tactical plans,** which involve upper and middle management, are shorter-range plans for implementing specific aspects of strategic plans. (3) **Operational plans,** which are developed by mid- and lower-level managers, set short-term targets for daily, weekly, or monthly performance.

Companies often develop alternative plans in case things go awry. There are two common methods of dealing with the unforeseen: (1) **Contingency planning** is planning for change: It seeks to identify factors, both external and internal, that might change and states how a company will respond to changes. (2) **Crisis management** involves an organization's methods for dealing with emergencies requiring immediate response.

2. ***Describe the four activities that constitute the* management process.**

Management is the process of planning, organizing, directing, and controlling all of a firm's resources to achieve its goals. (1) **Planning**—determining what the organization needs to do and how best to get it done—has three main components: (i) Managers first set goals; (ii) then they develop a strategy for achieving them; (iii) finally, they devise tactical and operational plans for implementing the strategy. (2) The process of arranging resources and activities into a coherent structure is called **organizing.** (3) When **directing,** a manager guides and motivates employees to meet the firm's objectives. (4) **Controlling** is the process of monitoring performance to make sure that a firm is meeting its goals.

3. ***Identify* types of managers *by level and area.***

Not all managers have the same degree of responsibility for all activities. Thus, it's helpful to classify managers according to levels and areas of *responsibility.* There are three levels of management: (1) The few executives who are responsible for the overall performance of large companies are **top managers** (including *president, chief executive officer [CEO], chief financial officer [CFO],* and so on. They set policies, formulate strategies, approve decisions, and represent the company in dealings with other firms and with government bodies. (2) Just below top managers are **middle managers,** including *plant, operations,* and *division managers,* who implement strategies, policies, and decisions made by top managers. (3) *Supervisors* and *office managers* are the **first-line managers** who work with and supervise the employees who report to them.

In any large company, most managers work in one of five areas: (1) *Human resource managers* hire and train employees, assess performance, and fix compensation. (2) *Operations managers* are responsible for production, inventory, and quality control. (3) *Marketing managers* are responsible for getting products from producers to consumers. (4) *Information managers* design and implement systems to gather, organize, and distribute information. Some firms have a top manager called a *chief information officer (CIO).* (5) *Financial managers,* including the *chief financial officer* (top), *division controllers* (middle), and *accounting supervisors* (first-line), oversee accounting functions and financial resources.

4. ***Describe the five basic* management skills.**

Effective managers must develop skills in five areas: (1) **Technical skills** are skills needed to perform specialized tasks. (2) **Human relations skills** are skills in understanding and getting along with other people. (3) **Conceptual skills** refer to the ability to think abstractly as well as diagnose and analyze different situations. (4) **Decision-making skills** include the ability to define problems and select the best courses of action. Decision-making consists of three steps: (i) Define the problem, gather facts, and identify alternative solutions. (ii) Evaluate each alternative and select the best one. (iii) Implement the chosen alternative, periodically evaluating the effectiveness of the choice. (5) **Time management skills** refer to the productive use of time. Managers must address four leading causes of wasted time: (i) paperwork; (ii) telephone; (iii) meetings; and (iv) e-mail.

In the twenty-first century, skills in two areas will be more important: (1) *Global management skills*: Managers will need to know how to compete in a global environment, including knowledge of foreign markets, cultural differences, and international operations. (2) *Technology management skills*: Because of technology, managers will have to organize ever-increasing amounts of input. They'll have to work in an environment in which decisions are made more quickly and more people are directly involved.

5. ***Describe the development and explain the importance of* corporate culture.**

Every company has a unique identity called **corporate culture:** its shared experiences, stories, beliefs, and norms. It helps define the work and business climate of an organization. A strong corporate culture directs efforts and helps everyone work toward the same goals.

It also influences management style and behavior. To use a firm's culture to its advantage, managers must accomplish several tasks, all of which hinge on communication. (1) Managers themselves must have a clear understanding of the culture; (2) they must transmit the culture to others in the organization; (3) they can maintain the culture by rewarding and promoting those who understand it and work toward maintaining it.

If an organization must change its culture, it must communicate the nature of the change to both employees and customers. This process usually goes through three stages: Top managers (1) identify extensive change as the best response to a firm's problems; (2) formulate a vision of a new company; and (3) set up new systems for appraising and compensating employees who enforce the firm's new values.

KEY TERMS

goal (p. 161)
strategy (p. 161)
corporate strategy (p. 161)
business (or competitive) strategy (p. 161)
functional strategy (p. 161)
mission statement (p. 162)
long-term goal (p. 163)
intermediate goal (p. 163)
short-term goal (p. 163)
strategy formulation (p. 163)
strategic goal (p. 164)
SWOT (p. 164)
environmental analysis (p. 164)
organizational analysis (p. 165)
strategic plan (p. 165)
tactical plan (p. 166)
operational plan (p. 166)
contingency planning (p. 166)
crisis management (p. 167)
management (p. 169)
planning (p. 169)
organizing (p. 170)
directing (p. 170)
controlling (p. 170)
top manager (p. 172)
middle manager (p. 172)
first-line manager (p. 172)
technical skills (p. 174)
human relations skills (p. 174)
conceptual skills (p. 175)
decision-making skills (p. 175)
time management skills (p. 176)
corporate culture (p. 178)

QUESTIONS AND EXERCISES

Questions for Review

1. What are the four main purposes of setting goals in an organization?
2. Identify and explain the three basic steps in strategy formulation.
3. Relate the five basic management skills to the four activities in the management process. For example, which skills are most important in directing?
4. What is corporate culture? How is it formed? How is it sustained?

Questions for Analysis

5. Select any group of which you are a member (your company, your family, or a club or organization, for example). Explain how planning, organizing, directing, and controlling are practiced in that group.
6. Identify managers by level and area at your school, college, or university.
7. In what kind of company would the technical skills of top managers be more important than human relations or conceptual skills? Are there organizations in which conceptual skills are not important?
8. What differences might you expect to find in the corporate cultures of a 100-year-old manufacturing firm based in the Northeast and a 1-year-old e-commerce firm set in Silicon Valley?

Application Exercises

9. Interview the manager at any level of a local company. Identify that manager's job according to level and area. Show how planning, organizing, directing, and controlling are part of this person's job. Inquire about the manager's education and work experience. Which management skills are most important for this manager's job?
10. Compare and contrast the corporate cultures of two companies that do business in most communities. Be sure to choose two companies in the same industry—for example, a Sears department store and a Wal-Mart discount store.

Building Your Business Skills

SPEAKING WITH POWER

This exercise enhances the following SCANS workplace competencies: demonstrating basic skills, demonstrating thinking skills, exhibiting interpersonal skills, and working with information.

Goal

To encourage students to appreciate effective speaking as a critical human relations skill.

Background

A manager's ability to understand and get along with supervisors, peers, and subordinates is a critical human relations skill. At the heart of this skill, says Harvard University professor of education Sarah McGinty, is the ability to speak with power and control. McGinty defines "powerful speech" in terms of the following characteristics:

- The ability to speak at length and in complete sentences
- The ability to set a conversational agenda
- The ability to deter interruptions
- The ability to argue openly and to express strong opinions about ideas, not people

- The ability to make statements that offer solutions rather than pose questions
- The ability to express humor

Taken together, says McGinty, "all this creates a sense of confidence in listeners."

Method

Step 1

Working alone, compare your own personal speaking style with McGinty's description of powerful speech by taping yourself as you speak during a meeting with classmates or during a phone conversation. (Tape both sides of the conversation only if the person to whom you are speaking gives permission.) Listen for the following problems:

- Unfinished sentences
- An absence of solutions
- Too many disclaimers ("I'm not sure I have enough information to say this, but. . . ")
- The habit of seeking support from others instead of making definitive statements of personal conviction (saying, "I recommend consolidating the medical and fitness functions," instead of, "As Emily stated in her report, I recommend consolidating the medical and fitness functions")
- Language fillers (saying, "you know," "like," and "um" when you are unsure of your facts or uneasy about expressing your opinion)

Step 2

Join with three or four other classmates to evaluate each other's speaking styles. Finally,

- Have a 10-minute group discussion on the importance of human relations skills in business.
- Listen to other group members, and take notes on the "power" content of what you hear.
- Offer constructive criticism by focusing on what speakers say rather than on personal characteristics (say, "Bob, you sympathized with Paul's position, but I still don't know what you think," instead of, "Bob, you sounded like a weakling").

Follow-Up Questions

1. How do you think the power content of speech affects a manager's ability to communicate? Evaluate some of the ways in which effects may differ among supervisors, peers, and subordinates.
2. How do you evaluate yourself and group members in terms of powerful and powerless speech? List the strengths and weaknesses of the group.
3. Do you agree or disagree with McGinty that business success depends on gaining insight into your own language habits? Explain your answer.
4. In our age of computers and e-mail, why do you think personal presentation continues to be important in management?
5. McGinty believes that power language differs from company to company and that it is linked to the corporate culture. Do you agree, or do you believe that people express themselves in similar ways no matter where they are?

Exercising Your Ethics

MAKING ROOM FOR ALTERNATIVE ACTIONS

The Situation

Assume that you are the manager of a large hotel adjacent to a medical center in a major city. The medical center itself consists of 10 major hospitals and research institutes. Two of the hospitals are affiliated with large universities and two with churches. Three are public and three are private. The center has an international reputation and attracts patients from around the world.

Because so many patients and their families travel great distances to visit the medical center and often stay for days or weeks, there are also eight large hotels in the area, including three new ones. The hotel that you manage is one of the older ones and, frankly, is looking a bit shabby. Corporate headquarters has told you that the hotel will either be closed or undergo a major remodeling in about two years. In the meantime, you are expected to wring every last cent of profit out of the hotel.

The Dilemma

A tropical storm has just struck the area and brought with it major flooding and power outages. Three of the medical center hospitals have been shut down indefinitely, as have six of the nearby hotels. Fortunately, your hotel sustained only minor damage and is fully functional. You have just called a meeting with your two assistant managers to discuss what actions, if any, you should take.

One assistant manager has urged you to cut room rates immediately for humanitarian reasons. This manager also wants you to open the hotel kitchens 24 hours a day to prepare free food for rescue workers and meals to donate to the hospitals, whose own food service operations have been disrupted. The other assistant manager, meanwhile, has urged just the opposite approach: raise room rates by at least 20 percent and sell food to rescue workers and hospitals at a premium price. Of course, you can also choose to follow the advice of neither and continue doing business as usual.

Questions for Discussion

1. What are the ethical issues in this situation?
2. What do you think most managers would do in this situation?
3. What would you do?

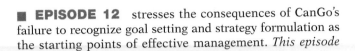

Mastering Business Essentials

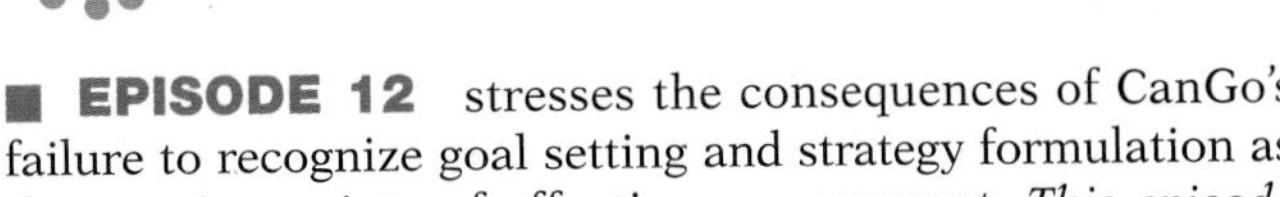

■ **EPISODE 12** stresses the consequences of CanGo's failure to recognize goal setting and strategy formulation as the starting points of effective management. *This episode demonstrates why evaluating plans is a necessary part of the process of improving operations.*

Crafting Your Business Plan

FURNISHING YOURSELF WITH MANAGEMENT SKILLS

The Purpose of the Assignment

1. To familiarize students with management-related issues that a sample firm may address in developing its business plan, in the planning framework of the *Business PlanPro* (*BPP*) software package.
2. To demonstrate how three chapter topics—business goals, business strategies, and management skills—can be integrated as components in the *BPP* planning environment.

Assignment

After reading Chapter 6 in the textbook, open the BPP software and search for information about business goals, business strategies, and management skills as they apply to a sample firm: Willamette Furniture. To find Willamette Furniture, do the following:

Open the *Business PlanPro.* If it asks if you want to "create a new business plan" or "open an existing plan," select "create a new business plan" (even though you are not going to create a plan at this time). You will then be taken to the *Business PlanPro EasyPlan Wizard.* On the screen, click on the option entitled **Research It.** You will then be presented with a new list of options, including **Sample Plan Browser.** After clicking on **Sample Plan Browser,** go down the alphabetical list of sample plans and double-click on **Furniture Mfr.—Office**, which is the location for *Willamette Furniture.* The screen you are looking at is the introduction page for *Willamette*'s business plan. Scroll down this page until you reach the **Table of Contents** for the company's business plan.

Now respond to the following items:

1. Evaluate Willamette Furniture's business objectives. Are they clearly stated? Are they measurable? [Sites to see in *BPP* (for this item): On the Table of Contents page, click on **1.1 Objectives.**]
2. Evaluate Willamette's mission and strategy statements. Do they clearly state how Willamette Furniture intends to achieve its purposes? [Sites to see in *BPP:* On the Table of Contents page, click on **1.0 Executive Summary.** Then click on **1.2 Mission.** Next, click on each of the following in turn: **5.0 Strategy and Implementation Summary** and **5.1 Strategy Pyramids.**]
3. In what areas of the business does each of Willamette's top managers work? [Sites to see in *BPP:* From the Table of Contents page, click on **6.0 Management Summary.** Now click on each of the following: **6.1 Organization Structure** and **6.2 Management Team.**]
4. What management skills areas are lacking in Willamette furniture's management team? Would you classify the missing skills as technical, human resources, conceptual, or decision-making skills? [Sites to see in *BPP:* On the Table of Contents page, click on **6.3 Management Team Gaps.**]

Video Exercise

IMAGINATIVE MANAGEMENT: CREATIVE AGE PUBLICATIONS

Learning Objectives

The purpose of this video is to help you:

1. Understand how and why managers set organizational goals.
2. Identify the basic skills that managers need to be effective.
3. Discuss ways in which corporate culture can affect an organization.

Synopsis

Creative Age Publications uses creativity in managing its beauty-industry publications. With offices or franchised operations in Europe, Japan, Russia, and other areas of the world, the company has expanded rapidly—thanks to sound management practices. In fact, one of the company's goals is to avoid overtaxing its management team by growing more slowly in the future. The CEO is working toward delegating most or all decisions to her management team, and as

Creative Age managers move up through the ranks, they hone both their technical skills and their skill in working with others. "Having heart" is a major part of the company's culture—an important element that, in the CEO's opinion, many companies lack.

Discussion Questions

1. *For analysis:* How does global growth affect Creative Age's emphasis on the management skill of interacting well with other people?
2. *For analysis:* How does moving managers up through the ranks help them develop conceptual skills?
3. *For application:* How would you suggest that the CEO spread the Creative Age culture throughout its global offices?
4. *For application:* How might the CEO manage growth through the process of controlling?
5. *For debate:* Do you agree with the CEO's policy of allowing managers and employees to work on any company magazine they choose? Support your position.

Online Exploration

Visit the Creative Age Web site at <www.creativeage.com> and follow the link to *Day Spa* magazine. Scan the magazine's home page and then click on **About Us** to read more about the magazine and its parent company. Why would Creative Age call attention to each magazine's goals and market rather than focusing on the parent company? How might Creative Age use a corporate Web site to communicate with other people and organizations that affect its ability to achieve its goals?

CHAPTER 7

Organizing the Business Enterprise

After reading this chapter, you should be able to:

1. Discuss the elements that influence a firm's *organizational structure.*
2. Explain *specialization* and *departmentalization* as the building blocks of organizational structure.
3. Distinguish among *responsibility, authority, delegation,* and *accountability* and explain the differences between decision making in *centralized* and *decentralized organizations.*
4. Explain the differences among *functional, divisional, matrix,* and *international organizational structures* and describe the most popular new forms of organizational design.
5. Describe the *informal organization* and discuss *intrapreneuring.*

A Supersonic Project Gets off the Ground (I)

Lockheed Martin <www.lockheedmartin.com> has been a major defense contractor for a long time. But while it's had its share of government contracts, it has all too often played second fiddle to competitors such as Boeing and Northrop Grumman. All that changed on October 21, 2001, a truly red-letter day for Lockheed and for Tom Burbage, aeronautics engineer, executive vice president, and head of the firm's Joint Strike Fighter program.

On that day, the Department of Defense chose Lockheed over rivals Boeing and McDonnell Douglas to develop and manufacture its new Joint Strike Fighter (JSF) jet. Lockheed immediately received $19 billion to begin design, and the 6,000-aircraft, 40-year contract should ultimately be worth as much as $200 billion. The contract made Lockheed the leading maker of fighter jets and main supplier of jet aircraft for the U.S. Air Force, Navy, and Marines, as well as for the Royal Air Force and Royal Navy of England.

How did a firm that has long been regarded as an industry also-ran come to win this highly lucrative defense contract? It might have something to do with the attitude expressed by Air Force acquisition chief Darleen Druyun: "This competition," explained Druyun, "is not about an airplane. It's about a management team." All three contract bidders boasted the excellent technical skills needed to manufacture an acceptable product. But the Pentagon was looking for management experience needed to coordinate an immensely costly and complex project.

Perhaps the key to Lockheed's victory was naming Burbage to head the program. Burbage, in turn, credits his time as a Navy test pilot with teaching him leadership and management skills. As a team commander on board an aircraft carrier he was known for flying top performing sailors to Italy for a weekend jaunt. His crew set numerous performance records.

". . . You can build a high-performing team in some pretty austere environments," says Burbage. "But first, you've got to take care of your people. And second, you've got to understand the difference between the carrot and the stick—and in my view, the former is a lot more useful than the latter. In the end, I stopped trying to motivate people. I learned that if you recognize and reward them, people will motivate themselves."

One problem that Burbage encountered almost immediately was a rift in Lockheed ranks. Two large and powerful divisions were competing for control of the project. "Lockheed wasn't known for pulling teams together," says a high-ranking manager at one of Lockheed's project partners. From the outset, then Burbage had to work tirelessly to get different units of his own company to adopt the idea of teamwork.

Meanwhile, another manager at Lockheed, Harry Blot, seeing that Lockheed lacked some of the skills needed to complete the project, recommended that the firm partner with rivals BAE systems and Northrop Grumman. At first, competitors were concerned. "Lockheed and Northrop have battled each other for 60 years," says Northrop Manager Martin McLaughlin. "At the time, I couldn't believe it: We're supposed to *partner* with these guys?" Representatives from the three firms met, and according to Taylor, "We expected the discussions to revolve around how to divide the work. But as it turned out, Lockheed was more interested in how we'd build a relationship." In fact, Lockheed put its money where its corporate mouth was by making the unheard-of decision to grant Northrop and BAE 30-percent financial and strategic shares in the program—effectively promoting them from subcontractors to equal partners.

Our opening story continues on page 211

"I stopped trying to motivate people. I learned that if you recognize and reward them, people will motivate themselves."

~Tom Burbage, executive VP, LOCKHEED MARTIN JOINT STRIKE FIGHTER PROJECT

What Is Organizational Structure?

What do we mean by the term *organizational structure*? Consider a simple analogy. In some ways, a business is like an automobile. All cars have engines, four wheels, fenders, and other structural components. They all have passenger compartments, storage areas, and various operating systems (fuel, braking, climate control). Although each component has a distinct purpose, it must also work in accord with the others. In addition, although the ways they look and fit may vary widely, all automobiles have the same basic components.

Similarly, all businesses have common structural and operating components, each composed of a series of *jobs to be done* and each with a *specific overall purpose*. From company to company, these components look different and fit together differently, but in every organization, components have the same fundamental purpose—each must perform its own function while working in concert with the others.

Although all organizations feature the same basic elements, each must develop the structure that is most appropriate for it. What works for Texas Instruments will not work for Shell Oil, Amazon.com, or the U.S. Department of Justice. The structure of the American Red Cross will probably not work for Union Carbide or the University of Minnesota. We define **organizational structure** as the specification of the jobs to be done within an organization and the ways in which those jobs relate to one another.

organizational structure

Specification of the jobs to be done within an organization and the ways in which they relate to one another

Determinants of Organization

How is an organization's structure determined? Does it happen by chance, or is there some logic that managers use to create structure? Does it develop by some combination of circumstance and strategy? Ideally, managers carefully assess a variety of important factors as they plan for and then create a structure that will allow their organization to function efficiently.

Many elements work together to determine an organization's structure. Chief among them are the organization's *purpose, mission,* and *strategy.* A dynamic and rapidly growing enterprise, for example, achieved that position because of its purpose and successful strategies for achieving it. Such a firm will need a structure that contributes to flexibility and growth. A stable organization with only modest growth will function best with a different structure.

Size, technology, and changes in the organization's environment also affect structure. As we saw in Chapter 6, organizing is a function of managerial planning. As such, it is conducted with an equal awareness of both a firm's external and internal environments. A large manufacturer operating in a strongly competitive environment—say, Boeing or Hewlett-Packard—requires a different structure than a local barbershop or video store. Moreover, even after a structure has been created, it is rarely free from tinkering—or even outright re-creation. Most organizations change their structures on an almost continuing basis.

Since it was first incorporated in 1903, Ford Motor Co. <www.ford.com> has undergone literally dozens of major structural changes, hundreds of moderate changes, and thousands of minor changes. In the last 10 years alone, Ford has initiated several major structural changes. In 1994, for instance, the firm announced a major restructuring plan called Ford 2000, which was intended to integrate all of Ford's vast international operations into a single, unified structure by the year 2000.

By 1998, however, midway through implementation of the grand plan, top Ford executives announced major modifications, indicating that (1) additional changes would be made, (2) some previously planned changes would not be made, and (3) some recently realigned operations would be changed again. I

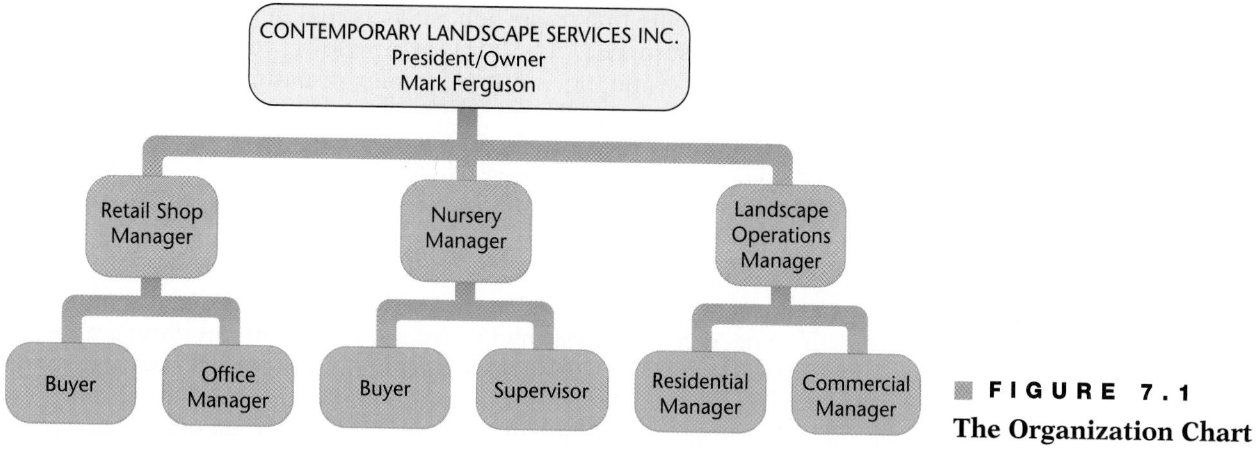

FIGURE 7.1
The Organization Chart

early 1999, managers announced another set of changes intended to eliminate corporate bureaucracy, speed decision making, and improve communication and working relationships among people at different levels of the organization.[1] Early in 2001, Ford announced yet more sweeping changes intended to boost the firm's flagging bottom line and stem a decline in product quality.[2]

Chain of Command

Most businesses prepare **organization charts** to clarify structure and to show employees where they fit into a firm's operations. Figure 7.1 is an organization chart for Contemporary Landscape Services Inc., a small but thriving business in Bryan, Texas. Each box in the chart represents a job. The solid lines define the **chain of command,** or *reporting relationships,* within the company. For example, the retail shop, nursery, and landscape operations managers all report to the owner and president, Mark Ferguson. Within the landscape operation is one manager for residential accounts and another for commercial accounts. Similarly, there are other managers in the retail shop and the nursery.

The organization charts of large firms are far more complex and include individuals at many more levels than those shown in Figure 7.1. Size prevents many large firms from even having charts that include all their managers. Typically, they create one organization chart showing overall corporate structure and separate charts for each division.

organization chart
Diagram depicting a company's structure and showing employees where they fit into its operations

chain of command
Reporting relationships within a company

The Building Blocks of Organizational Structure

The first step in developing the structure of any business, large or small, involves two activities:

- *Specialization:* determining who will do what
- *Departmentalization:* determining how people performing certain tasks can best be grouped together

These two activities are the building blocks of all business organizations.[3]

Specialization

The process of identifying the specific jobs that need to be done and designating the people who will perform them leads to **job specialization.** In a sense, all

job specialization
The process of identifying the specific jobs that need to be done and designating the people who will perform them

organizations have only one major job, such as making cars (Ford), selling finished goods to consumers (Wal-Mart), or providing telecommunications services (AT&T). Usually, the job is more complex in nature. For example, the job of Chaparral Steel <www.txi.com/steel> is converting scrap steel (such as wrecked automobiles) into finished steel products (such as beams and reinforcement bars).

To perform this one overall job, managers actually break it down, or specialize it, into several smaller jobs. Thus, some workers transport the scrap steel to the company's mill in Midlothian, Texas. Others operate shredding equipment before turning raw materials over to the workers who then melt them into liquid form. Other specialists oversee the flow of the liquid into molding equipment in which it is transformed into new products. Finally, other workers are responsible for moving finished products to a holding area before they are shipped out to customers. When the overall job of the organization is thus broken down, workers can develop real expertise in their jobs, and employees can better coordinate their work with that done by others.

Specialization and Growth In a very small organization, the owner may perform every job. As the firm grows, however, so does the need to specialize jobs so that others can perform them. To see how specialization can evolve in an organization, consider the case of the Walt Disney Company <www.disney.go.com>. When Walt Disney first opened his studio, he and his brother Roy did everything. For example, when they created the very first animated feature, *Steamboat Willy,* they wrote the story, drew the pictures, transferred the pictures to film, provided the voices, and then went out and sold the cartoon to theater operators.

Today, in sharp contrast, a Disney animated feature is made possible only through the efforts of hundreds of creators. The job of one cartoonist may be to draw the face of a single character throughout an entire feature. Another artist may be charged with erasing stray pencil marks inadvertently made by other illustrators. People other than artists are responsible for the subsequent operations that turn individual animated cells into a moving picture or for the marketing of the finished product.

Job specialization is a natural part of organizational growth. It also has certain advantages. For example, specialized jobs are learned more easily and can

Whether they're produced manually or digitally, the drawings that comprise a full-length cartoon such as Ice Age *are the result of highly coordinated job specialization.* Ice Age *was made by Blue Sky Studios* <www.blueskystudios.com>*, located in White Plains, New York, using its own software, CGI (for computer-generated imagery) Studio. To make its first full-length animated feature, Blue Sky reorganized as an assembly-line operation in which about 170 artists who were used to multitasking on commercials and special-effects jobs had to perform specialized tasks on a rigidly coordinated production schedule.*

be performed more efficiently than nonspecialized jobs, and it is also easier to replace people who leave an organization. However, jobs at lower levels of the organization are especially susceptible to overspecialization. If such jobs become too narrowly defined, employees may become bored and careless, derive less satisfaction from their jobs, and lose sight of their roles in the organization.[4]

Departmentalization

After jobs are specialized, they must be grouped into logical units, which is the process of **departmentalization.** Departmentalized companies benefit from the division of activities. Control and coordination are narrowed and made easier, and top managers can see more easily how various units are performing.

departmentalization
Process of grouping jobs into logical units

profit center
Separate company unit responsible for its own costs and profits

Departmentalization allows the firm to treat a department as a **profit center**—a separate company unit responsible for its own costs and profits. Thus, Sears <www.sears.com> can calculate the profits it generates from men's clothing, appliances, home furnishings, and every other department within a given store. Managers can then use this information in making decisions about advertising and promotional events, space allocation, and so forth.

Obviously, managers do not departmentalize jobs randomly. They group them logically, according to some common thread or purpose. In general, departmentalization may occur along *customer, product, process, geographic,* or *functional lines* (or any combination of these).

Customer Departmentalization Stores such as Sears and Macy's <www.macys.com> are divided into departments—a men's department, a women's department, a luggage department, and so on. Each department targets a specific customer category (men, women, people who want to buy luggage). **Customer departmentalization** makes shopping easier by providing identifiable store segments. Thus, a Sears customer shopping for a baby's playpen can bypass Lawn and Garden Supplies and head straight for Children's Furniture. Stores can also group products in locations designated for deliveries, special sales, and other service-oriented purposes. In general, the store is more efficient, and customers get better service because salespeople tend to specialize and gain expertise in their departments.

customer departmentalization
Departmentalization according to types of customers likely to buy a given product

product departmentalization
Departmentalization according to specific products or services being created

Product Departmentalization Manufacturers and service providers often opt for **product departmentalization**—dividing an organization according to the specific product or service being created. This approach is used at Lucent

SMILE WHEN YOU SAY THAT ABOUT MY DEPARTMENT, J.B.
YOU PEOPLE ARE BANKRUPTING THE COMPANY.
CBarsotti

*This "financial exploratorium" in New York is one of 5 opened by E*Trade <www.etrade.com> to accommodate customers in need of any one of the company's growing line of service products. Started in 1982 as a software service for brokers, E*Trade has grown by adding product departments to its core services and is now the No. 3 online brokerage, No. 3 ATM network, and No. 12 savings bank. Its goal is to become a financial-services supermarket: In addition to its brokerage business, E*Trade offers checking accounts and mortgages and will soon be in the credit-card and insurance businesses.*

Technologies. For example, the wireless communications department focuses on cellular telephones and services, while the optical networking department focuses on fiber optical and other cable and communications technologies. Because each of them represents a defined group of products or services, Lucent managers are able—in theory—to focus on specific product lines in a clear and defined way.

process departmentalization
Departmentalization according to production processes used to create a good or service

Process Departmentalization Other manufacturers favor **process departmentalization,** in which the organization is divided according to production processes. This principle is logical for the pickle maker Vlasic <www.vlasic.com>, which has separate departments to transform cucumbers into fresh-packed pickles, pickles cured in brine, and relishes. Cucumbers destined to become fresh-packed pickles must be packed into jars immediately, covered with a solution of water and vinegar, and prepared for sale. Those slated to be brined pickles must be aged in brine solution before packing. Relish cucumbers must be minced and combined with a host of other ingredients. Each process requires different equipment and worker skills.

geographic departmentalization
Departmentalization according to areas served by a business

Geographic Departmentalization Some firms are divided according to the areas of the country or the world that they serve. Levi Strauss, for instance, has one division for the United States <www.levi.com>, one for Europe <www.eu.levi.com>, one for the Asia Pacific region <www.levi.co.kr>, and one for Latin America <www.levi.com/lar>. Within the United States, **geographic departmentalization** is common among utilities. Pacific Power and Light is organized as four geographic departments—Southwestern, Columbia Basin, Mid-Oregon, and Wyoming.

functional departmentalization
Departmentalization according to a group's functions or activities

Functional Departmentalization Many service and manufacturing companies especially smaller ones, develop departments according to a group's functions or activities—a form of organization known as **functional departmentalization.** Such firms typically have production, marketing and sales, human resources, and accounting and finance departments. Departments may be further subdivided For example, the marketing department might be divided geographically or into separate staffs for market research and advertising.

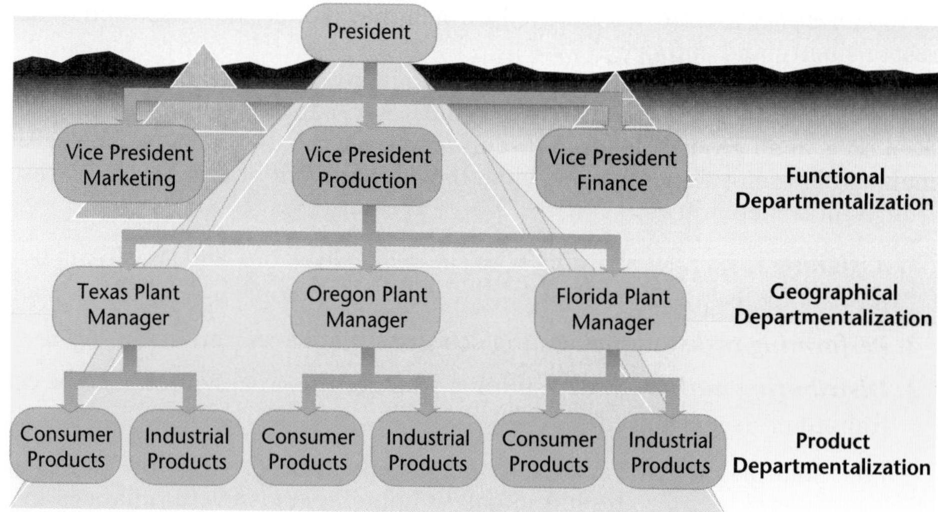

FIGURE 7.2
Multiple Forms of Departmentalization

Because different forms of departmentalization have different advantages, larger companies tend to adopt different types of departmentalization for various levels. The company illustrated in Figure 7.2 uses functional departmentalization at the top level. At the middle level, production is divided along geographic lines. At a lower level, marketing is departmentalized by product group.

Establishing the Decision-Making Hierarchy

After jobs have been appropriately specialized and grouped into manageable departments, the next step in organizing is to establish the decision-making hierarchy. That is, managers must explicitly define *reporting relationships* among positions so that everyone will know who has responsibility for various decisions and operations. The goal is to figure out how to structure and stabilize the organizational framework so that everyone works together to achieve common goals.

This truck-frame plant in Stockton, California, represents the commitment of Toyota Motor Co. <www.global.toyota.com> *to geography as a factor in the division of its activities. Operating in North America requires Toyota to forge relationships with such U.S. suppliers as Dana Corp.* <www.dana.com>*, an Ohio-based firm that furnishes Toyota with frame assemblies from its Parish Structural Products facility (which is also located in Stockton). At the same time, Toyota combines product with geographic departmentalization: At Stockton, it makes frames for its Tacoma-model trucks, not for its Highlander SUVs, Camry passenger cars, or even Tundra-model trucks.*

Companies vary greatly in the ways in which they handle the delegation of tasks, responsibility, and authority.

A major question that must be asked about any organization is this one: *Who makes which decisions?* The answer almost never focuses on an individual or even on a small group. The more accurate answer usually refers to the decision-making hierarchy. Generally speaking, the development of this hierarchy results from a three-step process:

1. ***Assigning tasks:*** determining who can make decisions and specifying how they should be made
2. ***Performing tasks:*** implementing decisions that have been made
3. ***Distributing authority:*** determining whether the organization is to be centralized or decentralized

For example, when Jack Greenberg took over as CEO of McDonald's <www.mcdonalds.com>, he immediately implemented several changes in the firm's decision-making hierarchy. McDonald's has always been—and continues to be—highly centralized. But Greenberg restructured both the company's decision-making process and its operations. He reduced staff at corporate headquarters in Oak Brook, Illinois, and established five regional offices throughout the United States. Now, many decisions are made at the regional level.

> **"For 40 years, all we did was open restaurants. That's not enough anymore."**
>
> **~Jack Greenberg, Former CEO of McDonald's**

Greenberg also clamped a lid on domestic growth and increased international expansion. In addition, he purchased stakes in three new restaurant chains with an eye on expansion: Donatos Pizza <www.donatos.com>, Chipotle Mexican Grill <www.chipotle.com>, and Aroma, a British coffee chain. Greenberg then installed four new managers, one to head up international operations and the others to oversee the three new restaurant partner groups. All four of these executives reported directly to Greenberg. Why the changes? "Maybe it was arrogance," said Greenberg. "For 40 years, all we did was open restaurants. That's not enough anymore."[5]

Self-Check Questions 1–3

*You should now be able to answer Self-Check Questions 1–3**

1. TRUE/FALSE Organizations create a stable *structure* for themselves and then seldom have to change it.

2. MULTIPLE CHOICE Which of the following jobs is likely to reflect the highest degree of *specialization?* [select one] **(a)** chief executive officer; **(b)** sales representative; **(c)** assembly line worker; **(d)** human resource manager; **(e)** public relations spokesperson.

3. MULTIPLE CHOICE Which of the following is **not** a common basis for *departmentalization?* [select one] **(a)** sequence; **(b)** function; **(c)** process; **(d)** product; **(e)** customer.

*Answers to Self-Check Questions 1–3 can be found on p. AN-4.

Assigning Tasks: Responsibility and Authority

The question of who is *supposed* to do what and who is entitled to do what in an organization is complex. In any company with more than one person, individuals must work out agreements about responsibilities and authority. **Responsibility** is the duty to perform an assigned task. **Authority** is the power to make the decisions necessary to complete the task.

responsibility
Duty to perform an assigned task

authority
Power to make the decisions necessary to complete a task

For example, imagine a midlevel buyer for Macy's department store who encounters an unexpected opportunity to make a large purchase at an extremely good price. Assume that an immediate decision is absolutely necessary—a decision that this buyer has no authority to make without confirmation from above. The company's policies on delegation and authority are inconsistent because the buyer is *responsible* for purchasing the clothes that will be sold in the upcoming season, but he or she lacks the *authority* to make the needed purchases.

Performing Tasks: Delegation and Accountability

Trouble occurs when appropriate levels of responsibility and authority are not clearly delineated in the working relationships between managers and subordinates. Here, the issues become delegation and accountability. **Delegation** begins when a manager assigns a task to a subordinate. **Accountability** falls to the subordinate, who must then complete the task. If tasks are effectively delegated and performed, the organization will function smoothly. But if the subordinate does not perform the task as assigned—perhaps doing a poor job or not getting the work done on time—problems can arise. The work unit may suffer, and the employee's performance abilities or motivation may be called into question.

delegation
Assignment of a task, responsibility, or authority by a manager to a subordinate

accountability
Liability of subordinates for accomplishing tasks assigned by managers

Fear of Delegating Unfortunately, many managers actually have trouble delegating tasks to others.[6] This is especially true in small businesses in which the owner-manager started out doing everything. Experts pinpoint certain reasons why some small-business managers may have trouble delegating effectively:[7]

- The feeling that employees can never do anything as well as you can
- The fear that something will go wrong if someone else takes over a job
- The lack of time for long-range planning because you are bogged down in day-to-day operations
- The sense of being in the dark about industry trends and competitive products because of the time you devote to day-to-day operations

To overcome these tendencies, small-business owners must begin by admitting that they can never go back to running the entire show and that they can in fact prosper—with the help of their employees—if they learn to let go. This problem, however, isn't always confined to small businesses. Some managers in big companies also don't delegate as much or as well as they should. There are also several reasons for this problem:

- The fear that subordinates don't really know how to do the job
- The fear that a subordinate might "show the manager up" in front of others by doing a superb job
- The desire to keep as much control as possible over how things are done
- A simple lack of ability as to how to effectively delegate to others

The remedies in these instances are a bit different. First, all managers should recognize that they can't do everything themselves. Second, if subordinates can't do a job, they should be trained so that they can assume more responsibility in the future. Third, managers should actually recognize that if a subordinate performs well, it also reflects favorably on the manager. Finally, a manager who simply

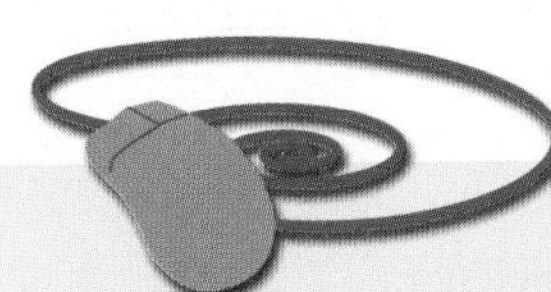

Mid-Chapter Internet Field Trip

"Organizing AOL"

In this chapter, we've introduced some of the many ways in which businesses are organized and shown how specialization and departmentalization affect organizational structure. We've also seen that its organization plays a large part in establishing a firm's procedures for decision making.

Although few companies disclose the details of their business processes, we can usually find some information about basic structure on their Web sites. AOL is one example. Let's explore AOL's corporate Web site at <www.corp.aol.com>. You probably know that AOL is the world leader in interactive and e-commerce services, Web brands, and Internet technologies. Its goal is to build a global medium as central to people's lives as the telephone or television. Founded in 1985, AOL also operates some of the most popular services on the Web, including MapQuest, AOL Instant Messenger, and AOL Moviefone, and is now a part of the world's largest communications company, AOL Time Warner. AOL's home page divides its coverage of the company into the following categories:

- Who We Are
- Press
- Member Services
- Foundation
- Careers

We'll start at the **Home** page (don't confuse this page with the home page for AOL's Internet service). First click on **New Corporate Web Site** at the bottom of the page and then select **Companies:**

1. Where does AOL appear to fit into the structure of its parent company, AOL Time Warner?

Look carefully at the way AOL Time Warner is organized:

2. Based on this Web page, what can you infer about the company's organizational structure?

Now return to the AOL corporate home page (you must return to the AOL Time Warner **Home** page first, choose **AOL,** and then select **Company Website**). Click on **Who We Are** and go to the **Who's Who** page:

3. What kind of organizational structure do you think is revealed by this list of AOL executives?

Under **Brand Support,** click on **President of Marketing:**

4. What can you deduce about this manager's levels of responsibility and authority and span of control?

Return to **Who's Who** and compare the list of **Business Support** executives with the positions listed under **AOL Products and Services:**

5. How do you think executive areas of responsibility might differ in these two groups?

To continue your Internet Field Trip, click on www.prenhall.com/griffin

doesn't know how to delegate might need specialized training in how to divide up and assign tasks to others.

Distributing Authority: Centralization and Decentralization

Delegation involves a specific relationship between managers and subordinates. Most businesses must also make decisions about general patterns of authority throughout the company. This pattern may be largely *centralized* or *decentralized* (or, usually, somewhere in between).

centralized organization
Organization in which most decision-making authority is held by upper-level management

Centralized Organizations

In a **centralized organization,** most decision-making authority is held by upper-level managers. Most lower-level decisions must be approved by upper management before they can be implemented.[8] As we noted earlier, McDonald's practices centralization as a way to maintain standardization. All restaurants must follow precise steps in buying products and making and packaging burgers and other menu items. Most advertising is handled at the corporate level, and any local advertising must be approved by a regional manager. Restaurants even have to follow prescribed schedules for facilities' maintenance and upgrades like floor polishing and parking lot cleaning.[9] Similarly, the CEO of J.C. Penney, Allen Questrom, has been systematically centralizing decision making as part of his efforts to revive the venerable retailer.[10] Centralized authority is also typical of small businesses.

The oil-industry giant ExxonMobil <www.exxon.mobil.com> *owns vast reserves of natural gas, like this field in the former Soviet republic of Turkmenistan. It does not, however, have much experience in the business of natural gas, which is becoming increasingly valuable as an alternative to coal and oil. In most respects, ExxonMobil is a highly centralized company, but in this less stable market, which tends to evolve and innovate rapidly, many experts are skeptical about the company's ability to decentralize the control that management exercises over corporate operations.*

Decentralized Organizations As a company gets larger, increasingly more decisions must be made; thus, the company tends to adopt a more decentralized pattern. In a **decentralized organization,** much decision-making authority is delegated to levels of management at various points below the top. The purpose of decentralization is to make a company more responsive to its environment by breaking the company into more manageable units, ranging from product lines to independent businesses. Reducing top-heavy bureaucracies is also a common goal. Jack Welch, former CEO of General Electric <www.ge.com/businesses>, is a longtime proponent of decentralized management. As he put it, "If you don't let managers make their own decisions, you're never going to be anything more than a one-person business." This logic also explains why cereal maker Kellogg Co. has been decentralizing. Top managers realize that in order to keep pace with today's eat-on-the-run lifestyles, lower level managers need more autonomy to make decisions and rush new products to market.[11]

decentralized organization

Organization in which a great deal of decision-making authority is delegated to levels of management at points below the top

"If you don't let managers make their own decisions, you're never going to be anything more than a one-person business."

~Jack Welch
FORMER CEO OF GENERAL ELECTRIC

Tall and Flat Organizations Related to the concept of centralized or decentralized authority are the concepts of tall and flat organizational structures. With relatively fewer layers of management, decentralized firms tend to reflect a **flat organizational structure** like that of the hypothetical law firm described in Figure 7.3(a). In contrast, companies with centralized authority systems typically require multiple layers of management and thus **tall organizational structures.** As you can see from Figure 7.3(b), the United States Army is a good example. Because information, whether upward or downward bound, must pass through so many organizational layers, tall structures are prone to delays in information flow.

As organizations grow in size, it is both normal and necessary that they become at least somewhat taller. For instance, a small firm with only an owner-manager and a few employees is likely to have two layers—the owner-manager and the employees who report to that person. But as the firm grows, more layers will be needed. Born Information Services <www.born.com>, for instance, is a small consulting firm created and run by Rick Born. At first, all his employees reported to him. But when the size of his firm had grown to more than 20 people, Born knew that he needed help in supervising and coordinating projects. As a result, he added a layer of management consisting of what he termed *staff managers* to serve as project coordinators.

flat organizational structure

Characteristic of decentralized companies with relatively few layers of management and relatively wide spans of control

tall organizational structure

Characteristic of centralized companies with multiple layers of management and relatively narrow spans of control

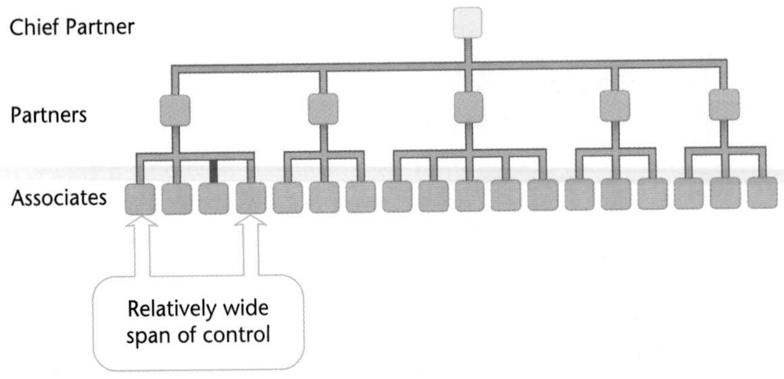

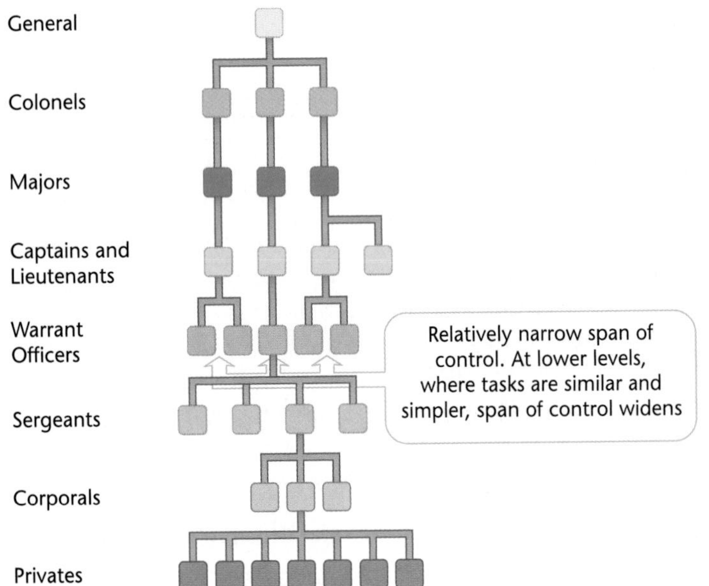

■ FIGURE 7.3
Organizational Structure and Span of Control

This move freed up time for Born to seek new business clients.[12] Like other managers, however, Born must ensure that he has only the number of layers his firm needs. Too few layers can create chaos and inefficiency, whereas too many layers can create rigidity and bureaucracy.

Span of Control As you can see from Figure 7.3, the distribution of authority in an organization also affects the number of people who work for any individual manager. In a flat organizational structure, the number of people managed by one supervisor—the manager's **span of control**—is usually wide. In tall organizations, span of control tends to be relatively narrower. Span of control, however, depends on many factors. Employees' abilities and the supervisor's managerial skills help determine whether span of control is wide or narrow, as do the similarity and simplicity of those tasks performed under the manager's supervision and the extent to which they are interrelated.[13]

span of control
Number of people supervised by one manager

If lower level managers are given more decision-making authority, their supervisors will thus have less work to do because some of the decisions they previously made will be transferred to their subordinates. By the same token, these managers may then be able to oversee and coordinate the work of more subordinates, resulting in an increased span of control. We have already seen that at McDonald's, the creation of five regional offices freed up time for the CEO, Jack Greenberg. In turn, reorganization allowed him to then create four new executive positions, one to oversee international expansion and the others to work with new restaurant partners.

Similarly, when several employees perform either the same simple task or a group of interrelated tasks, a wide span of control is possible and often desirable. For instance, because all the jobs are routine, one supervisor may well control an entire assembly line. Moreover, each task depends on another. If one station stops, everyone stops. Having one supervisor ensures that all stations receive equal attention and function equally well.

In contrast, when jobs are more diversified or prone to change, a narrow span of control is preferable. In Racine, Wisconsin, for example, the Case Corp. <www.casecorp.com> factory makes farm tractors exclusively to order in five to six weeks. Farmers can select from among a wide array of options, including engines, tires, power trains, and even a CD player. A wide assortment of machines and processes is used to construct each tractor. Although workers are highly skilled operators of their assigned machines, each machine is different. In this kind of setup, the complexities of each machine and the advanced skills needed by each operator mean that one supervisor can oversee only a small number of employees.[14]

Three Forms of Authority

Whatever type of structure a company develops, it must decide who will have authority over whom. As individuals are delegated responsibility and authority in a firm, a complex web of interactions develops. These interactions may take one of three forms of authority: *line, staff,* or *committee and team.* Like departmentalization, all three forms may be found in a given company, especially a large one.

Line Authority The type of authority that flows up and down the chain of command is **line authority.** Most companies rely heavily on **line departments**—those directly linked to the production and sales of specific products. For example, Clark Equipment Corp. has a division that produces forklifts and small earthmovers. In this division, line departments include purchasing, materials handling, fabrication, painting, and assembly (all of which are directly linked to production) along with sales and distribution (both of which are directly linked to sales).

line authority
Organizational structure in which authority flows in a direct chain of command from the top of the company to the bottom

line department
Department directly linked to the production and sales of a specific product

Each line department is essential to an organization's success. Line employees are the doers and producers in a company. If any line department fails to complete its task, the company cannot sell and deliver finished goods. Thus, the authority delegated to line departments is important. A bad decision by the manager in one department can hold up production for an entire plant. Say, for example, that the painting department manager at Clark Equipment changes a paint application on a batch of forklifts, which then show signs of peeling paint. The batch will have to be repainted (and perhaps partially reassembled) before the machines can be shipped.

Staff Authority Most companies also rely on **staff authority,** which is based on special expertise and usually involves counseling and advising line managers. Common staff members include specialists in areas such as law, accounting, and human resource management. A corporate attorney, for example, may be asked to advise the marketing department as it prepares a new contract with the firm's advertising agency. Legal staff members, however, do not actually make decisions that affect how the marketing department does its job. **Staff members,** therefore, aid line departments in making decisions but do not have the authority to make final decisions.

staff authority
Authority based on expertise that usually involves counseling and advising line managers

staff members
Advisers and counselors who aid line departments in making decisions but do not have the authority to make final decisions

Typically, the separation between line authority and staff responsibility is clearly delineated. As Figure 7.4 shows, this separation is usually indicated in organization charts by solid lines (line authority) and dotted lines (staff responsibility). It may help to understand this separation by remembering that whereas staff members generally provide services to management, line managers are directly involved in producing the firm's products.

Committee and Team Authority Recently, more and more organizations have started to use **committee and team authority**—authority granted to committees

committee and team authority
Authority granted to committees or work teams involved in a firm's daily operations

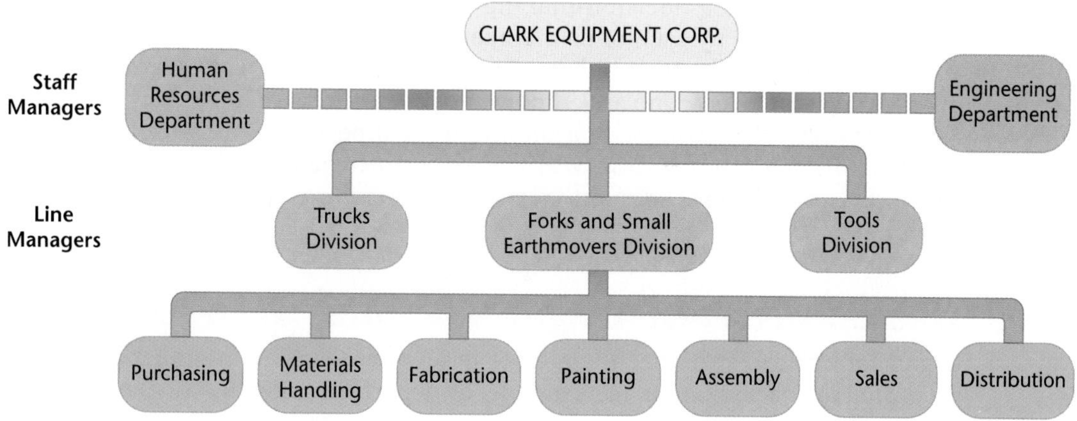

FIGURE 7.4
Line and Staff Organization

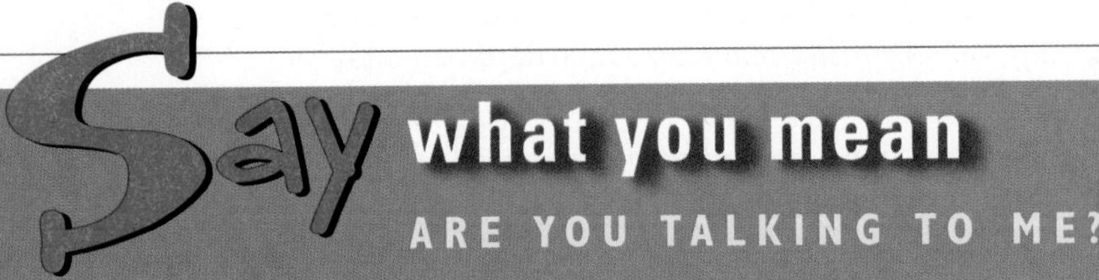

Say what you mean
ARE YOU TALKING TO ME?

One of the big reasons why global companies are organized in different ways is the culture of their home countries. Consequently, not only organization, but culture as well, influence the way decisions are made and communicated. In some companies, there's a big gap between senior management and those on the lower rungs, and communication across the gap is often quite formal. In other companies, because the vertical structure is less rigid, people tend to communicate in more familiar terms.

German companies, for example, tend to have fairly rigid structures, with jobs, authority, and responsibility clearly defined. Likewise, people in German organizations tend to respect status and titles. They're usually respectful of superiors and continue to use last names even when they're communicating with people they've known for years. Surprisingly, when it comes to decision-making, German companies like to keep everyone in the loop and be sure that people at all levels know what's going on.

In contrast, U.S. companies tend to have formal organizational structures while fostering communications—even between senior managers and easygoing lower level workers—that's often casual and easygoing, right down to the use of first names. Bosses command respect, but once they're outside the workplace, people from different levels interact easily.

In many Latin and South American cultures, bosses have a great deal of power and authority, and workers give them a corresponding degree of respect. Mexican workers sometimes call the boss *patrón*, and as the title suggests, the *patrón* is expected to provide employees with more than orders in the workplace: He's supposed to be a source of moral support and even material assistance and is a regular guest at weddings, funerals, and christenings (where he's often called upon to serve as godfather).

Sensitivity to local workplace behavior and attitudes—to the ways in which information is communicated and authority exercised and accepted—is one of the most important qualities that a global company can bring to its relationships with foreign organizations.

or work teams that play central roles in the firm's daily operations.[15] A committee, for example, may consist of top managers from several major areas. If the work of the committee is especially important and if the committee members will be working together for an extended time, the organization may even grant it special authority as a decision-making body that goes beyond the individual authority possessed by each of its members.

At the operating level, many firms today are also using work teams—groups of operating employees who are empowered to plan and organize their own work and to perform that work with a minimum of supervision. As with permanent committees, the organization will usually find it beneficial to grant special authority to work teams so that they may function more effectively.

Basic Forms of Organizational Structure

Organizations can structure themselves in an almost infinite number of ways—according to specialization, for example, or departmentalization or the decision-making hierarchy.[16] Nevertheless, it is possible to identify four basic forms of organizational structure that reflect the general trends followed by most firms: *functional, divisional, matrix,* and *international.*

Self-Check Questions 4–6

*You should now be able to answer Self-Check Questions 4–6**

4. MULTIPLE CHOICE The *decision-making hierarchy* includes all but which of the following? [select one] **(a)** assigning tasks; **(b)** performing tasks; **(c)** distributing authority; **(d)** creating obligations; **(e)** all of these are part of the decision-making hierarchy.

5. MULTIPLE CHOICE A *tall organization* usually has which of the following kinds of *span of control?* [select one] **(a)** wide; **(b)** hierarchical; **(c)** smooth; **(d)** top-down; **(e)** narrow.

6. TRUE/FALSE Organizations generally have *line authority, staff authority,* and *committee and team authority.*

*ANSWERS TO SELF-CHECK QUESTIONS 4–6 CAN BE FOUND ON P. AN-5.

Functional Organization

Functional organization is the approach to organizational structure used by most small to medium-size firms. Such organizations are usually structured around basic business functions (marketing, operations, finance). Thus, within the company, there is a marketing department, an operations department, and a finance department. The benefits of this approach include specialization within functional areas and smoother coordination among them. Experts with specialized training, for example, are hired to work in the marketing department, which handles all marketing for the firm.

functional organization
Form of business organization in which authority is determined by the relationships between group functions and activities

In large firms, coordination across functional departments becomes more complicated. Functional organization also fosters centralization (which may possibly be desirable) and makes accountability more difficult. As organizations grow, therefore, they tend to shed this form and move toward one of the other three structures.

Divisional Organization

A **divisional organization** relies on product departmentalization. The firm creates product-based divisions, each of which may then be managed as a separate enterprise. Organizations using this approach are typically structured around several **divisions**—departments that resemble separate businesses in that they produce and market their own products. The head of each division may be a corporate vice president or, if the organization is large, a divisional president. In addition, each division usually has its own identity and operates as a relatively autonomous business under the larger corporate umbrella.

divisional organization
Organizational structure in which corporate divisions operate as autonomous businesses under the larger corporate umbrella

division
Department that resembles a separate business in producing and marketing its own products

H. J. Heinz <www.heinz.com>, for example, is one of the world's largest food-processing companies. Heinz makes literally thousands of different products and markets them around the world. The firm is organized into seven basic divisions: food service (selling small packaged products such as mustard and relish to restaurants), infant foods, condiments (Heinz ketchup, steak sauce, and tomato sauce), Star-Kist tuna, pet foods, frozen-foods, and one division that handles miscellaneous products, including new lines being test marketed and soups, beans, and pasta products. Because of its divisional structure, Heinz can evaluate the performance of each division independently. Until recently, Heinz also had a division for its Weight Watchers business, but because this business was performing poorly, the company sold the Weight Watchers classroom program and folded its line of frozen foods into its existing frozen-foods division.[17] Because divisions are relatively autonomous, a firm can take such action with minimal disruption to its remaining business operations.

Like Heinz, other divisionalized companies are free to buy, sell, create, and disband divisions without disrupting the rest of their operations. Divisions can maintain healthy competition among themselves by sponsoring separate advertising campaigns, fostering different corporate identities, and so forth. They can also share certain corporate-level resources (such as market research data). Of course, if too much control is delegated to divisional managers, corporate managers may lose touch with daily operations. Competition between divisions can also become disruptive, and efforts in one division may be duplicated by those of another.

Matrix Organization

matrix structure
Organizational structure in which teams are formed and team members report to two or more managers

In a **matrix structure,** teams are formed in which individuals report to two or more managers. One manager usually has functional expertise, while the other has more of a product or project orientation. This structure was pioneered by the National Aeronautics and Space Administration (NASA) <www.nasa.gov> for use in developing specific programs. It is a highly flexible form that is readily adaptable to changing circumstances. Matrix structures rely heavily on committee and team authority.

In some companies, the matrix organization is a temporary measure, installed to complete a specific project and affecting only one part of the firm. In these firms, the end of the project usually means the end of the matrix—either a breakup of the team or a restructuring to fit it into the company's existing line-and-staff structure. Ford, for example, uses a matrix organization to design new models such as the new Ford Thunderbird, which was launched in 2001. A design team comprised of people from engineering, marketing, operations, and finance was created to design the new car. After its work was done, the team members moved back to their permanent functional jobs. Lockheed Martin also used a matrix structure to win its major government contract.

In other settings, the matrix organization is a semipermanent fixture. Figure 7.5 shows how Martha Stewart Living Omnimedia Inc. <www.marthastewart.com> has created a permanent matrix organization for its burgeoning lifestyle business. As you can see, the company is organized broadly into media and merchandising groups, each of which has specific product and product groups. Layered on top of this structure are teams of lifestyle experts organized into groups such as cooking, crafts, weddings, and so forth. Although each group targets specific customer needs, they all work, as necessary, across all product groups. A wedding expert, for example, might contribute to an article on wedding planning for a Martha Stewart magazine, contribute a story idea for a Martha Stewart cable television program, and supply content for a Martha Stewart Web site. This same individual might also help select fabrics suitable for wedding gowns that are to be retailed.[18]

International Organization

international organizational structures
Approaches to organizational structure developed in response to the need to manufacture, purchase, and sell in global markets

As we saw in Chapter 4, many businesses today manufacture, purchase, and sell in the world market. Thus, several different **international organizational structures** have emerged. Moreover, as competition on a global scale becomes more complex, companies often find that they must experiment with the ways in which they respond.[19]

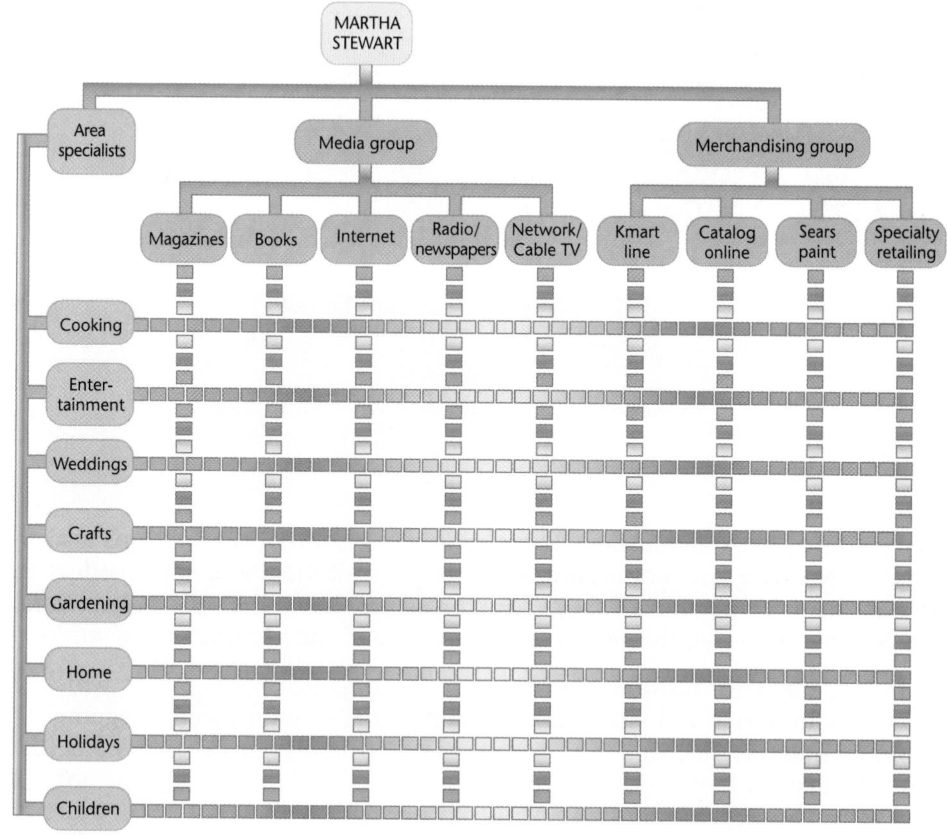

FIGURE 7.5
Matrix Organization at Martha Stewart

For example, when Wal-Mart <www.walmart.com> opened its first store outside the United States in 1992, it set up a special projects team to handle the logistics. As more stores were opened abroad in the mid-1990s, the firm created a small international department to handle overseas expansion. By 1999, however, international sales and expansion had become such a major part of Wal-Mart's operations that the firm created a separate international division headed up by a senior vice president. And by 2002, international operations had become so important to Wal-Mart that the international division was further divided into geographic areas where the firm does business, such as Mexico and Europe.[20]

Organizations with important international operations often begin with the form of organization outlined in Figure 7.6. Other firms have also developed a wide range of approaches to international organizational structure. The French food giant Danone Group <www.danonegroup.com>, for instance, has three major product groups: dairy products (Danone yogurts), bottled water (Evian), and cookies (Pim's). Danone's structure does not differentiate internationally but rather integrates global operations within each product group.[21]

Finally, some companies adopt a truly global structure in which they acquire resources (including capital), produce goods and services, engage in research and development, and sell products in whatever local market is appropriate, without any consideration of national boundaries. Until a few years ago, General Electric kept its international business operations as separate divisions. Now, however, the company functions as one integrated global organization. GE businesses around the world connect and interact with each other constantly, and managers freely move back and forth among them. This integration is also reflected in the top management team. The head of GE's audit team is French, the head of quality control is Dutch, and a German runs one of GE's core business groups.[22]

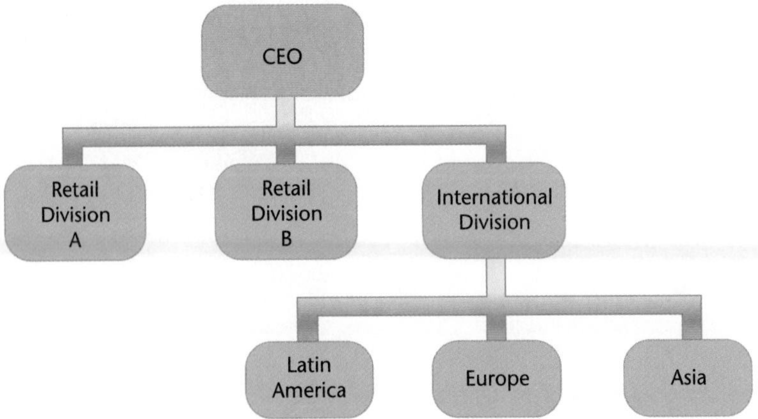

FIGURE 7.6
International Division Structure

Organizational Design for the Twenty-First Century

As the world grows increasingly complex and fast-paced, organizations also continue to seek new forms of organization that permit them to compete effectively. Among the most popular of these new forms are the *boundaryless organization*, the *team organization*, the *virtual organization*, and the *learning organization*.

Boundaryless Organization The *boundaryless organization* is one in which traditional boundaries and structures are minimized or eliminated altogether. For example, General Electric's fluid organization structure, in which people, ideas, and information flow freely between businesses and business groups, approximates this concept. Similarly, as firms partner with their suppliers in more efficient ways, external boundaries disappear. Some of Wal-Mart's key suppliers are tied directly into the retailer's vaunted information system. As a result, when Wal-Mart distribution centers start running low on Wrangler blue jeans, the manufacturer gets the information as soon as the retailer. Wrangler proceeds to manufacture new inventory and to restock the distribution center without Wal-Mart's having to place a new order.

As the term suggests, the boundaryless organization has erased certain boundaries. GE Power Systems <www.gepower.com/en_us>, *which sells electricity-generating turbines, uses the Internet to eliminate a boundary that once separated its traditional functions from those of its customers. Using the Web to connect with GE's turbine optimizer, any operator of a GE turbine can compare its performance with other turbines of the same model. GE will also calculate the long-term savings of a given improvement—another task that, in the pre–e-business era, would have been performed by the buyer-operator.*

The Technology of Personal Contact

Some observers worry that recent advances in communications signal the end of face-to-face dialogue, human interaction, collaboration, and teamwork. Surprisingly, however, many companies are finding that technology actually enhances and extends traditional interactions. "There's an opportunity for a whole new level of business-performance improvements in the collaborative redesign of processes, using the Internet," according to James A. Champy, chairman of consulting at Perot Systems.

Lockheed Martin uses a system of 90 Web software tools to coordinate its $200 billion project for building the next-generation stealth fighters. The manufacturer brings together 40,000 users, 80 subcontractors, and 187 locations around the world. Lockheed uses the Web to exchange documents and designs and to monitor project progress. "We're getting the best people, applying the best designs, from wherever we need them," says Mark Peden, Lockheed information systems vice president.

At General Motors, Web collaboration helps engineers and parts suppliers collaborate on product design. Complex designs might involve 14 worldwide sites in addition to the dozens of partner firms that design components and subsystems. Saving time allows the engineers to complete three or four alternative designs, instead of just one, and often still finish weeks sooner than anticipated.

Prospective students at Yale University <www.yale.edu/admit> use an Internet-based system to investigate the school, complete an application, and apply for financial aid. Admissions staff around the country share information about applicants, with online discussion and comments posted to documents. Yet admissions director James Stevens notifies every accepted applicant with a phone call. "[They'll] hear from me personally. It is very important to us for people to understand how personal the experience is here."

The Children's Hospital at Montefiore <www.montefiore.org> has integrated a facility-wide patient-information system. Patients and family members use smart cards for customized access to information about illness and treatment, for video games or movies on demand, and for Internet access. "It's about the patient's ability to control [the] environment," says software designer Jeb Weisman. The intent, says chief designer David Rockwell, is "to provide information, insight, and a sense of wonder and delight." Patients and their families thus become participants in their own treatment.

The technology is helpful, but of course it doesn't manage itself. Paul R. Gudonis, chairman and CEO of Genuity Inc., <www.genuity.com> says that while managers have made a good start in encouraging teams to use technology, "they've now found that it's going to take more effort off-line to integrate off-line and online processes to get the kind of changed behavior and benefits that they're looking for." Jon Katzenbach, consultant and author of *The Discipline of Teams,* reminds managers about the enduring value of hands-on management and face-to-face meetings. "Without meaningful personal interaction and doing 'real' work together," he warns, "it's hard to build understanding and accountability"

Team Organization *Team organization* relies almost exclusively on project-type teams, with little or no underlying functional hierarchy. People float from project to project as dictated by their skills and the demands of those projects. At Cypress Semiconductor <www.cypress.com>, T. J. Rodgers refuses to allow the organization to grow so large that it can't function this way. Whenever a unit or group starts getting too large, he simply splits it into smaller units. Therefore, the organization is composed entirely of small units. This strategy allows each unit to change direction, explore new ideas, and try new methods without having to deal with a rigid bureaucratic superstructure. Although few large organizations have actually reached this level of adaptability, Apple Computer <www.apple.com> and Xerox <www.xerox.com> are among those moving toward it.

"Without meaningful personal interaction and doing 'real' work together, it's hard to build understanding and accountability."

~Jon Katzenbach, consultant, AUTHOR OF *THE DISCIPLINE OF TEAMS*

Virtual Organization Closely related to the team organization is the *virtual organization*. A virtual organization has little or no formal structure. Typically, it has only a handful of permanent employees, a very small staff, and a modest administrative facility. As the needs of the organization change, its managers bring in temporary workers, lease facilities, and outsource basic support services to meet the demands of each unique situation. As the situation changes, the temporary workforce changes in parallel, with some people leaving the organization and others entering. Facilities and the subcontracted services also change. In other words, the virtual organization exists only in response to its own needs.[23]

Global Research Consortium (GRC) <www.worldvest.com> is a virtual organization. GRC offers research and consulting services to firms doing business in Asia. As clients request various services, GRC's staff of three permanent employees subcontracts the work to an appropriate set of several dozen independent consultants and researchers with whom it has relationships. At any given time, therefore, GRC may have several projects under way with 20 or 30 people working on various projects. As the projects change, so too does the composition of the organization. Figure 7.7 illustrates a hypothetical virtual organization.

Learning Organization The so-called *learning organization* works to integrate continuous improvement with continuous employee learning and development. Specifically, a learning organization works to facilitate the lifelong learning and personal development of all of its employees while continually transforming itself to respond to changing demands and needs.

While managers might approach the concept of a learning organization from a variety of perspectives, the most frequent goals are improved quality, continuous improvement, and performance measurement. The idea is that the most consistent and logical strategy for achieving continuous improvement is to constantly upgrade employee talent, skill, and knowledge. For example, if each employee in an organization learns one new thing each day and can translate that knowledge into work-related practice, continuous improvement will logically follow. Indeed, organizations that wholeheartedly embrace this approach believe that only through constant employee learning can continuous improvement really occur.

In recent years, many different organizations have implemented this approach on various levels. Shell Oil Co. <www.countonshell.com>, for example,

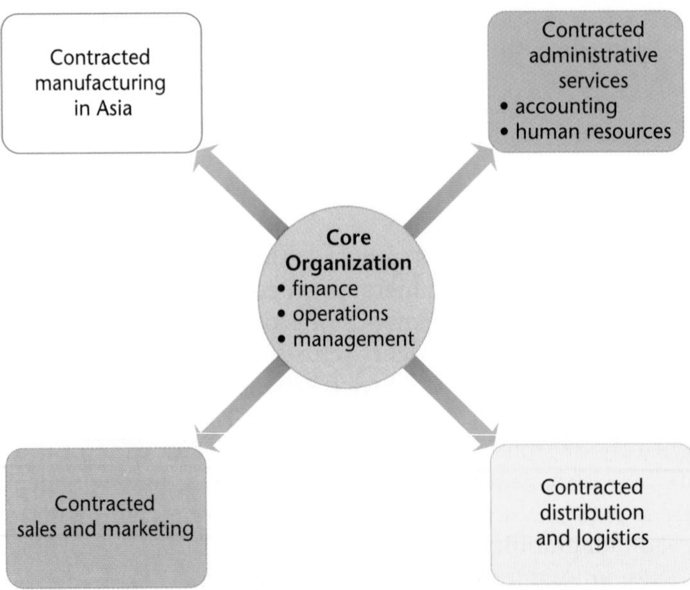

FIGURE 7.7
The Virtual Organization

recently purchased an executive conference center north of its headquarters in Houston. Called the Shell Learning Center, the facility boasts state-of-the-art classrooms and instructional technology, lodging facilities, a restaurant, and recreational amenities, such as a golf course, swimming pool, and tennis courts. Line managers at the firm rotate through the Center and serve as teaching faculty. Teaching assignments last anywhere from a few days to several months. At the same time, all Shell employees routinely attend training programs, seminars, and related activities, all the while gathering the latest information they need to have in order to contribute more effectively to the firm. Recent seminar topics have included time management, implications of the Americans with Disabilities Act, balancing work and family demands, and international trade theory.[24]

Informal Organization

Much of our discussion has focused on the organization's *formal structure*—its official arrangement of jobs and job relationships. In reality, however, all organizations also have another dimension—an *informal* organization within which people do their jobs in different ways and interact with other people in ways that do not follow formal lines of communication.

Formal Versus Informal Organizational Systems

The formal organization of a business is the part that can be seen and represented in chart form. The structure of a company, however, is by no means limited to the organization chart and the formal assignment of authority. Frequently, the **informal organization**—everyday social interactions among employees that transcend formal jobs and job interrelationships—effectively alters a company's formal structure. Indeed, this level of organization is sometimes just as powerful—if not more powerful—than the formal structure.

informal organization

Network, unrelated to the firm's formal authority structure, of everyday social interactions among company employees

On the negative side, the informal organization can reinforce office politics that put the interests of individuals ahead of those of the firm.[25] Likewise, a great deal of harm can be caused by distorted or inaccurate information communicated without management input or review. For example, if the informal organization is highlighting false information about impending layoffs, valuable employees may act quickly (and unnecessarily) to seek other employment. Among the more important elements of the informal organization are *informal groups* and the *organizational grapevine*.

Informal Groups *Informal groups* are simply groups of people who decide to interact among themselves. They may be people who work together in a formal sense or who just get together for lunch, during breaks, or after work. They may talk about business, the boss, or nonwork-related topics like families, movies, or sports. Their impact on the organization may be positive (if they work together to support the organization), negative (if they work together in ways that run counter to the organization's interests), or irrelevant (if what they do is unrelated to the organization).

Organizational Grapevine The **grapevine** is an informal communication network that can run through an entire organization.[26] Grapevines are found in all organizations except the very smallest, but they do not always follow the same patterns as formal channels of authority and communication, nor do they necessarily coincide with them. Moreover, because the grapevine typically passes information orally, such information often becomes distorted in the process.

grapevine

Informal communication network that runs through an organization

Attempts to eliminate the grapevine are fruitless, but, fortunately, managers do have some control over it. By maintaining open channels of communication and responding vigorously to inaccurate information, they can minimize the damage the grapevine can cause. In fact, the grapevine can actually be an asset.

By getting to know the key people in the grapevine, for example, the manager can partially control the information they receive and use the grapevine to sound out employee reactions to new ideas (for example, a change in human resource policies or benefit packages). The manager can also get valuable information from the grapevine and use it to improve decision making.

Intrapreneuring

Sometimes, organizations actually take steps to encourage the informal organization. They do so for a variety of reasons, two of which we have already discussed. First, most experienced managers recognize that the informal organization exists whether they want it or not. Second, many managers know how to use the informal organization to reinforce the formal organization. Perhaps more important, however, the energy of the informal organization can be harnessed to improve productivity.

intrapreneuring
Process of creating and maintaining the innovation and flexibility of a small-business environment within the confines of a large organization

Many firms, including Rubbermaid, 3M, and Xerox, support a process called **intrapreneuring:** creating and maintaining the innovation and flexibility of a small-business environment within the confines of a large, bureaucratic structure. The concept is basically sound. Historically, most innovations have come from individuals in small businesses (see Chapter 3). As businesses increase in size, however, innovation and creativity tend to become casualties in the battle for more sales and profits. In some large companies, new ideas are even discouraged, and champions of innovation have been stalled in midcareer.

Compaq <www.compaq.com>, which is now part of Hewlett-Packard, is an excellent example of how intrapreneuring works to counteract this trend. The firm has one major division, which is called the New Business Group. When a manager or engineer has an idea for a new product or product application, the individual takes it to the New Business Group and "sells" it. The managers in the group itself are then encouraged to help the innovator develop the idea for field-testing. If the product takes off and does well, it is then spun off into its own new business group or division. If it doesn't do as well as hoped, it may still be maintained as part of the New Business Group, or it may be phased out.

Self-Check Questions 7–9

*You should now be able to answer Self-Check Questions 7–9**

7. MULTIPLE CHOICE Which of the following is **not** a basic form of *organizational design?* [select one] **(a)** functional organization; **(b)** process organization; **(c)** divisional organization; **(d)** matrix organization; **(e)** international organization.

8. MULTIPLE CHOICE *Organizational designs for the twenty-first century* include which of the following? [select one] **(a)** boundaryless organization; **(b)** team organization; **(c)** virtual organization; **(d)** learning organization; **(e)** all of these.

9. TRUE/FALSE Few large businesses have informal organizations because of their formal and rigid organization charts.

*ANSWERS TO SELF-CHECK QUESTIONS 7–9 CAN BE FOUND ON P. AN-5.

Continued from page 189

How to Control for Vertical Lift

Throughout the project development process, Lockheed maintained a sharp focus on the needs of its customers, including the armed forces of the United States and United Kingdom. The U.S. Navy would be the biggest buyer, but the Marines were more assertive and had the most political and military influence. When the Marines demanded that the JFS jet be able to make vertical landings on smaller ships, Lockheed made that one of its top priorities requirements. Designing a vertical-lift system for such a large jet had never been done, and when it hit a snag, engineers worked around the clock for weeks to solve the problem.

Burbage's team also anticipated and planned strategies for addressing future problems. Managers from the three partner firms worked together to create an extensive list of lessons learned about building modern aircraft. In a technique that Burbage dubbed the "premortem," they compared the list to their 10-year schedule to identify high-risk points. Solutions for these high-risk points are already being worked out, years before they will be implemented. Preplanning gives the team confidence in meeting its deadlines, which are critical to the JSF program. "If you can't control your schedule," explains Burbage, "the implication is that you can't control costs. And if you can't control costs, you won't keep the [military] services interested in funding your program."

Lockheed is on track to reach its goal of a flying prototype by 2005. This accomplishment, while meaningful, is even more extraordinary in light of the challenges that had to be overcome to reach it. Loren Thompson, a defense analyst at the Lexington Institute, explains it best: "The Lockheed guys were like the patient who undergoes heart surgery while running for his life. They had to fix themselves in the midst of the biggest battle they'd ever been in."

Questions for Discussion

1. Describe the basic structural components at Lockheed Martin that are most relevant to the JSF project.
2. What role does specialization play at Lockheed Martin?
3. What kinds of authority are reflected in this case?
4. What kind of organizational structure does Lockheed Martin seem to have?
5. What role did the informal organization play in Lockheed's successful bid for the contract?

Summary of Learning Objectives

1. *Discuss the elements that influence a firm's* organizational structure.

Common structural and operating components in all businesses include a series of *jobs to be done* and a *specific overall purpose.* Each organization must develop the most appropriate **organizational structure**—the specification of the jobs to be done and the ways in which they relate to one another.

Managers assess many factors as they plan for and then create a structure that will allow an organization to function efficiently. Chief among elements that determine organizational structure are *purpose, mission,* and *strategy.* (Size, technology, and changes in environmental circumstances also affect structure.) Most organizations change structures almost continuously.

Firms prepare **organization charts** to clarify structure and to show employees where they fit into a firm's operations. Each box represents a job, and solid lines define the **chain of command,** or *reporting relationships.* The charts of large firms are complex and include individuals at many levels. Because size prevents them from charting every manager, they may create single organization charts for overall corporate structure and separate charts for divisions.

2. *Explain* specialization *and* departmentalization *as the building blocks of organizational structure.*

Two activities constitute the building blocks of all organizations: (1) The process of identifying specific jobs and designating people to perform them leads to **job specialization.** To perform one overall job, such as making cars (Ford) or providing telecommunications services (AT&T), managers specialize it into several smaller jobs. Workers can then develop real expertise and can better coordinate their work with that of others. Job specialization is a natural part of organizational growth and has certain advantages. Specialized jobs are learned more easily and can be performed more efficiently, and it's also easier to replace people who leave.

(2) After they're specialized, jobs are grouped into logical units—the process of **departmentalization.** Control and coordination are narrowed and made easier, and top managers can see more easily how units are performing. Firms can treat each department as a **profit center**—a separate unit responsible for its own costs and profits.

Departmentalization follows one (or any combination) of five forms: (i) **Customer departmentalization** divides stores into segments, making them more efficient and providing better customer service because salespeople tend to specialize. (ii) Manufacturers and service providers often use **product departmentalization**—dividing an organization according to specific products or services. (iii) Other manufacturers favor **process departmentalization**—dividing the organization according to production processes. (iv) With **geographic departmentalization,** a firm is divided according to the areas that it serves. (v) Many service and manufacturing companies rely on **functional departmentalization**—a division into such group functions as production, marketing and sales, human resources, or accounting and finance. Larger companies take advantage of different types of departmentalization for various levels.

3. *Distinguish among* responsibility, authority, delegation, *and* accountability *and explain the differences between decision making in* centralized *and* decentralized organizations.

After jobs have been specialized and departmentalized, firms establish decision-making hierarchies. They define *reporting relationships* so everyone will know who has responsibility for various decisions and operations. The development of this hierarchy results from a three-step process: (1) *Assigning tasks*: determining who can make decisions and specifying how they're to be made. (2) *Performing tasks*: implementing decisions that have been made. (3) *Distributing authority*: deciding whether the organization is to be centralized or decentralized

Individuals in organizations must work out agreements about responsibilities and authority. **Responsibility** is the duty to perform an assigned task. **Authority** is the power to make the decisions necessary to complete the task. Trouble occurs when levels of responsibility and authority are not clearly delineated. The issues then become delegation and accountability. **Delegation** begins when a manager assigns a task to a subordinate. **Accountability** falls to the subordinate, who must complete the task. If tasks are effectively delegated and performed, things will go smoothly.

In addition to specific relationships between managers and subordinates, firms must also decide on companywide patterns of authority. This pattern may be one of two types (or somewhere in between): (1) In a **centralized organization,** most decision-making authority is held by upper-level managers. Lower level decisions must be approved. (2) But as a company gets larger and must make more decisions, it tends toward a **decentralized organization,** in which decision-making authority is delegated to levels of management below the top. Decentralization makes a company more flexible by breaking it into manageable units.

With fewer management layers, decentralized firms reflect a **flat organizational structure.** Centralized companies require multiple layers of management and thus **tall organizational structures.** Growing organizations naturally become taller. Distribution of authority also affects the number of people under any individual manager. In a flat organizational structure, the number of people under one supervisor—the manager's **span of control**—is usually wide. In tall organizations, it's narrower.

Regardless of structure, every firm must decide who will have authority over whom. As responsibility and authority are delegated, a web of interactions develops into one of three forms of authority: (1) **Line authority** flows up and down the chain of command. Most companies rely on **line departments**—those directly linked to production and sales. (2) **Staff authority** is based on special expertise and usually involves advising line managers. Staff members include specialists in areas such as law and accounting. **Staff members** help line departments make decisions but have no authority to make them. (3) More organizations now use **committee and team authority**—authority granted to committees or work teams. Work teams are groups of operating employees who are empowered to plan and organize their own work and to perform it with little supervision.

4. *Explain the differences among* functional, divisional, matrix, *and* international organizational structures *and describe the most popular new forms of organizational design.*

Most firms rely on one of four basic forms of organizational structure: (1) **Functional organization** is used by most small to medium-size firms, which are usually structured around basic functions—a marketing department, an operations department, a finance department, and so on. (2) A **divisional organization** relies on product-based divisions, each of which may be managed as a separate enterprise. Companies are typically structured around several **divisions**—departments that resemble separate businesses because they produce and market their own products. They operate as relatively autonomous businesses under the larger corporate umbrella.

(3) In a **matrix structure,** individuals on teams report to two or more managers, one with functional expertise and one with a product or project orientation. Flexible and adaptable to changing circumstances, matrix structures rely on committee and team authority. Sometimes, they are temporary measures. (4) Because many businesses operate in the world market, different **international organizational structures** have emerged. As global competition becomes more complex, companies may experiment with ways to respond. Some adopt truly global structures, acquiring resources and producing and selling products in local markets without consideration of national boundaries.

Organizations continue to seek new forms of organization that permit them to compete effectively. Following are four of the most popular new forms: (1) In the *boundaryless organization*, traditional boundaries and structures are minimized or eliminated. (2) *Team organization* relies on project-type teams, with little or no functional hierarchy. People float from project to project due to their skills or project demands.

(3) A *virtual organization* has little formal structure, but rather a handful of permanent employees, a small staff, and a modest administrative facility. To keep up with changing needs or the demands of unique situations, managers hire temporary workers, lease facilities, and outsource support services. (4) The *learning organization* works to facilitate employees' lifelong learning and personal development while continually transforming itself to meet changing demands and needs. Upgrading employee talent, skill, and knowledge is treated as a strategy for continuous improvement.

5. ***Describe the* informal organization, *and discuss* intrapreneuring.**

The formal organization is the part that can be represented in chart form. The **informal organization**—everyday social interactions among employees that transcend formal jobs and job interrelationships—may alter formal structure. There are two important elements in most informal organizations: (1) *Informal groups* consist of people who decide to interact among themselves. Their impact on a firm may be positive, negative, or irrelevant. (2) The **grapevine** is an informal communication network that can run through an entire organization. Because it can be harnessed to improve productivity, some organizations encourage the informal organization. Many firms support **intrapreneuring**—creating and maintaining the innovation and flexibility of a small business within the confines of a large, bureaucratic one.

KEY TERMS

organizational structure (p. 190)
organization chart (p. 191)
chain of command (p. 191)
job specialization (p. 191)
departmentalization (p. 192)
profit center (p. 192)
customer departmentalization (p. 193)
product departmentalization (p. 193)
process departmentalization (p. 194)
geographic departmentalization (p. 194)
functional departmentalization (p. 194)
responsibility (p. 197)
authority (p. 197)
delegation (p. 197)
accountability (p. 197)
centralized organization (p. 198)
decentralized organization (p. 199)
flat organizational structure (p. 199)
tall organizational structure (p. 199)
span of control (p. 200)
line authority (p. 201)
line department (p. 201)
staff authority (p. 201)
staff members (p. 201)
committee and team authority (p. 201)
functional organization (p. 203)
divisional organization (p. 203)
division (p. 203)
matrix structure (p. 204)
international organizational structures (p. 204)
informal organization (p. 209)
grapevine (p. 209)
intrapreneuring (p. 210)

QUESTIONS AND EXERCISES

Questions for Review

1. What is an organization chart? What purpose does it serve?
2. Explain the significance of size as it relates to organizational structure. Describe the changes that are likely to occur as an organization grows.
3. What is the difference between responsibility and authority?
4. Why do some managers have difficulties in delegating authority? Why does this problem tend to plague smaller businesses?
5. Why is a company's informal organization important?

Questions for Analysis

6. Draw up an organization chart for your college or university.
7. Describe a hypothetical organizational structure for a small printing firm. Describe changes that might be necessary as the business grows.
8. Compare and contrast the matrix and divisional approaches to organizational structure. How would you feel personally about working in a matrix organization in which you were assigned simultaneously to multiple units or groups?

Application Exercises

9. Interview the manager of a local service business—a fast-food restaurant. What types of tasks does this manager typically delegate? Is the appropriate authority also delegated in each case?
10. Using books, magazines, or personal interviews, identify a person who has succeeded as an intrapreneur. In what ways did the structure of the intrapreneur's company help this individual succeed? In what ways did the structure pose problems?

Building Your Business Skills

GETTING WITH THE PROGRAM

This exercise enhances the following SCANS workplace competencies: demonstrating basic skills, demonstrating thinking skills, exhibiting interpersonal skills, and working with information.

Goal

To encourage students to understand the relationship between organizational structure and a company's ability to attract and keep valued employees.

Situation

You are the founder of a small but growing high-technology company that develops new computer software. With your current workload and new contracts in the pipeline, your business is thriving except for one problem: You cannot find computer programmers for product development. Worse yet, current staff members are being lured away by other high-tech firms. After suffering a particularly discouraging personnel raid in which competitors captured three of your most valued employees, you schedule a meeting with your director of human resources to plan organizational changes designed to encourage worker loyalty. You already pay top dollar, but the continuing exodus tells you that programmers are looking for something more.

Method

Working with three or four classmates, identify some ways in which specific organizational changes might improve the working environment and encourage employee loyalty. As you analyze the following factors, ask yourself the obvious question: If I were a programmer, what organizational changes would encourage me to stay?

- *Level of job specialization.* With many programmers describing their jobs as tedious because of the focus on detail in a narrow work area, what changes, if any, would you make in job specialization? Right now, for instance, few of your programmers have any say in product design.
- *Decision-making hierarchy.* What decision-making authority would encourage people to stay? Is expanding employee authority likely to work better in a centralized or decentralized organization?
- *Team authority.* Can team empowerment make a difference? Taking the point of view of the worker, describe the ideal team.
- *Intrapreneuring.* What can your company do to encourage and reward innovation?

Follow-Up Questions

1. With the average computer programmer earning nearly $70,000, and with all competitive firms paying top dollar, why might organizational issues be critical in determining employee loyalty?
2. If you were a programmer, what organizational factors would make a difference to you? Why?
3. As the company founder, how willing would you be to make major organizational changes in light of the shortage of qualified programmers?

Exercising Your Ethics

MINDING YOUR OWN BUSINESS

The Situation

Assume that you have recently gone to work for a large high-tech company. You have discovered an interesting arrangement in which one of your coworkers is engaging. Specifically, he blocks his schedule for the hour between 11:00 A.M. and 12:00 noon each day and does not take a lunch break. During this one-hour interval, he is actually running his own real estate business.

The Dilemma

You recently asked him how he manages to pull this off. "Well," he responded, "the boss and I never talked about it, but she knows what's going on. They know they can't replace me, and I always get my work done. I don't use any company resources. So, what's the harm?" Interestingly, you also have a business opportunity that could be pursued in the same way.

Questions for Discussion

1. What are the ethical issues in this situation?
2. What do you think most people would do in this situation?
3. What would you do in this situation?

Mastering Business Essentials

■ **EPISODE 7** describes the formation of a work team given responsibility for making an extremely important presentation. It shows why organizations sometimes find it beneficial to delegate responsibility and authority for special projects to committees or teams. *This episode illustrates the issues that arise when managers must be flexible within an existing organizational structure.*

Crafting Your Business Plan

DOCTORING THE ORGANIZATION

The Purpose of the Assignment

1. To provide an example that illustrates ways in which organizational options can be presented in a business plan, in the framework of the *Business PlanPro (BPP)* software package.
2. To demonstrate how three chapter topics—organization structure, departmentalization, and authority and responsibility—can be integrated as components in the *BPP* planning environment.

Assignment

After reading Chapter 7 in the textbook, open the BPP *software and look around for information about organizational structure, departmentalization, and authority and responsibility as they apply to a sample firm:* Medquip Inc. *To find* Medquip, Inc., *do the following:*

Open the *Business PlanPro.* If it asks if you want to "create a new business plan" or "open an existing plan," select "create a new business plan" (even though you are not going to create a plan at this time). You will then be taken to the *Business PlanPro EasyPlan Wizard.* On the screen, click on the option entitled "**Research It.**" You will then be presented with a new list of options, including **Sample Plan Browser.** After clicking on the **Sample Plan Browser,** go down the alphabetical list of sample plans and double-click on **Medical Equipment Development—Instruments,** which is the location for *Medquip Inc.* The screen you are looking at is the introduction page for *Medquip's* business plan. Next, scroll down until you reach the **Table of Contents** for the *Medquip* business plan.

Now respond to the following questions:

1. Construct an organization chart for Medquip Inc. [Sites to see in *BPP* for this item: On the Table of Contents page, click on each of the following in turn: **6.0 Management Summary, 6.1 Organizational Structure, 6.2 Management Team,** and **6.4 Personnel Plan,** including **Table: Personnel.**]
2. Explain how Medquip's organizational structure is set up to take advantage of its competitor's weakness in product innovation. [Sites to see in *BPP:* On the Table of Contents page, click on **4.2.4 Main Competitors.**]
3. Which type of departmentalization—customer, product, functional, or process—does Medquip use? Give examples from Medquip's business plan to support your answer.
4. For each job position at Medquip, how clearly are authority and responsibility delineated in the business plan?

Video Exercise

JUICING UP THE ORGANIZATION: NANTUCKET NECTARS

Learning Objectives

The purpose of this video is to help you:

1. Recognize how growth affects an organization's structure.
2. Discuss the reasons why businesses departmentalize.
3. Understand how flat organizations operate.

Synopsis

Tom Scott and Tom First founded Nantucket Nectars in 1989 when they had an idea for a peach drink. In the early days, the two ran the entire operation from their boat. Now, Nantucket Nectars has more than 130 employees split between headquarters in Cambridge, Massachusetts, and several field offices. As a result, management has developed a more formal structure, and the company relies on cross-functional teams to handle special projects, such as the implementation of new accounting software. This and other strategies have helped Nantucket Nectars successfully manage rapid growth.

Discussion Questions

1. *For analysis:* What type of organization is in place at Nantucket Nectars?
2. *For analysis:* How would you describe the top-level span of management at Nantucket Nectars?
3. *For application:* Nantucket Nectars may need to change its organizational structure as it expands into new products and new markets. Under what circumstances might some form of divisional organization be appropriate?
4. *For application:* Assume that Nantucket Nectars is purchasing a well-established beverage company with a tall structure stressing top-down control. What are some of the problems that management might face in integrating the acquired firm into the existing organizational structure of Nantucket Nectars?
5. *For debate:* Assume that someone who is newly promoted into a management position at Nantucket Nectars cannot adjust to the idea of delegating work to lower level employees. Should this new manager be demoted? Support your chosen position.

Online Exploration

Visit the Nantucket Nectars site at <www.juiceguys.com> and follow the links about the company and its products. Then use Hoover's Online at <www.hoovers.com> to search for the latest news about the company, which is formally known as Nantucket Allserve. Has it been acquired by a larger company, or has it acquired one or more smaller firms? What are the implications for the chain of command and decision-making and organizational structure of Nantucket Nectars?

CHAPTER

Managing Human Resources and Labor Relations

After reading this chapter, you should be able to:

1. Define *human resource management* and explain how managers plan for human resources.
2. Identify the tasks in *staffing* a company and discuss ways in which organizations *select, develop,* and *appraise* employee performance.
3. Describe the main components of a *compensation system.*
4. Describe some of the key legal issues involved in hiring, compensating, and managing workers in today's workplace.
5. Discuss *workforce diversity,* the management of *knowledge workers,* and the use of a *contingent workforce* as important changes in the contemporary workplace.
6. Explain why workers organize and what *labor unions* do for their members.
7. Explain the *collective bargaining* process and its possible outcomes.

From Hard Bargains to Hard Times

During the economic boom times of just a few years ago, workers had the advantage in the employment equation. A general labor shortage combined with an acute shortage of knowledge and other skilled workers to make the labor market a seller's market. Top college graduates had multiple offers, and skilled technical workers could take their pick of jobs. Moreover, businesses began rolling out new benefits, perquisites, and incentives to attract and retain the best and the brightest.

SAS Institute <www.sas.com>, a North Carolina software firm, offered employees unlimited sick days, on-site childcare, flexible work schedules, and free beverages. In Houston, BMC Software <www.bmc.com> greeted employees each morning with a pianist in the lobby and provided fresh vegetables for lunch from the firm's own garden. Other employers offered concierges, laundry pickup and delivery, and even on-site pet care. Some companies offered cash or new cars as signing bonuses.

But as the economy slowed in 2001 and into 2002, the advantage shifted to employers. Throughout the 1990s, as it turns out, companies had relied on technological advances ranging from robotics to the Internet to reduce costs in areas as diverse as advertising, production, and purchasing. When the economy turned sour, they realized that they had cut as many costs as possible from most areas of their operations, and not surprisingly, many turned to their labor forces for the next round of cuts.

Many firms have reduced or stopped hiring, and the hardest hit have even started layoffs. (Many of the dot-coms, among the most aggressive employers in terms of new and innovative benefits, have disappeared altogether.) This trend stems in part from the realization that workers have fewer options, either in finding or leaving jobs. One of the first areas hit was perquisites, or "perks." Among the lost amenities: the employee bowling alley at an Austin-based high-tech firm and Xerox's "Plant Caretaker" (employees must now water their own plants). But don't be fooled into thinking that these are trivial issues. "There is a huge dent in morale when you take anything away from employees, no matter how miniscule it may look," says workplace consultant Sharon Jordan-Evans.

Next in line have been more traditional benefits. Many firms have either reduced contributions to benefits programs or eliminated them altogether. Ford Motors and Lucent Technologies are just two of the many organizations that now pay less for health insurance or retirement plans. Bonuses, sick leave, and vacation time are also being squeezed. As a last resort, some firms are even asking workers to accept pay cuts. Pay at Agilent Technology has dropped 10 percent, and Disney has cut some pay rates by 30 percent.

Our opening story is continued on page 241.

"There is a huge dent in morale when you take anything away from employees, no matter how miniscule it may look."

~Sharon Jordan-Evans
WORKPLACE CONSULTANT

The Foundations of Human Resource Management

human resource management (HRM)
Set of organizational activities directed at attracting, developing, and maintaining an effective workforce

Human resource management (HRM) is the set of organizational activities directed at attracting, developing, and maintaining an effective workforce. Human resource management takes place within a complex and ever-changing environmental context and is increasingly being recognized for its strategic importance.[1]

The Strategic Importance of HRM

Human resources are critical for effective organizational functioning. HRM (or *personnel,* as it is sometimes called) was once relegated to second-class status in many organizations, but its importance has grown dramatically in the last several years. This new importance stems from increased legal complexities, the recognition that human resources are a valuable means for improving productivity, and the awareness today of the costs associated with poor human resource management.

Indeed, managers now realize that the effectiveness of their HR function has a substantial impact on a firm's bottom-line performance. Poor human resource planning can result in spurts of hiring followed by layoffs—costly in terms of unemployment compensation payments, training expenses, and morale. Haphazard compensation systems do not attract, keep, and motivate good employees, and outmoded recruitment practices can expose the firm to expensive and embarrassing legal action. Consequently, the chief human resource executive of most large businesses is a vice president directly accountable to the CEO, and many firms are developing strategic HR plans that are integrated with other strategic planning activities.

Human Resource Planning

As you can see in Figure 8.1, the starting point in attracting qualified human resources is planning. In turn, HR planning involves job analysis and forecasting the demand for and supply of labor.

job analysis
Systematic analysis of jobs within an organization

job description
Outline of the duties of a job, working conditions, and the tools, materials, and equipment used to perform it

job specification
Description of the skills, abilities, and other credentials required by a job

Job Analysis **Job analysis** is a systematic analysis of jobs within an organization.[2] A job analysis results in two things:

- The **job description** lists the duties and responsibilities of a job; its working conditions; and the tools, materials, equipment, and information used to perform it.
- The **job specification** lists the skills, abilities, and other credentials and qualifications needed to perform the job effectively.

Job analysis information is used in many HR activities. For instance, knowing about job content and job requirements is necessary to develop appropriate selection methods and job-relevant performance appraisal systems and to set equitable compensation rates.

Forecasting HR Demand and Supply After managers fully understand the jobs to be performed within an organization, they can start planning for the organization's future HR needs. The manager starts by assessing trends in past HR usage, future organizational plans, and general economic trends. A good sales forecast is often the foundation, especially for smaller organizations. Historical ratios can then be used to predict demand for types of employees, such as operating employees and sales representatives. Large organizations use much more complicated models to predict HR needs.

Forecasting the supply of labor is really two tasks:

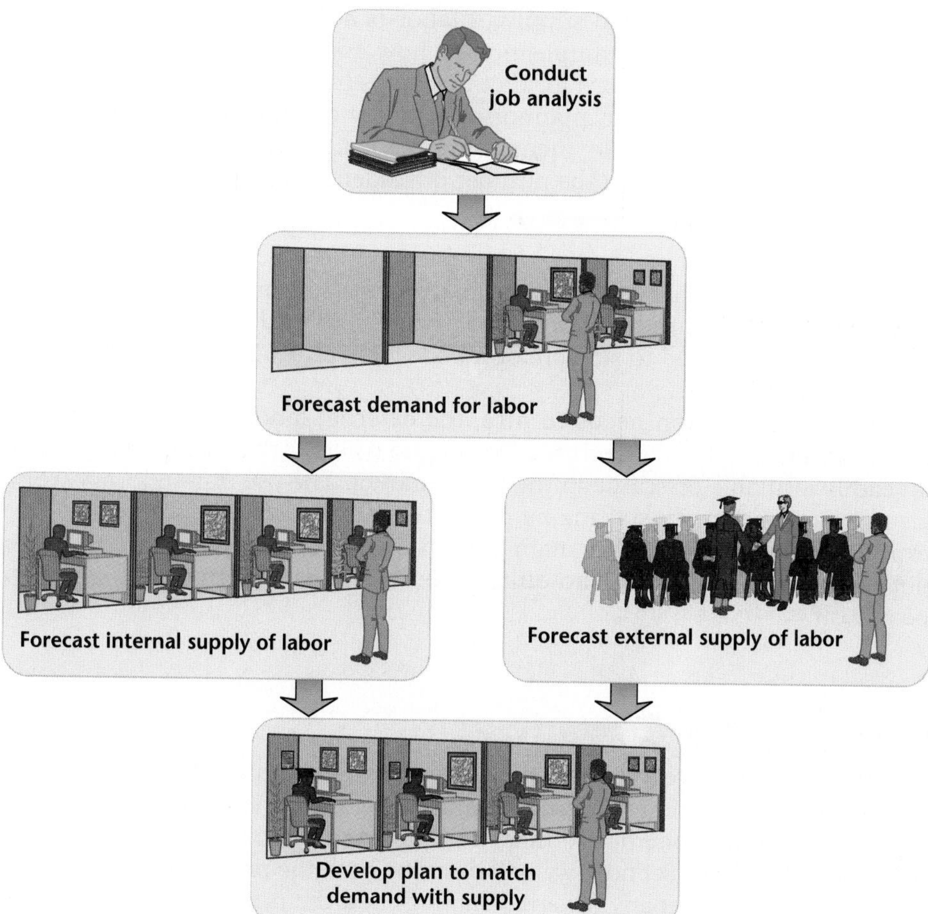

FIGURE 8.1
The Human Resource Planning Process

- Forecasting *internal supply*—the number and type of employees who will be in the firm at some future date.
- Forecasting *external supply*—the number and type of people who will be available for hiring from the labor market at large.

The simplest approach merely adjusts present staffing levels for anticipated turnover and promotions. Again, however, large organizations use extremely sophisticated models to make these forecasts.

Replacement Charts At higher levels of the organization, managers plan for specific people and positions. The technique most commonly used is the **replacement chart,** which lists each important managerial position, who occupies it, how long that person will probably stay in it before moving on, and who (by name) is now qualified or soon will be qualified to move into it. This technique allows ample time to plan developmental experiences for people identified as potential successors to critical managerial jobs.[3] Charles Knight, the former CEO of Emerson Electric Co. <www.emersonelectric.com>, maintained an entire room for posting the credentials of his top 700 executives.

replacement chart
List of each management position, who occupies it, how long that person will likely stay in the job, and who is qualified as a replacement

Skills Inventories To facilitate both planning and identifying people for transfer or promotion, some organizations also have **employee information systems,** or **skills inventories.** These systems are usually computerized and contain information on each employee's education, skills, work experience, and career aspirations. Such a system can quickly locate every employee who is qualified to fill a position requiring, for example, a degree in chemical engineering, three years of experience in an oil refinery, and fluency in Spanish.

employee information system (skills inventory)
Computerized system containing information on each employee's education, skills, work experience, and career aspirations

Forecasting the external supply of labor is a different problem altogether. How does a manager, for example, predict how many electrical engineers will be seeking work in California or Florida three years from now? To get an idea of the future availability of labor, planners must rely on information from outside sources, such as state employment commissions, government reports, and figures supplied by colleges on the number of students in major fields.

Matching HR Supply and Demand After comparing future demand and internal supply, managers can make plans to manage predicted shortfalls or overstaffing. If a shortfall is predicted, new employees can be hired, present employees can be retrained and transferred into understaffed areas, individuals approaching retirement can be convinced to stay on, or labor-saving or productivity-enhancing systems can be installed.

If the organization needs to hire, the external labor-supply forecast helps managers plan on how to recruit according to whether the type of person needed is readily available or scarce in the labor market. The use of temporary workers also helps managers in staffing by giving them extra flexibility. If overstaffing is expected to be a problem, the main options are transferring the extra employees, not replacing individuals who quit, encouraging early retirement, and laying people off.[4]

Staffing the Organization

When managers have determined that new employees are needed, they must then turn their attention to recruiting and hiring the right mix of people. Staffing the organization is one of the most complex and important tasks of good HR management. In this section, we will describe both the process of acquiring staff from outside the company (*external staffing*) and the process of promoting staff from within (*internal staffing*). Both external and internal staffing, however, start with effective *recruiting*.

recruiting
Process of attracting qualified persons to apply for jobs an organization is seeking to fill

internal recruiting
Considering present employees as candidates for openings

Recruiting Human Resources Once an organization has an idea of its future HR needs, the next phase is usually recruiting new employees. **Recruiting** is the process of attracting qualified persons to apply for the jobs that are open. Where do recruits come from? Some recruits are found internally, while others come from outside of the organization.

Internal Recruiting **Internal recruiting** means considering present employees as candidates for openings. Promotion from within can help build morale and keep high-quality employees from leaving. In unionized firms, the procedures for notifying employees of internal job-change opportunities are usually spelled out in the union contract. For higher-level positions, a skills inventory system may be used to identify internal candidates, or managers may be asked to recommend individuals who should be considered.

external recruiting
Attracting persons outside of the organization to apply for jobs

External Recruiting **External recruiting** involves attracting people outside of the organization to apply for jobs. External recruiting methods include advertising, campus interviews, employment agencies or executive search firms, union hiring halls, referrals by present employees, and hiring "walk-ins" or "gate-hires" (people who show up without being solicited). A manager must select the most appropriate method for each job. The manager might, for instance, use the state employment service to find a maintenance worker but not a nuclear physicist. Private employment agencies can be a good source of clerical and technical employees, and executive search firms specialize in locating top-management talent. Newspaper ads are often used because they reach a wide audience and thus allow minorities equal opportunity to find out about and apply for job openings.

As we noted at the beginning of this chapter, during the late 1990s, recruiters faced a difficult job as unemployment plummeted. By early 1998, for example, unemployment had dropped to a 23-year low of 4.6 percent. As a result, recruiters at firms such as Sprint, PeopleSoft, and Cognex had to stress how much "fun" it was to work for them, reinforcing this message with ice cream socials, karaoke contests, softball leagues, and free-movie nights. By 2001, however, the situation had begun to change. Unemployment began to creep back up, many larger employers (such as AT&T and Hewlett-Packard) announced major job cutbacks, and recruiters were again able to attract highly qualified employees. While most companies have tried to maintain the innovative benefits programs that they had inaugurated in the 1990s, they were also able to avoid costly new programs and could afford to be more selective in the employees they chose to hire.[5]

Selecting Human Resources

Once the recruiting process has attracted a pool of applicants, the next step is to select someone to hire. The intent of the selection process is to gather from applicants information that will predict their job success and then to hire the candidates likely to be most successful. Of course, the organization can only gather information about factors that can be used to predict future performance. The process of determining the predictive value of information is called **validation.**[6]

validation
Process of determining the predictive value of a selection technique

Application Forms The first step in selection is usually asking the candidate to fill out an application. An application form is an efficient method of gathering information about the applicant's previous work history, educational background, and other job-related demographic data. It should not contain questions about areas unrelated to the job such as gender, religion, or national origin. Application form data are generally used informally to decide whether a candidate merits further evaluation, and interviewers use application forms to familiarize themselves with candidates before interviewing them.

Tests Tests of ability, skill, aptitude, or knowledge that is relevant to a particular job are usually the best predictors of job success, although tests of general intelligence or personality are occasionally useful as well. In addition to being

Employees of Cingular Wireless <www.cingular.com>, *a specialist in mobile voice and data communications, gather at the hometown Atlanta Zoo. Cingular markets itself as a company that "enhances the customer experience," and it wants to send a comparable message when communicating to employees and potential employees. "We want customers to use the wireless device as a tool to express themselves," says a vice president for human resources, "and we want to give our employees the opportunity to be just as expressive." The point, of course, is to foster productivity and loyalty in an era of impermanence in employer-employee relations.*

validated, tests should be administered and scored consistently. All candidates should be given the same directions, allowed the same amount of time, and offered the same testing environment (temperature, lighting, distractions).[7]

Interviews Although a popular selection device, the interview is sometimes a poor predictor of job success. For example, biases inherent in the way people perceive and judge others on first meeting affect subsequent evaluations. Interview validity can be improved by training interviewers to be aware of potential biases and by tightening the structure of the interview. In a structured interview, questions are written in advance and all interviewers follow the same question list with each candidate. Such structure introduces consistency into the interview procedure and allows the organization to validate the content of the questions. For interviewing managerial or professional candidates, a somewhat less structured approach can be used. Although question areas and information-gathering objectives are still planned in advance, specific questions vary with the candidates' backgrounds.

Other Techniques Organizations also use other selection techniques that vary with circumstances. Polygraph tests, once popular, are declining in popularity. On the other hand, organizations occasionally require applicants to take physical exams (being careful that their practices are consistent with the Americans with Disabilities Act). More organizations are using drug tests, especially in situations in which drug-related performance problems could create serious safety hazards. Applicants at a nuclear power plant, for example, will probably be tested for drugs. Some organizations also run credit checks on prospective employees.

Developing the Workforce

After a company has hired new employees, it must acquaint them with the firm and their new jobs. Managers also take steps to train employees and to further develop necessary job skills. In addition, every firm has some system for performance appraisal and feedback. Unfortunately, the results of these assessments sometimes require procedures for demoting or terminating employees.

Self-Check Questions 1–3

*You should now be able to answer Self-Check Questions 1–3**

1. TRUE/FALSE A *job analysis* is used to determine how much someone should be paid to perform a particular job.

2. MULTIPLE CHOICE Which of the following is a useful technique for planning for managerial positions? [select one] **(a)** skills inventory; **(b)** replacement chart; **(c)** job description; **(d)** job specification; **(e)** application blank.

3. MULTIPLE CHOICE Which of the following is **not** a common *selection tool*? [select one] **(a)** test; **(b)** interview; **(c)** polygraph exam; **(d)** interview; **(e)** drug test.

*ANSWERS TO SELF-CHECK QUESTIONS 1–3 CAN BE FOUND ON P. AN-5.

Training

As its name suggests, **on-the-job training** occurs while the employee is at work. Much of this training is informal, as when one employee shows another how to use the photocopier. In other cases, it is quite formal. For example, a trainer may teach secretaries how to operate a new e-mail system from their workstations.

Off-the-job training takes place at locations away from the work site. This approach offers a controlled environment and allows focused study without interruptions. For example, the petroleum equipment manufacturer Baker-Hughes uses classroom-based programs to teach new methods of quality control. Chaparral Steel's training program includes four hours a week of general education classroom training in areas such as basic math and grammar.

Other firms use **vestibule training** in simulated work environments to make off-the-job training more realistic. American Airlines, for example, trains flight attendants through vestibule training, and AT&T uses it to train telephone operators. Finally, many organizations today are increasingly using computerized and/or Web-based training.[8]

on-the-job training
Training, sometimes informal, conducted while an employee is at work

off-the-job training
Training conducted in a controlled environment away from the work site

vestibule training
Off-the-job training conducted in a simulated environment

Performance Appraisal

In some small companies, **performance appraisal** takes place when the owner tells an employee, "You're doing a good job." In larger firms, performance appraisals are designed to show more precisely how well workers are doing their jobs. Typically, the appraisal process involves a written assessment issued on a regular basis. As a rule, however, the written evaluation is only one part of a multistep process.

The appraisal process begins when a manager defines performance standards for an employee. The manager then observes the employee's performance. If the standards are clear, the manager should have little difficulty comparing expectations with performance. For some jobs, a rating scale like the abbreviated one in Figure 8.2 is useful in providing a basis for comparisons. In addition to scales for initiative, punctuality, and cleanliness, a complete form will include several other scales directly related to performance. Comparisons drawn from such scales form the basis for written appraisals and for decisions about raises, promotions, demotions, and firings. The process is completed when the manager and employee meet to discuss the appraisal.[9]

performance appraisal
Evaluation of an employee's job performance in order to determine the degree to which the employee is performing effectively

Compensation and Benefits

Most workers today also expect certain benefits from their employers. Indeed, a major factor in retaining skilled workers is a company's **compensation system**—the total package of rewards that it offers employees in return for their labor.[10]

Although wages and salaries are key parts of all compensation systems, most also include *incentives* and *employee benefits programs*. We discuss these and other types of employee benefits in this section. Remember, however, that finding the right combination of compensation elements is always complicated by the need to make employees feel valued while holding down company costs. Thus, compensation systems differ widely, depending on the nature of the industry, the company, and the types of workers involved.

compensation system
Set of rewards that organizations provide to individuals in return for their willingness to perform various jobs and tasks within the organization

Wages and Salaries

Wages and salaries are the dollar amounts paid to employees for their labor. **Wages** are paid for time worked. For example, workers who are paid by the hour receive wages. A **salary** is paid for discharging the responsibilities of a job. A salaried executive earning $100,000 per year is paid to achieve results even if that

wages
Compensation in the form of money paid for time worked

salary
Compensation in the form of money paid for discharging the responsibilities of a job

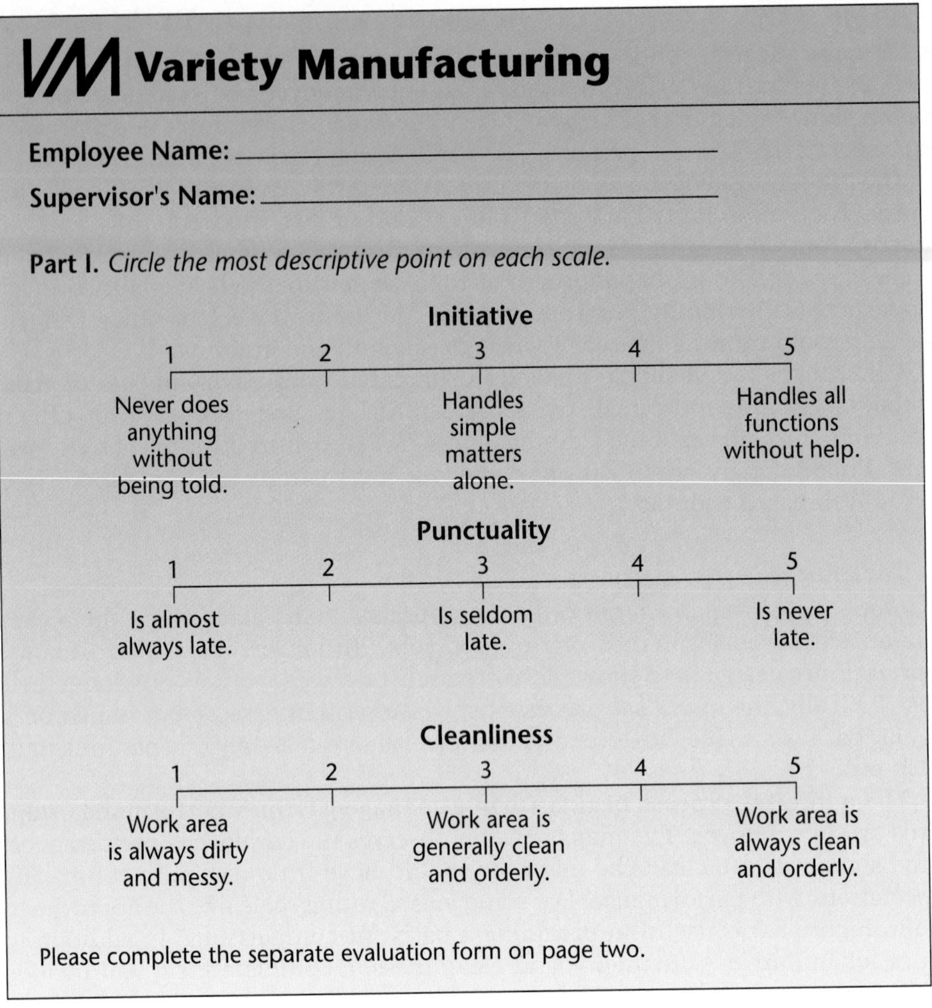

FIGURE 8.2
Performance Rating Scale

means working 5 hours one day and 15 the next. Salaries are usually expressed as an amount paid per year or per month.

In setting wage and salary levels, a company may start by looking at its competitors' levels. A firm that pays less than its rivals knows that it runs the risk of losing valuable personnel. Conversely, to attract top employees, some companies pay more than their rivals. M&M/Mars, for example, pays managerial salaries about 10 percent above the average in the candy and snack food industry.

A firm must also decide how its internal wage and salary levels will compare for different jobs. For example, Sears must determine the relative salaries of store managers, buyers, and advertising managers. In turn, managers must decide how much to pay individual workers within the company's wage and salary structure. Although two employees may do exactly the same job, the employee with more experience may earn more. Moreover, some union contracts specify differential wages based on experience.

> "What was once a smushy, subjective effort by finger-in-the wind managers is hitting new levels of scientific precision."
> —BUSINESS WEEK, ON THE ROLE OF TECHNOLOGY IN ASSESSING WORKER PERFORMANCE

Incentive Programs

Naturally, employees feel better about their companies when they believe that they are being fairly compensated; however, studies and experience have shown that beyond a certain point, more money will not produce better performance. Indeed, neither across-the-board nor cost-of-living wage increases cause peopl

From the Smushy to the Scientific

Advances in technology permit companies to gather, analyze, report, and apply information in ways that would have been impossible a decade ago. One area that has long cried out for better use of information is worker performance measurement. "[W]hat was once a smushy, subjective effort by finger-in-the-wind managers is hitting new levels of scientific precision," reports *Business Week*.

Consider the technology revolution in performance measurement at household goods retailer Pier 1 Imports <www.pier1.com>. In the past, because daily sales reports could be calculated only at the end of the day, employees didn't know how well they were doing until it was too late to do anything about it. Now, Pier 1 uses technology to tabulate sales continuously. In cities where Pier 1 has multiple stores, the same technology pits one store against the others by allowing employees to see not only their own results, but also results from other stores. Employees check performance regularly, and use improvement goals to increase their bonuses.

At British Airways <www.britishairways.com>, software monitors employees to ensure that coffee breaks and personal phone calls don't get charged to the company. Progress toward corporate goals, such as ticket sales and complaint resolutions, is also tracked. Workers have instant access to performance scores and can see the impact of incentive compensation on their daily pay. Other firms, however, are using even more intrusive technologies, such as entry card data (to determine what time workers arrive and leave) and security cameras (sometimes without notification to the employees) that are placed in cubicles, hallways, and even restrooms. Software also allows managers to receive reports of every Web site accessed and can even record workers' every keystroke on company PCs. Many workers see the benefits of accurate and objective performance measurement, but some, not surprisingly, claim that technology is invading their privacy. As technology continues to progress, the debate is sure to continue.

to work harder. Money motivates employees only if it is tied directly to performance. The most common method of establishing this link is the use of **incentive programs**—special pay programs designed to motivate high performance. Some programs are available to individuals, whereas others are distributed on a companywide basis.[11]

incentive program
Special compensation program designed to motivate high performance

Individual Incentives A sales bonus is a typical incentive. Employees receive **bonuses**—special payments above their salaries—when they sell a certain number or certain dollar amount of goods for the year. Employees who fail to reach this goal earn no bonuses. **Merit salary systems** link raises to performance levels in nonsales jobs.[12] For example, many baseball players have contract clauses that pay them bonuses for hitting over .300, making the All-Star team, or being named Most Valuable Player.

bonus
Individual performance incentive in the form of a special payment made over and above the employee's salary

merit salary system
Individual incentive linking compensation to performance in nonsales jobs

Executives commonly receive stock options as incentives. Disney CEO Michael Eisner, for example, can buy several thousand shares of company stock each year at a predetermined price.[13] If his managerial talent leads to higher profits and stock prices, he can buy the stock at a price lower than the market value for which, in theory, he is largely responsible. He is then free to sell the stocks at market price, keeping the profits for himself. Executive stock options have, unfortunately, been at the center of some of the recent accounting scandals plaguing some businesses today. In a nutshell, firms have chosen to not treat them as expenses at the time they were granted, contrary to what accountants suggest. In response to growing criticism, some companies, such

Discovery Communications Inc. <www.discovery.com> *faced a morale problem because its fixed-pay system meant that people doing a job in one division did not receive raises even when the pay scale for the same job description went up in another division. Employees saw the system as unfair, and so Discovery, which runs 33 cable networks out of its headquarters in Bethesda, Maryland, switched to a pay-for-performance compensation system that allows for healthy bonuses based on supervisors' evaluations and overall corporate performance.*

as Coca-Cola, have announced plans to change how they account for stock options.

pay for performance (or variable pay)
Individual incentive that rewards a manager for especially productive output

A newer incentive plan is called **pay for performance,** or **variable pay.** In essence, middle managers are rewarded for especially productive output—for producing earnings that significantly exceed the cost of bonuses. Such incentives have long been common among top-level executives and factory workers, but variable pay goes to middle managers on the basis of companywide performance, business unit performance, personal record, or all three factors.

The number of variable pay programs in the United States has been growing consistently for the last decade, and most experts predict that they will continue to grow in popularity. Eligible managers must often forgo merit or entitlement raises (increases for staying on and reporting to work every day), but many firms say that variable pay is a better motivator because the range between generous and mediocre merit raises is usually quite small anyway. Merit raises also increase fixed costs: They are added to base pay and increase the base pay used to determine the retirement benefits that the company must pay out.

profit-sharing plan
Incentive plan for distributing bonuses to employees when company profits rise above a certain level

gainsharing plan
Incentive plan that rewards groups for productivity improvements

pay-for-knowledge plan
Incentive plan to encourage employees to learn new skills or become proficient at different jobs

Companywide Incentives Some incentive programs apply to all the employees in a firm.[14] Under **profit-sharing plans,** for example, profits earned above a certain level are distributed to employees. Conversely, **gainsharing plans** distribute bonuses to employees when a company's costs are reduced through greater work efficiency. **Pay-for-knowledge plans** encourage workers to learn new skills and to become proficient at different jobs. They receive additional pay for each new skill or job that they master.

benefits
Compensation other than wages and salaries

workers' compensation insurance
Legally required insurance for compensating workers injured on the job

Benefits Programs

A growing part of nearly every firm's compensation system is its benefits program. **Benefits**—compensation other than wages and salaries offered by a firm to its workers—comprise a large percentage of most compensation budgets. Most companies are required by law to provide social security retirement benefits and **workers' compensation insurance** (insurance for compensating workers injured on the job). Most businesses also voluntarily provide health, life, and disability insurance. Many also allow employees to use payroll deductions to buy stock at discounted prices. Another common benefit is paid time-off for vacations and holidays. Counseling services for employees with alcohol, drug, or emotional problems are also becoming more common. On-site child-care centers are also becoming popular.[15]

Retirement Plans Retirement plans are also an important—and sometimes controversial—benefit that is available to many employees. Most company-sponsored retirement plans are set up to pay pensions to workers when they retire. In some cases, the company contributes all the money to the pension fund. In others, contributions are made by both the company and employees. Currently, about 60 percent of U.S. workers are covered by pension plans of some kind.

Containing the Costs of Benefits As the range of benefits has grown, so has concern about containing their costs. Many companies are experimenting with cost-cutting plans under which they can still attract and retain valuable employees. One approach is the **cafeteria benefits plan.** A certain dollar amount of benefits per employee is set aside so that each employee can choose from a variety of alternatives.

cafeteria benefit plan
Benefit plan that sets limits on benefits per employee, each of whom may choose from a variety of alternative benefits

Another area of increasing concern is health-care costs. Medical procedures that once cost several hundred dollars now cost several thousand dollars. Medical expenses have increased insurance premiums, which in turn have increased the cost to employers of maintaining benefits plans.

Many employers are looking for new ways to cut those costs. One increasingly popular approach is for organizations to create their own networks of health-care providers. These providers agree to charge lower fees for services rendered to employees of member organizations. In return, they enjoy established relationships with large employers and thus more clients and patients. Because they must make lower reimbursement payments, insurers also charge less to cover the employees of network members.

The Legal Context of HR Management

As much or more than any area of business, HR management is heavily influenced by federal law and judicial review. In this section, we summarize some of the most important and far-reaching areas of HR regulation.

Equal Employment Opportunity

The basic goal of all **equal employment opportunity** regulation is to protect people from unfair or inappropriate discrimination in the workplace.[16] Let's begin by noting that discrimination in itself is not illegal. Whenever one person is given a pay raise and another is not, for example, the organization has made a decision to distinguish one person from another. As long as the basis for this discrimination is purely job related (made, for instance, on the basis of performance or seniority) and is applied objectively and consistently, the action is legal and appropriate.

equal employment opportunity
Legally mandated nondiscrimination in employment on the basis of race, creed, sex, or national origin

Problems arise when distinctions among people are not job related. In such cases, the resulting discrimination is illegal. Various court decisions, coupled with interpretations of the language of various laws, suggest that illegal discrimination actions by an organization or its managers cause members of a "protected class" to be unfairly differentiated from other members of the organization.

Protected Classes in the Workplace Illegal discrimination is based on a stereotype, belief, or prejudice about classes of individuals. At one time, for example, common stereotypes regarded black employees as less dependable than white

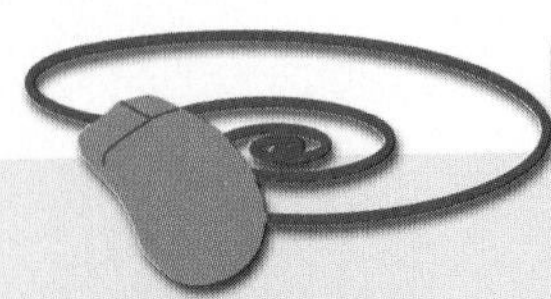

Mid-Chapter Internet Field Trip

"One of the 100 Best"

In this chapter, we've discussed some of the challenges that companies face in hiring, evaluating, and compensating employees, as well as some of the legal and safety issues that arise in the course of managing human resources.

Many companies manage these functions very well, maintaining safe workplaces where qualified employees are appraised and compensated fairly. Still other companies manage human resources *exceptionally* well, earning reputations as "the best places to work." Continental Airlines is one of these employers. Let's take a closer look at some of Continental's HR challenges and see how it meets them by exploring the airline's Web site at <www.continental.com>. From the home page go immediately to **About Continental,** where you will find pages on several topics, including:

- Career Opportunities
- Global Alliances
- Investor Relations
- News Releases
- Company Profile
- Company History

From the list at **About Continental,** click on **Career Opportunities** and then select **Benefits and Incentives:**

1. What are some of the benefits of working at Continental Airlines?
2. Which of these listed benefits are also incentives designed to help motivate employee performance?

Return to **About Continental** and select **Company Profile.** Now click on **Diversity:**

3. How does Continental use the diversity of its workforce to its best advantage?

Return to **Company Profile** and select **Awards:**

4. How do other organizations judge Continental as a place to work?

Go back again to **About Continental** and select **Career Opportunities** once more. This time, chose either **Airport and Reservations Positions** or **Corporate Positions.** Select a job and read the description:

5. How does Continental use its Web site as a staffing tool?

To continue your Internet Field Trip, click on www.prenhall.com/griffin

employees, women as less suited to certain types of work than men, and disabled individuals as unproductive employees.

Based on these stereotypes, some organizations routinely discriminated against blacks, women, and the disabled. To combat discrimination, laws have been passed to protect various classes of individuals. A **protected class** consists of all individuals who share one or more common characteristics as indicated by a given law. The most common criteria for defining protected classes include race, color, religion, gender, age, national origin, disability status, and status as a military veteran.[17]

protected class
Set of individuals who by nature of one or more common characteristics are protected under the law from discrimination on the basis of that characteristic

Equal Employment Opportunity Commission (EEOC)
Federal agency enforcing several discrimination-related laws

Enforcing Equal Employment Opportunity The enforcement of equal opportunity legislation is handled by two agencies. The **Equal Employment Opportunity Commission,** or **EEOC** <www.eeoc.gov>, is a division of the Department of Justice. It was created by Title VII of the 1964 Civil Rights Act and has specific responsibility for enforcing Title VII, the Equal Pay Act, and the Americans with Disabilities Act.

The other agency charged with monitoring equal employment opportunity legislation is the Office of Federal Contract Compliance Programs, or OFCCP <www.dol.gov/dol/esa/public/of_org.htm>. The OFCCP is responsible for enforcing executive orders that apply to companies doing business with the federal government. A business with government contracts must have on file a written **affirmative action plan**—that is, a written statement of how the organization intends to actively recruit, hire, and develop members of relevant protected classes.

affirmative action plan
Practice of recruiting qualified employees belonging to racial, gender, or ethnic groups who are underrepresented in an organization

Legal Issues in Compensation As we noted earlier, most employment regulations are designed to provide equal employment opportunity. Some legislation

"I see by your résumé that you're a woman."

however, goes beyond equal employment opportunity and really deals more substantively with other issues. One such area is legislation covering compensation.

Contemporary Legal Issues in HR Management

In addition to these established areas of HR legal regulation, there are several emerging legal issues that will likely become more and more important with the passage of time. These include employee safety and health, various emerging areas of discrimination law, employee rights, and employment-at-will.

Employee Safety and Health The **Occupational Safety and Health Act of 1970, or OSHA** <www.osha.gov>, is the single most comprehensive piece of legislation ever passed regarding worker safety and health. OSHA holds that every employer has an obligation to furnish each employee with a place of employment that is free from hazards that cause or are likely to cause death or physical harm. It is generally enforced through inspections of the workplace by OSHA inspectors. If an OSHA compliance officer believes that a violation has occurred, a citation is issued. Nonserious violations may result in fines of up to $1,000 for each incident. Serious or willful and repeated violations may incur fines of up to $10,000 per incident.

Occupational Safety and Health Act of 1970 (OSHA)
Federal law setting and enforcing guidelines for protecting workers from unsafe conditions and potential health hazards in the workplace

Emerging Areas of Discrimination Law There are also several emerging areas of discrimination law that managers must also be familiar with. In this section, we will discuss some of the most important.

AIDS in the Workplace Although AIDS is considered a disability under the Americans with Disabilities Act of 1990, the AIDS situation itself is sufficiently severe enough that it warrants special attention. Employers cannot legally require an AIDS or any other medical examination as a condition for making an offer of employment. Organizations must treat AIDS like any other disease covered by law. They must maintain the confidentiality of all medical records. They cannot discriminate against a person with AIDS, and they should try to educate coworkers about AIDS. They cannot discriminate against AIDS victims in training or in consideration for promotion, and they must accommodate or make a good-faith effort to accommodate AIDS victims.

sexual harassment

Practice or instance of making unwelcome sexual advances in the workplace

Sexual Harassment Sexual harassment has been a problem in organizations for a long time and is a violation of Title VII of the Civil Rights Act of 1964. **Sexual harassment** is defined by the EEOC as unwelcome sexual advances in the work environment. If the conduct is indeed unwelcome and occurs with sufficient frequency to create an abusive work environment, the employer is responsible for changing the environment by warning, reprimanding, or perhaps firing the harasser.[18]

The courts have ruled and defined that there are two types of sexual harassment:

quid pro quo harassment

Form of sexual harassment in which sexual favors are requested in return for job-related benefits

hostile work environment

Form of sexual harassment deriving from off-color jokes, lewd comments, and so forth

- In cases of **quid pro quo harassment,** the harasser offers to exchange something of value for sexual favors. A male supervisor, for example, might tell or suggest to a female subordinate that he will recommend her for promotion or give her a raise in exchange for sexual favors.
- The creation of a **hostile work environment** is a subtler form of sexual harassment. A group of male employees who continually make off-color jokes and lewd comments and perhaps decorate the work environment with inappropriate photographs may create a hostile work environment for a female colleague, who becomes uncomfortable working in that environment. As we noted earlier, it is the organization's responsibility for dealing with this sort of problem.

Regardless of the pattern, the same bottom-line rules apply: Sexual harassment is illegal, and the organization is responsible for controlling it.

employment-at-will

Principle, increasingly modified by legislation and judicial decision, that organizations should be able to retain or dismiss employees at their discretion

Employment-at-Will The concept of **employment-at-will** holds that both employer and employee have the mutual right to terminate an employment relationship anytime for any reason and with or without advance notice to the other. Specifically, it holds that an organization employs an individual at its own will and can, therefore, terminate that employee at any time for any reason. Over the last two decades, however, terminated employees have challenged the employment-at-will doctrine by filing lawsuits against former employers on the grounds of wrongful discharge.

In the last several years, such suits have put limits on employment-at-will provisions in certain circumstances. In the past, for example, organizations were guilty of firing employees who filed workers' compensation claims or took excessive time off to serve on jury duty. More recently, however, the courts have ruled that employees may not be fired for exercising rights protected by law.

New Challenges in the Changing Workplace

As we have seen throughout this chapter, human resource managers face several ongoing challenges in their efforts to keep their organizations staffed with effective workforces. To complicate matters, new challenges arise as the economic and social environments of business change. In the following sections, we take a look at several of the most important human resource management issues facing business today.

Managing Workforce Diversity

workforce diversity

Range of workers' attitudes, values, beliefs, and behaviors that differ by gender, race, and ethnicity

One extremely important set of human resource challenges centers on **workforce diversity**—the range of workers' attitudes, values, beliefs, and behaviors that differ by gender, race, age, ethnicity, physical ability, and other relevant characteristics. In the past, organizations tended to work toward homogenizing their workforces getting everyone to think and behave in similar ways. Partly as a result of affirmative action efforts, however, many U.S. organizations are now creating more

Self-Check Questions 4–6

*You should now be able to answer Self-Check Questions 4–6**

4. MULTIPLE CHOICE Which of the following is a common training method today? [select one] **(a)** on-the-job training; **(b)** off-the-job training; **(c)** vestibule training; **(d)** Web-based training; **(e)** all of these.

5. MULTIPLE CHOICE Both Jason Giambi of the New York Yankees and Sheryl Swoopes of the Houston Comets have contract clauses that pay them extra if they are voted Most Valuable Player of their respective leagues. This clause is an example of which of the following? [select one] **(a)** individual incentive; **(b)** profit-sharing plan; **(c)** gainsharing plan; **(d)** pay-for-knowledge plan; **(e)** cafeteria benefit.

6. TRUE/FALSE As long as hiring rules are applied uniformly, an employer can choose to not hire members of a protected class.

*ANSWERS TO SELF-CHECK QUESTIONS 4–6 CAN BE FOUND ON P. AN-5.

diverse workforces, embracing more women, ethnic minorities, and foreign-born employees than ever before.

Figure 8.3 helps put the changing U.S. workforce into perspective by illustrating changes in the percentages of different groups of workers—males and females, whites, African Americans, Hispanics, Asians, and others—in the total workforce in the years 1986, 1996, and (as projected) 2006. The picture is clearly one of increasing diversity. By 2006, say experts, almost half of all workers in the labor force will be women and almost one-third will be blacks, Hispanics, Asian Americans, and others.

Today, organizations are recognizing not only that they should treat everyone equitably, but also that they should acknowledge the individuality of each person they employ. They are also recognizing that diversity can be a competitive advantage.[19] For example, by hiring the best people available from every single group rather than hiring from just one or a few groups, a firm can develop a higher quality labor force. Similarly, a diverse workforce can bring a wider array of information to bear on problems and can provide insights on marketing products to a wider range of consumers. Says the head of workforce diversity at IBM, "We think it is important for our customers to look inside and see people like them. If they can't . . . the prospect of them becoming or staying our customers declines."

"We think it is important for our customers to look inside and see people like them. If they can't, the prospect of them becoming or staying our customers declines."

~Head of workforce diversity at IBM

Managing Knowledge Workers

Traditionally, employees added value to organizations because of what they did or because of their experience. In the Information Age, however, many employees add value because of what they know.[20]

The Nature of Knowledge Work These employees are usually called **knowledge workers,** and the skill with which they are managed is a major factor in determining which firms will be successful in the future. Knowledge workers, including computer scientists, engineers, and physical scientists, provide special challenges for the HR manager. They tend to work in high-technology firms and are

knowledge workers
Employees who are of value because of the knowledge they possess

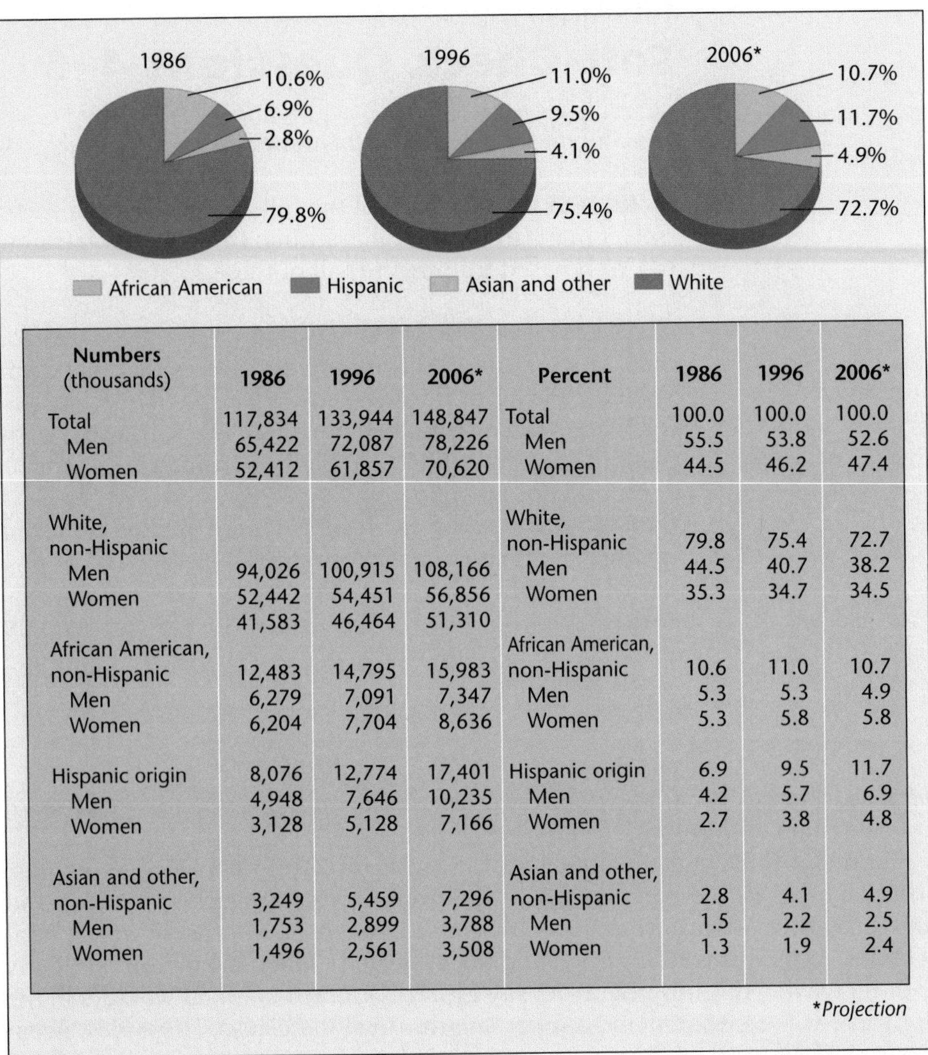

Numbers (thousands)	1986	1996	2006*	Percent	1986	1996	2006*
Total	117,834	133,944	148,847	Total	100.0	100.0	100.0
Men	65,422	72,087	78,226	Men	55.5	53.8	52.6
Women	52,412	61,857	70,620	Women	44.5	46.2	47.4
White, non-Hispanic				White, non-Hispanic	79.8	75.4	72.7
Men	94,026	100,915	108,166	Men	44.5	40.7	38.2
Women	52,442	54,451	56,856	Women	35.3	34.7	34.5
	41,583	46,464	51,310				
African American, non-Hispanic	12,483	14,795	15,983	African American, non-Hispanic	10.6	11.0	10.7
Men	6,279	7,091	7,347	Men	5.3	5.3	4.9
Women	6,204	7,704	8,636	Women	5.3	5.8	5.8
Hispanic origin	8,076	12,774	17,401	Hispanic origin	6.9	9.5	11.7
Men	4,948	7,646	10,235	Men	4.2	5.7	6.9
Women	3,128	5,128	7,166	Women	2.7	3.8	4.8
Asian and other, non-Hispanic	3,249	5,459	7,296	Asian and other, non-Hispanic	2.8	4.1	4.9
Men	1,753	2,899	3,788	Men	1.5	2.2	2.5
Women	1,496	2,561	3,508	Women	1.3	1.9	2.4

*Projection

FIGURE 8.3
Changing Composition of the U.S. Workforce

usually experts in some abstract knowledge base. They often like to work independently and tend to identify more strongly with their professions than with any organization—even to the extent of defining performance in terms recognized by other members of their professions.

As the importance of information-driven jobs grows, the need for knowledge workers continues to grow as well. But these employees require extensive and highly specialized training, and not every organization is willing to make the human capital investments necessary to take advantage of these jobs. In fact, even after knowledge workers are on the job, retraining and training updates are critical to prevent their skills from becoming obsolete. It has been suggested, for example, that the half-life of a technical education in engineering is about three years. The failure to update such skills will not only result in the loss of competitive advantage but will also increase the likelihood that the knowledge worker will go to another firm that is more committed to updating the worker's skills.

Knowledge Worker Management and Labor Markets In recent years, the demand for knowledge workers has grown at a dramatic rate. Even the economic downturn in 2000 only slowed the demand for highly skilled knowledge workers. As a result, organizations that need these workers must introduce regular market

Say what you mean

TOP-DOWN SENSITIVITY

By definition, global companies must communicate with employees in many different countries and cultures, and a firm's success in communicating with local workers can mean success or failure in an overseas operation. The most successful global companies know how to talk to the people who work for them.

In some countries, the gap between managers and workers is quite wide, and managers are used to bridging it with orders that are simply to be followed. In many Asian cultures, for example, you simply don't question the boss' decisions or the policies of the company. In the United States, by contrast, people are often encouraged to provide feedback and to say what they think. The gap is relatively narrow, and communication channels tend to be informal and wide open.

The same arrangements usually apply when it comes to dealing with workplace disputes. In some countries, such as Germany and Sweden, there's a formal system for ensuring that everyone involved gets a say in resolving workplace disputes. In these countries, although communication channels are always open, they're also highly structured.

But being culturally sensitive to local employees means much more than just knowing how to settle workplace disputes. As a rule, companies also need to convey a sense of good "citizenship" through their behavior in the host country. This means respecting the social and cultural values of employees and communicating to them the fact that the company cares about the things that they care about.

adjustments (upward) in order to pay them enough to keep them. This is especially critical in areas in which demand is still growing, since even entry-level salaries for these employees are continuing to escalate. Once an employee accepts a job with a firm, the employer faces yet another dilemma. Once hired, workers are more subject to the company's internal labor market, which is not likely to be growing as quickly as the external market for knowledge workers as a whole. Consequently, the longer employees remain with a firm, the further behind the market their pay falls—unless it is regularly adjusted upward.

The continuing demand for these workers has inspired some fairly extreme measures for attracting them in the first place.[21] High starting salaries and sign-on bonuses are common. British Petroleum Exploration <www.bpamoco.com> was recently paying starting petroleum engineers with undersea platform-drilling knowledge—not experience, just knowledge—salaries in the six figures, plus sign-on bonuses of over $50,000 and immediate profit sharing. Even with these incentives, HR managers complain that in the Gulf Coast region, they cannot retain specialists because young engineers soon leave to accept even more attractive jobs with competitors. Laments one HR executive, "We wind up six months after we hire an engineer having to fight off offers for that same engineer for more money."[22]

> **"We wind up six months after we hire an engineer having to fight off offers for that same engineer for more money."**
>
> ~Eric Campbell,
> HR EXECUTIVE AT DOCENT INC.

Contingent and Temporary Workers

A final contemporary HR issue of note involves the use of contingent and temporary workers. Indeed, recent years have seen an explosion in the use of such workers by organizations.

Trends in Contingent and Temporary Employment In recent years, the number of contingent workers in the workforce has increased dramatically. A **contingent**

contingent worker
Employee hired on something other than a full-time basis to supplement an organization's permanent workforce

worker is a person who works for an organization on something other than a permanent or full-time basis. Categories of contingent workers include independent contractors, on-call workers, temporary employees (usually hired through outside agencies), and contract and leased employees. Another category is part-time workers. The financial services giant Citigroup <www.citigroup.com>, for example, makes extensive use of part-time sales agents to pursue new clients. About 10 percent of the U.S. workforce currently uses one of these alternative forms of employment relationships. Experts suggest, however, that this percentage is increasing at a consistent pace.

Managing Contingent and Temporary Workers Given the widespread use of contingent and temporary workers, HR managers must understand how to use such employees most effectively. That is, they need to understand how to manage contingent and temporary workers.

One key is careful planning. Even though one of the presumed benefits of using contingent workers is flexibility, it still is important to integrate such workers in a coordinated fashion. Rather than having to call in workers sporadically and with no prior notice, organizations try to bring in specified numbers of workers for well-defined periods of time. The ability to do so comes from careful planning.

A second key is understanding contingent workers and acknowledging their advantages and disadvantages. That is, the organization must recognize what it can and can't achieve from the use of contingent and temporary workers. Expecting too much from such workers, for example, is a mistake that managers should avoid.

Third, managers must carefully assess the real cost of using contingent workers. We noted previously that many firms adopt this course of action to save labor costs. The organization should be able to document precisely its labor-cost savings. How much would it be paying people in wages and benefits if they were on permanent staff? How does this cost compare with the amount spent on contingent workers? This difference, however, could be misleading. We also noted, for instance, that contingent workers might be less effective performers than permanent and full-time employees. Comparing employee for employee on a direct-cost basis, therefore, is not necessarily valid. Organizations must learn to adjust the direct differences in labor costs to account for differences in productivity and performance.

Finally, managers must fully understand their own strategies and decide in advance how they intend to manage temporary workers, specifically focusing on how to integrate them into the organization. On a very simplistic level, for example, an organization with a large contingent workforce must make some decisions about the treatment of contingent workers relative to the treatment of permanent full-time workers. Should contingent workers be invited to the company holiday party? Should they have the same access to such employee benefits as counseling services and child care? There are no right or wrong answers to such questions. Managers must understand that they need to develop a strategy for integrating contingent workers according to some sound logic and then follow that strategy consistently over time.[23]

labor union

Group of individuals working together to achieve shared job-related goals, such as higher pay, shorter working hours, more job security, greater benefits, or better working conditions

labor relations

Process of dealing with employees who are represented by a union

Dealing with Organized Labor

A **labor union** is a group of individuals working together to achieve shared job-related goals, such as higher pay, shorter working hours, more job security, greater benefits, or better working conditions.[24] **Labor relations** describes the process of dealing with employees who are represented by a union.

Labor unions grew in popularity in the United States in the nineteenth and early twentieth centuries. The labor movement was born with the Industrial

Revolution, which also gave birth to a factory-based production system that carried with it enormous economic benefits. Job specialization and mass production allowed businesses to create ever greater quantities of goods at ever lower costs.

But there was also a dark side to this era. Workers became more dependent on their factory jobs. Eager for greater profits, some owners treated their workers like other raw materials: resources to be deployed with little or no regard for the individual worker's well-being. Many businesses forced employees to work long hours—60-hour weeks were common, and some workers were routinely forced to work 12 to 16 hours a day. With no minimum-wage laws or other controls, pay was also minimal and safety standards virtually nonexistent. Workers enjoyed no job security and received few benefits. Many companies, especially textile mills, employed large numbers of children at poverty wages. If people complained, nothing prevented employers from firing and replacing them at will.

Unions appeared and ultimately prospered because they constituted a solution to the worker's most serious problem: They forced management to listen to the complaints of all their workers rather than to just the few who were brave (or foolish) enough to speak out. The power of unions, then, comes from collective action. **Collective bargaining** (which we discuss more fully later in this chapter) is the process by which union leaders and managers negotiate common terms and conditions of employment for the workers represented by unions. Although collective bargaining does not often occur in small businesses, many midsize and larger businesses must engage in the process.

collective bargaining
Process by which labor and management negotiate conditions of employment for union-represented workers

Unionism Today

Although understanding the historical context of labor unions is important, so too is appreciating the role of unionism today, especially trends in union membership, union–management relations, and bargaining perspectives. We discuss these topics in the sections that follow.

Trends in Union Membership Since the mid-1950s, U.S. labor unions have experienced increasing difficulties in attracting new members. As a result, although millions of workers still belong to labor unions, union membership *as a percentage of the total workforce* has continued to decline at a very steady rate. In 1980, for example, nearly 25 percent of U.S. wage and salary employees belonged to labor unions. Today, that figure is about 14 percent. Figure 8.4(a) traces the decades-long decline in union membership. Moreover, if public employees are excluded from consideration, then only around 11 percent of all private industry wage and salary employees currently belong to labor unions. Figure 8.4(b) illustrates the different trends in membership for public employees versus private nonfarm employees.

Furthermore, just as union membership has continued to decline, so has the percentage of successful union-organizing campaigns. In the years immediately following World War II and continuing through the mid-1960s, most unions routinely won certification elections. In recent years, however, labor unions have been winning certification fewer than 50 percent of the time in which workers are called upon to vote. By the same token, of course, unions still do win. Meat cutters at a Florida Wal-Mart

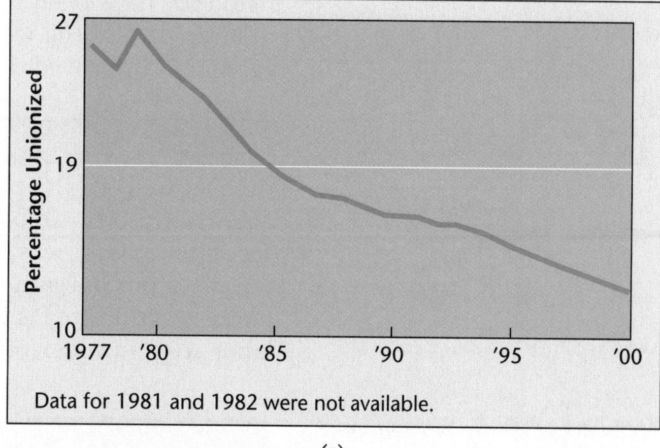

(a)

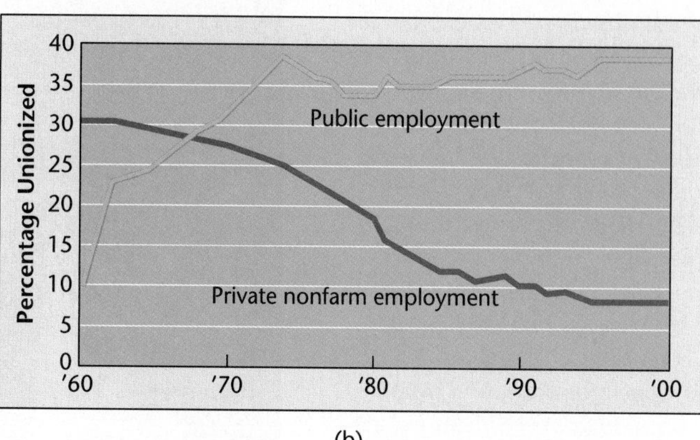

(b)

FIGURE 8.4
Trends in Union Membership

store recently voted to unionize—the first-ever successful organizing campaign against the retailing giant. "You'll see a lot more attention to Wal-Mart now," exulted one AFL-CIO official. "It's not like Wal-Mart stands out as some unattainable goal."[25]

From most indications, however, the power and significance of U.S. labor unions, while still quite formidable, are also measurably lower than they were just a few decades ago.

Trends in Union–Management Relations The gradual decline in unionization in the United States has been accompanied by some significant trends in union–management relations. In some sectors of the economy, perhaps most notably the automobile and steel industries, labor unions still remain quite strong. In these areas, unions have large memberships and considerable power in negotiating with management. The United Auto Workers (UAW), for example, is still one of the strongest unions in the United States.

In most sectors, however, unions are clearly in a weakened position, and as a result, many have taken much more conciliatory stances in their relations with management. This situation contrasts sharply with the more adversarial relationship that once dominated labor relations in this country. Increasingly, for instance, unions recognize that they don't have as much power as they once held and that it is in their own best interests, as well as in those of the workers that they represent, to work with management instead of working against it. Ironically, then, union–management relations are in many ways better today than they have been in many years. Admittedly, the improvement is attributable in large part to the weakened power of unions. Even so, however, most experts agree that improved union–management relations have benefited both sides.

Trends in Bargaining Perspectives Given the trends described in the two previous sections, we should not be surprised to find changes in bargaining perspectives as well. In the past, most union–management bargaining situations were characterized by union demands for dramatic increases in wages and salaries. A secondary issue was usually increased benefits for members. Now, however, unions often bargain for different benefits, such as job security. Of particular interest in this area is the trend toward relocating jobs to take advantage of lower labor costs in other countries. Unions, of course, want to restrict job movement,

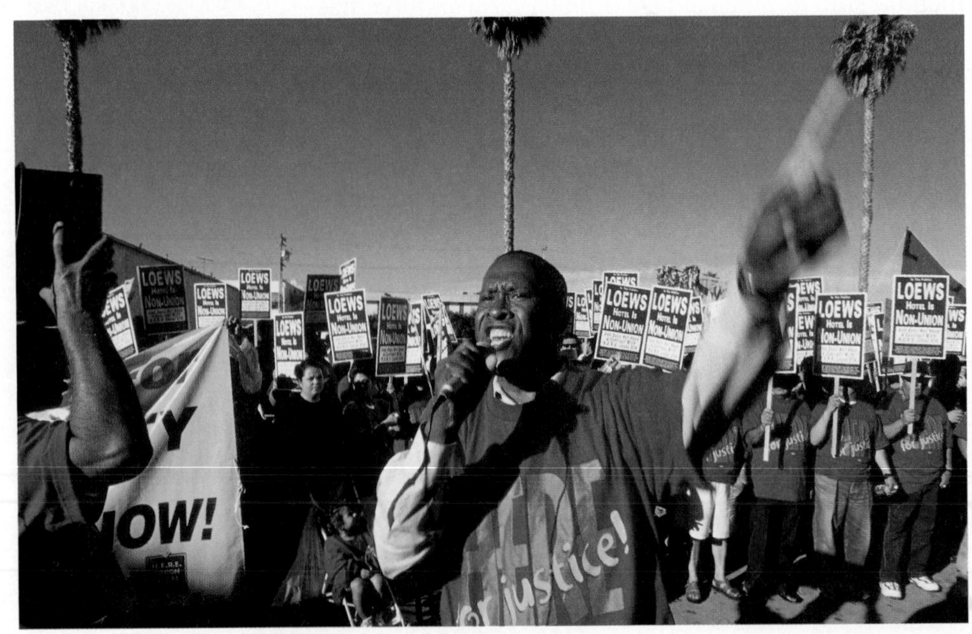

Members of the Hotel Employees and Restaurant Employees union (HERE) at a rally in California. What's the issue? As is often the case, it's saving jobs, but this time the problem is unusually severe for both hotel owners and hotel employees. Since 9/11, no less than 40 percent of the union's 175,000 North American members have been laid off, and another 20 percent are working short weeks. Because laid-off workers don't pay dues, HERE is strapped for cash, and union president John Wilhelm has cut his own salary by 20 percent.

whereas companies want to save money by moving facilities—and jobs—to other countries.

As a result of organizational downsizing and several years of relatively low inflation in this country, many unions today find themselves fighting against wage cuts rather than striving for wage *increases*. Similarly, as organizations are more likely to seek lower health care and other benefits, a common goal of union strategy is to preserve what's already been won. Unions also place greater emphasis on improved job security. A trend that has become especially important in recent years is the effort to improve pension programs for employees.

Unions have also begun increasingly to set their sights on preserving jobs for workers in the United States in the face of business efforts to relocate production in some sectors to countries where labor costs are lower. For example, the AFL-CIO has been an outspoken opponent of efforts to normalize trade relations with China, fearing that more businesses might be tempted to move jobs there. General Electric <www.ge.com> has been targeted for union protests recently because of its strategy to move many of its own jobs—and those of key suppliers—to Mexico.[26]

The Future of Unions Despite declining membership and some loss of power, labor unions remain a major factor in the U.S. business world. The 86 labor organizations in the AFL-CIO, as well as independent major unions such as the Teamsters and the National Education Association (NEA), still play a major role in U.S. business. Moreover, some unions still wield considerable power, especially in the traditional strongholds of goods-producing industries. Labor and management in some industries, notably airlines and steel, are beginning to favor contracts that establish formal mechanisms for greater worker input into management decisions. Inland Steel <www.inland.com>, for instance, recently granted its major union the right to name a member to the board of directors. Union officers can also attend executive meetings.

Collective Bargaining

When a union has been legally certified, it assumes the role of official bargaining agent for the workers whom it represents. Collective bargaining is an ongoing process involving both the drafting and the administering of the terms of a labor contract.[27]

Reaching Agreement on Contract Terms

The collective bargaining process begins when the union is recognized as the exclusive negotiator for its members. The bargaining cycle itself begins when union leaders meet with management representatives to agree on a contract. By law, both parties must sit down at the bargaining table and negotiate in good faith.

When each side has presented its demands, sessions focus on identifying the *bargaining zone*. The process is shown in Figure 8.5. For example, although an employer may initially offer no pay raise, it may expect to grant a raise of up to 6 percent. Likewise, the union may initially *demand* a 10-percent pay raise while *expecting* to accept a raise as low as 4 percent. The bargaining zone, then, is a raise between 4 and 6 percent. Ideally, some compromise is reached between these levels, and then the new agreement is submitted for a ratification vote by union membership.

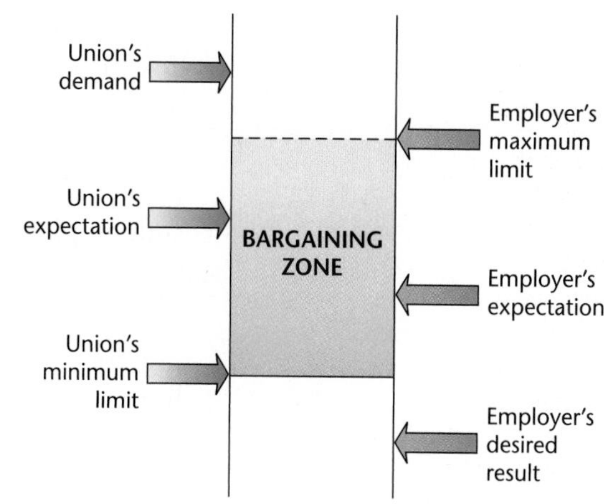

FIGURE 8.5
The Bargaining Zone

Sometimes this process goes quite smoothly. At other times, however, the two sides cannot—or will not—agree. The speed and ease with which such an impasse is resolved depend in part on the nature of the contract issues, the willingness of each side to use certain tactics, and the prospects for mediation or arbitration.[28]

Contract Issues

The labor contract itself can address an array of different issues. Most of these concern demands that unions make on behalf of their members. In this section, we will survey the categories of issues that are typically most important to union negotiators: *compensation, benefits,* and *job security.* Although few issues covered in a labor contract are company sponsored, we will also describe the kinds of management rights that are negotiated in most bargaining agreements.

Compensation The most common issue is compensation. One aspect of compensation is current wages. Obviously, unions want their employees to earn higher wages and try to convince management to raise hourly wages for all or some employees.

Of equal concern to unions is future compensation: wage rates to be paid during subsequent years of the contract. One common tool for securing wage increases is a **cost-of-living adjustment (COLA).** Most COLA clauses tie future raises to the *Consumer Price Index (CPI),* a government statistic that reflects changes in consumer purchasing power. The premise is that as the CPI increases by a specified amount during a given period of time, wages will automatically be increased. Almost half of all labor contracts today include COLA clauses.

cost-of-living adjustment (COLA)
Labor contract clause tying future raises to changes in consumer purchasing power

wage reopener clause
Clause allowing wage rates to be renegotiated during the life of a labor contract

Wage reopener clauses are now included in almost 10 percent of all labor contracts. Such a clause allows wage rates to be renegotiated at preset times during the life of the contract. For example, a union might be uncomfortable with a long-term contract based solely on COLA wage increases. A long-term agreement might be more acceptable, however, if management agrees to renegotiate wages every two years.

Benefits Employee benefits are also an important component in most labor contracts. Unions typically want employers to pay all or most of the costs of insurance for employees. Other benefits commonly addressed during negotiations include retirement benefits, paid holidays, and working conditions.

Job Security Nevertheless, the UAW's top priority in its most recent negotiations with U.S. automakers has been job security, an increasingly important agenda item in many bargaining sessions today. In some cases, demands for job security entail the promise that a company not move to another location. In others, the contract may dictate that if the workforce is reduced, seniority will be used to determine which employees keep their jobs.

Other Union Issues Other possible issues might include such things as working hours, overtime policies, rest period arrangements, differential pay plans for shift employees, the use of temporary workers, grievance procedures, and allowable union activities (dues collection, union bulletin boards, and so forth).

Management Rights Management wants as much control as possible over hiring policies, work assignments, and so forth. Unions, meanwhile, often try to limit management rights by specifying hiring, assignment, and other policies. At a DaimlerChrysler plant in Detroit, for example, the contract stipulates that three workers are needed to change fuses in robots: a machinist to open the robot, an electrician to change the fuse, and a supervisor to oversee the process. As in this case, contracts often bar workers in one job category from performing work that falls in the domain of another. Unions try to secure jobs by defining as many different categories as possible (the DaimlerChrysler plant has over 100). Of course, management resists the practice, which limits flexibility and makes it difficult to reassign workers.

When Bargaining Fails

An impasse occurs when, after a series of bargaining sessions, management and labor have failed to agree on a new contract or a contract to replace an agreement that is about to expire. Although it is generally agreed that both parties suffer when an impasse is reached and some action by one part, against the other is taken, each side can use several tactics to support its cause until the impasse is resolved.[29]

Union Tactics When their demands are not met, unions may bring a variety of tactics to the bargaining table. Chief among these are the *strike,* which may be supported by *pickets* and *boycotts,* and the *slowdown.*

The Strike A **strike** occurs when employees temporarily walk off the job and refuse to work. Most strikes in the United States are **economic strikes,** triggered by stalemates over mandatory bargaining items, including such noneconomic issues as working hours. For example, the Teamsters union struck United Parcel Service (UPS) a few years ago over several noneconomic issues. Specifically, the union wanted the firm to transform many of its temporary and part-time jobs into permanent and full-time jobs. Strikers returned to work only when UPS agreed to create 10,000 new jobs. More recently, the same union struck Union Pacific Corp. <www.up.com> in January 2000 over wages and new jobs. In April 2000, machinists at a Lockheed-Martin <www.lmco.com> plant in Fort Worth, Texas, staged a two-week strike. Reflected the president of the union local, "I think our people gained a lot of respect for taking a stand. We had a good strike."

strike
Labor action in which employees temporarily walk off the job and refuse to work

economic strike
Strike usually triggered by stalemate over one or more mandatory bargaining items

Still, there are far fewer strikes today than there were in previous years. For example, there were 222 strikes in the United States in 1960 involving a total of 896,000 workers. In 1970, 2,468,000 workers took part in 381 strikes. But in 1990, there were only 44 strikes involving 185,000 workers. Since 1990, the annual number of strikes has ranged from a high of 45 (in 1994) to a low of 29 (in 1997).[30]

Not all strikes are legal. **Sympathy strikes** (also called **secondary strikes**), which occur when one union strikes in sympathy with action initiated by another, may violate the sympathetic union's contract. **Wildcat strikes**—strikes unauthorized by the union that occur during the life of a contract—deprive strikers of their status as employees and thus of the protection of national labor law.

sympathy strike (or **secondary strike**)
Strike in which one union strikes to support action initiated by another

wildcat strike
Strike that is unauthorized by the strikers' union

Other Labor Actions To support a strike, a union faced with an impasse has recourse to additional legal activities:

- In **picketing,** workers march at the entrance to the employer's facility with signs explaining their reasons for striking.
- A **boycott** occurs when union members agree not to buy the products of a targeted employer. Workers may also urge consumers to boycott the firm's products.
- Another alternative to striking is a work **slowdown.** Instead of striking, workers perform their jobs at a much slower pace than normal. A variation is the *sickout,* during which large numbers of workers call in sick. Pilots at American Airlines engaged in a massive sickout in early 1999, causing the airline to cancel thousands of flights before a judge ordered them back into the cockpit.

picketing
Labor action in which workers publicize their grievances at the entrance to an employer's facility

boycott
Labor action in which workers refuse to buy the products of a targeted employer

slowdown
Labor action in which workers perform jobs at a slower than normal pace

Management Tactics Like workers, management can respond forcefully to an impasse:

lockout
Management tactic whereby workers are denied access to the employer's workplace

- **Lockouts** occur when employers deny employees access to the workplace. Lockouts are illegal if they are used as offensive weapons to give management a bargaining advantage. However, they are legal if management has a legitimate business need (for instance, avoiding a buildup of perishable inventory). Although rare today, ABC <www.abc.go.com> locked out its off-camera employees in 1998 because they staged an unannounced one-day strike during a critical broadcasting period. Likewise, almost half of the 1998–1999 NBA season was lost when team owners <www.nba.com> locked out their players over contract issues.

strikebreaker
Worker hired as permanent or temporary replacement for a striking employee

- A firm can also hire temporary or permanent replacements called **strikebreakers.** However, the law forbids the permanent replacement of workers who strike because of unfair practices. In some cases, an employer can also obtain legal injunctions that either prohibit workers from striking or prohibit a union from interfering with its efforts to use replacement workers.

mediation
Method of resolving a labor dispute in which a third party suggests, but does not impose, a settlement

voluntary arbitration
Method of resolving a labor dispute in which both parties agree to submit to the judgment of a neutral party

compulsory arbitration
Method of resolving a labor dispute in which both parties are legally required to accept the judgment of a neutral party

Mediation and Arbitration Rather than wield these often unpleasant weapons against one another, labor and management can agree to call in a third party to help resolve the dispute:

- In **mediation,** the neutral third party (the mediator) can suggest but cannot impose a settlement on the other parties.
- In **voluntary arbitration,** the neutral third party (the arbitrator) dictates a settlement between the two sides, which have agreed to submit to outside judgment.
- In some cases, arbitration is legally required to settle bargaining disputes. **Compulsory arbitration** is used to settle disputes between the government and public employees such as firefighters and police officers.

Self-Check Questions 7–9

*You should now be able to answer Self-Check Questions 7–9**

7. Multiple Choice In general, which of the following is **true** about workforce diversity? [select one] **(a)** It is decreasing. **(b)** It is increasing. **(c)** It remains constant. **(d)** It is becoming less important to business. **(e)** none of these.

8. Multiple Choice Which of the following is **true** about union membership in recent years? [select one] **(a)** It has generally remained constant. **(b)** It has generally become more diverse. **(c)** Generally, it has steadily increased. **(d)** Generally, it has steadily declined. **(e)** It has generally changed in unknown ways because of new privacy laws.

9. True/False In recent years, the number of contingent workers has sharply increased.

*Answers to Self-Check Questions 7–9 can be found on p. AN-6.

Continued from page 217

Time Out on the Labor Front

As we explained at the beginning of this chapter, many firms have reduced or frozen hiring, and some are reducing or eliminating benefits and perquisites. These firms are seeking ways to lower costs, and they've found that current economic conditions give them more flexibility than they had just a few years ago. But while these actions may lower costs and protect profits in the short term, firms that follow this path may face problems when the economy rebounds. In particular, they may find that they've tarnished their reputations as employers and find it more difficult to attract workers when they need them again.

The repercussions may include low morale, reduced productivity, or worse. When the Indiana Social Services Administration left job vacancies unfilled in 1990, the state soon led the country in welfare fraud cases. And the effects can be long-lasting. Says one executive whose company instituted pay cuts, "People are lying low, but when the economy improves, they'll be out of here." Workers complain that they shouldn't bear a disproportionate share of the cost cutting burden, and studies verify that median CEO compensation rose seven percent in 2001 and worker pay just three percent. Company profits fell 35 percent.

The good news for struggling firms is that there are still effective incentives. The most powerful, and least expensive, perk can be time off. Experts suggest, for example, that up to 20 percent of workers would be willing to work fewer hours for lower pay. Siemens, a German electronics firm, is offering workers a year-long "time-out," with reduced pay and a guaranteed job when they return. "It's a possibility for us not to lose good workers despite bad times," says Siemens' spokesperson Axel Heim. Firms are also finding that technology workers and professionals, who need to stay on the leading edge of their fields, want more training and increased job responsibilities. Many people, warns Patti Wilson, founder of a high-tech career-management firm, "will jump jobs to learn more or stay if they feel that they're being challenged."

Questions for Discussion

1. What are the basic human resource issues reflected in labor force reductions and other HR cutbacks?
2. What benefits seem to be the most valuable to employees, and what benefits seem trivial and/or extravagant?
3. Aside from laying off workers, what other costs might be cut in managing an organization's labor force?
4. What other incentives besides benefits might a company be able to offer its best workers in order to retain them?
5. How might current employment trends affect unionization? Why?

"It's a possibility for us not to lose good workers despite bad times."

~Siemens executive

ON THE COMPANY'S POLICY OF OFFERING EMPLOYEES A YEAR-LONG "TIME-OUT"

Summary of Learning Objectives

1. *Define* human resource management, *and explain how managers plan for human resources.*

Human resource management (HRM) is the set of organizational activities directed at attracting, developing, and maintaining an effective workforce. Because of the importance of HRM, many firms integrate strategic HR plans with other strategic planning activities.

HR planning involves two tasks: (1) *Job analysis:* **Job analysis** is a systematic analysis of jobs within an organization. It has two parts: (i) The **job description** lists the duties of a job, working conditions, and needed tools, materials, and equipment; (ii) the **job specification** lists the skills, abilities, and other credentials needed to do a job. Job analysis includes developing selection methods, performance appraisal systems, and compensation rates.

(2) *Forecasting HR demand and supply*: Managers must plan for future HR needs by assessing past trends, future plans, and general economic trends. Forecasting labor supply is really two tasks: (i) Forecasting *internal supply*—the number and type of employees who will be in the firm at some future date; (ii) forecasting *external supply*—the number and type of people who will be available from the labor market at large.

Large organizations use sophisticated models to make forecasts, including the following: (i) **Replacement charts** list such items as important managerial positions, who occupies them, and who is or will be qualified to move into them. (ii) **Employee information systems,** or **skills inventories,** are computerized systems which contain information on each employee and which can locate any employee who is qualified to fill a position.

The next step in HR planning is *matching HR supply and demand*—dealing with predicted shortfalls or overstaffing. If a shortfall is predicted, new employees can be hired. The external labor forecast helps managers recruit on the basis of which type of workers are available or scarce.

2. *Identify tasks in* staffing *a company and discuss ways in which organizations* select, develop, *and* appraise *employee performance.*

Staffing an organization means recruiting and hiring the right mix of people. **Recruiting** is the process of attracting qualified persons to apply for open jobs. **Internal recruiting** means considering present employees as candidates—a policy that helps build morale and keep high-quality employees. **External recruiting** involves attracting people from outside the organization. Methods include advertising, campus interviews, employment agencies or executive search firms, union hiring halls, and referrals by present employees.

The next step is the *selection* process—gathering information that will predict applicants' job success and then hiring the most promising candidates. The process of analyzing gathered information is called **validation.** The first step in selection is asking the candidate to fill out an *application form* (to find out work history, educational background, and so forth). Next, recruiters may give *tests* of ability, aptitude, or knowledge relevant to a particular job. Finally, in a structured *interview,* questions are written in advance, and all interviewers follow the same format. Some organizations also use such selection techniques as polygraphs and drug tests.

New employees must be trained and allowed to develop job skills. **On-the-job training** occurs while the employee is at work. **Off-the-job training** takes place at off site locations where controlled environments allow focused study. Some firms use **vestibule training**—off-the-job training in simulated work environments.

In larger firms, **performance appraisals** show how well workers are doing their jobs. Typically, appraisal involves a regular written assessment as part of a multistep process that begins when a manager defines performance standards for an employee. The manager then observes the employee, and the process ends when manager and employee meet to discuss the appraisal.

3. *Describe the main components of a* compensation system.

A **compensation system** is the total package that a firm offers employees in return for their labor. The right combination of compensation elements will make employees feel valued while holding down company costs. Systems differ widely, but the dollar amounts paid to employees are key parts of all systems. **Wages** are paid for time worked (for example, by the hour). A **salary** is paid for discharging the responsibilities of a job. In setting levels, companies look at competitors' levels and also decide how internal levels should compare for different jobs.

Beyond a certain point, money motivates employees only when tied directly to performance. One way to establish this link is the use of **incentive programs**—special pay programs designed to motivate high performance. They may be applied on two different levels: (1) *Individual incentives*: Employees receive sales **bonuses**—special payments above their salaries—when they sell a certain number or certain dollar amount of goods. **Merit salary systems** link raises to performance levels in nonsales jobs. Under **pay for performance,** or **variable pay,** plans, middle managers are rewarded for especially productive output. (2) *Companywide incentives* apply to all of a firm's employees. Under **profit-sharing plans,** profits above a certain level go to employees. **Gainsharing plans** give out bonuses when costs are reduced through greater work efficiency. **Pay-for-knowledge plans** give additional pay to workers who learn new skills or different jobs.

Benefits—compensation other than wages and salaries—comprise a large percentage of most compensation budgets. The law requires most companies to provide social security retirement benefits and **workers' compensation insurance** (insurance for compensating workers injured on the job). Most companies provide health, life, and disability insurance; *retirement plans* pay pensions to workers when they retire. Sometimes, the company puts all the money in the pension fund; sometimes, it comes from both company and employees. Many companies are experimenting with cost-cutting plans, such as the **cafeteria benefit plan,** in which a certain dollar amount of benefits per employee is set aside so that each employee can choose from a variety of alternatives.

4. *Describe some of the key legal issues involved in hiring, compensating, and managing workers in today's workplace.*

HR management is heavily influenced by the law. One area of HR regulation is **equal employment opportunity**—regulation to protect people from unfair or inappropriate discrimination in the workplace. Discrimination in the workplace is illegal when distinctions among people are not job related. Because illegal discrimination is based on a prejudice about classes of individuals, laws protect various classes. A **protected class** consists of all individuals who share one or more common characteristics as indicated by a given law (such as race, color, religion, gender, age, national origin, and so forth). Enforcement of equal opportunity legislation is handled by the **Equal Employment Opportunity Commission,** or **EEOC,** which is responsible for federal regulations, and the Office of Federal Contract Compliance Programs, or OFCCP, which is responsible for executive orders applying to companies doing business with the government. Such a business must file an **affirmative action plan**—a written statement of how it intends to recruit, hire, and develop members of protected classes.

Other legislation deals with emerging legal issues, including the following: (1) *Employee safety and health*: The **Occupational Safety and Health Act of 1970,** or **OSHA,** guarantees that places of employment are free from hazard and is enforced by OSHA inspectors. (2) *Emerging areas of discrimination law*: There are three such areas: (i) *AIDS in the workplace*: Employers can't require an AIDS exam as a condition of employment and must treat AIDS like any other disease. (ii) *Sexual harassment:* **Sexual harassment** is defined as unwelcome sexual advances in the work environment. Employers will be held responsible for changing an environment by warning or perhaps firing harassers. The courts recognize two types of sexual harassment: (a) In cases of **quid pro quo harassment,** the harasser offers to exchange something of value for sexual favors. (b) A **hostile work environment** may develop, for example, when a group of male employees makes the work environment uncomfortable for a female colleague. (iii) *Employment-at-will*: Under the concept of **employment-at-will,** an organization employs an individual at its own will and can terminate employment at any time for any reason. Lawsuits, however, have limited employment-at-will provisions in certain circumstances.

5. *Discuss* workforce diversity, *the management of* knowledge workers, *and the use of a* contingent workforce *as important changes in the contemporary workplace.*

Three of the most important issues in HR management are the following: (1) **Workforce diversity** refers to the range of workers' attitudes, values, beliefs, and behaviors that differ by gender, race, age, ethnicity, physical ability, and other relevant characteristics. Many U.S. organizations regard diversity as a competitive advantage. (2) Employees who add value because of what they know are usually called **knowledge workers,** and managing them skillfully helps to determine which firms will be successful in the future. Knowledge workers generally require extensive specialized training.

(3) **Contingent workers,** including independent contractors, on-call workers, temporary employees, contract and leased employees, and part time employees, work for organizations on something other than a permanent or full-time basis. Managers must integrate such workers in a coordinated fashion, and they must carefully assess the real cost of using contingent workers, learning to adjust the direct differences in labor costs to account for differences in performance.

6. *Explain why workers organize and what* labor unions *do for their members.*

A **labor union** is a group of individuals working together to achieve shared job-related goals (higher pay, more job security, and so forth). **Labor relations** describes the process of dealing with employees represented by a union. Unions appeared and prospered because they forced management to listen to the complaints of all their workers rather than to just the few who were brave (or foolish) enough to speak out. Their power comes from collective action, such as **collective bargaining**—the process by which union leaders and company managers negotiate conditions of employment for unionized workers. Although millions of workers still belong to unions, membership *as a percentage of the total workforce* has declined at a steady rate since the mid-1950s. Thus union power is much lower than it was just a few decades ago, and this decline has led to some significant trends in union–management relations.

In the past, most bargaining situations featured union demands for increases in wages and salaries. Now, however, unions often bargain for different benefits, such as job security. Another recent trend is union emphasis on improved pension programs. Unions now negotiate to preserve jobs for American workers in the face of business efforts to relocate to countries with lower labor costs.

7. *Explain the* collective bargaining *process and its possible outcomes.*

The collective bargaining process begins when the union is recognized as the negotiator for its members. The bargaining cycle begins when union leaders and management meet to agree on a contract. By law, both parties must bargain in good faith. Each presents its demands, and then the two sides focus on identifying the *bargaining zone.* When a compromise is reached, the new agreement is submitted to a vote by union membership.

Among issues that are important to union negotiators are the following: (1) *Compensation*: Unions try to convince management to raise current hourly wages and to secure good future compensation—wage rates to be paid during subsequent years of the contract. One tool for getting increases is a **cost-of-living adjustment (COLA)**—a contract clause tying future raises to changes in consumer purchasing power. **Wage reopener clauses** allow wage rates to be renegotiated at preset times during the life of a contract. (2) *Benefits*: Unions want employers to pay all or most of the costs of employees' insurance and also work to secure such benefits as retirement programs, paid holidays, and better working conditions. (3) *Job security*: Job security is an increasingly important issue. Unions may want employers to promise not to move or to reduce the workforce, but if they do, to use seniority to determine which employees keep their jobs.

An impasse occurs when management and labor fail to agree on a contract. Each side can use several tactics to support its cause until the impasse is resolved. The most important union tactic is the **strike,** which occurs when employees temporarily walk off the job and refuse to work. Most strikes are **economic strikes** resulting from stalemates over both economic and noneconomic issues (such as working hours). Illegal **sympathy strikes** (also called **secondary strikes**) occur when one union strikes in support of another. **Wildcat strikes**—strikes unauthorized by the union that occur during the life of a contract—deprive strikers of the protection of national labor law. Unions may also use **picketing,** in which workers march at an employer's facility to explain their reasons for striking. Under a **boycott,** union members agree not to buy the products of a targeted employer. During a work **slowdown,** workers perform their jobs at a much slower pace than normal. During a *sickout,* large numbers of workers call in sick.

Management may resort to **lockouts**—denying employees access to the workplace. A firm can also hire temporary or permanent replacements called **strikebreakers,** but the law forbids the permanent replacement of workers who strike because of unfair practices. An employer might also get a legal injunction to prohibit workers from striking or to prohibit a union from interfering with replacement workers.

Rather than use these tactics, labor and management can call in a third party to help resolve the dispute. In **mediation,** the neutral third party (the mediator) can suggest but can't impose a settlement. In **voluntary arbitration,** the third party (the arbitrator) dictates a settlement between the two sides, which have agreed to submit to outside judgment. **Compulsory arbitration,** which may be legally required, settles disputes between the government and public employees such as firefighters and police officers.

KEY TERMS

human resource management (HRM) (p. 218)
job analysis (p. 218)
job description (p. 218)
job specification (p. 218)
replacement chart (p. 219)
employee information system (skills inventory) (p. 219)
recruiting (p. 220)
internal recruiting (p. 220)
external recruiting (p. 220)
validation (p. 221)
on-the-job training (p. 223)
off-the-job training (p. 223)
vestibule training (p. 223)
performance appraisal (p. 223)
compensation system (p. 223)
wages (p. 223)
salary (p. 223)
incentive program (p. 225)
bonus (p. 225)
merit salary system (p. 225)
pay for performance (*or* ***variable pay***) (p. 226)
profit-sharing plan (p. 226)
gainsharing plan (p. 226)
pay-for-knowledge plan (p. 226)
benefits (p. 226)
workers' compensation insurance (p. 226)
cafeteria benefit plan (p. 227)
equal employment opportunity (p. 227)
protected class (p. 228)
Equal Employment Opportunity Commission (EEOC) (p. 228)
affirmative action plan (p. 228)
Occupational Safety and Health Act of 1970 (OSHA) (p. 229)
sexual harassment (p. 230)
quid pro quo harassment (p. 230)
hostile work environment (p. 230)
employment-at-will (p. 230)
workforce diversity (p. 230)
knowledge workers (p. 231)
contingent worker (p. 233)
labor union (p. 234)
labor relations (p. 234)
collective bargaining (p. 235)
cost-of-living adjustment (COLA) (p. 238)
wage reopener clause (p. 238)
strike (p. 239)
economic strike (p. 239)
sympathy strike (*or* ***secondary strike***) (p. 239)
wildcat strike (p. 239)
picketing (p. 239)
boycott (p. 239)
slowdown (p. 239)
lockout (p. 240)
strikebreaker (p. 240)
mediation (p. 240)
voluntary arbitration (p. 240)
compulsory arbitration (p. 240)

QUESTIONS AND EXERCISES

Questions for Review

1. What are the advantages and disadvantages of internal and external recruiting? Under what circumstances is each more appropriate?
2. Why is the formal training of workers so important to most employers? Why don't employers simply let people learn about their jobs as they perform them?
3. What different forms of compensation do firms typically use to attract and keep productive workers?
4. Why do workers in some companies unionize whereas workers in others do not?

Questions for Analysis

5. What are your views on drug testing in the workplace? What would you do if your employer asked you to submit to a drug test?
6. Workers at Ford, GM, and DaimlerChrysler are represented by the UAW. However, the UAW has been unsuccessful in its attempts to unionize U.S. workers employed at Toyota, Nissan, and Honda plants in the United States. Why do you think this is so?
7. What training do you think you are most likely to need when you finish school and start your career?

8. How much will benefit considerations affect your choice of an employer after graduation?

Application Exercises

9. Interview an HR manager at a local company. Focus on a position for which the firm is currently recruiting applicants, and identify the steps in the selection process.
10. Interview the managers of two local companies, one unionized and one nonunionized. Compare the wage and salary levels, benefits, and working conditions of employees at the two firms.

Building Your Business Skills

A LITTLE COLLECTIVE BRAINSTORMING

This exercise enhances the following SCANS workplace competencies: demonstrating basic skills, demonstrating thinking skills, exhibiting interpersonal skills, and working with information.

Goal

To encourage students to understand why some companies unionize and others do not

The Situation

You've been working for the same nonunion company for five years. Although there are problems in the company, you like your job and have confidence in your ability to get ahead. Recently, you've heard rumblings that a large group of workers wants to call for a union election. You're not sure how you feel about this because none of your friends or family are union members.

Method

Step 1

Come together with three other "coworkers" who have the same questions as you. Each person should target four companies to learn about their union status. Avoid small businesses—choose large corporations such as General Motors, Intel, and Sears. As you investigate, answer the following questions:

- Is the company unionized?
- Is every worker in the company unionized or just selected groups of workers? Describe the groups.
- If a company is unionized, what is the union's history in that company?
- If a company is unionized, what are the main labor–management issues?
- If a company is unionized, how would you describe the current status of labor–management relations? For example, is it cordial or strained?
- If a company is not unionized, what factors are responsible for its nonunion status?

To learn the answers to these questions, contact the company, read corporate annual reports, search the company's Web site, contact union representatives, or do research on a computerized database.

Step 2

Go to the Web site of the AFL-CIO <www.aflcio.org/> to learn more about the current status of the union movement. Then with your coworkers, write a short report about the advantages of union membership.

Step 3

Research the disadvantages of unionization. A key issue to address is whether unions make it harder for companies to compete in the global marketplace.

Follow-Up Questions

1. Based on everything you learned, are you sympathetic to the union movement? Would you want to be a union member?
2. Are the union members you spoke with satisfied or dissatisfied with their union's efforts to achieve better working conditions, higher wages, and improved benefits?
3. What is the union's role when layoffs occur?
4. Based on what you learned, do you think the union movement will stumble or thrive in the years ahead?

Exercising Your Ethics

OPERATING TACTICALLY

The Situation

Assume that you work as a manager for a medium-size nonunion company that is facing its most serious union organizing campaign in years. Your boss, who is determined to keep the union out, has just given you a list of things to do in order to thwart the efforts of the organizers. For example, he has suggested each of the following tactics:

- Whenever you learn about a scheduled union meeting, you should schedule a "worker appreciation" event at the same time. He wants you to offer free pizza and barbecue and to give cash prizes (that winners have to be present to receive).

- He wants you to look at the most recent performance evaluations of the key union organizers and to terminate the one with the lowest overall evaluation.
- He wants you to make an announcement that the firm is seriously considering such new benefits as on-site child care, flexible work schedules, telecommuting options, and exercise facilities. Although you know that the firm is indeed looking into these benefits, you also know that, ultimately, your boss will provide far less lavish benefits than he wants you to intimate.

The Dilemma

When you questioned the ethics—and even the legality—of these tactics, your boss responded by saying, "Look, all's fair in love and war, and this is war." He went on to explain that he was seriously concerned that a union victory might actually shut down the company's domestic operations altogether, forcing it to move all of its production capacities to lower-cost foreign plants. He concluded by saying that he was really looking out for the employees, even if he had to play hardball to help them. You easily see through his hypocrisy, but you also realize that there is some potential truth in his warning: If the union wins, jobs may actually be lost.

Questions for Discussion

1. What are the ethical issues in this situation?
2. What are the basic arguments for and against extreme measures to fight unionization efforts?
3. What do you think most managers would do in this situation? What would you do?

Crafting your Business Plan

TAKING THE OCCASION TO DEAL WITH LABOR

The Purpose of the Assignment

1. To acquaint students with the labor and management relations issues faced by a sample start-up firm as it develops its business plan in the framework of the *Business PlanPro (BPP)* software package.
2. To stimulate students' thinking about the application of the textbook's concepts and methods on labor and management relations to the preparation of a business plan in the *BPP* planning environment.

Assignment

After reading Chapter 8 in the textbook, open the BPP *software and search for information about labor and management relations as it applies to a sample firm: Occasions, The Event Planning Specialists. To find Occasions, do the following:*

Open *Business PlanPro.* If it asks if you want to "create a new business plan" or "open an existing plan," select "create a new business plan" (even though you are not going to create a plan at this time). You will then be taken to the *Business PlanPro EasyPlan Wizard.* On the screen, click on the option entitled **Research It.** You will then be presented with a new list of options, including **Sample Plan Browser.** After clicking on the **Sample Plan Browser,** go down the alphabetical list of sample plans and double-click on **Event Planning—Personal**, which is the location for *Occasions, The Event Planning Specialists.* The screen you are looking at is the introduction page for the *Occasions* business plan. Next, scroll down until you reach the **Table of Contents** for *Occasion's* business plan.

Now respond to the following items:

1. Explore the business plan for this company, paying special attention to its product line and the types of clients who will be buying its products. Do you suspect that there will be union members among the employees of some Occasions customers? [Sites to see in *BPP* for this item: On the Table of Contents page, click on each of the following in turn: **1.0 Executive Summary**, **1.1 Objectives,** and **1.2 Mission.** After returning to the Table of Contents page, examine each of the following: **Table 2.2: Startup** (beneath **2.2 Startup Summary**), **3.0 Products and Services, 3.1 Competitive Comparison,** and **4.1 Market Segmentation.**]
2. Considering Occasion's growth projections, do you foresee increasing likelihood for unionization of its employees? Why or why not? What should Occasions do to accommodate clients' unions? [Sites to see in *BPP:* In the Table of Contents page, click on **1.1 Objectives.** Also look at both **2.0 Company Summary** and **6.1 Organization Structure.**]
3. Explain why some experience with labor laws and management–union contract issues would be valuable for Occasions' salespeople in their dealings with clients. [Sites to see in *BPP* for this item: In the Table of Contents page, click on each of the following in turn: **1.0 Executive Summary, 3.0 Products and Services,** and **4.1 Market Segmentation.** After returning to the Table of Contents page, examine each of the following: **4.2 Target Market Segment Strategy** and **4.3 Industry Analysis.** After returning once again to the Table of Contents page, click on **1.3 Keys to Success.**]

Video Exercise

MANAGING THE HUMAN SIDE OF BUSINESS: PARK PLACE ENTERTAINMENT

Learning Objectives

The purpose of this video is to help you

1. Recognize the ways in which human resource management contributes to organizational performance.
2. Understand how and why HR managers make plans and decisions about staffing.
3. Identify some of the ways in which HR managers handle evaluation and development.

Synopsis

Park Place Entertainment owns and operates resorts and casinos around the world. Its human resource department is responsible for hiring, training, and managing a diverse group of more than 52,000 employees. Because its customers come from many countries and speak many languages, the company seeks employees from diverse backgrounds and varies the recruitment process for different properties in different areas. HR managers have created specific job descriptions for each position, instituted programs for employee and management development, and established incentive programs to reward good performance. Park Place's 360-degree evaluation method allows supervisors to get performance feedback from the employees they supervise.

Discussion Questions

1. *For analysis:* What are the advantages and disadvantages of centralizing the recruiting process at a company such as Park Place Entertainment?
2. *For analysis:* Why did Park Place begin the restructuring of its HR department by standardizing training for supervisors?
3. *For application:* What steps might Park Place HR managers take to reduce employee turnover at particular resorts?
4. *For application:* How might Park Place encourage employees to refer friends as candidates for open positions?
5. *For debate:* Rather than hiring employees when business booms and then laying them off when it slumps, should Park Place temporarily rehire retired employees during peak periods? Support your chosen position.

Online Exploration

Visit the Park Place Entertainment Web site at <www.ballys.com> and browse the home page to find the names and locations of the company's resorts and casinos. Then follow the company information link to find information on career opportunities and company benefits. What kinds of jobs are featured on the Web site? Why does Park Place arrange jobs by region? How does the firm make it convenient for applicants to submit résumés online? Why would Park Place put so much emphasis on Internet recruiting?

CHAPTER

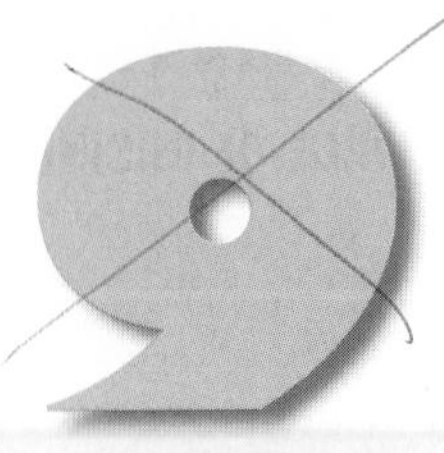

Motivating, Satisfying, and Leading Employees

After reading this chapter, you should be able to:

1. Describe the nature and importance of *psychological contracts* in the workplace.
2. Discuss the importance of *job satisfaction* and *employee morale* and summarize their roles in human relations in the workplace.
3. Identify and summarize the most important *theories of employee motivation.*
4. Describe some of the strategies used by organizations to improve *job satisfaction* and *employee motivation.*
5. Discuss different managerial styles of *leadership* and their impact on human relations in the workplace.

The Psychological Contract; or, the Manager as Brainwasher

The term *Fortune 500* is synonymous with size and power—the biggest and most important companies in the world. Wal-Mart <www.walmart.com> made history when it topped the list in April 2002. The feat was historically significant because the discount giant was the first service company ever to reach the top. When *Fortune* began publishing its list in 1955 (long before Wal-Mart was founded), the largest firm was General Motors. Almost ever since, General Motors and Exxon (now ExxonMobil) have dominated the number one and number two spots.

By virtually any measure, Wal-Mart's growth has been phenomenal. The firm was started by Sam Walton in 1960 and pursued a strategy of opening discount stores in rural communities across the country. Walton stressed two policies—everyday low prices and reasonable service. In 1979, annual sales first topped $1 billion, and by 1993, the company was averaging $1 billion in sales *every week*. In 2001, Wal-Mart averaged $1 billion *every day*.

Throughout the 1990s, the chain sustained an eight- to nine-percent annual increase in sales and a 23- to 25-percent increase in profits. In 2001, however, Wal-Mart sales growth dipped under six percent, and profits grew just nine percent. That's still much higher than the rates of major competitors, but Wal-Mart's reduced growth was disappointing to senior managers. The company stresses the fact that expenses must continuously be reduced to maintain target profit margins.

The good news is that Wal-Mart has long enjoyed an unusually harmonious relationship with its employees. The firm pays less than many of its competitors, but its corporate culture gives workers a sense that the company cares about them and their families. Indeed, Wal-Mart's psychological contract with its employees is a product of founder Sam Walton's values. "If you're good to people, and fair with them," said Walton, "they will eventually decide that you're on their side."

During Walton's tenure as CEO, Wal-Mart employees enjoyed numerous family-friendly policies and a wide array of benefits. Starting pay always above minimum wage, and everyone got time-and-a-half pay for working on Sunday. There was a liberal internal promotion policy (70 percent of store managers were once hourly associates) and even low-wage workers had an opportunity to own stock and receive retirement benefits.

Unfortunately, the constant pressure to reduce expenses, large store sizes, and 24-hour store openings have made it hard for Wal-Mart managers to maintain the personal touch that Sam Walton employed so well. Today, many Wal-Mart employees and managers have come to believe that their contract with workers isn't being honored or just isn't working. Says former manager Stan Fortune, "My job was brainwashing. My job was to take you from your job across town and make you want to work for me, regardless of the pay. I'm almost embarrassed to say it, but that's what I did."

Our opening story continues on page 271.

"My job was brainwashing. My job was to take you from your job across town and make you want to work for me, regardless of the pay."

~Former Wal-Mart manager

ON EMPLOYEE RECRUITING, POST-SAM WALTON

Psychological Contracts in Organizations

psychological contract

Set of expectations held by an employee concerning what he or she will contribute to an organization (referred to as *contributions*) and what the organization will in return provide the employee (referred to as *inducements*)

Whenever we buy a car or sell a house, both buyer and seller sign a contract that specifies the terms of the agreement—who pays what to whom, when it's paid, and so forth. In some ways, a psychological contract resembles a legal contract. On the whole, however, it's less formal and less rigidly defined. A **psychological contract** is the set of expectations held by employees concerning what they will contribute to an organization (referred to as *contributions*) and what the organization will provide the employees (referred to as *inducements*) in return.[1]

For example, consider Christine Choi, a programmer for BMC Software in Houston. Choi contributes her education, skills, effort, time, and energy. In return for these contributions, BMC provides various inducements for her to remain with the firm—a good place to work, nice benefits, and a nice salary. Both BMC and Choi seem to be satisfied with the relationship and are thus likely to maintain it—at least for the time being.

In other situations, however, things might not work out as well. If either party perceives an inequity in the contract, that party may seek a change. The employee, for example, might ask for a pay raise, promotion, or a bigger office. Also, the employee might put forth less effort or look for a better job elsewhere. The organization can also initiate change by training workers to improve their skills, transferring them to new jobs, or terminating them.

human relations

Interactions between employers and employees and their attitudes toward one another

All organizations face the basic challenge of managing psychological contracts. They want value from their employees, and they must give employees the right inducements. Valuable but underpaid employees may perform below their capabilities or leave for better jobs. Conversely, overpaying employees who contribute little incurs unnecessary costs. The foundation of good **human relations**—the interactions between employers and employees and their attitudes toward one another—is a satisfied and motivated workforce.[2]

If psychological contracts are created, maintained, and managed effectively, the result is likely to be workers who are satisfied and motivated. On the other hand, poorly managed psychological contracts may result in dissatisfied, unmotivated workers. Although most people have a general idea of what job satisfaction is, both job satisfaction and high morale can be elusive in the workplace. Because they are critical to an organization's success, we now turn our attention to discussing their importance.

The Importance of Satisfaction and Morale

job satisfaction

Degree of enjoyment that people derive from performing their jobs

morale

Overall attitude that employees have toward the workplace

Broadly speaking, **job satisfaction** is the degree of enjoyment that people derive from performing their jobs. If people enjoy their work, they are relatively satisfied; if they do not enjoy their work, they are relatively dissatisfied. In turn, satisfied employees are likely to have high **morale**—the overall attitude that employees have toward the workplace. Morale reflects the degree to which they perceive that their needs are being met by their jobs. It is determined by a variety of factors, including job satisfaction and satisfaction with such things as pay, benefits, coworkers, and promotion opportunities.[3]

Companies can improve morale and job satisfaction in a variety of ways. Some large firms, for example, have instituted companywide programs designed specifically to address employees' needs. Some of *Fortune*'s "100 Best Companies to Work For" offer take-home meals for employees who don't have time to cook. Others provide personal concierge services to help harried employees with everything from buying birthday gifts and organizing social events to planning vacations and maintaining cars.[4]

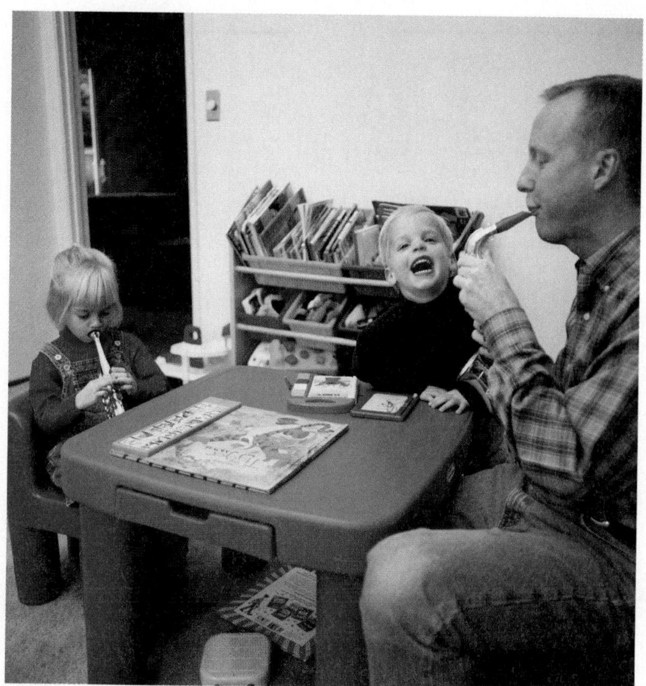

When Curtis Barthold needed 7 months to stay at home with a terminally ill wife and 2 children, he got help from his employer, investment broker Charles Schwab & Co. <www.schwab.com>. *As a member of Schwab's Life-Threatening Illness program, Barthold received a 2-month sabbatical and 5 months of unused sick and vacation days donated by co-workers. The program obviously promotes loyalty among Schwab employees, 90 percent of whom say that they can count on co-workers for help in time of need.*

Managers at Hyatt Hotels <www.hyatt.com> report that conducting frequent surveys of employee attitudes, soliciting employee input, and—most important—acting on that input give the company an edge in recruiting and retaining productive workers. Managers of smaller businesses realize that the personal touch can reap big benefits in employee morale. For example, First Tennessee <www.ftb.com>, a midsize regional bank, believes that work and family are so closely related that family considerations should enter into job design. Thus, it offers such benefits as on-site child care.

Unfortunately, today's tough economic times have caused some firms to rethink the benefits they offer to employees, and many have reduced some of the more extreme benefits. But others, especially those committed to remaining one of *Fortune*'s "100 Best Companies to Work For" remain convinced that a comprehensive benefits program makes good business sense.

When workers are satisfied and morale is high, the organization benefits in many ways. Compared with dissatisfied workers, for example, satisfied employees are more committed and loyal. Such employees are more likely to work hard and to make useful contributions. In addition, they tend to have fewer grievances and engage in fewer negative behaviors (complaining, deliberately slowing their work pace, and so forth) than dissatisfied counterparts. Finally, satisfied workers tend not only to come to work every day but also to remain with the organization. By promoting satisfaction and morale, then, management is working to ensure more efficient operations.

Conversely, the costs of dissatisfaction and poor morale are high.[5] Dissatisfied workers are far more likely to be absent for minor illnesses, personal reasons, or a general disinclination to go to work. Low morale may also result in high **turnover**—the percentage of an organization's workforce that leaves and must be replaced. High levels of turnover have many negative consequences, including the disruption of production schedules, high retraining costs, and decreased productivity. On the other hand, a moderate level of turnover may be beneficial: Organizations can eliminate the jobs of low-performing workers and/or bring in new ideas and fresh talent.

turnover

Annual percentage of an organization's workforce that leaves and must be replaced

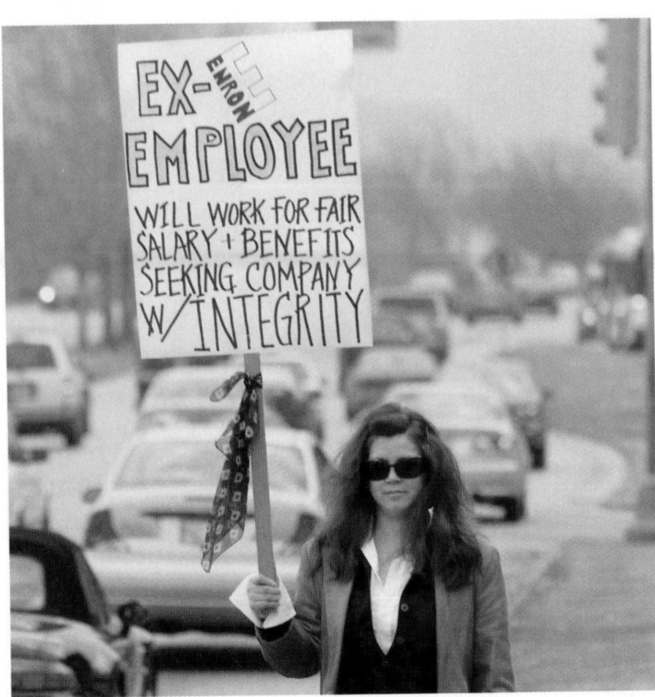

Morale at Enron Corp. reached a low point in January 2002, about a month after the giant energy trader filed for bankruptcy. For one thing, there were suddenly 4,000 employees in the 50-story headquarters instead of 7,000. "It's been dead here for a while," reported one survivor who found himself the lone occupant of the 27th floor. Sonia Garcia, who went job hunting in rush-hour Houston traffic, wasn't even one of the 4,000 survivors of the first round of layoffs.

Recent Trends in Managing Satisfaction and Morale

Achieving high levels of job satisfaction and morale seems like a reasonable organizational goal, especially given their potential impact on organizational performance. From the late 1980s through the mid-1990s, many major companies went through periods of massive layoffs and cutbacks. AT&T, for example, eliminated 40,000 jobs during this time. After a growth period in the late 1990s, many companies have again begun to institute job cuts as a way to remain competitive. In 2002, for instance, American Airlines, Ford Motor Company, and Kmart each

Self-Check Questions 1–3

*You should now be able to answer Self-Check Questions 1–3**

1. TRUE/FALSE A *psychological contract* consists of employee contributions and organizational inducements.

2. MULTIPLE CHOICE Which of the following describes the level of enjoyment that people derive from their jobs? [select one] **(a)** morale; **(b)** job enjoyment; **(c)** job satisfaction; **(d)** job empowerment; **(e)** human relations.

3. TRUE/FALSE Job cuts and the elimination of employee benefits has had which of the following effects on *morale*? [select one] **(a)** increased it; **(b)** maintained it; **(c)** affected it in unpredictable ways; **(d)** reduced it; **(e)** none of these.

*Answers to Self-Check Questions 1–3 can be found on p. AN-6.

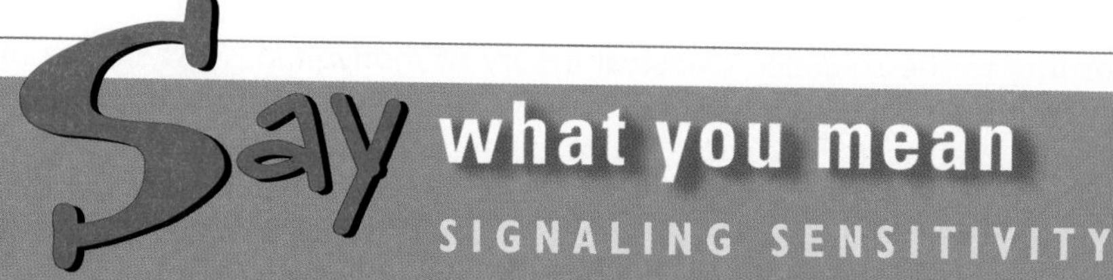

SIGNALING SENSITIVITY

These days, there's a lot of pressure on global companies to be "good corporate citizens"—to treat employees with dignity, to be sensitive to local cultures, and to ensure that the laws of host countries are respected.

It's a rule of thumb that the happier the employee, the more productive and dedicated he or she will be. But *communicating* the fact that a firm has a stake in the satisfaction of its employees and the prosperity of its community isn't always easy. For one thing, because global companies employ people all over the world, there's really no group of people who share all the same values and harbor all the same attitudes. In addition, people take jobs for a huge range of different reasons and may have very different expectations when it comes to pay and benefits and to the degree of commitment they're prepared to make to a corporate entity.

One way companies are trying to communicate more effectively with employees is through Web sites and in-house publications. The aim is to give employees around the world a sense of belonging to a community whose members have shared interests. At the same time, however, companies want to send the message that they're sensitive to *differences*—to the cultural and other forms of diversity that characterize their workforces and the communities in which they operate. Many global firms, for example, sponsor extensive outreach programs in which they provide assistance to various local community groups.

There are still a lot of questions about the role of the corporation in an increasingly globalized world, and of course, there have always been questions about the degree to which companies should exercise social responsibility in host communities. One thing, however, seems certain: Global companies are going to become a good deal more sophisticated in the way they communicate their intentions to both groups of stakeholders.

ɿad major job cuts. Not surprisingly, then, satisfaction and morale plummeted in ɳany companies. Workers feared for their job security, and even those who kept heir jobs were unhappy about their less fortunate colleagues and friends.[6] As a ·esult, then, most workers today seem satisfied enough, but for the most part this s due to the fact that they have a job. When the economy begins to grow again, heir attitudes may become more negative, and employers might again be forced o reinstate benefit programs that have recently been phased out.

Motivation in the Workplace

lthough job satisfaction and morale are important, employee motivation is even nore critical to a firm's success. As we saw in Chapter 6, motivation is one part f the managerial function of directing. Broadly defined, **motivation** is the set of orces that cause people to behave in certain ways. One worker may be motivated o work hard to produce as much as possible, whereas another may be motivated o do just enough to survive. Managers must understand these differences in ehavior and the reasons for them.

motivation
The set of forces that cause people to behave in certain ways

Over the years, a steady progression of theories and studies has attempted to ddress these issues. In this section, we survey the major studies and theories of mployee motivation. In particular, we focus on three approaches to human elations in the workplace that reflect a basic chronology of thinking in the area: 1) *classical theory* and *scientific management,* (2) *behavior theory,* and (3) *contmporary motivational theories.*[7]

Classical Theory

classical theory of motivation
Theory holding that workers are motivated solely by money

According to the so-called **classical theory of motivation**, workers are motivated solely by money. In his seminal 1911 book, *The Principles of Scientific Management,* industrial engineer Frederick Taylor proposed a way for both companies and workers to benefit from this widely accepted view of life in the workplace. If workers are motivated by money, Taylor reasoned, then paying them more should prompt them to produce more. Meanwhile, the firm that analyzed jobs and found better ways to perform them would be able to produce goods more cheaply, make higher profits, and thus pay and motivate workers better than its competitors.

Taylor's approach is known as *scientific management.* His ideas captured the imagination of many managers in the early twentieth century. Soon, plants across the United States were hiring experts to perform *time-and-motion studies:* Industrial engineering techniques were applied to each facet of a job in order to determine how to perform it most efficiently. These studies were the first scientific attempts to break down jobs into easily repeated components and to devise more efficient tools and machines for performing them.

Behavior Theory: The Hawthorne Studies

In 1925, a group of Harvard researchers began a study at the Hawthorne works of Western Electric outside Chicago. With an eye to increasing productivity, they wanted to examine the relationship between changes in the physical environment and worker output.

Hawthorne effect
Tendency for productivity to increase when workers believe they are receiving special attention from management

The results of the experiment were unexpected, even confusing. For example, increased lighting levels improved productivity. For some reason, however, so did lower lighting levels. Moreover, against all expectations, increased pay *failed* to increase productivity. Gradually, the researchers pieced together the puzzle. The explanation lay in the workers' response to the attention that they were receiving. The researchers concluded that productivity rose in response to almost any management action that workers interpreted as special attention. This finding, known widely today as the **Hawthorne effect**, had a major influence on human relations theory, although in many cases it amounted simply to convincing managers that they should pay more attention to employees.

Contemporary Motivational Theories

Following the Hawthorne studies, managers and researchers alike focused mor attention on the importance of good human relations in motivating employe performance. Stressing the factors that cause, focus, and sustain workers' behav ior, most motivation theorists are concerned with the ways in which manage ment thinks about and treats employees. The major motivation theories includ the *human resources model,* the *hierarchy of needs model, two-factor theory, expectancy theory,* and *equity theory.*

Theory X
Theory of motivation holding that people are naturally irresponsible and uncooperative

Theory Y
Theory of motivation holding that people are naturally responsible, growth-oriented, self-motivated, and interested in being productive

Human Resources Model: Theories X and Y In an important study, behaviora scientist Douglas McGregor concluded that managers had radically differen beliefs about how best to use the human resources employed by a firm. He classi fied these beliefs into sets of assumptions that he labeled "Theory X" and "Theor Y." The basic differences between these two theories are highlighted in Table 9.1

Managers who subscribe to **Theory X** tend to believe that people are naturall lazy and uncooperative and must therefore be either punished or rewarded to b made productive. Managers who are inclined to accept **Theory Y** tend to believ that people are naturally energetic, growth-oriented, self-motivated, and inter ested in being productive.

McGregor generally favored Theory Y beliefs. Thus, he argued that Theory managers are more likely to have satisfied and motivated employees. Of cours Theory X and Y distinctions are somewhat simplistic and offer little concret

Theory X	Theory Y
People are lazy.	People are energetic.
People lack ambition and dislike responsibility.	People are ambitious and seek responsibility.
People are self-centered.	People can be selfless.
People resist change.	People want to contribute to business growth and change.
People are gullible and not very bright.	People are intelligent.

TABLE 9.1
Theory X and Theory Y

basis for action. Their value lies primarily in their ability to highlight and classify the behavior of managers in light of their attitudes toward employees.

Maslow's Hierarchy of Needs Model Psychologist Abraham Maslow's **hierarchy of human needs model** proposed that people have several different needs that they attempt to satisfy in their work. He classified these needs into five basic types and suggested that they be arranged in the hierarchy of importance as shown in Figure 9.1. According to Maslow, needs are hierarchical because lower-level needs must be met before a person will try to satisfy higher-level needs.

hierarchy of human needs model
Theory of motivation describing five levels of human needs and arguing that basic needs must be fulfilled before people work to satisfy higher-level needs

Once a set of needs has been satisfied, it ceases to motivate behavior. This is the sense in which the hierarchical nature of lower- and higher-level needs affects employee motivation and satisfaction. For example, if you feel secure in your job, a new pension plan will probably be less important to you than the chance to make new friends and join an informal network among your coworkers.

If, however, a lower-level need suddenly becomes unfulfilled, most people immediately refocus on that lower level. Suppose, for example, that you are seeking to meet your self-esteem needs by working as a divisional manager at a major company. If you learn that your division and, consequently, your job may be eliminated, you might very well find the promise of job security at a new firm as motivating as a promotion once would have been at your old company.

Maslow's theory recognizes that because different people have different needs, they are motivated by different things. Unfortunately, it provides few specific guidelines for action in the workplace. Furthermore, research has found that the hierarchy varies widely, not only for different people but also across different cultures.

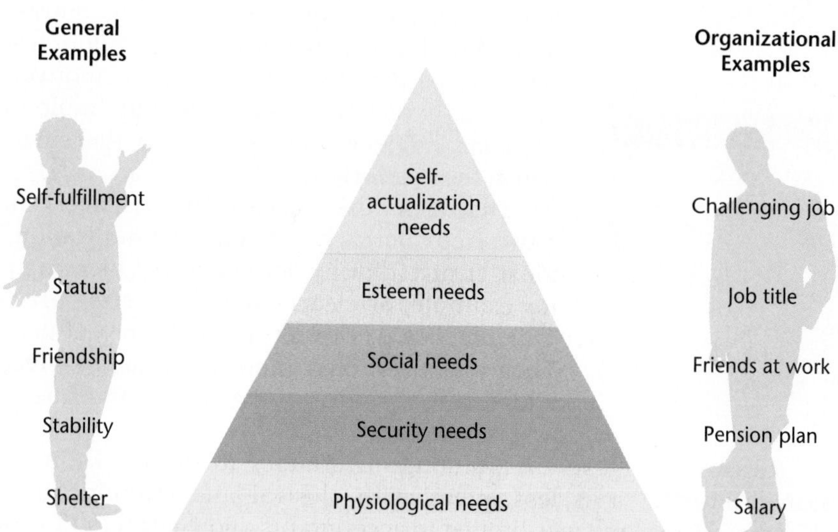

FIGURE 9.1
Maslow's Hierarchy of Needs

"Made on the inside to be sold on the outside" is the slogan of Prison Blues clothing <www.prisonblues.com>*, operated by the Array Corp. of Pendleton, Oregon, from the Eastern Oregon Correctional Institute. Array employs inmates but needs no armed guards because inmates are highly motivated. Even though the pay is paltry—and much of it is garnished for victim relief and other expenses—a day of hard work builds sef-esteem and teaches skills that can be applied when inmates leave prison.*

two-factor theory

Theory of motivation holding that job satisfaction depends on two types of factors: hygiene and motivation

Two-Factor Theory After studying a group of accountants and engineers, psychologist Frederick Herzberg concluded that job satisfaction and dissatisfaction depend on two factors: *hygiene factors,* such as working conditions, and *motivation factors,* such as recognition for a job well done.

According to the **two-factor theory**, hygiene factors affect motivation and satisfaction only if they are absent or fail to meet expectations. For example, workers will be dissatisfied if they believe that they have poor working conditions. If working conditions are improved, however, they will not necessarily become satisfied; they will simply not be dissatisfied. I workers receive no recognition for successful work, they may be neither dissatisfied nor satisfied. If recognition is provided, they will likely become more satisfied.

Motivation Factors
- achievement
- recognition
- the work itself
- responsibility
- advancement and growth

Dissatisfaction ⟷ No dissatisfaction

Hygiene Factors
- supervisors
- working conditions
- interpersonal relations
- pay and security
- company policies and administration

FIGURE 9.2
Two-Factor Theory of Motivation

Figure 9.2 illustrates the two-factor theory. Note tha motivation factors lie along a continuum from *satisfactio* to *no satisfaction.* Hygiene factors, in contrast, are likel to produce feelings that lie on a continuum from *dissatisf action* to *no dissatisfaction.* Whereas motivation factor are directly related to the work that employees actuall perform, hygiene factors refer to the environment i which they perform it.

This theory thus suggests that managers should follow a two-step approach to enhancing motivation. First, the must ensure that hygiene factors—working conditions for example, or clearly stated policies—are acceptable This practice will result in an absence of dissatisfactio Then they must offer motivation factors—recognition c added responsibility—as a way to improve satisfactio and motivation.

Research suggests that although two-factor theory works in some profes sional settings, it is less effective in clerical and manufacturing setting. (Herzberg's research was limited to accountants and engineers.) In addition, or

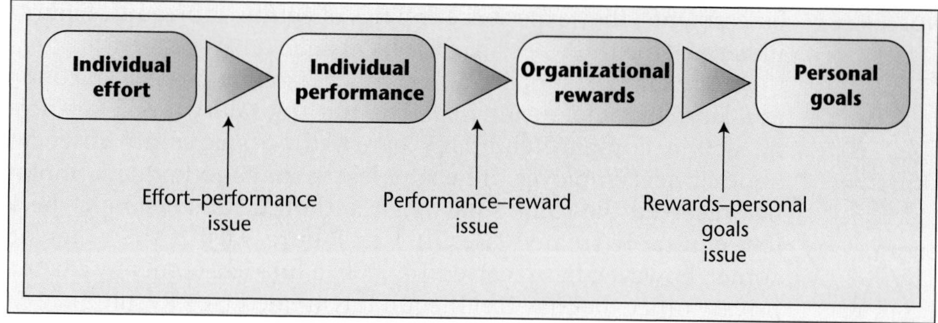

FIGURE 9.3
Expectancy Theory Model

person's hygiene factor may be another person's motivation factor. For example, if money represents nothing more than pay for time worked, it may be a hygiene factor for one person. For another person, however, money may be a motivation factor because it represents recognition and achievement.

Expectancy Theory The **expectancy theory** suggests that people are motivated to work toward rewards that they want and that they believe they have a reasonable chance—or expectancy—of obtaining. A reward that seems out of reach is likely to be undesirable even if it is intrinsically positive. Figure 9.3 illustrates expectancy theory in terms of issues that are likely to be considered by an individual employee.

expectancy theory
Theory of motivation holding that people are motivated to work toward rewards that they want and that they believe they have a reasonable chance of obtaining

Consider the case of an assistant department manager who learns that her firm needs to replace a retiring division manager two levels above her in the organization. Even though she wants the job, she does not apply because she doubts that she will be selected. In this case, she raises the *performance–reward issue:* For some reason, she believes that her performance will not get her the position. Note that she may think that her performance merits the new job but that performance alone will not be enough; perhaps she expects the reward to go to someone with more seniority.

Assume that our employee also learns that the firm is looking for a production manager on a later shift. She thinks that she could get this job but does not apply because she does not want to change shifts. In this instance, she raises the *rewards–personal goals issue.* Finally, she learns of an opening one level higher—department manager—in her own division. She may well apply for this job because she both wants it and thinks that she has a good chance of getting it. In this case, her consideration of all the issues has led to an expectancy that she can reach a given goal.

Expectancy theory helps explain why some people do not work as hard as they can when their salaries are based purely on seniority. Paying employees the same whether they work very hard or just hard enough to get by removes the financial incentive for them to work harder. In other words, they ask themselves, "If I work harder, will I get a pay raise?" and conclude that the answer is no. Similarly, if hard work will result in one or more undesirable outcomes—say, a transfer to another location or a promotion to a job that requires unpleasant travel—employees will not be motivated to work hard.

Equity Theory The **equity theory** focuses on social comparisons—people evaluating their treatment by the organization relative to the treatment of others. This approach holds that people begin by analyzing *inputs* (what they contribute to their jobs in terms of time, effort, education, experience) relative to *outputs* (what they receive in return—salary, benefits, recognition, security). The result is a ratio of contribution to return. Then they compare their own ratios with those of other employees; they ask whether their ratios are *equal to, greater than,* or *less than* those of the people with whom they are comparing themselves. Depending on their

equity theory
Theory of motivation holding that people evaluate their treatment by employers relative to the treatment of others

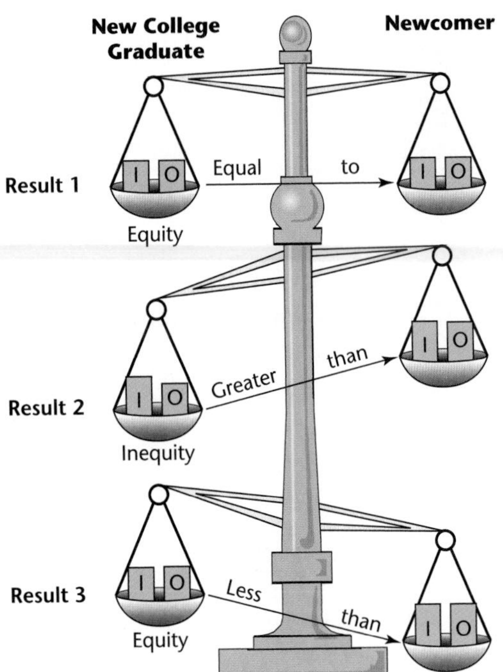

FIGURE 9.4
Equity Theory: Possible Assessments

assessments, they experience feelings of equity or inequity. Figure 9.4 illustrates the three possible results of such an assessment.

For example, suppose a new college graduate gets a starting job at a large manufacturing firm. His starting salary is $35,000 a year, he gets a compact company car, and he shares an office with another new employee. If he later learns that another new employee has received the same salary, car, and office arrangement, he will feel equitably treated (Result 1 in Figure 9.4). If the other newcomer, however, has received $40,000, a full-size company car, and a private office, he may feel inequitably treated (see Result 2).

Note, however, that for an individual to feel equitably treated, the two ratios do not have to be the same, only *fair*. Assume, for instance, that our new employee has a bachelor's degree and two years of work experience. Perhaps he learns subsequently that the other new employee has an advanced degree and 10 years of experience. After first feeling inequity, the new employee may conclude that the person with whom he compared himself is actually contributing more to the organization. That employee is equitably entitled, therefore, to receive more in return (Result 3).

When people feel they are being inequitably treated, they may do various things to restore fairness. For example, they may ask for raises, reduce their efforts, work shorter hours, or just complain to their bosses. They may also rationalize ("Management succumbed to pressure to promote a woman/Asian American"), find different people with whom to compare themselves, or leave their jobs.

Virtually perfect examples of equity theory at work can be found in professional sports. Each year, for example, rookies, sometimes fresh out of college, are often signed to lucrative contracts. No sooner is the ink dry than veteran players start grumbling about raises or revised contracts.

Strategies for Enhancing Job Satisfaction and Morale

Deciding what provides job satisfaction and motivates workers is only one part of human resource management. The other part is applying that knowledge. Experts have suggested—and many companies have implemented—a range of programs designed to make jobs more interesting and rewarding and to make the work environment more pleasant.

Reinforcement/Behavior Modification Theory

Many companies try to control—and even alter or modify—workers' behavior through systematic rewards and punishments for specific behaviors. In other words, such companies first try to define the specific behaviors that they want their employees to exhibit (working hard, being courteous to customers, stressing quality) and the specific behaviors they want to eliminate (wasting time, being rude to customers, ignoring quality). Then they try to shape employee behavior by linking reinforcement with desired behaviors and punishment with undesired behaviors.

reinforcement
Theory that behavior can be encouraged or discouraged by means of rewards or punishments

Reinforcement is used when a company pays *piecework* rewards—when workers are paid for each piece or product completed. In reinforcement strategies, rewards refer to all the positive things that people get for working (pay, praise, promotions, job security, and so forth). When rewards are tied directly to performance, they serve as *positive reinforcement*. For example, paying large cash bonuses to salespeople who exceed quotas prompts them to work even harder

"O.K., I messed up. He didn't have to rub my nose in it."

during the next selling period. John Deere <www.deere.com> has adopted a reward system based on positive reinforcement. The firm gives pay increases when its workers complete college courses and demonstrate mastery of new job skills.

Punishment is designed to change behavior by presenting people with unpleasant consequences if they fail to change in desirable ways. Employees who are repeatedly late for work, for example, may be suspended or have their pay docked. Similarly, when the National Football League or Major League Baseball fines or suspends players found guilty of substance abuse, the organization is seeking to change players' behavior.

Extensive rewards work best when people are learning new behavior, new skills, or new jobs. As workers become more adept, rewards can be used less frequently. Because such actions contribute to positive employer–employee relationships, managers generally prefer giving rewards and placing positive value on performance. Conversely, most managers dislike doling out punishment, partly because workers may respond with anger, resentment, hostility, or even retaliation. To reduce this risk, many managers couple punishment with rewards for good behavior.

Management by Objectives

Management by objectives (MBO) is a system of collaborative goal setting that extends from the top of an organization to the bottom. As a technique for managing the planning process, MBO is concerned mainly with helping managers implement and carry out their plans. As you can see from Figure 9.5, MBO involves managers and subordinates in setting goals and evaluating progress. Once the program is set up, the first step is establishing overall organizational goals. It is also these goals that will ultimately be evaluated to determine the success of the program. At the same time, however, collaborative activity—communicating, meeting, controlling,

management by objectives (MBO)

Set of procedures involving both managers and subordinates in setting goals and evaluating progress

FIGURE 9.5
Management by Objectives

and so forth—is the key to MBO. Therefore, it can also serve as a program for improving satisfaction and motivation.

According to many experts, motivational impact is the biggest advantage of MBO. When employees sit down with managers to set upcoming goals, they learn more about companywide objectives, come to feel that they are an important part of a team, and see how they can improve companywide performance by reaching their own goals. If an MBO system is used properly, employees should leave meetings not only with an understanding of the value of their contributions, but also with fair rewards for their performances. They should also accept and be committed to the moderately difficult and specific goals they have helped set for themselves.

Participative Management and Empowerment

participative management and empowerment

Method of increasing job satisfaction by giving employees a voice in the management of their jobs and the company

In **participative management and empowerment**, employees are given a voice in how they do their jobs and in how the company is managed—they become *empowered* to take greater responsibility for their own performance. Not surprisingly, participation and empowerment make employees feel more committed to organizational goals they have helped to shape.

Participation and empowerment can be used in large firms or small firms, both with managers and operating employees. For example, managers at General Electric <www.ge.com> who once needed higher level approval for any expenditure over $5,000 have the autonomy to make their own expense decisions up to as much as $50,000. At Adam Hat Co., a small firm that makes men's dress, military, and cowboy hats, workers who previously had to report all product defects to supervisors now have the freedom to correct problems themselves or even return products to the workers who are responsible for them.

Team Management

At one level, employees may be given decision-making responsibility for certain narrow activities, such as when to take lunch breaks or how to divide assignments with coworkers. On a broader level, employees are also being consulted on such decisions as production scheduling, work procedures and schedules, and the hiring of new employees. Among the many organizations actively using teams today are Texas Instruments <www.ti.com>, Lucent Technologies <www.lucent.com>, and Ford Motor Co. <www.ford.com>.

Although some employees thrive in participative programs, such programs are not for everyone. Many people will be frustrated by responsibilities they are not equipped to handle. Moreover, participative programs may actually result in dissatisfied employees if workers see the invitation to participate as more symbolic than substantive. One key, say most experts, is to invite participation only to the extent that employees want to have input and only if participation will have real value for an organization.

Managers, therefore, should remember that teams are not for everyone. Levi Strauss <www.levi.com>, for example, encountered major problems when it tried to use teams. Individual workers previously performed repetitive, highly specialized tasks, such as sewing zippers into jeans, and were paid according to the number of jobs they completed each day. In an attempt to boost productivity, company management reorganized everyone into teams of 10 to 35 workers and assigned tasks to the entire group. Each team member's pay was determined by the team's level of productivity. In practice, however, faster workers became resentful of slower workers because they reduced the group's total output. Slower workers, meanwhile, resented the pressure put on them by faster-working coworkers. As a result, motivation, satisfaction, and morale all dropped, and Levi's eventually abandoned the teamwork plan altogether.[8]

By and large, however, participation and empowerment in general, and team management in particular, continue to be widely used as enhancers of employee motivation and company performance. Although teams are often less effective in traditional and rigidly structured bureaucratic organizations, they often help smaller, more flexible organizations make decisions more quickly and effectively, enhance companywide communication, and encourage organizational members to feel more like a part of an organization. In turn, these attitudes usually lead to higher levels of both employee motivation and job satisfaction.[9]

Job Enrichment and Job Redesign

Whereas MBO programs and empowerment can work in a variety of settings, *job enrichment* and *job redesign programs* are generally used to increase satisfaction in jobs significantly lacking in motivating factors.[10]

job enrichment
Method of increasing job satisfaction by adding one or more motivating factors to job activities

Job Enrichment Programs

Job enrichment is designed to add one or more motivating factors to job activities. For example, *job rotation programs* expand growth opportunities by rotating employees through various positions in the

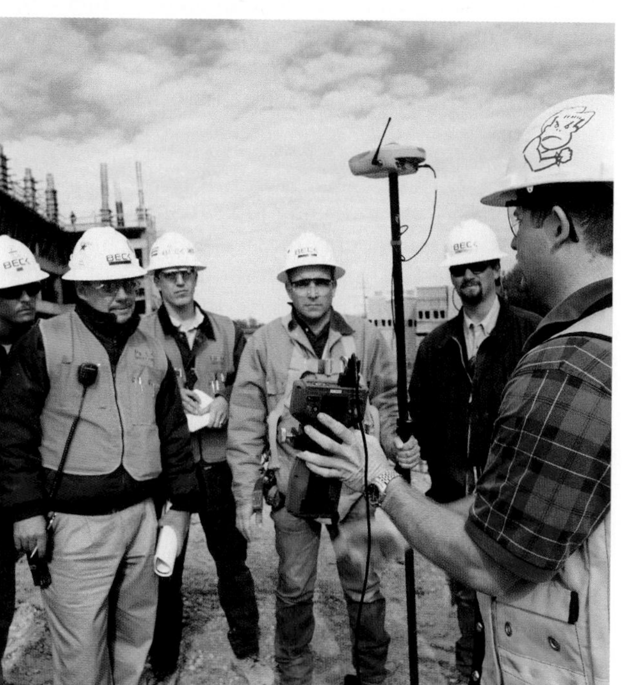

When employees of the Beck Group <www.beckgroup.com>, a Dallas-based construction and real estate development company, go to work on a project, they enjoy a great deal of autonomy in applying their decision-making and other skills. The approach works because the company encourages continuous training, reimbursing workers up to $4,500 a year for higher-education courses. Bonuses are paid out when customers are happy, and apparently the job satisfaction of Beck employees translates into customer satisfaction: 80% of the firm's clients are repeats.

same firm. Workers gain not only new skills but also broader overviews of their work and their organization. Other programs focus on increasing responsibility or recognition. At Continental Airlines <www.continental.com>, for example, flight attendants now have more control over their own scheduling. The jobs of flight service managers were enriched when they were given more responsibility and authority for assigning tasks to flight crew members.

Job Redesign Programs Job redesign acknowledges that different people want different things from their jobs. By restructuring work to achieve a more satisfactory fit between workers and their jobs, **job redesign** can motivate individuals with strong needs for career growth or achievement. Job redesign is usually implemented in one of three ways: through *combining tasks, forming natural work groups,* or *establishing client relationships.*

job redesign
Method of increasing job satisfaction by designing a more satisfactory fit between workers and their jobs

Combining Tasks The job of combining tasks involves enlarging jobs and increasing their variety to make employees feel that their work is more meaningful. In turn, employees become more motivated. For example, the job done by a programmer who maintains computer systems might be redesigned to include some system design and system development work. While developing additional skills, then, the programmer also gets involved in the overall system package.

Forming Natural Work Groups People who do different jobs on the same projects are candidates for natural work groups. These groups are formed to help employees see the place and importance of their jobs in the total structure of the firm. They are valuable to management because the people working on a project are usually the most knowledgeable about it and thus the most capable problem solvers.

Establishing Client Relationships Establishing client relationships means letting employees interact with customers. This approach increases job variety. It gives workers both a greater sense of control and more feedback about performance than they get when their jobs are not highly interactive.

For example, software writers at Microsoft <www.microsoft.com> watch test users work with programs and discuss problems with them directly rather than receive feedback from third-party researchers. In Fargo, North Dakota, Great Plains Software <www.greatplains.com> has employee turnover of less than 7 percent, compared with an industry average of 15 to 20 percent. The company recruits and rewards in large part according to candidates' customer service skills and their experience with customer needs and complaints.

Modified Work Schedules

As another way of increasing job satisfaction, many companies are experimenting with *modified work schedules*—different approaches to working hours and the workweek. The two most common forms of modified scheduling are *work-share programs* and *flextime programs,* including *alternative workplace strategies.*[11]

Work-Share Programs At Steelcase Inc. <www.steelcase.com>, the country's largest maker of office furnishings, two very talented women in the marketing division both wanted to work only part-time. The solution: They now share a single full-time job. With each working 2.5 days a week, both got their wish and the job gets done—and done well. In another situation, one person might work mornings and the other afternoons. The practice, known as **work sharing** (or **job sharing**), has "brought sanity back to our lives," according to at least one Steelcase employee.

work sharing (or **job sharing**)
Method of increasing job satisfaction by allowing two or more people to share a single full-time job

Job sharing usually benefits both employees and employers. Employees, for instance, tend to appreciate the organization's attention to their personal needs. At the same time, the company can reduce turnover and save on the cost of ben

Motivation and the Machine

There was a time when blue-collar manufacturing jobs were ideal for people with no interest in high technology. Through the 1970s, some people chose production work because they didn't care to earn a college degree. Says David Erb, a technician at Techneglas Inc., "When I finished high school, I said, 'Enough.'" But those days are gone. Today, advances in high-tech manufacturing have made factory-floor occupations among the most technology intensive in the business world. Not surprisingly, while some workers welcome the change, others are less enthused.

At first glance, the Columbus, Ohio, plant of Techneglas <www.techneglas.com> seems to be a throwback—it makes the glass funnels for television picture tubes. (Right now, the demand for TVs is robust, but flat-screen TVs—which don't need conventional picture tubes—are beginning to find their way into homes.) On the plant floor, however, a technology revolution has taken place. New equipment includes electronic quality monitoring machines and computers.

All employees are under constant pressure to learn new skills, and some older workers have taken early retirement rather than upgrade computer and math skills. The plant has a learning center, but Heidi LoRash-Neuenschwander, who runs it, reports that "older workers often demand to know exactly what they're going to get out of learning new skills, while younger workers just want to learn." As a rule, younger workers already have better technology skills; after all, most of them used PCs in high school. Erb sees another difference, too. "Younger employees," he says, "often want the latest and greatest technology, even when the upgrade confers no real benefit."

One explanation for this generational technology divide is the difference in motivating factors for older workers and younger workers. Older workers, often nervous about retirement, tend to look for job stability and security. They say that younger workers look for labor-saving devices because they're "lazy." Younger workers claim that learning technology is fun and motivating in itself. Perhaps the difference can be explained by motivation theory. Older workers want to be motivated first, and then they will achieve high performance. For younger employees, achievement may occur first, leading to higher motivation.

·fits. On the negative side, job-share employees generally receive fewer benefits han their full-time counterparts and may be the first to be laid off when cut-›acks are necessary.

'lextime Programs and Alternative Workplace Strategies **Flextime programs** ıllow people to choose their working hours by adjusting a standard work sched-ıle on a daily or weekly basis. Indeed, there was a significant boom in flextime ›rograms in the late 1990s as part of the escalation of employee benefits that we nentioned before. There are, of course, limits. The Steelcase program, for nstance, requires all employees to work certain core hours. This practice allows ·veryone to reach coworkers at a specified time of day. Employees can then lecide whether to make up the rest of the standard eight-hour day by coming in .nd leaving early (by working 6:00 A.M. to 2:00 P.M. or 7:00 A.M. to 3:00 P.M.) or late 9:00 A.M. to 5:00 P.M. or 10:00 A.M. to 6:00 P.M.).

flextime programs
Method of increasing job satisfaction by allowing workers to adjust work schedules on a daily or weekly basis

Figure 9.6 shows a hypothetical flextime system that could be used by three lifferent people. The office is open from 6:00 A.M. until 7:00 P.M. Core time is 9:00 .M. to 11:00 A.M. and 1:00 P.M. to 3:00 P.M. Joe, an early riser, comes in at 6:00, akes an hour for lunch between 11:00 and noon, and finishes his day by 3:00. ›ue, a working mother, prefers a later day. She comes in at 9:00, takes a long ınch from 11:00 to 1:00, and then works until 7:00. Pat works a more traditional -to-5 schedule.

"Older workers often demand to know exactly what they're going to get out of learning new skills, while younger workers just want to learn."

~Manager of the learning center, TECHNEGLASS INC.

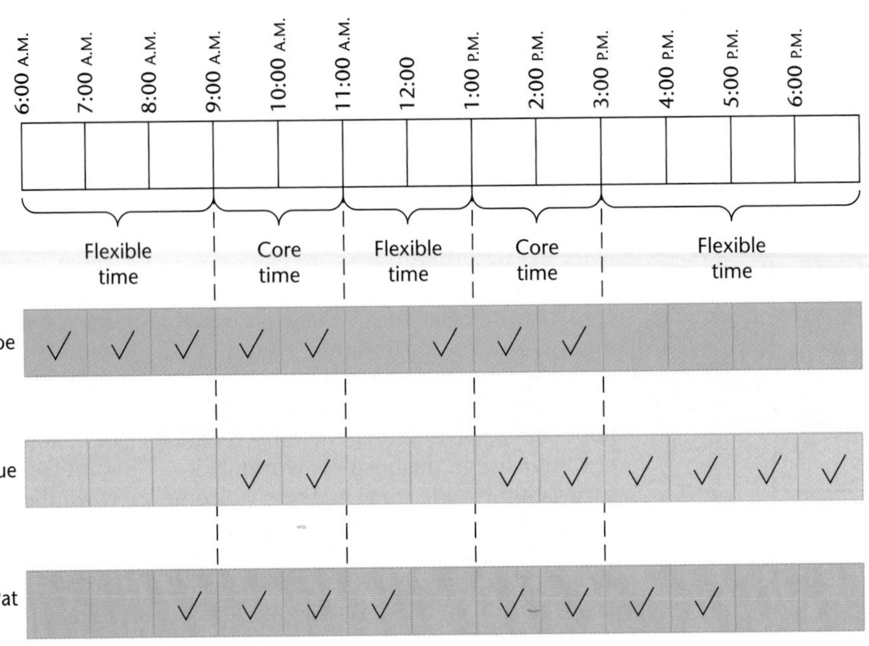

FIGURE 9.6
Sample Flextime Schedule

In one variation, companies may also allow employees to choose four, five, or six days on which to work each week. Some, for instance, may choose Monday through Thursday, others Tuesday through Friday. Still others may work Monday–Tuesday and Thursday–Friday and take Wednesday off. By working 10 hours over four workdays, employees still complete 40-hour weeks.

Telecommuting and Virtual Offices Kelly Ramsey-Dolson is an accountant employed by Ernst & Young <www.ey.com>. Because she has a young son, she does not want to be away from home more than she absolutely must. Ramsey-Dolson and the company have worked out an arrangement whereby she works at home two or three days a week and comes into the office the other days. Her home office is outfitted with a PC, modem, and fax machine, and she uses this technology to keep abreast of everything going on at the office.

Ramsey-Dolson is one of a rapidly growing number of U.S. workers who do a significant portion of their work on the basis of a relatively new version of flextime known as **telecommuting**—performing some or all of a job away from standard office settings. Among salaried employees, the telecommuter workforce grew by 21.5 percent in 1994—to 7.6 million—and then to 11 million in 1997; the number of telecommuters in 2001 exceeded 25.4 million employees.

telecommuting
Form of flextime that allows people to perform some or all of a job away from standard office settings

The key to telecommuting is technology. The availability of networked computers, fax machines, cellular telephones, and overnight-delivery services makes it possible for many professionals to work at home or while traveling. Cisco Systems <www.cisco.com>, the Internet networking giant, is at the forefront of telecommuting arrangements for its workers. The firm estimates that by allowing employees to do some of their work at home, it has boosted productivity by 25 percent, lowered overhead costs by $1 million, and achieved a higher retention rate among key knowledge workers who might have otherwise left for more flexibility elsewhere.[12]

Other companies have experimented with so-called *virtual offices*. They have redesigned conventional office space to accommodate jobs and schedules that are far less dependent on assigned spaces and personal apparatus. At the advertising firm of TBWA/Chiat/Day <www.chiatday.com> in Los Angeles, California, only about one-third of the salaried workforce is in the office on any given day. The office building features informal work carrels or nooks and open areas

Martin Gertel used to commute three hours a day, five days a week from Virginia to Washington, DC, to work as an auditor for the Transportation Department <www.dot.gov>. *Now he telecommutes, working on Mondays and Fridays from his home office. Gertel's arrangement is unusual: Telecommuting among government workers lags behind private-sector practices because much government work doesn't adapt very well, the costs of home offices are high, and federal managers have been slow to encourage change. Congress is now looking at legislation that would make more government employees eligible to telecommute.*

available to every employee. "The work environment," explains Director of Operations Adelaide Horton, "was designed around the concept that one's best thinking isn't necessarily done at a desk or in an office. Sometimes it's done in a conference room with other people. Other times it's done on a ski slope or driving to a client's office."

"Sometimes one's best thinking is done in a conference room with other people. Other times it's done on a ski slope or driving to a client's office."

~Director of Operations Adelaide Horton, TBWA/CHIAT/DAY ADVERTISING FIRM

Advantages and Disadvantages of Modified Schedules and Alternative Workplaces

Flextime gives employees more freedom in their professional and personal lives. It allows workers to plan around the work schedules of spouses and the school schedules of young children. Studies show that the increased sense of freedom and control reduces stress and thus improves individual productivity.

Companies also benefit in other ways. In urban areas, for example, such programs can reduce traffic congestion and similar problems that contribute to stress and lost work time. Furthermore, employers benefit from higher levels of commitment and job satisfaction. John Hancock Insurance <www.jhancock.com>, Atlantic Richfield <www.arco.com>, and Metropolitan Life <www.metlife.com> are among the major American corporations that have successfully adopted some form of flextime.

Conversely, flextime sometimes complicates coordination because people are working different schedules. In the schedules shown in Figure 9.6, for instance, Sue may need some important information from Joe at 4:30 P.M., but because Joe is working an earlier schedule, he leaves for the day at 3:00. In addition, if workers are paid by the hour, flextime may make it difficult for employers to keep accurate records of when employees are actually working.

As for telecommuting and virtual offices, although they may be the wave of the future, they may not be for everyone. For example, consultant Gil Gordon points out that telecommuters are attracted to the ideas of "not having to shave and put on makeup or go through traffic, and sitting in their blue jeans all day." However, he suggests that would-be telecommuters ask themselves several other questions: "Can I manage deadlines? What will it be like to be away from the social context of the office five days a week? Can I renegotiate the rules of the family, so my spouse doesn't come home every night expecting me to have a four-course meal on the table?" One study has shown that even though telecommuters

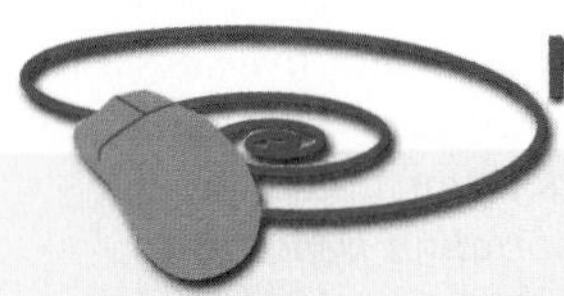

Mid-Chapter Internet Field Trip

"All About Teleworking"

This chapter discusses what we know about motivating employees in terms of both theories and the strategies designed to put those theories into practice. These strategies include participative management, teams, job enrichment, and modified work schedules that allow employees to share jobs, stagger hours, and work full time or part time from home through telecommuting.

Let's find out more about telecommuting by visiting the Web site of the International Telework Association and Council (ITAC) at <www.telework.org>. Once you've logged on, you'll find several topics on the home page, including:

- About ITAC
- Telework America
- e-Work Guide
- Membership
- Resources

Select **About ITAC** and go to the **Mission Statement**:

1. What is the mission of this organization?

Return to **About ITAC** and select **Alive and Well**. Read the first few paragraphs of this item.

2. How does ITAC define the term "telework"?

Read the first few **Q&As** in the second part of the item:

3. Why isn't teleworking for everyone?

Return once again to **About ITAC** and select **Committees**:

4. What are some of ITAC's initiatives and activities?

Now return to the home page and select **Membership**:

5. Who belongs to ITAC?

To continue your Internet Field Trip, click on www.prenhall.com/griffin

> **"Managers always ask, 'How can I tell if someone is working when I can't see them?' That's based on the erroneous assumption that if you can see them, they are working."**
>
> ~HR consultant
> ON MANAGERIAL QUALMS ABOUT TELECOMMUTING

may be producing results, those with strong advancement ambitions may miss networking and rubbing elbows with management on a day-to-day basis.

Another obstacle to establishing a telecommuting program is convincing management that it can be beneficial for all involved. Telecommuters may have to fight the perception from both bosses and coworkers that if they are not being supervised, they are not working. Managers, admits one experienced consultant, "usually have to be dragged kicking and screaming into this. They always ask, 'How can I tell if someone is working when I can't see them?'" By the same token, he adds, "that's based on the erroneous assumption that if you can see them, they are working." Most experts agree that reeducation and constant communication are requirements of a successful telecommuting arrangement. Both managers and employees must determine expectations in advance.

Managerial Styles and Leadership

leadership
Process of motivating others to work to meet specific objectives

In trying to enhance morale, job satisfaction, and motivation, managers can use many different styles of leadership. **Leadership** is the process of motivating others to work to meet specific objectives. Leading is also one of the key aspects of a manager's job and an important component of the directing function.[13]

Joe Liemandt, for example, dropped out of Stanford in 1990 to start a software company in Austin, Texas. As part of his strategy, he was determined to develop and maintain a workforce of creative people who worked well in teams, adapted to rapid change, and felt comfortable taking risks. A decade later, people with these qualities—now numbering nearly 1,000—have helped build Liemandt's company Trilogy Software Inc. <www.trilogy.com>, into a profitable maker of industry-leading software for managing product pricing, sales plans, and commissions.

When Trilogy hires a new group of employees, Liemandt himself oversees their training. He sees himself as the firm's leader and believes that, as such, it is

Self-Check Questions 4–6

*You should now be able to answer Self-Check Questions 4–6**

4. MULTIPLE CHOICE Which of the following is **not** a popular *motivational theory*? [select one] **(a)** equity theory; **(b)** expectancy theory; **(c)** two-factor theory; **(d)** hierarchy of needs model; **(e)** all are popular motivational theories.

5. MULTIPLE CHOICE In Maslow's *hierarchy of needs model*, an important job title can generally help satisfy which of the following set of needs? **(a)** self-actualization needs; **(b)** esteem needs; **(c)** social needs; **(d)** security needs; **(e)** physiological needs.

6. TRUE/FALSE *Team management* is an important form of *job enrichment*.

*ANSWERS TO SELF-CHECK QUESTIONS 4–6 CAN BE FOUND ON P. AN-6.

his responsibility to ensure that every employee shares his vision and understands his way of doing business. Training takes several weeks, starting with a series of classes devoted to the technical aspects of Trilogy's products and methods of software development. Then recruits move into areas in which Liemandt truly believes they make a real difference—developing risk-taking skills and the ability to recognize new opportunities.

Recruits are formed into teams, and each team is given three weeks to complete various projects, ranging from the creation of new products to the development of marketing campaigns for existing products. Teams actually compete with one another and are scored on such criteria as risk and innovation, goal setting, and goal accomplishment. Evaluations are completed by Liemandt, other Trilogy managers, and some of the firm's venture capital backers. Winners get free trips to Las Vegas. Losers go straight to work.

Liemandt's leadership doesn't stop there, even for those who go to Las Vegas, where Liemandt challenges everyone to place a $2,000 bet at the roulette wheel. He argues that $2,000 is a meaningful sum and one that can cause real pain, but it is not so much that it will cause financial disaster for anyone. Actually, Liemandt puts up the money, which losers pay back through payroll deductions of $400 over five months. Not everyone, of course, decides to take the chance, but enough do to make the message clear: Liemandt aims to succeed by taking chances, and he expects employees to share the risks. Those who do so stand to earn bigger returns on more intrepid investments.[14]

In this section, we begin by describing some of the basic features of and differences in managerial styles and then focus on an approach to managing and leading that, like Joe Liemandt's, understands those jobs as responses to a variety of complex situations.

Managerial Styles

Early theories of leadership tried to identify specific traits associated with strong leaders. For example, physical appearance, intelligence, and public speaking skills were once thought to be leadership traits. Indeed, it was once believed that taller people made better leaders than shorter people. The trait approach, however, proved to be a poor predictor of leadership potential. Ultimately, attention shifted from managers' traits to their behaviors, or **managerial styles**—patterns of behavior that a manager exhibits in dealing with subordinates. Managerial styles run the gamut from autocratic to democratic to free rein. Naturally, most managers do not clearly conform to any one style, but these three major types of styles involve very different kinds of responses to human relations problems. Under different circumstances, any given style or combination of the following three styles may prove appropriate.[15]

managerial style
Pattern of behavior that a manager exhibits in dealing with subordinates

- Managers who adopt an **autocratic style** generally issue orders and expect them to be obeyed without question. The military commander prefers and usually needs the autocratic style on the battlefield. Because no one else is consulted, the autocratic style allows for rapid decision making. It may, therefore, be useful in situations testing a firm's effectiveness as a time-based competitor.
- Managers who adopt a **democratic style** generally ask for input from subordinates before making decisions, but they retain final decision-making power. For example, the manager of a technical group may ask other group members to interview and offer opinions about job applicants. The manager, however, will ultimately make the hiring decision.
- Managers who adopt a **free-rein style** typically serve as advisers to subordinates who are allowed to make decisions. The chairperson of a volunteer committee to raise funds for a new library may find a free-rein style most effective.

autocratic style
Managerial style in which managers generally issue orders and expect them to be obeyed without question

democratic style
Managerial style in which managers generally ask for input from subordinates but retain final decision-making power

free-rein style
Managerial style in which managers typically serve as advisers to subordinates who are allowed to make decisions

According to many observers, the free-rein style of leadership is currently giving rise to an approach that emphasizes broad-based employee input into decision making and the fostering of workplace environments in which employees increasingly determine what needs to be done and how.

Regardless of theories about the ways in which leaders ought to lead, the relative effectiveness of any leadership style depends largely on the desire of subordinates to share input or to exercise creativity. Whereas some people, for example, are frustrated by autocratic managers, others prefer them because they don't want a voice in making decisions. The democratic approach, meanwhile, can be disconcerting both to people who want decision-making responsibility and to those who do not. A free-rein style lends itself to employee creativity and thus to creative solutions to pressing problems. This style also appeals to employees who like to plan their own work. Not all subordinates, however, have the necessary background or skills to make creative decisions. Others are not sufficiently self-motivated to work without supervision.

The Contingency Approach to Leadership

Because each managerial style has both strengths and weaknesses, most managers vary their responses to different situations. Flexibility, however, has not always characterized managerial style or responsiveness. For most of the twentieth century, in fact, managers tended to believe that all problems yielded to preconceived, pretested solutions. If raising pay reduced turnover in one plant, for example, it followed that the same tactic would work equally well in another.

More recently, however, managers have begun to adopt a **contingency approach to managerial style**. They have started to view appropriate managerial behavior in any situation as dependent, or contingent, on the elements unique to that situation. This change in outlook has resulted largely from an increasing appreciation of the complexity of managerial problems and solutions. For example, pay raises may reduce turnover when workers have been badly underpaid. The contingency approach, however, recognizes that raises will have little effect when workers feel adequately paid but ill treated by management. This approach

contingency approach to managerial style
Approach to managerial style holding that the appropriate behavior in any situation is dependent (contingent) on the unique elements of that situation

also recommends that training managers in human relations skills may be crucial to solving the problem in the second case.[16]

The contingency approach also acknowledges that people in different cultures behave differently and expect different things from their managers. A certain managerial style, therefore, is more likely to be successful in some countries than in others. Japanese workers, for example, generally expect managers to be highly participative and to give them input in decision making. In contrast, many South American workers actually balk at participation and want take-charge leaders. The basic idea, then, is that managers will be more effective when they adapt their styles to the contingencies of the situations they face.[17]

Motivation and Leadership in the Twenty-First Century

Motivation and leadership remain critically important areas of organizational behavior. As times change, however, so do the ways managers motivate and lead their employees.

Changing Patterns of Motivation From the motivational side, today's employees want rewards that are often quite different from those valued by earlier generations. Money, for example, is no longer the prime motivator for most people. In addition, because businesses today cannot offer the degree of job security that many workers want, motivating employees to strive toward higher levels of performance requires skillful attention from managers.

One recent survey asked workers to identify those things they most wanted at work. Among the things noted were flexible working hours (67 %), casual dress (56 %), unlimited Internet access (51 %), opportunities to telecommute (43 %), nap time (28 %), massages (25 %), daycare (24 %), espresso machines (23 %), and the opportunity to bring a pet to work (11 %). In another study focusing on fathers, many men also said they wanted more flexible working hours in order to spend more time with their families. Managers, then, must recognize the fact that today's workers have a complex set of needs and must be motivated in increasingly complicated ways.

Finally, the diversity inherent in today's workforce also makes motivating behavior more complex. The reasons why people work reflect more varying goals than ever before, and the varying lifestyles of diverse workers mean that managers must first pay closer attention to what their employees expect to get for their efforts and then try to link rewards with job performance.[18]

Changing Patterns of Leadership Leadership, too, is taking different directions as we head into the twenty-first century. For one thing, today's leaders are finding it necessary to change their own behavior. As organizations become flatter and workers more empowered, managers naturally find it less acceptable to use the autocratic approach to leadership. Instead, many are becoming more democratic—functioning more as coaches than as bosses. Just as an athletic coach teaches athletes how to play and then steps back to let them take the field, many leaders now try to provide workers with the skills and resources they need to perform at their best before backing off to let them do their work with less supervision.

Diversity, too, is also affecting leadership processes. In earlier times, most leaders were white males who were somewhat older than the people they supervised—people who were themselves relatively similar to one another. But as organizations become more and more diverse, leaders are also becoming increasingly diverse—women, African Americans, and Hispanics are entering the managerial ranks in ever greater numbers. They are also increasingly likely to be younger than some of the people they are leading. Leaders, therefore, must have greater sensitivity to the values, needs, and motives of a diverse group of people as they examine their own behavior in its relation to other people.

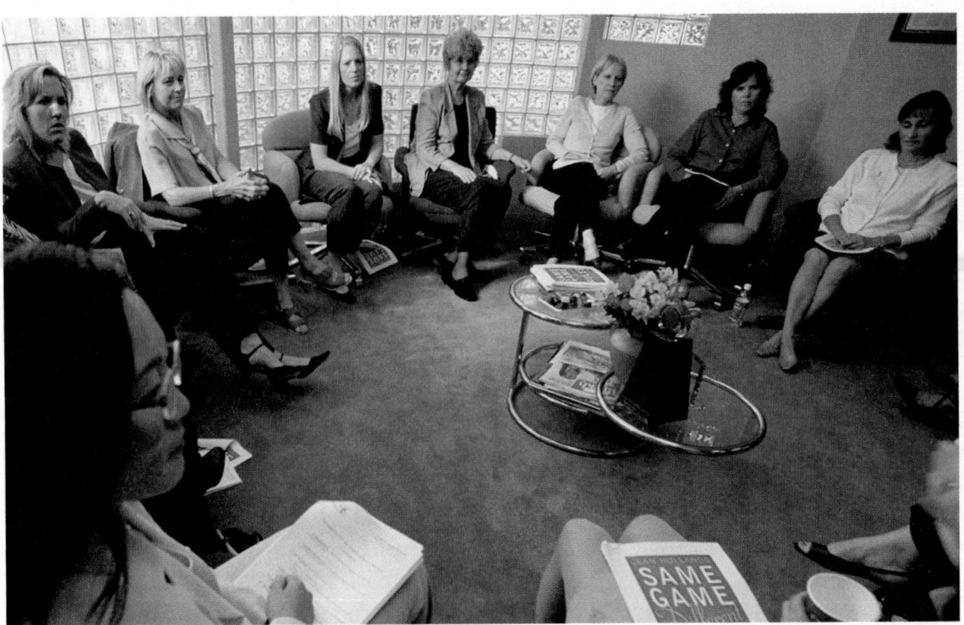

These female executives are all clients of the Growth and Leadership Center <www.glcweb.com> in Mountain View, California, because the same toughness that got them up the corporate ladder is keeping them from climbing any higher. Or so say their employers (mostly men). Program founder Jean A. Hollands calls it "Bully Broads" and recommends that female executives back off from the assertive stance they were taught in the 1980s and return to a "softer" approach to interpersonal relationships. Many people, of course, think that Hollands' approach is all wrong. "I think women in many cases need to be more aggressive," says Alexandra Lebenthal, CEO of the brokerage firm Lebenthal & Co.

Finally, leaders must also adopt more of a network mentality than a hierarchical one. As long as people worked in the same place at the same time, the organizational hierarchy had a clear vertical chain of command and lines of communication. But now people work in different places and at different times. New forms of organization design may call for one person to be the leader on one project and a team member on another. Thus, people need to get comfortable with leadership based more on expertise than on organizational position and with interaction patterns not tied to specific places or times. The leader of tomorrow, then, will need a different set of skills and a different point of view than did the leader of yesterday.[19]

Self-Check Questions 7–9

*You should now be able to answer Self-Check Questions 7–9**

7. MULTIPLE CHOICE Which of the following is a common *managerial style*? [select one] **(a)** autocratic; **(b)** democratic; **(c)** free-rein; **(d)** all of these are common managerial styles; **(e)** none of these are common managerial styles.

8. TRUE/FALSE According to the *contingency approach to leadership,* there is usually one approach to leadership that should always be used.

9. MULTIPLE CHOICE When Sam supervises Mike, he uses an *autocratic style* because he knows that Mike wants to be told what to do. But when he supervises Ashley, he uses a *democratic style* because he knows she wants to have a voice in how she does her work. To which of the following theories of workplace behavior is Sam adhering? [select one] **(a)** contingency approach to leadership; **(b)** trait approach to leadership; **(c)** expectancy theory of motivation; **(d)** equity theory of motivation; **(e)** behavioral approach to leadership.

*Answers to Self-Check Questions 7–9 can be found on p. AN-6.

Continued from page 249

Moral Integrity and Morale

Wal-Mart is changing the way it relates to its workers. But as it turns out, some of those workers aren't living up to their end of the bargain either. With little personal contact with managers, some workers miss work frequently or quit unexpectedly. "We had five call in and quit one day," says Stephanie Haynes, manager of the Madisonville, Texas, store. Sam Walton himself noted that as more stores were built in urban areas, "We have [had] more trouble coming up with educated people who want to work in our industry, or with people of the right moral character and integrity."

There are some signs that the retailing giant may be returning to more profitable times. Wal-Mart's stock price has increased 41 percent since September 2001. (Compared to a 33-percent improvement for all retail operations.) The company's growth over the next five years will rely on international markets, and according to stock analyst Jeff Klinefelter, "I have no doubt they can [become the dominant retailer] globally. But it's going to change the profile of the company."

Unhappy employees are less optimistic. Once, every Wal-Mart employee wore a blue apron that said, "Our people make the difference." Today, that slogan has been changed to "How may I help you?" For Wal-Mart workers, that change signals a shift in focus away from the worker and toward the customer. To ensure its success, Wal-Mart must find a way to provide what employees need, motivating them to continue providing quality customer service. Meanwhile, while the firm is still almost exclusively non-unionized, there have been a few union victories in recent years. A unionized workforce would clearly change the entire character of Wal-Mart's business.

Questions for Discussion

1. Discuss the role of psychological contracts at Wal-Mart.
2. How important are job satisfaction and morale to a large retailer such as Wal-Mart?
3. Show how various theories of motivation apply to Wal-Mart.
4. What strategies might Wal-Mart use to revive employee satisfaction?
5. What role do you think leadership may have played in events at Wal-Mart?

"We had five call in and quit one day."

~Wal-Mart store manager

ON INCREASING EMPLOYEE DISSATISFACTION

Summary of Learning Objectives

1. *Describe the nature and importance of* **psychological contracts** *in the workplace.*

The foundation of good **human relations**—the interactions between employers and employees and their attitudes toward one another—is a satisfied and motivated workforce. Satisfaction and motivation depend on a **psychological contract** between organizations and employees: the set of expectations held by employees concerning what they will contribute and what the organization will provide in return. If contracts are managed effectively, workers will probably be satisfied and motivated. If not, they are likely to be dissatisfied and unmotivated.

2. *Discuss the importance of* **job satisfaction** *and* **employee morale** *and summarize their roles in human relations in the workplace.*

Job satisfaction is the degree of enjoyment that people get from doing their jobs. If they enjoy their work, they are relatively satisfied. Satisfied employees are likely to have high **morale**—the overall attitude that employees have toward their workplace. Morale reflects the degree to which they perceive that their needs are being met by their jobs. It is determined by such factors as pay, benefits, coworkers, and promotion opportunities.

When workers are satisfied and morale is high, the organization benefits in many ways. Satisfied employees are more committed and loyal and more likely to make useful contributions. They tend to have fewer grievances and engage in fewer negative behaviors (complaining, deliberately slowing their work pace, and so forth). Satisfied workers tend to come to work every day and to remain with the organization. By promoting satisfaction and morale, then, management helps to ensure more efficient operations. Conversely, low morale may result in high **turnover**—the percentage of an organization's workforce that leaves and must be replaced. High levels of turnover result in the disruption of production schedules, high retraining costs, and decreased productivity.

3. *Identify and summarize the most important* **theories of employee motivation.**

Motivation is the set of forces that cause people to behave in certain ways. A steady progression of theories has attempted to explain motivation. The three major approaches to human relations in the workplace are as follows: (1) According to the so-called **classical theory of motivation**, workers are motivated solely by money. Frederick Taylor reasoned that if workers are motivated by money, paying them more should prompt them to produce more. In addition, the firm that found better ways to perform jobs would be able to pay and motivate workers better than competitors. Taylor's approach is known as *scientific management,* which encouraged *time-and-motion studies:* the application of industrial engineering techniques to determine how to perform a job most efficiently. (2) In 1925, a group of researchers concluded that productivity rose in response to almost any management action that workers interpreted as special attention. This finding, known widely today as the **Hawthorne effect**, had a major influence on human relations theory.

(3) Managers and researchers now focus on the importance of good human relations in motivating employee performance. Most motivation theorists are now concerned with the ways in which management treats employees. There are five major *motivation theories:* (i) *Human resources model: Theories X and Y.* Douglas McGregor classified beliefs about human behavior into two sets of assumptions. Managers who subscribe to **Theory X** believe that people are naturally lazy and must be punished or rewarded. Managers who accept **Theory Y** believe that people are naturally interested in being productive and are more likely to have satisfied and motivated employees.

(ii) *Maslow's hierarchy of needs model.* Abraham Maslow's **hierarchy of human needs model** holds that people at work try to satisfy one or more of five different needs, ranging from lower-level needs (such as physiological needs) to higher-level needs (including esteem and self-actualization). (iii) *Two-factor theory.* Frederick Herzberg's **two-factor theory** argues that satisfaction and dissatisfaction depend on *hygiene factors,* such as working conditions, and *motivation factors,* such as recognition for a job well done. Managers should thus follow a two-step approach: ensure that hygiene factors (such as working conditions) are acceptable and offer motivation factors (such as added responsibility) to improve satisfaction and motivation.

(iv) *Expectancy theory.* **Expectancy theory** suggests that people are motivated to work toward rewards that they have a reasonable expectancy of getting. A reward that seems out of reach is likely to be undesirable even if it is intrinsically positive. This is why some people do not work as hard as they can when salaries are based on seniority. (v) *Equity theory.* **Equity theory** focuses on social comparisons—people evaluating their treatment by the organization relative to the treatment of others. This approach holds that people begin by analyzing *inputs* (what they contribute to their jobs) relative to *outputs* (what they receive in return). They compare their own ratios of contribution to return with those of other employees and ask whether their ratios are *equal to, greater than,* or *less than* those of other people. Depending on their answers, they experience feelings of equity or inequity.

4. *Describe some of the strategies used by organizations to improve* **job satisfaction** *and* **employee motivation.**

The following five major programs are designed to make jobs more interesting and rewarding. (1) *Reinforcement/behavior modification theory.* Many companies try to control—and even alter or modify—workers' behavior through systematic rewards and punishments for specific behaviors. They try to shape behavior by linking **reinforcement** with desired behaviors and punishment with undesired behaviors. *Rewards* refer to positive things that people get for working (pay, promotions). When they're tied directly to performance, they serve as *positive reinforcement. Punishment* is designed to change behavior by imposing unpleasant consequences for undesirable behavior.

(2) **Management by objectives (MBO)** is a system of collaborative goal setting that extends from the top of an organization to the bottom. MBO involves managers and subordinates in setting goals and evaluating progress. As the key to MBO, collaborative activity is a program for improving satisfaction and motivation. (3) In **participative management and empowerment**, employees are given a voice in how they do their jobs and in how the company is managed—they become *empowered* to take greater responsibility for their own performance. Employees feel more committed to organizational goals they have helped to shape.

(4) *Job enrichment and job redesign.* **Job enrichment** adds motivating factors to job activities. Thus, *job rotation programs* expand growth opportunities by rotating employees through various positions. By restructuring work to achieve a more satisfactory fit between workers and their jobs, **job redesign** motivates individuals with strong needs for career growth or achievement. It is implemented in one of three ways: (i) *Combining tasks.* Enlarging jobs and

increasing variety makes employees feel that their work is more meaningful. (ii) *Forming natural work groups*. Natural work groups help employees see the importance of their jobs in the total structure of the firm. (iii) *Establishing client relationships*. Establishing client relationships means letting employees interact with customers. This approach increases job variety and gives workers a greater sense of control over and more feedback about their performance.

(5) Many companies are experimenting with *modified work schedules*—different approaches to working hours. (i) **Work sharing** (or **job sharing**) allows two or more people to share a single full-time job. (ii) **Flextime programs** allow people to choose their working hours by adjusting a standard work schedule. (iii) **Telecommuting** is a type of flextime that allows some or all of a job to be done away from standard settings. The key to telecommuting is technology (networked computers, fax machines, and so forth). The increased sense of freedom and control provided by flextime reduces stress and improves productivity, but it is sometimes hard to coordinate people who are working different schedules. In creating *virtual offices*, companies redesign conventional office space to accommodate jobs and schedules that are less dependent on assigned spaces and equipment.

5. ***Discuss different managerial styles of* leadership *and their impact on human relations in the workplace.***

An important component of the manager's directing function, **leadership** is the process of motivating others to work to meet specific objectives. Contemporary theories of leadership focus on **managerial styles**—patterns of behavior that a manager exhibits in dealing with subordinates. (1) Managers who adopt an **autocratic style** issue orders and expect them to be followed. This style allows for rapid decision making. (2) Managers who adopt a **democratic style** ask for input from subordinates before making decisions, but they retain final decision-making power. (3) Managers who adopt a **free-rein style** advise subordinates who are allowed to make decisions. The relative effectiveness of any leadership style depends on the desire of subordinates to share input or to exercise creativity.

Recently, managers have begun to adopt a **contingency approach to managerial style**: viewing appropriate managerial behavior in any situation as dependent, or contingent, on the elements unique to that situation. This approach recognizes the complexity of managerial problems and acknowledges that people in different cultures expect different things from their managers.

KEY TERMS

psychological contract (p. 250)
human relations (p. 250)
job satisfaction (p. 250)
morale (p. 250)
turnover (p. 251)
motivation (p. 253)
classical theory of motivation (p. 254)
Hawthorne effect (p. 254)
Theory X (p. 254)
Theory Y (p. 254)
hierarchy of human needs model (p. 255)
two-factor theory (p. 256)
expectancy theory (p. 257)
equity theory (p. 257)
reinforcement (p. 258)
management by objectives (MBO) (p. 259)
participative management and empowerment (p. 260)
job enrichment (p. 261)
job redesign (p. 262)
work sharing (or ***job sharing***) (p. 262)
flextime programs (p. 263)
telecommuting (p. 264)
leadership (p. 266)
managerial style (p. 268)
autocratic style (p. 268)
democratic style (p. 268)
free-rein style (p. 268)
contingency approach to managerial style (p. 268)

QUESTIONS AND EXERCISES

Questions for Review

1. Describe the psychological contract you currently have or have had in the past with an employer. If you have never worked, describe the psychological contract that you have with the instructor in this class.
2. Do you think that most people are relatively satisfied or dissatisfied with their work? Why are they mainly satisfied or dissatisfied?
3. Compare and contrast Maslow's hierarchy of needs with the two-factor theory of motivation.
4. How can participative management programs enhance employee satisfaction and motivation?

Questions for Analysis

5. Some evidence suggests that recent college graduates show high levels of job satisfaction. Levels then drop dramatically as they reach their late twenties, only to increase gradually once they get older. What might account for this pattern?
6. As a manager, under what sort of circumstances might you apply each of the theories of motivation discussed in this chapter? Which would be easiest to use? Which would be hardest? Why?
7. Suppose you realize one day that you are dissatisfied with your job. Short of quitting, what might you do to improve your situation?
8. List five U.S. managers who you think would also qualify as great leaders.

Application Exercises

9. At the library, research the manager or owner of a company in the early twentieth century and the manager or owner of a company in the 1990s. Compare and contrast the two in terms of their times, leadership styles, and views of employee motivation.
10. Interview the manager of a local manufacturing company. Identify as many different strategies for enhancing job satisfaction at that company as you can.

Building Your Business Skills

TOO MUCH OF A GOOD THING

This exercise enhances the following SCANS workplace competencies: demonstrating basic skills, demonstrating thinking skills, exhibiting interpersonal skills, working with information, and applying systems knowledge.

Goal

To encourage students to apply different motivational theories to a workplace problem involving poor productivity

Background

For years, working for the George Uhe Co., a small chemicals broker in Paramus, New Jersey, made employees feel as if they were members of a big family. Unfortunately, this family was going broke because too few members were working hard enough to make money for it. They were happy, comfortable, complacent—and lazy.

With sales dropping in the pharmaceutical and specialty-chemicals division, Uhe brought in management consultants to analyze the situation and to make recommendations. The outsiders quickly identified a motivational problem affecting the sales force: Reps were paid a handsome salary and received automatic, year-end bonuses regardless of performance. They were also treated to bagels every Friday and regular group birthday lunches that cost as much as $200. Employees felt satisfied but had little incentive to work very hard.

Eager to return to profitability, Uhe's owners waited to hear the consultants' recommendations.

Method

Step 1

In groups of four, step into the role of Uhe's management consultants. Start by analyzing your client's workforce-motivation problems from the following perspectives (our questions focus on key motivational issues):

- *Job satisfaction and morale.* As part of a 77-year-old family-owned business, Uhe employees were happy and loyal, in part, because they were treated so well. Can high morale have a downside? How can it breed stagnation, and what can managers do to prevent stagnation from taking hold?
- *Theory X versus Theory Y.* Although the behavior of these workers seems to make a case for Theory X, why is it difficult to draw this conclusion about a company that focuses more on satisfaction than on sales and profits?
- *Two-factor theory.* Analyze the various ways in which improving such motivational factors as recognition, added responsibility, advancement, and growth might reduce the importance of hygiene factors, including pay and security.
- *Expectancy theory.* Analyze the effect on productivity of redesigning the company's sales force compensation structure—namely, by paying lower base salaries while offering greater earnings potential through a sales-based incentive system. Why would linking performance with increased pay that is achievable through hard work motivate employees? Why would the threat of a job loss also motivate greater effort?

Step 2

Writing a short report based on your analysis, make recommendations to Uhe's owners. The goal of your report is to change the working environment in ways that will motivate greater effort and generate greater productivity.

Follow-Up Questions

1. What is your group's most important recommendation? Why do you think it is likely to succeed?
2. Changing the corporate culture to make it less paternalistic may reduce employees' sense of belonging to a family. If you were an employee, would you consider a greater focus on profits to be an improvement or a problem? How would it affect your motivation and productivity?
3. What steps would you take to improve the attitude and productivity of longtime employees who resist change?

Exercising Your Ethics

PRACTICING CONTROLLED BEHAVIOR

The Situation

As we noted in the text, some companies try to control—and even alter—workers' behavior through systematic rewards and punishments for specific behaviors. In other words, they first try to define the specific behaviors that they want their employees to exhibit (such as working hard, being courteous to customers, stressing quality) and the specific behaviors they want to eliminate (wasting time, being rude to customers, ignoring quality). Then they try to shape employee behavior by linking reinforcement to desired behaviors and punishment to undesired behaviors.

The Dilemma

Assume that you are the new human resources manager in a medium-size organization. Your boss has just ordered you to implement a behavior-modification program by creating an intricate network of rewards and punishments to be linked to specific desired and undesired behaviors. You, however, are uncomfortable with this approach. You regard behavior-modification policies to be too much like experiments on laboratory rats. Instead, you would prefer to use rewards in a way that is consistent with expectancy theory—that is, by letting employees know in advance how they can most effectively reach the rewards they most want. You have tried to change your boss's mind, but to no avail. She says to proceed with behavior modification with no further discussion.

Questions for Discussion

1. What are the ethical issues in this case?
2. What do you think most managers would do in this situation?
3. What would you do?

Mastering Business Essentials

■ **EPISODE 5** In this episode, the CanGo management team must motivate employees to take on a set of new and challenging tasks. *This episode puts motivational theories, such as hierarchy of needs and Theories X and Y, into a real-world context.*

EPISODE 6 The CEO of CanGo faces a specific leadership challenge: how to lead two decidedly different groups—a group of experienced senior managers and a group of younger employees—toward a common goal. *This episode illustrates the reasons why so many leadership situations are contingent upon unique and variable factors.*

Crafting Your Business Plan

MAKING RESERVATIONS AND OTHER PLANS

The Purpose of the Assignment

1. To familiarize students with the ways in which employee considerations (morale, motivation, and job satisfaction) enter into the development of a sample business plan, using the planning framework of the *Business PlanPro* (*BPP*) software package.
2. To stimulate students' thinking about the application of textbook information on employee morale, motivation, job satisfaction, and leadership to the preparation of a *BPP* business plan.

Assignment

After reading Chapter 9 in the textbook, open the BPP *software and look around for information about the plans being made by a sample firm,* Puddle Jumpers Airlines Inc. *To find* Puddle Jumpers, *do the following:*

Open the *Business PlanPro.* If it asks if you want to "create a new business plan" or "open an existing plan," select "create a new business plan" (even though you are not going to create a plan at this time). You will then be taken to the *Business PlanPro EasyPlan Wizard.* On the screen, click on the option entitled **Research It**. You will then be presented with a new list of options, including **Sample Plan Browser**. After clicking on the **Sample Plan Browser**, go down the alphabetical list of sample plans and double-click on **Airline—Regional**, which is the location for *Puddle Jumpers Airlines Inc.* The screen that you are looking at is the introduction page the business plan for *Puddle Jumpers.* Next, scroll down until you reach the **Table of Contents** for the company's business plan. Familiarize yourself with this firm by clicking on **1.0 Executive Summary**.

Then respond to the following items:

1. Consider *Puddle Jumpers,* plans to lower costs by using its flight crews more effectively than its competition does. If implemented, how might these plans affect employee morale? Job Satisfaction? [Sites to see in *BPP* for this item: On the Table of Contents page, click on each of the following in turn: **1.2 Mission** and **1.3 Keys to Success**. After returning to the Table of Contents page, click on **3.2 Competitive Comparison**. Finally, return to the Table of Contents page, and explore any listed categories in which you would expect to find information about employee motivation and job satisfaction.]
2. Consider both *Puddle Jumpers* plans for dealing with the high turnover among airline reservationists and its plans for training reservationists. Do you think the planned redesign will enrich the reservationist's job? Will it affect job satisfaction? Explain. [Sites to see in *BPP* for this item: On the Table of Contents page, click on each of the following in turn: **3.2 Competitive Comparison** and **3.5 Technology**. After returning to the Table of Contents page, click on **5.0 Strategy and Implementation Summary**.]
3. Consider the qualifications of Judy Land, director of reservations. Based on her background, would you say that she is qualified to lead and motivate employees under the new reservations system? Explain. [Sites to see in *BPP:* From the Table of Contents page, click on **6.2 Management Team**.]

Video Exercise

COMPUTING FAMILY VALUES: KINGSTON TECHNOLOGY

Learning Objectives

The purpose of this video is to help you

1. Understand the importance of motivating employees.
2. Consider ways in which financial and non-financial rewards can motivate employees.
3. Explain how high morale can positively affect organizational performance.

Synopsis

California-based Kingston Technology is the world's largest independent manufacturer of computer memory products. Founded by John Tu and David Sun, Kingston employs more than 1,500 people but tries to make each employee feel like part of a family. Besides returning 10 percent of its profits to employees every year through a profit-sharing program, the company fosters mutual trust and respect between employees and management. Senior managers stay in touch with employees at all levels and conduct surveys to obtain employee feedback. For their part, employees report high job satisfaction and develop both personal and professional connections with their colleagues—boosting morale and motivation.

Discussion Questions

1. *For analysis:* After Kingston's sale to Softbank, employees learned from news reports that Kingston's $100 million profit-sharing distribution was one of the largest in U.S. history. What was the likely effect of this publicity on employee morale?
2. *For analysis:* Are Kingston's managers applying Theory X or Theory Y in their relations with employees? How do you know?
3. *For application:* What kinds of survey questions should Kingston ask in order to gauge satisfaction and morale?
4. *For application:* What might Kingston management do to help employees satisfy higher level needs such as self-actualization?
5. *For debate:* Do you agree with Kingston's policy of giving new employees profit-sharing bonuses even when they join the company just one week before profits are distributed? Support your position.

Online Exploration

Visit Kingston Technology's Web site at <www.kingston.com> and follow the links to company information about its awards. From the company information page, follow the links to learn about the organization's values. How do these values support the founders' intention to create a family feeling within the company? How do they support employee satisfaction of higher level needs? Why would Kingston post a list of corporate milestones (including the company's founding and the honors bestowed on it) on its Web site?

PART 3

Understanding Principles of Marketing

CHAPTER

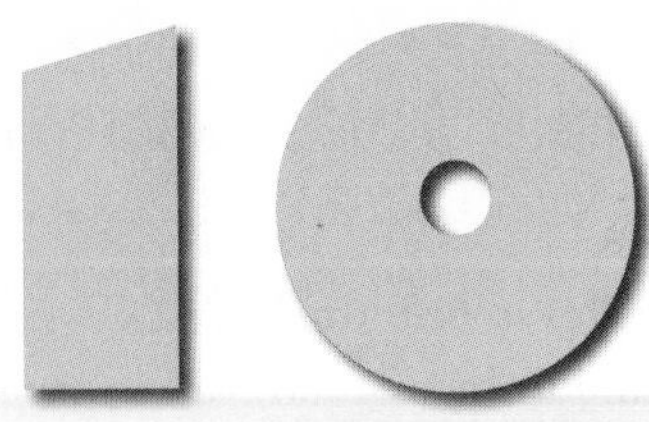

Understanding Marketing Processes and Consumer Behavior

After reading this chapter, you should be able to:

1. Explain the concept of *marketing* and describe the five forces that constitute the *external marketing environment.*
2. Explain the purpose of a *marketing plan* and identify the four components of the *marketing mix.*
3. Explain *market segmentation* and show how it is used in *target marketing.*
4. Explain the purpose and value of *marketing research.*
5. Describe the key factors that influence the *consumer buying process.*
6. Discuss the three categories of *organizational markets* and explain how *organizational buying behavior* differs from consumer buying behavior.
7. Describe the *international* and *small business marketing mixes.*

Xbox Spots the Market

Once the domain of teenage boys, interactive games now lure a much broader audience, including younger kids and adults. It's easy to become addicted: With cinematically realistic graphics and challenging action sequences, games require split-second timing and rapid-fire reactions. Today's communications technology allows real-time interaction among gaming enthusiasts, either in side-by-side competition or among opponents anywhere in the world.

Consider one such enthusiast, Josh Bell, a Grammy Award-winning violinist and one of *People* magazine's "50 Most Beautiful People" for 2001. Bell spends 20 hours a week gaming, sometimes at the expense of violin practice. He uses a wireless keyboard hooked into a 50-inch plasma wall TV. Six speakers provide surround sound for total immersion in such virtual games as "Quake III" and "Defense," an Internet game. To justify time away from the violin, admits Bell, "I used to tell my mother it would improve my hand–eye coordination." At 32, Bell is at the older end of the gaming-enthusiast spectrum. The mainstream is in its mid-20s, late and early teens, and, at the youngest end of the demographic spectrum, 10 years old.

Computer- and video-game sales have grown 15 percent a year for four years. By 2001, they had caught up with sales of DVDs and videotapes. Sales of game hardware and software in the three biggest markets—the United States, Europe, and Japan—reached $16.5 billion in 2001 and will top $20 billion by 2003. It's no surprise that the prospect of such a vast market has attracted the attention of Microsoft.

Before its launch in November 2001, Xbox—Microsoft's entry into console gaming—was one of the industry's most anticipated products. Its $500 million marketing budget included a prelaunch Web site <www.xbox.com>, to tantalize players with the most advanced hardware and hottest graphics in the industry. Microsoft intends for the site to become *the* gathering place for players and to promote enthusiasm among gamers everywhere. Thus far, Xbox.com has succeeded both in establishing relationships among gamers and in forming new bonds between gamers and the Xbox brand. Microsoft wants gamers to become loyal members of an Xbox community.

But industry experts know that it takes more than relationship building and nifty hardware to succeed in this market. Success depends on a steady flow of exciting software—games that capture players' imaginations. Xbox hardware, reports Phaedra Boinodiris, head of Womengamers.com, "far outweighs the competition for speed and memory," but she adds that "there's a serious problem with the lineup [of games] so far." The initial launch featured 12 to 20 games, most of them action and sports oriented. By early 2002, the list had grown to 56 but included only two—"Shrek" and "Rise of Parethi"—that cater to the market for adventure and strategy games.

Nevertheless, Microsoft's start-up marketing has already had an impact: By December 2001, more than 1.4 million Xbox units had been sold, many of them even before reaching store shelves.

Our opening story continues on page 298

"I used to tell my mother it would improve my hand–eye coordination."

~ Josh Bell
VIOLINIST AND ELECTRONIC GAMER

What Is Marketing?

Because we are all consumers and because we all buy goods and services, we are influenced by the marketing activities of companies that want us to buy their products rather than those of competitors. But as consumers, we are in fact *the* essential ingredients in the marketing process. Every day, we express *needs* for such essentials as food, clothing, and shelter and *wants* for such nonessentials as entertainment and leisure activities. Our needs and wants are the forces that drive marketing.

Most of us think of marketing as advertisements for detergents and soft drinks. Marketing, however, encompasses a much wider range of activities. The American Marketing Association <www.ama.org> defines **marketing** as "the process of planning and executing the conception, pricing, promotion, and distribution of ideas, goods, and services to create exchanges that satisfy individual and organizational goals."[1] In this section, we begin by looking at how marketing focuses on providing value and utility for consumers. We then explore the marketing environment and the development of marketing strategy. Finally, we focus on the four activities that comprise the *marketing mix:* developing, pricing, promoting, and placing products.

marketing
The process of planning and executing the conception, pricing, promotion, and distribution of ideas, goods, and services to create exchanges that satisfy individual and organizational goals

Providing Value and Satisfaction

What attracts buyers to one product instead of another? While our desires for the many goods and services available to us may be unbounded, limited financial resources force most of us to be selective. Accordingly, consumers buy products that offer the best value when it comes to meeting their needs and wants.

value
Relative comparison of a product's benefits versus its costs

Value and Benefits **Value** compares a product's benefits with its costs. The benefits of a *high-value* product are much greater than its costs. *Benefits* include not only the functions of the product, but also the emotional satisfactions associated with owning, experiencing, or possessing it. But, of course, every product has costs, including sales price, the expenditure of the buyer's time, and even the emotional costs of making a purchase decision. The satisfied buyer perceives the benefits derived from the purchase to be greater than its costs. Thus the simple but important ratio for value:

$$\text{Value} = \frac{\text{Benefits}}{\text{Costs}}$$

The marketing strategies of leading firms focus on increasing value for customers. Marketing resources are deployed to add value to products in order to satisfy customers' needs and wants. Satisfying customers may mean developing an entirely new product that performs better (provides greater benefits) than existing products. Or it may entail keeping a store open extra hours during a busy season (adding the benefit of greater shopping convenience). Some firms simply offer price reductions (the benefit of lower cost). Customers may also gain benefits from an informational promotion that explains how a product can be used in new ways.

utility
Ability of a product to satisfy a human want or need

Value and Utility To understand how marketing creates value for customers, we need to know the kind of benefits that buyers get from a firm's goods or services. Products provide consumers with **utility**—the ability of a product to satisfy a human want or need.

Marketing strives to provide four kinds of utility:

- When a company turns out ornaments in time for Christmas, it creates *time utility:* It makes products available when consumers want them.
- When a department store opens its annual Christmas department, it creates *place utility:* It makes products available where customers can conveniently purchase them.

- When the store sells ornaments, it provides *ownership utility* by conveniently transferring ownership from store to customer.
- By making products available in the first place—by turning raw materials into finished ornaments—the ornament maker creates *form utility.*

Marketing plays a role in all four areas—determining the timing, place, terms of sale, and product features that provide utility and add value for customers. Marketers, therefore, must begin with an understanding of customers' wants and needs. Their methods for creating utility are described in this and the following three chapters.

Goods, Services, and Ideas

The marketing of tangible goods is obvious in everyday life. You walk into a department store and a woman with a clipboard asks if you would like to try a new cologne. A pharmaceutical company proclaims the virtues of its new cold medicine. Your local auto dealer offers an economy car at an economy price. These products—the cologne, the cold medicine, and the car—are all **consumer goods:** products that you, the consumer, may buy for personal use. Firms that sell products to consumers for personal consumption are engaged in *consumer marketing.*

consumer goods
Products purchased by consumers for personal use

Marketing also applies to **industrial goods:** products used by companies to produce other products. Surgical instruments and earthmovers are industrial goods, as are such components and raw materials as integrated circuits, steel, and unformed plastic. Firms that sell products to other manufacturers are engaged in *industrial marketing.*

industrial goods
Products used by companies to produce other products

Marketing techniques can also be applied to **services**—intangible products such as time, expertise, or some activity that you can purchase. *Service marketing* has become a major growth area in the United States. Insurance companies, airlines, investment counselors, health clinics, and public accountants all engage in service marketing, both to individuals and to other companies.

services
Intangible products, such as time, expertise, or an activity that can be purchased

Finally, marketers also promote ideas. Television ads, for example, can remind us that teaching is an honorable profession and that teachers are "heroes." Other ads stress the importance of driving only when sober and the advantages of not smoking.

Relationship Marketing Although marketing often focuses on single transactions for products, services, or ideas, marketers also take a longer-term perspective. Thus **relationship marketing** emphasizes lasting relationships with customers and suppliers. Stronger relationships—including stronger economic and social ties—can result in greater long-term satisfaction and customer loyalty.[2]

relationship marketing
Marketing strategy that emphasizes lasting relationships with customers and suppliers

Commercial banks, for example, offer *economic* incentives to encourage longer-lasting relationships. Customers who purchase more of the bank's products (for example, checking accounts, savings accounts, and loans) accumulate credits toward free or reduced-price services, such as free traveler's checks.

The Marketing Environment

Marketing strategies are not determined unilaterally by any business, not even by marketers as experienced as Coca-Cola <www.coke.com> and Procter & Gamble <www.pg.com>. Rather, they are strongly influenced by powerful outside forces. As you can see in Figure 10.1, every marketing program must recognize the factors in a company's **external environment.** In this section, we describe five of these environmental factors: the *political–legal, social–cultural, technological, economic,* and *competitive environments.*

external environment
Outside factors that influence marketing programs by posing opportunities or threats

Political and Legal Environment Political activities, both foreign and domestic, have profound effects on business. Legislation on the use of cell phones in

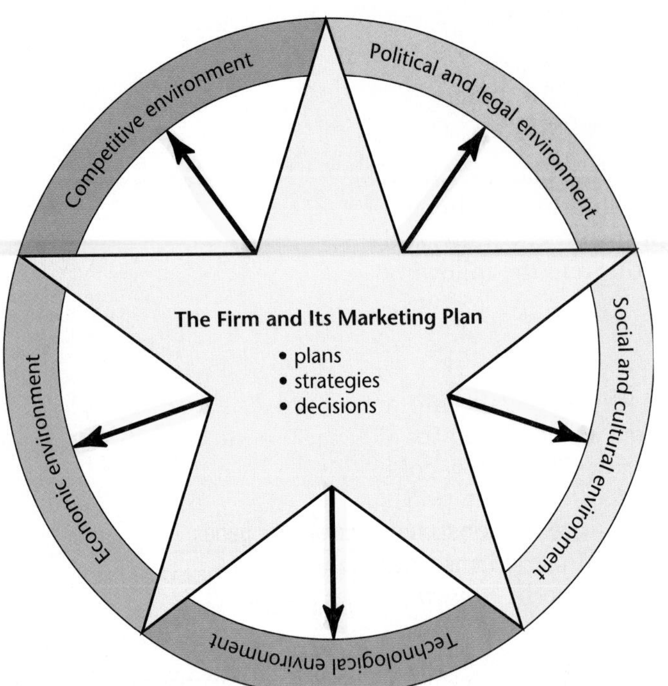

FIGURE 10.1
The External Marketing Environment

cars and the Clean Air Act have determined the destinies of entire industries. Marketing managers thus try to maintain favorable political–legal environments in several ways. To gain public support for products and activities, marketers use ad campaigns to raise public awareness of local, regional, or national issues. Companies contribute to political candidates and frequently support the activities of political action committees (PACs) maintained by their respective industries.

Social and Cultural Environment More people are working in home offices, the number of single-parent families is increasing, and food preferences reflect a growing concern for healthy lifestyles. These and other trends reflect the values, beliefs, and ideas that shape U.S. society.

Changing social values force companies to develop and promote new products for both individual consumers and industrial customers. For example, although most of us value privacy, Web surfers are discovering that a loss of privacy is often a price for the convenience of Internet shopping. Dot-com sites regularly collect personal information which they use for marketing purposes and which they often sell to other firms. Responding to the growing demand for better privacy protection, firms like iNetPrivacy <www.inetprivacy.com> offer such new products as Anonymity 4 Proxy software, which allows you to surf the Net anonymously.

Technological Environment New technologies create new goods (the satellite dish) and services (home television shopping). New products make existing products obsolete (compact disks are replacing audiotapes), and many products change our values and lifestyles. In turn, lifestyle changes often stimulate new products not directly related to the new technologies themselves. Cell phones, for example, not only facilitate business communication but free up time for recreation and leisure. The Internet is a new medium for selling, buying, and distributing products from your own home to customers around the world.

Economic Environment Because they determine spending patterns by consumers, businesses, and governments, economic conditions influence marketing plans for product offerings, pricing, and promotional strategies. Marketers are concerned with such economic variables as inflation, interest rates, and recession. Thus they must monitor the general business cycle, which typically features a pattern of transition from periods of prosperity to recession to recovery. Not surprisingly, consumer spending increases as consumer confidence in economic conditions grows during periods of prosperity.

Traditionally, economic analysis focused on the national economy. Increasingly, however, as nations form more complex economic connections, the global economy is becoming more prominent in the thinking of marketers everywhere.[3] At Wal-Mart <www.walmartstores.com>, for example, 17 percent of all sales revenue comes from the retailer's international division. Although overall international sales were up 41 percent for 2001, sales in some Latin American countries stalled. Why? Because economic conditions in such markets as Argentina and Brazil differ significantly from those in Mexico, which, in turn, differ from those in China, South Korea, and Germany.

Say what you mean

WHEN IT COMES TO PRIVACY, IT'S A SMALL WORLD AFTER ALL

E-mail has virtually become the standard method of communication in the business world. Most people enjoy its speed, ease, and casual nature. But e-mail also has its share of problems and pitfalls. One challenge, of course, is privacy. Many people assume that the contents of e-mail are private, but any number of people may in fact be authorized to see your e-mail. Like postcards sent through the U.S. mail, e-mail messages pass through a lot of hands and before a lot of eyes.

The courts, for example, have held that e-mail messages sent and/or received during working hours and on company equipment are the property of the business. Compaq Computer Corporation has one full-time employee who does nothing but randomly scan e-mail messages

Aside from organizational scrutiny, people also face the threat of hackers breaking into a company's computer network, including its e-mail system. Indeed, e-mail is one of the easiest routes for hackers to gain access to other parts of a computer system. Once inside, they can destroy sensitive e-mail messages or send them to outsiders.

Finally, many users are their own worst enemies. A surprisingly common error is inadvertently sending e-mail to the wrong address—even to a large group of people. A careless click of the mouse can send a sensitive message intended for a single recipient to everyone in the company.

Other concerns have arisen concerning privacy over the Internet. For consumers, Internet privacy is an especially important issue. Companies, for instance, can monitor which Web sites individuals visit, how long they stay there, what they buy, and how frequently they return. They can use information to make referrals to other firms to target new advertising to unsuspecting consumers. Not surprisingly, then, concerns about the shrinking world in which we can enjoy privacy are beginning to take on an increasingly higher profile with each passing day.

The euro, *the common currency of the European Union, is a variable in Great Britain's economic environment. On the one hand, for member-nation companies doing international business, it eliminates* exchange-rate risk*—the risk that changes in rates might adversely affect a firm's transactions. That's why multinationals and banks in England—a non-euro nation—favor the euro. On the other hand, protestors fear that in order to keep the British economy in line with those of euro nations, Britain would have to enact labor and other regulations like those of other EU countries.*

Competitive Environment In a competitive environment, marketers must convince buyers that they should purchase one company's products rather than those of some other seller. Because both consumers and commercial buyers have limited resources, every dollar spent on one product is no longer available for other purchases. Each marketing program, therefore, seeks to make its product the most attractive. Theoretically, a failed program loses the buyer's dollar forever (or at least until it is time for the next purchase decision).

Marketers must decide how to position products for three types of competition:

- **Substitute products** differ from those of competitors but can fill the same need. Your cholesterol level may be controlled with either a physical fitness program or a drug regimen. The fitness program and the drugs are substitute products.
- **Brand competition** occurs between similar products, such as the auditing services provided by large accounting firms. Competition is based on buyers' perceptions of the benefits of products offered by particular companies.
- **International competition** matches the products of domestic marketers against those of foreign competitors—say, a flight on Swissair <www.swissair.com> versus one on Delta Airlines <www.delta-air.com>.

Strategy: The Marketing Mix

A company's **marketing managers** are responsible for planning and implementing all the activities that result in the transfer of goods or services to its customers. These activities culminate in the **marketing plan**—a detailed strategy for focusing marketing efforts on consumer needs and wants. Therefore, marketing strategy begins when a company identifies a consumer need and develops a product to meet it.

In planning and implementing strategies, marketing managers develop the four basic components (often called the "Four P's") of the **marketing mix.** In this section we describe each of those components: *product, pricing, place,* and *promotion.*

Product Marketing begins with a **product**—a good, a service, or an ide designed to fill a consumer need or want. Conceiving and developing new product is a constant challenge for marketers, who must always consider the factor o change—changing technology, changing consumer wants and needs, and chang ing economic conditions. Meeting consumer needs, then, often means changin existing products to keep pace with emerging markets and competitors.

Product Differentiation Producers often promote particular features of product in order to distinguish them on the marketplace. **Product differentiation** is the cre ation of a feature or image that makes a product differ enough from existing prod ucts to attract consumers. For example, Volvo automobiles <www.volvo.com> pro vide newer, better safety features to set them apart from competitors. Customers o E*TRADE™ <www.etrade.com>, the online investment service, gain value fron after-hours trading not offered by conventional investment-service firms.

Pricing *Pricing* a product—selecting the best price at which to sell it—is often balancing act. On the one hand, prices must support a variety of costs—operat ing, administrative, and research costs as well as marketing costs. On the othe hand, prices can't be so high that consumers turn to competitors. Successful pric ing means finding a profitable middle ground between these two requirements.

Both low- and high-price strategies can be effective in different situation Low prices, for example, generally lead to larger sales volumes. High prices usu ally limit market size but increase profits per unit. High prices may also attrac customers by implying that a product is of high quality. We discuss pricing i more detail in Chapter 11.

substitute product
Product that is dissimilar to those of competitors but that can fulfill the same need

brand competition
Competitive marketing that appeals to consumer perceptions of similar products

international competition
Competitive marketing of domestic products against foreign products

marketing manager
Manager who plans and implements the marketing activities that result in the transfer of products or services from producer to consumer

marketing plan
Detailed strategy for focusing marketing efforts on consumer needs and wants

marketing mix
The combination of product, pricing, promotion, and distribution (place) strategies used to market products

product
Good, service, or idea that is marketed to fill consumer needs and wants

product differentiation
Creation of a feature or image that makes a product differ enough from existing products to attract consumers

Jann Wenner started Rolling Stone magazine in 1967, and it's been the cash cow of Wenner Media <www.rollingstone.com> *ever since. In 1985, Wenner bought* Us *magazine and set out to compete with* People, *perhaps the most successful magazine ever published. Wenner's latest strategy calls for greater differentiation between the two products.* People *is news driven, reporting on ordinary people as well as celebrities, and Wenner intends to punch up* Us *with more coverage of celebrity sex and glitter. So far, he hasn't been successful:* People *reaches 3.7 million readers,* Us *about 900,000.*

Place (Distribution) In the marketing mix, *place* refers to **distribution.** Placing a product in the proper outlet—say, a retail store—requires decisions about several activities, all of which are concerned with getting the product from the producer to the consumer. Decisions about warehousing and inventory control are distribution decisions, as are decisions about transportation options.

distribution
Part of the marketing mix concerned with getting products from producers to consumers

Firms must also make decisions about the *channels* through which they distribute products. Many manufacturers, for instance, sell goods to other companies which, in turn, distribute them to retailers. Others sell directly to major retailers such as Sears, Wal-Mart, or Safeway. Still others sell directly to final consumers. We explain distribution decisions further in Chapter 12.

Self-Check Questions 1–3

*You should now be able to answer Self-Check Questions 1–3**

1. MULTIPLE CHOICE Marketers know that consumers buy products which offer the best *value.* Which of the following **is not** true regarding value for the buyer? [select one] **(a)** It is related to the buyer's wants and needs. **(b)** It compares a product's benefits with its costs. **(c)** It is intangible and cannot be measured. **(d)** It depends on product price. **(e)** Market strategies focus on increasing it.

2. MULTIPLE CHOICE A program in which a bank offers free services to long-standing customers is an example of which of the following? [select one] **(a)** industrial marketing; **(b)** services marketing; **(c)** brand competition; **(d)** product differentiation; **(e)** relationship marketing.

3. MULTIPLE CHOICE All of the following are elements in the *marketing mix* (the "Four Ps" of marketing) **except** [select one]: **(a)** product differentiation; **(b)** place (or distribution); **(c)** promotion; **(d)** product; **(e)** pricing.

*ANSWERS TO SELF-CHECK QUESTIONS 1–3 CAN BE FOUND ON P. AN-6.

Promotion The most highly visible component of the marketing mix is no doubt *promotion,* which refers to techniques for communicating information about products. The most important promotional tools include advertising, personal selling, sales promotions, and public relations. We describe promotional activities more fully in Chapter 13.

Target Marketing and Market Segmentation

target market

Group of people that has similar wants and needs and that can be expected to show interest in the same products

market segmentation

Process of dividing a market into categories of customer types

Marketers have long known that products cannot be all things to all people. Buyers have different tastes, goals, lifestyles, and so on. The emergence of the marketing concept and the recognition of consumer needs and wants led marketers to think in terms of **target markets**—groups of people with similar wants and needs. Selecting target markets is usually the first step in the marketing strategy.

Target marketing requires **market segmentation**—dividing a market into categories of customer types or "segments." Once they have identified segments, companies may adopt a variety of strategies. Some firms market products to more than one segment. General Motors <www.gm.com>, for example, offers compact cars, vans, trucks, luxury cars, and sports cars with various features and at various price levels. GM's strategy is to provide an automobile for nearly every segment of the market.

In contrast, some businesses offer a narrower range of products, each aimed toward a specific segment. Note that segmentation is a strategy for analyzing consumers, not products. The process of fixing, adapting, and communicating the nature of the product itself is called *product positioning.*

Identifying Market Segments

By definition, members of a *market segment* must share some common traits that affect their purchasing decisions. In identifying segments, researchers look at several different influences on consumer behavior. Four of the most important are *geographic, demographic, psychographic,* and *behavioral variables.*[4]

geographic variables

Geographical units that may be considered in developing a segmentation strategy

Geographic Variables Many buying decisions are affected by the places people call home. The heavy rainfall in Washington State, for instance, means that people there buy more umbrellas than people in the Sun Belt. Urban residents don't need agricultural equipment, and sailboats sell better along the coasts than on the Great Plains. **Geographic variables** are the geographical units, from countries to neighborhoods, that may be considered in a segmentation strategy.

These patterns affect decisions about marketing mixes for a huge range of products. For example, consider a plan to market down-filled parkas in rural Minnesota. Demand will be high and price competition intense. Local newspaper ads may be effective, and the best retail location may be one that is easily reached from several small towns.

Although the marketability of some products is geographically sensitive, others enjoy nearly universal acceptance. Coke, for example, gets more than 70 percent of its sales from international markets. It is the market leader in Great Britain, China, Germany, Japan, Brazil, and Spain. Pepsi's international sales are about 15 percent of Coke's. In fact, Coke's chief competitor in most countries is some local soft drink, not Pepsi, which earns 78 percent of its income at home.

demographic variables

Characteristics of populations that may be considered in developing a segmentation strategy

Demographic Variables **Demographic variables** describe populations by identifying such traits as age, income, gender, ethnic background, marital status, race, religion, and social class. For example, several general consumption characteristics can be attributed to certain age groups (*18–25, 26–35, 36–45,* and so on). A marketer can thus divide markets into age groups. Table 10.1 lists some possible demographic breakdowns. Depending on the marketer's purpose, a segment can be a single classification (*aged 20–34*) or a combination of categories (*aged 20–34, married*

TABLE 10.1
Demographic Variables

Age	Under 5, 5–11, 12–19, 20–34, 35–49, 50–64, 65+
Education	Grade school or less, some high school, graduated high school, some college, college degree, advanced degree
Family life cycle	Young single, young married without children, young married with children, older married with children under 18, older married without children under 18, older single, other
Family size	1, 2–3, 4–5, 6+
Income	Under \$9,000, \$9,000–\$14,999, \$15,000–\$24,999, \$25,000–\$34,999, \$35,000–\$45,000, over \$45,000
Nationality	African, American, Asian, British, Eastern European, French, German, Irish, Italian, Latin American, Middle Eastern, Scandinavian
Race	American Indian, Asian, Black, White
Religion	Buddhist, Catholic, Hindu, Jewish, Muslim, Protestant
Sex	Male, female

with children, earning \$25,000–\$34,999). Foreign competitors, for example, are gaining market share in U.S. auto sales by appealing to young buyers (under age 30) with limited incomes (under \$30,000). While companies such as Hyundai <www.hyundai.net>, Kia <www.kia.com>, and Daewoo <www.daewoous.com> are winning entry-level customers with high-quality and generous warranties, Volkswagen <www.vw.com> targets under-35 buyers with its entertainment-styled VW Jetta.[5]

Psychographic Variables Markets can also be segmented according to such **psychographic variables** as lifestyles, interests, and attitudes. Take, for example, Burberry <www.burberry.com>, whose raincoats have been a symbol of British tradition since 1856. Burberry has repositioned itself as a global luxury brand, like Gucci <www.gucci.com> and Louis Vuitton <www.vuitton.com>. The strategy, which recently resulted in a 31-percent sales increase, calls for attracting a different type of customer—the top-of-the-line, fashion-conscious individual—who shops at such stores as Neiman Marcus and Bergdorf Goodman.[6]

psychographic variables
Consumer characteristics, such as lifestyles, opinions, interests, and attitudes, that may be considered in developing a segmentation strategy

Psychographics are particularly important to marketers because, unlike demographics and geographics, they can be changed by marketing efforts. For

Although Nike <www.nike.com> leads the \$15.5 billion athletic-footwear industry and had revenues of \$9 billion last year, it still has a serious problem: Women's footwear accounts for 33 percent of industrywide sales but generates only 20 percent of Nike's. Nike is going after this demographic segment with a marketing campaign that focuses on differences between the way men and women think about sports and the way they shop for clothing. According to Nike marketers, for example, women are more interested in image trends and active lifestyles than in athletic competition and sports celebrities.

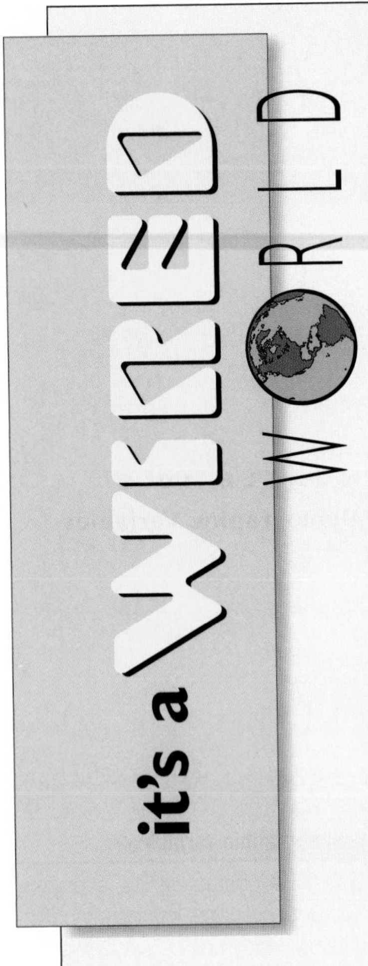

High-Tech Hits the Highway

Nicole Gunther's four-year-old daughter is happy in the back seat of the family's Honda minivan. There are no more whining cries of "When are we going to get there?" With the rear-seat DVD player delivering Disney films, Nicole is absorbed in entertainment that lets Mom concentrate on after-school traffic. Other services, such as a satellite-controlled navigation system, keep drivers from getting lost and alert them to road or traffic conditions. Competitors are also getting in on the act. Cadillac's OnStar navigation service offers satellite radio services in more than 30 GM car and truck models, and satellite feeds are linked into dozens of Ford, GM, and DaimlerChrysler models.

Telematics, automobile versions of the electronic entertainment systems that have become staples in many homes, were packaged in about 2 percent of new vehicles sold in 2002, but the industry is on the verge of a boom: Wireless communications for the highway had total sales of $1.6 billion in 2001 but will reach $20 billion annually in 2006.

Industry demographics are changing, too. Currently, buyers consist mostly of middle- to upper-class drivers who can afford pricey upscale vehicles—DVD players and navigation systems cost up to $2,000—and, especially, families with younger children. Electronic services are a welcome stress reliever for today's busy suburban lifestyles in which many parents find themselves staffing dawn-to-dusk transportation services.

Launched in Cadillacs during the 1999 to 2001 model years, the first in-car communications systems offered on-road monitoring of performance and location and traffic-guidance advisories for high-income drivers. But that target audience, say industry experts, will change by 2007, when 80 percent of all new cars will contain factory-installed telematics. For model years 2002–2004, the target is active families in midrange- and higher-income groups who have young children and who use in-car technology for safety and entertainment. Even midrange, lower-priced cars will be equipped with a variety of wireless appliances—hands-free cell phones, monitoring systems for roadside assistance, and satellite radios. Satellite subscription fees, currently ranging from $200 to $400 per year for GM's OnStar, will permit technology-oriented drivers to receive music and movies from home and elsewhere.

Still another target group for 2003–2006 is high-income professionals who use in-car communications technologies for business and personal transactions. Business-minded drivers will have at their fingertips palm-held computers, Web-connected PCs, voice-activated e-mail, and satellite-transmitted stock market reports.

example, Polish companies have overcome consumer resistance by promoting the safety and desirability of using credit rather than depending solely on cash. One product of changing attitudes is a booming economy and the emergence of a robust middle class. The increasing number of Polish households with TVs, appliances, automobiles, and houses is defining the status of Poland's middle class as the most stable in the former Soviet bloc.[7]

behavioral variables
Consumer characteristics based on the use of a product, benefits expected from it, reasons for purchasing it, and loyalty to it

Behavioral Variables The term **behavioral variables** refers to the ways in which consumers use a product, the benefits they expect from it, their reasons for purchasing it, and their loyalty to it.[8] A women's shoemaker might identify three segments—wearers of athletic, casual, and dress shoes. Each segment is looking for different benefits in a shoe. A woman buying an athletic shoe may not care about its appearance but may care a great deal about arch support and traction in the sole. A woman buying a casual shoe will want it to look good and feel comfortable. A woman buying a dress shoe may require a specific color or style and may even accept some discomfort. Consumers who always buy one brand are classified as *hard-core loyalists,* whereas *switchers* buy various brands.

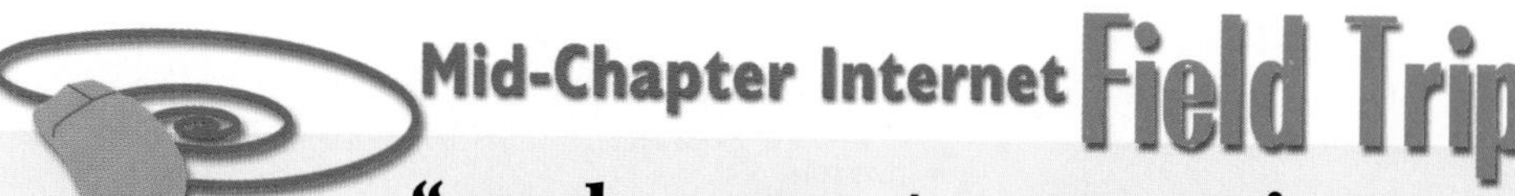

Mid-Chapter Internet Field Trip

"welcome to marriott.com"

In the first part of this chapter, we discussed the concept of marketing products to meet the needs and wants of customers in both consumer and industrial markets. We also saw how relationship marketing promotes customer loyalty and found that a sound marketing strategy involves the entire marketing mix—product, pricing, place (distribution), and promotion.

Let's look further into these marketing practices by exploring the Web site of a successful international company—Marriott International Inc., at <www.marriott.com>. The home page has five sections that we will use for exploring the marketing function at Marriott:

- **View Our 13 Lodging Brands** (see selection box at top of the page)
- **Explore & Plan** (box at middle of the page)
- **Marriott Rewards** (box at middle of the page)
- **Events & Meetings** (small box at bottom of the page)
- **Vacation Ownership** (small box at bottom of the page)

Begin by clicking on each of the following—**View Our 13 Lodging Brands, Events & Meetings,** and **Explore & Plan**—and examine their contents:

❶ What types of products does Marriott offer in its marketing mix?

On the home page, go to **View Our 13 Lodging Brands** and select **Marriott Hotels, Resorts & Suites.** Then drop down to the bottom of the page and click on **For Getaways.** Finally, click on **Marriott Resorts** and examine the information on that page:

❷ Which type of customer—consumer or industrial—is the target for information on this page?

At the home page, go to **View Our 13 Lodging Brands** and select **ExecuStay.** On the **Marriott ExecuStay** screen, go to the left side and click on **About ExecuStay.** Examine the information on that page:

❸ What product features on this page indicate the type of customer—consumer or industrial—that Marriott is targeting for this product?

On the home page, click on **Marriott Rewards.** After examining the contents of this page, go to the left side of the screen, click on **Elite Membership,** and read its contents:

❹ Is the Marriott Rewards program an example of relationship marketing? Give examples of incentives that Marriott uses to build relationships with its clients.

Briefly review the material at the Web pages entitled **Marriott Resorts** and **Executstay:**

❺ Which segmentation variables—demographic, geographic, psychographic, or behavioral—has Marriott used for differentiating its Marriott Resorts and ExecuStay products?

For the second leg of this Internet Field Trip, go to www.prenhall.com/griffin.

The "Wired World" box in this chapter shows how automobile companies use emographics and consumer variables to identify target markets for new techology applications.

Marketing Research

Marketing decisions are seldom perfect, and the consequences of a firm's choices f marketing mix and segmentation strategy can be long lasting. Effective decisions are customer focused and based on timely, valid information about maretplace trends. A powerful tool is **marketing research**—the study of what cusomers need and want and how best to meet those needs and wants.[9]

marketing research
The study of consumer needs and wants and the ways in which sellers can best meet them

The relationship of research to the overall marketing process is shown in igure 10.2. Ultimately, its role is to increase competitiveness by clarifying the nteractions among a firm's stakeholders (including consumers), marketing variables, environmental factors, and marketing decisions. Researchers use numerus methods to obtain, interpret, and apply information about customers. They etermine the kinds of information needed for decisions on marketing strategy, oal setting, and target-market selection. In doing so, they may conduct studies n customer responses to proposed changes in the marketing mix. One esearcher, for example, might study response to an experimental paint formula

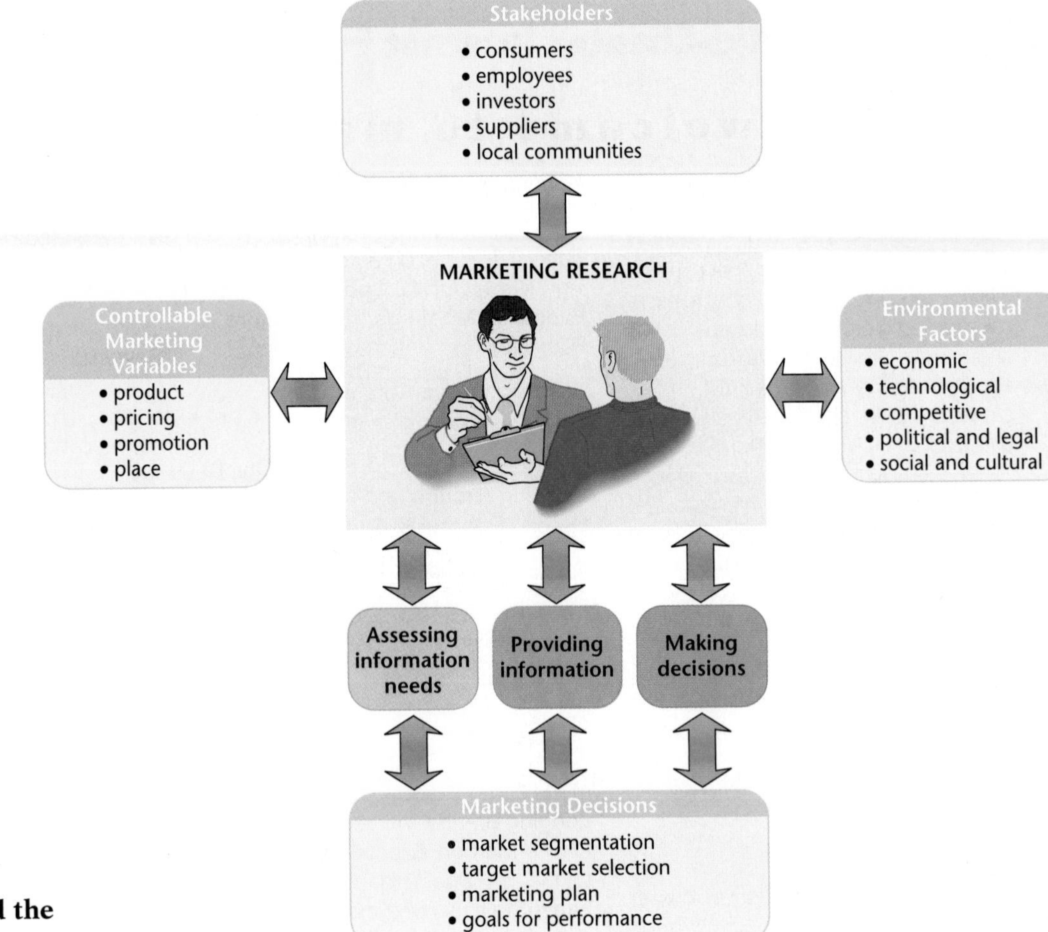

FIGURE 10.2
Market Research and the Marketing Process

(new product). Another might explore the response to a price reduction (new price) on calculators. Still a third might check responses to a proposed advertising campaign (new promotion). Marketers also try to learn whether customers will more likely purchase a product in a specialty shop or on the Internet (new place).

The importance of selling products in international markets is expanding the role of marketing research. For example, when a company decides to sell goods or services overseas, it must decide whether to standardize products or to specialize them by offering different versions for each market.[10]

The Research Process

Market research can occur at almost any point in a product's life cycle. Typically, however, it's used in developing new or altered products. These are the five steps in performing market research:[11]

1. ***Study the current situation.*** What is the need and what is being done to meet it?
2. ***Select a research method.*** In choosing from a wide range of methods, marketers must consider the effectiveness and costs of different options.
3. ***Collect data.*** There are two types of research data. **Secondary data** are already available from previous research. For example, the *Statistical Abstract of the United States* <www.census.gov/statab.www> offers data on geographic and demographic variables. Secondary data can save time,

secondary data
Data readily available as a result of previous research

"I'd get out of children and into older people."

effort, and money. When they are unavailable or inadequate, **primary data**—new data from newly performed research—must be obtained.

primary data

Data developed through new research

4. ***Analyze the data.*** Data are of no use until organized into information.
5. ***Prepare a report.*** This report should sum up the study's methodology and findings. It should also identify alternative solutions and, where appropriate, make recommendations on a course of action.

Research Methods

The success of a research study often depends on the method used. There are four basic methods of market research:

- **Observation** involves watching and recording consumer behavior. Today, computerized systems allow marketers to observe consumer preferences rapidly and with incredible accuracy. For example, electronic supermarket scanners allow managers to see what is and is not selling without having to check shelves.[12]

observation

Market research technique that involves watching and recording consumer behavior

- Sometimes, marketers must go a step further and ask questions. One way to get answers is by taking **surveys,** either mailing out questionnaires or conducting interviews. United Parcel Service <www.ups.com> surveyed customers to find out how to improve service. Clients wanted more interaction with drivers because they can offer practical advice on shipping. UPS thus added extra drivers, allowing drivers to spend time with customers.[13]

survey

Market research technique using a questionnaire that is either mailed to individuals or used as the basis of telephone or personal interviews

- In a **focus group,** people are gathered in one place, presented with an issue, and asked to discuss it. The researcher takes notes but provides only a minimal amount of structure. This technique allows researchers to explore issues too complex for questionnaires and can produce creative solutions.[14]

focus group

Market research technique in which a group of people is gathered, presented with an issue, and asked to discuss it in depth

experimentation

Market research technique that attempts to compare the responses of the same or similar people under different circumstances

Experimentation compares the responses of the same or similar people under different circumstances. For example, a firm trying to decide whether to include walnuts in a new candy bar probably wouldn't learn much by asking people what they thought of the idea. But if it asked some people to try bars with nuts and some without, the responses could be helpful.[15]

Data Warehousing and Data Mining

data warehousing

Process of collecting, storing, and retrieving data in electronic files

Almost everything you do leaves a trail of information about you. Your preferences in movie rentals, television viewing, Internet sites, and groceries; the destinations of your phone calls, your credit-card charges, your financial status; personal information about age, gender, marital status, and even health—these are just a few of the items in a huge cache of data that are stored about each of us. The collection, storage, and retrieval of such data in electronic files is called **data warehousing.** For marketing researchers, the data warehouse is a gold mine of clues about consumer behavior.[16]

data mining

Application of electronic technologies for searching, sifting and reorganizing data in order to collect marketing information and target products in the marketplace

The Uses of Data Mining After collecting information, marketers use **data mining**—the application of electronic technologies for searching, sifting, and reorganizing pools of data to uncover useful marketing information and to plan for new products that will appeal to target segments in the marketplace.[17] Using data mining, for example, the insurance company Farmers Group discovered that a sports car is not an exceptionally high insurance risk if it's not the only family car. The company thus issued more liberal policies on Corvettes and Porches and so generated more revenue without significantly increasing payout claims. Among retailers, Wal-Mart has long been a data-mining pioneer, maintaining perhaps the world's largest privately held data warehouse. Data include demographics, markdowns, returns, inventory, and other data for forecasting sales and the effects of marketing promotions.[18]

Understanding Consumer Behavior

Although marketing managers can tell us what qualities people want in a new VCR, they cannot tell us *why* they buy particular VCRs. What desire are con

Self-Check Questions 4–6

*You should now be able to answer Self-Check Questions 4–6**

4. TRUE/FALSE *Target marketing* requires *market segmentation.*

5. MULTIPLE CHOICE Suppose you have a product that you believe will appeal to politically liberal young adults in Asia and Eastern Europe. The *segmentation variable* that you are **not using** is [select one]: (a) psychographic; (b) geographic; (c) behavioral; (d) demographic.

6. MULTIPLE CHOICE Which of the following is **not true** regarding *marketing research?* [select one] **(a)** It can reveal what customers need and how to meet those needs. **(b)** It nearly always relies on experimentation. **(c)** It often involves collecting data. **(d)** It can use any of several different research methods. **(e)** It is commonly used in developing new or altered products.

*ANSWERS TO SELF-CHECK QUESTIONS 4–6 CAN BE FOUND ON P. AN-6.

sumers fulfilling? Is there a psychological or sociological explanation for why they purchase one product and not another? These questions and many others are addressed in the study of **consumer behavior**—the study of the decision process by which people buy and consume products.

consumer behavior
Study of the decision process by which people buy and consume products

Influences on Consumer Behavior

To understand consumer behavior, marketers draw heavily on such fields as psychology and sociology. The result is a focus on four major influences on consumer behavior: *psychological, personal, social,* and *cultural.* By identifying which influences are most active in certain circumstances, marketers try to explain consumer choices and predict future buying behavior.

1. ***Psychological influences*** include an individual's motivations, perceptions, ability to learn, and attitudes.[19]
2. ***Personal influences*** include lifestyle, personality, and economic status.
3. ***Social influences*** include family, opinion leaders (people whose opinions are sought by others), and such reference groups as friends, coworkers, and professional associates.[20]
4. ***Cultural influences*** include culture (the way of living that distinguishes one large group from another), subculture (smaller groups, such as ethnic groups, with shared values), and social class (the cultural ranking of groups according to such criteria as background, occupation, and income).[21]

Although these factors can have a strong impact on a consumer's choices, their effect on actual purchases is sometimes weak or negligible. Some consumers, for example, exhibit high **brand loyalty**—they regularly purchase products because they are satisfied with their performance. Such people (for example, users of Maytag appliances) are less subject to influence and stick with preferred brands. On the other hand, the clothes you wear and the food you eat often reflect social and psychological influences on your consuming behavior.

brand loyalty
Pattern of regular consumer purchasing based on satisfaction with a product

The Consumer Buying Process

Students of consumer behavior have constructed various models to help show how consumers decide to buy products. Figure 10.3 presents one such model. At the core of this and similar models is an awareness of the psychosocial influences

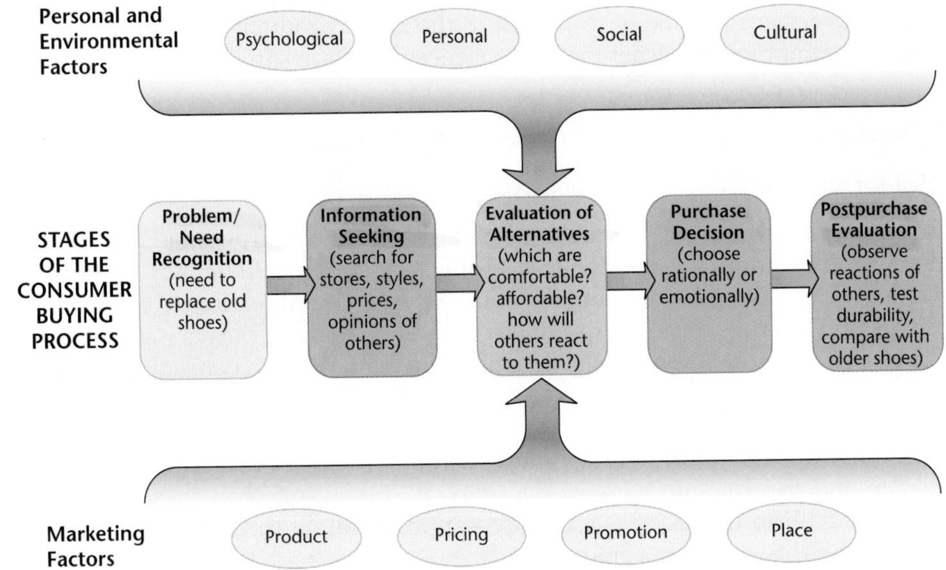

FIGURE 10.3
Consumer Buying Process

that lead to consumption. Ultimately, marketers use this information to develop marketing plans.[22]

- **Problem/need recognition** The process begins when the consumer recognizes a problem or need. After strenuous exercise, for example, you may realize that you are thirsty. Need recognition also occurs when you have a chance to change your buying habits. When you obtain your first job after graduation, your new income may let you purchase items that were once too expensive for you. You may find that you need professional clothing, apartment furnishings, and a car. American Express and Sears cater to such shifts in needs when they market credit cards to college seniors.
- **Information seeking** Having recognized a need, consumers often seek information. The search is not always extensive, but before making major purchases, most people seek information from personal sources, public sources, and their own experience. Before buying an exercise bike, you may read about bikes in *Consumer Reports* <www.consumerreports.org>, or you may test-ride several bikes.
- **Evaluation of alternatives** If you are in the market for skis, you probably have some idea of who makes skis and how they differ. Perhaps accumulated knowledge during the information-seeking stage is combined with what you already knew. By analyzing product attributes (color, price, prestige, quality, service record), you will compare products before deciding which one best meets your needs.
- **Purchase decision** Ultimately, consumers make purchase decisions. "Buy" decisions are based on rational motives, emotional motives, or both.[23] **Rational motives** involve the logical evaluation of product attributes: cost, quality, and usefulness. **Emotional motives** involve nonobjective factors and include sociability, imitation of others, and aesthetics. For example, you might buy the same brand of jeans as your friends to feel comfortable in a certain group, not because your friends happen to have the good sense to prefer durable, comfortably priced jeans.

rational motives

Reasons for purchasing a product that are based on a logical evaluation of product attributes

emotional motives

Reasons for purchasing a product that are based on nonobjective factors

- **Postpurchase evaluations** Marketing does not stop with the sale of a product. What happens *after* the sale is important. Marketers want consumers to be happy after buying products so that they are more likely to buy them again. Because consumers do not want to go through a complex decision process for every purchase, they often repurchase products they have used and liked. Not all consumers, of course, are satisfied with their purchases. These buyers are not likely to purchase the same product(s) again and are much more apt to broadcast their experiences than are satisfied customers.

Organizational Marketing and Buying Behavior

In the consumer market, buying and selling transactions are visible to the public Equally important, though far less visible, are *organizational* (or *commercial* *markets*. Some 23 million U.S. organizations buy goods and services to be used in cre ating and delivering consumer products. Marketing to these buyers involves variou kinds of markets and buying behaviors different from those in consumer markets.

Organizational Markets

Organizational or commercial markets fall into three categories: *industrial* *reseller*, and *government/institutional markets*. Taken together, these markets d about $8 trillion in business annually—approximately three times the amoun done in the U.S. consumer market.

Industrial Market The **industrial market** includes businesses that buy goods to be converted into other products or goods that are used up during production. It includes farmers, manufacturers, and some retailers. For example, Seth Thomas <www.seththomas.com> buys electronics, metal components, and glass to make clocks for the consumer market. The company also buys office supplies, tools, and factory equipment—items never seen by clock buyers—that are used during production.

Reseller Market Before products reach consumers, they pass through a **reseller market** consisting of intermediaries, including wholesalers and retailers, who buy and resell finished goods. As a leading distributor of parts and accessories for the pleasure boat market, The Coast Distribution System buys lights, steering wheels, and propellers and resells them to marinas and boat-repair shops. On resold products, 750,000 U.S. wholesalers have annual sales of $2.4 trillion. Some 2.5 million U.S. retailers purchase merchandise that, when resold, is valued at $2.6 trillion per year.[24]

Government and Institutional Market In addition to federal and state governments, there are some 87,000 local governments (municipalities, counties, and school districts) in the United States. State and local governments annually spend $1.3 trillion for durable goods, nondurables, services, and construction. The **institutional market** consists of nongovernmental organizations, such as hospitals, churches, museums, and charities, which also use supplies and equipment as well as legal, accounting, and transportation services.

Organizational Buying Behavior

In some respects, organizational buying behavior bears little resemblance to consumer buying practices. Differences include the buyers' purchasing skills and an emphasis on buyer–seller relationships.

Differences in Buyers Unlike most consumers, organizational buyers are professional, specialized, and expert (or at least well informed):

- As *professionals,* organizational buyers are trained in methods for negotiating purchase terms. Once buyer–seller agreements have been reached, they also arrange for formal contracts.
- As a rule, industrial buyers are company *specialists* in a line of items. As one of several buyers for a large bakery, for example, you may specialize in food ingredients. Another buyer may specialize in baking equipment (industrial ovens and mixers), while a third may buy office equipment and supplies.
- Industrial buyers are often *experts* about the products they buy. On a regular basis, organizational buyers study competing products and alternative suppliers by attending trade shows, by reading trade magazines, and by conducting technical discussions with sellers' representatives.

Differences in the Buyer–Seller Relationship Consumer–seller relationships are often impersonal, short-lived, one-time interactions. In contrast, industrial situations often involve frequent and enduring buyer–seller relationships. The development of a long-term relationship provides each party with access to the technical strengths of the other as well as the security of knowing what future business to expect. Thus, a buyer and a supplier may form a design team to create products of benefit to both. Accordingly, industrial sellers emphasize personal selling by trained representatives who understand the needs of each customer.

industrial market
Organizational market consisting of firms that buy goods that are either converted into products or used during production

reseller market
Organizational market consisting of intermediaries that buy and resell finished goods

institutional market
Organizational market consisting of such nongovernmental buyers of goods and services as hospitals, churches, museums, and charities

The International Marketing Mix

Marketing internationally means mounting a strategy to support global business operations. Foreign customers, for example, differ from domestic buyers in language, customs, business practices, and consumer behavior. If they go global, marketers must reconsider each element of the marketing mix—product, pricing, place, and promotion.[25]

International Products Some products can be sold abroad with virtually no changes. Budweiser, Coca-Cola, and Marlboros are exactly the same in Peoria, Illinois, and Paris, France. In other cases, U.S. firms have had to create products with built-in flexibility—for instance, electric shavers that adapt to either 115- or 230-volt outlets.

Sometimes a redesigned product will satisfy foreign buyers. To sell computers in Japan, for example, Apple had to develop a Japanese-language operating system. Whether they are designed for unique or universal markets, the branding and labeling of products are especially important for communicating global messages.

International Pricing When pricing for international markets, marketers must consider the higher costs of transporting and selling products abroad. Because of the higher costs of buildings, rent, equipment, and imported meat, a McDonald's Big Mac that sells for $2.43 in the United States has a price tag of $3.58 in Denmark.

International Distribution In some industries, delays in starting new distribution networks can be costly. Therefore, companies with existing systems often enjoy an advantage. Likewise, many companies have gained advantages by buying existing businesses. Procter & Gamble, for example, bought Revlon's Max Factor and Betrix cosmetics, both of which have distribution and marketing networks in foreign markets.

International Promotion Occasionally, a good ad campaign is a good campaign just about everywhere else. Quite often, however, U.S. promotional tactics do not succeed in other countries. In fact, many Europeans believe that a product must be inherently shoddy if a company resorts to any advertising, particularly the American hard-sell variety.

International marketers must also be aware that cultural differences can cause negative reactions to improperly advertised products. Some Europeans, for example, are offended by television commercials that show weapons or violence. Meanwhile, cigarette commercials that are banned from U.S. television thrive in many Asian and European markets. Product promotions must be carefully matched to local customs and cultural values.

Because of the need to adjust the marketing mix, success in international markets is hard won. But whether a firm markets in domestic or international markets, the basic principles of marketing still apply; only their implementation changes.

Small Business and the Marketing Mix

Many of today's largest firms were yesterday's small businesses. Behind the success of many small firms lies a skillful application of the marketing concept and an understanding of each element in the marketing mix.[26]

Small-Business Products Some new products and firms are doomed at the start because few consumers want or need what they have to offer. Many fail to estimate realistic market potential, and some offer new products before they have clear pictures of their target segments.

In contrast, a thorough understanding of what customers want has paid off for many small firms. Take, for example, the case of Little Earth Productions Inc. <www.littlearth.com>, a company that makes fashion accessories such as handbags. Originally, the company merely considered how consumers would use its handbags. But after examining shopping habits, Little Earth redesigned for better store display. Because stores can give handbags better visibility by hanging them instead of placing on floors or low countertops, Little Earth added small handles specifically for that purpose.[27]

Small-Business Pricing Haphazard pricing can even sink a firm with a good product. Small-business pricing errors usually result from a failure to estimate operating expenses accurately. Owners of failing businesses have often been heard to say, "I didn't realize how much it costs to run the business!" But when small businesses set prices by carefully assessing costs, many earn satisfactory profits.

Small-Business Distribution Perhaps the most critical aspect of distribution for small businesses is facility location, especially for new service businesses. The ability of many small businesses to attract and retain customers depends partly on the choice of location.

In distribution as in other aspects of the marketing mix, however, smaller companies may have advantages over larger competitors, even in highly complex industries. Everex Systems Inc. of Fremont, California <www.everex.com>, sells personal computers to wholesalers and dealers through a system that the company calls *zero response time.* Because Everex is small and flexible, phone orders can be reviewed every two hours and factory assembly adjusted to match demand.

Small-Business Promotion Successful small businesses plan for promotional expenses as part of start-up costs. Some hold down costs by using less expensive promotional methods. Local newspapers, for example, are sources of publicity when they publish articles about new or unique businesses. Other small businesses identify themselves and their products with associated groups, organizations, and events. Thus, a crafts gallery might join with a local art league to organize public showings of their combined products.

Self-Check Questions 7–9

*You should now be able to answer Self-Check Questions 7–9**

7. MULTIPLE CHOICE The following is **not** a stage in the *consumer buying process* [select one]: **(a)** substitution purchase; **(b)** evaluation of alternatives; **(c)** postpurchase evaluation; **(d)** information seeking; **(e)** problem/need recognition.

8. TRUE/FALSE In terms of market size, *organizational buying* in the United States is economically much more significant than *consumer buying.*

9. MULTIPLE CHOICE Which of the following is **not** true of the *international marketing mix* [select one]: **(a)** Products that sell for a given price in the United States may sell at a different price in another country. **(b)** The International Standards Act ensures the existence of uniform advertising practices in most countries. **(c)** A company can speed up its international distribution activities by buying an existing business in another country. **(d)** Some products can be sold abroad with virtually no changes. **(e)** Cultural differences can cause negative reactions to products that are advertised improperly.

*Answers to Self-Check Questions 7–9 can be found on p. AN-7.

Continued from page 279

Microsoft's Great Xpectations

Xbox is Microsoft's first venture into game consoles, and the company's marketing strategy differs from that of competitors, especially Nintendo, which targets the younger end of the market. Xbox, says product-team leader Robbie Rash, targets a different audience. "Let's face it," he says, "Nintendo's system is for kids. We're for sophisticated gamers. I don't know any 30-year-olds who want a GameCube [by Nintendo]." Both Xbox and PlayStation 2 (by Sony) are aimed at the 16- to 26-year-old audience. Nintendo, however, wants to shed its "kids only" image and attract more players in the 20s age group, too. Both Xbox and GameCube would like to bump Sony's PlayStation 2 (PS2) from the top spot in the console market.

With its current selling price of $199, the revenue from each Xbox doesn't begin to cover the cost of making it. In fact, Microsoft will lose about $125 on every box it sells. Because the consoles cost so much to make, the profits for console makers—Sony and Nintendo as well as Microsoft—depend on software sales. Thus, the console maker that fails to supply a constant stream of new titles is doomed. Reports indicate that Microsoft will have more than 200 Xbox games with a total of 300 titles in development by the next holiday season. For international appeal, Sega's participation also gives Xbox an important boost: Many Japanese gamers doubted Xbox's credibility until they learned of Microsoft's alliance with Sega's respected game publishers.

The Xbox product itself is also different from competing products. Sony's PS2 plays music CDs and DVD movies right out of the box. Xbox can also play music and movies—in fact, it delivers theater-quality 3D sound—but if you want DVD, you need a separate remote controller. Nintendo plays games only—no movies or CDs. Xbox also offers broadband multiplayer gaming and lets players take advantage of high-speed networks by playing online. By uniting gamers on the Internet via the Xbox, Microsoft is laying the groundwork for a future home-networking strategy that will use Xbox console as a hub.

"Nintendo's system is for kids. We're for sophisticated gamers. I don't know any 30-year-olds who want a Nintendo GameCube."

~ Robbie Rash
XBOX PRODUCT TEAM LEADER

Questions for Discussion

1. What social and technological factors have influenced the growth of the interactive entertainment market?
2. What demographics would you use to define the Xbox target market? How about the target market for Nintendo's GameCube?
3. Do you agree or disagree with Microsoft's strategy of featuring hardware, sound, and graphics rather than immediately offering lots of game titles?
4. Which is more important to Xbox's success—the product itself or Microsoft's marketing program for it? Explain your reasoning.
5. Why do you suppose Sega's participation was so meaningful for Japanese customers?

Summary of Learning Objectives

1. *Explain the concept of marketing and describe the five forces that constitute the external marketing environment.*

Marketing is "the process of planning and executing the conception, pricing, promotion, and distribution of ideas, goods, and services to create exchanges that satisfy individual and organizational goals." Consumers buy products that offer the best **value**—the comparison of a product's benefits to its costs—when it comes to meeting their needs and wants. *Benefits* include the product's functions, and the emotional satisfactions associated with it. The satisfied buyer perceives that the benefits derived from a purchase outweigh its costs.

Products provide consumers with **utility**—the ability of a product to satisfy a human want or need. There are four basic kinds of utility: (1) *Time utility* means that products are available when consumers want them. (2) *Place utility* means that products are available where customers can conveniently purchase them. (3) *Ownership utility* occurs when ownership of a product is transferred from seller to customer. (4) By turning raw materials into finished products—the seller creates *form utility.*

Marketing can be used for many different types of products. **Consumer goods** are products that consumers may buy for personal use. Firms that sell products for personal consumption are engaged in *consumer marketing.* Marketing also applies to **industrial goods**—products used by companies to produce other products. Firms that sell products to other manufacturers are engaged in *industrial marketing.* Marketing techniques can also be applied to **services**—intangible products such as time, expertise, or an activity that can be purchased. This application is called *service marketing.* Marketing is also relevant to the promotion of ideas. Rather than emphasizing a single transaction, **relationship marketing** emphasizes lasting relationships with customers and suppliers.

Every marketing program must recognize five outside factors that comprise a company's **external environment** and influence its marketing programs by posing opportunities or threats. (1) *Political and legal environment*: Political activities have profound effects on business. (2) *Social and cultural environment*: The values, beliefs, and ideas that form the fabric of U.S. society affect business. (3) *Technological environment*: New technologies create new products that change our values and lifestyles. (4) *Economic environment*: Economic conditions determine spending patterns by consumers, businesses, and governments. (5) *Competitive environment*: In a competitive environment, marketers must convince buyers that they should purchase their products rather than those of some other seller.

Each marketing program positions its products for three types of competition: (1) **Substitute products** are dissimilar from those of competitors but can fulfill the same need. (2) **Brand competition** occurs between similar products and is based on buyers' perceptions of differences in benefits. (3) **International competition** matches the products of domestic marketers against those of foreign competitors.

2. *Explain the purpose of a marketing plan and identify the four components of the marketing mix.*

Marketing managers plan and implement all the marketing activities that result in the transfer of products to customers. These activities culminate in the **marketing plan**—a detailed strategy for focusing the effort to meet consumer needs and wants.

Marketing managers rely on the "Four P's" of marketing, or the **marketing mix.** (1) *Product*: Marketing begins with a **product,** a good, a service, or an idea designed to fill a consumer need or want. **Product differentiation** is the creation of a feature or image that makes a product differ from competitors. (2) *Pricing*: *Pricing* is the strategy of selecting the most appropriate price at which to sell a product. (3) *Place (Distribution)*: All **distribution** activities are concerned with getting a product from the producer to the consumer. (4) *Promotion*: Promotion refers to techniques for communicating information about products and includes advertising.

3. *Explain market segmentation and show how it is used in target marketing.*

Marketers think in terms of **target markets**—groups of people who have similar wants and needs and who can be expected to show interest in the same products. Target marketing requires **market segmentation**—dividing a market into customer types or "segments."

Members of a *market segment* must share some common traits that affect purchasing decisions. Researchers look at several different influences on consumer behavior. Following are four of the most important influences: (1) **Geographic variables** are the geographical units that may be considered in developing a segmentation strategy. (2) **Demographic variables** describe populations by identifying such traits as age, income, gender, ethnic background, marital status, race, religion, and social class. (3) Members of a market can be segmented according to such **psychographic variables** as lifestyles, interests, and attitudes. (4) **Behavioral variables** refer to the ways in which consumers use a product, the benefits they expect from it, their reasons for purchasing it, and their loyalty to it.

4. *Explain the purpose and value of marketing research.*

Effectiveness in choosing marketing mix and segmentation strategies are based on timely information about trends in the marketplace. **Marketing research** is the study of what customers need and want and how best to meet those needs.

Market research is typically used in developing new or altered products. There are five basic steps in performing market research: (1) *Study the current situation*: What is the need and what is being done to meet it? (2) *Select a research method.* (3) *Collect data*: **Secondary data** are available as a result of previous research. When such data are unavailable or inadequate, **primary data**—new data from new research—must be obtained. (4) *Analyze the data*: Data are of no use until organized into information. (5) *Prepare a report*: Sum up the study's findings, identify solutions, and make recommendations.

The success of marketing research often depends on which of four basic methods is used: (1) **Observation** means watching and recording consumer preferences and behavior. (2) The heart of any **survey** is a *questionnaire*. (3) In a **focus group,** people are gathered in one place, presented with an issue, and asked to discuss it. (4) **Experimentation** compares the responses of the same or similar people under different circumstances.

Almost everything we do leaves a huge cache of data about each of us, and the collection, storage, and retrieval of data in electronic files is called **data warehousing.** For marketing researchers, the data warehouse is a gold mine of clues about consumer behavior. After collecting information, marketers use **data mining—**the application of electronic technologies for searching, sifting, and reorganizing pools of data to uncover useful marketing information.

5. *Describe the key factors that influence the consumer buying process.*

Consumer behavior is the study of the process by which customers decide to purchase products. The result is a focus on four major influences on consumer behavior: (1) *Psychological influences* include motivations, perceptions, ability to learn, and attitudes. (2) *Personal influences* include lifestyle, personality, and economic status. (3) *Social influences* include family, opinion leaders, and such reference groups as friends, coworkers, and professional associates. (4) *Cultural influences* include culture, subculture, and social class. By identifying which influences are most active in certain circumstances, marketers try to explain consumer choices and predict future purchasing behavior. Some consumers exhibit high **brand loyalty,** which means they regularly purchase products because they are satisfied with their performance.

Students of consumer behavior have constructed various models to help marketers understand how consumers decide to purchase products. One model considers four influences that lead to consumption: (1) *Problem/need recognition*: The buying process begins when the consumer recognizes a problem or need. (2) *Information seeking*: Having recognized a need, consumers seek information. (3) *Evaluation of alternatives*: By analyzing the attributes that apply to a given product, consumers compare products in deciding which product best meets their needs. (4) *Purchase decision*: "Buy" decisions are based on rational motives, emotional motives, or both. **Rational motives** involve the logical evaluation of product attributes such as cost, quality, and usefulness. **Emotional motives** involve nonobjective factors and include sociability, imitation of others, and aesthetics. (5) *Postpurchase evaluations*: Marketers want consumers to be happy after the consumption of products so that they are more likely to buy them again.

6. *Discuss the three categories of organizational markets and explain how organizational buying behavior differs from consumer buying behavior.*

Organizational (or *commercial*) *markets*, in which organizations buy goods and services to be used in creating and delivering consumer products, fall into three categories. (1) The **industrial market** consists of businesses that buy goods to be converted into other products or goods that are used during production. (2) Before products reach consumers, they pass through a **reseller market** consisting of intermediaries that buy finished goods and resell them. (3) *Government and institutional market*: Federal, state, and local governments buy durable and nondurable products. The **institutional market** consists of nongovernmental buyers such as hospitals, churches, museums, and charities.

Organizational buying behavior differs from consumer buyer behavior in two major ways: (1) *Differences in buyers*: Organizational buyers are *professionals* trained in arranging buyer–seller relationships and negotiating purchase terms. They are usually *specialists* in a line of items and are often *experts* about the products they are buying. (2) *Differences in the buyer–seller relationship*: Whereas consumer–seller relationships are often fleeting one-time interactions, industrial situations often involve frequent, enduring buyer–seller relationships.

7. *Describe the international and small business marketing mixes.*

When they decide to go global, marketers must reconsider each element of the marketing mix. (1) *International products*: Whereas some products can be sold abroad with virtually no changes, sometimes only a redesigned product will meet the needs of foreign buyers. (2) *International pricing*: When pricing for international markets, marketers must consider the higher costs of transporting and selling products abroad. (3) *International distribution*: In some industries, companies have gained advantages by buying businesses already established in foreign markets. (4) *International promotion*: Occasionally, a good ad campaign can be transported to another country virtually intact. Quite often, however, standard U.S. promotional tactics do not succeed in other countries.

Behind the success of many small firms lies an understanding of each element in the marketing mix. (1) *Small-business products*: Understanding of what customers need and want has paid off for many small firms. (2) *Small-business pricing*: Haphazard pricing can sink even a firm with a good product. Small-business pricing errors usually result from failure to project operating expenses accurately. But when small businesses set prices by carefully assessing costs many earn satisfactory profits. (3) *Small-business distribution*: Perhaps the most critical aspect of distribution is facility location: The ability of many small businesses to attract and retain customers depends partly on the choice of location. (4) *Small-business promotion*: Successful small businesses plan for promotional expenses as part of start-up costs. Some take advantage of less expensive promotional methods.

KEY TERMS

marketing (p. 280)
value (p. 280)
utility (p. 280)
consumer goods (p. 281)
industrial goods (p. 281)
services (p. 281)
relationship marketing (p. 281)
external environment (p. 281)
substitute product (p. 284)
brand competition (p. 284)
international competition (p. 284)
marketing manager (p. 284)
marketing plan (p. 284)
marketing mix (p. 284)
product (p. 284)
product differentiation (p. 284)
distribution (p. 285)
target market (p. 286)
market segmentation (p. 286)
geographic variables (p. 286)
demographic variables (p. 286)
psychographic variables (p. 287)
behavioral variables (p. 288)
marketing research (p. 289)
secondary data (p. 290)
primary data (p. 291)
observation (p. 291)
survey (p. 291)
focus group (p. 291)
experimentation (p. 292)
data warehousing (p. 292)
data mining (p. 292)
consumer behavior (p. 293)
brand loyalty (p. 293)
rational motives (p. 294)
emotional motives (p. 294)
industrial market (p. 295)
reseller market (p. 295)
institutional market (p. 295)

QUESTIONS AND EXERCISES

Questions for Review

1. What are the key similarities and differences between consumer buying behavior and organizational buying behavior?
2. Why and how is market segmentation used in target marketing?
3. How do the needs of organizations differ as a result of the various organizational markets of which they are members?
4. How are data mining and data warehousing useful in finding new information for marketing research?

Questions for Analysis

5. Select an everyday product (books, CDs, skateboards, dog food, or shoes, for example). Show how different versions of your product are aimed toward different market segments. Explain how the marketing mix differs for each segment.
6. Select a second everyday product and describe the consumer buying process that typically goes into its purchase.
7. Consider a service product, such as transportation, entertainment, or healthcare. What are some ways that more customer value might be added to this product? Why would your improvements add value for the buyer?
8. If you were starting your own small business (say, marketing a consumer good that you already know something about), which of the forces in the external marketing environment do you think would have the greatest impact on your success?

Application Exercises

9. Interview the marketing manager of a local business. Identify the degree to which this person's job is focused on each element in the marketing mix.
10. Select a product made by a foreign company and sold in the United States. What is the product's target market? What is the basis on which the target market is segmented? Do you think that this basis is appropriate? How might another approach, if any, be beneficial? Why?

Extra Exercise

11. Break the class into small groups and assign each group a specific industry. Have each group discuss the strategies that it believes are important to the marketing of products in that industry.

Building Your Business Skills

DEALING WITH VARIABLES

This exercise enhances the following SCANS workplace competencies: demonstrating basic skills, demonstrating thinking skills, exhibiting interpersonal skills, and working with information.

Goal

To encourage students to analyze the ways in which various market segmentation variables affect business success.

The Situation

You and four partners are thinking of purchasing a heating and air conditioning (H/AC) dealership that specializes in residential applications priced between $2,000 and $40,000. You are now in the process of deciding where that dealership should be located. You are considering four locations: Miami, Florida; Westport, Connecticut; Dallas, Texas; and Spokane, Washington.

Method

Step 1

Working with your partnership group, do library research to learn how H/AC makers market residential products. Check for articles in the *Wall Street Journal, Business Week, Fortune,* and other business publications.

Step 2

Continue your research. This time, focus on the specific marketing variables that define each prospective location. Check Census Bureau and Department of Labor data at your library and on the Internet and contact local chambers of commerce (by phone and via the Internet) to learn about the following factors for each location:

1. Geography
2. Demography (especially age, income, gender, family status, and social class)
3. Psychographic factors (lifestyles, interests, and attitudes)

Step 3

As a group, determine which location holds the greatest promise as a dealership site. Base your decision on your analysis of market segment variables and their effects on H/AC sales.

Follow-Up Questions

1. Which location did you choose? Describe the segmentation factors that influenced your decision.
2. Identify the two most important variables that you believe will affect the dealership's success. Why are these factors so important?
3. Which factors were least important? Why?
4. When equipment manufacturers advertise residential H/AC products, they often show them in different climate situations (winter, summer, or high-humidity conditions). Which market segments are these ads targeting? Describe these segments in terms of demographic and psychographic characteristics.

Exercising Your Ethics

DRIVING A LEGITIMATE BARGAIN

The Situation

A firm's marketing methods are sometimes at odds with the consumer's buying process. This exercise illustrates how ethical issues can become entwined with personal selling activities, product pricing, and customer relations.

The Dilemma

In buying his first-ever new car, Matt visited showrooms and Web sites for every make of SUV. After weeks of reading and test-driving, he settled on a well-known Japanese-made vehicle with a manufacturer's suggested retail price of $34,500 for the 2002 model. The price included accessories and options that Matt considered essential. Because he planned to own the car for at least five years, he was willing to wait for just the right package rather than accept a lesser-equipped car already on the lot. Negotiations with Gary, the sales representative, continued for two weeks. Finally, a sales contract was signed for $30,600, with delivery due no more than two or three months later if the vehicle had to be special-ordered from the factory, earlier if Gary found the exact car when he searched other dealers around the country. On April 30, to close the deal, Matt had to write a check for $1,000.

Matt received a call on June 14 from Angela, Gary's sales manager: "We cannot get your car before October," she reported, "so it will have to be a 2003 model. You will have to pay the 2003 price." Matt replied that the agreement called for a stated price and delivery deadline for 2002, pointing out that money had exchanged hands for the contract. When asked what the 2003 price would be, Angela responded that it had not yet been announced. Angrily, Matt replied that he would be foolish to agree now on some unknown future price. Moreover, he didn't like the way the dealership was treating him. He told Angela to send back to him everything he had signed; the deal was off.

Questions for Discussion

1. Given the factors involved in the consumer buying process, how would you characterize the particular ethical issues in this situation?
2. From an ethical standpoint, what are the obligations of the sales rep and the sales manager regarding the pricing of the product in this situation?
3. If you were responsible for maintaining good customer relations at the dealership, how would you handle this matter?

Mastering Business Essentials

■ **EPISODE 9** stresses the importance of developing a marketing strategy that identifies and makes the best use of a company's competitive advantage: A firm must not only develop one or more capabilities that are superior to those of competitors, but must also turn its advantage into an effective marketing strategy and growth plan. *This episode illustrates and enhances the chapter discussion of marketing strategy.*

■ **EPISODE 10** reminds us that the consumer buying process is complex and unpredictable. *This episode builds on the chapter discussion of personal, psychological, social, and cultural influences on consumer behavior.*

Crafting Your Business Plan

PICKING AND PACKAGING THE RIGHT PRODUCTS

The Purpose of the Assignment

1. To familiarize students with the various marketing issues that a sample firm faces in developing its business plan, in the framework of *Business PlanPro (BPP) 2002* software package.
2. To demonstrate how four chapter topics—consumer versus organizational marketing, relationship marketing, market segmentation, and product differentiation—can be integrated as components of the *BPP* planning environment.

Assignment

After reading Chapter 10 in the textbook, open the BPP *software and look around for information about the marketing plan for a sample firm, a promotional products manufacturer called* Elsewares Promotional Products & Packaging. *To find* Elsewares, *do the following:*

Open *Business PlanPro 2002.* If you are asked if you want to "create a new business plan" or to "open an existing plan," select "create a new business plan" (even though you are not going to create a plan at this time). You will then be taken to the *Business PlanPro EasyPlan Wizard.* On the screen, click on the option entitled **Research It.** You will then be presented with a new list of options, including **Sample Plan Browser.** After clicking on **Sample Plan Browser**, scan its alphabetical list of sample plans and double-click on **Promotional Products Manufacturer**, which is the location for *Elsewares Promotional Products & Packaging.* The screen you are looking at is the introduction page for the *Elsewares* business plan. Next, scroll down this page until you reach the **Table of Contents** for the *Elsewares* business plan.

Now respond to the following items:

1. Is Elsewares involved in *consumer marketing* or *organizational marketing*? [Sites to see in *BPP* (for this item): On the Table of Contents page, click on and read **1.0 Executive Summary**. After returning to the Table of Contents page, click on and read each of the following: **1.1 Objectives, 1.2 Mission,** and **1.3 Keys to Success.**]
2. Identify Elsewares' strategy and methods for *building relationships with its customers.* [Sites to see in *BPP*: On the Table of Contents page, click on and read **5.0 Strategy and Implementation Summary.** Also visit **5.1.4 Service and Support.** Then read **1.0 Executive Summary** and **1.3 Keys to Success.**]
3. What basis—geographic, demographic, psychographic, or behavioral—does Elsewares plan to use for its *market segmentation* strategy? [Sites to see in *BPP*: On the Table of Contents page, click on and read each of the following in turn: **4.0 Market Analysis Summary** and **4.1 Market Segmentation.**]
4. Describe Elsewares' plans for differentiating its product. Is the plan clear enough on this matter? Why or why not? [Sites to see in *BPP*: On the Table of Contents page, click on and read **4.0 Market Analysis Summary.** Then go to **4.2 Industry Analysis,** and explore the information in that section.]

Video Exercise

IN CONSUMERS' SHOES: SKECHERS USA

Learning Objectives

The purpose of this video is to help you:

1. Describe the role of the "Four P's" in a company's marketing mix.
2. Explain how a company shapes its market research to fit its marketing goals.
3. Discuss the effectiveness of target marketing and segmentation in analyzing consumers.

Background Information

Skechers USA <www.skechers.com> enjoys a reputation for producing footwear that combines comfort with innovative design. It has built its product line into a globally recognized brand distributed in more than 110 countries. From its corporate headquarters in Manhattan Beach, California, Skechers has engineered steady growth in market share while competing against some powerful players in the high-ticket, branded athletic shoe industry.

Since its start in 1992, Skechers has burnished its image as a maker of hip footwear through a savvy marketing strategy that calls for catering to a closely targeted consumer base. Maintaining brand integrity and its reputation for innovation is a crucial goal in all of Skechers' product development and marketing activities.

The Video

Director of public relations Kelly O'Connor discusses her work and the marketing activities that are critical to maintaining Skechers' edge in the highly competitive footwear marketplace. She describes the company's goal of creating a megabrand with an image, personality, and "feel" that can be translated and marketed globally. Skechers has been successful in brand building by means of an "Ask, Don't Tell" approach to product development and marketing: It aims to find out what the market wants and then appeal to customers' wants rather than trying to influence the market with the products that it makes available.

Discussion Questions

1. Which of the "Four P's" of the marketing mix seems to govern Skechers' marketing strategy? Why? How do you suppose Skechers alters elements of its American marketing mix to attract consumers in international markets?
2. Skechers collects a lot of *primary data* in its market research. What kinds of primary data does the company prefer to gather? Why does this kind of data suit its marketing goals? How does it suit the firm's consumer base? Given Skechers' fairly limited

consumer base, are there other types of research data that you would recommend?

3. Describe Skechers' target market and explain how company marketers segment it. How effective is this strategy in analyzing customers? How successful are Skechers' marketing efforts among 12- to 24-year-olds (and consumers wishing they were in that demographic segment)?
4. Discuss the impact of brand loyalty on the sale of Skechers products. Building brand loyalty is a major effort that presents both opportunities and challenges to marketers and product developers. What are some of the opportunities and challenges encountered by Skechers marketing managers?

Follow-up Assignment

Go online to find out about the product lines and target markets of such companies as Nike <www.nike.com>, Reebok <www.reebok.com>, Lady Foot Locker <www.ladyfootlocker.com>, and FUBU <wwwl.fubu.com>. How does the approach to segmentation at these companies compare with that of Skechers?

For Further Exploration

How do you think Skechers might expand its current product lines? What other new products might Skechers research, such as clothing or accessories? How could the company go about investigating the market potential for such products?

CHAPTER

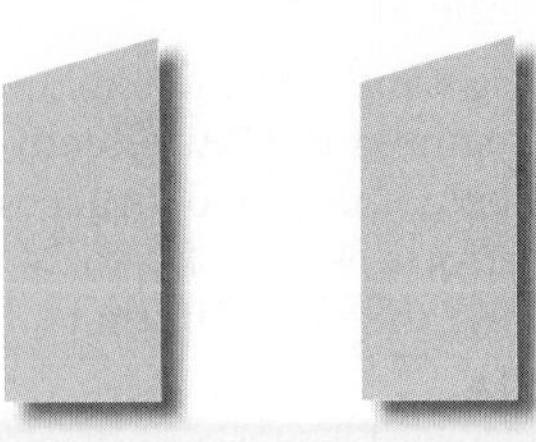

Developing and Pricing Products

After reading this chapter, you should be able to:

1. Identify a *product,* distinguish between *consumer* and *industrial products,* and explain the *product mix.*
2. Describe the *new product development process* and trace the stages of the *product life cycle.*
3. Explain the importance of *branding, packaging,* and *labeling.*
4. Identify the various *pricing objectives* that govern *pricing decisions* and describe the *price-setting tools* used in making these decisions.
5. Discuss *pricing strategies* and *tactics* for both existing and new products.

Who Wants to Be a Survivor?

It's more often famine than feast in the struggle for survival in the network-TV jungle. Consider both the weight that ABC was able to throw around because of Regis Philbin's *Who Wants to Be a Millionaire?* and, more recently, the show's anemic performance in the ratings. The game show that propelled ABC into the network ratings lead just a year earlier suffered a whopping 50-percent ratings drop at the end of the 2001 viewing season. The network's most reliable sitcoms—*The Drew Carey Show* and *Dharma & Greg*—have also tumbled in the ratings that measure program viewership.

Like other products, it seems, even the very best programs go through life cycles, and for TV shows, the end comes when viewers stop watching. The relationship between viewers and programs is simply a matter of demand and supply. Tastes change and, eventually, even producers of the top shows can only watch helplessly as viewers channel surf for more interesting or exciting programs. The financial aspect of this phenomenon is fairly simple: Without enough viewers, networks lose money, as executives at Disney-owned ABC <http://abc.go.com> have recently been forced to remind themselves. Viewers lost interest in the network's lineup, and with no new hit shows to boost ratings, ABC plummeted from a $150-million profit in 2001 to a projected $300-million loss in 2002—a reversal in fortunes of nearly half a billion dollars. The network's ill-fated attempt to replace Ted Koppel and *Nightline* with David Letterman and *The Late Show* from CBS was an effort to attract a larger audience—especially younger viewers—during the evening hours. ABC also opted to refurbish another old warhorse, *Monday Night Football,* by bringing in John Madden, the popular football commentator from Fox.

Unfortunately, a TV network's lifeblood is *new* programming. To turn things around, ABC needs a viewer-friendly mix of new shows, upgrades of existing programs, and successful properties purchased from competitors. ABC's last in-house megahit was 1999's *Who Wants to Be a Millionaire?,* which, according to some critics, the network mishandled in two ways. First, *Millionaire* probably suffered from overexposure when ABC began airing four episodes a week during the 2000 season. Especially among younger viewers, familiarity quickly bred contempt. "Just over a year ago," lamented ABC co-chairman Lloyd Braun, "we were No. 1 . . . and had four shows in the top 10. Of course . . . all four shows were *Millionaire.*" ABC further compounded the problem, not only by putting too many eggs in its *Millionaire* basket, but also by failing to look to the future with other programs to help carry the ratings load. Seduced by *Millionaire*'s initial blockbuster ratings and envisioning it as a hit for years to come, network executives cut its investment in other new shows. "They rode it like the Pony Express," says one industry analyst, "and then had no horse to jump to" when they had ridden *Millionaire* into the ground.

Now, ABC's prime-time audience is down 23 percent, far behind NBC and CBS and only slightly ahead of Fox. The network has no shows in the Top 10, and its only Top 30 shows—*NYPD Blue* and *The Practice*—are on the downside of their life cycles. Translated into bottom-line terms, the ratings hemorrhage means that for every available minute of prime-time advertising, the network is generating $100,000 less than it was a year ago.

As one of television's all-time most profitable shows—earning more than half a billion dollars in profits for ABC—does *Millionaire*'s demise spell doomsday

"They rode it like the Pony Express and then had no horse to jump to."

~Investment banker Jeffrey Logsdon
ON ABC'S HANDLING OF *WHO WANTS TO BE A MILLIONAIRE?*

or just a bump in the road for ABC? CEO Michael Eisner of ABC's parent company, Disney <http://disney.go.com>, says that the problem can be solved. And after all, concedes Goldman Sachs analyst Richard Greenfield, "It only takes one or two hit shows to jump-start a network." But coming up with a new show is doubtful when spending has been cut on program development. It's going to take time for ABC to rebuild its entertainment lineup. As ABC's Braun admits, "This won't be fixed overnight." Stay tuned.

Our opening story is continued on page 327.

Recent developments at ABC remind us that all products—including wildly popular TV shows—eventually reach the end of their life cycles and expire. This story also recalls a basic rule of thumb for developing new products in any industry: Begin by identifying the changing demands of your target audience and then develop new products to meet those demands. As you will see in this chapter, marketers can meet their goals only by making the right choices in both developing and pricing products.

Let's begin by looking at the way in which three well-known companies compete successfully in the same marketing environment. Oracle Corp., IBM, and Microsoft Corp. all are major players in database-software products—computer programs that other companies use for storing and manipulating massive volumes of internal data. Oracle <www.oracle.com> holds the top position, with a near 34-percent share of the market; IBM <www.ibm.com> is next, with more than 30 percent, and Microsoft <www.microsoft.com> is a distant third, with about 15 percent. While all are successful, surveys show that they rely on quite different strategies. Oracle is the hands-down winner in terms of product innovation, specializing in cutting-edge features that substantially improve performance. Microsoft products rate lower in both reliability and performance, but they are priced below Oracle software and cost less to operate. IBM gets high marks for satisfaction with technical and customer support. So whose product is best? Says one industry analyst, "It's hard to say who is the technological leader in this market, since it depends on what you value and how you want it delivered."[1]

"It's hard to say who is the technological leader in this market, since it depends on what you value and how you want it delivered."

~Carl Olofson
SOFTWARE INDUSTRY ANALYST

In Chapter 10, we introduced the four components of the marketing mix: product, price, promotion, and place (distribution). In making their strategic decisions, Oracle, IBM, and Microsoft face a basic fact of business reality: It is virtually impossible to focus on one element of the marketing mix (in this case, product design) without encountering other marketing variables (product price, after-sale service, and brand image). We start this chapter by looking more closely at the complex nature of the product. In particular, we will show why managers must keep in mind such a wide variety of possibilities when developing, naming, packaging, labeling, and pricing products.

What Is a Product?

In developing the marketing mix for any product, whether goods or services, marketers must consider what consumers really buy when they purchase products. Only then can these marketers plan strategies effectively. We begin this section where product strategy begins: by understanding that every product is a *value package* which provides benefits to satisfy the needs and wants of customers. Next, we describe the major *classifications of products,* both consumer and industrial. Finally, we discuss the most important component in the offerings of any business: its *product mix.*

The Value Package

Whether it is a physical good, a service, or some combination of the two, customers get value from the various benefits, features, and even intangible rewards associated with a product. Product **features** are the qualities, tangible and intan-

feature

Tangible and intangible qualities that a company builds into a product gible, that a company builds into its products, such as a 12-horsepower motor on a lawn mower. But to attract buyers, features also must provide *benefits:* The mower must produce an attractive lawn. The owner's pleasure in knowing that the mower is nearby when needed is an intangible reward.

Today's consumer regards a product as a bundle of attributes which, taken together, marketers call the **value package.** Increasingly, buyers expect to receive products with greater *value*—with more benefits at reasonable costs. Consider, for example, the possible attributes in a personal computer value package:

value package
Product marketed as a bundle of value-adding attributes, including reasonable cost

- Easy access to understandable prepurchase information
- Choices in keyboards, monitors, and processing capacities
- Choices of color
- Attractive software packages
- Attractive prices
- Fast, simple ordering via the Internet
- Protection for credit card purchasing
- Assurance of speedy delivery
- Warranties
- Easy access to around-the-clock postpurchase technical support
- Internet chat room capability
- Prestige of owning a state-of-the art system

Although the computer includes physical *features*—processing devices and other hardware—most items in the value package are services or intangibles which, collectively, add value by providing *benefits* that increase the customer's satisfaction. Reliable data processing is certainly a benefit, but so too are pride of ownership, access to technical support, and a feeling of security. Today, more and more firms compete on the basis of enhanced value packages. They find that the addition of a simple new service often pleases customers far beyond the cost of providing it. Just making the purchase transaction more convenient, for example, adds value by sparing customers long waits and cumbersome paperwork.[2]

Look carfully at the ad in Figure 11.1 for SAS Institute <www.sas.com>, a major designer of statistical software. SAS emphasizes not the technical features of its products, nor even the criteria that companies use in selecting software—efficiency, compatibility, support. Rather, the ad focuses on the customer-oriented benefits that a buyer of SAS software can expect from using the firm's products: "Only SAS provides you with a complete view of your customers." These benefits are being marketed as part of a complete value package.

Classifying Goods and Services

We can classify products according to expected buyers, who fall into two groups: buyers of *consumer products* and buyers of *industrial products.*[3] As we saw in Chapter 10, the consumer and industrial buying processes differ significantly. Not surprisingly, marketing products to consumers is vastly different from marketing them to other companies.

Classifying Consumer Products Consumer products are commonly divided into three categories that reflect buyer behavior:

convenience good/service
Inexpensive good or service purchased and consumed rapidly and regularly

shopping good/service
Moderately expensive, infrequently purchased good or service

- **Convenience goods** (such as milk and newspapers) and **convenience services** (such as those offered by fast-food restaurants) are consumed rapidly and regularly. They are inexpensive and are purchased often and with little output of time and effort.
- **Shopping goods** (such as stereos and tires) and **shopping services** (such as insurance) are more expensive and are purchased less often than convenience

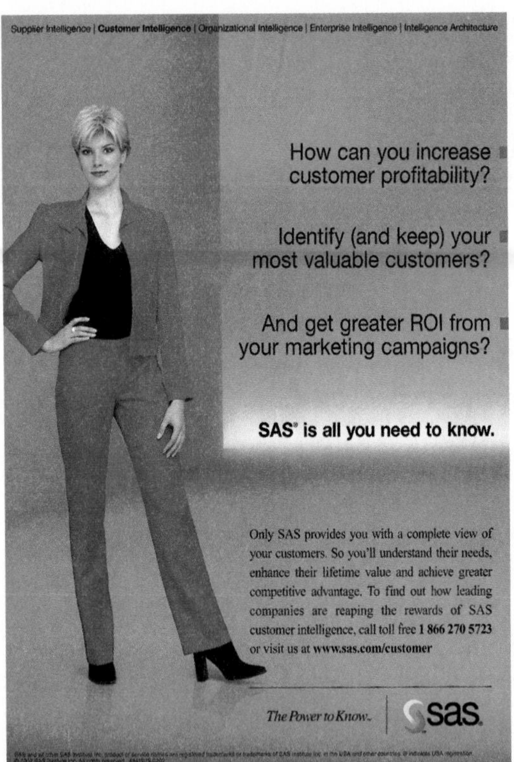

Supplier Intelligence | Customer Intelligence | Organizational Intelligence | Enterprise Intelligence | Intelligence Architecture
How can you increase customer profitability?
Identify (and keep) your most valuable customers?
And get greater ROI from your marketing campaigns?
SAS® is all you need to know.
Only SAS provides you with a complete view of your customers. So you'll understand their needs, enhance their lifetime value and achieve greater competitive advantage. To find out how leading companies are reaping the rewards of SAS customer intelligence, call toll free 1 866 270 5723 or visit us at www.sas.com/customer
The Power to Know.
sas.

FIGURE 11.1

products. Consumers often compare brands, sometimes in different stores. They may also evaluate alternatives in terms of style, performance, color, price, and other criteria.

- **Specialty goods** (such as wedding gowns) and **specialty services** (such as catering for wedding receptions) are extremely important and expensive purchases. Consumers usually decide on precisely what they want and will accept no substitutes. They often go from store to store, sometimes spending a great deal of money and time to get a specific product.

Classifying Industrial Products Depending on how much they cost and how they will be used, industrial products can be divided into two categories:

- **Expense items** are goods or services that are consumed within a year by firms producing other goods or supplying other services. The most obvious expense items are industrial goods used directly in the production process (for example, bulkloads of tea processed into tea bags).
- **Capital items** are permanent (expensive and longlasting) goods and services. They have expected lives of more than a year and, typically, of several years. Buildings (offices, factories), fixed equipment (water towers, baking ovens), and accessory equipment (computers, airplanes) are *capital goods*. *Capital services* are those for which long-term commitments are made, such as building and equipment maintenance or legal services. Because capital items are expensive and purchased infrequently, they often involve decisions by high-level managers.

specialty good/service
Expensive, rarely purchased good or service

expense item
Industrial product purchased and consumed rapidly and regularly for daily operations

capital item
Expensive, long-lasting, infrequently purchased industrial good, such as a building, or industrial service, such as building maintenance

The Product Mix

The group of products that a company makes available for sale, whether consumer, industrial, or both, is its **product mix.**[4] Black & Decker <www.blackanddecker.com>, for example, makes toasters, vacuum cleaners, electric drills, and a variety of other appliances and tools. 3M Corp. <www.3m.com> makes everything from Post-it notes to laser optics.

Product Lines Many companies begin with a single product, such as simple iced tea. Over time, they find that the initial product fails to suit every consumer shopping for the product type. To meet market demand, they introduce similar products—such as flavored teas—designed to reach more consumers. ServiceMaster <www.servicemaster.com> was among the first successful home services that offered mothproofing and carpet cleaning. Subsequently, the company expanded into other home services—lawn care (TruGreen, ChemLawn), pest control (Terminix), and cleaning (Merry Maids). A group of similar products intended for a group of similar buyers who will use them in similar ways is a **product line.**

product mix
Group of products that a firm makes available for sale

product line
Group of similar products intended for a similar group of buyers who will use them in similar ways

Companies may extend their horizons and identify opportunities outside existing product lines. The result—*multiple* (or *diversified*) *product lines*—is evident at firms such as ServiceMaster. After years of serving residential customers, ServiceMaster has added business and industry services (landscaping and janitorial), education services (management of schools and institutions, including physical facilities and financial and personnel resources), and health-care services (management of support services—plant operations, asset management, laundry/linen supply—for long-term–care facilities). Multiple product lines allow a company to grow rapidly and can help to offset the consequences of slow sales in any one product line.

Developing New Products

To expand or diversify product lines—in fact, just to survive—firms must develop and introduce streams of new products. Faced with competition and shifting consumer preferences, no firm can count on a single successful product to carry it forever. Even products that have been popular for decades need constant renewal.

Consider one of America's most popular brands—Levi's <www.levistrauss.com>. Its riveted denim styles were once market leaders, but the company failed to keep pace with changing tastes, fell behind new products from competitors, and lost market share among 14- to 19-year–old males during the 1990s. By 1999, at least one industry analyst was forced to report that Levi's "hasn't had a successful new product in years." More recently, the company may have gotten back on track by recognizing that female consumers in various sizes need special attention. In 2001, instead of trying to market women's jeans merely as variations on denim pants for men, Levi's introduced the Superlow line of jeans that emphasized femininity.[5]

In the next section, we focus on the process by which companies develop new goods and services.

The New Product Development Process

The demand for food and beverage ingredients has grown more than 6 percent per year, reaching $5 billion in the year 2000. Flavors and flavor enhancers are the biggest part of that growth, especially artificial sweeteners. However, companies that develop and sell these products face a big problem: It costs between $30 million and $50 million and can take as long as 8 to 10 years to get a new product through the approval process at the Food and Drug Administration (FDA) <www.fda.gov>.

Testing, both for FDA approval and for marketing, can be the most time-consuming stage of development. Acesulfame K beverage sweetener, which is made by Hoechst Celanese Corp. <www.hoechst.com>, has been through more than 90 safety studies and 1,000 technical studies to see how it performs in various kinds of beverages. After the testing process, additional stages include advertising and demonstration to food producers.[6] Cashing in on the growth of the food- and beverage-ingredients market requires an immense amount of time, patience, and money.

Product development is a long and expensive process, and like Hoechst, many firms have research and development (R&D) departments for exploring new product possibilities. Why do they devote so many resources to exploring product possibilities, rejecting many seemingly good ideas along the way? In this section, we focus on two answers to this question. First, we see that high *mortality rates* for new ideas means that only a few new products reach the market. Second, for many companies, *speed to market* with a product is as important as care in developing it.

Product Mortality Rates It is estimated that it takes 50 new product ideas to generate one product that finally reaches the market. Even then, only a few of these survivors become *successful* products. Many seemingly great ideas have failed as products. Indeed, creating a successful new product has become increasingly more difficult—even for the most experienced marketers. Why? The number of new products hitting the market each year has increased dramatically: More than 25,000 new household, grocery, and drugstore items are introduced annually. In 2001, the beverage industry alone launched 3,800 new products.[7] At any given time, however, the average supermarket carries a total of only 20,000 to 25,000 different items. Because of lack of space and customer demand, about 9 out of 10 new products will fail. Those with the best chances are innovative and deliver unique benefits.

speed to market
Strategy of introducing new products to respond quickly to customer or market changes

Speed to Market The more rapidly a product moves from the laboratory to the marketplace, the more likely it is to survive. By introducing new products ahead of competitors, companies establish market leadership. They become entrenched in the market before being challenged by newer competitors. How important is **speed to market**—that is, a firm's success in responding to customer demand or market changes? One study reports that a product which is only three months late to market (three months behind the leader) loses 12 percent of its lifetime profit potential. At six months, it will lose 33 percent.

The Seven-Step Development Process

To increase their chances of developing a successful new product, many firms adopt some version of a seven-step process (which is not the same for goods and service producers).

1. ***Product ideas.*** Product development begins with a search for ideas for new products. Ideas can come from consumers, the sales force, R&D people, or engineering personnel.
2. ***Screening.*** This stage is designed to eliminate all ideas that do not mesh with the firm's abilities or objectives. Representatives from marketing, engineering, and production have input at this stage.
3. ***Concept testing.*** Once ideas have been screened, companies use market research to get consumers' input about benefits and prices.
4. ***Business analysis.*** After gathering consumer opinions, marketers compare manufacturing costs and benefits to see whether the product meets minimum profitability goals.
5. ***Prototype development.*** Once the firm has determined the potential profitability of a product, engineering or R&D produce a prototype. This can be extremely expensive, often requiring extensive tooling and parts development.
6. ***Product testing and test marketing.*** Applying lessons from the prototype, the company goes into limited production. It then tests the product to see whether it meets performance requirements. If it does, it is sold in limited areas. Because promotional campaigns and distribution channels must be established for test markets, this stage is quite costly.
7. ***Commercialization.*** If test marketing proves positive, the company begins full-scale production and marketing. Gradual commercialization, with the firm providing the product to more and more areas over time, prevents undue strain on initial production capabilities. On the other hand, delays in commercialization may give other firms a chance to bring out competing products.

Variations in the Process for Services

The development of services involves many of the same stages.[8] Basically, steps 2, 3, 4, 6, and 7 are the same. There are, however, important differences in steps 1 and 5:

service package
Tangible and intangible features that characterize a service product

1. ***Service ideas.*** The search for service ideas includes defining the **service package:** identifying the tangible and intangible features that characterize the service (see Chapter 14) and stating service specifications. For example, a firm that wants to offer year-end cleaning services to office buildings might commit itself to the following specifications: The building interior will be cleaned by midnight, January 5, including carpets swept free of all

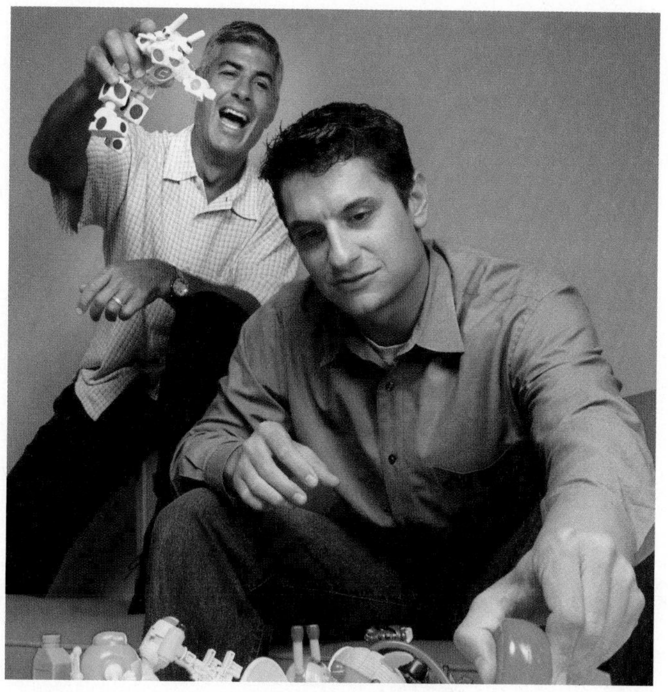

At Equity Marketing <www.equity-marketing.com> *in Los Angeles, engineers like Mike Barbato and Frank Kautzman used to design toys by sculpting models out of lumps of clay. Now they design promotional toys by means of "rapid prototyping," using technology that allows several employees to work simultaneously on three-dimensional "models" that can then be printed and faxed for review by clients anywhere in the world. It now takes five days instead of three weeks to make an initial sculpture, and problems can be spotted and corrected much more quickly.*

dust and debris and washbowls and lavatory equipment polished with no interference in customer service.

2. ***Service process design.*** Instead of prototype development, services require a three-part **service process design.** *Process selection* identifies each step in the service, including sequence and timing. *Worker requirements* states employee behaviors, skills, capabilities, and interactions with customers during the service encounter. *Facility requirements* designates all the equipment that supports service delivery.

service process design
Three aspects (process selection, worker requirements, facilities requirements) of developing a service product

The Product Life Cycle

When a product reaches the market, it enters the **product life cycle (PLC),** a series of stages through which it passes during its profit-producing life. Depending on the product's ability to attract and keep customers, its PLC may be a matter of months, years, or decades. Strong, mature products (such as Clorox bleach and H&R Block tax preparation) have had long productive lives.

product life cycle (PLC)
Series of stages in a product's profit-producing life

Stages in the Product Life Cycle The life cycle for both goods and services is a natural process in which products are born, grow in stature, mature, and finally decline and die.[9] Look at the two graphics in Figure 11.2. In Figure 11.2(a), the four phases of the PLC are applied to several products with which you are familiar:

1. ***Introduction.*** This stage begins when the product reaches the marketplace. Marketers focus on making potential consumers aware of the product and its benefits. Extensive promotional and development costs erase all profits.
2. ***Growth.*** If the new product attracts enough consumers, sales start to climb rapidly. The product starts to show a profit, and other firms move rapidly to introduce their own versions.
3. ***Maturity.*** Sales growth starts to slow. Although the product earns its highest profit level early in this stage, increased competition eventually forces price cutting and lower profits. Toward the end of the stage, sales start to fall.

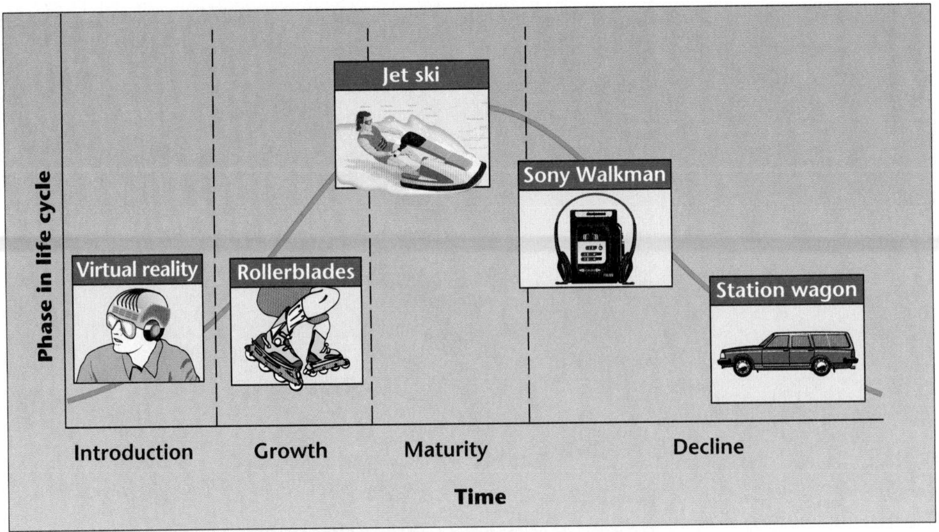

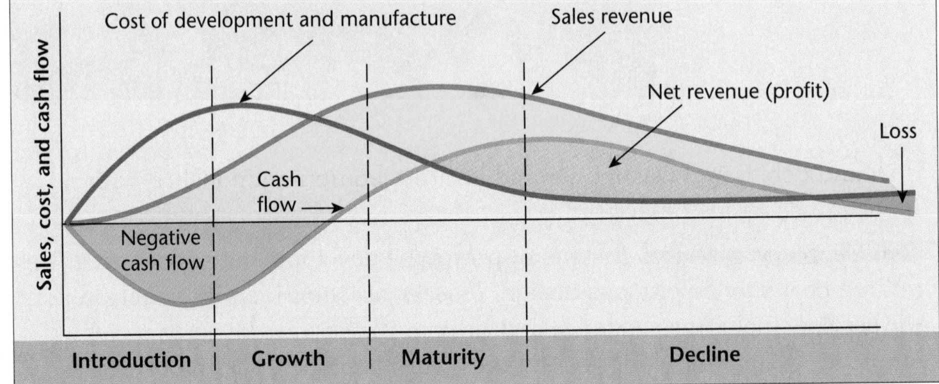

■ **FIGURE 11.2**

Products in Life Cycle: Stages, Sales, Cost, and Profit

4. ***Decline.*** Sales and profits continue to fall as new products in the introduction stage take away sales. Firms end or reduce promotional support (ads and salespeople) but may let the product linger to provide some profits.

Figure 11.2(b) plots the relationship of the PLC to a product's typical sales, costs, and profits. Although the early stages of the PLC often show negative cash flows, successful products usually recover those losses and, in fact, continue to generate profits until the decline stage. For most products, profitable life spans are short—thus, the importance placed by so many firms on the constant replenishment of product lines.

Extending Product Life: An Alternative to New Products Obviously, companies try to keep products in the maturity stage as long as they can. Sales of TV sets for example, have been revitalized by such feature changes as color, portability, miniaturization, and stereo capability. In fact, companies can extend product life through a number of creative means. Foreign markets, for example, offer three approaches to longer life cycles:

product extension
Existing, unmodified product that is marketed globally

product adaptation
Product modified to have greater appeal in foreign markets

1. In **product extension,** an existing product is marketed globally instead of just domestically. Coca-Cola and Levi's 501 jeans are prime examples of international product extensions.
2. With **product adaptation,** the product is modified for greater appeal in different countries. In Germany, a McDonald's meal includes beer, and Ford

Self-Check Questions 1–3

*You should now be able to answer Self-Check Questions 1–3**

1. MULTIPLE CHOICE When viewed as a *value package* for the buyer, a product is a bundle of attributes consisting of the following [select one]: **(a)** benefits; **(b)** features; **(c)** intangible rewards; **(d)** reasonable price; **(e)** all of the above.

2. TRUE/FALSE The *product mix* is the group of products which a company makes available for sale and within which it may have several *product lines.*

3. MULTIPLE CHOICE All of the following are considered *stages in the product life cycle* **except** [select one]: **(a)** introduction; **(b)** growth; **(c)** retention; **(d)** maturity; **(e)** decline.

*ANSWERS TO SELF-CHECK QUESTIONS 1–3 CAN BE FOUND ON P. AN-7.

puts the steering wheel on the right side for exports to Japan. Because it involves product changes, this approach is usually more costly than product extension.

3. **Reintroduction** means reviving, for new markets, products that are becoming obsolete in older ones. NCR, for instance, has reintroduced manually operated cash registers in Latin America.

reintroduction
Process of reviving for new markets products that are obsolete in older ones

Thus, the beginning of a sales downturn in the maturity stage is not necessarily the time to abandon a product. Rather, it is often a time to replace an old marketing approach with a new one.

Identifying Products

As we noted earlier, developing a product's features is only part of a marketer's job. Marketers must also identify products so that consumers recognize them. Three important tools for this task are *branding, packaging,* and *labeling.*

Branding Products

Coca-Cola <www.coca-cola.com> is the best-known brand in the world. Indeed, some Coke executives claim that if all the company's other assets were obliterated, they could go to the bank and borrow $100 billion on the strength of the brand name alone. Brand names such as Coca-Cola and emblems such as the McDonald's golden arches are symbols that characterize products and distinguish them from one another. **Branding** is a process of using symbols to communicate the qualities of a particular product made by a particular producer. Brands are designed to signal uniform quality: Customers who try and like a product can return to it by remembering its name.

branding
Process of using symbols to communicate the qualities of a product made by a particular producer

Adding Value Through Brand Equity Many companies that once measured assets in terms of cash, buildings, equipment, and inventories now realize that a

It's pronounced a little differently—STAH-buks-zu)—but the brand means pretty much the same: large cups of gourmet coffee served in comfortable surroundings to the sound of hip-hop and reggae. In Japan, Starbucks <www.starbucks.co.jp/en/home.htm> *has opened 300 stores since 1996 and plans another 180 over the next three years. In a depression-ridden country of traditional tea drinkers, volume per store is twice that of U.S. outlets. The brand has become so popular that Starbucks earned $242 million last year (twice the previous year's total) even though it has yet to advertise in Japan.*

brand equity

Degree of consumers' loyalty to and awareness of a brand and its resultant market share

strong brand is an equally important asset. Widely known and admired brands are valuable because of their power to attract customers. Those with higher **brand equity** have greater brand awareness and loyalty on the part of consumers and larger market shares than competing brands (and are perceived to have greater quality). Because a brand adds value to a product, marketers manage brands in order to increase that value. In other words, they build equity in a brand by maintaining or improving brand awareness and perceived quality in much the same manner that you build up ownership equity in your house by maintaining or improving its condition and features.[10]

Table 11.1 shows the rankings of the top global brands according to estimates of each brand's dollar value. It reflects the *earnings boost* that each brand delivers—that is, an index of a brand's power to increase sales and earnings, both present and the future—and shows how much those future earnings are worth today. Only *global brands*—those with sales of at least 20 percent outside the home country—are included.[11]

TABLE 11.1

The World's 10 Most Valuable Brands

Rank	Brand	2001 Brand Value ($ billions)
1	Coca-Cola	$68.9
2	Microsoft	65.1
3	IBM	52.8
4	GE	42.4
5	Nokia	35.0
6	Intel	34.7
7	Disney	32.6
8	Ford	30.1
9	McDonald's	25.3
10	AT&T	22.8

Source: Gerry Khermouch, Stanley Holmes, and Moon Ihlwan, "The Best Global Brands, *Business Week,* August 6, 2001, pages 50–57.

Several factors are involved in brand equity, including *brand loyalty* (which we discussed in Chapter 10) and **brand awareness**—the brand name that first comes to mind when you consider a particular product category. What company, for example, comes to mind when you need to send a document a long way on short notice? For many people, FedEx has the necessary brand awareness.

brand awareness
Extent to which a brand name comes to mind when the consumer considers a particular product category

E-Business Branding It takes a long time to establish national or global brand recognition.[12] After years of work, Cisco Systems Inc. <www.cisco.com>, the network-equipment manufacturer, reached new heights in branding for business-to-business, or B2B, e-commerce. The company's "Cisco Internet Generation" promotional campaign for 2001 stressed reliability and innovation, and in analyzing the campaign, Cisco found that its brand awareness increased by 80 percent (boosting it past rivals Lucent Technologies and Nortel Networks). The campaign also lifted Cisco's reputation as an Internet expert above that of Microsoft, IBM, and Lucent.[13]

The expensive, sometimes fierce struggle for brand recognition is perhaps nowhere more evident than in the current branding battles among dot-com firms. Collectively, the top Internet brands—America Online, Yahoo!, and Amazon.com—spend billions a year even though they have just barely cracked the ranks of top-60 global brands. Even with 210 million visitors each month, Yahoo! still faces formidable competitors in AOL Time Warner and Microsoft. Moreover, the costs of branding promotions are hitting all dot-coms at a time when they are trying to survive the near collapse of the industry.[14] The mounting costs of brand identity mean that many more would-be e-businesses will probably fail.[15]

Types of Brand Names Just about every product has a brand name. Generally, different types of brand names—national, licensed, or private—increase buyers' awareness of the nature and quality of competing products. When consumers are satisfied with a product, marketers try to build brand loyalty among the largest possible segment of repeat buyers.

National Brands **National brands** are produced by, widely distributed by, and carry the name of the manufacturer. These brands (for example, Scotch tape or Scope mouthwash) are often widely recognized by consumers because of national advertising campaigns, and they are, therefore, valuable assets. Because the costs of developing a national brand are high, some companies use a national brand on several related products. Procter & Gamble <www.pg.com> now markets Ivory shampoo, capitalizing on the name of its bar soap and dishwashing liquid.

national brand
Brand-name product produced by, widely distributed by, and carrying the name of a manufacturer

Licensed Brands We have become used to companies (and even personalities) selling the rights to put their names on products. These are called **licensed brands.** The logo "2002 Winter Olympic Games—Salt Lake City" generated millions in revenues for the International Olympic Committee, which licensed its name on license plates, clothing, tableware, coins, and countless other merchandise items. Harley-Davidson's famous logo—emblazoned on boots, eyewear, gloves, purses, lighters, and watches—brings the motorcycle maker more than 150 million annually. Along with brands such as Coors and Ferrari, licensing for character-based brands—Blade, Spiderman, Pokémon—are equally lucrative. Marketers exploit brands because of their public appeal—the image and status that consumers hope to gain by associating with them. The free advertising that comes with some licensing, such as T-shirts and other clothing, is an added bonus.

licensed brand
Brand-name product for whose name the seller has purchased the right from an organization or individual

Private Brands When a wholesaler or retailer develops a brand name and has a manufacturer put it on a product, the resulting name is a **private brand (or private label).** Sears, which carries such lines as Craftsman tools <www.craftsman.com>, Canyon River Blues denim clothing, and Kenmore appliances <www.kenmore.com>, is a well-known seller of private brands.

private brand (or private label)
Brand-name product that a wholesaler or retailer has commissioned from a manufacturer

packaging

Physical container in which a product is sold, advertised, or protected

Packaging Products

With a few exceptions (such as fresh fruits and vegetables and structural steel), products need some form of **packaging.** A package also serves as an in-store advertisement that makes the product attractive, displays the brand name, and identifies features and benefits. It also reduces the risk of damage, breakage, or spoilage, and it increases the difficulty of stealing small products. Recent advances in materials have created added uses for packaging. A paper-based material that doubles as a cooking container has made Budget Gourmet dinners <www.budgetgourmet.com> a low-cost entry in the dinner-entrée market. No-drip bottles have enhanced sales of Clorox bleach <www.clorox.com>.

label

Part of a product's packaging that identifies its name, manufacturer, and contents

Labeling Products

Every product has a **label** on the package. Like packaging, labeling can help market the product. First, it *identifies* the product or the brand, as do the names *Campbell* on a can or *Chiquita* on a banana. Labels also *promote* products by getting consumers' attention; attractive colors and graphics provide visual cues to products that otherwise might be overlooked on the shelf. Finally, the label *describes* the product: It provides information about nutritional content, directions for use, proper disposal, and safety.

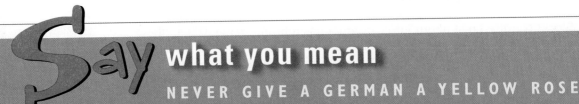

NEVER GIVE A GERMAN A YELLOW ROSE

Good things come in small packages—right? Not in cultures in which the size of the package says a lot about its value. More is better in some places, while big is wasteful in others. Color is important, too. White signifies death and mourning in China, while red means good luck and prosperity. Never give a German an even number of roses; it's bad luck. And don't give a German any number of yellow roses because yellow is associated with jealousy. In Japan, the number four is bad luck; so avoid putting any four things in any single package.

What does all of this superstition have to do with business? Packaging, color, quantity, and the way a product is presented can determine whether something's going to sell or sit on the shelf.

Almost all cultures have an unwritten set of rules when it comes to using words, colors, numbers, and images to sell products. Displaying images of animate objects—humans or otherwise—is frowned on in some Islamic cultures, while in Italy and Brazil, nakedness (or even near nakedness) always sells. Americans like to see their flag on packages; it's a good way of displaying one's patriotism. In some cultures, however, commercializing the national emblem is in bad taste.

If you're giving someone a package in Japan, don't expect the recipient to open it in front of you; it's not polite. But if someone gives you something in the United States, it's rude not show your delight immediately. Be careful of what you call things, too. Even in English-speaking countries, you can get into a lot of trouble by using culturally inaccurate names. If you want to market flip-flops in New Zealand, you'd better call them *jandals.* How about cookies in England? Put *biscuits* on the label.

And finally, speaking of food, beef in a hamburger in India is taboo, but you can't go wrong with a lamb burger in Saudi Arabia. Americans use chopsticks in Thai restaurants, but you won't find too many Thais using them. If you want to keep something cool in Australia, put it in an *eskie*—which is what we in America call a *cooler.* Sometimes, the name says it all, and sometimes it doesn't.

Know the culture and you'll know something about its market. Nothing beats a little research and a lot of cultural sensitivity.

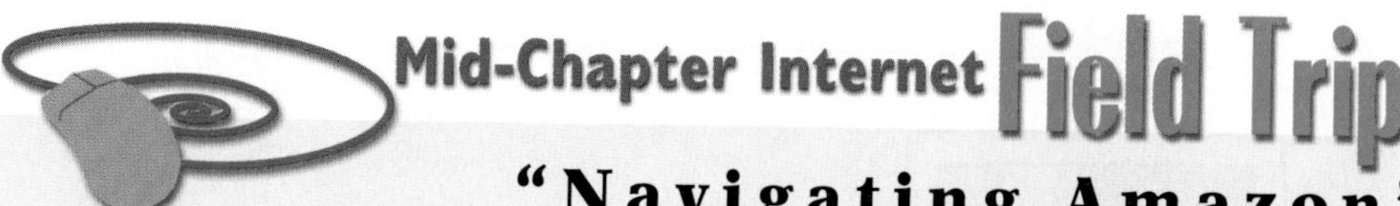

"Navigating Amazon"

In the first part of this chapter, we defined a *product* as a good or service that provides value by meeting a customer's needs, wants, and desires. Collectively, the tangible and intangible *features* and *benefits* of a product are called the *value package*. We also discussed the *product mix*: the group of products that a company makes available for sale. How easy or difficult is it to identify the products of an Internet company? How can we classify its product mix? What does the value package of its major services contain?

Let's look further into these questions by exploring the Web site of a successful Internet company—Amazon.com, at <www.amazon.com>. Scroll to the bottom of the homepage and click on **About** Amazon.com. Now scroll down to **What We Offer.**

❶ Are the general product categories on this page primarily goods or services?

Now go back to the homepage at <www.amazon.com>. At the top-right of the page, click on **See More Stores.**

❷ There are nearly 30 categories of stores listed here. Do any of them provide convenience goods? Shopping goods? Specialty goods?

❸ Are any store categories targeted to business buyers rather than to consumers?

❹ Based on this page of the Web site, how would you describe Amazon.com's product mix?

Return once again to the homepage, and scroll down to near the bottom of the page. Near the line "Turn Your Past Purchases into $$$," click on **Learn More About Selling At** Amazon.com **Today!**

❺ Identify at least six features or benefits that customers gain from Amazon.com's selling-service value package.

To continue your Internet Field Trip, click on www.prenhall.com/giffin

Determining Prices

In product development, managers decide what products a company will offer to customers. In **pricing,** the second major component of the marketing mix, managers decide what the company will get in exchange for its products. In this section, we first discuss the objectives that influence a firm's pricing decisions. Then we describe the major tools that companies use to meet those objectives.

pricing
Process of determining what a company will receive in exchange for its products

Pricing to Meet Business Objectives

Companies often price products to maximize profits, but they often hope to satisfy other **pricing objectives** as well. Some firms want to dominate the market or secure high market share. Pricing decisions are also influenced by the need to compete in the marketplace, by social and ethical concerns, and even by corporate image.[16]

pricing objectives
Goals that producers hope to attain in pricing products for sale

Profit-Maximizing Objectives Pricing to maximize profits is tricky. If prices are set too low, the company will probably sell many units of a product but may miss the chance to make additional profits on each unit (and may even lose money on each exchange). If prices are set too high, the company will make a large profit on each item but will sell fewer units. Again, the firm loses money. It may also be left with excess inventory and may have to reduce or even close production operations. To avoid these problems, companies try to set prices to sell the number of units that will generate the highest possible total profits.

In calculating profits, managers weigh sales revenues against costs for materials and labor. However, they also consider the capital resources (plant and equipment) that the company must tie up to generate a given level of profit. The

"O.K., who can put a price on love? Jim?"

costs of marketing (such as maintaining a large sales staff) can also be substantial. To use these resources efficiently, many firms set prices to achieve a targeted level of return on sales or capital investment.

Pricing for E-Business Objectives When pricing for Internet sales, marketers must consider different kinds of costs and different forms of consumer awareness. Many e-businesses reduce both costs and prices because of the Web's unique marketing capabilities. Because the Web provides a more direct link between producer and consumer, buyers avoid the added costs of wholesalers and retailers.

Another factor is the ease of comparison shopping: Obviously, point-and-click shopping is much more efficient than driving from store to store in search of the best price. Moreover, both consumers and business buyers can get lower prices by joining together for greater purchasing power. Numerous small businesses, for example, are joining forces on the Web to negotiate lower prices for employee healthcare.

Market Share Objectives In the long run, a business must make a profit to survive. Even so, companies often set initially low prices for new products. Because they are willing to accept minimal profits, even losses, to get buyers to try products, they use pricing to establish **market share**—a company's percentage of total market sales for a specific product type.[17] Even with established products, market share may outweigh profit as a pricing objective. For a product such as Philadelphia Brand Cream Cheese, dominating a market means that consumers are more likely to buy because they are familiar with a well-known, highly visible product. Market domination means the continuous sales of more units and thus higher profits even at lower unit prices.

market share

As a percentage, total of market sales for a specific company or product

Other Pricing Objectives In some instances, neither profit maximizing nor market share is the best objective. During difficult economic times, loss containment and survival may become a firm's main objectives. In the mid-1980s, for instance, John Deere priced agricultural equipment low enough to ensure survival in a severely depressed farm economy.

Price-Setting Tools

Whatever a company's objectives, managers must measure the potential impact before deciding on final prices. Two tools may be used for this purpose: *cost-oriented pricing* and *breakeven analysis.* They are combined to determine prices that will allow the company to reach its objectives.

Cost-Oriented Pricing Cost-oriented pricing considers the firm's desire to make a profit and its need to cover production costs. A music store manager would price CDs by calculating the cost of making them available to shoppers. He or she would include the costs of store rent, employee wages, utilities, product displays, insurance, and, of course, the manufacturer's price.

Let's assume that the manufacturer's price is $8 per CD. If the store sells CDs for $8, it won't make any profit. Nor will it make a profit if it sells CDs for $8.50 each—or even $10 or $11. We must charge enough to cover product and other costs in order to make a profit. Together, these factors determine our **markup.** In this case, a reasonable markup of $7 over costs means a $15 selling price. Markup is usually stated as a percentage of selling price and is calculated as follows:

markup

Amount added to an item's cost to sell it at a profit

$$\text{Markup percentage} = \frac{\text{Markup}}{\text{Sales price}}$$

For our CD retailer, the markup percentage is 46.7:

$$\text{Markup percentage} = \frac{\$7}{\$15} = 46.7\%$$

Out of every dollar taken in, $.467 will be gross profit. Out of this profit, the store must still pay rent, utilities, insurance, and all other costs. Markup can also be expressed as a percentage of cost: The $7 markup is 87.5 percent of the $8 cost of a CD ($7/$8).

Breakeven Analysis: Cost-Volume-Profit Relationships Using cost-oriented pricing, a firm will cover **variable costs**—costs that change with the number of units of a product produced and sold. It will also make some money to pay

variable cost

Cost that changes with the quantity of a product produced or sold

In the northeast United States, where more than a third of all houses are heated by oil, homeowners can take out fixed-price contracts in the spring to lock in the heating oil prices they'll pay during the winter. In some years, it's a good bet; in others, it's not. Two years ago, the homeowner receiving this delivery locked in at $1.15 per gallon and saved about $1,000 over the winter because open-market prices went up to $1.80. The next year, she locked in at $1.25 in June. Unfortunately, prices dropped to about 85 cents. "It's like buying insurance," says one analyst. "When you buy a fixed-price deal, you're saying you want the peace of mind."

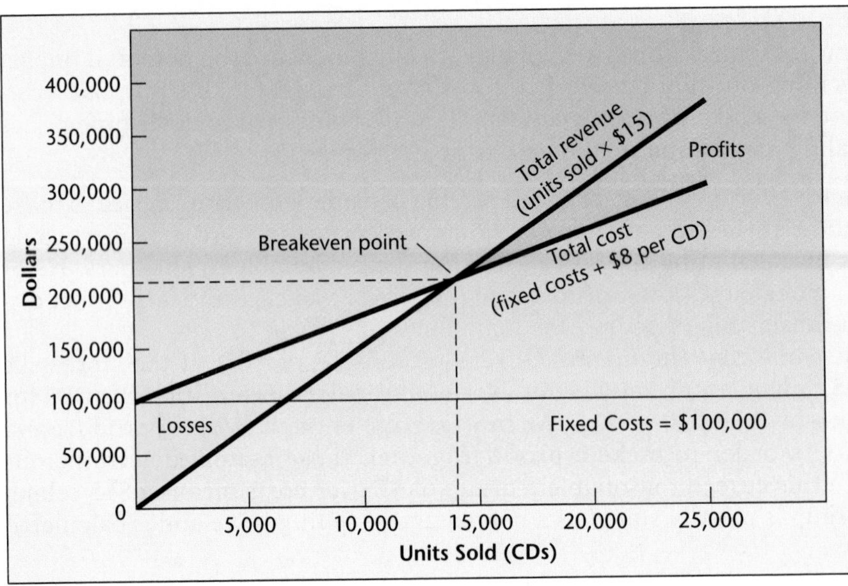

■ FIGURE 11.3
Breakeven Analysis

fixed cost
Cost unaffected by the quantity of a product produced or sold

breakeven analysis
For a particular selling price, assessment of the seller's costs versus revenues at various sales volumes

breakeven point
Sales volume at which the seller's total revenue from sales equals total costs (variable and fixed) with neither profit nor loss

fixed costs: costs that are unaffected by the number of units produced and sold. But how many units must the company sell before *all* costs, both variable and fixed, are covered and it begins to make a profit? What if *too few* units are sold? And what happens if sales are *greater* than expected? The answers depend on costs, selling price, and number of units sold. **Breakeven analysis** assesses costs versus revenues for various sales volumes. It shows, at any particular selling price, the financial result—the amount of loss or profit—for each possible volume of sales.[18]

To continue our music store example, suppose that the *variable cost* for each CD (in this case, the cost of buying the CD from the producer) is $8. This means that the store's annual variable costs depend on how many CDs are sold—the number of CDs sold times the $8 cost for each CD. Say that *fixed costs* for keeping the store open for one year are $100,000. The number of CDs sold does not affect these costs. Costs for lighting, rent, insurance, and salaries are steady no matter how many CDs are sold. Therefore, what we want to know is this: How many CDs must be sold *so that revenues exactly cover both fixed and variable costs*? The answer is the **breakeven point,** which is 14,286 CDs. We arrive at this number through the following equation:

$$\text{Breakeven point (in units)} = \frac{\text{Total fixed costs}}{\text{Price} - \text{Variable}} = \frac{\$100{,}000}{\$15 - \$8} = 14{,}286 \text{ CDs}$$

Look at Figure 11.3. If the store sells fewer than 14,286 CDs, it loses money for the year. If sales go over 14,286, profits grow by $7 for each CD. If the store sells exactly 14,286 CDs, it will cover all its costs but earn zero profit.

Pricing Strategies and Tactics

The pricing tools discussed in the previous section help managers set prices on specific goods. They do not, however, help them decide on pricing philosophies. In this section, we discuss pricing *strategy*—pricing as a planning activity. We then describe some basic pricing *tactics:* ways in which managers implement a firm's pricing strategies.

Self-Check Questions 4–6

*You should now be able to answer Self-Check Questions 4–6**

4. MULTIPLE CHOICE Which of the following is **true** regarding *brand equity* [select one]? (a) A company is more valuable with it than without it. (b) It exists when all of a company's brands are approximately equal in value. (c) It applies to domestic but not to international brands. (d) As a new concept, it has little significance for marketing.

5. MULTIPLE CHOICE At Kroger supermarkets, you will find canned peaches bearing the Kroger *label* alongside those with the Del Monte *brand.* Which of the following is **not true** regarding Kroger peaches [select one]? **(a)** It is a national brand. **(b)** It is a licensed brand. **(c)** It is a private brand. **(d)** The Kroger label is used to simplify the consumer's buying process. **(e)** It carries nutritional information about the product.

6. TRUE/FALSE The purpose of *breakeven analysis* is to identify the volume of sales at which total revenue from sales equals the cost of operations.

*ANSWERS TO SELF-CHECK QUESTIONS 4–6 CAN BE FOUND ON P. AN-7.

Pricing Strategies

How important is pricing as an element in the marketing mix and in the marketing plan? Because pricing has a direct impact on revenues, it is extremely important. Moreover, it is a very flexible tool. It is certainly easier to change prices than to change products or distribution channels. In this section, we focus on the ways in which pricing strategies can result in widely differing prices for very similar products.[19]

Pricing Existing Products A firm has three options for pricing existing products:

- Pricing above prevailing market prices for similar products
- Pricing below market prices
- Pricing at or near market prices

Pricing above the market takes advantage of the common assumption that higher price means higher quality. Curtis Mathes <www.curtismathes.com>, which manufactures consumer electronics, including Internet-enabled televisions, admits that it sells the most expensive TV set in the United States but promotes its product on the grounds that it's worth it. Godiva Chocolates <www.godiva.com> and Patek Phillipe watches <www.patek.com> also price high by promoting prestige and quality images.

In contrast, both Budget <www.budget.com> and Dollar <www.dollar.com> car-rental companies promote themselves as low-priced alternatives to Hertz <www.hertz.com> and Avis <www.avis.com>. Pricing below prevailing market price works if a firm offers a product of acceptable quality while keeping costs below those of competitors.

Pricing New Products When introducing new products, companies must often choose between two pricing policy options: very high prices or very low prices.

price skimming
Setting an initial high price to cover new product costs and generate a profit

penetration pricing
Setting an initial low price to establish a new product in the market

Price skimming—setting an initially high price to cover costs and generate a profit—may generate a large profit on each item sold. The revenue is often needed to cover development and introduction costs. Skimming works only if marketers can convince consumers that a new product is truly different from existing products. In contrast, **penetration pricing**—setting an initially low price to establish a new product in the market—seeks to create consumer interest and stimulate trial purchases.[20]

Fixed versus Dynamic Pricing for E-Business The electronic marketplace has introduced a highly variable pricing system as an alternative to more conventional—and more stable—pricing structures for both consumer and B2B products. *Dynamic pricing* works because information flow on the Web notifies millions of buyers of instantaneous changes in product availability. In order to attract sales that might be lost under traditional fixed-price structures, sellers can alter prices privately, on a one-to-one, customer-to-customer basis.[21]

At present, fixed pricing is still the most common option for cybershoppers. E-tail giant Amazon.com has maintained the practice as the pricing strategy for its 16 million retail items. That situation, however, is beginning to change as dynamic-price challengers, such as eBay (the online, person-to-person auction Web site) and Priceline.com (the online clearinghouse for person-to-business, price negotiation), grow in popularity.

An even more novel approach is taken by NexTag.com Inc. Instead of asking buyers to bid up prices against each other, NexTag asks customers to state the prices that they are willing to pay for products. Merchants then compete for the sales. Unlike Priceline customers, NexTag customers do not commit in advance to sale prices: They wait to see how low the price goes. NexTag gathers offers from merchants, each of whom decides how low to price a product. The customer then chooses the lowest price. According to one expert, NexTag's dynamic pricing may be the trend of the future. "Fixed prices," she points out, "are only a 100-year-old phenomenon. I think they will disappear online, simply because it is possible—cheap and easy—to vary prices online."[22]

The "Wired World" box in this chapter discusses the methods of online pricing used by FreeMarkets, an Internet auction firm.

"Fixed prices will disappear online, simply because it is possible—cheap and easy—to vary prices online."

~Patti Maes
MIT Media Lab

Pricing Tactics

Regardless of its pricing strategy, a company may adopt one or more *pricing tactics,* such as *price lining* or *psychological pricing.* Managers must also decide whether to use *discounting* tactics.

price lining
Setting a limited number of prices for certain categories of products

psychological pricing
Pricing tactic that takes advantage of the fact that consumers do not always respond rationally to stated prices

odd-even pricing
Psychological pricing tactic based on the premise that customers prefer prices not stated in even dollar amounts

Price Lining Companies selling multiple items in a product category often use **price lining**—offering all items in certain categories at a limited number of prices. A department store, for example, carries thousands of products. Setting separate prices for each brand and style of suit, glassware, or couch would take far too much time. With price lining, a store predetermines three or four *price points* at which a particular product will be sold. If price points for men's suits are $175, $250, and $400, all men's suits will be priced at one of these three levels. The store's buyers, therefore, must select suits that can be purchased and sold profitably at one of these three prices.

Psychological Pricing **Psychological pricing** takes advantage of the fact that customers are not completely rational when making buying decisions. One type of psychological pricing, **odd-even pricing,** is based on the theory that customers prefer prices that are not stated in even dollar amounts. Thus customers regard prices of $1,000, $100, $50, and $10 as significantly higher than $999.95, $99.95, $49.95, and $9.95, respectively.

The World of Cyberprice Bidding

Sometimes, a company is better off outsourcing some activities to an e-business rather than doing them all itself. Consider the experience of United Technologies Corp. (UTC) <www.utc.com>. The Connecticut-based conglomerate needed to renew contracts with the eight suppliers from whom it bought the printed circuit boards for UTC elevators, air conditioners, and other products. Before accepting supplier estimates, UTC hoped to cut overall prices by four percent and, based on the going rate, expected to pay out $74 million. It also decided to outsource the entire bidding process to FreeMarkets Inc. <www.freemarkets.com>, an Internet auction company. The results were stunning. FreeMarkets received bids from 29 circuit-board suppliers in the United States, Europe, and Asia. Winning suppliers ultimately signed contracts for $42 million—some 43 percent below UTC's projections.

As an auction marketplace for industrial goods, the Net has changed the rules for price setting by firms selling to industrial customers. Conventional price-setting methods generally follow established patterns:

- Incumbent suppliers have the inside edge for the new contracts.
- Closed bids prohibit suppliers from knowing competitors' prices.
- Only a few suppliers are invited to submit bids.
- If a firm's bid is rejected, it has no opportunity to revise it.

FreeMarkets is changing these patterns and, in so doing, saving client companies an average of 15 percent on the costs of purchases. By 2002, FreeMarkets had helped customers outsource the purchase of more than $30 billion in products, with savings of $6.4 billion. H.J. Heinz expects savings of more than $50 million, and the savings potential in the $5 trillion industrial-parts market is obvious. That's why FreeMarkets is now attracting customers such as Raytheon, Quaker Oats, Emerson Electric, and Owens Corning.

To get suppliers on board, FreeMarkets does not charge sellers for placing bids. Instead, large industrial buyers pay fixed subscription fees of up to $4 million a year. The auction package includes the software and computer technology necessary to conduct the bidding and standardizes all technical requirements. Delivery quantities and schedules, inventory quantities, and quality standards are all clarified before bidding starts. In a recent auction, the client set the most recent price for the parts it needed, $745,000, as a starting point. Twenty-five suppliers instantly saw each bid as it was received and posted at FreeMarkets' communications headquarters, and then an official 20-minute deadline for submitting better prices was set. The low bid dropped to $612,000 after 10 minutes and then to $585,000 with 30 seconds left. When a bid is received in the last minute of regulation time, the auction kicks into a series of 60-second overtime periods. After 13 minutes of overtime bidding, the final price came in at $518,000—31 percent below the client's expectations. In this environment, the fixed-price approach to selling industrial goods is quickly becoming a thing of the past.

Discounting Of course, the price set for a product is not always the price for which it sells. Often, a seller must resort to price reductions—**discounts**—to stimulate sales. Hyatt Hotels <www.hyatt.com> offers discount room prices to stimulate demand during off-peak seasons. Hyatt also offers commercial room discounts for frequent business users and for large-scale events such as conventions, trade shows, and special events. For other products, such as B2B sales of raw materials and equipment, discounts are frequently negotiated for large quantities.

discount
Price reduction offered as an incentive to purchase

International Pricing

When Procter & Gamble (P&G) <www.pg.com> reviewed its prospects for marketing products in new overseas markets, it encountered an unsettling fact:

If the manufacturer (say, JVC or Sony) says a product should retail for $349.00, why does every retailer (such as Best Buy or Amazon.com) sell it for (say) $229.00? Such discrepancies between manufacturer's suggested retail price (M.S.R.P.) and actual retail price are the norm in the electronics industry, and consumers have come to expect discounted prices. "You can't have a discount until there's a price to discount it from," explains an editor at Consumer Reports. *Nor should it be surprising that retailers routinely advertise M.S.R.P. "If they're willing to take a lower margin," says one analyst, "they at least would like the consumer to know it." All of this, of course, raises an interesting question: If no one charges M.S.R.P., is anyone really giving discounts?*

Because it typically priced products to cover hefty R&D costs, profitably priced items were out of reach for too many foreign consumers. The solution was, in effect, to reverse the process. Now P&G conducts research to find out what foreign buyers can afford and then develops products that they can buy. P&G penetrates markets with lower-priced items and encourages customers to trade up as they become able to afford higher-quality products.

As P&G's experience shows, pricing products for other countries is complicated because additional factors are involved. Income and spending trends must be analyzed. In addition, the number of intermediaries varies from country to

Self-Check Questions 7–9

*You should now be able to answer Self-Check Questions 7–9**

7. MULTIPLE CHOICE Suppose your main *pricing objective* is twofold: to establish a new product and to gain market share. The appropriate *pricing strategy* for this objective is [select one]: **(a)** market-share pricing; **(b)** dynamic pricing; **(c)** fixed pricing; **(d)** psychological pricing; **(e)** penetration pricing.

8. TRUE/FALSE With *dynamic pricing for e-business,* buyers do not bid up prices by bidding against one another. Rather, they tell sellers the price that they are willing to pay so that sellers can lower selling prices as they bid against one another to make the sale.

9. TRUE/FALSE Consider the *pricing tactics* in the clothing department of a department store. If the department uses *price lining,* then it cannot also use *odd-even pricing.*

*Answers to Self-Check Questions 7–9 can be found on p. AN-7.

country, as does their effect on a product's cost. Exchange rates change daily, there may be shipping costs, import tariffs must be considered (Chapter 4), and different types of pricing agreements may be permitted.

Another strategy calls for increasing foreign market share by pricing products below cost. As a result, a given product is priced lower in a foreign market than in its home market. As we saw in Chapter 4, this practice is called *dumping,* which is illegal. In recent years, the U.S. International Trade Commission (ITC) <www.usitc.gov> has ruled that Honda and Kawasaki motorcycles were being dumped on the U.S. market, as were computer memory chips. As a result, the United States imposed special tariffs on these products.

Continued from page 308

The ABCs of 18–49s

As it struggles for higher Nielson ratings, ABC, rather than seeking the widest possible audience, is looking for programs that appeal to younger viewers. Why? Because the 18–49 age group generates more lucrative ad revenue than do older audiences. ABC's plight was underscored when its overall ratings dropped to third, behind NBC and CBS, and its ratings among 18–49s to fourth, behind NBC, CBS, and Fox. When *Nightline* and its companion program, *Politically Incorrect,* consistently fell behind Letterman's *Late Show* and Jay Leno's *Tonight Show* among young adults, the signal for change could no longer be ignored.

Sponsors—who, of course, pay for advertising—are the driving force in programming for younger audiences. They want to reach consumers who are hard to reach by other methods, and they are willing to pay premium fees for ads that do the trick. Explains NBC West Coast President Scott Sassa, "As they get older, people watch more TV and are easier to reach, versus the 18-to-24-year-old male, who is impossible to reach." Even so, some networks appear to be attaining—or at least approaching—the impossible. In March 2002, for example, an episode of Fox's *That 70s Show,* a comedy about teenagers, drew just 9.9 million viewers, while CBS's *JAG,* a drama with a military background, boasted 17.1 million. But fewer than 2 million *JAG* viewers were 18-to-34-year-olds, whereas 4.5 million *That 70s Show* viewers fell into the coveted age group. To reach those profitable 18-to-34-year-olds, sponsors will pay more to advertise on *That 70s Show* even though more people watch *JAG.*

When it comes to television programming, it is difficult to separate the design of the programming from the methods that will be used to advertise products to viewers. Marketing researchers know which shows various demographic groups watch, which products they prefer, and which advertising methods will reach them. The challenge, therefore, is to develop new programs that will appeal to the target audience. Let's face it: The 18-to-49 group represents nearly 50 percent of the U.S. population above the age of one. Moreover, they're willing to change brands, and they tend to buy more of the kinds of products that are advertised on television: beer, SUVs, fast food, computers, movies, and soft drinks.

Older viewers, although they typically have more money to spend than their younger counterparts, are more limited in the scope of their purchasing, usually buying such products as travel, retirement plans, and cars. Not surprisingly, they don't watch the same TV shows as 18–49s. Recent ratings, for instance, reveal some important differences in the programs favored by different demographic groups. For example, among 18-to-49-year-olds, NBC's *Will & Grace* ranked 4th (versus 10th among all viewers), while NBC's *Just Shoot Me* ranked 8th (versus 19th among all viewers).

After the heyday of *Who Wants to Be a Millionaire?,* ABC currently finds itself behind rivals NBC and CBS in overall markets—and in fourth place behind Fox among young adults. It comes as no surprise, then, that ABC is focusing its resources with near-crisis intensity on developing new programming that will raise both ratings and ad revenues.

Questions for Discussion

1. How would you describe the pattern of life cycles among TV programs? What social factors affect program life cycles?
2. What methods for new product development are most common in this industry? Cite some examples.
3. Some people might argue that the age and spending considerations in this case seem illogical. ABC, for example, seems intent on attracting younger viewers even though older people have more money. Does that make good business sense? Explain.
4. From a cost-and-profit standpoint, which strategy makes more sense—developing new television programs starting from scratch or buying successful programs from other networks?
5. If you were a network executive, what factors would you consider in pricing programs for various sponsors?

"As they get older, people watch more TV and are easier to reach, versus the 18-to-24-year-old male, who is impossible to reach."

—NBC West Coast President Scott Sassa

Summary of Learning Objectives

1. *Identify a* product, *distinguish between* consumer *and* industrial products, *and explain the* product mix.

A *product* is a good, service, or idea that is marketed to fill consumer needs and wants. Customers buy products because of the *value* that they offer. Thus, a successful product is a **value package** that provides the right *features* and offers the right *benefits*. **Features** are the qualities, tangible and intangible, that a company builds into its products (such as a 12-horsepower motor on a lawn mower). To be sellable, features also must provide *benefits* (say, an attractive lawn).

We can classify products according to two groups of expected buyers: (1) *Consumer products* are divided into three categories that reflect buyer behavior: (i) **Convenience goods** (such as milk and newspapers) and **convenience services** (such as those offered by fast-food restaurants) are inexpensive and purchased often and with little expenditure of time and effort. (ii) **Shopping goods** (such as stereos and tires) and **shopping services** (such as insurance) are more expensive; consumers often compare brands and evaluate alternatives. (iii) **Specialty goods** (such as wedding gowns) and **specialty services** (such as catering for wedding receptions) are important and expensive purchases; consumers usually decide on precisely what they want and accept no substitutes.

(2) Depending on how much they cost and how they will be used, *industrial products* can be divided into two categories: (i) **Expense items** are goods and services consumed within a year by firms producing other goods or services. (ii) **Capital items** are permanent (expensive and long-lasting) goods and services. *Capital services* are those for which long-term commitments are made.

The group of products that a company makes available for sale, whether consumer, industrial, or both, is its **product mix.** A group of similar products intended for similar but not identical buyers who will use them in similar ways is a **product line.** When companies expand beyond existing product lines, the result is *multiple* (or *diversified*) *product lines,* which allow a company to grow rapidly and can help to offset the consequences of slow sales in any one product line.

2. *Describe the* new product development process, *and trace the stages of the* product life cycle.

To expand or diversify product lines, firms must develop and introduce new products. **Speed to market**—the strategy of introducing new products in quick response to customer or market changes—is often key to a product's survival. Faced with competition and shifting consumer preferences, many firms maintain research and development (R&D) departments for exploring new product possibilities. To increase their chances of developing successful new products, many firms adopt some version of a basic seven-step process: (1) *Product ideas:* Searching for ideas for new products. (2) *Screening:* Eliminating all product ideas that do not mesh with the firm's abilities or objectives. (3) *Concept testing:* Using market research to get consumers' input about product benefits and prices. (4) *Business analysis*: Comparing manufacturing costs and benefits to see whether a product meets minimum profitability goals. (5) *Prototype development*: Producing a preliminary version of a product. (6) *Product testing and test marketing*: Going into limited production, testing the product to see if it meets performance requirements, and, if so, selling it on a limited basis. (7) *Commercialization*: Beginning full-scale production and marketing.

In the development of services, there are two important differences in the seven-step model: (1) *Service ideas*: The search for service ideas means defining the **service package:** identifying the tangible and intangible features that characterize the service and stating service specifications. (2) *Service process design*: Instead of prototype development, services require a three-part **service process design.** *Process selection* identifies each step in the service, including the sequence and the timing, as well as *worker requirements* and *facility requirements*.

A product in the market has entered the **product life cycle (PLC):** a series of four stages or phases characterizing its profit-producing life: (1) *Introduction*: Marketers focus on making potential consumers aware of the product and its benefits. (2) *Growth*: Sales begin to climb and the product begins to show a profit. (3) *Maturity*: Although the product earns its highest profit level, increased competition eventually leads to price cutting and lower profits; sales start to fall. (4) *Decline*: Sales and profits are further lost to new products in the introduction stage.

Each aspect of the marketing mix—product, price, place (distribution), promotion—is reexamined during each stage of the life cycle. In this way, many companies can extend product life. Foreign markets offer three approaches to longer life cycles: (1) In **product extension,** an existing product is marketed globally instead of just domestically. (2) With **product adaptation,** the basic product is modified to give it greater appeal in different countries. (3) **Reintroduction** means reviving for new markets products that are becoming obsolete in older ones.

3. *Explain the importance of* branding, packaging, *and* labeling.

Branding is a process of using symbols to communicate the qualities of a particular product made by a particular producer. There are three types of brand names: (1) **National brands** are produced and widely distributed by and carry the name of the manufacturer; they are often widely recognized because of national advertising campaigns. (2) **Licensed brands** are brand names purchased from the organizations or individuals who own them. (3) When a wholesaler or retailer develops a brand name and has a manufacturer place it on a product, the product name is a **private brand (or private label).** Brands with high **brand equity** are valuable assets because of their power to attract customers.

With a few exceptions, a product needs some form of **packaging**—a physical container in which it is sold, advertised, or protected. A package makes the product attractive, displays the brand name, and identifies features and benefits. It also reduces the risk of damage, breakage, or spoilage, and it lessens the likelihood of theft. Every product has a **label** on its package that identifies its name, manufacturer, and contents; like packaging, labeling can help market a product.

4. *Identify the various* pricing objectives *that govern* pricing decisions *and describe the* price-setting tools *used in making these decisions.*

In **pricing,** managers decide what the company will get in exchange for its products. **Pricing objectives** refer to the goals that producers hope to attain as a result of pricing decisions. These objectives can be divided into two major categories:

(1) *Pricing to maximize profits*: If prices are too low, the company will probably sell many product units but miss the chance to make additional profits on each one. If prices are set too high, it will make a large profit on each unit but will sell fewer units. In calculating profits, managers weigh sales revenues against costs for materials and labor. They also consider the costs of capital resources (such as equipment and sales staffs) needed to generate a given level of profit. Many e-businesses are lowering both costs and prices because the Web provides a more direct link between producer and consumer; buyers thus avoid the costs entailed by wholesalers and retailers.

(2) *Market share objectives*: Many companies are willing to accept minimal profits, even losses, to get buyers to try products. They may use pricing to establish **market share**—a company's percentage of the total market sales for a specific product type. Sometimes, neither profit maximizing nor market share is the best objective. During difficult economic times, loss containment and survival may be the main objectives.

Managers must measure the potential impact before deciding on final prices. For this purpose, they use two basic tools (which are often combined): (1) *Cost-oriented pricing*: This tool considers both the firm's desire to make a profit and need to cover production costs. Managers price products by calculating the cost of making them available to shoppers (including rent, wages, and manufacturer's cost). When they total these costs and add a figure for profit, they arrive at a **markup.**

(2) *Breakeven analysis*: Using cost-oriented pricing, a firm will cover its **variable costs:** costs that change with the number of goods or services produced or sold. It will also make some money to pay **fixed costs:** costs that are unaffected by the number of goods or services produced or sold. **Breakeven analysis** assesses total costs versus revenues for various sales volumes. It shows, at any particular sales price, the financial result—the amount of loss or profit—for each possible sales volume. The number of units that must be sold for total revenue to equal total costs is the **breakeven point,** which results in neither a profit nor a loss.

5. *Discuss* pricing strategies *and* tactics *for both existing and new products.*

Pricing tools such as breakeven analysis help managers set prices on specific goods but do not help in setting pricing *strategy,* which is a planning activity. Pricing strategy is important because pricing has a direct impact on revenues and is very flexible.

There are three options for *pricing existing products:* (1) *Pricing above the market* takes advantage of the common assumption that higher price means higher quality. (2) *Pricing below the market* works if a firm can offer a product of acceptable quality while keeping costs below those of higher priced competitors. (3) *Pricing at or near market prices* is often another option.

Companies *pricing new products* must often choose between two pricing policy options: (1) **Price skimming**—setting an initially high price to cover costs and generate a profit—may allow a firm to earn a large profit on each item sold; marketers must convince consumers that a product is truly different from existing products. (2) **Penetration pricing**—setting an initially low price to establish a new product in the market—seeks to generate consumer interest and stimulate trial purchase.

In the electronic marketplace, *dynamic pricing* works because the flow of information on the Web notifies millions of buyers of instantaneous changes in product availability. In order to attract sales that might be lost under traditional fixed-price structures, this strategy allows sellers to alter prices privately, on a one-to-one, customer-to-customer basis.

Regardless of its pricing strategy, a company may adopt *pricing tactics:* (1) Companies selling multiple items in a product category often use **price lining,** offering all items in certain categories at a limited number of prices. With price lining, a store predetermines three or four *price points* at which a product will be sold. (2) **Psychological pricing** takes advantage of the fact that customers are not completely rational when making buying decisions. **Odd-even pricing** is based on the theory that customers prefer prices not stated in even-dollar amounts. (3) Often a seller must offer price reductions—**discounts**—to stimulate sales.

KEY TERMS

feature (p. 308)
value package (p. 309)
convenience good/service (p. 309)
shopping good/service (p. 309)
specialty good/service (p. 310)
expense item (p. 310)
capital item (p. 310)
product mix (p. 310)
product line (p. 310)
speed to market (p. 312)
service package (p. 312)
service process design (p. 313)
product life cycle (PLC) (p. 313)
product extension (p. 314)
product adaptation (p. 314)
reintroduction (p. 315)
branding (p. 315)
brand equity (p. 316)
brand awareness (p. 317)
national brand (p. 317)
licensed brand (p. 317)
private brand (or private label) (p. 317)
packaging (p. 318)
label (p. 318)
pricing (p. 319)
pricing objectives (p. 319)
market share (p. 320)
markup (p. 321)
variable cost (p. 321)
fixed cost (p. 322)
breakeven analysis (p. 322)
breakeven point (p. 322)
price skimming (p. 324)
penetration pricing (p. 324)
price lining (p. 324)
psychological pricing (p. 324)
odd-even pricing (p. 324)
discount (p. 325)

QUESTIONS AND EXERCISES

Questions for Review

1. What are the various classifications of consumer and industrial products? Give an example of a good and a service for each category other than those discussed in the text.
2. List the four stages in the product life cycle, and discuss some of the ways in which a company can extend product life cycles.
3. Explain how brand names and packaging can be used to foster brand loyalty.
4. How do cost-oriented pricing and breakeven analysis help managers measure the potential impact of prices?
5. What is the overall goal of price skimming? Of penetration pricing?

Questions for Analysis

6. How would you expect the branding, packaging, and labeling of convenience, shopping, and specialty goods to differ? Why? Give examples to illustrate your answers.
7. Suppose that a small publisher selling to book distributors has fixed operating costs of $600,000 each year and variable costs of $3.00 per book. How many books must the firm sell to break even if the selling price is $6.00? If the company expects to sell 50,000 books next year and decides on a 40-percent markup, what will the selling price be?
8. Suppose your company produces industrial products for other firms. How would you go about determining the prices of your products? Describe the method you would use to arrive at a pricing decision.

Application Exercises

9. Interview the manager of a local manufacturing firm. Identify the company's different products according to their positions in the product life cycle.
10. Select a product with which you are familiar, and analyze various possible pricing objectives for it. What information would you want to have if you were to adopt a profit-maximizing objective? A market-share objective? An image objective?

Building Your Business Skills

WHAT'S BRAND NEWS?

This exercise enhances the following SCANS workplace competencies: demonstrating basic skills, demonstrating thinking skills, exhibiting interpersonal skills, and working with information.

Goal

To encourage students to evaluate the ways in which branding affects their personal awareness of products

Method

Step 1

Working individually, examine a recent Sunday newspaper from a nearby large city. Focusing on paid advertisements, list the brands of various products. For example, you may see food-store ads, a Saturn ad, an ad for an HMO, and so on. Draw up a *selective* list of the various brands that are featured in the ads, including only those that attract your attention for one reason or another. Then divide the items on your list into two columns—national brands and private brands.

Step 2

Join with three or four classmates to compare lists. Analyze the extent to which private brands versus national brands are more prominent in the newspaper. Which brands are more familiar to you? Less familiar? Discuss the reasons for your familiarity or nonfamiliarity with specific brands.

Follow-Up Questions

1. What do you think motivated the makers of national brands on your list to advertise in this newspaper rather than elsewhere? For those brands, are you influenced by brand reputation or advertising?
2. Can you say what attracted you to select the private brands that you put on your list? Were you influenced mainly by price? By visual appeal? Were other factors involved?
3. Find a national brand that appears on the list of just one group member. Given the fact that only one member listed a brand that other members ignored, what factors were responsible for the different choices?
4. Based on this exercise, are you likely to change the way you look at brands? Will you be attracted more to national brands or to private brands? Explain your answer.

Exercising Your Ethics

THE COLLECTIVE CONSCIENCE

The Situation

Designing a new product, whether a service or a good, involves collective creative thinking; and original designs—the results of that collective thinking—become the property of either the designer or the organization that sponsors the design project. Because numerous people may be involved in any new product-development effort, numerous ethical issues can arise. This exercise encourages you to examine some of the ethical issues that can surface when an advertising theme is developed by a team.

The Dilemma

Suppose the term project for your introduction-to-business course is to develop an advertising product: Your four-person team must create an original advertising campaign for a hypothetical client who is launching a revolutionary new bird feeder. Your report to this client must specify a national ad theme designed to reach a targeted group of consumers. It must also present a plan for selecting advertising media—magazines, television, and radio—along with a proposed advertising budget. You should also include advertising content—samples of phrases for radio scripts, graphics for printed media, and concepts for television visuals. Your project report, including professional-quality printing along with photos and color graphics, is due on the last day of class. The project counts as 50 percent of your course grade.

Let's say that after several agonizing meetings, an exciting theme finally emerges. One team member proposes an extraterrestrial setting. Floating in outer space are five astronauts, each holding the client's bird feeder in outstretched hands. On the astronauts' shoulders sits a variety of otherworldly birds, all of them admiring the bird feeder of the future.

Once the theme is accepted, the rest of the project falls into place over the next eight weeks, during which each team member carries out specific assignments. One of your end-of-semester tasks is to collect all of the team's materials from other members, assemble the parts into a coherent presentation, and type up the final report. On the weekend before the project is due, your mother proofreads your report for spelling errors and says, "I like your astronaut theme; I've seen it before in a magazine ad for women's undergarments." Thumbing through an upscale fashion magazine, she shows you an identical ad, except that where yours features birds, the magazine ad displays fashionable lingerie. Your team's theme, it seems, isn't so original after all.

Questions for Discussion

1. As a member acting in the interests of your team, what are your ethical obligations, if any, in this situation?
2. From an ethical standpoint, what actions should you take? What actions should the team take.
3. Do you think that the ethical lessons learned from this situation have any application to product-development activities in the business world? Explain.

Crafting Your Business Plan

SPICING UP THE PRODUCT DEVELOPMENT PROCESS

The Purpose of the Assignment

1. To familiarize students with certain product development and product pricing issues that a sample firm addresses in developing its business plan within the framework of *Business PlanPro* (*BPP*) software package.
2. To demonstrate how four chapter topics—product line, product pricing, breakeven analysis, and packaging—affect the *BPP* planning environment.

Assignment

After reading Chapter 11 in the textbook, open the BPP software and look around for information about product line, product pricing, packaging, and breakeven analysis as they apply to a sample firm, a salsa manufacturer called Salvadore's Sauces *(Salvadore's, Inc.). To find* Salvadore's, *do the following:*

Open the *Business PlanPro*. If you are asked if you want to "create a new business plan" or to "open an existing plan," select "create a new business plan" (even though you are not going to create a plan at this time). You will then be taken to the *Business PlanPro EasyPlan Wizard*. On the screen, click on the option entitled **Research It.** You will then be presented with a new list of options, including **Sample Plan Browser.** After clicking on the **Sample Plan Browser**, scan its alphabetical list of sample plans and double-click on **Salsa Manufacturer**, which is the location for *Salvadore's Sauces*. The screen you are looking at is the introduction page for the *Salvadore's Sauces* business plan. Next, scroll down from this page until you reach the **Table of Contents** for the *Salvadore's Sauces* business plan.

Now respond to the following items:

1. Is Salvadore's Sauces planning to offer consumer products or industrial products? How would you describe its product line? [Sites to see in *BPP* (for this item): In the Table of Contents page, click on **4.0 Market Analysis Summary,** and read its contents. After returning to the Table of Contents page, click on **4.1 Market Segmentation.** After returning to the Table of Contents page, click on each of the following in turn: **5.1 Marketing Strategy, 5.2 Sales Strategy,** and **5.3 Strategic Alliances.**]
2. How would you describe the pricing strategy that Salvadore's Sauces plans to use? [Sites to see in *BPP:* In the Table of Contents page, click on **5.2.1 Sales Forecast** and read it. After returning to the Table of Contents page, click on **5.1.1 Pricing Strategy.**]
3. Suppose you want to help Salvadore's Sauces set prices on the basis of cost-oriented pricing. Does the plan contain enough data to allow this method of pricing? Explain why or why not. [Sites to see in *BPP:* In the Table of Contents page, click on and read **7.4 Projected Profit and Loss** (including the **Table: Profit and Loss**).]
4. What role does packaging play in Salvadore's plan? [Sites to see in *BPP*: In the Table of Contents page, click on **4.3 Industry Analysis.** See also **4.3.1 Industry Participants.** After returning to the Table of Contents page, click on each of the following: **3.0 Products** and **3.2 Competitive Comparison.**]
5. Explain how product pricing relates to breakeven analysis in Salvadore's plan. [Sites to see in *BPP:* In the Table of Contents page, click on **7.3 Breakeven Analysis.**]

Video Exercise

SENDING PRODUCTS INTO SPACE: MCCI

Learning Objectives

The purpose of this video is to help you

1. Understand why and how a company develops specialized products for organizational customers.
2. Describe some of the decisions that a company faces in pricing specialized products under long-term contracts for organizational customers.
3. Understand how a company can use quality to differentiate its products.

Synopsis

MCCI, a 55-person company based in California, designs and produces highly specialized products customized to the detailed specifications of organizational customers. When a telecommunications company or government agency needs a radio frequency filter for a new satellite, it calls on MCCI to design one especially for the product in question. Custom-made from tiny components and precious materials, the filter must be top-quality to withstand powerful vibration and temperature extremes in space. It must also continue to perform exactly as promised for 20 years. Because some contracts cover products purchased over a decade or more, MCCI must carefully assess the risks of designing a product and pricing it for long-term profit. Yet speed is also a factor: To win a contract from an important customer, MCCI once developed a new product over a single weekend.

Discussion Questions

1. *For analysis:* Are MCCI's products capital or expense items? How do you know?
2. *For analysis:* Given its in-depth knowledge of its market, why does MCCI develop new products for individual customers rather than creating new products to meet general industry needs?
3. *For application:* The price of gold can fluctuate widely, depending on market conditions. How might fluctuations affect MCCI's pricing decisions for products with components made from gold?
4. *For application:* What factors must MCCI analyze as it prices a custom-designed product?
5. *For debate:* At the start of a long-term contract, should MCCI price a product to return little or no profit in the hope that the firm can generate profit from products sold to the customer later in the contract period? Support your chosen position.

Online Exploration

One of MCCI's products went to Mars on NASA's Sojourner Rover. What other kinds of goods and services does NASA buy? Visit NASA's procurement Web site at <acquisition.jpl.nasa.gov> and follow the links to find out about some of the proposal requests posted by the agency. Do any contain documents with questions and answers? Why would MCCI need to read such a document before preparing a proposal to develop a product for NASA? Now examine the listing of other links. How could MCCI use information from the sites on this list in planning a product for NASA?

CHAPTER 12

Distributing Products

After reading this chapter, you should be able to:

1. Explain the *distribution mix,* the different *channels of distribution,* and different *distribution strategies.*
2. Explain the differences between *merchant wholesalers* and *agents/brokers* and explain the activities of *e-intermediaries.*
3. Identify the different types of *retailing* and *retail stores.*
4. Define *physical distribution* and describe the major activities in *warehousing* operations.
5. Compare the five basic forms of *transportation* and explain how distribution can be used as a marketing strategy.

Changing Channels on the Local News

Unlike retailers of most products, news services can't choose their distribution channels. Most of us don't think twice about how we get our local news—whether through broadcast or print media. But if we take a closer look at the methods by which the news gets to us, we find the industry in the throes of a controversy that could change both the format and the content of the information we receive. There are conflicting views on how the news should be delivered to local markets, and numerous issues are involved—industry history, federal regulation, technological change, the proliferation of distribution media, and questions of corporate responsibility.

A core concern is anchored in the U.S. Constitution—namely, the twofold proposition that (1) an informed public must have access to unfettered news and information and that (2) we need constant vigilance to protect the flow of news and information, whether from government, business, or any other institution. Long-standing Federal Communication Commission <www.fcc.gov> regulations against cross-ownership, the FCC's so-called duopoly rules, require that local media sources—radio, television, newspapers—be owned by different firms. The goal, of course, is to ensure independent reporting. Current rules, for example, bar a company from owning two TV stations in a single market in which there are fewer than eight independently owned stations. The FCC also forbids ownership by one firm of a newspaper and a TV station in the same market.

Thus, the media that make up the distribution mix of most companies are highly regulated. Some regulations, however, are now being challenged. In bringing court action against the FCC, some industry members argue that the news business is under significant economic pressure that has only been worsened by the outdated policies of the FCC. They cite the FCC's seemingly arbitrary refusal to acknowledge that newer channels of distribution—notably cable TV, satellite broadcasting, and the Internet—present just as much competition as the traditional outlets of radio, newsprint, and network TV.

These complaints have been supported in a string of court decisions, most recently in February 2002 by a U.S. Court of Appeals ruling that the FCC must justify (or do away with) its bans on media cross-ownership. Plaintiffs argued that when assessing the level of competition in a given market, the FCC considered only traditional distribution channels and ignored the newer technologies that have dramatically changed the industry's environment. The court agreed. FCC policy, it ruled, is not in the public interest. The recent rulings were welcome news for the plaintiffs—Sinclair Broadcast Group Inc. <www.sbgi.net>, News Corporation <www.newscorp.com>, Viacom <www.viacom.com>, and AOL Time Warner <www.aoltimewarner.com>—which, like other media companies, are eager to add more stations to their broadcast networks.

Not everyone, however, favors relaxing ownership rules. Some insiders insist that proposed changes would only further concentrate channel ownership—a situation that conflicts directly with the broader public interest. The recent rulings, warns Frank Blethen, CEO and publisher of the *Seattle Times* <http://seattletimesnwsource.com>, are not a good omen. "This is a dangerous moment for American democracy," warns Blethen. Relaxed rules "will dramatically accelerate the country's already narrow concentration of media control, as well as the channels of information distribution, into the hands of an elite few. It will directly lead to the loss of an independent press and the diversity of voices essential to the survival of a

"We would love to own a TV station in Seattle. But we believe it would be bad public policy if we were allowed to do so."

~Frank Blethen
***SEATTLE TIMES* PUBLISHER**

democracy." Blethen argues that the increasing concentration of media ownership is motivated by profit. "From a purely business perspective," he admits, "we would love to own a TV station in Seattle. And, yes, it would significantly increase the value of our company. But we don't believe we need it to survive and compete. Indeed, we believe it would be bad public policy if we were allowed to do so."

But with calls for change ringing through the courts, most media-industry observers expect the FCC to repeal such rules as the prohibition of single ownership of community newspapers and broadcast TV stations. When they get their wish, will controlling companies act responsibly in influencing the content of the news they deliver? Or will they promote the kind of self-serving manipulation of information that inspired FCC regulations against cross-ownership in the first place? Stay tuned.

Our opening story continues on page 355.

Just as companies in broadcasting use various media for delivering news, firms in other industries use different channels to get products to customers. As the third element in the marketing mix, distribution (place) takes many forms. In this chapter, we will describe those forms and explain the importance of distribution in the marketing process.

The Distribution Mix

We have already seen that a company needs a good *product mix.* But the success of any product also depends on its **distribution mix**: the combination of distribution channels by which a firm gets products to end users. In this section, we will consider some of the many factors in the distribution mix. First, we will look at the role of the target audience and explain the need for intermediaries. We will then discuss basic distribution strategies. Finally, we will consider some special issues in channel relationships—namely, conflict and leadership.

distribution mix
The combination of distribution channels by which a firm gets its products to end users

Intermediaries and Distribution Channels

Once called *middlemen,* **intermediaries** help to distribute a producer's goods, either by moving them or by providing information that stimulates their movement from sellers to customers. **Wholesalers** are intermediaries who sell products to other businesses for resale to final consumers. **Retailers** sell products directly to consumers. While some firms rely on independent intermediaries, others employ their own distribution networks and sales forces.[1]

intermediary
Individual or firm that helps to distribute a product

wholesaler
Intermediary who sells products to other businesses for resale to final consumers

retailer
Intermediary who sells products directly to consumers

Distribution of Consumer Products A **distribution channel** is the path that a product follows from producer to end user. Figure 12.1 shows how eight primary distribution channels can be identified according to the kinds of channel members involved in getting products to buyers. Note first that all channels begin with a producer and end either with a consumer or an industrial (business) user. Channels 1 through 4 are most often used to distribute consumer products.

distribution channel
Network of interdependent companies through which a product passes from producer to end user

Channel 1: Direct Distribution of Consumer Products In a **direct channel**, the product travels from the producer to the consumer without intermediaries. Using their own sales forces, companies such as Avon, Fuller Brush, and Tupperware use this channel.

direct channel
Distribution channel in which a product travels from producer to consumer without intermediaries

This direct channel is also prominent on the Internet for thousands of products ranging from books and automobiles to insurance and vacation packages sold directly by producers to consumers. The Gateway 2000 Internet storefront <www.gateway.com>, for example, handles annual sales of more than $6 billion in computers and related products for home and workplace. Likewise, you can purchase airline reservations directly from such Internet sites as American Airlines <www.aa.com>, Southwest <www.southwestairlines.com>, and Delta <www.deltaairlines.com>.

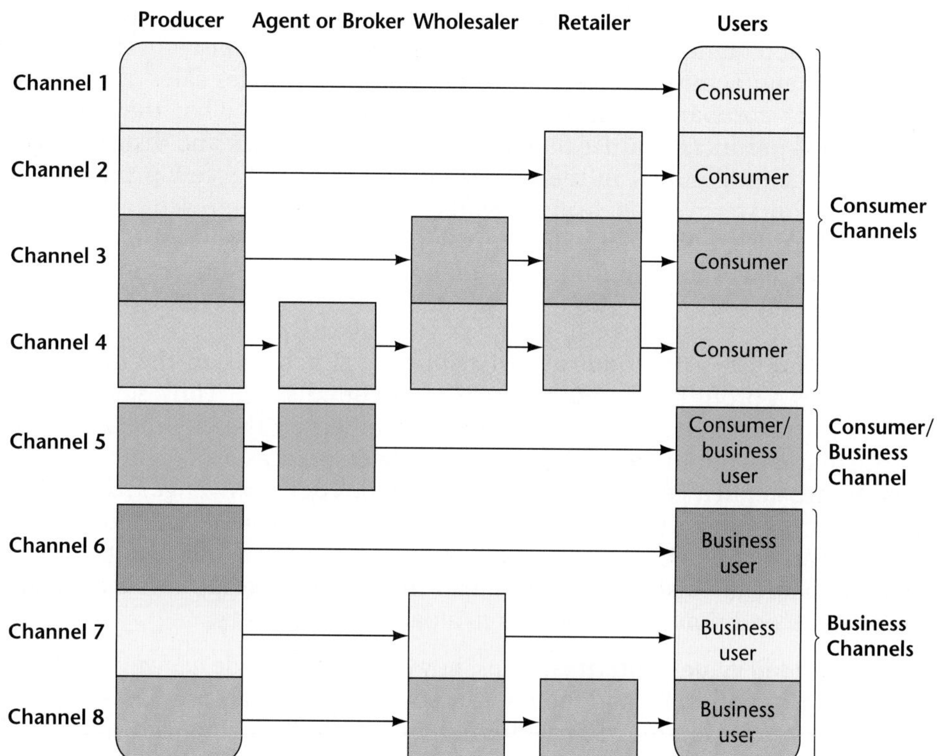

FIGURE 12.1
Channels of Distribution

Channel 2: Retail Distribution of Consumer Products In Channel 2, producers distribute products through retailers. Goodyear, for example, maintains its own system of retail outlets. Levi's has its own outlets but also produces jeans for other retailers such as Gap Inc. Many retailers offer Internet sales. Grocery shoppers, for example, can browse the electronic aisles of the Kroger Co. <www.kroger.com>, one of America's largest grocery chains. Kroger's grocery list is actually compiled and delivered under agreements with specialty service providers, such as PeaPod.com, which partner with the retail chain in delivering goods to consumers.[2]

Channel 3: Wholesale Distribution of Consumer Products Once the most widely used method of nondirect distribution, Channel 2 requires a large amount of floor space, both for storing merchandise and for displaying it in stores. Faced with the rising cost of store space, many retailers found that they could not afford both retail and storage space. Thus, wholesalers entered the distribution network to take over more of the storage function. The combination convenience store/gas station is an example of Channel 3. With approximately 90 percent of the space used to display merchandise, only 10 percent is left for storage and office facilities. Wholesalers store merchandise and restock it frequently.

Wholesalers are prominent in e-commerce because Internet stores give customers access to information and product displays 24 hours a day. Buyers can also place orders electronically and confirm delivery almost instantaneously. In the diamond industry, retail companies can access wholesalers such as Diasqua Group <www.gemkey.com/diasqua>, visually examine diamonds, place orders, and receive delivery dates.

Channel 4: Distribution Through Sales Agents or Brokers Channel 4 uses **sales agents**, or **brokers**, who represent producers and sell to wholesalers, retailers, or both. They receive commissions based on the prices of the goods they sell.

sales agent/broker
Independent intermediary who usually represents many manufacturers and sells to wholesalers or retailers

Lafferty and Co. Food Brokers Inc. <www.laffertyandco.com> represents several prominent food manufacturers—Pillsbury, Old El Paso, Sunkist—in the Midwest. To relieve manufacturers of sales activities, Lafferty arranges sales of their products to other companies, allowing manufacturers to do what they do best—process food products—rather than divert resources to sales and distribution.

Agents generally deal in the related product lines of a few producers and work on a long-term basis. Travel agents, for example, represent airlines, car-rental companies, and hotels. In contrast, brokers match sellers and buyers as needed. The real estate industry relies on brokers to match buyers and sellers of property.

The Pros and Cons of Nondirect Distribution Each link in the distribution chain makes a profit by charging a markup or commission. Thus, nondirect distribution means higher prices: The more members in the channel—the more intermediaries—the higher the final price. Calculated as a percentage of cost, *markups* are applied each time a product is sold. They may range from 10 to 40 percent for manufacturers, from 2 to 25 percent for wholesalers, and from 5 to 100 percent for retailers. *E-intermediaries*—wholesalers and agents who use Internet channels—also charge markups. In general, markup levels depend on competitive conditions and practices in a particular industry.

Creating Added Value Intermediaries, however, can provide *added value* by saving consumers both time and money. Moreover, the value accumulates with each link in the supply chain. Intermediaries provide time-saving information and make the right quantities of products available where and when you need them. Consider Figure 12.2, which illustrates the problem of making chili without benefit of a common intermediary—the supermarket. As a consumer/buyer, you would obviously spend a lot more time, money, and energy if you tried to gather all the ingredients from one retailer at a time. In any case, even if we did away with intermediaries, you would not eliminate either their tasks or the costs entailed by performing those tasks. They exist because they do necessary jobs in cost-efficient ways.

"On the one hand, eliminating the middleman would result in lower costs, increased sales, and greater consumer satisfaction; on the other hand, we're the middleman."

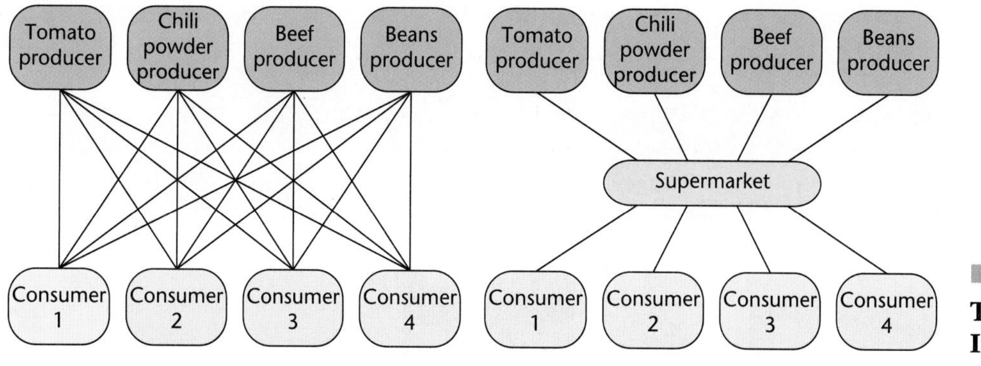

FIGURE 12.2
The Value-Adding Intermediary

Channel 5: Distribution by Agents to Consumers and Businesses Channel 5 differs from previous channels in two ways: (1) An agent functions as the sole intermediary and (2) the agent distributes to both consumers and business customers. Consider Vancouver-based Uniglobe Travel International, a travel agent representing airlines, car-rental companies, and hotels. Uniglobe books flight reservations and arranges complete recreational-travel services for consumers. The firm also services companies whose employees need lodging and transportation for business travel.

E-commerce works well in this channel because it directly informs more people about products. At Uniglobe, for instance, a new online subsidiary (<www.uniglobe.com>) combines a high-tech Web site with an old-fashioned human touch in a specialty market—booking cruises. Customers can scan for destinations, cruise lines, restaurants, and cabin locations for any of 70 ships. Using Uniglobe's online chat function, travelers can simply open a window to speak in real time with one of 75 cruise specialists. The strategy has paid off: Uniglobe.com leads the market in online cruise bookings.[3]

Distribution of Business Products Industrial channels are important because every company is also a customer that buys other companies' products. The Kellogg Co. <www.kelloggs.com> buys grain to make breakfast cereals, and Humana Inc. <www.humana.com>, a chain of for-profit hospitals, buys medicines and other supplies to provide medical services. **Industrial (business) distribution** is the network of channel members involved in the flow of manufactured goods to business customers. Unlike consumer products, business products are traditionally distributed through Channels 6, 7, and 8, as shown in Figure 12.1.

industrial (business) distribution
Network of channel members involved in the flow of manufactured goods to business customers

Channel 6: Direct Distribution of Business Products Most business goods are sold directly by the manufacturer to the industrial buyer. Lawless Container Corp., for instance, produces packaging containers for direct sale to Fisher-Price (toys), Dirt Devil (vacuum cleaners), Peak antifreeze, and Mr. Coffee (coffeemakers). Many manufacturers maintain **sales offices** as contact points with customers and headquarters for salespeople.

sales office
Office maintained by a manufacturer as a contact point with its customers

Intermediaries are often unnecessary because goods distributed through Channel 6 are usually purchased in large quantities. In some cases, however, brokers or agents may enter the chain between manufacturers and buyers. Finally, e-commerce technologies have also popularized Channel 6. Dell Computer Corp. <www.dell.com>, a pioneer in direct Internet sales, now gets about two-thirds of its $32 billion in sales from other businesses, governments, and schools.[4]

Channel 7: Wholesale Distribution of Industrial Products Wholesalers function in only a few industrial channels. Brokers and agents are even rarer. Channel 7 mostly handles accessory equipment (computers, fax machines, and other office

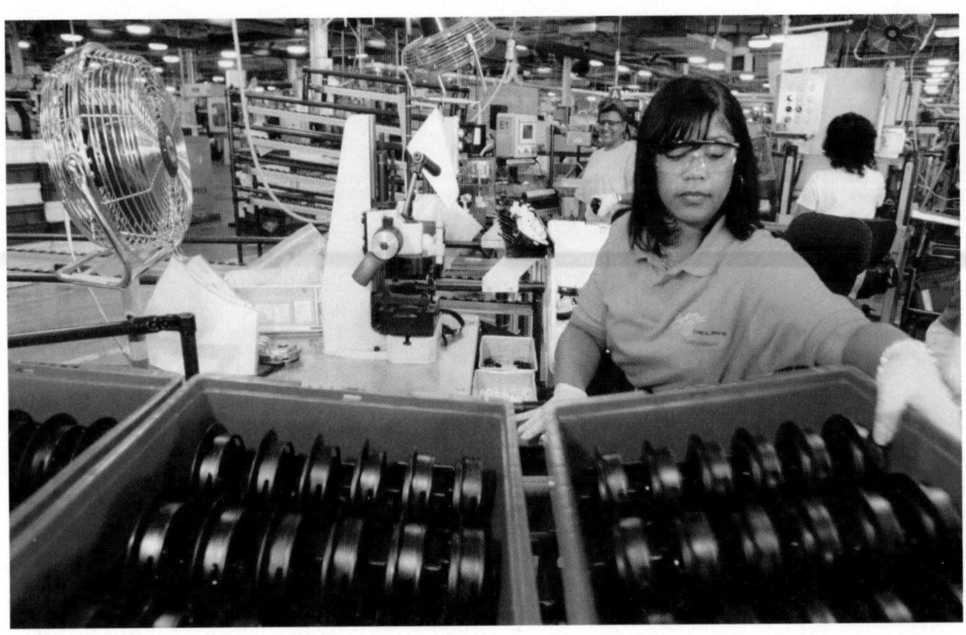

At the Flint, Michigan, plant of Delphi Automotive Systems <www.delphi.com>, *the world's largest auto parts supplier, Jessica V. Prince assembles fuel pumps according to a process that she helped engineers and consultants design. Radically increased efficiency has become an absolute necessity in the direct distribution of auto parts to car makers: There are now about 12,000 auto parts makers, down from 30,000 in 1980, and the number may plummet to about 200 in just a few decades.*

equipment) and supplies (floppy disks, pencils, copier paper). Manufacturers produce these items in large quantities, but companies buy them in small quantities. For example, few companies order truckloads of paper clips. Intermediaries, then, help end users by breaking down large quantities into smaller sales units. Thus, the traditional office-supply store wholesales a variety of goods to other businesses.

Channel 8: Wholesale Distribution to Business Retailers In some industries, the roles of channel members are changing. In the office-products industry, Channel 7 is being displaced by a channel that looks very much like Channel 3 for consumer products: Instead of buying office supplies from wholesalers (Channel 7), many businesses are now shopping at office discount stores such as Staples, Office Depot, and Office Max. Before selling to large companies, these warehouse-like superstores originally targeted retail consumers and small businesses that bought supplies at retail stores (and at retail prices). Today, however, small-business buyers shop at discount stores designed for industrial users, selecting from 7,000 items at prices 20 to 75 percent lower than retail.

E-commerce is fueling the rapid growth in the office-superstore industry. In the United States, Staples Inc., the office-superstore pioneer, relies on e-business for rapid growth. In Japan, customers of the largest office supplier, Askul <club.askul.co.jp>, can shop the Internet in real time and receive orders within 24 hours. Askul can charge low prices because it locates high-tech distribution warehouses on cheap land and uses electronic transactions to reduce the workforce needed for face-to-face selling.

Distribution Strategies

Selecting an appropriate distribution network is a strategic decision: It determines both the amount and cost of *market coverage* that a product gets—that is how many of any kind of intermediary will be used.[5] Generally, strategy depends on the type of product and the degree of market coverage that is most effective in getting it to the greatest number of customers. Marketers strive to make a product accessible in just enough locations to satisfy customers' needs. You can buy milk, for instance, in numerous retail outlets, but there is only one Rolls-Royce

KEEPING CHANNELS CLEAR

Merely securing a distributor is no guarantee of success in any market. Distributors often carry a huge range of products and usually have different incentives for getting different products to market. Using intermediaries to distribute products around the world requires an understanding of cultural differences, especially when it comes to communicating with channel partners whose cultural values—such as what's an incentive and what's not—may not be the same as your own.

Most communication with distributors is written—e-mails, faxes, letters, and so forth. Obviously, your distributor must be able to understand what you need, so here are a few tips for communicating with foreign members of your distribution channel. Don't be too casual or informal when you're e-mailing businesspeople in Germany; you may give them the wrong idea about your commitment to the partnership and even turn them off to you and your firm. German businesspeople expect to be addressed by *Mr., Mrs.,* and other appropriate titles, and they expect you to observe a certain level for formality in all communications. Latin Americans, on the other hand, tend to appreciate a personal touch—say, a reference to family or health early in the communication. If you're an American, you probably expect succinct, matter-of-fact messages; you don't even mind bulleted lists of things to be discussed.

If distributors don't understand the value or benefits of your new product features, they're less likely to market them successfully. In many cases, explaining things in culturally specific slang or jargon just confuses foreign distributors. Do not, however, expect Singaporeans or Filipinos to tell you voluntarily that they don't understand your technical terms. They'd lose face. You're better off anticipating communication challenges and focusing on such questions as how they would recommend improving your sales in their markets. You're bound to get a list of polite suggestions that may not only be useful, but which should help you determine whether your communications are coming across.

Finally, remember that your distributor is probably the best person to ask about the local market. Thus, you may want to consider translating your marketing and product materials to ensure that foreign distributors understand the features and benefits of your products. Typically, they're representing numerous products and communicating clearly with them will make it easier for them to represent yours.

distributor in any city or region. Three strategies—*intensive, exclusive,* and *selective distribution*—provide different degrees of market coverage.

Intensive distribution means distributing through as many channels and channel members as possible (both wholesalers and retailers). It is normally used for low-cost consumer goods with widespread appeal, such as candy and magazines. M&M's candies <www.mms.com> enter the market through all suitable retail outlets—supermarkets, candy machines, drugstores, and so forth.

intensive distribution
Strategy by which a product is distributed through as many channels as possible

With **exclusive distribution**, a manufacturer grants the exclusive right to distribute or sell a product to a limited number of wholesalers or retailers, usually in a given geographic area. Such agreements are most common for high-cost prestige products. Rolex watches <www.rolex.com> are sold only by "Official Rolex Jewellers."

exclusive distribution
Strategy by which a manufacturer grants exclusive rights to distribute or sell a product to a limited number of wholesalers or retailers in a given geographic area

Using **selective distribution**, a producer selects only wholesalers and retailers that will give a product special attention in sales effort, display advantage, and so forth. Selective distribution is used most often for consumer products

selective distribution
Strategy by which a company uses only wholesalers and retailers who give special attention to specific products

such as furniture and appliances. General Electric <www.ge.com> uses selective distribution for appliances in order to cement relationships with wholesalers who will market GE over other brands. GE also keeps costs lower while giving its products good market coverage.

Channel Conflict and Channel Leadership

Manufacturers may distribute through more than one channel, and many retailers (for example, RiteAid drugstores) are free to strike agreements with as many producers (the makers of Tylenol, Advil, and Bayer) as capacity permits. In such cases, channel conflict may arise. Conflicts are resolved through better coordination, and a key factor in coordinating the activities of organizations is *channel leadership*.

channel conflict
Conflict arising when the members of a distribution channel disagree over the roles they should play or the rewards they should receive

Channel Conflict **Channel conflict** occurs when members of the channel disagree over roles or rewards. John Deere would object to its dealers distributing Japanese tractors. Likewise, a manufacturer-owned outlet store runs the risk of alienating independent retailers when it discounts the company's products. Conflict may arise if one member has more power or is perceived as getting preferential treatment. Such conflicts, of course, defeat the purpose of the system by disrupting the flow of goods.

channel captain
Channel member who is most powerful in determining the roles and rewards of other members

Channel Leadership Usually, one channel member—the **channel captain**—can determine the roles and rewards of the others. Often, this is a manufacturer. The jewelry of New Orleans artisan Thomas Mann is in such demand that wholesalers and retailers wait years for the chance to distribute it. Mann <www.thomasmann.com> selects channel members, sets prices, and determines product availability. In other industries, an influential wholesaler or a large retailer such as Wal-Mart or Sears may be a channel captain because of large sales volume.

The dresses being shipped from this Kahn-Lucas factory are bound for department-store retail shelves. If they don't arrive when promised, there may be conflict in the distribution channel: In fact, the buyer could charge Kahn-Lucas 5% on every item in the shipment. Such penalties are called charge backs, *and retailers can charge suppliers for putting bar codes in the wrong place, attaching labels improperly, and unloading boxes out of order. Retailers say they're holding down costs by being efficient. Some suppliers say retailers are wrong anywhere from 25% to 50% of the time and reply that, to offset losses, they have to raise prices.*

Self-Check Questions 1–3

*You should now be able to answer Self-Check Questions 1–3**

1. TRUE/FALSE The *distribution mix* is the combination of products that a firm offers for distribution to end users.

2. MULTIPLE CHOICE Which of the following is **not true** regarding *intermediaries* and *distribution channels* [select one]: **(a)** Wholesalers sell products to other businesses, which resell them to final customers. **(b)** Intermediaries are retailers who move goods or information to customers. **(c)** Intermediaries provide added value for customers. **(d)** Distribution channels for consumer products are often different from those for industrial products.

3. MULTIPLE CHOICE Which of the following is **true** regarding *distribution strategies* and *distribution channels* [select one]: **(a)** Distribution strategies—intensive, exclusive, and selective distribution—differ in kinds of products and degree of market coverage. **(b)** The direct channel of distribution for consumer products employs, at most, two intermediaries. **(c)** Agents are intermediaries for distribution to businesses but not to consumers. **(d)** Channel conflict is less of a concern today because the number of distribution channels is diminishing.

*ANSWERS TO SELF-CHECK QUESTIONS 1–3 CAN BE FOUND ON P. AN-7.

Wholesaling

Now that you know something about distribution channels, we can consider more closely the role of intermediaries. Wholesalers, for example, provide a variety of services to buyers of products for resale or business use. In addition to storing and providing an assortment of products, some wholesalers offer delivery, credit, and product information.[6] The range of services depends on the type of intermediary: *merchant wholesaler, agent/broker,* or *e-intermediary.*

Merchant Wholesalers

Most wholesalers are independent operations that sell various consumer or business goods produced by a variety of manufacturers. The largest group, **merchant wholesalers**, buys products from manufacturers and sells them to other businesses. They own the goods that they resell and usually provide storage and delivery. In the United States, the merchant wholesaling industry employs six million people with a total yearly payroll of $210 billion.

Full-service merchant wholesalers (about 80 percent of all merchant wholesalers) provide credit, marketing, and merchandising services. **Limited-function merchant wholesalers** provide fewer services, sometimes merely storage. Customers are normally small operations that pay cash and pick up their own goods. **Drop shippers** don't even carry inventory or handle products: They take orders from customers, negotiate with producers to supply goods, take title to

merchant wholesaler
Independent wholesaler who takes legal possession of goods produced by a variety of manufacturers and then resells them to other businesses

full-service merchant wholesaler
Merchant wholesaler who provides credit, marketing, and merchandising services in addition to traditional buying and selling services

limited-function merchant wholesaler
Merchant wholesaler that provides a limited range of services

drop shipper
Limited-function merchant wholesaler that receives customer orders, negotiates with producers, takes title to goods, and arranges for shipment to customers

rack jobber
Limited-function merchant wholesaler that sets up and maintains display racks in retail stores

them, and arrange for shipment. **Rack jobbers** market consumer goods (mostly nonfood items) directly to retail stores, marking prices and setting up displays in a variety of stores. Procter & Gamble <www.pg.com> uses rack jobbers to distribute products such as Pampers diapers.

Agents and Brokers

Agents and brokers, including Internet e-agents, serve as independent sales representatives for many companies' products. They work on commission, usually about four to five percent of net sales. Unlike merchant wholesalers, they do not own their merchandise. Rather, they serve as sales and merchandising arms for producers who do not have their own sales forces.

Consider the role of On Air Digital Audio as an *e-agent* (or *shopping agent*). Corporate clients need the right kind of voices for radio ads; likewise, on-air voice talents are looking for jobs. As an intermediary between clients and artists, On Air Digital <www.mediadog.net/Portfolio/small4index.html> saves clients' time by transmitting ad scripts and artists' readings electronically. Clients scan samples from On Air's voice bank to select the best voices. On Air then arranges for the recording and sends it electronically to the client, thus avoiding the cost of mailing CDs and tapes back and forth.[7]

The value of agents and brokers lies in their knowledge of markets and their merchandising expertise. They also provide such services as shelf and display merchandising and advertising layout. They remove open, torn, or dirty packages, arrange products neatly, and generally keep goods attractively displayed. Many supermarket products are handled through brokers.

The Advent of the E-Intermediary

e-intermediary
Internet distribution channel member that assists in moving products through to customers or that collects information about various sellers to be presented in convenient format for Internet customers

syndicated selling
E-commerce practice whereby a Web site offers other Web sites commissions for referring customers

The ability of e-commerce to bring together millions of widely dispersed consumers and businesses is changing the types and roles of intermediaries. **E-intermediaries** are Internet-based channel members who perform one or both of two functions: (1) They collect information about sellers and present it to consumers, or (2) they help deliver Internet products to buyers.[8] We will examine three types of e-intermediaries: *syndicated sellers, shopping agents,* and *business-to-business brokers.*

Syndicated Sellers **Syndicated selling** occurs when one Web site offers another a commission for referring customers. Here's how it works. With 9.2 million users each month, Expedia.com is a heavily visited travel-services Web site. Expedia has given Dollar Rent A Car <www.dollarcar.com> a special banner on its Web page. When Expedia customers click on the banner for a car rental, they are transferred from the Expedia site to the Dollar site. Dollar pays Expedia a fee for each booking that comes through this channel. Although the new intermediary increases the cost of Dollar's supply chain, it adds value for customers. Travelers avoid unnecessary cyberspace searches and are efficiently guided to a car-rental agency.[9]

shopping agent (or **e-agent**)
E-intermediary (middleman) in the Internet distribution channel that assists users in finding products and prices but that does not take possession of products

Shopping Agents **Shopping agents** (or **e-agents**) help Internet consumers by gathering and sorting information. Although they don't take possession of products, they know which Web sites and stores to visit, give accurate comparison prices, identify product features, and help consumers complete transactions by presenting information in a usable format—all in a matter of seconds. PriceScan <www.pricescan.com> is a well-known shopping agent for computer products. For CDs and tapes, evenbetter.com searches for vendors, does price comparisons, lists prices from low to high, and then transfers you to the Web sites of 50 different e-stores.

Business-to-Business Brokers E-commerce intermediaries have also emerged for business customers. The start-up Internet company Efdex (which stands for

"Brick and Mortar to Fill Your Order"

Up to this point, our discussion of *distribution channels* and *wholesaling* has shown us various ways in which products get from producers to customers. We have seen that along the way, *intermediaries* perform a variety of services that facilitate the movement of goods from upstream sources to ultimate destinations. What are some specific activities of intermediaries? What kinds of clients need the services of intermediaries? Why do clients hire intermediaries rather than perform certain activities themselves?

We begin to answer these and related questions by exploring the Web site of a real company—American Fulfillment LLC(AF), at < afllc.com>—that specializes in intermediary activities for client companies. As you can see, the AF homepage contains six section headings: **Home, Company Profile, Services, Contact Us, Case Study,** and **Request Information.**

Let's begin near the top of the homepage. Click on **Company Profile** and then scroll down the page to the list entitled **Clients Include.** After reading the list of clients, move to the right side of the screen and click on **See Our Company History.** Once you are on the AF history page, scroll down to the section headed **American Fulfillment LLC's Client List Includes** and examine the types of industries that AF serves.

1. Who are AF's customers? Are AF's services available to consumers, or are they intended for other businesses?

Returning to the homepage, look at the section entitled **What Is Fulfillment?**

2. How would you describe or classify American Fulfillment's role as an intermediary in distribution channels?
3. This chapter describes eight channels of distribution. Based on the information that you've gathered so far, in which of these eight channels might American Fulfillment fit as an intermediary? In which channels would it not fit?

Return once more to the AF homepage. Click on **Company Profile,** scroll down to the bottom of the page, and read in the last paragraph the description of basic services that AF performs for its customers.

4. Instead of performing the services itself, why might a client company hire American Fulfillment to perform them?

To continue your Internet Field Trip, click on www.prenhall.com/giffin

electronic food and drink exchange) is a massive food exchange for buying and selling foodstuffs among food manufacturers, restaurants, grocers, and farmers. Established first in the United Kingdom in early 2000, the Web site <www.efdex.com> provides up-to-date market information and price and product data from both suppliers and buyers. Efdex lets businesses buy and sell from one another and confirm transactions electronically. As a broker, Efdex does not take possession of products. Rather, it brings together timely information and links businesses to one another.[10]

Retailing

There are more than 1.6 million retail establishments in the United States. Most of them are small, often consisting of owners and part-time help. Indeed, over one-half of the nation's retailers account for less than 10 percent of all retail sales. Retailers also include huge operations such as Wal-Mart, the largest employer in the United States, and Sears. Although there are large retailers in many other countries—Kaufhof <www.kaufhof.de> in Germany, Carrefour in France <www.carrefour.com>, and Daiei in Japan <www.cybercitykobe.com/daiei/index.htm>—most of the world's largest retailers are U.S. businesses.

Types of Retail Outlets

U.S. retail operations vary widely by type as well as size. We can classify them in various ways: by pricing strategies, location, range of services, or range of product

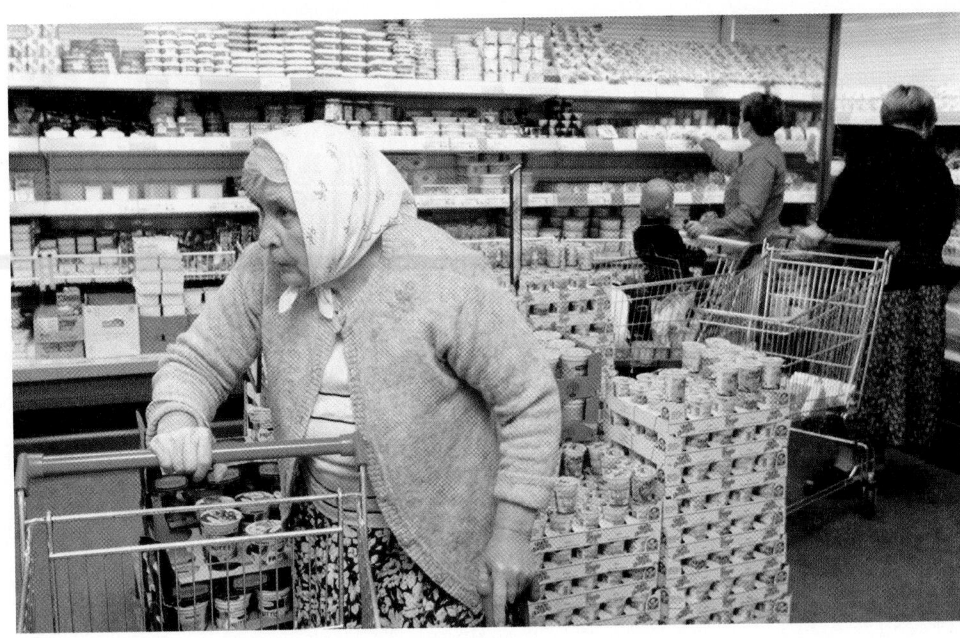

It took a few years after the fall of Communism before entrepreneurs braved the uncertain economic climate of Russia and opened supermarkets and other retail chains. Ikea, the Swedish home-furnishings seller, has been successful in Moscow, as has Kopeika <www.kopeika.ru>, a home-owned discount chain that models itself after Wal-Mart. Russian shoppers (who used to go to drab stores called "Food" and "Furniture") are enthusiastic, and more companies are opening outlets in Moscow, which has more people than all of Belgium.

lines. Choosing the right types of retail outlets is a crucial aspect of every seller' distribution strategy. In this section, we describe U.S. retail stores by using tw classifications: *product line retailers* and *bargain retailers.*[11]

Product Line Retailers Retailers featuring broad product lines includ **department stores**, which are organized into specialized departments: shoes, fu niture, women's petite sizes, and so on. Stores are usually large, handle a wid range of goods, and offer a variety of services, such as credit plans and deliver Similarly, **supermarkets** are divided into departments of related products: foo products, household products, and so forth. They stress low prices, self-servic and wide selection.

In contrast, **specialty stores** are small stores that carry one line of relate products. They serve specific market segments with full product lines in narro product fields and often feature knowledgeable sales personnel. Sunglass Hu International <www.sunglasshut.com>, for instance, has 1,600 outlets with deep selection of competitively priced sunglasses.

Bargain Retailers **Bargain retailers** carry wide ranges of products and come i many forms. The first **discount houses** sold large numbers of items (such a televisions and other appliances) at substantial price reductions to certain cu tomers. As name-brand items became more common, they offered better pro uct assortments while still transacting cash-only sales in low-rent facilities. A they became firmly entrenched, they began moving to better locations, impro ing decor, and selling better-quality merchandise at higher prices. They als began offering a few department store services, such as credit plans and no cash sales.

Catalog showrooms mail catalogs to attract customers into showrooms view display samples, place orders, and wait briefly while clerks retrieve orde from attached warehouses. **Factory outlets** are manufacturer-owned stores th avoid wholesalers and retailers by selling merchandise directly from factory

department store
Large product line retailer characterized by organization into specialized departments

supermarket
Large product line retailer offering a variety of food and food-related items in specialized departments

specialty store
Small retail store carrying one product line or category of related products

bargain retailer
Retailer carrying a wide range of products at bargain prices

discount house
Bargain retailer that generates large sales volume by offering goods at substantial price reductions

catalog showroom
Bargain retailer in which customers place orders for catalog items to be picked up at on-premises warehouses

factory outlet
Bargain retailer owned by the manufacturer whose products it sells

consumer. The **warehouse club** (or **wholesale club**) offers large discounts on a wide range of brand-name merchandise to customers who pay annual membership fees. Neighborhood food retailers such as 7-Eleven and Circle K stores are **convenience store** chains, which offer ease of purchase: They stress easily accessible locations, extended store hours, and speedy service. They differ from most bargain retailers in that they do not feature low prices. Like bargain retailers, they control prices by keeping in-store service to a minimum.

warehouse club (or **wholesale club**)
Bargain retailer offering large discounts on brand-name merchandise to customers who have paid annual membership fees

convenience store
Retail store offering easy accessibility, extended hours, and fast service

Nonstore and Electronic Retailing

Some of the nation's largest retailers sell all or most of their products without brick-and-mortar stores. Certain types of consumer goods—soft drinks, candy, and cigarettes—sell well from vending machines. But even at $107 billion per year, vending machine sales still make up less than 4 percent of all U.S. retail sales. In e-retailing, sales reached $42 billion in 2001, as some 63 million households with PCs went online to shop.[12]

Nonstore retailing also includes **direct-response retailing**, in which firms contact customers directly to inform them about products and to receive sales orders. **Mail order** (or **catalog marketing**), such as that practiced by Spiegel <www.spiegel.com> and its Eddie Bauer <www.eddiebauer.com> subsidiary, is a form of direct-response retailing. So is **telemarketing**—the use of the telephone to sell directly. Telemarketing is growing rapidly in the United States, Canada, and Great Britain, and experts estimate that U.S. sales alone could top $800 billion in 2004.[13] Finally, more than 600 U.S. companies use **direct selling** to sell door-to-door or through home-selling parties. Avon Products has 465,000 independent U.S. sales reps.[14]

direct-response retailing
Nonstore retailing by direct interaction with customers to inform them of products and to receive sales orders

mail order (or **catalog marketing**)
Form of nonstore retailing in which customers place orders for catalog merchandise received through the mail

telemarketing
Nonstore retailing in which the telephone is used to sell directly to consumers

direct selling
Form of nonstore retailing typified by door-to-door sales

The Boom in Electronic Retailing **Electronic retailing** is made possible by communications networks that let sellers post product information on consumers' PCs. With over 3.6 million subscribers, Prodigy Communications Corp. <www.prodigy.com> is among the largest home networks. As an *Internet service provider* (*ISP*), Prodigy employs a network of more than 850 U.S. locations that can be accessed by 90 percent of the population with a local telephone call. Prodigy gives members access to the Internet and displays of products ranging from travel packages to financial services to consumer goods. Home PC users can examine detailed descriptions, compare brands, send for free information, or purchase by credit card.[15]

electronic retailing
Nonstore retailing in which information about the seller's products and services is connected to consumers' computers, allowing consumers to receive the information and purchase the products in the home

Internet-Based Stores Use of the Internet to interact with customers—to inform, sell to, and distribute to them—is booming. Internet use by American small businesses doubled in 1998, nearly doubled again in 1999, and added another 2.1 million Web sites during 2000. Figure 12.3 tells the story of this growth by showing the percentages of small businesses with Web sites (Figure 12.3[a]), of those planning to post Web sites (Figure 12.3[b]), and of the marketing functions that owners expect sites to perform (Figure 12.3[c]).[16]

The rampant growth of e-commerce is undoubtedly just the beginning. B2B e-commerce is already a $1.2 *trillion* industry and is expected to reach $4.8 trillion in 2004. In addition, while e-retail sales were 15 times higher in 2001 than in 1997, at $42 billion they were still less than 4 percent of total retail sales. There is a lot of room for growth, and huge growth prospects are spurring the scramble among firms to get into e-business.[17]

Electronic Catalogs **E-catalogs** use the Internet to display products for both retail and business customers. By sending electronic versions (instead of traditional mail catalogs), firms give millions of users instant access to pages of product information. The seller avoids mail-distribution and printing costs, and once an

e-catalog
Nonstore retailing in which the Internet is used to display products

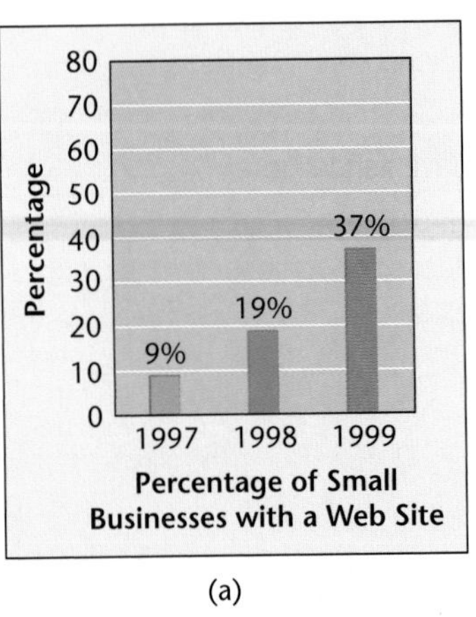

Percentage of Small Businesses with a Web Site

(a)

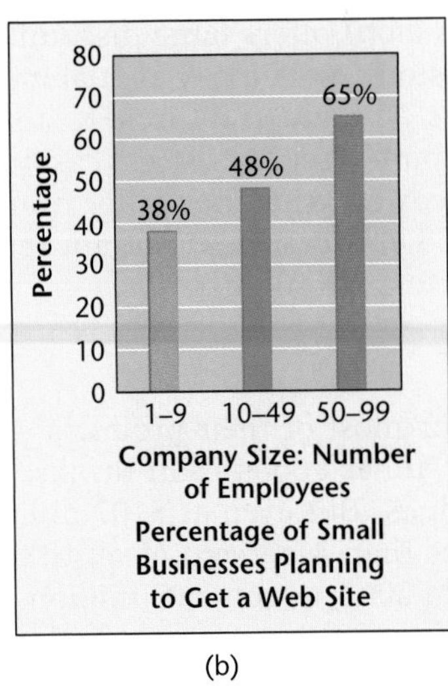

Percentage of Small Businesses Planning to Get a Web Site

(b)

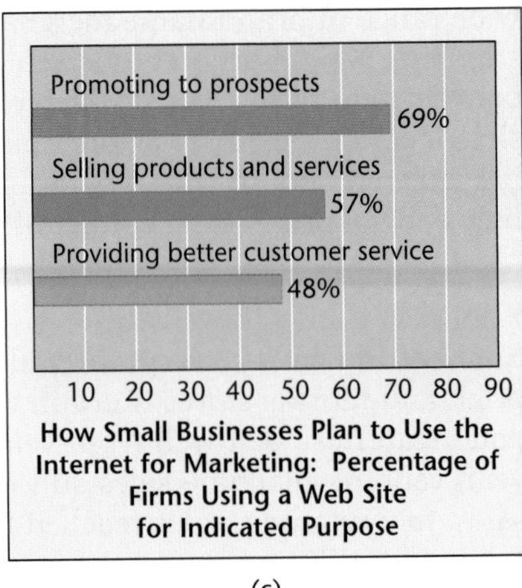

How Small Businesses Plan to Use the Internet for Marketing: Percentage of Firms Using a Web Site for Indicated Purpose

(c)

FIGURE 12.3
Small Business and the Web

online catalog is in place, there is little cost in maintaining and accessing it. Recognizing these advantages, about 85 percent of all catalogers are now on the Internet, with sales via Web sites accounting for 10 percent of all catalog sales. The top 10 consumer e-catalogs include JCPenney (number 1), Fingerhut (number 3) L.L. Bean (number 7), and Victoria's Secret (number 8). Top B2B e-catalogs include Dell Computer (number 1) and Office Depot (number 5).[18]

electronic storefront
Commercial Web site in which customers gather information about products and buying opportunities, place orders, and pay for purchases

Electronic Storefronts and Cybermalls Today, a seller's Web site is an **electronic storefront** (or *virtual storefront*) from which consumers collect information abou products and buying opportunities, place orders, and pay for purchases. Producers of large product lines, such as Dell Computer <www.dell.com>, dedicate storefronts to their own product lines. Other sites, such as CDNOW <www.cdnow.com>, which offers CDs and audio and videotapes, are category sellers whose storefronts feature products from many manufacturers.

cybermall
Collection of virtual storefronts (business Web sites) representing a variety of products and product lines on the Internet

Search engines like Yahoo! <www.yahoo.com> serve as **cybermalls**: collections of virtual storefronts representing diverse products. After entering a cybermall, shoppers can navigate by choosing from a list of stores (Eddie Bauer or Macy's), product listings (Pokémon or MP3 players), or departments (apparel o bath/beauty). When your virtual shopping cart is full, you check out and pay you bill. The value-added properties of cybermalls are obvious: speed, convenience 24-hour access, and, most important, efficient searching that avoids the "click 'til-you-drop" syndrome—the endless wandering through cyberspace experienced by early Internet users.[19]

multilevel marketing
Distribution channel consisting of self-employed distributors who receive commissions for selling products to customers and for recruiting new distributors

From Door-to-Door to E-Sales? Not surprisingly, cyberspace is encroaching on door-to-door distribution. Amway is famous for a **multilevel marketing** channel in which self-employed distributors get commissions for recruiting new customer and new Amway reps. Now Amway is expanding this system to the Internet wit a spinoff called Quixstar <www.quixstar.com>. With help from Quixstar, you ca start your own at-home Internet business. You will be paid for directing new customers to the Quixstar site and for encouraging others to become Quixstar reps The Internet's huge at-home sales potential is also luring other famous door-to door names—Tupperware, Avon, and Mary Kay. Such firms are racing to boar the Internet train even though they are courting potential channel conflic

Millions of loyal door-to-door sales reps stand to lose customers to their own companies' Internet outlets.[20]

Interactive and Video Marketing Today, both retail and B2B customers interact with multimedia Web sites using voice, graphics, animation, film clips, and access to live human advice. One good example of **interactive marketing** is LivePerson <www.liveperson.com>, a leading provider of real-time sales and customer service for over 450 Web sites. When customers log on to the sites of e-Loan, Playboy, CBS Sportsline's IgoGolf, or USABancShares—all of which are LivePerson clients—they enter a live chat room where a service operator initiates a secure one-on-one text chat. Questions and answers go back and forth to help customers with answers to specific questions that must be answered before they decide on a product. Another form of interaction is the so-called *banner ad* that changes as the user's mouse moves about the page, revealing new drop-down, check, and search boxes.[21]

interactive marketing
Nonstore retailing that uses a Web site to provide real-time sales and customer service

Video marketing, a long-established form of interactive marketing, lets viewers shop at home from TV screens. Most cable systems offer video marketing through home-shopping channels that display and demonstrate products and allow viewers to phone in or e-mail orders. One network, QVC <www.qvc.com>, operates in the United Kingdom, Germany, Mexico, and South America and has also launched iQVC as an interactive Web site.

video marketing
Nonstore retailing to consumers via standard and cable television

Physical Distribution

Physical distribution refers to the activities needed to move products from manufacturer to consumer. Its purpose is to make goods available when and where consumers want them, keep costs low, and provide services that keep customers satisfied. Thus, physical distribution includes *warehousing* and *transportation operations* as well as *distribution for e-customers.*

physical distribution
Activities needed to move a product efficiently from manufacturer to consumer

Warehousing Operations

Storing, or **warehousing**, is a major part of distribution management. In selecting a strategy, managers must keep in mind both the different characteristics and costs of warehousing operations.

warehousing
Physical distribution operation concerned with the storage of goods

Types of Warehouses There are two basic types of warehouses: *private* and *public.* Facilities can be further divided according to use as *storage warehouses* or *distribution centers.*

Public and Private Warehouses **Private warehouses** are owned by a single manufacturer, wholesaler, or retailer. Most are run by large firms that deal in mass quantities and need regular storage. JCPenney, for example, facilitates the movement of products to retail stores by maintaining its own warehouses.

private warehouse
Warehouse owned by and providing storage for a single company

Public warehouses are independently owned and operated. Because companies rent only the space they need, they are popular with firms needing storage only during peak periods. They are also used by manufacturers who need multiple storage locations to get products to multiple markets.

public warehouse
Independently owned and operated warehouse that stores goods for many firms

Storage Warehouses and Distribution Centers **Storage warehouses** provide storage for extended periods. Producers of seasonal items, such as agricultural crops, use this type of warehouse. **Distribution centers** provide short-term storage of products whose demand is both constant and high. They are used by retail chains, wholesalers, and manufacturers who need to break down large quantities of merchandise into the smaller quantities that stores or customers demand.

storage warehouse
Warehouse providing storage for extended periods of time

distribution center
Warehouse providing short-term storage of goods for which demand is both constant and high

"Going to School" Takes On a New Meaning

Education has traditionally been a fixed distribution channel: Students go to classrooms, where they interact with teachers, and they have access to libraries, books, and study halls from 7:30 A.M. to 3:00 P.M. But electronic and digital technology is about to change things. Today's student can already use an at-home PC to call up a classroom from a place of work. More parents are relying on the Internet for home schooling, and many adults with full-time jobs and family obligations are getting college degrees without setting foot in classrooms, without worrying about how they're dressed, and without face-to-face interaction with fellow students and teachers. They're taking advantage of *distance learning*—the newest means for distributing educational services from providers to consumers.

More than a million American students take classes this way—either for credit or for personal development—and the number is growing rapidly. With a potential market of over $10 billion a year, what is the key competitive advantage of distance? The answer is simple: convenience. Distance learning is a portable, flexible resource. Internet-based courses are not tied down to fixed locations or times, and support resources, such as library materials, are readily at hand: Just call up reference sources from the Internet. Taking a trip? Take your computer along to receive and submit assignments, and use electronic chat rooms to meet with classmates.

Going beyond student-teacher interactions and chat rooms, online education offers a variety of support resources, including curricula, testing, test preparation, film libraries and reading materials, tutoring, and even school management. One company, California-based Tutor.com, offers online interaction with tutors for everyone from fifth-graders to college freshmen, and it targets online-educational products for different market segments: pre-K through grade 12, higher education, continuing education, home school, government, certificate programs, and corporate training.

Because it can deliver programs economically, online education is growing most rapidly as a corporate-training tool. The savings are so great that online corporate training in the United States should increase from $2.2 billion in 2000 to $15 billion by 2005. Dow Chemical, for example, has invested $1.3 million in an e-learning system for 40,000 employees in 70 countries. By contrast, traditional training often involves expensive travel, hotel, and food bills and enrollment fees (not to mention the employee's absence from the workplace). But with the recession that began in 2001, fallout from the September 11th tragedy, and tighter time constraints, many firms are searching for nontravel alternatives that will keep employees at work even while they're getting job or management training. The downside, of course, is lack of human interaction. That, however, is a tradeoff that both employers and employees are willing to make in exchange for convenience and cost savings. NEC America <www.necamerica.com>, a maker of communications products, contracts with a supplier for more than 100 online courses. The cost is about $800 per seat, compared with $2,000 for off-site training.

The University of Phoenix <www.phoenix.edu> is the largest online university, with about 20 accredited programs. But nonuniversity programs are growing too. One distance-learning program—School at Work (SAW)—is designed for low-skilled workers. It gives low-wage earners a chance to learn basic skills (math, communications, writing) that will help them become more promotable in their jobs. Employers provide classroom space and let employees attend on company time. An educational network delivers a live TV feed with instructors who use workbooks, videos, and Web resources from remote locations. Both students and companies see courses as advancement and promotion tools, and for many employees, online education is widening the channel to a better-paying future.

Self-Check Questions 4–6

*You should now be able to answer Self-Check Questions 4–6**

4. MULTIPLE CHOICE Which of the following is **true** about *e-intermediaries* and *electronic retailing* [select one]: **(a)** Electronic retailing is rapidly surpassing brick-and-mortar retailing in the United States. **(b)** Consumers become discouraged with e-catalogs because product images are not readily available on the Internet. **(c)** Most syndicated selling is accomplished without the use of Web sites. **(d)** Electronic storefronts provide Internet shoppers added value from speed, convenience, and 24-hour access.

5. TRUE/FALSE Some *merchant wholesalers* provide a variety of services to customers, whereas other merchant wholesalers provide only one or a few services.

6. MULTIPLE CHOICE Which of the following is **false** regarding *retailing* and *retail outlets* [select one]: **(a)** Factory outlets and warehouse clubs, but not specialty stores, are examples of bargain retailers. **(b)** Department stores offer a wide range of goods and customer services. **(c)** Product line retailers, such as catalog showrooms, offer deep price discounts. **(d)** Electronic retailing relies on communication networks connecting sellers to buyers' computers.

*ANSWERS TO SELF-CHECK QUESTIONS 4–6 CAN BE FOUND ON P. AN-8.

Distribution centers are common in the grocery and food industry. Kellogg's, for example, stores virtually no products at its plants. Instead, it ships cereals from factories to regional distribution centers. As wholesalers place orders for combinations of products, warehouses fill and ship them. Because warehouses are regional, wholesalers receive orders quickly.

Warehousing Costs Typical warehouse costs include such obvious expenses as storage-space rental or mortgage payments (usually computed on a square-foot basis), insurance, and wages. They also include the costs of *inventory control* and *materials handling*.

Inventory Control **Inventory control** means more than keeping track of what is on hand at any time. It often involves the tricky balancing act of ensuring that although an adequate supply of a product is in stock at all times, excessive supplies are avoided.

inventory control
Warehouse operation that tracks inventory on hand and ensures that an adequate supply is in stock at all times

Materials Handling Most warehouse personnel are involved in **materials handling**: the transportation, arrangement, and orderly retrieval of inventoried goods. Holding down materials-handling costs means developing a strategy that takes into account product placement within the warehouse. Other considerations include packaging decisions (whether to store products as individual units, in multiple packages, or in sealed containers).

materials handling
Warehouse operation involving the transportation, arrangement, and orderly retrieval of goods in inventory

The strategy known as *unitization* calls for standardizing the weight and form of materials. A GE warehouse in Kentucky, for instance, receives apartment-size refrigerators from Europe in containers of 56 refrigerators each. Dealing with the huge containers rather than individual boxes not only makes handling easier but reduces theft and damage. It also optimizes shipping space and makes restocking easier.

Transportation Operations

Because the highest cost faced by many companies is that of physically moving a product, cost is a major factor in choosing transportation methods. But firms must also consider other factors: the nature of the product, the distance it must travel, the speed with which it must be received, and customer wants and needs.

Transportation Modes

The major transportation modes are trucks, railroads, planes, water carriers, and pipelines. Differences in cost are most directly related to delivery speed.

Trucks The advantages of trucks include flexibility, fast service, and dependability. Nearly all areas of the United States can be reached by truck. Because less breakage occurs than with railroad transport, trucked goods need less packing—a major cost savings. Trucks are a good choice for short-distance distribution and for expensive products, and they carry more freight than any other form of transport except trains.

Railroads Railroads are now used primarily to transport heavy, bulky items such as cars, steel, and coal. To regain market share from trucks, they have expanded services to include faster delivery times and *piggyback service,* in which truck trailers are placed on railcars. This service alone can save shippers up to one-half the cost of shipping by truck.

Planes Besides being the fastest mode of transportation, air boasts much lower costs in handling and packing and unpacking. Inventory carrying costs can also be reduced by eliminating the need to store items that might deteriorate. Shipments of fresh fish, for example, can be picked up by restaurants each day, avoiding the risk of spoilage from packaging and storing. Air freight, however, is the most expensive form of transportation.

Water Carriers Water, by contrast, is the least expensive, and modern networks of waterways, locks, rivers, and lakes let water carriers reach many areas in the United States and throughout the world. But because water transport is also slow, boats and barges are used mostly for heavy, bulky materials and products (such as sand, gravel, oil, and grain), for which delivery speed is unimportant. Today, many ships are specially constructed to hold large standardized containers.

Specializing in long-haul shipping, U.S. Xpress Enterprises <www.usxpress.com> *employs nearly 6,000 drivers to operate 5,300 trucks and 12,000 trailers. The company has used satellite technology to communicate with drivers since the 1980s, and trucks now have anticollision radar, vehicle-detection sensors, and computers for shifting through ten speeds. Roomy cabs have sleepers, refrigerators, and microwaves because driver comfort is a top priority. "Drivers," explains a company executive, "can lose you a $100 million account with words, actions, and how they do business."*

Pipelines Like water transport, pipelines are slow. Used to transport liquids and gases, they are also inflexible. The Trans-Alaska Pipeline, however, provides a constant flow of oil from Alaska to the lower 48 states and is unaffected by weather. Lack of adaptability to other products makes pipelines an unimportant transportation method for most industries.

Changes in Transportation Operations For many years, U.S. transport companies specialized in one mode or another. Since deregulation in 1980, however, this pattern has changed. New developments in cost-efficiency and competitiveness include *intermodal transportation, containerization,* and *order fulfillment through e-commerce channels.*

Intermodal Transportation **Intermodal transportation**—the combined use of different transport modes—is now widespread. For example, shipping by a combination of air and rail or truck is called *birdyback* transport. Large railroads, such as Burlington Northern and Union Pacific, have merged with trucking, air, and shipping lines in order to offer simplified source-to-destination delivery by any necessary combination of methods.

intermodal transportation
Combined use of several different modes of transportation

Containerization To make intermodal transport more efficient, **containerization** uses standardized heavy-duty containers in which many items are sealed at points of shipment and opened at final destinations. Containers may be stowed on ships for ocean transit, transferred to trucks, loaded onto railcars (piggyback service), and delivered to final destinations by other trucks. Unloaded containers are then returned for future use.

containerization
Transportation method in which goods are sealed in containers at shipping sources and opened when they reach final destinations

Physical Distribution and E-Customer Satisfaction New e-commerce companies often focus on sales, only to discover that delays in after-sale distribution cause customer dissatisfaction. Any delay in physical distribution is a breakdown in fulfillment. **Order fulfillment** begins when the sale is made: It involves getting the product to each customer in good condition and on time. But the volume of a firm's transactions can be huge—Web retailers shipped 300 million packages in 2001—and fulfillment performance has been disappointing for many e-businesses.

order fulfillment
All activities involved in completing a sales transaction, beginning with making the sale and ending with on-time delivery to the customer

To improve on-time deliveries, many businesses, such as Amazon.com, maintain distribution centers and ship from their own warehouses. Other e-tailers, however, entrust order-filling to distribution specialists such as the giant UPS e-logistics <www.e-logistics.ups.com> and the much smaller Atomic Box <www.atomicbox.com>. Atomic Box clients range from manufacturers to dot-coms such as BODUM Inc. (an e-tailer of coffee and tea appliances), Decora Inc. (an e-tailer of window dressings), and Innovon LLC (an e-tailer of specially designed bags and storage devices). The company maintains 325,000 square feet of warehousing through which it annually delivers products worth more than $200 million. It handles the flow of goods and information in both B2B and business-to-consumer transactions.

Both Atomic Box and UPS e-logistics process customer orders, ship goods, provide information about product availability, inform customers about the real-time status of orders, and handle returns. To perform these tasks, the client's computer system must be integrated with that of the distribution specialist. In deciding whether to build their own distribution centers or to use third-party distributors, clients must consider fixed costs as well as the need for shipping expertise. Because the capital investment required for a one-million-square-foot distribution center is $60 to $80 million, only high-volume companies can afford it. The alternative is paying a third-party distributor about 10 percent of each sale to fulfill orders.[22]

Distribution as a Marketing Strategy

Distribution is an increasingly important way of competing for sales. Instead of just offering advantages in product features and quality, price, and promotion, many firms have turned to distribution as a cornerstone of business strategy.

This approach means assessing and improving the entire stream of activities—wholesaling, warehousing, and transportation—involved in getting products to customers.

hub
Central distribution outlet that controls all or most of a firm's distribution activities

The Use of Hubs To streamline distribution systems, some companies use **hubs**: central distribution outlets that control all or most of a firm's distribution activities. Two contrasting strategies have emerged from this approach: *supply-side and prestaging hubs* and *distribution-side hubs*.

Supply-Side and Prestaging Hubs *Supply-side hubs* make sense when large shipments flow regularly to a single industrial user, such as a large manufacturer. They are used by auto factories, where thousands of supplies can arrive by train, truck, and air. Even so, incoming shipments can create a nightmare of loading dock congestion, storage-space shortages, and paperwork logjams.

To clear this congestion, some firms resort to *prestaging hubs*. Saturn maintains such a facility—managed by Ryder System <www.ryder.com>—located two miles from its factory. All incoming transportation is managed by Ryder to satisfy one requirement: meeting Saturn's production schedules. The long-haul tractors at the hub are disconnected from trailers and sent on return trips to any of 339 suppliers in 39 states. Responding to Saturn's up-to-the-minute needs, hub headquarters arranges transport for presorted and preinspected materials to the factory by loading them onto specially designed tractors.

The chief job of the hub, then, is to coordinate the customer's material needs with supply-chain transportation. If the hub is successful, factory inventories are virtually eliminated, storage-space requirements reduced, and long-haul trucks kept moving instead of queued up at the unloading dock. By outsourcing distribution activities to its hub, Saturn can focus on what it does best: manufacturing. Meanwhile, Ryder, the nation's largest logistics-management firm, is paid for its specialty: handling transportation flows.

Self-Check Questions 7–9

*You should now be able to answer Self-Check Questions 7–9**

7. TRUE/FALSE *Order fulfillment* involves all activities from receiving an order to getting it to the customer.

8. MULTIPLE CHOICE Which of the following is **false** regarding *transportation* and *physical distribution* [select one]: **(a)** The choice of transportation mode has an effect on the cost of distribution. **(b)** Industrial customers prefer some transportation modes over others because of differences in delivery speed. **(c)** Physical distribution delays have been a source of disappointment for many Web retail customers. **(d)** Intermodal transportation is used when merchandise is shipped back and forth between warehouses for storage and packaging.

9. TRUE/FALSE In using *distribution as a marketing strategy*, the purpose of *supply-side hubs* and *distribution-side hubs* is to reduce the costs of distribution, thus lowering prices and increasing sales.

*Answers to Self-Check Questions 7–9 can be found on p. AN-8.

Distribution-Side Hubs Whereas supply-side hubs are located near industrial customers, *distribution-side hubs* may be located much farther away, especially if customers are geographically dispersed. National Semiconductor <www.national.com>, one of the world's largest chip makers, is an example. Finished silicon microchips are produced in plants around the world and shipped to customers such as IBM, Toshiba, Siemens, Ford, and Compaq, which also run factories around the globe. Chips originally sat waiting at one location after another—on factory floors, at customs, in distributors' facilities, and in customers' warehouses. Typically, they traveled 20,000 different routes on as many as 12 airlines and spent time in 10 warehouses before reaching customers. National has streamlined the system by shutting down six warehouses and now airfreights chips worldwide from a single center in Singapore. Every activity—storage, sorting, and shipping—is run by Federal Express <www.fedex.com>. As a result, distribution costs have fallen, delivery times have been reduced by half, and sales have increased.

Continued from page 336

What Price News?

Like other products, news information is produced, assembled, packaged, and delivered to customers, and in return, revenues flow to the service provider. The industry's distribution channels are the various media through which news is delivered: radio, newsprint, television, cable TV, satellite broadcasting, and, more recently, the Internet. The dynamics of this system of channels not only poses problems for both news suppliers and the FCC, but it raises questions about the public interest as well.

From the news producer's standpoint, distribution strategies are especially challenging for four reasons:

1. Companies in the news industry are not free to choose distribution channels; the choice is constrained by federal regulations.
2. Restrictive regulations are periodically subject to change.
3. Forces in the business environment, such as new technology and legal challenges by businesses or consumers, can stimulate changes in regulations.
4. Once regulations change, news suppliers must rethink distribution strategies and make choices regarding distribution channels.

To illustrate item 4, let's consider the implications of anticipated FCC rule changes that will allow multiple-media ownership. Media companies such as PostNewsweek TV Stations <www.postnewsweektech.com>, Sinclair Broadcasting, Disney, Scripps Howard Broadcasting <www.scripps.com>, AOL Time Warner, Emmis Communications <www.emmis.com>, and Gannett <www.gannett.com> will be facing two strategic alternatives: (1) Concentrate news-reporting activities by operating *various* distribution channels in *one* market, or (2) redirect distribution activities into *one* medium with *national* coverage. Observes industry analyst Blair Levin, "If you look at how most of the ownership regulations have been falling, any sensible company will want to stand back and rethink how it would restructure its . . . empire. It's like a chess game, only with several opponents. You really have to pause and think out your moves." Each company in the industry, then, faces the possibility of revising its distribution strategy.

The industry's distribution dynamics also raise questions about protecting the public interest. As we have seen, *Seattle Times* CEO Frank Blethen fears that profit-driven consolidation will further threaten the institution of an independent press. As if to underscore Blethen's concerns, Sinclair Broadcast Group is considering a centralized news service to produce news for delivery to all of its 63 stations. In fact, Sinclair has shut down local newscasts from three stations. "We're in the business of making money and serving our shareholders in the public interest," says Sinclair CEO David Smith. "News is a great business—as long as it makes money."

Centralized distribution would replace more expensive local news coverage with more profitable standardized news programming—a move that critics like Blethen consider a threat to a diverse and open flow of news. Indeed, some people argue that more, not less, FCC regulation is needed to protect the public interest.

Questions for Discussion

1. What do you think should be the FCC's role, if any, in controlling distribution channels in the news industry?
2. Consider traditional versus newer channels of distribution. Do newer media truly bring additional competition into local markets? Explain how they affect competition.
3. Comments by Frank Blethen (CEO of the *Seattle Times*) and David Smith (CEO of Sinclair Broadcast Group) suggest differing views on what elements comprise "the public interest" when it comes to the regulation of news distribution. Compare and contrast their motivations.
4. Companies will face two strategic alternatives if the FCC revises ownership regulations. Explain why these alternatives do not currently exist.
5. Consider again the two strategic alternatives that will emerge if the FCC revises ownership regulations. For each alternative, identify ways in which a news supplier's marketing activities will be affected. How will its financial and marketing resources be allocated under the one strategy versus the other?
6. Regulatory changes by the FCC might increase consolidation of media ownership in companies such as the Sinclair Broadcast Group. Would repositioning of Sinclair's distribution channels raise any ethical issues or social responsibility concerns?

"News is a great business—as long as it makes money."

~David Smith,
CEO OF SINCLAIR BROADCAST GROUP

Summary of Learning Objectives

1. *Explain the* distribution mix, *the different* channels of distribution, *and different* distribution strategies.

The success of any product depends on its **distribution mix**: the combination of distribution channels that a firm uses to get products to end users. **Intermediaries** help to distribute a producer's goods. **Wholesalers** sell products to other businesses, which resell them to final consumers. **Retailers** sell products directly to consumers. Some firms rely on independent intermediaries, and others employ their own distribution networks and sales forces.

A **distribution channel** is the path that a product follows from producer to end user. We can identify eight primary distribution channels according to the kinds of members who participate in getting products to their destinations. All channels begin with a producer and end either with a consumer or an industrial (business) user. Channels 1 through 4 are most common in distributing consumer goods and services.

Channel 1: Direct distribution of consumer products: In a **direct channel** (which is prominent on the Internet), the product travels from the producer to the consumer without intermediaries. *Channel 2: Retail distribution of consumer products*: In Channel 2, producers distribute products through retailers (many of whom offer Internet sales). *Channel 3: Wholesale distribution of consumer products*: Because many retailers can't afford both retail and storage space, wholesalers have entered the network to take over more of the storage service. They are prominent in e-commerce because Internet stores can provide information and product displays 24 hours a day. They also make it possible to place and confirm orders electronically. *Channel 4: Distribution through sales agents or brokers*: Channel 4 uses **sales agents**, or **brokers**, who represent producers and sell to wholesalers, retailers, or both and who receive commissions based on the prices of goods sold. This channel is well suited to e-commerce because it provides widespread and direct information about products.

Each link in the distribution chain makes a profit by charging a *markup* or commission. Nondirect distribution channels mean higher prices for end users: The more members in the channel—the more intermediaries—the higher the final price. But intermediaries provide *added value* for customers by providing time-saving information and by making the right quantities of products available where and when customers need them.

Channel 5: Distribution by Agents to Consumers and Businesses: Channel 5 differs from previous channels in two ways: (1) An agent functions as the sole intermediary and (2) The agent distributes to both consumers and business customers.

Industrial channels are important because every company is a customer that buys other companies' products. **Industrial (business) distribution** is the network of channel members involved in the flow of manufactured goods to business customers. Business products are traditionally distributed through Channels 6, 7, and 8.

Channel 6: Direct distribution of business products: Most business goods are sold directly by the manufacturer to the industrial buyer. As contact points with customers, manufacturers maintain **sales offices**. *Channel 7: Wholesale distribution of industrial products*: Intermediaries help end users by representing manufacturers or by breaking down large quantities into smaller sales units. It is most often used for accessory equipment (such as office equipment) and supplies. *Channel 8: Wholesale distribution to business retailers*: Instead of buying office supplies from wholesalers (Channel 7), many businesses now shop at office discount stores such as Staples.

The goal of distribution strategy is to make a product accessible in just enough locations to satisfy customers' needs. Different degrees of market coverage are available through three distribution strategies: (1) **Intensive distribution** entails distributing a product through as many channels and channel members as possible. (2) With **exclusive distribution**, a manufacturer grants the exclusive right to distribute or sell a product to a limited number of wholesalers or retailers. (3) Using **selective distribution**, a producer selects only wholesalers and retailers that will give a product special attention.

Because manufacturers may distribute through more than one channel, *channel conflict* may arise. **Channel conflict** often occurs when members disagree over roles or rewards. It may also arise if one member has more power or is perceived as getting preferential treatment. Such conflicts defeat the purpose of the system by disrupting the flow of goods. Conflicts are resolved through better coordination, and a key factor in coordinating activities is *channel leadership*. Usually, one channel member—the **channel captain**—can determine the roles and rewards of the others.

2. *Explain the differences between* merchant wholesalers *and* agents/brokers *and explain the activities of* e-intermediaries.

Services offered by wholesalers to buyers of products for resale depend on the type of intermediary involved: (1) *Merchant wholesalers*: **Merchant wholesalers** buy products from manufacturers and sell them to other businesses, usually providing storage and delivery. A **full-service merchant wholesaler** also provides credit, marketing, and merchandising. **Limited-function merchant wholesalers** provide only a few services, sometimes merely storage. **Drop shippers**, for example, merely take customer orders, purchase goods from producers, and arrange for shipment. **Rack jobbers** market consumer goods directly to retail stores. (2) *Agents and brokers*: Agents and brokers are independent representatives of many companies and work on commissions. They serve as sales and merchandising arms of producers that don't have sales forces.

E-intermediaries are Internet-based channel members who perform one or both of two functions: (1) They collect information about sellers and present it to consumers; (2) they help deliver Internet products. There are three types of e-intermediaries: (1) **Syndicated selling** occurs when a Web site offers other Web sites a commission for referring customers. (2) **Shopping agents** (or **e-agents**) help Internet consumers by gathering and sorting information (such as comparison prices and product features) for making purchases. (3) **Business-to-business brokers** are e-commerce intermediaries for business customers. They may provide up-to-date market information and price and product data.

3. *Identify the different types of* retailing *and* retail stores.

U.S. retail operations fall under two classifications: (1) *Product line retailers*: Retailers featuring broad product lines include **department stores**, which are organized into specialized departments. They are usually large, handle a wide range of goods, and offer a variety of services. **Supermarkets** are divided into departments of related products. Small **specialty stores** serve clearly defined market segments by offering full product lines in narrow product fields.

(2) *Bargain retailers*: **Bargain retailers** carry wide ranges of products and come in many forms. **Discount houses** offer product assortments on a cash-only basis and a few department store services. **Catalog showrooms** mail out catalogs to attract customers into showrooms where they can view display samples, place orders, and receive goods from attached warehouses. **Factory outlets** are manufacturer-owned stores that avoid wholesalers and retailers by selling merchandise directly from factory to consumer. The **warehouse club** (or **wholesale club**) gives discounts on brand-name products to customers who pay membership fees. **Convenience stores** are neighborhood food retailers offering easily accessible locations with extended store hours and speedy service.

Important forms of nonstore retailing include **direct-response retailing**, in which firms make direct contact with customers to inform them about products and take sales orders. **Mail order** (or **catalog marketing**) is a form of direct-response retailing, as is **telemarketing**—using the telephone to sell directly to consumers. **Direct selling** is still used by companies that sell door-to-door or through home-selling parties.

Electronic retailing uses communications networks that allow sellers to connect to consumers' computers. Sellers provide members with Internet access to product displays. Buyers can examine detailed descriptions, compare brands, send for free information, or purchase by credit card. **E-catalogs** use the Internet to display products for both retail and business customers. Today, a seller's Web site is an **electronic**

storefront in which consumers collect information about products, place orders, and pay for purchases. Search engines such as Yahoo! serve as **cybermalls**: collections of *virtual storefronts* representing diverse products and offering such added value as speed, convenience, and efficient searching.

Cyberspace is encroaching on door-to-door distribution channels. In a **multilevel marketing** channel, self-employed distributors get commissions for recruiting new customers and reps. Both retail and B2B customers participate in **interactive marketing**: They interact with multimedia Web sites featuring voice, graphics, animation, film clips, and access to live human advice. The so-called *banner ad*, for example, changes as the user's mouse moves about the page. **Video marketing** lets viewers shop at home from television screens.

4. ***Define* physical distribution, *and describe the major activities in* warehousing *operations.***

Physical distribution refers to the activities needed to move products from manufacturer to consumer. These activities make goods available when and where consumers want them, keep costs low, and provide customer services. They include **warehousing**, or the storage of goods. There are two types of warehouses: **Private warehouses** are owned and used by a single manufacturer, wholesaler, or retailer. **Public warehouses** are independently owned and operated and permit companies to rent only the space they need. Facilities can be further divided according to their uses: **Storage warehouses** provide storage for extended periods. **Distribution centers** store products whose market demand is constant and high. Retail chains, wholesalers, and manufacturers use them to break down large quantities of merchandise into the smaller quantities that stores or customers demand.

Typical warehouse operations include two important costs: In addition to keeping track of what is on hand at any time, **inventory control** involves the balancing act of ensuring that although an adequate supply of a product is in stock at all times, excessive supplies are avoided. **Materials handling** refers to the transportation, arrangement, and orderly retrieval of inventoried goods.

5. ***Compare the five basic forms of* transportation, *and explain how distribution can be used as a marketing strategy.***

The highest cost faced by many companies is the cost of physically moving a product. But firms must consider other factors: the nature of the product, the distance it must travel, the speed with which it must be received, and customer wants and needs. There are five different modes of transportation, and differences in cost are most directly related to delivery speed. (1) *Trucks*: The advantages of trucks include flexibility, fast service, and dependability. (2) *Railroads*: Railroads are now used primarily to transport heavy, bulky items such as cars and steel. Railroad services now include faster delivery and *piggyback* service, in which truck trailers are placed on railcars. (3) *Planes*: Air is the fastest available mode of transportation and also boasts lower costs in handling and packing and unpacking. However, air freight is the most expensive form of transportation. (4) *Water carriers*: Water is the least expensive and the slowest. (5) *Pipelines*: Used to transport liquids and gases, pipelines are slow and inflexible but do provide a constant flow of products and are unaffected by weather.

Important developments in cost-efficiency and competitiveness include **intermodal transportation**—combining different modes of transportation. The goal is to offer simplified source-to-destination delivery by any combination necessary. **Containerization** uses standardized heavy-duty containers in which goods are sealed at points of shipment and opened at final destinations. To improve **order fulfillment**—all activities involved in sales transactions—many e-businesses maintain distribution centers and ship their own products from warehouses near major shipping hubs. Others entrust order filling to distribution specialists.

Many firms regard distribution as a cornerstone of business strategy. This approach means assessing and streamlining the entire range of activities involved in getting products to customers. One approach to streamlining is the use of **hubs**: central distribution outlets that control all or most of a firm's distribution activities. Two contrasting strategies have emerged from this approach: (1) *Supply-side hubs* make the most sense when large shipments flow regularly to a single industrial user. To clear congestion, some firms operate *prestaging hubs* at which all incoming supplies are managed in order to meet production schedules. (2) Whereas supply-side hubs are located near industrial customers, *distribution-side hubs* may be located much farther away, especially if customers are geographically dispersed. From these facilities, finished products, which may be produced in plants throughout the world, can be shipped to customer locations around the globe.

KEY TERMS

distribution mix (p. 336)
intermediary (p. 336)
wholesaler (p. 336)
retailer (p. 336)
distribution channel (p. 336)
direct channel (p. 336)
sales agent/broker (p. 337)
industrial (business) distribution (p. 339)
sales office (p. 339)
intensive distribution (p. 341)
exclusive distribution (p. 341)
selective distribution (p. 341)
channel conflict (p. 342)
channel captain (p. 342)
merchant wholesaler (p. 343)
full-service merchant wholesaler (p. 343)

limited-function merchant wholesaler (p. 343)
drop shipper (p. 343)
rack jobber (p. 344)
e-intermediary (p. 344)
syndicated selling (p. 344)
shopping agent **(or** *e-agent***)** (p. 344)
department store (p. 346)
supermarket (p. 346)
specialty store (p. 346)
bargain retailer (p. 346)
discount house (p. 346)
catalog showroom (p. 346)
factory outlet (p. 346)
warehouse club **(or** *wholesale club***)** (p. 347)
convenience store (p. 347)
direct-response retailing (p. 347)
mail order **(or** *catalog marketing***)** (p. 347)
telemarketing (p. 347)
direct selling (p. 347)
electronic retailing (p. 347)
e-catalog (p. 347)
electronic storefront (p. 348)
cybermall (p. 348)
multilevel marketing (p. 348)
interactive marketing (p. 349)
video marketing (p. 349)
physical distribution (p. 349)
warehousing (p. 349)
private warehouse (p. 349)
public warehouse (p. 349)
storage warehouse (p. 349)
distribution center (p. 349)
inventory control (p. 351)
materials handling (p. 351)
intermodal transportation (p. 353)
containerization (p. 353)
order fulfillment (p. 353)
hub (p. 354)

QUESTIONS AND EXERCISES

Questions for Review

1. From the manufacturer's point of view, what are the advantages and disadvantages of using intermediaries to distribute products? From the end user's point of view?
2. Identify the eight channels of distribution. In what key ways do the four channels used only for consumer products differ from the channels used only for industrial products?
3. Identify and explain the differences between the three distribution strategies.
4. Explain the different roles played by merchant wholesalers and agents/brokers.
5. Explain how the activities of e-agents (Internet shopping agents) or brokers differ from those of traditional agents/brokers.
6. Identify the five modes of transportation used in product distribution. What factors lead companies to choose one over the others to deliver products to end users?

Questions for Analysis

7. Give three examples (other than those in the chapter) of products that use intensive distribution. Do the same for products that use exclusive distribution and selective distribution. For which category was it easiest to find examples? Why?
8. Consider the various kinds of nonstore retailing. Give examples of two products that typify the products sold to at-home shoppers through each form of nonstore retailing. Explain why different products are best suited to each form of nonstore retailing.
9. If you could own a firm that transports products, would you prefer to operate an intermodal transportation business or one that specializes in a single mode of transportation (say, truck or air)? Explain your choice.

Application Exercises

10. Interview the manager of a local manufacturing firm. Identify the firm's distribution strategy and the channels of distribution that it uses. Where applicable, describe the types of wholesalers or retail stores used to distribute the firm's products.
11. Choose any consumer item at your local supermarket, and trace the chain of physical distribution activities that brought it to the store shelf.

Building Your Business Skills

ARE YOU SOLD ON THE NET?

This exercise enhances the following SCANS workplace competencies: demonstrating basic skills, demonstrating thinking skills, exhibiting interpersonal skills, and working with information.

Goal

To encourage students to consider the value of online retailing as an element in a company's distribution system.

The Situation

As the distribution manager of a privately owned clothing manufacturer whose specialty is camping gear and outdoor clothing, you are convinced that your product line is perfect for online distribution. But the owner of the company is reluctant to expand from a successful network of retail stores and a catalog operation. Your challenge is to convince the boss that retailing via the Internet can boost sales.

Method

Step 1

Join with four or five classmates to research the advantages and disadvantages of an online distribution system for your company. Among the factors to consider are the following:

- The likelihood that target consumers are Internet shoppers. Camping gear is generally purchased by young, affluent consumers who are comfortable with the Web.
- The industry trend to online distribution. Are similar companies doing it? Have they been successful?
- The opportunity to expand inventory without increasing the cost of retail space or catalog production and mailing charges.
- The opportunity to maintain a store that never closes.
- The lack of trust many people have about doing business on the Web. (Many consumers are reluctant to provide credit card data over the Internet.)
- The difficulty that electronic shoppers have in finding a Web site when they don't know the store's name.
- The frustration and waiting time entailed by Web searches.
- The certainty that the site will not reach consumers who don't use computers or who are uncomfortable with the Web.

Step 2

Based on your findings, write a persuasive memo to the boss detailing your position on expanding to an online distribution system. Include information that will counter expected objections.

Follow-Up Questions

1. What place does online distribution have in the distribution network of this company?
2. In your view, is online distribution the wave of the future? Is it likely to increase in importance as a distribution system for apparel companies? Why or why not?

Exercising Your Ethics

THE CHAIN OF RESPONSIBILITY

The Situation

Because several stages are involved when distribution chains move products from supply sources to end consumers, the process offers ample opportunity for ethical issues to arise. This exercise encourages you to examine some of the ethical issues that can emerge during transactions among suppliers and customers.

The Dilemma

A customer bought an expensive wedding gift at a local store and asked that it be shipped to the bride in another state. Several weeks after the wedding, the customer contacted the bride because she had sent no word confirming the arrival of the gift. In fact, it hadn't arrived. Charging that the merchandise had not been delivered, the customer requested a refund. The store manager uncovered the following facts:

- All shipments from the store are handled by a well-known national delivery firm.
- The delivery firm verified that the package had been delivered to the designated address two days after the sale.
- Normally, the delivery firm does not obtain recipient signatures; deliveries are made to the address of record, regardless of the name on the package.

The gift giver argued that even though the package had been delivered to the right address, it had not been delivered to the named recipient. It turns out that, unbeknownst to the gift giver, the bride had moved. It stood to reason, then, that the gift was in the hands of the new occupant of the bride's former address. The manager informed the gift giver that the store had fulfilled its obligation. The cause of the problem, she explained, was the incorrect address given by the customer. She refused to refund the customer's money and suggested that the customer might want to recover the gift by contacting the stranger who received it at the bride's old address.

Questions for Discussion

1. What are the responsibilities of each party—the customer, the store, the delivery firm—in this situation?
2. From an ethical standpoint, in what ways is the store manager's action right? In what ways is it wrong?
3. If you were appointed to settle this matter, what actions would you take?

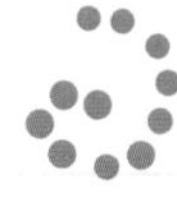

Crafting Your Business Plan

GETTING THE CAFFEINE INTO YOUR CUP

The Purpose of the Assignment

1. To acquaint students with product distribution issues that a sample firm addresses in developing its business plan, in the framework of the *Business PlanPro* (*BPP*) *2002* software package.
2. To demonstrate how channels of distribution, supply chains, and warehousing can be integrated as components in the *BPP* planning environment.

Follow-Up Assignment

After reading Chapter 12 in the textbook, open the BPP *software and look around for information about plans for sup-ply chains and channels of distribution as they apply to a sam-ple firm, a coffee exporter:* Silvera & Sons Ltd. *To find* Silvera, *do the following:*

Open the *Business PlanPro.* If it asks if you want to "create a new business plan" or to "open an existing plan," select "create a new business plan" (even though you are not going to create a plan at this time). You will then be taken to the *Business PlanPro EasyPlan Wizard.* On the screen, click on the option entitled **Research It**. You will then be presented a new list of options, including **Sample Plan Browser**. After click-ing on the **Sample Plan Browser**, scan its alphabetical list of sample plans and double-click on **Export—Coffee**, which is the location for *Silvera & Sons Ltd.* The screen you are look-ing at is the introduction page for the *Silvera* business plan. Next, scroll down from this page until you reach the **Table of Contents** for the *Silvera* business plan.

Now respond to the following items:

1. Describe Silvera's products and customers. Then identify the steps in the supply chain, beginning from raw materials to the final consumer. [Sites to see in *BPP* for this item: In the Table of Contents page, click on **1.0 Executive Summary**. Then click on each of the following in turn: **1.1 Objectives**, **2.0 Company Summary**, **2.2 Company History**, and **3.0 Products**.]
2. Where is Silvera's main warehouse located? What are its activities? [Sites to see in *BPP:* In the Table of Contents page, click on **2.3 Company Locations and Facilities**. After returning to the Table of Contents page, click on **3.0 Products**.]
3. Describe the equipment and warehousing activities that are needed to prepare coffee beans for shipment. [Sites to see in *BPP:* From the Table of Contents page, click on each of the following in turn: **3.1 Competitive Comparison** and **3.4 Technology**.]
4. What steps are involved in getting the product from Silvera's plant in Ouro Fino to Miami? Who is responsible for paying the distribution charges? [Sites to see in *BPP:* In the Table of Contents page, click on **4.2.2 Distribution Patterns**. After returning to the Table of Contents page, click on **5.3.4 Distribution Strategy**.]

Video Exercise

THROUGH THE GRAPEVINE: CLOS DU BOIS WINERY

Learning Objectives

The purpose of this video is to help you

1. Understand how a company works with wholesalers and retailers to make its products available to consumers.
2. Discuss the factors that affect a company's distribution strategy.
3. Consider the goals and challenges of physical distribution.

Synopsis

Riding a tidal wave of U.S. consumer interest in California wines, Clos du Bois Winery sells its wines from coast to coast. The company now ships more than one million cases of wine every year, although less than 20 percent is sold in California. The winery works through a network of statewide and regional distributors that sell to retailers and restaurants which, in turn, serve the wine to consumers. For efficient order fulfillment and inventory management, Clos du Bois ships from a central warehouse to more than 00 wholesaler warehouses around the United States. To ensure that quality is not compromised by temperature extremes, the company also pays close attention to the details of physical distribution. Now it is tapping the infra-structure of parent company Allied Domecq to arrange for wider distribution in Europe.

Discussion Questions

1. *For analysis:* Why does Clos du Bois sell through wholesalers rather than selling directly to retailers and restaurants?
2. *For analysis:* How does the U.S. pattern of table wine consumption affect the winery's domestic distribution strategy?
3. *For application:* What might Clos du Bois do if its supply of a certain vintage runs low?
4. *For application:* What effect does the cost of storing and shipping Clos du Bois wine have on the prices paid by retailers and, ultimately, consumers?
5. *For debate:* Given its long-term relationships with established wholesalers, should Clos du Bois lobby against direct sales of wine to U.S. consumers through Internet channels? Support your position.

Online Exploration

Visit the Web site of the Clos du Bois Winery at <www.closdubois.com/home.html> and (if you are of legal drinking age in your state) enter and read what the company says about its wines, winery, and wine club. Also follow the link to explore the trade site and find out where Clos du Bois wines are sold. Considering the winery's dependence on distribu-tors, why would it invest so heavily in a consumer-oriented Web site? What channel conflict might be caused by this site? If you cannot legally enter the winery's Web site, use your favorite search engine (such as Google.com) to see whether other online retailers are selling this wine. If so, why would Clos du Bois make its wine available through these intermediaries?

CHAPTER 13

Promoting Products

After reading this chapter, you should be able to:

1. Identify the important objectives of *promotion* and discuss the considerations entailed in selecting a *promotional mix.*
2. Discuss the most important *advertising strategies* and describe the key *advertising media.*
3. Outline the tasks involved in *personal selling* and list the steps in the *personal selling process.*
4. Describe the various types of *sales promotions* and distinguish between *publicity* and *public relations.*
5. Show how small businesses use promotional activities.
6. Describe the development of *international promotional strategies.*

Congested? Stuffed Up? Try DTC

There was a time when patients didn't care about the name of the drug that the doctor prescribed—so long as it cured the ailment. Not so in today's consumer-empowered environment. If you watch television, you know the names of such medicines as Vioxx, Prilosec, Zocor, Viagra, Celebrex, and Allegra whether you need them or not. What's more, a lot of people *want* to know more about them. It's all part of a revolutionary marketing movement known as *direct-to-consumer (DTC) marketing.*

DTC is a form of "pull" marketing in which ads tell consumers about a prescription drug and encourage them to ask their doctors about it. Some ads, for example, target the approximately 45 million allergy sufferers in the United States: "Congested? Stuffed Up? Watery Eyes? Talk to your doctor about Allegra-D, send in for your rebate, and start enjoying real relief today."

In using DTC, drug makers are appealing to end users—today's informed health-care consumers—who, instead of passively entrusting themselves to a doctor's care, not only expect educational information about available treatments, but also often engage in self-diagnosis. The concept behind DTC is to motivate the consumer, rather than the MD, to initiate the consumption a specific drug. Ads are designed to increase consumer awareness, thereby stimulating more inquiries to MDs who, in turn, will prescribe the advertised drug more often than its competitors.

It works. Since 1997, industry spending on DTC ads has tripled and now tops $2.5 billion annually. At the same time, of course, prescription takers are feeling the side effects of higher prices at the pharmacy. Why? To help defray the cost of DTC advertising. During the same period, spending on prescription drugs tripled, topping $116 billion in 2000. Major media growth has been in television, whose share of DTC spending is now 64 percent.

Generating a flurry of spiraling ad expenditures and skyrocketing drug prices, DTC advertising is the most prominent and expensive—and controversial—promotional method in the history of pharmaceuticals. Drug companies argue that DTC encourages patients to see their doctors and informs them about the latest health news. Critics counter that DTC drives up prices and stimulates excessive spending on drugs. They also charge that ads often contain incomplete or misleading information that could lead to misuse.

And how do physicians feel about such changes in promotional conditions? In many cases, they are less than enthusiastic. "It's catastrophic in my office, with people coming in and demanding a drug they saw on television," Dr. David Priver of San Diego told a meeting of the American Medical Association (AMA). Other MDs complain that ads are biased, circulate incomplete information, and have already degenerated into a competition to see who can sell the most antihistamines or nasal sprays. The patient, says New Jersey Dr. Angelo Agro, "is at best incompletely informed and at worst . . . deluded." Agro also argues that DTC ads undermine the MD's credibility, especially if the doctor disagrees with the patient's choice among advertised drugs.

The medical profession has considered a resolution asking the Food and Drug Administration (FDA) to ban DTC ads, but health-care professionals can't seem to agree among themselves. The proposed resolution was defeated at the 2001 meeting of the AMA. "It's too late to ban direct-to-consumer advertising," laments Dr. Sandra Adamson Fryhofer. "The cat's out of the bag." Moreover, some doctors point to the upside of DTC.

"The Zyban ads began and all of a sudden people came to me and said: 'Help me stop smoking.'"

~Stuart Gitlow,
ADDICTION PSYCHIATRIST

Ads, they say, help patients remember to take their medicine. They also prompt more patients to talk about health conditions. "I like DTC advertising," says Stuart Gitlow, an addiction psychiatrist in Providence, RI. "The Zyban ads began and all of a sudden people came to me and said: 'Help me stop smoking.'"

Some physicians not only approve of DTC advertising, but they also actively support it with computer-interactive kiosks in their waiting rooms. Moments before entering the office, patients are exposed to ads on consumer-friendly touch-screen displays sponsored by pharmaceutical companies. In effect, drug makers are betting that customers familiar with on-site ads are more likely to request a particular product. "It's location, location, location," says Mark Pavao, VP of marketing for Helios Healthcare's eStations. "We're reaching people when they're thinking about their health care—when they're sitting in the doctor's office."

Controversy and confusion continue to surround DTC advertising. One thing, however, is clear: Physician-patient relationships are being redefined. Ad expenditures and health-care costs are climbing, while consumer access to health-care information is at an all-time high. As of mid-2002, both Congress and a number of state legislatures were investigating the fallout from DTC advertising, looking at both the public-health benefits and health-care costs. Critics are adamant in pointing to the drawbacks of DTC, while advocates proclaim its benefits. The question, however, may not be whether DTC is a cure-all or a prescription for disaster. Many observers contend that it works both ways. Says Drew Altman, president of the Kaiser Family Foundation, a California think tank, "Drug ads may drive up [health-care] costs and drug company profits. But the drugs people get may also make them healthier."

Our opening story continues on page 383.

The pharmaceutical industry has adopted a new—and effective—promotional strategy for prescription products. Although TV is the primary advertising medium, other media are also used to broaden advertisers' reach. As you will see in this chapter, the challenge of marketing is to meet strategic goals by making the right promotional choices in all media.

The Importance of Promotion

promotion

Aspect of the marketing mix concerned with the most effective techniques for selling a product

As we noted in Chapter 10, **promotion** is any technique designed to sell a product. It is part of the *communication mix:* the total message any company sends to consumers about its product. Promotional techniques, especially advertising, must communicate the uses, features, and benefits of products. Sales promotions also include various programs that add value beyond the benefits inherent in the product. It's nice to get a quality product at a good price but even better when you get a rebate or a bonus pack with "20 percent more free."

In this chapter, we will look at the different objectives of and approaches to promotion. We will show when and why companies use particular strategies and tools, and then we'll describe some promotional problems faced by both small and international businesses. First, however, we will explain the two general values to be gained from any promotional activity: *communicating information* and *creating more satisfying exchanges.*

Information and Exchange Values

In free-market systems, a business uses promotional methods to communicate information about itself and its products. The purpose is to influence purchase decisions. From an information standpoint, promotions seek to accomplish four goals:

1. Make potential customers aware of products
2. Make them knowledgeable about products
3. Persuade them to like products
4. Persuade them to purchase products

The buyer gains from the exchange (a more attractive product), as does the seller (more unit sales or higher prices).

Successful promotions, therefore, provide information about products and create exchanges that satisfy both customers' and the sellers' needs. But because promotions are expensive, choosing the best promotional mix is critical. A company's promotional program, whether at the introduction stage (promoting new-product awareness) or maturity stage (promoting brand benefits and customer loyalty), can determine the success or failure of any business or product.

Promotional Objectives

The ultimate objective of any promotion is to increase sales. In addition, marketers may use promotion to *communicate information, position products, add value,* and *control sales volume.*

Communicating Information Consumers cannot buy products unless they know about them. Information may thus advise customers that a product exists, or it may educate them about the product's features. If, for example, you want to connect your business to the Internet economy, a KPMG Consulting <www.kpmg.com> advertisement in the *Wall Street Journal* not only tells you about the availability of KPMG consultants but also educates you about the need to integrate e-strategy, e-branding, and e-services. Information may be communicated in writing (in newspapers and magazines), verbally (in person or over the telephone), or visually (on television, matchbook covers, or billboards). Today, communication about a company's products is so important that marketers try to communicate everywhere consumers can be found: Experts estimate that the average consumer encounters about 1,500 bits of promotional information each day.

Positioning Products As we saw in Chapter 10, **positioning** is the process of establishing an easily identifiable product image in the minds of consumers. Positioning a product is difficult because a company is trying to appeal to a specific segment of the market rather than to the market as a whole. First, the firm must identify which segments are likely to purchase its product and who are its competitors. Only then can it focus its strategy on differentiating its product while still appealing to its target audience.[1]

positioning
Process of establishing an identifiable product image in the minds of consumers

Panera Bread Co. <www.panerabread.com>, for example, has used positioning to differentiate its restaurants from competitors' throughout the eastern half of the United States. It offers a limited menu for morning, noon, and early-evening meals. The "light and healthy" theme of the menu—fresh baked goods, soups, salads, sandwiches, and flavored coffees—is complemented by quiet surroundings, fresh flowers, light classical music, and cleanliness. Sites are chosen so that each Panera outlet is easily accessible to upper-middle-class professionals looking for quick, wholesome, reasonably priced meals in a pleasant atmosphere.[2]

Adding Value Promotional mixes are often designed to communicate a product's value-added benefits. Burger King <www.burgerking.com> shifted its promotional mix by cutting back on advertising dollars and using the money for customer discounts: Getting the same food at a lower price is a value-added benefit. Promotion is also a chief means of establishing a product's perceived value. Customers, after all, perceive value when they know about the value-adding benefits—warranties, repair contracts, and after-purchase service—that they get with one product but not with its competitors.

Controlling Sales Volume Many companies, such as Hallmark Cards <www.hallmark.com>, experience seasonal sales patterns. By increasing promotions during slow periods, these firms can keep production and distribution systems running evenly and stabilize sales volume throughout the year. Promotions can even turn slow seasons into peak sales periods. Greeting card companies and florists, for instance, have actively fostered Grandparents' Day. The result has been increased consumer demand for cards and flowers during what was once a slow season for both industries.

Promotional Strategies

Once its larger marketing objectives are clear, a firm must develop a promotional strategy to achieve them. There are two types of strategies:[3]

pull strategy
Promotional strategy designed to appeal directly to consumers who will demand a product from retailers

push strategy
Promotional strategy designed to encourage wholesalers or retailers to market products to consumers

- A **pull strategy** appeals directly to consumers who will demand the product from retailers. In turn, retailers will demand the product from wholesalers. When publishing a Stephen King novel, for example, Doubleday directs its promotions at horror-story fans. If a bookstore doesn't stock the book, requests from readers will prompt it to order copies from Doubleday.
- Using a **push strategy,** a firm markets its product to wholesalers and retailers who then persuade consumers to buy it. Brunswick Corp., for instance, uses a push strategy to promote Bayliner boats, directing its promotions at dealers and persuading them to order more inventory. Dealers are then responsible for stimulating demand among boaters in their respective districts.

Many large firms combine pull and push strategies. General Foods, for instance, advertises to create consumer demand (pull) for cereals. At the same time, it pushes wholesalers and retailers to stock them.

The Promotional Mix

promotional mix
Combination of tools used to promote a product

As we noted in Chapter 10, there are four types of promotional tools: *advertising, personal selling, sales promotions,* and *publicity and public relations.* The best combination of these tools—the best **promotional mix**—depends on many factors. The most important is the target audience.

The Target Audience: Promotion and the Buyer Decision Process In establishing a promotional mix, marketers match promotional tools with the five stages in the buyer decision process:

1. Buyers must first recognize the need to make a purchase. At this stage, marketers must make sure that buyers are aware of their products. Advertising and publicity, which can reach many people quickly, are important.
2. Buyers also want to learn more about available products. Advertising and personal selling are important because both can be used to educate consumers.
3. Buyers compare competing products. Personal selling can be vital. Sales representatives can demonstrate product quality and performance in comparison with competitors' products.
4. Buyers choose products and purchase them. Sales promotion is effective because it can give consumers an incentive to buy. Personal selling can help by bringing products to convenient purchase locations.
5. Buyers evaluate products after purchase. Advertising, or even personal selling, is sometimes used to remind consumers that they made wise purchases.[4]

Figure 13.1 summarizes the effective promotional tools for each stage of the consumer buying process.

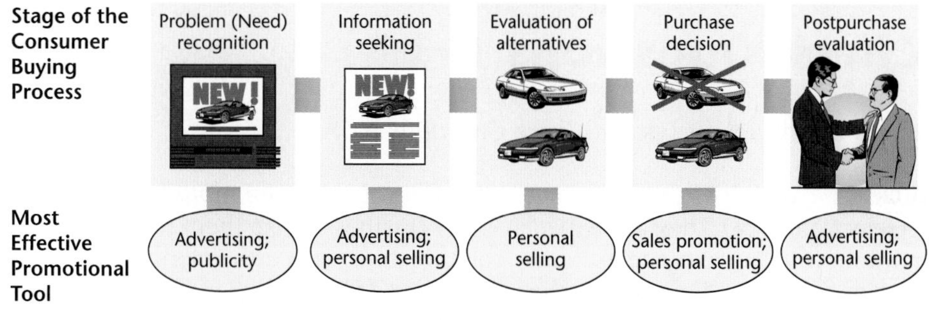

FIGURE 13.1
The Consumer Buying Process and the Promotional Mix

Advertising Promotions

Advertising is paid, nonpersonal communication, by which an identified sponsor informs an audience about a product. In 2000, U.S. firms spent $243 billion on advertising—$83 billion of it by just 100 companies.[5] In this section, we will begin by describing some key elements in advertising strategy. Then we will describe the types of advertising media, noting the advantages and limitations of each one. Then we will discuss advertising campaigns and the role of advertising agencies in designing them.

advertising
Promotional tool consisting of paid, nonpersonal communication used by an identified sponsor to inform an audience about a product

Advertising Strategies

Like promotional tools, advertising strategies usually depend on which stage of the product life cycle (see Chapter 10) a product is in.[6] During the introduction stage, for example, informative advertising can help develop an awareness of the product and help establish a demand for it. When a new textbook is published, instructors receive direct-mail advertisements that notify them of contents and availability.

As products become established and competition increases, strategies change. During the growth and maturity stages, marketers may choose one of three approaches:

- **Persuasive advertising** seeks to influence consumers to buy a company's products rather than its rivals', usually by stressing quality. Goodyear advertises its Eagle #1 NASCAR street tires <www.goodyear.com/us/tires/tirecatalog/EAG1NAS.html> by emphasizing year-round traction, responsive cornering, and similarity to the Goodyear Racing Eagles used in the Daytona 500.[7]
- Also useful during the maturity stage is **comparative advertising,** in which two or more products are directly compared. The goal is to take sales from the competition. In a Pepsi One ad, for example, ferry passengers sit side by side while, unnoticed, Coca-Cola and Pepsi One cans slide from person-to-person on the swaying boat. The message? Inasmuch as people can't taste any difference, why not switch to Pepsi One?[8]
- During the late part of the maturity stage and throughout the decline stage, **reminder advertising** helps to keep the product name in the consumer's mind. Atari <www.atari.com> continues to advertise home video games even though market attention has shifted to competitors such as Nintendo and Sega Genesis.

persuasive advertising
Advertising strategy that tries to influence consumers to buy one company's products instead of those of its rivals

comparative advertising
Advertising strategy that directly compares two or more products

reminder advertising
Advertising strategy that tries to keep a product's name in the consumer's mind

Advertising Media

Consumers tend to ignore the bulk of advertising messages that bombard them. Marketers must find out who their customers are, which media they pay attention to, what messages appeal to them, and how to get their attention. Thus, marketers use several different **advertising media**—specific communication devices

advertising media
Variety of communication devices for carrying a seller's message to potential customers

Self-Check Questions 1–3

*You should now be able to answer Self-Check Questions 1–3**

1. MULTIPLE CHOICE Which of the following is **not true** about *promotional methods* for marketing [select one]: **(a)** They are expensive. **(b)** Businesses use them to communicate information. **(c)** They replace exchange relationships with customers. **(d)** They seek to persuade people to like and purchase products. **(e)** They are intended to make products more attractive.

2. TRUE/FALSE The *positioning* of a product cannot be accomplished until a specific market segment has been identified.

3. MULTIPLE CHOICE In regard to *marketing promotions,* all of the following are correct **except** [select one]: **(a)** The ultimate objective of any promotion is to provide information. **(b)** The promotional mix can provide value-added benefits. **(c)** Some firms use a combination of push and pull strategies. **(d)** The choice of a promotional mix should consider the target audience. **(e)** Personal selling can be effective when potential buyers are evaluating competing products.

*ANSWERS TO SELF-CHECK QUESTIONS 1–3 CAN BE FOUND ON P. AN-8.

for carrying a seller's message to potential customers. IBM <www.ibm.com> uses television ads to keep its name fresh in the minds of consumers, newspaper and magazine ads to educate them about product features, and trade publications to introduce new software. The following are the most common advertising media. Each medium has its own advantages and disadvantages.

Television Figure 13.2 shows network-TV advertising expenditures for some U.S. firms.[9] With 24 percent of all advertising outlays, television is the most widely used medium. In addition to the major networks, cable television increased ad revenues from $3.4 billion in 1995 to more than $14 billion in 2000.[10]

Combining sight, sound, and motion, television appeals to an array of the consumer's senses. In addition, information on viewer demographics for particular programs allows advertisers to aim their commercials at target audiences. Television reaches more people than any other medium, but the welter of TV ads often causes viewers confusion. (Most people can't recall whether a tire commercial sang the praises of Firestone, Goodyear, or B. F. Goodrich.) The brevity of TV ads makes television a poor medium in which to educate viewers, and TV is also the most expensive medium. Companies such as Pepsi, Anheuser-Busch, Levi Strauss, E-Trade, and Monster.com paid an average of $1.9 million for 30-second spots during Super Bowl XXXVI.[11]

Newspapers Newspapers account for about 20 percent of all advertising outlays. Because each local market has at least one daily newspaper, newspapers provide excellent coverage, reaching more than 171 million U.S. adults daily.

Newspaper ads are flexible—they can easily be changed from day to day. By the same token, newspapers are generally thrown out after one day, and because their readership is so broad, they don't allow advertisers to target audiences very well.

direct mail
Advertising medium in which messages are mailed directly to consumers' homes or places of business

Direct Mail **Direct mail** advertisements account for 18 percent of all advertising outlays. Direct mail involves printed ads mailed directly to consumers' homes or

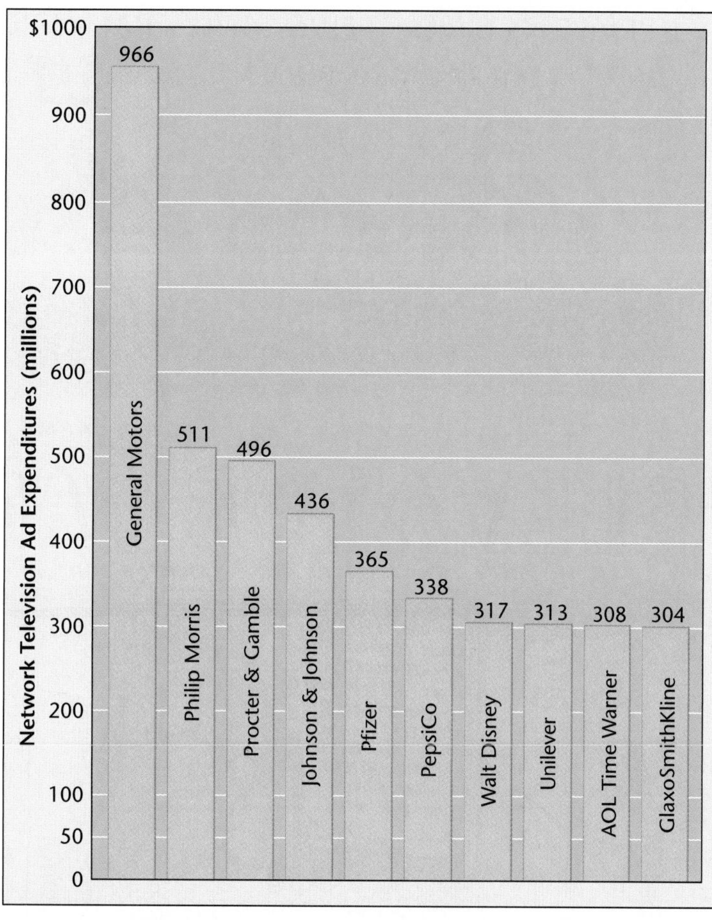

FIGURE 13.2
Top 10 Network TV Advertisers

places of business. It allows a company to select its audience and personalize its message. Although many people discard junk mail, advertisers can predict in advance how many recipients will take a mailing seriously. Moreover, such recipients display stronger-than-average interest in an advertised product and are more likely than most to buy it. Although direct mail involves the largest advance costs of any technique, it also appears to have the highest cost-effectiveness—and it generated $582 million in U.S. sales for 2001.[12]

Radio About eight percent of all advertising outlays go to radio. Over 227 million people—or 96 percent of all persons aged 12 and older in the United States—listen to the radio each day, and radio ads are inexpensive. A small business in a Midwestern town of 100,000 people pays about $20 for a 30-second local radio spot. (A television spot costs over $250.) In addition, because stations are usually segmented into categories such as rock 'n' roll, country and western, jazz, talk, or news, audiences are largely segmented. Unfortunately, radio ads, like TV ads, go by quickly, and people tend to use the radio as background while doing other things.

Magazines Magazine ads account for roughly five percent of all advertising. The huge variety of magazines provides a high level of ready market segmentation. Magazines also allow plenty of space for detailed information, and they can nicely reproduce photographs and artwork. Because they have long lives and tend to be passed around, ads get increased exposure. They must, however, be submitted well in advance, and there is rarely a guarantee of where an ad will appear in a magazine. Magazines are so effective for reaching some targeted audiences that advertisers—including Philip Morris, American Automobile Association, Mercedes-Benz, and Sears & Roebuck—have sponsored their own magazines.

Outdoor Advertising Outdoor advertising—billboards, signs, and advertisements on buses, street furniture, taxis, stadiums, and subways—makes up about one percent of all advertising. Ads are inexpensive, face little competition for consumers' attention, and provide high repeat exposure. They were once regarded as visually inferior to more glamorous media, but new technology has enhanced outdoor advertising and fueled a revival in spending. At 8 percent per year, it's growing faster than newspapers, magazines, and television.

Many of the 400,000 billboards in the United States now experiment with animation and changing images, and today's billboard messages are cheaper because they can be digitally color-printed in large quantities. On the down side, outdoor ads can present only limited information, and sellers have little control over audiences.[13]

Internet Advertising The most recent advertising medium is the Internet, where such well-known names as 3M Corp., Burlington Coat Factory, Miller Genuine Draft, MCI Communications, Reebok, and thousands of lesser-known

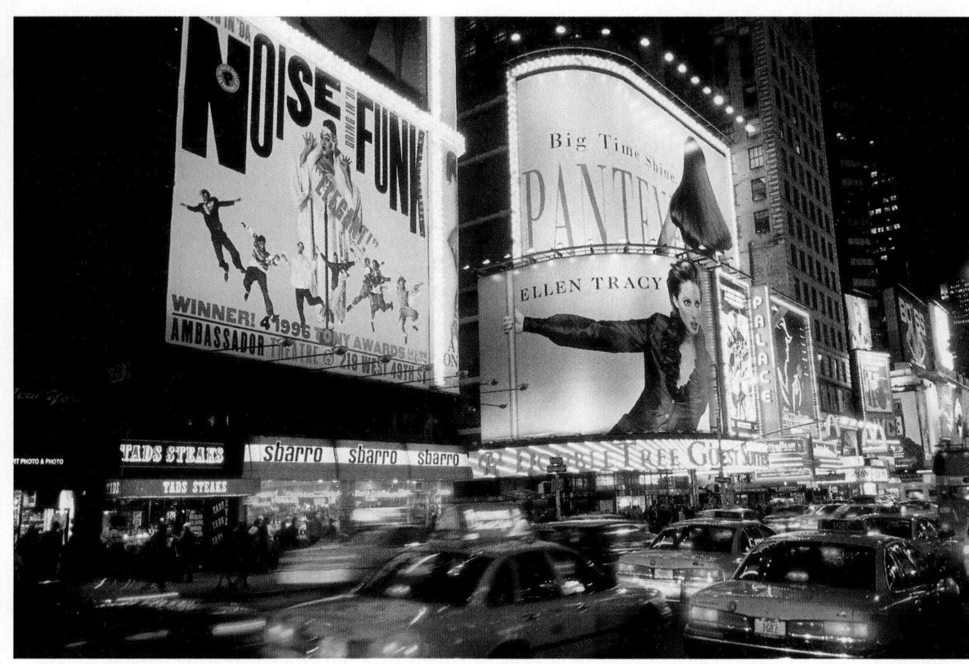

Speed and creativity have given billboards like these in New York's Times Square a new prominence in the world of advertising media. Instead of relying on highly skilled human artists, outdoor ad sellers can now commission digital creations that not only turn heads but still cost less than most other media. Whereas it used to take a month to launch a billboard-based campaign, it now takes just days.

firms have all placed ads. Although Internet advertising is still in its infancy and has great potential, many marketers recognize its limitations. In particular, consumers don't want to wade through electronic pages looking at hundreds of products. Some experts contend that most commercial ads on the Internet are never read by anyone, but Internet advertising accounts for nearly two percent of U.S. ad expenditures.[14]

Targeted advertising, however, is appealing because Internet advertisers can measure the success of messages: They count how many people see each ad and track the number of click-throughs to the advertiser's own Web site. Electronic tracking devices relay such information as which ads generate more purchases, what sales margins result from each sale, and which ads attract the most attention from target audiences. DoubleClick <www.doubleclick.com>, a global Internet advertising firm, was one of the first companies to help other advertisers take advantage of the Web's unique capacity for tailoring ad messages and tracking user behavior online. DoubleClick also sells ad space that allows advertisers to reach as many as 80 million users worldwide on thousands of Web sites, such as Nasdaq.com, Zagat.com, TravelWeb, Macromedia, and Hollywood.com.[15]

Although still an immature marketing medium, the Internet's potential for reaching customers continues to lure more advertisers. In 2000, for example, U.S. companies spent $4.3 billion on Internet ads—an upsurge of 53 percent over 1999. General Motors led the way with $52 million.[16] The "Wired World" box in this chapter tells the story of one company that hired an e-marketing specialist to help it devise and implement an Internet marketing strategy.

Data Mining and Data Warehousing for Internet Advertising The Internet fosters targeting because volumes of data can be gathered electronically from users. The behavior patterns of millions of users can be traced by analyzing files of information gathered over time. By means of *data mining* and *data warehousing* (see Chapter 10), vast pools of data on user behavior reveal who has bought which products and how many, over what Web site individuals bought products, how they paid, and so on. By analyzing what consumers actually do, e-marketers can determine what subsequent purchases they are likely to make and then send them tailor-made ads.[17]

The Sound Approach to Internet Marketing

You may not recognize the name Altec Lansing Technologies Inc., but you've probably listened to its products. Altec designs, manufactures, and markets high-quality sound systems for personal computers and home-entertainment systems. Its customers are mostly other companies—Compaq, Dell Computer, IBM, Fujitsu—that use Altec industrial products to make consumer products. Altec has built strategic partnerships with such leading companies as Intel Corp., Dolby® Labs, and Microsoft, but Altec managers decided they could use some outside help getting into Internet marketing. They selected Agency.Com Ltd., experts in e-business marketing, to determine how to best promote the company to competitive advantage on the Net.

Step 1 called for an overall Internet strategy: Altec and Agency.Com had to identify the firm's basic goal in Net marketing and then devise a way to implement the best strategy for achieving that goal. One consideration was Altec's intention to maintain long-lasting relationships with business customers. Another consideration was changing industry trends. At the time, the markets for home computing, office computing, and home entertainment were converging, and the technology was changing from analog to digital. To address these considerations, Altec and Agency.Com proposed a strategy featuring five elements:

1. Altec would go online and stress relationship marketing to ensure ongoing relationships with customers.
2. Altec would position its products on quality—to provide the best audio experience possible.
3. Altec would secure current customers and encourage further sales.
4. Altec would seek new customers.
5. Altec would strive for greater brand recognition.

The company's Web site <www.alteclansing.com> is now the focal point for all of its online activity. It is a commerce center featuring information pages, and, along with e-mail, it provides an online communication channel for building and maintaining customer relationships. Customers can access product listings, assess system requirements and performance specs, download speaker-system software, link directly to Altec distributors, and make online purchases. The site includes pages devoted to customer support and a feature called System Builders, which provides special services to companies that buy Altec systems for computers and sound systems. Altec also purchases space on third-party sites and uses comarketing to bring new customers to the Web site.

"All we're doing," says Howard Draft, chairman of Draft Worldwide in Chicago <www.draftworldwide.com>, "is using information we have on our customers, with overlays of demographic or psychographic information, to enhance our knowledge of them and market back to them." Instead of using one advertisement to blanket all consumers, data mining makes it feasible to use niche advertising that is targeted to individual consumers.[18]

> **"All we're doing is using information we have on our customers... to enhance our knowledge of them."**
>
> ~Howard Draft, ADVERTISING EXECUTIVE ON THE USE OF DATA MINED FROM THE INTERNET

Virtual Advertising Even newer than Internet advertising, *virtual advertising* digitally implants brands or products into live or taped programming, giving the illusion that the implant is part of the show. With this technique, products appear as part of TV shows themselves—when viewers are paying more attention—instead of during commercial breaks. In a televised basketball game, the image of a brand—say, a Rolex watch or an Acura hubcap—can be enlarged and superimposed on center court, where it will be seen for the whole game. Digital images can also be inserted into taped movies. A Kmart shopping bag can be set on the table during a kitchen scene, a Philips Flat TV can be hung on the wall during a scene in the den, and your favorite stars can be redressed in Polo and other brand-name clothing.[19]

Other Advertising Channels A combination of other media, including catalogs, sidewalk handouts, Yellow Pages, skywriting, telephone calls, special events, and

Industry*	Magazine	Newspaper	Outdoor	Television	Radio
Retail	15.2%	41.1%	1.7%	38.1%	3.9%
Telecommunications	7.9	28.6	2.7	54.2	6.6
Restaurants	1.1	2.6	4.7	87.5	4.1
Apparel	68.6	2.1	1.4	27.3	0.6
Manufacturing equipment, and freight	31.5	11.8	1.0	54.2	1.5

*Comparative Internet figures not available

TABLE 13.1
Media Mix by Industry

door-to-door communication, make up the remaining 22 percent of all U.S. advertising. The combination of media through which a company advertises is called its **media mix.** As Table 13.1 suggests, different industries use different mixes, and most depend on a variety of media for reaching target audiences.

media mix
Combination of advertising media chosen to carry a message about a product

Preparing the Campaign with an Advertising Agency

An **advertising campaign** is the arrangement of ads in selected media to reach target audiences. It includes several activities that, taken together, constitute a program for meeting a marketing objective, such as introducing a new product or changing a company's image. A campaign typically includes six steps:

advertising campaign
Arrangement of ads in selected media to reach targeted audiences

1. Identify the target audience.
2. Establish the advertising budget.
3. Define the objectives of the advertising messages.
4. Create advertising messages.
5. Select the appropriate media.
6. Evaluate the advertising effectiveness.

Advertising agencies—independent companies that provide some or all of their clients' advertising needs—help to develop ad campaigns by providing specialized services. They work with clients to determine a campaign's central message, create detailed message content, identify ad media, and negotiate media purchases.

advertising agency
Independent company that provides some or all of a client firm's advertising needs

The advantages of agencies include expertise in developing ad themes, message content, and artwork as well as in coordinating ad production and advising on legal matters. Today, there are specialized agencies to cater to clients with specific goals in specific industries or market segments. Some agencies, for instance, specialize in pharmaceuticals. Burrell Communications Group <www.hoovers.com/co/capule/4/0,2163,52144,00.html?>, one of the largest African-American–owned agencies in the United States, specializes in ads aimed at African-American consumers.

As payment, agencies usually receive a percentage, traditionally 15 percent of media purchase cost. In other words, if an agency buys a $1 million television commitment for a client's campaign, it will be paid $150,000.[20]

Personal Selling

In **personal selling,** a salesperson communicates one-to-one with potential customers to identify their needs and align them with the seller's products. The oldest form of selling, it lends credibility to a firm because it allows buyers to interact

personal selling
Promotional tool in which a salesperson communicates one-on-one with potential customers

MUSIC UP AND UNDER
THROUGHOUT
BROOKS V/O: I learned from...

David Brooks
Pagosa Springs, CO
my father and my grandfather,

don't think about trying to buy

STIHL
but concentrate on buying the best.

You work hard for your money.

You've got to put it where you know it's gonna do the best.

That have held their quality.

But for my money,

STIHL®
I would go out and buy a Stihl chainsaw.

A company hires an advertising agency to identify the target audience for its product and to ensure that the whole range of its advertising is aimed at that market. The agency is also responsible for planning the campaign and selecting the appropriate media. In this campaign for Stihl Power Tools <www.stihl.com>*, the agency of Howard, Merrell & Partners* <www.merrellgroup.com> *uses television as the best medium for putting the product in the most effective context. That context, in turn, is determined by the agency's understanding of the product and the crucial message that it wants to get across. For Stihl, the message is the importance of buying the best possible equipment.*

with and ask questions of the seller. This professional intimacy is especially effective in relationship marketing. It gives the seller a clearer picture of the buyer's business and allows salespeople to provide buyers with value-adding services.[21]

Because it involves personal interaction, personal selling requires some trust between buyer and seller—a relationship that must often be established over time. Moreover, because presentations are generally made to only one or two individuals at a time, personal selling is the most expensive form of promotion per contact. Expenses may include salespeople's compensation and overhead—usually travel, food, and lodging. The average cost of a single industrial sales is approximately $300.

Self-Check Questions 4–6

*You should now be able to answer Self-Check Questions 4–6**

4. MULTIPLE CHOICE Which of the following is **true** about *advertising media* [select one]? (a) TV is the most-used media and reaches the most people. (b) TV ads are more effective than radio ads. (c) Advertisers who want fast, immediate impact prefer magazines. (d) The success of an Internet ad cannot be measured as easily as the success of ads in other media.

5. MULTIPLE CHOICE Which of the following is **not** true about Internet advertising [select one]? **(a)** The Internet is the most recent advertising medium. **(b)** Consumers like it because it provides electronic pages with lots of interesting and attractive ads. **(c)** Marketers recognize it as having great promotional potential. **(d)** It is a source for volumes of data about consumer behavior.

6. TRUE/FALSE Large *retailers* have more difficulty advertising to target markets than do sellers of *industrial products*.

*ANSWERS TO SELF-CHECK QUESTIONS 4–6 CAN BE FOUND ON P. AN-8.

Say what you mean

THE MEDIUM, THE MESSAGE, AND THE MARKET

In the past decade or so, we've witnessed a worldwide explosion of media and the technology that powers our communications systems. In its wake, we've also seen a vast expansion in the opportunities to advertise and otherwise promote products of every kind. The advent of enhanced cable and satellite TV, the Internet, and satellite radio—all of these new communications media are also new avenues for advertisers to reach ever-expanding markets.

The ability of marketers to reach targeted audiences is more critical than ever before. For one thing, the contemporary market is more segmented (read: fragmented). Ethnic and cultural background; urban, suburban, and rural lifestyles; discrepancies in age and differences in gender—all of these factors enter into the complex demographic mix to which marketers must now communicate in the United States alone.

Take the Spanish-speaking market. People of Hispanic origin now account for a sizeable proportion of the U.S. consumer market. In some states, such as California, they constitute the largest minority group. The phenomenal growth of Spanish-language newspapers, magazines, Internet sites, and TV channels shows just how important this market is to American business. To ignore it is clearly to miss a wealth of opportunities in an increasingly lucrative market. The most savvy advertisers know their markets well and understand the most effective ways to take advantage of their opportunities by connecting with a diverse customer base.

Of course, communicating with culturally and ethnically diverse consumers means revising one's notions about buyers and what they want. Expectations and assumptions about a product may be quite different from group to group, and advertisers also need to be aware of cultural sensibilities. How important is family to one group and religion to another? In what ways do two different groups perceive gender roles? How do different groups regard and use their leisure time?

Of course, the medium is important, too. Does your targeted audience get most of its information from TV, the Internet, or print media? To what extent can advertisers compile accurate socioeconomic profiles of targeted audiences? At best, trying to promote a product without considering such issues will doom it to poor sales. At worst, a culturally uninformed campaign can even backfire and turn opportunities into public-relations nightmares.

We all like to feel that our core values are respected in the marketplace. Besides, it makes good business sense for marketers to know their customers' likes and dislikes. For advertisers, the bottom line is to know your market and to use the most appropriate media for communicating a message that's been well researched and designed. Today's advertisers must also be prepared to fine-tune their campaigns, no matter how subtle or comprehensive the overhaul needs to be.

Telemarketing and Personal Sales Costs have prompted many companies to turn to *telemarketing:* using telephone solicitations to conduct the personal selling process. Telemarketing is useful in handling any stage of this process and in arranging appointments for salespeople. For example, it cuts the cost of personal sales visits to industrial customers, each of whom requires about four visits to complete a sale. Telemarketing has saved some sellers $1,000 or more in sales visits. Such savings are stimulating the growth of telemarketing, which, in the United States, placed 40 billion phone calls and sold $668 billion in goods and services in 2001. Employing some six million people in the United States, the industry's growth makes sense. It averages more than a $7 return for every dollar invested.[22]

Mid-Chapter Internet Field Trip

"Marketing Help Is Just a Click Away"

In the first part of this chapter, we discussed *advertising promotions,* including advertising *strategies* and *media.* The choice of media, or the *media mix,* includes both *direct mail* and *Internet* advertising for reaching specific markets. We saw also that firms sometimes call upon outside specialists to help formulate effective advertising campaigns. In what ways can such outside specialists help a company plan its advertising? What services do they offer, and what value do those services provide? What kinds of results might a client firm expect from such specialists?

Let's look further into these questions by exploring the Web site of a successful Internet company—DoubleClick Inc.—at <www.doubleclick.com>. At the top of the homepage are several boxes, including those labeled **Marketers, Publishers, Corporate,** and **International.** In this exercise, we will be mostly, though not exclusively, concerned with **Marketers.**

Begin at the top of the homepage by clicking on the **Corporate** box. Then, in the drop-down menu, select **About DoubleClick** and read that page:

1. What is DoubleClick's main line of business?

Now return to the top of the homepage and click on **Marketers.** In the drop-down menu, select **Direct Marketing.** Scan the categories of available services:

2. Of what value is *Abacus* for developing an advertising campaign?
3. In what ways might DoubleClick's Direct Mail services be of value to an advertiser?

After returning again to the homepage, click on **Marketers.** In the drop-down menu, select **Products/Services,** and scan the list of available services:

4. In what ways might a client expect to benefit from the DoubleClick Brand Network?

Return to the homepage and click once again on **Marketers.** In the drop-down menu, select **Media Buying.** Examine the contents of this page, especially **Marketing Tools:**

5. What kinds of advertising services are available under the heading of "Marketing Tools"?

To continue your Internet Field Trip, click on www.prenhall.com/griffin

Sales Force Management

Sales force management means setting goals at the top levels of an organization, setting practical objectives for salespeople, organizing a sales force that can meet those objectives, and implementing and evaluating the success of the overall sales plan. Obviously, it is an important factor in meeting the marketing objectives of any large company. In this section, we begin by describing the basic types of *personal selling situations.* Then we discuss the *personal selling tasks* for which managers set objectives and the *personal selling process* whose success managers judge.

Personal Selling Situations Managers of both telemarketers and traditional salespeople must consider the ways in which personal sales activities are affected by the differences between consumer and industrial products:

retail selling
Personal selling situation in which products are sold for buyers' personal or household use

industrial selling
Personal selling situation in which products are sold to businesses, either for manufacturing other products or for resale

- **Retail selling** is selling a consumer product for the buyer's personal or household use.
- **Industrial selling** is selling products to other businesses, either for the purpose of manufacturing other products or for resale.

Levi's <www.levi.com>, for instance, sells jeans to the retail clothing operation Gap Inc. <www.gap.com> (industrial selling). In turn, consumers purchase Levi's jeans at one of The Gap's stores (retail selling).

Each of these situations has distinct characteristics. In retail selling, the buyer usually comes to the seller, whereas the industrial salesperson typically calls on the prospective buyer. An industrial decision may take longer than a retail decision because it involves more money, decision makers, and weighing of alternatives. As we saw in Chapter 10, industrial buyers are professional *purchasing agents* accustomed to dealing with salespeople. Consumers in retail stores, on the other hand, may actually be intimidated by salespeople.

Personal Selling Tasks An important aspect of sales force management is overseeing salespeople as they perform the three basic tasks of personal selling: *order processing, creative selling,* and *missionary selling.* Depending on the product and company, sales jobs usually require individuals to perform all three tasks to some degree.

Order Processing In **order processing,** a salesperson receives an order and sees to its handling and delivery. Route salespeople, who call on regular customers to check inventories, are often order processors. With the customer's consent, they may decide on the sizes of reorders, fill them directly from their trucks, and even stock shelves.

order processing
Personal selling task in which salespeople receive orders and see to their handling and delivery

Creative Selling When the benefits of a product are not entirely clear, **creative selling** can help to persuade buyers. Thus, any new product can benefit from creative selling that differentiates it from a competitor's. Most industrial products involve creative selling, especially when a buyer is unfamiliar with a product or with the features of a specific brand. Personal selling is also crucial for high-priced consumer products, such as homes and cars, for which buyers comparison shop.

creative selling
Personal selling task in which salespeople try to persuade buyers to purchase products by providing information about their benefits

Missionary Selling A company may use **missionary selling** when it wants to promote itself and its products rather than simply to close a sale. Drug company representatives promote drugs to doctors who, in turn, prescribe them to patients. The sale, then, is actually made at the drugstore. In this case, the goal may be to promote the company's long-term image as much as any given product. Another form of missionary selling is after-sale technical assistance for complex products. IBM uses after-sale missionary selling to ensure that customers know how to use equipment and to promote goodwill.

missionary selling
Personal selling tasks in which salespeople promote their firms and products rather than try to close sales

The Personal Selling Process Perhaps the most complicated of these three sales tasks is creative selling. The creative salesperson is responsible for starting and following through on most of the steps in the personal selling process:

1. ***Prospecting and qualifying.*** A salesperson must first have a potential customer, or prospect. **Prospecting** is the process of identifying potential customers. Salespeople find prospects through company personnel records and customers, friends, relatives, and business associates. Prospects must then be **qualified** to determine whether they have the authority to buy and the ability to pay.
2. ***Approaching.*** The *approach* refers to the first few minutes of a salesperson's contact with a qualified prospect. Because it affects the salesperson's credibility, the success of later stages depends on the prospect's first impression. A salesperson must, therefore, present a professional appearance and greet prospects in a confident manner.
3. ***Presenting and demonstrating.*** Next, the salesperson makes a *presentation* to the prospect—a full explanation of the product, its features, and its uses. Most important, the presentation links product benefits to the prospect's needs. A presentation may or may not include a demonstration.
4. ***Handling objections.*** No matter what product is for sale, prospects will have some objections. At the very least, they may angle for discounts by objecting

prospecting
Step in the personal selling process in which salespeople identify potential customers

qualifying
Step in the personal selling process in which salespeople determine whether prospects have the authority to buy and ability to pay

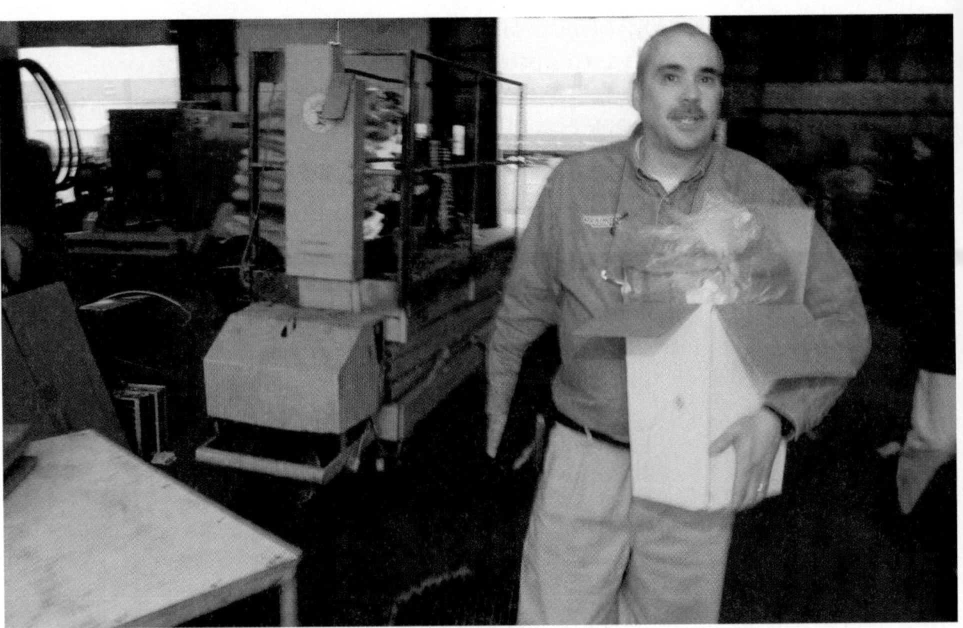

Tom Giorgio sells tools and other industrial supplies for W.W. Grainger Inc. <www.grainger.com>. *About two years ago, the business of his best clients started to slump. Things got worse after September 11, and Giorgio has made some changes in his selling strategies. He used to spend 80% of his time with 20% of his customers—the ones who bought big-ticket items, such as hydraulic coolers and belt-driven generators. Now his presentations feature more modest products from the Grainger catalog, such as light fixtures and janitorial supplies, and he calls more often on the prospects who are likely to buy them. "I'm out looking for new customers," says Giorgio. "People unaffected, like school systems, food companies."*

to price. Objections, however, not only indicate that the buyer is interested but also pinpoint the parts of the presentation that trouble the buyer.

closing

Step in the personal selling process in which salespeople ask prospective customers to buy products

5. ***Closing.*** The most critical part of the selling process is the **closing,** in which the salesperson asks the prospect to buy the product. Successful salespeople recognize the signs that a customer is ready to buy. Prospects who start to figure out monthly payments are clearly indicating readiness to buy. Salespeople should then try to close the sale, either asking directly for the sale or implying a close indirectly. Questions such as "Could you take delivery Tuesday?" and "Why don't we start you off with an initial order of 10 cases?" are implied closes. Indirect closes place the burden of rejecting the sale on the prospect, who may find it a little harder to say no.
6. ***Following up.*** Follow-up is a key activity, especially in relationship marketing. For lasting relationships with buyers, good salespeople don't end the sales process with the closing. They want sales to be so successful that customers will buy from them again. Thus, they supply additional services—after-sale support that provides convenience and added value. Follow-ups include quick processing of customer orders, on-time delivery, and speedy repair service.

Sales Promotions

sales promotion

Short-term promotional activity designed to stimulate consumer buying or cooperation from distributors, sales agents, or other members of the trade

Sales promotions are short-term promotional activities designed to stimulate either consumer buying or cooperation from distributors, sales agents, or other members of the trade. They are important because they increase the likelihood that buyers will try products. They also enhance product recognition and can increase purchase size and amount.[23]

Successful sales promotions are convenient and accessible when the decision to buy occurs. If Harley-Davidson holds a one-week motorcycle promotion and you have no local dealer, the promotion is useless to you and you won't buy. If Folgers offers a $1-off coupon that you can save and use later, the promotion is both convenient and accessible.

Types of Sales Promotions

The best-known forms of promotions are coupons, point-of-purchase displays, purchasing incentives (especially free samples and premiums), trade shows, and contests and sweepstakes.

- Certificates entitling bearers to savings off regular prices are **coupons.** They may be used to encourage customers to try new products, to lure customers away from competitors, or to induce customers to buy more of a product. They appear in newspapers and magazines, are included with other products, and often arrive by direct mail.

coupon
Sales promotion technique in which a certificate is issued entitling the buyer to a reduced price

- To grab customers' attention as they move through stores, companies use **point-of-purchase (POP) displays.** Located at the ends of aisles or near checkout counters, POP displays make it easier for customers to find products and easier for sellers to eliminate competitors from consideration.

point-of-purchase (POP) display
Sales promotion technique in which product displays are located in certain areas to stimulate purchase

- Free samples and premiums are *purchasing incentives.* Free samples let customers try products without risk. They may be given out at retail outlets or sent by direct mail. **Premiums** are free or reduced-price items, such as pens, pencils, calendars, and coffee mugs, given to consumers in return for buying a specified product. Retailers and wholesalers also receive premiums for carrying some products.

premium
Sales promotion technique in which offers of free or reduced-price items are used to stimulate purchases

- Periodically, industries sponsor **trade shows** for members and customers. Trade shows allow companies to rent booths to display and demonstrate products to customers who have a special interest or who are ready to buy. They are inexpensive and, because the buyer is already interested in a given type of product, are quite effective.

trade show
Sales promotion technique in which various members of an industry gather to display, demonstrate, and sell products

- Customers, distributors, and sales representatives may all be induced to increase sales by means of *contests.* For example, consumers may be asked to enter their cats in the Purina Cat Chow calendar contest by submitting entry blanks from the backs of cat food packages.

Publicity and Public Relations

To the delight of marketers with tight budgets, **publicity** is free. Marketers usually have little control over publicity, but because it is presented in a news format, consumers often regard it as objective and credible.[24]

publicity
Promotional tool in which information about a company or product is transmitted by general mass media

Consider the case of Tyco International Ltd. <www.tyco.com>, a diversified conglomerate in electronics, security systems, medical supplies, commercial cable, and other interests. Tyco received a series of jolts in early 2002, when investors reacted to publicity about two actions taken by the company. In January, executives announced plans to break the company into four businesses. This plan was developed in response to the growing public mistrust—stemming from the collapse of Enron Corp. over accounting irregularities—of diversified companies which, like Tyco, encouraged complex accounting procedures. Then in April, the company reversed itself, announcing it had scrapped the plan to break up. The next day, as word spread about the firm's actions and financial condition, Tyco stock fell 20 percent. From early January to late April, it tumbled more than 60 percent, losing $72 billion in market value.[25]

Public relations is company-influenced publicity that seeks either to build good relations with the public or to deal with unfavorable events. A firm will try to establish goodwill with customers (and potential customers) by performing and publicizing its public-service activities.

public relations
Company-influenced publicity directed at building goodwill with the public or dealing with unfavorable events

The World Trade Center, for example, was home to 2,500 employees of Citigroup, which is best known as a credit-card issuer with 90 million card members worldwide. Both Citigroup's annual report and the company's Web site

Best Buy <www.bestbuy.com>, a 1,900-store chain once known for consumer electronics and appliances, has added software and entertainment to its inventory and is now the country's biggest retailer of CDs and DVDs. To promote its entertainment products, Best Buy uses promotional tie-ins, such as deals to become the exclusive retailer of U2's latest DVD. In return, Best Buy spent $10 million to put U2 <www.u2.com> in newspaper circulars and on the sides of buses. Meanwhile, CEO Richard Schultze (right) pursues his strategy of putting electronics and entertainment under one roof. "Consumers," he explains, "are telling us they want to depend increasingly on one guy."

<www.citigroup.com> describe Citigroup Relief Fund scholarships for children of parents killed or permanently disabled in the September 11th terrorist attack on the World Trade Center. The company endowed the fund with $15 million, and with other contributors following its lead, the fund has grown to more than $20 million. To cover administrative costs, Citigroup maintains a Web site <www.citigroup.com/citigroup/relieffund/>, at which the public can monitor the fund's status and find out about contribution options.[26]

Promotional Practices in Small Business

From our discussion so far, you may think that only large companies can afford to promote their products. Although small businesses generally have fewer resources, cost-effective promotions can improve sales and allow small firms to compete with much larger firms.

Small-Business Advertising

Has any other development in modern history provided more advertising opportunities than the Internet? Cheaper access to computing equipment, to online services, and to Web-site expertise puts cyberspace within the grasp of nearly every firm. Still, owners must decide which audiences to target and what messages to send. And even though the Web can instantaneously reach distant customers, other methods depend on the market that the small business is trying to reach: local, national, or international.

Non-prime–time ads on local or cable TV have good impact at costs within the reach of many small firms. More often, however, they use newspaper, radio, and, increasingly, direct mail to reach local markets. For year-round advertising, the Yellow Pages are popular for both industrial and consumer products. However, many small businesses, especially those selling to consumer markets, rely more on seasonal advertising.

Many businesses (such as Sears and L.L. Bean) have grown by using direct mail, particularly catalogs. By purchasing mailing lists from other companies, small firms can cut costs with targeted mailings. The ability to target an audience also makes specialized magazines attractive to small businesses. Georgetown Galleries of Bethesda, Maryland, and Omaha Steaks of Omaha, Nebraska, reach for upscale nationwide audiences in the *Smithsonian* magazine. When it comes to international markets, television, radio, and newspapers are too expensive for small businesses. Most small firms find direct mail and carefully targeted magazine ads the most effective tools.

The Role of Personal Selling in Small Business

As with advertising, small-business personal-selling strategies depend on intended markets. Some small firms maintain sales forces, especially in local markets, where clients can be quickly visited. Others contract with *sales agencies*—companies that act on behalf of several clients. Because the costs of a national sales force are high, small companies prefer sales agencies and such methods as telemarketing. By combining telemarketing with catalogs or other print media, small businesses can sometimes compete with larger companies on a national scale. Syncsort Inc. <www.syncsort.com> combined a telemarketing staff with eight national sales reps to become the number-one developer of computer software for sorting data into convenient formats. Number two is IBM.

Small-Business Promotions

Small companies use the same sales promotion incentives as larger companies. Large firms tend to rely on coupons, POP displays, and sales contests, but because these tools are expensive and difficult to manage, small firms prefer premiums and special sales.[27] An automobile dealership, for example, might offer you a fishing reel if you come in to road-test a new four-wheel-drive vehicle. Service companies ranging from martial arts centers to dry cleaners frequently feature special sale prices.

International Promotional Strategies

In recent decades, we have witnessed a profound shift from home-country marketing to multicountry and now to global marketing. Nowhere is this rapidly growing global orientation more evident than in the area of promotions, especially advertising.

Emergence of the Global Perspective

Every company that markets products in several countries faces a basic choice: use a *decentralized approach,* maintaining separate marketing management for each country, or adopt a *global perspective,* directing a coordinated marketing program at one worldwide audience. Thus, the **global perspective** is a philosophy that directs marketing toward a worldwide rather than toward local or regional markets. American companies such as IBM, PepsiCo, and the accounting firm KPMG International are in the forefront of global orientation in advertising.

global perspective

Company's approach to directing its marketing toward worldwide rather than local or regional markets

The Movement Toward Global Advertising A truly global perspective means designing products for multinational appeal—that is, genuinely global products.[28] A few brands, such as Coca-Cola, McDonald's, Mercedes Benz, Rolex, and Xerox, enjoy global recognition and have become truly global brands. Not surprisingly,

Marlboro is the number-one cigarette in the world and one of the world's most successful brands. Why does the Marlboro Man succeed in selling cigarettes in Hanoi, the capital of Vietnam? Marlboro's maker, Philip Morris <www.philipmorris.com>, *has known for a long time that the image of the cowboy, coupled with an appeal to the urge for independence and an association with wide open spaces, is not merely an American image: These themes apparently strike a chord that's nearly universal. It also doesn't hurt that Marlboro is an American cigarette: Among consumers around the world, American cigarettes inspire confidence in quality as readily as Japanese electronics and German cars.*

globalization is affecting the promotional activities of such firms. In effect, they have already posed the question, "Is it possible to develop global advertising?"

Certainly, one universal advertising program would be more efficient and cost-effective than developing different programs for each of many countries. For several reasons, however, global advertising is not feasible for many companies. Four factors make global advertising a challenging proposition:

- ***Product variations.*** Even if a product has universal appeal, some variations, or slightly different products, are usually preferred in different cultures. In the magazine business, Hearst Corp. <www.hearst.com> has expanded to 33 editions of *Cosmopolitan* magazine, including one for Central America; English and Spanish editions for the United States; and local editions for Italy, Turkey, Russia, Hong Kong, and Japan. *Reader's Digest* <www.readersdigest.com> has 48 editions in 19 languages.
- ***Language differences.*** Compared with those in other languages, ads in English require less print space and airtime because English is a more efficient and precise language than most others. Moreover, translations are often inexact and confusing: When Coke first went to China, the direct translation of "Coca-Cola" came out "Bite the wax tadpole." Advertising agencies have set up worldwide agency networks that can coordinate a campaign's central theme while allowing regional variations.
- ***Cultural receptiveness.*** There is a lot of difference across nations regarding the mass advertising of sensitive products (such as birth control or personal hygiene products), not to mention those for which advertising may be legally restricted (alcohol, cigarettes). An American in Paris may be surprised to see nudity in billboard ads and even more surprised to find that France is the only country in the European Union (EU) that bans advertising or selling wine on the Internet. In the EU and through much of Asia, comparative advertising is considered distasteful or even illegal.
- ***Image differences.*** Any company's image can vary from nation to nation, regardless of any advertising appeals for universal recognition. American

Self-Check Questions 7–9

*You should now be able to answer Self-Check Questions 7–9**

7. MULTIPLE CHOICE Suppose your chief *personal selling* strategy is to *persuade* buyers that there are benefits to your company's product, especially buyers who are unfamiliar with its features and uses. The appropriate name for this type of selling is [select one]: **(a)** order extraction; **(b)** missionary selling; **(c)** prospecting; **(d)** psychological selling; **(e)** creative selling.

8. TRUE/FALSE The most critical stage in the *personal selling process* is the *closing.* In closing, the salesperson should ask the client indirectly to close the sale rather than ask directly.

9. TRUE/FALSE Even if it has done nothing to deserve bad publicity, a company can suffer adverse publicity because of the actions of other firms.

*ANSWERS TO SELF-CHECK QUESTIONS 7–9 CAN BE FOUND ON P. AN-9.

Express, IBM, and Nestlé have better images in the United States than in the United Kingdom, where Heinz, Coca-Cola, and Ford have better images.

Universal Messages and Regional Advertising Skills Although universal advertising themes are cost-effective and promote brand awareness, major companies have found that without a local or national identity, universal ads don't cause consumers to buy. Coca-Cola's "think global, act local" strategy and Nestlé's approach to small-scale local advertising call for ads tailored to different areas. Such ads are designed to toy with variations on a universal theme while appealing to local emotions, ideas, and values.

Continued from page 364

Do We Need Relief From DTC?

The pharmaceuticals business is risky because it involves expensive research and development (R&D) for new drugs. Sales revenues must recover not only the costs of developing successful drugs, but also the costs of unsuccessful research. To stimulate sales, drug companies have historically relied on various methods for persuading doctors to prescribe products, such as sponsoring educational events, providing promotional gifts, and funding medical research. But the shift to DTC promotions is an expensive multimedia thrust that embraces TV—national and cable—radio, telephone (for instance, 1-800-for-Nexium), Internet <www.purplepill.com>, magazines, newspapers, Sunday supplements, and outdoor advertising. Both advertising costs and drug prices are skyrocketing, while product information—sometimes informative, sometimes misleading—is at an all-time high.

In 2002, the National Health Council (NHC), a nonprofit group of 118 U.S. health-related organizations, concluded that, on balance, DTC marketing is more beneficial than detrimental to most patients and doctors. Says the NHC report, "The Council recognizes that DTC advertising provides important information to consumers and patients, which often is beneficial to their health." It adds, however, that while some ads are merely unclear about the conditions that drugs are supposed to treat, others fail to report product risks. Some even make drugs seem more effective than they are. The NHC also reports that one-third of MDs are concerned about the negative effects of DTC advertising on physician-patient relationships.

Aside from questions of consumer motivation and patient-doctor relationships, controversy rages over how to curb the rising prices of prescription drugs. A 2002 study of health-care managers reported that DTC advertising—the fastest-growing expense in the industry's promotional budget—is the number-one factor in the explosion of drug costs. It is greater even than the cost of developing new drugs. The study overwhelmingly singles out pharmaceutical companies—rather than consumers, government, or health-care organizations—as responsible for high drug costs.

At the same time, it advises caution in dealing with the problem. Most respondents dislike the idea of government management of prices, arguing that bureaucrats aren't qualified to set prices and would just make matters worse. Let the free market, say these experts, correct itself. A dissenting minority, however, noted that runaway costs must be kept down—and that the only way to do this is to regulate the industry. DTC advertising, they contend, should be banned, and price controls should be put in place. The FDA, they suggest, should loosen regulations governing the introduction of new drugs so that more choices become available to consumers.

How do matters look to observers outside the United States? Foreign observers are wary about the U.S. experience and the danger posed by DTC to health-care inside their own borders. In Canada, for example, DTC ads are banned. Officials in the European Union have also banned DTC ads, but they are experimenting with a pilot plan to "ensure the availability of better, clear, and reliable information" on authorized drugs. The EU allows drug makers to supply limited information—and only when patients request it. While protecting the public from misleading information is a prime goal, officials also worry that U.S.-style DTC advertising could spur both higher prescription costs and the use of unsafe and unnecessary drugs. Gradually, the ban on DTC broadcast ads may be softened, because health-conscious Europeans are already getting doses of medical information from other sources, especially from the Internet.

Even the proponents of DTC ads recognize the dangers of misleading or biased information. Every year, the U.S. FDA demands that drug makers alter certain ads. Recently, for example, Pharmacia Corp., maker of the arthritis medicine Celebrex, was chided for television ads claiming "powerful 24-hour relief." The ad, charged the FDA, "suggests that Celebrex is more effective than has been demonstrated by substantial evidence." The allergy drugs Claritin, Flonase, and Flovent have been cited 10 or more times each.

So is DTC advertising good, bad, or a little of both? The FDA isn't sure and wants more information before making additional decisions. Accordingly, the FDA's Division of Drug Marketing, Advertising & Communications (DDMAC) launched a 2002 survey to get the views of doctors and patients. Although the results may help, industry experts expect to see a mixture of pros and cons rather than a sure cure for any DTC malady.

Questions for Discussion

1. Why do you suppose TV is the industry's medium of choice for DTC promotions?
2. In addition to prescription drugs, can you think of any other industry that uses a DTC promotional strategy? What elements must be present in the marketing environment for such a strategy to be successful?
3. Why are physicians concerned about the effect of DTC advertising on doctor-patient relationships? List some ways in which those relationships might be changed. Are the changes you listed good or bad?
4. List at least four measures that drug companies might take to hold down consumer prices. What are the disadvantages and advantages of each measure?
5. What might the federal government do to prevent the rise of prescription drug prices? Outline the pros and cons for each action you identify. Which action(s) do you recommend?
6. Has the emergence of DTC advertising created any ethical or social-responsibility issues for physicians? Explain why or why not.

Summary of Learning Objectives

1. *Identify the important objectives of* promotion *and discuss the considerations entailed in selecting a* promotional mix.

Promotion is any technique designed to sell a product. It is part of the *communication mix:* the total message any company sends to consumers about its products. Promotional techniques must communicate the uses, features, and benefits of products. There are two general values to be gained from any promotional activity: (1) *Communicating information:* Using promotional methods to communicate information about a producer and its products to potential buyers. This activity has four goals: (i) To make potential buyers aware of products; (ii) to make them knowledgeable about products; (iii) to persuade them to like products; and (iv) to persuade them to purchase products. (2) *Creating more satisfying exchanges*: Trying to make a product more attractive, so that both buyer and seller gain more from the exchange (a more attractive product and more unit sales or higher prices, respectively).

Besides the ultimate objective of increasing sales, marketers may use promotion to accomplish any of the following four goals: (1) *Communicating information*: Information tells customers that a product exists or educates them about its features. (2) *Positioning products*: **Positioning** is the process of establishing an easily identifiable product image in the minds of consumers. (3) *Adding value*: Not only is promotion the main means of establishing a product's perceived value, but customers gain when the promotional mix includes value-added benefits (say, consumer discounts). (4) *Controlling sales volume:* Firms can compensate for seasonal sales patterns and achieve more stable sales volume throughout the year.

Once its larger marketing objectives are clear, a firm must develop a promotional strategy to achieve them. Two strategies are available: (1) A **pull strategy** appeals directly to consumers who will demand the product from retailers who, in turn, will demand it from wholesalers. (2) A **push strategy** aggressively markets a product to wholesalers and retailers who then persuade consumers to buy it. Many large firms use a combination of pull and push strategies.

There are four types of promotional tools: *advertising, personal selling, sales promotions,* and *publicity and public relations.* The best combination of these tools—the best **promotional mix**—depends on several factors, the most important of which is *the target audience and buyer decision process*: Marketers try to match promotional tools with stages in the buyer decision process. This process can be broken down into five steps: (i) *Buyers recognize the need to make a purchase.* Marketers must make sure that buyers are aware that a products exist. (ii) *Buyers want to learn more about products.* Advertising and personal selling, for example, can be used to educate the customer. (iii) *Buyers compare competing products.* Personal selling can be vital because sales reps can demonstrate product quality and performance. (iv) *Buyers decide on and purchase specific products.* Sales promotion is effective because it gives consumers incentives to buy. (v) *Buyers evaluate products after purchasing them.* After the sale, advertising or personal selling can be used to remind consumers that they made a wise purchase.

2. *Discuss the most important* advertising strategies *and describe the key* advertising media.

Advertising is paid, nonpersonal communication used by an identified sponsor to inform an audience about a product. The advertising strategies used for a product most often depend on the stage of the product life cycle the product is in. As products become established and competition increases, advertisers may choose one of three strategies: (1) **Persuasive advertising** seeks to influence consumers to buy a company's products rather than those of rivals. (2) In **comparative advertising,** in which two or more products are directly compared, the goal is to take away competitors' business. (3) **Reminder advertising** helps to keep a product's name in the public mind.

Marketers use several different **advertising media**—specific communication devices for carrying a seller's message to potential customers. The following are the most common advertising media:

(1) *Television*: The most widely-used medium, TV reaches the most people. Knowledge of demographics for a show lets advertisers aim at target audiences. But TV is expensive, and because there are so many TV commercials, viewers often confuse products.

(2) *Newspapers*: Newspapers are flexible, and ads can be changed from day to day. However, they are generally thrown out after one day, and broad readership makes it hard to target audiences.

(3) *Direct Mail*: **Direct mail** involves fliers or other types of printed ads mailed directly to homes or places of business. Messages can be personalized, and interested recipients are more likely than most people to buy. Direct mail, however, is not very cost effective.

(4) *Radio*: A lot of people listen to radio, and ads are inexpensive. In addition, audiences are largely segmented according to listener preferences (such as rock 'n' roll, music, or talk shows). Unfortunately, ads are quick, and people tend to use the radio as background noise while doing other things.

(5) *Magazines*: The huge variety of magazines provides segmentation. They allow plenty of space for detailed information, and because they have long lives and are passed from person to person, ads get constant exposure. Ads, however, must be submitted in advance, and there is often no guarantee of where an ad will appear.

(6) *Outdoor Advertising*: Outdoor ads are inexpensive and subject to high repeat exposure. New technology has also made outdoor advertising more creative. However, outdoor ads can present only limited amounts of information, and sellers have little control over audiences.

(7) *Internet Advertising*: Although consumers don't want to wade through electronic pages to look at hundreds of products, targeted Internet advertising is gaining favor because user data can be gathered electronically. Through *data mining* and *data warehousing,* e-marketers can amass vast pools of data on buyer behavior and then send tailor-made ads for products that consumers are likely to buy.

(8) *Virtual Advertising*: Virtual advertising digitally implants brands or products into live or taped programming. An advertiser's product can thus appear as part of a TV show, when viewers are paying more attention, instead of during commercial breaks.

Other advertising channels include catalogs, sidewalk handouts, Yellow Pages, skywriting, telephone calls, special events, and door-to-door communication. The combination of media through which a company advertises is its **media mix.** Different industries use different mixes, and most depend on a variety of media rather than on just one to reach target audiences.

An **advertising campaign** is the arrangement of ads in selected media to reach target audiences. It includes several activities that, taken together, constitute a program for meeting a marketing objective. A campaign includes six steps: (1) Identify the target audience; (2) establish the advertising budget; (3) define the objectives of the advertising messages; (4) create advertising messages; (5) select the appropriate media; and (6) evaluate the effectiveness. **Advertising agencies**—independent companies that provide some or all of a client's advertising needs—provide specialized services to help develop campaigns.

3. *Outline the tasks involved in* personal selling *and list the steps in the* personal selling process.

In **personal selling,** a salesperson communicates one to one with potential customers to identify their needs and align them with a seller's products. It adds to a firm's credibility because it allows buyers to interact with and ask questions of the seller. Unfortunately, expenses are high, and high costs have turned many companies to *telemarketing*—the use of telephone solicitations to conduct the personal selling process.

Sales force management means setting goals at the top levels of the organization, setting practical objectives for salespeople, organizing a sales force that can meet those objectives, and implementing and evaluating the success of the overall plan. Managers of both telemarketers and traditional salespeople must always consider the ways in which personal sales are affected by the differences between consumer and industrial products: (1) **Retail selling** promotes a consumer product for the buyer's own personal or household use. (2) **Industrial selling** promotes products to other businesses, either for the purpose of manufacturing other products or for resale. In retail selling, the buyer usually comes to the seller; the industrial salesperson typically goes to the prospect's place of business. Industrial decisions take longer because more money, decision makers, and a weighing of alternatives are involved.

There are three basic tasks in personal selling: (1) In **order processing,** a salesperson receives an order and sees to its handling and delivery. (2) When the benefits of a product are not entirely clear, sellers may use **creative selling**—providing buyers with information about a product's benefits. (3) A company may use **missionary selling** when its purpose is to promote itself and its products rather than simply to close a sale.

The creative salesperson goes through most of the following six steps in the personal selling process. (1) *Prospecting and qualifying*: **Prospecting** identifies potential customers, who are then **qualified** to determine whether they have the authority to buy and ability to pay. (2) *Approaching*: The first few minutes of a contact with a qualified prospect make up the approach. (3) *Presenting and demonstrating*: After the approach, the salesperson makes a presentation—a full explanation of the product, its features, and its uses. (4) *Handling objections:* Objections pinpoint the parts of the presentation with which the buyer has a problem and which the salesperson must overcome. (5) *Closing*: In the **closing,** the salesperson asks the prospective customer to buy the product. (6) *Following up*: To cement lasting relationships with buyers, sellers supply additional after-sale services.

4. *Describe the various types of* sales promotions *and distinguish between* publicity *and* public relations.

Sales promotions are short-term promotional activities designed to stimulate consumer buying or cooperation from members of the trade. They increase the likelihood that buyers will try products; they also enhance product recognition and can increase purchase size and amount.

The following are the best-known forms of promotions. (1) Certificates entitling bearers to savings off regular prices are **coupons.** (2) To grab customers' attention as they move through stores, companies use **point-of-purchase (POP) displays.** (3) Free samples and premiums are *purchasing incentives* that allow customers to try products without risk. (4) **Premiums** are gifts to consumers in return for buying certain products. (5) Industries sponsor **trade shows,** at which companies rent booths to display and demonstrate products to customers with a special interest in them. (6) Customers, distributors, and sales reps may all be persuaded to increase sales by means of *contests*.

Publicity is a promotional tool in which information about a company or product is created and transmitted by general mass media. It is free, and because it is presented in a news format, consumers often see it as objective and credible. However, marketers often have little control over it, and it can be as easily detrimental as beneficial. **Public relations** is company-influenced publicity that seeks to build good relations with the public and to deal with unfavorable events.

5. *Show how small businesses use promotional activities.*

Although small businesses generally have fewer resources, cost-effective promotions can improve sales and allow small firms to compete with larger firms. Advertising opportunities abound more than ever because of the Internet, cheaper access to computing equipment, and online service that puts cyberspace within the grasp of even the smallest firms. Although the Web can instantaneously reach distant customers, other advertising methods depend on the market that the small business is trying to reach. Non-prime-time ads on local TV have good impact at low costs. More often, however, small businesses use newspaper, radio, and direct mail to reach local markets. When it comes to international markets, television, radio, and newspapers are too expensive for small businesses. Most find direct mail and carefully targeted magazine ads the most effective tools.

Some small firms maintain sales forces, especially in local markets. Others contract with *sales agencies*—companies that act on behalf of several clients. For national markets, sales agencies and such methods as telemarketing are used. By combining telemarketing with catalogs or other print advertising, small businesses can sometimes compete against larger companies. Small companies use the same sales promotion incentives as larger companies but rely mostly on premiums and special sales.

6. *Describe the development of* international promotional strategies.

Recent decades have witnessed a profound shift from home-country marketing to global marketing. Every company that markets its products in several countries faces a basic choice: use a decentralized approach, with separate marketing management for each country, or adopt a **global perspective,** directing marketing toward a worldwide rather than toward a local or regional market.

Although globalization is affecting many firms' promotional activities, global advertising is not always feasible. Four factors make global advertising challenging: (1) *Product variations*: Even if a basic product has universal appeal, at least modest variations, or slightly different products, are usually preferred in different cultures. (2) *Language differences*: Translations are often inexact and confusing. (3) *Cultural receptiveness*: Another variable is cultural receptiveness to foreign ideas, products, and practices. There is a lot of difference across nations regarding the acceptability of mass advertising for certain products. Marketing methods, too, must be carefully selected. (4) *Image differences*: A company's image can vary from nation to nation, regardless of any advertising appeals for universal recognition and acceptance.

In recognizing national differences, many global marketers try to build on a universal advertising theme that nevertheless allows for variations. In doing so, they rely on help from different advertising agencies in various geographic regions.

KEY TERMS

promotion (p. 364)
positioning (p. 365)
pull strategy (p. 366)
push strategy (p. 366)
promotional mix (p. 366)
advertising (p. 367)
persuasive advertising (p. 367)
comparative advertising (p. 367)
reminder advertising (p. 367)
advertising media (p. 367)
direct mail (p. 368)
media mix (p. 373)
advertising campaign (p. 373)
advertising agency (p. 373)
personal selling (p. 373)
retail selling (p. 376)
industrial selling (p. 376)
order processing (p. 377)
creative selling (p. 377)
missionary selling (p. 377)
prospecting (p. 377)
qualifying (p. 377)
closing (p. 378)
sales promotion (p. 378)
coupon (p. 379)
point-of-purchase (POP) display (p. 379)
premium (p. 379)
trade show (p. 379)
publicity (p. 379)
public relations (p. 379)
global perspective (p. 381)

QUESTIONS AND EXERCISES

Questions for Review

1. What are the differences between push and pull strategies? Why would a firm choose one over the other?
2. Compare the advantages and disadvantages of different advertising media.
3. What are the advantages of personal selling over other promotional tools?
4. Which promotional tools have proven most useful in mounting global advertising campaigns? Why?
5. Is publicity more or less available to small firms than to larger firms? Why?

Questions for Analysis

6. Take a look at some of the advertising conducted by locally based businesses in your area. Choose two campaigns: one that you think is effective and one that you think is ineffective. What differences in the campaigns make one better than the other?
7. Select a good or a service that you have purchased recently. Try to retrace the relevant steps in the buyer decision process as you experienced it. Which steps were most important to you? Least important?
8. Find some examples of publicity about some business, either a local firm or a national firm. Did the publicity

have—or is it likely to have—positive or negative consequences for the business involved? Why?

Application Exercises

9. Select a product that is sold nationally. Identify as many media used in its promotion as you can. Which medium is used most? On the whole, do you think the campaign is effective? Why or why not?
10. Interview the owner of a local small business. Identify the company's promotional objectives and strategies and the elements in its promotional mix. What (if any) changes would you suggest? Why?

Building Your Business Skills

GREETING START-UP DECISIONS

This exercise enhances the following SCANS workplace competencies: demonstrating basic skills, demonstrating thinking skills, exhibiting interpersonal skills, and working with information.

Goal

To encourage students to analyze the potential usefulness of two promotional methods—personal selling and direct mail—for a start-up greeting card company

Situation

You are the marketing adviser for a local start-up company that makes and sells specialty greeting cards in a city of 400,000. Last year's sales totaled 14,000 cards, including personalized holiday cards, birthday cards, and special-events cards for individuals. Although revenues increased last year, you see a way of further boosting sales by expanding into card shops, grocery stores, and gift shops. You see two alternatives for entering these outlets:

1. Use direct mail to reach more individual customers for specialty cards.
2. Use personal selling to gain display space in retail stores.

Your challenge is to convince the owner of the start-up company which alternative is the more financially sound decision.

Method

Step 1

Get together with four or five classmates to research the two kinds of product segments: *personalized cards* and *retail store cards*. Find out which of the two kinds of marketing promotions will be more effective for each of the two segments. What will be the reaction to each method by customers, retailers, and card company owners?

Step 2

Draft a proposal to the company owner. Leaving budget and production details to other staffers, list as many reasons as possible for adopting direct mail. Then list as many reasons as possible for adopting personal selling. Defend each reason. Consider the following reasons in your argument:

- *Competitive environment:* Analyze the impact of other card suppliers that offer personalized cards and cards for sale in retail stores.
- *Expectations of target markets:* Who buys personalized cards, and who buys ready-made cards from retail stores?
- *Overall cost of the promotional effort:* Which method—direct mail or personal selling—will be more costly?
- *Marketing effectiveness:* Which promotional method will result in greater consumer response?

Follow-Up Questions

1. Why do you think some buyers want personalized cards? Why do some consumers want ready-made cards from retail stores?
2. Today's computer operating systems provide easy access to software for designing and making cards on home PCs. How does the availability of this product affect your recommendation?
3. What was your most convincing argument for using direct mail? For using personal selling?
4. Can a start-up company compete in retail stores against industry giants such as Hallmark and American Greetings?

Exercising Your Ethics

CLEANING UP IN SALES

The Situation

Selling a product—whether a good or a service—requires the salesperson to believe in it, to be confident of his or her own sales skills, and to keep commitments made to clients. Because so many people and resources are involved in making and delivering a product, numerous uncertainties and problems arise that can raise ethical issues. This exercise encourages you to examine some of the ethical issues that can surface in the personal selling process for industrial products.

The Dilemma

Along with 16 other newly hired graduates, Ethel Skilsel has just completed the sales training program for a new line of high-tech machinery that ABC Technologies manufactures for industrial cleaners. As an aspiring salesperson, Ethel is eager to get on the road and meet potential clients, all of whom are professional buyers for companies—such as laundries and dry cleaners, carpet cleaners, and military cleaners—that use ABC products or those of ABC's competitors. Ethel is especially enthusiastic about several facts that she learned during training: ABC's equipment is the most technically advanced in the industry, carries a 10-year performance guarantee, and is safe—both functionally and environmentally.

The first month was difficult but successful: In visits to seven firms, Ethel successfully closed three sales, earning handsome commissions (her pay is based on sales results) as well as praise from her sales manager. Moreover, after listening to her presentations, two more potential buyers had given verbal commitments and were about to sign for much bigger orders than any Ethel had closed to date. But as she was catching her flight to close those sales, Ethel received two calls—one from a client and one from a competitor. The client was just getting started with ABC equipment and was having some trouble: Employees stationed nearby were getting sick when the equipment was running. The competitor told Ethel that the U.S. Environmental Protection Agency (EPA) had received complaints that ABC's new technology was environmentally unsafe because of noxious emissions.

Questions for Discussion

1. As a sales professional, does Ethel have any ethical obligations to ABC Technologies?
2. From an ethical standpoint, what should Ethel say to the two client firms she is scheduled to visit? What would you say to those clients?
3. Are there any ethical issues involved when an employee of one company calls a competitor's employee, as in this case of an ABC competitor calling Ethel? Explain.

Mastering Business Essentials

■ **EPISODE 10** focuses on the ways that marketers communicate with consumers at each stage in the buying process. It also shows how advertisers use different strategies to inform consumers about products they may need or want. *This episode enhances the coverage of promotions, especially advertising, as a means of both informing consumers and appealing to their changing needs and wants.*

Crafting Your Business Plan

HITTING THE SAUCE CUSTOMER

The Purpose of the Assignment

1. To familiarize students with promotion-related issues that a sample firm addresses in developing its business plan, within the framework of *Business PlanPro* (*BPP*) software package.
2. To demonstrate how four chapter topics—promotional strategy, product positioning, personal selling, and advertising—can be integrated as components of the *BPP* planning environment.

Assignment

After reading Chapter 13 in the textbook, open the BPP *software and look around for information on plans for promotion as it applies to a sample firm, a salsa manufacturer:* Salvadore's Sauces *(Salvadore's, Inc.). To find* Salvadore's, *do the following:*

Open *Business PlanPro.* If you are asked whether you want to "create a new business plan" or to "open an existing plan," select "create a new business plan" (even though you are not going to create a plan at this time). You will then be taken to the *Business PlanPro EasyPlan Wizard.* On the screen, click on the option entitled **Research It.** You will then be presented with a new list of options, including **Sample Plan Browser.** After clicking on the **Sample Plan Browser,** go down its alphabetical list of sample plans and double-click on **Salsa Manufacturer**, which is the location for *Salvadore's Sauces.* The screen you are looking at is the introduction page for the business plan of *Salvadore's Sauces.* On this page, scroll down until you reach the **Table of Contents** for *Salvadore's Sauces* business plan.

Now respond to the following items:

1. As we saw in Chapter 13, product positioning is an important promotional objective. What are Salvadore's Sauces' plans for positioning its products? [Sites to see in *BPP* (for this item): On the Table of Contents page, click on **4.1 Market Segmentation** and read its contents. After returning to the Table of Contents page, click on each of the following in turn: **4.3.1 Industry Participants, 4.3.2 Distribution Patterns, 4.3.3 Competition and Buying Patterns,** and **4.3.4 Main Competitors.**]
2. Describe Salvadore's Sauces' promotional strategy. [Sites to see in *BPP:* On the Table of Contents page, click on and read **5.1.2 Promotion Strategy.** After returning to the Table of Contents page, click on **5.1.1 Pricing Strategy.**]
3. What kinds of advertising does Salvadore's Sauces plan to use? Do you agree or disagree with the firm's advertising plans? Explain. [Sites to see in *BPP:* On the Table of Contents page, click on each of the following in turn: **4.0 Market Analysis Summary** and **5.0 Strategy and Implementation Summary.**]
4. What role does personal selling play in the promotional plans at Salvadore's? Who will do the personal selling? Are these individuals qualified for the job? [Sites to see in *BPP* (for this assignment): On the Table of Contents page, click on **5.2 Sales Strategy** and **5.2.2 Sales Programs.** After returning to the Table of Contents page, click on each of the following: **6.0 Management Summary** and **6.2 Management Team.**]

Video Exercise

REVVING UP PROMOTION: BMW MOTORCYCLES

Learning Objectives

The purpose of this video is to help you

1. Describe the purpose of product promotion.
2. Understand how and why a company must coordinate the elements in its promotional mix.
3. Explain how message and media work together in an effective advertising campaign.

Synopsis

Although U.S. car buyers are quite familiar with the BMW brand, it enjoys much lower awareness among motorcycle buyers. This low profile is a major challenge for BMW Motorcycles, which has been producing high-end motorcycles for more than 80 years. The company's main promotional goal is to attract serious riders who are looking for an exceptional riding experience. To meet this objective, marketers carefully coordinate every promotional detail to convey a unified brand message positioning the BMW as "the ultimate riding machine." Using print and television advertising, personal selling by dealers, sales promotion, and a virtual showroom on the Web, BMW is driving its brand message home to motorcycle enthusiasts across the United States.

Discussion Questions

1. *For analysis:* What are the advantages of using more personal advertising copy and encouraging customers to become missionaries for BMW motorcycles?
2. *For analysis:* Why would BMW use its Web site as a virtual showroom rather than as a site for selling for directly to consumers?
3. *For application:* What are some ways that BMW might use public relations to build brand awareness?
4. *For application:* How might BMW use direct mail to bring potential buyers into dealerships?
5. *For debate:* Should BMW develop and promote a new brand to differentiate its motorcycles not only from competing brands but from BMW cars as well? Support your position.

Online Exploration

Visit the BMW Motorcycle site at <www.bmwmotorcycle.com> and observe the links on the home page. Go to the pages promoting new models and pre-owned motorcycles. Finally, follow the link to the contact page. Which elements of the promotional mix are evident on this site? How does the site support the company's message about the "ultimate riding machine"? How does the site make it easy for customers to obtain more information and ask questions about BMW motorcycles and dealer services?

PART 4

Managing Operations and Information

CHAPTER

Producing Goods and Services

After reading this chapter, you should be able to:

1. Explain the meaning of the term *production* or *operations.*
2. Describe the four kinds of *utility* provided by production and explain the two classifications of *operations processes.*
3. Identify the characteristics that distinguish *service operations* from *goods production* and explain the main differences in the *service focus.*
4. Describe the factors involved in *operations planning.*
5. Explain some factors in *operations scheduling* and describe some activities involved in *operations control,* including *materials management* and the use of certain *operations control tools.*

A Supersonic Project Gets off the Ground

When the battle ended on October 26, 2001, Lockheed Martin Aeronautics Co. <www.lockheedmartin.com> had been given the green light to launch one of the biggest production projects in U.S. history. Cheers erupted at Lockheed's Forth Worth, Texas, conference center as Air Force Secretary James Roche announced that Lockheed had won the $200 billion Joint Strike Fighter (JSF) contract. Capping a five-year, winner-take-all competition with rival Boeing, Lockheed had captured the largest defense contract in history—one that could be worth more than $320 billion over the next two or three decades.

Intended to meet the needs not only of the U.S. Navy, Air Force, and Marines, but of Britain's Royal Air Force and Royal Navy and the armed forces of several other nations, Lockheed's design for the next generation of supersonic, radar-evading combat jet was just the beginning. The contract was awarded on the basis of experimental versions of the aircraft. Now the real work—detailed planning for production and then production itself—begins.

Many observers think that the next phase—System Development & Demonstration (SDD)—will be the most difficult. Says Michael Burkett, a Boston technology consultant, "Lockheed Martin and its partners have to firm up the design, detail all components, [and] put in the manufacturing process and the supply chain to support it." SDD calls for building and demonstrating 22 aircraft (known in the United States as the F-35) to be delivered by 2005. The next phase—gearing up to full production—begins in 2008, with plans calling for the production of 3,000 planes—each worth from $28 million to $38 million—by 2040. During each phase, the U.S. Defense Department <www.defenselink.mil> will insist that aircraft perform reliably, that deliveries be on time, and that costs be met.

To get started, Lockheed's JSF team needs about 4,500 more personnel (up from 500) during the first 18 months. But organizing the project goes far beyond Lockheed's walls because Lockheed, as prime contractor, is collaborating with Northrop Grumman Corp. <www.northgrum.com> and Britain's BAE Systems PLC <www.baesystems.com>. More than 70 U.S. and 18 international subcontractors at some 187 locations are involved in the SDD phase. Pratt & Whitney <www.pratt-whitney.com>, for example, is developing the engines. All told, more than 1,500 firms will supply everything from radar systems to bolts. Not surprisingly, the program for production planning will be as futuristic as the airplane itself. Teamwork and technology will be key elements in tracking hundreds of thousands of components, and by 2005, specialists sitting at some 40,000 remote computers will be collaborating on the project.

Of course, the JSF aircraft is more than just hardware. Computers provide onboard brainpower for the advanced-performance capabilities of this electronic weapons platform. Such features as short takeoff and helicopter-like vertical-landing capabilities rely as much on software as on pilot performance. So, too, do real-time views of the battlefield (a major advance for combat pilots). The system depends on software-driven integration of various radar and sensor inputs. Electro-optic and infrared sensor inputs will track targets, and other electronic systems include communications-navigation-and-identification (CNI), targeting, and electronic warfare. Combining huge arrays of electronic and software

"The challenge will be to keep an organization intact, not lose momentum through confusion and inexperience, integrate various demands from outside parties, and keep the huge customer set engaged, onboard, and excited."

~Tom Burbage,
Lockheed Manager on the Joint Strike Fighter Project

systems is the name of the game for JSF. For example, the software-intensive CNI system, built by Cleveland-based TRW Inc. <www.trw.com>, must be integrated with other modules, such as electronic countermeasures, which will be built by Britain's BAE.

Lockheed Martin is responsible for final integration, and although the technical hurdles are enormous, managerial logistics is also an area of concern. Reflecting on the number of people that his team must hire, Lockheed program manager Tom Burbage admits, "We've got a big scaling up to do. The challenge will be trying to keep an organization intact, not lose momentum through confusion and inexperience, integrate various demands from outside parties, and keep the huge customer set engaged, onboard, and excited about the airplane."

Satisfying multiple customers won't be easy. The three U.S. armed services want different versions of the fighter, as do customers from Britain, Italy, Canada, Denmark, and Norway—all of whom want their own defense industries to share in the program. About 80 percent of all parts will be common to each model, but the rest will vary. The JSF production system, therefore, will have to be flexible enough to produce multiple models on schedule and within budget. Such requirements call for suppliers who can provide reliable components and subsystems—and the right ones for each model—to ensure a final assembly that meets delivery commitments.

Our opening story is continued on page 417.

You're always involved in business activities that provide goods and services to customers. You wake up to the sound of your favorite radio station and pick up a newspaper on your way to the bus stop, where you catch your ride to work or school. Your instructors, the bus driver, the clerk at the 7-Eleven store, and the morning radio announcer all work in **service operations.** They provide intangible and tangible service products, such as entertainment, transportation, education, and food preparation. Firms that make tangible products—radios, newspapers, buses, textbooks—are engaged in **goods production.**

service operations
Activities producing intangible and tangible products, such as entertainment, transportation, and education

goods production
Activities producing tangible products, such as radios, newspapers, buses, and textbooks

What Does "Production" Mean Today?

Although the term *production* has historically referred to companies engaged in goods production, the concept as we now use it also means services. Many of the things that we need or want, from health care to fast food, are produced by service operations. As a rule, service-sector managers focus less on equipment and technology than on the human element in operations. Why? Because success or failure may depend on provider-customer contact. Employees who deal directly with customers affect customer feelings about the service, and as we will see, a key difference between production and service operations is the customer's involvement in the latter.

Today, however, customers are increasingly involved in all kinds of production because electronic communications are key components in winning and keeping customers in a huge range of competitive industries. Orders are placed faster, schedules are accelerated, and delivery times are shrinking. Internet buyers can be linked to the production floor itself, where their orders for products ranging from cell phones to automobiles are launched and filled in real time. B2B customers also expect real-time response and online delivery. "Our biggest pitfall," says Gerhard Schulmeyer, former CEO of U.S. operations for the German electronics firm Siemens Corp. <www.siemens.de>, "is that we go [off-line] and make plans. The customer is online, and he doesn't care about your plan. He wants what he wants now and is always one click away from your competitor."[1]

"The customer is online, and he doesn't care about your plan. He wants what he wants now and is always one click away from your competitor."

~Gerhard Schulmeyer, CEO of U.S. Operations for Siemens Corporation

The Growth of Global Operations

Global competition has made production a faster-paced, more complex activity. Although the factory remains the centerpiece in manufacturing, it bears little resemblance to its counterpart of a decade ago. Smoke and grease and the clang

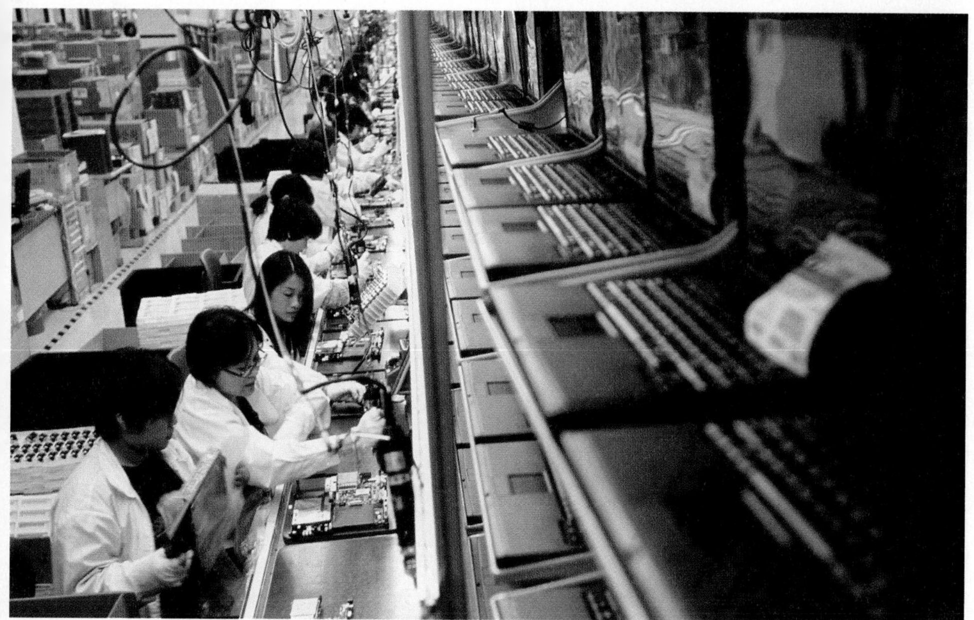

Quanta Computer Inc. <www.quantata.com> *of Taiwan supplies Dallas-based Dell Computer* <www.dell.com> *with 55% of its notebook PCs. The world's number-one notebook maker does just about everything for Dell's notebook unit and pretty much does it by matching Dell's renowned skill at just-in-time manufacturing: Quanta can assemble the hardware, install the software, test the final product and ship to Dell in 48 hours. The key is the Internet, which allows Dell and other customers much greater freedom in placing customized orders around the clock.*

of steel on steel have been replaced by computers and other high-tech machines in contaminant-free, climate-controlled "clean rooms."

Today's firm may no longer face the pressures of continuous mass production, but it does face constant change. New technologies make machines that run cleaner, faster, and safer and that operate on a global scale. For online manufacturing, machines can log on to the Internet, adjust their own settings, and make minor decisions without human help. They can communicate with other machines in the company (via an intranet) and with other companies' machines (via the Internet). With the Internet, producers of both services and goods can integrate their production activities with those of far-off suppliers and customers.

Growth in the Service and Goods Sectors

Following the September 11th terrorist attacks, employment in the U.S. manufacturing sector fell to about 19 percent of all private-sector jobs. Even so, the number has remained steady, hovering around 20 percent for four decades, and the economic significance of manufacturing is going up. For example, real income from manufacturing has increased by over 30 percent in the past 10 years. So effective are new manufacturing methods—and so committed are U.S. manufacturers to using them—that in 2001, the United States remained ahead of Germany and Japan in manufactured exports, retaining the number-one spot for the eighth straight year.

Of course, both goods and service industries are important, but as you can see from Figure 14.1, employment has risen significantly in the service sector while remaining stagnant in goods production. By 2002, service employment accounted for 81 percent of the U.S. private-sector workforce—107 million jobs. Much of this growth comes from e-commerce and from business services, health care, amusement and recreation, and education. Employment projections indicate that services will remain the faster-growing job source in the immediate future.[2] The gap in average wages between the two sectors has closed to just $19 per week more for goods-producing workers. More important, the distribution of high-paying and low-paying jobs in each sector is now equal.

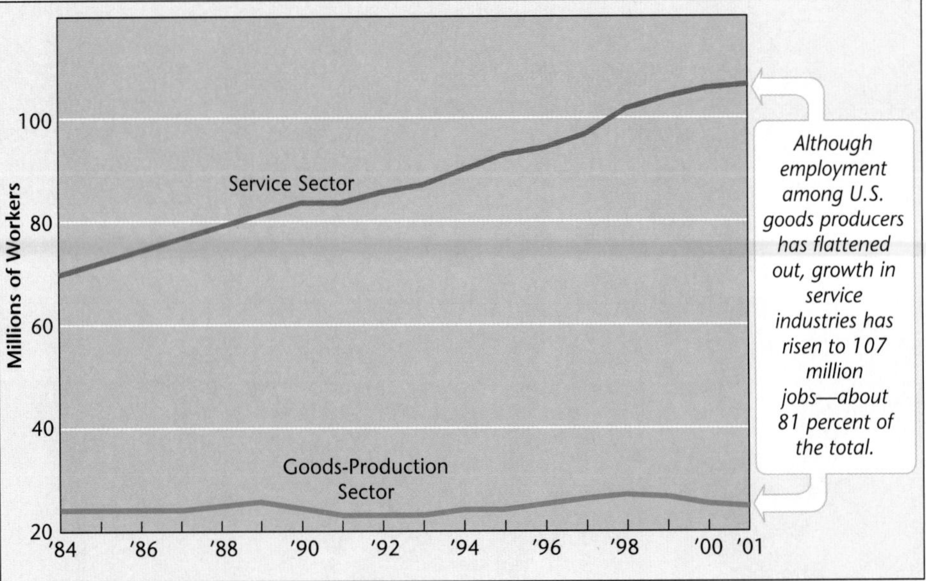

Millions of Workers
100
80
60
40
20
Service Sector
Goods-Production Sector
'84 '86 '88 '90 '92 '94 '96 '98 '00 '01
Although employment among U.S. goods producers has flattened out, growth in service industries has risen to 107 million jobs—about 81 percent of the total.

■ FIGURE 14.1
Employment in Goods and Service Sectors

By 2001, the service sector also provided 52 percent of national income, as opposed to about 50 percent in 1947. As Figure 14.2 shows, the service-sector's greater percentage of gross domestic product (GDP)—the value of all the goods and services produced by the economy, excluding foreign income—has climbed since 1984 until it is now 33 percent more than goods-producing GDP. At the same time, the 19 percent of the workforce in manufacturing produces nearly 40 percent of the nation's GDP.[3] In China, by contrast, manufacturing employs 70 percent of the urban labor force but produces only 30 percent of the national income.[4]

Although companies are typically classified as either goods producers or service providers, the distinction is often blurred. For one thing, all businesses are ser-

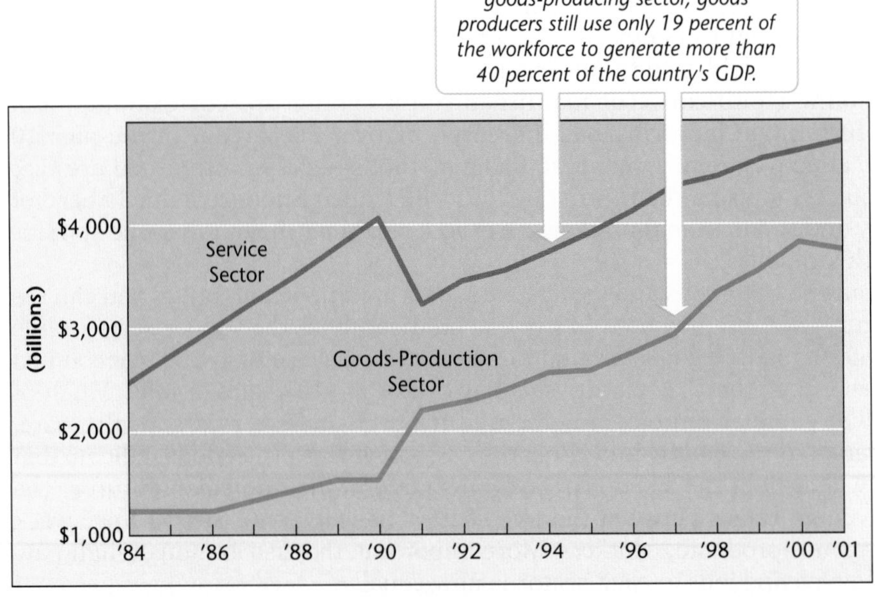

Although the service sector is now almost 33 percent greater than the goods-producing sector, goods producers still use only 19 percent of the workforce to generate more than 40 percent of the country's GDP.
(billions)
$4,000
$3,000
$2,000
$1,000
Service Sector
Goods-Production Sector
'84 '86 '88 '90 '92 '94 '96 '98 '00 '01

■ FIGURE 14.2
GDP from Goods and Services

PROJECTING CULTURE

When you're trying to prosper in highly diversified and volatile markets, good project management is indispensable in contemporary operations. Efficient project management is also important because so many products, both goods and services, are offered for sale in such a variety of countries and cultures, and it is increasingly the case that products are finally assembled just before the consumer has access to them.

For many large companies who operate internationally, a major challenge is managing the production of goods and services across a wide range of geographic locations. Employees may come from a host of differing cultures, bringing with them a diverse array of attitudes toward management and hierarchy, power and authority, and even work and leisure. Workplaces in some countries, for instance, are highly regulated by governments, unions are strong, and employee expectations are high. Elsewhere, the management style is more autocratic and decisions are rarely questioned.

Such differences add up to a complex set of relationships that must be analyzed and managed with care and skill if operations are to proceed smoothly and efficiently. North Americans, for example, like to get things done quickly and on time, and consumers will shift brand loyalties if expectations aren't met. But a lot of North American companies rely on production facilities in other countries where rules and regulations are quite different, both from those in the United States and from each other. Even time may be viewed differently, and overseas workers don't necessarily feel the same pressure to get things done as promptly as their U.S. counterparts.

Leadership is the number-one criterion when it comes to successful project management. The best project managers are people who understand how teams work and who recognize differences in workers' cultural perspectives. Recognizing the cultural perspectives of the people who make up a team helps managers to find the most appropriate ways to get things done and adjust assignments accordingly.

At the same time, of course, every company has its own unique corporate culture, and employees with different national and ethnic backgrounds need to feel that they can fit into that culture. Usually, it's the job of managers to ensure that the company's aims, ideals, and expectations are communicated clearly to everyone involved in a project, no matter how widely dispersed their workplaces or how different their workplace attitudes and values.

vice operations to some extent. Consider General Electric <www.ge.com>, which inspires thoughts of appliances (and jet engines). But GE is not just a goods producer. According to its own annual report, "The General Electric Company is the world's largest diversified services company as well as a provider of high-quality, high-technology industrial and consumer products."[5] GE service operations include broadcasting (NBC), finance, insurance, investment, and real estate.

Creating Value Through Operations

To understand a firm's production processes, we need to know what kinds of benefits its production provides, both for itself and for its customers. Production, of course, provides businesses with economic results: profits, wages, and goods purchased from other companies. At the same time, it provides consumers with **utility**—the ability of a product to satisfy a want or need. Although production can contribute to all four kinds of utility—*time, place, possession,* and *form*—its

utility
A product's ability to satisfy a human want

operations (or production) management

Systematic direction and control of the processes that transform resources into finished products that create value for and provide benefits to customers

operations (or production) managers

Managers responsible for ensuring that operations processes create value and provide benefits

role in two areas is most obvious. It provides *time utility* by making products available when consumers want them and *form utility* by converting raw materials and human skills into finished goods and services.

Because the term *production* has long been associated with manufacturing, writers have recently replaced it with *operations,* a term reflecting both service and goods production. **Operations** (or **production**) **management** is the systematic direction and control of the processes that transform resources into finished services and goods which create value for and provide benefits to customers. In overseeing production, inventory, and quality control, **operations** (or **production**) **managers** are responsible for ensuring that operations processes create value and provide benefits.[6]

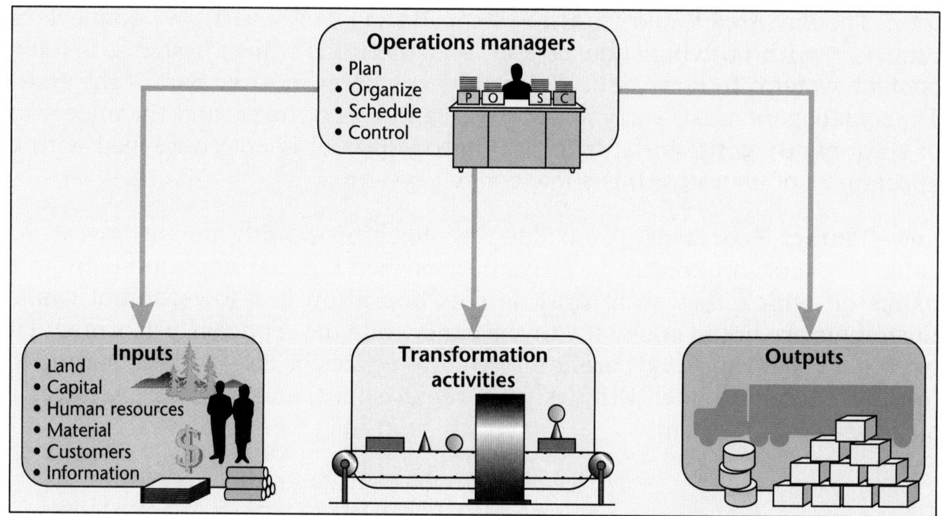

FIGURE 14.3
Resource Transformation Process

As Figure 14.3 shows, operations managers draw up plans to transform resources into products. First, they bring together basic resources: knowledge, physical materials, equipment, and labor. Then they put them to effective use in the production facility. As demand for a product increases, they schedule and control work to produce the required amount. Finally, they control costs, quality levels, inventory, and facilities and equipment.

Some operations managers work in factories; others work in offices and stores. Farmers are operations managers who create utility by transforming soil, seeds, fuel, and other inputs into soybeans, milk, and other outputs. They may hire crews of workers to plant and harvest, opt instead for automated machinery, or prefer some combination of workers and machinery. These decisions affect costs, the role of buildings and equipment in operations, and the quality and quantity of goods produced.

Operations Processes

An **operations process** is a set of methods and technologies used to produce a good or a service. We classify types of production according to differences in operations processes. We can classify goods by asking whether an operations process combines resources or breaks them into component parts. We can classify services according to the *extent of customer contact* required.[7]

operations process
Set of methods and technologies used in the production of a good or service

Goods-Manufacturing Processes: Analytic versus Synthetic Processes All goods-manufacturing processes can be classified by the *analytic* or *synthetic* nature of the transformation process. An **analytic process** breaks down resources into components (as Tyson reduces whole chickens to packaged parts for the meat counter). A **synthetic process** combines raw materials to produce a finished product (as GE shapes steel to produce a refrigerator; then adds motors, light bulbs, and shelves; and finally packages the complete refrigerator in a shipping carton).

analytic process
Production process in which resources are broken down into components to create finished products

synthetic process
Production process in which resources are combined to create finished products

Service Processes: Extent of Customer Contact In classifying services, we may ask whether a service can be provided without the customers being part of the production system. In answering this question, we classify services according to *extent of customer contact.*[8]

High-Contact Processes Think about your local public transit system. The service is transportation, and when you purchase transportation, you board a bus or

high-contact system

Level of customer contact in which the customer is part of the system during service delivery

low-contact system

Level of customer contact in which the customer need not be a part of the system to receive the service

train. The Bay Area Rapid Transit System (BART) <www.bart.gov> connects San Francisco with outlying suburbs and, like all public transit systems, is a **high-contact system:** To receive the service, the customer must be part of the system. Thus, managers must worry about the cleanliness of trains and the appearance of stations. By contrast, a firm that that ships coal is not concerned with the appearance of its trains. It is a low-contact system.

Low-Contact Processes Consider the check-processing operations at your bank. Workers sort checks that have been cashed that day and send them to the banks on which they were drawn. This operation is a **low-contact system:** Customers are not in contact with the bank while the service is performed. They receive the service—funds are transferred to cover checks—without setting foot in the processing center. Utilities, auto repair shops, and lawn-care services are also low-contact systems.

Differences Between Service and Manufacturing Operations

Both service and manufacturing operations transform raw materials into finished products. In service operations, however, the raw materials, or inputs, are not glass or steel. Rather, they are people who have either unsatisfied needs or possessions needing care or alteration. In service operations, then, finished products or outputs are people with needs met and possessions serviced.[9]

Focus on Performance Thus, there is at least one obvious difference between service and manufacturing operations. Whereas goods are *produced,* services are *performed.* Therefore, customer-oriented performance is a key factor in measuring the effectiveness of a service company. The reputation of Wal-Mart <www.walmart.com> stems in part from a policy of speedy product delivery that measures efficiency not in days but in minutes and seconds. A strong customer-focus strategy means getting fast supplier responses, streamlining transactions, and keeping the right merchandise on store shelves. To implement this strategy, Wal-Mart has made technology—namely, its vaunted computer and telecommunications system—a core competency.[10]

There are three areas of service operations that often make them more complex than goods production: *Focus on process and outcome, focus on service characteristics,* and *focus on service quality considerations.*

Focus on Process and Outcome Manufacturing operations focus on the outcome of the production process—for example, on the finished refrigerator. But the products of most service operations are really combinations of goods and services. Services, therefore, must focus on the transformation *process* as well as on its *outcome*—both on making a pizza and on delivering it.[11] Service workers thus need different skills. Gas company employees may need interpersonal skills to calm frightened customers who have reported gas leaks. The job, therefore, can mean more than just repairing pipes. Factory workers who install gas pipes in mobile homes don't need such skills.

Focus on Service Characteristics Service transactions reflect the fact that service products are characterized by three qualities: *intangibility, customization,* and *unstorability.*[12]

1. ***Intangibility.*** Often, services can't be touched, tasted, smelled, or seen. An important value, therefore, is the *intangible* value that the customer receives in the form of pleasure, satisfaction, or a feeling of safety. When you hire an attorney, you purchase not only the intangible quality of legal expertise but also the equally intangible reassurance that help is at hand. Some services

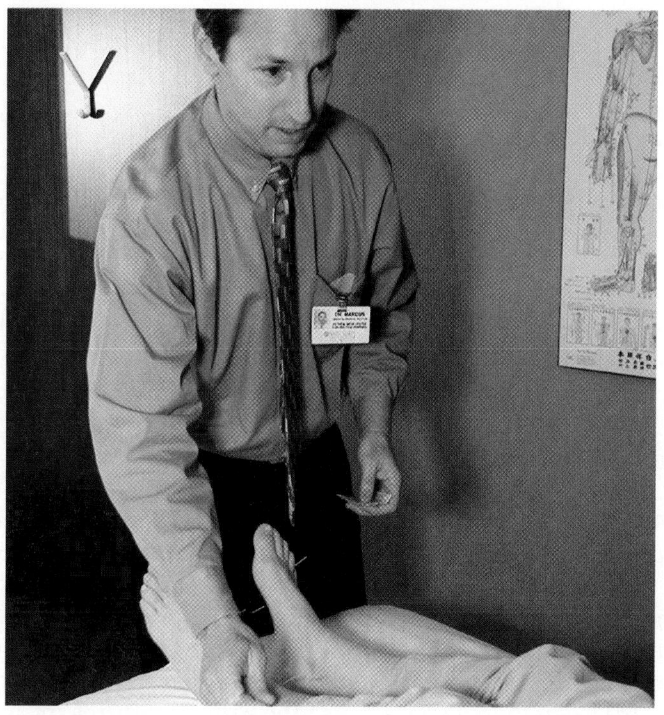

Studies have shown that acupuncture can help relieve nausea, pain, and headaches, and hospitals looking for a competitive edge through a wider array of services now offer alternative forms of medicine, including chiropractic, homeopathy, and herbal medicine. There's also a treatment called "remote healing," in which therapeutic prayers are sent to distant patients, but most alternative treatments, like most traditional treatments, are customized, high-contact services: They're tailored to meet the needs of a specific patient who must schedule a visit to a specialized service center.

also provide tangible elements. Your attorney, for instance, can draw up a will that you can keep in your safe-deposit box.

2. ***Customization.*** When you visit a doctor, you expect to be treated for *your* symptoms, not someone else's. Likewise, when you buy insurance or get your hair cut, you expect these services to be meet *your* needs. They must, in other words, be *customized.*
3. ***Unstorability.*** Many services—trash collection, transportation, child care, and house cleaning—can't be produced ahead of time and then stored. If a service isn't used when available, it's usually wasted. Services, then, are typically characterized by a high degree of *unstorability.*

Focus on the Customer-Service Link Because they transform customers or their possessions, service operations often treat the customer as part of the operations process itself. To get a haircut, for example, most of us have to go to the barbershop or beauty salon.

As physical participants in the operations process, consumers can affect it. As a customer, you expect the salon to be conveniently located, to be open for business at convenient times, and to offer needed services at reasonable prices. Accordingly, the manager sets hours of operation, available services, and an appropriate number of employees to meet customer requirements.

E-Commerce: The "Virtual Presence" of the Customer E-commerce introduces a "virtual," as opposed to the physical, presence of customers. Consumers interact with sellers electronically and in real time, collecting information about product features, delivery schedules, and postsale service. You enjoy 24-hour access to information via automated call centers, and if you want human interaction, you can talk with live respondents or log on to chat rooms. Many companies invite virtual customers into the system by building customer-communications relationships. The online travel agency Expedia.com responds to your personalized profile with an e-mail greeting, presents you with a tailor-made Web page the

*You should now be able to answer Self-Check Questions 1–3**

1. TRUE/FALSE Whereas the term *production* refers primarily to the creation of physical goods, the term *operations* refers to activities for providing services to customers.

2. MULTIPLE CHOICE Which of the following is **not** true regarding *operations processes* [select one]: (a) In high-contact service processes, the customer is a part of the process. (b) All goods-manufacturing processes may be classified as either analytic or synthetic. (c) A chicken-processing plant (one that prepares chickens for grocery stores) is a good example of an analytic process. (d) Foot surgery is a good example of a low-contact operation.

3. MULTIPLE CHOICE Which of the following is **true** regarding *differences between service and manufacturing operations* [select one]: (a) Whereas manufacturing operations focus on the outcome of the production process, service operations focus on both the transformation process and its outcome. (b) The products offered by most service operations are intangible and do not involve physical goods. (c) Whereas service operations are customized for customers, manufacturing operations focus on mass-production processes. (d) Customers generally use the same measures for judging the quality of service products and physical goods products.

*ANSWERS TO SELF-CHECK QUESTIONS CAN BE FOUND ON P. AN-9.

next time you sign on, maintains chat rooms where you can compare notes with other customers, and notifies you of upcoming special opportunities.[13]

Internet technology also lets firms build relationships with industrial customers. Electronic Data Systems (EDS) <www.eds.com> helps client firms develop networks among desktop computers. In managing more than 700,000 desktops for clients throughout the world, EDS has created a special service called Renasence <www.eds.com/geographic_sites/new_zealand/offerings/nz_renascence> that links clients, suppliers, and employees in a private 500,000-computer electronic marketplace. Some 2,000 software products can be viewed, purchased, tracked, and delivered if you are a member of the network.[14]

Focus on Service Quality Considerations Consumers use different measures to judge services and goods. Most service managers know that quality of work and quality of service are not necessarily the same thing. Your car, for example, may have been flawlessly repaired, but you'll probably be unhappy with the service if you're forced to pick it up a day later than promised.

Operations Planning

Now that we've contrasted goods and services, let's turn to a general discussion of production as an activity that results in both goods *and* services. Like all good managers, we start with planning. Managers from many departments contribute to decisions about operations. As Figure 14.4 shows, however, no matter how many decision makers are involved, the process is a series of logical steps. Success depends on the final result of this logical sequence of decisions.

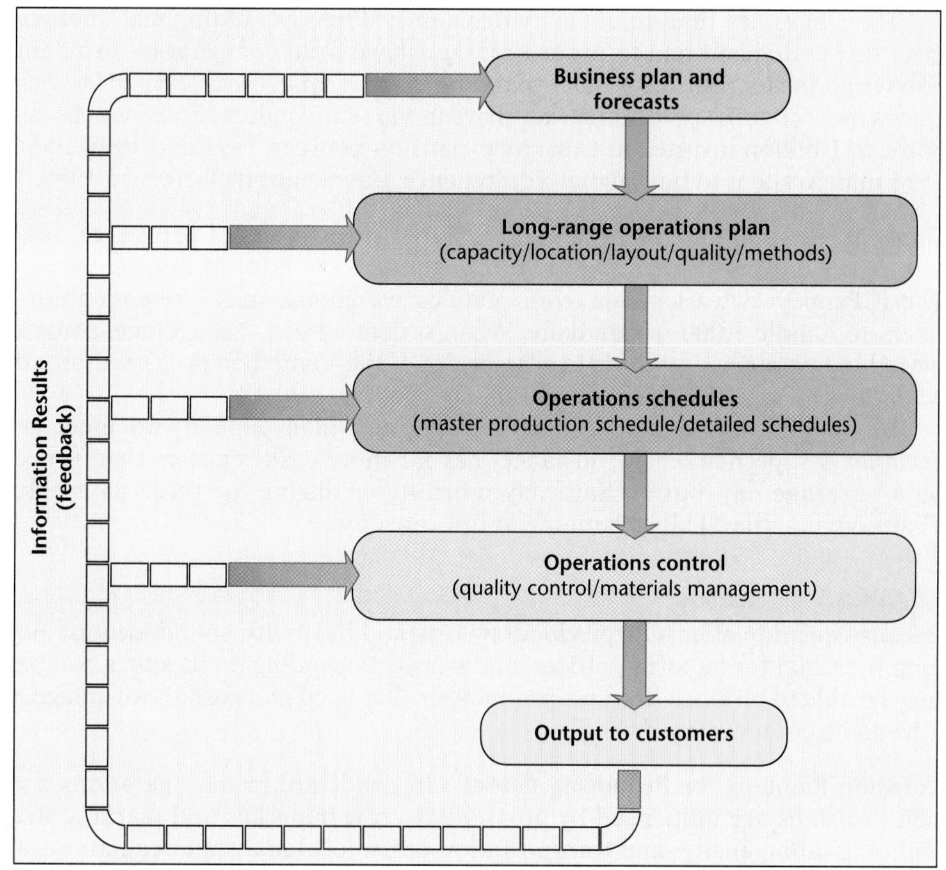

FIGURE 14.4

Operations Planning and Control

The business plan and forecasts developed by top managers guide operations planning. The business plan outlines goals and objectives, including the specific goods and services that the firm will offer. Managers also develop a long-range production plans through **forecasts** of future demand for both new and existing products. Covering a two-to-five-year period, the production plan specifies the number of plants or service facilities and the amount of labor, equipment, transportation and storage that will be needed to meet demand. It also specifies how resources will be obtained.

forecast

Facet of a long-range production plan that predicts future demand

In this section, we survey the main elements of operations planning, discussing the planning activities that fall into one of five categories: *capacity, location, layout, quality,* and *methods planning.*

Capacity Planning

The amount of a product that a company can produce under normal conditions is its **capacity.** A firm's capacity depends on how many people it employs and the number and size of its facilities. Long-range planning considers both current and future capacity.[15]

capacity

Amount of a product that a company can produce under normal working conditions

Capacity Planning for Producing Goods Capacity planning for goods means ensuring that a firm's capacity slightly exceeds normal demand for its product. To see why this is the best policy, consider the alternatives. If capacity is too small for demand, the company must turn away customers—a situation that cuts into profits and alienates both customers and salespeople. If capacity greatly exceeds demand, the firm is wasting money by maintaining a plant that's too large, by keeping excess machinery online, or by employing too many workers.

The stakes are high in capacity decisions: While expanding fast enough to meet future demand and to protect market share from competitors, firms must also weigh the increased costs of expanding. In part, Intel Corp. <www.intel.com> enjoys more than 70-percent market share in the semiconductor business because of the $11 billion invested in capacity expansion between 1991 and 1995 and the $625 million spent to buy Digital Equipment's Massachusetts factory in 1998.[16]

Capacity Planning for Producing Services In low-contact processes, maintaining inventory lets managers set capacity at the level of *average demand.* The JCPenney <www.jcpenney.com> catalog warehouse may hire enough order fillers to handle 1,000 orders daily. When orders exceed this average, some are placed in inventory—set aside in a "to be done" file—and then processed on a day when fewer than 1,000 orders come in.

In high-contact processes, managers must plan capacity to meet *peak demand.* A supermarket, for instance, has far more cash registers than it needs on an average day, but on Saturday morning or during the three days before Thanksgiving, they'll all be running at full capacity.

Location Planning

Because location affects its production costs and flexibility, sound location planning is crucial for factories, offices, and stores. Depending on its site, a company may be able to produce low-cost products or find itself at a cost disadvantage relative to its competitors.[17]

Location Planning for Producing Goods In goods-producing operations, location decisions are influenced by proximity to raw materials and markets, availability of labor, energy and transportation costs, local and state regulations and taxes, and community living conditions. At General Motors in Brazil, for example, GM and its suppliers operate a highly efficient assembly plant that relies on outside producers to supply large components such as fully assembled dashboards. Operations are more efficient because each supplier specializes in one component, and to resupply parts and reduce transportation costs, the factories of 16 suppliers share on-site floor space. They reduce needless inventory by delivering customized modules in just-in-time sequence to the nearby final assembly line.[18]

Location Planning for Producing Services Low-contact services can be located either near to or far from resource supplies, labor, or transportation outlets. At Wal-Mart, for example, distribution managers regard Wal-Mart outlets as their customers. In order to ensure that truckloads of merchandise flow quickly to stores, distribution centers are located near the hundreds of Wal-Mart stores that they supply, not near the companies that supply them.

High-contact services must locate near the customers who participate in the system. Thus fast-food restaurants such as Taco Bell and McDonald's now locate in nontraditional locations with high traffic—dormitories, hospital cafeterias, and shopping malls. They can also be found in Wal-Mart outlets and Meijer Supermarkets that draw large crowds. Some McDonald's outlets are located at highway rest stops, and Domino's Pizza and KFC restaurants can be found on military bases.

Layout Planning

Layout of machinery, equipment, and supplies determines whether a company can respond efficiently to demand for more and different products or whether it finds itself unable to match competitors' speed and convenience.[19]

Mid-Chapter Internet Field Trip

"Copying a Formula for Success"

In the first part of this chapter, we have seen how operations create goods and services that provide value for consumers and other businesses. We found that operations processes for producing goods often differ from those which provide services. But in many firms, operations provide a combination of goods and services. Of course, basic production issues are always involved: What must production do in order to provide utility for customers? What are some considerations for deciding where to locate a production facility? What resource inputs are required for the production process? What role does the customer play, if any, in the operations process?

Let's address such questions by exploring the Web site of a rags-to-riches success story that began in 1970, when Paul Orfalea, just out of college, borrowed money to open a tiny photocopy shop near the University of California at Santa Barbara. He called it "Kinko's," the nickname given to the curly-headed Orfalea by his college buddies. Today, Kinko's has more than 1,100 branches in the United States, Canada, and seven other countries in the Middle East, Asia, and Europe. Let's look at Kinko's Web site at <www.kinkos.com>.

First, browse the homepage. Near the top of the page, note the five selection categories: **Home, Our Services, Locations, Search Site,** and **Help.** Click on **Our Services** and examine Kinko's service products. Then respond to the following items:

1. Who are Kinko's customers? Are they mostly individual consumers or other businesses? Explain.
2. Is Kinko's product line primarily goods or services? Explain using examples.
3. Consider the four kinds of *utility*—time, place, possession (ownership), form—through which all operations systems provide benefits to customers. Identify a Kinko's product that provides form utility. Explain using an example. Do the same for time, place, and possession (ownership) utility.

On the **Our Services** page, scroll down to the bottom section, **Store Services,** and examine each of the four categories: *Copying & Finishing, Computer & Facilities, Paper & Supplies,* and *Shipping & Delivery:*

4. Think about location planning for Kinko's stores. Identify the main factors that must be considered.

On the **Store Services** page, go into **Copying & Finishing** and then click on **Express Copying:**

5. Identify the resource inputs that Kinko's uses to make Express Copying services available to customers. What is the customer's role in the production process?

To continue your Internet Field Trip, click on www.prenhall.com/griffin

Layout Planning for Producing Goods In facilities that produce goods, layout must be planned for three types of space:

1. ***Productive facilities:*** for example, workstations and equipment for transforming raw materials
2. ***Nonproductive facilities:*** storage and maintenance areas
3. ***Support facilities:*** offices, restrooms, parking lots, cafeterias, and so forth

In this section, we focus on productive facilities. Alternatives include *process, cellular,* and *product layouts.*

Process Layouts In a **process layout,** which is well suited to *job shops* specializing in custom work, equipment and people are grouped according to *function.* In a custom bakery, machines blend batter in an area devoted to mixing, baking occurs in the oven area, and cakes are decorated on tables in a finishing area.

process layout
Spatial arrangement of production activities that groups equipment and people according to function

The job shop produces many one-of-a-kind products, and each product, as you can see from Figure 14.5(a), requires different kinds of work. Whereas Product X needs three steps prior to packaging, Product Y needs four. When there is a large number of products, there will be many flow paths and potentially much congestion. Machine, woodworking, and dry cleaning shops often use process layouts.

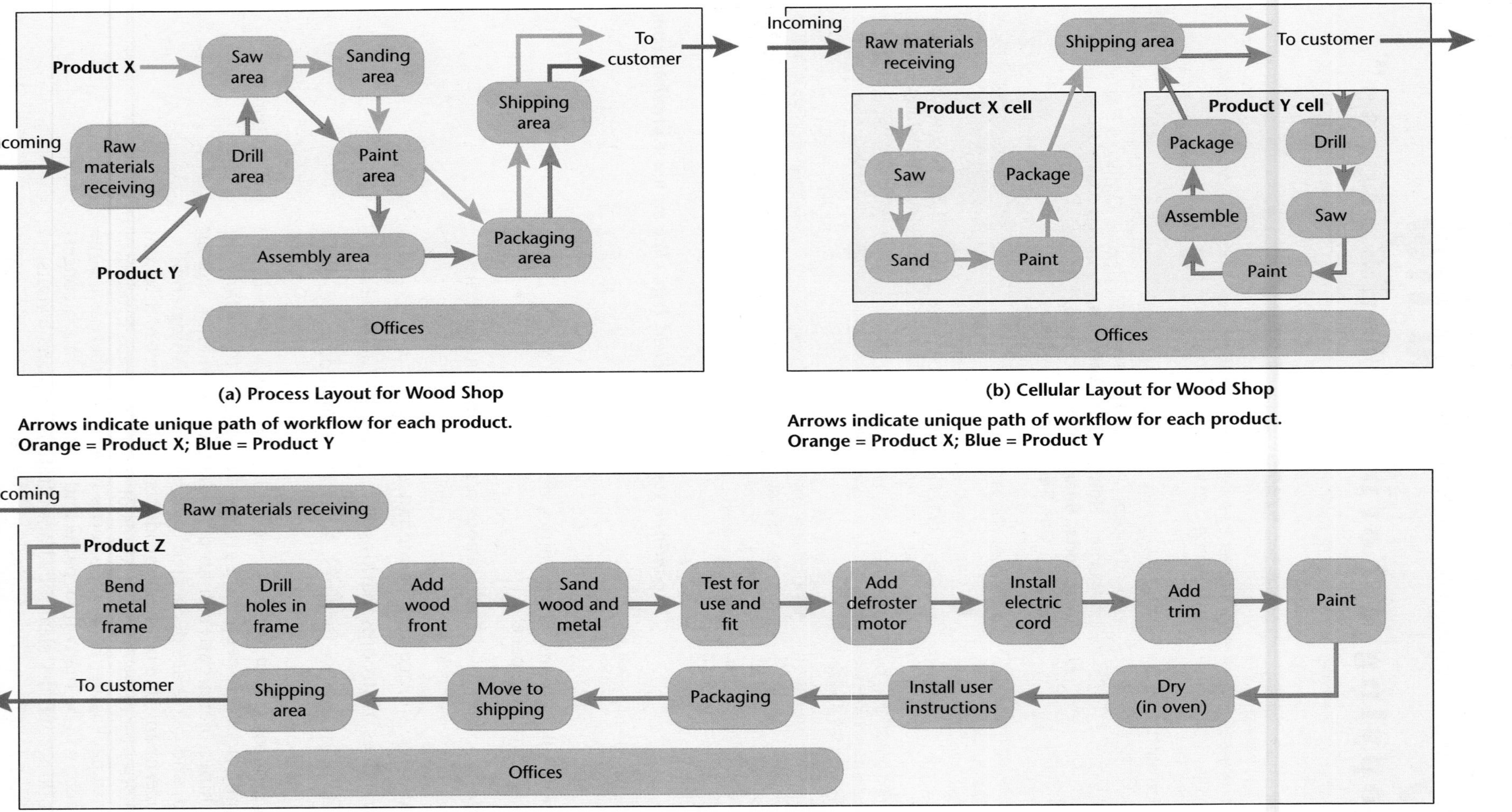

(a) Process Layout for Wood Shop

Arrows indicate unique path of workflow for each product.
Orange = Product X; Blue = Product Y

(b) Cellular Layout for Wood Shop

Arrows indicate unique path of workflow for each product.
Orange = Product X; Blue = Product Y

(c) Product Layout—Assembly Line

Arrows indicate the fixed path of workflow for all units of Product Z

FIGURE 14.5
Layouts for Producing Goods

Cellular Layouts **Cellular layouts** work well when a family (or similar group) of products follows a fixed flow path. A clothing manufacturer may dedicate a *cell*, or designated area, to making pockets—pockets for shirts, coats, blouses, trousers, and slacks. Although each type of pocket is unique in shape, size, and style, all go through the same steps. Within the cell, various types of equipment (for cutting, trimming, and sewing) are arranged close together in the appropriate sequence. All pockets pass stage by stage through the cell from beginning to end in a nearly continuous flow.

cellular layout
Spatial arrangement of production facilities designed to move families of products through similar flow paths

In plants that make a variety of products, one or two high-volume products may justify separate cells. Figure 14.5(b) shows two production cells, one each for Products X and Y, while all other smaller-volume products are made elsewhere in the plant.

Cellular layouts have several advantages. Because similar products require less machine adjustment, equipment setup time is less than that entailed by process layouts. Because flow distances are usually shorter, there is less material handling and transit time. Inventories of goods in progress are lower and paperwork is simpler because material flows are more orderly.

Product Layouts A **product layout** is set up to make one type of product in a fixed sequence and is arranged according to its production requirements. It is efficient for producing large volumes of product quickly and often uses an **assembly line:** A partially finished product moves step-by-step through the plant on conveyor belts or other equipment, often in a straight line, until the product is completed. Figure 14.5(c) shows the sequence of identical steps performed, from start to finish, on all units of Product Z as they move through the line. Automobile, food-processing, and television-assembly plants use product layouts.

product layout
Spatial arrangement of production activities designed to make one type of product in a fixed sequence

assembly line
Product layout in which a product moves step-by-step through a plant on conveyor belts or other equipment until it is completed

They are efficient because the work skill is built into the equipment, allowing unskilled labor to perform simple tasks. But they are often inflexible, especially if they require specialized equipment that's hard to rearrange for new applications. Workers can also get bored, and when someone is absent or overworked, those farther down the line can't help out.

Other Developments in Layout Flexibility In addition to variations on product layouts, there have been experiments in ways to make standard production lines more flexible. Some firms have adopted **U-shaped production lines:** Rather than stretching out in a straight line, machines are placed in a narrow *U* shape, with workers working from within the *U*. Because machines are close together, one worker in slow periods can complete all the tasks needed to make a product by moving from one side of the *U* to the other. In busier times, workers can be added until there is one per machine.

U-shaped production line
Product layout in which machines and workers are placed in a narrow *U* shape rather than a straight line

Another development is the **flexible manufacturing system (FMS):** Using computer-controlled instructions, one factory can make a wide variety of products. By integrating sales information with factory production activities, a manufacturer can adapt both automation and human resources to meet changes in customer demand.

flexible manufacturing system (FMS)
Production system in which a single factory uses automation to produce a wide variety of products

Because many companies find large FMS operations to be too complex and prone to breakdowns, some have experimented with so-called *soft manufacturing*—reducing huge FMS operations to smaller, more manageable groups of machines. Automation is less likely to fail when relegated to jobs it does best, while human workers perform the assembly-line jobs that require dexterity and decision making. Both are supported by networks of computers programmed to assist in all sorts of tasks.

In Cologne, Germany, the igus Inc. <www.igus.de> plant takes flexibility as far as possible. Everything—from assembly lines to furniture and employees—is adaptable and can be rearranged at a moment's notice. In a large open space about the size of three football fields, the igus factory makes 28,000 different industrial components for sale to other companies. While workers ride from task to task on motor scooters, modular furniture and movable machines allow the plant to be reshaped and entire departments relocated 24 hours a day, seven days a week.

"The beauty of the building," says igus President Frank Blasé, "is that it allows us to see where the business is growing and to react." Because customer needs are unpredictable, the firm has to react quickly. Up to 90 percent of all orders require customization. Rapid product innovation is also a way of life at igus, which develops about 2,500 new products and model variations each year. The strategy of being fast and agile has paid off. Annual revenue has increased tenfold to $100 million in the past seven years, and its workforce has more than tripled.[20]

"The beauty of the building is that it allows us to see where the business is growing and to react."

~ Frank Blasé,

PRESIDENT OF IGUS INC. ON HIS COMPANY'S FLEXIBLE FACILITY

Layout Planning for Producing Services Service firms use some of the same layouts as goods producers. In a low-contact system, the facility should be arranged to enhance the performing of the service. A mail-processing facility at UPS or Fed Ex, therefore, looks very much like a factory product layout. Machines and people are arranged in the order in which they help to mass-process mail. In contrast, Kinko's Copy Centers <www.kinkos.com> use process layouts for custom jobs. Specific functions such as photocopying, computing, binding, photography, and laminating are performed in specialized areas of the store.

High-contact systems should be arranged to meet customer needs. Piccadilly Cafeterias <www.piccadilly.com> focuses both layout and services on the groups that eat there most: families and elderly people. As you can see in Figure 14.6, customers enter to find high chairs and rolling baby beds for wheeling children through the line. Servers carry trays for the elderly and those pushing strollers. Note that customers must pass by the whole serving line before making selections. Not only does this layout help them make up their minds; it also tempts them to select more.

Quality Planning

Every operations plan must ensure that products meet the firm's quality standards. The American Society for Quality <www.asq.org> defines *quality* as the combination of "characteristics of a product or service that bear on its ability to satisfy stated or implied needs."[21] Such features may include a reasonable price and consistent performance in delivering the benefits it promises.

Methods Planning

In designing operations systems, managers must identify each production step and the specific methods for performing it. They can then reduce waste and inefficiency by examining procedures on a step-by-step basis—an approach sometimes called *methods improvement*.

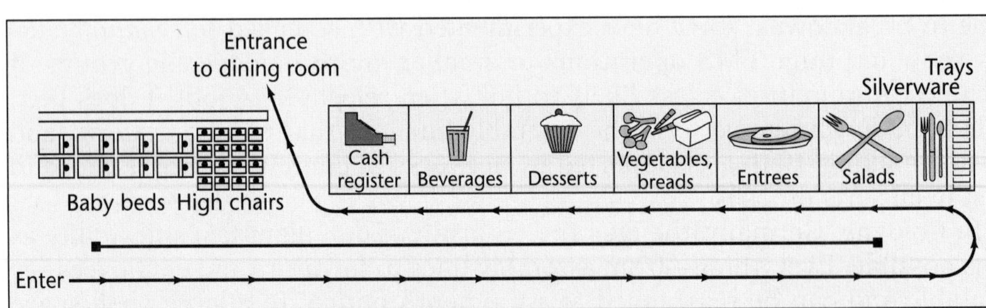

FIGURE 14.6

Layout of a Typical Piccadilly Cafeteria

Methods Improvement in Goods To improve goods production, a manager begins by documenting current methods. A detailed description, often using a diagram called the *process flowchart,* is helpful in organizing and recording information. The flowchart identifies the sequence of production activities, movements of materials, and work performed at each stage of the process. It can then be analyzed to isolate wasteful activities, sources of delay, and other inefficiencies. The final step is implementing improvements.

At Mercury Marine <www.mercurymarine.com>, a study of the process flow from raw materials to assembly (the final production step) revealed inefficiencies in the production of stern-drive units for power boats. Each product passed through 122 steps, traveled nearly 21,000 feet (almost four miles), and was handled by 106 people. Analysis revealed that only 27 steps added value to the product (for example, drilling, painting). Work methods were revised to eliminate nonproductive activities. Mercury ultimately saved money in labor, inventory, paperwork, and space requirements. Customer orders were also filled much faster.

Methods Improvement in Services In a low-contact process, methods improvements can speed up services ranging from mowing lawns to drawing up legal documents. At Dell Computer <www.dell.com>, for example, methods analysis eliminates unnecessary steps so that orders for computers, whether received online or by phone, are processed quickly. Committed to efficient selling by means of electronic technology, Dell can boast extremely fast delivery as a specific value of its products.

Service Flow Analysis By showing the flow of processes that make up a given service, **service flow analysis** helps managers decide whether every process is needed. Moreover, because each process is a potential source of good or bad service, analysis also helps isolate potential problems (known as *fail points*). In Figure 14.7, the manager of a photofinishing shop knows that it takes 48.5 minutes to develop a role of film. She also knows that the "develop film" stage is most likely to delay service because it's the most complex. She has thus flagged it as a potential fail point—a reminder to give it special attention.

service flow analysis
Method for analyzing a service by showing the flow of processes that constitute it

Designing to Control Employee Discretion in Services So far, we have stressed the importance of the human factor in service activities—the direct contact of

This control room operates a steel mill in Luxembourg that employees 1,000 people to produce just as much steel as a nearby traditional mill that needed 5,000 people (and which is out of business). Minimills like those run by Luxembourg's Arcelor <www.arcelor.com> *melt down scrap iron exclusively, and almost every operation in the facility is automated. From the control room, for example, computers move raw materials through electric-arc furnaces, pour liquid steel into copper molds, and cut strips of molded steel into desired lengths. The workforce is really a skeleton crew of technicians.*

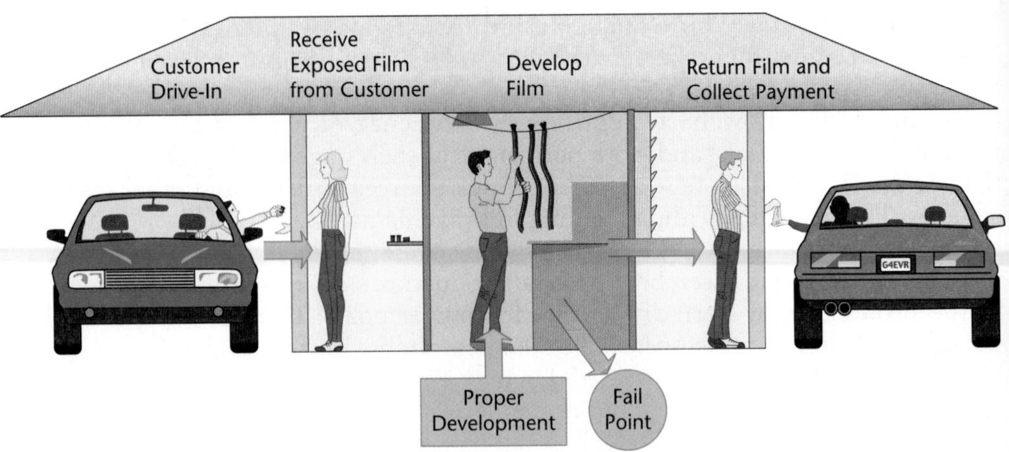

FIGURE 14.7
Service Flow Analysis

server and customer. In some cases, however, the purpose of service design is to *limit* the activities of both employees and customers. Managers can, for instance, make services more customer oriented by ensuring that processes—and not the people who operate them—make services consistent.

By automating processes that would otherwise rely on human judgment, McDonald's <www.mcdonalds.com> can provide consistent products and service from a staff with little specialized training. At a central supply house, hamburger patties are automatically measured and packed. Specially designed scoops measure French fries and other items into standard containers. All drawers, shelves, and bins are designed to hold only ingredients for McDonald's standard product mixes.

Design for Customer Contact in Services In high-contact services, managers must develop procedures that clearly spell out the ways in which workers interact with customers. Procedures must cover such activities as exchanging information or money, delivering and receiving materials, and even making physical contact. The next time you visit your dentist's office, notice how dental hygienists scrub and wear disposable gloves. They also scrub after patient contact and rescrub before working on the next patient. This high-contact system depends on strict procedures for avoiding contact that can transmit disease.

Operations Scheduling

Once they have determined the needed production resources, managers must develop timetables for acquiring and using them. This aspect of operations is called *scheduling.*[22]

Scheduling Goods Operations

master production schedule
Schedule showing which products will be produced, when production will take place, and what resources will be used

Scheduling of goods production occurs at different levels. First, a top-level **master production schedule** shows which products will be produced, when production will take place, and what resources will be used during specified time periods.[23] Logan Aluminum Inc., for example, makes coils of aluminum that its main customers, Atlantic Richfield and Alcan Aluminum, use to make aluminum cans. Logan's master schedule covers 60 weeks and shows how many coils will be made each week. For various types of coils, it specifies how many of each will be produced. "We need this planning and scheduling system," says material manager Candy McKenzie, "to determine how much of what product we can produce each and every month."

This information, however, is not complete. Manufacturing personnel must also know the location of all coils on the plant floor and their various stages of

Self-Check Questions 4–6

*You should now be able to answer Self-Check Questions 4–6**

4. MULTIPLE CHOICE Which of the following is **true** about *layout planning* [select one]: **(a)** Most high-contact services have facilities with product layouts. **(b)** Process layouts, also called *assembly lines,* are well suited for high-volume, continuous-flow operations. **(c)** Cellular layouts are useful for making a family of similar (though not identical) products that follow a fixed flow path. **(d)** Flexible layouts are appropriate for manufacturing operations but not for service operations.

5. TRUE/FALSE *Capacity planning* for low-contact service operations differs from capacity planning for high-contact services because of the inventory of waiting jobs in a low-contact facility.

6. MULTIPLE CHOICE Which of the following is **not true** for *operations planning* [select one]: **(a)** Location planning for both goods-producing facilities and for services producers is influenced by proximity to suppliers and customers. **(b)** Methods improvements are feasible in goods-producing operations but are often impossible in service operations because of the unpredictability of customer behavior. **(c)** Operations planning should ensure that customers are satisfied by ensuring that products meet the firm's quality standards. **(d)** The firm's overall business plan, along with forecasts of future demand for current and existing products, should be the driving forces behind operations planning.

*ANSWERS TO SELF-CHECK QUESTIONS 4–6 CAN BE FOUND ON P. AN-9.

production. Start-up and stop times must be assigned, and employees need scheduled work assignments. Detailed short-term schedules fill in these blanks; they allow managers to use customer orders and information about equipment status to update sizes and variety of coils to be made each day.

Scheduling Service Operations

Service scheduling may involve both work and workers. In a low-contact service, work scheduling may be based either on desired completion dates or on the time of order arrivals. Let's say, for example, that several cars are scheduled for repairs at your local garage. If your car is not scheduled until 3:30, it may sit idle for several hours even if it was the first to be dropped off. In such businesses, reservations and appointments smooth ups and downs in demand.

But if a hospital emergency room is overloaded, patients can't be asked to make appointments and come back later. In high-contact services, the customer must be accommodated as part of the system and its processes. Precise scheduling may not be possible.

In scheduling workers, managers must also consider efficiency and costs. McDonald's guarantees workers that they will be scheduled for at least four hours at a time. To accomplish this goal, McDonald's uses overlapping shifts. The ending hours for some employees overlap the beginning hours for others. The overlap provides maximum coverage during peak periods.

Tools for Scheduling Special projects, such as plant renovations or relocations, often require close coordination and precise timing. In these cases, scheduling is facilitated by special tools, such as *Gantt* and *PERT charts.*

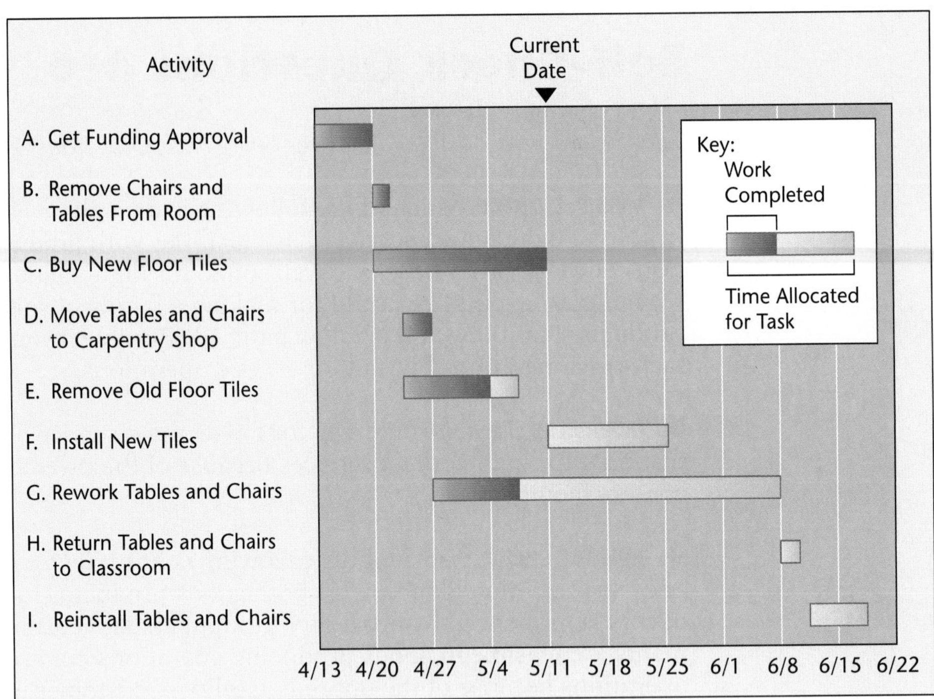

FIGURE 14.8
Gantt Chart

Gantt chart
Production schedule diagramming the steps in a project and specifying the time required for each

Gantt Charts A **Gantt chart** diagrams steps to be performed and specifies the time required to complete each step. The manager lists all activities needed to complete the work, estimates the time required for each step, and checks the progress of the project against the chart. If it's ahead of schedule, some workers may be shifted to another project. If it's behind schedule, workers may be added or completion delayed.[24]

Figure 14.8 shows a Gantt chart for the renovation of a college classroom. It shows progress to date and schedules for the remaining work. The current date is 5/11. Note that workers are about one-half week behind in removing old floor tiles and reworking tables and chairs.

PERT chart
Production schedule specifying the sequence and critical path for performing the steps in a project

PERT Charts *PERT*—short for *Program Evaluation and Review Technique*—is useful for customized projects in which numerous activities must be coordinated. Like Gantt charts, **PERT charts** break down large projects into steps and specify the time required to perform each one. Unlike Gantt charts, however, PERT not only shows the necessary *sequence* of activities but identifies the *critical path* for meeting project goals.[25]

Figure 14.9 shows a PERT chart for the classroom renovation that we visited above. The critical path consists of activities *A, B, D, G, H,* and *I.* It's critical because any delay in completing any activity will cause workers to miss the completion deadline (nine and one half weeks after start-up). First, no activity can be started until all preceding activities are done. Chairs and tables can't be returned to the classroom (*H*) until after they've been reworked (*G*) and after new tiles are installed (*F*). Second, the chart identifies activities that will cause delays unless special action is taken at the right time. By reassigning workers and equipment, managers can speed up potentially late activities and keep on schedule.

Operations Control

operations control
Process of monitoring production performance by comparing results with plans

Once long-range plans have been put into action and schedules drawn up, **operations control** requires managers to monitor performance by comparing results with detailed plans and schedules. If schedules or quality standards aren't

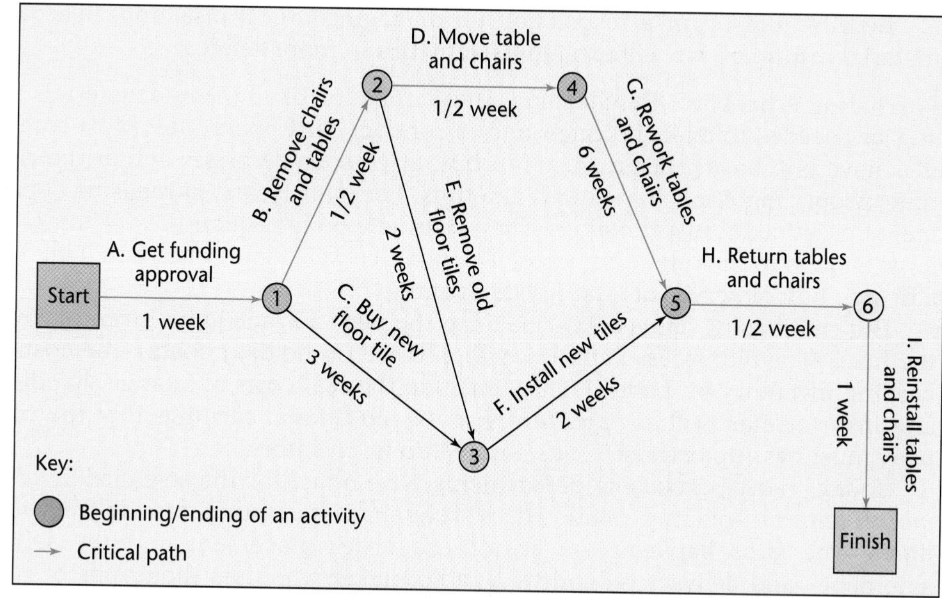

FIGURE 14.9
PERT Chart

met, managers must take corrective action. **Follow-up**—checking to ensure that production decisions are being implemented—is a key and ongoing facet of operations control.

follow-up
Production control activity for ensuring that production decisions are being implemented

Operations control includes *materials management* and *operations process control.* Both activities ensure that schedules are met and production goals fulfilled, both in quantity and in quality. In this section, we consider the nature of materials management and look at some important methods of process control.

Materials Management

All companies use materials. For many manufacturing firms, materials costs make up 50 to 75 percent of total product costs. For goods whose production uses little labor, such as petroleum refining, this percentage is even higher. Thus, companies have good reasons for emphasizing materials management.

The process of **materials management** allows managers not only to control but also to plan and organize materials flow. Even before production starts, materials management focuses on product design by emphasizing **standardization**—the use of standard and uniform components rather than new or different ones for related products.[26] Law firms keep standardized forms and data files for estate wills, trust agreements, and various contracts that can be adjusted easily to meet individual needs. Ford's engine plant in Romeo, Michigan, uses common parts for several different kinds of engines. Standardization also simplifies paperwork, reduces storage requirements, and eliminates unnecessary material flows.

materials management
Planning, organizing, and controlling the flow of materials from design through distribution of finished goods

standardization
Use of standard and uniform components in the production process

Once a product has been designed, materials managers purchase the necessary materials and monitor the production process through the distribution of finished goods. Thus, there are four major areas in materials management:

- *Transportation* includes the means of transporting resources to the manufacturer and finished goods to buyers.
- *Warehousing* is the storage of both incoming materials for production and finished goods for distribution to customers.
- **Inventory control** includes the receiving, storing, handling, and counting of all raw materials, partly finished goods, and finished goods. It ensures that enough materials inventories are available to meet production schedules.[27]

inventory control
In materials management, receiving, storing, handling, and counting of all raw materials, partly finished goods, and finished goods

Because *purchasing* is responsible for managing large transactions to acquire material resources, we will explain its activities in more detail.

purchasing

Acquisition of the raw materials and services that a firm needs to produce its products

Purchasing Processes **Purchasing** is the acquisition of all the raw materials and services needed to make products and to conduct daily operations. Most companies have purchasing departments to buy, at reasonable prices and at the right time, proper materials in required amounts. For many years, purchasing departments practiced *forward buying*. They routinely bought quantities of materials large enough to fill long-term needs. The practice was popular because it allowed a firm to buy materials at quantity discounts.

holding costs

Costs of keeping extra supplies or inventory on hand

But purchasing agents must balance the need for adequate inventory with the need to avoid excess supplies, which drive up **holding costs**—the costs of keeping inventory on hand.[28] These include the real costs of storage, handling, and insurance as well as *opportunity costs*—additional earnings that the company must pass up because funds are tied up in inventory.

lead time

In purchasing control, the gap between the customer's placement of an order and the seller's shipment of merchandise

Today, many purchasing departments have opted for the so-called *hand-to-mouth pattern*—placing small orders frequently. It requires fast delivery **lead times**—the gaps between the customer's order placement and the seller's shipment—and delivery reliability. A radio maker who uses thousands of standard components may significantly reduce holding costs by ordering only what it needs for a coming day or week.

supplier selection

Process of finding and selecting suppliers from whom to buy

Supplier Selection Purchasing departments also handle **supplier selection**—deciding which suppliers to buy from. The process typically has four stages:

1. Investigating possible suppliers
2. Evaluating and isolating the best candidates
3. Negotiating terms of service with a final choice
4. Maintaining a positive buyer-seller relationship.

Maintaining multiple supplier relationships is expensive. It takes time to survey, contact, and evaluate potential suppliers and build good relationships. In addition, fewer suppliers mean stronger, mutually dependent purchaser-supplier relationships. Today, therefore, most purchasers try to reduce their number of suppliers. In the first year of a supplier-reduction program, one 3M factory trimmed its supplier list from 2,800 to 600—and then reduced it to 300 the following year. Dana Corp. <www.dana.com>, one of the world's largest suppliers of automobile components, is dropping half of its 86,000 suppliers.[29]

Finally, think about the cost-cutting possibilities for industrial buyers who band together on the Internet. By forming online buying groups, they can purchase materials in huge quantities at big discounts. Online brokerage sites, such as PurchasingCenter.com <www.purchasing.about.com>, also unite buyers and sellers in a single Internet marketplace, where it is easier for companies to negotiate.[30] The "Wired World" box in this chapter recounts the experiences of several companies that have experimented with online purchasing.

Tools for Operations Process Control

Numerous tools assist managers in controlling operations. Chief among these are *worker training, lean production systems* (including *just-in-time operations*), *material requirements planning*, and *quality control*.

Worker Training Customer satisfaction depends largely on the employees who provide the service. In service-product design, employees are often both the providers of the product and the salespeople. Naturally, good customer relationships don't happen by accident: Service workers can be trained in customer-oriented attitudes.

Who's Buying Into E-Procurement?

Online purchasing, or *e-procurement,* has gained in popularity by promising savings over traditional purchasing and payment processes. E-procurement is expected to reach a staggering $3 trillion by 2003, using both public and private exchanges as well as so-called *reverse auctions,* in which purchasers use Web sites to invite potential suppliers to submit price bids.

One source reports that, on average, companies can cut purchased-goods costs by 15 to 20 percent via e-procurement. Testimonials abound: Owens Corning <www.owenscorning.com>, the maker of glass products and building materials, claims savings of 10 percent on annual purchases of $3.4 billion. Lucent Technologies <www.lucent.com> also relies on e-procurement as a means of cost reduction. Says Robert Piconi, general manager of Lucent's supply-chain strategy. "Every dollar we can save through e-purchasing is like receiving $5 to $7 of revenue." Hewlett-Packard <www.hp.com> has cut both materials and energy costs. E-procurement slashed HP's San Diego-area electrical bill from $2.2 to $1.3 million annually.

Various electronic tools are available to assist buyers and supply-chain strategists. Dutch Railways NS <http://mercurio.iet.unipi.it/ns/ns.html> uses Spend Management Suite, software from Ariba Inc. <www.ariba.com>, to automate the spending of nearly $1.5 billion on parts, fuel, and equipment. It helps company purchasers find suppliers and negotiate contracts, and it also analyzes the firm's overall purchasing process to find ways to save money with both new and existing suppliers. Savings, of course, come from lower prices on purchased materials, but transactions are also a big savings area. Streamlining eliminates duplicated activities, and automating the process cuts costs.

Some firms, however, have had less satisfactory experiences with e-procurement. A report from the National Association of Purchasing Management <www.napm.org> and Forrester Research Inc. <www.forrester.com> notes that online collaboration with suppliers among large-volume-buying organizations recently decreased by 10 percent. Why such a falloff? Forrester's Bruce Tomkin says that high technology is both a boon and a bane to Internet purchasing. Buyers, he explains, "realize that e-procurement takes more than surfing on supplier Web sites. That's why we're seeing a growing number of organizations . . . running into difficulties integrating their purchasing systems." Buyers and suppliers must thoroughly integrate their electronic systems, and doing so is time-consuming and expensive. Thus, although 84 percent of survey respondents report that they plan to use Internet purchasing, 47 percent admit that they're only at the earliest stages of introducing such systems.

Then there's the problem of inflated hopes. Many early adopters saw e-procurement as a way to downsize. One person with a mouse could do the job of an army of purchasers. But ironically, because of the Internet, supplier networks grew. Suddenly able to contact a vast pool of online suppliers, buyers began accumulating vendors, often duplicating and complicating services. Labor savings were offset by the costs of managing vendor relationships. In the health-care industry, unrealistic expectations have dampened the initial excitement over Internet purchasing.

Are there any solutions? IBM <www.ibm.com>—itself an e-procurement pioneer and promoter—recommends that firms start with a strategy and end with a technology. Translation: Think first about your procurement strategy and don't worry yet about the technology. Clarify the relationship of your company to your suppliers and customers. Then you can identify the most important elements in your buying process. Until you've taken these steps, say IBM experts, it's too early to think about the technology.

Says Kip Tindell, chief operating officer at the Container Store <www.containerstore.com>, a Dallas-based retailer of storage products, "We are just wild-eyed fanatics when it comes to human resources and training." While admitting that human resources and training are "the most difficult . . . part of the retail business," Tindell attributes the Container Store's success to its employees.[31] Like

lean system
Production system designed for smooth production flows that avoid inefficiencies, eliminate unnecessary inventories, and continuously improve production processes

just-in-time (JIT) production
Production method that brings together all materials and parts needed at each production stage at the precise moment they are required

material requirements planning (MRP)
Production method in which a bill of materials is used to ensure that the right amounts of materials are delivered to the right place at the right time

bill of materials
Production control tool that specifies the necessary ingredients of a product, the order in which they should be combined, and how many of each are needed to make one batch

manufacturing resource planning (MRP II)
Advanced version of MRP that ties together all parts of an organization into its production activities

Tindell, human resource experts now realize that without employees trained in customer-relationship skills, businesses such as airlines and hotels can lose customers to better-prepared competitors.

Lean Production Systems: Just-in-Time Operations **Lean systems** are designed for smooth production flows that avoid inefficiencies, eliminate unnecessary inventories, and continuously improve production processes. **Just-in-time (JIT) production,** a type of lean system, brings together all needed materials at the precise moment they are required for each production stage, not before, thus creating fast and efficient responses to customer orders. All resources flow continuously—from arrival as raw materials to final assembly and shipment of finished products.

JIT reduces to practically nothing the number of *goods in process* (goods not yet finished). It thus minimizes inventory costs and saves money by replacing stop-and-go production with smooth movement. Once smooth flow is the norm, disruptions are more visible and thus get resolved more quickly. Finding and eliminating disruptions by the continuous improvement of production is a major objective of JIT.[32]

Material Requirements Planning Like JIT, **material requirements planning (MRP)** seeks to deliver the right amounts of materials at the right place and the right time. MRP uses a **bill of materials** as a "recipe" for the finished product. It specifies necessary ingredients (raw materials and components), the order for combining them, and the quantity of each for making one batch (say, 2,000 finished telephones). The recipe is fed into a computer that controls inventory and scheduling at each stage of production. The result is fewer stock shortages and lower storage costs. MRP is most valuable when products require complicated assembly, such as the production of cars, appliances, and furniture.[33]

Manufacturing resource planning (MRP II) is an advanced version of MRP that ties all parts of an organization into its production activities. Inventory and production schedules, for example, are translated into cost requirements for financial managers and into personnel requirements for the human resource managers.

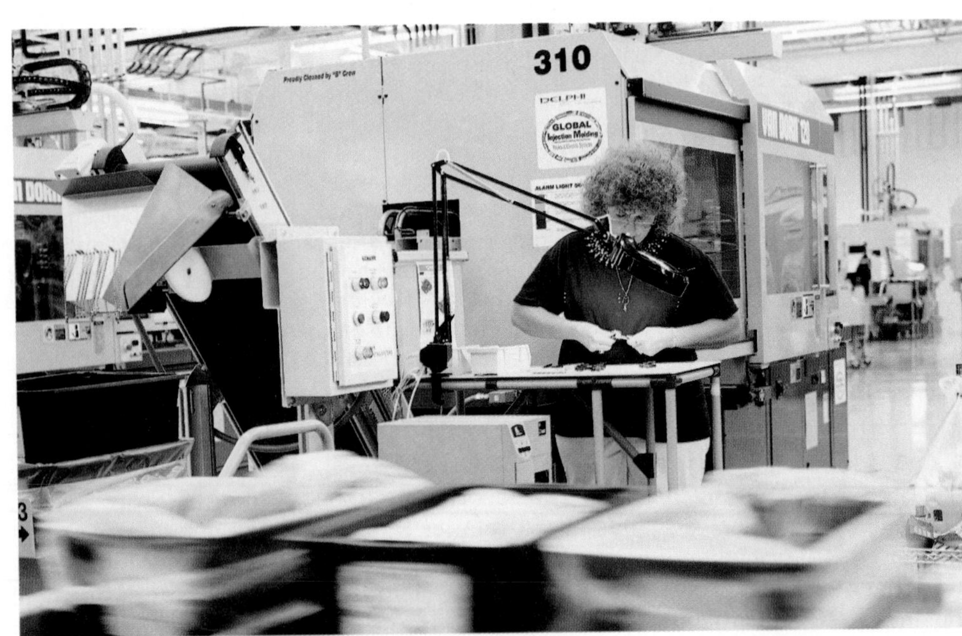

At this plant in Courtland, Ohio, Delphi Automotive Systems <www.delphi.com>*, which makes plastic housings for electrical connectors in cars and telecom equipment, quality checkers are among the members of an increasingly small human workforce. Since 1999, Delphi has spent $30 million for new production equipment, computers, software, and an e-manufacturing network that's so efficient that the plant superintendent can work at home from his own PC. As for these quality checkers, their work is made easier by a defect rate of about 14 parts per million.*

Self-Check Questions 7–9

*You should now be able to answer Self-Check Questions 7–9**

7. TRUE/FALSE Internet purchasing, or *e-procurement,* is superior to traditional purchasing because it allows faster contact with more suppliers.

8. MULTIPLE CHOICE Which of the following is **not true** for *just-in-time operations* and *material requirements planning* [select one]: (a) The main purpose of just-in-time systems is to reduce inventories. (b) In addition to managing materials flows, manufacturing resource planning (MRP II) systems provide information for financial management and human resource planning. (c) The bill of materials for MRP is basically a recipe for the finished product. (d) A primary objective of JIT is continuous improvement of production by eliminating disruptions and waste.

9. TRUE/FALSE Service operations present special *production control problems* arising from the customized nature of services, the unstorability of services, and customer involvement in services production..

*ANSWERS TO SELF-CHECK QUESTIONS 7–9 CAN BE FOUND ON P. AN-9.

Quality Control **Quality control** means managing the operations process in order to produce goods or supply services that meet specific quality standards. United Parcel Service Inc. (UPS) < www.ups.com> delivers 13 million packages every day (mostly to business clients) and promises that all of them will arrive on schedule. It keeps this promise by tracking the locations, schedules, and on-time performance of 500 aircraft and 150,000 vehicles as they carry packages through the delivery system. Quality control is essential because delivery reliability—namely, avoiding late deliveries—is critical for customer satisfaction.[34] (Our discussion of quality control is continued in Chapter 15.)

quality control
Management of the production process designed to manufacture goods or supply services that meet specific quality standards

Continued from page 394

Sharing "A Lot of Neat Stuff"

Linking all of JSF's companies, customers, and suppliers in real time would be impossible without Web-design and project-management tools. Keeping projects on schedule and holding down costs depend on both. Located all around the globe, thousands of design engineers, equipment engineers, logistics specialists, production planners, suppliers, and customers must move hundreds of thousands of components and share product designs, production schedules, and workflows.

With so many participants, information exchanges are essential in order to avoid lost time and duplicated effort. To save alliance members both time and money, Lockheed Martin hosts a Web collaboration network or *product data management system.* For instance, because all engineers working on a particular component are automatically notified when anyone makes a change, no one wastes time working on an outdated design. The system is also accessible to the Department of Defense for tracking progress in real time.

As the cornerstone of this project, Lockheed's Internet-based system does more than help to design the aircraft. It also makes it simple for Lockheed and its suppliers to link inventory and production systems. "The scale of this program is unprecedented," says Mike Brown, senior vice president of PTC <www.ptc.com>, a project software supplier. Project managers can quickly check on inventory status and production schedules as well as determine whether suppliers will have trouble meeting delivery deadlines. In addition to keeping materials flowing throughout the supply chain, the system features shop-floor–management tools to help identify delays, quality problems, and areas for process improvement.

The system also supports the 3D-solid–modeling program that underlies both design and production. Digital definition of the aircraft provides instantaneous information needed for making production tools and for assembling parts and components. Initial plans call for building one airplane every five months, but that time span will be reduced as the team gains experience with new materials and processes.

"We're using a lot of neat stuff," says Martin McLaughlin, Northrop Grumman's chief executive for the JSF product team. "Our use of 3D-solid modeling has revolutionized the machining of parts: [L]asers in the factory ceiling can read the 3D-solid–model data and project directly onto a machine tool an outline of exactly where the mechanic should place the next ply of composite material." Laser imaging cuts production time in half, guarantees precise control over composite materials, and trims inspection time by a whopping 90 percent. Laser technology also rigs assembly fixtures digitally (rather than manually), reduces the number of required parts by 50 percent, and eliminates 90 percent of the tools that would once have been needed to build the JSF. The team expects that manufacturing flow time will eventually be reduced by half.

Finally, the task of coordinating members and activities also falls on the project's Net-collaboration systems. Although separated by oceans, partners must communicate as if they were in the same room, and this intensive level of communication must be maintained for years to come. The sharing of real-time data is essential for more than just cost control. As the project progresses, the collaboration system will build stronger customer relationships and promote deeper political ties among members.

Questions for Discussion

1. How would you describe the time utility and form utility that customers will receive from the Joint Strike Fighter? List examples of each kind of utility.
2. How might scheduling tools, such as Gantt and PERT charts, be useful for the JSF project? Using examples from the JSF case description, show how Gantt and PERT charts might be used.
3. Suppose you are responsible for planning a full-scale production process slated to begin in 2008. You are concerned about the number of parts and systems suppliers who are scattered around the globe. What are some major production-planning problems posed by your supply chain and its geographic dispersion?
4. How would you describe the kinds of production or operations that will take place in the next phase of the JSF project, which will be System Development & Demonstration? Are the main products mostly services or mostly physical goods? Explain.
5. Because Lockheed Martin is responsible for overall project coordination, it must maintain sufficient capacity to fulfill its contract with the Defense Department. How would you describe the kinds of production capacity that will be needed for the next phase of the project, SDD? What kinds of capacity will be needed for the full-scale production phase?

Summary of Learning Objectives

1. *Explain the meaning of the term* **production** *or* **operations.**

Service operations provide intangible and tangible services products, such as entertainment, transportation, education, and food preparation. Firms that make tangible products—radios, newspapers, buses, textbooks—are engaged in **goods production.** Because the term *production* is associated just with manufacturing, we now use *operations* to refer to both service and goods production. **Operations** (or **production**) **management** is the systematic direction and control of the processes that transform resources into finished services and goods which create value for and provide benefits to customers. In overseeing production, inventory, and quality control, **operations** (or **production**) **managers** are responsible for ensuring that operations processes create value and provide benefits.

Today, operations reflect changes in two important areas: (1) *Growth in global operations*: Many countries compete globally, and instead of having to maintain continuous mass production, firms now face constant change. (2) *Relative growth in the service and goods sectors:* Although manufacturing still accounts for 19 percent of all private-sector jobs in the United States, the number of jobs has held steady for four decades. Service industries have grown far more rapidly since 1984. Employment has risen in the service sector, but it has remained stagnant in goods production. The service sector provides 52 percent of national income, and its share of the U.S. GDP is 33 percent greater than that of the goods-producing sector. (But the 19 percent of the U.S. workforce in manufacturing produces 40 percent of the nation's GDP.)

2. ***Describe the four kinds of* utility *provided by production and explain the two classifications of* operations processes.**

Products provide businesses with economic results: profits, wages, and goods purchased from other companies. They also provide consumers with **utility**—the ability of a product to satisfy a human want. There are four kinds of production-based utility: (1) *Time utility.* Production makes products available when consumers want them. (2) *Place utility*: Production makes products available where they are convenient for consumers. (3) *Ownership or possession utility*: Production makes products available for consumers to own and use. (4) *Form utility*: By turning raw materials into finished goods, production makes products available in the first place.

An **operations process** is a set of methods and technologies used in the production of a good or a service. There are two types of operations processes for goods: (1) An **analytic process** breaks down resources into components. (2) A **synthetic process** combines raw materials to produce a finished product. We classify services according to the *extent of customer contact*: (1) *High-contact processes*: To receive the service in a **high-contact system,** the customer must be a part of the system. (2) *Low-contact processes*: In a **low-contact system,** customers are not in contact with the provider while the service is performed.

3. ***Identify the characteristics that distinguish* service operations *from* goods production *and explain the main differences in the* service focus.**

Both service and manufacturing operations transform raw materials into finished products. In service production, the raw materials are people who have either unsatisfied needs or possessions needing some form of care or alteration. "Finished products" are, thus, people with needs met and possessions serviced. The focus of service operations differs from that of goods production in five ways: (1) *Focus on performance*: Because goods are *produced* and services *performed,* customer-oriented performance is crucial to a service company. (2) *Focus on process and outcome*: Because most service products are combinations of goods and services, services focus on both the transformation *process* and its *outcome.*

(3) *Focus on service characteristics*: Service transactions reflect the three key qualities of service products: (i) *Intangibility*: Because services usually can't be touched, tasted, smelled, or seen, they provide *intangible* value experienced as pleasure, satisfaction, or a feeling of safety. (ii) *Customization*: Each customer expects a service to be designed (customized) for his or her specific needs. (iii) *Unstorability*: Because many services can't be produced ahead of time and then stored, they have a high degree of *unstorability.*

(4) *Focus on the customer-service link*: Because service operations often acknowledge the customer as part of the process, consumers can directly affect that process. (5) *Focus on service quality considerations*: Service providers know that quality of work and quality of service are not necessarily the same thing (a properly repaired car is one thing, but getting it back when you need it is another).

4. ***Describe the factors involved in* operations planning.**

The operations-management process is as a series of logical steps. Whereas the business plan outlines goals and objectives, managers also develop long-range production plans through **forecasts** of future demand for both new and existing products.

Operations planning then focuses on five major categories: (1) *Capacity planning*: The amount of a product that a company can produce under normal working conditions is its **capacity.** The capacity of a goods or service firm depends on how many people it employs and the number and size of its facilities. Capacity planning for goods means ensuring that capacity slightly exceeds normal demand. In low-contact services, maintaining inventory lets managers set capacity at the level of *average demand.* In high-contact processes, managers plan capacity to meet *peak demand.*

(2) *Location planning*: In location planning, managers in goods-producing operations consider such factors as proximity to raw materials and markets; availability of labor; energy and transportation costs; regulations and taxes; and community living conditions. Low-contact services can be located either near to or far from supplies, labor, or transportation. High-contact services must locate near customers who are a part of the system.

(3) *Layout planning*: Layout of machinery, equipment, and supplies determines how quickly a company can respond to customer demand for more and different products. In goods production, layout can be planned for three different types of space: (i) *Productive facilities:* workstations and equipment for transforming raw materials; (ii) *nonproductive facilities:* storage and maintenance areas (iii) *support facilities:* offices, restrooms, parking lots, cafeterias, and so forth.

There are three types of layout for facilities: (i) In a **process layout,** which is well suited to *job shops* specializing in custom work, equipment and people are grouped according to *function.* (ii) **Cellular layouts** take groups of similar products through fixed flow paths. Equipment setup is easier, flow distances are shorter, and material handling and transit time are reduced. (iii) In a **product layout,** equipment and people are set up to produce one type of product in a fixed sequence. It produces large volumes quickly and often uses **assembly lines** in which partially finished products move step by step through the plant until they are completed. With more flexible **U-shaped production lines,** machines are placed in a narrow *U* shape, with workers operating them from within the *U.* One worker can complete all the tasks needed to make a product by easily moving from one side of the *U* to the other.

In a low-contact service system, the facility should be arranged to enhance the production of the service. High-contact systems (such as cafeterias) should be arranged according to customer needs.

(4) *Quality planning*: Products must meet standards of quality—"the totality of features and characteristics of a product or service that bear on its ability to satisfy stated or implied needs." Such features may include reasonable price and consistent performance.

(5) *Methods planning*: When managers reduce waste and inefficiency by identifying every production stage and the specific methods for performing it, they are practicing *methods improvement*. A *process flowchart* can identify the sequence of production activities, movements of materials, and work performed at each stage. The flow can then be analyzed to identify wasteful activities, sources of delay, and other inefficiencies. **Service flow analysis** helps managers decide which processes in a service are necessary. It also helps isolate potential problems known as *fail points*.

5. *Explain some factors* in operations scheduling *and describe some activities involved in* operations control, *including* materials management *and the use of certain* operations control tools.

Once plans identify needed resources, managers must develop timetables for acquiring them. This aspect of operations is called *scheduling*. In goods production, a **master production schedule** shows which products will be produced, when production will take place, and what resources will be used during specified periods. For scheduling special projects, two tools—**Gantt Charts** and **PERT charts**—assist managers in maintaining close coordination and timing.

Once schedules have been drawn up, **operations control** requires managers to monitor performance by comparing results with detailed plans and schedules. If schedules or quality standards are not met, managers take corrective action. **Follow-up**—checking to ensure that decisions are being implemented—is an essential facet of operations control.

Operations control features two processes that ensure that schedules are met and production goals fulfilled: (1) *Materials management*: Both goods-producing and service companies use materials. The process of **materials management** not only controls but also plans and organizes the flow of materials. Materials management may focus on product design by stressing **standardization**—the use of standard and uniform components.

There are four areas in materials management: (i) *Transportation* includes the means of transporting resources to the company and finished goods to buyers. (ii) *Warehousing* is the storage of incoming materials and finished goods for distribution to customers. (iii) **Inventory control** includes the receiving, storing, handling, and counting of all raw materials, partly finished goods, and finished goods. It ensures that enough materials inventories are available to meet production schedules. (iv) **Purchasing** is the acquisition of all the raw materials and services that a company needs for production. It includes **supplier selection**—choosing suppliers of services and materials.

Various tools assist managers in controlling operations: (i) *Worker training*: Customer satisfaction is closely linked to the employees who provide the service. This is especially true in service systems, in which employees are both product producers and salespeople. (ii) **Lean systems** are designed for smooth production flows that avoid inefficiencies, eliminate unnecessary inventories, and continuously improve production processes. One such system, the **just-in-time (JIT) production system,** brings together materials at the precise moment they are needed for each production stage. All resources flow continuously, and JIT drastically reduces *goods in process* (goods not yet finished), thereby reducing inventory costs. (iii) **Material requirements planning (MRP)** seeks to deliver the right amounts of materials at the right place and the right time. It uses a **bill of materials**—a "recipe" specifying necessary ingredients, the order for combining them, and the quantity of each needed to make one batch of the product. **Manufacturing resource planning (MRP II)** is an advanced version of MRP that ties all of its functions into the company's production activities. (iv) **Quality control** is the management of the operations process in order to make goods or supply services that meet specific quality standards.

KEY TERMS

service operations (p. 394)
goods production (p. 394)
utility (p. 397)
operations (or production) management (p. 398)
operations (or production) managers (p. 398)
operations process (p. 399)
analytic process (p. 399)
synthetic process (p. 400)
high-contact system (p. 400)
low-contact system (p. 400)
forecast (p. 403)
capacity (p. 403)
process layout (p. 405)
cellular layout (p. 407)
product layout (p. 407)
assembly line (p. 407)
u-shaped production line (p. 407)
flexible manufacturing system (fms) (p. 407)
service flow analysis (p. 409)
master production schedule (p. 410)
Gantt chart (p. 412)
PERT chart (p. 412)
operations control (p. 412)
follow-up (p. 413)
materials management (p. 413)
standardization (p. 413)
inventory control (p. 413)
purchasing (p. 414)
holding costs (p. 414)
lead times (p. 414)
supplier selection (p. 414)
lean system (p. 416)
just-in-time (JIT) production (p. 416)
material requirements planning (MRP) (p. 416)
bill of materials (p. 416)
manufacturing resource planning (MRP II) (p. 416)
quality control (p. 417)

QUESTIONS AND EXERCISES

Questions for Review

1. What are the four different kinds of production-based utility?
2. What are the major differences between goods-production operations and service operations?
3. What are the major differences between high-contact and low-contact service systems?
4. What are the five major categories of operations planning?

Questions for Analysis

5. What are the resources and finished products in the following services?
   - Real estate firm
   - Child-care facility
   - Bank
   - City water and electric department
   - Hotel
6. Analyze the location of a local firm where you do business (perhaps a restaurant, a supermarket, or a manufacturing firm). What problems do you see with this location? What recommendations would you make to management?
7. Find good examples of a synthetic production process and an analytic process. Explain your choices.
8. Develop a service flow analysis for some service that you use frequently, such as buying lunch at a cafeteria, having your hair cut, or riding a bus. Identify areas of potential quality or productivity failures in the process.

Application Exercises

9. Interview the manager of a local service business, such as a laundry or dry-cleaning shop. Identify the major decisions involved in planning its service operations. Prepare a class report suggesting areas for improvement.
10. Select a high-contact industry. Write an advertisement seeking workers for a company in this industry. Draw up a plan for motivating workers to produce high-quality services.

Building Your Business Skills

THE ONE-ON-ONE ENTREPRENEUR

This exercise enhances the following SCANS workplace competencies: demonstrating basic skills, demonstrating thinking skills, exhibiting interpersonal skills, and working with information.

Goal

To encourage students to apply the concept of customization to an entrepreneurial idea

Situation

You are an entrepreneur who wants to start your own service business. You are intrigued with the idea of creating some kind of customized one-on-one service that would appeal to baby boomers, who traditionally have been pampered, and working women, who have little time to get things done.

Method

Step 1

Get together with three or four other students to brainstorm ideas for services that would appeal to harried working people. Here are just a few:

- A concierge service in office buildings that would handle such personal and business services as arranging children's birthday parties and booking guest speakers for business luncheons.
- A personal-image consultation service aimed at helping clients improve appearance, etiquette, and presentation style.
- A mobile pet-care network through which vets and groomers make house calls.

Step 2

Choose one of these ideas or one that your team thinks of. Then write a memo explaining why you think your idea will succeed. Research may be necessary as you target any of the following:

- A specific demographic group or groups (Who are your customers, and why would they buy your service?)
- The features that make your service attractive to this group
- The social factors in your local community that would contribute to success

Follow-Up Questions

1. Why is the customization of and easy access to personal services so desirable in the twenty-first century?
2. As services are personalized, do you think quality will become more or less important? Why?
3. Why does the trend toward personalized, one-on-one service present unique opportunities for entrepreneurs?
4. In a personal one-on-one business, how important are the human relations skills of those delivering the service? Can you make an argument that they are more important than the service itself?

Exercising Your Ethics

PROMISES, PROMISES

The Situation

Unfortunately, false promises are not uncommon when managers feel pressure to pump up profits. Many operations managers no doubt recall times when excited marketing managers asked for unrealistic commitments from production in order to get a new customer contract. This exercise will introduce you to some ethical considerations pertaining to such promises and commitments.

The Dilemma

You are operations manager for a factory that makes replacement car mufflers and tailpipes. Your plant produces these items for all makes and models and sells them throughout the country to muffler-repair shops that install them on used vehicles. After several years of modest but steady growth, your company has recently suffered a downturn and must shut down five percent of the factory's production capacity. Two supervisors and 70 production workers have been laid off. All of the company's stakeholders—employees, managers, the union, suppliers, and owners—are concerned about prospects for the immediate future.

After returning from lunch, you receive a phone call from the general manager of King Kong Mufflers, one of the nation's top three muffler-repair chains. He says the following:

> I suppose you know that we're about to sign a contract under which your firm will supply us with replacement parts in large volumes, beginning two months from now. Your sales manager has assured me that you can reliably meet my needs, and I just want to confirm that promise with you before I sign the contract.

This is the first you've heard about this contract. While your potential customer is talking, you realize that meeting his needs will involve a 20-percent increase in your current production capacity. Two months, however, isn't enough time to add more equipment, acquire tools, hire and train workers, and contract for supplies. In fact, an increase this large might even require a bigger building (which would, of course, take considerably more than two months to arrange). On the other hand, you also know how much your firm needs the business. Your thoughts are interrupted when the caller says, "So what's your production situation insofar as meeting our needs?" The caller waits in silence while you gather your thoughts.

Questions for Discussion

1. What are the underlying ethical issues in this situation?
2. From an ethical standpoint what is an appropriate response to the customer's question? What steps should you take in responding to it? Explain.
3. What would you say on the phone at this time to this customer?

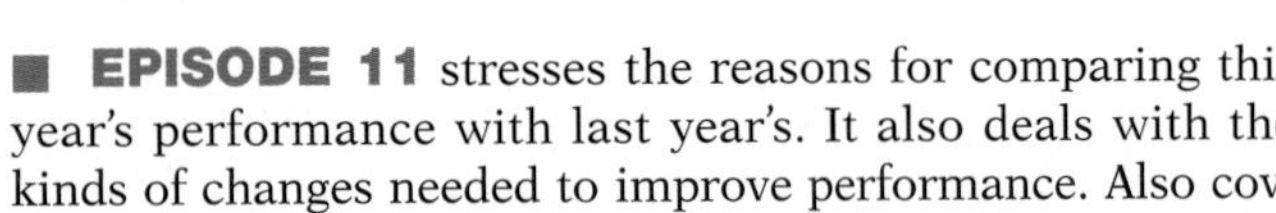

Mastering Business Essentials

■ **EPISODE 11** stresses the reasons for comparing this year's performance with last year's. It also deals with the kinds of changes needed to improve performance. Also covered is the fit between an organization's overall strategy and its approach to operations. *This episode deals with the issues of capacity planning, quality planning, materials management, and operations control.*

Crafting Your Business Plan

SPORTING A FRIENDLIER ATMOSPHERE

The Purpose of the Assignment

1. To acquaint students with production and operations issues that a sample firm addresses in developing its business plan, in the framework of the *Business PlanPro* (*BPP*) software package.
2. To demonstrate how choices of goods and services, characteristics of the transformation process, facilities and equipment, and product quality considerations can be integrated as components in the *BPP* planning environment.

Assignment

After reading Chapter 14 in the textbook, open the BPP *software and look around for information about plans for operations processes as they apply to a sample firm, a sports bar:* Take Five Sports Bar & Grill. *To find* Take Five, *do the following:*

Open *Business PlanPro.* If you are asked whether you want to "create a new business plan" or to "open an existing plan," select "create a new business plan" (even though you are not going to create a plan at this time). You will then be taken to the *Business PlanPro EasyPlan Wizard.* On the screen, click on the option entitled **Research It.** You will then be presented a new list of options, including **Sample Plan Browser.** After clicking on the **Sample Plan Browser,** go down its alphabetical list of sample plans and double-click on **Bar—Sports,** which is the location for *Take Five Sports Bar & Grill.* The screen you are looking at is the introduction page for the business plan of *Take Five.* On this page, scroll down until you reach the **Table of Contents** for the *Take Five* business plan.

Now respond to the following items:

1. What type of product—physical good or service—is Take Five Sports Bar & Grill creating in its operations process? Explain. [Sites to see in *BPP* for this item: On the Table of Contents page, click on **1.0 Executive Summary.** Then click on each of the following in turn: **1.2 Mission, 2.3 Company Locations and Facilities.**]
2. Describe the characteristics of the transformation (operations) process that results in this company's products. Be sure to include in your description some comments on the level of customer contact and its implications for the transformation process. [Sites to see in *BPP:* On the Table of Contents page, click on **4.0 Strategy and Implementation Summary.** After returning to the Table of Contents page, click on each of the following in turn: **4.1.2 Promotion Strategy** and **5.1 Organizational Structure.**]
3. Describe the equipment and facilities needed by a typical Take Five unit. [Sites to see in *BPP:* From the Table of Contents page, scan any headings that you expect will contain information on equipment and facilities specifications.]
4. How many Take Five stores are planned for the future? What steps can be taken in the interest of quality—that is, to ensure that the same consistent services are provided regardless of store location? [Sites to see in *BPP*: On the Table of Contents page, click on **1.1 Objectives.** After returning to the Table of Contents page, click on each of the following in turn: **2.3 Company Locations and Facilities, 4.3 Milestones,** and **5.3 Management Team Gaps.**]

Video Exercise

MANAGING GLOBAL PRODUCTION: BODY GLOVE

Learning Objectives

The purpose of this video is to help you

1. Recognize some of the operations challenges faced by a growing company.
2. Understand the importance of quality in operations processes.
3. Discuss how and why a company may shift production operations to other countries and other companies.

Synopsis

Riding the wave of public interest in water sports, Body Glove began manufacturing wetsuits in the 1950s. The founders, dedicated surfers and divers, came up with the idea of making the wetsuits from neoprene, which offered more comfortable insulation than the rubber wetsuits of the time. The high costs of both neoprene and labor were major considerations in Body Glove's eventual decision to do its manufacturing in Thailand. The company's constant drive for higher quality was also a factor. Now company management can focus on building Body Glove's image as a California-lifestyle brand without worrying about inventory and other production issues. In licensing its brand for a wide range of goods and services—from cell-phone cases and footwear to flotation devices and vacation resorts—Body Glove has also created a network of partners around the world.

Discussion Questions

1. *For analysis:* Even though Body Glove makes its products in Thailand, why must managers continually research the ways in which American customers use them?
2. *For analysis:* With which aspects of product quality are wetsuit buyers most likely to be concerned?
3. *For application:* When deciding whether to license its name for a new product, what production issues might Body Glove managers research in advance?
4. *For application:* How might Body Glove's Thailand facility use forecasts of seasonal demand to plan production?
5. *For debate:* Should the products that Body Glove does not manufacture be labeled to alert buyers that they are produced under license? Support your position.

Online Exploration

Visit the Body Glove Web site at <www.bodyglove.com>, read the Body Glove story, and look over the variety of products, including electronics products, sold under the Body Glove brand. Then browse the contacts listing to find out which U.S. and international companies have licensed the Body Glove brand. How do various licensed products fit with the Body Glove brand image? What challenges might Body Glove face in coordinating its operations with so many different companies and licensed products?

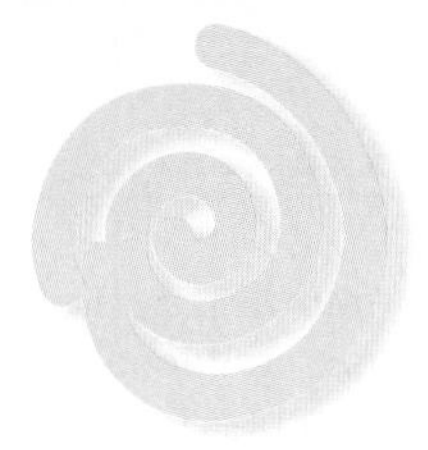

CHAPTER 15

Managing for Productivity and Quality

After reading this chapter, you should be able to:

1. Describe the connection between *productivity* and *quality.*
2. Explain the decline and recovery in U.S. productivity that has occurred in the last 30 or 35 years.
3. Identify the activities involved in *total quality management* and describe six tools that companies can use to achieve it.
4. Identify three trends in productivity and quality management, including *supply chain management.*
5. Discuss four strategies that companies use to improve productivity and quality.

Marshaling the Arts of Quality

If it's been around since the 1980s, it's too old-fashioned to be much good, right? Not necessarily. With new proponents seeking better products, happier customers, greater productivity, and higher profits, he Six Sigma concept of quality is just hitting its stride. ntroduced at Motorola Inc. <www.motorola.com> in 1987, Six Sigma works continuously o capture, measure, and eliminate defects in every companywide process—from financial ransactions and accounting practices, to R&D and production processes, to marketing nd human resources activities. It strives for excellence in very facet of the business. Materials from suppliers, for xample, must contain no efects; press releases should ontain purely valid information; and, of course, customers hould get error-free products nd get them on time.

Is error-free performance really possible? Before ix Sigma came along, most companies could only ream about it. But Motorola and other leading Six igma firms have made the dream an organizational eality. Today, the gates of higher quality are defended y so-called Six Sigma Black Belts—trained experts who implement quality-improvement programs, project by project and company by company. Before Black Belts, companies thought about quality in terms of ercentages of defective-free parts or defective parts er hundred. In approaching perfection, Motorola's ix Sigma target of 99.99966 percent, or 3.4 defects per *illion*, renders such measures virtually meaningless.

What does such a target mean in practical terms? onsider the fact that a company deals with customers, both internally and externally, through thousands of activities and transactions. There are thus housands of opportunities to make mistakes (which Iotorola calls *defectives*). Six Sigma strives to reduce efectives to 3.4 *per million opportunities*. In fact, Iororola plans to reach the point at which it makes ense only to count defectives per *billion*.

Naturally, Six Sigma has caught the eye of other uality-conscious companies. 3M, for instance, has ade Six Sigma its top priority. "Our other initiatives," ays 3M director of marketing David Powell, "are shorter-term, tied to our three-year strategic plan, but Six Sigma is forever. It's the umbrella." The International Society of Six Sigma Professionals <www.isssp.org> has grown to more than 8,000 members from over 600 companies. In addition to Fortune 500 firms, hundreds of other organizations are in various stages of instituting Six Sigma. Why? It is a proven fact that as quality goes up, other benefits soon follow—not the least of which are lower costs and higher productivity.

Getting started, however, can mean major organizational changes. The driving force behind Six Sigma is a customer focus aimed ultimately at bottom-line results. Motorola, explains Senior VP Dennis Sester, "views quality from a customer perspective, meaning we have only one opportunity per each product we deliver to favorably impact a customer. If the product doesn't meet expectations, we run the risk of losing that customer. It isn't enough to simply meet industry averages—every single product that reaches a customer should exhibit a uniform standard of quality."

Other major proponents of Six Sigma include former General Electric CEO Jack Welsh and CEO Lawrence Bossidy of Honeywell (formerly Allied-Signal). Early adopters were primarily manufacturing firms, such as Ford, DuPont, and Dow Chemical. But as more and more Black Belts arrived on the scene, Six Sigma methods began spreading to service firms such as CitiGroup, McKesson HBOC, American Express, and GE Capital Services. In fact, it's gaining strength precisely at a time when service-sector firms, especially, need a boost in quality and productivity.

Our opening story is continued on page 446.

"We have only one opportunity per each product to favorably impact a customer."

~ Dennis Sester,
MOTOROLA SENIOR VP

It is no secret that *productivity* and *quality* are watchwords in today's competitive environment. Companies are not only measuring productivity and insisting on improvements, but they are also insisting on quality that brings satisfaction to customers, improves sales, and boosts profits. By focusing on the learning objectives of this chapter, you will better understand the important concepts of productivity and quality.

The Productivity-Quality Connection

productivity

Measure of economic performance that compares how much a system produces with the resources needed to produce it

quality

A product's fitness for use; its success in offering features that consumers want

Productivity is a measure of economic performance: It compares how much we produce with the resources we use to produce it. The formula is fairly simple. The more we can produce while using fewer resources, the more productivity grows and the more everyone—the economy, businesses, and workers—benefits.

However, productivity also refers to the *quantity* and *quality* of what we produce. When resources are used more efficiently, the quantity of output is certainly greater. But experience has shown marketers of goods and services that unless the resulting products are of satisfactory quality, consumers will reject them. Producing **quality**, then, means creating fitness for use—offering features that consumers want.

Responding to the Productivity Challenge

Productivity has both international and domestic ramifications. Obviously, when one country is more productive than another, it will accumulate more wealth. Similarly, a nation whose productivity fails to increase as rapidly as that of competitor nations will see its standard of living fall.

A Reality Check for International Business Survival For decades, U.S. products dominated world markets because U.S. businesses were so successful in producing goods and distributing them in both domestic and foreign markets. The 1960s found U.S. manufacturers unchallenged as the world's industrial leaders, but by the 1970s, U.S. productivity had begun a dramatic downslide that continued into the 1980s. Then a remarkable turnaround in productivity occurred, and by 1994, American businesses had regained significant market shares in several large industries. As of 2001, U.S. companies were once again the leading exporters in several major industries, and today more and more Asian and European firms are once again forced to catch up with American competitors.

How did this change in fortunes come about? For one thing, U.S. businesses concentrated on understanding the true meaning of *productivity* and devised means of measuring it. Once learning that *quality* must be defined in terms of value to the customer, they redesigned organizations and marketing efforts to cultivate a more customer-oriented focus. As quality-improvement practices were implemented, more and more firms began to realize payoffs from these efforts. These successes highlighted the interdependence of four key ingredients: *customers, quality, productivity,* and *profits.*

labor productivity

Partial productivity ratio calculated by dividing total output by total labor inputs

Measuring Productivity How do we know when a nation is being more or less productive? Using the following formula, most countries use **labor productivity** to measure national productivity:

$$\text{labor productivity of a country} = \frac{\text{gross domestic product}}{\text{total number of workers}}$$

This equation reflects the general idea of productivity. It compares a country's total annual output of goods and services to the resources used to produce that output. The focus on labor, rather than on other resources (such as capital or

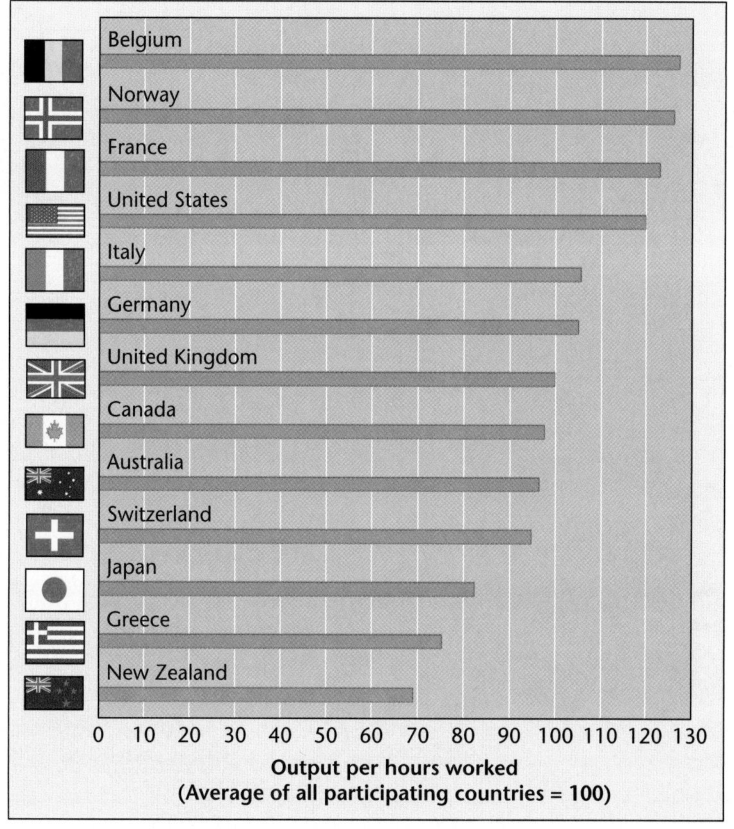

FIGURE 15.1
International Productivity Comparisons

energy), is preferred because most countries keep accurate records on employment and hours worked. For example, the U.S. Bureau of Labor Statistics <www.bls. gov> and the U.S. Bureau of Economic Analysis <www.bea.gov> compile updated monthly labor and economic output statistics.

Productivity Among Global Competitors A study by the Organization for Economic Cooperation and Development (OECD) <www.oecdwash.org> reports productivity levels in 23 participating countries. Figure 15.1 compares productivity among several OECD countries. As you can see, economic output per hour worked in Belgium is about 28 percent higher than the average for OECD members. At 31 percent below average, output in New Zealand is lowest among the nations listed in Figure 15.1.

Why such differences from nation to nation? The answer lies in many factors: technologies, human skills, economic policies, natural resources—and even in traditions. Consider, for example, just one industrial sector—food production (see <www.foodservice.com>). In Japan, the food-production industry employs more workers than the automotive, computer, consumer-electronics, and machine-tool industries combined. It is a fragmented, highly protected industry—and, compared with U.S. food production, it is extremely inefficient. The average U.S. worker produces 3.5 times as much food as his or her Japanese counterpart. Overall, data show that in the time that it takes a U.S. worker to produce $100 worth of goods, Japanese workers produce about $68 worth. Belgian workers, on the other hand, produce $107 worth.[1]

Domestic Productivity Nations must be concerned about domestic productivity regardless of their global standing. A country that improves its ability to make something out of its existing resources can increase the wealth of all its inhabitants. Conversely, a decline in productivity shrinks a nation's total wealth.

Say what you mean

TO BE OR NOT TO BE ON TIME

We all use time to organize our lives, and in the United States, we're particularly avid clock watchers. In some cultures, however, people think a little differently about time, and the differences can have a big impact on the way business is conducted around the world. When we call a friend or business associate in the United States, we expect a quick reply. Not necessarily so in countries where different priorities can mean different time frames for doing things.

If you're supposed to be at an 8:00 A.M. meeting in the United States or northern Europe, you'd better be on time (say, 8:05 at the latest). We expect people to be punctual, whether it's for a board meeting or a family picnic. Time is one of our ways of imposing order on our activities, and we regard regulated activity as something necessary to our workday productivity. But in some countries, thinking about time is, well, less timely. In Latin America, the Mediterranean, and the Middle East, for example, people generally do business according to relaxed timetables. They're likely to schedule a number of things at once, and if this habit means that schedules get ignored and some things get delayed, it doesn't really matter.

There are, of course, advantages as well as disadvantages. Sometimes, a more relaxed attitude toward making productive use of your time means taking time to develop relationships and getting to know someone instead of just achieving a specific goal in a specific time frame. Whatever the case, if you're operating in another country and culture, you need to know how people regard time and timeliness. Not only will you know when to show up at meetings and other events, but you may also have a better idea of how to devise production and delivery schedules. The most successful companies know their host cultures and are prepared to make allowances for local conditions.

Therefore, an increase in one person's wealth comes only at the expense of others with whom he or she shares a social-economic system.

For example, additional wealth from higher productivity can be shared among workers (as higher wages), investors (as higher profits), and customers (as stable prices). When productivity drops, however, wages can be increased only by reducing profits (penalizing investors) or by increasing prices (penalizing customers). It is understandable, then, that investors, suppliers, managers, and workers are all concerned about the productivity of specific industries and companies.

level of productivity
Dollar value of goods and services produced by each U.S. worker

National Productivity Trends The United States remains one of the most productive nations in the world. At $65,900, our **level of productivity**—the value of goods and services produced by each U.S. worker—is the highest in the world. (In second place, Belgian workers produced $64,200 per worker, followed by Italian workers at $61,700.[2]) For the most part, the U.S. level of productivity rose steadily throughout the 1980s and 1990s.

Growth Rate of U.S. Productivity Many observers treat productivity trends as indicators of national economic health. In the 1980s, for example, the United States suffered a slowdown in the *growth rate of productivity*—the annual increase in a nation's output over the previous year. Productivity was not increasing as quickly as it had in the past. Then, however, recovery began, continued through the 1990s, and is projected to increase in the decade ahead.

Uneven Growth in the Manufacturing and Service Sectors A comparison of the manufacturing and service sectors reveals important productivity differences. Throughout most of the 1970s, the manufacturing sector trailed slightly behind the service sector. But from 1978 to 1990, service productivity averaged zero improvement. By 1993, while service productivity was once again on the upswing, growth in manufacturing productivity more than doubled that of services (a margin sustained through 2001).[3]

Thus, manufacturing is primarily responsible for the recent increases in overall productivity. In 2001, for instance, the value of goods produced by each U.S. manufacturing worker was $156,000, compared with $72,100 for each service worker.[4] As we saw in Chapter 14, however, services are growing faster than goods production as a proportion of all U.S. business and now account for about 60 percent of national income.

Industrywide Productivity Industries also differ vastly in terms of productivity. During the 1990s, for instance, the productivity of electric utilities (see <www.eei.org>) increased by 48 percent, while grocery store productivity (see <www.progressivegrocer.com>) declined by 1 percent. Producers of men's and boys' furnishings increased productivity by more than 80 percent, whereas plywood manufacturing productivity (see <www.hpva.org>) fell by nearly 8 percent. Figure 15.2 shows contrasting productivity levels for several selected services and manufacturing industries.[5]

Let's consider the response of the U.S. textile industry (see <www.atmi.org>) to recent competitive pressures. Two decades ago, lower-priced foreign labor and European innovations threatened to cripple the U.S. textile industry. During the past decade, however, U.S. yarn and fabric makers have improved productivity at an annual rate of 3.4 percent per year. The industry spends $2 billion a year on modernized equipment and processes, and today's mills weave cloth four times faster than they did a decade ago. Fewer workers are needed, and some highly

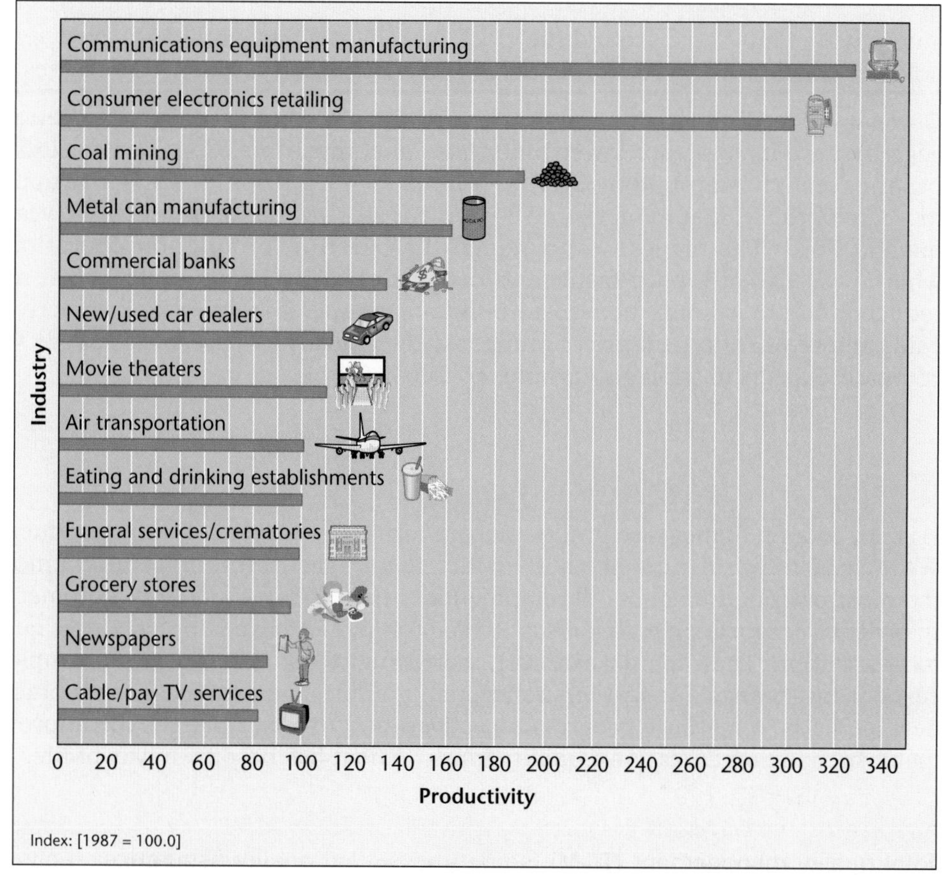

FIGURE 15.2
Productivity in Selected U.S. Industries

On the left, workers at International Truck & Engine Corp. <www.internationaldelivers.com> *of Springfield, Ohio, assemble a truck the old way, manually lowering and bolting frames on to axles. Today (right), the process is highly automated (and safer), with robotic grippers to flip and align the bulky frames. International has also shifted to modular design—combining standardized components to create a variety of products. The whole productivity-improvement program is costing $900 million, but the company intends to hold on to its number-one share in medium-size trucks by using 40 percent less labor to build them.*

automated plants work around the clock with hardly any employees. New technologies consume 50 percent less water and energy than outmoded processes.[6]

Companywide Productivity High productivity gives a company a competitive edge because its costs are lower than those of competitors. Consider, for example, the recent turnaround by General Motors <www.gm.com>, which has upped its share of the U.S. auto market to 31 percent and, for the first time in 11 years, outsold Ford. The biggest improvement has been in production operations, where processes are both faster and better. Between 1997 and 2001, GM had reduced the labor hours needed to build a car to 40.3 from 48.3. Productivity gains allowed GM to trim prices and boost earnings by 17 percent for 2002. The company expects to triple its earnings by 2005.[7]

Total Quality Management

It is not enough to measure productivity in terms of numbers of items produced. We must also consider quality; and, in fact, the "quality revolution" ranks among the most profound business developments in the history of modern commerce. In order to compete on a global scale, U.S. companies have adopted a new quality orientation. They are, for example, increasingly customer-driven. All employees, not just managers, participate in quality efforts, and firms have embraced new methods to measure progress objectively and to identify areas for improvement. In many organizations, quality improvement has become a way of life.

total quality management (TQM) (or **quality assurance**)

The sum of all activities involved in getting high-quality products into the marketplace

Managing for Quality

Total quality management (TQM) (sometimes called **quality assurance**) includes all of the activities necessary for getting high-quality goods and services into the

Self-Check Questions 1–3

*You should now be able to answer Self-Check Questions 1–3**

1. TRUE/FALSE An increase in *labor productivity* means that output is higher because workers are working harder and faster.

2. MULTIPLE CHOICE Which of the following is **not** true regarding *U.S. labor productivity?* [select one]: **(a)** Federal government productivity is lower than private business productivity. **(b)** Manufacturing productivity has been losing ground to services productivity. **(c)** Some manufacturing industries have lower productivity than some service industries. **(d)** Overall, productivity for services is lower than productivity in manufacturing.

3. MULTIPLE CHOICE Which of the following is **true** regarding *productivity* and *productivity measurement?* [select one]: **(a)** Although productivity and quality are sometimes related, they are generally separate and independent concepts. **(b)** The general form for measuring productivity is "resource inputs" divided by "outputs." **(c)** Companies are required to report labor productivity so that the government can calculate national productivity. **(d)** Labor-productivity measurement is popular because most countries keep accurate records on employment and hours worked, thus making labor productivity easy to calculate and compare.

*ANSWERS TO SELF CHECK QUESTIONS 1–3 CAN BE FOUND ON P. AN-10.

marketplace. It must consider all aspects of a business, including customers, suppliers, and employees. The strategic approach to TQM begins with leadership and a desire for TQM. This approach means getting people's attention, getting them to think in new ways about what they do, and then getting them to improve both processes and products.[8]

Customer focus is the starting point. Companies must develop methods to determine what customers want and need and then direct all their resources toward satisfying those wants and needs. Total participation is mandatory. Unless all employees are working to improve quality, a firm is wasting potential contributions from its human resources—and, thus, it is missing a chance to become a stronger competitor. TQM demands continuous improvement not only of products and services, but also of the company's internal processes, such as accounting, delivery, billing, and information flows.

Says John Kay, director of Oxford University's School of Management, "You can't run a successful company if you don't care about customers and employees, or if you are systematically unpleasant to suppliers." To marshal the interests of all these stakeholders, TQM involves planning, organizing, directing, and controlling.

"You can't run a successful company if you don't care about customers and employees, or if you are systematically unpleasant to suppliers."

~John Kay, Director, Oxford University School of Management

Planning for Quality To achieve high quality, managers must plan for production processes (including equipment, methods, worker skills, and materials). Planning for quality, however, begins *before* products are designed or redesigned. Early in the process, managers must set goals for both performance quality and quality reliability. **Performance quality** refers to the *performance features* of a product. For loyal buyers of Godiva premium chocolates <www.godiva.com>, performance quality includes such sensory delights such as aroma, flavor, and texture. "Truly fine chocolates," observes Master Chocolatier Thiery Muret, "are always fresh, contain high-quality ingredients like cocoa beans and butter . . .

performance quality
The performance features offered by a product

and feature unusual textures and natural flavors." Superior performance quality helps Godiva remain one of the world's top brands.[9]

quality reliability

Consistency of a product's quality from unit to unit

Performance quality is usually related to **quality reliability**—the *consistency* of product quality from unit to unit. Cars from Toyota <www.toyota.com>, for example, enjoy high-quality reliability. Consistency is achieved by controlling the quality of raw materials, encouraging conscientious work, and maintaining equipment. Naturally, some products offer both high-quality reliability and high-performance quality. Kellogg's <www.kelloggs.com>, for example, has a reputation for consistently producing cereals made of high-quality ingredients.

Organizing for Quality Producing high-quality goods and services requires an effort from all parts of an organization. A separate quality control department is no longer enough. Everyone—purchasers, engineers, janitors, marketers, machinists, and other personnel—must focus on quality. At Merrill Lynch Credit Corp. <www.ml.com>, for example, all employees are responsible for taking the initiative in responding to customers' credit needs. The overall goal is to reduce problems to a minimum by providing credit selectively and skillfully from the beginning of the process. The result: Both number of loans and market share are increasing while loan delinquencies are decreasing.

At the same time, many firms assign responsibility for specific aspects of TQM to specific departments or positions. Many companies have *quality assurance* or *quality control* departments staffed by quality experts. They may be called in to solve quality-related problems in any department, and they keep everyone informed about the latest developments in quality-related equipment and methods. They also monitor quality control activities to identify areas for improvement.

quality ownership

Principle of total quality management that holds that quality belongs to each person who creates it while performing a job

Directing for Quality Managers must motivate employees throughout the company to achieve quality goals. They must continually find ways to foster a quality focus by training employees, encouraging involvement, and tying compensation to work quality. If managers succeed, employees will ultimately accept **quality ownership**: the idea that quality belongs to each person who creates it while performing a job. At ITT Industries Inc. <www.itt.com>, for example, CEO Louis J. Giuliano implemented a quality program called Value-Based Six Sigma (VBSS) by organizing quality improvement teams and retraining employees to use quality-related equipment. The payoffs have been enormous: Between 1998 and 2001, earnings per share went up from $1.25 to $3.09—an annual growth rate of 35 percent despite a recession and repercussions from September 11th.[10]

Controlling for Quality By monitoring products and services, a company can detect mistakes and make corrections. First, however, managers must establish specific standards and measurements. At a bank, for example, the control system for teller services might require supervisors to observe employees periodically and evaluate their work according to a checklist. The results would then be reviewed with employees and either confirm proper performance or indicate changes for bringing performance up to standards.

Tools for Total Quality Management

competitive product analysis

Process by which a company analyzes a competitor's products to identify desirable improvements

Many companies rely on proven tools to manage quality. Ideas for improving both products and production processes often come from **competitive product analysis**. Toshiba, for example, might take apart a Xerox copier and test each component. The results would help managers decide which Toshiba product features are satisfactory, which features should be upgraded, and which operations processes need improvement.

In this section, we will survey six of the most commonly used tools for TQM: *value-added analysis, statistical process control, quality/cost studies, quality improvement teams, benchmarking,* and *getting closer to the customer.*

Value-Added Analysis **Value-added analysis** refers to the evaluation of all work activities, material flows, and paperwork to determine the value that they add for customers. It often reveals wasteful or unnecessary activities that can be eliminated without jeopardizing customer service. When Hewlett-Packard <www.helwett-packard.com>, for example, simplified its contracts and reduced them from 20 pages to as few as two, computer sales rose by more than 18 percent.

value-added analysis
Process of evaluating all work activities, materials flows, and paperwork to determine the value they add for customers

Statistical Process Control Although every company would like complete uniformity in its output, all firms experience unit-to-unit variations in products. Companies can, however, control product quality by understanding sources of variation. **Statistical process control (SPC)** refers to methods by which employees can gather data and analyze variations in production activities to determine needed adjustments.[11] At EZ Acres, a 500-cow dairy farm near Homer, New York, personnel use SPC to control the dryness and chemical composition of cattle feed, thereby reducing the costs of milk production. Steelcase <www.steelcase.com>, an office furniture manufacturer, uses SPC to control the thickness of paint on furniture cabinets. Excessive thickness increases costs and provides no added value for customers. Using SPC, Steelcase improved consistency from painting machines and cut the cost of paint by 15 percent.[12]

statistical process control (SPC)
Methods for gathering data to analyze variations in production activities to see when adjustments are needed

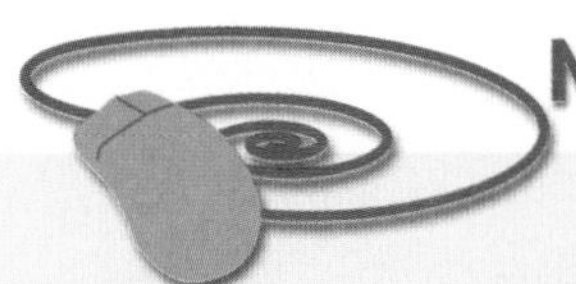

Mid-Chapter Internet Field Trip

"Is Quality Manageable?"

In the first part of this chapter, we examined basic ideas about *productivity* and *quality,* including the *productivity-quality connection.* We offered some examples of the ways companies increase productivity by improving *internal processes,* introduced the concept of *Six Sigma quality,* and described the activities involved in *quality management.*

Performing these activities effectively means that managers must maintain up-to-date skills and information on developments relating to quality and productivity. What sources for information are available? How do managers keep abreast of recent developments? What kinds of resources are available to assist managers in continuing their professional development as quality professionals?

Let's explore some of these questions by visiting the Web site of a preeminent association for quality professionals—the American Society for Quality (ASQ)—at <www.asq.org>. At the top of the home page, you will find that the Web site is divided into six categories: **Publications, Information, Certification, Training, Standards,** and **Networking.** Start by clicking on **Information.** The screen displays a page entitled **Why Quality?,** which includes a list of several reasons why quality is important. Much of this information will help you in responding to the following item:

❶ Are any of the items in the list related to *productivity*? Which items are not directly related to productivity? Explain.

After returning to the top of the home page, click on **Training.** On the **Training** page, scan down to the section entitled **Public Training Courses** and the drop-down menu labeled **Select a Course.** Scan the various courses in the **Select a Course** listing and then respond to the following item:

❷ Determine if any of ASQ's public training courses might be useful for improving productivity. Explain.

Go back to the top of the home page, and click on **Networking.** From among the new options appearing on the screen, select **Divisions,** which will give you access to a page entitled **Divisions and Interest Groups.** In the drop-down menu [**Go Directly to a Division**], click on **Quality Management Division,** and then respond to the following item:

❸ Who are members of the Quality Management Division of ASQ? What is the mission of the division? How might a quality manager benefit from membership in this division?

Now go to the bottom of the home page. Click on **About ASQ** and then on **What is ASQ?** Respond to the following item:

❹ Identify and briefly describe any five services that ASQ offers to professional members.

After returning to the top of the homepage, click on **Certification.** Next, click on **Certifications,** read the list of types of certifications, and then respond to the following item:

❺ From the listing of various types of certifications, choose any three and identify some of ASQ's requirements for each of the types you have chosen.

To continue your Internet Field Trip, click on www.prenhall.com/griffin

Two of the most common SPC methods are *process variation studies* and *control charts.*

process variation

Variation in products arising from changes in production inputs

Process Variations Variations in a firm's products arise from the changes in inputs used in the production process. As employees, materials, work methods, and equipment change, so do production outputs (that is, the company's products). These variations are called **process variations.** Although some amount of process variation is inevitable, too much can result in poor quality and excessive operating costs.

Consider the box-filling operation for Honey Nuggets, a hypothetical cereal maker. Each automated machine fills two 14-ounce boxes per second. Even under proper conditions, slight variations in weight from box to box are normal. Managers, however, want to know *how much* variation occurs. They also want to determine how much is acceptable.

Information about such variation can be obtained from a *process capability study.* At Honey Nuggets, boxes are taken from filling machines and weighed. The results are plotted, as in Figure 15.3, and compared for weight against upper and lower specification limits, which serve as acceptable quality limits. Boxes with over 14.2 ounces are considered wasteful giveaways of the company's prod-

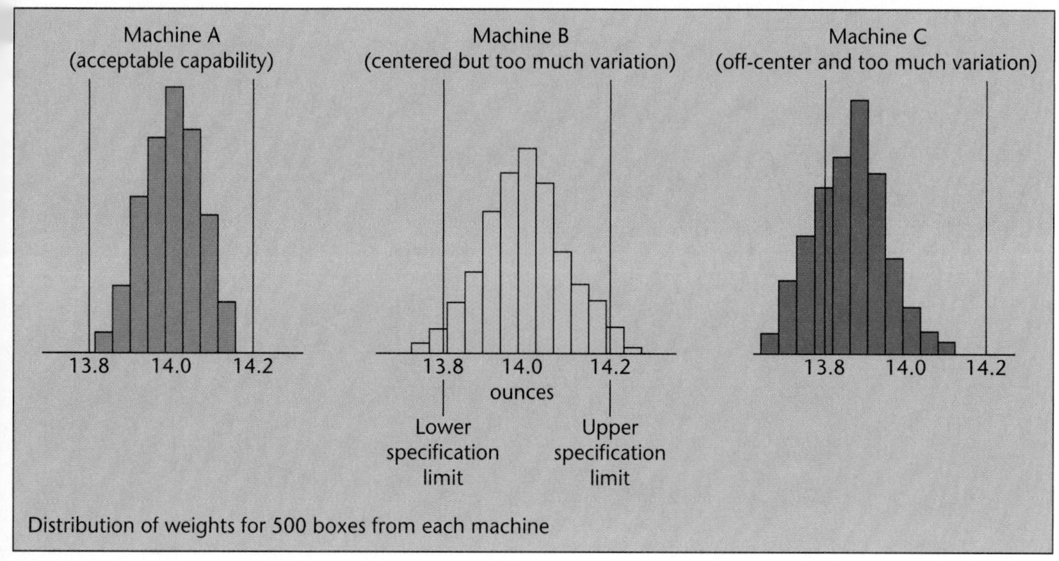

FIGURE 15.3

Process Variation Study at Honey Nuggets Cereal

uct. Boxes with less than 13.8 ounces are also costly, not only because they will anger a lot of buyers but also because they are unlawful.

The chart in Figure 15.3 reveals that Machine A's output is acceptable; none of its boxes violates quality limits. Machine A, then, is *capable* of meeting company standards. Machines B and C, however, have problems. Because neither machine reliably meets Honey Nuggets' standards, they are not capable. Unless Machines B and C are fixed, the company will continue to suffer from substandard production quality.

Control Charts Unfortunately, knowing that a process is capable of meeting quality standards is not enough. Managers must still monitor production processes to keep them from going astray. To detect the onset of departures from normal conditions, employees can check production and plot the results on a **control chart.**[13] Three or four times a day, for example, a Honey Nuggets machine operator might weigh several boxes of cereal to determine the average weight. That average is then plotted on the control chart.

control chart
Process control method that plots test sampling results on a diagram to determine when a process is beginning to depart from normal operating conditions

Figure 15.4 shows the control chart for Machine A at the Honey Nuggets plant. As you can see, the first five points are randomly scattered around the center line, indicating that the machine was operating well from 8 A.M. until noon. However, the points for samples 5 through 9 are all above the center line, indicating that something caused boxes to overfill. The last point falls outside the upper *control limit,* confirming that the process is out of control. At this point, the machine must be shut down so that someone can investigate the cause of the problem: Is it the equipment, people, materials, or work methods? Control is completed when the process is restored to normal.

Quality/Cost Studies SPC helps *maintain* existing capabilities, but in today's competitive environment, firms must consistently *raise* quality capabilities. Unfortunately, any improvement in products or processes means additional costs, whether for new facilities, equipment, training, or other changes. Managers must, therefore, identify the improvements that offer the greatest promise. **Quality/cost studies** not only identify a firm's current costs but also reveal areas with the largest cost-savings potential.[14]

quality/cost study
Method of improving quality by identifying current costs and areas with the greatest cost-saving potential

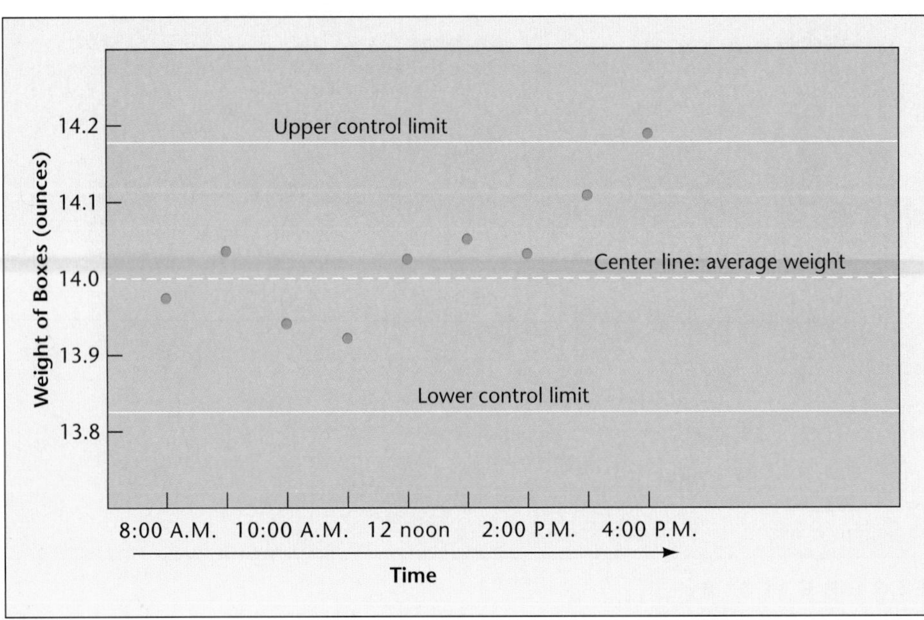

■ **FIGURE 15.4**
Process Control Chart at Honey Nuggets Cereal

Quality costs are associated with finding, repairing, or preventing defective products. All of these costs should be analyzed in a quality/cost study. Honey Nuggets, for example, must determine the costs of **internal failures.** These expenses include the costs of overfilling boxes and the costs of sorting out bad boxes incurred during production and before bad products leave the plant. For many U.S. manufacturers, internal-failures costs account for 50 percent of total costs.

internal failures
Reducible costs incurred during production and before bad products leave a plant

Unfortunately, some bad boxes may escape the factory, reach the customer, and generate complaints. These **external failures** are discovered outside the factory. The costs of correcting them (refunds to customers, transportation costs to return bad boxes to the factory, possible lawsuits, and factory recalls) should also be tabulated in the quality/cost study.

external failures
Reducible costs incurred after defective products have left a plant

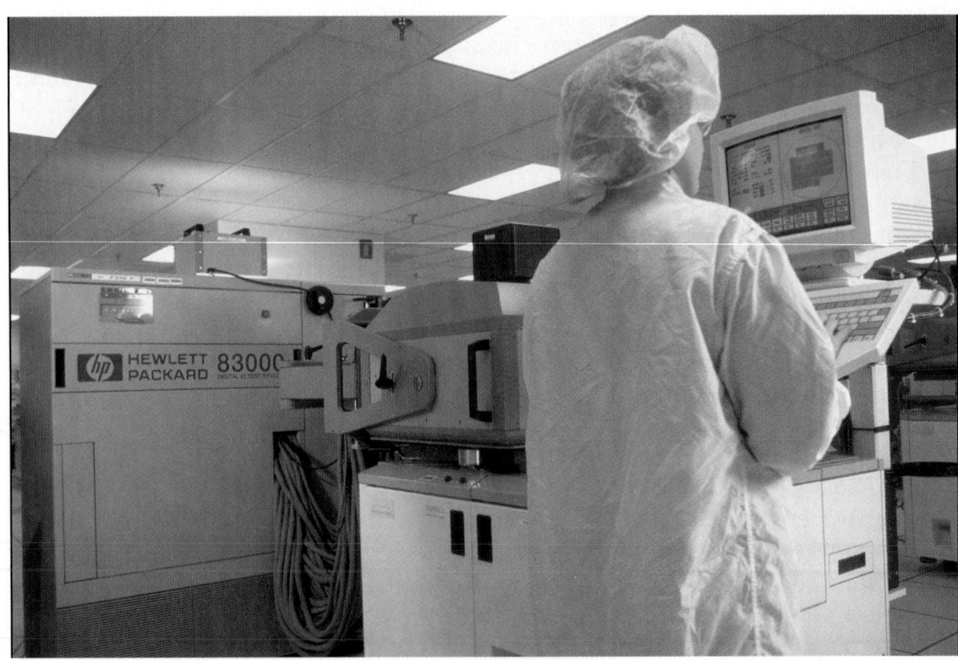

At Hewlett-Packard <www.hp.com>*, testing machines use miniscule probes to ensure that the electronic characteristics of every semiconductor are correct. Such systems are designed to check primarily for so-called "class defects"—problems that can affect a whole parade of products on the assembly line. One bad wafer at the end of the line can represent a waste of $10,000 in costs, and its commercial value is $0.00.*

Quality Improvement Teams Many U.S. businesses have adopted **quality improvement (QI) teams** (patterned after the Japanese concept of *quality circles*): groups of employees from various work areas who meet regularly to define, analyze, and solve common production problems. Their goal is to improve both their own work methods and the products they make.[15]

quality improvement (QI) team
TQM tool in which groups of employees work together to improve quality

Many QI teams organize their own work, select leaders, and address problems in the workplace. Motorola sponsors companywide team competitions to emphasize the value of the team approach, to recognize outstanding team performance, and to reaffirm the team's role in the company's continuous-improvement culture. Teams get higher marks for dealing with projects closely tied to Motorola's key initiatives. Over the years, competing teams have increased cellular phone production by 50 percent and cut electronic-circuit defects by 85 percent (for a one-year savings of $1.8 million).[16]

Benchmarking Another powerful TQM tool is called **benchmarking**: To improve its own products or processes, a company either compares its current performance against its own past performance or implements the best practices of other firms.[17] With *internal benchmarking,* a firm tracks its own performance over time to evaluate progress and set goals for improvement. Let's say that the percentage of customer calls requiring more than two minutes' response time is 15 percent this month. Compared with past months, that figure may be high or low. In short, past performance is the benchmark for evaluating recent results.

benchmarking
Process by which a company implements the best practices from its own past performance and those of other companies to improve its own products

External benchmarking begins with a critical review of competitors (or even companies in other lines of business) to determine which products perform best. These activities or products are called *best practices.* Why is one product better than another? Which features do customers like? Critical comparisons of a company's own products and processes with selected benchmarks often reveal specific areas where improvement will result in greater competitiveness. L.L. Bean <www.llbean.com>, for example, regularly attracts observers who want to see its world-class methods for processing customer orders.

Getting Closer to the Customer Says one advocate of quality improvement, "Customers are an economic asset. They're not on the balance sheet, but they should be." Struggling companies have often lost sight of customers as the driving force behind all business activity. Perhaps such companies waste resources designing products that customers do not want. Sometimes, they ignore customer reactions to existing products or fail to keep up with changing tastes. Meanwhile, successful businesses know what their customers want in the products they consume.

Los Alamos National Bank (LANB) of New Mexico <www.lanb.com> gathers public and industry data into 13 measures of customer needs and satisfaction. But because measurement alone does not improve performance, customer-service employees can match customer needs by modifying bank products—on the spot and without supervisory approval. Employees are trained in listening and learning techniques, enabling them to pick up cues about what customers want, how they think services can be improved, and what the competition is doing. LANB boasts satisfaction ratings of "excellent" from 87 percent of its customers. Not only is its customer satisfaction higher than that of both its competitors and the national average, but there are also bottom-line results: Net income and market share for deposits and loans have grown, and earnings per share have gone up 80 percent in just five years. Common stock price has increased 150 percent in five years.[18]

"Customers are an economic asset. They're not on the balance sheet, but they should be."

~Claess Fornell
QUALITY IMPROVEMENT ADVOCATE

Self-Check Questions 4–6

*You should now be able to answer Self-Check Questions 4–6**

4. MULTIPLE CHOICE Which of the following is **true** regarding *quality management*? [select one]: **(a)** *Total quality management (TQM)* focuses on production to ensure that products are produced according to specifications. **(b)** In *controlling* for quality, managers should establish specific standards and measurements. **(c)** Because it sets the tone for everything that follows, *planning* for quality is the most important stage in quality management. **(d)** Total quality management is sometimes called *quality insurance.*

5. TRUE/FALSE *Statistical process control* cannot be used to analyze and adjust business processes unless data are gathered and analyzed.

6. MULTIPLE CHOICE Which of the following is **not** true regarding the *tools of total quality management*? [select one]: **(a)** *Quality improvement teams* have proved to be effective for improving work methods and products in North American firms. **(b)** *Control charts* rely on sample averages that are plotted on charts to determine if a process is in or out of control. **(c)** *Benchmarking*—both internal and external—is a method for improving products or business procedures by comparing them against a firm's own past performance or the performance of competitors. **(d)** *Quality/cost studies* are conducted to determine how much a company is spending in order to prevent product failures.

*ANSWERS TO SELF-CHECK QUESTIONS 4–6 CAN BE FOUND ON P. AN-10.

Trends in Productivity and Quality Management

Intensified competition has stimulated new ideas regarding quality management. Among them are the international quality standards and the radical redesign of business processes to improve products. A third trend emphasizes gains in productivity and service quality through supply chain management.

ISO 9000:2000 and ISO 14000

Consider the following case in quality diagnosis and correction. The mission of the U.S. Transportation Security Administration (TSA) is to aid in preventing terrorist attacks by protecting U.S transportation systems. Following September 11, 2001, a unit known as AAR-500 <www.its.tc.faa.gov/aar500> was given responsibility for bolstering security at American airports. AAR-500 recognized a major quality problem: the need to train and certify individual employees to perform specific tasks in a revamped screening system. To train 28,000 new airport security personnel, AAR-500 turned to international quality standards that had been applied successfully in private service businesses. To instill public confidence in the new screening system, AAR-500 also adopted the principle of independent third-party certification of the system.[19]

ISO 9000

Program certifying that a factory, laboratory, or office has met the quality management standards of the International Organization for Standardization

Both the training and certification systems were based on the world-class standards of **ISO 9000**—a certification program attesting to the fact that a factory, a laboratory, or an office has met the rigorous quality management requirements set by the International Organization for Standardization <www.iso.ch>. ISO 9000 (pronounced *ICE-o nine thousand*) originated in Europe to standardize materials received from suppliers in such high-technology industries as electron ics, chemicals, and aviation. Today, more than 140 countries have adopted ISO 9000 as a national standard. More than 400,000 certificates have been issued in 160 countries, 40,000 of those in the United States.[20]

The latest version, *ISO 9000:2000,* indicates that it was revised in 2000. Revised standards allow firms to show that they follow documented procedures for testing products, training workers, keeping records, and fixing defects. To become certified, companies must document the procedures followed by workers during every stage of production. The purpose, according to the International Division of the U.S. Chamber of Commerce <www.uschamber.com>, is to ensure that a manufacturer's product is exactly the same today as it was yesterday and as it will be tomorrow. Ideally, standardized processes would ensure that goods are produced at the same level of quality even if all employees were replaced by a new set of workers. Says John Tye, quality manager at AAR-500, "We wanted to have a good quality standard to benchmark our processes and—at the same time—enforce that quality standard on the manufacturers of our equipment."

ISO 14000 The **ISO 14000** program certifies improvements in *environmental* performance. Extending the ISO approach into the arena of environmental protection and hazardous waste management, ISO 14000 requires a firm to develop an *environmental management system (EMS)*: a plan documenting how the company has acted to improve its performance in using resources (such as raw materials) and in managing pollution. A company must not only identify hazardous wastes that it expects to create, but it must also stipulate plans for treatment and disposal. ISO 14000 covers practices in environmental labeling—the use of such terms as *energy efficient* and *recyclable*—and assesses the total environmental impact of the firm's products, not just from manufacturing, but also from use and disposal.

ISO 14000

Certification program attesting to the fact that a factory, laboratory, or office has improved environmental performance

Process Reengineering

Every business consists of *processes*—activities that it performs regularly and routinely in conducting business. Examples abound: receiving and storing materials from suppliers, billing patients for medical treatment, filing insurance claims for auto accidents, inspecting property for termites, opening checking accounts for new customers, filling customer orders from Internet sales. Any business process can add value and customer satisfaction by performing processes well. By the same token, any business can disappoint customers and irritate business partners by managing them poorly.

Business process reengineering focuses on improving both the productivity and quality of business processes—rethinking each step of an organization's operations by starting from scratch. *Reengineering* is the fundamental rethinking and radical redesign of business processes to achieve dramatic improvements in measures of performance, such as cost, quality, service, and speed.[21] The calling-services company GTE <www.gte.com>, for example, found that its over-the-phone service was not user-friendly for customers wanting to correct service or billing problems. To provide fast, accurate one-stop service, GTE reengineered the whole service process by improving equipment, retraining employees, and connecting software to formerly inaccessible corporate databases.

business process reengineering

Redesigning of business processes to improve performance, quality, and productivity

The Reengineering Process Figure 15.5 shows the six steps involved in the reengineering process. It starts with a statement of the benefits envisioned for customers and the company and then flows logically through the next five steps:

1. Identify the business activity that will be changed.
2. Evaluate information and human resources to see if they can meet the requirements for change.

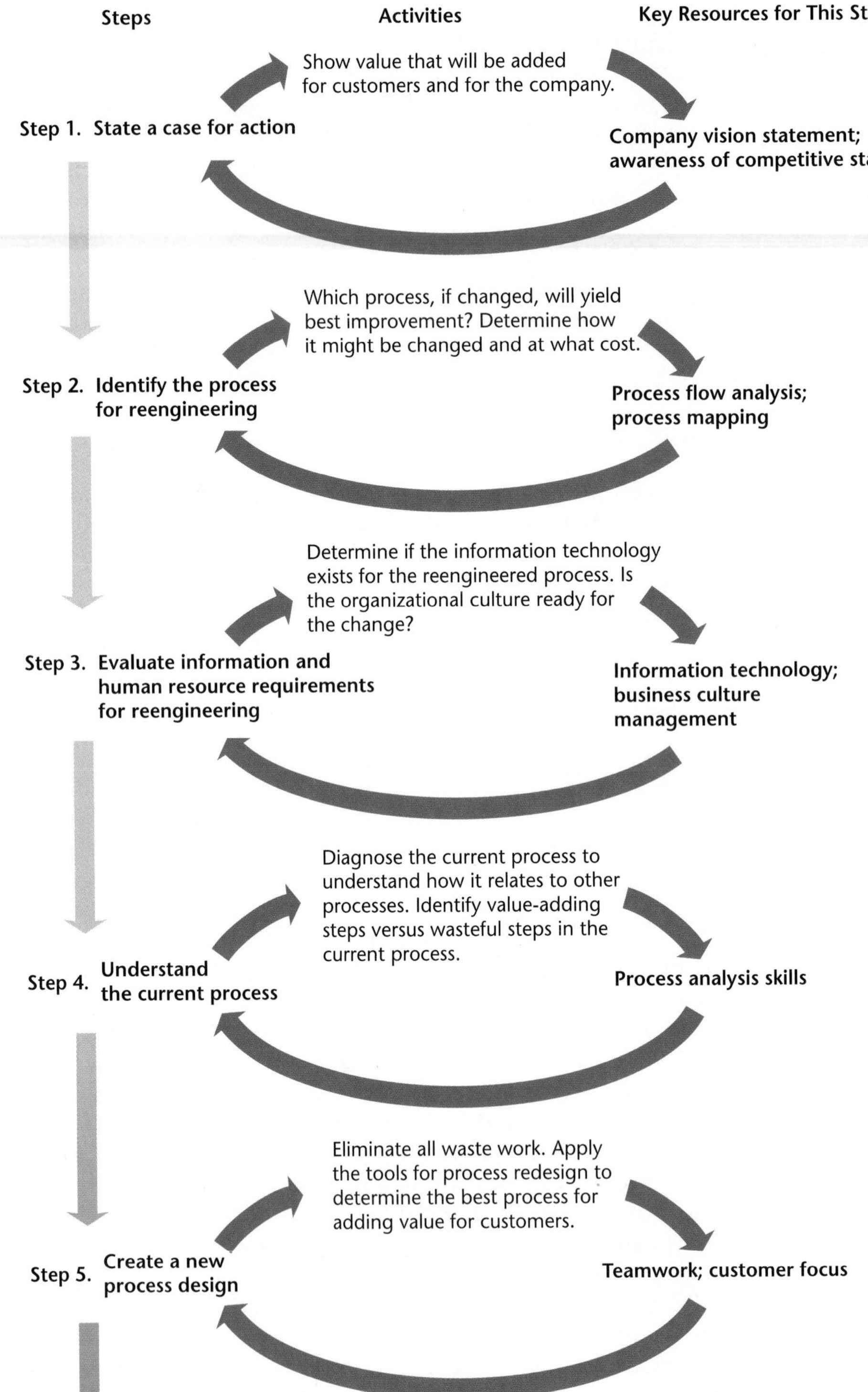
Steps
Activities
Key Resources for This Step
Show value that will be added for customers and for the company.
Step 1. State a case for action
Company vision statement; awareness of competitive status
Which process, if changed, will yield best improvement? Determine how it might be changed and at what cost.
Step 2. Identify the process for reengineering
Process flow analysis; process mapping
Determine if the information technology exists for the reengineered process. Is the organizational culture ready for the change?
Step 3. Evaluate information and human resource requirements for reengineering
Information technology; business culture management
Diagnose the current process to understand how it relates to other processes. Identify value-adding steps versus wasteful steps in the current process.
Step 4. Understand the current process
Process analysis skills
Eliminate all waste work. Apply the tools for process redesign to determine the best process for adding value for customers.
Step 5. Create a new process design
Teamwork; customer focus

FIGURE 15.5

Steps in the Reengineering Process

3. Diagnose the current process to identify its strengths and weaknesses.
4. Create the new process design.
5. Implement the new design.

As you can see, reengineering is a broad undertaking that requires know-how i technical matters, depends on leadership and management skills, and calls upo

Seagate Technology <www.seagate.com>, a California maker of computer hard drives, has reengineered itself. Up until a few years ago, Seagate built almost everything for itself—disks, motors for spinning disks, and tracking mechanisms for reading and writing on disks. Unfortunately, it needed factories from Minnesota to Malaysia and California to Ireland, each with its own suppliers and inventories. Seagate wasn't flexible enough to respond to either change or customers until it teamed up with a consulting firm called DesignShop <www.mgtaylor.com> and figured out how to reorganize itself. Now companywide operations are run by computer-based planning systems, the supplier list has been slashed, and even important components are being outsourced.

knowledge about customer needs and how well they are being met by the company and its competition. The bottom line in every reengineering process is adopting a companywide customer-first philosophy. Redesign is guided by a desire to improve operations so that goods and services are produced at the lowest possible cost and at the highest value for the customer.

Adding Value Through Supply Chains

Managers sometimes forget that a company belongs to a network of firms that must coordinate their activities. The term *supply chain* refers to the group of companies and stream of activities that work together to create a product. A **supply chain** for any product is the flow of information, materials, and services that starts with raw-materials suppliers and continues through other stages in the operations process until the product reaches the end customer.[22]

supply chain
Flow of information, materials, and services that starts with raw-materials suppliers and continues through other stages in the operations process until the product reaches the end customer

Figure 15.6 shows the supply chain activities involved in supplying baked goods to consumers. Each stage adds value for the final customer. Although a typical beginning stage is product design, our bakery example begins with raw materials (grain harvested from the farm). It also includes additional storage and transportation activities, factory operations for baking and wrapping, and distribution to retailers. Each stage depends on the others for success in getting fresh-baked goods to consumers.

The Supply Chain Strategy Traditional strategies assume that companies are managed as individual firms rather than as members of a coordinated supply system. Supply chain strategy is based on the idea that members of the chain, working as a coordinated unit, will gain competitive advantage. Although each company looks out for its own interests, it works closely with suppliers and customers throughout the chain. Everyone focuses on the entire chain of relationships rather than on the next stage in the chain.[23]

A traditionally managed bakery, for example, would focus simply on getting production inputs from flour millers and paper suppliers and supplying baked

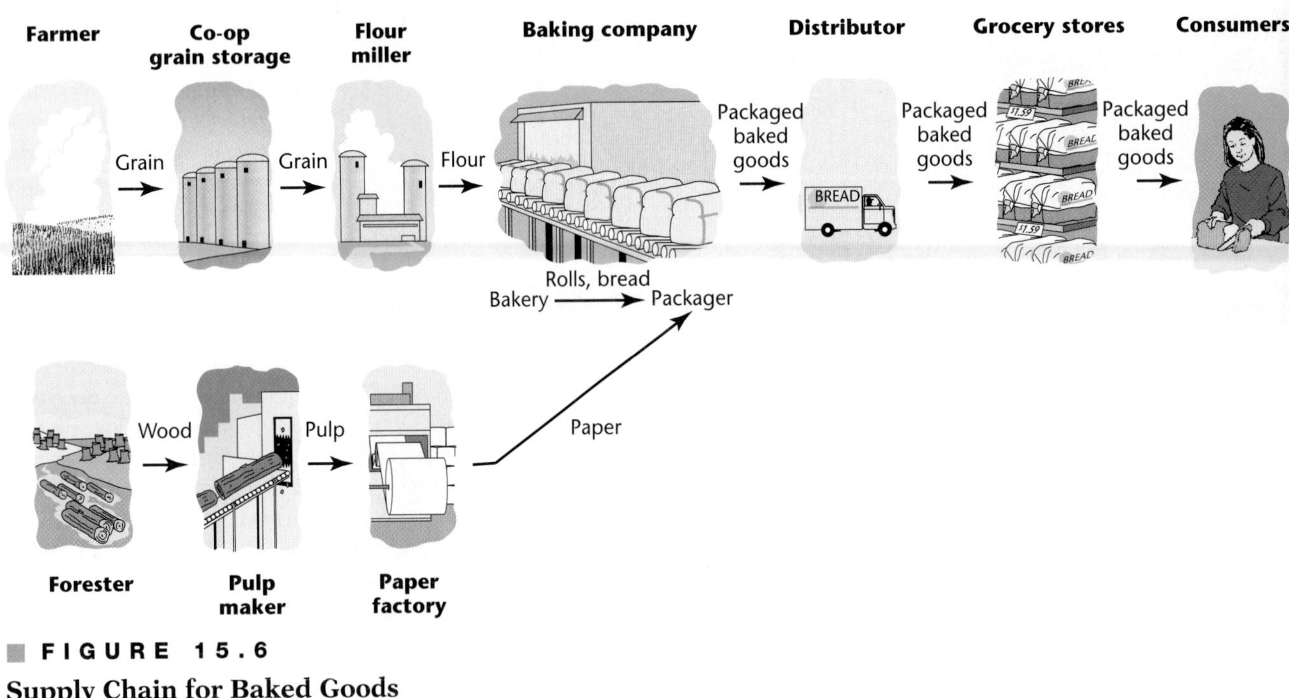

FIGURE 15.6

Supply Chain for Baked Goods

goods to distributors. Unfortunately, this approach limits the chain's performance and doesn't allow for possible improvements when activities are more carefully coordinated. Supply chain management can improve performance and, as a result, provide higher quality at lower prices.

supply chain management (SCM)

Principle of looking at the supply chain as a whole in order to improve the overall flow through the system

Supply Chain Management **Supply chain management (SCM)** looks at the chain as a whole in order to improve the overall flow through a system composed of companies working together. Because customers ultimately get better value, SCM gains competitive advantage for each supply-chain member.[24]

Dell Computer's supply chain, for example, improves performance by allowing people to share information. Dell shares long-term production plans and up-to-the-minute sales data with suppliers via the Internet. The process starts when customer orders are automatically translated into updated production schedules on the factory floor. These schedules are used not only by operations managers at Dell but also by such parts suppliers as Sony, which adjust their own production and shipping activities to better meet Dell's production needs. In turn, parts suppliers' updated schedules are transmitted to their materials suppliers, and so on. As Dell's requirements change, suppliers synchronize their schedules to produce the right materials and parts efficiently.

Because the smooth flow of accurate information along the chain reduces unwanted inventories, avoids delays, and cuts supply times, materials move faster to business customers and individual consumers. For both, the efficiency of SCM means faster deliveries and lower costs than customers could get if each member acted only according to its own operations requirements.

Reengineering Supply Chains for Better Results By lowering costs, speeding service, or coordinating flows of information and materials, process improvements and reengineering often improve supply chains. Consider, for example, the supply chain for transistor radios. For a long time, radio components made in both the United States and Asia were imported by Li&Fung, the largest export trading company in Hong Kong. After supplying these components to a Hong Kong assembly

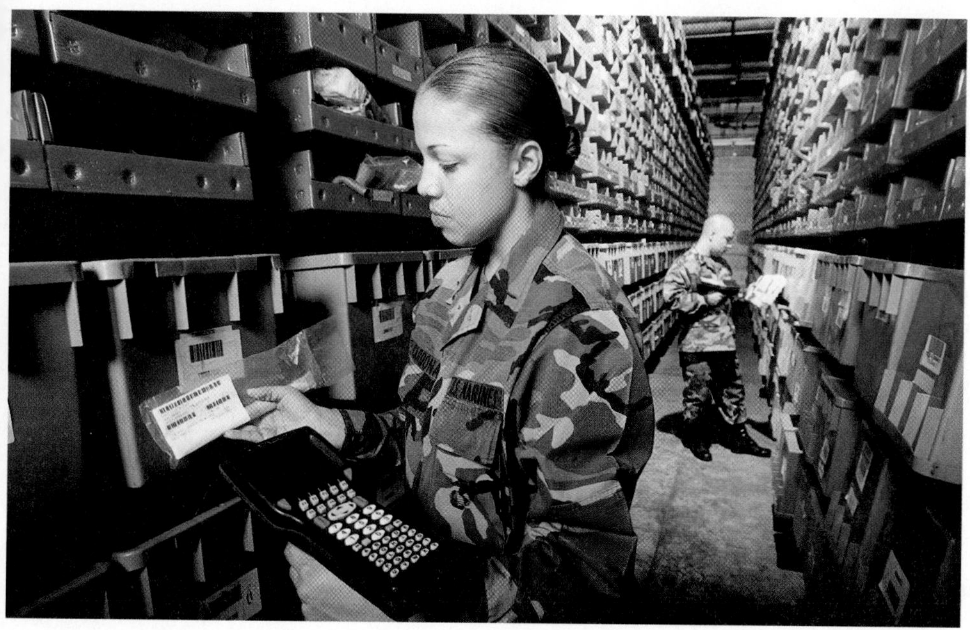

When it took a week to get a spare part from one side of Camp Pendleton to the other and 50 days to fix a jeep, the Marine Corps <www.usmc.mil> *realized that it needed to streamline its supply chain. Studying companies such as Wal-Mart and UPS, the Corps set out to replace warehouses full of overstocked inventory with systems full of information that would enable it to get supplies to troops within 24 hours anywhere in the world. Among other improvements, Marine warehouse workers now use handheld wireless scanners for real-time inventory tracking.*

factory, Li&Fung shipped finished radios to U.S. and European distributors. Gradually, however, rising wage rates in Hong Kong became a threat to Li&Fung. Increases in assembly costs would cut into its profits and market share. The company thus reengineered its supply chain. First, it added a new stage. It created little kits—plastic bags filled with all the components needed to make a radio. Second, one supply-chain link was replaced. The kits were shipped to a new assembler in southern China instead of to the old Hong Kong factory. Finally, another stage was added. After the Chinese supplier had completed the labor-intensive, low-wage assembly process, finished radios were shipped back to Hong Kong for final inspection and testing by Li&Fung before being shipped to customers. The result: lower prices and increased business for companies throughout the chain.

Productivity and Quality as Competitive Tools

A company's ability to compete by improving productivity and quality depends on participation by all parts of the firm. And total firm involvement stems from having companywide strategies that we consider in this section: the company's willingness to invest in innovation, its long-run perspective on its goals, its concern for the quality of work life, and the streamlining of its service operations.

Investing in Innovation and Technology

Many U.S. firms that have invested in innovative technology have enjoyed greater productivity and higher revenues. For example, while Steinway & Sons piano factory <www.steinway.com> maintains the highest quality in its products, it uses advanced technology to help woodworkers do traditional jobs more efficiently. "It still takes us a year to craft one of these things," says Steinway president Bruce Stevens, "but technology is assisting us in making more precise parts that our people can assemble. It's helping us create a better instrument."[25]

Investment in the Internet and information technology is rising, with new applications in every major industry from manufacturing to health care. GE, for

Selling the Idea of Culture Shift

When a firm decides to exchange its traditional operations for high-tech processes, more than just financial and technical considerations come into play. Consider, for example, a company whose successful sales procedures were established long before modern electronic-sales processes were available. What problems does it face in relocating its established (and highly personalized) sales process into the realm of Internet sales?

That's the issue at Mercury Marine <www.mercurymarine.com>, the market leader in recreational boat engines. Offering choices of engine types, horsepower ratings, and other options, Mercury sells about 400 different outboard engines and enjoys a 40-percent share of the U.S. market. Sales of inboard engines and stern drives are even better, with a market share of over 70 percent. Needless to say, Mercury's $1.4 billion annual sales are vital to its parent company, Brunswick Corp. <www.brunswickcorp.com>.

Mercury has two kinds of customers:

1. It sells outboard motors mainly to distributors and boat dealers, who resell them.
2. It sells inboard engines and stern drives to boat builders.

In addition to its current person-to-person selling process, Mercury wants to sell motors to outboard dealers and boat builders over the Internet. In other words, Mercury wants to use technology to make it easier for its customers to do business. Internet access can not only increase sales productivity but also promote better service.

So what's the problem? Resistance from the sales department, which felt threatened by changes. With person-to-person sales, salespeople can increase revenues by talking up the advantages of upgrading to more expensive motors (*upselling*). They can also talk customers into buying complementary products (*cross-selling*), such as propellers, inflatable boats, and other accessories. Salespeople, of course, are reluctant to give up these sales tools. Admits CIO Geof Storm, "There are a lot of culture changes involved when tightening the supply chain." Although the sales department still prefers the more personal touch, some resistance is being overcome—Mercury will proceed to sell inboard engines to boat builders over the Net. But until the internal climate changes further, any further use of the Internet as a selling tool is likely to remain on hold.

example, expects turbine-engine productivity to rise because customers can now use the Internet to compare the performance of various models before they buy. The Weyerhauser door factory in Marshfield, Wisconsin, uses the Internet to cut out its least valuable customers, thus cutting its customer list in half and allowing the firm to double order volumes for remaining customers.[26]

Adopting a Long-Run Perspective

continuous improvement
An ongoing commitment to improving products and processes in the pursuit of ever-increasing customer satisfaction

Many quality-oriented firms are committed to long-term efforts at **continuous improvement**: the ongoing commitment to improving products and processes, step by step, in pursuit of ever-increasing customer satisfaction.[27] Motorola is a good example. As we saw in our opening story, its Six Sigma program originally set a target of only 3.4 defects per million parts. By 1996, Motorola was thinking in terms of errors per *billion.* As of 2001, the company's production-monitoring software—Manufacturing Intellitrak—had helped to reduce errors in some applications to two defects per billion parts.[28]

Emphasizing Quality of Work Life

Business products represent such a large part of total national output that the well-being and participation of workers is crucial to improving national productivity. How can firms make jobs more challenging and interesting? As we saw in

Chapter 9, many companies enhance jobs with recreational facilities, counseling services, and other programs. In addition, more and more firms now sponsor programs to empower and train employees.

Employee Empowerment Many firms now maintain worker-oriented environments that foster loyalty, teamwork, and commitment. Trident Precision Manufacturing <www.tridentprecision.com>, for example, now accepts over 95 percent of employee recommendations for process improvements. Employee turnover has fallen from 41 percent to less than 5 percent, and sales per employee has more than doubled.

employee empowerment

Concept that all employees are valuable contributors to a firm's business and should be entrusted with decisions regarding their work

Firms like Trident have discovered the value of **employee empowerment:** the principle that all employees are valuable contributors to a business and should be entrusted with certain decisions regarding their work.[29] The Hampton Inns motel chain <www.hampton-inn.com> started a program of refunds to customers who were dissatisfied with their stays. The refund policy created far more additional business than it cost, but a surprise bonus was the increased morale when employees—everyone from front-desk personnel to maids—were empowered to grant refunds. With greater participation and job satisfaction, employee turnover fell by more than one-half. Confidence in employee involvement breaks sharply with traditional concepts of managers as an organization's only decision makers and problem solvers.

Employee Training Employee involvement is effective when it is implemented with preparation and intelligence. *Training* is a key method of preparing employees for productivity-improvement programs. In fact, a recent American Management Association survey found a direct relationship between training and greater productivity profitability: Firms that increased training activities were 66 percent more likely to report improved productivity and three times more likely to report increased profits. Moreover, waste diminishes and quality increases. Finally, team training not only teaches employees to work in groups, but it also acquaints them more fully with the company's markets and operations.[30]

Improving the Service Sector

Employee attitude is even more crucial to service production than to goods production. In services, after all, employees often *are* the service. Although the U.S. service sector has grown rapidly, growth has often been accompanied by high levels of inefficiency. Many newly created service jobs have not been streamlined, and although some companies, such as UPS and Fed Ex, operate effectively, many are so inefficient that they drag down overall U.S. productivity. Fortunately, increased competition is forcing service providers to operate more productively and to stress service quality.[31]

Many companies have discovered five criteria that customers use to judge service quality:[32]

- ***Reliability.*** Perform the service as promised, both accurately and on time.
- ***Responsiveness.*** Be willing to help customers promptly.
- ***Assurance.*** Maintain knowledgeable and courteous employees who will earn the confidence of customers.
- ***Empathy.*** Provide caring, individualized attention.
- ***Tangibles.*** Maintain a pleasing appearance among personnel and in materials and facilities.

In one recent study, 1,600 customers cited reliability most often as the essence of good service. For customers, reliability means "sameness"—consistency from day to day and location to location—so that service quality is predictable.

Self-Check Questions 7–9

*You should now be able to answer Self-Check Questions 7–9**

7. TRUE/FALSE *ISO 9000* certification signifies to customers that a firm's products meet the quality standards for its industry.

8. MULTIPLE CHOICE Which of the following is **not** true regarding *supply chains* and *supply chain management?* [select one]: **(a)** Supply chains involve the flow of information as well as materials and services. **(b)** A company using supply chain strategy always focuses on the next stage (either incoming or outgoing) in the chain. **(c)** Efficiency in supply chains means faster on-time deliveries and lower costs. **(d)** Reengineering is used to improve supply chains by cutting costs and by better coordinating flows of materials and information.

9. TRUE/FALSE *Employee empowerment* is based on the idea that all employees are valuable contributors and should be entrusted with work-related decisions.

*Answers to Self Check Questions 7–9 can be found on p. AN-10.

Consistency is especially important with multiple-branch companies, such as car-rental agencies and fast-food restaurants. Customers want to be sure of the same treatment and service no matter where they are. Ruth's Chris Steak House uses simple 4-by-8–inch reminder cards that slide easily into employees' pockets. Each card lists ways to perform tasks and quality reminders for each job. The same cards are used at every location, and after employees have studied the appropriate cards, everyone is tested and certified.[33]

Continued from page 425

The Penalty for 99.99 Percent Perfection

First Data Resources of Omaha, Nebraska <www.firstdatacorp.com>, is a recent convert to Six Sigma. The firm ships six million credit cards a month from its warehouse for such customers as MasterCard and Visa. Workers personalize each card, attach a label with an activation phone number, and prepare envelopes and paper inserts for mailing. Finally, they assure that each card is mailed to the right person. One misplaced card can cost hundreds of thousands of dollars. Warehouse accuracy, then, is crucial.

Back in 1999, First Data had no system for tracking quality, and warehousing activities were in disarray. The possibility of expensive mistakes was high. "With the volumes we handle and the amount of material we put out, we could say we are at 99.99 percent," says materials manager Cliff Radcliff, "but the banks are saying that's not good enough."

Aiming for zero tolerance for errors, the warehouse inventory team implemented Six Sigma and improved quality by 40 percent in 2000, followed by another 30 to 40 percent in 2001. Warehouse accuracy is now 99.9969 percent, and although the figure is not quite Six Sigma quality, Radcliff was *Warehousing Management*'s 2001 Peak Performer. "By going to Six Sigma," explains Radcliff, "we can't rest on our laurels at 99.99, and it makes it easier to focus in on where we need to go to get to near perfection."

How can Radcliff earn a Six-Sigma Black Belt? As in the disciplined self-defense system, candidates begin as novices and work their way through the ranks. They earn promotions by demonstrating skills, passing proficiency tests, and getting on-the-job results. Some companies have their own training and testing programs, but industrywide acceptance usually goes to certification programs sponsored by professional associations, most notably the American Society for Quality (ASQ) <www.asq.org>. The ASQ e-Learning Center offers a series of Web-based Six Sigma courses, beginning with "Introduction to Six Sigma" (an overview of method, concepts, and language) and culminating in "Black Belt Certification Review" (a preparatory course for the certification exam). Interactive courses emphasize practice exercises and online assessments.

Many firms insist that Six Sigma deliver certain financial benefits. In 2002, for example, the financial-services firm Conseco Services LLC. <www.conseco.com> expects to see $100 million in first-year savings by improving customer-service and internal operations. Spearheaded by a team of 170 Six Sigma professionals, Conseco's program started with 230 projects designed to reduce customer dissatisfaction and ineffective processes. Project teams are led by 145 Black Belts in sales, finance, information technology, and customer service. Twenty-three Master Black Belts spend four weeks training other Black Belts and then oversee projects and coach the project leaders. After two weeks of training, 18 Green Belts serve as project leaders.

Of course, having a title means being responsible for results: Each Black Belt has an annual cost-saving goal of $500,000. Each Master Black Belt is expected to save $5 million a year, and every Black Belt is required to prove that project savings are real by submitting results to the Finance Department. "We don't want just the Black Belts saying a project will save a million dollars," says Ruth Fattori, executive VP for process and productivity. "We want Finance saying it. . . . We don't want Black Belts giving us the theoretical savings; we want Finance to tell us what in fact we have saved."

Questions for Discussion

1. Of what significance is leadership for a Six Sigma program? Give some examples of ways that leadership might affect such a program.
2. List some of the main elements in training for a Six Sigma Black Belt. What skills does such training teach?
3. Consider the kinds of improvements made by companies cited in this case. Did improvements relate merely to quality, merely to productivity, or to both? Explain.
4. Do you believe that Six Sigma programs have a better chance for success in manufacturing or service firms? Explain.
5. Suppose you want to start a Six Sigma program for your company. Identify the managerial skills that will be most important for a successful program. Explain why you chose those particular skills over certain others.

". . . We don't want Black Belts giving us the theoretical savings; we want Finance to tell us what in fact we have saved."

~Ruth Fattori, Executive VP FOR PROCESS AND PRODUCTIVITY AT CONSECO

Summary of Learning Objectives

1. *Describe the connection between* productivity *and* quality.

Productivity is a measure of economic performance: It compares how much we produce with the resources we use to produce it. Thus, the more we can produce with fewer resources, the more productivity grows and the more everyone benefits. Productivity also refers to the *quantity* and *quality* of what we produce. When resources are used more efficiently, the quantity of output is certainly greater. But unless the resulting products are of satisfactory quality, consumers will reject them. Producing **quality**, then, means creating fitness for use—offering features that consumers want.

2. *Explain the decline and recovery in U.S. productivity that has occurred in the last 30 or 35 years.*

When one country is more productive than another, it will accumulate more wealth. Similarly, when a nation's productivity fails to increase as rapidly as that of competitor nations, its standard of living will fall. By the 1960s, U.S. products dominated world markets because U.S. businesses were so successful in producing goods and distributing them in both domestic and foreign markets. In the 1970s, however, U.S. productivity began a downslide that continued into the 1980s. Then, a turnaround in productivity occurred in the years leading up to 1994, when American businesses regained significant market shares in several large industries. By 2001, U.S. companies remained the world's leading exporters in several major industries. Today, many Asian and European firms are again forced to catch up with U.S. competitors.

This change in fortunes occurred for several reasons. First, U.S. business concentrated on understanding the true meaning of *productivity* and devised means of measuring it. Soon learning that *quality* must be defined in terms of value to the customer, they redesigned organizations and marketing efforts to cultivate a more customer-oriented focus. As quality-improvement practices were implemented, more and more firms began to realize payoffs. These successes highlighted the interdependence of four key ingredients: customers, quality, productivity, and profits.

Most countries use **labor productivity** to measure national productivity by comparing a country's total annual output of goods and services to the resources used to produce that output. The focus on labor, rather than other resources, is preferred because most countries keep accurate records on employment and hours worked. By this and other measures, the U.S. **level of productivity** is higher than that of any other country. Output per hour worked also rose steadily in the United States throughout most of the 1980s and 1990s. Many observers consider the trends in productivity to be an indicator of a nation's economic health. In the 1980s, for example, there was a slowdown in the *growth rate of U.S. productivity*—the annual increase in a nation's output over the previous year. Then, recovery began, continued through the 1990s, and is projected to increase in the decade ahead.

Finally, throughout most of the 1970s, productivity in the manufacturing sector trailed slightly behind that of the service sector. But U.S. service productivity averaged zero improvement in the years between 1978 and 1990. By 1993, service productivity was once again growing, but manufacturing productivity growth was more than double that of services, a margin sustained through 2001. Thus, manufacturing is primarily responsible for the recent increases in overall U.S. productivity.

3. *Identify the activities involved in* total quality management, *and describe six tools that companies can use to achieve it.*

Total quality management (TQM) (sometimes called **quality assurance**) includes all of the activities necessary for getting high-quality goods and services into the marketplace. It must consider all parts of the business, including customers, suppliers, and employees. The strategic approach to TQM begins with customer focus. It includes methods for determining what customers want and then directing all the company's resources toward satisfying those wants and needs. Total participation is mandatory, and TQM is more than part-time. It demands continuous improvement of products, services, and improvement in all of the company's internal processes, such as accounting, delivery, billing, and information flows.

Finally, TQM involves four basic managerial activities: (1) *Planning for quality*: Planning for quality begins *before* products are designed or redesigned. In the predesign stage, managers must set goals for both **performance quality** (which refers to the *performance features* of a product) and **quality reliability** (the *consistency* of product quality from unit to unit). (2) *Organizing for quality*: Because producing high-quality products requires an effort from all parts of the organization, having a separate "quality control" department is no longer enough. Although everyone in a company contributes to product quality, responsibility for specific aspects of TQM is often assigned to specific departments and jobs.

(3) *Directing for quality*: Managers must motivate employees to achieve quality goals. They must help employees see how they affect quality and how quality affects both their jobs and the company. Leaders must also find ways to foster a quality orientation by training employees, encouraging involvement, and tying compensation to work quality. They want employees to accept **quality ownership**: the idea that quality belongs to each person who creates it while performing a job. (4) *Controlling for quality*: First, managers must establish specific quality standards and measurements. Then, by monitoring its products and services, they can detect mistakes and make corrections.

Many companies rely on proven tools to manage quality. Often, ideas for improving both the product and the production process come from **competitive product analysis**: the process of analyzing a competitor's products to identify desirable improvements in a firm's own products. In addition, there are six commonly used tools for total quality management: (1) **Value-added analysis** is the evaluation of all work activities, material flows, and paperwork to determine the value that they add for customers. (2) Although every business experiences unit-to-unit variations in products, they can better control product quality by understanding sources of variation. **Statistical process control** (**SPC**) refers to methods by which employees can gather data and analyze variations in production activities to determine when adjustments are needed. There are two common SPC methods: (i) **Process variations** arise from the inputs used in the production process. Although some amount of process variation is inevitable, too much can result in poor quality and excessive operating costs. Information about variation in a process can be obtained from a *process capability study*. Results can be plotted and compared to acceptable quality limits. (ii) To detect incipient departures from the normal conditions of a production process, employees can check production periodically and plot the results on **control charts**.

(3) Any improvement means additional costs. **Quality/cost studies** are useful because they not only identify a firm's

current costs but also reveal areas with the largest cost-savings potential. Quality costs are associated with finding, repairing, or preventing defective goods and services. They may result either from **internal failures** (which occur during production and before bad products leave a plant) or from **external failures** (which are discovered after defective products have left the factory). The costs of correcting failures are also tabulated in the quality/cost study.

(4) Many U.S. businesses have adopted **quality improvement (QI) teams**: groups of employees from various work areas who meet regularly to define, analyze, and solve common production problems. Their goal is to improve both their own work methods and the products they make.

(5) With **benchmarking**, a company improves its own products or business procedures by comparing them to either its own past performance or the best practices of others. With *internal benchmarking,* a firm tracks its own performance over time to evaluate its progress and to set goals for further improvement. *External benchmarking* begins with a review of competitors (or even companies in other lines of business) to determine which goods or services perform the best; these activities and products are called *best practices.* (6) *Getting closer to the customer:* Struggling companies often lose sight of customers as the driving force for all business activity; the most successful businesses keep close to their customers and know what they want in the products they consume.

4. *Identify three trends in productivity and quality management, including* supply chain management.

Three trends in productivity and quality management have emerged as firms learn to deal with intensified competition. (1) **ISO 9000** is a certification program attesting to the fact that a factory, a laboratory, or an office has met the rigorous quality-management requirements set by the International Organization for Standardization. *ISO 9000:2000* reflects revisions made in 2000. It allows firms to show that they follow documented procedures for testing products, training workers, keeping records, and fixing product defects. To become certified, companies must document the procedures that workers follow during every stage of production. **ISO 14000** certifies improvements in *environmental* performance. Extending ISO into the arena of environmental protection and hazardous waste management, ISO 14000 requires a firm to develop an *environmental management system (EMS)*: a plan documenting how the company has acted to improve performance in using resources and managing pollution. ISO 14000 standards also cover areas such as environmental labeling—the use of such terms as *energy efficient* and *recyclable*—and they assess the total environmental impact of the firm's products.

(2) Every business consists of *processes*—activities that it performs regularly and routinely in conducting business. **Business process reengineering** focuses on improving both the productivity and quality of business processes—rethinking each step of an organization's operations by starting from scratch. *Reengineering* is the fundamental rethinking and redesign of processes to achieve dramatic improvements in measures of performance. Managers first justify the proposed reengineering based on benefits envisioned for customers and the company. Then there are five steps in the reengineering process itself: (i) Identify the business activity that will be changed. (ii) Evaluate information and human resources to see if they meet the requirements for change. (iii) Diagnose the current process to identify strengths and weaknesses. (iv) Create the new process design. (v) Implement the new design.

(3) The **supply chain** refers to the group of companies and stream of activities that operate together to create a product. Traditional strategies assume that companies are managed as individual firms rather than as members of a coordinated supply chain. **Supply chain management (SCM)** looks at the chain as a whole in order to improve the overall flow through a system composed of companies working together. Because customers ultimately get better value, SCM gives chain members a competitive advantage.

5. *Discuss four strategies that companies use to improve productivity and quality.*

A company's ability to compete by improving productivity and quality depends on participation by all parts of the firm. Total firm involvement stems from adopting companywide strategies, which include the following: (1) *Investing in innovation and technology*: Many U.S. firms that have continued to invest in innovative technology have enjoyed rising productivity and rising incomes. Increasingly, investments in the Internet and information technology are rising, with new applications in every major industry. (2) *Adopting a long-run perspective*: Many quality-oriented firms are committed to long-term efforts at **continuous improvement**: the ongoing commitment to improving products and processes, step by step, in pursuit of ever-increasing customer satisfaction.

(3) *Emphasizing quality of work life*: Business products and services represent such a large part of total national output that the well-being and participation of workers is crucial to improving national productivity. Thus, many companies enhance jobs with recreational facilities, counseling services, and other programs. In addition, more and more firms are committed to worker-oriented environments that foster loyalty, teamwork, and commitment. One approach to achieving these goals is the concept of *employee empowerment*: the principle that all employees are valuable contributors to a business and should be entrusted with certain work-related decisions. Companies have also learned that *training* is a key method of preparing employees for productivity-improvement programs.

(4) *Improving the service sector*: As important as employee attitude is to goods production, it is even more crucial to service production, where employees often *are* the service. In trying to offer more satisfactory services, many companies have discovered five criteria that customers use to judge service quality: (i) *Reliability*: Perform the service as promised, both accurately and on time. (ii) *Responsiveness*: Be willing to help customers promptly. (iii) *Assurance*: Train knowledgeable and courteous employees who will earn the confidence of customers. (iv) *Empathy*: Provide caring, individualized attention. (v) *Tangibles*: Maintain a pleasing appearance among personnel and in materials and facilities.

KEY TERMS

productivity (p. 426)
quality (p. 426)
labor productivity (p. 426)
level of productivity (p. 428)
total quality management (TQM) (or quality assurance) (p. 430)
performance quality (p. 431)
quality reliability (p. 432)
quality ownership (p. 432)
competitive product analysis (p. 432)
value-added analysis (p. 433)
statistical process control (SPC) (p. 433)
process variation (p. 434)
control chart (p. 435)
quality/cost study (p. 435)
internal failures (p. 436)
external failures (p. 436)
quality improvement (QI) team (p. 437)
benchmarking (p. 437)
ISO 9000 (p. 438)
ISO 14000 (p. 439)
business process reengineering (p. 439)
supply chain (p. 440)
supply chain management (SCM) (p. 442)
continuous improvement (p. 444)
employee empowerment (p. 445)

QUESTIONS AND EXERCISES

Questions for Review

1. What is the relationship between productivity and quality?
2. Why do labor unions care about the productivity of an industry?
3. What part do inputs and outputs play in the basic equation for measuring labor productivity?
4. What activities are involved in total quality management?
5. What are the essential steps in process engineering?

Questions for Analysis

6. How would you suggest that benchmarking be used to increase productivity in the service sector?
7. Why is employee empowerment essential to successful quality improvement teams?
8. Why is high productivity in the service sector so difficult to achieve?

Application Exercises

9. Using a local company as an example, show how you would conduct a quality/cost study. Identify the cost categories and give some examples of the costs in each category. Which categories do you expect to have the highest and lowest costs? Why?
10. Select a company of interest to you and consider the suggestions for competing that are detailed in this chapter. Which of these suggestions apply to this company? What additional suggestions would you make to help this company improve its overall quality and productivity?

Building Your Business Skills

MAKING YOUR BENCHMARK IN THE BUSINESS WORLD

This exercise enhances the following SCANS workplace competencies: demonstrating basic skills, demonstrating thinking skills, exhibiting interpersonal skills, and working with information.

Goal

To encourage students to understand ways in which benchmarking can improve quality and productivity

Situation

As the director of maintenance for a regional airline, you are disturbed to learn that the cost of maintaining your 100-plane fleet is skyrocketing. A major factor is repair time: When maintenance or repairs are required, work often proceeds slowly. As a result, additional aircraft must be pressed into service to meet the schedule. To address the problem, you decide to use a powerful total quality management tool called benchmarking: You will approach your problem by studying ways in which other companies have successfully managed similar problems. Your goal is to apply the best practices to your own maintenance and repair operation.

Method

Step 1

Working with three or four other students, choose your benchmarking target from among the following choices:

- The maintenance and repair operations of a competing airline
- The pit crew operations of an Indianapolis 500 race car team
- The maintenance and repair operations of a nationwide trucking company

Write a memo explaining the reasons for your choice.

Step 2

Write a list of benchmarking questions that will help you learn the best practices of your targeted company. Your goal is to ask questions that will help you improve your own operation. These questions will be asked during on-site visits.

Step 3

As part of a benchmarking project, you will be dealing with your counterparts in other companies. You have a responsibility to prepare for these encounters, and you must remember that what you learn during the exchange process is privileged information. Given these requirements, describe the steps that you would take before your first on-site visit, and outline your benchmarking code of ethics.

Follow-Up Questions

1. Why is benchmarking an important method for improving quality?
2. Why did you make your benchmarking choice? Explain why the company you selected holds more promise than other companies in helping you solve your internal maintenance problems.
3. What kind of information would help you improve the efficiency of your operations? Are you interested in management information, technical information, or both?
4. In an age of heightened competition, why do you think companies are willing to benchmark with each other?

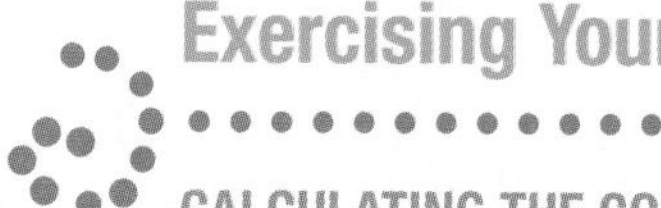

Exercising Your Ethics

CALCULATING THE COST OF CONSCIENCE

The Situation

Product quality and cost affect every firm's reputation and profitability as well as the satisfaction of customers. This exercise will expose you to some ethical considerations that pertain to certain cost and service decisions that must be made by operations managers.

The Dilemma

As director of quality for a major appliance manufacturer, Ruth was reporting to the executive committee on the results of a recent program for correcting problems with a newly redesigned rotary compressor that the company had recently begun putting in its refrigerators. After receiving several customer complaints, the quality lab and the engineering department had determined that some of the new compressor units ran more loudly than expected. Some remedial action was needed. One option was simply waiting until customers complained and responding to each complaint if and when it occurred. Ruth, however, had decided that this approach was inconsistent with the company's policy of offering the highest quality in the industry. Deciding that the firm's reputation called for a proactive, "pro-quality" approach, Ruth had initiated a program for contacting all customers who had purchased refrigerators containing the new compressor.

Unfortunately, her "quality-and-customers-first" policy was expensive. Local service representatives had to phone every customer in each area of the country, make appointments for home visits, and replace original compressors with a newer model. But because replacement time was only one-half hour, customers were hardly inconvenienced, and food stayed refrigerated without interruption. Customer response to the replacement program was overwhelmingly favorable.

Near the end of Ruth's report, an executive vice president was overheard to comment, "Ruth's program has cost this company $400 million in service expenses." Two weeks later, Ruth was fired.

Questions for Discussion

1. What are the underlying ethical issues in this situation?
2. What are the respective roles of profits, obligations to customers, and employee considerations for the firm in this situation?
3. Suppose you were an employee who realized that your company was selling defective appliances. Suppose that the cost of correction might put the firm out of business. What would you do?

Crafting Your Business Plan

ENSURING STRUCTURAL INTEGRITY

The Purpose of the Assignment

1. To acquaint students, within the framework of *Business PlanPro* (*BPP*) software package, with some of the quality considerations that a sample firm addresses in developing its business plan.
2. To demonstrate how customers' expectations of service quality, the role of quality in a firm's business strategy, the dimensions of service quality, and methods for ensuring quality can be integrated as components of the *BPP* planning environment.

Assignment

After reading Chapter 15 in the textbook, open the BPP *software and look around for information about plans for service quality as they apply to a sample firm called* StructureAll Ltd.*, a consulting firm that specializes in structural engineering services. To find* StructureAll*, do the following:*

Open the *Business PlanPro*. If it asks if you want to "create a new business plan" or to "open an existing plan," select "create a new business plan" (even though you are not going to create a plan at this time). You will then be taken to the *Business PlanPro EasyPlan Wizard*. On the screen, click on the option entitled **Research It**. You will then be presented with a new list of options, including **Sample Plan Browser**. After clicking on the **Sample Plan Browser**, go down the alphabetical list of sample plans, and double-click on **Engineering—Consulting**, which is the location for *StructureAll Ltd.* The screen at which you are now looking is the introduction page to the *StructureAll* business plan. Next, scroll down this page until you reach the **Table of Contents** for the *StructureAll* business plan.

Now respond to the following items:

1. Who are StructureAll's customers? What do you suppose they expect from the quality of services received from StructureAll? What aspects of quality are important to them? [Sites to see in *BPP* for this item: On the Table of Contents page, click on **1.0 Executive Summary**. Then click on each of the following in turn: **1.2 Mission**, **1.3 Keys to Success**, **3.1 Service Description**, **3.2 Competitive Comparison**, **4.0 Market Analysis Summary**, and **4.1 Market Segmentation**.]
2. What role does quality play in StructureAll's business strategy? [Sites to see in *BPP*: On the Table of Contents page, click on each of the following in turn: **1.2 Mission**, **1.3 Keys to Success**, and **3.2 Competitive Comparison**.]
3. What are some specific dimensions of quality in the services offered by StructureAll? [Sites to see in *BPP*: From the Table of Contents page, click on **1.0 Executive Summary**. Then click on each of the following in turn: **3.1 Service Description** and **3.2 Competitive Comparison**.]
4. What are some of the procedures, methods, and policies by which StructureAll ensures quality? [Sites to see in *BPP*: On the Table of Contents page, click on **3.1 Service Description**. After returning to the Table of Contents page, click on each of the following in turn: **3.4 Fulfillment**, **3.5 Technology**, **3.6 Future Services** and **5.1 Competitive Edge**.]

Video Exercise

GLOWING WITH QUALITY: LIQUID LAB

Learning Objectives

The purpose of this video is to help you

1. Consider the quality decisions made by a U.S. manufacturer.
2. Understand how quality and productivity affect a company's global competitiveness.
3. Discuss the ways in which a company can use quality assurance to produce high-quality goods that satisfy customers.

Synopsis

The CEO of Liquid Lab invented and patented the process for making the glowing multi-chambered neon necklaces that you can buy at sporting events, amusement parks, and concerts. As the patents expired, however, Liquid Lab faced an onslaught of competition from global rivals selling cheaper versions, especially manufacturers in China, where lower labor costs make production less expensive. Through years of experience, Liquid Lab has found ways to boost productivity while maintaining high quality. In order to compete on the basis of quality, the company rigorously tests materials and accommodates the few customers who want to return necklaces.

Discussion Questions

1. *For analysis:* Why must Liquid Lab pay close attention to performance quality as well as to quality reliability?

2. *For analysis:* If Liquid Lab never sells directly to consumers, how can it determine what they want in terms of product quality?
3. *For application:* How might Liquid Lab use external benchmarking to identify ideas for reducing returns due to breakage in transit?
4. *For application:* Which total quality management tools might Liquid Lab use to find opportunities for cost-cutting while maintaining high quality?
5. *For debate:* Given the increase in competition, should Liquid Lab seek ISO 9000 certification to showcase its emphasis on quality? Support your position.

Online Exploration

Use your favorite search engine (such as Ixquick.com <www.ixquick.com>) to search for sites promoting "Made in America" products. What kinds of quality claims do these sites make about their products? How do they back up those claims? Do any sites explain their quality-assurance techniques or compare their American-made products to those of foreign competitors? What kind of information would persuade you, as a consumer, to buy from a U.S.-based company if competing foreign-made products cost much less?

CHAPTER

Managing Information Systems and Communication Technology

After reading this chapter, you should be able to:

1. Explain why businesses must manage *information* and show how computer systems and communication technologies have revolutionized *information management*.
2. Identify and briefly describe three elements of *data communication networks*—the Internet, the World Wide Web, and intranets.
3. Describe five *new options for organizational design* that have emerged from the rapid growth of information technologies.
4. Identify and briefly describe the *main elements of an information system*.
5. Discuss different information-system *application programs* that are available for users at various organizational levels.

More Productive than a Speeding Locomotive

Locomotive manufacturing: Is it a twilight industry? Yes and no. At GE Transportation Systems, a unit of General Electric Co., the core business of making locomotives is in a severe downturn. Sales of 911 locomotives in 1999 had plummeted to 350 by 2002. So why is CEO John Krenicki Jr. so upbeat about the future? One reason is an industrywide shift toward improving railroad services rather than just buying more trains.

Railroads want to raise productivity, improve on-time delivery, and cut costs—and GE is in a position to help with its *remote monitoring diagnostics.* Developed at GE's corporate R&D center, the technology has been used in GE Medical Systems products and aircraft engines. Now it's being customized for the locomotive business. For 2002, revenues from Transportation Systems services, including remote diagnostics applications, was \$1.5 billion—triple the 1996 total. New technologies, reports Krenicki, are changing the industry. "We're also digitizing all of our workflows—not just in our own factories but in customers' service shops. We want to run service shops like an Indianapolis pit crew." If shops run smoothly, freight rolls on time and at lower cost.

What does remote diagnostics do? It's designed to anticipate breakdowns before they happen. An unexpected breakdown can cost hundreds of thousands of dollars in lost operations, rescheduling, and unhappy customers. Remote sensing—sensing from afar—transmits signals from equipment to a satellite and then to the Internet, where specialists anywhere can view data, perform tests, predict maintenance needs, and troubleshoot equipment operating in out-of-the-way places. Monitoring key components can catch failures ahead of time so that they can be repaired less expensively, with less disruption to schedules, and with shorter downtimes. The ideal is just-in-time maintenance: performing work when it's needed, not before or too late. "There are two kinds of mistakes," says Gerald Hahn, retired founder of GE's Applied Statistics Program. "Replacing too soon and replacing too late. We want to minimize both."

Remote monitoring is possible because of two advances in technology. First is the miniaturization of sensors—the devices that attach to components and detect system characteristics (temperature, pressure, and so forth). New devices are easier to install, take up little room, and don't interfere with normal operation. Second, advanced computing power makes it easier to process data for diagnosis. Today's 6,000-horsepower locomotive engine is controlled by two dozen microprocessors that monitor such variables as speed, horsepower output, and voltage. Sensor data are relayed from a satellite to GE's service center in Erie, Pennsylvania, where technicians monitor 300 locomotives around the country.

Let's say that GE's diagnostics team detects a clogged fuel filter, which can cut horsepower by 30 percent. Even the engineer wouldn't detect the loss if the train were pulling a light load, but it would slow down a heavily loaded train on an uphill grade, and the effect would soon be felt throughout the entire rail system. Other trains would fall behind, and the rescheduling would be expensive. With remote monitoring, technicians can check real-time data on hundreds of variables and detect problems that would otherwise go unsuspected. Much of the rail industry's increase in effectiveness, therefore, is due not to bigger or even better equipment, but rather to advanced technology and better information.

Our opening story continues on page 479.

"We want to run service shops like an Indianapolis pit crew."

~John Krenicki Jr.,

CEO, GE TRANSPORTATION SYSTEMS

Information Management: An Overview

Business today relies on information management in ways that no one could foresee a decade ago. Managers now treat digital technology as a basic organizational resource for conducting daily business. At major firms, every activity—designing services, ensuring product delivery and cash flow, evaluating personnel—is linked to information systems. Managing systems is a core business activity that can no longer be delegated to technical personnel.

Most businesses also regard their information as a private resource—an asset that's planned, developed, and protected. It's not surprising that they have **information managers,** who operate systems for gathering, organizing, and distributing information, just as they have production, marketing, and finance managers. **Information management** is the internal operation that arranges information resources to support business performance and outcomes. At Chaparral Steel <www.chaparralsteel.com>, delivery times, sales, profits, and (last, but by no means least) customer service and loyalty have been boosted by an information system that gives customers electronic access to the mill's inventories. The technology that lets customers shop electronically through its storage yards makes Chaparral more agile in responding to their needs, and because it responds faster than its competitors, Chaparral enjoys more sales.

information manager
Manager responsible for designing and implementing systems to gather, organize, and distribute information

information management
Internal operations for arranging a firm's information resources to support business performance and outcomes

To find information, managers must often sift through mountains of reports, memos, and phone messages. Thus, the question facing so many businesses today: how to channel useful information to the right people at the right time. In this section, we will explore the ways in which companies manage information with computers and related information technologies.

Data Versus Information

Although businesspeople often complain that they get too much information, what they usually mean is that they get too many **data**—raw facts and figures. **Information** is usefully interpreted data.

data
Raw facts and figures

information
Meaningful, useful interpretation of data

Here, for example, are some data:

- Last year, 53 million Americans visited gambling casinos, averaging one visit every two months (about the same number they made to amusement and theme parks).
- Seventy-nine percent of all Americans believe that casino entertainment is acceptable for themselves or others.
- The lottery is the number-one form of gambling, followed by casino gambling and sports betting.
- The Western states account for the largest number of casino visits (33 percent), followed by the North Central (27 percent), Southern (23 percent), and Northeastern states (17 percent).
- Gross revenues from casino gambling rose from $8.3 billion in 1990 to $24.3 billion in 2000. Revenues from all forms of gambling rose from $26.6 billion to $61.4 billion.[1]

If we collect these data in a meaningful way, we might get a good idea of what sells gaming. We might even be able to say whether entertainment companies should build new hotels and casinos to meet increasing demand. The challenge for businesses is always the same: turning a flood of data into a manageable flow of information.

Information Systems

information system (IS)
System for transforming raw data into information that can be used in decision making

One response to this challenge has been the growth of the **information system (IS)**—a system for transforming raw data into information and transmitting it for use in decision making. IS managers must first determine what information is needed. Then they must gather the data and apply the technology to convert data into information. They must also control the flow of information so that it goes only to those people who need it.[2]

Supplied information varies according to such factors as the functional areas in which people work (say, accounting or marketing) and their management levels. At all levels, informational quality depends on an organization's technological resources and on the people who manage them. In the following section, we discuss the evolution of information-processing technology and then describe the information requirements of today's organization.

New Business Technologies in the Information Age

Employees at every level—from operational specialists to top executives—use the IS to improve performance. Information systems aid in scheduling trips, evaluating employees, and formulating strategy. The widening role of IS is due to rapid developments in electronic technologies that allow faster and broader communications and information flows. But as we shall see, the networked enterprise is more than a firm equipped with the latest technology. Technology has inspired new organizational designs, innovative relationships with other organizations, and new management processes for improved competitiveness.

The Expanding Scope of Information Systems

The relationship between the IS and the organization is among the fastest-changing aspects of business. At one time, IS applications were narrow in scope and technically oriented—processing payroll data, simulating engineering designs, compiling advertising expenditures. But as you can see in Figure 16.1, managers soon began using IS not merely to solve technical problems, but also to analyze management problems, especially for control purposes—applying quality standards to production, comparing costs against budgets, and keeping records on absences and turnover.

Today, information systems are also crucial in planning. Managers routinely use the IS to decide on products and markets for the next 5 to 10 years. The same database that helps marketing analyze demographics is used for financial planning, materials handling, and electronic funds transfers with suppliers and customers.

Another basic change is greater interdependence between a company's strategy and its IS. In addition to choosing a strategy—say, to be the lowest-cost, most flexible, or highest-quality provider—the firm needs an IS that can support that

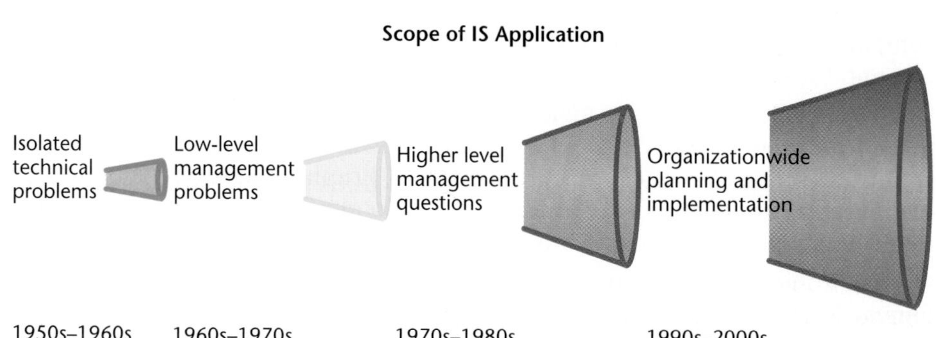

FIGURE 16.1
Evolution of IS Scope

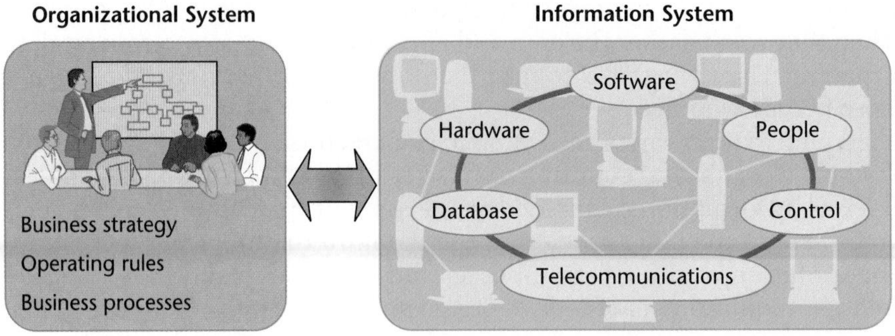

Organizational System

Business strategy
Operating rules
Business processes

Information System

Software
Hardware
People
Database
Control
Telecommunications

FIGURE 16.2
Aligning Business Strategy and the IS

strategy. As Figure 16.2 shows, a strategy will fail if a system's components are not integrated to support it. Consider a strategy that calls for the rapid receipt of customer orders and fast order fulfillment. Unless IS components are specifically designed to handle these tasks, the best-laid plans are probably doomed to failure.

Electronic Business and Communications Technologies

The need for better communications and information systems is growing as competition intensifies and as companies go global and expand into e-business. Firms like Ralston Purina Co. <www.ralston.com> need instantaneous communications among managers in countries where they either sell products or buy raw materials, including China, Colombia, Canada, and Brazil. Such needs are being met by new electronic information technologies and advanced data communication networks.

electronic information technologies (EIT)
Information-systems applications, based on telecommunications technologies, that use networks of appliances or devices to communicate information by electronic means

fax machine
Machine that can transmit copies of documents (text and graphics) over telephone lines

voice mail
Computer-based system for receiving and delivering incoming telephone calls

electronic mail (e-mail)
Computer system that electronically transmits letters, reports, and other information between computers

electronic conferencing
Computer-based system that allows people to communicate simultaneously from different locations via software or telephone

Electronic Information Technologies

Electronic information technologies (EIT) are IS applications based on telecommunications technologies. EITs use networks of devices (such as computers and satellites) to communicate information by electronic means. They enhance performance and productivity by serving two functions:

1. By providing coordination and communication within the firm
2. By speeding up transactions with other firms

Following are six of the most widely used innovations in digital business systems:

- The **fax machine** (short for *facsimile machine*) transmits and receives digitized images of texts, drawings, and photographs over telephone lines, thus permitting written communication over long distances. Fax machines are popular with both large and small firms because of their speed and low cost.
- **Voice mail** refers to a computer-based system for receiving and delivering incoming telephone calls. Incoming calls are never missed because a voice responds to the caller, invites a message, and stores it for later retrieval. A company with voice mail networks each employee's phone for receiving, storing, and forwarding calls.
- An **electronic mail** (or **e-mail**) system transmits memos and other information between computers, whether in the same building or in different countries. It can also send voice transmission, graphics, and videos between computers. E-mail thus substitutes for the flood of paper and phone calls that threatens to engulf many offices.
- **Electronic conferencing** allows groups of people to communicate simultaneously from various locations via e-mail or phone. One form, called *dataconferencing,* allows people in remote locations to work simultaneously on

"Ah, here is your fax now."

one document: Working as a team, they can revise a marketing plan or draft a press release. *Videoconferencing* allows participants to see one another on video screens while the conference is in progress. Teleconferencing is attractive because it eliminates travel and thus saves money.[3]

- Collaborative work is made easier by **groupware**—software that connects group members for e-mail distribution, electronic meetings, message storing, appointments and schedules, and group writing. Linked by groupware, people can collaborate from their own desktop PCs even if they're remotely located. It is especially useful when people work together regularly and rely heavily on information sharing. Groupware products include Lotus Development Corp.'s Lotus Notes <www.lotus.com/home.nsf/welcome/lotusnotes>, and Netscape Communicator <http://home.netscape.com/communicator/v4.5/index.html>.

groupware
Software that connects members of a group for shared e-mail distribution, electronic meetings, appointments, and group writing

- Outside information can be linked to a firm's electronic network and the information can be made available at every workstation. Commercial *digital information services* provide online information for both special-purpose and general topics. Lexis <www.lexis-nexis.com>, for instance, is designed for legal research, while America Online <www.aol.com> offers a range of business and general-interest information.[4]

A sluggish economy (and a lingering post-9/11 reluctance to fly) is hampering business travel. More and more companies are thus turning to videoconferencing as a means of holding meetings among people located in distant places. In the weeks following September 11, the law firm of Mintz, Levin, Cohen, Feris, Glovsky & Popeo managed to "virtually" link its Boston, Washington, and New York offices through teleconferencing. The firm's human resource director notes that the technology allows her to analyze participants' body language—something she couldn't do over the telephone or through e-mail.

data communication network

Global network (such as the Internet) that permits users to send electronic messages and information quickly and economically

Internet

Global data communication network serving millions of computers with information on a wide array of topics and providing communication flows among certain private networks

Data Communication Networks **Data communication networks** carry streams of digital data (electronic documents and other forms of video and sound) back and forth over telecommunication systems. The most prominent network, the Internet, and its companion system, the World Wide Web, have emerged as powerful communication technologies. Let's look a little more closely at each of these networks.

The Internet The largest public data communications network, the **Internet** (or "the Net") is a gigantic system of networks that both serves millions of computers with information on business, science, and government and provides communication flows among more than 170,000 separate networks around the world.[5] Originally commissioned by the Pentagon <www.defenselink.mil> as a wartime communication tool, the Internet allows personal computers in virtually any location to be linked. Because it can transmit information fast and at lower cost than long-distance phone service and postal delivery, the Net is also the most important e-mail system in the world. For thousands of businesses, it has joined—and is even replacing—the telephone, fax machine, and express mail as a communications tool.

Individuals can't connect directly to the Internet, but for small monthly usage fees, they can subscribe to the Net via an **Internet service provider (ISP),** such as Prodigy <www.prodigy.com>, America Online, or Earthlink <www.earthlink.com>. An ISP is a commercial firm that maintains a permanent connection to the Net and sells temporary connections to subscribers.

Internet service provider (ISP)
Commercial firm that maintains a permanent connection to the Net and sells temporary connections to subscribers

By 2002, more than 700 million Net users were active in more than 180 countries. In North America, more than 95 million users over the age of 16 were on the Net every day. Its power to change the way business is conducted has been amply demonstrated in both large and small firms. Consider how it's changing just one industry—financial markets. By 2003, 25 million U.S. households will be trading stocks and 32 million banking online, and many online brokerages have already appeared to meet growing demand.[6]

The World Wide Web Thanks to the subsystem of computers known as the **World Wide Web** (WWW or "the Web"), the Internet allows users around the world to communicate electronically with little effort. The Web is a system with universally accepted standards for storing, retrieving, formatting, and displaying information.[7] It provides the common language that allows us to surf the Net and makes it available to a general audience, not merely to technical users such as computer programmers. To access a Web site, the user specifies the *Uniform Resource Locator* (*URL*) that points to the unique Web address of the resource. Thus, American Airlines' URL is <www.aa.com>—a designation that specifies the storage location of American's Web pages.

World Wide Web
Subsystem of computers providing access to the Internet and offering multimedia and linking capabilities

Servers and Browsers Each Web site opens with a *home page*—a screen display that introduces the visitor and may include graphics, sound, and visual enhancements. Additional *pages* present the sponsor's products and explain how to get help in using the site. They often furnish URLs for related Web sites that the user can link into by simply pointing and clicking. The person who is responsible for maintaining an organization's Web site is usually called a *Webmaster.* Large sites use dedicated workstations—large computers—known as **Web servers,** which are customized for managing and supporting such sites.

Web server
Dedicated workstation customized for managing, maintaining, and supporting Web sites

With hundreds of thousands of new Web pages appearing each day, cyberspace now posts billions of pages of information. Sorting through this maze would be impossible without a Web **browser**—the software that permits users to access information on the Web. A browser runs on the user's PC and supports the graphics and linking capabilities needed to navigate the Web. Netscape Navigator <home.netscape.com/browsers/index.html> once enjoyed an 80-percent market share but is now being challenged by other browsers, including its own Netscape Communicator and Microsoft's Internet Explorer <www.microsoft.com/windows/ie>.

browser
Software supporting the graphics and linking capabilities necessary to navigate the World Wide Web

Directories and Search Engines Browsers offer additional tools—Web site directories and search engines—for navigating on the Web. Among the most successful cyberspace enterprises are companies such as Yahoo! <www.yahoo.com> that maintain free-to-use *directories* of Web content. When Yahoo! is notified about new Web sites, it classifies them in its directory. Users enter one or two keywords (for example, "compact disk"), and the directory retrieves a list of sites with titles containing those words.

In contrast, a **search engine** scans millions of Web pages without preclassifying them into a directory. It merely searches for pages containing the same words

search engine
Tool that searches Web pages containing the user's search terms and then displays pages that match

as the user's search terms, displaying addresses for those that come closest to matching, then the next closest, and so on. A search engine, such as AltaVista <www.altavista.com> or Lycos <www.lycos.com>, may respond to more than 10 million inquiries a day. Not surprisingly, both directories and search engines are packed with paid ads.[8]

intranet
Private network of internal Web sites and other sources of information available to a company's employees

firewall
Software and hardware system that prevents outsiders from accessing a company's internal network

Intranets Many companies have extended Net technology internally by maintaining internal Web sites linked throughout the firm.[9] These private networks, or **intranets,** are accessible only to employees through electronic **firewalls**—hardware and software security systems inaccessible to outsiders.[10] The Ford Motor Co. <www.ford.com> intranet connects 120,000 workstations in Asia, Europe, and the United States to thousands of Ford Web sites containing private information on Ford activities in production, engineering, distribution, and marketing. Sharing information has reduced the lead time for getting models into production from 36 to 24 months, and it has shortened customer delivery times. Ford expects to save billions in inventory and fixed costs.[11]

extranet
Internet allowing outsiders limited access to a firm's internal information system

Extranets **Extranets** allow outsiders limited access to a firm's internal information system. The most common application allows buyers to enter a system to see which products are available for sale and delivery, thus providing convenient product-availability information. Industrial suppliers are often linked into customers' intranets so that they can see planned production schedules and prepare supplies for customers' upcoming operations.

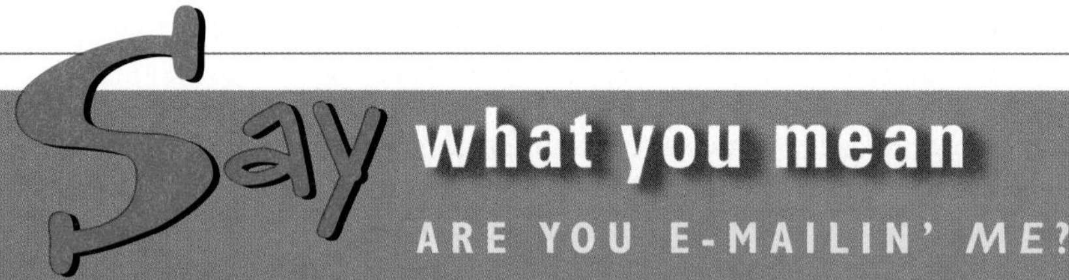

ARE YOU E-MAILIN' ME?

The Internet may be a global phenomenon, but that doesn't mean we can ignore cultural differences when we use it to communicate. Remember that the person who's getting mail on the receiving end of an Internet message may be interpreting it from an entirely different cultural perspective.

Americans are notoriously informal when addressing each other. The same habit shows up in their e-mail, and with the Internet, many Americans now feel free to be informal when addressing people all over the world. Unfortunately, being *too* informal in e-mail can send the wrong message. Depending on your correspondent, you may come across as either too familiar or too aggressive. In some cultures, including those of the United Kingdom, Germany, and Japan, people *like* a little formality in their e-mail.

Be careful about using first names or being too casual in other ways. Review your grammar and even the structure of your note. Sloppy language is a turnoff for a lot of people, and many others see it as a sign of poor education. In some cultures, an Internet message should be like a letter, with a formal structure and sign-off.

In addition, don't always expect people to reply immediately. Different cultures have different concepts of time, and their perceptions of time affect people's sense of when they need to respond to their mail. Demanding an immediate response from a Brazilian or a Mexican is the surest way to send your message to the bottom of the electronic pile.

Finally, remember that these days, people are bombarded with Internet messages. Many businesspeople regard responding to all of them as a drain on their time. As a rule, communicate electronically only when you have something that needs to be said or you need a question answered.

Self-Check Questions 1–3

*You should now be able to answer Self-Check Questions 1–3**

1. MULTIPLE CHOICE All of the following are considered to be *electronic information technologies* **except** [select one]: **(a)** computers; **(b)** voice mail; **(c)** groupware; **(d)** electronic conferencing; **(e)** e-mail.

2. TRUE/FALSE *A search engine,* such as AltaVista or Lycos, will search millions of Web pages and then classify them into free-to-use directories of Web content.

3. MULTIPLE CHOICE All of the following are **true** of the *World Wide Web* **except** [select one]: (a) It uses Uniform Resource Locators (URLs) to identify unique Web addresses. (b) It has uniform standards for formatting and displaying information. (c) It maintains orderly flows by prohibiting Web sites from listing URLs for related sites. (d) Its accessibility is facilitated by Web browsers.

* Answers to Self-Check Questions 1–3 can be found on p. AN-10.

New Options for Organizational Design: The Networked Enterprise

The rapid growth of information technologies has changed the very structure of business organizations. We begin this section by discussing changes wrought by technology in the workforces and structures of many organizations. We then examine ways that electronic networks contribute to greater flexibility in dealing with customers. After discussing the growing importance of workplace collaboration, we look at ways in which information networks help to free the workplace from the constraints of physical location. Finally, we describe new management processes inspired by the availability of electronic networks.

Leaner Organizations Information networks are leading to leaner companies with fewer employees and simpler structures. Because a networked firm can maintain information links among both employees and customers, more work can be accomplished with fewer people. Bank customers can dial into a 24-hour information system and find out their current balances from a digital voice. Assembly workers at IBM once got instructions from supervisors or special staff. Now these instructions are delivered to workstations electronically.

Reducing middle-management spots and eliminating layers of organizational structure are possible because information networks provide direct communications between the top managers and lower level workers. The operating managers who once forwarded policies, procedures, or instructions to lower-level employees are being replaced by information networks.

More Flexible Operations Electronic networks let businesses offer customers greater variety and faster delivery cycles.[12] Products such as cellular phones, PCs, and audio systems can be custom-ordered, with choices of features and next-day delivery. The principle is called **mass-customization:** Although companies produce in large volumes, each unit features the unique options preferred by the customer.[13] As you can see in Figure 16.3, flexible production and fast delivery depend on an integrated network to coordinate all the transactions and

mass-customization
Flexible production process that generates customized products in high volumes at low cost

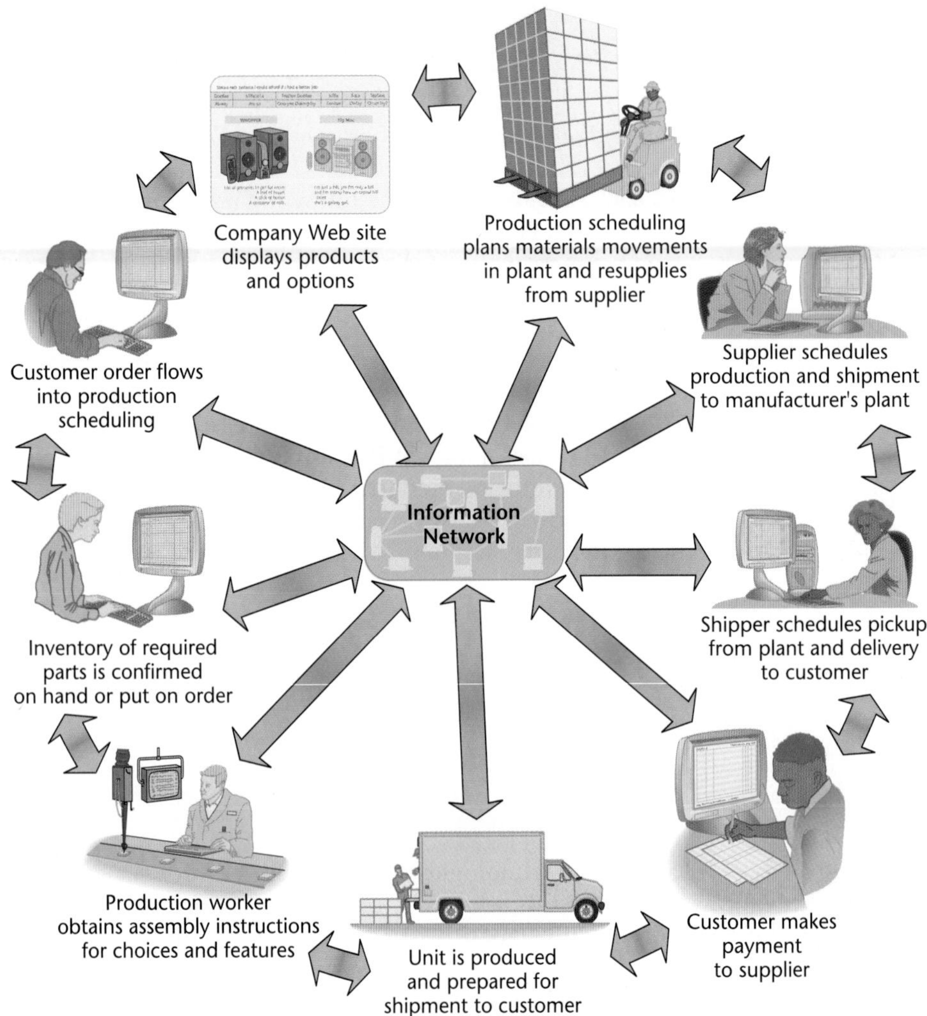

FIGURE 16.3
Networking for Mass-Customization

processes needed to make quick adjustments in production. The ability to organize and store massive volumes of information is crucial, as are the electronic links among customers, manufacturers, suppliers, and shippers.

Increased Collaboration Collaboration, both among internal units and with outside firms, is on the rise because networked systems make it cheaper and easier to contact everyone. Aided by intranets, companies are learning that complex problems can be better solved through collaboration, either by means of formal teams or spontaneous interaction. Decisions once made by individuals are now shared among people and departments. The design of new products, for example, was once an engineering responsibility. Now it can be shared because so much information is available from and accessible to people in different functional areas: Marketing, finance, production, engineering, and purchasing can share stores of information and determine the best design.[14]

Networking and the Virtual Company Networked systems can also improve collaboration between organizations through the so-called *virtual company.* We noted in Chapter 7 that this can be a temporary team assembled by a single organization, but a virtual company can also be created by several allied firms.[15] Each contributes different skills and resources that collectively result in a competitive business that wouldn't be feasible for any one of them working alone. A company with marketing and promotional skills, for example, may team up with firms with expertise in warehousing and distribution, engineering, and production. Networking lets collaborators exchange ideas, plan strategy, share customer information, and otherwise coordinate efforts, even if their respective facilities are far apart.

Greater Independence of Company and Workplace Geographic separation of the workplace from headquarters is now more common. Employees no longer work only at the office or the factory, nor are all of a company's operations performed at one place. A sales manager for an ad agency may visit the New York office twice a month, preferring instead to use the firm's electronic network from home in Florida.

Likewise, company activities may be geographically scattered but highly coordinated through a networked system. Many e-businesses conduct no activities at

Mid-Chapter Internet Field Trip

"On the Cutting Edge with Experts"

In the first part of this chapter, we discussed issues involved in aligning a firm's business strategy with its information system, including its communications technologies. We have seen how today's networked enterprise provides new options for organizational design that allow a firm to be more effective in meeting the needs of customers and employees. But because keeping pace with fast-changing technologies is a challenge that most companies can't meet by themselves, many rely on outside firms for expert advice. Whether addressed internally or externally, however, several basic issues are always involved: What are the company's information needs? How might the IS help employees and increase productivity? Is the firm's IS consistent with its basic orientation? Are communications links adequate for networking among the departments and branches of the business? What kinds of equipment does the firm's IS need?

Let's look further into these questions by exploring the Web site of Cisco Systems Inc., the worldwide leader in networking. Cisco's product line includes just about everything needed for networking, and by examining Cisco's products—hardware, software, and services—we can learn more about the needs of Internet users and some of the leading-edge information-technology solutions available to them. To find out more about Cisco, its products, and its customers, go the firm's Web site at <www.cisco.com>.

First, to get an idea of the variety of Cisco products and services, browse the home page, including the various subject gates located around the page. Then go to the subject gate entitled **Solutions for Your Network,** and from the sublistings, select the category **Home Networking.** After exploring the various pages under **Home Networking,** respond to the following item:

1. "Greater Independence of Company and Workplace" is a topic discussed in the first part of this chapter. What does its Web site say about products and services that Cisco offers for the geographic separation of the workplace from company headquarters?

Beginning again from the homepage, return to the subject gate entitled **Solutions for Your Network,** and from the sublistings, select the category **Small/Medium Business.** From here, go to the left-side panel and select **Business Solutions.** This page has a drop-down menu entitled **Select a Business Solution.** Enter the menu and choose **Internet Business Roadmap.** After reading the page entitled **Cisco Internet Business Roadmap,** respond to the following question:

2. Of what value is the information on this page to Cisco's potential customers? What is the purpose of this page?

Return to the **Small/Medium Business** page. On the left-side panel, select **Technology Solutions.** Enter the drop-down menu entitled **Select a Technology Solution,** and click on **Branch-Office Connectivity.** After reading this page, respond to the following question:

3. What is "branch-office connectivity," and what information requirements does it have?

Return to the drop-down menu entitled **Select a Technology Solution,** and click on **Telecommuting/Remote Access.** Read the page and then respond to the following question:

4. How does this Web page information relate to this chapter's textbook discussion?

Go back once more to the drop-down menu entitled **Select a Technology Solution,** and click on and read the page entitled **Internet Access.** Next, go back to the menu and read the page on **Internet Security.** After reading these pages, respond to the following question:

5. What kinds of Internet access and security assistance does Cisco offer?

To continue your Internet Field Trip, click on www.prenhall.com/griffin

one centralized location. When you order furniture from an Internet storefront—say, a chair, a sofa, a table, and two lamps—the chair may come from a warehouse in Philadelphia and the lamps from a manufacturer in California; the sofa and table may be direct-shipped from different mills in North Carolina. Every activity begins instantaneously with the customer's order and is coordinated through the network just as if the whole order were being processed at one place.

Improved Management Processes Networked systems have changed the nature of the management process. The activities and methods of today's manager differ significantly from those that were common just a few years ago. At one time, upper-level managers didn't concern themselves with all of the detailed information filtering upward in the workplace. Why? Because it was expensive to gather, it was slow in coming, and it quickly became out of date. Workplace management was delegated to middle and first-line managers.

With networked systems, however, instantaneous information is accessible and useful. Consequently, more upper managers use it routinely for planning, leading, directing, and controlling operations. Today, a top manager can find out the current status of any customer order, inspect productivity statistics for each workstation, and analyze the delivery performance of any vehicle. More important, managers can better coordinate companywide performance. They can identify departments that are working well together and those that are creating bottlenecks.

enterprise resource planning (ERP)

Large information system for integrating all the activities of a company's business units

Enterprise Resource Planning One type of networked system is **enterprise resource planning (ERP)**—a large information system for integrating the activities of all of a company's units.[16] It is supported by one large database through which everyone shares the same information when any transaction occurs. The biggest supplier of commercial ERP packages is Germany's SAP AG <www.sap.com>, followed by Oracle <www.oracle.com>. Hershey Foods <www.hersheys.com> uses the SAP system. It identifies the status of any order and traces its progress from order entry through customer delivery and receipt of payment. Progress and delays at intermediate stages—materials ordering, inventory availability, production scheduling, packaging, warehousing, distribution—can be checked continuously to determine which operations should be more closely coordinated with others to improve overall performance.

Types of Information Systems

In a sense, the term *information system* may be a misnomer. It suggests that there is one system when, in fact, employees have many different responsibilities and decision-making needs. One IS can't handle such a range of requirements. In reality, the information system is a complex of several information systems that share information while serving different levels of the organization, different departments, or different operations.

User Groups and System Requirements

knowledge worker

Employee who uses information and knowledge as raw materials and who relies on information technology to design new products or business systems

Four user groups are identified in Figure 16.4, which also indicates the kinds of systems best suited to each user level. We include **knowledge workers**—employees for whom information and knowledge are the raw materials of their work. They are specialists, usually professionally trained and certified—engineers, scientists, information technology specialists—who rely on information technology to design new products or create new processes.

Managers at Different Levels Because they work on different kinds of problems, top managers, middle managers, knowledge workers, and first-line managers have different information needs. First-line (or operational) managers need information to oversee the day-to-day details of departments or projects. Knowledge workers need information in order to conduct technical projects. Middle managers need summaries and analyses for setting intermediate and long-range goals for activities under their supervision. Top management analyzes trends in the business environment and overall company performance in order to make long-range plans.

Consider the information needs for a flooring manufacturer. Sales managers (first-level managers) supervise salespeople and handle customer service and delivery problems. They need current information on the sales and delivery of products: lists of incoming customer orders and daily delivery schedules. Regional managers (middle managers) set sales quotas for sales managers and prepare budgets. They need information on monthly sales by product and region. To develop new materials, knowledge workers need information on the chemical properties of adhesives. Top managers need both external and internal information. Internally, they compare current sales data, summarized by product and geographic region, to data from previous years. Equally important is external information on consumer trends and economic forecasts.

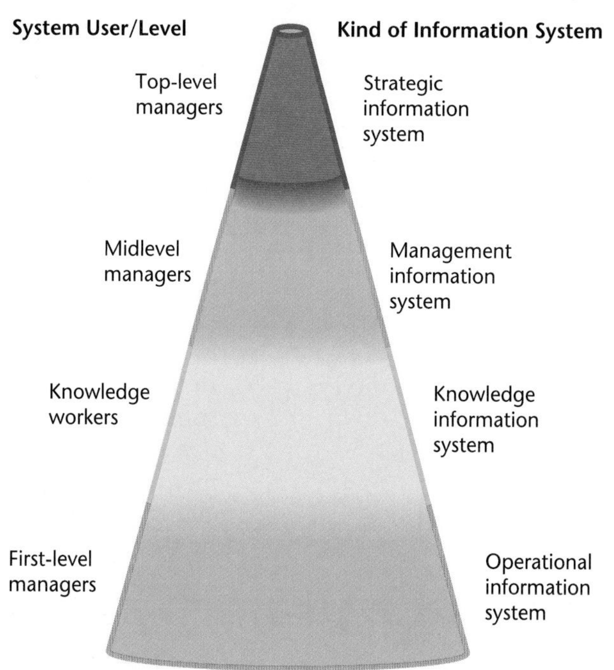

FIGURE 16.4
Matching Information Users and Systems

Functional Areas and Business Processes Each business *function*—marketing, human resources, accounting, production, finance—has its own information needs. In addition, in businesses organized according to business processes, process groups need special information. Each user group and department is represented by an IS. Now add to these systems the four systems needed by the four levels of users that we just discussed: The total number of systems and applications increases significantly.

Each cell on the left side of Figure 16.5 represents a potential IS associated with a given functional group. Top-level finance managers, for instance, plan long-range spending for facilities and equipment, and they determine sources of

	Organization Function			Business Process			
	Marketing	Finance	Production	Strategic planning	Product development	Order fulfillment	Supply chain management
Top-level managers				↕	↕	↕	↕
Midlevel managers							
Knowledge workers							
First-level managers							

FIGURE 16.5
Matching User Levels with Functional Areas and Business Processes

capital. The arrows on the right side of Figure 16.5 show that a business-process group will include users, both managers and employees, drawn from all organizational levels. The supply chain management group, for instance, may need to cut the number of suppliers. The IS supporting this project would contain information cutting across different functions and management levels. The group will need information on and expertise in marketing, warehousing and distribution, production, communications technology, purchasing, and finance. It will also need input on operational, technical, and managerial issues—say, technical requirements for new suppliers and future financial requirements.

Major Systems by Level

In this section, we discuss different kinds of systems that provide applications at some levels but not at others. For routine, repetitive transactions, such as day-to-day order taking by online retailers, specialized applications will do. But requirements for knowledge workers will vary because they usually face a variety of specialized problems. IS applications for middle- and top-level managers must also be flexible because they use a broad range of information collected from both external and internal sources.

transaction processing system (TPS)
Information-processing application for routine business activities involving well-defined processing steps

Transaction Processing Systems **Transaction processing systems (TPS)** apply information processing to routine business transactions involving well-defined steps. Order taking by online retailers, claims approval at insurance companies, payroll processing and bill payment at almost every company—all are routine business processes. Typically, the TPS for first-level (operational) activities has predetermined data needs and follows the same steps for every transaction.

Figure 16.6 is a diagram of TPS for a customer-billing process. The process begins when ordered products are packed for shipment. Using data from the company's master files, billing staffers match the customer's identification number (from the billing master file) with product code numbers (from the jobs master file). The system tallies the amount due (including the shipping bill plus any past-due payments), creates the invoice, and issues status reports to system users with online access. Information from the billing and jobs master files flows electronically to the accounting system, where it updates accounts receivables and inventory accounts.

Systems for Knowledge Workers and Office Applications Many systems and office applications support the activities of both knowledge workers and clerical workers. They aid in data processing and other activities, including the creation of communications documents. Like other departments, the IS department includes both *knowledge workers* and *data workers.*

IS Knowledge Workers IS knowledge workers include both systems analysts and application or systems programmers:

- *Systems analysts* deal with the entire computer system. They learn users' requirements and design systems that meet them, deciding on types and sizes of computers and how to set up links to form a network.
- *Programmers* write the software instructions that tell computers what to do. Application programmers, for example, write instructions to address particular problems. Systems programmers ensure that a system can handle the requests made by application programs.

system operations personnel
Information-systems employees who run a company's computer equipment

Operations Personnel (Data Workers) **System operations personnel** run the company's computer equipment. They make sure that the right programs are run in the correct sequence and monitor equipment to see that it's operating properly. Many organizations also have personnel to enter data for processing in the system.

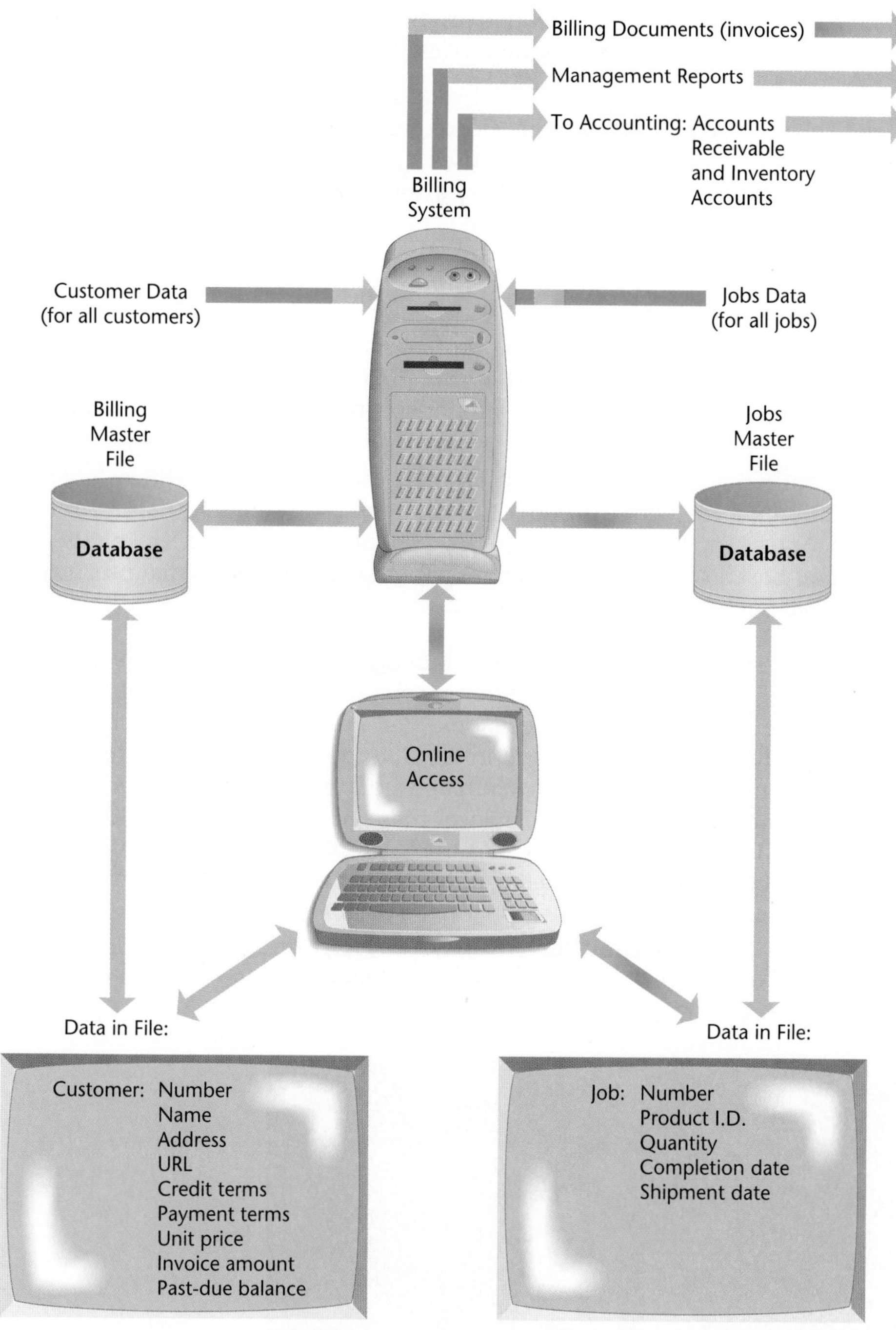

FIGURE 16.6
Flow Diagram for Customer-Billing TPS

Knowledge-Level and Office Systems New support systems—word processing, desktop publishing, computer-aided design, simulation modeling—have increased the productivity of both office and knowledge workers. We will discuss *word processing*—systems for formatting, editing, and storing documents—later in this chapter. *Desktop publishing,* also discussed later, combines graphics and word processing to publish professional-quality documents. *Document imaging systems* scan paper documents and images, convert them into digital form for storage on disks, retrieve them, and transmit them electronically to workstations throughout the network.

World-class firms such as Harley-Davidson <www.harley-davidson.com>, John Deere <www.deere.com>, and GE <www.ge.com> rely on knowledge-level system applications that help reduce product-design times and production-cycle times and make faster customer deliveries.[17]

computer-aided design (CAD)
Computer-based electronic technology that assists in designing products by simulating a real product and displaying it in three-dimensional graphics

Computer-aided design (CAD) helps design products by simulating them and displaying them in three-dimensional graphics. Immersion's MicroScribe-3D software <www.immersion.com> uses a penlike tool to scan the surface of any three-dimensional object, such as a football helmet, and electronically transforms it into a 3D graphic. The designer then tries different shapes and surfaces in the computer and analyzes them on a video monitor. Products ranging from cell phones to auto parts are created with CAD because it creates faster designs at lower cost than manual modeling methods. The older method—making handcrafted prototypes (trial models) from wood, plastic, or clay—is replaced with *rapid prototyping* (*RP*): The CAD system electronically transfers instructions to a computer-controlled machine that builds the prototype.

computer-aided manufacturing (CAM)
Computer system used to design and control equipment needed in the manufacturing process

Computer-aided manufacturing (CAM) is used to design facilities, layouts, and equipment for better product flows. *Computer operations control* refers to any system for managing day-to-day production activities. Hospitals use computer-based scheduling to prepare patients' meals, just as manufacturers do for making cars, clocks, and paper products.

management information system (MIS)
System used for transforming data into information for use in decision making

Management Information Systems **Management information systems (MIS)** support managers by providing daily reports, schedules, plans, and budgets that can then be used for making decisions. Each manager's information activities vary according to his or her functional area (accounting or marketing and so forth) and management level. Whereas midlevel managers focus on internal activities and information, higher level managers are also engaged in external activities. Middle managers, the largest MIS user group, need information to plan such activities as personnel training, materials movements, and cash flows. They also need to know the status of the jobs and projects assigned to their departments. What stage is a job at now? When will it be finished? Is there an opening so we can start the next job? Many management information systems—

Even as late as the 1980s, computing hadn't had much impact on industrial automation, largely because there were no good software programs for computer operated manufacturing. Working in the 1970s to help set up Unix operating systems for various manufacturers, Myron Zimmerman recognized a need, and in 1980, he founded VenturCom <www.plantautomation.com/storefronts/venturcominc.html>, *which develops programs for controlling industrial production equipment like this metal-cutting machine at Hillside Industries in Middletown, Connecticut.*

cash flow, sales, production scheduling, shipping—are indispensable for helping managers find answers to such questions.[18]

Decision Support Systems Middle- and top-level managers get assistance from **decision support systems (DSS)**—interactive systems that find and present information needed for the decision-making process. Whereas some DSSs handle specific problems, others are general purpose, allowing managers to analyze different types of problems. A firm faced with decisions on plant capacity may have a *capacity DSS.* The manager inputs data on anticipated sales, working capital, and customer-delivery requirements. Then built-in transaction processors manipulate the data and make recommendations on the best levels of plant capacity for each future time period.

decision support system (DSS)
Interactive computer-based system that locates and presents information needed to support decision making

Executive Support Systems An **executive support system (ESS)** is an easy-access IS application specially designed for upper level managers. ESSs are designed to assist with executive-level problems ranging from "What lines of business should we be in five years from now?" to "Based on forecasted developments in electronic technologies, to what extent should our firm be globalized in five years? In 10 years?" The ESS uses a wide range of both internal and external sources, such as industry reports, global economic forecasts, and reports on competitors.

executive support system (ESS)
Quick-reference information-system application designed specially for instant access by upper level managers

Artificial Intelligence and Expert Systems **Artificial intelligence (AI)** is the construction of computer systems to imitate human behavior—in other words, systems that perform physical tasks, use thought processes, and learn. In developing AI systems, business specialists, modelers, and information-technology experts try to design computer-based systems capable of reasoning so that computers, instead of people, can perform certain activities. A credit-evaluation system may

artificial intelligence (AI)
Computer-system application that imitates human behavior by performing physical tasks, using thought processes, sensing, and learning

*You should now be able to answer Self-Check Questions 4–6**

4. MULTIPLE CHOICE Suppose you are a *knowledge worker* in a major industrial firm. Which of the following types of information do you most likely need from an IS [select one]? **(a)** data on broad economic trends and overall company performance for long-range planning; **(b)** summaries and analyses for setting intermediate-range goals for a group of departments; **(c)** special information for conducting technical projects on specific problems; **(d)** daily production schedules and work-shift assignments.

5. TRUE/FALSE The development of next year's business plan is an example of an activity that can be conducted by a *transaction processing system.*

6. MULTIPLE CHOICE The *networked enterprise*—one that adopts information technologies—can be expected to have all of the following characteristics **except** [select one]: **(a)** shrinkage of layers in organizational structure; **(b)** more departments and firms participating in designing products; **(c)** more employees working at home rather than at the office, **(d)** upper level managers' avoidance of detailed information about specific operations; **(e)** increased likelihood of participating with other workers in a virtual company.

* Answers to Self-Check Questions 4–6 can be found on p. AN-11.

decide which loan applicants are creditworthy and which too risky, and it may then compose acceptance and rejection letters accordingly.[19]

robotics

Combination of computers and industrial robots for use in manufacturing operations

Robotics—the combination of computers with industrial robots—is a category of AI. With certain reasoning capabilities, robots can "learn" repetitive tasks such as painting, assembling components, and inserting screws. They also avoid repeating mistakes by "remembering" the causes of past mistakes and, when those causes reappear, adjusting or stopping until adjustments are made.

expert system

Form of artificial intelligence that attempts to imitate the behavior of human experts in a particular field

Expert Systems A special form of AI, the **expert system,** is designed to imitate the thought processes of human experts in a particular field. Expert systems incorporate the rules that an expert applies to specific types of problems, such as a doctor's judgments in diagnosing illness. In effect, they endow everyday users with instant expertise.

Elements of the Information System

We know that an IS is a group of interconnected devices that exchange information from different locations. We also know that *networking*—connecting these devices—allows decentralized computers to exchange data quickly and easily. A key component of the IS is its **computer network**—all the computer and information technology devices which, working together, drive the flow of digital information through the system.

computer network

All the computer and information technology devices that, by working together, drive the flow of digital information throughout a system

The computer is a powerful machine, but it is only one part of the IS. Every system has six components:

- Hardware
- Software
- Control
- Database
- People
- Telecommunications

In this section, we will describe the first four components in detail. We have already described the fifth element, the people at various levels who use and prepare the system. We'll reserve our discussion of telecommunications for the next section. Remember that all six components must be properly coordinated for a networked IS to function effectively.

Hardware

hardware

Physical components of a computer system

input device

Part of the computer system that enters data into it

central processing unit (CPU)

Part of the computer system where data processing takes place

main memory

Part of the computer CPU that houses the memory of programs that the CPU needs to operate

program

Set of instructions used by a computer used to perform specified activities

Figure 16.7 shows the systems and components that make up IS **hardware**—the physical components of a computer system. The functioning of this hardware is not as complicated as it looks. To get an insider's view, suppose that you are a piece of data (say, the number *3*).

- To get into the computer, data must be entered by an **input device.** Optical scanners, CD drives, and computer mice are all input devices, but let's assume that you're entered by the most common input device, a keyboard. When the user punches *3* on the keyboard, an electronic signal goes to the **central processing unit (CPU),** where actual data processing takes place.
- You're now inside the CPU in a form that the computer can handle. Now what happens? As a piece of data, you must go first to **main memory**—the part of the CPU that stores the programs that the computer needs to operate.
- Now the CPU searches through its memory for instructions—**programs**—on what to do with you. Using the appropriate instructions, it then performs

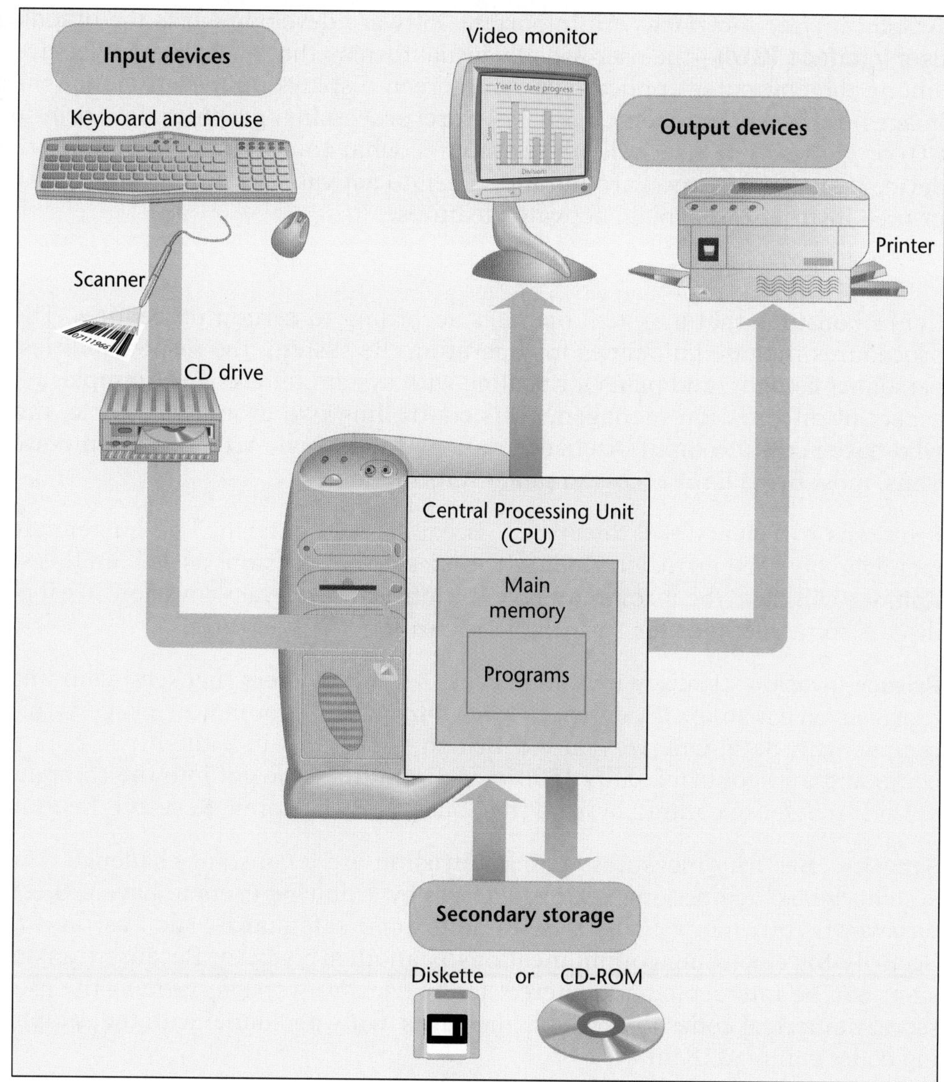

■ **FIGURE 16.7**
Hardware Components of an IS

calculations and comparisons as directed by the program. Finally, it sends the results into one or more **output devices:** a video monitor, a printer, or a voice output.

output device
Part of a computer system that presents results, either visually or in printed form

Software

Although hardware is a vital component, it needs programs—**software**—to function. There are two types of software programs:

software
Programs that instruct a computer in what to do

- **System programs** tell the computer what resources to use and how. For example, an *operating* system program tells the computer how and when to transfer data from secondary to primary storage and return information to the user.
- Most computer users do not write programs but rather use **application programs:** software packages written by others. Each different type of application (such as financial analysis, word processing, or Web browsing) uses a program that meets that need. Thus, a computer system usually has many application programs available, such as Lotus 1-2-3, Quicken, and WordPerfect. We review some of these later in this chapter.

system program
Software that tells the computer what resources to use and how to use them

application program
Software (such as Word for Windows) that processes data according to a user's special needs

graphical user interface (GUI)
Software that provides a visual display to help users select applications

icon
Small image in a GUI that enables users to select applications or functions

Graphical User Interface An important software development is the **graphical user interface (GUI)**—the user-friendly visual display that helps users select from among the computer applications. The screen displays numerous **icons** (small images) representing such choices as word processing, graphics, fax, printing, CD, or games. The user tells the computer what to do by moving a pointing device (usually an arrow) around the screen to activate the desired icon. Simple printed instructions explain activated features.

Control

Control ensures that a system operates according to certain procedures. These procedures include guidelines for operating the system, the responsibilities of personnel using it, and plans for dealing with system failure. For example, a key aspect of information management is controlling two groups of people: those who have access to input or change data and those who receive system output. Thus, most firms limit access to salary information.

Problems of Privacy and Security "Breaking and entering" no longer refers merely to physical intrusion. Today, it applies to IS intrusions as well. In this section, we will describe a common form of intrusion—privacy invasion. We'll also discuss some methods for ensuring IS security.[20]

Privacy Invasion Privacy invasion occurs when intruders (hackers) gain unauthorized access to an IS, either to steal information, money, or property or to tamper with data. One 16-year-old British hacker got into the Air Force's top command-and-control facility 150 times. From there, he got into the computers of several defense contractors and the South Korean Atomic Research Institute.

Security Security measures against intrusion are a constant challenge. Many systems guard against unauthorized access by requiring users to have protected passwords, but many firms rely on additional safeguards, such as *firewalls*. Security for electronic communications is another concern. Because transmissions can be intercepted and altered, many firms rely on *encryption*—the use of secret numerical codes to scramble messages. Only personnel with the deciphering codes can read them.

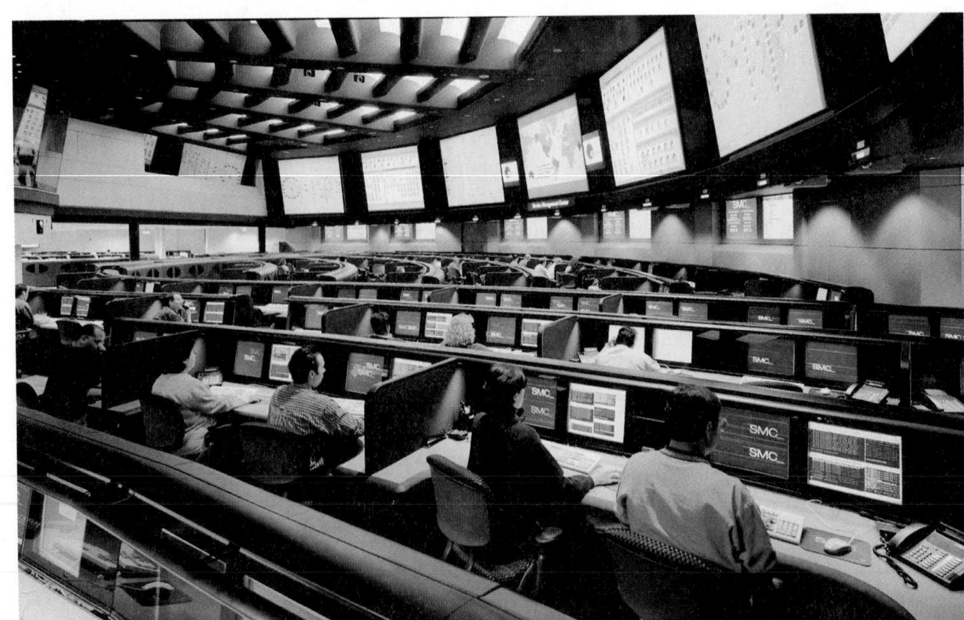

Network security is a serious matter at Electronic Data Systems (EDS) <www.eds. com> *of Plano, Texas. The company not only provides security services for 2,500 clients but must also secure its own information systems. That's why it keeps data centers small, spreads operations across 38 states, and continually tests its networks. Today, EDS partners with EMC Corp.* <www.emc. com> *to run networks that instantaneously "mirror" databases to backup crucial information in case of network failure or cyber terrorism.*

The most important security factor in an IS is people. Most firms train personnel in the responsibilities of computer use and warn them about violating security. Each time the computer boots up, for instance, a notice reminds users that software and data are protected and spells out penalties for unauthorized use.

Databases and Application Programs

All computer processing is the processing of data. It is carried out by programs—instructions that tell the system to perform certain functions. In this section, we begin by describing data and databases. We then discuss a few specialized applications programs designed for business use.

Data and Databases Computers convert data into information by organizing them in some meaningful manner. Within the system, chunks of data—numbers, words, and sentences—are stored in a series of related collections called *fields, records,* and *files.* Together, data files constitute a **database**—a central, organized collection of related data.[21]

database
Centralized, organized collection of related data

Application Programs Most computer users don't write programs. Programs are available for a huge range of business-related tasks. Some address such common, long-standing needs as accounting and inventory control, while others have been developed for an endless variety of specialized needs. Most business programs fall into one of four categories—*word processing, spreadsheets, database management,* and *graphics.* Of all PC software applications, 70 percent are designed for the first three types of programs.[22]

Word Processing Popular **word-processing programs,** such as Microsoft Word for Windows <www.microsoft.com/windows> and Lotus's Word Pro <www.lotus.com/home/nsf/welcome/smartsuite>, allow computer users to store, edit, display, and print documents. Sentences and paragraphs can be added or deleted without retyping or restructuring an entire document, and mistakes are easily corrected.

word-processing program
Applications program that allows computers to store, edit, and print letters and numbers for documents created by users

Spreadsheets **Electronic spreadsheets** spread data across and down the page in rows and columns. Users enter data, including formulas, at row and column intersections, and the computer automatically performs the necessary calculations. Payroll records, sales projections, and a host of other financial reports can be prepared in this manner.

Spreadsheets are good planning tools because they let managers see how making a change in one item affects related items. For example, you can insert operating-cost percentages, tax rates, or sales revenues into the spreadsheet. The computer will automatically recalculate all the other figures and determine net profit. Popular spreadsheet packages include Lotus 1-2-3, Quattro Pro, <www.corel/products/wordperfect/cqp>, and Microsoft Excel for Windows.[23]

electronic spreadsheet
Applications program with a row-and-column format that allows users to store, manipulate, and compare numeric data

Database Management Another popular type of personal-productivity software is a **database management program.** Such programs as Microsoft Access for Windows and Borland's InterBase <www.borland.com> are popular for desktop applications. Oracle9i <www.oracle.com> is a popular database for Internet computing. These systems can create, store, sort, and search through data and integrate a single piece into several different files.

database management program
Applications program for creating, storing, searching, and sorting an organized collection of data

Graphics **Computer graphics programs** convert numeric and character data into pictorial information, such as charts and graphs. They make computerized information easier to use and understand in two ways. First, graphs and charts summarize data and allow managers to detect problems, opportunities, and relationships more easily. Second, graphics contribute to clearer and more persuasive reports and presentations.

computer graphics program
Applications program that converts numeric and character data into pictorial information, such as graphs and charts

presentation graphics software

Applications that enable users to create visual presentations that can include animation and sound

Presentation graphics software, such as CorelDRAW, Microsoft PowerPoint for Windows, and Microsoft Visio 2002, lets users assemble graphics for visual displays, slides, video, and even sound splices for professional presentations. Varying color and size and using pictures and charts with three-dimensional effects and shading with animation and sound make for far more visually interesting presentations.

Computer graphics capabilities go beyond data presentation. They also include stand-alone programs for artists, designers, and special effects engineers. Everything from simple drawings to motion picture special effects are now created by computer graphics software. The sinking ship in *Titanic,* the aliens in *Men in Black II,* and the dog in *Scooby-Doo* were all created with computer graphics.

desktop publishing

Process of combining word-processing and graphics capability to produce virtually typeset-quality text from personal computers

Some software allows firms to publish sales brochures, in-house magazines, and annual reports. The latest **desktop publishing** packages for the PC combine word-processing and graphics to produce typeset-quality text with stimulating visual effects. They also eliminate printing costs for reports and proposals. QuarkXPress <www.quark.com>, which can manipulate text, tables of numbers, graphics, and full-color photographs, is used by ad agencies such as J. Walter Thompson because its computer-generated designs offer greater control over color and format. Other packages include Microsoft Publisher and Adobe Systems PageMaker <www.adobe.com/products/pagemaker/main.html>.

Telecommunications and Networks

Communications systems are constantly evolving, but certain basic elements are well established: computers, communications devices, and networking. The most powerful vehicle for using these elements to their full potential is the marriage of computers and communication technologies.

A *network* organizes telecommunications components into an effective system. When a company decides how to organize its equipment and facilities, it also determines how its information resources will be shared, controlled, and applied by network users. In this section, we will first discuss *multimedia communications technologies* and some of the devices found in today's systems. We will then describe different ways of organizing information resources into networks.

Multimedia Communication Systems

multimedia communication system

Connected network of communication appliances (such as faxes or TVs) that may be linked to forms of mass media (such as print publications or TV programming)

Today's IS includes not only computers but also **multimedia communication systems**—connected networks of communication appliances, such as faxes, televisions, sound equipment, cell phones, printers, and photocopiers, that may also be linked by satellite with other networks. The integration of these elements is changing the way we manage our businesses.

A good example is the modern grocery store. The checkout scanner reads the bar code on the product you buy. Data are then transmitted to the store's inventory-control system, which updates the number of available units. If inventory falls below a given level, more product is ordered. Meanwhile, the correct price is added to your bill and appropriate checkout coupons are printed. Your debit card transfers funds, sales reports are generated for store management, and all the while, satellite transmissions are dispatching trucks loaded with replacement inventory.

Communication Devices Today's technology lets people conduct business across large distances and from places where communications were once unavailable. *Global positioning systems (GPSs),* for example, use satellite transmissions to track the geographic locations of targets, such as boats or even people. When you're linked to a GPS network, your firm can know your whereabouts at all times. *Personal digital assistants (PDAs)* are tiny hand-held computers with wireless telecommunications capabilities. Many can access the Internet, even receiving and sending e-mail messages from the most primitive locations. *Paging systems* and *cellular telephones* connect us instantly with distant networks.

Communication Channels *Communication channels,* including wired and wireless transmission, are the media that make all these transmissions possible.[24] Most of us use communication channels when we use wired telephone systems, but today most telephone transmissions are data, not conversations. Fax data account for 90 percent of all telephone signals between the United States and Japan.

Meanwhile, microwave systems transmit wireless radio signals between transmission stations. Satellite communications has also gained popularity with the growth in demand for wireless transmission. Accessible through satellite networks built by McCaw <www.mccaw.com>, Hughes <www.hns.com>, Motorola <www.gi.com>, AT&T <www.attws.com>, and Loral <www.loral.com>, the Net is available in remote areas where underground cable isn't feasible.

System Architecture

There are several ways to organize computer and network components. As we see in the next section, one way to classify networks is according to *geographic scope.*[25]

Going to School in Networking

Ninety percent of freshmen arriving at the University of Michigan are PC owners. More than 41 percent have already created at least one Web site, and 39 percent say they're on the cell phone 250 hours a month. At nearby drinking spots, students are just as apt to pull out laptops as they are to order up brews. They love hi-tech gadgets, especially when they're networked. Josh Michaels, a senior at the University of Illinois, keeps a laptop on his nightstand. "I want to be able to control every device in this apartment without getting out of my bed," he explains. Those devices include two lamps, a TiVo, a coffee grinder and espresso machine, an Xbox, a DVD player, and a homemade security camera, all of which are wired into a private network.

Michaels's devotion to gadgetry may be extreme, but communications technology is as much a part of campus life today as classes, coffee breaks, and the library. Many campuses guarantee fast network access, and some, like Pittsburgh's Carnegie Mellon, have already gone wireless.

For keeping in touch with friends and classmates, *instant messaging* (*IM*) is replacing e-mail and phone calls. Because it's real-time and instant, IM tells you who else is connected at a given moment. Allowing the immediate exchange of messages and documents among networked "others," IM is a great means of staying connected with family and friends. As for entertainment, although Napster may be dead, file sharing is still alive and well. Sites like Morpheus <www.morpheussoftware.net> and Kazaa <www.kazaa.com> post loads of fun stuff—TV hits, software, movies, and music—for downloading at home or school. Both video games for solitary play—such as Snood, a puzzle game—and fantasy games played with others have become a popular activity at so-called LAN (for local area network) parties.

Living quarters are also showing the effects of networking. On many campuses, dorms are enjoying renewed attention because they're usually wired (thereby forcing off-campus houses to remodel and get wired if they want to compete for tech-savvy students). "I considered moving off campus," says a University of Chicago junior, "but then I realized I'd lose my Internet access. So I dropped that idea!"

What about overloading a school's information system, especially with an upsurge of nonacademic applications? You might be surprised. Administrators at the University of California at San Diego actually encourage students to network in full force. In fact, they're handing out wireless PDAs in the hope that students will use them to IM one another, check e-mail, and surf the Web. What's in it for the school? University officials want to see how students learn to use technology so that they can design classes to attract technology-savvy students.

Local and Wide Area Networks Networked systems may be either local or wide area networks. Computers may be linked statewide or even nationwide through telephone lines, microwave, or satellite communications, as in a **wide area network (WAN).** Firms can lease lines from communications vendors or maintain private WANs. Wal-Mart, for example, depends heavily on a private satellite network that links more than 2,000 retail stores to its Bentonville, Arkansas, headquarters.

wide area network (WAN)
Network of computers and workstations located far from one another and linked by telephone wires, microwave, or by satellite

Limited internal networks may link all of a firm's nearby computers, as in a **local area network (LAN).** Computers within a building, for example, can be linked by cabling (fiber-optic, coaxial, or twisted wire) or by wireless technology. Internally networked computers share processing duties, software, storage areas, and data. On cable TV's *Home Shopping Network* <www.hsn.com>, hundreds of operators are united by a LAN for entering call-in orders. The arrangement requires only one computer system with one database and software system.

local area network (LAN)
Network of computers and workstations, usually within a company, that are linked together by cable

Wireless Networks Wireless technologies use airborne electronic signals for linking network appliances. In addition to mobile phones, wireless technology extends to laptops, hand-held computers, and applications in cars (including Internet access and music players, map terminals, and game machines). Businesses benefit by avoiding webs of wires crisscrossing facilities. Ford, for example, uses an innovative industrial information system—WhereNet—for tracking inventory by means of identification tags that transmit radio waves. Antennas mounted on the factory ceiling receive transmissions and send information to a central computer that locates tags in the plant. The system saves time and money by coordinating the delivery of hundreds of parts to assembly lines.[26]

Client-Server Systems An obvious advantage of networks is resource sharing—and thus avoiding costly duplication. In a **client-server network,** clients are the users of services. They are the points of entry, usually laptop or desktop computers or workstations. The server provides the services shared by users.

client-server network
Information-technology system consisting of clients (users) that are electronically linked to share network resources provided by a server, such as a host

Self-Check Questions 7–9

*You should now be able to answer Self-Check Questions 7–9**

7. MULTIPLE CHOICE All of the following are *components of the information system* **except** [select one]: **(a)** hardware, including a central processing unit; **(b)** software, including system and application programs; **(c)** control, including arrangements for security; **(d)** a centralized database that includes all of a firm's data files; **(e)** the people at various levels who use and prepare the system.

8. TRUE/FALSE If you're preparing a professional presentation for a business audience, an information system can be helpful by providing *application programs* such as word processing, electronic spreadsheets, and computer graphics software.

9. MULTIPLE CHOICE Suppose your pickup-and-delivery vehicles cover the countryside making trips to and from customers' facilities. Which of the following telecommunications devices and characteristics would be most helpful for continuous tracking of truck locations? [select one]: **(a)** a wide area network (WAN); **(b)** fiber-optic cable; **(c)** a client-server network; **(d)** a paging system; **(e)** a global positioning system (GPS).

* Answers to Self-Check Questions 7–9 can be found on p. AN-11.

Larger and more sophisticated than your PC, a powerful minicomputer at the network hub may be the server for client PCs in an office network. As a *file server,* the minicomputer has a large-capacity disk for storing the database and word-processing, graphics, and spreadsheet programs used by all network PCs. As a *print server,* it controls the printer, stores printing requests from client PCs, and routes jobs as the printer becomes available. As the *fax server,* it receives and sends and controls fax activities. Thus, an entire system of users needs only one disk drive, one printer, and one fax. Internet computing uses the client-server arrangement.

Continued from page 455

Remote Damage Control

As it flies from Tokyo to San Francisco, the jet engines on an Airbus 340 are monitored and readings are collected by onboard computers transmitted to a GE monitoring station in Cincinnati, Ohio. By detecting impending component failures, airlines can avoid not only expensive repairs, but also flight diversions and delays. An aircraft engine costs $5 million to $10 million, and remote monitoring also helps with maintenance scheduling. Each engine needs an overhaul—costing between $500,000 and $2 million—every three to five years. Using software that runs statistical tests on monitored data, GE's Engine Services team can predict when engines will deteriorate to the point at which servicing is justified. By forecasting how many engines will need repair, service teams can anticipate how many spare engines and parts will be needed, thereby avoiding delays from shortages and the costs of storing too many expensive extras. In factories, too, remote monitoring tools are used for advanced maintenance programs on pumps, motors, machining centers, assembly lines, and automated painting systems.

The goal of remote monitoring is early detection. In the trucking industry, wireless communications combine data from onboard sensors with real-time data gathered from global positioning systems (GPSs). Detecting low pressure in tire number seven of a fleet truck in Montana, a dispatcher in Chicago may signal the driver that a repair station is located 15 miles ahead, thus avoiding tire failure and lost road time. Diagnostics also monitor other potential breakdowns—low coolant, alternator failure, engine oil or lube depletion, electrical system deterioration.

There will soon be similar applications for consumer products, not only for household appliances—washers, dryers, refrigerators, and air conditioners—but also for cars and home alarm systems. Studded with computing chips, tiny sensors, and communications ports, your refrigeration compressor will detect and report potential failures before breakdown spoils a week's worth of food. GE, Whirlpool, Samsung, IBM, and several carmakers are working on systems that will detect and report maintenance problems over the Internet.

Whatever the application, the key is the diagnostics center, including data inflow and the software needed to extract useful information from it. Specialists must create the diagnostics software that receives data, discovers and stores correlations among variables, interprets the data, and reports findings in a format that's useful to maintenance personnel. As applications expand, don't be surprised if signals from your new car, television set, or refrigerator are being monitored at some diagnostics center far, far away.

Questions for Discussion

1. What role, if any, does human judgment play in GE's remote monitoring diagnostics system?
2. What are the financial risks, if any, in subscribing to the GE system? What are risks of *not* subscribing?
3. Consider the kinds of software that might be useful in remote monitoring and diagnosis. What kinds of software might be needed, and what functions would it have to perform?

4. Do you foresee any potential ethical issues in the use of remote monitoring and diagnostics? Explain.
5. Recall some equipment and conveniences on which you rely in your everyday activities. What are some potential applications for remote monitoring and diagnostics?

Summary of Learning Objectives

1. *Explain why businesses must manage* information, *and show how computer systems and communication technologies have revolutionized* information management.

Every firm's activities are linked to information systems, and most treat information as an asset. Thus, they have **information managers,** just as they have production, marketing, and finance managers. **Information management** arranges a firm's information resources to support performance and outcomes. The challenge is to turn a flood of **data,** or raw facts and figures, into manageable **information,** which is the useful interpretation of data.

One response to this challenge is the growth of the **information system (IS)**—a system for transforming raw data into information and making it useful to decision makers. IS managers decide upon what information they need, gather data, and provide the technology to convert it into information. They also ensure that information flows only to people who need it. The role of IS is growing because of developments in electronic technologies that allow faster and broader flows of information and communications. At one time, IS applications were narrow in scope and technically oriented. But managers soon began using IS to analyze management problems, and it is now crucial in developing strategy.

With intensified competition and expanded global and e-business operations, companies need more advanced data communication networks and new **electronic information technologies (EITs)**—IS applications based on telecommunications technologies. EITs use networks of devices (such as computers and satellites) to communicate information and enhance productivity by serving two functions: (1) by providing coordination and communication within the firm; and (2) by speeding up transactions with other firms

Six innovations in EIT are widely used today: (1) The **fax machine** permits written communication over long distances by transmitting and receiving digitized images of documents, drawings, and photographs over telephone lines. (2) **Voice mail** is a system for receiving and delivering incoming phone calls. (3) **Electronic mail** (or **e-mail**) transmits letters, reports, and other information (including graphics and videos) between computers. (4) **Electronic conferencing** allows groups of people to communicate simultaneously from various locations via telephone or e-mail. With *data-conferencing,* people can work simultaneously on the same document. *Videoconferencing* allows participants to see one another on a video screen. (5) Collaborative work by groups is made easier by **groupware**—software that connects members for e-mail distribution, electronic meetings, and other functions. (6) With *digital information services,* outside information can be linked to a firm's electronic network and accessed from every workstation.

2. *Identify and briefly describe three elements of* data communication networks*—the Internet, the World Wide Web, and intranets.*

Data communication networks are global networks that use telecommunication systems to carry streams of digital data back and forth quickly and economically. The largest communications network, the **Internet** (or "the Net"), is a system of networks serving millions of computers, offering a vast range of information, and providing communication flows among more than 170,000 separate networks. It allows PCs virtually anywhere to be linked and has also become the most important e-mail system in the world. Individuals can't connect directly, but monthly usage fees permit them to subscribe to it via an **Internet service provider (ISP)**—a commercial firm that maintains a permanent connection to the Net and sells temporary connections.

The **World Wide Web** (WWW or "the Web") lets users around the world communicate with little effort. The Web supports standards for storing, retrieving, formatting, and displaying information. It provides the "common language" that makes the Internet available to a general audience and not just technical users. To access a Web site, the user specifies the *Uniform Resource Locator* (*URL*) that points to the resource's unique Web address. Each site opens with a *home page*—a screen that may include graphics, sound, and visuals to introduce the site. Additional *pages* detail the sponsor's products and other useful information. A *Webmaster* is usually responsible for maintaining an organization's site. Large sites are managed and maintained by dedicated computers known as **Web servers.**

A Web **browser**—the software that permits the user to access information on the Web—runs on the user's PC and supports the graphics and linking needed to navigate the Web. Companies such as Yahoo! maintain *directories* of Web content where preclassified lists of sites can be located and retrieved. A **search engine** scans for millions of Web pages without preclassifying them into a directory.

Intranets allow users to browse internal sites containing a firm's information. Only employees can get in by penetrating electronic **firewalls**—hardware and software security systems that can't be breached by outsiders. **Extranets** give outsiders limited access to a firm's internal information system. The most common application allows buyers to enter a seller's system to examine products. Industrial suppliers are often linked to customers' intranets so that they can see production schedules and prepare supplies as needed.

3. *Describe five* new options for organizational design *that have emerged from the rapid growth of information technologies.*

(1) *Leaner organizations*: Because today's networked firm can link information among employees and customers, fewer people can do more work than before. Reductions in middle-management positions and layers of structure are possible because information networks provide direct communications between top managers and lower level workers.

(2) *More flexible operations*: Electronic networks allow firms to offer greater variety and faster delivery. Thanks to **mass-customization,** many products can be custom ordered with a choice of features and next-day delivery. Although companies produce in large volumes, each unit features variations and options preferred by each customer. Flexible production and fast delivery depend on a network that coordinates all the activities necessary to make quick adjustments in the production process.

(3) *Increased collaboration*: Collaboration is on the rise because networked systems make it cheaper and easier to connect people. Aided by intranets, companies are learning that complex problems can be solved by means of collaboration, and in networked organizations, decisions that were once made by individuals are now shared among people and departments. Networked systems also foster collaboration between firms, creating *virtual companies* in which each partner contributes different skills and resources to more competitive operations.

(4) *Greater independence of company and workplace*: Networked organizations have made the geographic separation of workplace and headquarters more common. Employees no longer work solely at the office or the factory; nor are all operations performed at one location.

(5) *Improved management processes*: At one time, upper level managers didn't concern themselves with detailed information that filtered upward. Workplace management was delegated to middle and first-line managers. But with networked systems, instantaneous information is accessible in convenient formats. Thus, more upper level managers use it routinely for planning, leading, directing, and controlling operations. A popular form of networked systems is **enterprise resource planning (ERP)**—a large IS for integrating the activities of all of a company's units. Because the system is supported by a shared database, everyone gets the same updated information when transactions occur.

4. *Identify and briefly describe the* main elements of an information system.

An *information system* (IS) is a group of interconnected devices that can exchange information from different locations. *Networking*—connecting these devices—lets computers exchange data quickly and easily. A key component of the IS is its **computer network**—all the computer and information technology devices that work together to drive the flow of digital information. Every system has six components:

(1) *Hardware*: IS **hardware** refers to the physical components of a system. Data is entered by an **input device,** such as a keyboard or mouse. When data have been input, an electronic signal goes to the **central processing unit (CPU),** where the actual processing takes place. The data go first to **main memory,** where the CPU stores the programs it needs to operate. The CPU then searches its memory for instructions—**programs**—on what to do with the data. Having followed the appropriate instructions, the CPU sends the results into one or more **output devices,** such as a video monitor or printer.

(2) *Software*: Hardware needs programs—**software**—to function. There are two types of software programs: (i) **System programs** tell the computer what resources to use and how. For example, an operating system program tells the computer how and when to transfer data from secondary to primary storage and return it as information to the user. (ii) **Application programs** are software packages written by others. Each type of application (such as word processing or Web browsing) uses a program that meets that need. An important software development is the **graphical user interface (GUI)**—the user-friendly visual display that helps users choose applications. Typically, the screen displays numerous **icons** (small images), and the user directs the computer by moving a pointing device (usually an arrow) to activate the desired icon.

(3) *Control*: Control ensures that the system is operating according to specific procedures. These include guidelines for operating the system, the responsibilities of personnel, and plans for handling system failure. *Privacy invasion* occurs when intruders (hackers) gain unauthorized access, either to steal something or to tamper with data. To protect against intrusion, companies use such security devices as *firewalls.* To prevent unauthorized access to information, many rely on *encryption*—secret numerical coding to scramble the characters in a message during transmission.

(4) *Database*: All computer processing is the processing of data. Computers convert data into information by organizing the data into meaningful information. Within a computer system, chunks of data—numbers, words, and sentences—are stored in a series of collections called *fields, records,* and *files.* Together, data files constitute a **database**—a central, organized collection of related data. All data processing is carried out by *programs*—instructions that tell a system to perform certain functions.

Most business application programs fall into one of four categories: (i) **Word-processing programs** allow users to store, edit, display, and print documents. (ii) **Electronic spreadsheets** spread data across and down the page in rows and columns. Users enter data, including formulas, and the computer automatically performs the necessary calculations. (iii) **Database management programs** can store, sort, and search data and integrate a single piece into different files. (iv) **Computer graphics programs** convert numeric and character data into pictorial information such as charts and graphs. They include **presentation graphics software,** which assembles graphics for visual displays, slides, video, and even sound splices for presentations. Computer graphics capabilities extend to stand-alone programs for artists, designers, and special effects designers. **Desktop publishing** packages combine word-processing and graphics to produce typeset-quality text enhanced by visual effects.

(5) *People*: IS people fall into four user groups, including the **knowledge worker**—the employee whose job involves the use of information and knowledge as raw materials. Because they work on different kinds of problems, top managers, middle managers, knowledge workers, and first-line managers have different information needs. First-line (or operational) managers need information to oversee the day-to-day details of departments or projects. Knowledge workers need information for technical projects. Middle managers need summaries and analyses for setting department or project goals. Top managers analyze trends in the economy, the business environment, and overall company performance in order to conduct companywide, long-range planning. Each business *function*—marketing, human resources, accounting, production, finance—also has its own information requirements.

(6) *Telecommunications*: Today's information systems include not only computers but also **multimedia communication systems**—connected networks of communication appliances (faxes, televisions, cell phones, printers, and so forth) that may also be linked by satellite with other networks. The use of personal communications devices is also increasing. *Global positioning systems* (*GPSs*) use satellite transmissions to track the geographic locations of targets. *Personal digital assistants* (*PDAs*) are tiny hand-held computers with wireless telecommunications capabilities. *Paging systems* and *cellular telephones* provide instant connections within communications networks. *Communication channels,* such as microwave and satellite systems, are the media that make both wired and wireless transmissions possible.

One way to organize network components is according to *geographic scope.* Computers may be linked statewide or even nationwide through telephone lines, microwave, or satellite communications, as in a **wide area network (WAN).** Internal networks covering limited distances may link nearby computers in a **local area network (LAN).** Wireless technologies use airborne transmission of electronic signals instead of wires. In a **client-server network,** clients are the users of services—points of entry from laptops, desktops, or workstations. The server provides the services shared by users.

5. *Discuss different information-system* application programs *that are available for users at various organizational levels.*

System requirements for knowledge workers vary because they often face specialized problems. IS applications for middle- or top-level management decisions must also be flexible because they depend on a broader range of information collected from both external and internal sources. There are seven categories of IS applications:

(1) *Transaction processing systems*: **Transaction pro cessing systems (TPS)** are applications for daily transac tions (such as customer order taking). The TPS for first-leve activities is well defined and follows the same steps on al transactions.

(2) *Systems for knowledge workers and office applica tions*: IS systems require people in two different capacities (i) *IS knowledge workers* include systems analysts and appli cation or systems programmers. *Systems analysts* decide or types of computers and on how to set up links to form a net work. *Programmers* write the software instructions that tel computers what to do. *Systems programmers* ensure that a system can handle the requests made by application pro grams. (ii) *Operations personnel (data workers)*: **System operations personnel** make sure that the right program are run in the correct sequence and monitor equipment t ensure proper operation.

(3) *Knowledge-level and office systems*: Knowledge-leve systems include the following: (i) By simulating real product and displaying them in three-dimensional graphics **computer-aided design (CAD)** creates faster designs at lowe cost than manual modeling methods. With *rapid prototypin (RP)*, CAD transfers instructions to a computer-controlle machine that builds a prototype. (ii) **Computer-aided manu facturing (CAM)** is used to design equipment, facilities, an layouts for better flows and productivity. (iii) *Computer opera tions control* refers to any system for managing daily produc tion activities.

(4) *Management information systems*: **Managemen information systems (MIS)** support managers by provic ing reports, schedules, plans, and budgets. Each manager information activities vary according to his or her func tional area (for example, accounting or marketing) an management level.

(5) *Decision support systems*: Middle- and top-level mar agers can use a **decision support system (DSS)**—an inte active system that finds and presents information to suppo the decision-making process.

(6) *Executive support systems*: An **executive support sy tem (ESS)** is specially designed for instant access by uppe level managers. Using a wide range of internal and extern information sources, an ESS helps make top-manageme decisions and solve executive-level problems.

(7) *Artificial intelligence and expert systems*: **Artifici intelligence (AI)** is the construction of computer systems t imitate human behavior—systems that perform physic tasks, use thought processes, and learn. **Robotics**—combi ing computers with industrial robots that can perform repe itive tasks—is a form of AI. Another form, the **expert sy tem,** imitates the thought processes of human experts in particular field by incorporating the rules that experts app to specific types of problems.

KEY TERMS

information manager (p. 456)
information management (p. 456)
data (p. 456)
information (p. 456)
information system (IS) (p. 456)
electronic information technologies (EIT) (p. 458)

fax machine (p. 458)
voice mail (p. 458)
electronic mail (e-mail) (p. 458)
electronic conferencing (p. 458)
groupware (p. 459)
data communication network (p. 460)
Internet (p. 460)
Internet service provider (ISP) (p. 461)
World Wide Web (p. 461)
Web server (p. 461)
browser (p. 461)
search engine (p. 461)
intranet (p. 462)
firewall (p. 462)
extranet (p. 462)
mass-customization (p. 463)
enterprise resource planning (ERP) (p. 466)
knowledge worker (p. 466)
transaction processing system (TPS) (p. 468)
system operations personnel (p. 468)
computer-aided design (CAD) (p. 470)
computer-aided manufacturing (CAM) (p. 470)
management information system (MIS) (p. 470)
decision support system (DSS) (p. 471)
executive support system (ESS) (p. 471)
artificial intelligence (AI) (p. 471)
robotics (p. 472)
expert system (p. 472)
computer network (p. 472)
hardware (p. 472)
input device (p. 472)
central processing unit (CPU) (p. 472)
main memory (p. 472)
program (p. 472)
output device (p. 473)
software (p. 473)
system program (p. 473)
application program (p. 473)
graphical user interface (GUI) (p. 474)
icon (p. 474)
database (p. 475)
word-processing program (p. 475)
electronic spreadsheet (p. 475)
database management program (p. 475)
computer graphics program (p. 475)
presentation graphics software (p. 476)
desktop publishing (p. 476)
multimedia communication system (p. 476)
wide area network (WAN) (p. 478)
local area network (LAN) (p. 478)
client-server network (p. 478)

QUESTIONS AND EXERCISES

Questions for Review

1. Why must a business manage information as a resource?
2. How can an electronic conferencing system increase productivity and efficiency?
3. Why do the four levels of user groups in an organization need different kinds of information from the IS?
4. In what ways are local area networks (LANs) different from or similar to wide area networks (WANs)?
5. What are the main types of electronic information technologies being applied in business information systems?

Questions for Analysis

6. Give two examples (other than those in this chapter) for each of the major types of business application programs.
7. Describe three or four activities in which you regularly engage that might be made easier by multimedia technology.
8. Give three examples (other than those in this chapter) of how a company can become leaner by adopting a networked IS.

Application Exercises

9. Describe the IS at your school. Identify its components and architecture. What features either promote or inhibit collaboration?
10. Visit a small business in your community to investigate the ways it's using communication technologies and the ways it plans to use them in the future. Prepare a report for class presentation.

Building Your Business Skills

THE ART AND SCIENCE OF POINT-AND-CLICK RESEARCH

This exercise enhances the following SCANS workplace competencies: demonstrating basic skills, demonstrating thinking skills, exhibiting interpersonal skills, working with information, applying system knowledge, and using technology.

Goal

To introduce students to World Wide Web search sites.

Background

In a recent survey of nearly 2,000 Web users, two-thirds said they used the Web to obtain work-related information. With an estimated 320 million pages of information on the Web, the challenge for business users is fairly obvious: how to find what they're looking for.

Method

You'll need a computer and access to the World Wide Web to complete this exercise.

Step 1

Get together with three classmates and decide on a business-related research topic. Choose a topic that interests you—for example, "Business Implications of the Year 2000 Census," "Labor Disputes in Professional Sports," or "Marketing Music Lessons and Instruments to Parents of Young Children."

Step 2

Search the following sites for information on your topic (dividing them among group members to speed the process):

- Yahoo! <www.yahoo.com>
- Hotbot <www.hotbot.lycos.com>
- Alta Vista <www.altavista.com>
- Excite <www.excite.com>
- Infoseek <www.infoseek.go.com>
- Lycos <www.lycos.com>
- Metacrawler <www.metacrawler.com>
- Dogpile <www.dogpile.com>
- Ask Jeeves <www.askjeeves.com>
- Northern Light <www.northernlight.com>

Take notes as you search so that you can explain your findings to other group members.

Step 3

Working as a group, answer the following questions about your collective search:

1. Which sites were the easiest to use?
2. Which sites offered the most helpful results? What specific factors made these sites better than the others?
3. Which sites offered the least helpful results? What were the problems?
4. Why is it important to learn the special code words or symbols, called operators, that target a search? (Operators are words like AND, OR, and NOT that narrow search queries. For example, using AND in a search tells the system that *all* words must appear in the results—American AND Management AND Association.)

Follow-Up Questions

Research the differences between search engines *and search* directories. *Then place the sites listed in Step 2 in the proper category. Did you find search engines or directories more helpful in this exercise?*

1. Why is it important to learn how to use the search-site "Help" function?
2. Based on your personal career goals, how do you think that mastering Web-research techniques might help you in the future?
3. How has the Web changed the nature of business research?

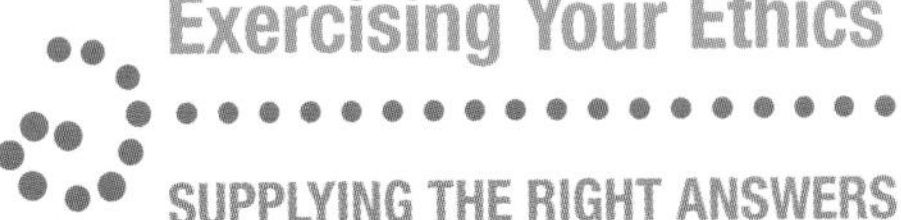

Exercising Your Ethics

SUPPLYING THE RIGHT ANSWERS

The Situation

Networked systems facilitate information sharing among companies and often involve sensitive customer data. This exercise asks you to consider ethical issues that might arise when firms are developing information technologies for use in networked systems.

The Dilemma

Home Sweet Home-e (HSH-e) was an e-business start-up that sold virtually everything in home furnishings—from linens and towels to cleaning supplies and furniture. From home computers, HSH-e members could shop in virtual storefronts, chat online with other shoppers, talk live with virtual store clerks, and pay electronically at a one-stop Web site. In reality, HSH-e was a *virtual store:* a network of numerous suppliers located around the country, each specializing in a particular line of goods. The network was connected by a centrally controlled information technology that HSH-e developed, owned, and operated. Once a customer's order was placed, suppliers instantaneously received information on what to ship, where to ship it, and how much to charge.

HSH-e chose only suppliers who guaranteed fast, reliable deliveries and promised to supply HSH-e exclusively. The linen supplier, for example, could not supply products to other home-furnishings e-businesses. In return, the supplier was guaranteed all HSH-e orders for linen products. As HSH-e grew, suppliers stood to gain more business and prosper in an expanding e-tail industry. As it turns out, some prospective suppliers refused to join the network and others in the network were discontinued by HSH-e for failing to expand fast enough to keep up with demand.

Questions for Discussion

1. For a potential HSH-e supplier of a specialized product line, what are the ethical issues in this situation?
2. Consider past suppliers who have been discontinued or have withdrawn from the HSH-e network. Do they face any ethical issues involving HSH-e customers? Involving HSH-e operations? Involving other HSH-e suppliers?
3. Suppose you work at HSH-e and discover a nonnetwork supplier that is more attractive than one of the company's existing suppliers. What ethical considerations do you face in deciding whether or not to replace an existing supplier?

Crafting your Business Plan

GETTING WIRED INTO BETTER INFORMATION

The Purpose of the Assignment

1. To acquaint students with issues involving information systems that a sample firm faces in developing its business plan, in the framework of *Business PlanPro* (*BPP*) software package.
2. To demonstrate how communications technologies, the Internet, and database considerations can be integrated as components in the *BPP* planning environment.

Assignment

After reading Chapter 16 in the textbook, open the BPP *software and look around for information about plans for computer and communications technologies as they apply to a sample firm, a travel agency called* Adventure Travel International (ATI). *To find* Adventure Travel, *do the following:*

Open the *Business PlanPro*. If it asks if you want to "create a new business plan" or "open an existing plan," select "create a new business plan" (even though you are not going to create a plan at this time). You will then be taken to the *Business PlanPro EasyPlan Wizard.* Click on the option entitled **Research It.** You will then be presented with a new list of options, including **Sample Plan Browser.** After clicking on **Sample Plan Browser,** go down the alphabetical list of sample plans and double-click on **Travel Agency—Adventure**; which is the location for ATI. The screen that you are looking at is the introduction page for the ATI business plan. Next, scroll down from this page until you reach the **Table of Contents** for the ATI business plan.

Now respond to the following items:

1. How have the Internet and related communications technologies changed the travel agency industry? [Sites to see in *BPP* for this question: On the Table of Contents page, click in turn on each of the following: **3.2 Competitive Comparison** and **4.3.1 Business Participants.**]
2. How might databases be used to advantage at ATI? [Sites to see in *BPP:* On the Table of Contents page, click in turn on each of the following: **3.3 Sales Literature, 3.5 Technology, 4.1 Market Segmentation, 5.0 Strategy and Implementation Summary,** and **5.3.5 Marketing Programs.**]
3. What are the advantages in ATI's Computerized Reservation System? [Sites to see in *BPP:* From the Table of Contents page, click in turn on each of the following: **3.5 Technology** and **4.3.2 Distributing a Service.**]
4. How can ATI's distribution system benefit from the Web? After exploring the ATI plan, what suggestions would you make about using the Web? [Sites to see in *BPP:* In the Table of Contents page, click on **5.3.4 Distribution Strategy** and **5.5 Strategic Alliances.**]

Video Exercise

SPACE AGE INFORMATION SYSTEMS: BOEING SATELLITE SYSTEMS

Learning Objectives

The purpose of this video is to help you

1. Understand why a business must manage information.
2. Consider the role of information systems in an organization.
3. Understand how information systems and communications technology contribute to efficiency and performance.

Synopsis

The world's leading manufacturer of commercial communications satellites, Boeing Satellite Systems is a wholly owned subsidiary of Boeing and serves customers in 14 countries. Boeing's information system collects and analyzes data from all departments and then disseminates the results to help management make decisions for boosting performance, productivity, and competitiveness. The chief information officer also oversees security precautions, disaster recovery plans, and procedures for safeguarding valuable data. In addition, each of the company's more than 8,000 employees is equipped with a personal computer or laptop that can also serve as a television to receive broadcasts about company activities.

Discussion Questions

1. *For analysis:* What role do information systems play at Boeing Satellite Systems?
2. *For analysis:* What are some of the ways in which IT can improve productivity and performance at Boeing Satellite Systems?
3. *For application:* What potential problems might Boeing Satellite Systems have encountered when introducing computer kiosks into factory operations?
4. *For application:* In addition to scenes of Boeing-made satellite launches, what else should the company broadcast over employee computers? Why?
5. *For debate:* Should Boeing Satellite Systems try to prevent potential abuses by using software for monitoring employee use of PCs and laptops? Support your position.

Online Exploration

Visit the Boeing Satellite Systems Web site at <www.boeing.com/satellite> and search for more information about the firm's state-of-the-art integration and test facility. Also browse the site to see what the company says about its use of information systems and communication technology. Why would the company discuss technology in detail on a public Web site? What specific benefits of IS does Boeing Satellite Systems highlight? Why are these benefits important to customers who buy satellites?

CHAPTER 17

Understanding Principles of Accounting

After reading this chapter, you should be able to:

1. Explain the role of accountants and distinguish between the kinds of work done by *public* and *private accountants*.
2. Discuss the *CPA Vision Project* and explain how the CPA profession is changing.
3. Explain how the following concepts are used in accounting: the *accounting equation* and *double-entry accounting*.
4. Describe the three basic *financial statements* and show how they reflect the activity and financial condition of a business.
5. Explain the key standards and principles for reporting financial statements.
6. Show how computing key *financial ratios* can help in analyzing the financial strengths of a business.
7. Explain some of the special issues facing accountants at firms that do international business.

Humpty-Dumpty Time at Arthur Andersen

Rarely does a single event shake a whole industry as dramatically as Arthur Andersen's failed attempts to cover up the role of accounting in iding and abetting the dubious and self-destructive ctivities of oil-trading giant Enron. With employee and tockholder losses totaling tens f billions of dollars, the Enron reakdown certainly caused ıonumental damage to this ountry's business psyche. But ı many ways, it's really small tuff compared with the wide-pread failure of confidence ıat Andersen has spawned. As ınron's auditors, Andersen's PAs were supposed to assess ınron's financial status, evalu-te its financial statements, and eport on its adherence to gener-lly accepted accounting prac-ces. Had it done what it 'as supposed to, how could ndersen have failed to see ırough the bookkeeping sleight f hand that soon led to Enron's mammoth collapse? nd what if Andersen *did* foresee the collapse? Vhat if its accountants had actually *helped* Houston-ased Enron hide its financial shortfalls and ethical ıortcomings?

In March 2002, the Department of Justice (DOJ) led obstruction-of-justice charges against Andersen, ccusing the firm of shredding tons of Enron docu-ıents that should have been preserved as legal ecords. Andersen executives denied that any crimes ad been committed. Prosecutors argued that months efore Enron's collapse, Andersen knew that its econd-biggest client was in an accounting mess. To nplement damage control, Chicago-based Andersen xecutives moved to Houston, but it was too late. "It as Humpty Dumpty time for Arthur Andersen," says .S. Prosecutor Samuel Buell. "They brought all the ng's horses and all the king's men, and they couldn't ıt Humpty together again. Enron's accounting was ade up of eggshells."

Meanwhile, a pall of cynicism has fallen over the ccounting industry: If it can happen at Andersen, hat's to keep it from happening to anyone else in the ccounting industry? Such questions lead, at best, to a ofound skepticism about the profession's methods and mores, and, at worst, to further questions of possible corruption. As of mid-2002, suspicious investors were questioning the accounting practices of thousands of firms, and people are still extremely skeptical about the honesty of independent auditors who are supposed to keep clients honest. Without unbiased audits, how much can investors know about a company's financial health and trust its financial reports? Long among the world's most trusted professionals, accountants have been regarded as providers of valid information on corporate performance and as watchdogs of the public interest. Almost single-handedly, Andersen has changed all that. The public is suspicious. If a firm with Andersen's reputation can't be trusted, how much confidence can be placed in the paperwork spewing from anywhere else in Corporate America? Loss of confidence—on the part of investors, employees, retirees, unions, and government—has contributed to a plunging stock market, with losses in the hundreds of billions since Enron's demise. Corporate mischief and the willingness of accountants to cover it up have done untold damage to public trust. "We all too often forget," says one securities analyst, "that markets depend on trust to operate. Enron and the . . . corporate scandals that followed have all but destroyed that trust. What it all means is that the U.S. must get its house in order and fast."

Our opening story continues on page 510.

"They brought all the king's horse's and all the king's men, and they couldn't put Humpty together again."

~U.S. Prosecutor Samuel Buell,
ON ENRON EXECUTIVES' LAST-DITCH EFFORT TO CLEAN UP THEIR ACCOUNTING MESS

What Is Accounting and Who Uses Accounting Information?

accounting
Comprehensive system for collecting, analyzing, and communicating financial information

bookkeeping
Recording of accounting transactions

accounting information system (AIS)
Organized means by which financial information is identified, measured, recorded, and retained for use in accounting statements and management reports

Accounting is a comprehensive system for collecting, analyzing, and communi cating financial information. It measures business performance and translate the findings into information for management decisions. Accountants also pre pare performance reports for owners, the public, and regulatory agencies. T perform these functions, they keep records of taxes paid, income received, an expenses incurred, and they assess the effects of these transactions on busines activities. By sorting and analyzing thousands of such transactions, accountant can determine how well a business is being managed and how financially stron it is.[1] **Bookkeeping** is just one phase of accounting—the recording of transac tions. Accounting itself is much more comprehensive than bookkeeping becaus it involves more than merely recording information.

Because businesses engage in thousands of transactions, ensuring consis tent, dependable financial information is mandatory. This is the job of th **accounting information system (AIS)**—an organized procedure for identifyin measuring, recording, and retaining financial information so that it can be use in accounting statements and management reports. The system includes all c the people, reports, computers, procedures, and resources that are needed t compile financial transactions.[2]

There are numerous users of accounting information:

- *Business managers* use it to develop goals and plans, set budgets, and evaluate future prospects.
- *Employees and unions* use it to plan for and receive compensation and such benefits as health care, vacation time, and retirement pay.
- *Investors and creditors* use it to estimate returns to stockholders, determine growth prospects, and decide whether a firm is a good credit risk.
- *Tax authorities* use it to plan for tax inflows, determine the tax liabilities of individuals and businesses, and ensure that correct amounts are paid on time.
- *Government regulatory agencies* rely on it to fulfill their duties toward the public. The Securities and Exchange Commission (SEC), for example, requires firms to file financial disclosures so that potential investors have valid information about their financial status.

Who Are Accountants and What Do They Do

controller
Person who manages all of a firm's accounting activities (chief accounting officer)

At the head of the AIS is the **controller,** who manages a firm's accounting acti ities. As chief accounting officer, the controller ensures that the AIS provid the reports and statements needed for planning, controlling, decision makin and other management activities. This range of activities requires differe types of accounting specialists. In this section, we begin by distinguishi between the two main fields of accounting: *financial* and *managerial.* Then v discuss the different functions and activities of *certified public accountants* a *private accountants.*

Financial Versus Managerial Accounting

In any company, two fields of accounting—financial and managerial—can be d tinguished by the users they serve. It is both convenient and accurate to classi users as those outside the company and those inside the company. We can u this same distinction to classify accounting systems as *financial* or *managerial.*

Financial Accounting A firm's **financial accounting system** is concerned with external information users: consumer groups, unions, stockholders, and government agencies. It regularly prepares income statements and balance sheets as well as other financial reports published for shareholders and the public. All of these documents focus on the activities of the company as a whole rather than on individual departments or divisions.[4]

financial accounting system
Field of accounting concerned with external users of a company's financial information

Managerial Accounting **Managerial** (or **management accounting**) serves internal users. Managers at all levels need information to make departmental decisions, monitor projects, and plan future activities. Other employees also need accounting information. Engineers need to know certain costs in order to make product or operations improvements. To set performance goals, salespeople need past sales data by geographic region. Purchasing agents use information on materials costs to negotiate terms with suppliers.

managerial (or **management**) **accounting system**
Field of accounting that serves internal users of a company's financial information

Certified Public Accountants

Certified public accountants (CPAs) offer accounting services to the public. They are licensed by the state after passing an exam prepared by the American Institute of Certified Public Accountants (AICPA) <www.aicpa.org>, which also provides technical support and discipline in matters of ethics.

certified public accountant (CPA)
Accountant licensed by the state and offering services to the public

Professional Practice Whereas some CPAs work as individual practitioners, many form partnerships or professional corporations. There are more than 40,000 CPA firms in the United States, but one-half of the total revenues go to the four biggest firms: Deloitte Tohmatsu Touche <www.deloitte.com>, Ernst & Young <www.ey.com>, KPMG LLP <www.kpmg.com>, and Price Waterhouse-Coopers <www.pwcglobal.com>. In addition to their prominence in the United States, international operations are important for all four of these companies.

CPA Services Virtually all CPA firms, whether large or small, provide auditing, tax, and management services. Larger firms earn up to 60 percent of their revenue from auditing services, and consulting services constitute another growth area. Smaller firms earn most of their income from tax and management services.

Auditing An **audit** examines a company's AIS to determine whether financial reports reliably represent its operations.[5] Organizations must provide audit reports when applying for loans or selling stock or when going through a major restructuring. Auditors ensure that clients' accounting systems follow **generally accepted accounting principles (GAAP)**—rules and procedures governing the content and form of financial reports. GAAP is formulated by the Financial Accounting Standards Board (FASB) of the AICPA and should be used to determine whether a firm has controls to prevent errors and fraud.[6] Ultimately, the auditor will certify whether the client's reports comply with GAAP.

audit
Systematic examination of a company's accounting system to determine whether its financial reports fairly represent its operations

generally accepted accounting principles (GAAP)
Accepted rules and procedures governing the content and form of financial reports

Sometimes, however, companies ignore GAAP, and sometimes auditors fail to disclose violations. In the WorldCom accounting scandal of 2002, the telecommunications giant violated the most basic of GAAPs by disguising (hiding) operating expenses and thereby overstating profits in its annual reports. Again, Arthur Andersen was the responsible auditor and has been roundly criticized for failing to report the alleged fraud. Some observers even suspect Andersen of taking part in the deception. Andersen's erroneous certification of WorldCom's financial reports was uncovered by one of WorldCom's own internal auditors.[7]

Tax Services Tax services include assistance not only with tax-return preparation but also with tax planning. A CPA's advice can help a business structure (or restructure) operations and investments and perhaps save millions of dollars in taxes. Staying abreast of tax-law changes is no simple matter. Legislators made

Although employees at telecommunications giant WorldCom <www.worldcom.com> *were surprised to hear about the company's $3.8 billion restatement of 2002 earnings, many were also shocked when they were laid off a short time later. The largest bankruptcy in U.S. history put some 17,000 people out of work. Many of them blamed auditor Arthur Andersen* <www.arthurandersen.com> *for failing to uncover WorldCom's accounting problems. Government officials and financial analysts questioned whether Andersen could have maintained any objectivity as an auditor while collecting millions of dollars in consulting fees from the same client.*

more than 70 pages of technical corrections to the 1986 Tax Reform Act before it even became law.

management advisory services
Specialized accounting services to help managers resolve a variety of problems in finance, production scheduling, and other areas

Management Advisory Services As consultants, accounting firms provide **management advisory services** ranging from personal financial planning to planning corporate mergers. Other services include production scheduling, computer-feasibility studies, and AIS design. Some firms even assist in executive recruitment. On the staffs of the largest CPA firms are engineers, architects, mathematicians, and psychologists, who are available for consulting.

Noncertified Public Accountants Many accountants don't take the CPA exam; others work in the field while getting ready for it or while meeting requirements for state certification. Many small businesses, individuals, and even larger firms rely on these noncertified public accountants for income tax preparation, payroll accounting, and financial-planning services.

Private Accountants

private accountant
Salaried accountant hired by a business to carry out its day-to-day financial activities

To ensure integrity in reporting, CPAs are always independent of the firms they audit. As employees of accounting firms, they provide services for many clients. However, many businesses also hire their own salaried employees—**private accountants**—to perform day-to-day activities.

Private accountants perform numerous jobs. An internal auditor at Phillips Petroleum might fly to the North Sea to confirm the accuracy of oil-flow meters on offshore drilling platforms. A supervisor responsible for $2 billion in monthly payouts to vendors and employees may never leave the executive suite. Large businesses employ specialized accountants in such areas as budgets, financial planning, internal auditing, payroll, and taxation. In small businesses, a single person may handle all accounting tasks. Most private accountants are management accountants who provide services to support managers in various activities (marketing, production, engineering, and so forth).

The CPA Vision Project

The CPA Vision Project <www.cpavision.org> is a professionwide program that was established to assess the future of accounting.[8] A prime reason for the project is a disturbing decline in the number of young people who entered the profession

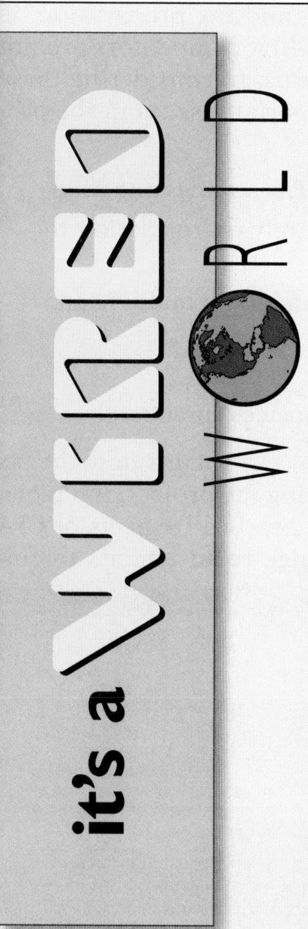

A Roundabout Look at Conflicting Interests

With all the new dot-coms popping up, things are looking up for accountants. Because all those e-businesses need accounting services, prospects are good for an upsurge of new clients. Or are they? Two factors are getting in the way, one having to do with the shallow pockets of many dot-coms and the other with the structure of large accounting firms. As a result, CPA firms are running into roadblocks in the pursuit of dot-com clients.

Many dot-coms are short on cash, most of them still operating in the red even though future prospects may be bright. But some of today's financially strapped dot-coms will be tomorrow's e-commerce giants. Naturally, CPA firms want them to become giant clients in need of accounting services for years to come. Price Waterhouse Coopers expects that about half of its consulting revenues will eventually come from e-businesses. Unfortunately, would-be e-giants need management advisory services to help formulate strategies, target markets, and improve operations *now,* while they're getting started, not later. The trouble is, they can't pay now.

The answer? Increasingly, accounting firms are accepting equity positions instead of cash payment. In return for its services, the CPA becomes part owner of the dot-com. Generally speaking, it's a good arrangement. While the CPA gets a new client (and stands to gain future revenues from its ownership position), the dot-com gets timely management help without laying out badly needed cash.

But there's a problem. What the CPA gains in today's consulting partner, it may lose in tomorrow's auditing client. Public accounting firms are not allowed to make ownership-investment arrangements *and also* provide auditing (or some other financial accounting) services for the same company-as-a-client. Both the accounting profession and federal regulations frown on potential conflicts of interest. Auditors can have no investment stake in companies they audit. And, in fact, it stands to reason that allowing a CPA to audit a company in which it has an ownership stake is an invitation to financial mischief. It would be like asking a bank to audit itself rather than to hire an independent auditor.

Nor do the problems stop here. As part owner, a CPA must also steer away from other part owners. Let's say that a number of other firms, such as a shipping company, an investment banker, and a wholesaler, also have ownership interests in the same dot-com. The CPA must decline to audit those firms as well. Again, there is conflict of interest: The CPA could make the dot-com look good financially in order to improve the financial positions of its fellow partners.

Therefore, it looks as if the dot-com explosion, which seems to be a terrific opportunity for CPAs, may be much more limited. Currently, accountants are forced to make a choice: Take on the dot-com *either* as an auditing client *or* as a client for consulting services, but not both. And whatever choice it makes, the accounting firm also has to make sure that its auditors on the one hand and consultants on the other know what the others are doing.

in the 1990s. The talent shortage has forced the profession to rethink its culture and lifestyle.[9] With grassroots participation from CPAs, educators, and industry leaders, the AICPA has undertaken a comprehensive long-term project to define the role of the accountant in the world economy of the twenty-first century. In recognizing a rapidly changing business world, the project focuses on certain desired goals for the profession and identifies the changes that will be needed to accomplish them.

Identifying Issues for the Future First, the Vision Project has identified key forces, both domestic and global, affecting the profession. Why are fewer students choosing to become CPAs? Technology is replacing many traditional CPA skills, the new borderless business world requires that accountants (like everybody else) offer new skills and services, and the perceived value of some traditional accounting services, including auditing and tax preparation, is declining. In addition, an increasing number of non-CPA competitors are not bound by the accounting profession's code of standards. In considering these forces, the Vision Project has identified the most important issues in the profession's future:

- Success will depend on public perceptions of the CPA's abilities and roles.
- CPAs must respond to market needs rather than rely on regulation to keep them in business.
- The market demands more high-value consulting and fewer auditing and accounting services.
- Specialization will be vital.
- CPAs must be familiar with global strategies and business practices.

Global Forces as Drivers of Change The Vision Project explains how the six classes of global forces shown in Figure 17.1 are driving the profession's reorientation. The wide range of these forces touches on nearly all aspects of CPA work—everything from working hours and knowledge requirements to cultural flexibility.

Economic forces
- globalization of capital markets
- electronic movement of capital
- interdependent worldwide system of trade, finance, management

Political forces
- spread of democracy
- democratized management styles
- public interest groups
- globalization of politics

Technical forces
- displacement of human activity by expert systems and automation
- advent of digital technology, new ways of working, different points of decision, and more complicated decision tasks

Social forces
- new educational methods
- new global standards for conducting business
- changing worldwide demographics
- colliding and merging of ethnic groups

The new CPA profession

Human resource forces
- fragmentation of traditional employer–employee relationships
- growth in outsourcing, permanent temporaries, and just-in-time employment
- advent of multiple jobs and multiple careers
- premium pay for knowledge workers and digital-tech employees

Regulatory forces
- influence of globalized corporations, public interest groups, and professional organizations
- collaboration of organizations and groups to shape reform for the future
- collaboration of organizations and companies to force viewpoints onto political agendas

FIGURE 17.1
Global Forces in the Changing CPA Profession

Recommendations for Change What, precisely, needs to be done? The Vision Project indicates that accounting educators and accounting professionals must make changes in the functioning of the profession. Among the top recommendations for change:

- The profession should adopt a broader focus beyond "numbers" that includes "strategic thinking."
- The profession should provide more value to society by expanding knowledge, education, and experience.
- CPA education must be revitalized to meet the demands of the future.
- To attract qualified members, the profession must increase opportunities for advancement, rewards, and lifestyle preferences.

A New Direction Responses from participants in the Vision Project reveal the profession's views of its own future. They are summarized in two categories—*Core Services* and *Core Competencies*—that are designed to shape and guide the CPA profession in the twenty-first century.

Core Services *Core services* refer to the work that the CPA performs. The Vision Project reports a stark departure from the traditional range of accounting activities and strongly recommends a broader perspective that encompasses areas traditionally outside the accounting realm. As you can see in Table 17.1, CPAs must develop new skills to deal with the range of business activities that affect performance. Financial planning, for instance, arguably falls beyond accounting's traditional role of reporting on historical financial performance. The distinction is largely one of perspective: futuristic outlook (financial planning) versus the historical (financial performance reporting). But many companies feel that they could get a clearer picture of their competitive health if the two areas were integrated. It will require a major commitment of organizational resources for a CPA firm to move in this direction.

Core Competencies The Vision Project identifies a unique combination of skills, technology, and knowledge—called *core competencies*—that will be necessary for the future CPA. As Table 17.2 shows, those skills go far beyond the ability to "crunch numbers": They include certain communications skills, along with skills in critical thinking and leadership. Indeed, the Vision Project foresees CPAs

TABLE 17.1
Core Services in Accounting

- *Assurance and Information Integrity*

  A variety of services that improve and assure the quality of information for business activities
- *Technology*

  Services that utilize technology—new business applications in knowledge management, system security, and new-business practices—to improve business activities
- *Management Consulting and Performance Management*

  Broad business knowledge and judgment to supply advice on an organization's strategic, operational, and financial performance
- *Financial Planning.*

  Various services—in tax planning, financial transactions, investment portfolio structuring, financial statement analysis—that help clients better understand, interpret, and utilize the full range of financial information
- *International Business*

  Services that enhance performance in global operations and facilitate global commerce.

TABLE 17.2

Core Competencies in Accounting

- *Strategic and Critical Thinking Skills*

  The accountant can provide competent advice for strategic action by combining data, knowledge, and insight
- *Communications and Leadership Skills*

  The accountant can exchange information meaningfully in a variety of business situations with effective delivery and interpersonal skills
- *Focus on the Customer, Client, and Market*

  The accountant can meet the changing needs of clients, customers, and employers better than the competition and can anticipate those needs better than competitors
- *Skills in Interpreting Converging Information*

  The accountant can interpret new meaning by combining financial and nonfinancial information into a broader understanding that adds more business value
- *Technology Skills*

  The accountant can use technology to add value to activities performed for employers, customers, and clients

who combine specialty skills with a broad-based orientation in order to communicate more effectively with people in a broad range of business activities.

Tools of the Accounting Trade

All accountants rely on record keeping, either manual or electronic, to enter and track transactions. Underlying all record-keeping procedures are the two key concepts of accounting: the *accounting equation* and *double-entry accounting.*

Self-Check Questions 1–3

*You should now be able to answer Self-Check Questions 1–3**

1. TRUE/FALSE *Auditing services*, as provided by CPA firms for client companies, are primarily concerned with managerial accounting.

2. MULTIPLE CHOICE *CPA firms* provide all of the following services **except** [select one]: **(a)** auditing for clients owned by the CPA firm; **(b)** financial planning for government and business firms; **(c)** management advisory services for companies and individuals; **(d)** tax services; **(e)** advice on AIS design.

3. MULTIPLE CHOICE Which of the following is **not** a motivating factor for development of the *CPA Vision Project*? [select one]: **(a)** an increasing number of non-CPA competitors who are not bound by the profession's standards; **(b)** fewer students choosing to become CPAs; **(c)** a variety of forces—economic, political, regulatory, cultural—that urge a reorientation; **(d)** today's accounting systems, which require fundamental revisions in generally accepted accounting principles (GAAP) for auditing; **(e)** professionals who believe that new core CPA services and core CPA competencies will be required in the future.

*Answers to Self-Check Questions 1–3 can be found on p. AN-11.

The inventory at this Boston-area Volkswagen dealership is among the company's assets: The cars constitute an economic resource because the firm will benefit financially as it sells them. When (and if) they are sold, at the end of the company's accounting period, the dealership will convert the cost of the cars as expenses and show them as costs of goods sold.

The Accounting Equation

At various points in the year, accountants use the following equation to balance the data pertaining to financial transactions:

Assets = Liabilities + Owners' equity

To understand the importance of this equation, we must first understand the terms *assets, liabilities*, and *owners' equity.*[10]

Assets and Liabilities An **asset** is any economic resource that is expected to benefit a firm or an individual who owns it. Assets include land, buildings, equipment, inventory, and payments due the company (accounts receivable). A **liability** is a debt that the firm owes to an outside party.

asset
Any economic resource expected to benefit a firm or an individual who owns it

liability
Debt owed by a firm to an outside organization or individual

owners' equity
Amount of money that owners would receive if they sold all of a firm's assets and paid all of its liabilities

Owners' Equity You may have heard of the equity that a homeowner has in a house—that is, the amount of money that could be made by selling the house and paying off the mortgage. Similarly, **owners' equity** is the amount of money that owners would receive if they sold all of a company's assets and paid all of its liabilities. We can rewrite the accounting equation to highlight this definition:

Assets − Liabilities = Owners' equity

If a company's assets exceed its liabilities, owners' equity is *positive;* if the company goes out of business, the owners will receive some cash (a gain) after selling assets and paying off liabilities. If liabilities outweigh assets, owners' equity is *negative;* assets are insufficient to pay off all debts. If the company goes out of business, the owners will get no cash and some creditors won't be paid. Owners' equity is meaningful for both investors and lenders. Before lending money to owners, for example, lenders want to know the amount of owners' equity in a business. Owners' equity consists of two sources of capital:

1. The amount that the owners originally invested
2. Profits earned by and reinvested in the company

When a company operates profitably, its assets increase faster than its liabilities. Owners' equity, therefore, will increase if profits are retained in the business instead of paid out as dividends to stockholders. Owners' equity also

"Setting the Standard for Professionalism"

In the first part of this chapter, we have discussed the *financial accounting systems* that provide reports for external users, such as unions, stockholders, and government agencies. We've also explored the CPA's role in ensuring that external users can trust the financial information they're given. Equally important, though less visible, is the *management accounting system* that serves *internal* users—managers, boards of directors, department heads, and project teams. These users rely on internal information, such as budgets, financial plans, and cost reports, that are never seen by external users. *Management accountants* perform all of the internal accounting activities that provide accurate information for timely decisions. As professionals, they must meet standards set forth by a professional association—the *Institute of Management Accountants (IMA)*—of which most management accountants are members. How large is the IMA and what's its purpose? What kinds of certification does it offer? What are the requirements for certification and what are its advantages? What skills should members have?

We can address these questions and learn more about IMA services by exploring the IMA Web site at <www.imanet.org>.

First, to get an idea of the variety of information available about the IMA, browse the various subject gates on the home page. Then click on the subject gate entitled **About IMA,** examine the page entitled **About IMA Overview,** and then respond to the following item:

1. What is IMA's purpose?

Return to the page entitled **About IMA Overview.** Scan down to the section labeled **Join Us** and find the sentence containing the underlined word **introduction**. When you click on **introduction**, a new document will appear. Scan its contents and then respond to the following questions:

2. What kinds of certifications are available from IMA?
3. How many members are affiliated with IMA, and what are some advantages of IMA certification?
4. What are the requirements for CMA certification?
5. What categories of skills are suggested for future success as a CMA and CFM?

To continue your Internet Field Trip, click on www.prenhall.com/griffin

increases if owners invest more of their own money to increase assets. However, owners' equity can shrink if the company operates at a loss or if owners withdraw assets.

Double-Entry Accounting

If your business buys inventory with cash, you decrease your cash and increase your inventory. Similarly, if you buy supplies on credit, you increase your supplies and increase your accounts payable. If you invest more money in your business, you increase the company's cash and increase your owners' equity. In other words, *every transaction affects two accounts.* Accountants thus use a **double-entry accounting system** to record the dual effects of transactions.[11] This practice ensures that the accounting equation always balances.

double-entry accounting system

Bookkeeping system that balances the accounting equation by recording the dual effects of every financial transaction

Financial Statements

As we noted earlier, the job of accounting is to summarize the results of a firm's transactions and to issue reports to help managers make informed decisions. Among the most important reports are **financial statements,** which fall into three broad categories—*balance sheets, income statements,* and *statements of cash flows.*[12] In this section, we will discuss these three types of financial statements, as well as the function of the budget as an internal financial statement. We'll conclude by explaining the most important reporting practices and the standards that guide accountants in drawing up financial statements.

financial statement

Any of several types of reports summarizing a company's financial status to aid in managerial decision making

Perfect Posters, INC.
555 RIVERVIEW, CHICAGO, IL 60606

Perfect Posters, Inc.
Balance Sheet
As of December 31, 2002

Assets		
Current Assets:		
Cash		$7,050
Marketable securities		2,300
Accounts receivable	$26,210	
Less: Allowance for doubtful accounts	(650)	25,560
Merchandise inventory		21,250
Prepaid expenses		1,050
Total current assets		**$ 57,210**
Fixed assets:		
Land		18,000
Building	65,000	
Less: Accumulated depreciation . .	(22,500)	42,500
Equipment	72,195	
Less: Accumulated depreciation . .	(24,815)	47,380
Total fixed assets		**$ 107,880**
Intangible assets:		
Patents	7,100	
Trademarks	900	
Total intangible assets		**8,000**
Total assets		**$173,090**

Liabilities and Owners' Equity		
Current liabilities:		
Accounts payable	$16,315	
Wages payable	3,700	
Taxes payable	1,920	
Total current liabilities		**$ 21,935**
Long-term liabilities:		
Notes payable, 8% due 2003. .	10,000	
Bonds payable, 9% due 2005 .	30,000	
Total long-term liabilities . . .		**40,000**
Total liabilities		**$ 61,935**
Owners' Equity:		
Common stock, $5 par	40,000	
Additional paid-in capital	15,000	
Retained earnings	56,155	
Total owners' equity		**$ 111,155**
Total liabilities and owners' equity		**$173,090**

Perfect Posters' balance sheet as of December 31, 2002. Perfect Posters' balance sheet shows clearly that the firm's total assets equal its total liabilities and owners' equity.

FIGURE 17.2
Perfect Posters' Balance Sheet

Balance Sheets

Balance sheets supply detailed information about the accounting equation factors: *assets, liabilities,* and *owners' equity.* Because they also show a firm's financial condition at one point in time, they are sometimes called *statements of financial position.* Figure 17.2 is the balance sheet for a hypothetical wholesaler called Perfect Posters.

balance sheet
Financial statement detailing a firm's assets, liabilities, and owners' equity

Assets As we have seen, an asset is any economic resource that a company owns and from which it expects to get some future benefit. From an accounting standpoint, most companies have three types of assets: *current, fixed,* and *intangible.*

Current Assets **Current assets** include cash and assets that can be converted into cash within a year. They are normally listed in order of **liquidity**—the ease of converting them into cash. Debts, for example, are usually paid in cash. A company that needs but cannot generate cash—a company that's not liquid—may be forced to sell assets at reduced prices or even go under.

current asset
Asset that can or will be converted into cash within the following year

liquidity
Ease with which an asset can be converted into cash

By definition, cash is completely liquid. *Marketable securities* purchased as short-term investments are slightly less liquid but can be sold quickly. These include stocks or bonds of other companies, government securities, and money market certificates. Many companies hold three other important nonliquid assets: *accounts receivable, merchandise inventory,* and *prepaid expenses.*

account receivable (or **receivables**)
Amount due from a customer who has purchased goods on credit

1. ***Accounts Receivable:*** **Accounts receivable** (or **receivables**) are amounts due from customers who have purchased goods on credit. Most businesses

expect to receive payment within 30 days of a sale. In our example, the entry *Less: Allowance for doubtful accounts* in Figure 17.2 indicates $650 in receivables that Perfect Posters doesn't expect to collect. Total receivable assets are decreased accordingly.

2. ***Merchandise Inventory*** Following accounts receivable on the Perfect Posters' balance sheet is **merchandise inventory**—the cost of merchandise that's been acquired for sale to customers and is still on hand.[13] Accounting for the value of inventories is difficult because they're always flowing in and out. We must, therefore, make assumptions about which ones were sold and which ones remain in storage.

merchandise inventory

Cost of merchandise that has been acquired for sale to customers and is still on hand

3. ***Prepaid Expenses*** **Prepaid expenses** include supplies on hand and rent paid for the period to come. They are assets because they've been paid for and are available to the company. In all, Perfect Posters' current assets as of December 31, 2002, totaled $57,210.

prepaid expense

Expense, such as prepaid rent, that is paid before the upcoming period in which it is due

Fixed Assets **Fixed assets** (such as land, buildings, and equipment) have long-term use or value. But as buildings and equipment wear out or become obsolete, their value decreases, and accountants use **depreciation** to spread the cost of an asset over the years of its useful life. To reflect decreasing value, they calculate its useful life in years, divide its worth by that many years, and subtract the resulting amount each year. Every year, therefore, the remaining value decreases on the books. In Figure 17.2, Perfect Posters shows fixed assets of $107,880 after depreciation.

fixed asset

Asset with long-term use or value, such as land, buildings, and equipment

depreciation

Process of distributing the cost of an asset over its life

Intangible Assets Although their worth is hard to set, **intangible assets** have monetary value in the form of expected benefits. These usually include the cost of obtaining rights or privileges such as patents, trademarks, copyrights, and franchise fees. **Goodwill** is the amount paid for an existing business beyond the value of its other assets. A purchased firm, for example, may have a particularly good reputation or location.[14]

Perfect Posters has no goodwill assets, but it does own trademarks and patents for specialized storage equipment. These intangible assets are worth $8,000. Larger companies, of course, have much more valuable intangible assets.

intangible asset

Nonphysical asset, such as a patent or trademark, that has economic value in the form of expected benefit

goodwill

Amount paid for an existing business above the value of its other assets

Liabilities Like assets, liabilities are often separated into different categories. **Current liabilities** are debts that must be paid within one year. These include **accounts payable**—unpaid bills to suppliers for materials as well as wages and taxes that must be paid in the coming year. Perfect Posters has current liabilities of $21,935.

Long-term liabilities are debts that are not due for at least a year. These normally represent borrowed funds on which the company must pay interest. Perfect Posters' long-term liabilities are $40,000.

current liability

Debt that must be paid within the year

accounts payable

Current liability consisting of bills owed to suppliers, plus wages and taxes due within the upcoming year

long-term liability

Debt that is not due for at least one year

Owners' Equity The final section of the balance sheet in Figure 17.2 shows owners' equity broken down into *common stock, paid-in capital,* and *retained earnings.* When Perfect Posters was formed, the declared legal value of its common stock was $5 per share. By law, this $40,000 ($5 × 8,000 shares) can't be distributed as dividends. **Paid-in capital** is additional money invested by owners. Perfect Posters has $15,000 in paid-in capital.

Retained earnings are net profits kept by a firm rather than paid out as dividend payments to stockholders. They accumulate when profits, which can be distributed to stockholders, are kept instead for the company's use. At the close of 2002, Perfect Posters had retained earnings of $56,155.[15]

paid-in capital

Additional money, above proceeds from stock sale, paid directly to a firm by its owners

retained earnings

Earnings retained by a firm for its use rather than paid as dividends

Income Statements

The **income statement** is sometimes called a **profit-and-loss statement** because its description of revenues and expenses results in a figure showing the firm's annual profit or loss. In other words,

Revenues − Expenses = Profit (or Loss)

Popularly known as "the bottom line," profit or loss is probably the most important figure in any business enterprise. Figure 17.3 shows the 2002 income statement for Perfect Posters, whose bottom line was $12,585. Like the balance sheet, the income statement is divided into three major categories: *revenues, cost of goods sold,* and *operating expenses.*

Revenues When a law firm receives $250 for preparing a will or a supermarket collects $65 from a grocery shopper, both are receiving **revenues**—the funds that flow into a business from the sale of goods or services. In 2002, Perfect Posters reported revenues of $256,425 from the sale of art prints and other posters.

Cost of Goods Sold In Perfect Posters' income statement, the **cost of goods sold** section shows the costs of obtaining materials to make the products sold during the year. Perfect Posters began 2002 with posters valued at $22,380. Over the year, it spent $103,635 on materials to make posters. During 2002, then, it had $126,015 worth of merchandise available to sell. By the end of the year, it had sold all but $21,250 of those posters, which remained as merchandise inventory. The cost of obtaining the goods that it sold was thus $104,765.

Perfect Posters, INC.
555 RIVERVIEW, CHICAGO, IL 60606

Perfect Posters, Inc.
Income Statement
Year Ended December 31, 2002

Revenues (gross sales)			**$256,425**
Cost of goods sold:			
Merchandise inventory, January 1, 2002.	$22,380		
Merchandise purchases during year	103,635		
Goods available for sale		$126,015	
Less: Merchandise inventory December 31, 2002	21, 250		
Cost of goods sold			104,765
Gross profit			151,660
Operating expenses:			
Selling and repackaging expenses:			
Salaries and wages	49,750		
Advertising	6,380		
Depreciation—warehouse and repackaging equipment	3,350		
Total selling and repackaging expenses		59,480	
Administrative expenses:			
Salaries and wages	55,100		
Supplies	4,150		
Utilities	3,800		
Depreciation—office equipment	3,420		
Interest expense	2,900		
Miscellaneous expenses	1,835		
Total administrative expenses		71,205	
Total operating expenses			130,685
Operating income (income before taxes)			20,975
Income taxes			8,390
Net income			$12,585

Perfect Posters' income statement for year ended December 31, 2002. The final entry on the income statement, the bottom line, reports the firm's profit or loss.

FIGURE 17.3
Perfect Posters' Income Statement

Gross Profit (or Gross Margin) To calculate **gross profit** (or **gross margin**), subtract cost of goods sold from revenues obtained from goods sold. Perfect Posters' gross profit in 2001 was $151,660 ($256,425 − $104,765). Expressed as a percentage of sales, gross profit is 59.1 percent ($151,660 / $256,425).

Gross profit percentages vary widely across industries. In retailing, Home Depot <www.homedepot.com> reports 30 percent. In manufacturing, Harley-Davidson <www.harley-davidson.com> reports 34 percent; and in pharmaceuticals, American Home Products <www.ahp.com> reports 75 percent. For companies with low gross margins, product costs are a big expense. If a company has a high gross margin, it probably has low cost-of-goods-sold but high selling and administrative expenses.

Operating Expenses In addition to costs directly related to acquiring goods, every company has general expenses ranging from erasers to the CEO's salary. Like cost of goods sold, **operating expenses** are resources that must flow out of a company if it is to earn revenues. As you can see from Figure 17.3, Perfect Posters had 2002 operating expenses of $130,685—$59,480 in selling and repackaging expenses and $71,205 in administrative expenses.

Selling expenses result from activities related to selling goods or services, such as sales force salaries and advertising expenses. *General and administrative expenses,* such as management salaries and maintenance costs, are related to the general management of the company.

income statement (or **profit-and-loss statement**)
Financial statement listing a firm's annual revenues and expenses so that a bottom line shows annual profit or loss

revenues
Funds that flow into a business from the sale of goods or services

cost of goods sold
Total cost of obtaining materials for making the products sold by a firm during the year

gross profit (or **gross margin**)
Revenues obtained from goods sold minus cost of goods sold

operating expenses
Costs, other than the cost of goods sold, incurred in producing a good or service

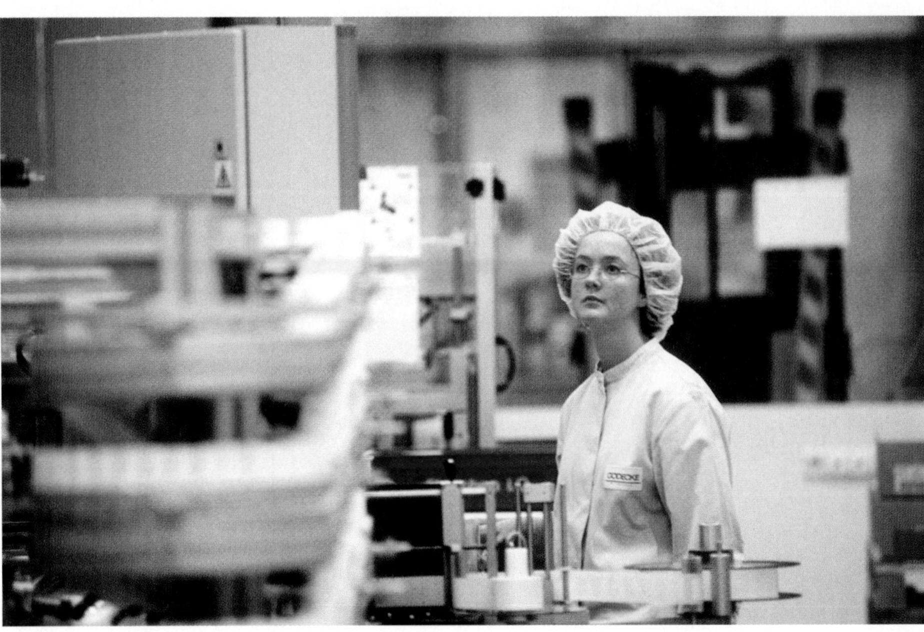

At the end of its accounting period, this pharmaceuticals company will subtract the cost of making the goods that it sold from the revenues received from sales. The difference will be its gross profit (or gross margin). Cost of goods sold does not include the firm's operating expenses, including such selling expenses as advertising and sales commissions. In part, gross margins in the pharmaceuticals industry are high because they do not account for high selling expenses.

operating income
Gross profit minus operating expenses

net income (or **net profit or net earnings**)
Gross profit minus operating expenses and income taxes

statement of cash flows
Financial statement describing a firm's yearly cash receipts and cash payments

Operating and Net Income **Operating income** compares the gross profit from operations against operating expenses. This calculation for Perfect Posters ($151,660 − $130,685) reveals an operating income, or income before taxes, of $20,975. Subtracting income taxes from operating income ($20,975 − $8,390) reveals **net income** (also called **net profit** or **net earnings**). In 2002, Perfect Posters' net income was $12,585.

Statements of Cash Flows

Some companies prepare only balance sheets and income statements. The Securities and Exchange Commission <www.sec.gov>, however, requires all firms whose stock is publicly traded to issue a third report: The **statement of cash flows** describes yearly cash receipts and cash payments.[16] It shows the effects on cash of three activities:

- *Cash flows from operations.* This part of the statement concerns main operating activities: cash transactions involved in buying and selling goods and services. It reveals how much of the year's profits result from the firm's main line of business (for example, Jaguar's sales of automobiles) rather than from secondary activities (say, licensing fees paid to Jaguar by a clothing firm that puts the Jaguar logo on shirts).
- *Cash flows from investing.* This section reports net cash used in or provided by investing. It includes cash receipts and payments from buying and selling stocks, bonds, property, equipment, and other productive assets.
- *Cash flows from financing.* The final section reports net cash from all financing activities. It includes cash inflows from borrowing or issuing stock as well as outflows for payment of dividends and repayment of borrowed money.

The overall change in cash from these three sources provides information to lenders and investors. When creditors and stockholders know how a firm obtained and used funds during the course of a year, it's easier for them to interpret year-to-year changes in the balance sheet and income statement.

This concession stand at Dodger Stadium is operated by the Los Angeles Dodgers Inc. <www.dodgers.com>. *It sells products manufactured mostly by members of the Sporting Goods Manufacturers Association (SGMA)* <www.sportlink.com>, *who make apparel, footwear, and equipment. Much of this merchandise is licensed from Major League Baseball Properties Inc.* <www.mlb.com>, *which distributes licensing revenues to the sport's 30 franchises. Both MLB teams (who own logos and uniform designs) and MLB Properties treat sales of licensed products as cash flows from operations.*

The Budget: An Internal Financial Statement

For planning, controlling, and decision making, the most important internal financial statement is the **budget**—a detailed report on estimated receipts and expenditures for a future period of time.[17] Although that period is usually one year, some companies also prepare three- or five-year budgets, especially when considering major capital expenditures.

budget
Detailed statement of estimated receipts and expenditures for a period of time in the future

Budgets are also useful for keeping track of weekly or monthly performance. Procter & Gamble evaluates business units monthly by comparing actual financial results with monthly budgets. Discrepancies signal potential problems and spur action to improve financial performance.

Although the accounting staff coordinates the budget process, it needs input from many areas regarding proposed activities and required resources. In preparing a sales budget like the one in Figure 17.4, accounting must obtain from the sales group projections for units to be sold and expected expenses for the coming year. Then accounting draws up the final budget and, throughout the year, compares the budget to actual expenditures and revenues.

Reporting Standards and Practices

Accountants follow standard reporting practices and principles when they prepare external reports. The common language dictated by standard practices is designed to give external users confidence in the accuracy and meaning of financial information. Spelled out in GAAP, these principles cover a range of issues, such as when to recognize revenues from operations, how to *match* revenues and expenses, and how to make full public disclosure of financial information. Without such standards, users of financial statements wouldn't be able to compare information from different companies, and thus they would misunderstand—or be led to misconstrue—a company's true financial status.

Revenue Recognition As we noted earlier, revenues are funds that flow into a business as a result of operating activities during an accounting period. *Revenue recognition* is the formal recording and reporting of revenues in financial statements.[18] Although a firm earns revenues continuously as it makes sales, earnings

Perfect Posters, INC.
555 RIVERVIEW, CHICAGO, IL 60606

Perfect Posters, Inc.
Sales Budget
First Quarter, 2003

	January	February	March	Quarter
Budgeted sales (units)	7,500	6,000	6,500	20,000
Budgeted selling price per unit	$3.50	$3.50	$3.50	$3.50
Budgeted sales revenue	$ 26,250	$ 21,000	$ 22,750	$ 70,000
Expected cash receipts:				
From December sales	$26,210[a]			$26,210
From January sales	17,500[b]	$8,750		26,250
From February sales		14,000	$7,000	21,000
From March sales			15,200	15,200
Total cash receipts:	$ 43,710	$ 22,750	$ 22,200	$ 88,660

[a]This cash from December sales represents a collection of the accounts receivable appearing on the December 31, 2002, balance sheet.
[b]The company estimates that two-thirds of each month's sales revenues will result in cash receipts during the same month. The remaining one-third is collected during the following month.

FIGURE 17.4

Perfect Posters' Sales Budget

are not reported until the *earnings cycle* is completed. This cycle is complete under two conditions:

1. The sale is complete and the product delivered.
2. The sale price has been collected or is collectible (accounts receivable).

The end of the earning cycle determines the timing for revenue recognition in a firm's financial statements. Revenues are recorded for the accounting period in which sales are completed and collectible (or collected). This practice assures the users that the statement gives a fair comparison of what was gained in return for the resources that were given up.

Matching Net income is calculated by subtracting expenses from revenues. The *matching principle* states that expenses will be matched with revenues to determine net income for an accounting period.[19] Why is this principle important? It permits the statement user to see how much net gain resulted from the assets that had to be given up in order to generate revenues during a given period. Thus, when we match revenue recognition with expense recognition, we get net income for the period.

Consider the hypothetical case of Little Red Wagon Co. Let's see what happens when the books are kept in two different ways:

1. *Correct method*: Revenue recognition is matched with expense recognition to determine net income when the earnings cycle is *completed.*
2. *Incorrect method*: Revenue recognition occurs *before* the earnings cycle is completed.

Suppose that 500 wagons are produced and delivered to customers at $20 each during 2001. In the next year, 600 wagons are produced and delivered. In part (A) of Table 17.3, we use the correct matching method: Revenues are recorded for

TABLE 17.3

Revenue Recognition and the Matching Principle

(A) The Correct Method Reveals each Accounting Period's Activities and Results

	Year Ended December 31, 2001	*Year Ended December 31, 2002*
Revenues	$10,000	$12,000
Expenses	8,000	9,000
Net income	2,000	3,000

(B) The Incorrect Method Disguises each Accounting Period's Activities and Results

	Year Ended December 31, 2001	*Year Ended December 31, 2002*
Revenue	$14,000	$8,000
Expenses	8,000	9,000
Net income	6,000	(1,000)

Self-Check Questions 4–6

*You should now be able to answer Self-Check Questions 4–6**

4. MULTIPLE CHOICE The end-of-year *financial statement* for Millie's fruit stand includes the following data: assets = $20,000; owner's equity = $4,500; liabilities = $17,500. Given this information, which of the following is **true**? [select one]: **(a)** Assets are increasing faster than liabilities. **(b)** Profits are being reinvested in the firm. **(c)** Assets are mostly fixed rather than current. **(d)** An accounting error has occurred. **(e)** Retained earnings for the current year have increased.

5. MULTIPLE CHOICE Which of the following is **not true** regarding *assets on the balance sheet*? [select one]: **(a)** Next year's book value for a fixed asset will be less than this year's value after depreciation is subtracted. **(b)** Cash is the most liquid of all current assets. **(c)** Merchandise inventory is a current asset. **(d)** Prepaid expenses are increased by paying next year's rent this year. **(e)** Allowance for doubtful accounts increases the book value of accounts receivable.

6. TRUE/FALSE Because *gross profit* (or gross margin) is calculated by subtracting the cost of goods sold from revenues, the result (gross profit) must always be a positive number.

*ANSWERS TO SELF-CHECK QUESTIONS 4–6 CAN BE FOUND ON P. AN-11.

the period in which sales are completed and collectible from customers. So are the expenses of producing and delivering the products that were sold. When sales revenues are matched against the expenses of making sales, we see how much better off the company is at the end of each accounting period as a result of that period's operations. Little Red Wagon earned $2,000 net income for the first year and did even better in 2002.

In part (B) of Table 17.3, the principles of revenue recognition and matching have been violated. Certain activities of the two accounting periods are disguised and mixed together rather than separated by period. The result is a distorted performance report showing (incorrectly) that 2001 was better than 2002.

Here's what Red Wagon's accountants did wrong. The sales department sold 200 wagons (with revenues of $4,000) to a customer late in 2001. Those *revenues* are included in the $14,000 for 2001. But because the 200 wagons were produced and delivered to the customer in 2002, the *expenses* are recorded, as in (A), for 2002. The result is a distorted picture of operations: It looks as if expenses for 2002 are very high for such a low sales level and as if expenses (compared to revenues) were better kept under control during 2001. Accountants violated the matching principle by ignoring *the period during which the earnings cycle was completed.* Although $4,000 in sales of wagons occurred in 2001, the earnings cycle for those wagons is not completed until they were produced and delivered, which occurred in 2002. Accordingly, both revenues and expenses for those 200 wagons should have been reported *in the same period*—namely, in 2002. They were properly reported in part (A), where we can see clearly what was gained and what was lost on activities completed in an *accounting period.* By requiring this practice, the matching principle avoids financial distortions.

Full Disclosure *Full disclosure* means that financial statements should not include just numbers. They should also furnish management's interpretations and explanations of those numbers so that users can better understand information in the statements. Because they know about events inside the company, the people in management prepare additional information to explain certain events or transactions or to disclose the circumstances behind certain results.

Analyzing Financial Statements

Financial statements present a lot of information, but what does it all *mean*? How, for example, can statements help investors decide what stock to buy or help lenders decide whether to extend credit? Statements provide data, which can in turn be applied to various *ratios* (comparative numbers). We can then use these ratios to analyze a firm's financial health or to check its progress by comparing current and past statements.[20]

Ratios are normally grouped into three major classifications:

- **Solvency ratios,** both short- and long-term, estimate risk.
- **Profitability ratios** measure potential earnings.
- **Activity ratios** reflect management's use of assets.

Depending on the decisions to be made, a user may apply none, some, or all of the ratios in a classification.

solvency ratio
Financial ratio, either short- or long-term, for estimating the risk in investing in a firm

profitability ratio
Financial ratio for measuring a firm's potential earnings

activity ratio
Financial ratio for evaluating management's use of a firm's assets

liquidity ratio
Solvency ratio measuring a firm's ability to pay its immediate debts

current ratio
Solvency ratio that determines a firm's creditworthiness by measuring its ability to pay current liabilities

Short-Term Solvency Ratios

In the short run, survival depends on a company's ability to pay its immediate debts. Such payments require cash. Short-term solvency ratios measure a company's relative liquidity and thus its ability to pay immediate debts. The higher a firm's **liquidity ratios,** the lower the risk to investors.

Current Ratio The most commonly used liquidity ratio, the current ratio or "banker's ratio," concerns a firm's creditworthiness. The **current ratio** measures a company's ability to meet current obligations out of current assets. It thus reflects a firm's ability to generate cash to meet obligations through the normal, orderly process of selling inventories and collecting accounts receivable. It is calculated by dividing current assets by current liabilities.

As a rule, a current ratio is satisfactory at 2:1 or higher—that is, if current assets more than double current liabilities. A smaller ratio may indicate that a firm will have trouble paying its bills. Note, however, that a larger ratio may imply that assets are not being used productively and should be invested elsewhere.

How does Perfect Posters measure up? Look again at the balance sheet in Figure 17.2. Judging from current assets and current liabilities at the end of 2002, we see that

$$\frac{\text{Current assets}}{\text{Current liabilities}} = \frac{\$57{,}210}{\$21{,}935} = 2.61$$

How does this ratio compare with those of other companies? Not bad: It's lower than O'Reilly Automotive <www.oreillyauto.com> (2.94) and higher than those of Gillette <www.gillette.com> (1.56), Cisco Systems <www.cisco.com> (2.14), and Starwood Hotels & Resorts Worldwide <www.sheraton.com> (0.23). Perfect Posters may be holding too much uninvested cash, but it looks like a good credit risk.

working capital
Difference between a firm's current assets and current liabilities

Working Capital A related measure is **working capital**—the difference between a firm's current assets and current liabilities. Working capital indicates a firm's ability to pay short-term debts (liabilities) owed to outsiders. At the end of 2002,

Perfect Posters' working capital was $35,275 (that is, $57,210 − $21,935). Because current liabilities must be paid off within one year, current assets are more than enough to meet current obligations.

Long-Term Solvency Ratios

To survive in the long run, a company must meet both its short-term (current) debts and its long-term liabilities. These latter debts usually involve interest payments. A firm that can't meet them is in danger of collapse or takeover—a risk that makes creditors and investors quite cautious.

Debt-to-Owners' Equity Ratio To measure a company's risk of running into this problem, we use **debt ratios.** The most common debt ratio is the **debt-to-owners' equity ratio** (or **debt-to-equity ratio**), which describes the extent to which a firm is financed through borrowed money. It is calculated by dividing **debt**—total liabilities—by owners' equity. Companies with debt-to-equity ratios above 1 are probably relying too much on debt. Such firms may find themselves owing so much debt that they lack the income needed to meet interest payments or to repay borrowed money.

In the case of Perfect Posters, we can use the balance sheet in Figure 17.2 to work out the debt-to-equity ratio as follows:

$$\frac{\text{Debt}}{\text{Owners' equity}} = \frac{\$61{,}935}{\$111{,}155} = 0.56$$

debt ratio
Solvency ratio measuring a firm's ability to meet its long-term debts

debt-to-owners' equity ratio (or **debt-to-equity ratio**)
Solvency ratio describing the extent to which a firm is financed through borrowing

debt
A firm's total liabilities

Leverage Sometimes, however, a high debt-to-equity ratio can be not only acceptable but also desirable. Borrowing funds gives a firm **leverage**—the ability to make otherwise unaffordable investments. In *leveraged buyouts* (*LBOs*), firms have willingly taken on sometimes huge debt in order to buy out other companies. But when owning the purchased company generates profits above the cost of borrowing the purchase price, leveraging makes sense, even if it raises the buyer's debt-to-equity ratio. Unfortunately, many buyouts have caused problems because profits fell short of expected levels or because rising interest rates increased payments on the buyer's debt.

leverage
Ability to finance an investment through borrowed funds

Profitability Ratios

It's important to know whether a company is solvent in both the long and the short term, but risk alone is not an adequate basis for investment decisions. Investors also want some measure of the returns they can expect. *Return on equity* and *earnings per share* are two common profitability ratios.

Return on Equity Investors want to know the net income earned for each dollar invested. **Return on equity** measures this performance by dividing net income (recorded in the income statement, Figure 17.3) by total owners' equity (recorded in the balance sheet, Figure 17.2).[21] For Perfect Posters, we calculate 2002 return on equity as follows:

$$\frac{\text{Net income}}{\text{Total owners' equity}} = \frac{\$12{,}585}{\$111{,}155} = 11.3\%$$

return on equity
Profitability ratio measuring income earned for each dollar invested

Is this figure good or bad? There's no set answer. If Perfect Posters' ratio for 2002 is higher than in previous years, owners and investors should be encouraged. But if 11.3 percent is lower than the ratios of other companies in the same industry, they should be concerned.

Earnings per Share Defined as net income divided by the number of shares of common stock outstanding, **earnings per share** determines the size of the dividend that a firm can pay shareholders. Investors use this ratio to decide whether

earnings per share
Profitability ratio measuring the size of the dividend that a firm can pay shareholders

Say what you mean

TECHNICALLY SPEAKING

The meeting for department heads began when the general manager asked, "Well, how did we do last month compared to the budget?" "On a static-budget basis," replied the head of accounting, "unfavorable variances were realized for variable expenses and total expenses. Favorable budget variances were realized for units sold, sales revenues, and operating income." She paused and then continued: "On a flexible-budget basis, unfavorable variances were realized on variable expenses, fixed expenses, total expenses, and operating income." After a moment of silence, the general manager said, "What does all that mean?"

An interesting situation. The key element—and the problem—is specialization. Companies form specialized units—whether departments, teams, or other groups—to foster expertise. But specialization can be both a blessing and a curse. On the one hand, specialists tend to develop their own languages so that they can communicate with one another efficiently and clearly. Communicating with outsiders, however—non-specialists and specialists with other specialties—presents problems, because specialists then have to communicate in the "foreign" languages of other specialists. What happens when, say, a team includes engineers and accountants and people from sales, purchasing, and production? Team effectiveness depends on specialists finding a common language.

In our sample meeting, the general manager asked for information from a specialist (an accountant) in front of other specialists. The answer, though technically accurate, didn't inform anyone who didn't understand the special language of accountants. Matters could have gotten worse if, in heeding a call for clarification, the accountant had launched into even more technical detail—perhaps by offering a quick course on static versus flexible budgets and favorable versus unfavorable variances. Obviously, this meeting was neither the time nor place for a tutorial on budgeting technicalities. In fact, it was probably called to focus on budgeting as a tool for managing performance across the entire organization—to explain, for instance, why budgets are important in every department. The technical detail just sidetracked everyone.

How could this situation have been avoided from the outset? Step one is recognizing the existence of specialized languages and working to foster communications across specialty areas. Second, the general manager should have let accounting know beforehand the purpose of the meeting, perhaps giving the accountant advance notice of the question with which he intended to start things off. This way, the accountant could have come up with alternative answers based on the manager's purpose in asking the question. Step three—adopting a language to be used by everyone—is optional. It suggests that there are occasions when specialized language should be spoken throughout the organization. This approach, for example, would have been useful if our general manager had decided that all of his departments should know more about the technicalities of the budgets for which they're responsible.

to buy or sell a company's stock. As the ratio goes up, stock value increases because investors know that the firm can better afford to pay dividends. Naturally, stock loses market value if financial statements report a decline in earnings per share. For Perfect Posters, we can use the net income total from the income statement in Figure 17.3 to calculate earnings per share as follows:

$$\frac{\text{Net income}}{\text{Number of common shares outstanding}} = \frac{\$12{,}585}{8{,}000} = \$1.57 \text{ per share}$$

As a baseline for comparison, note that Gucci's <www.gucci.com> recent earnings were $3.31 per share. Phillips Petroleum Co. <www.phillips66.com> earned $7.26.

Activity Ratios

The efficiency with which a firm uses resources is linked to profitability. As a potential investor, then, you want to know which company gets more mileage from its resources. Activity ratios measure this efficiency. Let's say, for example, that two firms use the same amount of resources or assets. If Firm A generates greater profits or sales, it's more efficient and so enjoys a better activity ratio.

Inventory Turnover Ratio Certain specific measures can be used to explain *how* one firm earns more profit than another. The **inventory turnover ratio** measures the average number of times that inventory is sold and restocked during the year—that is, how quickly it is produced and sold.[22] To find this ratio, you first need to know your *average inventory*—the typical amount of inventory on hand during the year. You can calculate average inventory by adding end-of-year inventory to beginning-of-year inventory and dividing by 2. You can now find your inventory turnover ratio, which is expressed as the cost of goods sold divided by average inventory:

inventory turnover ratio
Activity ratio measuring the average number of times that inventory is sold and restocked during the year

$$\frac{\text{Cost of goods sold}}{\text{Average inventory}} = \frac{\text{Cost of goods sold}}{(\text{Beginning inventory} + \text{Ending inventory})/2}$$

High inventory turnover means efficient operations. Because less investment money is tied up in inventory, funds can be put to work elsewhere to earn greater returns. But inventory turnover must be compared with both prior years and industry averages. A rate of 5, for example, might be excellent for an auto supply store but disastrous for a supermarket, where a rate of about 15 is common. Rates can also vary within a company that markets a variety of products. To calculate Perfect Posters' inventory turnover ratio for 2002, we take the merchandise inventory figures for the income statement in Figure 17.3. The ratio can be expressed as follows:

$$\frac{\$104,765}{(\$22,380 + \$21,250)/2} = 4.8 \text{ times}$$

In other words, new merchandise replaces old merchandise every 76 days (365 days/4.8). The 4.8 ratio is below the average of 7.0 for comparable operations, indicating that the business is slightly inefficient.

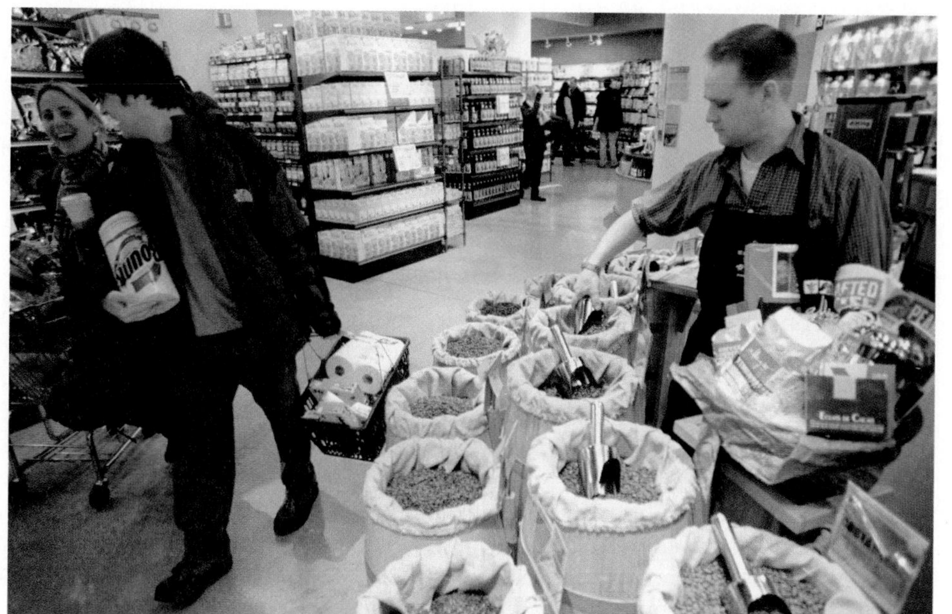

Inventory turnover ratio measures the average number of times that a store sells and restocks its inventory in one year. The higher the ratio, the more products that get sold and the more revenue that comes in. Supermarkets—even upscale outlets like this Whole Foods Market <www.wholefoodsmarket.com> *in New York City—must have a much higher turnover ratio than, say, auto-supply or toy stores. In almost all retail stores, products with the highest ratios get the shelf spaces that generate the most customer traffic and sales.*

"It's up to you now, Miller. The only thing that can save us is an accounting breakthrough."

International Accounting

More U.S. companies are buying and selling in other countries. Coca-Cola and Boeing receive large portions of their revenues from overseas sales, while Sears and Kmart buy goods from other countries for sale in the United States. In addition, more and more companies own foreign subsidiaries. Obviously, accounting for foreign transactions involves special procedures. One of the most basic is translating the values of the different currencies.

Foreign Currency Exchange

A unique consideration in international accounting is the value of currencies and exchange rates.[23] As we saw in Chapter 4, the value of any country's currency is subject to change. Political and economic conditions, for instance, affect the stability of a currency and its value relative to other currencies.

As it's traded around the world, a currency's value is determined by market forces—what buyers are willing to pay for it. The resulting values are called **foreign currency exchange rates.** When a currency becomes unstable—that is, when its value changes frequently—it is regarded as a *weak currency.* The value of the Brazilian real, for example, fluctuated between 0.416 and 0.957—a variation range of 130 percent in U.S. dollars—during the period from 1997 to 2002.

foreign currency exchange rate
Value of a nation's currency as determined by market forces

On the other hand, a *strong currency* historically rises or holds steady in comparison to the U.S. dollar. As changes occur, they must be considered by accountants when recording international transactions. They will affect, perhaps profoundly, the amount that a firm pays for foreign purchases and the amount it gains from sales to foreign buyers.

International Transactions

International purchases, credit sales, and accounting for foreign subsidiaries all involve transactions affected by exchange rates. When a U.S. company called Village Wine and Cheese Shops imports Bordeau wine from a French company called Pierre Bourgeois, its accountant must be sure that Village's books reflect its true costs. The amount owed to Pierre Bourgeois changes daily along with the exchange rate between euros and dollars. Thus, our accountant must identify the actual rate *on the day that payment in euros is made* so that the correct U.S.-dollar cost of the purchase is recorded.

International Accounting Standards

Professional accounting groups from about 80 countries are members of the International Accounting Standards Board (IASB) <www.iasb.org.uk>, which is trying to eliminate national differences in financial reporting procedures.[24] Bankers, investors, and managers want procedures that are comparable from country to country and applicable to all firms regardless of home nation. Standardization is occurring in some areas but is far from universal. IASB financial statements include an income statement, balance sheet, and statement of cash flows similar to those issued by U.S. accountants. International standards, however, do not require a uniform format, and variety abounds.

Self-Check Questions 7–9

*You should now be able to answer Self-Check Questions 7–9**

7. TRUE/FALSE In 2002, Kiddie Kar Kompany received orders for 400 red wagons at a purchase price of $80 per wagon. The wagons were delivered to customers in 2003. According to the *revenue recognition principle*, Kiddie Kars should report the $32,000 as revenue for year 2003 rather than for 2002.

8. MULTIPLE CHOICE Which of the following statements about *financial ratios* is **not true**? [select one]: **(a)** An *inventory turnover ratio* of 6.5 means that the firm has enough inventory on hand to supply its sales requirements for the next 6.5 months. **(b)** A *current ratio* of 10.4 strongly suggests that the firm is able to meet immediate (short-term) debts. **(c)** A company with a *debt-to-equity ratio* of 4.8 is probably risky because it's relying too much on debt. **(d)** A *return on equity* of 16 percent indicates that the firm is earning net income of 16 percent on each dollar invested. **(e)** *Solvency ratios*, both short- and long-term, estimate risk.

9. TRUE/FALSE *Earnings per share* is a more reliable indicator of profitability than is *return on equity.*

*ANSWERS TO SELF-CHECK QUESTIONS 7–9 CAN BE FOUND ON P. AN-12.

Continued from page 487

Is Anybody Holding Auditors Accountable?

Although Andersen executives claimed that no one had committed any crimes, that story turned to fiction when a former partner pleaded guilty to obstruction charges. As a witness for the government, David Duncan admitted that he'd broken the law by destroying documents. Even more damning for Andersen was news that the Enron affair wasn't its first brush with charges of shady auditing. Four years earlier, the firm's Fort Lauderdale office had destroyed sensitive documents when the SEC came to look into Andersen's restatment of Sunbeam's earnings following a barrage of lawsuits by Sunbeam stockholders. According to another Andersen partner, employees were ordered to destroy anything that didn't agree with the CPA's final statement of Sunbeam's earnings.

In a case involving another client—Waste Management—Andersen agreed in 2001 to pay $7 million to settle federal charges of filing false auditing reports dating back to before the Sunbeam case. In assessing the largest civil penalty ever levied against a major accounting firm, the SEC claimed that Andersen had filed false audits of its client's books from 1992 to 1996. Andersen claimed that all financial statements were prepared according to GAAP, but income was, in fact, overstated by more than $1 billion.

In an even larger action—one of the largest nonprofit frauds in history—Andersen agreed in 2002 to a $217 million settlement involving the Baptist Foundation of Arizona. The Foundation, with Andersen as its auditor, allegedly swindled elderly people out of $590 million. The suit accused Andersen of ignoring danger signs, falsifying documents, and destroying records.

In June 2002, Andersen was convicted of obstructing justice in the Enron case by destroying files while on notice of a federal investigation. Both accountants and clients began bailing on Andersen once its entanglement with Enron came to light. Hundreds of accountants, many of them partners in the firm, have jumped to other major firms, and many others have started their own consulting or accounting firms. Even before the conviction in June, more than 500 clients, including the 15 biggest publicly traded firms that Andersen had audited the year before, had found new CPAs.

Before long, wrongdoing at Enron, Tyco, WorldCom, Rite Aid, Adelphia Communications, Dynegy, and ImClone Systems—including a wide range of practices that should have been noticed by vigilant CPAs—had spooked investors and strained public trust to the breaking point. By late June 2002, the U.S. stock market, buried under an avalanche of reports of fraud and deceit, had lost more than 20 percent of its value—amounting to hundreds of billions in losses for retirees and other investors.

What can we do to recover? As part of the settlement in the Baptist Foundation case, one Andersen partner and one auditing manager had to give up their CPA licenses. The Arizona Board of Accountancy appointed a three-person panel to monitor Andersen's audits of Arizona companies for two years. In effect, this last action reveals the sad state of affairs in contemporary accounting: We need auditors to monitor auditors. And unfortunately, we don't yet have an answer to the next obvious question: How many layers of monitors monitoring monitors will we need to restore public trust in the accounting profession?

Questions for Discussion

1. Why do you suppose Andersen auditors were reluctant to disclose deficiencies in clients' financial statements and accounting practices?
2. Do you think that Arizona authorities were overly harsh with the penalties they imposed on Andersen? Why or why not?
3. Consider the obligations of CPAs employed by Arthur Andersen. Is the CPA's first obligation to Andersen or to the accounting profession? Explain your reasoning.
4. Suppose that you're a CPA at a major accounting firm, where you suspect that a client isn't abiding by GAAP. You also get the impression that your boss would prefer you to keep your suspicions under wraps. How would you handle this situation?
5. What changes, if any, do you recommend be made by the accounting profession or by regulatory agencies to restore public confidence in the business of financial reporting?

Summary of Learning Objectives

1. *Explain the role of accountants, and distinguish between the kinds of work done by* public *and* private accountants.

Accounting is a comprehensive system for collecting, analyzing, and communicating financial information. It measures business performance and translates the results into information for management decisions. It also prepares performance reports for owners, the public, and regulatory agencies. To meet these objectives, accountants keep records of income, expenses, and taxes, and they analyze the effects of these transactions on particular business activities. **Bookkeeping** (just one phase of accounting) is the recording of transactions. Ensuring consistent, dependable financial information is the job of the **accounting information system (AIS)**—an organized procedure for identifying, measuring, recording, and retaining financial information so that it can be used in accounting statements and management reports. Users of such information include: (1) business managers, (2) employees and unions, (3) investors and creditors, (4) tax authorities, and (5) government regulatory agencies. At the head of the AIS, the **controller** manages all accounting activities.

There are two main fields in accounting: (1) A **financial accounting system** deals with external information users (consumer groups, unions, stockholders, and government agencies). It regularly prepares income statements, balance sheets, and other financial reports published for shareholders and the public. (2) **Managerial** (or **management**) **accounting** serves internal users, such as managers at all levels.

Certified public accountants (CPAs) offer accounting services to the public. They are licensed at the state level after passing a written exam prepared by the American Institute of Certified Public Accountants (AICPA). Virtually all CPA firms, large or small, provide all or most of the following services: (1) *Auditing:* An **audit** examines a company's AIS to determine whether financial reports reliably represent operations. It also ensures that the AIS follows **generally accepted accounting principles (GAAP)**—rules and procedures governing the content and form of financial reports. (2) *Tax services*: Because tax laws are quite complex, tax services include tax planning as well as tax-return preparation. (3) *Management advisory services*: As consultants, CPAs provide **management advisory services** ranging from personal financial planning to planning corporate mergers.

CPAs are always independent of the firms they audit. But many businesses, large as well as small, rely on noncertified public accountants (those who don't take the CPA exam) to handle income tax, payroll, accounting, and financial planning. Many businesses hire their own salaried employees—**private accountants.**

2. *Discuss the* CPA Vision Project, *and explain how the CPA profession is changing.*

With participation from CPAs, educators, and industry leaders, the CPA Vision Project is a comprehensive project to define the role of accountants in the twenty-first century world economy. It has identified the following as the most important issues in the profession's future: (1) Success will depend on public perceptions of CPA abilities and roles. (2) CPAs must respond to market needs rather than rely on regulation to stay in business. (3) The market demands more high-value consulting and fewer auditing and accounting services. (4) Specialization will be vital. (5) CPAs must be conversant in global strategies and business practices.

Among the Vision Project's top recommendations for change are the following: (1) The profession should adopt a focus beyond "numbers" that includes "strategic thinking." (2) The profession should provide more value by expanding knowledge, education, and experience. (3) CPA education should address the demands of the future. (4) The profession must increase opportunities for advancement and rewards.

The profession's views of its own future are summarized in two categories: (1) *Core services* refer to the CPA's work. The Project recommends a move toward *core services* that have traditionally remained outside the accounting realm. CPAs should develop skills in a variety of business activities. (2) The Project also identifies a unique combination of skills, technology, and knowledge—called *core competencies*—that will be necessary for the future CPA.

3. *Explain how the following concepts are used in accounting: the* accounting equation *and* double-entry accounting.

Accountants use the following equation to balance the data pertaining to financial transactions:

$$\text{Assets} = \text{Liabilities} + \text{Owners' equity}$$

(1) An **asset** is any economic resource that is expected to benefit its owner (such as buildings, equipment, inventory, and payments due the company). (2) A **liability** is a debt that the firm owes to an outside party. (3) **Owners' equity** is the amount of money that owners would receive if they sold all of a company's assets and paid all of its liabilities. We can rewrite the accounting equation to show this definition:

$$\text{Assets} - \text{Liabilities} = \text{Owners' equity}$$

If assets exceed liabilities, owners' equity is *positive;* if the firm goes out of business, owners will receive some cash (a gain) after selling assets and paying off liabilities. If liabilities outweigh assets, owners' equity is *negative;* assets aren't enough to pay off debts. If the company goes under, owners will get no cash and some creditors won't be paid.

Owners' equity consists of two sources of capital: (i) The amount that owners originally invested; and (ii) profits earned and reinvested. When a firm operates profitably, assets increase faster than liabilities, and owners' equity will increase if profits are kept in the business instead of being paid out as dividends. It can also increase if owners invest more of their own money.

Because every transaction affects two accounts, accountants use a **double-entry accounting system** to record the dual effects. Because the double-entry system requires at least two bookkeeping entries for each transaction, it keeps the accounting equation in balance.

4. ***Describe the three basic* financial statements, *and show how they reflect the activity and financial condition of a business.***

Accounting summarizes the results of a firm's transactions and issues reports to help managers make informed decisions. The class of reports known as **financial statements,** are divided into three categories—*balance sheets, income statements*, and *statements of cash flows*.

Balance sheets (sometimes called *statements of financial position*) supply detailed information about the accounting-equation factors: *assets, liabilities*, and *owners' equity*. (1) *Assets*: In accounting, companies can have three types of assets: (i) **Current assets** include cash and assets that can be converted into cash within a year, and they are listed in order of **liquidity**—the ease with which they can be converted into cash. Cash is completely liquid, but most companies also hold three important nonliquid assets: (a) **Accounts receivable** (or **receivables**) are amounts due from customers who have bought goods on credit. (b) **Merchandise inventory** is the cost of merchandise that has been acquired for sale to customers and is still on hand. (c) **Prepaid expenses** include supplies on hand and rent paid for the period to come. They are assets because they have been paid for and are available.

(ii) The next major classification on the balance sheet is usually **fixed assets.** These items have long-term use or value (say, land, buildings, and equipment). As they wear out or become obsolete, their value decreases. To reflect decreasing value, accountants use **depreciation** to spread the cost of an asset over the years of its useful life. (iii) **Intangible assets** usually include the cost of obtaining rights or privileges (patents, trademarks, copyrights, franchise fees). **Goodwill** is the amount paid for an existing business beyond the value of its other assets.

(2) *Liabilities*: Liabilities are often separated into different categories. (i) **Current liabilities** are debts that must be paid within a year. These include **accounts payable**—unpaid bills for materials as well as wages and taxes due within the year. (ii) **Long-term liabilities** are debts not due for at least a year (usually from borrowed funds on which interest is due).

(3) *Owners' equity*: Owners' equity can be broken down into three categories. (i) *Common stock* means the declared value of the company's shares when it was formed. (ii) **Paid-in capital** is additional money invested by owners. (iii) **Retained earnings** consist of net profits minus dividends paid to stockholders.

The **income statement** (sometimes called a **profit-and-loss statement**) describes revenues and expenses to show a firm's annual profit or loss:

Revenues − Expenses = Profit (or Loss)

It is divided into three major categories: (1) **Revenues** are the funds that flow in from the sale of goods or services. (2) **Cost of goods sold** means the costs of obtaining materials to make products sold during the year. To calculate **gross profit** (or **gross margin**), subtract cost of goods sold from revenues (a figure that can be expressed as a percentage of sales). (3) In addition to costs directly related to acquiring goods, every firm has general expenses. **Operating expenses** are resources that must flow out in order for a firm to earn revenues. **Operating income,** or income before taxes, compares the gross profit from operations against operating expenses. Subtracting income taxes from operating income reveals **net income** (also called **net profit** or **net earnings**).

A publicly traded firm must issue a **statement of cash flows,** which describes its yearly cash receipts and payments. It shows the effects on cash of three activities: (1) *Cash flows from operations*: This part of the statement concerns cash transactions involved in buying and selling goods and services. It shows how much of the year's profits come from the main line of business. (2) *Cash flows from investing*: This section reports net cash used in or provided by investing (say, payments from buying and selling stocks). (3) *Cash flows from financing*: This section reports net cash from all financing activities. The overall change in cash from these three sources provides information to lenders and investors.

Another financial statement is the **budget**—a detailed statement of estimated receipts and expenditures for a future period of time. Budgets help to keep track of weekly or monthly performance. Discrepancies in actual versus budget totals signal problems and stir action to get performance back on track.

5. ***Explain the key standards and principles for reporting financial statements.***

Accountants follow standard reporting practices and principles when they prepare financial statements. Otherwise, users wouldn't be able to compare information from different companies, and they might misunderstand—or be led to misconstrue—a company's true financial status. The following are three of the most important standard reporting practices and principles:

(1) *Revenue recognition* is the formal recording and reporting of revenues in the financial statements. All firms earn revenues continuously as they make sales, but earnings are not reported until the *earnings cycle* is completed. This cycle is complete under two conditions: (i) The sale is complete and the product delivered; (ii) The sale price has been collected or is collectible. This practice assures interested parties that the statement gives a fair comparison of what was gained for the resources that were given up.

(2) The *matching principle* states that expenses will be matched with revenues to determine net income. It permits users to see how much net gain resulted from the assets that had to be given up in order to generate revenues.

(3) Because they have inside knowledge, management prepares additional information that explains certain events or transactions or discloses the circumstances behind certain results. *Full disclosure* means that financial statements include management interpretations and explanations to help external users understand information contained in statements.

6. ***Show how computing key* financial ratios *can help in analyzing the financial strengths of a business.***

Financial statements provide data that can be applied to *ratios* (comparative numbers). Ratios can then be used to analyze the financial health of one or more companies. They can also be used to check a firm's progress by comparing current with past statements. Ratios are grouped into three major classifications:

(1) **Solvency ratios** estimate risk. *Short-term solvency ratios* measure relative liquidity and thus a company's ability to pay immediate debts. The higher a firm's **liquidity ratios,** the lower the risk for investors. The most common liquidity ratio is the **current ratio,** which measures ability to meet current obligations out of current assets. It thus reflects a firm's ability to generate cash to meet obligations through the normal process of selling inventories and collecting accounts receivable. **Working capital** is the difference between current assets and current liabilities. It indicates ability to pay off short-term debts (liabilities) owed to outsiders. *Long-term solvency ratios* measure ability to meet long-term liabilities consisting of interest payments. **Debt ratios** are long-term solvency ratios. The most common debt ratio is the **debt-to-owners' equity ratio** (or **debt-to-equity ratio**), which describes the extent to which a firm is financed through borrowed money. It is calculated by dividing **debt**—total liabilities—by owners' equity. A fairly high debt-to-equity ratio may sometimes be desirable because borrowing funds provides **leverage**—the ability to make otherwise unaffordable purchases.

(2) **Profitability ratios** measure potential earnings. **Return on equity** measures income earned for each dollar invested; it's calculated by dividing net income by total owners' equity. Defined as net income divided by the number of shares of common stock outstanding, **earnings per share** determines the size of the dividend that a company can pay shareholders. Investors use it when deciding whether to buy or sell a company's stock. As it gets higher, stock value increases, because investors know that the firm can better afford to pay dividends.

(3) **Activity ratios** reflect management's use of assets by measuring the efficiency with which a firm uses its resources. The **inventory turnover ratio** measures the average number of times that inventory is sold and restocked annually—that is, how quickly it is produced and sold. A high inventory turnover ratio means efficient operations: Because a smaller amount of investment is tied up in inventory, the firm's funds can be put to work elsewhere to earn greater returns.

7. ***Explain some of the special issues facing accountants at firms that do international business.***

Accounting for foreign transactions involves special procedures, such as translating the values of different countries' currencies and accounting for the effects of exchange rates. Moreover, currencies are subject to change: As they're traded each day around the world, their values are determined by market forces—what buyers will to pay for them. The resulting values are **foreign currency exchange rates,** which can be fairly volatile. When a currency becomes unstable—when its value changes frequently—it is called a *weak currency.* The value of a *strong currency* historically rises or holds steady in comparison to the U.S. dollar.

International purchases, sales on credit, and accounting for foreign subsidiaries all involve transactions affected by exchange rates. When a U.S. company imports a French product, its accountant must be sure that its books reflect its true costs. The amount owed to the French seller changes daily along with the exchange rate between euros and dollars. The American accountant must therefore identify the actual rate on the day that payment in euros is made so that the correct U.S.-dollar cost of the product is recorded.

With accounting groups from 80 countries, the International Accounting Standards Board (IASB) is trying to eliminate national differences in financial reporting. Bankers, investors, and managers want financial reporting that is comparable from country to country and across all firms regardless of home nation. Standardization governs some areas but is far from universal.

KEY TERMS

accounting (p. 488)
bookkeeping (p. 488)
accounting information system (AIS) (p. 488)
controller (p. 488)
financial accounting system (p. 489)
managerial (or management) accounting system (p. 489)
certified public accountant (CPA) (p. 489)
audit (p. 489)
generally accepted accounting principles (GAAP) (p. 489)
management advisory services (p. 490)
private accountant (p. 490)
asset (p. 495)
liability (p. 495)
owners' equity (p. 495)
double-entry accounting system (p. 496)
financial statement (p. 496)
balance sheet (p. 497)
current asset (p. 497)
liquidity (p. 497)
account receivable (or receivable) (p. 497)
merchandise inventory (p. 498)
prepaid expense (p. 498)
fixed asset (p. 498)
depreciation (p. 498)
intangible asset (p. 498)
goodwill (p. 498)
current liability (p. 498)
accounts payable (or payable) (p. 498)
long-term liability (p. 498)
paid-in capital (p. 498)
retained earnings (p. 498)
income statement (or profit-and-loss statement) (p. 499)
revenues (p. 499)
cost of goods sold (p. 499)

gross profit (or gross margin) (p. 499)
operating expenses (p. 499)
operating income (p. 500)
net income (or net profit or net earnings) (p. 500)
statement of cash flows (p. 500)
budget (p. 501)
solvency ratio (p. 504)
profitability ratio (p. 504)
activity ratio (p. 504)
liquidity ratio (p. 504)
current ratio (p. 504)
working capital (p. 504)
debt ratio (p. 505)
debt-to-owners' equity ratio (or debt-to-equity ratio) (p. 505)
debt (p. 505)
leverage (p. 505)
return on equity (p. 505)
earnings per share (p. 505)
inventory turnover ratio (p. 507)
foreign currency exchange rate (p. 508)

QUESTIONS AND EXERCISES

Questions for Review

1. Identify the three types of services performed by CPAs.
2. How does the double-entry system reduce the chances of mistakes or fraud in accounting?
3. What are the three basic financial statements, and what major information does each contain?
4. Identify the three major classifications of financial statement ratios, and give an example of one ratio in each category.
5. Explain how financial ratios allow managers to monitor efficiency and effectiveness.
6. Explain the ways in which financial accounting differs from managerial (management) accounting.

Questions for Analysis

7. If you were planning to invest in a company, which of the three types of financial statements would you most want to see? Why?
8. Dasar Co. reports the following data in its September 30, 2001, financial statements:

Gross sales	$225,000
Current assets	40,000
Long-term assets	100,000
Current liabilities	16,000
Long-term liabilities	44,000
Owners' equity	80,000
Net income	7,200

Compute the following ratios: current ratio, debt-to-equity ratio, and return on owners' equity.

Application Exercises

9. Interview an accountant at a local manufacturing firm. Trace the process by which budgets are developed in the company. How does it use budgets? How does budgeting help managers plan business activities? How does budgeting help them control activities? Give examples.
10. Interview the manager of a local retail or wholesale business about taking inventory. What is the firm's primary purpose in taking inventory? How often is it done?

Building Your Business Skills

PUTTING THE BUZZ IN BILLING

This exercise enhances the following SCANS workplace competencies: demonstrating basic skills, demonstrating thinking skills, exhibiting interpersonal skills, working with information, and applying system knowledge.

Goal

To encourage students to think about the advantages and disadvantages of using an electronic system for handling accounts receivable and accounts payable.

Method

Step 1

Study Figure 17.5. The outside circle depicts the seven steps involved in the issuance of paper bills to customers, the payment of these bills by customers, and the handling by banks of debits and credits for the two accounts. The inside circle shows the same bill process handled electronically.

Step 2

As the chief financial officer of a Midwestern utility company, you are analyzing the feasibility of switching from a paper to an electronic system. You decide to discuss the ramifications of the choice with three associates (choose three classmates to take on these roles). Your discussion requires that you research electronic payment systems now being developed. Specifically, using online and library research, you must find out as much as you can about the electronic bill-paying systems being developed by Visa International, Intuit, IBM, and the Checkfree Corp. After you have

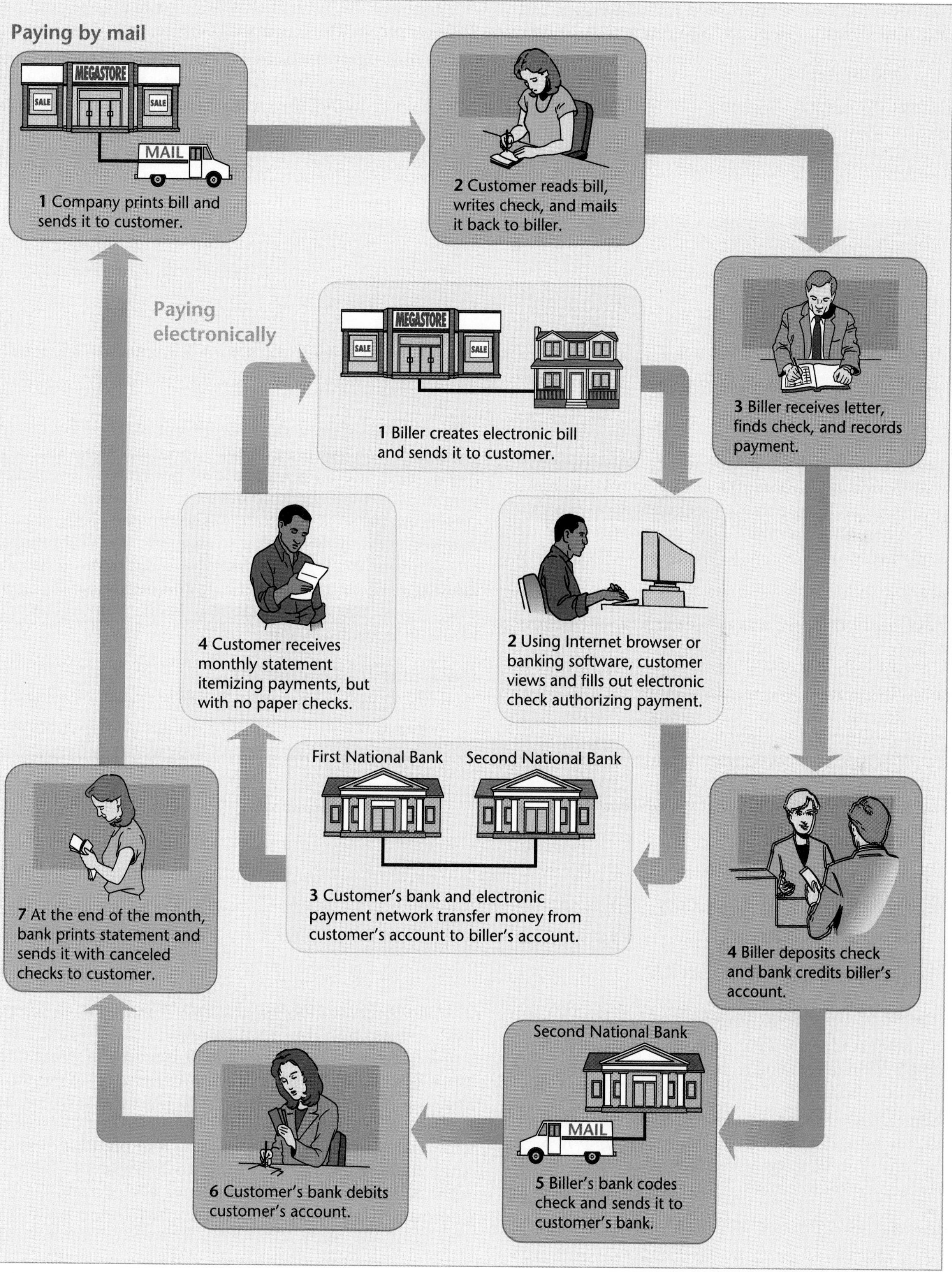
Paying by mail
MEGASTORE
SALE
SALE
MAIL
1 Company prints bill and sends it to customer.
2 Customer reads bill, writes check, and mails it back to biller.
3 Biller receives letter, finds check, and records payment.
4 Biller deposits check and bank credits biller's account.
Second National Bank
MAIL
5 Biller's bank codes check and sends it to customer's bank.
6 Customer's bank debits customer's account.
7 At the end of the month, bank prints statement and sends it with canceled checks to customer.
Paying electronically
MEGASTORE
SALE
SALE
1 Biller creates electronic bill and sends it to customer.
2 Using Internet browser or banking software, customer views and fills out electronic check authorizing payment.
First National Bank
Second National Bank
3 Customer's bank and electronic payment network transfer money from customer's account to biller's account.
4 Customer receives monthly statement itemizing payments, but with no paper checks.

FIGURE 17.5
vo Ways of Handling Accounts Receivable

researched this information, brainstorm the advantages and disadvantages of switching to an electronic system.

Follow-Up Questions

1. What cost savings are inherent in the electronic system for both your company and its customers? In your answer, consider such costs as handling, postage, and paper.
2. What consequences would your decision to adopt an electronic system have on others with whom you do business, including manufacturers of check-sorting equipment, the U.S. Postal Service, and banks?
3. Switching to an electronic system would mean a large capital expense for new computers and software. How could analyzing the company's income statement help you justify this expense?
4. How are consumers likely to respond to paying bills electronically? Are you likely to get a different response from individuals than you get from business customers?

Exercising Your Ethics

CONFIDENTIALLY YOURS

The Situation

Accountants are often entrusted with private, sensitive information that should be used confidentially. In this exercise, you're encouraged to think about ethical considerations that might arise when an accountant's career choices come up against a professional obligation to maintain confidentiality.

The Dilemma

Assume that you're the head accountant in a large electronics firm. Your responsibilities include preparing income statements and balance sheets for financial reporting to stockholders. In addition, you regularly prepare confidential budgets for internal use by managers responsible for planning departmental activities, including future investments in new assets. You've also worked with auditors and supplied sensitive information to consultants from a CPA firm that assesses financial problems and suggests solutions.

Now let's suppose that you're approached by another company—one of the electronics industry's most successful firms—and offered a higher-level position. If you accept, your new job will include developing financial plans and serving on the strategic planning committee. Thus, you'd be involved not only developing strategy but also evaluating the competition. You'll undoubtedly be called upon to use your knowledge of your previous firm's competitive strengths and weaknesses. You realize that your insider knowledge could be useful in your new job.

Questions for Discussion

1. What are the roles of financial accounting, managerial accounting, and accounting services in this scenario?
2. What are the chief ethical issues in this situation?
3. As the central figure in this scenario, how would you handle this situation?

Crafting Your Business Plan

THE PROFITABILITY OF PLANNING

The Purpose of the Assignment

1. To acquaint students with accounting issues faced by a sample firm in developing its business plan, in the framework of *Business PlanPro* (*BPP*) software package.
2. To demonstrate how three chapter topics—accounting skills, financial data reports, and the profit-and-loss statement—can be integrated as components in the *BPP* planning environment.

Assignment

After reading Chapter 17 in the textbook, open the BPP software and search for information about plans for accounting as it applies to a sample firm: AMT Computer Store *(American Management Technology). To find* AMT Computer Store, *do the following:*

Open *Business PlanPro.* If it asks if you want to "create a new business plan" or "open an existing plan," select "create a new business plan" (even though you are not going to create a plan at this time). You will then be taken to the *Business PlanPro EasyPlan Wizard.* On the screen, click on the option entitled **Research It.** You will then be presented with a new list of options, including **Sample Plan Browser.** After clicking on the **Sample Plan Browser**, go down the alphabetical list of sample plans and double-click on **Computer Hardware—Reseller**, which is the location for *AMT Computer Store.* The screen that you're now looking at is the introduction page for the *AMT Computer Store* business plan. Next, scroll down until you reach the **Table of Contents** for *AMT*'s business plan.

Now respond to the following items:

1. What is your assessment of the accounting skills possessed by AMT's management team? What do you recommend? [Sites to see in *BPP* for this item: On the **Table of Contents** page, click on each of the following, in turn: **6.1 Organizational Structure, 6.2 Management Team**, and **6.3 Management Team Gaps.**]
2. Use *BPP*'s computer graphics to explore AMT's financial data reports. Describe the kinds of accounting information you find in the charts. [Sites to see in *BPP*: Beginning on the **Table of Contents** page, go to the outline section entitled **7.2 Key Financial Indicators**, including **Benchmark Comparison Chart.**]
3. At the time of this plan, AMT Computer Store was expecting large changes in annual net profits during the next three years. Based on the company's planned profit-and-loss statement, identify the key factors—changes in revenues and expenses—that account for changes in expected net profits from year to year. [Sites to see in *BPP*: From the **Table of Contents** page, click on **7.4 Projected Profit and Loss**, including **Table: Profit and Loss (Planned).**]

Video Exercise

ACCOUNTING FOR BILLIONS OF BURGERS: MCDONALD'S

Learning Objectives

The purpose of this video is to help you

1. Understand the challenges that a company may face in managing financial information from operations in multiple countries.
2. Consider ways in which managers and investors use financial information reported by a public company.
3. Understand how different laws and monetary systems can affect the accounting activities of a global corporation.

Synopsis

Collecting, analyzing, and reporting financial data from 27,000 restaurants in 119 countries is no easy task, as the accounting experts at McDonald's are well aware. Every month, individual restaurants send their sales figures to be consolidated with data from other restaurants at the local or country level. From there, the figures are sent to country-group offices and then to one of three major regional offices before going to their final destination at McDonald's headquarters in Oak Brook, Illinois. In the past, financial information arrived in Illinois in bits and pieces, sent by courier, mail, or fax. Today, local and regional offices enter month-end figures into a special secure Web site, enabling the corporate controller to produce financial statements and projections for internal and external use.

Discussion Questions

1. *For analysis:* Why does McDonald's use "constant currency" comparisons when reporting its financial results?
2. *For analysis:* What types of assets might McDonald's list under depreciation in its financial statements?
3. *For application:* What effect do corporate income tax rates in the countries where it operates have on the income statements prepared at McDonald's local offices?
4. *For application:* What problems might arise if individual restaurants were required to enter sales data directly on the company's centralized accounting Web site instead of following the current procedure of sending it through country and regional channels?
5. *For debate:* To help investors and analysts better assess the company's worldwide financial health, should McDonald's be required to disclose detailed financial results for every country and region? Support your position.

Online Exploration

Visit the McDonald's corporate Web site at <www.mcdonalds.com/corporate>. Locate the most recent financial report (quarterly or annual) and examine both overall and regional results. What aspects of its results does McDonald's highlight in this report? Which regions are doing particularly well? Which are lagging? How does management explain any differences in performance? What does McDonald's say about its use of constant currency reporting?

PART 5

Understanding Financial Issues

CHAPTER

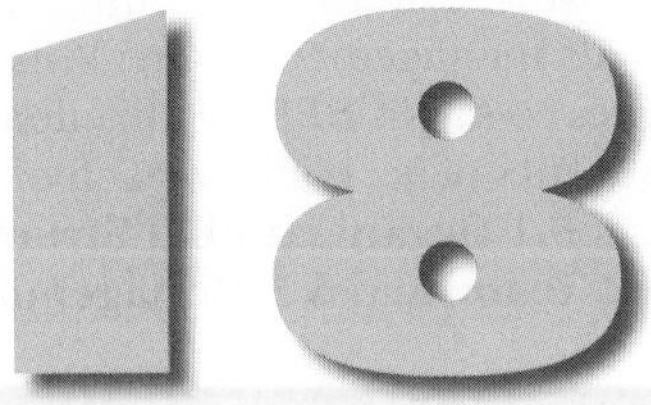

Understanding Money and Banking

After reading this chapter, you should be able to:

1. Define *money* and identify the different forms that it takes in the nation's money supply.
2. Describe the different kinds of *financial institutions* that comprise the U.S. financial system and explain the services they offer.
3. Explain how banks create money and describe the means by which they are regulated.
4. Discuss the functions of the *Federal Reserve System* and describe the tools that it uses to control the money supply.
5. Identify three important ways in which the financial industry is changing.
6. Understand some of the key concepts and activities in *international banking and finance.*

Argentines No Longer Bank on the Peso

They get in line before dawn. Peaceful at first, they become unruly when they have to protect their places in line. No, they're not jockeying for seats at a rock concert or a World Cup soccer game. These frenzied people are customers at one of the largest banks in Buenos Aires, a bank that, like every other bank in the country's depleted system, has to say no to angry account holders. Denied access to their life savings, many will return tomorrow (and be rejected again). In one day, panicked depositors had yanked \$2 billion, and to stop the bleeding, the government has temporarily limited withdrawals to \$250 a week regardless of the size of the account. Transfers abroad are limited to \$1,000 a month, and even the accounts of the wealthiest patrons are frozen. The result? Not surprisingly, a serious shortage of money. "As long as I live, I shall never again put a peso in a bank in Argentina," says Buenos Aires real estate agent Pablo Pechague. "I'm going to put everything in Uruguay where there is a much more serious banking system."

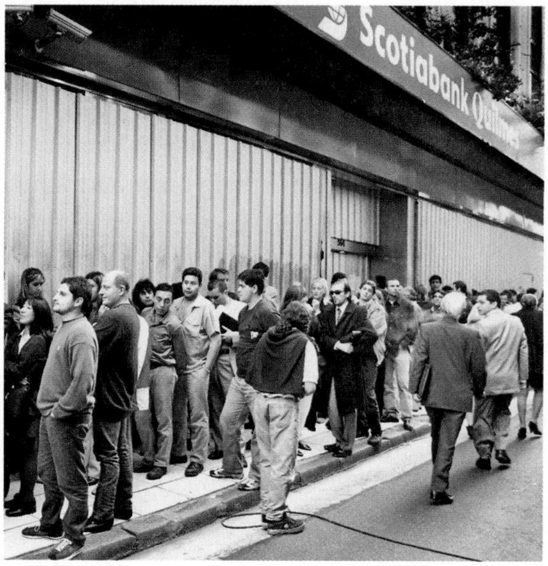

Argentina's currency—the peso—was long known as the most stable in Latin America. The country's free-market economy, South America's second largest (after Brazil), was the darling of emerging markets with its fast-paced economic growth during the 1990s. Billions of investment dollars flowed in from abroad as Argentina undertook the privatization of state industries by selling off hundreds of inefficient businesses.

A healthy nine percent growth rate and low unemployment meant economic prosperity—until a turnaround started in the late 1990s, with a recession that worsened into 2002. With unemployment reaching 18 percent, investors from the United States and Europe feared that Argentina would devalue the peso to help the economy and, by doing so, would slash investors' profits and, perhaps, even cause the government to protect local industry by reverting back to old policies that are less market friendly than the recent privatization movement.

As the recession lingered, the peso, long considered the foundation of Argentina's steady economy, gradually came to be viewed as overvalued, making the country's exports too expensive and uncompetitive in foreign markets. In late 2001, worried investors and savers started a run on the banks in hopes of reclaiming their money rather than risking financial loss if the economy failed. By year-end 2001, Argentines had withdrawn 17 percent of all bank deposits, or \$14.5 billion, causing a sharp decline in the central bank reserves. In early 2002, Economy Minister Jorge Remes Lenicov broke the news: "We are devaluing; we are in collapse. Argentina is bankrupt."

The currency devaluation could cause further job cuts and inflation for Argentina's citizens. As the threat of further instability continued, fears mounted that a steep drop in the peso's value could trigger huge losses for foreign companies in telecommunications, oil, banks, and utilities. And those fears were justified: By mid-2002, foreign creditors, too, were taking a financial beating. Citigroup, for example, the New York-based financial giant, reported losses of \$470 million in one calendar quarter from economic problems in Argentina. J.P. Morgan Chase & Co. was hurt even worse, and FleetBoston Financial Corp. took the rare step of postponing its regularly-scheduled earnings report until it could sort out the full financial impact of its Argentine losses. Meanwhile, frustrated Argentines, starved for cash, have to rely on bank debit cards, credit cards, and checks to pay for day-to-day purchases.

Our opening story continues on page 541.

What Is Money?

When someone asks you how much money you have, do you count the dollar bills and coins in your pockets? Do you include your checking and savings accounts? What about stocks and bonds? Do you count your car? Taken together, the value of all these things is your personal wealth. Not all of it, however, is "money." In this section, we consider more precisely what *money* is and does.

The Characteristics of Money

money

Any object that is portable, divisible, durable, and stable and that serves as a medium of exchange, a store of value, and a unit of account

Modern money often takes the form of stamped metal or printed paper—U.S. dollars, British pounds, Japanese yen—issued by governments. Theoretically, however, just about any object can serve as **money** if it is *portable, divisible, durable,* and *stable.* To appreciate these qualities, imagine using something that lacks them—say, a 70-pound salmon:

- ***Portability.*** Try lugging 70 pounds of fish from shop to shop. In contrast, modern currency is light and easy to handle.
- ***Divisibility.*** Suppose that you want to buy a hat, a book, and some milk from three different stores. How would you divide your fish-money? Is a pound of its head worth as much as, say, two gills? Modern currency is easily divisible into smaller parts, each with a fixed value. A dollar, for example, can be exchanged for four quarters. More important, units of money can be easily matched with the value of all goods.
- ***Durability.*** Regardless of whether you "spend" it, your salmon will lose value every day (in fact, it will eventually be too smelly to be worth anything). Modern currency, however, neither dies nor spoils, and if it wears out, it can be replaced. It is also hard to counterfeit—certainly harder than catching more salmon.
- ***Stability.*** If salmon were in short supply, you might be able to make quite a deal for yourself. In the middle of a salmon run, however, the market would be flooded with fish. Sellers of goods would soon have enough fish and would refuse to produce anything for which they could get only salmon. Goods would become scarcer, but the salmon would continue (or cease) running, regardless of the plenitude or scarcity of buyable goods. The value of our paper money also fluctuates, but it is considerably more stable than salmon. Its value is related to what we can buy with it.

The Functions of Money

Imagine a successful fisherman who needs a new sail for his boat. In a barter economy—one in which goods are exchanged directly for one another—he would have to find someone who not only needs fish but who is also willing to exchange a sail for it. If no sail maker wants fish, the fisherman must find someone else—say, a shoemaker—who does want fish. Then the fisherman must hope that the sail maker will trade for his new shoes. Clearly, barter is inefficient in comparison with money. In a money economy, the fisherman would sell his catch, receive money, and exchange the money for such goods as a new sail.

Money serves three functions:[1]

1. ***Medium of exchange.*** Like the fisherman "trading" money for a new sail, we use money as a way of buying and selling things. Without money, we would be bogged down in a system of barter.
2. ***Store of value.*** Pity the fisherman who catches a fish on Monday and wants to buy a few bars of candy on, say, the following Saturday, by which time the fish would have spoiled and lost its value. In the form of currency, however, money can be used for future purchases and so "stores" value.

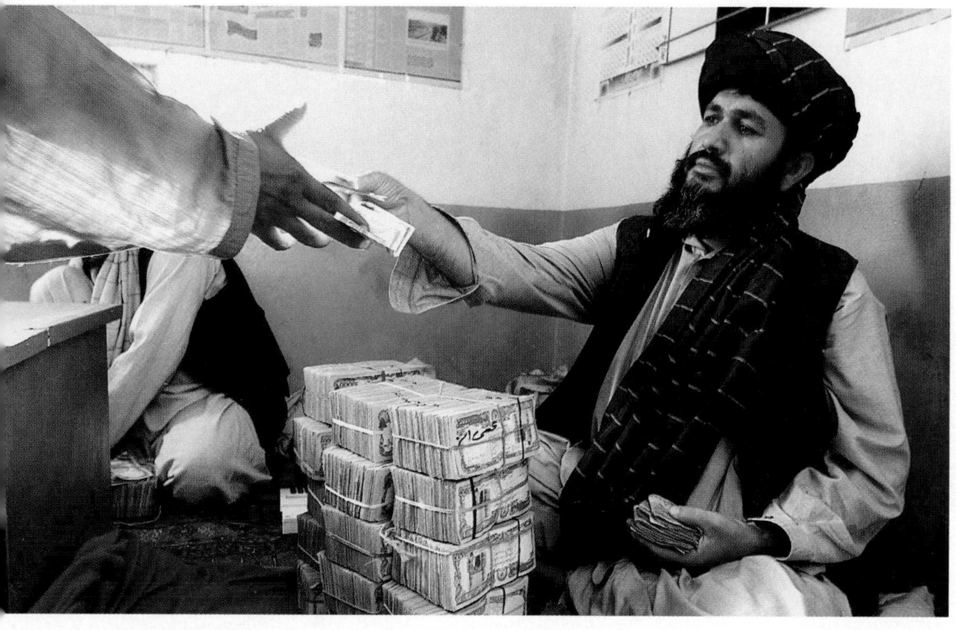

In the modern world, we've become used to highly structured monetary systems. But in some places, centuries-old systems still survive. In Quetta, Pakistan, for example. traders like Mohammad Essa transfer funds through handshakes and code words. The system is called hawala, *which means "trust" in Arabic. The worldwide hawala system, though illegal in most countries, moves billions of dollars past regulators annually and is alleged to be the system of choice for terrorists because it leaves no paper trail.*

3. ***Unit of account.*** Money lets us measure the relative values of goods and services. It acts as a unit of account because all products can be valued and accounted for in terms of money. For example, the concepts of "$1,000 worth of clothes" or "$500 in labor costs" have universal meaning because everyone deals with money every day.

'he Spendable Money Supply: M-1

'or money to serve its basic functions, both buyers and sellers must agree on its alue. That value depends in part on its *supply*—on how much money is in circu-ıtion. When the money supply is high, the value of money drops. When it is low, ıat value increases.

Unfortunately, it is not easy to measure the supply of money. One of the most ommonly used measures, known widely as **M-1,** counts only the most liquid, or pendable, forms of money: currency, demand deposits, and other checkable eposits. These are all non-interest–bearing or low–interest-bearing forms of ıoney. As of May 2002, M-1 totaled $1.18 trillion.[2]

M-1
Measure of the money supply that includes only the most liquid (spendable) forms of money

Paper money and metal coins are **currency** issued by the government. urrency is widely used for small exchanges, and the law requires creditors to ccept it in payment of debts. As of May 2002, currency in circulation in the 'nited States amounted to $605 billion, or about 51 percent of M-1.[3]

currency
Government-issued paper money and metal coins

A **check** is essentially an order instructing a bank to pay a given sum to a ɔayee." Although not all sellers accept them as payment, many do. Checks are sually acceptable in place of cash because they are valuable only to specified ayees and can be exchanged for cash. Checking accounts, which are known as **emand deposits,** are counted in M-1 because its funds may be withdrawn at any me—"on demand." In May 2002, demand deposits in the United States totaled 306 billion (26 percent of M-1).[4]

check
Demand deposit order instructing a bank to pay a given sum to a specified payee

demand deposit
Bank account funds that may be withdrawn at any time

1-1 Plus the Convertible Money Supply: M-2

1-2 includes everything in M-1 plus items that cannot be spent directly but are asily converted to spendable forms. The major components of M-2 are M-1, *time eposits, money market mutual funds,* and *savings deposits.* Totaling over $5.5 tril-on in May 2002, M-2 accounts for nearly all of the nation's money supply.[5] Thus, measures the store of monetary value available for financial transactions. As

M-2
Measure of the money supply that includes all the components of M-1 plus the forms of money that can be easily converted into spendable forms

MONEY TALKS

Money makes the world go round. Or so they say. But in different cultures, people put different spins on monetary transactions. In some countries—Japan is a good example—money is exchanged with a good deal of respect, even down to the way it's physically handled. You'll often find little trays and dishes next to cash registers where notes and coins are placed for people to pick up. Rarely is money passed from hand to hand. In Japan, too, it's not good form to talk too much about how much you make or have in the bank. These are private matters. The same goes in the United Kingdom, where it's often considered bad manners to talk about money.

In some places, of course—and the United States is one of them—attitudes toward money and talking about it are far more relaxed. You'll find people freely discussing how much they make, how much they paid for their houses, and how much they're worth. Notes and coins themselves are exchanged with very little formality. Typically, people pitch bills on a counter or slap them into someone's hand with little ceremony.

In many countries—America included—money is an important element of national identity: It helps to distinguish a country from its neighbors, and people often feel a touch of pride toward their national currencies. A lot of people don't like to see denominations of national currency removed from circulation or altered in design.

Ironically, those are precisely the changes that swept across much of Europe beginning in January 2002, when the currencies of twelve nations were replaced by a new currency called the *euro.* At first, officials worried that many Europeans would be reluctant to give up their unique currencies in favor of common notes and coins. After all, the German Deutschmark and the French franc had long been important symbols of national identity. But when the time came to make the switch, old currencies disappeared rapidly, and Europeans quickly became used to the cash and coinage. Ultimately, of course, what's important is what you can buy with your money.

this overall level of money increases, more is available for consumer purchases and business investment. When the supply is tightened, less money is available, and financial transactions, spending, and business activity, thus, slow down.

time deposit
Bank funds that cannot be withdrawn without notice or transferred by check

Unlike demand deposits, **time deposits,** such as certificates of deposit (CDs) and savings certificates, require prior notice of withdrawal and cannot be transferred by check. However, time deposits pay higher interest rates. Time deposits in M-2 include only accounts of less than $100,000 that can be redeemed on demand with small penalties.

money market mutual fund
Fund of short-term, low-risk financial securities purchased with the pooled assets of investor-owners

Operated by investment companies that bring together pools of assets from many investors, **money market mutual funds** buy a collection of short-term, low-risk financial securities. Ownership of and profits (or losses) from the sale of these securities are shared among the fund's investors. In May 2002, these funds held $942 billion in assets.[6] In the wake of new, more attractive investments, traditional savings deposits, such as passbook savings accounts, have declined in popularity. Totaling a little over $2.5 trillion, savings deposits represented 44 percent of M-2 in May 2002.[7]

Figure 18.1 shows how the two measures of money, M-1 and M-2, have grown since 1959. For many years, M-1 was the traditional measure of liquid money. Because it was closely related to gross domestic product, it served as a

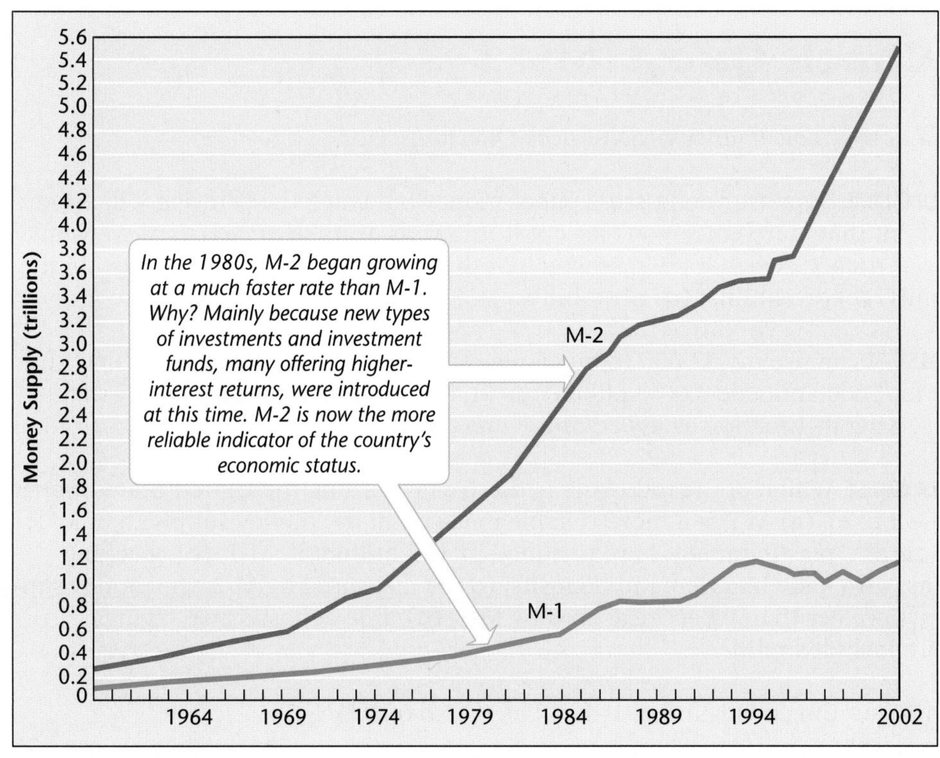

FIGURE 18.1
Money-Supply Growth

reliable predictor of the nation's economic health. As you can see, however, this situation changed in the early 1980s, with the introduction of new types of investments and the easier transfer of money among investment funds to gain higher interest returns. As a result, M-2 today is a more reliable measure than M-1 and is often used by economists for economic planning.

Credit Cards: Plastic Money?

Citi Cards <www.citigroup.com> is the world's largest credit card issuer, with more than 100 million accounts in North America alone. It is estimated that more than 160 million U.S. cardholders carry 1.5 billion cards. Spending with general-purpose credit cards in the United States is estimated at $1.7 trillion—almost half of all transactions—for the year 2001.[8] Indeed, the use of cards such as Visa <www.visa.com>, MasterCard <www.mastercard.com>, American Express <www.americanexpress.com>, Discover <www.discover.com>, and Diners Club <www.dinersclub.com> has become so widespread that many people refer to them as "plastic money." Credit cards, however, are not money and, accordingly, are not included in M-1 or M-2 when measuring the nation's money supply.

Credit cards are big business for two basic reasons. First, they are convenient. Second, they are extremely profitable for issuing companies. Profits derive from two sources:

1. Some cards charge annual fees to holders. All charge interest on unpaid balances. Depending on the issuer—and on certain state regulations—cardholders pay interest rates ranging from 11 to 20 percent.
2. Merchants who accept credit cards pay fees to card issuers. Depending on the merchant's agreement with the issuer, 2 to 5 percent of total credit sales dollars goes to card issuers.

Self-Check Questions 1–3

*You should now be able to answer Self-Check Questions 1–3**

1. MULTIPLE CHOICE Suppose you possess paper money on which the printing will eventually be so faint that merchants won't accept it. In terms of its *characteristics,* we would say that your money does not possess which of the following [select one]: **(a)** stability; **(b)** durability; **(c)** divisibility; **(d)** portability.

2. TRUE/FALSE "I can use my $2,000 to buy a new stereo system, or I can buy a new suit of clothes for $600 and a deluxe road bike for $1,400." In this example, we say that money is serving its function as a *medium of exchange.*

3. MULTIPLE CHOICE Which of the following is **not** true regarding the United States *money supply* [select one]: **(a)** M-2 is a more reliable measure of the money supply than M-1; **(b)** credit cards ("plastic money") are included in M-2 but not in M-1; **(c)** checking accounts are also known as demand deposits; **(d)** as measured by M-2, the money supply is always greater than when measured by M-1; **(e)** time deposits and savings deposits are included in M-2.

ANSWERS TO SELF CHECK QUESTIONS 1–3 CAN BE FOUND ON P. AN-12.

The U.S. Financial System

Many forms of money, especially demand deposits and time deposits, depend on the existence of financial institutions to provide a broad spectrum of services to both individuals and businesses. Just how important are these financial institutions to both businesses and individuals? In the sections that follow, we describe the major types of financial institutions, explain how they work, and survey some of the special services that they offer. We also explain their role as creators of money and discuss the regulation of the U.S. banking system.

Financial Institutions

The main function of financial institutions is to ease the flow of money from sectors with surpluses to those with deficits. They do this by issuing claims against themselves and using the proceeds to buy the assets of—and thus invest in—other organizations. A bank, for instance, can issue financial claims against itself by making available funds for checking and savings accounts. In turn, its assets will be mostly loans invested in individuals and businesses and perhaps government securities. In this section, we discuss each of the major types of financial institutions: *commercial banks, savings and loan associations, mutual savings banks, credit unions,* and various organizations known as *nondeposit institutions.*

commercial bank

Federal- or state-chartered financial institution accepting deposits that it uses to make loans and earn profits

Commercial Banks The United States today boasts nearly 10,000 **commercial banks**—companies that accept deposits that they use to make loans and earn profits. Commercial banks range from the very largest institutions in New York, such as Bank of America and Chase Manhattan, to tiny banks dotting the rural landscape. Bank liabilities include checking accounts and savings accounts. Assets consist of a wide variety of loans to individuals, businesses, and governments.

Diversification and Mergers Many observers today believe that traditional banking has become a mature industry, one whose basic operations have expanded as broadly as they can. For instance, 1993 marked the first year in which the money invested in mutual funds—almost $2 trillion—equaled the amount deposited in U.S. banks. Thus, financial industry competitors in areas such as mutual funds are growing, sometimes rapidly.

As consumers continue to look for alternatives to traditional banking services, commercial banks and savings and loan associations find themselves with a dwindling share of the market. The investment bank Merrill Lynch <www.ml.com> has originated billions of dollars in commercial loans, formerly the province of commercial banks. Savers, too, have been putting their savings into money market funds, stocks, and bonds that are offered by companies such as Charles Schwab <www.schwab.com> instead of into the traditional savings accounts offered by banks. Many observers contend that to compete, banks, too, must diversify their offerings. The only way that they can compete, says banking analyst Thomas Brown, "is to transform themselves into successful retailers of financial services, which involves dramatic, not incremental change."

"The only way banks can compete is to transform themselves into successful retailers of financial services, which involves dramatic, not incremental change."

~Thomas Brown, BANKING ANALYST

A related option seems to be to get bigger. In efforts to regain competitiveness, banks were merging at a record-setting pace in the 1990s. When commercial banks merge with investment banks, the resulting companies hold larger shares of the financial market, and the lines become blurred between traditional banking and nonbank financial institutions. Citigroup Inc. <www.citigroup.com>, for example, was formed as the result of a 1998 merger between Citicorp (a commercial bank) and Travelers Group (which includes investment bank Salomon Smith Barney <www.smithbarney.com>). Still, Citicorp is the largest U.S. retail bank, with $902 billion in assets in 2001. Citigroup, the parent company, offers one-stop shopping on a global scale for both consumers and businesses, including private banking, credit card services, mortgages, mutual funds, stock brokerage services, insurance, and loans.

Mergers are the trend, and fewer but larger banks are offering a wide range of financial products. The strategy streamlines operations to reduce costs and focuses on providing products that will win back customers from nonbank competitors.

Commercial Interest Rates Every bank receives a major portion of its income from interest paid on loans by borrowers. As long as terms and conditions are

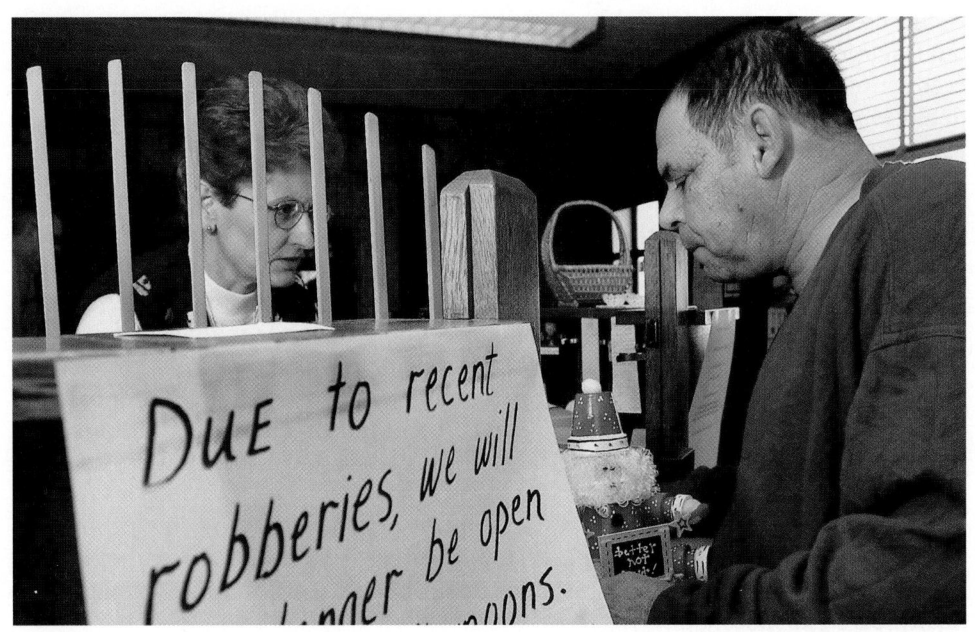

Think your bank is robbing you blind? Actually, it's often just the opposite in rural America, where robberies at small town banks are on the rise, thanks in part to an increase in suburban sprawl and all the changes that have come with it. Better roads, for example, make for easier getaways. "It's easier to hit and run," explains one expert in rural crime. This bank in Plevna, Kansas, went 99 years without a robbery, only to be hit twice in a span of two months in 2001 and 2002. Despite cutting back its Friday afternoon hours and hiring an armed guard, the bank eventually went out of business.

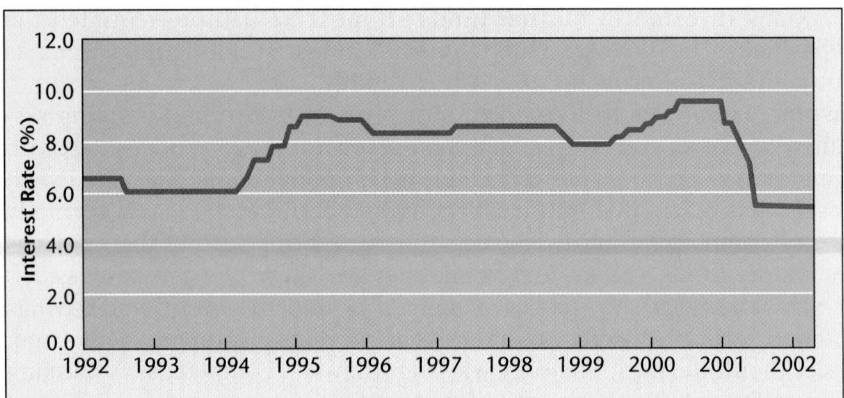

FIGURE 18.2
The Prime Rate

clearly revealed to borrowers, banks are allowed to set their own interest rates. Traditionally, the lowest rates were made available to the bank's most creditworthy commercial customers. That rate is called the **prime rate.** Most commercial loans are set at markups over prime. However, the prime rate is no longer a strong force in setting loan rates. Borrowers can now get funds less expensively from other sources, including foreign banks that set lower interest rates. To remain competitive, U.S. banks now offer some commercial loans at rates below prime.[9] Figure 18.2 shows the changes in the prime rate since 1992.[10]

prime rate
Interest rate available to a bank's most creditworthy customers

Savings and Loan Associations Like commercial banks, **savings and loan associations (S&Ls)** accept deposits and make loans. They lend money primarily for home mortgages. Most S&Ls were created to provide financing for homes. Many of them, however, have ventured into other investments, with varying degrees of success. S&Ls in the United States now hold $1.2 trillion in assets and deposits of $738 billion.[11]

savings and loan association (S&L)
Financial institution accepting deposits and making loans primarily for home mortgages

Mutual Savings Banks and Credit Unions In **mutual savings banks,** all depositors are considered owners of the bank. All profits, therefore, are divided proportionately among depositors, who receive dividends. Like S&Ls, mutual savings banks attract most of their funds in the form of savings deposits, and funds are loaned out in the form of mortgages.

mutual savings bank
Financial institution whose depositors are owners sharing in its profits

In **credit unions,** deposits are accepted only from members who meet specific qualifications, usually working for a particular employer. Most universities run credit unions, as do the U.S. Navy <www.navy.mil> and the Pentagon <www.defenselink.mil>. Credit unions make loans for automobiles and home mortgages as well as other types of personal loans. Currently, U.S. credit unions hold $442 billion in assets.[12]

credit union
Financial institution that accepts deposits from, and makes loans to, only its members, usually employees of a particular organization

Nondeposit Institutions A variety of other organizations take in money, provide interest or other services, and make loans. Four of the most important are *pension funds, insurance companies, finance companies,* and *securities dealers.*

A **pension fund** is essentially a nondeposit pool of funds managed to provide retirement income for its members. *Public pension funds* include Social Security <www.ssa.gov> and $3.1 trillion in retirement programs for state and local government employees. *Private pension funds,* operated by employers, unions, and other private groups, cover about 100 million people and have total assets of $9 trillion.[13]

pension fund
Nondeposit pool of funds managed to provide retirement income for its members

Insurance companies collect large pools of funds from the premiums charged for coverage. Funds are invested in stocks, real estate, and other assets. Earnings pay for insured losses, such as death benefits, automobile damage, and health-care expenses.

insurance company
Nondeposit institution that invests funds collected as premiums charged for insurance coverage

"And, hey, don't kill yourself trying to pay it back. You know our motto—'What the hell, it's only money.'"

Finance companies are nondeposit institutions that specialize in making loans to businesses and consumers. *Commercial finance companies* lend to businesses needing capital or long-term funds. They may, for instance, lend to a manufacturer that needs new assembly-line equipment. *Consumer finance companies* devote most of their resources to small noncommercial loans to individuals.

finance company
Nondeposit institution that specializes in making loans to businesses and consumers

Securities investment dealers (brokers), such as Merrill Lynch <www.ml.com> and A.G. Edwards & Sons <www.agedwards.com>, buy and sell stocks and bonds on the New York and other stock exchanges for client-investors. They also invest in securities—they buy stocks and bonds for their own accounts in hopes of reselling them later at a profit. These companies hold large sums of money for transfer between buyers and sellers. (We discuss the activities of brokers and investment bankers more fully in Chapter 19.)

securities investment dealer (broker)
Nondeposit institution that buys and sells stocks and bonds both for investors and for its own accounts

Special Financial Services

The finance business today is a highly competitive industry. No longer is it enough for commercial banks to accept deposits and make loans. Most, for example, now offer bank-issued credit cards and safe-deposit boxes. In addition, many offer pension, trust, international, and brokerage services and financial advice. Most offer ATMs and electronic money transfer.

Pension and Trust Services Most banks help customers establish savings plans for retirement. **Individual retirement accounts (IRAs)** are tax-deferred pension funds that wage earners and their spouses can set up to supplement other retirement funds. All wage earners can invest up to $2,000 of earned income annually in an IRA. IRAs offer a significant tax benefit: Under many circumstances, taxes on principal and earnings are deferred until funds are withdrawn upon retirement.

individual retirement account (IRA)
Tax-deferred pension fund with which wage earners supplement other retirement funds

Under the 1997 tax changes, some IRAs are entirely tax-free. Banks serve as financial intermediaries by receiving funds and investing them as directed by customers. They also provide customers with information on investment vehicles available for IRAs (deposit accounts, mutual funds, stocks, and so forth).[14]

trust services

Bank management of an individual's investments, payments, or estate

Many commercial banks offer **trust services**—the management of funds left "in the bank's trust." In return for a fee, the trust department will perform such tasks as making your monthly bill payments and managing your investment portfolio. Trust departments also manage the estates of deceased persons.

International Services The three main international services offered by banks are *currency exchange, letters of credit,* and *banker's acceptances.* Suppose a U.S. company wants to buy a product from a British supplier. For a fee, it can use one or more of three services offered by its bank:

1. It can exchange U.S. dollars for British pounds at a U.S. bank and then pay the British supplier in pounds.
2. It can pay its bank to issue a **letter of credit**—a promise by the bank to pay the British firm a certain amount if specified conditions are met.
3. It can pay its bank to draw up a **banker's acceptance,** which promises that the bank will pay some specified amount at a future date.

letter of credit

Bank promise, issued for a buyer, to pay a designated firm a certain amount of money if specified conditions are met

banker's acceptance

Bank promise, issued for a buyer, to pay a designated firm a specified amount at a future date

A banker's acceptance requires payment by a particular date. Letters of credit are payable only after certain conditions are met. The British supplier, for example, may not be paid until shipping documents prove that the merchandise has been shipped from England.

Financial Advice and Brokerage Services Many banks, both large and small, help their customers manage their money. Depending on the customer's situation, the bank may recommend different investment opportunities. The recommended mix might include CDs, mutual funds, stocks, and bonds. Many banks also serve as securities intermediaries, using their own stockbrokers to buy and sell securities and their own facilities to hold them. Bank advertisements often stress the role of banks as financial advisers.

automated teller machine (ATM)

Electronic machine that allows customers to conduct account-related activities 24 hours a day, 7 days a week

Automated Teller Machines Electronic **automated teller machines (ATMs)** allow customers to withdraw money and make deposits 24 hours a day, seven days a week. They also allow transfers of funds between accounts and provide information on account status. Some banks offer cards that can be used in affiliated nationwide systems. About 324,000 machines are now located at U.S. bank buildings, grocery stores, airports, shopping malls, and other locations. Bank of America, with 12,000 units, is this country's leading owner of ATMs. U.S. bank customers conduct more than 13 billion ATM transactions a year, with each machine being used an average of 3,500 times a month.[15]

Increasingly, ATMs are also becoming global fixtures. In fact, among the world's nearly one million ATMs, 68 percent are located outside the United States. Asia, with 32 percent of the world's total, is the leading region for ATMs, followed by North America (31 percent), western Europe (25 percent), and Latin America (8 percent). Many U.S. banks now offer international ATM services. Citicorp installed Shanghai's first 24-hour ATM and is the first foreign bank to receive approval from the People's Bank of China to issue local currency through ATMs. Elsewhere, Citibank machines feature touch screens that take instructions in any of 10 languages.

electronic funds transfer (EFT)

Communication of fund-transfer information over wire, cable, or microwave

Electronic Funds Transfer ATMs are the most popular form of **electronic funds transfer (EFT).** These systems transfer many kinds of financial information via electrical impulses over wire, cable, or microwave. In addition to ATMs, EFT systems include automatic payroll deposit, bill payment, and automatic funds trans-

Citibank <www.citibank.com> *now has consumer banking outlets in 41 countries, where it strives to make once specialized products universal. One of the key functions of overseas ATMs is to attract customers to the bank's retail branches, and the strategy has been particularly successful in Japan. Since 1986, Citibank Japan* <www.citibank.co.jp/en/> *has offered Japanese customers such services as free ATM and telephone banking and multi-currency accounts. Aftertax profits in Asia now top $700 million a year.*

fer. Such systems can help a businessperson close an important business deal by transferring money from San Francisco to Miami within a few hours.[16]

Banks as Creators of Money

In the course of their activities, financial institutions provide a special service to the economy—they create money. This is not to say that they mint bills and coins. Rather, by taking in deposits and making loans, they *expand the money supply.*[17]

As Figure 18.3 shows, the money supply expands because banks are allowed to loan out most (although not all) of the money they take in from deposits. Suppose that you deposit $100 in your bank. If banks are allowed to loan out 90 percent of all their deposits, then your bank will hold $10 in reserve and loan $90 of your money to borrowers. (You, of course, still have $100 on deposit.) Meanwhile, borrowers—or the people they pay—will deposit the $90 loan in their own banks. Together, the borrowers' banks will then have $81 (90 percent of $90) available for new loans. Banks, therefore, have turned your original $100

Deposit	Money Held in Reserve by Bank	Money to Lend	Total Supply
$100.00	$10.00	$90.00	$190.00
90.00	9.00	81.00	271.00
81.00	8.10	72.90	343.90
72.90	7.29	65.61	409.51
65.61	6.56	59.05	468.56

FIGURE 18.3
How Banks Create Money

into $271 ($100 + $90 + $81). The chain continues, with borrowings from one bank becoming deposits in the next.

Regulation of Commercial Banking

Because commercial banks are critical to the creation of money, the government regulates them to ensure a sound and competitive financial system. Later in this chapter, we will see how the Federal Reserve System regulates many aspects of U.S. banking. Other federal and state agencies also regulate banks to ensure that the failure of some banks as a result of competition will not cause the public to lose faith in the banking system itself.

Federal Deposit Insurance Corporation (FDIC)

Federal agency that guarantees the safety of all deposits up to $100,000 in the financial institutions that it insures

Federal Deposit Insurance Corporation The **Federal Deposit Insurance Corporation (FDIC)** insures deposits in member banks. More than 99 percent of the nation's commercial banks pay fees for membership in the FDIC <www.fdic.gov>. In return, the FDIC guarantees, through its Bank Insurance Fund (BIF), the safety of all deposits up to the current maximum of $100,000. If a bank collapses, the FDIC promises to pay its depositors—through the BIF—for losses up to $100,000 per account. (A handful of the nation's 10,000 commercial banks are insured by states rather than by the BIF.)

To insure against multiple bank failures, the FDIC maintains the right to examine the activities and accounts of all member banks. Such regulation was effective from 1941 through 1980, when fewer than 10 banks failed per year. At the beginning of the 1980s, however, banks were deregulated, and between 1981 and 1990, losses from nearly 1,100 bank failures depleted the FDIC's reserve fund. In recent years, the FDIC has thus raised the premiums charged to member banks to keep up with losses incurred by failed banks.

Self-Check Questions 4–6

*You should now be able to answer Self-Check Questions 4–6**

4. TRUE/FALSE *Loans* are available from all of the following financial institutions: credit unions, mutual savings banks, savings and loan associations, commercial banks, and finance companies.

5. MULTIPLE CHOICE Suppose you have accumulated substantial wealth that you want to leave to your now-infant children when they reach age 40. Which of the following *financial services* is most appropriate for your purposes? [select one]: **(a)** individual retirement account (IRA); **(b)** pension fund; **(c)** banker's acceptance; **(d)** banker's trust; **(e)** commercial loan.

6. MULTIPLE CHOICE Suppose that you deposit $250 in your local bank, which is allowed to loan out 85 percent of its deposits. Suppose, further, that the following events occur: Your bank loans out the maximum allowable money to borrowers who, in turn, deposit the borrowed money in their banks. These banks also loan out the maximum allowable funds. In total, banks, as *creators of money,* have turned your original $250 into which of the following amounts [select one]: **(a)** $643.13; **(b)** $319.75; **(c)** $750.00; **(d)** $487.37; **(e)** none of the above.

ANSWERS TO SELF-CHECK QUESTIONS 4–6 CAN BE FOUND ON P. AN-12.

The Federal Reserve System

Perched atop the U.S. financial system and regulating many aspects of its operation is the Federal Reserve System. Established by Congress in 1913, the **Federal Reserve System** (or the **Fed**) <www.federalreserve.gov> is the nation's central bank. In this section, we describe the structure of the Fed, its functions, and the tools that it uses to control the nation's money supply.

Federal Reserve System (the Fed)
Central bank of the United States, which acts as the government's bank, serves member commercial banks, and controls the nation's money supply

The Structure of the Fed

The Federal Reserve System consists of a board of governors, a group of reserve banks, and member banks. As originally established by the Federal Reserve Act of 1913, the system consisted of 12 relatively autonomous banks and a seven-member committee whose powers were limited to coordinating the activities of those banks. By the 1930s, however, both the structure and function of the Fed had changed dramatically.

The Board of Governors The Fed's board of governors consists of seven members appointed by the president for overlapping terms of 14 years. The chair of the board serves on major economic advisory committees and works actively with the administration to formulate economic policy. The board plays a large role in controlling the money supply. It alone determines the reserve requirements, within statutory limits, for depository institutions. It also works with other members of the Federal Reserve System to set discount rates and handle the Fed's sale and purchase of government securities.

Reserve Banks The Federal Reserve System consists of 12 administrative areas and 12 banks. Each Federal Reserve bank holds reserve deposits from and sets the discount rate for commercial banks in its region. Reserve banks also play a major role in the nation's check-clearing process.

Member Banks All nationally chartered commercial banks are members of the Federal Reserve System, as are some state-chartered banks. The accounts of all member bank depositors are automatically covered by the FDIC/BIF. Although many state-chartered banks do not belong to the Federal Reserve System, most pay deposit insurance premiums and are covered by the FDIC.

The Functions of the Fed

In addition to chartering national banks, the Fed serves as the federal government's bank and the "bankers' bank," regulating a number of banking activities. Most important, it controls the money supply. In this section, we describe these functions in some detail.

The Government's Bank Two of the Fed's activities are producing the nation's paper currency and lending money to the government. The Fed decides how many bills to produce and how many to destroy. To lend funds to the government, the Fed buys bonds issued by the Treasury Department <www.ustreas.gov>. The borrowed money is then used to help finance the national deficit.

The Bankers' Bank Individual banks that need money can borrow from the Federal Reserve and pay interest on the loans. In addition, the Fed provides storage for commercial banks, which are required to keep funds on reserve at a Federal Reserve bank.

Check Clearing The Fed also clears checks, some 69 million of them each day, for commercial banks. To understand the check-clearing process, imagine that you are a photographer living in New Orleans. To participate in a workshop in

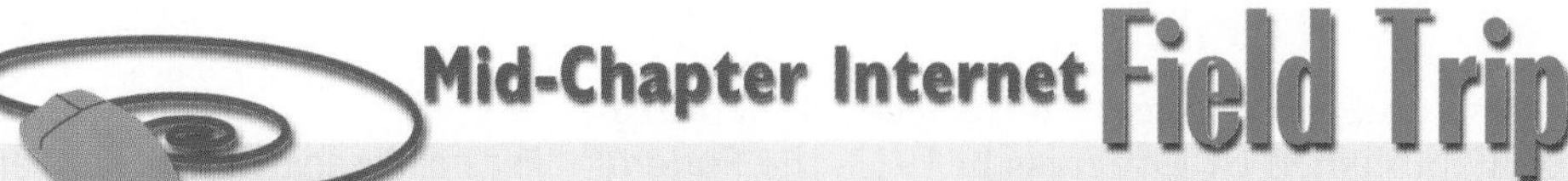

"Controlling the Money Supply"

In the first part of this chapter, we discussed the nature of money, its purposes, and its various forms. We've seen the importance of maintaining a sound banking system that includes different kinds of financial institutions for safely moving funds among people and organizations. We have just begun our discussion of the U.S. Federal Reserve System, which is the nation's central bank. As we examine its activities, we'll raise several questions about the Fed: What geographic areas are served by each Federal Reserve district? How much coin and currency are received and shipped by the Fed? What happens to currency once it deteriorates and can no longer be used?

Let's pursue these questions by exploring the Web site of one Fed bank, the Federal Reserve Bank of Minneapolis. To learn about its services and history as well as its role in the Federal Reserve System, let's visit its Web site at <www.mpls.frb.org>.

First, to get an idea of what kind of information is available, browse the home page, including the various subject gates located up, down, and across the page. Notice especially the categories across the top, including **About the Fed, Banking Information, Community Development,** and several other content areas. In exploring these pages, you'll see that the Minneapolis Fed's Web site contains not only information unique to the Minneapolis District, but also information about the entire system. In this field trip, we'll start with the Minneapolis district and then find out some information about U.S. currency.

Begin at the top of the home page by clicking on **About the Fed**. After reading information about the Minneapolis Fed, respond to the following items:

1. Where is the Minneapolis Fed located? Which Federal Reserve District does it serve? What geographic areas does it serve?
2. What are the functions of the Federal Reserve Bank of Minneapolis?

Now return to the top of the home page, and enter the gate entitled **Consumer Information.** Scroll down the panel to the section on **U.S. Money,** read about the Fed's role in distributing currency and coin, and respond to the following questions:

3. How much currency and coin is received and sent by the Minneapolis Fed? How much unfit currency is destroyed?
4. Identify at least three security features in the $20 note.

Go back to the top of the home page, and reenter the gate entitled **Consumer Information.** Scroll down to the section on **Consumer Banking.** Within that section, look at **Bank Products,** and then respond to the following question:

5. What categories of bank products are listed?

To continue your Internet Field Trip, click on www.prenhall.com/griffin

Detroit, you must send a check for $50 to the Detroit studio. Figure 18.4 traces your check through the clearing process:

1. You send your check to the Detroit studio, which deposits it in its Detroit bank.
2. The Detroit bank deposits the check in its own account at the Federal Reserve Bank of Chicago.
3. The check is sent from Chicago to the Atlanta Federal Reserve Bank for collection because you, the check writer, live in the Atlanta district.
4. Your New Orleans bank receives the check from Atlanta and deducts the $50 from your personal account.
5. Your bank then has $50 deducted from its deposit account at the Atlanta Federal Reserve Bank.
6. The $50 is shifted from Atlanta to the Chicago Federal Reserve Bank. The studio's Detroit bank gets credited, whereupon the studio's account is then credited $50. Your bank mails the canceled check back to you.

Depending on the number of banks and the distances between them, a check will clear in two to six days. Until the process is completed, the studio's Detroit

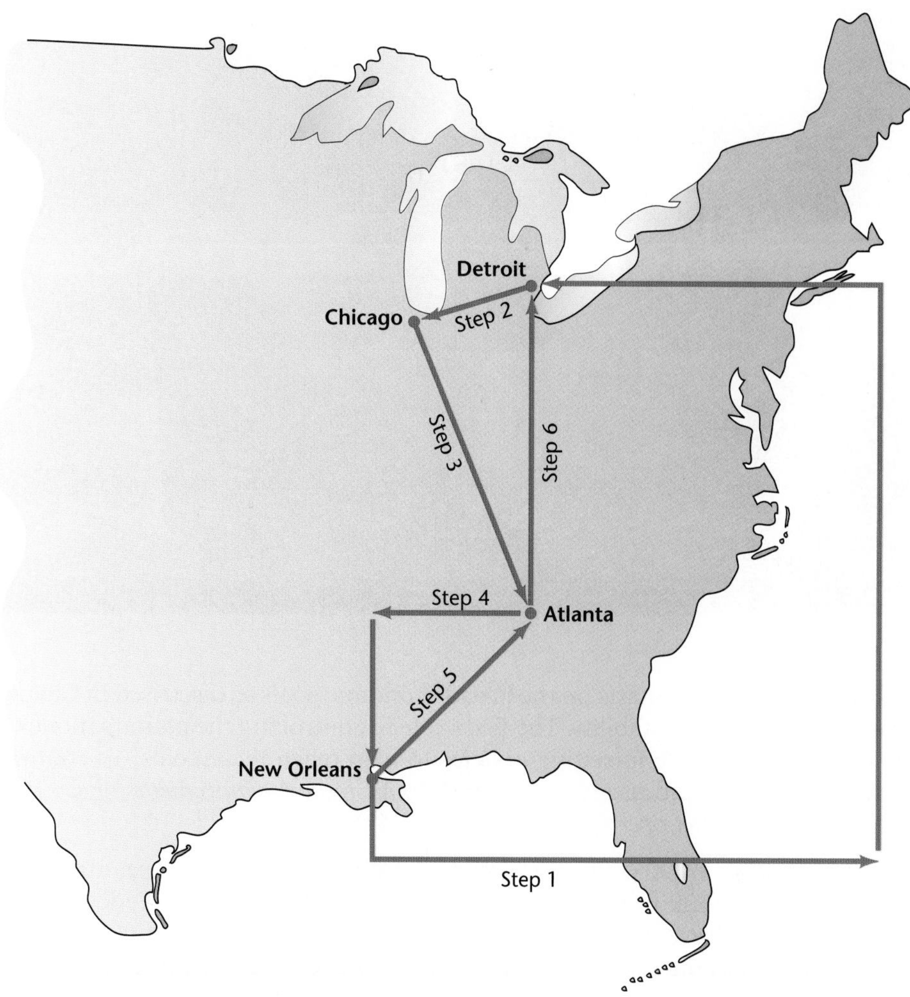

■ FIGURE 18.4
Clearing a Check

bank cannot spend the $50 deposited there. Meanwhile, your bank's records will continue to show $50 in your account. Each day, approximately $1 billion in checks is processed by the system. The term **float** refers to all of the checks in the process at any one time.

float
Total amount of checks written but not yet cleared through the Federal Reserve

Controlling the Money Supply The Federal Reserve System is responsible for the conduct of U.S. **monetary policy**—the management of the nation's economic growth by managing money supply and interest rates. By controlling these two factors, the Fed influences the ability and willingness of banks throughout the country to loan money.

monetary policy
Policies by which the Federal Reserve manages the nation's money supply and interest rates

Inflation Management As we defined it in Chapter 2, *inflation* is a period of widespread price increases throughout an economic system. It occurs if the money supply grows too large. Demand for goods and services increases, and the prices of everything rise. (In contrast, too little money means that an economy will lack the funds to maintain high levels of employment.) Because commercial banks are the main creators of money, much of the Fed's management of the money supply takes the form of regulating the supply of money through commercial banks.

The Tools of the Fed

According to the Fed's original charter, its primary duties were to supervise banking and to manage both the currency and commercial paper. The duties of the Fed evolved, however, along with a predominant philosophy of monetary policy. That

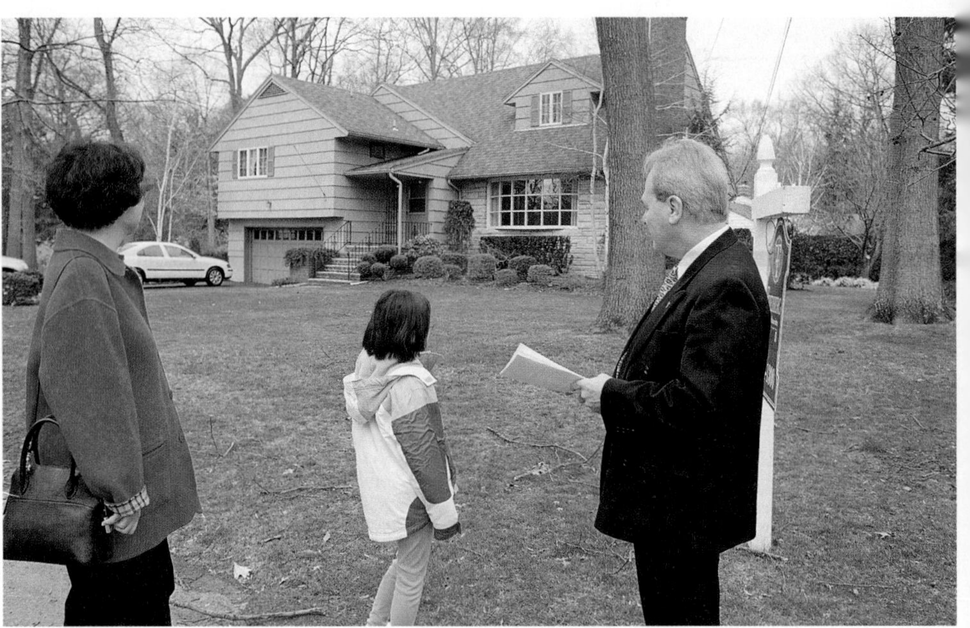

In 2001, the Fed <www.federalreserve.gov>*cut the discount rate eleven times in an effort to bolster a sagging U.S. economy. Although it's hard to calculate the effects on the overall economy, the immediate impact on the housing market was profound. Because banks could lower mortgage rates, the number of people who could afford to buy houses went up by three million. "People keep buying the darn things," reported one economist, and in so doing they strengthened the economy by adding $2 trillion to $3 trillion to total homeowner wealth.*

policy includes an emphasis on the broad economic goals as discussed in Chapter 2, especially growth and stability. The Fed's role in controlling the nation's money supply stems from its role in setting policies to help reach these goals. To control the money supply, the Fed uses four primary tools: *reserve requirements, discount rate controls, open-market operations,* and *selective credit controls.*[18]

reserve requirement
Percentage of its deposits that a bank must hold in cash or on deposit with the Federal Reserve

Reserve Requirements The **reserve requirement** is the percentage of its deposits that a bank must hold, in cash or on deposit, with a Federal Reserve bank. High requirements mean that banks have less money to lend. Thus, a high reserve requirement reduces the money supply. Conversely, low requirements permit the supply to expand. Because the Fed sets requirements for all depository institutions, it can adjust them to make changes to the overall supply of money in the economy.

discount rate
Interest rate at which member banks can borrow money from the Federal Reserve

Discount Rate Controls As the "bankers' bank," the Fed loans money to banks. The interest rate on these loans is known as the **discount rate.** If the Fed wants to reduce the money supply, it increases the discount rate, making it more expensive for banks to borrow money and less attractive for them to loan it. Conversely, low rates encourage borrowing and lending and expand the money supply. The Fed used a series of discount rate decreases—from 6.0 percent beginning in May 2000 down to 1.25 percent in December 2001—to speed up the sagging U.S. economy.[19]

open-market operations
The Federal Reserve's sales and purchases of securities in the open market

Open-Market Operations The third instrument for monetary control is probably the Fed's most important tool. **Open-market operations** refer to the Fed's sale and purchase of securities (usually U.S. Treasury notes and bonds) in the open market. Open-market operations are particularly effective because they act quickly and predictably on the money supply. How so? The Fed buys securities from dealers. Because the dealer's bank account is credited for the transaction, its bank has more money to lend, and so this transaction expands the money supply. The opposite happens when the Fed sells securities.[20]

selective credit controls
Federal Reserve authority to set both margin requirements for consumer stock purchases and credit rules for other consumer purchases

Selective Credit Controls The Federal Reserve can exert considerable influence over business activity by exercising **selective credit controls.** The Fed may set special requirements for consumer stock purchases as well as credit rules for other consumer purchases.

As we will see in Chapter 19, investors can set up credit accounts with stockbrokers to buy stocks and bonds. A margin requirement set by the Fed stipulates the amount of credit that the broker can extend to the customer. For example, a 60 percent margin rate means that approved customers can purchase stocks having $100,000 market value with $60,000 in cash (60 percent of $100,000) and $40,000 in loans from the dealer. If the Fed wants to increase securities transactions, it can lower the margin requirement. Customers can then borrow greater percentages of their purchase costs from dealers, thus increasing their purchasing power and the amount of securities that they can buy.

Within stipulated limits, the Fed is also permitted to specify the conditions of certain credit purchases. This authority extends to such conditions as allowable down payment percentages for appliance purchases and repayment periods on automobile loans. The Fed has chosen to not use these powers in recent years.

The Changing Money and Banking System

The U.S. money and banking systems have changed in recent years and continue to change today. Deregulation and interstate banking, for example, have increased competition not only among banks but also between banks and other financial institutions. Electronic technologies affect how you obtain money and how much interest you pay for it.

Deregulation

The Depository Institutions Deregulation and Monetary Control Act (DIDMCA) of 1980 brought many changes to the banking industry. Before its passage, there were clear distinctions between the types of services offered by different institutions. Although all institutions could offer savings accounts, only commercial banks could offer checking accounts, and S&Ls and mutual savings banks generally could not make consumer loans. The DIDMCA and subsequent laws sought to promote competition by eliminating many such restrictions.

Under deregulation, many banks were unable to survive in the new competitive environment. In the 1980s, more than 1,000 banks—more than 7 percent of the total—failed, as did 835 savings and loans. Many economists, however, regard some bank closings as a beneficial weeding out of inefficient competitors.

Interstate Banking

Although interstate banking is commonplace, it is a relatively new development. The Interstate Banking Efficiency Act was passed into law in September 1994, thus allowing banks to enter (gradually) into interstate banking—the operation of banks or branches across state lines. It also mandates regulation by government agencies to ensure proper operation and competition. The key provisions in this act include the following:

- Limited nationwide banking is permitted, beginning in 1995. Bank holding companies can acquire subsidiaries in any state.
- The ultimate *size* of any company is limited. No one company can control more than 10 percent of nationwide insured deposits. No bank can control more than 30 percent of a state's deposits (each state is empowered to set its own limit).
- Beginning in 1995, banks can provide limited transactions for affiliated banks in other states. They can thus accept deposits, close loans, and accept

loan payments on behalf of other affiliated banks. (They cannot, however, originate loans or open deposit accounts for affiliates.)

- Beginning in June 1997, banks can convert affiliates into full-fledged interstate branches.

Interstate banking offers certain efficiencies. For example, it allows banks to consolidate services and eliminate duplicated activities. Opponents, however, remain concerned that some banks will gain undue influence, dominate other banks, and hinder competition.

The Impact of Electronic Technologies

Like so many other businesses, banks are increasingly investing in technology as a way to improve efficiency and customer service levels. Many banks offer ATMs and EFT systems. Some offer TV banking, in which customers use television sets and terminals—or home computers—to make transactions. The age of electronic money has arrived. Digital money is replacing cash in stores, taxicabs, subway systems, and vending machines. Each business day, more than $2 trillion exists in and among banks and other financial institutions in purely electronic form. Each year, the Fed's Fedwire funds transfer system transfers electronically more than $390 trillion in transactions.

Debit Cards One of the electronic offerings from the financial industry that has gained popularity is the debit card. Unlike credit cards, **debit cards** allow only the transfer of money between accounts. They do not increase the funds at an individual's disposal. They can, however, be used to make retail purchases. The number of cards in use more than doubled from 173 million in 1990 to more than 400 million in 2001, with transactions exceeding $400 billion. Debit card purchases are expected to reach $1 trillion in 2005. In stores with **point-of-sale (POS) terminals,** customers insert cards that transmit to terminals information relevant to their purchases. The terminal relays the information directly to the bank's computer system. The bank automatically transfers funds from the customer's account to the store's account.

debit card
Plastic card that allows an individual to transfer money between accounts

point-of-sale (POS) terminal
Electronic device that allows customers to pay for retail purchases with debit cards

Smart Cards The so-called **smart card** is a credit-card-size plastic card with an embedded computer chip that can be programmed with "electronic money." Also known as electronic purses or stored-value cards, smart cards have existed for more than a decade. Phone callers and shoppers in Europe and Asia are the most avid users, holding the majority of the nearly two billion cards in circulation in 2001. Although small by European standards, card usage in North America grew by more than 40 percent since 2000, reaching more than 50 million cards in 2002. They are most popular in financial services, followed by prepaid long distance or wireless phone cards.[21]

smart card
Credit-card-size plastic card with an embedded computer chip that can be programmed with electronic money

Why are smart cards increasing in popularity today? For one thing, the cost of producing them has fallen dramatically, from as much as $10 to as little as $1. Convenience is equally important, notes Donald J. Gleason, president of Smart Card Enterprise, a division of Electronic Payment Services <www.eps.com.hk>. "What consumers want," Gleason contends, "is convenience, and if you look at cash, it's really quite inconvenient."

> **"What customers want is convenience, and if you look at cash, it's really quite inconvenient."**
>
> ~Donald J. Gleason, President, Smart Card Enterprise

Smart cards can be loaded with money at ATM machines or, with special telephone hookups, even at home. After using your card to purchase an item, you can then check an electronic display to see how much money your card has left. Analysts predict that in the near future, smart cards will function as much more than electronic purses. For example, travel industry experts predict that people will soon book travel plans at home on personal computers and then transfer their reservations onto their smart cards. The cards will then serve as airline tickets and boarding passes. As an added benefit, they will allow travelers to avoid waiting in lines at car rental agencies and hotel front desks.

E-Cash A new, revolutionary world of electronic money has begun to emerge with the rapid growth of the Internet. Electronic money, known as **e-cash,** is money that moves along multiple channels of consumers and businesses via digital electronic transmissions. E-cash moves outside of the established network of banks, checks, and paper currency overseen by the Federal Reserve. Companies as varied as new start-up Mondex <www.mondex.com> and giant Citicorp are developing their own forms of electronic money that allow consumers and businesses to spend money more conveniently, quickly, and cheaply than they can through the banking system. In fact, some observers predict that by the year 2005, as much as 20 percent of all household expenditures will take place on the Internet. "Banking," comments one investment banker, "is essential to the modern economy, but banks are not."

e-cash
Electronic money that moves between consumers and businesses via digital electronic transmissions

"Banking is essential to the modern economy, but banks are not."

~Investment banker

How does e-cash work? Traditional currency is used to buy electronic funds, which are downloaded over phone lines into a PC or a portable "electronic wallet" that can store and transmit e-cash. E-cash is purchased from any company that issues (sells) it, including companies such as Mondex, Citicorp, and banks. When shopping online—for example, to purchase jewelry—a shopper sends digital money to the merchant instead of using traditional cash, checks, or credit cards. Businesses can purchase supplies and services electronically from any merchant that accepts e-cash. It flows from the buyer's into the seller's e-cash funds, which are instantaneously updated and stored on a microchip. One system, operated by CyberCash <www.cybercash.com>, tallies all e-cash transactions in the customer's account and, at the end of the day, converts the e-cash balance back into dollars in the customer's conventional banking account.

Although e-cash transactions are cheaper than handling checks and the paper records involved with conventional money, there are some potential problems.[22] Hackers, for example, may break into e-cash systems and drain them instantaneously. Moreover, if the issuer's computer system crashes, it is conceivable that money "banked" in memory may be lost forever. Finally, regulation and control of e-cash systems remain largely nonexistent; there is virtually none of the protection that covers government-controlled money systems.

International Banking and Finance

Along with international banking networks, electronic technologies now permit nearly instantaneous financial transactions around the globe. The economic importance of international finance is evident from both the presence of foreign banks in the U.S. market and the sizes of certain banks around the world. In addition, each nation tries to influence its currency exchange rates for economic advantage in international trade. The subsequent country-to-country transactions result in an *international payments process* that moves money between buyers and sellers on different continents.

International Banking at U.S. Banks

The United States is heavily involved in international transactions that often entail exchanges between U.S. banks and other banks around the world. In 2001, these transactions amounted to some $2.4 trillion. Such sums have obviously attracted foreign banks to the U.S. market, where many now maintain a significant presence. In their U.S. branches and agencies, these banks hold $694 billion in assets and $371 billion in loans, mostly in New York, California, and Illinois. Meanwhile, foreign branches of U.S. banks, most

Why Aren't We Cashing In on E-Cash?

Whatever became of the e-cash craze that advocates just a few years ago were predicting would replace paper money? Cybercash still has a ways to go before it catches up with old-fashioned coin and paper currency. Contrary to predictions, the demand for currency seems to be increasing rather than decreasing. Consider the following data for the end of 2001: U.S. currency held by the public was more than $620 billion, or about $2,200 for every woman, man, and child in the United States. Sixty-five percent of it was held in $100 bills, and yet a Federal Reserve survey reports that the typical family doesn't hold even a single $100 bill. And, clearly, most people never have $2,200 in cash on hand.

So where's the money? Experts estimate that most of it—up to 75 percent—is probably held abroad by foreigners who want the security of U.S. dollars, while the rest is stashed away by U.S. businesses and citizens. The Japanese people are even greater currency lovers, with per capita cash (in yen) of more than $4,000 per person. Unlike the U.S. dollar, holdings of the yen outside Japan are relatively small. Europeans, in contrast, have somewhat smaller currency holdings, with Austrians and Germans holding over $1,800 per person, while on the lower end of cash keepers, the average four-person French family held the equivalent of just $3,000.

Because it circulates outside the U.S. Federal Reserve System, unregulated e-cash is regarded as somewhat risky. Some would-be customers are frightened away by prospects of e-money getting drained away and lost forever in cyberspace; others fear Internet intrusions into personal privacy; while still others are concerned with possibilities for electronic counterfeiting, fraud, and money laundering. While some regulatory efforts are underway to require uniform reporting and record-keeping among the more than 200,000 money services businesses (MSBs) in the United States alone, further assurances, apparently, will be required to brighten e-money's image sufficiently to keep pace with hard currency's popularity. Unlike brick-and-mortar banks and financial institutions, MSBs do not accept deposits, and they offer consumers alternative methods to make payments and to obtain cash through stored value cards and through Internet-based payments, money transfers, and foreign currency exchange.

But regardless of assurances from cryptography, e-cash creators have yet to devise guarantees of transaction anonymity. Banks, for example, can electronically identify the person who originally withdraws money from the bank, and they can then track some of the electronic money as it moves through the economy. Many consumers and businesses don't want outsiders knowing what they do with private money. Instead, they prefer to hold cash because it can move through the system without leaving trails, electronic or otherwise. And, likewise, paper currency has a "feel-good" quality that's hard to duplicate electronically.

notably in the United Kingdom, the Bahamas, and the Cayman Islands, hold $738 billion in assets.[23]

Exchange Rates and International Trade

As we saw in Chapter 4, every country's currency exchange rate affects its ability to buy and sell on the global market. The value of a given currency (say, the Canadian dollar) reflects the overall supply and demand for Canadian dollars both at home and abroad. This value changes with economic conditions. Worldwide, therefore, firms will watch those trends, and decisions about doing business in Canada will be affected by more or less favorable exchange rates.

How do firms determine when exchange rates are favorable? When a country's currency becomes overvalued, its exchange rate is higher than warranted by its economic conditions. Its high costs make it less competitive. Because its products are too expensive to make and buy, fewer are purchased by other countries. The likely result is a trade deficit (see Chapter 4). In contrast, an undervalued currency means low costs and low prices: It attracts purchases by other countries, usually leading to a trade surplus.

Government Influences on Exchange Rates What happens when a currency becomes overvalued or undervalued? A nation's economic authorities may take action to correct its balance-of-payments conditions. Typically, they will devalue or revalue the nation's currency. The purpose of devaluing is to cause a decrease in the home country's exchange value. It will then be less expensive for other countries to buy the home country's products. As more of its products are purchased, the home country's payment deficit goes down. The purpose of revaluation, of course, is the reverse: to increase the exchange value and reduce the home country's payment surplus.

In 2001, for instance, the exchange rate was 1.0 Argentine peso per U.S. dollar throughout the year. Then, in January 2002, the Argentine government devalued the peso to 1.4 pesos per dollar. By July 2002, the rate had gone to 3.57 on the world market, meaning that each peso was worth just $0.28. Argentine officials seek the more favorable exchange rate to encourage other countries to buy more Argentine products, thereby reducing Argentina's payments deficit.

The International Payments Process

Now we know why a nation tries to control its balance of payments and what it can do about an unfavorable balance. When transactions are made between buyers and sellers in different countries, exactly how are payments made? Payments are simplified through the services provided by their banks.[24] For example, payments from buyers flow through a local bank that converts them from the local currency into the foreign currency of the seller. The local bank receives and converts incoming money from the banks of foreign buyers. The payment process is shown in Figure 18.5.

- ***Step 1.*** A U.S. olive importer withdraws $1,000 from its checking account to buy olives from a Greek exporter. The local U.S. bank converts those dollars into Greek drachmas at the current exchange rate (230 drachmas per dollar).
- ***Step 2.*** The U.S. bank sends a check for 230,000 drachmas (230 × 1,000) to the exporter in Greece.

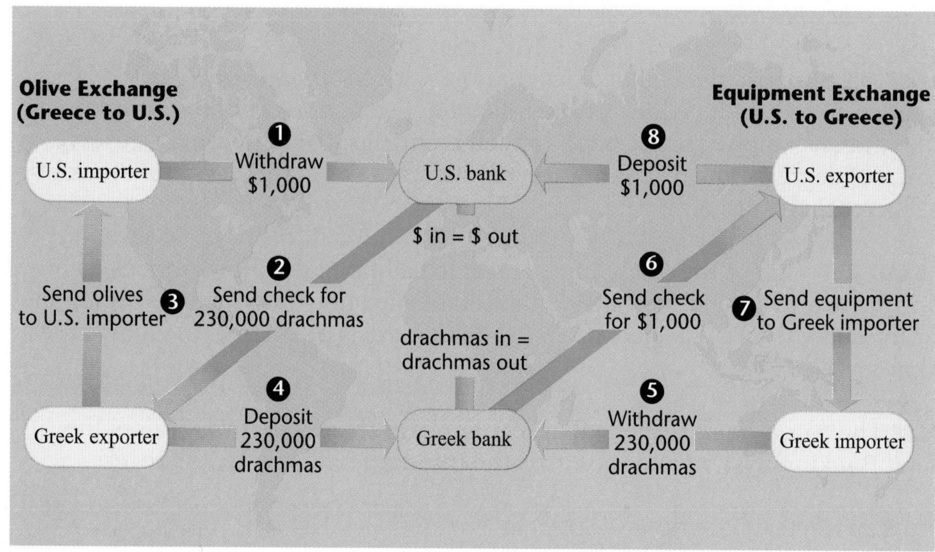

FIGURE 18.5
International Payments Process

- ***Steps 3 and 4.*** The exporter sends olives to its U.S. customer and deposits the check in its local Greek bank. The exporter now has drachmas that can be spent in Greece, and the importer has olives to sell in the United States.

At the same time, a separate transaction is being made between a U.S. machine exporter and a Greek olive oil producer. This time, importer/exporter roles are reversed between the two countries: The Greek firm needs to import a $1,000 olive oil press from the United States.

- ***Steps 5 and 6.*** Drachmas (230,000) withdrawn from a local Greek bank account are converted into U.S. $1,000 and sent via check to the U.S. exporter.
- ***Steps 7 and 8.*** The olive oil press is sent to the Greek importer, and the importer's check is deposited in the U.S. exporter's local bank account.

In this example, trade between the two countries is in balance. Money inflows and outflows are equal for both countries. When such a balance occurs, *money does not actually have to flow between the two countries.* Within each bank, the dollars spent by local importers offset the dollars received by local exporters. In effect, therefore, the dollars have simply flowed from U.S. importers to U.S. exporters. Similarly, the drachmas have moved from Greek exporters to Greek importers.

International Bank Structure

There is no worldwide banking system that is comparable, in terms of policy making and regulatory power, to the system of any industrialized nation. Rather, worldwide banking stability relies on a loose structure of agreements among individual countries or groups of countries.

World Bank

United Nations agency that provides a limited scope of financial services, such as funding national improvements in undeveloped countries

The World Bank and the IMF Two United Nations agencies, the World Bank and the International Monetary Fund, help to finance international trade.[25] Unlike true banks, the **World Bank** (technically the International Bank for Reconstruction and Development) <www.worldbank.org>, a U.N. agency, provides only a very limited scope of services. For instance, it funds national improvements by making loans to build roads, schools, power plants, and hospi-

Self-Check Questions 7–9

*You should now be able to answer Self-Check Questions 7–9**

7. MULTIPLE CHOICE Suppose the Fed decides that the nation's *money supply* is too large and takes action to reduce it. Which of the following Fed actions is **not** appropriate for reducing the money supply? [select one]: **(a)** sell securities; **(b)** increase the reserve requirement; **(c)** decrease the discount rate; **(d)** increase the margin rate for stock purchases; **(e)** increase the discount rate.

8. MULTIPLE CHOICE Which of the following electronic technologies allows money to move among consumers and businesses outside the established network of banks and money supplies overseen by the Fed? [select one]: **(a)** debit cards; **(b)** e-cash; **(c)** smart cards; **(d)** credit cards; **(e)** ATMs.

9. TRUE/FALSE The *World Bank* is the global regulatory authority that supervises the International Banking System and monitors the international payments process.

ANSWERS TO SELF-CHECK QUESTIONS 7–9 CAN BE FOUND ON P. AN-12.

tals. The resulting improvements eventually enable borrowing countries to increase productive capacity and international trade.

Another U.N. agency, the **International Monetary Fund (IMF)** <www.imf.org>, is a group of some 150 nations that have combined resources for the following purposes:

International Monetary Fund (IMF)
United Nations agency consisting of about 150 nations that have combined resources to promote stable exchange rates, provide temporary short-term loans, and serve other purposes

- To promote the stability of exchange rates
- To provide temporary, short-term loans to member countries
- To encourage members to cooperate on international monetary issues
- To encourage development of a system for international payments

The IMF makes loans to nations suffering from temporary negative trade balances. By making it possible for these countries to continue buying products from other countries, the IMF facilitates international trade. However, some nations have declined IMF funds rather than accept the economic changes that the IMF demands. For example, some developing countries reject the IMF's requirement that they cut back social programs and spending in order to bring inflation under control.

Continued from page 519

There's No Accounting for Financial Systems

As the run on Argentina's banks continued into 2002, unpopular banking restrictions were tightened even further, triggering widespread street protests. Bank accounts were frozen by the government. All checking accounts with money over $10,000 were switched into fixed-term deposits, meaning the money was not available to depositors for at least a year. The same was true for savings accounts of $3,000 or more. "We want our money and we want it now," shouted Rubin Orlando, a 46-year-old doctor, as he slammed two trash can lids together. Angry vandals set fires in downtown Buenos Aires, shattered windows, and destroyed ATMs. The economic and social chaos led to a government turnover that included five presidents in two weeks. So intense and violent was public unrest that Roque Maccarone, the head of Argentina's central bank, resigned.

As economist Raul Buonuome of SBS Brokerage noted, however, "Simply changing the head of the bank would not be enough by itself to bolster confidence of Argentines in the banking system." Overall, he says, the government has two main tasks: revamping Argentina's financial system and restructuring debt. President Eduardo Duhalde's government has taken two steps to rescue the country: First, devaluing the currency should help increase Argentina's exports, and second, temporarily halting debt payments should help stabilize the domestic economy.

In a move to assist in the crisis, the IMF granted Argentina a one-year extension for repaying a nearly $1 billion loan due early in 2002, hoping the reprieve will help restart the economy and calm social unrest. Meanwhile, Horst Koehler, Managing Director of IMF, is offering more than just short-term assistance for getting Argentina's economy back on track: "We have been in close contact with the government of President Duhalde from the beginning. We have sent technical experts for the banking sector there, for the debt operation and for fiscal measures, so everything is offered to Argentina if [it wants] to get our technical assistance to work on a comprehensive strategy."

In addition to the government defaulting on its $132 billion debt, companies, too, are joining in nonpayment on obligations. In the country's biggest corporate default to date, Telecom Argentina, the nation's No. 2 phone carrier, announced it would suspend principal payments on its $3.2 billion in debt. Most of the debt is in the form of bonds and bank loans. Telecom Argentine issued most of its debt in dollars during the past decade, while the peso was stable. When the Argentine government devalued the peso by 30 percent to 1.4 pesos per dollar in January 2002, it continued to fall on the world markets and quickly lost 65 percent of its value as the recession deepened, so there are not enough funds to pay what is owed. It is paying interest—$200 million in interest is due in 2002—but it will not be paying the $900 million in principal that is due. And the firm cannot raise prices to cover its debt because the government froze prices—in pesos—that utility companies can charge customers.

As the downslide continues, additional defaults include $1 billion by Argentina's wireless unit of Verizon, $1 billion by CTI Holdings, and $425 million by Metrogas SA, a giant natural gas company.

Questions for Discussion

1. Assume for a moment that you're a consumer of retail goods in Argentina. Can you identify any problems you might expect to encounter during your country's transition to the devalued peso?
2. Suppose you are manager of an Argentine retail store that sells imported clothing. What preparations would you make to ensure that your business is ready for the transition to the devalued peso?
3. Identify the advantages to be gained—for both individuals and companies—by the payment of all debt by the Argentine government and businesses, instead of both sectors defaulting on debt payments. What are the disadvantages?
4. Consider the actions taken by the government to stop the run on cash from the Argentine banking system. Do you think the actions were effective? Can you propose alternative actions that might have been better than those that were implemented?
5. Consider the risks that foreign banks and businesses took by investing in Argentina. In consideration of their financial losses and other economic and political factors, do you expect those businesses will invest again in Argentine-based ventures? Explain why or why not.

Summary of Learning Objectives

1. ***Define* money *and identify the different forms that it takes in the nation's money supply.***

Almost any object can serve as **money** if it meets four criteria: (1) *Portability*: It can be carried around and distributed. (2) *Divisibility*: It can easily be broken down into smaller parts, each with a fixed value. (3) *Durability*: It is replaceable and not easily worn out or counterfeited. (4) *Stability*: It has a value determined by what it can buy. Money serves three functions: (1) *Medium of exchange*: It's a way of buying and selling things, and without it, we'd be bogged down in a system of barter. (2) *Store of value*: As currency, it can be used for future purchases, and so it "stores" value. (3) *Unit of account*: It lets us measure the relative values of goods and services and acts as a unit of account because all products can be valued and accounted for in terms of it.

Both buyers and sellers must agree on the value of money, which depends on its *supply*—on how much money is in circulation. When the supply is high, value drops. When it's low, value increases. The measure known as **M-1** counts only the most liquid, or spendable, forms of money, including the following: (1) Government-issued **currency,** which must be accepted for the payment of debts. (2) **Checks**—orders instructing banks to pay given sums to "payees." (3) Checking accounts or **demand deposits,** which may be withdrawn at any time—"on demand."

M-2 includes everything in M-1 plus items that cannot be spent directly but are easily converted to spendable forms. There are three major components of M-2: (1) **Time deposits,** such as certificates of deposit (CDs), which require prior notice of withdrawal. (2) **Money market mutual funds,** which buy short-term, low-risk financial securities whose returns are shared by investors. (3) Traditional *savings deposits.*

2. ***Describe the different kinds of* financial institutions *that comprise the U.S. financial system and explain the services they offer.***

Financial institutions ease the flow of money from sectors with surpluses to those with deficits. They do this by issuing claims against themselves and investing in other organizations. There are four major types: (1) **Commercial banks** accept deposits which they use to make loans and earn profits. Liabilities include checking and savings accounts, and assets consist of loans. Every bank gets a major portion of its income from interest paid on loans. The lowest rate, called the **prime rate,** was traditionally granted to the most credit-worthy commercial customers, but to remain competitive, U.S. banks now offer some commercial loans at rates below prime. Many observers contend that commercial banks must also diversify offerings.

(2) **Savings and loan associations (S&Ls)** also accept deposits and make loans, primarily for home mortgages. (3) In **mutual savings banks,** all depositors are owners of the bank, and all profits are divided proportionately among them. Most funds are in the form of savings deposits and are loaned out as mortgages. (4) In **credit unions,** deposits are accepted only from members.

Numerous other organizations called *nondeposit institutions* take in money, provide interest or other services, and make loans. Four of the most important are: (1) A **pension fund,** whether *public* (such as Social Security) or *private,* is a pool of funds managed to provide retirement income for members. (2) **Insurance companies** collect and invest large pools of funds from premiums charged for coverage. (3) **Finance companies,** whether *commercial* or *consumer,* make loans to businesses and consumers. (4) **Securities investment dealers (brokers)** buy and sell stocks and bonds on stock exchanges for client investors or for their own accounts in hopes of reselling them later at a profit.

In the competitive finance business, most commercial banks offer a wide range of special services: (1) *Pension and trust services*: Most banks help customers establish savings plans for retirement, such as **individual retirement accounts (IRAs)**—pension funds that wage earners and their spouses can set up to supplement other retirement funds. In return for a fee, banks will perform such **trust services** as managing investments.

(2) *International services*: Banks offer three main international services: (i) They can exchange U.S. dollars for foreign currency. (ii) Firms can pay them to issue **letters of credit**—promises to pay foreign firms under specified conditions. (iii) Firms can pay banks to draw up **bankers acceptances,** which promise that a specified amount will be paid at a future date.

(3) *Financial advice and brokerage services*: Many banks help customers manage their money. (4) *Automated teller machines*: **Automated teller machines (ATMs)** allow customers to withdraw money and make deposits 24 hours a day, 7 days a week. They also allow transfers of funds and provide information on account status. (5) *Electronic funds transfer*: ATMs are a form of **electronic funds transfer (EFT)**—systems that transfer many kinds of financial information via electrical impulses. EFT systems also include automatic payroll deposit and bill payment.

3. *Explain how banks create money, and describe the means by which they are regulated.*

The money supply expands because banks can loan out most (although not all) of the money they take in from deposits. Out of a deposit of $100, the bank may hold $10 in reserve and loan 90 percent—$90—to borrowers. There will still be $100 on deposit, and borrowers will also deposit the $90 loan in their banks. Now the borrowers' banks have $81 (90 percent of $90) available for new loans. Banks, therefore, have turned the original $100 into $271 ($100 + $90 + $81).

The government regulates commercial banks to ensure a sound financial system. The **Federal Deposit Insurance Corporation (FDIC)** insures deposits and guarantees, through its Bank Insurance Fund (BIF), the safety of all deposits up to the current maximum of $100,000. It also examines the activities and accounts of all member banks.

4. *Discuss the functions of the* Federal Reserve System *and describe the tools that it uses to control the money supply.*

As the nation's central bank, the **Federal Reserve System** (or the **Fed**) has three major components: (1) *Board of governors*: The board determines the reserve requirements for depository institutions, sets discount rates, and handles transactions in government securities. (2) *Reserve banks*: Each of the 12 Federal Reserve banks holds reserve deposits from and sets the discount rate for commercial banks in its region. These Federal Reserve banks also play a major role in the nation's check-clearing process. (3) *Member banks*: All nationally chartered commercial banks are members of the Fed, and all member accounts are covered by the FDIC/BIF.

In addition to chartering national banks, the Fed plays three major roles: (1) *The government's bank*: The Fed decides how many bills to produce and destroy. It also buys Treasury Department bonds, which it then lends to the government to help finance the national deficit. (2) *The bankers' bank*: Banks can borrow from the Fed, which also provides storage for their reserve funds. The Fed clears checks for commercial banks; the term **float** refers to all of the checks in the process at any one time.

(3) *Controller of the money supply*: The Fed conducts the U.S. **monetary policy,** management of economic growth by managing the money supply and interest rates. In so doing, it influences the ability and willingness of banks to loan money. Thus, one of its most important jobs is managing inflation, which occurs when the money supply grows too large, demand for goods and services increases, and the prices of everything rise. The Fed manages the money supply primarily by regulating its flow through commercial banks.

To control the money supply, the Fed uses four tools: (1) *Reserve requirements:* The **reserve requirement** is the percentage of its deposits that a bank must hold in a Federal Reserve bank. The Fed can adjust requirements to affect the overall supply of money to the economy. (2) *Discount rate controls*: The Fed loans money to banks at an interest rate known as the **discount rate.** It can reduce the money supply by increasing the discount rate and making it more expensive for banks to borrow and loan money. Low rates encourage borrowing and lending and expand the money supply.

(3) *Open-market operations*: **Open-market operations** refer to the Fed's sale and purchase of securities. The Fed buys securities from dealers, whose banks are credited for the transactions. With more money to lend, the banks expand the money supply. The opposite happens when the Fed sells securities. (4) *Selective credit controls*: The Fed can exercise **selective credit controls** by setting requirements and credit rules for consumer purchases.

5. *Identify three important ways in which the financial industry is changing.*

(1) *Deregulation*: The Depository Institutions Deregulation and Monetary Control Act (DIDMCA) of 1980 and subsequent laws sought to promote competition by eliminating many restrictions on banking services. (2) *Interstate banking*: The Interstate Banking Efficiency Act (1994) allows banks to operate across state lines. It also limits the size of any banking company and the kinds of transactions between affiliated banks.

(3) *The impact of electronic technologies*: Banks are increasingly investing in technology as a way to improve efficiency and customer service levels: (i) **Debit cards** allow the transfer of money between accounts and can be used to make retail purchases at **point-of-sale (POS) terminals,** which relay purchase information directly to the bank's computer system for automatic transfer to the store's account.

(ii) The **smart card** can be programmed with "electronic money" at ATM machines or even at home. (iii) **E-cash** is money that moves along multiple channels via digital electronic transmissions. It moves outside the established network of banks, checks, and paper currency overseen by the Fed. Traditional currency is used to buy electronic funds, which are downloaded over phone lines into a PC or a portable "electronic wallet" that can store and transmit e-cash. The online shopper pays by sending digital money into the seller's e-cash funds, which are instantaneously updated.

6. *Understand some of the key concepts and activities in* international banking and finance.

Every country's *currency exchange rate* affects its ability to buy and sell globally. The value of its currency reflects the supply and demand for a currency and the products that a country creates with it. When a currency is overvalued, its exchange rate is higher than warranted by its economic conditions. Its high costs make the currency less competitive: Because a country's products are too expensive to make and buy, fewer are purchased by other countries. The likely result is a trade deficit. In contrast, an undervalued currency means low costs and low prices: It attracts purchases by other countries, usually leading to a trade surplus. Thus, the purpose of devaluing a currency is to reduce its exchange value: It will then be less expensive for other countries to buy a country's products, and as more of its products are purchased, its payment deficit goes down. International payments are simplified through the services provided by banks. For example, payments from buyers flow through a local bank that converts them from the local currency into the foreign currency of the seller.

Two United Nations agencies help to finance international trade: (1) The **World Bank** funds national improvements by making loans to build roads, schools, and so forth. Improvements enable borrowers to increase productive capacity and international trade. (2) In the **International Monetary Fund (IMF),** some 150 nations have combined resources for the following purposes: (i) To promote the stability of exchange rates; (ii) to provide temporary, short-term loans to member countries; (iii) to encourage cooperation on international monetary issues; and (iv) to encourage development of a system for international payments.

KEY TERMS

money (p. 520)
M-1 (p. 521)
currency (p. 521)
check (p. 521)
demand deposit (p. 521)
M-2 (p. 521)
time deposit (p. 522)
money market mutual fund (p. 522)
commercial bank (p. 524)
prime rate (p. 526)
savings and loan association (S&L) (p. 526)
mutual savings bank (p. 526)
credit union (p. 526)
pension fund (p. 526)
insurance company (p. 526)
finance company (p. 527)
securities investment dealer (broker) (p. 527)
individual retirement account (IRA) (p. 527)
trust services (p. 528)
letter of credit (p. 528)
banker's acceptance (p. 528)
automated teller machine (ATM) (p. 528)
electronic funds transfer (EFT) (p. 528)
Federal Deposit Insurance Corporation (FDIC) (p. 530)
Federal Reserve System (the Fed) (p. 531)
float (p. 533)
monetary policy (p. 533)
reserve requirement (p. 534)
discount rate (p. 534)
open-market operations (p. 534)
selective credit controls (p. 534)
debit card (p. 536)
point-of-sale (POS) terminal (p. 536)
smart card (p. 536)
e-cash (p. 537)
World Bank (p. 540)
International Monetary Fund (IMF) (p. 541)

QUESTIONS AND EXERCISES

Questions for Review

1. What are the components of M-1? Of M-2?
2. Explain the roles of commercial banks, savings and loan associations, and nondeposit institutions in the U.S. financial system.
3. Explain the types of pension services that commercial banks provide for their customers.
4. Describe the structure of the Federal Reserve System.
5. Show how the Fed uses the discount rate to manage inflation in the U.S. economy.

uestions for Analysis

5. Do you think credit cards should be counted in the money supply? Why or why not? Support your argument by using the definition of money.
7. Should commercial banks be regulated, or should market forces be allowed to determine the money supply? Why?
8. Identify a purchase made by you or a family member in which payment was made by check. Draw a diagram to trace the steps in the clearing process followed by that check.

Application Exercises

9. Start with a $1,000 deposit and assume a reserve requirement of 15 percent. Now trace the amount of money created by the banking system after five lending cycles.
10. Interview the manager of a local commercial bank. Identify several ways in which the Fed either helps the bank or restricts its operations.

Building Your Business Skills

FOUR ECONOMISTS IN A ROOM

ıis exercise enhances the following SCANS workplace compe-ıcies: demonstrating basic skills, demonstrating thinking ills, exhibiting interpersonal skills, working with informa-ɔn, and applying system knowledge.

oal

encourage students to understand the economic factors nsidered by the Federal Reserve Board in determining cur-nt interest rates

ackground

ıe of the Federal Reserve's most important tools in setting ɔnetary policy is the adjustment of the interest rates it arges member banks to borrow money. To determine inter-t rate policy, the Fed analyzes current economic conditions ɔm its 12 districts. Its findings are published eight times a ar in a report commonly known as the *Beige Book.*

ethod

Step 1

ɔrking with three other students, access the Federal serve Web site at <www.federalreserve.gov>. Look for the ading "Monetary Policy," and then look for "Federal Open ırket Committee." Next, click on the subheading "Beige ok". When you reach that page, click on "Summary of the rrent Report."

Step 2

ɔrking with group members, study each of the major sum-ıry sections:

- Consumer spending
- Manufacturing
- Construction and real estate
- Banking and finance
- Nonfinancial services
- Labor market, wages, and pricing
- Agriculture and natural resources

Working with team members, discuss ways in which you think that key information contained in the summary might affect the Fed's decision to raise, lower, or maintain interest rates.

Step 3

At your library, find back issues of *Barron's* <www.barrons.com>, the highly respected weekly financial publication. Look for the issue published immediately following the appearance of the most recent *Beige Book.* Search for articles analyzing the report. Discuss with group members what the articles say about current economic conditions and interest rates.

Step 4

Based on your research and analysis, what factors do you think the Fed will take into account to control inflation? Working with group members, explain your answer in writing.

Step 5

Working with group members, research what the Federal Reserve chairperson says about interest rates. Do the chairperson's reasons for raising, lowering, or maintaining rates agree with your group's analysis?

Follow-Up Questions

1. What are the most important factors in the Fed's interest rate decision?
2. Consider the old joke about economists that goes like this: When there are four economists in a room analyzing current economic conditions, there are at least eight different opinions. Based on your research and analysis, why do you think economists have such varying opinions?

Exercising Your Ethics

TELLING THE ETHICAL FROM THE STRICTLY LEGAL

The Situation

When upgrading services for convenience to customers, commercial banks are concerned about setting prices that cover all costs so that, ultimately, they make a profit. This exercise challenges you to evaluate one banking service—ATM transactions—to determine if there are also ethical issues that should be considered in a bank's pricing decisions.

The Dilemma

A regional commercial bank in the western United States has more than 300 ATMs serving the nearly 400,000 checking and savings accounts of its customers. Customers are not charged a fee for their 30 million ATM transactions each year, so long as they use their bank's ATMs. For issuing cash to noncustomers, however, the bank charges a $2 ATM fee. The bank's officers are reexamining their policies on ATM surcharges because of public protests against other banks in Santa Monica, New York City, and Chicago. Iowa has gone even further, becoming the first state to pass legislation that bans national banks from charging ATM fees for noncustomers. To date, the courts have ruled that the access fees are legal, but some organizations—such as the U.S. Public Interest Research Group (PIRG)—continue to fight publicly against them.

In considering its current policies, our western bank's vice president for community relations is concerned about more than mere legalities. She wants to ensure that her company is "being a good citizen and doing the right thing." Any decision on ATM fees will ultimately affect the bank's customers, its image in the community and industry, and its profitability for its owners.

Questions for Discussion

1. From the standpoint of a commercial bank, can you find any economic justification for ATM access fees?
2. Based on the scenario described for our bank, do you find any ethical issues in this situation? Or do you find the main issues legal and economic rather than ethical?
3. As an officer for this bank, how would you handle this situation?

Mastering Business Essentials

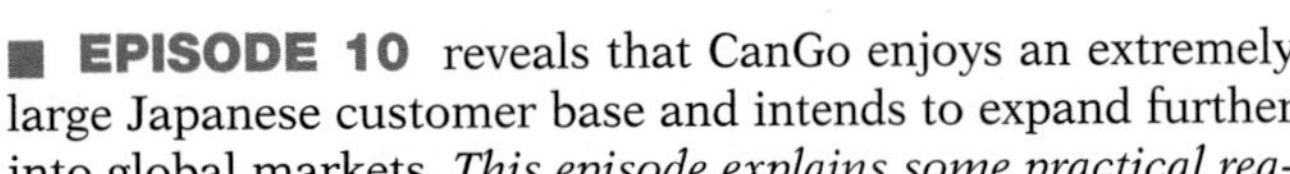

EPISODE 10 reveals that CanGo enjoys an extremely large Japanese customer base and intends to expand further into global markets. *This episode explains some practical reasons why a small company may need to understand international banking and finance.*

Crafting Your Business Plan

HOW TO BANK ON YOUR MONEY

The Purpose of the Assignment

1. To familiarize students with banking issues that a sample firm faces in developing its business plan, in the framework of *Business PlanPro* (*BPP*) software package.
2. To demonstrate how two chapter topics—bank services and interest rates—can be integrated as components in the *BPP* planning environment.

Assignment

After reading Chapter 18 in the textbook, open the BPP software and search for information about the financial plans of a sample firm: Fantastic Florals Inc. *To find* Fantastic Florals, *do the following:*

Open the *Business PlanPro.* If it asks if you want to "create a new business plan" or "open an existing plan," select "create a new business plan" (even though you are not going to create a plan at this time). You will then be taken to the *Business PlanPro EasyPlan Wizard.* Click on the option entitled **Research It**. You will then be presented a new list of options, including **Sample Plan Browser.** After clicking on the **Sample Plan Browser**, go down the alphabetical list of sample plans and double-click on **Import—Artificial Flowers**, which is the location for *Fantastic Florals Inc.* (FFI). The screen you are looking at is the introduction page for the *Fantastic Florals* business plan. Now scroll down until you reach the **Table of Contents** for the *Fantastic Florals* business plan.

Now respond to the following items:

1. Consider interest rates that are assumed in the business plan. Are the short-term and long-term rates reasonable in today's economy? Explain. [Sites to see in *BPP* for this item: On the Table of Contents page, click on **7.1 Important Assumptions**.]
2. Identify some international banking services that would benefit FFI in its daily operations. [Sites to see in *BPP:* On the Table of Contents page, click on **1.0 Executive Summary**. Return to the Table of Contents page, and click on each of the following in turn: **3.4 Sourcing** and **3.6 Future Products**.]
3. From FFI's financial plan, can you see any need for bank credit? When, during the planning horizon, might the firm need a line of credit, and how much might it need? [Sites to see in *BPP:* From the Table of Contents page, click on each of the following in turn: **7.0 Financial Plan** and **7.5 Projected Cash Flow**.]
4. Does FFI plan to have excess cash that can be deposited in the bank to earn interest? When, during the planning horizon, might the firm accumulate excess cash, and how much might it have? [Sites to see in *BPP:* On the Table of Contents page, click on **5.2.1 Sales Forecast**. Return to the Table of Contents page, and click on **7.5 Projected Cash Flow**. Observe the cash balance at the bottom of the table.]

Video Exercise

FUNDING THE BUSINESS WORLD: COAST BUSINESS CREDIT

Learning Objectives

The purpose of this video is to help you to:

1. Recognize how and why banks use customer deposits as the basis of loans.
2. Understand the role of banks and financial services firms in providing funding for business expansion, operations, and acquisitions.
3. Identify the risks that financial services firms take when loaning money to businesses.

Synopsis

Coast Business Credit, a division of Southern Pacific Bank, provides money for business. When evaluating the risk that a loan will not be repaid, Coast carefully considers the borrower's collateral, cash flow, and management. Business customers may apply for a short-term line of credit, a long-term loan, or other types of financing for a variety of purposes. One company may need operating capital; another may need money to make a major acquisition or to expand. Coast analyzes each lending opportunity in terms of potential risk, potential profit, and—in some cases—the ability to create or save jobs and thus benefit the community at large.

Discussion Questions

1. *For analysis*: How might the amount of time deposits gathered by parent company Southern Pacific Bank affect the loans made by Coast Business Services?
2. *For analysis*: If the Federal Reserve lowers the discount rate by a significant amount, what would be the likely effect on business loan rates?
3. *For application*: What type of collateral might Coast Business Credit prefer when considering a loan application?
4. *For application*: In addition to collateral, Coast Business Credit looks at cash flow and management when considering a loan application. Why is management such an important element?
5. *For debate*: Should Coast Business Credit establish a separate lending department specifically for financing Internet start-ups? Support your chosen position.

Online Exploration

Visit the Coast Business Credit Web site at <www.coastbusinesscredit.com>. After browsing the home page, follow the links to learn more about Coast Business Credit. What types of loans will Coast make? To what types of businesses? Why does Coast explain its financial offerings in such detail? Why would it mention the names of its parent company, its affiliates, and its FDIC coverage on its Web site? How does Coast make it easy for businesses to make contact?

CHAPTER

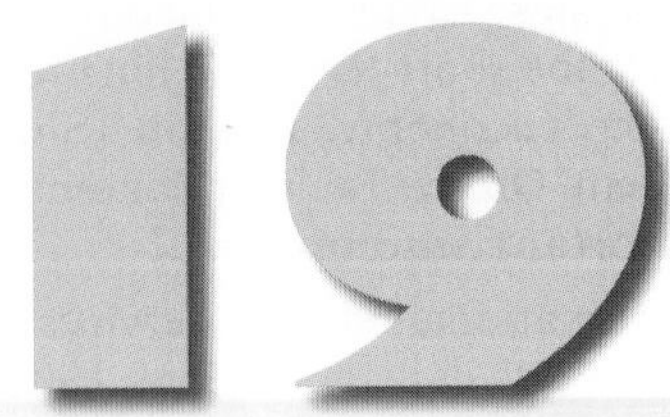

Understanding Securities and Investments

After reading this chapter, you should be able to:

1. Explain the difference between *primary* and *secondary securities markets.*
2. Discuss the value to shareholders of *common* and *preferred stock* and describe the secondary market for each type of security.
3. Distinguish among various types of *bonds* in terms of their issuers, safety, and retirement.
4. Describe the investment opportunities offered by *mutual funds* and *commodities.*
5. Explain the process by which securities are bought and sold.
6. Explain how securities markets are regulated.

And the Wall (Street) Came Tumbling Down

In the late 1990s, tens of thousands of U.S. investors became new millionaires in a booming economy spurred by a vibrant stock market. Annual returns of 15 to 25 percent were commonplace as investors pumped money into the market at a record pace. Major market indexes—the Dow Jones Industrials, the Nasdaq Composite, and the S&P 500—continued an unstinting climb to record highs. Dot-coms and other beneficiaries of the new economy led a parade toward record levels of wealth and prosperity. Government revenues grew so fast that legislators struggled to figure out how to spend the nation's newfound wealth. As investor assets accumulated, older workers began planning for early retirement. Young parents could rest assured that their kids' educations would be paid for.

Then something happened: A slowdown that had first surfaced in late 1999 gradually gained momentum and began to dampen stock prices in mid-2000. Soon the slowdown became a calm but unmistakable retreat. With unprofitable dot-coms failing, unemployment started to climb and the stock market was hit by further economic downturns that continued throughout 2001, even before the devastating blow of September 11. To further depress an already downcast market, more setbacks came in a series of corporate scandals involving well-known firms—Global Crossings, Enron, Arthur Andersen, ImClone, WorldCom, and a host of others—that struck both fear and anger in retirees, employees, investors, and the entire U.S. public. As reports rolled in, the public's trust dwindled until, by fall 2002, the market had tumbled to its lowest level in years as wary investors pulled money out of stocks and went looking for safer investments. "It's very volatile out there," commented one executive at UBS Warburg. "There seems to be a disaster a day, and investors are frustrated."

In the wake of Wall Street's precipitous fall, many erstwhile millionaires began assessing the damage. How bad was it? One prominent publication pointed out that if you owned 500 shares of JDS Uniphase Corp., California, producer of components for fiber-optic networks, in March 2000, you could have bought a new Porsche 911 Carrera. By July 2002, those same shares would have bought you a 1990 Dodge Omni Hatchback with 100,000 miles and no air conditioning. Aside from millionaires, blue-collar investors were also hit hard. Some would-be early retirees began replanning to delay retirements. Others were left with no retirement funds at all. Young parents started saving all over again for their children's education; legislators scrambled to figure out how to cover suddenly growing government deficits.

Our opening story continues on page 575.

"There seems to be a disaster a day, and investors are frustrated."

~Robert Harrington,
WALL STREET TRADER

Securities Markets

securities
Stocks and bonds representing secured, or asset-based, claims by investors against issuers

Stocks and bonds are known as **securities** because they represent *secured,* or *asset-based,* claims on the part of investors. In other words, holders of stocks and bonds have a stake in the business that issued them. As we saw in Chapter 3, stockholders have claims on some of a corporation's assets (and a say in how the company is run) because each share of stock represents part ownership.

In contrast, *bonds* represent strictly financial claims for money owed to holders by a company. Companies sell bonds to raise long-term funds. The markets in which stocks and bonds are sold are called *securities markets.*[1]

Primary and Secondary Securities Markets

primary securities market
Market in which new stocks and bonds are bought and sold

In **primary securities markets,** new stocks and bonds are bought and sold by firms and governments. Sometimes, new securities are sold to single buyers or small groups of buyers. These so-called *private placements* are desirable because they allow issuers to keep their plans confidential.[2]

In 2001, more than $9 billion in new private placements were purchased in the United States by large pension funds and other institutions that privately negotiate prices with sellers.[3] Because private placements cannot be resold in the open market, buyers generally demand higher returns from the issuers.

Securities and Exchange Commission (SEC)
Federal agency that administers U.S. securities laws to protect the investing public and maintain smoothly functioning markets

investment bank
Financial institution engaged in issuing and reselling new securities

Investment Banking Most new stocks and some bonds are sold on the wider public market. To bring a new security to market, the issuing firm must get approval from the **Securities and Exchange Commission (SEC)** <www.sec.gov>—the government agency that regulates securities markets. It also needs the services of an **investment bank**—a financial institution that specializes in issuing and reselling new securities. Such investment banking firms as Merrill Lynch <www.ml.com> and Morgan Stanley <www.msdw.com> provide three important services:

1. They advise companies on the timing and financial terms of new issues.
2. By *underwriting*—that is, buying—new securities, they bear some of the risks of issuing them.
3. They create the distribution networks for moving new securities through groups of other banks and brokers into the hands of individual investors.

secondary securities market
Market in which stocks and bonds are traded

In 2001, U.S. investment bankers brought to the market $128 billion in new corporate stocks and $1.2 trillion in new corporate bonds.[4] New securities, however, represent only a minute portion of traded securities. Existing stocks and bonds are sold in the **secondary securities market,** which is handled by such familiar bodies as the New York Stock Exchange. We consider the activities of these markets later in this chapter.

Stocks

Each year, financial managers, with millions of individual investors, buy and sell the stocks of thousands of companies. This widespread ownership has become possible because of the availability of different types of stocks and because markets have been established that enable individuals to conveniently buy and sell them. In this section, we focus on the value of *common* and *preferred stock* as securities. We also describe the *stock exchanges* on which they are bought and sold.[5]

Common Stocks

Individuals and other companies purchase a firm's common stock in the hope that it will increase in value, provide dividend income, or both. But how is the value of a common stock determined? Stock values are expressed in three different ways—as par, market, and book value.

- The face value of a share of stock at the time it is originally issued is the **par value.** To receive their corporate charters, all companies must declare par values for their stocks. Each company must preserve the par value money in its retained earnings, and it cannot be distributed as dividends.
- A stock's real value is its **market value**—the current price of a share in the stock market. Market value reflects buyers' willingness to invest in a company.
- Recall from Chapter 17 our definition of *stockholders' equity*—the sum of a company's common stock par value, retained earnings, and additional paid-in capital. The **book value** of common stock represents *stockholders' equity* (see Chapter 17) divided by the number of shares. Book value is used as a comparison indicator because, for successful companies, the market value is usually greater than its book value. Thus, when market price falls to near book value, some investors buy the stock on the principle that it is underpriced and will increase in the future.

par value

Face value of a share of stock, set by the issuing company's board of directors

market value

Current price of a share of stock in the stock market

book value

Value of a common stock expressed as total stockholders' equity divided by the number of shares of stock

Investment Traits of Common Stock Common stocks are among the riskiest of all securities. Uncertainties about the stock market itself, for instance, can quickly change a given stock's value. Furthermore, when companies have unprofitable years, they often cannot pay dividends. Shareholder income, therefore—and perhaps share price—drops. At the same time, however, common stocks offer high growth potential. Naturally, the prospects for growth in various industries change from time to time, but the **blue-chip stocks** of well-established, financially sound firms such as Ralston Purina <www.ralston.com> and Exxon Mobil <www.exxon.mobil.com> have historically provided investors steady income through consistent dividend payouts.

blue-chip stock

Common stock issued by a well-established company with a sound financial history and a stable pattern of dividend payouts

The "Old" Economy versus the "New": What's a "Blue Chip" Now? Because the very nature of the stock market is continuously changing, the future performance of any stock is often unpredictable. With the proliferation of Internet and start-up dot-coms, experts realize that many of the old rules for judging the market prospects of stocks are changing. Conventional methods don't seem to apply to the surprising surges in "new economy" stock prices. Old performance yardsticks—a company's history of dividend payouts, steady growth in earnings per

At Cerner Corp. <www.cerner.com>, a healthcare software company, CEO Neal L. Patterson e-mailed managers to complain, among other things, that empty parking lots at 8 A.M. and 5 P.M. reflected a lazy workforce: "You have a problem and you will fix it, or I will replace you," warned Patterson. "You have two weeks. Tick, tock." Unfortunately, the message found its way on to the Internet. When investors and analysts read it, they deduced that Cerner was struggling to make its quarterly goals by working overtime. In a three-day period, Cerner stock went down 22 percent.

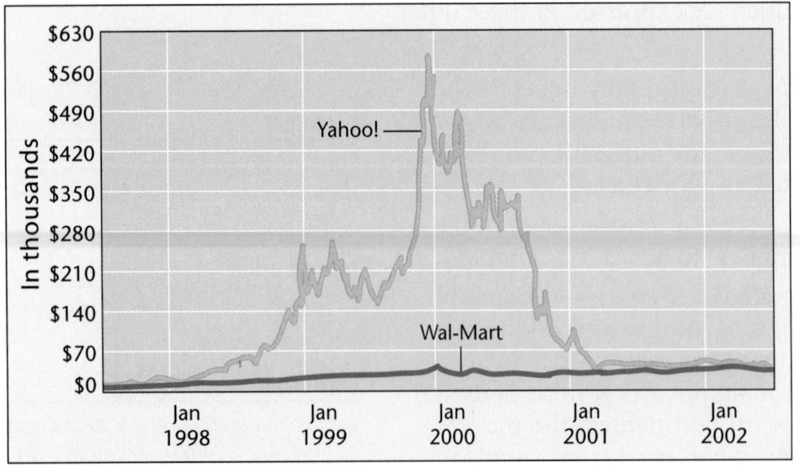

FIGURE 19.1
Market Value Growth: Wal-Mart versus Yahoo!

share, and a low price-earnings ratio (current stock price divided by annual earnings per share)—do not seem to measure the value of new economy stocks. In some cases, market prices are soaring for start-ups that have yet to earn a profit.

While some of the newcomers—America Online, Amazon, eBay, Yahoo!—are regarded by many on Wall Street as Internet Blue Chips, their financial performance is quite different from that of traditional blue-chip stocks.[6] Let's compare Yahoo! and Wal-Mart. If you had invested $10,000 in Wal-Mart stock in July 1997, the market value of this blue chip would have increased to more than $35,000 in just five years (see Figure 19.1). The same investment in Yahoo! would have also grown to about $35,000. At peak value during the five-year period, however, the Yahoo! investment surged to nearly $600,000 versus Wal-Mart's nearly $40,000.

Could this gigantic difference be predicted from indicators traditionally used by market experts? Hardly. The initial public offering (IPO) of Yahoo! stock in 1996 was priced at $13 per share. It quickly jumped to $43, then settled down to close the day at $33 even though the company had not yet turned a profit. Subsequently, because Yahoo! was the leading Internet portal brand name, investors were betting that it would become a profitable business in the future—a bet that many traditionalists would view as extremely risky.

Consider the fact that Wal-Mart's book value is more than double that of Yahoo!. Even more glaring is the fact that entering 2002, Yahoo! has had zero or negative earnings per share for the last six years, whereas Wal-Mart's net earnings have grown steadily during the previous 10 years. The comparison is similar for dividends: Whereas Wal-Mart has a steady history of payouts to stockholders, Yahoo! has never paid a cash dividend. Over all, then, the traditional performance yardsticks favor Wal-Mart heavily. Nevertheless, investors are betting the future on Yahoo!. As recently as July 2000, the original $10,000 investment had accumulated in three years to a market value more than 10 times that of the same investment in Wal-Mart.[7]

Preferred Stock

Preferred stock is usually issued with a stated par value, and dividends are typically expressed as a percentage of par value. If a preferred stock with a $100 par value pays a 6 percent dividend, holders will receive an annual dividend of $6 per share.

Some preferred stock is *callable*. The issuing firm can call in shares by requiring preferred stockholders to surrender them in exchange for cash payments. The amount of this payment—the *call price*—is specified in the purchase agreement between the firm and its preferred stockholders.

cumulative preferred stock

Preferred stock on which dividends not paid in the past must be paid to stockholders before dividends can be paid to common stockholders

Investment Traits of Preferred Stock Because preferred stock has first rights to dividends, income is less risky than income from the same firm's common stock. Most preferred stock is **cumulative preferred stock,** which means that any missed dividend payments must be paid as soon as the firm is able to do so. In addition, the firm cannot pay any dividends to common stockholders until it has made up all late payments to preferred stockholders. Let's take the example of a firm with preferred stock having a $100 par value and paying a 6 percent divi-

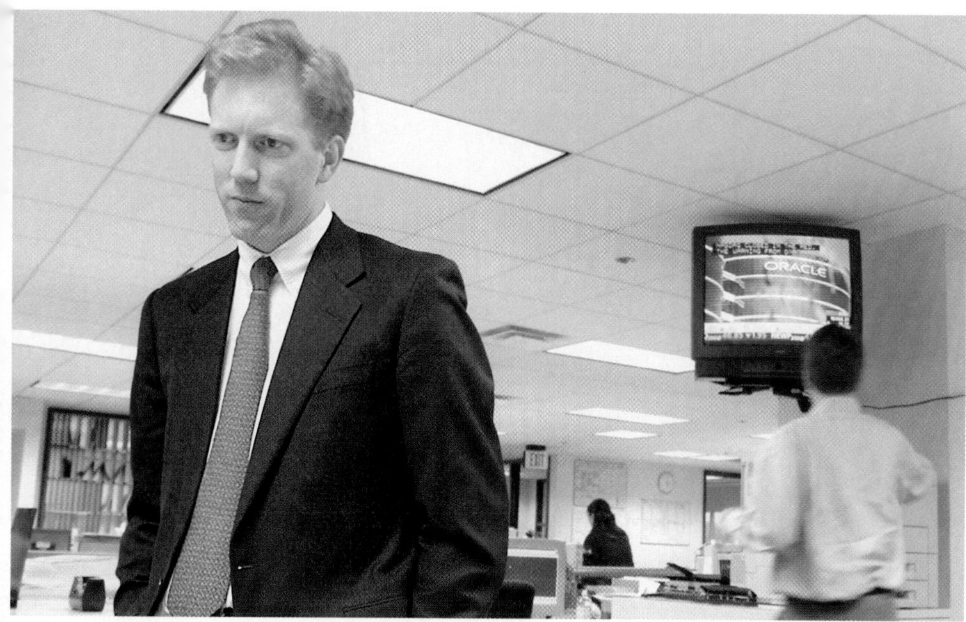

Back in 1998, when Henry Blodget, an analyst at brokerage firm Merrill Lynch <www.ml.com>, predicted (correctly) that the stock of Amazon.com would climb from $240 to $400 a share, Merrill's leading Internet analyst at the time laughed. But the laugh, it turns out, was on every other analyst, as the value of Amazon—and that of hundreds of dot-coms—soared until early 2000. Then came the so-called "dot-com crash." In March 2001, Amazon.com had dropped to $9.56; as of this writing, it was at $18.58. Still a leading analyst, Blodget maintains that he and Merrill Lynch rode but did not fuel the Internet euphoria of the late 1990s.

dend. If the firm fails to pay that dividend for two years, it must make up arrears of $12 per share to preferred stockholders before it can pay dividends to common stockholders.

Stock Exchanges

Most of the secondary market for stocks is handled by organized stock exchanges. In addition, a dealer in the over-the-counter market handles the exchange of some stocks. A **stock exchange** is an organization of individuals formed to provide an institutional setting in which stock can be bought and sold. The exchange enforces certain rules to govern its members' trading activities. Most exchanges are nonprofit corporations established to serve their members.

stock exchange
Organization of individuals formed to provide an institutional setting in which stock can be traded

To become a member, an individual must purchase one of a limited number of memberships, called *seats,* on the exchange. Only members (or their representatives) are allowed to trade on the exchange. In this sense, because all orders to buy or sell must flow through members, members of the exchange have a legal monopoly. Memberships can be bought and sold like other assets.

The Trading Floor Each exchange regulates the places and times at which trading may occur. Trading is allowed only at an actual physical location called the trading floor. The floor is equipped with a vast array of electronic communications equipment for conveying buy-and-sell orders or confirming completed trades. A variety of news services furnish up-to-the-minute information about world events and business developments. Any change in these factors, then, may be swiftly reflected in share prices.

Brokers Some of the people on the trading floor are employed by the exchange. Others are trading stocks for themselves. Many, however, are **brokers,** who earn commissions by executing buy-and-sell orders from nonexchange members. Although they match buyers with sellers, brokers do not own the securities. They earn commissions from the individuals and organizations for whom they place orders.[8]

broker
Individual or organization who receives and executes buy-and-sell orders on behalf of other people in return for commissions

Discount Brokers Like many products, brokerage assistance can be purchased at either discount or at full-service prices. Buying 200 shares of a $20 stock in 2002 cost the investor $8 at Ameritrade <www.ameritrade.com>, $14.99 to $19.99

"Our stock just went up ten points on the rumor that I was replacing you all with burlap sacks stuffed with straw."

at E*Trade <www.etrade.com>, $29.95 at Charles Schwab <www.schwab.com>, and more than $100 at a full-service brokerage firm. Price differences are obvious even among the discount brokers—Ameritrade, E*Trade, and Schwab—but the highest discount price is well below the price of the full-service broker.[9]

Discount brokers offer well-informed individual investors a fast, low-cost way to participate in the market. Charles Schwab's customers are do-it-yourself investors. They know what they want to buy or sell, and they usually make trades by using personal computers or Schwab's automated telephone order system

On September 17, 2001, the trading floor of the New York Stock Exchange <www.nyse.com> *reopened after a six-day shutdown following the September 11 attacks. As experts looked on to see whether the market would rebound, trading followed the day's news events: Prices fell just after President Bush announced that he wanted Osama bin Laden "dead or alive," prompting fears of future violence. At closing, stocks had slid seven percent but still remained above what many investors had feared. "Bad Numbers," said a* New York Times *headline, "Still Felt Good."*

without talking with a broker. Why are discount brokerage services low cost? For one thing, sales personnel receive fees or salaries, not commissions. Unlike many full-service brokers, they do not offer investment advice or person-to-person sales consultations. They do, however, offer automated online services, such as stock research, industry analysis, and screening for specific types of stocks.

Online Trading The popularity of online trading stems from convenient access to the Internet, fast no-nonsense transactions, and the opportunity for self-directed investors to manage their own portfolios while paying low fees for trading. Although only 14 percent of all equity trades were executed online in 1998, that number was growing rapidly until the market slowdown in the 2000–2002 period. The Internet, says Gideon Sasson, head of Schwab's electronic brokerage unit, "is fundamentally changing the story of investing."[10] As you can see in Figure 19.2, the volume of online trading is increasing as competition among brokers drives prices further downward.

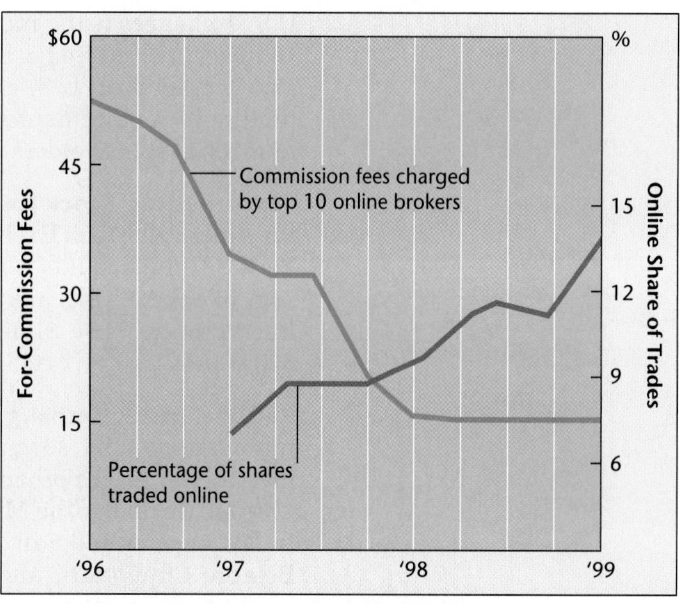

FIGURE 19.2
Growth of Online Trading

"The Internet is fundamentally changing the story of investing."
~Gideon Sasson,
HEAD OF ELECTRONIC BROKERAGE,
CHARLES SCHWAB & COMPANY

Full-Service Brokers Despite the growth in online investing, there remains an important market for full-service brokerages, both for new, uninformed investors and for experienced investors who don't have time to keep up with all the latest developments. When you deal with busy people who want to invest successfully, says Joseph Grano of UBS PaineWebber <www.ubspainewebber.com>, "you can't do it through a telephone response system. In a world that's growing more and more complicated, the advice and counsel of a broker will be more important, not less important."

With full lines of financial services, firms such as Merrill Lynch can offer clients consulting advice in personal financial planning, estate planning, and tax strategies, along with a wider range of investment products. IPOs of stock, for example, are generally not available to the public through online retail brokers. Rather, a full-service broker, who is also the investment banker that sells the IPO shares, can sell IPO shares to its clients. Financial advisers also do more than deliver information: They offer interpretations of and suggestions on investments that clients might overlook when trying to sift through an avalanche of online financial data.

The Major Exchanges and the OTC Market The two major stock exchanges that operate on trading floors in the United States are the New York and American stock exchanges. The New York Stock Exchange, for many years the largest exchange in the United States, has recently begun to face stiff competition from both the electronic market in the United States and large foreign exchanges, especially in London and Tokyo.

The most important differences between exchanges and the electronic market are (1) the activity of *dealers* and (2) the geographic location of the market. On the trading floor of an exchange, one dealer, called a *specialist,* is appointed by the exchange to control trading for each stock. The specialist not only buys and sells that stock for his or her own inventory but also acts as exclusive auctioneer for it.[11] The electronic market, on the other hand, conducts trades electronically among thousands of dealers in remote locations around the world.

The New York Stock Exchange For many people, "the stock market" means the New York Stock Exchange (NYSE) <www.nyse.com>. Founded in 1792 and located at the corner of Wall and Broad Streets in New York City, the largest of all

U.S. exchanges is the model for exchanges worldwide. An average of 1.24 billio shares valued at $42.3 billion change hands each day. About 41 percent of a shares traded on U.S. exchanges are traded here. Only firms meeting certai minimum requirements—earning power, total value of outstanding stock, an number of shareholders—are eligible for listing on the NYSE.[12]

The American Stock Exchange The second-largest floor-based U.S. exchang the American Stock Exchange (AMEX) <www.amex.com>, is also located in Ne York City. It accounts for about 2 percent of all shares traded on U.S. exchange and, like the NYSE, has minimum requirements for listings. They are, howeve less stringent. The minimum number of publicly held shares, for example, i 500,000—versus 1.1 million for the NYSE.

Regional Stock Exchanges Established long before the advent of modern com munications, the seven regional stock exchanges were organized to serv investors in places other than New York. The largest regional exchanges are th Chicago (formerly the Midwest) Stock Exchange and the Pacific Stock Exchang in Los Angeles and San Francisco. Other exchanges are located in Philadelphi Boston, Cincinnati, and Spokane, Washington. Many corporations list the stocks both regionally and on either the NYSE or the AMEX.

Foreign Stock Exchanges As recently as 1980, the U.S. market accounted fo more than half the value of the world market in traded stocks. Indeed, as late a 1975, the equity of IBM alone <www.ibm.com> was greater than the nation market equities of all but four countries. Market activities, however, have shifte as the value of shares listed on foreign exchanges continues to grow. The annu dollar value of trades on exchanges in London, Tokyo, and other cities is in th trillions. In fact, the London exchange exceeds even the NYSE in number o stocks listed. In market value, however, transactions on U.S. exchanges remai larger than those on exchanges in other countries. Relatively new exchanges a also flourishing in cities from Shanghai to Warsaw.

over-the-counter (OTC) market
Organization of securities dealers formed to trade stock outside the formal institutional setting of the organized stock exchanges

Over-the-Counter Market The **over-the-counter (OTC) market** is so calle because its original traders were somewhat like retailers. They kept supplies o shares on hand and, as opportunities arose, sold them over the office counter t interested buyers. Even today, the OTC market has no trading floor. Rather, consists of many people in different locations who hold an inventory of secur ties that are not listed on any of the national U.S. securities exchanges. Th **over-the-counter market** consists of independent dealers who own the secur ties that they buy and sell at their own risk. Although OTC activities are of inte est from an historical perspective, trading volume is small in comparison t other markets.[13]

National Association of Securities Dealers Automated Quotation (Nasdaq) system
Organization of over-the-counter dealers who own, buy, and sell their own securities over a network of electronic communications

Nasdaq and NASD In the 1960s, an SEC study reported that the OTC, on whic the shares of thousands of companies were traded, was unduly fragmented. O proposal recommended automation of the OTC, calling for a new system to b implemented by the National Association of Securities Dealers Inc. (NASD). Th resulting automated OTC system, launched in 1971, is known as the **Nation Association of Securities Dealers Automated Quotation**—or **Nasdaq**—**syste** the world's first electronic stock market.[14] In 2001, NASD became a separa organization from the Nasdaq system so that NASD could focus solely on secu ties regulation.

With more than 5,500 member firms, NASD <www.nasd.com> is the large private-sector securities-regulation organization in the world. Every broker/deal in the United States who conducts securities business with the public is requir by law to be a member of the NASD.[15] NASD includes dealers (not just broker who must pass qualification exams and meet certain standards for financi soundness. The privilege of trading in the market is granted by federal regulators and by NASD.

Meanwhile, the Nasdaq telecommunications system operates the Nasdaq Stock Market by broadcasting trading information on an intranet to over 350,000 terminals worldwide. Whereas orders at the NYSE are paired on the trading floor, Nasdaq orders are paired and executed on a computer network. Currently, Nasdaq is working with officials in an increasing number of countries who want to replace the trading floors of traditional exchanges with electronic networks like Nasdaq.

The stocks of nearly 4,100 companies are traded by Nasdaq. Newer firms are often listed here when their stocks first become available in the secondary market. Current listings include Starbucks and such well-known technology stocks as Intel <www.intel.com>, Dell Computer <www.dell.com>, Oracle Technology <www.oracle.com>, and Microsoft <www.microsoft.com>.

In early 2001, Nasdaq, the fastest-growing U.S. stock market, set a record volume of over three billion shares traded in one day. Its 2001 volume of 471 billion shares traded was the industry leader, and it is the leading U.S. market for non-U.S. listings, with a total of 461 non-U.S. companies. Although the volume of shares traded surpasses that of the New York Stock Exchange, the total market value of Nasdaq's U.S. stocks is only about one-half of that of the NYSE.

Steps Toward a Global Stock Market With its electronic telecommunication system, Nasdaq possesses an infrastructure that could eventually lead to a truly global stock market—one that would allow buyers and sellers to interact from any point in the world. Currently, Nasdaq provides equal access to both the market and market information via simultaneous broadcasts of quotes from more than 1,000 participating firms. Nasdaq communication networks enter customer orders and then display new quotes reflecting those orders.

In laying the groundwork for a system that would connect listed companies and investors for worldwide 24-hour-a-day trading, Nasdaq is taking the following steps:

- The Nasdaq Japan Market was launched in 2000 in partnership with the Osaka Securities Exchange <www.ose.or.jp/e>. In 2001, it captured nearly 30 percent of Japan's new public stock offerings. This electronic securities market uses a technology that can eventually link Europe and the United States as well.
- Nasdaq-Europe, an Internet-accessible stock market patterned after Nasdaq, was opened in June 2001. It offers European traders access to the stocks of listed U.S. and Asian companies.
- In 2001, Nasdaq opened offices in Shanghai, China, primarily for educational purposes, and in Bangladore, India.
- It has agreed to a deal with the government of Quebec to launch Nasdaq Canada.
- An agreement with the Hong Kong Stock Exchange allows some of Nasdaq's shares to trade in Hong Kong and some of Hong Kong's shares to trade in the United States.
- News reports indicate that Nasdaq has established relationships with Sydney, Australia's, stock market and that negotiations are underway with South Korea's stock market.[16]

Although these initiatives are promising, it will take several years to resolve differences in market regulation and trading practices that currently separate various countries.

Self-Check Questions 1–3

*You should now be able to answer Self-Check Questions 1–3**

1. TRUE/FALSE Suppose you're thinking about buying 100 common shares of a particular stock on the secondary securities market. Is the following statement true or false? The *par value* of a share of that stock is a good indicator of the purchase price you will have to pay.

2. MULTIPLE CHOICE Suppose your firm has decided to raise capital by issuing new *securities*. Which of the following services or institutions will be most useful for your purposes? [select one]: **(a)** a discount broker; **(b)** a full-service broker; **(c)** New York Stock Exchange; **(d)** an investment bank; **(e)** secondary securities market.

3. MULTIPLE CHOICE Which of the following items regarding *organized stock exchanges* is **not** true? [select one]: **(a)** buy-and-sell orders at the New York Stock Exchange are paired on the trading floor; **(b)** trading volume on the NYSE far exceeds that on the American Exchange; **(c)** the number of shares traded on the floor at the Nasdaq Stock Market is greater than at the NYSE; **(d)** the over-the-counter market has no trading floor; **(e)** the NYSE is facing increasing competition from electronic and foreign stock exchanges.

*Answers to Self-Check Questions 1–3 can be found on p. AN-13.

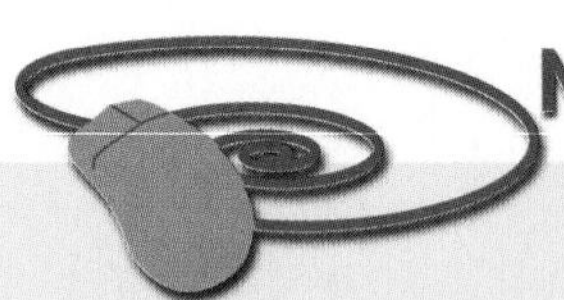

Mid-Chapter Internet Field Trip

"Securities Regulation"

In the first part of this chapter, we examined the basics of stocks and bonds. We explored both primary and secondary markets and explained why companies issue securities, why investors buy them, and what risks are associated with trading them. Trillions of dollars are at stake in securities trading, and various stock exchanges provide organized settings for buying and selling efficiently, both online and on the trading floor. How can markets operate so smoothly and quickly? On what basis can investors place trust in strangers—brokers, dealers, and companies—to buy and sell on their behalf? How does the designated regulatory body oversee all U.S. stock market activities to ensure the safety of traders and investors?

Let's explore some of these questions by visiting the Web site of the government agency that's responsible for securities market safety—the United States Securities and Exchange Commission (SEC)—at <www.sec.gov>. The Web site home page includes several major sections, including **About the SEC, Investor Information, Filings and Forms, News and Public Statements, Regulatory Actions,** and **Litigation.**

Start by clicking on **About the SEC.** The screen will then display a page with several selections, including **What We Do.** When you select **What We Do,** you will be taken to a Web page entitled "The Investor's Advocate," which contains the information that you'll need to respond to the following questions:

1. What is the primary mission of the SEC?
2. What were the economic and social conditions that led to the creation of the SEC?
3. How many SEC Commissioners are there, who appoints them, and what are the terms of appointment?
4. What topics and issues do SEC Commissioners discuss at their meetings?
5. What activities by the SEC's Division of Corporation Finance might be of assistance to the investing public?

To continue your Internet Field Trip, click on www.prenhall.com/griffin

Bonds

A **bond** is an IOU—a promise by the issuer to pay the buyer a certain amount of money by a specified future date, usually with interest paid at regular intervals. The U.S. bond market is supplied by three major sources—the U.S. government, municipalities, and corporations. Bonds differ in terms of maturity dates, tax status, and level of risk versus potential yield.[17]

bond
Security through which an issuer promises to pay the buyer a certain amount of money by a specified future date

To aid bond investors in making purchase decisions, several services rate the quality of bonds. Table 19.1, for example, shows the systems of two well-known services, Moody's <www.moodys.com> and Standard & Poor's <www.standardpoors.com>. Ratings measure default risk—the chance that one or more promised payments will be deferred or missed altogether. The highest grades are *AAA* and *Aaa,* the lowest are *C* and *D.* Low-grade bonds are usually called *junk bonds.*

U.S. Government Bonds

The U.S. government is the world's largest debtor. New federal borrowing from the public actually decreased by $90 billion in 2001. In other words, the federal government's repayments of loans exceeded the funds it raised in new loans. Nevertheless, the total U.S. debt at the beginning of 2002 hovered near $6 trillion.[18] To finance its debt, the federal government issues a variety of government bonds. The U.S. Treasury issues Treasury bills (T-bills), Treasury notes, and Treasury bonds (including U.S. savings bonds). Many government agencies (for example, the Federal Housing Administration, or FHA) also issue bonds.

Government bonds, issued by the federal government, are among the safest investments available. Securities with longer maturities are somewhat riskier than short-term issues because their longer lives expose them to more political, social, and economic changes. All federal bonds, however, are backed by the U.S. government. Government securities are sold in large blocks to institutional investors who buy them to ensure desired levels of safety in their portfolios. As investors' needs change, they may buy or sell government securities to other investors.

government bond
Bond issued by the federal government

Municipal Bonds

State and local governments issue **municipal bonds** to finance school and transportation systems and a variety of other projects. In 2001, new municipal bonds were issued at a value of more than $270 billion.

municipal bond
Bond issued by a state or local government

Some bonds, called *obligation bonds,* are backed by the issuer's taxing power. A local school district, for example, may issue $50 million in obligation bonds to fund new elementary and high schools. The issuer intends to retire the bonds from future tax revenues. In contrast, *revenue bonds* are backed only by the revenue generated by a specific project.

The most attractive feature of municipal bonds is the fact that investors do not pay taxes on interest received. Commercial banks invest in bonds nearing maturity because they are relatively safe, liquid investments. Pension funds, insurance companies, and even private citizens also make longer-term investments in municipals.

	High Grades	Medium Grades (Investment Grades)	Speculative	Poor Grades
Moody's	Aaa, Aa	A, Baa	Ba, B	Caa to C
Standard & Poor's	AAA, AA	A, BBB	BB, B	CCC to D

TABLE 19.1
Bond Rating Systems

Corporate Bonds

corporate bond
Bond issued by a company as a source of long-term funding

Although the U.S. government and municipalities are heavy borrowers, corporate long-term borrowing is even greater. **Corporate bonds** issued by U.S. companies are a large source of financing, involving more money than government and municipal bonds combined.[19] U.S. companies raised nearly $1.4 trillion from new bond issues in 2001. Bonds have traditionally been issued with maturities ranging from 20 to 30 years. In the 1980s, 10-year maturities came into wider use.

Like municipal bonds, longer-term corporate bonds are somewhat riskier than shorter-term bonds. To help investors evaluate risk, Standard & Poor's and Moody's rate both new and proposed issues on a weekly basis. Remember, however, that negative ratings do not necessarily keep issues from being successful. Rather, they raise the interest rates that issuers must offer. Corporate bonds may be categorized in terms of the method of interest payment or in terms of whether they are *secured* or *unsecured.*

registered bond
Bond bearing the name of the holder and registered with the issuing company

bearer (or coupon) bond
Bond requiring the holder to clip and submit a coupon to receive an interest payment

secured bond
Bond backed by pledges of assets to the bondholders

debenture
Unsecured bond for which no specific property is pledged as security

Interest Payment: Registered and Bearer Bonds **Registered bonds** register the names of holders with the company, which simply mails out checks. Certificates are of value only to registered holders. **Bearer (or coupon) bonds** require bondholders to clip coupons from certificates and send them to the issuer to receive an interest payment. Coupons can be redeemed by anyone, regardless of ownership.

Secured Bonds With **secured bonds,** issuers can reduce the risk to holders by pledging assets in case of default. Bonds can be backed by first mortgages, other mortgages, or other specific assets. In 1994, the Union Pacific Railroad Co. <www.uprr.com> issued $76 million in bonds to finance the purchase and renovation of equipment. Rated *Aaa* (prime) by Moody's and maturing in 2012, the bonds are secured by the newly purchased and rehabilitated equipment itself—80 diesel locomotives, 1,300 hopper cars, and 450 auto-rack cars.

Debentures Unsecured bonds are called **debentures.** No specific property is pledged as security. Rather, holders generally have claims against property not otherwise pledged in the company's other bonds. Thus, debentures are said to have inferior claims on a corporation's assets. Financially strong firms often use debentures. An example is the $175 million debenture issued by Boeing <www.boeing.com> in 1993, with maturity on April 15, 2043. Similar issues by weaker companies often receive low ratings and may have trouble attracting investors.

The Retirement of Bonds

Maturity dates on bonds of all kinds may be very long. Of course, all bonds must be paid off, or retired, at some point. With regard to maturity dates, there are three types of bonds: *callable, serial,* and *convertible.*

callable bond
Bond that may be called in and paid for by the issuer before its maturity date

Callable Bonds The issuer of **callable bonds** may call them in and pay them off at a price stipulated in the indenture, or contract, before the maturity date. Usually, the issuer cannot call the bond for a certain period of time after issue. For example, most Treasury bonds cannot be called within the first five years.

Issuers usually call in existing bonds when prevailing interest rates are lower than the rate being paid on the bond. The issuer must still pay a *call price* in order to call in the bond. The call price usually gives a premium to the bondholder. The premium is merely the difference between the face value and call price. For example, a bond offered by the Wisconsin Power Co. <www.wpl.com> bears a $100 face value and can be called by the firm for $108.67 any time during the first year after issue. The call price and the premium decrease annually as bonds approach maturity.

Sinking Funds Callable bonds are often retired by the use of **sinking fund provisions.** The issuing company is required annually to put a certain amount of money into a special bank account. At the end of a certain number of years, the money (including interest) will be sufficient to redeem the bonds. Failure to meet the sinking fund provision places the issue in default. Obviously, such bonds are generally regarded as safer investments than many other bonds.

sinking fund provision
Method for retiring bonds whereby the issuer puts enough money into a banking account to redeem the bonds at maturity

Serial and Convertible Bonds Some corporations issue serial or convertible bonds. With a **serial bond,** the firm retires portions of the bond issue in a series of different preset dates. For example, a company with a $100 million issue maturing in 20 years may retire $5 million each year. Serial bonds are most popular among local and state governments.

serial bond
Bond retired when the issuer redeems portions of the issue at different preset dates

Only corporations, however, can issue **convertible bonds.** These bonds can be converted into the common stock of the issuing company. At the option of the holder, payment is made in stock instead of in cash. When holders are given such flexibility and because of the potential benefits of converting bonds into stock, firms can offer lower interest rates when the bonds are issued. However, because holders cannot be forced to accept stock instead of cash, conversion works only when the bond buyer also regards the issuing corporation as a good investment.

convertible bond
Bond that can be retired by converting it to common stock

Secondary Markets for Bonds Nearly all secondary trading in bonds occurs in the OTC market rather than on organized exchanges. Thus, precise statistics about annual trading volumes are not recorded. As with stocks, however, market values and prices change daily. The direction of bond prices and interest rates move in opposite directions. As interest rates move up, bond prices tend to go down. The prices of riskier bonds fluctuate more widely than those of higher grade bonds.

Other Investments

Stocks and bonds are not the only marketable securities available to businesses. Financial managers are also concerned with financial opportunities in *mutual funds* and *commodities.* In striking the right balance for *risk* among investment alternatives, financial managers use *diversification* and *asset allocation.*

Mutual Funds

Companies called **mutual funds** pool investments from individuals and organizations to purchase a portfolio of stocks, bonds, and other securities. Investors are thus part owners of the portfolio.[20] If you invest $1,000 in a mutual fund with a portfolio worth $100,000, you own 1 percent of that portfolio. Investors in **no-load funds** are not charged sales commissions when they buy into or sell out of funds. Investors in **load funds** generally pay commissions of 2 to 8 percent.

mutual fund
Company that pools investments from individuals and organizations to purchase a portfolio of stocks, bonds, and other securities

no-load fund
Mutual fund in which investors pay no sales commissions when they buy in or sell out

load fund
Mutual fund in which investors are charged sales commissions when they buy in or sell out

Reasons for Investing The total assets invested in U.S. mutual funds grew significantly every year from 1991 to 2000—to a total of $7 trillion in more than 10,000 different funds. The total fell, however, to $6.9 trillion with the economic downturn and reports of corporate scandals by mid-2002.[21] Why do investors find mutual funds so attractive? Remember first of all that they vary in their investment goals. Naturally, different funds are designed to appeal to the different motives and goals of investors. Funds stressing safety often include money market mutual funds and other safe issues offering immediate income. Investors seeking higher current income must generally sacrifice some safety. Typically, these people look to long-term municipal bonds, corporate bonds, and income mutual funds that invest in common stocks with good dividend-paying records.

Mutual funds that stress growth include *balanced mutual funds*—portfolios of bonds and preferred and common stocks, especially the common stocks of established firms. Aggressive growth funds seek maximum capital appreciation. They sacrifice current income and safety and invest in stocks of new (and even troubled) companies and other high-risk securities.

Commodities

futures contract
Agreement to purchase specified amounts of a commodity at a given price on a set future date

commodities market
Market in which futures contracts are traded

Individuals and businesses can buy and sell commodities as investments. **Futures contracts**—agreements to purchase specified amounts of commodities at given prices on set dates—can be bought and sold in the **commodities market.** These contracts are available not only for stocks but also for commodities ranging from coffee beans and hogs to propane and platinum. Because selling prices reflect traders' estimates of future events and values, futures prices are quite volatile, and trading is risky.

To clarify the workings of the commodities market, let us look at an example. On December 12, 2001, the price of gold on the open market was $274 per ounce. Futures contracts for July 2002 gold were selling for $275 per ounce. This price reflected investors' judgment that gold prices would be higher the following July. Now suppose that you purchased a 100-ounce gold futures contract in December for $27,500 ($275 × 100). If in February 2002, the July gold futures sold for $299 (which they really did), you could sell your contract for $29,900. Your profit after the two months would be $2,400.

margin
Percentage of the total sales price that a buyer must put up to place an order for stock of futures contracts

Margins Usually, buyers of futures contracts need not put up the full purchase amount. Rather, the buyer posts a smaller amount—the **margin**—that may be as little as $3,000 for contracts up to $100,000. Let us look again at our gold futures example. As we saw, if you had posted a $3,000 margin for your July gold contract, you would have earned a $2,400 profit on that investment of $3,000 in only two months.

However, you also took a big risk involving two big *ifs*: If you had held onto your contract until July *and* if gold had dropped, say to $240, you would have lost $3,500 ($27,500 − $24,000). If you had posted a $3,000 margin to buy the contract, you would have lost all of that margin and would owe an additional $500. As

Back when Terri Clynes was trading commodities for Enron <www.enron.com>, the company's trading portfolio boasted tens of thousands of contracts for commodities ranging from paper and metals to crude oil and power. At one time, Enron assessed the value of its commodities holdings at more than $12 billion. Within two months of its bankruptcy filing in December 2001, that figure had fallen to a mere $1.3 billion. Why the dramatic drop in value? In part because of ups and down in the market and in part because of the collapse of Enron's strategy of overestimating the value of its contracts in order to inflate profits.

it turns out, July gold prices increased to $315, so your investment of $27,500 would have gained $4,000 in July. In fact, however, between 75 and 90 percent of all small-time investors lose money in the futures market. For one thing, the action is fast and furious, with small investors trying to keep up with professionals ensconced in seats on the major exchanges. Although the profit potential is exciting, experts recommend that most novices retreat to safer stock markets. Of course, as one veteran financial planner puts it, commodities are tempting. "After trading commodities," he reports, "trading stocks is like watching the grass grow."

"After trading commodities, trading stocks is like watching the grass grow."

~Veteran financial planner

Making Choices for Diversification, Asset Allocation, and Risk Reduction

Investors seldom take an extreme approach—total risk or total risk avoidance—in selecting their investments. Extreme positions attract extreme results, and most investors have a preference toward either risk or risk avoidance, but they are not totally immersed at either end of the risk spectrum. Instead, they select a mixture, or *portfolio,* of investments—some riskier and some more conservative—that, collectively, provides the level of risk and financial stability at which they are comfortable. They do this in two ways: through *diversification* and *asset allocation.*

SWIMMING AGAINST THE TIDES OF TRUST

These are tough times for both global financial markets and Corporate America. Over the last few years, there's been a dramatic drop in public confidence both in the ability of financial markets to perform at desired levels and in the capacity of Corporate America to perform in ethically responsible ways. The assault on the public trust has been two-pronged.

Financial markets, of course, have always fluctuated. The difference is that never before have so many people had a stake in the system. Over the past few years, millions of Americans have invested their life savings in 401(k) plans and other financial instruments. In fact, the latest data suggest that over 50 percent of all U.S. households now own shares of stock. Unfortunately, some of the companies they've invested in haven't done much to bolster their confidence in Corporate America. Among other practices, issuing bogus balance sheets and false financial-health reports has prefigured some spectacular declines in stock prices and corresponding losses of investors' money.

In addition, the always volatile world of business and finance has been further agitated by an enormous amount of media attention. Since the early 1990s, our supply of investment information has exploded, especially with the advent of new media outlets devoted entirely to market analysis and other business coverage. The media attention means that corporations must communicate more regularly and more clearly with larger stakeholder audiences, ranging from individual investors to large pension funds that control huge blocks of company stock. Because it's not easy to get a coherent message across to an audience with widely differing expectations, many large corporations employ financial communications experts whose job is to project accurate and up-to-date images. They're also responsible for ensuring that certain legal obligations are met in the reporting of the financial data on which investors rely.

In the end, of course, it's hard for companies to buck financial trends, and even the best financial communications specialists have a hard time convincing investors that things are going well when sentiment about the state of the market—not to mention public opinion of corporate ethics—is running against them.

Self-Check Questions 4–6

*You should now be able to answer Self-Check Questions 4–6**

4. MULTIPLE CHOICE Which of the following is **not** true about *bonds*? [select one]: **(a)** Government bonds are among the safest investments available. **(b)** Corporate bonds issued by U.S. companies involve less money than U.S. government and municipal bonds. **(c)** Secured bonds can reduce risk to holders because the issuing firms pledge assets in case of default. **(d)** Only corporations can issue convertible bonds. **(e)** Bonds can be traded on the secondary market.

5. TRUE/FALSE Suppose a well-respected corporation has decided to issue bonds for raising capital but also wants to minimize future interest payments. Is the following statement true or false? A *convertible bond* is well-suited to this firm's objectives.

6. MULTIPLE CHOICE Suppose you're the superintendent of a local school district. You want to issue *debt securities* that will be repaid reliably over a number of years and that holders will regard as safe investments. Which of the following would be suitable for meeting your objectives? [select one]: **(a)** debentures; **(b)** bearer bonds; **(c)** futures contracts; **(d)** mutual funds with no-load provisions; **(e)** callable bonds with sinking fund provisions.

*ANSWERS TO SELF-CHECK QUESTIONS 4–6 CAN BE FOUND ON P. AN-13.

diversification

Purchase of several different kinds of investments rather than just one

Diversification **Diversification** means buying several different kinds of investments rather than just one. Diversification as applied to common stocks means, for example, that you invest in stocks of several different companies, such as IBM, Cisco Systems, and Boeing, rather than put all your money into just one of them. The risk of loss is reduced by spreading the total investment across more stocks because, while any one stock may tumble, there is less chance that all of them will fall. Even more diversification is gained when funds are spread across more kinds of investment alternatives—stocks, bonds, mutual funds, real estate, and so on. Among the tragedies resulting from the scandals at Enron and WorldCom are the life-long employees who did not diversify their 401(k) investments and, instead, had all their retirement funds invested in their firm's stock. This was an extremely risky position, as they sorrowfully learned. When their firm's stock took a free-fall to near zero, their retirement funds disappeared.

asset allocation

Relative amount of funds invested in (or allocated to) each of several investment alternatives

Asset Allocation **Asset allocation** is the proportion—the relative amounts—of funds invested in (or allocated to) each of the investment alternatives. You may decide for example, to allocate $20,000 to common stocks, $10,000 to a money market mutual fund, and $10,000 to a U.S. Treasury Bond mutual fund. Ten years later, the same investor may decide on a less risky asset allocation of $10,000, $15,000, and $15,000 in the same investment categories, respectively. As one's investment objectives change, in this example from moderate risk to lower risk for capital preservation, the asset allocation must be changed accordingly.

Buying and Selling Securities

The process of buying and selling securities is complex. First, you need to find out about possible investments and match them to your investment objectives. Then you must select a broker and open an account. Only then can you place orders and make different types of transactions.

Financial Information Services

Have you ever looked at the financial section of your daily newspaper and wondered what all those tables and numbers mean? It is a good idea to know how to read stock, bond, and mutual fund quotations if you want to invest in issues. Fortunately, this skill is easily mastered.

Stock Quotations Daily transactions for NYSE and Nasdaq common stocks are reported in most city newspapers. Figure 19.3 shows part of a listing from the *Wall Street Journal,* with columns numbered 1 through 11. Let us analyze the listing for the company at the top, Gap Inc. <www.gap.com>:

1	2	3	4	5	6	7	8	9	10	11
YTD % Chg	52 Weeks High	52 Weeks Low	Stock	Sym	Div	Yld %	PE	Vol 100s	Last	Net Chg
- 1.4	30.68	11.12	Gap Inc	GPS	.09	.7	dd	27593	13.74	-0.20
-11.5	28	18.35	GardnrDenvr	GDI		...	14	279	19.75	...
-24.0	13.70	8.20	Gartner	IT		...	dd	2657	8.88	-0.29
-23.6	13.50	8.05	GartnerB	ITB		...	...	346	8.56	-0.44
-49.0	16.20	3.80	Gateway	GTW		...	dd	18600	4.10	0.11
-18.4	**29.26**	**18.49**	**GaylEnt**	GET		...	**dd**	**160**	**20.08**	**-1.17**
-15.7	16.25	10.50	GenCorp	GY	.12	1.0	4	1413	11.90	-0.21
-45.2	**58.95**	**25.10**	**Genentech**	DNA		...	**dd**	**33696**	**29.75**	**1.61**
-53.8	19.24	5.59	GenlCbl	BGC	.20	3.3	dd	1699	6.05	-0.20
20.9	111.18	74.90	GenDynam	GD	1.20	1.2	21	28126	96.31	-2.29
-28.6	47.75	26.40	GenElec	GE	.72	2.5	20	479987	28.60	1.25

FIGURE 19.3
Reading a Stock Quotation

- The first column ("YTD % CHG") shows the stock price percentage change for the calendar year to date. Gap's common stock price has decreased 1.4 percent for 2002 (as of mid-July).
- The next two columns ("High" and "Low") show the highest and lowest prices paid for one share of Gap stock *during the past year.* Note that stock prices throughout are expressed in dollars per share. In the past 52 weeks, then, Gap's stock ranged in value from \$30.68 to \$11.12 per share. This range reveals a fairly volatile stock price.
- The fourth column ("Stock") is the abbreviated company name.
- The NYSE *symbol* for the stock is listed in column 5 ("Sym").
- The sixth column ("Div") indicates that Gap pays an annual *cash dividend* of \$0.09 per share. This amount can be compared with payouts by other companies.
- Column 7 ("Yld %") is the *dividend yield* expressed as a percentage of the stock's current price (shown in column 10). Gap's dividend yield is 0.7 percent (0.09/13.74, rounded). Potential buyers can compare this yield with returns they might get from alternative investments.
- Column 8 ("PE") shows the **price-earnings ratio**—the current price of the stock divided by the firm's current annual earnings per share. On this day, Gap's PE is indicated as *dd,* a code meaning that the Gap had negative earnings for the past four quarters. If, in contrast, the Gap's PE had been 20, for example, it means that investors are willing to pay \$20 for each dollar of reported profits to own Gap stock. This figure can be compared with PE ratios of other stocks when deciding which is the best investment.
- The last three columns detail the day's trading. Column 9 ("Vol 100s") shows the *number of shares* (in hundreds) that were traded—in this case, 27,953. Some investors interpret increases in trading volume as an indicator of forthcoming price changes in a stock.
- Column 10 ("Last") shows that Gap's *last sale of the day* was for \$13.74.
- The final column ("Net Chg") shows the *difference between the previous day's close and the close on the day being reported.* The closing price of Gap stock is \$0.20 lower than it was on the previous business day. Day-to-day changes are indicators of recent price stability or volatility.

price-earnings ratio
Current price of a stock divided by the firm's current annual earnings per share

The listings also report unusual conditions of importance to investors. An *s* next to the stock symbol, for example, would indicate either a *stock split* (a division of stock that gives stockholders a greater number of shares but that does not change each individual's proportionate share of ownership) or an *extra stock dividend* paid by the company during the past 52 weeks. An *n* accompanying a stock symbol would indicate that this stock was *newly issued* during the past 52 weeks. A downward-pointing marker (▼) next to a stock symbol would indicate a new 52-week low in the price of that stock. The stock listings contain an index explaining the various codes for unusual conditions.

Reports on daily transactions for preferred stocks use a format similar to that for common stocks.

①	②	③	④	⑤	⑥	⑦	⑧	⑨
52 Weeks High	52 Weeks Low	Bond Identifier	Cur Yld	Sales $1,000	Weekly High	Weekly Low	Weekly Last	Net Chg
105⅜	77	ATT 8⅝31	10.5	1272	82¾	79⅞	82⅜	+ 3⅜
191	80	Aquila 6⅝11	cv	28	94⅛	93½	93½	+ ½
103	89¼	BayView 9s07	9.1	45	99½	98	99	– ½
103	99½	Dole 7s03	6.9	21	102	101 23/32	101 23/32	– 9/32
107⅞	104⅜	Fortune 8½03	8.1	54	105⅛	105⅛	105⅛	– ⅛
53	38	HewlPkd zr17	...	20	44¾	44¾	44¾	+ 6¾
98½	49	Hexcel 7s03	cv	221	85	79	85	...
99	80½	Hilton 5s06	cv	418	94½	92⅝	92⅝	– 2
105⅞	91½	Hollngr 9¼06	9.1	53	102	101	102	+ 1
96½	87⅝	Honywll zr03	...	15	95½	95½	95½	+ ¼

FIGURE 19.4

Reading a Bond Quotation

Bond Quotations Daily quotations on corporate bonds from the NYSE are also widely published. As you can see in Figure 19.4, bond quotations contain essentially the same type of information as stock quotations. One difference is that the year in which it is going to mature is listed beside each bond. Again, let's focus on the first bond listed, ATT.

- The first two columns ("High" and "Low") show the highest and lowest prices paid for the ATT bond during the past year. The bond's price is expressed in terms of dollars, and it ranged from a low of $77 to a high of $105⅜.
- Column 3 is the *bond identifier:* the abbreviation for both the company and a specific bond issue. Here, we see that the ATT bond bears an annual interest payment of 8⅝ percent of the bond's face value. The digits 31 mean that the bond matures in the year 2031. (The *s* that sometimes appears between the rate and maturity year is meaningless; it simply keeps numbers from running together.)
- Column 4 shows the *current yield:* the annual dollar coupon amount divided by the current market price. For every $100 worth of bonds they own, holders will receive $8⅝ ($8.70) in cash. If we jump ahead momentarily to column 8 ("Last"), we see that the same bond (and remaining coupons) can now be purchased for $82⅜. This means that the bond currently yields an annual return of 10.50 percent (8⅝ divided by 82⅜, rounded off). (The designation *CV* in column 4 means that the bond is *convertible.*)
- Columns 5, 8, and 9 refer to the *current day's activities.* Under "Sales," for example, we see that $1.272 million in ATT bonds were traded. "Last" (col. 8) is the particular bond's *closing price.* Note that this price, 82⅜, is expressed as a percentage of the bond's par value. Let's say that ATT had set a par value of $1,000. Today's closing price means that the actual price to a buyer would be 82.375 percent of par value: that is, $823.75 instead of $1,000. "Net Chg" refers to the *difference between today's closing price and yesterday's.* This bond is currently up 3⅜ of a dollar, or $3.375.
- Columns 6 and 7 refer to the *current week's activities.* The bond's highest price was $82.75; the low was $79.875.

Mutual Funds Quotations Selling prices for mutual funds are reported daily in most city newspapers. Additional investor information is also available in the financial press. Figure 19.5 shows how to read a typical weekly mutual funds quotation.

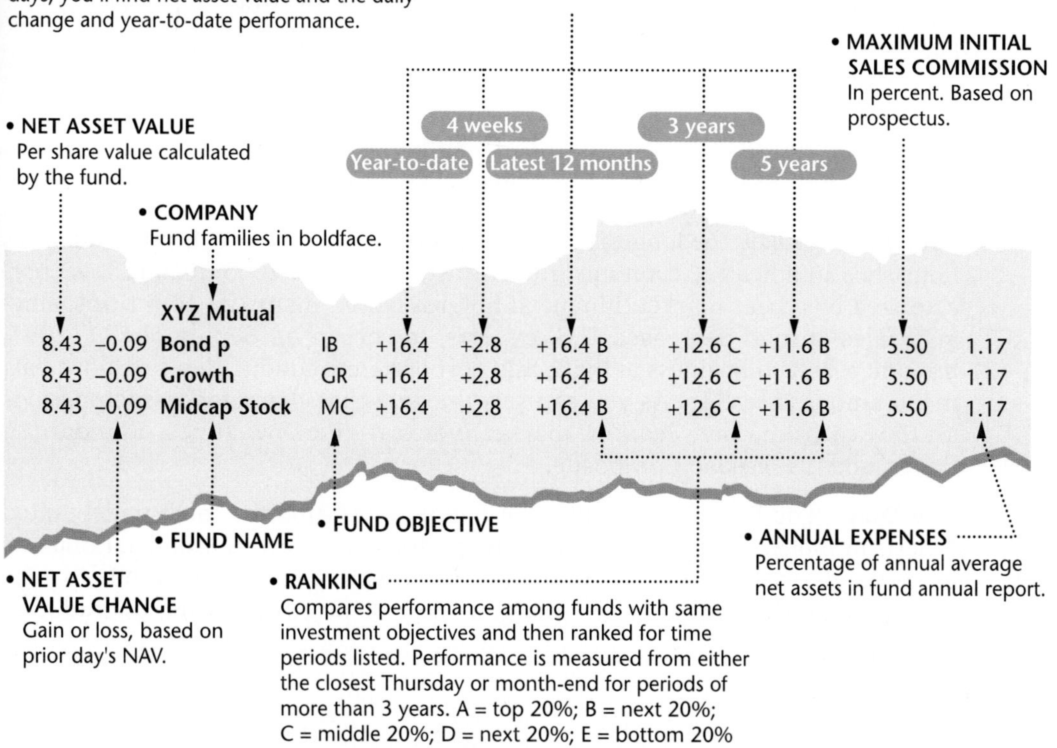
Performance calculations assume reinvestment of all distributions and are after subtracting annual expenses. But figures don't reflect sales charges ("loads") or redemption fees.
These expanded tables appear Fridays. Other days, you'll find net asset value and the daily change and year-to-date performance.
• TOTAL RETURN
NAV change plus accumulated income for the period, in percent. Assumes reinvestment of all distributions. Percentages are annualized for periods exceeding one year. Calculations are based on latest data from fund.
• MAXIMUM INITIAL SALES COMMISSION
In percent. Based on prospectus.
• NET ASSET VALUE
Per share value calculated by the fund.
4 weeks
3 years
Year-to-date
Latest 12 months
5 years
• COMPANY
Fund families in boldface.
XYZ Mutual
8.43 -0.09 Bond p IB +16.4 +2.8 +16.4 B +12.6 C +11.6 B 5.50 1.17
8.43 -0.09 Growth GR +16.4 +2.8 +16.4 B +12.6 C +11.6 B 5.50 1.17
8.43 -0.09 Midcap Stock MC +16.4 +2.8 +16.4 B +12.6 C +11.6 B 5.50 1.17
• FUND NAME
• FUND OBJECTIVE
• ANNUAL EXPENSES
Percentage of annual average net assets in fund annual report.
• NET ASSET VALUE CHANGE
Gain or loss, based on prior day's NAV.
• RANKING
Compares performance among funds with same investment objectives and then ranked for time periods listed. Performance is measured from either the closest Thursday or month-end for periods of more than 3 years. A = top 20%; B = next 20%; C = middle 20%; D = next 20%; E = bottom 20%

FIGURE 19.5
Reading a Mutual Fund Quotation

- Column 1 is the *net asset value* (NAV), or the value of a single share as calculated by the fund.
- Column 2 shows the *net asset value change*—the gain or loss based on the previous day's NAV.
- Column 3 lists the *fund family* at the top and the individual fund names beneath the family name.
- Column 4 reports *each fund's objective.* The "IB" code stands for an intermediate-term bond fund; "GR" indicates a growth stock fund. This allows readers to compare the performance of funds with similar objectives.
- The next five columns report *each fund's recent and long-term performance,* and they rank the funds within each investment objective. These numbers reflect the percentage change in NAV plus accumulated income for each period, assuming that all distributions are reinvested in the fund. These five columns show the return of the fund for the year to date, the last 4 weeks, 12 months, 3 years, and 5 years. The numbers for periods exceeding a year show an average annual return for the period, and they are followed by letters indicating the fund's performance relative to other funds with the same objective. "A" means the fund was among the top 20 percent of funds in that category, "B" indicates the second 20 percent, and so on.

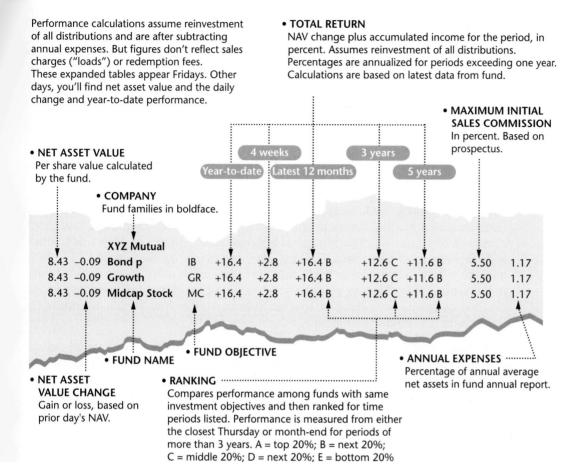

- The next column reports the *maximum initial sales commission,* expressed in percent, which the investor would have to pay to purchase shares in the fund.
- The last column shows the fund's *average annual expenses* as a percentage of the fund's assets, paid annually by investors in the fund.

market index
Summary of price trends in a specific industry and/or the stock market as a whole

bull market
Period of rising stock prices

bear market
Period of falling stock prices

Market Indexes Although they do not indicate the status of particular securities, **market indexes** provide useful summaries of price trends, both in specific industries and in the stock market as a whole. Market indexes, for example, reveal bull and bear market trends. **Bull markets** are periods of rising stock prices. Periods of falling stock prices are called **bear markets.**

As Figure 19.6 shows, the years 1981 to the beginning of 2000 boasted a strong bull market, the longest in history. Inflation was under control as business flourished in a healthy economy. In contrast, the period 2000 to 2002 was characterized by a bear market. Financial failures closed many dot-com firms, sluggish sales abroad decreased U.S. exports, terrorism on September 11, 2001, brought a halt to business activity, and corporate misconduct led to a downcast mood among investors. As you can see, the data that characterize such periods are drawn from three leading market indexes—the Dow Jones, Standard & Poor's, and the Nasdaq Composite.

Dow Jones Industrial Average (DJIA)
Market index based on the prices of 30 of the largest industrial firms listed on the NYSE

The Dow The **Dow Jones Industrial Average (DJIA)** is the most widely cited American index. The Dow measures the performance of U.S. financial markets by focusing on 30 blue-chip companies as reflectors of economic health. The Dow is an average of the stock prices for these 30 large firms and, by tradition,

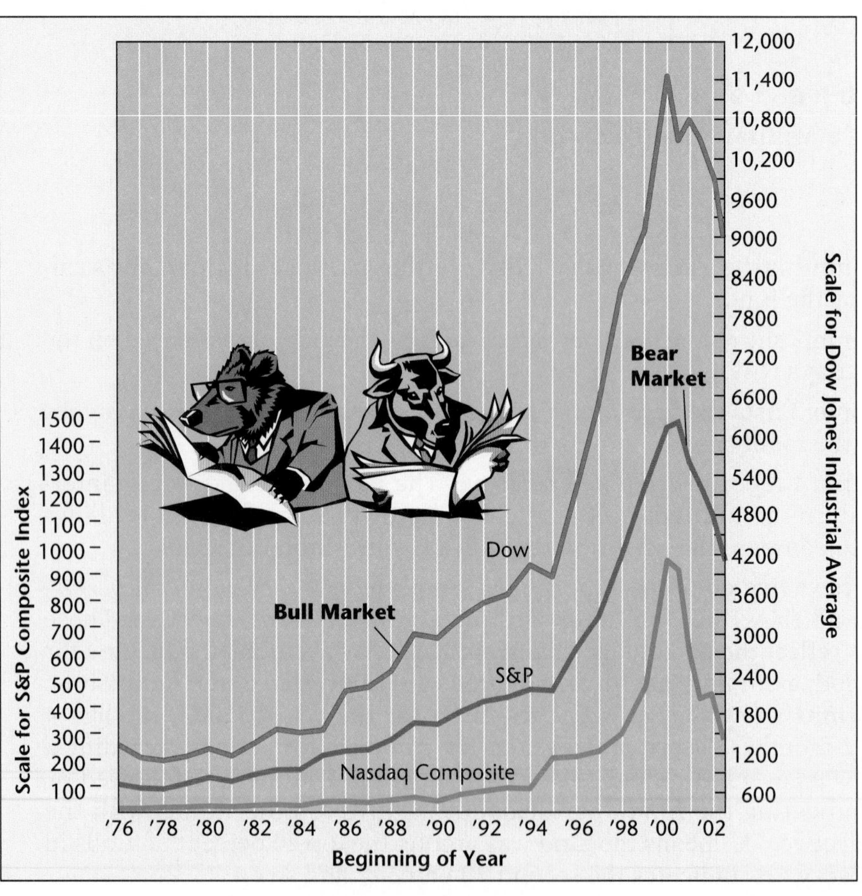

FIGURE 19.6
Bull and Bear Markets

traders and investors use it as a barometer of the market's overall movement. Because it includes only 30 of the thousands of companies on the market, the Dow is only an approximation of the overall market's price movements.

Over the decades, the Dow has been revised and updated to reflect the changing composition of U.S. companies and industries. The most recent modification occurred in November 1999, when four companies were added—Home Depot <www.homedepot.com>, Intel, Microsoft, and SBC Communications <www.sbc.com>—replacing Chevron <www.chevron.com>, Goodyear <www.goodyear.com>, Sears <www.sears.com>, and Union Carbide <www.unioncarbide.com>. These changes not only reflect the increasing importance of technology stocks, but also include for the first time two stocks from the Nasdaq market rather than only companies listed on the NYSE.

The Dow average is computed as the sum of the current prices of the 30 stocks divided not by 30 (as might be expected) but rather by a number that compensates for stock splits and each stock's available number of shares. On July 15, 2002, the value of that divisor was 0.14445. Each day, the divisor's value is printed in the *Wall Street Journal,* as is the DJIA.

The S&P 500 Because it considers very few firms, the Dow is a limited gauge of the overall U.S. stock market. **Standard & Poor's Composite Index** is a broader report. It consists of 500 stocks, including 400 industrial firms, 40 utilities, 40 financial institutions, and 20 transportation companies. Because the index average is weighted according to the total market values of each stock, the more highly valued companies exercise a greater influence on the index.

Standard & Poor's Composite Index
Market index based on the performance of 400 industrial firms, 40 utilities, 40 financial institutions, and 20 transportation companies

The Nasdaq Composite Because it considers more stocks, some Wall Street observers regard the **Nasdaq Composite Index** as the most important of all market indexes. Unlike the Dow and the S&P 500, all Nasdaq-listed companies, not just a selected few, are included in the index, for a total of over 4,000 firms (both domestic and foreign)—more than most other indexes.

Nasdaq Composite Index
Value-weighted market index that includes all Nasdaq-listed companies, both domestic and foreign

The popularity of the Nasdaq Index goes hand-in-hand with investors' growing interest in technology and small-company stocks. Compared with other markets, the Nasdaq market has enjoyed a remarkable level of activity. By 1998, so many shares were being traded on Nasdaq that its share-of-market surpassed that of the NYSE. Figure 19.7 shows the steady growth in the dollar volume of Nasdaq trades, which continue to capture market share. In a further display of Nasdaq's emerging role in the stock market, it has also overtaken the NYSE in terms of investor awareness. NYSE's historical dominance as the market's flagship brand is being challenged by the newer Nasdaq, which, according to one study, even enjoys greater name recognition among U.S. investors.

Placing Orders

After doing your own research and getting recommendations from your broker, you can choose to place several different types of orders:[22]

- A **market order** requests that a broker buy or sell a certain security at the prevailing market price at the time of the order. For example, look again at Figure 19.3. On that day, your broker would have sold your Gap stock at a price near $13.74.

market order
Order to buy or sell a security at the market price prevailing at the time the order is placed

- Note that when you gave your order to sell, you did not know exactly what the market price would be. This situation can be avoided with limit and stop orders, which allow for buying and selling only if certain price conditions are met.

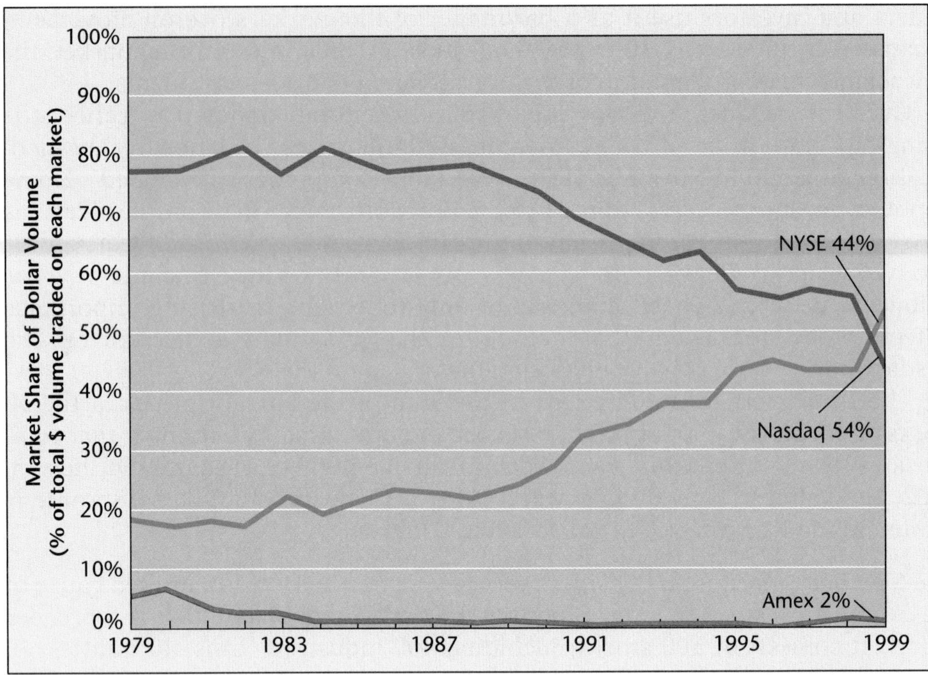

FIGURE 19.7
The Stock Markets: Comparative Dollar Volume of Trades

limit order
Order authorizing the purchase of a stock only if its price is equal to or less than a specified amount

stop order
Order authorizing the sale of a stock if its price falls to or below a specified level

round lot
Purchase or sale of stock in units of 100 shares

odd lot
Purchase or sale of stock in fractions of round lots

A **limit order** authorizes the purchase of a stock only if its price is less than or equal to a specified limit. For example, an order to buy at $15 a share means that the broker is to buy if and only if the stock becomes available for a price of $15 or less. A **stop order** instructs the broker to sell if a stock price falls to a certain level. For example, an order of $10 on a particular stock means that the broker is to sell that stock if and only if its price falls to $10 or below.

Orders also differ by size. An order for a **round lot** requests 100 shares of a particular stock or some multiple thereof. Fractions of round lots are called **odd lots.** Because an intermediary—an *odd-lot broker*—is often involved, odd-lot trading is usually more expensive than round-lot trading.

Financing Purchases

When you place a buy order of any kind, you must tell your broker how you will pay for the purchase. For example, you might maintain a cash account with your broker. Then, as you buy and sell stocks, your broker adds proceeds to your account while deducting commissions and purchase costs. Like almost every product in today's economy, securities can also be purchased on credit.

Margin Trading Like futures contracts, stocks can be bought *on margin*—that is, the buyer can put down a portion of the stock's price. The rest is borrowed from the buyer's broker, who secures special-rate bank loans with stock. Controlled by the Federal Reserve Board, the *margin requirement* has remained fixed at 50 percent since 1974.

Margin trading offers several advantages. Suppose you purchased $100,000 worth of stock in Intel Corp. Let's also say that you paid $50,000 of your own money and borrowed the other $50,000 from your broker at 10 percent interest. Valued at its market price, your stock serves as your collateral. If shares have risen in value to $115,000 after one year, you can sell them and pay your broker $55,000 ($50,000 principal plus $5,000 interest). You will have $60,000 left over.

Your original investment of $50,000 will have earned a 20 percent profit of $10,000. If you had paid the entire price out of your own pocket, you would have earned only a 15 percent return.

Although investors often recognize possible profits to be made in margin trading, they sometimes fail to consider that losses, too, can be amplified. The rising use of margin credit by investors had become a growing concern during the recent bull market. Investors who seemed focused on the upside benefits were confident that the market trend would continue upward, and they were less sensitive to the downside risks of margin trading. Especially at online brokerages, inexperienced traders were borrowing at an alarming rate, and some were using the borrowed funds for risky and speculative day trading. So-called *day traders* visited Web sites online to buy and sell a stock in the same day (so-called *intraday trades*), seeking quick in-and-out fractional gains on large volumes (many shares) of each stock. While some day traders were successful, most ended up financial losers. With more investors buying on debt, more of them were headed for a serious accelerated crash. Bradley Skolnick, president of the North American Securities Administrators Association, voices the opinion held by many investment experts: "A lot of people are purchasing rather speculative, high-risk stocks with borrowed money, and that's a source of concern for me. In a volatile market, trading on margin can find you in a whole lot of hurt very quickly."[23]

"In a volatile market, trading on margin can find you in a whole lot of hurt very quickly."

~Bradley Skolnick, President, NORTH AMERICAN SECURITIES ADMINISTRATORS ASSOCIATION

Short Sales In addition to lending money, brokerages also lend securities. A **short sale** begins when you borrow a security from your broker and sell it (one of the few times that it is legal to sell something that you do not own). At a given point in the future, you must restore an equal number of shares of that issue to the brokerage, along with a fee.

short sale
Stock sale in which an investor borrows securities from a broker to be sold and then replaced at a specified future date

We now return to our Gap example. Suppose that in January, you believe the price of Gap stock will soon fall. You, therefore, order your broker to "sell short" 100 shares at the market price of $13.74 per share. Your broker will make the sale and credit $1,374 to your account. If Gap's price falls to $8 per share in July, you can buy 100 shares for $800 and use them to repay your

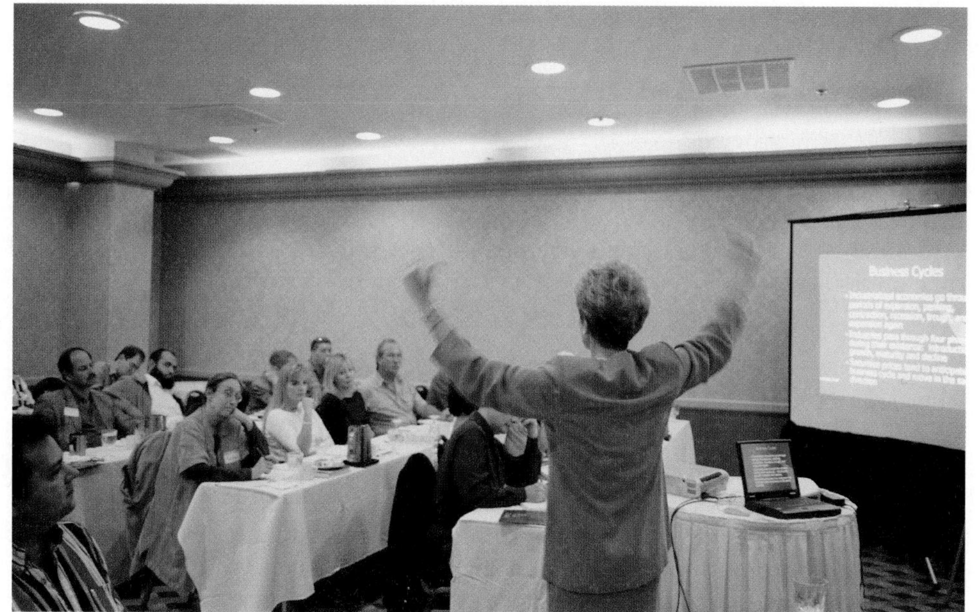

In a packed Orlando classroom, customers have paid $595 each for a one-day class with Toni Turner <www.toniturner.com>. *What special message makes Turner worth that much? Turner teaches a type of day trading called "swing trading": She discourages buying and selling stocks in a matter of minutes (the strategy of the typical day trader) and explains when and why it's better to study price and patterns over the course of days. If you're interested in day trading, there are a number of Web sites that can tell you about the perils and perks. See* <www.daytradingworld.com/> *as a start.*

The Daily Grind of Keystroking

Want some excitement? Try day trading. Especially if you enjoy the thrill of risking your money, have the courage to trust your own judgment, and like to make split-second decisions. You'll also need a computer that's wired for real-time stock market transactions. These are some of the difference between day traders and other investors. Investors buy or sell securities with longer-term price changes in mind. Day traders count price volatility—on within-day price changes—as opportunities for buying and selling within a single day. Each day is an adventure. In fact, there's an adventure to be had hundreds or even thousands of times during a fatiguing six-hour trading period, as day traders scour computer monitors for second-to-second changes in market prices for soybeans, S&P 500 Index funds, Treasury bonds, common stocks, or even foreign currencies. And when they find something, they buy and sell in rapid-fire transactions, some lasting only a matter of seconds.

Because daily price variations of 10 percent or more are commonplace for most stocks and commodities, day traders thrive on within-day changes. You'll find them focused on monitors, scrolling numbers, watching TV financial news, and browsing chat rooms. News flashes about companies, economic events, and even the weather might signal momentary price swings that quickly disappear. Judging the timing, direction, and size of those changes is what day trading is all about.

It's all made possible by lightening-fast computer networks and real-time information. If traders expect a stock will rise, they buy and resell shares in a matter of seconds. The strategy for falling prices is buying short, then immediately reselling. At Swift Trade Securities in Toronto, Canada, for example, short selling lets some day-trading clients walk home with $20,000 in a single day. Of course, when prices move in the wrong direction, traders lose money and for every day trader, wrong movements are a daily fact of life. The final tally—pluses versus minuses—at day's end is all that matters. Although the popularity of day trading has slackened in recent years, avid traders still regard it as capitalism's last bastion of fast and vast riches.

If you'd like to see the range of within-day price swings for your favorite stock or commodity, visit a popular securities market Web site (for example, <www.cnnfn.com>). Among other data for each stock, an intraday bar chart shows the time-phased pattern of prices that are so alluring to the day trader. Interested in trying it? All you need to do to enter the world of day trading is to establish a computer connection to real-time market data, set up an account of about $20,000, learn a little about particular stocks and commodities, muster the courage to buy and sell at breath-taking speeds, and then use rapid keystroking to move your money around. At day's end, you can go home, relax, and, if you survived, get ready for tomorrow's action.

broker. You will have made a $574 profit (before commissions). Your risk, of course, is that Gap's price will not fall. If it holds steady or rises, you will take a loss.

Securities Market Regulation

In addition to regulation by government agencies, both the NASD and the NYSE exercise self-regulation to maintain the public trust and to assure professionalism in the financial industry. A visible example is the NYSE's actions in establishing so-called *circuit breakers*—trading rules for reducing excessive market volatility and promoting investor confidence—that suspend trading for a preset length of time. Adopted first in October 1988, with the approval of the SEC, the rules suspend trading on the NYSE whenever the market begins spiraling out of control during a single day. The 1988 rules stipulated that trading would halt for one hour on any day when the Dow Jones Industrial Average dropped 250 points and would close for two hours with any 400-point decline. The interruption provides a "cooling off" period that slows trading activity, gives investors time to reconsider their trading positions, and allows computer programs to be revised or shut down.[24]

Because circuit-breaker thresholds are updated periodically to keep up with the Dow's growth, as of April 2000 the following single-day declines will halt trading marketwide:

- A 1,050-point drop in the DJIA before 2 P.M. halts trading for one hour.
- A 2,100-point drop before 1 P.M. halts trading for two hours.
- A 3,150-point drop at any time halts trading for the day.

Although circuit breaker rules were initiated in response to severe market plunges in October 1987 and October 1988, they have been triggered only once—on October 27, 1997, when the DJIA fell 350 points at 2:35 P.M. and 550 points at 3:30 P.M., for an overall seven percent plunge that shut down trading for the day.

One oft-cited cause of sudden market fluctuations is **program trading**—the portfolio trading strategy involving the sale or purchase of a group of stocks valued at $1 million or more, often triggered by computerized trading programs that can be launched without human supervision or control. It works in the following way. As market values change and economic events transpire during the course of a day, computer programs are busy recalculating the future values of stocks. Once a calculated value reaches a critical point, the program automatically signals a buy or sell order. Because electronic trading could cause the market to spiral out of control, it has contributed to the establishment of circuit breakers.

program trading
Large purchase or sale of a group of stocks, often triggered by computerized trading programs that can be launched without human supervision or control

The Securities and Exchange Commission

To protect the investing public and to maintain smoothly functioning markets, the SEC oversees many phases of the process through which securities are issued. The SEC regulates the public offering of new securities by requiring that all companies file prospectuses before proposed offerings commence. To protect investors from fraudulent issues, a **prospectus** contains pertinent information about both the offered security and the issuing company. False statements are subject to criminal penalties.

prospectus
Registration statement filed with the SEC before the issuance of a new security

Insider Trading The SEC also enforces laws against **insider trading**—the use of special knowledge about a firm for profit or gain. In June 2002, for example, the SEC filed suit in federal court in New York against Samuel Waksal, the former CEO of ImClone Systems, Inc. on charges of using insider information to gain illegal profits. The suit charged that Waksal received disappointing news in late December 2001 that the U.S. Food and Drug Administration (FDA) would soon reject ImClone's application to market its cancer treatment drug, Erbitux. The next day, before the FDA was scheduled to notify ImClone of its rejection, Waksal's family members sold more than $9 million in ImClone stock. For two days, Waksal himself tried to sell his shares, which were worth nearly $5 million, but two brokerage firms refused to execute the orders. The following day, after the stock market had closed, ImClone publicly announced the FDA decision. The next trading day, ImClone's stock price dropped 16 percent—from $55.25 to $46.46. Family members, the suit alleges, avoided millions in losses by

insider trading
Illegal practice of using special knowledge about a firm for profit or gain

illegally using the insider information. News reports further indicate that Federal prosecutors are investigating Martha Stewart, the home décor entrepreneur and a friend of Waksal, who sold 3,900 shares at $58 each the day before ImClone made its public announcement. Stewart commented, "In placing my trade I had no improper information." By mid-2002, ImClone's stock had plummeted to $8 per share. [25]

The SEC also offers a bounty to any person who provides information leading to a civil penalty for illegal insider trading. The courts can render such a penalty of up to three times the illegal profit that was gained, and the bounty can, at most, be 10 percent of that penalty.

Along with the SEC's enforcement efforts, the stock exchanges and securities firms, as members of NASD, cooperate in detecting and stopping insider action. In any given year, NASD may refer more than 100 cases to the SEC for charges of possible insider trading. In addition, NASD's self-regulation results in actions ranging from fining member firms and officers to barring or suspending them.

blue-sky laws

Laws requiring securities dealers to be licensed and registered with the states in which they do business

Blue-Sky Laws State governments also regulate the sale of securities. For example, commenting that some promoters would sell stock "to the blue sky itself," one legislator's speech led to the phrase **blue-sky laws** and the passage of statutes requiring securities to be registered with state officials. In addition, securities dealers must be registered and licensed by the states in which they do business. Finally, states may prosecute for the sale of fraudulent securities.

Self-Check Questions 7–9

*You should now be able to answer Self-Check Questions 7–9**

7. MULTIPLE CHOICE Suppose you want to buy a particular stock at a price lower than current market value. Once it's purchased, you intend to hold it for future price gains. After you buy shares, however, you also want to protect yourself by being able to sell quickly if the market price should suddenly fall. To accomplish all of this, which of the following arrangements should you use with your broker? [select one]: **(a)** place a limit order and a stop order; **(b)** trade only in round lots; **(c)** place a market order now and another market order later; **(d)** use margin trading; **(e)** place an order to sell short.

8. TRUE/FALSE The *Dow Jones Industrial Average* is the most widely-cited American index because it approximates the market's overall price movements more accurately than other indexes.

9. MULTIPLE CHOICE Which of the following is **not** true about printed *stock quotations* like those published in the *Wall Street Journal*? [select one]: **(a)** the percentage change in the stock's price for the year is shown; **(b)** the company's annual cash dividend is reported; **(c)** a stock's high- and low-prices for any given day are reported; **(d)** the difference between closing prices on successive days is shown; **(e)** the stock's closing price for the day is given.

*Answers to Self-Check Questions 7–9 can be found on p. AN-13.

Continued from page 549

Bearing Up

Many investors, having experienced only bull market years during the 1970s to 1999, were unprepared for the bear that greeted them in the 2001–2002 period. By mid-July 2002, losses in U.S. market values amounted to a resounding $7.7 trillion—more than $28,000 for every woman, man, and child in the United States. Dazed traders and market analysts were using words like "crash" and "panic," and the numbers bore them out: The Nasdaq composite fell from a record-high 5,100 in 2000 to just above 1,300 in mid-July 2002, losing 74 percent of its value. In that same period, the Dow fell 32 percent, the S&P 500 44 percent. In just one week in mid-July 2002, the Dow fell 7.7 percent, the Nasdaq 4 percent, and the S&P 500 8 percent.

So, what will it take for the market to recover? How do you restore the public's faith in corporations and the market? There was some talk about the Fed stepping in to cut interest rates to generate money for investment; but many analysts argued that any Fed action would only stoke concerns about the market. President Bush and Fed Chairman Alan Greenspan cited positive economic signs—increases in sales and industrial production, low inflation, strong consumer spending—but investors continued to retreat to safer ground as new reports surfaced about conniving CEOs cooking corporate books. On August 14, 2002, more than 1,000 U.S. corporations were required to resubmit financial statements revised to reflect financial conditions as certified by CEOs, who can now be held criminally liable for misstatements. Unfortunately, the impact of this policy has not yet registered on overall economic activity.

Meanwhile, individual investors still have their own problems. After 2½ years of losses, those still brave enough to remain in the market faced the possibility of sinking even farther or pulling out. Should they hang on or get out? Should they put their money in money market mutual funds? Should they gamble on further downfalls by selling short? How about taking the stance—that currently low prices present bargain buying opportunities? Although the answers to these and other questions are by no means clear, there is general agreement that an important lesson has been learned: Because it's volatile and unpredictable, the market is a comfortable home for some investors but a very disturbing place for those who can't deal with economic uncertainty.

Questions for Discussion

1. In a volatile stock market, why is it important for investors to assess their reactions to financial risk and to put together short-term and long-term financial plans?
2. What do you think about the media's role in stock market volatility?
3. As the market was falling during the 2000–2002 period, why do you suppose that some market indexes experienced larger changes than others?
4. What factors will be most significant—economic, social, political, psychological—for reversing the market crash of 2002?
5. Suppose your retirement account had reached $500,000 in 2000 and was invested half-and-half in a bond mutual fund and an S&P 500 index mutual fund. By mid-July 2002, the index fund had fallen to $150,000 in market value, while the bond fund was worth $280,000. At mid-July 2002, what would be your investment strategy?

Summary of Learning Objectives

1. ***Explain the difference between* primary *and* secondary securities markets.**

Stocks and bonds are **securities** because they represent *secured,* or *asset-based,* claims on the part of investors. Stockholders have claims on some of a corporation's assets because each share of stock represents part ownership. In contrast, *bonds* represent financial claims for money owed to holders. Both stocks and bonds are sold in *securities markets.* In **primary securities markets,** new stocks and bonds are bought and sold by firms and governments. Although some new securities are sold to small groups, most new stocks and some bonds are sold to the wider public. To issue a new security, a firm must get approval from the **Securities and Exchange Commission (SEC)**—the government agency that regulates securities.

It also needs an **investment bank**—a financial institution that specializes in issuing and reselling new securities. These firms provide three services: (1) They advise on timing and financial terms. (2) By *underwriting*—that is, buying—new securities, they bear some of the risks. (3) They create distribution networks for moving new securities into the hands of investors. Existing stocks and bonds are sold in the **secondary securities market,** including such firms as the New York Stock Exchange.

2. ***Discuss the value to shareholders of* common *and* preferred stock *and describe the secondary market for each type of security.***

Investors purchase common stock in the hope that it will increase in value, provide dividend income, or both. Stock values are expressed in three different ways: (1) The face value of a share of stock at the time it is originally issued is its **par value.** (2) A stock's real value is its **market value**—the current price of a share in the stock market. (3) The **book value** of common stock represents *stockholders' equity* (the sum of a company's common stock par value, retained earnings, and additional paid-in capital) divided by the number of shares.

Although common stocks are risky, they offer high growth potential. The **blue-chip stocks** of well-established firms have historically provided investors steady income. With the proliferation of Internet and start-up dot-coms, however, many of the old rules for judging stocks are changing. The financial performance of so-called "Internet Blue Chips" is different from that of traditional blue-chip stocks because many investors believe that they will become profitable businesses in the future—a bet that traditionalists view as risky.

Preferred stock is issued with a stated par value, and dividends are expressed as a percentage of par value. Some preferred stock is *callable:* The issuing firm can call in shares by requiring preferred stockholders to surrender them in exchange for cash. The amount of this payment—the *call price*—is specified in the purchase agreement. Most preferred stock is **cumulative preferred stock,** which means that any missed dividend payments must be paid as soon as the firm can do so. The firm can't pay dividends to common stockholders until it has made up all late payments to preferred stockholders.

Most of the secondary market for stocks is handled by **stock exchanges:** institutional settings in which stock can be bought and sold. Most exchanges are nonprofit corporations established to serve members holding *seats.* Trading is allowed only on the *trading floor.* Many of the people on the floor are **brokers,** who execute buy-and-sell orders from nonexchange members. They match buyers with sellers but don't own securities. They earn commissions from the clients for whom they place orders. *Full-service brokers* offer consulting advice in financial planning, along with a wider range of investment products. *Discount brokers* offer a fast, low-cost way to trade on the market. The popularity of *online trading* stems from convenient access to the Internet and fast transactions.

There are two key differences between exchanges and the electronic market: (1) the activity of *dealers* and (2) the geographic location of the market. On the floor of an exchange, a *specialist* controls trading for each stock, buying and selling it for his own inventory and acting as its exclusive auctioneer. The electronic market conducts trades electronically among thousands of dealers in remote locations.

The two major *stock exchanges* in the United States are the New York and American. Seven regional stock exchanges serve investors outside of New York City, and the value of shares listed on foreign exchanges continues to grow. The **over-the-counter (OTC) market** consists of people in different locations who hold securities not listed on national U.S. exchanges. The OTC consists of independent dealers who own the securities that they buy and sell at their own risk. The National Association of Securities Dealers Inc. (NASD) operates an automated OTC system known as the **National Association of Securities Dealers Automated Quotation—** or **Nasdaq—system** as the world's first electronic stock market. Whereas NYSE orders are fulfilled on the trading floor, Nasdaq orders are handled on a computer network.

3. ***Distinguish among various types of* bonds *in terms of their issuers, safety, and retirement.***

A **bond** is an IOU—a promise by the issuer to pay the buyer a certain amount of money by a specified future date, usually with interest paid at regular intervals. Bonds differ in terms of maturity dates, tax status, and level of risk versus potential yield. Several services rate the quality of bonds according to *default risk*—the chance that promised payments will be deferred or missed altogether. Nearly all secondary trading in bonds occurs in the OTC market.

The U.S. bond market is supplied by three major sources: (1) *U.S. government*: The the world's largest debtor, the federal government issues **government bonds** to finance its debt. They're safe because they're backed by the U.S. government. (2) *Municipalities*: State and local governments issue **municipal bonds** to finance school and transportation systems and other projects. *Obligation bonds* are backed by the issuer's taxing power. *Revenue bonds* are backed only by the revenue from a specific project. Municipal bonds are attractive because investors don't pay taxes on interest.

(3) *Corporations*: Like municipal bonds, longer-term **corporate bonds** are riskier than shorter-term bonds. They can be classified by method of interest payment: **Registered bonds** register the names of holders with the company, which simply mails out checks. **Bearer** (or **coupon) bonds** require bondholders to clip coupons and send them to the issuer. Bonds are also secured or unsecured: (1) With **secured bonds,** issuers reduce the risk by pledging assets (such as mortgages) in case of default. (2) Unsecured bonds are called **debentures.** Holders have claims against property not pledged in other bonds.

With regard to maturity dates, there are three types of bonds: (1) The issuer of **callable bonds** may call them in and pay them off at a price stipulated in the contract. They do so when interest rates are lower than the rate being paid on the bond but must still pay a *call price* in order to call in the bond. Callable bonds are often retired by the use of **sinking fund provisions.** The issuing company must put a certain amount of money into a special bank account. At the end of a certain period, the money will be enough to redeem the bonds. (2) With a **serial bond,** the issuer retires portions of the bond issue in a series of preset dates. (3) Only corporations can issue **convertible bonds,** which can be converted into their own common stock. The holder may request payment in stock instead of in cash.

4. *Describe the investment opportunities offered by* **mutual funds** *and* **commodities.**

Mutual funds pool investments from individuals and organizations to purchase portfolios of securities. Investors are thus part owners of the portfolio. Investors in **no-load funds** are not charged sales commissions when they buy in or sell out. Those in **load funds** pay commissions of 2 to 8 percent. Different funds are designed to appeal to the different goals of investors. Those that stress growth include *balanced mutual funds*—portfolios of bonds and preferred and common stocks, especially those of established firms.

Futures contracts—agreements to purchase specified amounts of commodities at given prices on set dates—are bought and sold in the **commodities market.** Contracts are available not only for stocks but also for commodities ranging from coffee beans and hogs to propane and platinum. Because selling prices reflect estimates of future events and values, prices are volatile and trading is risky. Buyers need not put up the full purchase amount but can post a smaller amount called the **margin.**

Investors usually select a mixture, or *portfolio,* of investments—some riskier and some more conservative—in one of two ways. (1) **Diversification** means buying several different kinds of investments rather than just one. You might invest in stocks of several different companies, or you can diversify even further by spreading your funds across different investment alternatives—stocks, bonds, mutual funds, real estate, and so on. (2) **Asset allocation** refers to the relative amounts of funds invested in (or allocated to) each investment alternative. As your investment objectives change, you can change your asset allocation accordingly.

5. *Explain the process by which securities are bought and sold.*

First, you need to match investments to your investment objectives. Then you must select a broker and open an account so that you can make transactions. It's also a good idea to know how to read stock, bond, and mutual fund quotations. Daily transactions are reported in newspapers.

Market indexes provide useful summaries of price trends, both in specific industries and in the stock market as a whole. Market indexes, for example, reveal bull and bear market trends. **Bull markets** are periods of rising prices. Periods of falling stock prices are **bear markets.** There are three key market indexes: (1) The **Dow Jones Industrial Average (DJIA)** measures the performance of U.S. financial markets by focusing on 30 blue-chip companies as reflectors of economic health; the index is an average of the stock prices for these 30 large firms. (2) The broader **Standard & Poor's Composite Index** consists of 500 stocks, including 400 industrial firms, 40 utilities, 40 financial institutions, and 20 transportation companies. (3) Because it considers more stocks, some experts regard the **Nasdaq Composite Index** as the most important of all market indexes. All Nasdaq-listed companies are included in the index—for a total of over 4,000 firms (both domestic and foreign).

After doing research and getting recommendations, you can place different types of orders: (1) A **market order** requests that a broker buy or sell a certain security at the prevailing market price at the time of the order. (2) A **limit order** authorizes the purchase of a stock only if its price is less than or equal to a specified limit, and a **stop order** instructs the broker to sell if price falls to a certain level. (3) A **round lot** requests 100 shares of a particular stock or some multiple thereof. Fractions of round lots are called **odd lots.**

When you place a buy order, you must decide how you will pay. You might maintain a cash account with your broker, but like futures contracts, stocks can be bought *on margin*—you can put down a portion of the price. The rest is borrowed from your broker, who secures special-rate bank loans with stock. Brokers also lend securities. A **short sale** begins when you borrow a security from your broker and sell it. At a given point in the future, you must restore an equal number of shares to the brokerage, along with a fee.

6. *Explain how securities markets are regulated.*

In addition to government regulation, both the NASD and the NYSE exercise self-regulation. For example, one cause of sudden market fluctuations is **program trading**—a strategy involving the sale or purchase of a group of stocks valued at $1 million or more, often triggered by computerized trading programs with no human supervision. Because such trading could cause the market to spiral out of control, it has led to *circuit breakers*—trading rules for reducing excessive volatility and promoting investor confidence

The SEC protects investors from fraudulent issues by requiring all companies to file prospectuses before proposed offerings commence. A **prospectus** contains information about both the offered security and the issuing company. The SEC also enforces laws against **insider trading**—the use of special knowledge for profit or gain. The stock exchanges help in stopping insider action, fining member firms and officers and barring or suspending them. State governments enforce so-called **blue-sky laws,** and securities dealers must be licensed by the states in which they do business.

KEY TERMS

securities (p. 550)
primary securities market (p. 550)
Securities and Exchange Commission (SEC) (p. 550)
investment bank (p. 550)
secondary securities market (p. 550)
par value (p. 551)
market value (p. 551)
book value (p. 551)
blue-chip stock (p. 551)

cumulative preferred stock (p. 552)
stock exchange (p. 553)
broker (p. 553)
over-the-counter (OTC) market (p. 556)
National Association of Securities Dealers Automated Quotation (Nasdaq) system (p. 556)
bond (p. 559)
government bond (p. 559)
municipal bond (p. 559)
corporate bond (p. 560)
registered bond (p. 560)
bearer (or ***coupon***) ***bond*** (p. 560)
secured bond (p. 560)
debenture (p. 560)
callable bond (p. 560)
sinking fund provision (p. 561)
serial bond (p. 561)
convertible bond (p. 561)
mutual fund (p. 561)
no-load fund (p. 561)
load fund (p. 561)
futures contract (p. 562)
commodities market (p. 562)
margin (p. 562)
diversification (p. 564)
asset allocation (p. 564)
price-earnings ratio (p. 565)
market index (p. 568)
bull market (p. 568)
bear market (p. 568)
Dow Jones Industrial Average (DJIA) (p. 568)
Standard & Poor's Composite Index (p. 569)
Nasdaq Composite Index (p. 569)
market order (p. 569)
limit order (p. 570)
stop order (p. 570)
round lot (p. 570)
odd lot (p. 570)
short sale (p. 571)
program trading (p. 573)
prospectus (p. 573)
insider trading (p. 573)
blue-sky laws (p. 574)

QUESTIONS AND EXERCISES

Questions for Review

1. What are the purposes of the primary and secondary markets for securities?
2. Which one of the three measures of common stock value is most important? Why?
3. How do government, municipal, and corporate bonds differ from one another?
4. How might an investor lose money in a commodities trade?
5. How does the Securities and Exchange Commission regulate securities markets?
6. Which U.S. stock market has the largest volume of trade?

Questions for Analysis

7. Suppose you decide to invest in common stocks as a personal investment. Which kind of broker—full service or online discount—would you use for buying and selling? Why?
8. Which type of mutual fund would be most appropriate for your investment purposes at this time? Why?
9. Using a newspaper, select an example of a recent day's transactions for each of the following: a stock on the NYSE, a stock on the AMEX, a Nasdaq stock, a bond on the NYSE, and a mutual fund. Explain the meaning of each element in the listing.

Application Exercises

10. Interview the financial manager of a local business or your school. What are the investment goals of this person's organization? What securities does it use? What advantages and disadvantages do you see in its portfolio?
11. Either in person or through a toll-free number, contact a broker, and request information about setting up a personal account for trading securities. Prepare a report on the broker's policies regarding the following: buy/sell orders, credit terms, cash account requirements, services available to investors, and commissions/fees schedules.

Building Your Business Skills

MARKET UPS AND DOWNS

This exercise enhances the following SCANS workplace competencies: demonstrating basic skills, demonstrating thinking skills, exhibiting interpersonal skills, and working with information.

Goal

To encourage students to understand the forces that affect fluctuations in stock prices.

Background

Investing in stocks requires an understanding of the various factors that affect stock prices. These factors may be intrinsic to the company itself or part of the external environment.

- Internal factors relate to the company itself, such as an announcement of poor or favorable earnings, earn-ngs that are more or less than expected, major layoffs, abor problems, management issues, and mergers.

- External factors relate to world or national events, such as a threatened war in the Persian Gulf, the Asian currency crisis, weather conditions that affect sales, the Federal Reserve Board's adjustment of interest rates, and employment figures that were higher or lower than expected.

By analyzing these factors, you will often learn a lot about why a stock did well or why it did poorly. Being aware of these influences will help you anticipate future stock movements.

Method

Step 1

Working alone, choose a common stock that has experienced considerable price fluctuations in the past few years. Here are several examples (but there are many others): IBM, J.P. Morgan, AT&T, Amazon.com, Oxford Health Care, and Apple Computer. Find the symbol for the stock (for example, J.P. Morgan is JPM) and the exchange on which it is traded (JPM is traded on the New York Stock Exchange).

Step 2

At your library, find the *Daily Stock Price Record,* a publication that provides an historical picture of daily stock closings. There are separate copies for the New York Stock Exchange, the American Stock Exchange, and the Nasdaq markets. Find your stock, and study its trading pattern.

Step 3

Find four or five days over a period of several months or even a year when there have been major price fluctuations in the stock. (A two- or three-point price change from one day to the next is considered major.) Then research what happened on that day that might have contributed to the fluctuation. The best place to begin is with the *Wall Street Journal* or on the business pages of a national newspaper, such as the *New York Times* or the *Washington Post.*

Step 4

Write a short analysis that links changes in stock price to internal and external factors. As you analyze the data, be aware that it is sometimes difficult to know why a stock price fluctuates.

Step 5

Get together with three other students who studied different stocks. As a group, discuss your findings, looking for fluctuation patterns.

Follow-Up Questions

1. Do you see any similarities in the movement of the various stocks during the same period? For example, did the stocks move up or down at about the same time? If so, do you think the stocks were affected by the same factors? Explain your thinking.
2. Based on your analysis, did internal or external factors have the greater impact on stock price? Which factors had the more long-lasting effect? Which factors had the shorter effect?
3. Why do you think it is so hard to predict changes in stock price on a day-to-day basis?

Exercising Your Ethics

ARE YOU ENDOWED WITH GOOD JUDGMENT?

The Situation

Every organization faces decisions about whether to make conservative or risky investments. Let's assume that you have been asked to evaluate the advantages and drawbacks of conservative versus risky investments, including all relevant ethical considerations, by Youth Dreams Charities (YDC), a local organization that assists low-income families in gaining access to educational opportunities. YDC is a not-for-profit firm that employs a full-time professional manager to run daily operations. Overall governance and policy making reside with a board of directors—10 part-time community-minded volunteers who are entrusted with carrying out YDC's mission.

For the current year, 23 students receive tuition totaling $92,000 paid by YDC. Tuition comes from annual fund-raising activities (a white-tie dance and a seafood carnival) and from financial returns from YDC's $2.1 million endowment. The endowment has been amassed from charitable donations during the past 12 years, and this year, it has yielded some $84,000 for tuitions. The board's goal is to increase the endowment to $4 million in five years in order to provide $200,000 in tuition annually.

The Dilemma

Based on the Finance Committee's suggestions, the board is considering a change in YDC's investment policies. The current, rather conservative approach invests the endowment in CDs and other low-risk instruments that have consistently yielded a 6-percent annual return. This practice has allowed the endowment to grow modestly (at about 2 percent per year). The remaining investment proceeds (4 percent) flow out for tuitions. The proposed plan would invest one-half of the endowment in conservative instruments and the other half in blue-chip stocks. Finance Committee members believe that with market growth, the endowment has a good chance of reaching the $4 million goal within five years. While some board members like the prospects of faster growth, others think the proposal is too risky. What happens if, instead of increasing, the stock market collapses and the endowment shrinks? What will happen to YDC's programs then?

Questions for Discussion

Your opinion has been asked on the following issues:

1. Why might a conservative versus risky choice be different at a not-for-profit organization than at a for-profit organization?
2. What are the main ethical issues in this situation?
3. What action should the board take?

Mastering Business Essentials

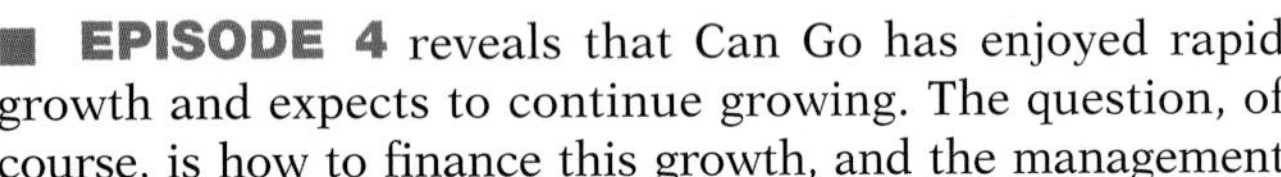

■ **EPISODE 4** reveals that Can Go has enjoyed rapid growth and expects to continue growing. The question, of course, is how to finance this growth, and the management team examines the company's options. *This episode provides a context for the study of stock issues, including initial public offerings.*

Crafting your Business Plan

A CAPITAL IDEA

The Purpose of the Assignment

1. To familiarize students with securities and investment issues that a sample firm may face in developing its business plan, in the framework of *Business PlanPro* (*BPP*) software package.
2. To demonstrate how three chapter topics—issuing stock, issuing bonds, and making securities-market transactions—can be integrated as components in the *BPP* planning environment.

Assignment

After reading Chapter 19 in the textbook, open the BPP *software, and search for information about financial plans, equity financing (stocks), and debt financing via bonds as they apply to a sample firm:* Sample Software Company *(Sample Software Inc.). To find* Sample Software, *do the following:*

Open the *Business PlanPro.* If it asks if you want to "create a new business plan" or "open an existing plan," select "create a new business plan" (even though you are not going to create a plan at this time). You will then be taken to the *Business PlanPro EasyPlan Wizard.* Click on the option entitled **Research It.** You will then be presented with a new list of options, including **Sample Plan Browser.** After clicking on the **Sample Plan Browser**, go down the alphabetical list of sample plans, and double-click on **Software Publishing—Printing and. . .** , which is the location for *Sample Software Company.* The screen you are looking at is the introduction page for the *Sample Software* business plan. Scroll down until you reach the **Table of Contents** for the company's business plan.

Now respond to the following items:

1. Evaluate Sample Software's plans for financing its operations. Does the company have any outstanding stock? Does it plan to issue stock or bonds in the future? [Sites to see in *BPP* for this question: On the Table of Contents page, click on **7.0 Financial Plan.**]
2. What sources of capital have been used to meet Sample Software's financial requirements? What equity (stock) sources are available for meeting the firm's financial needs? What debt sources are available? [Sites to see in *BPP:* On the Table of Contents page, click on **1.0 Executive Summary.** Return to the Table of Contents page, and click on each of the following in turn: **2.1 Company Ownership, 2.2 Company History,** and **7.1 Important Assumptions.**]
3. Based on the company's net profit projections, at what points in time will Sample Software be able to pay dividends or repay its debt obligations? How much financing will be needed according to this plan, and at what points in time? [Sites to see in *BPP:* From the Table of Contents page, click on **7.4 Projected Profit and Loss.**]

Video Exercise

INFORMATION PAYS OFF: MOTLEY FOOL

Learning Objectives

The purpose of this video is to help you to:

1. Identify the wide variety of investments available to individuals.
2. Describe the process by which securities are bought and sold.
3. Recognize the risks involved in commodities and other investments.

Synopsis

Despite news reports about lottery winners and other overnight millionaires, individuals have a better chance of getting rich if they learn to select investments that are appropriate for their long-term financial goals. Experts advise looking for investments that will beat inflation and keep up with or—ideally—beat general market returns. You can invest in preferred or common stock, newly issued stock from IPOs, managed or index mutual funds, bonds, or commodities. These investments, however, are far from risk-free. Commodities and IPOs can be particularly risky. Thus, if you're planning to invest, you might want to educate yourself about securities and investment strategies by surfing Web sites such as the Motley Fool <www.fool.com>.

Discussion Questions

1. *For analysis*: Why is the SEC concerned about stock rumors that circulate on the Internet?
2. *For application*: What should you consider when deciding whether to buy and sell stock through a broker, through a Web-based brokerage, or directly through the company issuing the stock?
3. *For application*: If you were about to retire, why might you invest in preferred stock rather than common stock?
4. *For debate*: Should stock rumors that circulate on the Internet be covered by the individual's constitutional right to freedom of speech rather than be regulated by the SEC? Support your chosen position.

Online Exploration

Mutual funds that seek out environmentally and socially conscious firms in which to invest are becoming more popular because they offer investors a way to earn returns that don't offend their principles. Investigate the following Web sites: <www.efund.com>, <www.ethicalfunds.com>, and <www.domini.com>. What types of firms does each fund avoid? What type does each prefer? Would you choose one of these funds if you wanted to invest in a mutual fund? Explain your answer.

CHAPTER 

Understanding Financial and Risk Management

After reading this chapter, you should be able to:

1. Describe the responsibilities of a *financial manager.*
2. Distinguish between *short-term (operating)* and *long-term (capital) expenditures.*
3. Identify four sources of *short-term financing* for businesses.
4. Distinguish among the various sources of *long-term financing* and explain the risks entailed by each type.
5. Discuss some key issues in financial management for small business.
6. Explain how *risk* affects business operations and identify the five steps in the *risk management process.*
7. Explain the distinction between *insurable* and *uninsurable risks* and distinguish among the different *types of insurance* purchased by businesses.

Getting a Kick Out of the Soccer Business

The challenge of World Cup soccer isn't just for sports fans. Just as challenging as playing the games themselves is planning, financing, and scheduling all the activities that go into mounting the world's premier sporting event. While fans are concerned about the strengths of the next opponent and the health of key players, organizers worry about insurance coverage and other precautions against financial loss from weather, terrorism, hooliganism, and other risks to the success of the tournament.

Financial and risk management, as well as a host of other business decisions in preparing for the tournament, are prominent concerns for the Federation Internationale de Football Associations (FIFA) <www.fifa.com>, soccer's world governing body. In addition to television rights, FIFA sells the rights to its brand name to consumer-products companies around the world that want to enhance their products—soft drinks, transportation, clothing, sporting goods, shoes, soap—with World Cup symbols and the FIFA logo. These rights alone are worth more than $300 million, money that FIFA uses to help cover its costs for the competition that it holds once every four years.

To improve cash flow and avoid excessive borrowing, FIFA changed its strategy for 2002. It sold the rights to its brand to International Sports and Leisure (ISL), a Swiss marketing firm. The deal called for ISL to make all the arrangements for worldwide marketing, collect the revenues, make payments to FIFA, and pocket a residual fee for its services. In addition to stabilizing FIFA's cash inflows, the deal with ISL was cheaper than borrowing from banks, FIFA's traditional means of financing the World Cup.

With fans from around the world supporting teams from 32 nations, the 2002 event held in Japan and South Korea ultimately generated about $475 million. Before the games began, however, organizers bought insurance to protect against interruptions to the income flow from the tournament. Individual businesses, too, upped insurance protection—especially against hooliganism—for the revenues they expected from fans and tourists.

Past World Cup hosts, including France in 1998, had suffered considerable damage from rampaging hooligans both before and after Cup games, and Japan's culture was especially unprepared for the rowdiness typical of some European fans. Japanese venues were not geared for increased security demands. According to Kazuyuki Hoshi of the World Cup Preparation Office in Sendai, "Although this is the world's biggest sporting event, we not only have to construct new stadiums but prepare access and security strategies that Europe and South America, for example, have been developing for decades. The Japanese do not think in terms of security measures, like fencing and separate access for supporters." But he also noted that for the World Cup, Japan knew what to expect. "When it comes to crisis management, to think that hooligans won't travel to Japan is being too optimistic."

In setting up security measures, the Japanese started from scratch. Restaurants and retail shops bought protection against the hooliganism that rowdy fans traditionally ignited before and after their teams took the field. Seoul-based Hyundai Fire & Marine Insurance sold more than 1,000 policies to local business for protection of up to $40,000 from damages related to vandalism. While hoping they wouldn't have to collect on their various policies, businesses in the host countries placed their trust in the old adage: Better safe than sorry.

Our opening story is continued on page 606.

"When it comes to crisis management, to think that hooligans won't travel to Japan is being too optimistic."

~Kazuyuki Hoshi,
WORLD CUP 2002 OFFICIAL

The Role of the Financial Manager

finance (or **corporate finance**)
Activities concerned with determining a firm's long-term investments, obtaining the funds to pay for them, conducting the firm's everyday financial activities, and managing the firm's risks

The business activity known as **finance** (or **corporate finance**) typically entails four responsibilities:

1. Determining a firm's long-term investments
2. Obtaining funds to pay for those investments
3. Conducting the firm's everyday financial activities
4. Helping to manage the risks that the firm takes

financial manager
Manager responsible for planning and controlling the acquisition and dispersal of a firm's financial resources

As we saw in Chapter 14, production managers plan and control the output of goods and services. In Chapter 10, we saw that marketing managers plan and control the development and marketing of products. Similarly, **financial managers** plan and control the acquisition and dispersal of a firm's financial resources. In this section, we will see in some detail how those activities are channeled into specific plans for protecting—and enhancing—a firm's financial well-being.

Responsibilities of the Financial Manager

Financial managers collect funds, pay debts, establish trade credit, obtain loans, control cash balances, and plan for future financial needs. But a financial manager's overall objective is to increase a firm's value—and thus stockholders' wealth. Whereas accountants create data to reflect a firm's financial status, financial managers make decisions for improving that status. Financial managers, then, must ensure that a company's earnings exceed its costs—in other words, that it earns a profit. In sole proprietorships and partnerships, profits translate directly into increases in owners' wealth. In corporations, profits translate into an increase in the value of common stock.

The various responsibilities of the financial manager in increasing a firm's wealth fall into general categories: *cash-flow management* and *financial control and planning*.

cash-flow management
Management of cash inflows and outflows to ensure adequate funds for purchases and the productive use of excess funds

Cash-Flow Management To increase a firm's value, financial managers must ensure that it always has enough funds on hand to purchase the materials and human resources that it needs to produce goods and services. At the same time, of course, there may be funds that are not needed immediately. These must be invested to earn more money for the firm. This activity—**cash-flow management**—requires careful planning. If excess cash balances are allowed to sit idle instead of being invested, a firm loses the cash returns that it could have earned.

How important to a business is the management of its idle cash? One study has revealed that companies averaging $2 million in annual sales typically hold $40,000 in non-interest–bearing accounts. Larger companies hold even larger sums. More and more companies, however, are learning that these idle funds can become working funds. By locating idle cash and putting it to work, for instance, they can avoid borrowing from outside sources. The savings on interest payments can be substantial.

financial control
Process of checking actual performance against plans to ensure that desired financial results occur

Financial Control Because things rarely go exactly as planned, financial managers must make adjustments for actual financial changes that occur each day. **Financial control** is the process of checking actual performance against plans to ensure that desired financial results occur. For example, planned revenues based on forecasts usually turn out to be higher or lower than actual revenues because sales are largely unpredictable. Control involves monitoring revenue inflows and making appropriate financial adjustments. Excessively high revenues, for instance, may be deposited in short-term interest-bearing accounts. Or they may be used to pay off short-term debt. In contrast, lower-than-expected revenues may necessitate short-term borrowing to meet current debt obligations.

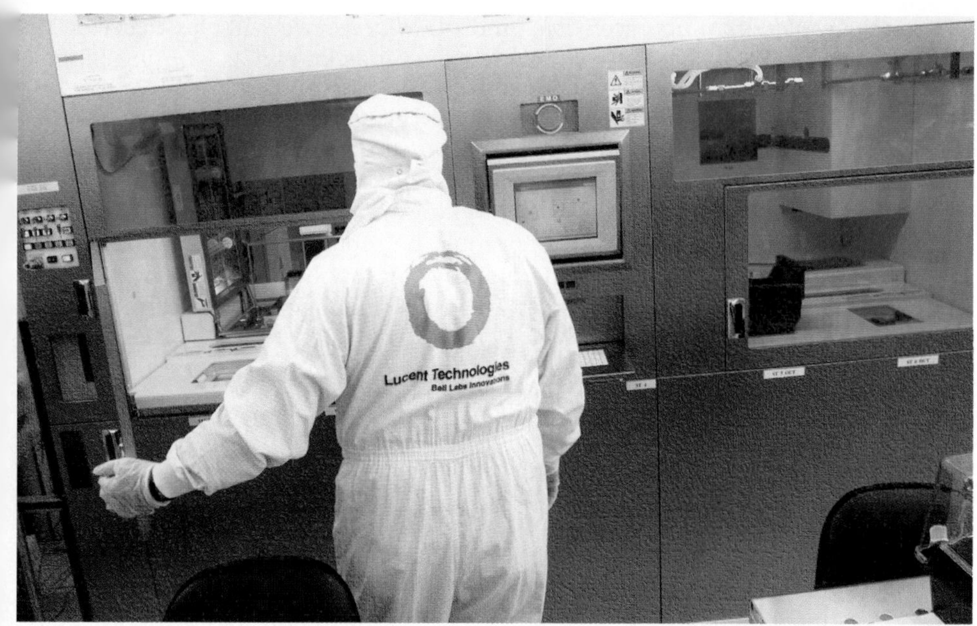

There's always room for creative cash-flow management. Analysts report, for example, that Lucent Technologies <www.lucent.com> *has added employee compensation that's paid out in stock options instead of cash into its operating cash flow. Technically, that category should include only money that's earned from operating activities such as manufacturing microchips. But when operating cash flow is inflated in this manner (which, by the way, is perfectly legal), unwary investors may be led to believe that the company's earnings are higher than they really are. In Lucent's case, the apparent increase was $1 billion in 9 months.*

Budgets (as we saw in Chapter 17) are often the backbone of financial control. The budget provides the measuring stick against which performance is evaluated. The cash flows, debts, and assets not only of the whole company but also of each department are compared at regular intervals against budgeted amounts. Discrepancies indicate the need for financial adjustments so that resources are used to the best advantage.

Financial Planning The cornerstone of effective financial management is the development of a financial plan. A **financial plan** describes a firm's strategies for reaching some future financial position. In constructing the plan, a financial manager must ask several questions:

financial plan
A firm's strategies for reaching some future financial position

- What amount of funds does the company need to meet immediate needs?
- When will it need more funds?
- Where can it get the funds to meet both its short- and long-term needs?

To answer these questions, a financial manager must develop a clear picture of why a firm needs funds. Managers must also assess the relative costs and benefits of potential funding sources. In the sections that follow, we will examine the main reasons for which companies generate funds, and we will describe the main sources of business funding, both for the short term and the long term.

Why Do Businesses Need Funds?

Every company must spend money to survive. According to the simplest formula, funds that are spent on materials, wages, and buildings eventually lead to the creation of products, revenues, and profits. In planning for funding requirements, financial managers must distinguish between two different kinds of expenditures: *short-term (operating)* and *long-term (capital) expenditures.*

Short-Term (Operating) Expenditures

Short-term expenditures are incurred regularly in a firm's everyday business activities. To manage these outlays, managers must pay special attention to *accounts payable, accounts receivable,* and *inventories.* We will also describe the measures used by some firms in managing the funds known as *working capital.*

Accounts Payable In Chapter 17, we defined *accounts payable* as unpaid bills owed to suppliers plus wages and taxes due within the upcoming year. For most companies, this is the largest single category of short-term debt. To plan for funding flows, financial managers want to know *in advance* the amounts of new accounts payable as well as when they must be repaid. For information about such obligations and needs—say, the quantity of supplies required by a certain department in an upcoming period—financial managers must rely on other managers.

Accounts Receivable As we also saw in Chapter 17, *accounts receivable* consist of funds due from customers who have bought on credit. A sound financial plan requires financial managers to project accurately both how much credit is advanced to buyers and when they will make payments on their accounts. For example, managers at Kraft Foods must know how many dollars' worth of cheddar cheese Kroger's supermarkets will order each month; they must also know Kroger's payment schedule. Because accounts receivable represent an investment in products for which a firm has not yet received payment, they temporarily tie up its funds. Clearly, the seller wants to receive payment as quickly as possible.

credit policy
Rules governing a firm's extension of credit to customers

Credit Policies Predicting payment schedules is a function of **credit policy:** the rules governing a firm's extension of credit to customers. This policy sets standards as to which buyers are eligible for what type of credit. Typically, credit is extended to customers who have the ability to pay and who honor their obligations. Credit is denied to firms with poor payment histories. Information about such histories is available from many sources, including the Credit Interchange developed by the National Association of Credit Management.

Credit policy also sets payment terms. For example, credit terms of "2/10, net 30" mean that the selling company offers a 2-percent discount if the customer pays within 10 days. The customer has 30 days to pay the regular price. Under these terms, the buyer would have to pay only $980 on a $1,000 invoice on days 1 to 10, but all $1,000 on days 11 to 30. The higher the discount, the more incentive buyers have to pay early. Sellers can thus adjust credit terms to influence when customers pay their bills.

inventory
Materials and goods which are held by a company but which will be sold within the year

Inventories Between the time a firm buys raw materials and the time it sells finished products, it ties up funds in **inventory**—materials and goods that it will sell within the year. Failure to manage inventory can have grave financial consequences. Too little inventory of any kind can cost a firm sales. Too much inventory means tied-up funds that cannot be used elsewhere. In extreme cases, a company may have to sell excess inventory at low profits simply to raise cash.

working capital
Difference between a firm's current assets and current liabilities

Working Capital As we saw in Chapter 17, **working capital** is the difference between a firm's current assets and current liabilities. It is a liquid asset out of which current debts can be paid. A company calculates its working capital by adding up the following:

- Inventories—that is, raw materials, work-in-process, and finished goods on hand
- Accounts receivable (minus accounts payable)

How much money is tied up in working capital? Fortune 500 companies typically devote 20 cents of every sales dollar—about $800 billion total—to working capital. What are the benefits of reducing these sums? There are two very important pluses:

1. Every dollar that is not tied up in working capital becomes a dollar of more useful cash flow.
2. Reduction of working capital raises earnings permanently.

The second advantage results from the fact that money costs money (in interest payments and the like). Reducing working capital, therefore, means saving money.

Long-Term (Capital) Expenditures

In addition to needing funds for operating expenditures, companies need funds to cover long-term expenditures on fixed assets. As we saw in Chapter 17, *fixed assets* are items with long-term use or value, such as land, buildings, and machinery.

Long-term expenditures are usually more carefully planned than short-term outlays because they pose special problems. They differ from short-term outlays in the following ways, all of which influence the ways that long-term outlays are funded:

- Unlike inventories and other short-term assets, they are not normally sold or converted into cash.
- Their acquisition requires a very large investment.
- They represent a binding commitment of company funds that continues long into the future.

Sources of Short-Term Funds

Firms can call on many sources for the funds they need to finance day-to-day operations and to implement short-term plans. These sources include *trade credit, secured* and *unsecured loans,* and *factoring accounts receivable.*

Trade Credit

Accounts payable are not merely expenditures. They also constitute a source of funds for the buying company. Until it pays its bill, the buyer has the use of both the purchased product and the price of the product. This situation results when the seller grants **trade credit,** which is effectively a short-term loan from one firm to another. Trade credit can take several forms:

- The most common form, **open-book credit,** is essentially a good-faith agreement. Buyers receive merchandise along with invoices stating credit terms. Sellers ship products on faith that payment will be forthcoming.
- When sellers want more reassurance, they may insist that buyers sign legally binding **promissory notes** before merchandise is shipped. The agreement states when and how much money will be paid to the seller.
- The **trade draft** is attached to the merchandise shipment by the seller and states the promised date and amount of payment due. To take possession of the merchandise, the buyer must sign the draft. Once signed by the buyer, the document becomes a **trade acceptance.** Trade drafts and trade acceptances are useful forms of credit in international transactions.

Secured Short-Term Loans

For most firms, bank loans are a very important source of short-term funding. Such loans almost always involve promissory notes in which the borrower promises to repay the loan plus interest. In **secured loans,** banks also require **collateral:** a legal interest in certain assets that can be seized if payments are not made as promised.

trade credit
Granting of credit by one firm to another

open-book credit
Form of trade credit in which sellers ship merchandise on faith that payment will be forthcoming

promissory note
Form of trade credit in which buyers sign promise-to-pay agreements before merchandise is shipped

trade draft
Form of trade credit in which buyers must sign statements of payment terms attached to merchandise by sellers

trade acceptance
Trade draft that has been signed by the buyer

secured loan
Loan for which the borrower must provide collateral

collateral
Borrower-pledged legal asset that may be seized by lenders in case of nonpayment

Secured loans allow borrowers to get funds when they might not qualify for unsecured credit. Moreover, they generally carry lower interest rates than unsecured loans. Collateral may be in the form of inventories or accounts receivable, and most businesses have other types of assets that can be pledged. Some, for instance, own marketable securities, such as stocks or bonds of other companies (see Chapter 19). Many more own fixed assets, such as land, buildings, or equipment. Fixed assets, however, are generally used to secure long-term rather than short-term loans. Most short-term business borrowing is secured by inventories and accounts receivable.

Inventory Loans When a loan is made with inventory as a collateral asset, the lender lends the borrower some portion of the stated value of the inventory. Obviously, inventory is more attractive as collateral when it provides the lender with real security for the loan amount. For example, if the inventory can be readily converted into cash, it is more valuable as collateral. Other inventory (say, boxes full of expensive, partially completed lenses for eyeglasses) is of little value on the open market. Meanwhile, 1,000 crates of boxed, safely stored canned tomatoes might well be convertible into cash.[1]

pledging accounts receivable

Using accounts receivable as loan collateral

Accounts Receivable as Collateral When accounts receivable are used as collateral, the process is called **pledging accounts receivable.** In the event of nonpayment, the lender may seize the receivables. If these assets are not enough to cover the loan, the borrower must make up the difference. Loans on receivables are granted only when lenders are confident that they can recover funds from the borrower's debtors. Receivables are especially important to service companies such as accounting firms and law offices because they do not maintain inventories of physical products; accounts receivable are their main source of collateral. Typically, lenders who will accept accounts receivable as collateral are financial institutions with credit departments capable of evaluating the quality of the receivables.[2]

Factoring Accounts Receivable

A firm can raise funds rapidly by *factoring:* selling the firm's accounts receivable. In this process, the purchaser of the receivables, usually a financial institution, is known as the factor. The factor pays some percentage of the full amount of receivables due to the selling firm. The seller gets this money immediately.[3]

For example, a factor might buy $40,000 worth of receivables for 60 percent of that sum ($24,000). The factor profits to the extent that the money it eventually collects exceeds the amount it paid. This profit depends on the quality of the receivables, the cost of collecting them, and interest rates.

Unsecured Short-Term Loans

unsecured loan

Loan for which collateral is not required

With an **unsecured loan,** the borrower does not have to put up collateral. In many cases, however, the bank requires the borrower to maintain a *compensating balance*—that is, the borrower must keep a portion of the loan amount on deposit with the bank in a non-interest–bearing account.

The terms of the loan—amount, duration, interest rate, and payment schedule—are negotiated between the bank and the borrower. To receive an unsecured loan, then, a firm must ordinarily have a good banking relationship with the lender. Once an agreement is made, a promissory note will be executed and the funds will be transferred to the borrower. Although some unsecured loans are one-time-only arrangements, many take the form of *lines of credit, revolving credit agreements,* or *commercial paper.*

line of credit

Standing arrangement in which a lender agrees to make available a specified amount of funds upon the borrower's request

Line of Credit A **line of credit** is a standing agreement between a bank and a business in which the bank promises to lend the firm a maximum amount of funds on request. Suppose, for example, that First National Bank gives Sunshine

Tanning Inc. a $100,000 line of credit for the coming year. Under this arrangement, Sunshine's borrowings can total up to $100,000 at any time, and Sunshine benefits by knowing in advance that the bank regards it as creditworthy and will lend funds on short notice.

Revolving Credit Agreement **Revolving credit agreements** are similar to consumer bank cards. A lender agrees to make some amount of funds available on a continuing basis. The lending institution guarantees that these funds will be available when sought by the borrower. In return for this guarantee, the bank charges the borrower a commitment fee for holding the line of credit open. This fee is payable even if the customer does not borrow any funds. It is often expressed as a percentage of the loan amount (usually .5 to 1 percent of the committed amount).

revolving credit agreement
Arrangement in which a lender agrees to make funds available on demand and on a continuing basis

Say, for example, that First National agrees to lend Sunshine Tanning up to $100,000 under a revolving credit agreement. If Sunshine borrows $80,000, it still has access to $20,000. If it pays off $50,000 and reduces its debt to $30,000, it then has $70,000 available. Sunshine pays interest on the borrowed funds, plus a fee on the unused funds in its line of credit.

Commercial Paper Some firms can raise short-term funds by issuing **commercial paper:** short-term securities, or notes, containing the borrower's promise to pay.[4] Because it is backed solely by the issuing firm's promise to pay, commercial paper is an option for only the largest and most creditworthy firms.

commercial paper
Short-term securities, or notes, containing a borrower's promise to pay

How does commercial paper work? Corporations issue commercial paper with a certain face value. Buying companies pay less than that value. At the end of a specified period (usually 30 to 90 days, but legally up to 270 days), the issuing company buys back the paper at face value. The difference between the price paid and the face value is the buyer's profit. For the issuing company, the cost is usually lower than prevailing interest rates on short-term loans.

If, for example, Consolidated Edison <www.coned.com> needs to borrow $10 million for 90 days, it might issue commercial paper with a face value of $10.2 million. Who will buy the paper? Among other investors, insurance companies with $10 million in available cash may buy it. After 90 days, Consolidated Edison will pay a total of $10.2 million to the insurance companies who invested.

Sources of Long-Term Funds

Firms need long-term funding to finance expenditures on fixed assets: the buildings and equipment needed to conduct their businesses. They may seek long-term funds through *debt financing* (that is, from outside the firm) or through *equity financing* (by drawing on internal sources). We will discuss both options in this section, as well as a middle ground called *hybrid financing.* We will also analyze some of the options that enter into decisions about long-term financing as well as the role of the *risk-return relationship* in attracting investors to a firm.

Debt Financing

Long-term borrowing from sources outside the company—**debt financing**—is a major component of most firms' long-term financial planning. Long-term debts are obligations that are payable more than one year after they are originally issued. The two primary sources of such funding are *long-term loans* and the sale of *corporate bonds.*

debt financing
Long-term borrowing from sources outside a company

Long-Term Loans Most corporations get long-term loans from commercial banks, usually those with which they have developed long-standing relationships. Credit companies (such as Household Finance Corp.), insurance companies, and pension funds also grant long-term business loans.

Self-Check Questions 1–3

*You should now be able to answer Self-Check Questions 1–3**

1. MULTIPLE CHOICE Which of the following items is **not** an example of the *financial manager's* responsibilities? [select one]: **(a)** ensuring that the firm has enough funds on hand to purchase the materials and human resources that it needs; **(b)** making adjustments when financial planning doesn't go as expected; **(c)** monitoring revenue inflows and paying off debt or borrowing funds; **(d)** planning for short-term investing of excess cash balances to earn more money; **(e)** ensuring that the firm abides by generally accepted accounting principles (GAAP) in preparing financial statements.

2. TRUE/FALSE Suppose a supplier tells a buyer that the *terms of payment* (*credit*) are 3/20, net 60. Under these terms, the buyer would have to pay only $9,700 on a $10,000 invoice on days 1 to 20, but all $10,000 on days 21 to 60.

3. MULTIPLE CHOICE Suppose your firm has decided to raise capital to expand a large building and furnish it with modern equipment. Which of the following *sources of funds* is most appropriate for your purposes? [select one]: **(a)** trade credit, such as open-book credit; **(b)** a long-term loan; **(c)** inventory loans; **(d)** factoring accounts receivable; **(e)** a revolving credit agreement.

*ANSWERS TO SELF-CHECK QUESTIONS 1–3 CAN BE FOUND ON P. AN-13.

Long-term loans are attractive to borrowers for several reasons:

- Because the number of parties involved is limited, loans can often be arranged very quickly.
- The firm need not make public disclosure of its business plans or the purpose for which it is acquiring the loan. (In contrast, the issuance of corporate bonds requires such disclosure.)
- The duration of the loan can easily be matched to the borrower's needs.
- If the firm's needs change, loans usually contain clauses making it possible to change terms.

Long-term loans also have some disadvantages. Borrowers, for instance, may have trouble finding lenders to supply large sums. Long-term borrowers may also face restrictions as conditions of the loan. For example, they may have to pledge long-term assets as collateral or agree to take on no more debt until the loan is paid.

Interest Rates Interest rates are negotiated between borrower and lender. Although some bank loans have fixed rates, others have floating rates tied to the prime rate that the bank charges its most creditworthy customers (see Chapter 18). A loan at one percent above prime, then, is payable at one percentage point higher than the prime rate. This rate may fluctuate, or float, because the prime rate itself goes up and down as market conditions change.

Corporate Bonds As we saw in Chapter 19, a *corporate bond,* like commercial paper, is a contract—a promise by the issuer to pay the holder a certain amount of money on a specified date. Unlike issuers of commercial paper, however, bond issuers do not pay off quickly. In many cases, bonds may not be redeemable for

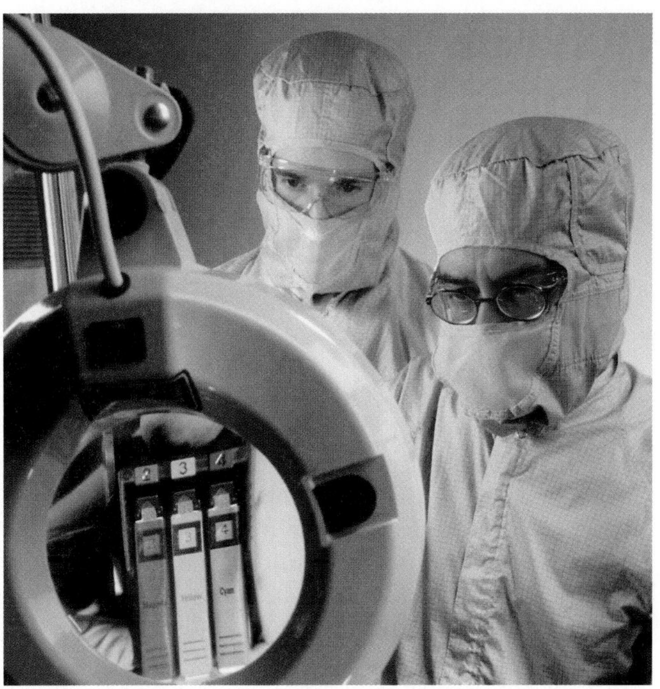

In 1999, Xerox stock hit an all-time high of $64 per share. It's now selling at about $7, and the company is worth $38 billion less. Xerox <www.xerox.com> *has been floundering for nearly a decade, and debt financing will make recovery even harder. The company has $1.7 billion in cash on hand, but it owes $17 billion. In one recent year, Xerox was unable to postpone payment on its* commercial paper *(short-term notes backed only by the promise to pay). Financial managers thus resorted to a* line of credit *(a bank loan) which, with interest, incurred $7 billion in debt. The most recent round of cost-saving layoffs at Xerox affected 4,000 people.*

30 years. Also, unlike commercial paper, most bonds pay bondholders a stipulated sum of annual or semiannual interest. If the company fails to make a bond payment, it is said to be *in default*.

Bonds are the major source of long-term debt financing for most corporations.[5] They are attractive when firms need large amounts for long periods of time. The issuing company also gains access to large numbers of lenders through nationwide bond markets and stock exchanges. On the other hand, bonds entail high administrative and selling costs. They may also require stiff interest payments, especially if the issuing company has a poor credit rating.

Bond Indentures The terms of a bond, including the amount to be paid, the interest rate, and the maturity date (the date when the principal is to be paid) differ from company to company and issue to issue. They are spelled out in the bond contract, or **bond indenture.** The indenture also identifies which of the firm's assets, if any, are pledged as collateral for the bonds.

bond indenture
Statement of the terms of a corporate bond

PPG Industries <www.ppg.com>, a leading manufacturer of fiberglass, industrial chemicals, and medical supplies, has a $150-million debt issue that matures on May 1, 2021. Until the maturity date, the bondholders, including those who purchased the initial offering in 1991, will be paid 9.12 percent interest each year. In addition, they will receive a total of $150 million, the principal amount owed by PPG, when the bonds mature and are retired. The bond indenture contains no specific pledge of particular assets for security.

Equity Financing

Although debt financing often has strong appeal, looking inside the company for long-term funding is sometimes preferable. In small companies, for example, founders may increase personal investments in their own firms. In most cases, **equity financing** means issuing common stock or retaining the firm's earnings. Both options involve putting the owners' capital to work.

equity financing
Use of common stock and/or retained earnings to raise long-term funding

Common Stock People who purchase common stock seek profits in two forms—dividends and appreciation. Overall, shareholders hope for an increase

■ TABLE 20.1

Stockholders' Equity for Sunshine Tanning

Common Stockholders' Equity, 1996	
Initial common stock (500 shares issued @ $20 per share, 1996)	$10,000
Total stockholders' equity	$10,000
Common Stockholders' Equity, 2002	
Initial common stock (500 shares issued @ $20 per share, 1996)	$10,000
Additional paid-in capital (500 shares issued @ $100 per share, 2002)	50,000
Total stockholders' equity	$60,000

in the market value of their stock (appreciation) because the firm has profited and grown. By issuing shares of stock, the company gets the funds it needs for buying land, buildings, and equipment.

Suppose that Sunshine Tanning's founders invested $10,000 by buying the original 500 shares of common stock (at $20 per share) in 1996. The company used these funds to buy equipment, and it succeeded financially. By 2002, then, it needed funds for expansion. A pattern of profitable operations and regularly paid dividends now allows Sunshine to raise $50,000 by selling 500 new shares of stock at $100 per share. This $50,000 would constitute *paid-in capital*—additional money, above the par value of its original stock sale, paid directly to a firm by its owners (see Chapter 19). As Table 20.1 shows, this additional paid-in capital would increase total stockholders' equity to $60,000.

Finally, we should note that the use of equity financing by means of common stock can be expensive because paying dividends is more expensive than paying bond interest. Why? Because interest paid to bondholders is a business expense and, therefore, a tax deduction for the firm. Stock dividends are not tax deductible.

Retained Earnings As we saw in Chapter 17, *retained earnings* are profits retained for the firm's use rather than paid out in dividends. If a company uses retained earnings as capital, it will not have to borrow money and pay interest. If a firm has a history of reaping profits by reinvesting retained earnings, it may be very attractive to some investors. Retained earnings, however, mean smaller dividends for shareholders. In this sense, then, the practice may decrease the demand for—and thus the price of—the company's stock.

For example, if Sunshine Tanning had net earnings of $50,000 in 2002, it could pay a $50-per-share dividend on its 1,000 shares of common stock. Let's say, however, that Sunshine plans to remodel at a cost of $30,000, intending to retain $30,000 in earnings to finance the project. Only $20,000—$20 per share—will be available for shareholders.

Financial Burden on the Firm As we have already noted, a firm cannot deduct paid-out dividends as business expenses, but it can deduct the interest that it pays on bonds. If equity funding can be so expensive, why do firms not rely entirely on debt financing? Loans and bonds carry fixed interest rates and represent fixed promises to pay, regardless of changes in economic conditions. If a firm defaults on its obligations, it may lose assets and may even go bankrupt. Indeed, a classic example is WorldCom, the nation's then-No. 2 long-distance phone company, which filed for bankruptcy protection in 2002. With $102 billion in assets, WorldCom's bankruptcy is the largest in U.S. history. Even with those massive assets, however, the firm was crushed by its $41 billion debt, $24 billion of which was in bonds. Facing prospects that the firm would default on upcoming interest payments, many of its creditors began withholding additional money unless loans were secured with WorldCom assets. With more than 1,000 creditors—including Citibank, J.P. Morgan Chase, and Credit Suisse First Boston—the firm is allowed to operate while in bankruptcy, but all of its financing must be approved by the bankruptcy court.[6]

Likewise, during the 2001–2002 Argentine financial crisis, banks around the world suffered when borrowers (large companies and government borrowers) could not repay outstanding debt. Some borrower companies went bankrupt, defaulting on obligations to foreign investors. Faced with a struggling economy, Argentina's government could not meet payments on its $132 billion debt. Argentine President Fernando de la Rua proposed a rescue plan that would require holders of the debt to swap their bonds for ones paying lower interest, leaving lenders no choice but to take losses on their original agreements. FleetBoston Financial Corp., the Boston-based banking company, attributed much of its $386 million second-quarter losses for 2002 to investments in Argentina. Similarly, U.S. and Spanish banks—Santander Central Hispano and Banco Bilbao Vizcaya Argentaria—have written off losses in Argentina. Credit Lyonnais and SocGen, two French banks, set aside more than 500 million francs to cover bad loans, while Lloyds of London lost more than £100 million pounds as a result of bad loans. Even as it defaults on current obligations, however, the Argentine government is seeking additional installments of new credit from the International Monetary Fund (IMF) to help make payments on existing debt.[7]

Because of the risk of default, debt financing appeals most strongly to companies in industries that have predictable profits and cash flow patterns. For example, demand for electric power is quite steady from year to year and predictable from month to month. Thus, electric utility companies enjoy steady streams of income and can carry substantial amounts of debt. Detroit Edison <www.detroitedison.com>, a major privately owned utility, is a representative example. About 61 percent of its long-term funding is in the form of debt. Equity from common stock provides only 37 percent. Some of the remaining 2 percent of Edison's long-term capital is equity from preferred stock, a topic discussed in the next section.

"It's simple enough, Langdon, but I'll explain again. To help pay off the debt that we incurred when we bought this company, we've sold some of you into slavery."

Hybrid Financing: Preferred Stock

A middle ground between debt financing and equity financing is the use of preferred stock (see Chapter 19). Preferred stock is a hybrid because it has some of the features of both corporate bonds and common stocks. As with bonds, for instance, payments on preferred stock are fixed amounts such as $6 per share per year. Unlike bonds, however, preferred stock never matures; like common stock, it can be held indefinitely. In addition, preferred stockholders have first rights (over common stockholders) to dividends.

A major advantage to the issuer is the flexibility of preferred stock. Because preferred stockholders have no voting rights, the stock secures funds for the firm without jeopardizing corporate control of its management. Furthermore, corporations are not obligated to repay the principal and can withhold payment of dividends in lean times.

Choosing Between Debt and Equity Financing

Needless to say, an aspect of financial planning is striking a balance between debt and equity financing. Because a firm relies on a mix of debt and equity to raise the cash needed for capital outlays, that mix is called its **capital structure.** Financial plans, thus, contain targets for capital structure; an example would be 40 percent debt and 60 percent equity. But choosing a target is not easy. A wide range of mixes is possible, and strategies range from conservative to risky.

capital structure
Relative mix of a firm's debt and equity financing

The most conservative strategy is all-equity financing and no debt: A company has no formal obligations to make financial payouts. As we have seen, however, equity is an expensive source of capital. The riskiest strategy is all-debt financing. Although less expensive than equity funding, indebtedness increases the risk that a firm will be unable to meet its obligations (and even go bankrupt). Somewhere between the two extremes, financial planners try to find mixes that will increase stockholders' wealth with a reasonable exposure to risk.

Indexes of Financial Risk To help understand and measure the amount of financial risk they face, financial managers often rely on published indexes for various investments. *Financial World,* for example, publishes independent appraisals of mutual funds (see Chapter 19), using risk-reward ratings of A (very good) to E

As we saw in Chapter 19, if agencies like Moody's and Standard & Poor's downgrade a company's ratings to low enough levels, its bonds become junk bonds. That's what happened to The Gap <www.gap.com> *in early 2002, after sales at virtually every store in the chain fell every single month for nearly two solid years. The reasons for the steep and rapid decline are complex, but now that it's been relegated to junk status, The Gap is finding it harder to raise money. Banks that were once willing to extend lines of credit now want collateral, such as inventory. In 2002 alone, the company paid $145 million* in interest *on debt of $2 billion.*

(poor) to indicate each fund's riskiness in comparison to its anticipated financial returns. An A-rated fund is judged to offer very good returns relative to the amount of risk involved. An E-rated fund carries the greatest risk, with smaller returns. Similarly, Standard & Poor's <www.standardpoor.com> publishes various indexes for numerous funds and for stocks that are available for purchase by financial managers.

By using such indexes, financial managers can determine how a particular investment compares to other opportunities in terms of its stability. A bond, for example, is considered investment grade if it qualifies for one of the top four ratings by either S&P or Moody's <www.moodys.com>. Bonds below investment grade are called junk bonds because they have unusually high default rates. Nonetheless, junk bonds appeal to many investors because they promise uncommonly high yields.

The Risk-Return Relationship

While developing plans for raising capital, financial managers must be aware of the different motivations of individual investors. Why, for example, do some individuals and firms invest in stocks while others invest only in bonds? Investor motivations, of course, determine who is willing to buy a given company's stocks or bonds. Investors give money to firms and, in return, anticipate receiving future cash flows. Thus, everyone who invests money is expressing a personal preference for safety versus risk.

In other words, some cash flows are more certain than others. Investors generally expect to receive higher payments for higher uncertainty. They do not generally expect large returns for secure investments like government-insured bonds. Each type of investment, then, has a **risk-return relationship** reflecting the principle that whereas safer investments tend to offer lower returns, riskier investments tend to offer higher returns. In early 2002, for example, rating agencies downgraded the Gap's debt from investment grade to junk status, meaning that raising money would become more difficult and expensive. Because greater risk is associated with the downgraded rating, banks and other lenders will demand higher interest payments; they will also demand that loans be secured by assets, such as the retailer's inventory, to protect against the risk of default.[8]

risk-return relationship
Principle that, whereas safer investments tend to offer lower returns, riskier investments tend to offer higher returns

Figure 20.1 shows the general risk-return relationship for various financial instruments, along with the types of investors they attract. Thus, conservative investors, who have a low tolerance for risk, will opt for high-grade corporate bonds that rate low in terms of risk on future returns but also low on the size of expected returns. The reverse is true of aggressive investors who prefer the higher risks and potential returns from junk bonds and common stocks.

Risk-return differences are recognized by financial planners, who try to gain access to the greatest funding at the lowest possible cost. By gauging investors' perceptions of their riskiness, a firm's managers can estimate how much they must pay to attract funds to their offerings. Over time, a company can reposition itself on the risk continuum by improving its record on dividends, interest payments, and debt repayment.

Financial Management for Small Business

As we saw in Chapter 3, new business success and failure are often closely related to adequate or inadequate funding. For example, one study of nearly 3,000 new companies revealed a survival rate of 84 percent for new businesses with initial investments of at least $50,000. Unfortunately, those with less funding have a much lower survival rate. Why are so many start-ups underfunded?

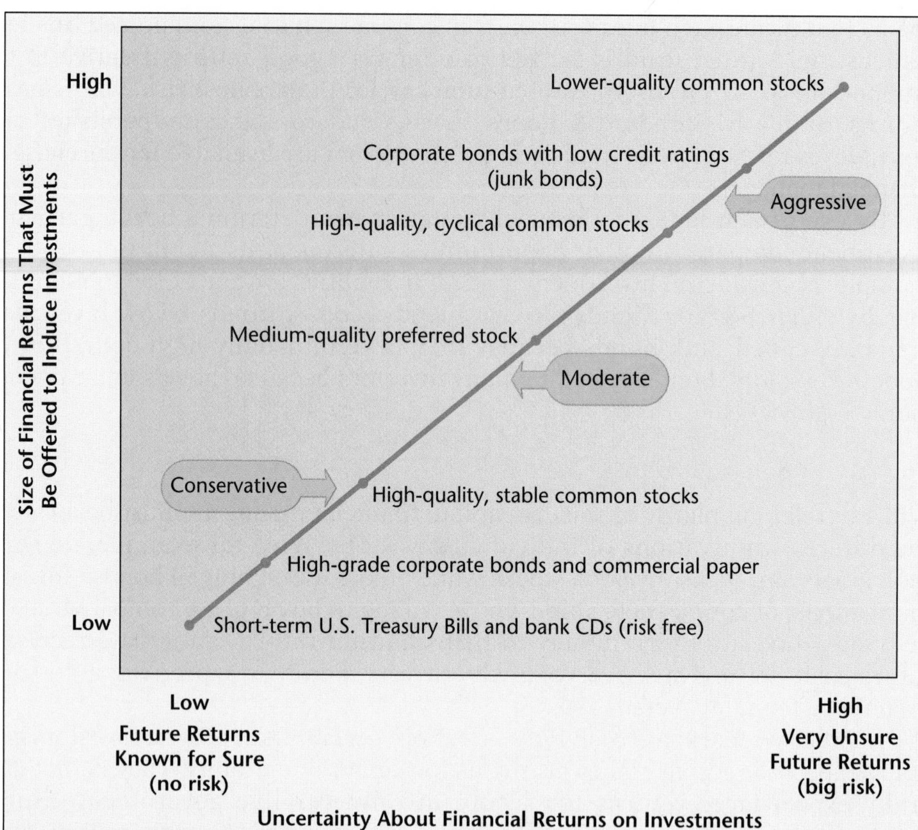

FIGURE 20.1
The Risk-Return Relationship

Self-Check Questions 4–6

*You should now be able to answer Self-Check Questions 4–6**

4. MULTIPLE CHOICE Which of the following is **not** true about *debt financing*? [select one]: **(a)** Sources of long-term loans include banks, credit companies, insurance companies, and pension funds. **(b)** The two primary sources of debt financing by U.S companies are corporate bonds and common stock. **(c)** Secured bonds can reduce risk to holders because the issuer pledges assets in case of default. **(d)** The terms and conditions of a bond are spelled out in the bond indenture. **(e)** If a company fails to make a bond payment, it is said to be *in default*.

5. TRUE/FALSE Suppose that you're a financial manager for a small business. You decide to retain $100,000 of its recent profits for the firm's use rather than pay it out as dividends to shareholders. This action is an example of *equity financing*.

6. MULTIPLE CHOICE Which of the following best describes the underlying pattern of the *risk-return relationship*? [select one]: **(a)** Investors generally expect to receive higher payments for higher uncertainty. **(b)** Equity financing is more expensive than debt financing. **(c)** The most conservative financing strategy for a firm is all-equity financing and no debt. **(d)** The mix of debt and equity used by a firm to raise cash for capital outlays is called its capital structure. **(e)** Investment grade bonds qualify for the top ratings by Moody's.

*ANSWERS TO SELF-CHECK QUESTIONS 4–6 CAN BE FOUND ON P. AN-14.

Mid-Chapter Internet Field Trip

"Taking Finances Personally"

The first part of this chapter explored basic financial management activities, including the role of the financial manager, cash flow management, financial planning and control, and debt and equity financing as sources of long-term funds. We discussed several activities of financial managers, such as clarifying financial goals, determining short-term and long-term funding requirements, and managing risk. Many of these issues in organizational finance are also issues in personal finance. In managing your own finances and pursuing your personal financial goals, you must consider cash management, financial planning and control, investment alternatives, and risk management. Questions, of course, will arise on your prospects for making or losing money with alternative investments. How about diversification? Can it provide some protection from financial risk? What kinds of diversification are available to individual investors from prominent financial services companies?

Let's explore some of these questions of personal financial management by visiting the Internet site of one of the world's leading financial services firms, The Vanguard Group, at <www.vanguard.com>. The opening page offers two choices—**Personal Investors** and **Institutional Investors.** Select **Personal Investors.** Look around the **Personal Investors** home page to learn about the company and the kinds of services it offers for personal investing. Five major sections across the top of the page include **Home, My Portfolios, Research Funds & Stocks, Planning & Advice,** and **Buy & Sell.**

Let's start by clicking on **Planning & Advice.** The screen then displays a page with several selections, including **Get a Financial Start.** After selecting **Get a Financial Start,** you will be shown a Web page with a section entitled **Frequently Asked Questions** (located near the bottom of the page). Select the question: **How do mutual fund investors make money?** Based on the information from that page, respond to the following questions:

1. What are the three ways in which an investor can make money from stock and bond mutual funds?
2. Is there any risk that an investor might lose money from stock and bond mutual funds?

Now return to the page entitled **Get a Financial Start**. In the section entitled **Frequently Asked Questions** (located near the bottom of the page), select this question: **Is it risky to have most or all of my investments with one mutual fund company?** Based on the information that you find on this page, respond to the following questions:

3. What role does diversification play in Vanguard's response to the issue of risk when investing with one company?
4. What is Vanguard's response to the question of risk associated with placing all investments with one company?
5. What is your evaluation of Vanguard's response?

To continued your Internet Field Trip , click on www.prenhall.com/griffin

For one thing, entrepreneurs often underestimate the value of establishing *bank credit* as a source of funds and use trade credit ineffectively. In addition, they often fail to consider *venture capital* as a source of funding, and they are notorious for not planning *cash flow needs* properly.

Establishing Bank and Trade Credit

Some banks have liberal credit policies and offer financial analysis, cash flow planning, and suggestions based on experiences with other local firms. Some provide loans to small businesses in bad times and work to keep them going. Some, of course, do not. Obtaining credit, therefore, begins with finding a bank that can—and will—support a small firm's financial needs. Once a *line of credit* is obtained, the small business can seek more liberal credit policies from other businesses. Sometimes, for instance, suppliers give customers longer credit periods—say, 45 or 60 days rather than 30 days. Liberal trade credit terms with their suppliers let firms increase short-term funds and avoid additional borrowing from banks.

Long-Term Funding Naturally, obtaining long-term loans is more difficult for new businesses than for established companies. With unproven repayment ability, start-up firms can expect to pay higher interest rates than older firms. If a new enterprise displays evidence of sound financial planning, however, the Small Business Administration, the SBA (see Chapter 3), may support a guaranteed loan.

The Business Plan as a Tool for Credit Start-up firms without proven financial success usually must present a business plan to demonstrate that the firm is a good credit risk.[9] The business plan is a document that tells potential lenders why the money is needed, the amount, how the money will be used to improve the company, and when it will be paid back.

Photographer David Cupp, for example, needed $50,000 in funding for his new firm, Photos Online Inc., in Columbus, Ohio, which displays and sells photos over the Internet. His business plan had to be rewritten many times until it became understandable, in financial terms, to potential lenders. The plan eventually reached 35 pages and contained information on the competition as well as cash flow projections. After four failed attempts, Cupp found a fifth bank that approved a $26,000 term loan and granted a $24,000 line of credit, to be used for computers, software, and living expenses to get the business started.[10]

Venture Capital

venture capital
Outside equity financing provided in return for part ownership of the borrowing firm

Many newer businesses—especially those undergoing rapid growth—cannot get the funds they need through borrowing alone. They may, therefore, turn to **venture capital:** outside equity funding provided in return for part ownership of the borrowing firm. As we saw in Chapter 3, venture capital firms actively seek chances to invest in new firms with rapid growth potential. Because failure rates are high, they typically demand high returns, which are now often 20 to 30 percent.

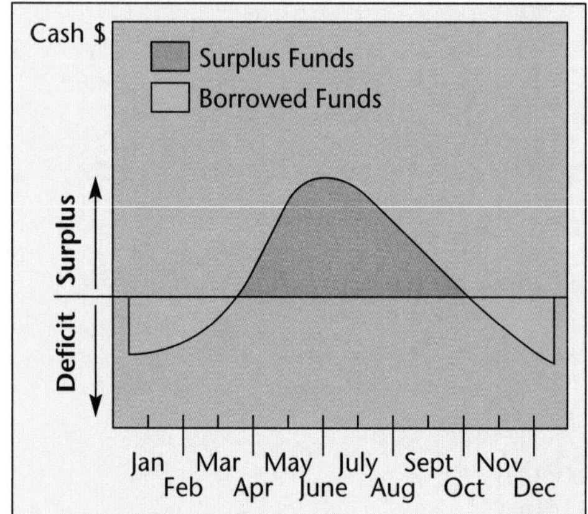

FIGURE 20.2
Projected Cash Flow for Slippery Fish Bait Supply Co.

Planning for Cash-Flow Requirements

Although all businesses should plan for their cash flows, this planning is especially important for small businesses. Success or failure may hinge on anticipating those times when either cash will be short or excess cash can be expected.

Figure 20.2 shows possible cash inflows, cash outflows, and net cash position (inflows minus outflows) month by month for Slippery Fish Bait Supply Co.—a highly seasonal business. As you can see, bait stores buy heavily from Slippery during the spring and summer months. Revenues outpace expenses, leaving surplus funds that can be invested. During the fall and winter, however, expenses exceed revenues. Slippery must borrow funds to keep going until revenues pick up again in the spring. Comparing predicted cash inflows from sales with outflows for expenses shows the firm's expected monthly cash-flow position.

Such knowledge can be invaluable for the small business manager. By anticipating shortfalls, for example, financial managers can seek funds in advance and minimize their costs. By anticipating excess cash, a manager can plan to put the funds to work in short-term, interest-earning investments.

Risk Management

risk
Uncertainty about future events

speculative risk
Risk involving the possibility of gain or loss

pure risk
Risk involving only the possibility of loss or no loss

Financial risks are not the only risks faced every day by companies (and individuals). In this section, we will describe various other types of risks that businesses face and analyze some of the ways in which they typically manage them.

Coping with Risk

Businesses constantly face two basic types of **risk**—that is, uncertainty about future events. **Speculative risks,** such as financial investments, involve the possibility of gain or loss. **Pure risks** involve only the possibility of loss or no loss.

Designing and distributing a new product, for example, is a speculative risk. The product may fail, or it may succeed and earn high profits. In contrast, the chance of a warehouse fire is a pure risk.

For a company to survive and prosper, it must manage both types of risk in a cost-effective manner. We can thus define the process of **risk management** as conserving the firm's earning power and assets by reducing the threat of losses due to uncontrollable events. In every company, each manager must be alert for risks to the firm and their impact on profits. The risk-management process usually entails the five steps outlined in Figure 20.3.

risk management
Process of conserving the firm's earning power and assets by reducing the threat of losses due to uncontrollable events

Step 1: Identify Risks and Potential Losses Managers analyze a firm's risks to identify potential losses. For example, a firm with a fleet of delivery trucks can expect that one of them will eventually be involved in an accident. The accident may cause bodily injury to the driver or others, may cause physical damage to the truck or other vehicles, or both.

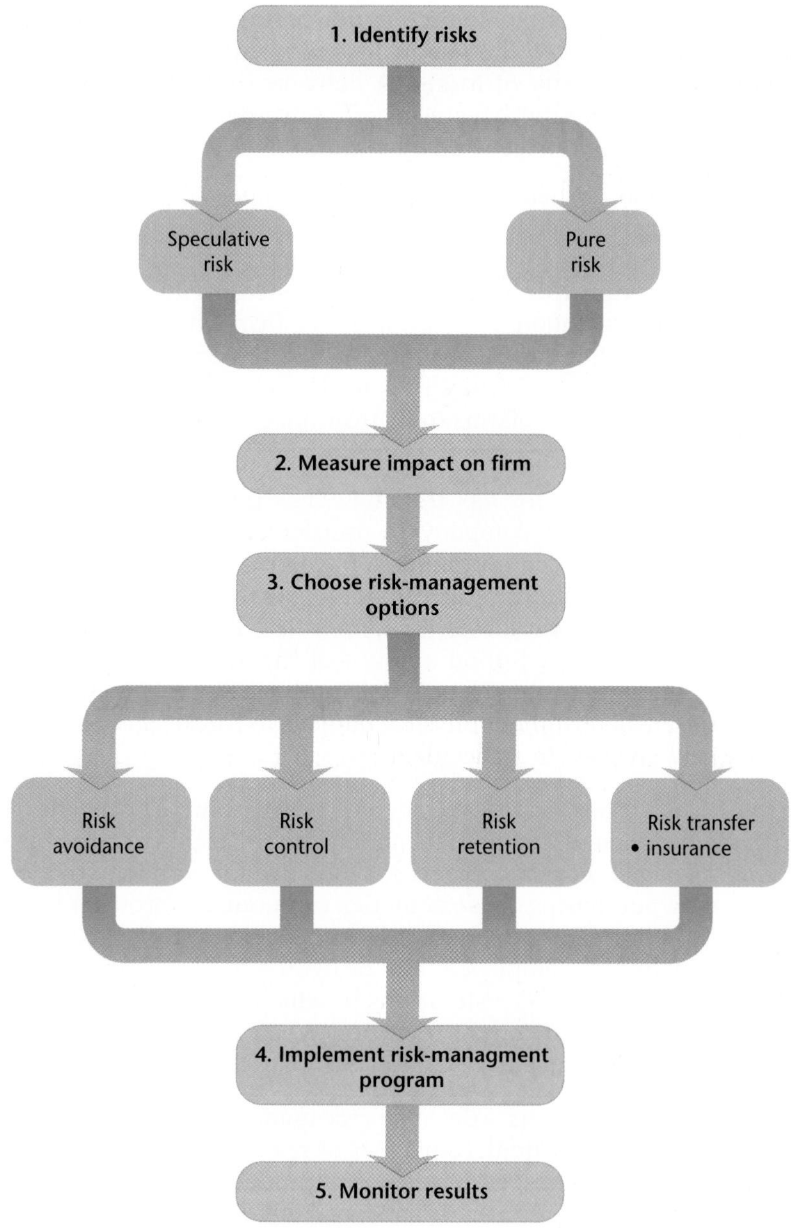

FIGURE 20.3
The Risk-Management Process

Step 2: Measure the Frequency and Severity of Losses and Their Impact To measure the frequency and severity of losses, managers must consider both past history and current activities. How often can the firm expect the loss to occur? What is the likely size of the loss in dollars? For example, our firm with the fleet of delivery trucks may have had two accidents per year in the past. If it adds trucks, however, it may reasonably expect the frequency of accidents to increase.

Step 3: Evaluate Alternatives and Choose the Techniques That Will Best Handle the Losses Having identified and measured potential losses, managers are in a better position to decide how to handle them. With this third step, they generally have four choices: *risk avoidance, control, retention,* or *transfer.*

risk avoidance
Practice of avoiding risk by declining or ceasing to participate in an activity

Risk Avoidance A firm opts for **risk avoidance** by declining to enter or by ceasing to participate in a risky activity. For example, the firm with the delivery trucks could avoid any risk of physical damage or bodily injury by closing down its delivery service. Similarly, a pharmaceutical maker may withdraw a new drug for fear of liability suits.

risk control
Practice of minimizing the frequency or severity of losses from risky activities

Risk Control When avoidance is not practical or desirable, firms can practice **risk control**—say, the use of loss-prevention techniques to minimize the frequency or severity of losses. A delivery service, for instance, can prevent losses by training its drivers in defensive-driving techniques, mapping out safe routes, and conscientiously maintaining its trucks.

risk retention
Practice of covering a firm's losses with its own funds

Risk Retention When losses cannot be avoided or controlled, firms must cope with the consequences. When such losses are manageable and predictable, the firm may decide to cover them out of company funds. The firm is thus said to assume or retain the financial consequences of the loss: hence the practice known as **risk retention.** For example, our firm with the fleet of trucks may find that vehicles suffer vandalism totaling $100 to $500 per year. Depending on its coverage, the company may find it cheaper to pay for repairs out-of-pocket rather than to submit claims to its insurance company.

risk transfer
Practice of transferring a firm's risk to another firm

Risk Transfer When the potential for large risks cannot be avoided or controlled, managers often opt for **risk transfer.** They transfer the risk to another firm—namely, an insurance company. In transferring risk to an insurance company, a firm pays a sum called a premium. In return, the insurance company issues an insurance policy—a formal agreement to pay the policyholder a specified amount in the event of certain losses. In some cases, the insured party must also pay a deductible—an agreed-upon amount of the loss that the insured must absorb prior to reimbursement. Thus, our hypothetical company may buy insurance to protect itself against theft, physical damage to trucks, and bodily injury to drivers and others involved in an accident.

Step 4: Implement the Risk-Management Program The means of implementing risk-management decisions depend on both the technique chosen and the activity being managed. For example, risk avoidance for certain activities can be implemented by purchasing those activities from outside providers—say, hiring delivery services instead of operating delivery vehicles. Risk control might be implemented by training employees and designing new work methods and equipment for on-the-job safety. For situations in which risk retention is preferred, reserve funds can be set aside out of revenues. When risk transfer is needed, implementation means selecting an insurance company and buying the right policies.

Step 5: Monitor Results Because risk management is an ongoing activity, follow-up is always essential. New types of risks, for example, emerge with changes in customers, facilities, employees, and products. Insurance regulations change, and new types of insurance become available. Consequently, managers must con-

Say what you mean

THE CULTURE OF RISK

Risk-taking is a defining feature of U.S. business culture and has been for centuries. From the early pioneers and prospectors heading west to find gold to the dot-com billionaires of the 1990s, Americans are known for their readiness to try out new ideas and for their willingness to risk everything for the chance to make it big. Those philosophies endure today, although they're stronger in certain regions than others.

The first oil drillers of the nineteenth century, for example, were known as wildcatters. You may hear people talking about how the "wildcatter" tradition persists in Texas, and not just in the oil industry.

Risk-taking has also become an important part of California's business culture, especially in the entertainment and high-tech industries. New York, too, is home to some very high risk takers, particularly in the world of finance. The Midwest stands in striking contrast. Here, where a more conservative approach prevails, risks are calculated from every angle.

Risk-taking in the U.S. differs by industry and by size of company, and it's often governed by the personalities on management teams. Small companies are more likely to be able to make snap decisions than large ones, where an elaborate vetting process may slow things down. Likewise, in publicly traded companies, stockholders usually keep a watchful eye on investments, making them less likely to be big risk-takers than privately held firms.

Patriarchal bosses running large companies in other countries, particularly in parts of Asia and Latin America, have as much power as American executives to make quick decisions. The difference is they choose not to, generally preferring that tried-and-tested business ideas. Americans are far more likely to plow ahead with change.

Americans' propensity to take risks is one of the reasons the so-called new economy sprouted here more quickly and confidently than it did elsewhere—and perhaps helps explain why the dot-com bust happened so quickly. The fledgling companies were helped along by rules and regulations designed to support a spirit of change. In fact, risk taking can be seen in the attitudes of authorities as much as in the entrepreneurial spirit of business people, particularly when it comes to tax policies and the financial markets system.

Easier access to capital is one encouraging factor for adventuresome entrepreneurs. Another is the country's attitude toward those who fail in their ventures. For people who lose their bets and end up bankrupt, systems are in place to help them get solvent again. It's not uncommon for a business to start up again under a new name and to resume operations soon after the previous one failed.

But even though failure is an accepted, almost time-honored, tradition in the U.S., that's not to say bankruptcy is taken lightly. Sure, businesspeople who fail can pick themselves up again, but they have a lot of rebuilding to do—from their reputations to the trust they shared with former customers and associates.

tinuously monitor a company's risks, reevaluate the methods used for handling them, and revise them as necessary.

The Contemporary Risk Management Program

Virtually all business decisions involve risks having financial consequences. As a result, the company's chief financial officer (CFO), along with managers in other areas, has a major voice in applying the risk management process. In some industries, most notably insurance, the companies' main line of business revolves around risk taking and risk management for themselves and their clients.

Today, many firms are taking a systematic approach to risk management. The key to that approach is developing a program that is both comprehensive and companywide. In the past, risk management was often conducted by different departments or by narrowly focused financial officers. Now, however, more and more firms have not only created high-level risk-management positions, but they are also stressing the need for middle managers to practice risk management on a daily basis. Advises one global risk-management expert, "The breadth of products offered, the complexity of those products, and the global nature of markets, all make top-down, centralized risk management a necessity."

Insurance as Risk Management

To deal with some risks, both businesses and individuals may choose to purchase one or more of the products offered by insurance companies. Buyers find insurance appealing for a very basic reason: In return for a relatively small sum of money, they are protected against certain losses, some of them potentially devastating. In this sense, buying insurance is a function of risk management. To define it as a management activity dealing with insurance, we can thus expand our definition of *risk management* to say that it is the logical development and implementation of a plan to deal with chance losses.

With insurance, then, individuals and businesses share risks by contributing to a fund out of which those who suffer losses are paid. But why are insurance companies willing to accept these risks for other companies? Insurance companies make profits by taking in more **premiums** than they pay out to cover policyholders' losses. Quite simply, although many policyholders are paying for protection against the same type of loss, by no means will all of them suffer such a loss.

premium
Fee paid by a policyholder for insurance coverage

Insurable versus Uninsurable Risks Like every business, insurance companies must avoid certain risks. Insurers thus divide potential sources of loss into *insurable* and *uninsurable risks*. Obviously, they issue policies only for insurable risks. Although there are some exceptions, an insurable risk must meet the four criteria described in the following sections.

1. ***Predictability:*** The insurer must be able to use statistical tools to forecast the likelihood of a loss. For example, an auto insurer needs information about the number of car accidents in the past year to estimate the expected number of accidents for the following year. With this knowledge, the insurer can translate expected numbers and types of accidents into expected dollar losses. The same forecast, of course, also helps insurers determine premiums charged to policyholders.
2. ***Casualty:*** A loss must result from an accident, not from an intentional act by the policyholder. Obviously, insurers do not have to cover damages if a policyholder deliberately sets fire to corporate headquarters. To avoid paying in cases of fraud, insurers may refuse to cover losses when they cannot determine whether policyholders' actions contributed to them.
3. ***Unconnectedness:*** Potential losses must be random and must occur independently of other losses. No insurer can afford to write insurance when a large percentage of those who are exposed to a particular kind of loss are likely to suffer such a loss. One insurance company, for instance, would not want all the hurricane coverage in Miami or all the earthquake coverage in Los Angeles. By carefully choosing the risks that it will insure, an insurance company can reduce its chances of a large loss or even insolvency.
4. ***Verifiability:*** Finally, insured losses must be verifiable as to cause, time, place, and amount. Did an employee develop emphysema because of a chemical to which she was exposed or because she smoked 40 cigarettes a day for 30 years? Did the policyholder pay the renewal premium before the

fire destroyed his factory? Were the goods stolen from company offices or from the president's home? What was the insurable value of the destroyed inventory? When all these points have been verified, payment by the insurer goes more smoothly.

The Insurance Product Insurance companies are often distinguished by the types of insurance coverage they offer. Whereas some insurers offer only one area of coverage—life insurance, for example—others offer a broad range. In this section, we describe the four major categories of business insurance: *liability, property, life,* and *health.*

Liability Insurance As we will see in Appendix I, *liability* means responsibility for damages in case of accidental or deliberate harm to individuals or property. **Liability insurance** covers losses resulting from damage to people or property when the insured party is judged liable.

liability insurance
Insurance covering losses resulting from damage to people or property when the insured is judged liable

Workers' Compensation A business is liable for any injury to an employee when the injury arises from activities related to occupation. When workers are permanently or temporarily disabled by job-related accidents or disease, employers are required by law to provide **workers' compensation coverage** for medical expenses, loss of wages, and rehabilitation services. U.S. employers now pay out approximately $60 billion in workers' compensation premiums each year, much of it to public insurers.

workers' compensation coverage
Coverage provided by a firm to employees for medical expenses, loss of wages, and rehabilitation costs resulting from job-related injuries or disease

Property Insurance Firms purchase **property insurance** to cover injuries to themselves resulting from physical damage to or loss of real estate or personal property. Property losses may result from fire, lightning, wind, hail, explosion, theft, vandalism, or other destructive forces. Losses from fire alone in the United States come to over $12 billion per year.

property insurance
Insurance covering losses resulting from physical damage to or loss of the insured's real estate or personal property

Business Interruption Insurance In some cases, loss to property is minimal in comparison to loss of income. A manufacturer, for example, may have to close down for an extended time while repairs to fire damage are being completed. During that time, of course, the company is not generating income. Even so, however, certain expenses—such as taxes, insurance premiums, and salaries for key personnel—may continue. To cover such losses, a firm may buy **business interruption insurance.**

business interruption insurance
Insurance covering income lost during times when a company is unable to conduct business

Life Insurance Insurance can also protect a company's human assets. As part of their benefits packages, many businesses purchase **life insurance** for employees. Life insurance companies accept premiums in return for the promise to pay beneficiaries after the death of insured parties. A portion of the premium is used to cover the insurer's own expenses. The remainder is invested in various types of financial instruments such as corporate bonds and stocks.

life insurance
Insurance paying benefits to the policyholder's survivors

Group Life Insurance Most companies buy **group life insurance,** which is underwritten for groups as a whole rather than for each individual member. The insurer's assessment of potential losses and its pricing of premiums are based on the characteristics of the whole group. Johnson & Johnson's benefit plan, for example, includes group life coverage with a standard program of protection and benefits—a master policy purchased by J&J—that applies equally to all employees.

group life insurance
Insurance underwritten for a group as a whole rather than for each individual in it

Health Insurance **Health insurance** covers losses resulting from medical and hospital expenses as well as income lost from injury or disease. It is, of course, no secret that the cost of health insurance has skyrocketed in recent years. In one recent year, for example, companies paid an average of more than $5,000 per employee on health insurance premiums to both commercial insurers like Prudential, Metropolitan, and Nationwide and special health insurance providers like Blue Cross/Blue Shield.

health insurance
Insurance covering losses resulting from medical and hospital expenses as well as income lost from injury or disease

disability income insurance
Insurance providing continuous income when disability keeps the insured from gainful employment

Disability Income Insurance **Disability income insurance** provides continuous income when disability keeps the insured from gainful employment. Many health insurance policies cover short-term disabilities, sometimes up to two years. Coverage for permanent disability furnishes some stated amount of weekly income—usually 50 to 70 percent of the insured's weekly wages—with payments beginning after a six-month waiting period. Group policies account for over 70 percent of all disability coverage in the United States.

Special Health Care Providers Instead of reimbursement for a health professional's services, Blue Cross/Blue Shield, which is made up of nonprofit health-care membership groups, provides specific service benefits to its subscribers. Many other commercial insurers do the same. What is the advantage to the subscriber or policyholder? No matter what the service actually costs, the special health-care provider will cover the cost. In contrast, when policies provide reimbursement for services received, the policyholder may pay for a portion of the expense if the policy limit is exceeded. Other important options include *health maintenance organizations, preferred provider organizations,* and *point-of-service plans.*

health maintenance organization (HMO)
Organized health-care system providing comprehensive care in return for fixed membership fees

preferred provider organization (PPO)
Arrangement whereby selected professional providers offer services at reduced rates and permit thorough review of their service recommendations

point-of-service plan (POS)
Health-care plan allowing members to select primary-care doctors who may provide services or refer patients to other plan providers

- A **health maintenance organization (HMO)** is an organized health-care system providing comprehensive medical care to its members for a fixed, prepaid fee. In an HMO, all members agree that, except in emergencies, they will receive their health care through the organization.
- A **preferred provider organization (PPO)** is an arrangement whereby selected hospitals and/or doctors agree to provide services at reduced rates and to accept thorough review of their recommendations for medical services. The objective of the PPO is to help control health-care costs by encouraging the use of efficient providers' health-care services.
- A **point-of-service (POS)** plan allows member-patients to select a primary-care doctor who provides medical services but may refer patients to other providers in the plan. In a POS plan, a member can refer themselves outside the plan if he or she is willing to pay an additional fee for services. If a plan doctor makes a referral out of network, the plan pays all or most of the bill.

Special Forms of Business Insurance Many forms of insurance are attractive to both businesses and individuals. For example, homeowners are as concerned about insuring property from fire and theft as are businesses. Businesses, how-

David Scott Sandoval, a technician at the University of Southern Colorado, isn't happy about the fact that his monthly health-insurance premium has just doubled, from $258 to $549. In the past 15 years, managed-care companies haven't been able to keep the promise that they would control employers' health-care costs. As a result, workers now face the largest increases in health-care rates in 10 years, and although most large employers are still absorbing their share of the increases, that policy is likely to become less common in the next few years.

A Healthy Approach Risk Response

An Internet-based system for health assessment called Network Health Systems™ (NHS) <www.nhsinfo.com> uses demographics and lifestyle data to evaluate the chances that any particular individual will experience various kinds of diseases or ailments. That same system also serves as an online resource for managing employee health programs. Many companies use it to assess the risk they run from poor employee health, the costs that they can expect to incur from those risks, and actions that they can take to counter those risks. Employee health is a pure risk for employers. Poor health results in the disruption of business and potentially high costs. Although risk transfer—usually in the form of health insurance for medical services—offsets part of the risk, there still remain health-related consequences (such as absenteeism) that insurance alone does not cover. To overcome these additional consequences, firms can turn to some form of risk control, usually an effective health-promotion program. Although such programs cannot guarantee against additional losses, they permit firms to minimize their harm by allowing them to respond with planned actions.

Armed with health profiles for all client-company employees, the NHS has created a system that collates them into a summary profile—a kind of "company health profile." NHS provides two kinds of organizational reports that are useful in the management of health risks:

1. The *Organizational Assessment* uses personal data collected from employees' responses to an NHS Questionnaire to provide a breakdown of the specific risks from unhealthy behaviors. It also itemizes predicted costs of care in terms of hospitalization, medical care, lost time, and replacement of employees. The client company is given detailed reports on 44 different risk factors (such weight, age at first pregnancy) and their impact on a possible 52 different diseases or conditions (nerve disorders, suicide). Finally, it lists potential problem areas applicable to this specific group of employees. The demographic information then breaks down the group by work type, gender, and specific health risks. The reports also provide information on various resources that the client company can adopt—intervention programs, education materials, benefit plans, and incentive systems—to influence lifestyle changes that will improve employee health.
2. *The Cost Analysis* evaluates the costs that the organization will incur over an upcoming 12-month period as a result of risk factors present and specifies the portion of those costs likely to be entailed by employee lifestyle. Further, it identifies which costs are nonreversible versus those that can be reversed through various wellness actions. It also cites the costs of implementing those actions. Using this data, the organization targets those areas of risk that offer savings justifying the program expense. The report makes specific recommendations on those areas that are most likely to realize the greatest savings.

In essence, therefore, health-profile reports provide a cost/benefit analysis in the area of health promotion which, until now, has been either neglected or, at best, an area of subjective decision making. In addition to helping to structure a company's benefit and insurance offerings, these reports thus form the basis for the planning of case management, employee-assistance programs, health promotion, and wellness programs, as well as structuring the company's benefit and insurance offerings.

ever, have some special insurable concerns. In this section, we will discuss two forms of insurance that apply to the departure or death of key employees or owners: *Key person insurance* and *business continuation agreements.*

Key Person Insurance Many businesses choose to protect themselves against loss of the talents and skills of key employees. For example, if a salesperson who annually rings up $2.5 million dies or takes a new job, the firm will suffer loss. It will also incur recruitment costs to find a replacement and training expenses once a replacement is hired. **Key person insurance** is designed to offset both lost income and additional expenses.

key-person insurance
Special form of business insurance designed to offset expenses entailed by the loss of key employees

Self-Check Questions 7–9

*You should now be able to answer Self-Check Questions 7–9**

7. MULTIPLE CHOICE Because you're concerned about on-the-job safety for your employees, you initiate a training program that emphasizes safe work practices in the office, in the use of operating equipment, and even for driving in the parking lot. This program is an example of which of the following *risk-management techniques*? [select one]: **(a)** risk avoidance; **(b)** risk control; **(c)** risk retention; **(d)** risk transfer; **(e)** none of the above.

8. TRUE/FALSE As the owner of a small business, you determine a temporary need for $15,000 to meet cash flow requirements for the next two months. At present, you have a line of credit at a neighborhood bank. You also have outstanding accounts payable to a supplier with whom you're on good financial terms. Given these circumstances, either the bank or the supplier, or both, are feasible *sources of credit* for the cash you need.

9. MULTIPLE CHOICE Potential for earthquakes was a risk for the 2002 World Cup Soccer Championships in Japan and South Korea. A consortium of insurance companies sold earthquake insurance for protection against loss of revenues to local businesses and the World Cup Federation. The use of a group of insurance firms, rather than just one company, illustrates which of the following *insurable risk* criteria? [select one]: **(a)** predictability; **(b)** casualty; **(c)** unconnectedness; **(d)** verifiability; **(e)** none of the above.

*ANSWERS TO SELF-CHECK QUESTIONS 7–9 CAN BE FOUND ON P. AN-14.

business continuation agreement
Special form of business insurance whereby owners arrange to buy the interests of deceased associates from their heirs

Business Continuation Agreements Who takes control of a business when a partner or associate dies? Surviving partners are often faced with the possibility of having to accept an inexperienced heir as a management partner. This contingency can be handled in **business continuation agreements,** whereby owners make plans to buy the ownership interest of a deceased associate from his or her heirs. The value of the ownership interest is determined when the agreement is made. Special policies can also provide survivors with the funds needed to make the purchase.

Continued from page 583

Betting Against Earthquakes

Hooliganism wasn't the only threat to the World Cup Championships. Weather, too, posed financial risks. FIFA and the host cities had to be prepared for Southeast Asia's rainy season, which coincided with the month-long tournament in June 2002. In addition to cities where the games were played, 22 other towns hosted training camps that would generate revenues for local businesses. All of this money could be lost if matches were rescheduled or cancelled due to bad weather. Thus businesses located near stadiums paid

$8,000 for coverage from Tokyo-based Mitsui Sumitomo Insurance Co., which would pay out $12,000 for each day that rain reached 0.4 inches (up to a limit of $120,000).

Aside from weather, the two host countries posed different kinds of risks. Earthquakes can hit in Japan, and political unrest poses a threat in South Korea. Earthquake insurance covered all 10 Japanese stadiums, with coverage applying to any quake measuring between 6.8 and 7.9 on the Richter scale. The cost for such insurance is high, but so are the potential losses from shutting down the World Cup games. As for the possibility of political unrest and terrorism, FIFA purchased event cancellation coverage, with payouts of up to $870 million for a shutdown due to terrorism, from a consortium of insurance firms led by Paris-based insurer AXA S.A. Citing "the current uncertain international climate," AXA terminated the coverage in October 2001, following the September 11 terrorist attacks in the United States, but FIFA was able to secure new coverage with U.S.-based National Indemnity Co.

Even with all of this insurance, FIFA took additional risk-management steps on several fronts. To reduce vandalism and hooliganism, French security strategies were studied; 5,500 riot police officers in Japan were trained to handle violent fans; and plans were developed with other nations to keep known hooligans away from the games. Above all, however, stadium location was a major factor in risk reduction. Many of the stadiums were located in rural venues, and railways and roads were built to take fans directly to and from hotels and stadiums without stopovers and crowd interference. "One of the main reasons for outbreaks of violence," explained a FIFA spokesman, "is the geographic layout of the city. In Europe, for example, the town center is within reachable distance of the stadium. It's easy for fans to get drunk, go to the stadium, and cause havoc."

Another way to protect against stadium shutdowns is to arrange for backup stadiums. Although the tournament could be played in seven stadiums, 20 were made available—10 in each host country. If an earthquake hit in one location, matches could be moved to replacement sites in the other so that the tournament would not have to be cancelled.

It turns out that terrorism and political unrest did not materialize during the 2002 championships. Hooliganism, too, was minimal. The rains came but caused little disruption and, overall, the games—won by Brazil—were successful from both a sporting and financial standpoint. But the game isn't over for Switzerland-based FIFA. It is now preparing for the 2006 competition, to be held in Germany, which will present its own set of risks.

Questions for Discussion

1. Give an example of the use of risk control and an example of risk transfer in the 2002 World Cup Championships.
2. What are some additional risks, other than those discussed in the case, that FIFA officials faced in choosing Japan and Korea as host countries for 2002?
3. From a financial-management standpoint, why was it a good idea for FIFA to hire a single firm to manage the marketing of worldwide branding rights?
4. Why might an insurance company prefer to participate in a consortium of insurers, rather than alone, in providing earthquake or terrorism coverage for the World Cup Championships?
5. In what ways might the risks for the 2002 venues in Japan and Korea differ from those for the 2006 World Cup in Germany?

Summary of Learning Objectives

1. ***Describe the responsibilities of a* financial manager.**

Finance (or **corporate finance**) entails four responsibilities: (1) Determining long-term investments; (2) obtaining funds to pay for those investments; (3) conducting everyday financial activities; and (4) helping to manage risks. **Financial managers** plan and control the acquisition and dispersal of financial resources. They collect funds, pay debts, establish trade credit, obtain loans, control cash balances, and plan for future financial needs. But a financial manager's overall objective is to increase a firm's value and stockholders' wealth. They must ensure that earnings exceed its costs—in other words, a profit.

The responsibilities of the financial manager fall into two general categories: (1) **Cash-flow management:** Financial managers must ensure that the company has enough funds on hand to purchase the resources that it needs to produce products. Funds not needed immediately must be invested to earn money. (2) **Financial control** is the process of checking actual performance against plans to ensure that desired financial results occur. Control involves monitoring revenue inflows and making appropriate financial adjustments. The budget is often the backbone of financial control because it provides the measuring stick against which performance is evaluated. Cash flows, debts, and assets are regularly compared against budgeted amounts. Discrepancies indicate the need for adjustments.

The cornerstone of financial management is the **financial plan** that describes a firm's strategies for reaching some future financial position. Financial managers must know the amount and sources of funds needed to meet both short- and long-term needs. They must develop a clear picture of why a firm needs funds, and they must assess the costs and benefits of different sources.

2. ***Distinguish between* short-term (operating) *and* long-term (capital) *expenditures.***

Short-term (operating) expenditures are incurred in a firm's everyday business activities. Managers must pay special attention to three areas of financial activity: (1) *Accounts payable*: Financial managers want to know *in advance* the amounts of new accounts payable—unpaid bills owed to suppliers and due within the upcoming year—as well as when each must be repaid.

(2) *Accounts receivable*: Because accounts receivable temporarily tie up funds, financial managers must project accurately both how much credit is advanced to buyers and when buyers who have bought on credit will make payments. Predicting payment schedules is a function of **credit policy:** the rules governing a firm's extension of credit to customers.

(3) *Inventories*: Between the time a firm buys raw materials and the time it sells finished products, it ties up funds in **inventory**—materials and goods that it will sell within the year. Too little inventory can cost sales; too much inventory means tied-up funds. **Working capital** is the difference between a firm's current assets and current liabilities. It is a liquid asset from which current debts can be paid. We calculate working capital by adding up (i) *inventories* (raw materials, work-in-process, and finished goods on hand) and (ii) *accounts receivable* (minus accounts payable). There are two advantages in reducing working capital: (i) Every dollar not tied up in working capital becomes a dollar of more useful cash flow; (ii) reduction of working capital raises earnings permanently.

Companies also need funds to cover *long-term (capital) expenditures* on *fixed assets*—items with long-term use or value, such as land, buildings, and machinery. Long-term expenditures differ from short-term outlays in the following ways: (i) They are not normally sold or converted into cash; (ii) their acquisition requires a large investment; (iii) they represent binding, long-term commitments of funds.

3. ***Identify four sources of* short-term financing *for businesses.***

(1) *Trade credit*: Until it pays its bill, a buyer has the use of both the purchased product and its purchase price. This situation results when the seller grants **trade credit,** which is really a short-term loan from one firm to another. It can take several forms: (i) With **open-book credit,** buyers receive merchandise along with invoices stating credit terms; sellers ship products on faith that payment will be forthcoming. (ii) Legally binding **promissory notes** state when and how much money will be paid to the seller. (iii) The **trade draft** is attached to the merchandise shipment by the seller and states the promised date and amount due. To take possession of the merchandise, the buyer must sign the draft. Once signed, it becomes a **trade acceptance.**

(2) *Secured short-term loans*: Bank loans usually involve promissory notes in which the borrower promises to repay the loan plus interest. Secured loans allow borrowers to get funds when they might not qualify for unsecured credit. In **secured loans,** banks also require **collateral:** a legal interest in assets that can be seized if payments are not made as promised. There are two forms of collateral: (i) *Inventory loans*: When inventory serves as a collateral asset, the lender lends the borrower some portion of the stated value of the inventory. (ii) *Accounts receivable*: When accounts receivable are used as collateral, the process is called **pledging accounts receivable.**

(3) *Factoring accounts receivable*: A firm can raise funds rapidly by *factoring*—selling the firm's accounts receivable. In this process, the purchaser of the receivables is known as the *factor.* Because the factor pays some percentage of the full amount due to the selling firm, the seller gets this money immediately.

(4) *Unsecured short-term loans*: With an **unsecured loan,** the borrower does not have to put up collateral. The bank may, however, require the borrower to maintain a *compensating balance*—a portion of the loan amount kept on deposit with the bank. Many unsecured loans take one of the following forms: (i) A **line of credit** is a standing agreement between a bank and a business in which the bank promises to lend the firm a maximum amount of funds on request. (ii) With a **revolving credit agreement,** a bank agrees to make some amount of funds available on a continuing basis. The lender guarantees that the funds will be available and charges a commitment fee. (iii) Some firms can raise short-term funds by issuing **commercial paper**—short-term securities, or notes, containing the borrower's promise to pay.

4. ***Distinguish among the various sources of* long-term financing *and explain the risks entailed by each type.***

Firms may seek long-term funds to pay for fixed assets through two channels:

(1) Long-term borrowing from sources outside the company is called **debt financing.** *Long-term* means that obligations are payable more than one year after originally issued. There are two primary sources of such funding: (i) Most corporations get *long-term loans* from commercial banks. These loans are attractive to borrowers because they can often be arranged quickly, and they are designed to meet borrowers' needs. On the other hand, borrowers may have trouble finding lenders for large sums and may have to pledge long-term assets as collateral. Interest rates are negotiated between borrower and lender.

(ii) A *corporate bond* is a promise by the issuer to pay the holder a certain amount of money on a specified date. Most bonds pay stipulated sums of annual or semiannual interest, and if a company fails to make a payment, it is *in default.* Bonds are attractive when firms need large amounts for long periods of time. The issuer gains access to large numbers of lenders through bond markets and stock exchanges but may also face stiff interest payments. The terms of a bond are spelled out in a contract called the **bond indenture.**

(2) Looking inside the company for long-term funding is sometimes preferable to debt financing. **Equity financing** usually means issuing common stock or retaining earnings. (i) *Common stock*: By issuing shares of common stock, a company gets funds from people seeking profits in two forms—dividends and appreciation. Equity financing by means of

common stock can be expensive because paying dividends is more expensive than paying bond interest. (ii) *Retained earnings*: **Retained earnings** are profits retained for the firm's use rather than paid out in dividends. If a company uses retained earnings as capital, it will not have to borrow money and pay interest. But because retained earnings mean smaller shareholder dividends, the practice may decrease the demand for—and thus the price of—the company's stock.

A middle ground between debt financing and equity financing is the use of *preferred stock*, which is a "hybrid" because it has features of both corporate bonds and common stocks. As with bonds, payments on preferred stock are fixed amounts. But like common stock, preferred stock can be held indefinitely.

A key aspect of financial planning is striking a balance between debt and equity financing. Because a firm relies on a mix of debt and equity to raise the cash needed for capital outlays, that mix is called its **capital structure.** A range of mixes is possible, and strategies range from conservative to risky. The most conservative strategy is all-equity financing and no debt; the riskiest strategy is all-debt financing. Somewhere between the two extremes, financial planners try to find mixes that will increase stockholders' wealth with a reasonable exposure to risk.

Financial managers often rely on published indexes, such as Standard & Poor's, to determine how a particular investment compares to other opportunities in terms of stability. Financial managers must also be aware of the different motivations of individual investors. Everyone who invests money is expressing a personal preference for safety versus risk, and investors generally expect to receive higher payments for higher uncertainty. Each type of investment, then, has a **risk-return relationship** reflecting the principle that whereas safer investments tend to offer lower returns, riskier investments tend to offer higher returns. By gauging investors' perceptions of these investments' riskiness, a firm's managers can estimate how much they must pay to attract funds to their offerings.

5. *Discuss some key issues in financial management for small business.*

Obtaining credit begins with finding a bank that will support a small firm's financial needs. Once a *line of credit* is obtained, the small business can seek more liberal credit policies from other businesses. Obtaining long-term loans is more difficult for new businesses than for established companies, and start-ups pay higher interest rates than older firms. To demonstrate that it's a good credit risk, a start-up must usually present a *business plan*—a document explaining why the money is needed, the amount, how it will be used to improve the company, and when it will be paid back.

Many newer businesses can't get needed funds through borrowing alone. They may turn to **venture capital:** outside equity funding provided in return for part ownership. But with high failure rates, such investors demand high returns. Planning for cash flows is especially important for small businesses. Success or failure may hinge on anticipating those times when either cash will be short or excess cash can be expected. By anticipating shortfalls, a financial manager can seek funds in advance and minimize the cost. By anticipating excess cash, a manager can put funds to work in short-term, interest-earning investments.

6. *Explain how* risk *affects business operations and identify the five steps in the* risk management process.

Businesses face two basic types of **risk**—that is, uncertainty about future events. (1) **Speculative risks,** such as financial investments, involve the possibility of gain or loss. (2) **Pure risks** (such as the chance of a warehouse fire) involve only the possibility of loss or no loss. **Risk management** entails conserving earning power and assets by reducing the threat of losses due to uncontrollable events. The process entails five steps: (1) *Step 1: Identify risks and potential losses*: Analyze risks to identify potential losses. A firm with a fleet of delivery trucks can expect one of them eventually to be in an accident. (2) *Step 2: Measure the frequency and severity of losses and their impact*: To measure the frequency and severity of losses, consider past history and current activities. (How often can the firm expect a loss to occur?)

(3) *Step 3: Evaluate alternatives, and choose the techniques that will best handle the losses*: Decide how to handle risks from among four choices: (i) A firm opts for **risk avoidance** by declining to enter or by ceasing to participate in a risky activity. (ii) Firms can practice **risk control** when they use loss-prevention techniques to minimize the frequency of losses. (iii) When unavoidable losses are manageable and predictable, firms may cover them out of company funds. Thus, they assume or retain the financial consequences through **risk retention.** (iv) When the potential for large risks can't be avoided or controlled, firms may opt for **risk transfer:** They transfer the risk to another firm—namely, an insurance company.

(4) *Step 4: Implement the risk-management program*: The means of implementing risk-management decisions depend on both the technique chosen and the activity being managed. (5) *Step 5: Monitor results*: Managers must monitor risks, reevaluate methods for handling them, and revise them as necessary.

7. *Explain the distinction between* insurable *and* uninsurable risks *and distinguish among the different* types of insurance *purchased by businesses.*

In return for a relatively small sum of money, insurance buyers are protected against certain losses. Thus, buying insurance is a function of *risk management,* which is the implementation of a plan to deal with chance losses. Insurance companies make profits by taking in more **premiums** than they pay out to cover policyholders' losses. Insurers divide potential losses into *insurable* and *uninsurable risks,* and an insurable risk must meet four criteria: (1) *Predictability:* The insurer must be able to use statistical tools to forecast the likelihood of a loss. (2) *Casualty:* A loss must result from an accident, not from an intentional act. (3) *Unconnectedness*: Potential losses must be random and occur independently of other losses. (4) *Verifiability:* Insured losses must be verifiable as to cause, time, place, and amount.

There are four major categories of business insurance: (1) *Liability insurance: Liability* means responsibility for damages in case of accidental or deliberate harm, and **liability insurance** covers losses resulting from damage to people or property when the insured party is held liable. The law requires most employers to provide employees injured on the job with **workers' compensation coverage** for medical expenses, loss of wages, and rehabilitation services.

(2) *Property insurance*: Firms purchase **property insurance** to cover injuries to themselves resulting from damage to or loss of real estate or personal property. A firm may buy **business interruption insurance** to cover expenses incurred when it is closed down and generating no income.

(3) *Life insurance*: **Life insurance** policies promise to pay beneficiaries after the death of insured parties. Most companies buy **group life insurance,** which is underwritten for groups as a whole rather than for each individual member.

(4) *Health insurance*: **Health insurance** covers losses resulting from medical and hospital expenses as well as income lost from injury or disease. **Disability income insurance** provides continuous income when disability keeps the insured from gainful employment. Health insurers include the following: (i) A **health maintenance organization (HMO)** is an organized health-care system providing comprehensive medical care for a fixed, prepaid fee. (ii) In a **preferred provider organization (PPO),** hospitals and/or doctors agree to provide services at reduced rates and to accept thorough review of their recommendations for services. (iii) A **point-of-service (POS)** plan allows patients to select a primary-care doctor who provides medical services but may refer patients to other providers in the plan.

Two forms of business insurance apply to the loss of key employees or owners: (1) Many businesses protect themselves against loss of the talents and skills of key employees by buying **key-person insurance.** (2) Certain contingencies are handled in **business continuation agreements,** in which owners make plans to transfer the ownership interest of a deceased associate.

KEY TERMS

finance (or ***corporate finance***) (p. 584)
financial manager (p. 584)
cash-flow management (p. 584)
financial control (p. 584)
financial plan (p. 585)
credit policy (p. 586)
inventory (p. 586)
working capital (p. 586)
trade credit (p. 587)
open-book credit (p. 587)
promissory note (p. 587)
trade draft (p. 587)
trade acceptance (p. 587)
collateral (p. 587)
secured loan (p. 587)
pledging accounts receivable (p. 588)
unsecured loan (p. 5588)
line of credit (p. 588)
revolving credit agreement (p. 589)
commercial paper (p. 589)
debt financing (p. 589)
bond indenture (p. 591)
equity financing (p. 591)
capital structure (p. 594)
risk-return relationship (p. 595)
venture capital (p. 598)
risk (p. 598)
speculative risk (p. 598)
pure risk (p. 598)
risk management (p. 599)
risk avoidance (p. 600)
risk control (p. 600)
risk retention (p. 600)
risk transfer (p. 600)
premium (p. 602)
liability insurance (p. 603)
workers' compensation coverage (p. 603)
property insurance (p. 603)
business interruption insurance (p. 603)
life insurance (p. 603)
group life insurance (p. 603)
health insurance (p. 603)
disability income insurance (p. 604)
health maintenance organization (HMO) (p. 604)
preferred provider organization (PPO) (p. 604)
point-of-service plan (POS) (p. 604)
key-person insurance (p. 605)
business continuation agreement (p. 606)

QUESTIONS AND EXERCISES

Questions for Review

1. What are four short-term sources of funds for financing day-to-day business operations? Identify the advantages and disadvantages of each.
2. In what ways do the two sources of debt financing differ from each other? How do they differ from the two sources of equity financing?
3. Describe the relationship between investment risk and return. In what ways might the risk-return relationship affect a company's financial planning?
4. Give two examples of risks that are uninsurable. Why are they uninsurable?
5. Describe the risk-management process. What are the major roles of a company's risk manager?

Questions for Analysis

6. How would you decide on the best mix of debt, equity, and preferred stock for a company?
7. Why is liability insurance important to business firms?

8. As a risk manager of a large firm, what risks do you think your firm faces? For a small firm? What accounts for the most important differences?

Application Exercises

9. Interview the owner of a small local business. Identify the types of short-term and long-term funding that this firm typically uses. Why has the company made the financial management decisions that it has?
10. Interview the owner of a small local business. Ask this person to describe the risk management process that he or she follows. What role, for example, is played by risk transfer? Why has the company made the risk-management decisions that it has?

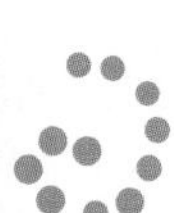

Building Your Business Skills

MINIMIZING THE NEGATIVES

This exercise enhances the following SCANS workplace competencies: demonstrating basic skills, demonstrating thinking skills, exhibiting interpersonal skills, working with information, and applying system knowledge.

Goal

To encourage students to better understand the major financial and risk management issues that face large companies

Background

In the 2001–2002 period, all of the following companies reported financial problems relating to risk management:

- Levi Strauss & Co. <www.levistrauss.com>
- UAL Corporation <www.ual.com>
- Halliburton Company <www.halliburton.com>
- EarthLink Inc. <www.earthlink.com>
- El Paso Energy Corp. <www.epenergy.com>

Method

Step 1

Working alone, research one of the companies listed here to learn more about the financial risks that were reported in the news.

Step 2

Write a short explanation of the financial and management issues that were faced by the firm that you researched.

Step 3

Join in teams with students who researched other companies and compare your findings.

Follow-Up Questions

1. Were there common themes in the "big stories" in financial management?
2. What have the various companies done to minimize future risks and losses?

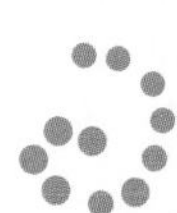

Exercising Your Ethics

DOING YOUR DUTY WHEN PAYABLES COME DUE

The Situation

Assume you work as a manager for one of the world's best-known conglomerates. As the end of the fiscal year approaches, you are attending an Executive Committee meeting at which the CEO, the firm's dominant leader, expresses concern that the firm's year-end cash position will be less favorable than projected. The firm has exceeded analysts' performance expectations in each of his eight years at the helm and he is determined that stockholders will never be disappointed as long as he is CEO. The purpose of the meeting is to find solutions to the cash problem and decide on a course(s) of action.

The Dilemma

To open the meeting, CEO Charles Z. announces, "We have just two weeks either to reduce expenses or to increase revenues; we need a $400 million swing to get us where market analysts predicted we'd be on cash flows for the year. Any suggestions?"

Discussion reveals that the firm has outstanding payables, amounting to hundreds of millions of dollars, owed to thousands of firms that supply manufacturing components and operating supplies. The payables are due before year-end. According to the financial officer, "Our cash outflows for the year will be lower if we delay paying suppliers, which will help the bottom line. And, it's like getting a free loan." The procurement director is concerned, however. "Our agreements with suppliers call for faithful payments at designated times, and many of the smaller firms depend on receiving that cash to meet their obligations. Also, we've worked hard for two years at improving relationships with all suppliers, and that effort could go down the drain if we don't meet our financial commitments as promised."

As the meeting drew to a close, Charles Z. announced, "Keep me posted on any unexpected developments, but if nothing helpful comes up in the next few days, let's go ahead and withhold supplier payments for three weeks."

Questions for Discussion

1. What are the ethical issues in this case?
2. What are the basic arguments for and against Charles Z.'s position on withholding payments?
3. What do you think most managers would do in this situation? What would you do?

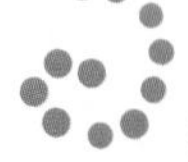

Crafting Your Business Plan

PICKING UP SPEED ON THE FAST TRACK

The Purpose of the Assignment

1. To familiarize students with financial and risk management issues that a sample firm may face in developing its business plan, in the framework of *Business PlanPro* (*BPP*) software package.
2. To demonstrate how three chapter topics—start-up financing, risk management, and pure risks—can be integrated as components in the *BPP* planning environment.

Assignment

After reading Chapter 20 in the textbook, open the BPP software and search for information about both financial risks for a start-up company and risk management as they apply to a sample firm: Southeast Racing Parts. *To find* Southeast Racing, *do the following:*

Open the *Business PlanPro 2002.* If it asks if you want to "create a new business plan" or "open an existing plan," select "create a new business plan" (even though you are not going to create a plan at this time). You will then be taken to the *Business PlanPro EasyPlan Wizard.* Click the option entitled **Research It.** You will then be presented with a new list of options, including **Sample Plan Browser.** After clicking on the **Sample Plan Browser,** go down the alphabetical list of sample plans, and double-click on **Automotive—Parts Mfr.,** which is the location for *Southeast Racing Parts.* The screen you are looking at is the introductory page for the *Southeast Racing* business plan. Next, scroll down from this page until you reach the **Table of Contents** for the company's business plan.

Now respond to the following items:

1. Based on its business plan, would you loan Southeast Racing the $60,625 start-up capital? What are your reasons? What payback terms would you require? Explain. [Sites to see in *BPP* (for this item): On the Table of Contents page, click on each of the following in turn: **1.1 Objectives, 2.1 Company Ownership, 2.2 Startup Summary, 6.1 Management Team,** and **7.0 Financial Plan.**]
2. Consider Southeast Racing's facility needs—specifically, 3,000 square feet in the office building. If you were the building manager, would you see any risks in leasing to Southeast Racing? If so, identify them. [Sites to see in *BPP*: On the Table of Contents page, click on each of the following in turn: **2.4 Company Facility** and **7.4 Projected Profit and Loss.**]
3. Chapter 20 discusses pure risks and ways to cope with them. Identify some pure risks and potential losses that Southeast Racing faces in its day-to-day operations. What techniques do you recommend for handling Southeast's potential losses? [Sites to see in *BPP:* From the Table of Contents page, click on each of the following in turn: **3.0 Products and Services, 3.1 Product and Service Description, 3.6 Future Products and Services, 4.2.2 Market Trends,** and **5.1.3 Distribution Strategy.**]

Video Exercise

NAILING DOWN FINANCIAL MANAGEMENT: SECHE INTERNATIONAL

Learning Objectives

The purpose of this video is to help you to:

1. Understand the financial consequences of protecting intellectual property such as patented product formulations and trademarks.
2. Identify some of the ways a small company can manage its funding requirements.
3. Discuss the role of the chief financial officer in a growing business.

Synopsis

Seche International makes innovative nail-care products used in salons around the world. But just two years after introducing its first product, the company learned that some rivals were copying the formula and others selling counterfeit versions of the product. To fight back, Seche management embarked on a legal battle to remove fakes from the market and to protect the company's patents. Unfortunately, the aftermath of the lengthy and expensive legal struggle found the firm faced with the daunting task of rebuilding its financial position. Through responsible and conscientious financial management, Seche emerged more secure and ready for the challenge of implementing an aggressive growth strategy.

Discussion Questions

1. *For analysis:* Why would Seche have a negative cash flow at the beginning of its production cycle?
2. *For analysis:* Why would venture capital firms be reluctant to invest in Seche during its legal battles?
3. *For application:* Which sources of short-term funds should Seche's CFO pursue now that the company's financial position is stronger?
4. *For application:* Which short-term expenditures would most likely increase as Seche implements an aggressive growth strategy?
5. *For debate:* Seche's management made a deliberate decision to take legal action against competitors who infringed on its patents and trademarks. Considering the huge financial burden that these legal battles placed on the company, do you agree with management's decision? Support your chosen position.

Online Exploration

Visit the Seche International site at <www.seche.com>. Browse various links to read about the company, its products, its global distributors, and its trademarks. Also read the question-and-answer section. Why would Seche post trademark details on its site? Why would Seche alert customers to ways of detecting counterfeit products? As a consumer, what concerns might you have about using a nail-care product that appeared to be made by Seche but turned out to be counterfeit?

Appendix

Understanding the Legal Context of Business

In this appendix, we describe the basic tenets of U.S. law and show how these principles work through the court system. We will also survey a few major areas of business-related law. By focusing on the learning objectives of this appendix, you will see that laws may create opportunities for business activity just as readily as they set limits on them.

The U.S. Legal and Judicial Systems

If people could ignore contracts or drive down city streets at any speed, it would be unsafe to do business on Main Street—or even to set foot in public. Without law, people would be free to act "at will," and life and property would constantly be at risk. **Laws** are the codified rules of behavior enforced by a society. In the United States, laws fall into three broad categories according to their origins: *common, statutory,* and *regulatory.* After discussing each of these types of laws, we will briefly describe the three-tier system of courts through which the judicial system administers the law in the United States.

laws
Codified rules of behavior enforced by a society

Types of Law

Law in the United States originates primarily with English common law. Its sources include the U.S. Constitution, state constitutions, federal and state statutes, municipal ordinances, administrative agency rules and regulations, executive orders, and court decisions.

Common Law Court decisions follow *precedents,* or the decisions of earlier cases. Following precedent lends stability to the law by basing judicial decisions on cases anchored in similar facts. This principle is the keystone of **common law:** the body of decisions handed down by courts ruling on individual cases. Although some facets of common law predate the American Revolution (and even hearken back to medieval Europe), common law continues to evolve in the courts today.

common law
Body of decisions handed down by courts ruling on individual cases

Statutory Law Laws created by constitutions or by federal, state, or local legislative acts constitute **statutory law.** For example, Article I of the U.S. Constitution is a statutory law that empowers Congress to pass laws on corporate taxation, the zoning authority of municipalities, and the rights and privileges of businesses operating in the United States.

statutory law
Law created by constitutions or by federal, state, or local legislative acts

State legislatures and city councils also pass statutory laws. Some state laws, for example, prohibit the production or sale of detergents containing phosphates, which are believed to be pollutants. Nearly every town has ordinances specifying sites for certain types of industries or designating areas where cars cannot be parked during certain hours.

Regulatory Law Statutory and common law have long histories. Relatively new is **regulatory (or administrative) law:** law made by the authority of administrative agencies. By and large, the expansion of U.S. regulatory law has paralleled the nation's economic and technological development. Lacking the technical expertise to develop specialized legislation for specialized business activities, Congress

regulatory (or administrative) law
Law made by the authority of administrative agencies

established the first administrative agencies to create and administer the needed laws in the late 1800s. Before the early 1960s, most agencies concerned themselves with the *economic* regulation of specific areas of business—say, transportation or securities. Since then, many agencies have been established to pursue narrower *social* objectives. They focus on issues that cut across different sectors of the economy—clean air, for example, or product testing.

Today a host of agencies, including the Equal Employment Opportunity Commission (EEOC), the Environmental Protection Agency (EPA), the Food and Drug Administration (FDA), the Federal Trade Commission (FTC), and the Occupational Safety and Health Administration (OSHA), regulate U.S. business practices.

In this section, we look briefly at the nature of regulatory agencies and describe some of the key legislation that makes up administrative law in this country. We also discuss an area of increasing importance in the relationship between government and business: regulation—or, more accurately, *deregulation*.

Agencies and Legislation Although Congress retains control over the scope of agency action, once passed, regulations have the force of statutory law. Government regulatory agencies act as a secondary judicial system, determining whether regulations have been violated and imposing penalties. A firm that violates OSHA rules, for example, may receive a citation, a hearing, and perhaps a heavy fine. Much agency activity consists of setting standards for safety or quality and monitoring the compliance of businesses. The FDA, for example, is responsible for ensuring that food, medicines, and even cosmetics are safe and effective.

Regulatory laws have been on the books for nearly a century. As early as 1906, for example, the Pure Food and Drug Act mandated minimum levels of cleanliness and sanitation for food and drug companies. More recently, the Children's Television Act of 1990 required that broadcasters meet the educational and informational needs of younger viewers and limit the amount of advertising broadcast during children's programs. In 1996, a sweeping new law to increase competition in the communications industry required television makers to install a "V-chip," which allows parents to block undesirable programming. And Congress continues to debate the possibility of regulating the Internet.

Congress has created many new agencies in response to pressure to address social issues. In some cases, agencies were established in response to public concern about corporate behavior. The activities of these agencies have sometimes forced U.S. firms to consider the public interest almost as routinely as they consider their own financial performance.

The Move Toward Deregulation Although government regulation has benefited U.S. business in many ways, it is not without its drawbacks. Businesspeople complain—with some justification—that government regulations require too much paperwork. To comply with just one OSHA regulation for a year, Goodyear once generated 345,000 pages of computer reports weighing 3,200 pounds. It now costs Goodyear $35.5 million each year to comply with the regulations of six government agencies, and it takes 36 employee-years annually (the equivalent of one employee working full time for 36 years) to fill out the required reports.

Not surprisingly, many people in both business and government support broader **deregulation**: the elimination of rules that restrict business activity. Advocates of both regulation and deregulation claim that each acts to control business expansion and prices, increase government efficiency, and right wrongs that the marketplace cannot or does not handle itself. Regulations such as those enforced by the EEOC, for example, are supposed to control undesirable business practices in the interest of social equity. In contrast, the court-ordered breakup of AT&T was prompted by a perceived need for greater market effi-

deregulation

Elimination of rules that restrict business activity

ciency. For these and other reasons, the federal government began deregulating certain industries in the 1970s.

It is important to note that the United States is the only industrialized nation that has deregulated key industries—financial services, transportation, telecommunications, and a host of others. A 1996 law, for instance, allowed the seven "Baby Bells"—regional phone companies created when AT&T was broken up—to compete for long-distance business. It also allowed cable television and telephone companies to enter each other's markets by offering any combination of video, telephone, and high-speed data communications services. Many analysts contend that such deregulation is now and will become an even greater advantage in an era of global competition. Deregulation, they argue, is a primary incentive to innovation.

According to this view, deregulated industries are forced to innovate in order to survive in fiercely competitive industries. Those firms that are already conditioned to compete by being more creative will outperform firms that have been protected by regulatory climates in their home countries. "What's important," says one economist, "is that competition energizes new ways of doing things." The U.S. telecommunications industry, proponents of this view say, is twice as productive as its European counterparts because it is the only such industry forced to come out from under a protective regulatory umbrella.

The U.S. Judicial System

Laws are of little use unless they are enforced. Much of the responsibility for law enforcement falls to the courts. Although few people would claim that the courts are capable of resolving every dispute, there often seem to be more than enough lawyers to handle them all. Indeed, there are 140 lawyers for every 100,000 people in the United States. Litigation is a significant part of contemporary life, and we have given our courts a voice in a wide range of issues, some touching profoundly personal concerns, some ruling on matters of public policy that affect all our lives. In this section, we look at the operations of the U.S. judicial system.

The Court System There are three levels in the U.S. judicial system—*federal, state,* and *local.* These levels reflect the federalist structure of a system in which a central government shares power with state or local governments. Federal courts were created by the U.S. Constitution. They hear cases on questions of constitutional law, disputes relating to maritime laws, and violations of federal statutes. They also rule on regulatory actions and on such issues as bankruptcy, postal law, and copyright or patent violation. Both the federal and most state systems embody a three-tiered system of *trial, appellate,* and *supreme courts.*

Trial Courts At the lowest level of the federal court system are the **trial courts,** general courts that hear cases not specifically assigned to another court. A case involving contract violation would go before a trial court. Every state has at least one federal trial court, called a district court.

trial court
General court that hears cases not specifically assigned to another court

Trial courts also include special courts and administrative agencies. Special courts hear specific types of cases, such as cases involving tax evasion, fraud, international disputes, or claims against the U.S. government. Within their areas of jurisdiction, administrative agencies also make judgments much like those of courts.

Courts in each state system deal with the same issues as their federal counterparts. However, they may rule only in areas governed by state law. For example, a case involving state income tax laws would be heard by a state special court. Local courts in each state system also hear cases on municipal ordinances, local traffic violations, and similar issues.

appellate court

Court that reviews case records of trials whose findings have been appealed

Appellate Courts A losing party may disagree with a trial court ruling. If that party can show grounds for review, the case may go before a federal or state **appellate court**. These courts consider questions of law, such as possible errors of legal interpretation made by lower courts. They, do not examine questions of fact. There are now 13 federal courts of appeal, each with 3 to 15 judges. Cases are normally heard by three-judge panels.

Supreme Courts Cases still not resolved at the appellate level can be appealed to the appropriate state supreme courts or to the U.S. Supreme Court. If it believes that an appeal is warranted or that the outcome will set an important precedent, the U.S. Supreme Court also hears cases appealed from state supreme courts. Each year, the U.S. Supreme Court receives about 5,000 appeals but typically agrees to hear fewer than 200.

Business Law

Most legal issues confronted by businesses fall into one of six basic areas: *contract, tort, property, agency, commercial,* or *bankruptcy law.* These areas cover a wide range of business activity.

Contract Law

contract

Agreement between two or more parties enforceable in court

A **contract** is any agreement between two or more parties that is enforceable in court. As such, it must meet six conditions. If all these conditions are met, one party can seek legal recourse from another if the other party breaches (that is, violates) the terms of the agreement.

capacity

Competence required of individuals entering into a binding contract

considerations

Any item of value exchanged between parties to create a valid contract

1. *Agreement.* Agreement is the serious, definite, and communicated offer and acceptance of the same terms. Let us say that an auto parts supplier offers in writing to sell rebuilt engines to a repair shop for $500 each. If the repair shop accepts the offer, the two parties have reached an agreement.
2. *Consent.* A contract is not enforceable if any of the parties has been affected by an honest mistake, fraud, or pressure. For example, a restaurant manager orders a painted sign, but the sign company delivers a neon sign instead.
3. *Capacity.* To give real consent, both parties must demonstrate legal **capacity** (competence). A person under legal age (usually 18 or 21) cannot enter into a binding contract.
4. *Consideration.* An agreement is binding only if it exchanges **considerations**, that is, items of value. If your brother offers to paint your room for free, you cannot sue him if he changes his mind. Note that items of value do not necessarily entail money. For example, a tax accountant might agree to prepare a homebuilder's tax return in exchange for a new patio. Both services are items of value. Contracts need not be rational, nor must they provide the best possible bargain for both sides. They need only include legally sufficient consideration. The terms are met if both parties receive what the contract details.
5. *Legality.* A contract must be for a lawful purpose and must comply with federal, state, and local laws and regulations. For example, an agreement between two competitors to engage in price fixing—that is, to set a mutually acceptable price—is not legal.
6. *Proper form.* A contract may be written, oral, or implied from conduct. It must be written, however, if it involves the sale of land or goods worth more than $500. It must be written if the agreement requires more than a year to

fulfill—say, a contract for employment as an engineer on a 14-month construction project. All changes to written contracts must also be in writing.

Breach of Contract What can one party do if the other fails to live up to the terms of a valid contract? Contract law offers a variety of remedies designed to protect the reasonable expectations of the parties and, in some cases, to compensate them for actions taken to enforce the agreement.

As the injured party to a breached contract, you may be entitled to demand any of the following actions:

- You might cancel the contract and refuse to live up to your part of the bargain. For example, you might simply cancel a contract for carpet shampooing if the company fails to show up.
- You might sue for damages up to the amount that you lost as a result of the breach. Thus, you might sue the original caterer if you must hire a more expensive caterer for your wedding reception because the original company canceled at the last minute.
- If money cannot repay the damage you suffered, you might demand specific performance—that is, require the other party to fulfill the original contract. For example, you might demand that a dealer in classic cars sell you the antique Stutz Bearcat he agreed to sell you and not a classic Jaguar instead.

Tort Law

Tort law applies to most business relationships *not governed by contracts.* A **tort** is a *civil*—that is, noncriminal—injury to people, property, or reputation for which compensation must be paid. For example, if a person violates zoning laws by opening a convenience store in a residential area, he or she cannot be sent to jail as if the act were a criminal violation. But a variety of other legal measures can be pursued, such as fines or seizure of property. Trespass, fraud, defamation, invasion of privacy, and even assault can be torts, as can interference with contractual relations and wrongful use of trade secrets. In this section, we explain three classifications of torts: *intentional, negligence,* and *product liability.*

tort
Civil injury to people, property, or reputation for which compensation must be paid

Intentional Torts **Intentional torts** result from the deliberate actions of another person or organization—for instance, a manufacturer knowingly fails to install a relatively inexpensive safety device on a product. Similarly, refusing to rectify a product design flaw, as in the case of the space shuttle *Challenger* disaster, can render a firm liable for an intentional tort. The actions of employees on the job may also constitute intentional torts—say, an overzealous security guard who wrongly accuses a customer of shoplifting. To remedy torts, courts will usually impose **compensatory damages**: payments intended to redress an injury actually suffered. They may also impose **punitive damages**: fines that exceed actual losses suffered by plaintiffs and that are intended to punish defendants.

intentional tort
Tort resulting from the deliberate actions of a party

compensatory damages
Monetary payments intended to redress injury actually suffered because of a tort

punitive damages
Fines imposed over and above any actual losses suffered by a plaintiff

Negligence Torts Ninety percent of tort suits involve charges of **negligence**, conduct falling below legal standards for protecting others against unreasonable risk. If a company installs a pollution-control system that fails to protect a community's water supply, it may later be sued by an individual who gets sick from drinking the water.

negligence
Conduct falling below legal standards for protecting others against unreasonable risk

Negligence torts may also result from employee actions. For example, if the captain of a supertanker runs aground and spills 11 million gallons of crude oil into coastal fishing waters, the oil company may be liable for potentially astronomical damages. Thus, in September 1994, a jury in Alaska ordered Exxon Corp. to pay $5 billion in punitive damages to 34,000 fishermen and other plaintiffs as a consequence of the *Exxon Valdez* disaster of 1989. (Plaintiffs had asked for $15 billion.) A month earlier, the jury had awarded plaintiffs $287 million in compensatory damages. In 1993, the firm responsible for pipeline operations a the Valdez, Alaska, terminal (which is partially owned by Exxon) agreed to pay plaintiffs in the same case $98 million in damages. In a separate case, Exxon paid $20 million in damages to villages whose food supply had been destroyed. A separate state jury will consider another $120 million in claims by Alaskan corporations and municipalities. Even before any of these awards were handed down Exxon had spent $2.1 billion on the cleanup effort and paid $1.3 billion in civi and criminal penalties.

product liability tort
Tort in which a company is responsible for injuries caused by its products

Product Liability Torts In cases of **product liability**, a company may be held responsible for injuries caused by its products. According to a special government panel on product liability, about 33 million people are injured and 28,000 killed by consumer products each year.

strict product liability
Principle that liability can result not from a producer's negligence but from a defect in the product itself

Strict Product Liability Since the early 1960s, businesses have faced a number of legal actions based on the relatively new principle of **strict product liability**: the principle that liability can result not from a producer's negligence but from a defect in the product itself. An injured party need show only that

1. The product was defective.
2. The defect was the cause of injury.
3. The defect caused the product to be unreasonably dangerous.

Many recent cases in strict product liability have focused on injuries or illnesses attributable to toxic wastes or other hazardous substances that were legally disposed of. Because plaintiffs need not demonstrate negligence or fault, these suits frequently succeed. Not surprisingly, the number of such suits promises to increase.

Property Law

As the name implies, *property law* concerns property rights. But what exactly is "property"? Is it the land under a house? The house itself? A car in the driveway? A dress in the closet? The answer in each case is yes: In the legal sense, **property** is anything of value to which a person or business has sole right of ownership. Indeed, property is technically those rights.

property
Anything of value to which a person or business has sole right of ownership

Within this broad general definition, we can divide property into four categories. In this section, we define these categories and then examine more fully the legal protection of a certain kind of property—intellectual property.

tangible real property
Land and anything attached to it

tangible personal property
Any movable item that can be owned, bought, sold, or leased

intangible personal property
Property that cannot be seen but that exists by virtue of written documentation

intellectual property
Property created through a person's creative activities

- **Tangible real property** is land and anything attached to it. A house and a factory are both tangible real property, as are built-in appliances or the machines inside the buildings.
- **Tangible personal property** is any movable item that can be owned, bought, sold, or leased. Examples are automobiles, clothing, stereos, and cameras.
- **Intangible personal property** cannot be seen but exists by virtue of written documentation. Examples are insurance policies, bank accounts, stocks and bonds, and trade secrets.

Intellectual property is created through a person's creative activities. Books, articles, songs, paintings, screenplays, and computer software are all intellectual property.

Protection of Intellectual Rights The U.S. Constitution grants protection to intellectual property by means of copyrights, trademarks, and patents. Copyrights and patents apply to the tangible expressions of an idea—not to the ideas themselves. Thus, you could not copyright the idea of cloning dinosaurs from fossil

DNA. Michael Crichton could copyright his novel *Jurassic Park,* which is a tangible result of that idea, and he could sell the film rights to producer-director Steven Spielberg. Both creators are entitled to the profits, if any, that may be generated by their tangible creative expressions.

Copyrights **Copyrights** give exclusive ownership rights to the creators of books, articles, designs, illustrations, photos, films, and music. Computer programs and even semiconductor chips are also protected. Copyrights extend to creators for their entire lives and to their estates for 70 years thereafter. All terms are automatically copyrighted from the moment of creation.

copyright
Exclusive ownership right belonging to the creator of a book, article, design, illustration, photo, film, or musical work

Trademarks Because the development of products is expensive, companies must prevent other firms from using their brand names. Often, they must act to keep competitors from seducing consumers with similar or substitute products. A producer can apply to the U.S. government for a **trademark**—the exclusive legal right to use a brand name or symbol.

trademark
Exclusive legal right to use a brand name or symbol

Trademarks are granted for 20 years and may be renewed indefinitely if a firm continues to protect its brand name. If a firm allows the brand name to lapse into common usage, it may lose protection. Common usage takes effect when a company fails to use the ® symbol to indicate that its brand name is a registered trademark. It also takes effect if a company seeks no action against those who fail to acknowledge its trademark. Recently, for example, the popular brand-name sailboard Windsurfer lost its trademark. Like *trampoline, yo-yo,* and *thermos, windsurfer* has become the common term for the product and can now be used by any sailboard company. In contrast, Formica Corp. successfully spent the better part of a decade in court to protect the name *Formica* as a trademark. The Federal Trade Commission had contended that the word had entered the language as a generic name for any similar laminate material.

Patents **Patents** provide legal monopolies for the use and licensing of manufactured items, manufacturing processes, substances, and designs for objects. A patentable invention must be *novel, useful,* and *nonobvious.* Since June 1995, U.S. patent law has been in harmony with that of most developed nations. For example, patents are now valid for 20 years rather than 17 years. In addition, the term now runs from the date on which the application was *filed,* not the date on which the patent itself was *issued.*

patent
Exclusive legal right to use and license a manufactured item or substance, manufacturing process, or object design

Although the U.S. Patent Office issues about 1,200 patents a week, requirements are stringent, and U.S. patents actually tend to be issued at a slow pace. While Japan and most European countries have installed systems to speed up patent filing and research, the U.S. system can extend the process to years. Other observers argue that American firms trail their foreign counterparts in patents because of the sluggishness with which U.S. companies move products through their own research and development programs.

Restrictions on Property Rights Property rights are not always absolute. For example, rights may be compromised under any of the following circumstances:

- Owners of shorefront property may be required to permit anglers, clam diggers, and other interested parties to walk near the water.
- Utility companies typically have rights called easements, such as the right to run wire over private property or to lay cable or pipe under it.
- Under the principle of **eminent domain**, the government may, upon paying owners fair prices, claim private land to expand roads or erect public buildings.

eminent domain
Principle that the government may claim private land for public use by buying it at a fair price

Agency Law

The transfer of property—whether the deeding of real estate or the transfer of an automobile title—often involves agents. An **agent** is a person who acts for,

agent
Individual or organization acting for, and in the name of, another party

principal
Individual or organization authorizing an agent to act on its behalf

and in the name of, another party, called the **principal**. The most visible agents are those in real estate, sports, and entertainment. Many businesses, however, use agents to secure insurance coverage and handle investments. Every partner in a partnership and every officer and director in a corporation is an agent of that business. Courts have also ruled that both a firm's employees and its outside contractors may be regarded as its agents.

Authority of Agents Agents have the authority to bind principals to agreements. They receive that authority, however, from the principals themselves; they cannot create their own authority. An agent's authority to bind a principal can be express, implied, or apparent.

express authority
Agent's authority, derived from written agreement, to bind a principal to a certain course of action

implied authority
Agent's authority, derived from business custom, to bind a principal to a certain course of action

apparent authority
Agent's authority, based on the principal's compliance, to bind a principal to a certain course of action

Let's say, for example, that Ellen is a salesperson in Honest Sam's Used Car Lot. Her written employment contract gives her **express authority** to sell cars, to provide information to prospective buyers, and to approve trade-ins up to $2,000. Derived from the custom of used-car dealers, she also has **implied authority** to give reasonable discounts on prices and to make reasonable adjustments to written warranties. Furthermore, Ellen may—in the presence of Honest Sam—promise a customer that she will match the price offered by another local dealer. If Honest Sam assents—perhaps merely nods and smiles—Ellen may be construed to have the **apparent authority** to make this deal.

Responsibilities of Principals Principals have several responsibilities to their agents. They owe agents reasonable compensation, must reimburse them for related business expenses, and should inform them of risks associated with their business activities. Principals are liable for actions performed by agents *within the scope of their employment.* Thus, if agents make untrue claims about products or services, the principal is liable for making amends. Employers are similarly responsible for the actions of employees. In fact, firms are often liable in tort suits because the courts treat employees as agents.

Businesses are increasingly being held accountable for *criminal* acts by employees. Court findings, for example, have argued that firms are expected to be aware of workers' propensities for violence, to check on their employees' pasts, and to train and supervise employees properly. Suppose, for instance, that a delivery service hires a driver with a history of driving while intoxicated. If the driver has an accident with a company vehicle while under the influence of alcohol, the company may be liable for criminal actions.

Commercial Law

Managers must be well acquainted with the most general laws affecting commerce. Specifically, they need to be familiar with the provisions of the *Uniform Commercial Code*, which sets down rules regarding *warranties.*

The Uniform Commercial Code For many years, companies doing business in more than one state faced a special problem: Laws governing commerce varied, sometimes widely, from state to state. In 1952, however, the National Conference of Commissioners on Uniform State Laws and the American Law Institute drew up the **Uniform Commercial Code (UCC)**. Subsequently accepted by every state except Louisiana, the UCC describes the rights of buyers and sellers in transactions.

Uniform Commercial Code (UCC)
Body of standardized laws governing the rights of buyers and sellers in transactions

For example, buyers who believe that they have been wronged in agreements with sellers have several options. They can cancel contracts, refuse deliveries, and demand the return of any deposits. In some cases, they can buy the same products elsewhere and sue the original contractors to recover any losses incurred. Sellers, too, have several options. They can cancel contracts, withhold deliveries, and sell goods to other buyers. If goods have already been delivered, sellers can repossess them or sue the buyers for purchase prices.

Warranties A **warranty** is a seller's promise to stand by its products or services if a problem occurs after the sale. Warranties may be *express* or *implied*. The terms of an **express warranty** are specifically stated by the seller. For example, many stereo systems are expressly warranted for 90 days. If they malfunction within that period, they can be returned for full refunds.

An **implied warranty** is dictated by law. Implied warranties embody the principle that a product should (1) fulfill the promises made by advertisements and (2) serve the purpose for which it was manufactured and sold. If you buy an advertised frost-free refrigerator, the seller implies that the refrigerator will keep your food cold and that you will not have to defrost it. It is important to note, however, that warranties, unlike most contracts, are easily limited, waived, or disclaimed. Consequently, they are the source of more and more tort action, as dissatisfied customers seek redress from producers.

warranty
Seller's promise to stand by its products or services if a problem occurs after the sale

express warranty
Warranty whose terms are specifically stated by the seller

implied warranty
Warranty, dictated by law, based on the principle that products should fulfill advertised promises and serve the purposes for which they are manufactured and sold

Bankruptcy Law

At one time, individuals who could not pay their debts were jailed. Today, however, both organizations and individuals can seek relief by filing for **bankruptcy**—the court-granted permission not to pay some or all debts.

Hundreds of thousands of individuals and tens of thousands of businesses file for bankruptcy each year, and their numbers continue to increase. Why do individuals and businesses file for bankruptcy? Cash-flow problems and drops in farm prices caused many farmers, banks, and small businesses to go bankrupt. In recent years, large enterprises such as United Airlines and Kmart have sought the protection of bankruptcy laws as part of strategies to streamline operations, cut costs, and regain profitability.

bankruptcy
Permission granted by the courts to individuals and organizations not to pay some or all of their debts

Three main factors account for the increase in bankruptcy filings:

1. The increased availability of credit
2. The "fresh-start" provisions in current bankruptcy laws
3. The growing acceptance of bankruptcy as a financial tactic

In some cases, creditors force an individual or firm into **involuntary bankruptcy** and press the courts to award them payment of at least part of what they are owed. Far more often, however, a person or business chooses to file for court protection against creditors. In general, individuals and firms whose debts exceed total assets by at least $1,000 may file for **voluntary bankruptcy**.

involuntary bankruptcy
Bankruptcy proceedings initiated by the creditors of an indebted individual or organization

voluntary bankruptcy
Bankruptcy proceedings initiated by an indebted individual or organization

Business Bankruptcy

A business bankruptcy may be resolved by one of three plans:

- Under a *liquidation plan,* the business ceases to exist. Its assets are sold and the proceeds used to pay creditors.
- Under a *repayment plan,* the bankrupt company simply works out a new payment schedule to meet its obligations. The time frame is usually extended, and payments are collected and distributed by a court-appointed trustee.

Reorganization is the most complex form of business bankruptcy. The company must explain the sources of its financial difficulties and propose a new plan for remaining in business. Reorganization may include a new slate of managers and a new financial strategy. A judge may also reduce the firm's debts to ensure its survival. Although creditors naturally dislike debt reduction, they may agree to the proposal, since 50 percent of one's due is better than nothing at all.

Legislation passed since 1994 has made some major revisions in bankruptcy laws. For example, it is now easier for individuals with up to $1 million in debt to make payments under installment plans instead of liquidating assets immediately. In contrast, the new law restricts how long a company can protect itself in bankruptcy while continuing to do business. Critics have charged, for instance, that many firms have succeeded in operating for many months under bankruptcy protection. During that time, they were able to cut costs and prices, not only competing with an unfair advantage but dragging down overall industry profits. The new laws place time limits on various steps in the filing process. The intended effect is to speed the process and prevent assets from being lost to legal fees.

The International Framework of Business Law

Laws can vary dramatically from country to country, and many businesses today have international markets, suppliers, and competitors. It follows that managers need a basic understanding of the international framework of business law that affects the ways in which they can do business.

National laws are created and enforced by countries. The creation and enforcement of international law is more complicated. For example, if a company shipping merchandise between the United States and Mexico breaks an environmental protection law, to whom is that company accountable? The answer depends on several factors. Which country enacted the law in question? Where did the violation occur? In which country is the alleged violator incorporated?

international law
Set of cooperative agreements and guidelines established by countries to govern actions of individuals, businesses, and nations

Issues such as pollution across borders are matters of **international law**: the very general set of cooperative agreements and guidelines established by countries to govern the actions of individuals, businesses, and nations themselves. In this section, we examine the various sources of international law. We then discuss some of the important ways in which international trade is regulated and place some key U.S. trade laws in the international context in which they are designed to work.

Sources of International Law

International law has several sources. One source is custom and tradition. Among countries that have been trading with each other for centuries, many customs and traditions governing exchanges have gradually evolved into practice. Although some trading practices still follow ancient unwritten agreements, there has been a clear trend in more recent times to approach international trade within a more formal legal framework. Key features of that framework include a variety of formal trade agreements.

Trade Agreements In addition to subscribing to international rules, virtually every nation has formal trade treaties with other nations. A *bilateral agreement* is one involving two countries; a *multilateral agreement* involves several nations.

General Agreement on Tariffs and Trade (GATT)
International trade agreement to encourage the multilateral reduction or elimination of trade barriers

GATT and the WTO The **General Agreement on Tariffs and Trade (GATT)** was first signed shortly after the end of World War II. Its purpose was to reduce or eliminate trade barriers, such as tariffs and quotas. It does so by encouraging nations to protect domestic industries within internationally agreed-upon limits and to engage in multilateral negotiations.

In December 1994, the U.S. Congress ratified a revision of GATT that had been worked out by 124 nations over a 12-year period. Still, many issues remain unresolved—for example, the opening of foreign markets to most financial services. Governments may still provide subsidies to manufacturers of civil aircraft, and no agreement was reached on limiting the distribution of American cultural exports—movies, music, and the like—in Europe. With those agreements that have been reached, however, one international economic group predicts that world commerce will have increased by $270 billion by 2002.

The **World Trade Organization (WTO)** came into being on January 1, 1995, as the result of a complex round of GATT negotiations lasting from 1986 to 1994. The 140 member countries are required to open their markets to international trade, and the WTO is empowered to pursue three goals:

World Trade Organization (WTO)
Organization through which member nations negotiate trading agreements and resolve disputes about trade policies and practices

1. Promote trade by encouraging member nations to adopt fair trade policies and practices
2. Reduce trade barriers by promoting multilateral negotiations among member nations
3. Establish fair procedures for resolving disputes among member nations

North American Free Trade Agreement The **North American Free Trade Agreement (NAFTA)** was negotiated to remove tariffs and other trade barriers among the United States, Canada, and Mexico. NAFTA also included agreements to monitor environmental and labor abuses. It took effect on January 1, 1994, and immediately eliminated some tariffs; others will disappear after 5-, 10-, or 15-year intervals.

North American Free Trade Agreement (NAFTA)
Agreement to gradually eliminate tariffs and other trade barriers between the United States, Canada, and Mexico

European Union Originally called the Common Market, the **European Union (EU)** includes the principal Western European nations. These countries have eliminated most quotas and have set uniform tariff levels on products imported and exported within their group. In 1992, virtually all internal trade barriers were eliminated, making the European Union the largest free marketplace in the world.

European Union (EU)
Agreement among major Western European nations to eliminate or make uniform most trade barriers affecting group members

Self-Concept Check: Answers

Chapter 1

1. (b) Buildings and equipment Items (a), (c), (d), and (e) can all be classified as basic resources that **businesses** can use to produce goods and services. Buildings and equipment, however, are not "basic"; rather, they have already been produced and may be used to produce other goods or services over time. As such, they are forms of **capital,** which is a **factor of production.**

2. (e) Input market On the **input market,** firms such as Rubbermaid buy resources from households such as yours: You are furnishing the resource of **capital,** for which Rubbermaid is paying in the form of dividends. The exchange flows in the opposite direction on the **output market** (d). The over-the-counter market (a) refers to an organization of securities dealers trading outside the formal setting of a stock exchange. Organizations buy and resell finished goods on the reseller market (b). You may have entered the **labor** market (c) to work and earn the money that you invested, but it is only one component of the input market.

3. False These numbers reflect the allocation of resources in the United States, which, although it does not have a *pure* free market economy (no one does), does have a free **mixed market economy**—one in which some economic functions are planned while most are determined by **demand** and **supply.**

4. True A lot of people think that pizza can be properly enjoyed only with a beer. If the price of pizza goes so high that these people prefer to find a substitute, they'll be buying both fewer pizzas and less of the beer that they normally consume with pizza.

5. (d) The law of demand Because the price of his portraits has come down, Pierre finds that buyers are willing to purchase *(demand)* more of them. Because Pierre has taken no action to control the number of portraits that he can or will paint (the number that he will *supply*), the **law of supply** is not directly involved; thus (b) is wrong. Likewise, because neither Pierre's ability or willingness to produce portraits has been reduced, no **shortage** is involved; (c), therefore, is not correct. *Discounting* (a) refers to the tactic of dropping prices to stimulate sales though not necessarily **demand.** *Economic justice* (e) is a nice-sounding but irrelevant term.

6. (c) Shoppers will buy fewer eggs This result follows the **law of demand:** buyers will purchase less of a product as its price goes up. The reverse result (d), therefore, cannot be true at the same time, because it would violate the law of demand. If both (c) and (d) cannot be correct, then (e) cannot be correct. If the price that they can get is going up, producers will not produce fewer eggs; rather, they will follow the **law of supply,** which holds that producers will offer *more* of a product as its price rises. As for (a), this situation might occur if importing more eggs were the only way to follow the law of supply (that is, by offering more eggs for sale); importing chicken eggs, however, is not common practice.

7. (d) Freedom of choice Private enterprise is based on roughly the same principles as the **market economy,** in which producers are free to decide what to make and how much to charge and consumers are free to decide what to buy. In nations with free market, free enterprise systems, adequate representation in government (a) is typical but not absolutely necessary. Under liberalized policies in China, for example, more free enterprise is encouraged, but the government remains a dictatorship. Free enterprise is characterized by **competition,** which encourages businesses to operate efficiently in order to secure needed resources and customers; as for (b), then, competition can be either domestic or foreign. Every nation's **economic system** has *some* natural resources (c) to allocate among its citizens, but they are more accurately regarded as a **factor of production** than as a requirement of free enterprise.

8. False Even though the town has only one newspaper, the newspaper has competitors. Newspapers from other cities can be trucked or flown in and sold at newsstands. If you're after news, you might also turn to news magazines or TV news. Likewise, advertisers can choose TV, radio, magazines, billboards, or the Yellow Pages. It is very hard to cite clear-cut examples of true **monopolies.**

9. (c) Charging a price that will not depress consumer demand Being the only seller in its industry, a monopolist has no **competition** to undercut (d). The only reason to offer bargain prices (b) would be to attract more buyers, but the monopolist already has all the buyers in the **market.** The same is essentially true for attracting buyers by improving quality or service (e). Not having to worry about being undercut by a competitor's prices, the **monopoly** could charge buyers whatever it wanted (a), but if the price were too high, customers would demand less of the product; in that case, the monopolist would suffer lower profits because it would sell less of its product. It thus charges the price at which it can generate maximum **profit.**

Chapter 2

1. False Boundaries between an organization and its environment are becoming more and more difficult to define. As firms interact with each other, it becomes difficult to tell where one organization ends and its environment begins.

2. (b) Inflation There are several ways to determine whether or not an economy is growing. **Aggregate output** (c) is the main measure of growth in a **business cycle;** it is the total quantity of goods and services produced by an economic system during a given period. **Standard of living** (a) is another measure of growth that refers to the total quantity *and* quality of goods and services that you can purchase with the currency used in your economic system. **Productivity** (d) measures growth by comparing how much a system produces with the resources needed to produce it. Finally, **gross domestic product** (e) refers to the total value of all goods and services produced within a given period by a national economy through domestic factors of production. **Inflation** (b) is not a measure of economic growth.

3. (c) They mean different things but are usually very similar While **gross domestic product (GDP)** and **gross national product (GNP)** *are* different, they are very similar. GDP refers to the total value of all goods and services produced within a given period by a national economy through domestic factors of production. GNP refers to the total value of all goods and services produced by a national economy within a given period of time *regardless of where the factors of production are located*. Thus the only difference has to do with the country in which products are actually produced. To figure in GDP, they must be produced *domestically;* they figure in GNP no matter where they are produced.

4. True The word *technology*, of course, has several meanings, but when we apply it to the business environment, we mean all the ways by which firms create value for their constituents. For any organization, the form and availability of its technology are usually determined by factors in its external environment.

5. (d) Enterprise resource planning **Enterprise resource planning** (d) is a large-scale information system that integrates and synchronizes many activities in the "extended enterprise." Such a system can manage company-wide processes that cut across product lines, departments, and geographic locations. ERP increases the efficiency and accuracy of business transactions because all processes are integrated in real time.

6. (e) Business taxes might be decreased During periods of antibusiness sentiment, firms may find that their competitive strategies are more restricted. If the government desires to restrict business activity, it will be less likely to encourage such activity by decreasing taxes (e).

7. (a) Consumer tastes The **sociocultural environment** includ es the customs (b), mores (c), values (d), and demographic characteristics (e) of the society in which an organization functions. Consumer tastes (a) are not part of the process that determines the types of products and the standards of business conduct that members of a society are likely to value and accept.

8. False An auditing accountant is expected to give an *objective* assessment of accounting and financial information. Thus when an accounting firm is also involved in management consulting, a conflict of interest may arise. In a desire to ensure that his or her accounting firm gets revenues from future consulting projects, an auditor may be tempted to ignore some of the findings of an audit.

9. (e) Attaching seat assemblies to the interior of new cars on the assembly line **Outsourcing** is becoming an increasingly popular way to conduct certain business without losing focus on a firm's core competencies. In outsourcing, a firm will hire another company to perform business operations such as payroll, employee training, transportation, or even research and development. In our example, a car manufacturer would be *least* likely to outsource the attachment of seat assemblies to the interior of a car (e). This process is part of the company's main business operations. The other available options are not.

Chapter 3

1. (e) One that is independently owned and managed and does not dominate its market It's hard to define a **small business** in strictly numerical terms (items [a] and [c]), because different agencies use different numerical classifications. Even if a business operates out of a single location or country (items [b] and [d]), it might still dominate its market. A small business, however, cannot dominate its market, nor can it be part of another business. Thus (e) is the best option.

2. (b) Manufacturing Ease of entry depends on the resources required to do business in an industry: The more costly the resources required, the harder it is to start a business. Items (a), (c), (d), and (e) all require fewer resources than (b). Because of the cost of resources, manufacturing generally (though not exclusively) lends itself to big business.

3. False Entrepreneurs and small business owners typically differ mainly in vision, aspiration, and strategy for growth and expansion. An **entrepreneur** is usually motivated to grow, expand, and build, while a small business owner often desires a secure and comfortable income that can be attained without dramatic growth in his or her business.

4. False A **business plan** is critical, both in helping you make the right decisions and forcing you to prepare thoroughly for the successful launching of your business. The plan defines your business **strategy** and **goals** and describes the match between your entrepreneurial abilities and the requirements of your business. It aids in strategic decision making and can also help you plan the financial aspects of your business.

5. (d) Personal resources Because of the risk associated with starting up a new business, **entrepreneurs** must often rely on their own resources. In fact, personal resources account for over two-thirds of all money invested in new small businesses. Lending institutions (items [a], [b], and [c]) are more likely to help finance the purchase of an existing business because there is less risk involved.

6. (d) Employee theft or sabotage Items (a), (b), (c), and (e) are all general factors that can contribute to small business failure. As for the success of a business, this requires dedication and the commitment to succeed. You must also learn the principles of management, especially how to make basic business decisions. You should establish effective controls to alert you to trouble, and you should realize that you may not make any money for some time. Employee theft or sabotage (d) is not one of the more common causes of business failure.

7. (d) All of the above Because a **sole proprietorship** has only one owner, you have the freedom to operate without answering to anyone but yourself. It's relatively simple to create a sole proprietorship, and there are tax benefits associated with being a sole proprietor.

8. False Because of their disadvantages, **general partnerships** are among the *least* popular forms of business. The greatest drawback is **unlimited liability,** which makes each partner potentially liable for all debts incurred in the name of the partnership. Approximately 1.86 million general partnerships in the United States account for only about 6 percent of total sales revenues.

9. (c) Master limited corporation Items (a), (b), (d), and (e) are all legitimate **corporations.** A **public corporation** (a) sells stock to the general public. In a **private corporation** (b) (the most common form in the United States), the stock is held by only a few people rather than the general public. A **limited liability corporation** (d) is a hybrid form of ownership in which owners are taxed as partners while enjoying the benefits of **limited liability** accorded to corporations. Finally, a **professional corporation** (e) is usually comprised of groups of professionals (doctors, lawyers, accountants).

Chapter 4

1. (c) Association of South American Agricultural Producers Although the Association of South American Agricultural Producers does affect the United States to some degree, this affect is not as great as that of the other choices. The **General Agreement on Tariffs and Trade** (a) is designed to help eliminate trade barriers, such as **tariffs** and **quotas.** As such, it influences U.S. trade, as does the **North American Free Trade Agreement** (d), which was designed to remove tariffs among the United States, Mexico, and Canada. The **World Trade Organization** (b) was created in 1995 to promote global trade, and the 140 members (including the United States) are required to open their markets to international trade. Finally, the **European Union** (e) is the largest free marketplace in the world, having eliminated most trade quotas among member nations.

2. (d) Movies and other filmed entertainment A **comparative advantage** exists when a company can produce a product more efficiently or better than it can produce other goods. The prolific U.S. film industry produces well-made movies quite efficiently. None of the other products on the list (a), (b), (c), and (e) is produced as efficiently as item (d); thus the United States has a comparative advantage in the production of movies.

3. False Countries are divided into three groups of the basis of per capita income, or average income per person. High-income countries are those with a per capita income greater than $9386; middle-income countries are those with a per capita income less than $9386 but greater than $765; low-income (or developing) countries have a per capita income of less than $765.

4. (b) Exchange rates When deciding whether or not to "go international," a company should consider many things. First of all, it must be sure that there's an international demand for its product. (a). If there is such demand, the company should decide how best to adapt the product for international consumption (d). The foreign business climate (c) must always be considered, and the firm must determine whether it has the knowledge and expertise to do business abroad (e). **Exchange rates** (b), which change frequently, are not an immediate concern when considering whether or not to go global.

5. (a) Foreign direct investment Because **foreign direct investment** (a) involves actually buying or establishing tangible assets in another country, it is the most complex form of international organizational structure; the company is making a significant investment of time and resources. **Independent agents** (b) (foreign individuals or organizations that agree to represent an exporter's interests in the host country) represent the least complex form. A **licensing arrangement** (c), by which firms give individuals or companies the exclusive rights to manufacture or market their products in another country, is a more complex commitment. Even more complex is a **branch office** (d) to which a firm sends some of its own managers to oversee foreign operations. Finally, setting up an international division in another country (e) is not generally as significant a step as foreign direct investment.

6. True The most basic level of international involvement is importing or exporting. An **exporter** makes products in one country and sells them in another; an **importer** buys products in foreign markets and resells them domestically. In both cases, then, most of the business is conducted in the home country.

7. (e) Transportation differences Social (a) and cultural barriers (b), ranging from differences in language to tastes in food and clothing, both arise from cultural differences. Economic barriers (c) may be due to economic conditions or to the role played by government in a nation's business activities. Political differences (d) may also derive from the role of government, which can discourage international activity by controlling the flow of **capital,** confiscating property, or levying taxes. Compared to these problems, transportation differences (e) are usually minor barriers to international involvement.

8. (b) Exchange rate parameters **Quotas** (restrictions on the quantity of products that can enter a country) and **tariffs** (taxes on imports) (a) adversely affect trade because they affect the prices and availability of foreign-made products. The same is true of **local content laws** (c), which require that foreign products must in part be made domestically. Likewise, **business practice laws** (d) erect bureaucratic obstacles to local business activity by foreign firms. **Subsides** (e), government payments to help domestic businesses compete with foreign firms, have the same effect as tariffs because they lower the price of the domestic product. **Exchange rate** parameters (b) are economic factors, not legal conditions.

9. False Protectionism refers to the protection of domestic, rather than international, business. It's the practice of protecting domestic business at the expense of free market competition and can be a source of friction between nations.

Chapter 5

1. (b) Employee behavior toward the organization If a manager cheats on an expense report, the breach is a matter of employee behavior toward the organization (b): Quite simply, the action benefits the individual at the employer's expense. Organizational behavior toward the employee (c) includes hiring and firing policies and wages and working conditions. In items (a), (d), and (e), *other economic agents* include customers, competitors, stockholders, suppliers, and unions.

2. (e) Regulation Items (a), (b), (c), and (d) are all normal criteria for assessing **ethical behavior.** The question of utility (a) asks if an action does what's best for those who are affected. The question of rights (b) implies that the individuals involved in an action possess certain rights. The norms of justice (c) and caring (d) refer to what we regard as fair and to people's responsibilities to each other, respectively. Regulation (e) implies that behavior is required, not ethically motivated.
3. False Although it's wise for a company to issue a code of **ethics,** it's not legally required. Many companies, of course, choose to establish clear ethical guidelines on how the firm and its employees will conduct business.
4. True Ethics affects individual behavior in the workplace, while **social responsibility** refers to a firm's overall efforts to balance its commitments to groups and individuals in the social environment. These groups and individuals are called **organizational stakeholders** because they are directly affected by the firm's practices and have a stake in its performance.
5. (e) All of these Organizational stakeholders generally include customers (a), employees (b), suppliers (c), investors (d), and the local community in which a firm does business.
6. (d) Growing skepticism and concern regarding responsible corporate governance In the 1980s and 1990s, most people viewed business as a positive social force—a sector in which self-control and free-market forces dictated socially conscious behavior. This *laissez-faire* attitude (e) was encouraged by economic prosperity, but today, attitudes toward businesses reflect growing skepticism and concern regarding responsible corporate governance (d). Although most companies are socially responsible, this attitude has become more deeply embedded in the wake of recent corporate scandals.
7. (a) Responsibility toward the board of directors When defining its sense of **social responsibility,** a firm typically looks at its responsibilities toward the environment (b), its customers (c), its employees (d), and its investors (e)—in other words, toward **organizational stakeholders** toward whom it must choose to behave in one way or another. As the governing body of a corporation, its board of directors (a) is one of the parties responsible for determining how it will behave.
8. (e) All of these Among the approaches that a firm can take toward **social responsibility,** it can take an **obstructionist stance** (a), doing as little as possible to address social problems. Or it can take **defensive stance** (b), doing everything legally required of it but nothing more. In taking an **accommodative stance** (c), a firm may voluntarily exceed legal requirements but solicitors must often be convinced that a particular program is worth its. A company taking a **proactive stance** (d) will take the initiative in seeking opportunities to act in a socially conscious manner.
9. False There is no reason that a small businesses can't take a stance on **social responsibility** that determines the ways in which it interacts with the stakeholders in its community.

Chapter 6

1. (a) Goals show the government what the firm hopes to achieve Goal setting serves four main purposes: providing direction and guidance for managers (b), including performance assessment (e); helping firms allocate resources (so that, for example, areas that are expected to grow will get first priority) (c); and helping to define the corporate culture (d). By and large, businesses don't have to tell the government what they hope to achieve (a).
2. False All **goals** should be consistent with the company's purpose and mission.
3. (d) Deciding which division to sell if a firm runs short of cash Contingency planning is planning for change; it recognizes the need to find solutions to specific problems. By determining ahead of time which division to sell if it runs short of cash (d), a firm is dealing with potential change, protecting itself from the consequences of decisions made without the benefit of planning. The other options are all plans that are made as a matter of normal business operations.
4. (c) Coordinating Planning (a) begins when managers determine the company's **goals,** develop a **strategy** for achieving them, and design plans for implementing the strategy. When **organizing** (b), they determine the best way to structure a firm's resources. In **leading** (d), they motivate employees to meet the firm's objectives. **Controlling** (e) means monitoring the firm's progress and performance to ensure that it's meeting its goals. Coordinating (c), while perhaps a function of any of the other activities, is not part of the management process.
5. True Most organizations have three basic levels of **management**: **top managers** typically make decisions and determine **strategies** affecting the entire company; **middle managers** generally implement the strategies, policies, and procedures set down by top-level managers; **first-line managers** oversee the work of employees under their supervision.
6. (e) All of these Virtually al managers—top, middle, and first-line—work in one or more of the areas listed.
7. (c) Conceptual skills When a manager thinks in abstract terms (say, in analyzing new market opportunities), he or she is using **conceptual skills** (c). **Technical skills** (a) are needed to perform specialized tasks. **Human relations skills** (b) help managers get along with other people, while **decision-making skills** (d) include the ability to define problems and select the best course of action. Managers need **time management skills** (e) to make the most productive use of their time.
8. (b) Global and technology Most experts agree that as more and more businesses enter the global market, they will need managers who can understand international operations. Managers will also need to use technology to gather vast and complex amounts of information.
9. False The shared experiences, stories, beliefs, and norms that characterize an organization constitute a culture that directs employee efforts toward shared goals and helps new employees learn accepted organizational behaviors.

Chapter 7

1. False Organizational structure is created as managers assess the organization's purpose, mission, and **strategies** and is influenced by its size

and technology. The structure of successful organization changes constantly to keep up with the normal and unexpected changes in the company.
2. (c) Assembly line worker Specialization is the determination of who will perform specific jobs in an organization. The more narrowly defined the duties of a job, the more specialized it is. In this question, assembly line worker (c) is the most specialized job because it's the most narrowly defined. The duties that come with all the other jobs tend to entail a variety of tasks.
3. (a) Sequence Departmentalization is the process of combining specialized jobs into logical groupings. This combination of jobs may result in **functional departmentalization** (according to the tasks performed by a group) (b); **process departmentalization** (according to the processes needed to make a product) (c); **product departmentalization** (according to the specific products being made) (d); or **customer departmentalization** (according to the likely buyers of a product) (e). Sequence (a) is not a common basis for departmentalizing jobs.
4. (d) Creating obligations The decision-making process helps determines who has responsibility for various tasks. It's generally a three-step process of assigning tasks (a), performing tasks (b), and delegating **authority** (assigning decision-making power) (c). Creating obligations (d) is not part of this three-step process.
5. (e) Narrow Span of control refers to the number of people managed by one supervisor. In a **tall organization,** it tends to be narrow (e)—fewer individuals are supervised by one manager. This level of control is desirable when jobs are entail diverse tasks or are prone to change.
6. True After developing its **organizational structure,** a company must decide which type of **authority** is needed to make and implement decisions. **Line authority** typically flows up and down the chain of command and conducts the operations of **line departments** (those directly linked to the production and sales of a product). **Staff authority** is based on special expertise and usually involves advising line managers. **Committee and team authority** is given to committees or work teams involved in daily operations. It's quite common for an organization to delegate all three types of authority.
7. (b) Process organization There are four basic forms of organizational structure. **Functional organization** (a) is used by most small to medium-size firms, which delegate **authority** according to group functions. **Divisional organizations** (c) manage a number of product-based divisions as if they were separate enterprises. In a **matrix structure** (d), members of teams report to two or more managers who typically have different types of expertise. An **international organizational structure** (e) is best for firms that compete on a global scale. Process organization (b) is not one of these basic forms.
8. (e) All of these As their environments change with the times, firms look to new forms of organization to maintain their effectiveness. These new forms include the **boundaryless organization** (a), which eliminates or minimizes traditional boundaries and structures; the **team organization** (b), which relies almost solely on project-oriented teams and has essentially no functional hierarchy; the **virtual organization** (c), which typically has only a few permanent employees, hiring temporary workers as conditions change; and the **learning organization** (d), which tries to integrate continuous improvement with continuous employee learning and development.
9. False An **informal organization** is structured by the everyday social interactions among employees that transcend formal jobs and job interrelationships. Because such interactions occur in every company, every company, regardless of size, has an informal organization. Informal groups of people who decide to interact among themselves and the organizational **grapevine** are both part of the informal organization.

Chapter 8

1. False Job analysis is a systematic analysis of jobs in an organization. It results in a **job description,** which outlines the duties and responsibilities of a job, and a **job specification,** which lists the skills and abilities entailed by it.
2. (b) Replacement chart A **replacement chart** (b) lists each managerial position, who occupies it, how long that person will probably stay before moving on, and who (by name) is now qualified or soon will be qualified to move into it. A **skills inventory** (a), which files each employee's education, skills, work experience, and career aspirations, helps identify people for transfer or promotion. Both **job descriptions** (c) and **job specifications** (d) are more general human resource planning tools. An application blank (e) is a staffing tool to collect information about job applicants.
3. (c) Polygraph exams Tests (a) assess ability, skill, aptitude, or knowledge relevant to a job. Interviews (b) are used in **recruiting,** although biases can influence the interviewer and render the interview an imperfect indicator. Physical exams (d) are used if the job requirements justify them. Drug tests (e) are used when performance problems could create a safety hazard. Polygraph exams (c) are not generally used in recruiting employees.
4. (e) All of these There are several techniques for training new employees. With **on-the-job training** (a), the trainee informally observes another employee while both are at work. **Off-the-job training** (b) takes place away from the work site and offers a controlled environment. **Vestibule training** (c) is a type of off-the-job training that simulates work environments. **Web-based training** (d) is conducted by computer.
5. (a) Individual incentive Because Giambi and Swoopes will receive a monetary reward if they perform exceptionally well, their contracts contain individual incentive clauses (a), which tie monetary rewards to individual performance. **Profit-sharing plans** (b) distributes profits above a certain level to employees, while **gainsharing plans** (c) distributes bonuses when costs are reduced through greater work efficiency. **Pay-for-knowledge plans** (d) compensate employees for learning new skills and becoming proficient at different jobs. **Cafeteria plans** (e) allow employees to choose **benefits** from a variety of alternatives.
6. True Equal Employment Opportunity (EEO) laws protect people from *unfair* discrimination in the

workplace by making it illegal to discriminate against someone of a **protected class** (which is defined race, religion, gender, national origin, color, age, military veteran status, or disability status). As long as a firm doesn't discriminate against people in a protected class, it's not required to hire them. These laws protect people's rights; they don't require companies to hire certain people. If a firm treats applicants fairly—doesn't discriminate—it can hire whomever it desires.

7. (b) It is increasing Partly because of **affirmative action plans, workforce diversity** is increasing (b) as organizations hire more women, ethnic minorities, and foreign-born employees.

8. (d) Generally, it has steadily declined Since the 1950s, **labor union** membership has steadily declined (d) as a percentage of the total workforce. In the private sector, membership is now only 11 percent of the workforce.

9. True A **contingent worker** works for an organization on something other than a permanent or full-time basis. The category includes independent contractors, on-call workers, temporary employees, and contract and leased employees. Because of the flexibility that the arrangement allows employers, the number of contingent workers has recently been on the rise.

Chapter 9

1. True A **psychological contract** is the set of expectations held by employees concerning what they will contribute to an organization (contributions) and what the organization will provide them (inducements) in return.

2. (c) Job satisfaction The degree of enjoyment that people receive from performing their jobs is called **job satisfaction** (c). Generally speaking, the more they enjoy their work (b), the more satisfied they are (d); the more satisfied they are, the more likely they are to have high **morale** (a), which refers to the overall attitude that people have toward their workplaces.

3. (d) Reduced it Job satisfaction and **morale** have decreased in many companies because of job cuts and the elimination of employee **benefits.** Under such circumstances, workers naturally worry about job security or become upset if a co-worker loses his or her job.

4. (e) All are popular motivational theories Four major motivational theories are concerned with the way management thinks about and treats employees. **Equity theory** (a) focuses on the fact that people tend to compare the ratios of their own contribution to those of others. **Expectancy theory** (b) suggests that people are more willing to work toward goals if they yield attainable, worthwhile rewards. **Two-factor theory** (c) holds that **job satisfaction** and dissatisfaction depend on hygiene factors (working conditions) and motivation factors (recognition). The **hierarchy of needs model** (d) argues that people's satisfaction needs can be isolated on a hierarchical scale.

5. (b) Esteem needs Esteem needs involve one's sense of self-worth and the need to feel good about oneself. These are the needs that will likely be satisfied by an important new job title.

6. False Job enrichment is designed to add one or more motivating factors to job activities. Job rotation, for example, allows employees to perform several different tasks. Team management is a technique that gives employees greater decision-making responsibility, but although it's successful with some employees, many others become frustrated and dissatisfied. Because motivation may decrease, team management is not necessarily a good strategy for job enrichment.

7. (d) All of these are common managerial styles Using an **autocratic style** (a), a manager usually dictates orders and expects them to be followed without question. A manager with a **democratic style** (b) will typically ask for input before making a decision. A **free-rein style** (c) is evident when a manager acts as an advisor while allowing subordinates to make final decisions.

8. False The **contingency approach** to leadership recognizes that managers have different styles and suggests that the appropriate style for a given situation is contingent on certain factors unique to that situation.

9. (a) Contingency approach to leadership Sam is using the **contingency approach** to leadership (a) because he changes his managerial style to fit each situation and individual.

Chapter 10

1. (c) It is intangible and cannot be measured Items (a) and (b) are true because they involve buyer perceptions and buyer perceptions determine **value.** Item (d) is true: From the buyer's perspective, price is the denominator in the value equation (value = benefits/costs). Item (e) is true: Value sells products, and benefits determine a product's value. The correct answer is (c). Although value is intangible, it can be measured. Thus the statement is false. Some companies, for example, measure one product's value versus another's by comparing the total sales of a product to sales of competing products.

2. (e) Relationship marketing Item (e) is correct because loyalty banking, a relationship marketing tool, reinforces lasting relationships by rewarding long-standing customers with incentives. Programs that encourage the building of such relationships are examples of relationship marketing. Items (a), (b), and (c) represent marketing concepts that are, at most, only tangentially related to the question on loyalty banking. As for Item (d), loyalty-banking benefits could be used to differentiate one bank's products from another's. However, a bank's motivation in offering loyalty incentives is more a matter of relationship building than of product differentiation; thus (d) is not as good an answer as (e).

3. (a) Product differentiation Items (b), (c), (d), and (e) comprise the "Four P's" of marketing: the four basic components on which marketing managers focus in planning and implementing marketing strategies. Accordingly, item (a) is the correct answer to the question: Although **product differentiation** is an important marketing concept, it is one of many specific marketing considerations within the major category of "product."

4. True The statement is true because **target markets** are groups of people with similar wants and needs, while **segmentation** involves dividing the market into categories of similar customers. Accordingly, target markets and market segmentation go together, like hands and gloves, in developing marketing strategies for target marketing.

5. (c) Behavioral Item (c) is correct because behavioral variables refer to the ways in which consumers use a product, the benefits they expect from it, and their loyalty to it. None of these factors apply to potential users as described in the question. Instead, the description refers to **psychographic** (politically liberal), **geographic** (Asia/Eastern Europe), and **demographic** (young adults) **variables** that are the bases for **segmentation.** Accordingly, Items (a), (b) and (d) designate variables that marketers would use in the situation described.

6. (b) It nearly always relies on experimentation Items (a), (c), (d), and (e) are all true statements about **marketing research.** Item (b) is not true, primarily because of the word *always*. **Experimentation** is indeed one form of marketing research and offers some decided advantages. But because it is an expensive method, marketers must weigh its costs against possible benefits; often they choose less expensive methods over experimentation.

7. (a) Substitution purchase The correct answer, Item (a), is pretty straightforward: In the context of the consumer buying process, "substitution purchase" is a nonsense phrase. All the other items—evaluation of alternatives, post-purchase evaluation, information seeking, and problem/need recognition—are in fact mainstream stages in the process.

8. True Each year, some 23 million organizations in the United States spend $8 trillion to buy goods and services. This dollar amount is about three times the amount spent in consumer markets.

9. (b) The International Standards Act ensures the existence of uniform advertising practices in most countries Items (a), (c), (d), and (e) all are true statements about the international marketing mix; in fact, examples for each are given in the discussion of this chapter. Item (b) is the correct answer for the question because it is *not* true: There is no such thing as the International Standards Act for advertising. The chapter actually emphasizes that advertising is by no means standardized across countries and regions.

Chapter 11

1. (e) All of the above Because value, from the buyer's perspective, includes both the benefits and costs of a product, items (a) and (d) are inherently included in the **value package.** Furthermore, the value package also includes the product's **features** (b) and intangible rewards (c) which, in combination with benefits and price, contribute to customer satisfaction. Accordingly, item (e) is the correct answer.

2. True The first part of the statement is correct: A **product mix** is the group of products—whether consumer, industrial, or both—that a company makes available for sale. The second part is also true: Within its product mix, a company may offer several **product lines** (multiple or diversified product lines). Although the products in any one product line are similar, each is a different product—a variation intended for a group of similar buyers who will use the product in similar ways. The total of all products, whether similar or very different, is the firm's product mix.

3. (c) Retention The classic **product life cycle** concept includes four stages: introduction, growth, maturity, and decline. The term *retention* is not one of these stages, nor is it defined in this self-check question. Theoretically, it could refer to the practice of a firm's *retaining* a product so its life is extended. That would certainly be a desirable marketing goal, but it is not an accepted stage in the life cycle concept.

4. (a) A company is more valuable with it than without it Brand equity refers to a brand's power to attract customers in the marketplace. Products with higher brand equity are more valuable because they enjoy greater consumer awareness, customer loyalty, and market share. Accordingly, item (a) is the correct answer. Item (b) is wrong because brand equity does not mean that "all brands are equal." Contrary to items (c) and (d), brand equity applies to all brands, both domestic and international, and the concept is significant for marketing.

5. (b) It is a licensed brand The presence of Kroger-brand peaches on a Kroger grocery shelf does not indicate a **licensed brand.** If a T-shirt company were to buy the right to put the Kroger brand on its shirts, then it would be licensing the brand from Kroger. Kroger, of course, does not license the brand from itself. Items (a), (c), (d), and (e) are all true statements: Kroger is a **national brand** produced and distributed by and carrying the name of the manufacturer (a). Kroger developed and retails its own brand, which is a **private brand** (c). A primary purpose of all **labels** is to simplify the consumer buying process (d). Finally, the label does in fact carry nutritional information (e).

6. False The statement is only partly true. Finding the breakeven sales volume is only one purpose of **breakeven analysis.** An equally important purpose is assessing revenue versus cost at other sales volumes: By doing this, we can show the amounts of financial loss for sales volumes below the **breakeven point** and the amounts of profit at sales volumes above the breakeven point.

7. (e) Penetration pricing Penetration pricing (e) is correct because it is used primarily for the stated objectives. Item (a) is a fictitious phrase with no general acceptance in marketing. **Dynamic pricing** (b) is a general term relevant to various objectives, not just to the objectives of establishing new products and gaining market share. **Fixed pricing** (c) applies mostly to pricing for Internet sales. **Psychological pricing** (d), which means that customers are not always rational in evaluating prices, is not at all consistent with the objective of gaining market share with new products. Item (e) is used primarily for the stated objectives and is the correct answer.

8. True The statement accurately reflects the way that **dynamic pricing** works. It also captures the contrast between classic buyer-auction bidding versus the newer practice of dynamic pricing. (This chapter's "Wired World" feature provides a vivid example of how one dynamic-pricing system is benefiting buyers from several major companies.)

9. False The statement is false because a company can use both **price lining** and **odd-even pricing.** A department store, for example, may decide to offer price lines at just three levels (low, medium, and high prices) for women's dresses. The specific sales prices may be set—using odd-even prices—at $39.95, $74.95, and $156.95.

Chapter 12

1. False The combination of products offered by a firm is its ***product* mix,** not its ***distribution* mix.** *Distribution*

mix means the combination of **distribution channels** that a firm uses to get its products to its customers.
2. (b) Intermediaries are retailers who move goods or information to customers Wholesalers sell products to other businesses, which resell them to final customers; **intermediaries** provide added value for customers; and, as we saw in Figure 12.1, **distribution channels** for consumer products are often different from those for industrial products. Thus items (a), (c), and (d) all are true. Item (b) is false (and thus the correct answer) because some intermediaries, including wholesalers, are not **retailers.**
3. (a) Distribution strategies—intensive, selective, and exclusive distribution—differ in terms of the kinds of products and degree of market coverage Item (a) is the correct response: the three distribution strategies differ in terms of kinds of products and degree of market coverage. Item (b) is false because the **direct channel** does not use **intermediaries.** Item (c) is false because Channels 4 and 5 can include **sales agents** for distribution to consumers. Item (d) is false because the number of **distribution channels** is not growing rather than diminishing.
4. (d) Electronic storefronts allow consumers on the Internet to receive added value from speed, convenience, and 24-hour access Items (a), (b), and (c) all directly contradict information in the text: **Electronic retailing** trails far behind brick-and-mortar retailing (a); product images are readily available for consumers on the Internet (b); and most **syndicated selling** relies on the use of Web sites (c). Item (d), the correct answer, is true: **Electronic storefronts** allow consumers on the Internet to receive added value from speed, convenience, and 24-hour access.
5. True Merchant wholesalers differ considerably in the kinds of services they offer. A **full-service merchant wholesaler,** in addition to reselling products to other businesses, provides storage, credit, marketing, and merchandising services. In contrast, **limited-function merchant wholesalers** offer fewer services, perhaps only storage.
6. (c) Product line retailers, such as catalog showrooms, offer deep price discounts Items (a), (b), and (d) all are true. Each of these statements accurately reflects the corresponding discussion in the text. Item (d), however, is false because it asserts that **catalog showrooms** are product line retailers (like department stores and supermarkets). They are not: A catalog showroom is a **bargain retailer.**
7. True Order fulfillment begins when the sale is made and continues through all follow-up activities, from receiving the order to getting it to the customer. While some companies perform order fulfillment activities themselves, others outsource those activities to outside specialists such as UPS e-logistics. By outsourcing fulfillment activities, a firm avoids the large investment required for building and operating its own **distribution center**.
8. (d) Intermodal transportation is used when merchandise is shipped back and forth between warehouses for storage and packaging Item (d) is the correct answer because the statement is false: It misses the main point about **intermodal transportation.** The intermodal approach uses a variety of transportation modes—a combination of air, rail, and trucking, for example—to simplify source-to-destination shipping. Its purpose is to combine whatever modes will get the job done most effectively. Items (a), (b), and (c) all are true statements.
9. False The advantages of using **hubs** go beyond mere cost reduction. Hubs provide better overall flows of materials and goods throughout the supply chain. *Supply-side hubs* eliminate congestion and coordinate the customer's incoming material needs with supply chain transportation. By streamlining outgoing transportation flows, *distribution-side hubs* not only speed deliveries but lower costs.

Chapter 13

1. (c) They replace exchange relationships with customers Items (a), (b), (d), and (e) all are mainstream characteristics of promotional methods as described in the opening pages of the chapter. Promotional methods, however, are never intended to replace the exchange relationship between buyer and seller. To the contrary, firms hope that **promotions** will *facilitate* the exchange relationship by providing the buyer with more information and a more attractive product.
2. True Positioning is the process of establishing an easily identifiable product image in the minds of consumers, and promotions provide methods for doing so. Obviously, the target audience in a particular market segment must be identified before marketers can determine promotional methods for appealing to it.
3. (a) The ultimate objective of any promotion is to provide information Items (b), (c), (d), and (e) are correct for various aspects of marketing **promotions:** They add value for customers, orient strategy, match promotional mix to target audience, and determine promotions for stages in the buyer decision process. But it's easy to lose sight of what promotions are all about—selling products. Thus (a) is false because the ultimate objective of any promotion is to increase sales.
4. (a) TV is the most-used medium and reaches the most people Firms spend more on TV advertising than on any other medium, and TV reaches more people than the other media. Item (b) is false because media effectiveness depends on audience (depending on audience and message, either TV or radio could be more effective). Item (c) is obviously incorrect because magazines take more time to produce and distribute while newspaper ads can be changed daily and reach readers quickly. Item (d) is wrong because electronic tracking allows Internet advertisers to measure the success of each ad they place, whereas most other media cannot be accurately tracked.
5. (b) Consumers like it because it provides electronic pages with lots of interesting and attractive ads. Item (b) is not true. In fact, exactly the opposite is the case: Marketers realize that consumers don't want to wade through electronic pages looking at hundreds of products. Hence, the abundance of ads is a limitation, rather than an advantage, for advertising on the Internet. The other items are, indeed, true as discussed in the chapter: **(a)** The Internet is the most recent advertising medium. **(c)** Marketers recognize Internet advertising as having great promotional potential. **(d)** Internet advertising provides volumes of data about consumer behavior.

6. True Retailers must reach a consumer base that is spread geographically and includes diverse demographics, lifestyles, and values. Thus various kinds of ad content and media will appeal more to some potential consumers than to others, and reaching all of them can be expensive as well as inefficient. Target markets for industrial products are easier to pinpoint because of professional buyers, trade associations, and the geographic concentrations of some industries.
7. (e) Creative selling *Order extraction* (a) is a nonsense phrase, although some salespeople may wish there was such a method. **Missionary selling** (b) promotes both the firm and its products. **Prospecting** (c) is the process of identifying potential customers. **Psychological selling** (d) is another nonsense phrase (or at least one not commonly used among marketers).
8. False The first part of the statement is true: In the **personal selling process** the most critical part is the **closing.** The second part, however, is incorrect. In performing the closing, the salesperson must exercise judgment to determine which is better: asking the client directly or indirectly to close the sale. There is no hard-and-fast rule.
9. True A good example is Tyco, the conglomerate cited in this chapter. Tyco, along with other diversified firms, suffered public skepticism from Enron's collapse in part because, like Enron, Tyco is a large conglomerate. Enron's adverse publicity generated a kind of "guilt by association," casting suspicion on all conglomerates. This is one of the downsides of **publicity:** No firm can control it.

Chapter 14

1. False Although the term ***production*** historically referred to the creation of physical **goods,** today it refers to the creation of both goods and **services.** In recent years, the term ***operations***—reflecting both services and goods production—has largely replaced the term *production*.
2. (d) Foot surgery is a good example of a low-contact operation Although foot surgery takes place on a lower part of your body, it is nevertheless a **high-contact process** because you, the customer (patient), must be intimately involved. For **low contact processes,** the customer needn't be present while the service is performed. Items (a), (b), and (c) are true, as discussed in the text.
3. (a) Whereas manufacturing operations focus on the outcome of the production process, service operations focus on both the transformation process and its outcome Manufacturing can focus more sharply on outcomes because customers are typically not present during the conversion process and don't take part in **operations.** In services production, however, customers participate in operations processes and so are affected not only by the eventual outcome, but also by the transformation process itself, as it's being performed. Item (b) is incorrect: The products offered by most service operations are combinations of goods and services. Item (c) is wrong because both goods and service providers can and do offer customization. As for item (d), customers use different criteria in judging goods versus services. In judging services, customers consider the processes because they witness them while participating in production. Conversely, they seldom see the process for physical goods production.
4. (c) Cellular layouts are useful for a family of similar (though not identical) products that follow a fixed flow path Although products are not identical, they all go through the same production steps. Thus equipment and workstations are arranged close together and in the correct sequence for making all products. Results include lower **inventories,** less **materials handling,** and less transit time through production. Item (a) is false: **Product layouts** are wrong for most **high-contact** services because they involve so much customization. Item (b) is also incorrect: Product layouts (not **process layouts**) include **assembly lines.** Item (d) is wrong because flexible layouts are not uniquely associated with either manufacturing or **service operations.**
5. True In **low-contact processes** (such as car-repair services), the customer drops off the work to be done, then leaves and returns later to pick it up when it's completed. The **inventory** of "to-be-done" jobs allows the manager to vary processing **capacity** throughout the day because jobs can be done in whatever sequence he or she chooses. More efficient sequences permit jobs to be completed more quickly and with fewer workers. But in **high-contact processes,** customers expect to be served when they arrive; thus capacity must be adequately staffed to meet peak demand.
6. (b) Methods improvements are feasible in goods-producing operations but are often impossible in service operations because of the unpredictability of customer behavior Granted that customer unpredictability poses difficulties, especially for **high-contact services,** but methods planning and methods improvements are nevertheless used quite effectively to eliminate unnecessary activities in service processes. Items (a), (c), and (d) are all true; you should recognize them as re-statements of some prominent operations-planning concepts discussed in the chapter.
7. False This is a controversial statement because it's partly true and partly false. Internet **purchasing,** or e-procurement, does allow faster contact with more suppliers. But that doesn't mean it's better than traditional purchasing. In fact, making "faster contact with more suppliers" has become a problem for some large firms, some of which have actually had to reduce their use of e-procurement. Other firms, however, are benefiting from online purchasing in the form of lower prices and more efficient relationships with suppliers.
8. (a) The main purpose of just-in-time systems is to reduce inventories Contrary to popular opinion, inventory reduction is not the main purpose of **just-in-time production.** Its main purpose is the one stated in item (d): continuous improvement of production by finding and eliminating disruptions and waste. Inventory reduction is just one way to accomplish these objectives. Other means include worker training and participation, **quality improvement,** and methods improvement. Items (b) and (c) both reflect key MRP concepts discussed in the chapter.
9. False The use of standard and uniform components is called **standardization. Materials management,** in contrast, is a broader process involving four major areas for materials

flows: transportation, warehousing, inventory control, and purchasing.

Chapter 15

1. False Although output may be higher due to workers' efforts, that's not necessarily the case. **Labor productivity** may increase because of other reasons, such as modernizing equipment, redesigning products, or using better materials, and not from workers working harder or faster.
2. (b) Manufacturing productivity has been losing ground to services productivity To the contrary, manufacturing **productivity** has grown faster for the past decade and far surpasses both services and federal government productivity. Item (a) is true: Government productivity (at least at last report) is lower than either services or manufacturing productivity in the private sector. Item (c) is true: Consumer electronics retailing, for example, has greater productivity than metal can manufacturing. Item (d) true, as discussed in the text.
3. (d) Labor-productivity measurement is popular because most countries keep accurate records on employment and hours worked, thus making labor productivity easy to calculate and compare The ease of measuring **labor productivity,** along with the availability of data in many countries, make it the measurement of choice for productivity assessment. Item (a) is clearly incorrect: **Productivity** and **quality** are nearly inseparable, both conceptually and in practice. Improved quality contributes directly to productivity, and, conversely, productivity improvements can contribute to greater quality. Item (b) is "upside down": The correct form is "outputs" divided by "resource inputs." Item (c) is pure fiction. There is no such requirement. The government can obtain the data from other sources.
4. (b) In controlling for quality, managers should establish specific standards and measurements Controlling is a process of comparing performance with goals; in **total quality management,** those goals should be specific standards and measurements. Item (a) is false because total quality management focuses on improving all parts of the organization, not just production and products. Item (c) is false: No stage of quality management—planning, organizing, directing, or controlling—is generally regarded as "the most important." Item (d) is incorrect: **TQM** is sometimes called **quality *assurance,*** but not "quality *insurance*."
5. True By definition, **statistical process control (SPC)** uses numerical data—statistics—that represent some characteristic of the process that a company wants to monitor and manage for good performance. Data from the process are gathered, measured, analyzed, and monitored to control the process at some desired level. Data and analysis can also reveal opportunities for improvement.
6. (d) Quality/cost studies are conducted to determine how much a company is spending in order to prevent product failures The statement is wrong. The scope of such studies goes beyond prevention costs. **Quality/cost studies** are useful for identifying how much the firm is spending for prevention, but they also isolate the costs for making and repairing defectives and the additional costs incurred if defectives reach the customer. Items (a), (b), and (c) are all true; you should recognize them as re-statements of prominent **TQM** tools discussed in this section of the chapter.
7. False Certification signifies nothing about the quality level of your products as compared to others in the same industry. It signifies that your firm has documented the procedures that it uses to achieve quality, such as testing products, training workers, keeping records, and fixing defects. Certification means that you are consistently applying the same quality procedures at all times, but it doesn't ensure that your products are up to the standards of other firms in your industry.
8. (b) A company using the supply chain strategy always focuses on the next stage (either incoming or outgoing) in the chain Supply chain strategies would reject item (b) because focusing on the next stage (either incoming or outgoing) is shortsighted and, consequently, doesn't allow the entire chain to work as a coordinated unit. Contrary to the supply chain concept, the approach suggested in item (b) would limit the chain's performance; it wouldn't allow for improvements in coordination that would benefit customers and suppliers throughout the chain. Items (a), (c) and (d) are true: Supply chains do involve the flow of information as well as flows of materials and services; efficiency in supply chains means faster on-time deliveries and lower costs; and reengineering is used for improving supply chains in order to lower costs and better coordinate flows of materials and information.
9. True Employee empowerment recognizes that everyone in the organization has potentially useful knowledge and skills and that, when they're put to use, employees gain **job satisfaction** while employers benefit from employee contributions.

Chapter 16

1. (a) Computers According to the chapter, **electronic information technologies (EIT),** such as items (b), (c), (d), and (e), are **IS** applications that use *networks of appliances or devices to communicate information by electronic means*. A computer is a hardware device that need not be part of a network, and it can be used for purposes other than to communicate information. Although computers manipulate **data** and assist in creating **information,** they are not EITs.
2. False Search engines will search cyberspace's millions of Web pages but won't pre-classifying them in directories. It searches for Web pages that contain the same words as the user's search terms and then displays addresses for the closest matches. Web site directories, such as those maintained by Yahoo!, classify new Web sites into directories (lists) of sites with titles containing the same key words.
3. (c) It maintains orderly flows by prohibiting Web sites from listing URLs for related Web sites Any Web user will quickly point out that the statement in (c) is wrong. Many (even most) sites have readily displayed colored links on which users can point-and-click to go to other related sites. Items (a), (b), and (d) are all correct, as discussed in the first part of the chapter.
4. (c) Special information for conducting technical projects on spe-

cific problems Knowledge workers** are specialists who rely on information technology for special needs in conducting specific projects, such as designing new products or installing new computer systems. Item (a) is more indicative of the kinds of information needed for top-level management. Items (b) and (d) describe the kinds of information needs typically associated with middle and first-line managers, respectively.

5. False Transaction processing systems apply information processing to basic day-to-day business transactions, such as order taking, payroll processing, and billing. In contrast, the processes for business planning involve a broader range of information and variables, including nonstandard information, and provide flexibility in choosing what factors to consider in the planning process. Because business planning is certainly not a standardized process, transaction processing systems are inappropriate for business-planning applications.

6. (d) Upper-level managers' avoidance of detailed information about specific operations In fact, the reverse is most likely true: Detailed information about individual work stations and operations has become easily accessible at low cost for higher-level managers using information technologies. Today's top manager uses such information more often to find out quickly the status of any customer order and to check on the performance of individual operators. This same reasoning applies to item (a): Leaner organizations are emerging because information networks provide direct communications between top managers and workers at lower levels, thus reducing the need for some middle-management positions. Items (b), (c), and (e) reflect increased collaboration, greater independence of company and workplace, and the use of networking in the virtual company, respectively. All are discussed in the chapter.

7. (d) A centralized database that includes all of a firm's data files Every information system includes a **database**—a centralized, organized collection of related **data.** A given firm, however, may have several IS systems, each with its own database. With multiple databases, all of a firm's data may not be consolidated into one centralized database. Accordingly, item (d) is not correct. Items (a), (b), (c), and (e) correctly identify four additional IS components—**hardware, software,** control, and people—along with brief examples or descriptions of each. An additional IS component—telecommunications—was not included in the question.

8. True The **application programs** listed in the statement—**word processing, electronic spreadsheets,** and **computer graphics software**—can help in creating professional-level, attractive, and stimulating presentations. Word processing is convenient for organizing content in word and symbol format that can then be displayed visually. Spreadsheets are handy for organizing numerical data and for manipulating relationships among categories of data so that the audience can see how changes in some numbers cause changes in others. Graphics programs and presentation software offer motion, color, and sound that not only display information in a useful format, but add some life to presentations.

9. (e) A global positioning system (GPS) GPSs use satellite transmissions to track and identify the geographic locations of targets, such as delivery vehicles. With continuous tracking, fleet managers monitor the locations of vehicles, report on weather conditions or road hazards, and re-direct drivers to nearby locations for new pickups. A **wide area network**—item (a)—does not provide continuous location tracking and so doesn't meet the needs described in the situation. Item (b), **fiber optic cable,** is merely one kind of material for linking telecommunications **hardware** in telecommunications networks and is thus irrelevant. Item (d), a paging system, might be a second choice, but even a wireless pager would require numerous back-and-forth communications between driver and dispatcher to achieve continuous tracking.

Chapter 17

1. False Although auditing services are provided by CPA firms for client companies, those services deal primarily with **financial accounting** matters rather than issues in **managerial accounting**. Whereas managerial accounting serves *internal* users, financial accounting is concerned with *external* users of financial information such as **income statements** and **balance sheets.**

2. (a) Auditing for clients owned by the CPA firm Auditing, one of the major products offered by **CPAs,** continues to be an important source of revenue for CPA firms. CPAs, however, are not permitted to perform **audits** for clients in which the CPA firm has an ownership interest. Both the accounting profession and federal regulations frown on the potential conflict of interest entailed by such an arrangement. The other items—financial planning (b), management advisory services (c), tax services (d), and advice on AIS design (e)—are all services offered to clients by CPA firms.

3. (d) Today's accounting systems require fundamental revisions in generally accepted accounting principles (GAAP) for auditing Nothing in the AICPA's reports even hint that changes are needed in **GAAP** standards for auditing. Indeed, those principles have been developed under close scrutiny and have withstood intense examination and testing for decades. Instead, the reports suggest as catalysts for rethinking the profession's future considerations the decline in the number of young people entering the profession (b) and the fact that an increasing number of non-**CPA** competitors are not bound by the profession's code of standards (a). As for (c), the "global forces" affecting the industry are prompting reconsiderations of core CPA services and competencies (e).

4. (d) An accounting error has occurred The accounting equation has been violated. Using Millie's data, we find that **assets** minus **liabilities** are not equal to **owner's equity** for the current year. Assets minus liabilities = $2,500, which should equal owner's equity; but the **financial statement** says that owner's equity is $4,500. Someone has incorrectly applied accounting procedures. Item (a) is not true because, from the data given, we have no way of knowing how fast assets versus liabilities are growing. Item (b) is not true because there is no way to know, from the given data, whether or not owner's equity is changing and, if so, what's causing the change. Items (c) and (e) are incorrect because the information given does not identify the kinds of assets, nor does it reveal last year's comparison numbers for **retained earnings.**

5. (e) Allowance for doubtful accounts increases the book value of accounts receivable The reverse, in fact, is true: Allowance for doubtful accounts decreases the book value of **accounts receivable.** Doubtful accounts are receivables judged to be uncollectable. In order for accounts receivable to reflect what the seller truly expects to happen, doubtful accounts should be deducted from total receivables on the books. All of the other items—**depreciation** (a), **liquidity** of **current assets** (b), types of current assets (c), and **prepaid expenses** (d)—are subject to accounting practices as discussed in the chapter.

6. False Although they wish that the statement was true, many firms discover to their dismay that it's not. Nothing in the arithmetic assures a positive **gross margin.** Whether it turns out to be a positive or negative amount depends on the way the business is managed. The only way to make it positive is by conducting the business so that its gross **revenues** are greater than the costs of buying or making the products that it sells **(cost of goods sold).** If revenues are too low or costs too high, the gross margin will be negative.

7. True The statement is true because the principle of revenue recognition stipulates that earnings are not reported in **financial statements** until the earnings cycle is completed. The earnings cycle is completed when the product has been delivered and the sales price is collected or is collectable. In this case, Kiddie Kar delivers the wagons in 2003 (accompanied by an invoice that makes the bills collectable). Thus the earnings cycle is completed in 2003.

8. (a) An inventory turnover ratio of 6.5 means that the firm has enough inventory on hand to supply its sales requirements for the next 6.5 months Inventory turnover ratio does not indicate how many months' worth of **inventory** is available. Rather, it measures the average number of times that inventory is sold and restocked during the year. In this case, inventory is sold and restocked 6.5 times per year. In other words, it goes through 6.5 complete inventory cycles every year. Items (b), (c), (d), and (e), as discussed in the chapter, all are true.

9. False Although **earnings per share** is an often-used indicator of profitability, we can't say that it's more or less reliable than **return on equity.** The two ratios measure two different things, and investors, of course, like to see high values for both. But when it comes to choosing which is the better indicator of profitability, it's a matter of investor preference. If earnings per share are low, for example, return on equity can still be high (and attractive to some investors) if owners have very little invested. Other investors, however, prefer high earnings per share with prospects for increased dividends regardless of equity.

Chapter 18

1. (b) Durability Loss of value from wear or deterioration indicates that **money** doesn't have the durability needed to withstand repeated use over time. Item (a), stability, refers to the absence of fluctuations in the value of money overtime. Money has divisibility (c) if it can be easily broken down into smaller parts. Portability (d) means that the money is lightweight and easy to handle.

2. False The example focuses on **money** as a *unit of account:* It serves as a measure of the relative values of products so that they can be accounted for in terms of money. Thus the suit and bike, combined, are worth the same amount as the stereo. *Medium of exchange* merely means that money is a way of buying and selling things instead of using a system of barter.

3. (b) Credit cards ("plastic money") are included in M-2 but not in M-1 Credit cards are not included in either **M-1** or **M-2.** In other words, in the U.S. money supply, they are not recognized as a form of **money.** Items (a), (c), (d), and (e), all are true, as discussed in the chapter.

4. True Although borrower eligibility and such terms as interest rate and collateral vary, loans are available from **credit unions, mutual savings banks, savings and loan associations, commercial banks,** and **finance companies.** Credit unions, for example, loan money to members but not to non-members. Commercial banks loan money to individuals and businesses with no such requirements.

5. (d) Banker's trust Trust departments in **commercial banks** can arrange and manage a trust that meets your specifications for holding and transferring assets to your children. Bank officers will provide financial advice, arrange for the legal documents, retain the trust document, and ensure that the terms of the document are implemented once the children reach age 40. The other alternatives—**IRA, pension fund, banker's acceptance,** and commercial loan—are financial services for purposes other than those described.

6. (a) $643.13 Your bank keeps $37.50 in reserve (15 percent of $250) and loans out $212.50 to borrowers. After the $212.50 is deposited by borrowers in their banks, those banks keep $31.857 in reserve (15 percent of $212.50) and loan out $180.625. Banks, therefore, have turned your original $250 into $643.13 ($250.00 + $212.50 + $180.625, rounded)

7. (c) Decrease the discount rate To control the money supply, **the Fed** uses four primary tools: **reserve requirements** (b), **discount rate** controls (c) and (e), **open-market operations** (a), and **selective credit controls** item (d). Item (c) is the correct choice because it takes the money supply in the wrong direction if the goal is to *decrease* it. If the discount rate is decreased, the lower rates will encourage borrowing and increase, rather than reduce, the money supply. The other proposed actions will have the desired effect.

8. (b) E-cash Many banks offer **ATMs** (e), **smart cards** (c), credit cards (d), and **debit cards** (a). **E-cash** (b), however, involves electronic money developed by individual firms or groups of companies that sell it to online shoppers who, in turn, use it to buy from merchants who accept it. E-cash transactions are convenient because they're cheaper than handling checks and avoid the record keeping entailed by conventional money. But they're also risky because e-cash is an unregulated money supply.

9. False There is no institution or organization that serves as a global regulatory authority for supervising the International Banking System or monitoring the international payments process. In fact, there is no "International Banking System"—at least nothing that's in any way comparable to the banking systems of individual countries. The **World Bank** is a United Nations agency that provides improvement loans for needy countries that want to improve productive capacity and increase international trade, but its services are limited in scope. The World Bank, for example, doesn't provide checking, savings, trust, and other services commonly offered by commercial banks.

Chapter 19

1. False Par value is the face value of a share at the time it was originally issued, which could have been recently or many years in the past. It is a fixed, unchanging value, whereas the current market price (the purchase price you will have to pay) reflects the amount that investors are currently willing to pay. It's usually much different (greater) than par value.
2. (d) An investment bank To bring a new **security** to market, the issuing firm often needs the services of an **investment bank**—a financial institution that specializes in issuing and reselling new securities. Investment banks advise on the timing and financial terms of the issue, buy it, and serve as a distribution network for it. **Discount brokers** (a), **full-service brokers** (b), and the NYSE (c), all cater more to **secondary securities markets** (e) than to new issues. Thus they're less useful when it comes to issuing new securities.
3. (c) The number of shares traded on the floor at the Nasdaq Stock Market is greater than at the NYSE The volume of shares traded at **Nasdaq** is greater than at NYSE. But the phrase "on the floor" makes (c) incorrect: Nasdaq orders are paired and executed on a computer network, whereas orders at the NYSE are paired on the trading floor (a). Items (b), (d), and (e) all are true, as discussed in the text.
4. (b) Corporate bonds issued by U.S. companies involve less money than U.S. government and municipal bonds To the contrary, **bonds** issued by U.S. companies are a major source of corporate financing, involving more money than **government bonds** and **municipal bonds** combined. U.S. government bonds (a) are among the safest investments available, and **secured bonds** (c) reduce risk by pledging assets against default. **Convertible bonds** (d) allow holders to exchange corporate bonds for shares of the company's **common stock.** Item (e) is true, as discussed in the chapter.
5. True If **bond** buyers regard the issuing firm as a good investment—as they probably do with a well-respected company—then **convertible bonds** are certainly among the instruments that the issuing firm should consider. Because it offers flexibility to the holders (they can convert the bond to **common stocks** at some future time), convertible bonds can pay lower interest rates than other kinds of bonds, thus meeting one of this firm's **securities** objectives.
6. (e) Callable bonds with sinking fund provisions Callable bonds can be called in (retired) over time, which is one of the superintendent's objectives. Because the **sinking fund provision** provides assurances that funds will be available to pay the holder, such a bonds are generally regarded as safer investments than many others. **Debentures** (a) are unsecured bonds that offer less safety. **Bearer bonds** (b) don't offer features that support the superintendent's objectives. **Futures contracts** and **mutual funds** are irrelevant to this investment situation.
7. (a) Place a limit order and a stop order If you place a **limit order,** the stock will be purchased only if its price is less than a specified limit, thus assuring that you will buy it only at the low price you've specified. By placing a **stop order,** you're instructing the **broker** to sell if, once you've bought the stock, its price falls to a specific level, thus saving yourself further losses. Trading in **round lots** (b) and using **margin trading** (d) are irrelevant to the objectives stated in the question. Item (c), using two market orders, merely tells the broker to first buy, then sell, at the prevailing market price and gives you no assurance of reaching the objectives in the question. Item (e)—selling short—is appropriate if you think that the price is going to fall in the future; the problem, however, implies that the price is expected to rise.
8. False Because it includes only 30 of the thousands of companies on the market, the **Dow** is regarded as a less accurate barometer of price movements than some other indexes. With 500 stocks, the **S&P** index represents a much broader range of types and sizes of firms. The **Nasdaq Composite Index** covers an even broader spectrum, with price averages for thousands of firms.
9. (c) A stock's high- and low-prices for any given day are reported Quotations do not report the intra-day high and low prices of each **stock.** Only the last price for the day (e) and the net change from the previous day's closing (d) are reported. Items (a) and (b) are true, as discussed in the chapter.

Chapter 20

1. (e) Ensuring that the firm abides by generally accepted accounting principles (GAAP) in preparing financial statements Because accountants, rather than **financial managers,** are responsible for ensuring adherence to **GAAP,** the situation doesn't encompass the financial manager's responsibilities. Items (a) and (d) are matters of **cash-flow management** that do fall within the financial manager's domain. Items (b) and (c) are part of the **financial control** process and, accordingly, the financial manager's responsibility.
2. True The "3" indicates a three-percent discount ($300 in this example) if the bill is paid within 20 days after receipt of the purchased goods or services. If it isn't paid within 20 days, the buyer must pay the full $10,000 within 60 days from date of receipt.
3. (b) A long-term loan A key consideration in this situation is the long-term nature of the project: Because expanding and equipping buildings is a long-term capital expenditure rather than short-term project, a long-term source of funds is appropriate. Item (b) is the only long-term source of funds among those listed in the question. All the other items—**trade credit,** inventory loans, factoring accounts receivable, and **revolving credit agreement**—involve short-term funding.

4. (b) The two primary sources of debt financing by U.S companies are corporate bonds and common stock Common stock is a form of **equity financing,** not **debt financing.** In contrast, all the other items—seeking long-term loans, securing bonds to reduce risk, providing information in the bond indenture, and defaulting from non-payment—are all activities related to debt financing.

5. True Retaining the firm's earnings is a form of **equity financing,** as is issuing **common stock,** that provides funds for meeting financial needs. But although retaining earnings provides financial benefits, it also has a drawback: Because every dollar retained is one less dollar paid out to **shareholders,** shareholder wealth decreases.

6. (a) Investors generally expect to receive higher payments for higher uncertainty Although all five items are correct statements, only one responds to the question on the **risk-return relationship:** item (a). Investors do not expect to receive large returns from safe investments such as government-insured bonds. Nor are they willing to expect small returns from high-risk investments such as junk bonds and **common stock.** In general, safer investments tend to offer lower returns and riskier investments higher returns.

7. (b) Risk control Risk control is the use of loss-prevention techniques to minimize the frequency of losses. Training programs provide an effective means for loss reduction by sensitizing employees to workplace dangers, demonstrating methods for reducing and avoiding them, and eliminating them by redesigning work methods and changing behaviors. Training is neither **risk avoidance** (a), which would eliminate employee-based activities, nor **risk retention** (c), which would cover accident costs internally rather than trying to reduce accident frequency. **Risk transfer** (d) would seek to cover losses via outside insurance coverage rather than attempting to reduce accident frequency.

8. True If your cash requirements are part of the normal business cycle rather than a condition of unusual stress, the bank is a logical source for borrowing cash for the two-month timeframe. Your supplier may also be willing to extend your credit period during which you must pay outstanding **accounts payable.** Both the bank and the supplier are potential sources of short-term credit.

9. (c) Unconnectedness
Unconnectedness is the principle that losses must be random and occur independently of other losses. No insurer can afford to write insurance when a large percentage of those parties (businesses, fans, and the soccer federation) who are exposed to a particular kind of loss, such as an earthquake in Japan during the World Cup Championships, are likely to suffer such a loss. Accordingly, by grouping together with other companies, a single insurance firm reduces its chances of a larger loss.

Notes, Sources, and Credits

Reference Notes

Chapter 1

[1]See Paul Heyne, Peter J. Boettke, and David L. Prychitko, *The Economic Way of Thinking,* 10th ed. (Upper Saddle River, NJ: Prentice Hall, 2003), 171–76.

[2]See Ricky W. Griffin and Michael W. Pustay, *International Business—A Managerial Perspective,* 3rd ed. (Upper Saddle River, NJ: Prentice Hall, 2002), 26–49.

[3]See Karl E. Case and Ray C. Fair, *Principles of Economics,* 6th ed., updated (Upper Saddle River, NJ: Prentice Hall, 2003), 47.

[4]See Robert A. Collinge and Ronald M. Ayers, *Economics by Design: Principles and Issues,* 2nd ed. (Upper Saddle River, NJ: Prentice Hall, 2000), 41–42; Michael J. Mandel, "The New Economy," *Business Week* (January 31, 2000), 73–77.

[5]See also Case and Fair, *Principles of Economics,* 224–25.

[6]See Marc Gunther, "AOL's Grand Unified Theory of the Media Cosmos," *Fortune* (January 8, 2001), 72, 74+; Catherine Yang with Ronald Grover and Ann Therese Palmer, "Showtime for AOL and Time Warner," *Business Week* (January 15, 2001), 56–62+.

[7]See Rick Kuhn, "Marxism Page" (June 18, 2002), at <www.anu.edu.au/polsci/marx/marx.html>.

[8]See Case and Fair, *Principles of Economics,* 103–5.

[9]Peter Burrows, "Personal Computers: Are the Glory Days Over?" *Business Week,* February 14, 2000, 50.

[10]See Case and Fair, *Principles of Economics,* 48–67.

[11]See also Heyne, Boettke, and Prychitko, *The Economic Way of Thinking,* Chapters 3 and 4.

[12]See Heyne, Boettke, and Prychitko, *The Economic Way of Thinking,* 190, 358–59.

[13]See Gina M. Larson, "bebe Bridges Style Gap" (July 10, 2001), at <www.office.com/global/0,2724,509-10386_1,FF.html>; Natural Fibers Information Center, "Ranking of Top U.S. Public Apparel Companies" (June 2001), at <www.utexas.edu/depts/bbr/natfiber>; "bebe.com Finishes #1," *Fashion Windows.com* (January 14, 2002), at <www.fashionwindows.com/beauty/2002/bebe.asp>.

[14]See Case and Fair, *Principles of Economics,* 300–9.

[15]*Hoover's Handbook of World Business 2002* (Austin, TX: Hoover's Business Press, 2002), 74–75.

[16]See Case and Fair, *Principles of Economics,* Chapter 12.

[17]See Henry R. Cheesman, *Business Law: Ethical, International, and E-Commerce Environment,* 4th ed. (Upper Saddle River, NJ: Prentice Hall, 2001), 965–66.

[18]See "Pamphlet: In Defence of Laissez-Faire," *Modern History Sourcebook* (June 18, 2002), at <www.fordham.edu/halsall/mod/1840laissezfaire.html>.

[19]See "Microsoft Case in Brief," *CNNMoney* (November 1, 2001), at <http://money.cnn.com/2001/11/01/news/microsoft_chronology/index.htm>; "Target Microsoft," *Time Digital* (June 18, 2002), at <ww\w.time.com/time/digital/microsoft>.

[20]See Griffin and Pustay, *International Business,* 12–18.

[21]See Efraim Turban et al., *Electronic Commerce: A Managerial Perspective* (Upper Saddle River, NJ: Prentice Hall, 2000), 17–30; Elias M. Awad, *Electronic Commerce* (Upper Saddle River, NJ: Prentice Hall, 2002), 42–50.

Chapter 2

[1]See Jay B. Barney and William G. Ouchi (Eds.), *Organizational Economics* (San Francisco: Jossey-Bass, 1986), for a detailed analysis of linkages between economics and organizations.

[2]Karl E. Case and Ray C. Fair, *Principles of Economics,* 6th ed., updated (Upper Saddle River, NJ: Prentice Hall, 2003), 432–33.

[3]Case and Fair, *Principles of Economics,* 15.

[4]Case and Fair, *Principles of Economics,* 15.

[5]Central Intelligence Agency, *The World Factbook 2000* (February 16, 2001), at <www.odci.gov/cia/publications/factbook/geos/us.html>.

[6]See Olivier Blanchard, *Macroeconomics,* 3rd ed. (Upper Saddle River, NJ: Prentice Hall, 2003), 24–26.

[7]See Jay Heizer and Barry Render, *Operations Management,* 6th ed. (Upper Saddle River, NJ: Prentice Hall, 2001), 15–16.

[8]United Auto Workers, *UAW Research Bulletin: Productivity and Growth* (March 9, 2001), at <http://uaw.com/publications/bobs_pay/0700/jpe03.html>.

[9]This section is based on Paul Heyne, Peter J. Boettke, and David L. Prychitko, *The Economic Way of Thinking,* 10th ed. (Upper Saddle River, NJ: Prentice Hall, 2003), 491–93.

[10]See Warren J. Keegan, *Global Marketing Management,* 7th ed. (Upper Saddle River, NJ: Prentice Hall, 2002), 39–42.

[11]This section follows Robert A. Collinge and Ronald M. Ayers, *Economics by Design: Principles and Issues,* 2nd ed. (Upper Saddle River, NJ: Prentice Hall, 2000), 356–58.

[12]See Heyne et al., *The Economic Way of Thinking,* 403–9, 503–4.

[13]See Collinge and Ayres, *Economics by Design,* 362–65.

[14]See Case and Fair, *Principles of Economics,* 416.

[15]Ram Charan and Geoffrey Colvin, "Managing for the Slowdown," *Fortune* (February 5, 2001), 78–88.

[16]See "Rethinking the Internet," *Business Week* (March 26, 2001), 116–36.

[17]Michael J. Mandel et al., "The 21st Century Economy," *Business Week* (August 31, 1998), 58–67. See also David Fairlamb and Gail Edmondson, "Work in Progress—Signs Abound of a Nascent New Economy," *Business Week* (January 31, 2000), 80–87.

[18]See also Brian Bremner and Moon Ihlwan, "Edging Toward the Information Age," *Business Week* (January 31, 2000), 90–91.

[19]Charan and Colvin, "Managing for the Slowdown," 78–88.

[20]Bremner and Ihlwan, "Edging Toward the Information Age," 91.

[21]Rich Miller et al., "How Prosperity Is Reshaping the American Economy," *Business Week* (February 14, 2000), 100–04.
[22]See Roberta S. Russell and Bernard W. Taylor III, *Operations Management,* 4th ed. (Upper Saddle River, NJ: Prentice Hall, 2003), Chapter 12.
[23]"Andersen Ends Role As Public Auditor," *USATODAY.com,* (September 4, 2002), at <www.usatoday.com>.
[24]See Lee J. Krajewski and Larry P. Ritzman, *Operations Management: Strategy and Analysis,* 6th ed. (Upper Saddle River, NJ: Prentice Hall, 2002), 102–6.
[25]See Anne T. Coughlin et al., *Marketing Channels,* 6th ed. (Upper Saddle River, NJ: Prentice Hall, 2001), 168–72.
[26]See Judy Strauss and Raymond Frost, *E-Marketing* (Upper Saddle River, NJ: Prentice Hall, 2001), 245–46.
[27]See Krajewski and Ritzman, *Operations Management,* 3–4.
[28]See Krajewski and Ritzman, *Operations Management,* Chapter 3.
[29]See especially "9.11.02," *Business Week* (September 16, 2002), 22–28+.

Chapter 3

[1]U.S. Department of Commerce, "Statistics about Business Size (Including Small Business)," *Statistical Abstract of the United States* (December 4, 2002), at <www.census.gov/epcd/www/smallbus.html>.
[2]Small Business Administration (SBA), "Learn about SBA" (September 6, 2001), at <www.sba.gov/aboutsba/>.
[3]See Jim McCartney, "Celebrity Endorsement: Vice President Dick Cheney Got Medtronic's Version of the Implantable Cardioverter Defibrillator," *Pioneer Planet* (July 3, 2001), at <http://mbbnbet.umn.edu/MBBNetNews/cheney.html>; John Heilemann, "Reinventing the Wheel," *Time.com* (December 2, 2001), at <www.time.com/time/business/article/0,8599,186660,00.html>.
[4]SBA, "Learn about SBA," at <www.sba.gov/aboutsba/>.
[5]See Thomas W. Zimmerer and Norman M. Scarborough, *Essentials of Entrepreneurship and Small Business,* 3rd ed. (Upper Saddle River, NJ: Prentice Hall, 2002), 4–6.
[6]See also Paulette Thomas, "A New Generation Re-Writes the Rules," *Wall Street Journal* (May 22, 2002), R4.
[7]Nicholas Stein, "The Renaissance Man of E-Commerce," *Fortune* (February 7, 2000), 181–82.
[8]Brian O'Reilly, "What It Takes to Start a Startup," *Fortune* (June 7, 1999), 135–40.
[9]See Zimmerer and Scarborough, *Essentials of Entrepreneurship and Small Business,* Chapter 10.
[10]See Zimmerer and Scarborough, *Essentials of Entrepreneurship and Small Business,* Chapter 8. See also Charles T. Horngren, Srikant M. Datar, and George Foster, *Cost Accounting: A Managerial Emphasis,* 11th ed. (Upper Saddle River, NJ: Prentice Hall, 2003), 195–99.
[11]See Zimmerer and Scarborough, *Essentials of Entrepreneurship and Small Business,* Chapter 5.
[12]Jim Hopkins, "Venture Capital Investments Plunge 23%," *USA Today* (May 1, 2002), 1B.
[13]See Norman M. Scarborough and Thomas W. Zimmerer, *Effective Small Business Management: An Entrepreneurial Approach,* 7th ed. (Upper Saddle River, NJ: Prentice Hall, 2003), Chapter 4.
[14]*Statistical Abstract of the United States: 2001,* (Austin, TX: Hoover's Business Press Edition, 2002), 491.
[15]See Efraim Turban et al., *Electronic Commerce: A Managerial Perspective* (Upper Saddle River, NJ: Prentice Hall, 2000), 449–51.
[16]Andy Serwer, "There's Something about Cisco," *Fortune* (May 15, 2000), 114–38.
[17]See U.S. Census Bureau, "Surveys of Minority- and Women-Owned Enterprises," *Statistical Abstract of the United States* (September 6, 2001), at <www.census.gov/csd/mwb>.
[18]Bill Meyers, "Women Increase Standing as Business Owners," *USA Today* (June 29, 1999), 1B.
[19]Noelle Knox, "Women Entrepreneurs Attract New Financing," *New York Times* (July 26, 1998), 10.
[20]Scarborough and Zimmerer, *Effective Small Business Management,* Chapter 12.
[21]See Scarborough and Zimmerer, *Effective Small Business Management,* 412–13.
[22]Jim Hopkins, "Expert Entrepreneur Got Her Show on the Road at an Early Age," *USA Today* (May 24, 2000), 5B.
[23]See Henry R. Cheeseman, *Contemporary Business Law* (Upper Saddle River, NJ: Prentice Hall, 2000), 553–55; and Scarborough and Zimmerer, *Effective Small Business Management,* 73–76.
[24]Department of Commerce, "Statistics about Business Size," *Statistical Abstract of the United States* (September 6, 2001), at <www.census.gov/epcd/www/smallbus.html>.
[25]See Cheeseman, *Contemporary Business Law,* 554–55.
[26]See Cheeseman, *Contemporary Business Law,* Chapter 24; and Scarborough and Zimmerer, *Effective Small Business Management,* 77–84.
[27]*Statistical Abstract of the United States: 2001,* 507.
[28]"Statistics about Business Size," at <www.census.gov/epcd/www/smallbus.html>.
[29]"Fortune Five Hundred Largest Corporations," *Fortune* (April 18, 2002), F1–F20.
[30]See Cheeseman, *Contemporary Business Law,* Chapter 25.
[31]See Cheeseman, *Contemporary Business Law,* 652–54.
[32]See Cheeseman, *Contemporary Business Law,* 611–13.
[33]See Cheeseman, *Contemporary Business Law,* Chapter 26.
[34]See John A. Byrne, "How to Fix Corporate Governance," *Business Week* (May 6, 2002), pp. 68–78.
[35]See Matthew Boyle, "The Dirty Half-Dozen: America's Worst Boards," *Fortune,* (May 14, 2001), pp. 249–52.
[36]See Thomas L. Wheelen and J. David Hunger, *Strategic Management and Business Policy,* 7th ed. (Upper Saddle River, NJ: Prentice Hall, 2000), 125–29.
[37]Go to The National Center for Employee Ownership (September 6, 2001), at <www.nceo.org/>.

Chapter 4

[1]*Hoover's Handbook of World Business 2002* (Austin, TX: Hoover's Business Press, 2002).
[2]See John J. Wild, Kenneth L. Wild, and Jerry C.Y. Han, *International Business,* 2nd ed. (Upper Saddle River, NJ: Prentice Hall, 2003), 14–21.
[3]See Stuart R. Lynn, *Economic Development: Theory and Practice for a Divided World* (Upper Saddle River, NJ: Prentice Hall, 2003), 2–4, 33–36; Ricky W. Griffin and Michael W. Pustay, *International Business: A Managerial Perspective,* 3rd ed. (Upper Saddle River, NJ: Prentice Hall, 2002), 27.

[4]Trade Partners UK, "Automotive Industries Market in Mexico" (July 10, 2001), at <www.tradepartners.gov/uk/automotive/mexico/opportunities/opportunities.shtml>; NAFTA Works, "Mexico Auto Sector Sees $15 Billion Investment in 5 Years" (July 10, 2001), at <www.naftaworks.org/papers/2000/automex.htm>.

[5]David Fairlamb and Gail Edmondson, "Work in Progress," *Business Week* (January 31, 2000), 80–81+.

[6]See Edmund L. Andrews, "The Metamorphosis of Germany Inc.," *New York Times,* March 12, 2000, sec. 3, 1, 12.

[7]See Mark Landler, "Mapping Out Silicon Valley East," *New York Times* (April 5, 1999), C1, C10; and Bruce Einhorn with Cathy Yang, "Portal Combat," *Business Week* (January 17, 2000), 96–97.

[8]Wild, Wild, and Han, *International Business,* 239.

[9]See Griffin and Pustay, *International Business,* 125–27. See also Steven Husted and Michael Melvin, *International Economics,* 5th ed. (Boston: Addison Wesley Longman, 2001), 54–61; and Karl E. Case and Ray C. Fair, *Principles of Economics,* 6th ed. (Upper Saddle River, NJ: Prentice Hall, 2002), 669–77.

[10]See Husted and Melvin, *International Economics,* 60–61.

[11]This section is based on Michael Porter, *The Competitive Advantage of Nations* (Boston: Harvard Business School Press, 1990), Chapters 3 and 4. See also Wild, Wild, and Han, *International Business,* 155–59; Warren J. Keegan and Mark C. Green, *Global Marketing,* 3rd ed. (Upper Saddle River, NJ: Prentice Hall, 2003), 380–88.

[12]J. Michael Donnelly, "U.S. Merchandise Trade Statistics: 1948–2000," *CRS Report for Congress* (March 15, 2001), at <www.cnie.org/NLE/CRSreports/Economics/econ-54.cfm>; Andrzej Zwaniecki, "U.S. Trade Deficit Down as Imports Slide and Exports Grow" (October 19, 2001), at <www.usconsulate.org.hk/usinfo/statis/ft/2001/08.htm>.

[13]*Hoover's Handbook of World Business 2002,* 56.

[14]See Griffin and Pustay, *International Business,* 171–81.

[15]See Case and Fair, *Principles of Economics,* 675–77; Griffin and Pustay, *International Business,* 189–91; Husted and Melvin, *International Economics,* 306–10.

[16]Robyn Meredith, "Dollar Makes Canada a Land of the Spree," *New York Times* (August 1, 1999), sec. 3, 1, 1. See also *Currencies Direct,* "Canada—Cautious Optimism" (July 10, 2001), at <www.currenciesdirect.com/mecklai/NTFxCanadaReport.html>; "Interest Rates," *Canada US Investment* (March 2002), at <www.canadausinvestment.com/Caninfo2.htm>; "The Canada/U.S. Exchange Rate," *FRB Cleveland* (March 2001), at <www.clev.frb.org/research/Et2001/0301/Html/CANEX.htm>.

[17]Jeremy Kahn, "Wal-Mart Goes Shopping in Europe," *Fortune* (June 7, 1999), 105–12; Wendy Zellner, "Someday, Lee, This May All Be Yours," *Business Week* (November 15, 1999), 84, 88, 92; and Michael McCarthy, "Wal-Mart Takes Slow Road in Germany," *USA Today* (May 10, 2000), 3B.

[18]See V. Kumar, *International Marketing Research* (Upper Saddle River, NJ: Prentice Hall, 2000), Chapter 4.

[19]"Worldwide BoxOffice" (August 14, 2002), at <www.worldwideboxoffice.com>.

[20]*Hoover's Handbook of World Business 2002,* 129.

[21]See Norman M. Scarborough and Thomas W. Zimmerer, *Effective Small Business Management: An Entrepreneurial Approach,* 7th ed. (Upper Saddle River, NJ: Prentice Hall, 2003), 349–66.

[22]Paola Hjelt, "The Fortune Global 500," *Fortune* (July 22, 2002), 144–47.

[23]See Keegan and Green, *Global Marketing,* 326–28.

[24]See Keegan and Green, *Global Marketing,* 330–44.

[25]See Wild, Wild, and Han, *International Business,* Chapter 7; Griffin and Pustay, *International Business,* 332–35.

[26]See Robert L. Simison and Scott Miller, "Ford Grabs Big Prize as Steep Losses Force BMW to Sell Rover," *Wall Street Journal* (March 17, 2000), A1, A8; Shelly Branch and Ernest Beck, "For Unilever, It's Sweetness and Light," *Wall Street Journal* (April 13, 2000), B1, B4.

[27]Bureau of Economic Analysis, "Foreign Direct Investment in the U.S." (July 11, 2001), at <www.bea.doc.gov/bea/di/di1fdibal.htm>; Progressive Policy Institute, "Foreign Direct Investment Is on the Rise around the World" (July 11, 2001), at <www.neweconomyindex.org/section1_page04.html>.

[28]World Trade Organization, "Foreign Direct Investment Seen as Primary Motor of Globalization" (July 11, 2001), at <www.wto.org/english/news_e/pres96_e/pr042_e.htm>.

[29]See Robert Frank, "In Paddies of Vietnam, Americans Once Again Land in Quagmire," *Wall Street Journal* (April 21, 2000), A1, A6.

[30]Anthony DePalma, "Chiquita Sues Europeans, Citing Banana Quota Losses," *New York Times* (January 26, 2001), C5; Brian Lavery, "Trade Feud on Bananas Not as Clear as It Looks," *New York Times* (February 7, 2001), W1; David E. Sanger, "Miffed at Europe, U.S. Raises Tariffs for Luxury Goods," *New York Times* (March 4, 1999), A1, A5.

[31]See Keegan and Green, *Global Marketing,* 441–45.

Chapter 5

[1]Constance L. Hays, "Aide Was Reportedly Ordered to Warn Stewart on Stock Sales," *New York Times* (August 6, 2002), C1, C2.

[2]William G. Symonds with Geri Smith, "The Tax Games Tyco Played," *Business Week,* (July 1, 2002), 40–41.

[3]Thomas Donaldson and Thomas W. Dunfee, "Toward a Unified Conception of Business Ethics: An Integrative Social Contracts Theory," *Academy of Management Review* 19, no. 2 (1994), 252–84.

[4]"Drug Companies Face Assault on Prices," *Wall Street Journal* (May 11, 2000), B1, B4.

[5]Jeremy Kahn, "Presto Chango! Sales are Huge," *Fortune* (March 20, 2000), 90–96; "More Firms Falsify Revenue to Boost Stocks," *USA Today* (March 29, 2000), 1B.

[6]This section follows the logic of Gerald F. Cavanaugh, *American Business Values with International Perspectives,* 4th ed. (Upper Saddle River, NJ: Prentice Hall, 1998), Chapter 3.

[7]See "Are Your Work Ethics in Line?" *CNN.com* (July 11, 2001), at <www.cnn.com/TECH/computing/9906/22/ethics.ent.idg/>.

[8]See Abagail McWilliams and Donald Siegel, "Corporate Social Responsibility: A Theory of the Firm Perspective," *Academy of Management Review* 26, no. 1, (2001), 117–27.

[9]Jeffrey S. Harrison and R. Edward Freeman, "Stakeholders, Social Responsibility, and Performance: Empirical Evidence and Theoretical Perspectives," *Academy of Management Journal* 42, no. 5, (1999), 479–85. See also David P. Baron, *Business and Its Environment*, 4th ed. (Upper Saddle River, NJ: Prentice Hall, 2003), Chapter 18.

[10]Mara Der Hovanesian and Heather Timmons, "For Small Banks, It's a Wonderful Life," *Business Week* (May 6, 2002), 83–84.

[11]Charles Haddad, "Woe Is WorldCom," *Business Week* (May 6, 2002), 86–90.

[12]Queena Sook Kim, "Once Skeptics, Builders See Green in 'Green,' " *Wall Street Journal* (July 10, 2002), B1, B6.

[13]Symonds with Smith, "The Games Tyco Played," 40–41.

[14]Gerald Seib, "What Could Bring 1930s-Style Reform of U.S. Business?" *Wall Street Journal* (July 24, 2002), A1, A8.

[15]Richard S. Dunham, "Bush's Softer Sell," *Business Week* (June 25, 2001), 34–37; Paul Raeburn, "Global Warming Needs More Than Just Another Study," *Business Week* (June 25, 2001), 36–37.

[16]Andrew C. Revkin, "Who Cares About a Few Degrees?" *New York Times* (December 12, 1997), F4.

[17]See Baron, *Business and Its Environment*, Chapter 11.

[18]Marilyn Adams, "Careless Cargo," *Danatec Educational Services* (July 11, 2001), at <www.danatec.com/freebie9.htm>; Cat Lazaroff, "American Airlines Guilty of Hazmat Storage, Shipment Violations," *Environment News Service* (July 11, 2001), at <http://ens.lycos.com/ens/dec99/1999L-12-17-06.html>.

[19]Susan Warren, "Recycler's Nightmare: Beer in Plastic," *Wall Street Journal* (November 16, 1999), B1, B4.

[20]U.S. Department of Health and Human Services, "Abbott Labs Signs Consent Decree with FDA," *SafetyAgent.com* (July 11, 2001), at <www.safetyagent.com/reports/P_99_17400.asp>.

[21]Richard B. Schmitt and Robert Langreth, "American Home Products Agrees to Pay Up to $3.75 Billion in Diet-Drug Lawsuits," *WSJ Interactive Edition* (July 11, 2001), at <www.productslaw.com/diet21.html>. See also Nancy Shute, "Pills Don't Come with a Seal of Approval," *U.S. News Online* (July 11, 2001), at <www.usnews.com/usnews/issue/970929/29fen.htm>.

[22]Department of Justice, "F. Hoffmann-La Roche and BASF Agree to Pay Record Criminal Fines for Participating in International Vitamin Cartel" (July 11, 2001), at <www.usdoj.gov/atr/public/press_releases/1999/2450.htm>; Alain L. Sanders, "The 'C' in Vitamin C No Longer Stands for Cartel," *Time.com* (July 11, 2001), at <www.time.com/time/nation/article/0,8599,25068,00.html>.

[23]Greg Farrell, "Enron Law Firm Called Accounting Practices 'Creative'," *USA Today* (January 16, 2002), 1B.

[24]See Jerald Greenberg and Robert A. Baron, *Behavior in Organizations: Understanding and Managing the Human Side of Work*, 7th ed. (Upper Saddle River, NJ: Prentice Hall, 2000), 374–75.

[25]Rick Lyman, "A Tobacco Whistle-Blower's Life Is Transformed," *New York Times* (October 15, 1999), A24.

[26]Cora Daniels, "'It's a Living Hell,'" *Fortune* (April 15, 2002), 367–68.

[27]See Henry R. Cheesman, *Business Law: Ethical, International, and E-Commerce Environment*, 4th ed. (Upper Saddle River, NJ: Prentice Hall, 2001), 144–45.

[28]Andy Pasztor and Peter Landers, "Toshiba to Pay $2B Settlement on Laptops," *ZD Net News* (July 12, 2001), at <www.zdnet.com/zdnn/stories/news/0,4586,2385037,00.html>.

[29]See Cheesman, *Business Law*, 809–11.

[30]Greg Farrell, "Enron Law Firm Called Accounting Practices 'Creative,'" *USA Today* (January 16, 2002), 1B.

[31]For a recent discussion of these issues, see Amy Hillman and Gerald Keim, "Shareholder Value, Stakeholder Management, and Social Issues: What's the Bottom Line?" *Strategic Management Journal* 22, no. 2, (2001), 125–39.

[32]David Bank and Martha Brannigan, "Battling 'Donor Dropsy,'" *Wall Street Journal* (July 19, 2002), B1, B4.

[33]Bruce Horovitz, "Employers Back Olympic Hopefuls," *USA Today* (February 7, 2000), 1B.

[34]See Michael E. Porter and Mark R. Kramer, "Philanthropy's New Agenda: Creating Value," *Harvard Business Review* (November–December 1999), 121–30.

[35]See Sandra Waddock and Neil Smith, "Corporate Responsibility Audits: Doing Well by Doing Good," *Sloan Management Review* (Winter 2000), 75–85.

Chapter 6

[1]Stanley Reed, "Can Scardino Get Pearson Out of This Pickle?" *Business Week* (July 22, 2002), 50–52.

[2]"The Top 25 Managers of the Year," *Business Week* (January 8, 2001), 62; Michael Ryan, "AmEx Charges Ahead," *ZD Net News* (July 17, 2001), at <www.zdnet.com/zdnn/stories/news/0,4586,2688779,00.html>.

[3]David Dorsey, "Andy Pearson Finds Love," *Fast Company* (August 2001), 78–86.

[4]See Thomas L. Wheelan and J. David Hunger, *Strategic Management and Business Policy*, 7th ed. (Upper Saddle River, NJ: Prentice Hall, 2000), 12–14; and Mary K. Coulter, *Strategic Management in Action*, 2nd ed. (Upper Saddle River, NJ: Prentice Hall, 2002), 9–12.

[5]Mike Hofman, "Two Guys and a Start-Up: The True-Life Adventures of First-Time Company Founders," *Inc.* (February 2001), 76–81.

[6]See Wheelan and Hunger, *Strategic Management*, 10–14.

[7]Janet Guyon, "Getting the Bugs Out at VW," *Fortune* (March 29, 1999), 96–102; and Dale Jewett, "Running near the Front," *Automotive Industries* (July 18, 2001), at <www.findarticles.com/m3012/4_180/61892631/p1/article.jhtml>.

[8]See Stephen P. Robbins and Mary Coulter, *Management*, 7th ed. (Upper Saddle River, NJ: Prentice Hall, 2002), 202–4; and Wheelan and Hunger, *Strategic Management and Business Policy*, 107.

[9]Melanie Wells, "Red Baron," *Forbes* (July 3, 2000), 150–60; Andrew Ross Sorkin, "Taking Virgin's Brand into Internet Territory," *New York Times* (February 14, 2000), C1, C17.

[10]"Cruise-Ship Delays Leave Guests High and Dry," *Wall Street Journal* (October 24, 1997), B1, B10; *Hoover's Handbook of American Business 2001* (Austin, TX: Hoover's Business Press, 2001), 1512–13.

[11]Peter Burrows, "The Radical—Carly Fiorina's Bold Management Experiment at HP," *Business Week* (February 19, 2001), 70–80.

[12]Brian O'Reilly, "The Mechanic Who Fixed Continental," *Fortune* (December 20, 1999), 176–86; David Field, "Fliers Give Continental Sky-High Marks," *USA Today* (May 10, 2000), 3B.

[13]See David A. Whetten and Kim S. Cameron, *Developing Management Skills,* 5th ed. (Upper Saddle River, NJ: Prentice Hall, 2002), Chapter 6.
[14]Frank Rose, "Vivendi's High Wireless Act," *Wired* (July 18, 2001), at <www.wired.com/wired/archive/8.12/vivendi.html>; Mike Trigg, "Vivendi Grabs Houghton Mifflin," *The Motley Fool* (July 18, 2001), at <www.fool.com/news/2001/v010601.htm>.
[15]"Rallying the Troops at P&G," *Wall Street Journal* (August 31, 2000), B1, B4.

Chapter 7

[1]Robert L. Simison, "Ford Rolls Out New Model of Corporate Culture," *Wall Street Journal* (January 13, 1999), B1, B4; Joann S. Lublin, "Place vs. Product: It's Tough to Choose a Management Model," *Wall Street Journal* (June 27, 2001), A1, A4.
[2]Joann Muller, "Ford: Why It's Worse Than You Think," *Business Week* (June 25, 2001), 80–84+.
[3]See Gregory Moorhead and Ricky W. Griffin, *Organizational Behavior: Managing People and Organizations,* 6th ed. (Boston: Houghton Mifflin, 2001), 420–79.
[4]See Amy Wrzesniewski and Jane Dutton, "Crafting a Job: Revisioning Employees as Active Crafters of Their Work," *Academy of Management Review* 26, no. 2, (2001), 179–201.
[5]Bruce Horovitz, "Restoring the Golden-Arch Shine," *USA Today* (June 16, 1999), 3B; "Industry Report: Restaurant Industry," *US Business Reporter* (July 19, 2001), at <www.activemediaguide.com/print_restaurant.htm>; Michael Arndt, "There's Life in the Old Bird Yet," *Business Week* (May 14, 2001), 77–78.
[6]See David A. Whetten and Kim S. Cameron, *Developing Management Skills,* 5th ed. (Upper Saddle River, NJ: Prentice Hall, 2002), 427–35.
[7]See also Gary Yukl, *Leadership in Organizations,* 5th ed. (Upper Saddle River, NJ: Prentice Hall, 2002), 100–2.
[8]Michael E. Raynor and Joseph L. Bower, "Lead From the Center," *Harvard Business Review* (May 2001), 93–102.
[9]Horovitz, op cit., 3B.
[10]Stephanie Forest, "Can an Outsider Fix J.C. Penney?" *Business Week* (February 12, 2001), 56–58.
[11]Joann Muller, "Thinking Out of the Cereal Box," *Business Week* (January 15, 2001), 54–55.
[12]Donna Fenn, "Redesign Work," *Inc.* (June 1999), 75–83.
[13]See Yukl, *Leadership in Organizations,* 35–36.
[14]"Multi-Tasking: Cost-Reduction Strategy at Case Corp.," *Machinery Systems Inc.* (July 20, 2001), at <www.machinerysystems.com/RavingFan/CaseCorp.html>.
[15]See Whetten and Cameron, *Developing Management Skills,* Chapter. 9; Yukl, *Leadership in Organizations,* Chapter 11.
[16]Lublin, "Place vs. Product," A1, A4.
[17]Robert Berner and Kevin Helliker, "Heinz's Worry: 4,000 Products, Only One Star," *Wall Street Journal* (September 17, 1999), B1, B4.
[18]Diane Brady, "Martha Inc.," *Business Week* (January 17, 2000), 62–66.
[19]Mitchell Lee Marks and Philip H. Mirvis, "Creating an Effective Transition Structure," *Organizational Dynamics* (Winter 2000), 35–44. See also Helen Deresky, *International Management: Managing across Borders and Cultures,* 3rd ed. (Upper Saddle River, NJ: Prentice Hall, 2000), Chapter 9.
[20]"Wal-Mart Acquires Interspar," *Management Ventures* (July 20, 2001) at <www.mventures.com/news/Key1998/flash98/wmtinters.asp>; Kerry Capell et al., "Wal-Mart's Not-So-Secret British Weapon," *Business Week Online* (July 20, 2001), at <www.businessweek.com:/2000/00_04/b3665095.htm>.
[21]Gail Edmondson, "Danone Hits Its Stride," *Business Week* (February 1, 1999), 52–53.
[22]Thomas A. Stewart, "See Jack. See Jack Run," *Fortune* (September 27, 1999), 124–271; Geoffrey Colvin, "America's Most Admired Companies," *Fortune* (February 21, 2000), 108–10.
[23]Leslie P. Willcocks and Robert Plant, "Getting from Bricks to Clicks," *Sloan Management Review* (Spring 2001), 50–60.
[24]Ethan Smith, "Business-Driven CUs Take Many Forms," *Corporate University Review* (July 20, 2001), at <www.traininguniversity.com/magazine/mar_apr97/starting.html>.
[25]See, for example, Denise M. Rousseau, "The Idiosyncratic Deal: Flexibility versus Fairness?" *Organizational Dynamics* 29, no. 4, (2001), 260–73.
[26]See Moorhead and Griffin, *Organizational Behavior,* 248–78.

Chapter 8

[1]See Angelo S. DeNisi and Ricky W. Griffin, *Human Resource Management* (Boston: Houghton Mifflin, 2001), 34–67.
[2]See Luis R. Gómez-Mejía, David B. Balkin, and Robert L. Cardy, *Managing Human Resources,* 3rd ed. (Upper Saddle River, NJ: Prentice Hall, 2001), 64–71.
[3]See Gary Dessler, *Human Resource Management,* 8th ed. (Upper Saddle River, NJ: Prentice Hall, 2000), 126.
[4]Matthew Boyle, "The Not-So-Fine Art of the Layoff," *Fortune* (March 19, 2001), 209–10.
[5]Associated Press, "Unemployment Steady but Hiring Slows," *WFAA.com* (August 21, 2001), at <http://www.wfaa.com/wfaa/articledisplay/1,1002,18294,00.html>.
[6]See Dessler, *Human Resource Management,* 177.
[7]See Dessler, *Human Resource Management,* Chapter 5.
[8]Kenneth Brown, "Using Computers to Deliver Training: Which Employees Learn and Why?" *Personnel Psychology* (Summer 2001), 271–96.
[9]Abby Ellin, "Training Programs Often Miss the Point on the Job," *New York Times* (March 29, 2000), C12.
[10]See Richard I. Henderson, *Compensation Management in a Knowledge-Based World,* 8th ed. (Upper Saddle River, NJ: Prentice Hall, 2000), 17–18.
[11]See Dessler, *Human Resource Management,* Chapter 12.
[12]See Gómez-Mejía, Balkin, and Cardy, *Managing Human Resources,* 366–69.
[13]See James Bateslos, "Eisner's Stock-Option Profit: $565 Million" (August 21, 2001), at <http://www.onlineathens.com/1997/120597/1205.a3eisnerdisney.html>.
[14]See Gómez-Mejía, Balkin, and Cardy, *Managing Human Resources,* 376–78.
[15]Barbara Carton, "In 24-Hour Workplace, Day Care Is Moving to the Night Shift," *Wall Street Journal* (July 6, 2001), A1, A4.
[16]See Henry R. Cheeseman, *Business Law: Ethical, International, and E-Commerce Environment,* 4th ed. (Upper Saddle River, NJ: Prentice Hall, 2001), Chapter 42.
[17]See Dessler, *Human Resource Management,* 44–46.
[18]See Cheeseman, *Business Law,* 843–47; Dessler, *Human Resource Management,* 40–44.

[19]Jeremy Kahn, "Diversity Trumps the Downturn," *Fortune* (July 9, 2001), 114–28.
[20]See Henderson, *Compensation Management,* 3–6.
[21]Thomas Stewart, "In Search of Elusive Tech Workers," *Fortune* (February 16, 1998), 171–72.
[22]Matt Richtel, "Need for Computer Experts Is Making Recruiters Frantic," *New York Times* (December 18, 1999), C1.
[23]Aaron Bernstein, "When Is a Temp Not a Temp?" *Business Week* (December 7, 1998), 90–92.
[24]See Michael R. Carrell and Christina Heavrin, *Labor Relations and Collective Bargaining: Cases, Practice, and Law,* 6th ed. (Upper Saddle River, NJ: Prentice Hall, 2001), Chapter 1.
[25]David Koenig, "Labor Unions Say Recent Victories Signal a Comeback," Associated Press news release published in *The Bryan-College Station Eagle* (June 11, 2000), E1, E6.
[26]Aaron Bernstein, "Welch's March to the South," *Business Week* (December 6, 1999), 74, 78.
[27]See Carrell and Heavrin, *Labor Relations and Collective Bargaining,* 90–91.
[28]See also Carrell and Heavrin, *Labor Relations and Collective Bargaining,* 189–97.
[29]See Carrell and Heavrin, *Labor Relations and Collective Bargaining,* 197–211.
[30]*New York Times Almanac 2000* (New York: Penguin Reference, 1999), 351.

Chapter 9

[1]Richard B. Chase and Sriram Dasu, "Want to Perfect Your Company's Service? Use Behavioral Science," *Harvard Business Review* (June 2001), 79–88.
[2]Daniel M. Cable and Charles K. Parsons, "Socialization Tactics and Person-Organization Fit," *Personnel Psychology* (Spring 2001), 1–24.
[3]Gregory Moorhead and Ricky W. Griffin, *Organizational Behavior,* 6th ed. (Boston: Houghton Mifflin, 2001), 95–99.
[4]Jerry Useem, "Welcome to the New Company Town," *Fortune* (January 10, 2000), 62–70.
[5]See Jerald Greenberg and Robert A. Baron, *Behavior in Organizations: Understanding and Managing the Human Side of Work,* 7th ed. (Upper Saddle River, NJ: Prentice Hall, 2000), 177–79.
[6]Anne Fisher, "Surviving the Downturn," *Fortune* (April 2, 2001), 98–106.
[7]See Moorhead and Griffin, op cit., Chapters 5 and 6.
[8]See Moorhead and Griffin, *Organizational Behavior,* Chapter 7.
[9]See Moorhead and Griffin, *Organizational Behavior,* Chapter 7.
[10]See Moorhead and Griffin, *Organizational Behavior,* Chapter 7.
[11]Ibid., Chapter 7.
[12]Robert Levering and Milton Moskowitz, "The 100 Best Companies to Work For," *Fortune* (January 8, 2001), 148–66.
[13]See Gary Yukl, *Leadership in Organizations,* 5th ed. (Upper Saddle River, NJ: Prentice Hall, 2002), Chapter 1.
[14]"Insanity, Inc.," *Fast Company* (January 1999), 100–8.
[15]See Francis J. Yammarino, Fred Dansereau, and Christina J. Kennedy, "A Multiple-Level Multidimensional Approach to Leadership," *Organizational Dynamics* 29, no. 3, (2001), 149–63.
[16]See Yukl, *Leadership in Organizations,* Chapter 8; Jon P. Howell and Dan L. Costley, *Understanding Behaviors for Effective Leadership* (Upper Saddle River, NJ: Prentice Hall, 2001), Chapter 3.
[17]See Moorhead and Griffin, *Organizational Behavior,* Chapters 13 and 14.
[18]See Greenberg and Baron, *Behavior in Organizations,* 193–99; Yukl, *Leadership in Organizations,* 418–20.
[19]Frederick F. Reichheld, "Lead for Loyalty," *Harvard Business Review,* July–August 2001, 76–86.

Chapter 10

[1]American Marketing Association, "Marketing Services Guide" (August 23, 2001), at <www.ama.org/about/ama/markdef.asp>.
[2]See Philip Kotler, *Marketing Management,* 11th ed. (Upper Saddle River, NJ: Prentice Hall, 2003), 76–78.
[3]See Warren J. Keegan and Mark C. Green, *Global Marketing,* 2nd ed. (Upper Saddle River, NJ: Prentice Hall, 2000), 7–15.
[4]See Leon G. Schiffman and Leslie Lazar Kanuk, *Consumer Behavior,* 7th ed. (Upper Saddle River, NJ: Prentice Hall, 2000), chap. 3; Kotler, *Marketing Management,* chap. 10.
[5]Alex Taylor III, "Detroit: Every Silver Lining Has a Cloud," *Fortune* (January 24, 2000), 92–93.
[6]"Burberry Earns Independence," *BBC News* (August 23, 2001), at <http://newsvote.bbc.co.uk/hi/english/business/newsid_1047000/1047772.stm>; GUS: The Retail and Services Business Group, "Reports and Accounts" (April 3, 2002), at <www.gusplc.com>.
[7]Kitty McKinsey, "Poland: Credit and Debit Cards Take Off," *Radio Free Europe* (August 23, 2001), at <http://www.rferl.org/nca/features/1997/03/F.RU.970303160756.html>; Jane Perlez, "Joy of Debts: Eastern Europe on Credit Fling," *New York Times* (May 30, 1998), A3.
[8]See Kotler, *Marketing Management,* 292–94.
[9]See Alvin C. Burns and Ronald F. Bush, *Marketing Research,* 3rd ed. (Upper Saddle River, NJ: Prentice Hall, 2000), 7–13; and American Marketing Association, "Marketing Services Guide" (March 1, 2000), at <www.ama.org/about/ama/markdef.asp>.
[10]See V. Kumar, *International Marketing Research* (Upper Saddle River, NJ: Prentice Hall, 2000), 15–22.
[11]See Burns and Bush, *Marketing Research,* 70–84.
[12]See Burns and Bush, *Marketing Research,* 232–37.
[13]See Burns and Bush, *Marketing Research,* chap. 9.
[14]See Burns and Bush, *Marketing Research,* 237–51.
[15]See Burns and Bush, *Marketing Research,* 140–48.
[16]See Kenneth C. Laudon and Jane P. Laudon, *Management Information Systems: Managing the Digital Firm,* 7th ed. (Upper Saddle River, NJ: Prentice Hall, 2002), 221–22.
[17]See Laudon and Laudon, *Management Information Systems,* 222–24.
[18]Paul S. Foote and Malini Krishnamurthi, "Forecasting Using Data Warehousing Model: Wal-Mart's Experience," *The Journal of Business Forecasting Methods & Systems* (Fall 2001), 13–17.
[19]See Schiffman and Kanuk, *Consumer Behavior,* chaps. 6, 7, 8.
[20]See Schiffman and Kanuk, *Consumer Behavior,* chap. 11.
[21]See Schiffman and Kanuk, *Consumer Behavior,* chap. 12.
[22]See Schiffman and Kanuk, *Consumer Behavior,* pp. 442–51.
[23]See Schiffman and Kanuk, *Consumer Behavior,* pp. 69–70.

[24]U.S. Department of Commerce, *Statistical Abstract of the United States: 1998* (Washington, DC: Bureau of the Census, 1999), 305–309, 547, 768, 776.
[25]See Warren J. Keegan, *Global Marketing Management,* 7th ed. (Upper Saddle River, NJ: Prentice Hall, 2002), esp. chaps. 11, 12, and 13.
[26]See Norman N. Scarborough and Thomas W. Zimmerer, *Effective Small Business Management: An Entrepreneurial Approach,* 6th ed. (Upper Saddle River, NJ: Prentice Hall, 2000), chap. 6.
[27]Paco Underhill, "What Shoppers Want," *Inc.* (July 1999), 76, 80.

Chapter 11

[1]Dan Verton, "Oracle Scraps Unpopular Database Pricing Model: Oracle Faces Challenges in the Marketplace," *Computerworld* (June 18, 2001), 6, 8.
[2]See Philip Kotler, *Marketing Management,* 11th ed. (Upper Saddle River, NJ: Prentice Hall, 2003), Chapter 3; Roger J. Best, *Market-Based Management: Strategies for Growing Customer Value and Profitability,* 2nd ed. (Upper Saddle River, NJ: Prentice Hall, 2000), 87–100.
[3]See Kotler, *Marketing Management,* 410–12.
[4]See Kotler, *Marketing Management,* 413–14.
[5]Kelly Barron, "Getting a Rise Out of Levi's," *Forbes* (November 26, 2001), 156–58; "Levi to Cut 3,600 Jobs," *CNNMoney* (April 8, 2002), at <http://money.cnn.com/2002/04/08/news/companies/levis>.
[6]See Chet Zelasko, "Acesulfame-K," *Better Life Institute* (May 17, 2001), at <www.blionline.com/HDB/Acesulfame-K.htm>.
[7]"The Best New Products," *Beverage Industry* (February 2002), 35–37.
[8]See also Cengiz Haksever et al., *Service Management and Operations,* 2nd ed. (Upper Saddle River, NJ: Prentice Hall, 2000), 193–201; Christopher Lovelock, *Services Marketing: People, Technology, Strategy,* 4th ed. (Upper Saddle River, NJ: Prentice Hall, 2001), 245–53.
[9]See Kotler, *Marketing Management,* 328–39.
[10]See Kotler, *Marketing Management,* 422–24.
[11]Gerry Khermouch, Stanley Holmes, and Moon Ihlwan, "The Best Global Brands," *Business Week* (August 6, 2001), 50–57.
[12]See Eloise Coupey, *Marketing and the Internet* (Upper Saddle River, NJ: Prentice Hall, 2001), 174–79.
[13]John Frook, "Cisco Scores with Its Latest Generation of Empowering Tools," *B to B* (August 20, 2001), 20.
[14]Marc Gunther, "The Cheering Fades for Yahoo," *Fortune* (November 12, 2001), 151–58.
[15]See Lori Mitchell, "Branding Equals Smart E-Business," *InfoWorld* (December 15, 2000), at <www.infoworld.com/articles/tc/xml/00/12/18/001218tcbranding.xml>; Robyn Greenspan, "Brand Opening," *ECommerce-Guide* (January 10, 2001), at <http://ecommerce.internet.com/news/insights/ectips/article/0,,6311_557131,00.html>; Kris Wadia, "Top 10 Myths of E-Branding," *Business-Minds* (May 17, 2001), at <www.business-minds.com/article.asp?item=68>.
[16]See Thomas T. Nagle and Reed K. Holden, *The Strategy and Tactics of Pricing: A Guide to Profitable Decision Making* (Upper Saddle River, NJ: Prentice Hall, 2002), Chapter 6.
[17]See Nagle and Holden, *The Strategy and Tactics of Pricing,* 123–24.
[18]See Nagle and Holden, *The Strategy and Tactics of Pricing,* 39–45, 67–72.
[19]See Nagle and Holden, *The Strategy and Tactics of Pricing,* Chapter 7.
[20]See Nagle and Holden, *The Strategy and Tactics of Pricing,* 166–73. See also Best, *op. cit.,* 189–91.
[21]Judy Strauss and Raymond Frost, *E-Marketing,* 2nd ed. (Upper Saddle River, NJ: Prentice Hall, 2001), 166–67; Eloise Coupey, *Marketing and the Internet* (Upper Saddle River, NJ: Prentice Hall, 2001), 281–83.
[22]Robert D. Hof and Linda Himelstein, "eBay vs. Amazon.com," *Business Week* (May 31, 1999), 128–32+; Janet Rae-Dupree and Diane Brady, "Let the Buyer Be in Control," *Business Week* (November 8, 1999), 100.

Chapter 12

[1]See also Anne T. Coughlan et al., *Marketing Channels,* 6th ed. (Upper Saddle River, NJ: Prentice Hall, 2001), 9–17.
[2]See "An Assessment of E-Grocers," E-Agribusiness Working Group (February 2002), at <http://aede.osu.edu/programs/e-biz>; Richard R. Johnson et al., "Online Grocery: How the Internet Is Changing the Grocery Industry," University of Virginia Darden School Foundation (2000), at <http://faculty.darden.virginia.edu/ebiz/documents/OnlineGrocery_8-25.pdf>.
[3]Ahmad Diba, "An Old-Line Agency Finds an Online Niche," *Fortune* (April 3, 2000), 258.
[4]*Dell Annual Report: FY2001 Year in Review* (April 22, 2002), at <www.dell.com>. See also Qiao Song, "Legend Outlines Role in China's Wireless Future," *Ebn* (March 25, 2002), 3; Faith Hung, "Legend Looks to Defend Its Turf—WTO Entry Will Force China's Top PC Maker to Fend Off Unrestricted Rivals," *Ebn* (December 17, 2001), 44; and Neel Chowdhury, "Dell Cracks China," *Fortune* (June 21, 1999), 120–24.
[5]See Coughlan et al., *Marketing Channels,* p 120; and Philip Kotler, *Marketing Management,* 11th ed. (Upper Saddle River, NJ: Prentice Hall, 2003), 513–14.
[6]See Coughlan et al., *Marketing Channels,* Chapter 15.
[7]Leigh Buchanan, "Best of the Small Business Web: Hear, Here," *Inc.com* (May 20, 2002), at <www.inc.com/incmagazine/archives/18990691.html>.
[8]See especially Eloise Coupey, *Marketing and the Internet* (Upper Saddle River, NJ: Prentice Hall, 2001), Chapter 11; Coughlin et al., *Marketing Channels,* 447–69.
[9]"Expedia.com" (July 8, 2002), at <www.expedia.com>.
[10]Diane Brady, "From Nabisco to Tropicana to . . . EFDEX?" *Business Week* (September 20, 1999), 100; "Efdex™" (April 19, 2000), at <www.efdex.com>.
[11]See also Barry Berman and Joel R. Evans, *Retail Management: A Strategic Approach,* 8th ed. (Upper Saddle River, NJ: Prentice Hall, 2001), Chapter 5.
[12]Quentin Hardy, "The Death and Life of Buy.com," *Forbes* (January 21, 2002), 86–89; Tobi Elkin, "AOL Time Warner Banks On Broadband Future," *Advertising Age* (February 11, 2002), 3.
[13]Gene Gray, "The Future of the Teleservices Industry—Are You Aware," *Telemarketing* (January 1999), 90–96.
[14]See Mary Jo Foley and Tom Steinert-Threlkeld, "The Ultimate CRM

Machine," *Baseline* (October 29, 2001), at <www.baselinemag.com/article/0,3658,a=17004,00.asp>.

[15]"Prodigy.com™" (April 8, 2002), at <www.prodigy.com>.

[16]"Small Biz Web Sites on the Rise, Yet Many Owners Slow to Embrace the Internet," *Prodigy.com* (April 19, 2000), at <www.prodigy.com/pcom/business/business/content>.

[17]"efdex Launches the First Global e-Market for the Food & Drink Industry," press release from Connors Communications, (April 19, 2000), at <www.connors.com/press/efdex>; Darren Noyce, "eB2B: Analysis of Business-to-Business e-Commerce and How Research Can Adapt to Meet Future Challenges," *International Journal of Market Research* (First Quarter 2002), 71–95.

[18]"Did You Know?" *Catalog News.com* (April 8, 2002), at <www.catalog-news.com>; Judy Strauss and Raymond Frost, *E-Marketing,* (Upper Saddle River, NJ: Prentice Hall, 2001), 140.

[19]See Carolyn Brackett, "Setting Up Shop in Cyberspace," *Inc.com* (May 20, 2002), at <www.inc.com/conducting_commerce/advice/15237.html>; David Radin, " 'Electronic Mall Syndrome' Gives Way to Unified Buying," *eBusiness News* (May 20, 2002), at <http://ebusiness.dci.com/articles/1998/05/14radin.htm>; Garrett Wasny, "Free Electronic Storefronts" (July, 2000), at <www.howtoconquertheworld.com/gohome111.htm>.

[20]Peter Elkind, "Shhhhh! Amway's on the Web," *Fortune* (March 6, 2000), 76.

[21]"LivePerson.com™" (April 19, 2000), at <www.liveperson.com>.

[22]See Coughlin et al., *Marketing Channels,* 458–62.

Chapter 13

[1]See Kenneth E. Clow and Donald Baack, *Integrated Advertising, Promotion, and Marketing Communications* (Upper Saddle River, NJ: Prentice Hall, 2002), 128–32.

[2]Amy Tsao, "Panera Bread: An Appetizing Stock," *Business Week Online* (March 25, 2002), at <www.businessweek.com/bw50/content/mar2002/a3776069.htm>; Kimberly Pfaff, "Panera Bread Co.: The Best Thing Since . . . ," *Retailing Today* (May 2002), at <www.icsc.org/srch/sct/current/page55.html>.

[3]See Philip Kotler, *Marketing Management,* 11th ed. (Upper Saddle River, NJ: Prentice Hall, 2003), 510–11.

[4]See Clow and Baack, *Integrated Advertising,* Chapter 5.

[5]*Advertising Age* (September 24, 2001), s1.

[6]See J. Thomas Russell and W. Ronald Lane, *Kleppner's Advertising Procedure,* 15th ed. (Upper Saddle River, NJ: Prentice Hall, 2002), 54–66.

[7]See Russell and Lane, *Kleppner's Advertising Procedure,* 161–62.

[8]See Russell and Lane, *Kleppner's Advertising Procedure,* 646–48.

[9]*Advertising Age* (September 24, 2001), s1.

[10]R. Craig Endicott, "100 Leading National Advertisers," *Advertising Age* (September 24, 2001), s1.

[11]Michael Mahoney, "Why Three Dot-Coms Did Not Ditch the Super Bowl," *E-Commerce Times* (January 25, 2002), at <www.ecommercetimes.com/perl/story/15986.html>.

[12]Cara B. Dipasquale, "Direct-Mail Sector Staying the Course," *Advertising Age* (March 11, 2002), 16.

[13]*Outdoor Advertising Association of America* (April 24, 2002), at <www.oaaa.org>. See also *Advertising Age* (September 24, 2001), s1.

[14]See Clow and Baack, *Integrated Advertising,* Chapter 16; Judy Strauss and Raymond Frost, *E-Marketing,* 2nd ed. (Upper Saddle River: Prentice Hall, 2001), 248–62; and Efraim Turban et al., *Electronic Commerce: A Managerial Perspective* (Upper Saddle River, NJ: Prentice Hall, 2000), Chapter 4.

[15]"BMCMedia Signs DART Contract with DoubleClick," *List-News.com* (May 1, 2001), at <http://listnews.com/articles/01may/20010508.html>.

[16]"100 Leading National Advertisers," *Advertising Age* (September 24, 2001), s1, s12.

[17]See Strauss and Frost, *E-Marketing,* 115–19.

[18]Stuart Elliott, "You've Got Mail, Indeed," *New York Times* (October 25, 1999), C1, C23.

[19]See Nikki Swartz, "Amphibian Firebrands," *Wireless Review* (July 15, 2001), 16–20; and David Goetzl, "TBS Tries Virtual Advertising," *Advertising Age* (May 21, 2001), 8.

[20]See Russell and Lane, *Kleppner's Advertising Procedure,* Chapter 5.

[21]See Michael D. Hutt and Thomas W. Speh, *Business Marketing Management,* 6th ed. (New York: Dryden Press, 1998), 504–5.

[22]Ira Teinowitz and Cara B. Dipasquale, "Direct Marketers Take Issue with Proposed FTC Rules," *Advertising Age* (January 28, 2002), 3, 29; Larry Neilson, "Look Out for Telemarketing Speed Bumps," *National Underwriter* (September 17, 2001), 12–14.

[23]See Clow and Baack, *Integrated Advertising,* Chapter 12; Russell and Lane, *Kleppner's Advertising Procedure,* Chapter 14.

[24]See Scott M. Cutlip, Allen H. Center, and Glen M. Broom, *Effective Public Relations,* 8th ed. (Upper Saddle River, NJ: Prentice Hall, 2000), 9–10.

[25]"Tyco Backs Off Breakup," *CNNmoney* (April 25, 2002), at <http://money.cnn.com/2002/04/25/news>.

[26]*2001 Annual Report: This is Citigroup* (New York, 2002), 5.

[27]See Norman M. Scarborough and Thomas W. Zimmerer, *Effective Small Business Management: An Entrepreneurial Approach,* 6th ed. (Upper Saddle River, NJ: Prentice Hall, 2000), Chapter 11.

[28]See Warren J. Keegan, *Global Marketing Management,* 7th ed. (Upper Saddle River, NJ: Prentice Hall, 2002), Chapter 14.

Chapter 14

[1]Thomas A. Stewart, "It's 10 P.M. Do You Know Where Your Business Is?" *Fortune* (April 3, 2000), 270.

[2]Jennifer L. Martel and Laura A. Kelter, "The Job Market Remains Strong in 1999," *Monthly Labor Review* (February 2000), 3–23.

[3]Martel and Kelter, "The Job Market Remains Strong," 3–23. See also *Employment & Earnings* (Washington, DC: U.S. Department of Labor: Bureau of Labor Statistics, June 2001), 70; and *Survey of Current Business* (Washington, DC: U.S. Department of Commerce, June 2001), D-4.

[4]Sarah Pence, "Workforce in China" (May 3, 2002), at <http://icdweb.cc.purdue.edu/~tstewart/ansc295K/Factsheets/Work_Force-Pence.htm>.

[5]*GE Annual Report: 2001* (Fairfield, CT: General Electric Co., 2002), 1–7.

[6]See Robert S. Russell and Bernard W. Taylor III, *Operations Management,* 4th ed. (Upper Saddle River, NJ: Prentice Hall, 2003), 3–5.

[7]See Lee J. Krajewski and Larry P. Ritzman, *Operations Management: Strategy and Analysis,* 6th ed. (Upper Saddle River, NJ: Prentice Hall, 2002), 9–11.
[8]See Christopher Lovelock, *Services Marketing: People, Technology, Strategy,* 4th ed. (Upper Saddle River, NJ: Prentice Hall, 2001), 56–59.
[9]See Lovelock, *Services Marketing,* 8–15.
[10]Catherine Valenti, "Low Prices, High Hopes," *ABCNews.com* (February 19, 2002), at <http://abcnews.go.com/sections/business/DailyNews/Wal-Mart_020219.html>. See also *Wal-Mart Annual Report 2001* (Bentonville, AR: Wal-Mart Stores, 2001), 6.
[11]See Lovelock, *Services Marketing,* 37–41.
[12]See Russell and Taylor, *Operations Management,* 104–5.
[13]See Judy Strauss and Raymond Frost, *E-Marketing,* 2nd ed. (Upper Saddle River, NJ: Prentice Hall, 2001), 280–325; and Elias Awad, *Electronic Commerce* (Upper Saddle River, NJ: Prentice Hall, 2002), 339–41.
[14]Strauss and Frost, *E-Marketing,* 266–71.
[15]See Krajewski and Ritzman, *Operations Management,* Chapter 8; and Russell and Taylor, *Operations Management,* Chapter 9.
[16]Dawn Kawamoto, "FTC Approves Digital-Intel Deal," *News.com* (August 9, 2001), at <http://news.cnet.com/news/0-1005-200-328663.html?tag= rltdnws>.
[17]See Krajewski and Ritzman, *Operations Management,* Chapter 9.
[18]Barbara McClellan, "Brazilian Revolution," *Ward's Auto World* (September 2000), 69–74. See also "E-GM Expands Its Online Sales Model," *ITWorld.com* (December 6, 2000), at <www.itworld.com/Tech/2397/IW001206hnehm>.
[19]See Krajewski and Ritzman, *Operations Management,* Chapter 10; and Russell and Taylor, *Operations Management,* Chapter 5.
[20]Chuck Salter, "This Is One Fast Company," *Fast Company* (August 2001), 32–33.
[21]"ASQ Glossary of Terms," *American Society for Quality* (June 10, 2002), at <www. asq.org/info/glossary/definition.html#q>.
[22]See Krajewski and Ritzman, *Operations Management,* Chapter 17; and Russell and Taylor, *Operations Management,* Chapter 13.
[23]See Russell and Taylor, *Operations Management,* 737–38.
[24]See Krajewski and Ritzman, *Operations Management,* 153–54, 828–29; and Russell and Taylor, *Operations Management,* 221–22, 593–95.
[25]See Russell and Taylor, *Operations Management,* 222–24.
[26]See Krajewski and Ritzman, *Operations Management,* 504–6.
[27]See Krajewski and Ritzman, *Operations Management,* 608–15; and Russell and Taylor, *Operations Management,* 459–64.
[28]See Krajewski and Ritzman, *Operations Management,* 595.
[29]Tom Murphy, "E Cyber Squeeze: The Pressure Is On," *Ward's Auto World* (December 2000), 44–47.
[30]See Kevin Ferguson, "Purchasing in Packs," *Business Week Online* (November 1, 1999), at <www.businessweek.com/1999/99_44/b3653024.htm>; and Bob Wallace, "Wireless Buying Service Targets Workers in the Field," *InformationWeek Online* (June 26, 2000), at <www.informationweek.com/792/wireless.htm>; and Jim Romeo, "U.S. B2B to Reach \$2.8 Trillion by 2003," *E-Commerce Times* (January 12, 2000), at <www.ecommercetimes.com/perl/story/2191.html>.
[31]See Sherry Alpert, "The Right 'Corporate Culture' Pays Off in Unseen Ways," *Kansas City Infozine* (March 5, 2002), at <www.infozine.com/news/stories/op/storiesView/sid/662/>; and Karen M. Kroll, "Container Store a Hit with Customers, Employees," *Shopping Centers Today* (May 1, 2000), at <www.icsc.org/srch/sct/current/sct0500/07a.html>.
[32]See Russell and Taylor, *Operations Management,* Chapter 11.
[33]See Russell and Taylor, *Operations Management,* 550–57.
[34]See *United Parcel Service 1999 Annual Report* (Atlanta, GA: United Parcel Service Inc., 2000); and "Fortune 500," *Fortune* (April 16, 2001), F-57.

Chapter 15

[1]Bart VanArk and Robert McGuckin, "International Comparisons of Labor Productivity and Per Capita Income," *Monthly Labor Review* (Washington, DC: U.S. Department of Labor, July 1999), 33–41.
[2]U.S. Department of Labor, "Comparative Real Gross Domestic Product per Capita and per Employed Person: Fourteen Countries, 1960–1998," (Washington, DC: Bureau of Labor Statistics, March 30, 2000).
[3]See *Monthly Labor Review* (Washington, DC: U.S. Department of Labor, February 2002), 124; "Data Table for Total Federal Government, Fiscal Years 1967–1994" (June 6, 2002), at <www.bls.gov/lpc>; and Ronald A. Wirtz, "Icebergs and Government Productivity," *The Region* (June 2001), 16–19+.
[4]Estimated from U.S. Bureau of Labor Statistics (Washington, DC: U.S. Department of Labor), Data Series PRS 84006163, EES 500001 and PRS 30006163 (June 6, 2002), at <www.data.bls.gov>; and Bureau of Economic Analysis, "Gross Domestic Product by Sector" (Washington, DC: U.S. Department of Commerce), Table 1.7 (June 6, 2002), at <www.bea.gov>.
[5]*Monthly Labor Review* (Washington, DC: U.S. Department of Labor, Bureau of Labor Statistics, February 2002), 125–27.
[6]Alicia Hills Moore, "U.S. Textiles Hand in Hand with High Tech," *Fortune* (April 16, 2001), 358(B)–358(Z).
[7]David Welch, "Finally, Skid Control at GM," *Business Week* (March 25, 2002), 54–55; Alex Taylor III, "Finally GM Is Looking Good," *Fortune* (April 1, 2002), 68–74.
[8]See S. Thomas Foster Jr., *Managing Quality: An Integrative Approach* (Upper Saddle River, NJ: Prentice Hall, 2001), 22–23.
[9]"Savoring Fine Chocolates" (June 7, 2002), at <www.godiva.com>.
[10]John S. McClenahen, "ITT's Value Champion," *Industry Week* (May 2002), 44–49.
[11]See Lee J. Krajewski and Larry P. Ritzman, *Operations Management: Strategy and Analysis,* 6th ed. (Upper Saddle River, NJ: Prentice Hall, 2002), Chapter 7; and Roberta S. Russell and Bernard W. Taylor III, *Operations Management,* 4th ed. (Upper Saddle River, NJ: Prentice Hall, 2003), Chapter 15.
[12]Thomas P. Tylutki and Danny G. Fox, "Mooooving toward Six Sigma," *Quality Progress* (February 2002), 34–41; "SPC Produces Big Savings at Steelcase," *Quality* (April 2002), 42.

[13]See Foster, *Managing Quality*, 354–71; and Russell and Taylor, *Operations Management*, 676–91.
[14]See Foster, *Managing Quality*, 106–9; and Russell and Taylor, *Operations Management*, 636–42.
[15]See Foster, *Managing Quality*, 325–39.
[16]James Evans and James Dean Jr., *Total Quality: Management, Organization, and Strategy*, 2nd ed. (Cincinnati, OH: South-Western, 2000), 230.
[17]See Foster, *Managing Quality*, 153–67.
[18]"2000 Award Recipients Applications Summaries" (June 8, 2002), at <www.quality.nist.gov/2000>.
[19]See "ISO 9001 Registration Helps Improve Airport Security," *Quality Digest* (June 9, 2002), at <www.qualitydigest.com/currentmag/html/news.html>; and "A Call for Consistency in the Quality of Airline Security Screening Services," *American Society for Quality* (December 18, 2002), at <www.asq.org/news/interest/airportsecurity.html>.
[20]See Russell and Taylor, *Operations Management*, 658–62; and Foster, *Managing Quality*, 85–86.
[21]See Russell and Taylor, *Operations Management*, 137–40.
[22]See Sunil Chopra and Peter Meindl, *Supply Chain Management: Strategy, Planning, and Operation*, 6th ed. (Upper Saddle River, NJ: Prentice Hall, 2001), 3–6; Krajewski and Ritzman, *Operations Management*, Chapter 11; Russell and Taylor, *Operations Management*, Chapter 7; and Foster, *Managing Quality*, Chapter 9.
[23]See Chopra and Meindl, *Supply Chain Management*, Chapter 2.
[24]See Chopra and Meindl, *Supply Chain Management*, 348–49.
[25]Catherine Greenman, "An Old Craft Learns New Tricks," *New York Times* (June 10, 1999), G1, G7.
[26]Jennifer Reingold, Marcia Stepanek, and Diane Brady, "Why the Productivity Revolution Will Spread," *Business Week* (February 14, 2000), 112–18.
[27]See Krajewski and Ritzman, *Operations Management*, 805–7.
[28]"Motorola." Online. Internet (accessed May 24, 2000), at <http://www.motorola.com>.
[29]See Ceasar Douglas, "Employee Empowerment in Organizations Today," ed. Gerald R. Ferris, M. Ronald Buckley, and Donald B. Fedor, *Human Resources Management: Perspectives, Context, Functions, and Outcomes*, 4th ed. (Upper Saddle River, NJ: Prentice Hall, 2002), 413–21.
[30]"Evaluate the Value of Training," *Quality* (April 2002), 48.
[31]See Cengiz Haksever et al., *Service Management and Operations*, 2nd ed. (Upper Saddle River, NJ: Prentice Hall, 2000), 357–72.
[32]Leonard L. Berry, A. Parasuraman, and Valerie A. Zeithaml, "Improving Service Quality in America: Lessons Learned," *Academy of Management Executive* 8, no. 2 (1994), 32–45.
[33]See Dina Berta, "Effective Employee Training Is in the Cards at Ruth's Chris Steak House," *Nation's Restaurant News* (October 8, 2001), 6; and Diane Ridge, "Training Culinary Talent," *Food Management* (November 2001), 20–28.

Chapter 16

[1]American Gaming Association (June 16, 2002), at <www.americangaming.org>.
[2]See Kenneth C. Laudon and Jane P. Laudon, *Management Information Systems: Managing the Digital Firm*, 7th ed. (Upper Saddle River, NJ: Prentice Hall, 2002), 7–11.
[3]See Laudon and Laudon, *Management Information Systems*, 252–53.
[4]See Larry Long and Nancy Long, *Computers: Information Technology in Perspective*, 9th ed. (Upper Saddle River, NJ: Prentice Hall, 2002), 241–42.
[5]See Long and Long, *Computers*, Chapter 7 and Chapter 8.
[6]"The Internet: Bringing Wall Street to Main Street," *Wall Street & Technology* (September 2001), 52–53.
[7]See Laudon and Laudon, *Management Information Systems*, 273–83.
[8]See Steve Jarvis, "Ain't Nothin' for Free," *Marketing News* (April 23, 2001), 3; and Alex Salkever and Sheridan Prasso, "Search Engines: Leading US Astray?" *Business Week (Industry/ Technology Edition)* (August 6, 2001), 8.
[9]See Laudon and Laudon, *Management Information Systems*, 122–27, 276–77.
[10]Jennifer Tanaka, "Don't Get Burned," *Newsweek* (August 20, 2001), 52–53.
[11]See Mary J. Cronin, "Ford's Intranet Success," *Fortune* (March 30, 1998), 158; and Rick Gurin, "Online System to Streamline Ford's Delivery Process," *Frontline Solutions* (April 2000), 1, 8.
[12]See Laudon and Laudon, *Management Information Systems*, 21–22.
[13]See Lee J. Krajewski and Larry P. Ritzman, *Operations Management: Strategy and Analysis*, 6th ed. (Upper Saddle River, NJ: Prentice Hall, 2002), 46–48.
[14]See Gary W. Dickson and Gerardine DeSanctis, *Information Technology and the Future Enterprise: New Models for Managers* (Upper Saddle River, NJ: Prentice Hall, 2001), Chapter 4.
[15]Krajewski and Ritzman, *Operations Management: Strategy and Analysis*, 106.
[16]See Krajewski and Ritzman, *Operations Management: Strategy and Analysis*, 205–10.
[17]See Krajewski and Ritzman, *Operations Management: Strategy and Analysis*, 232–33.
[18]See Laudon and Laudon, *Management Information Systems*, esp. 40–45.
[19]See Laudon and Laudon, *Management Information Systems*, 383–91.
[20]Heather Green et al., "It's Time for Rules in Wonderland," *Business Week* (February 21, 2000), 82–88; Ira Sager et al., "Cyber Crime," *Business Week* (February 21, 2000), 36–42; and Ira Sager, Neil Gross, and John Carey, "Locking Out the Hackers," *Business Week* (February 28, 2000), 32–34.
[21]See Long and Long, *Computers*, 24–26, 107–12.
[22]See esp. Long and Long, *Computers*, 52–54.
[23]See Long and Long, *Computers*, 101–6.
[24]See Laudon and Laudon, *Management Information Systems*, 237–44.
[25]See Laudon and Laudon, *Management Information Systems*, 270–71.
[26]Nathalie Raffray, "Portal Power," *Communications International* (August 2001), 30–35; and David Maloney, "The Newest Better Idea at Ford," *Modern Materials Handling* (June 2000), 34–39. See also Laudon and Laudon, *Management Information Systems*, 239–44.

Chapter 17

[1]Charles T. Horngren, Walter T. Harrison Jr., and Linda Smith Bamber, *Accounting*, 5th ed. (Upper Saddle River, NJ: Prentice Hall, 2002), 5.
[2]See Marshall B. Romney and Paul John Steinbart, *Accounting Information Systems*, 9th ed. (Upper Saddle River, NJ: Prentice Hall, 2003), Chapter 1; and Kumen H. Jones et al., *Introduction to Accounting: A User*

Perspective (Upper Saddle River, NJ: Prentice Hall, 2000), F-231.
[3]See Anthony A. Atkinson et al., *Management Accounting* (Upper Saddle River, NJ: Prentice Hall, 2001), 5–6.
[4]See Walter T. Harrison Jr. and Charles T. Horngren, *Financial Accounting,* 4th ed. (Upper Saddle River, NJ: Prentice Hall, 2000), 6.
[5]See Alvin A. Arens, Randal J. Elder, and Mark S. Beasley, *Essentials of Auditing and Assurance Services* (Upper Saddle River, NJ: Prentice Hall, 2003), 10–14.
[6]See Horngren, Harrison, and Bamber, *Accounting,* 9–11.
[7]See Kurt Eichenwald, "Auditing Woes at WorldCom Were Noted Two Years Ago," *New York Times* (July 15, 2002), C1, C9; Simon Romero and Alex Berenson, "WorldCom Says It Hid Expenses, Inflating Cash Flow $3.8 Billion," *New York Times* (June 26, 2002), A1, C2; Simon Romero and Riva D. Atlas, "WorldCom Files for Bankruptcy; Largest U.S. Case," *New York Times* (July 22, 2002), A1, A12; Mark M. Meinero and Parija Bhatnagar, "Woe From WorldCom," *CNNMoney* (June 26, 2002), at <www.cnnfn.com>; and Charles Hadda with Steve Rosenbush, "Woe Is WorldCom," *Business Week* (May 6, 2002), 86–88+.
[8]This section is based on material from the following sources: AICPA, "CPA Vision Project" (August 12, 2002), at <www.aicpa.org/vision/index.htm>; and AICPA, "CPA Vision Project: 2011 and Beyond" (August 12, 2002), at <www.cpavision.org>.
[9]Nanette Byrnes, "Where Have All the Accountants Gone?"*Business Week* (March 27, 1999), 203–4.
[10]See Horngren, Harrison, and Bamber, *Accounting,* 11–12, 39–41.
[11]See Horngren, Harrison, and Bamber, *Accounting,* 41–56.
[12]See Harrison and Horngren, *Financial Accounting,* 17–20.
[13]See Lawrence Revsine, Daniel W. Collins, and W. Bruce Johnson, *Financial Reporting and Analysis,* 2nd ed. (Upper Saddle River, NJ: Prentice Hall, 2002), 387.
[14]See Revsine, Collins, and Johnson, *Financial Reporting and Analysis,* 179–81, 468–70.
[15]See Revsine, Collins, and Johnson, *Financial Reporting and Analysis,* Chapter 15.
[16]See Horngren, Harrison, and Bamber, *Accounting,* Chapter 17.
[17]See Horngren, Harrison, and Bamber, *Accounting,* 927–40.
[18]See Jones et al., *Introduction to Accounting: A User Perspective,* F-187.
[19]See Horngren, Harrison, and Bamber, *Accounting,* 86.
[20]See Jones et al., *Introduction to Accounting: A User's Perspective,* F-454–F-479.
[21]See Horngren, Harrison, and Bamber, *Accounting,* 728–29; Arthur J. Keown et al., *Foundations of Finance: The Logic and Practice of Financial Management,* 3rd ed. (Upper Saddle River, NJ: Prentice Hall, 2001), 118–20.
[22]See Horngren, Harrison, and Bamber, *Accounting,* 186–88.
[23]See Frederick D. S. Choi, Carol Ann Frost, and Gary K. Meek, *International Accounting,* 4th ed. (Upper Saddle River: Prentice Hall, 2002), Chapter 6.
[24]See Choi, Frost, and Meek, *International Accounting,* 267–79.

Chapter 18

[1]See Arthur O'Sullivan and Steven M. Sheffrin, *Economics: Principles and Tools,* 2nd ed. (Upper Saddle River, NJ: Prentice Hall, 2001), 566–68.
[2]Federal Reserve Board of Governors, "M1 Money Stock Seasonally Adjusted" (July 2, 2002), at <www.federalreserve.gov>.
[3]Federal Reserve Board of Governors, "Currency Component of Money Stock" (July 2, 2002), at <www.federalreserve.gov>.
[4]Federal Reserve Board of Governors, "Demand Deposits at Commercial Banks" (July 2, 2002), at <www.federalreserve.gov>.
[5]Federal Reserve Board of Governors, "M2 Money Stock" (July 2, 2002), at <www.federalreserve.gov>.
[6]Federal Reserve Board of Governors, "Money Market Funds" (June 2, 2002), at <www.federalreserve.gov>.
[7]Federal Reserve Board of Governors, "Total Savings Deposits" (June 2, 2002), at <www.federalreserve.gov>.
[8]See Citigroup, "Global Consumer Business" (July 17, 2001), at <www.citigroup.com/citigroup/corporate/gcb_m.htm>; and U.S. Census Bureau, *Statistical Abstract of the United States* (2001), 1191, at <www.census.gov/statab/www>.
[9]See James C. Van Horne, *Financial Management and Policy,* 12th ed. (Upper Saddle River, NJ: Prentice Hall, 2002), 494–95.
[10]See "Prime Rate," *Money.café* (July 7, 2002), at <www.nfsn.com/library/prime.htm>.
[11]U.S. Census Bureau, *Statistical Abstract of the United States* (2001), 1163, 1183, at <www.census.gov/statab/www>.
[12]U.S. Census Bureau, *Statistical Abstract of the United States* (2001), 1163, at <www.census.gov/statab/www>.
[13]U.S. Census Bureau, *Statistical Abstract of the United States* (2001), 532, 1218, at <www.census.gov/statab/www>.
[14]See Gordon J. Alexander, William F. Sharpe, and Jeffery V. Bailey, *Fundamentals of Investments,* 3rd ed. (Upper Saddle River, NJ: Prentice Hall, 2001), 100–1.
[15]American Bankers Association, "ATM Fact Sheet" (July 8, 2002), at <www.aba.com/Press1 Room/ATMfacts2001.htm>.
[16]See Marshall B. Romney and Paul John Steinbart, *Accounting Information Systems,* 8th ed. (Upper Saddle River, NJ: Prentice Hall, 2000), 218–19.
[17]See Karl E. Case and Ray C. Fair, *Principles of Economics,* 6th ed. (Upper Saddle River, NJ: Prentice Hall, 2002), 483–89.
[18]See O'Sullivan and Sheffrin, *Economics,* 574–76.
[19]See "discount window," at (July 8, 2002), <www.frbdisountwindow.org>.
[20]See Case and Fair, *Principles of Economics,* 497–99.
[21]See Jim Middlemiss, "Banks Get Smart About Computer Chips," *Bank Systems & Technology* (April 2002), p. 44; and Lisa Daigle, "Beyond Expectations," *Credit Card Management* (May 2000), pp. 50–52.
[22]See Michael Froomkin, "The Unintended Consequences of E-Cash" (July 16, 2001), at <www.law.miami.edu/~froomkin/articles/cfp97.htm>.
[23]*Survey of Current Business* (Washington, DC: U.S. Dept. of Commerce, June 2002), p. D-53; *Federal Reserve Bulletin* (June 2002), pp. A64, A72.
[24]See Charles T. Horngren, Walter T. Harrison Jr., and Linda Smith Bamber, *Accounting,* 5th ed. (Upper Saddle River, NJ: Prentice Hall, 2002), 636–37.
[25]See Ricky W. Griffin and Michael W. Pustay, *International Business: A*

Managerial Perspective, 3rd ed. (Upper Saddle River, NJ: Prentice Hall, 2002), 159–61.

Chapter 19

[1]See Gordon J. Alexander, William F. Sharpe, and Jeffery V. Bailey, *Fundamentals of Investments,* 3rd ed. (Upper Saddle River, NJ: Prentice Hall, 2001), 2–7.
[2]See Arthur J. Keown et al., *Foundations of Finance: The Logic and Practice of Financial Management,* 3rd ed. (Upper Saddle River, NJ: Prentice Hall, 2001), 51–52; and Alexander, Sharpe, and Bailey, *Fundamentals of Investments,* 261, 478.
[3]*Flow of Funds Accounts of the United States* (Washington, DC: Board of Governors of the Federal Reserve System, June 6, 2002), Table F.2.
[4]See *Federal Reserve Bulletin* (May 2002), A31; and *Flow of Funds Accounts of the United States* (Washington, DC: Board of Governors of the Federal Reserve System, June 6, 2002), Table F.4.
[5]See Keown et al., *Foundations of Finance,* 230–38.
[6]Joseph Nocera, "Do You Believe? How Yahoo! Became a Blue Chip," *Fortune* (June 7, 1999), 76–81.
[7]See Cory Johnson, "The Internet Blue Chip," *The Industry Standard* (August 7, 2001), at <www.thestandard.com/article/0,1902,4088,00html>; and Chris Nerney "Yahoo!: Bargain or Big Trouble?" *The Internet Stock Report* (August 7, 2001), at <www.internetstockreport.com/column/print/0,,530021,00.html>.
[8]See Alexander, Sharpe, and Bailey, *Fundamentals of Investments,* 21–22.
[9]See Chilik Wollenberg, "How Does Your Broker Measure Up?" *Medical Economics* (May 28, 2001), 98–100; and Leah Nathans Spiro and Edward C. Baig, "Who Needs a Broker?" *Business Week* (February 22, 1999), 113–61.
[10]See Borzou Daragahi, "E-Finance Forecast," *Money* (March 2001), 129–33; and Joseph Kahn, "Schwab Lands Feet First on Net," *New York Times* (February 10, 1999), C1, C5.
[11]See Alexander, Sharpe, and Bailey, *Fundamentals of Investments,* 39.
[12]See Alexander, Sharpe, and Bailey, *Fundamentals of Investments,* 36–39.
[13]See Alexander, Sharpe, and Bailey, *Fundamentals of Investments,* 44–46.
[14]Nasdaq (June 25, 2000), at <www.nasdaq.com/about/timeline.stm>.
[15]NASD (June 25, 2000), at <www.nasd.com>.
[16]*Nasdaq 2001 Annual Report* (October 31, 2002), at <www.nasdaq.com/investorrelations/annualreport2001>. See also "The World in Its Hands," *The Economist* (May 6, 2000), 77; "The Nasdaq Japan Market Launches First Day of Trading; First Step in Creating Nasdaq Global Platform Is Achieved" (June 19, 2000), at <www.nasdaq.co.uk/reference>; and "Globalization and International Reach," at *Nasdaq Initiatives* (June 23, 2000), at <www.nasdaq.com>.
[17]See Frank J. Fabozzi, *Bond Markets, Analysis and Strategies,* 4th ed. (Upper Saddle River, NJ: Prentice Hall, 2000), Chapter 1; and Keown et al., *Financial Management,* Chapter 7.
[18]See *Federal Reserve Bulletin* (May 2002), A25, A27; and *Flow of Funds Accounts of the United States* (Washington, DC: Board of Governors of the Federal Reserve System, June 6, 2002), p. 1.
[19]*Federal Reserve Bulletin* (May 2002), A31.
[20]See George W. Tivoli, *Personal Portfolio Management: Fundamentals and Strategies* (Upper Saddle River, NJ: Prentice Hall, 2000), Chapter 5.
[21]*Wiesenberger Mutual Funds Update* (Rockville, MD: CDA Investment Technologies, August 31, 2000), iv–ix; *Mutual Funds Facts and Figures,* (July 14, 2002), at <www.ici.org/facts.figures>.
[22]See Alexander, Sharpe, and Bailey, *Fundamentals of Investments,* 39–43.
[23]See Gretchen Morgenson, "Buying on Margin Becomes a Habit," *New York Times* (March 24, 2000), C1, C7; and David Barboza, "Wall Street after Dark," *New York Times* (February 13, 2000), BU1, BU14–BU15.
[24]See Alexander, Sharpe, and Bailey, *Fundamentals of Investments,* 37–38.
[25]See U.S. Securities and Exchange Commission, "SEC Charges Former ImClone CEO Samuel Waksal with Illegal Insider Trading" (June 12, 2002), at <www.sec.gov/news/press>; Andrew Pollack, "ImClone's Ex-Chief in Talks with U.S. on Plea Agreement," *New York Times on the Web* (July 13, 2002), at <www.nytimes.com/2002/07/13/business>; and "Martha Scrutiny Heats Up," *CNNMoney* (June 14, 2002), at <www.cnnfn.com>.

Chapter 20

[1]See David F. Scott et al., *Basic Financial Management,* 8th ed. (Upper Saddle River, NJ: Prentice Hall, 1999), p. 627.
[2]See Scott et al., *Basic Financial Management,* pp. 625–26.
[3]See Scott et al., *Basic Financial Management,* pp. 626–27.
[4]See Scott et al., *Basic Financial Management,* pp. 624–25.
[5]See Frank J. Fabozzi, *Bond Markets, Analysis and Strategies,* 4th ed. (Upper Saddle River, NJ: Prentice Hall, 2000), Ch. 7.
[6]See Jake Ulick, "WorldCom's Financial Bomb," *CNNMoney* (June 26, 2002), at <www.cnnfn.com>; and Luisa Beltran, "WorldCom Files Largest Bankruptcy Ever," *CNNMoney* (July 22, 2002), at <www.cnnfn.com>.
[7]See "Britain's Third Biggest Bank Sees 2001 Net Profit Fall as Bad-Debt Provisions Rise," *CNNMoney* (February 15, 2002), at <www.cnnfn.com>; "SocGen, Abbey National Set Aside Money for Bad Loans, Profits Decline," *CNNMoney* (February 21, 2002), at <www.cnnfn.com>; and James Cox, "Argentina Pins Hope On Debt-Swap proposal," *World Business* (November 11, 2002), at <www.usatoday.com>.
[8]Julie Creswell, "Gap Got Junked: Now What?" *Fortune* (March 18, 2002), 93–94.
[9]See Norman M. Scarborough and Thomas W. Zimmerer, *Effective Small Business Management: An Entrepreneurial Approach,* 6th ed. (Upper Saddle River: Prentice Hall, 2000), esp. pp. 298–300.
[10]Susan Hodges, "One Big Step Toward a Loan," *Nation's Business* (August 1997), pp. 34–36.

Source Notes

Chapter 1 Introducing the Contemporary Business Environment

Megawatt Laundering and Other Bright Business Ideas/Blackouts and Other Dark Forces Chris Taylor, "California Scheming," *Time,* May 20, 2002, 42–44; Richard A. Oppel Jr., "How Enron Got California to Buy Power It Didn't Need," *New York Times,* May 8, 2002, C1, C6; Mark Gimein,

"Who Turned the Lights Out?" *Fortune* (February 5, 2001), 110–14+; Holman Jenkins Jr., "Enron for Beginners," *Wall Street Journal,* January 23, 2002, A1, A17; Delroy Alexander, "Keener Focus on Enron Deals," *Chicago Tribune,* February 20, 2002, C1; Brock N. Meeks, "Enron Sailed into a Perfect Storm," *QwestLightspeed* (January 23, 2002), at <www.msnbc.com/news/ 692391.asp>; Nelson D. Schwartz, "Is Energy Trading a Big Scam?" *Fortune,* June 10, 2002, 126–28+; Neela Banerjee, "Who Will Needle Regulators Now That Enron's Muzzled?" *New York Times,* January 20, 2002, Sec. 3, 1,12. **It's a Wired World: *Electronic B2B in the Auto Industry*** Keith Bradsher, "Carmakers to Buy Parts on Internet," *The New York Times,* February 26, 2000, A1, C14; David Welch, "E-Marketplace: Covisint," *BusinessWeek Online* (June 5, 2000), at <www.businessweek.com/2000/00_23/ b3684044.htm>; "Big Three Car Makers Plan Net Exchange," *Wall Street Journal,* February 28, 2000, A3, A16; Steve Konicki, "GM Buys $96 Billion in Materials via Covisint," *Informationweek.com* (August 16, 2001), at <www.informationweek.com/ story/IWK20010816S0001>; Jeff Bennett, "Measure of the Auto Industry: Covisint Refines Online Ways to Connect Buyers with Suppliers," *Auto.com* (February 19, 2002), at <www.auto.com/ industry/covi19_20020219.htm>; Beth Cox, "Covisint Brings Automakers Together," *Internetnews.com* (February 6, 2002), at <www.internetnews.com/ ec-news/article.php/4_969701>; "Covisint Creates Strategic Business Units" (company press release dated April 3, 2002) and "Covisint Chooses Southfield, Michigan for Corporate Headquarters" (company press release dated January 22, 2002), at <www.covisint.com>. **Figure 1.1** Adapted from Karl E. Case and Ray C. Fair, *Principles of Economics,* 6th ed., revised (Upper Saddle River, NJ: Prentice Hall, 2002), 47.

Chapter 2 Understanding the Environments of Business
Making the Grade/Firms That Flunked Matthew Boyle, "The Right Stuff," *Fortune,* March 4, 2002, 85–86; Boyle, "The Shiniest Reputations in Tarnished Times," *Fortune,* March 4, 2002, 70–72; Justin Fox, "What's So Great about GE?" *Fortune,* March 4, 2002, 64–67. **Figure 2.3** United Auto Workers, *AUW Research Bulletin: Productivity and Growth* (September 20, 2002), at <http://uaw.com/ publications/jobs_pay/0700/jpe.html>. Data from Bureau of Economic Analysis, U.S. Dept. of Commerce; Bureau of Labor Statistics, U.S. Dept. of Labor. **Table 2.3** Robert A. Collinge and Ronald M. Ayers, *Economics by Design: Principles and Issues* (Upper Saddle River, NJ: Prentice Hall, 2000), 357. Data from *1999 Economic Report of the President,* Table B-60. **Figure 2.4** Michael J. Mandel, "The New Economy," *Business Week,* January 31, 2000, 75. Data from *Computer Industry Almanac.* **Figure 2.5** Mandel, "The New Economy," 77. Data from International Data Corp. Figure 1.7 Mandel, "The New Economy," 75. Data from Standard & Poor's DRI. **Figure 2.7** Adapted from Cedric X. Scalle and Mark J. Cotteleer, *Enterprise Resource Planning (ERP).* (Boston: Harvard Business School Publishing, No. 9-699-020, 1999). **It's a Wired World: *Electronic Preplanning for Disruption Management*** Jens Clausen, Jesper Hansen, Jesper Larsen, and Allan Larsen, "Disruption Management," *ORMS Today,* October 2001, 40–43.

Chapter 3 Understanding Entrepreneurship and Ownership
The Big Cheese in Vermont/The Odd Couple of Cheese Paul Judge, "From Country Boys to Big Cheese," *Fast Company,* December 2001, 38–40; Sue Robinson, "Saving Our Farms," *BurlingtonFreePress.com* (November 27, 2001), at <www. burlingtonfreepress. com/specialnews/farms/5000h.htm>. **Figures 3.1, 3.2, & 3.6** Data from U.S. Department of Commerce, "Statistics about Business Size (Including Small Business) from the U.S. Census Bureau," *Statistical Abstract of the United States* (September 6, 2001), at <www.census.gov/epcd/www/smallbus. html>. **Figure 3.3** Data from U.S. Department of Commerce, "Statistics about Business Size," *Statistical Abstract of the United States* (Washington, DC: Bureau of the Census, 2001), 491 **Figure 3.4** Norman M. Scarborough and Thomas W. Zimmerer, *Effective Small Business Management: An Entrepreneurial Approach,* 6th ed. (Upper Saddle River, NJ: Prentice Hall, 2000), 15. Data from Forrester Research Inc. **It's a Wired World: *What Doth It Profit a Dot-Com?*** Timothy Mullaney, "Break Out the Black Ink," *Business Week,* May 13, 2002, 74–76; Robert Hof, "How E-Biz Rose, Fell, and Will Rise Anew," *Business Week,* May 13, 2002, 64–72. **Figure 3.5** Data from Catalyst; National Foundation for Women Business Owners.

Chapter 4 Understanding the Global Context of Business
"We Must Americanize"/National Identity Crisis in Toyota City Chester Dawson et al., "The Americanization of Toyota," *Business Week,* April 15, 2002, 52–54; Todd Zaun, "Auto Makers Look for Another Edge Farther from Home," *Wall Street Journal,* July 31, 2002, A1, A8. **Figure 4.1** David Hale, "A Second Chance," *Fortune,* November 22, 1999, 190. **Table 4.1** *Hoover's Handbook of World Business 2002* (Austin, TX: Hoover's Business Press, 2002), 52. Data from <http://www.ita.doc. gov/td/industry/otea/ustth/tabcon.html>. **Figure 4.5** Michael E. Porter, *The Competitive Advantage of Nations* (New York: Free Press, 1990), 72. **Table 4.2** Robyn Meredith, "Dollar Makes Canada a Land of the Spree," *The New York Times,* August 1, 1999, C11. **Figures 4.6 & 4.7** *Survey of Current Business,* July 2001 (Washington, DC: U.S. Department of Commerce), 88–89. **It's a Wired World: *Rolling in the Worldwide Dough*** Ron Lieber, "Give Us This Day Our Global Bread," *Fast Company,* March 2001, 164–67. **Building Your Business Skills: *Putting Yourself in Your Place*** Maria Atanasov, "Taking Her Business on the Road," *Fortune,* April 13, 1998, 158–60.

Chapter 5 Conducting Business Ethically and Responsibly
The Rules of Tipping/When Does a Stock Warrant Warrant a Warrant for Arrest? Geeta Anand, Jerry Markon, and Chris Adams, "ImClone's Ex-CEO Arrested, Charged with Insider Trading," *The Wall Street Journal,* June 13, 2002, A1, A8; Greg Farrell, "Waksal Indictment Unsealed," *USA Today,* August 8, 2002, 1B; Amy Barrett, "No Quick Cure," *Business Week,* May 6, 2002, 30–33; Andrew Pollack, "For ImClone Drug Entrepreneur, a Past of Celebrity and Notoriety," *New York Times,* January 24, 2002, C1, C9.

Figures 5.1 & 5.2 Based on Gerald S. Cavanaugh, *American Business Values: With International Perspectives,* 4th ed. (Upper Saddle River, NJ: Prentice Hall, 1998), 71, 84. **It's a Wired World: *On-Line Griping and Other Issues in High-Tech Ethics*** Daniel H. Pink, "America's Top Cybercop," *Fast Company,* February 2002, 28–35; John Simons, "Stop Moaning about Gripe Sites and Log On," *Fortune,* February 26, 2002, 95–98; Michael Shrage, "E-Mail or E-Sting? Your Boss Knows, but He's Not Telling," *Fortune,* March 20, 2000, 240; "OTG Software Introduces Transparent Email Surveillance for Policy Enforcement," *Business Wire,* December 5, 2001, 76. **Figure 5.3** David P. Baron, *Business and Its Environment,* 4th ed. (Upper Saddle River, NJ: Prentice Hall, 2003), 768. **Figure 5.5** Based on Andrew C. Revkin, "Who Cares about a Few Degrees?" *The New York Times,* December 12, 1997, F1. **Table 5.1** The Foundation Center, "Fifty Largest Corporate Foundations by Total Giving," *Researching Philanthropy* (August 12, 2002), at <fdncenter.org/research/ trends_analysis/top50giving.html>.

Chapter 6 Managing the Business Enterprise
"Our Business Isn't Really about Moving Freight" Chuck Salter, "Fresh Start 2002: On the Road Again," *Fast Company,* January 2002, 50–58; Matthew Boyle, "America's Most Admired Companies: The Right Stuff," *Fortune,* March 4, 2002; *Yellow Corporation 2000 Annual Report* (March 2001), at <www.yellowcorp.com>. **Wired World: *Always in Touch*** Chris Sandlund, "Stay Plugged In," *Fortune,* February 27, 2002, 24–26; Eyal Ravinovitch, "Life in the Fast Lane," *Fortune,* February 1, 2002, 98–104; "It Takes a Cell Phone," *Wall Street Journal,* June 25, 1999, B1, B6. **Figure 6.1** Based on Thomas L. Wheelen and J. David Hunger, *Strategic Management and Business Policy,* 7th ed. (Upper Saddle River, NJ: Prentice Hall, 2000), 13. **Figure 6.2** Based on Stephen P. Robbins and Mary Coulter, *Management,* 7th ed. (Upper Saddle River, NJ: Prentice Hall, 2002), 199. **Building Your Business Skills: *Speaking with Power*** Information from Justin Martin, "How You Speak Shows Where You Rank," *Fortune,* February 2, 1998, 156.

Chapter 7 Organizing the Business Enterprise
Getting a Supersonic Project Off the Ground (I)/How to Control for Vertical Lift Bill Breen, "High Stakes, Big Bets," *Fast Company,* April 2002, 66–78; Michael A. Dornheim, "Boeing: Lift Fan Put LockMart Over the Top in JSF Competition," *Aviation Week & Space Technology,* March 12, 2002; Massachusetts Institute of Technology's Engineering Systems Division, "Special Seminar: Lockheed Martin Aeronautics Company" (April 4, 2002), at <www.mit.edu/headline/seminar0306.htm>. **It's a Wired World: *The Technology of Personal Contact*** Anne Fisher, "Virtual Teams and Long-Distance Meetings: More on Staying Grounded," *Fortune,* October 15, 2001; Faith Keenan and Spencer E. Ante, "The New Teamwork," *Business Week,* February 18, 2002; Keenan, "Giants Can Be Nimble," *Business Week E.Biz,* September 18, 2000; Nadav Enbar, "Meet Yale's Admissions Director," *Business Week,* May 20, 2002; "Paul Gudonis, Chairman and CEO, Genuity Inc.," *Fast Company,* May 20, 2002; Polly LaBarre, "Strategic Innovation: The Children's Hospital at Montefiore," *Fast Company,* May 2002.

Chapter 8 Managing Human Resources and Labor Relations
From Hard Bargains to Hard Times/Time Out on the Labor Front David Leonhardt, "Did Pay Incentives Cut Both Ways?" *New York Times,* April 7, 2002, BU1-3; Dean Foust and Michelle Conlin, "A Smarter Squeeze?" *Business Week,* December 31, 2001, 42–44; John Strauss, "Agency Workers Mull Pay Cut for Time Off," *Indianapolis Star,* March 11, 2002; Rick Perera, "Siemens Offers Workers 'Time-Outs' to Save Cash," *The Industry Standard,* August 31, 2001; Tischelle George, "Bye-Bye, Employee Perks," *Information Week,* October 15, 2001. **Figure 8.2** *The Wall Street Journal Almanac 1999,* 226. Reprinted by Permission of Dow Jones Inc. via Copyright Clearance Center Inc. © 1999 Dow Jones and Co. Inc. All rights reserved. **It's a Wired World: *The Technology of Personal Contact*** Eric Wahlgren, "Have Investors Missed the Boat on Pier 1?" *Business Week,* December 21, 2001; James C. Cooper and Kathleen Madigan, "The Surprise Economy," *Business Week,* March 18, 2002; Karen E. Klein, "Making Performance Reviews Pay Off," *Business Week,* February 6, 2002; Michelle Conlin, "The Software Says You're Just Average," *BusinessWeek,* February 25, 2002. **Figure 8.4(a)** Adapted from David Whitford, "Labor's Lost Chance," *Fortune,* September 28, 1998, 180. **Figure 8.4(b)** Dan Seligman, "Driving the AFL-CIO Crazy," *Forbes,* November 1, 1999, 106. Data from Leo Troy and Neil Sheflin, *Union Sourcebook* (1985) and Barry T. Hirsch and David A. MacPherson, *Union Membership and Earnings Data Book* (1999).

Chapter 9 Motivating, Satisfying, and Leading Employees
The Psychological Contract; or, The Manager as Brainwasher/Moral Integrity and Morale Brian O'Keefe, "The High Price of Being No. 1," *Fortune,* April 15, 2002; Cait Murphy, "Now That Wal-Mart Is America's Largest Corporation, the Service Economy Wears the Crown," *Fortune,* April 15, 2002; "Fourteen Top CEOs (and One President) Gauge the Year Ahead," *Fortune,* April 15, 2002; Mark Gimein, "Sam Walton Made Us a Promise," *Fortune,* March 18, 2002, 120–130. **Figure 9.1** A.H. Maslow, *Motivation and Personality,* 2nd ed. (Upper Saddle River, NJ: Prentice Hall, 1970). Reprinted by permission of Prentice Hall Inc. **It's a Wired World: *Motivation and the Machine*** Aaron Bernstein, "Too Many Workers? Not for Long," *Business Week,* May 20, 2002; Timothy Aeppel, "Young and Old See Technology Sparking Friction on Shop Floor," *The Wall Street Journal,* April 7, 2000, A1, A10; Ed Michaels, Helen Handfield-Jones, and Beth Axelrod, *The War for Talent,* excerpt reprinted in *Business Week,* December 12, 2001.

Chapter 10 Understanding Marketing Process and Consumer Behavior
Xbox Spots the Market/Microsoft's Great Xpectations Chris Gaither, "Microsoft Explores a New Territory: Fun," *New York Times,* November 4, 2001, Sec. 3, 1, 7; Leslie P. Norton, "Toy

Soldiers," *Barron's,* May 14, 2001, 25–30; Chris Taylor, "The Battle of Seattle," *Time,* May 21, 2001, 58–59; N'Gai Croal, "Game Wars 5.0," *Newsweek,* May 28, 2001, 65+; Tobi Elkin, "The X Factor: Microsoft, Sony Prepare for E3," *Advertising Age,* April 23, 2001, 4+; Bill Powell, "Gamemakers Aren't Racking Up Bonus Points," *Fortune,* April 16, 2001, 58; Danny Bradbury, "Home Free," *Communications International,* February 2001, 41; Tobi Elkin, "Gearing Up for Xbox Lunch," *Advertising Age,* November 20, 2000, 16+; Arlene Weintraub, "Video Games: The Sky's the Limit," *Business Week,* January 14, 2002, 100–01. **It's a Wired World: *High-Tech Hits the Highway*** Associated Press, "High-Tech Hits the Road," *Columbia Daily Tribune,* February 25, 2002, 1B; *Fortune: Technology Guide,* Winter 2001, 37–38. **Figure 10.2** Erick Schonfield, "Changes in the U.S. Population: Betting on the Boomers," *Fortune,* December 25, 1995, 78–80. Reprinted from the December 25, 1995 issue of *Fortune* by special permission; © 1995, Time Inc. **Figure 10.3** Adapted from Naresh K. Malhorta, *Marketing Research: An Applied Orientation,* 3rd ed. (Upper Saddle River, NJ: Prentice Hall, 1999), 10.

Chapter 11 Developing and Pricing Products
Who Wants to Be a Survivor?/The ABCs of 18–49s David Lieberman, "ABC's Actions Reflect Network's Troubles," *USA Today,* March 6, 2002, 1B; Gary Levin, "Youth Served in Ratings Game," *USA Today,* March 6, 2002, 3D; Peter Johnson, " 'The View' from Here: News Deserves Respect," *USA Today,* March 6, 2002, 3D; Joe Schlosser, "Who Wants to Program ABC?" *Broadcasting & Cable,* December 3, 2001, 7; Peg Tyre, "A New Life Lyne?" *Newsweek,* January 21, 2002, 57; Johnnie Roberts, "Disney's Lost Magic," *Newsweek,* December 10, 2001, 52. **Figure 11.2** Jay Heizer and Barry Render, *Operations Management,* 6th ed. (Upper Saddle River, NJ: Prentice Hall, 2001), 135. **Table 11.1** Gerry Khermouch, Stanley Holmes, and Moon Ihlwan, "The Best Global Brands," *Business Week,* August 6, 2001, 50–57. **It's a Wired World: *The World of Cyberprice Bidding*** Shawn Tully, "The B2B Tool That Really Is Changing the World," *Fortune,* March 20, 2000, 132–34+; Ken Zapinsky, "FreeMarkets Is the Easy Winner in Having the Biggest Stock Price Increase," *Post-Gazette.com* (April 9, 2000), at <www.post-gazette.com/businessnews/20000409stock. asp>; "American Management Systems and FreeMarkets Form Strategic Alliance to eEmpower Public Sector Purchasing," *AMS News Room* (March 9, 2000), at <www3.amsinc.com/CMC/newsroom.nsf/prMBRY-4HQM3Z>; "FreeMarkets and webPLAN Form Strategic Alliance to Deliver Web-Based B2B eMarketplace and e-Supply Chain Solutions," *TechMall* (May 16, 2000), at <www8.techmall.com/techdocs/TS000516-html>; "The H.J. Heinz Company," *FreeMarkets* (April 3, 2002), at <www.freemarkets.com/benefits/case_studies/hjheinz.asp>.

Chapter 12 Distributing Products
Changing Channels on the Local News/What Price News? Mark Wigfield, "FCC Ordered by Court to Revisit Broadcast-Ownership Restrictions," *Wall Street Journal,* April 3, 2002, B2; Frank Blethen, "A 'Dangerous' Step," *Editor & Publisher,* March 18, 2002, 30; Doug Halonen, "Mr. Smith Goes After Washington," *Electronic Media,* December 31, 2001, 1, 20+; Alicia Mundy and Jeremy Murphy, "Ownership Limits Under Fire," *Mediaweek,* February 25, 2002, 4, 5; Murphy, "Bringing News In-House," *Mediaweek,* January 14, 2002, 8. **Figure 12.3** Prodigy, "Small Biz Web Sites on the Rise, Yet Many Owners Slow to Embrace the Internet" (April 13, 2000), at <www.prodigy.com/pcombusiness/business_content>. **It's a Wired World: *"Going to School" Takes On a New Meaning*** Mick O'Leary, "E-Global Library Advances the Virtual Library," *Information Today,* March 2002, 19–20; Elisabeth Goodridge, "Web-Based Training Speeds Delivery and Saves Money," *Informationweek,* February 11, 2002, 71; Stephanie Overby, "The World's Biggest Classroom," *CIO,* February 1, 2002, 56–60; Kathleen Melymuka, "Executive Education on a Shoestring," *Computerworld,* March 11, 2002, 24–25; Elisabeth Goodridge, "AOL's Online Campus," *Informationweek,* December 17, 2001, 59; Stephen P. Pizzo, "Master of the Knowledge Universe," *Forbes,* September 10, 2001, 64–69; Dirk Johnson, "Next Frontiers," *Newsweek,* October 29, 2001, 54–58; Matt Bolch, "School at Work," *Training,* February 2002, 50–54; Michael Rogers, "Tutor.com Online Help for Fifth Grade through College," *Library Journal,* April 1, 2002, 27.

Chapter 13 Distributing Products
Congested? Stuffed Up? Try DTC/Do We Need Relief from DTC? Paul Jung, "No Free Lunch," *Health Affairs,* March/April 2002, 226–31; Richard Haugh, "DTC Drug Advertising Soars," *Hospitals & Health Networks,* February 2002, 49; Lindsey Tanner, "U.S. Doctors Seek Ban on Prescription Drug Ads," *C-Health* (June 18, 2001), at <www.canoe.ca>; Victoria Stagg Elliott, "Questions Swirl Around Drug Ads for Patients," *amednews.com* (July 9/16, 2001), at <www.ama-assn.org>; *USA Weekend,* April 19–21, 2002, 9; Andra Brichacek and Sibyl Shalo, "Location, Location, Location," *Pharmaceutical Executive,* June 2001, 126; Jill Wechsler, "DDMAC Queries Docs, Patients about DTC Advertising," *Pharmaceutical Executive,* March 2002, 38; "National Health Council Backs DTC Advertising," *Medical Marketing and Media,* March 2002, 8; Sandra Levy, "Survey Says: DTC Advertising, R&D Driving Up Drug Costs," *Drug Topics,* April 1, 2002, 56; Kevin Gopal, Consumer Communication in Europe Stalls," *Pharmaceutical Executive,* February 2002, 38; Jackie Judd, "Truth in Advertising?" *ABCNews.com* (January 3, 2002), at <abcnews.go.com>; Kathleen Blankenhorn, Nancy Duckwitz, and Marjorie Sherr, "Power to the People," *Medical Marketing and Media,* August 2001, 66–70. **Figure 13.2** *Advertising Age,* September 24, 2001, s16. **Table 13.1** *Advertising Age,* September 24, 2001, s16. **It's a Wired World: *The Sound Approach to Internet Marketing*** Michelle Fradette and Heather Kelly, "Altec Lansing Unveils New Corporate Direction at CES 2002," Press Release (January 8, 2002), at <www.alteclansing.com>; Keith Shaw, "Car Tools," *Network World,* April 15, 2002, 46; Matt Beer, "Eight Extraordinary Gizmos Stand Out at the Fall Show," *San Francisco Examiner,* November 21, 1999, B5; "Agency.Com" and "Altec Lansing" (April

25, 2000), at <www.agency.com> and <www.altecmm.com>.

Chapter 14 Producing Goods and Services

Getting a Supersonic Project Off the Ground (II)/Sharing "A Lot of Neat Stuff" Bill Breen, "High Stakes, Big Bets," *Fast Company,* April 2002, 66–78; William H. Miller, "Reaching New Heights," *Industry Week,* February 2002, 61–62; Norm Alster, "Managing a Mega Project," *Electronic Business,* February 2002, 47–49; Chuck Moozakis, "Web Powers Fighter Project—Linking All the Contractors in Real Time Would Have Been Impossible without the Web, Says Northrop's Dave Torchia," *Internetweek,* November 12, 2001, 1, 49; Steve Konicki, "Collaboration is Cornerstone of $19 billion Defense Contract," *Informationweek,* November 12, 2001, 30; James Dao with Laura M. Holson, "Lockheed Wins $200 Billion Deal for Fighter Jet," *New York Times,* October 21, 2001, A1, A9; Holson, "Pushing Limits, Finding None," *New York Times,* November 1, 2001, C1, C6; Edward H. Phillips, "LockMart Bracing for JSF Transition Phase," *Aviation Space & Space Technology,* November 19, 2001, 86; Faith Keenan and Spencer E. Ante, "The New Teamwork," *BusinessWeek Online,* February 18, 2002. **Figure 14.1** Bureau of Labor Statistics, *Employment & Earnings,* March 2002 (Washington, DC: Dept. of Labor, 2002), 42. **Figure 14.2** Bureau of Economic Analysis, *Survey of Current Business,* March 2002 (Washington, DC: Dept. of Commerce, 2002), D4. **It's a Wired World: *Who's Buying Into E-Procurement?*** Michael A. Verespej, "E-Procurement Explosion," *Industry Week,* March 2002, 24–28; Steve Konicki, "E-Procurement: From (Shop) Rags to Riches," *Informationweek,* March 4, 2002, 26; "B2B Outlook Mixed," *Industrial Distribution,* September 2001, 15–16; Karen Tourigny and Steve Sidorchuk, "Exploding the Myth of E-Procurement," *Semiconductor International,* November 2001, S10–S12; Paul DeJohn, "Buyers Impatient with E-Commerce Delays," *Hospital Materials Management,* May 2001, 2.

Chapter 15 Managing for Quality and Productivity

Marshaling the Arts of Quality/The Penalty for 99.99% Perfection Wayne Sander, "Six Sigma Project Management: A Pocket Guide," *Quality Progress,* May 2002, 114; "E-Learning Center Offers New Six Sigma Courses," *Quality Progress,* May 2002, 17; "Green Belt Training Starts Feb. 4," *Quality Progress,* February 2002, 13; Dennis Sester, "Motorola: A Tradition of Quality," *Quality,* October 2001, 30–34; Roxanne O'Brasky, "Translating Six Sigma Methodology," *Best's Review,* November 2001, 56–57; "Six Sigma Continues as a Hot Media Topic," *Quality Progress,* January 2002, 25; John R. Johnson, "Giving Credit Where Credit is Due," *Warehousing Management,* January/February 2002, 26–32; Ron Panko, "Stealth Solution," *Best's Review,* November 2001, 53–57; "Conseco Moves Full Speed Ahead with Six Sigma," *Best's Review,* November 2001, 58–62. **Figure 15.1** Bart Van Ark and Robert McGuckin, "International Comparisons of Labor Productivity and Per Capita Income," *Monthly Labor Review,* July 1999, 33–41. **Figure 15.2** Data from *Monthly Labor Review,* February 2000, 98. **Figure 15.5** Adapted from Richard B. Chase, Nicholas J. Aquilano, and F. Robert Jacobs, *Production and Operations Management,* 8th ed. (Boston: Irwin McGraw Hill, 1998), 771. **It's a Wired World: *Selling the Idea of Culture Shift*** Philip Siekman, "Mercury Marine: Focusing on the Demand Side," *Fortune [Industrial Management & Technology],* November 8, 1999, 272[N]-272[O]; "Mercury: The Water Calls" (May 22, 2000), at <www.mercurymarine.com/ mercuryhome/ merchome.cfm>; Lynne M. Almvig, "Robotics Milling Department," *Robotics Today,* First Quarter 2000, 1–4.

Chapter 16 Managing Information Systems and Communications Technology

More Productive Than a Speeding Locomotive/Remote Damage Control Larry Adams, "Diagnostics from Afar," *Quality,* November 2001, 26–28; Robert Pool, "If It Ain't Broke, Fix It," *Technology Review,"* September 2001, 64–69; Richard Baxter, "Remote M&D Leverages Expertise," *Power,* March 20, 2002, 44–52; Jim Mele, "Diagnostics on the Fly," *Fleet Owner,* September 2001, 73–78; Chuck Moozakis, "Planes, Trains, Autos, Monitored from Afar," *Internetweek,* March 12, 2001, 1, 70; "Working on the Railroad: A Talk with John Krenicki," *Business Week,* April 29, 2002, 28b. **Figure 16.2** Adapted from Kenneth C. Laudon and Jane P. Laudon, *Essentials of Management Information Systems: Managing the Digital Firm,* 5th ed. (Upper Saddle River, NJ: Prentice Hall, 2003), 16. **Figure 16.4** Adapted from Laudon and Laudon, *Essentials of Management Information Systems,* 39. **Figure 16.6** Adapted from Laudon and Laudon, *Essentials of Management Information Systems,* 44. **It's a Wired World: *Going to School in Networking*** Scott Sonneborn, "33 Days, 8 Campuses, 127 Kids, and an Infinity of Gizmos," *Fortune,* June 24, 2002, 126–132; Johna Till Johnson, "Boosting Your IM IQ Will Pay Off," *Network World,* March 11, 2002, 48; "New Palm Targets Wireless Enterprise," *Frontline Solutions,* March 2002, 44; Scott Kirsner, "IM Is Here, RU Prepared?" *Darwin,* February 2002, 22–24.

Chapter 17 Understanding Principles of Accounting

Humpty-Dumpty Time at Arthur Andersen/Is Anybody Holding Auditors Accountable? John A. Byrne, "Fall from Grace," *Business Week,* August 12, 2002, 50–56; Kurt Eichenwald, "Andersen Witnesses Defend Intent of Shredding," *New York Times,* June 1, 2002, C1, C2; Eichenwald, "Andersen Guilty in Effort to Block Inquiry on Enron," *New York Times,* June 16, 2002, 1, 20; Eichenwald, "Andersen Trial Yields Evidence in Enron's Fall," *New York Times,* June 17, 2002, A1, A14; Mark M. Meinaro and Parija Bhatnagar, "Andersen Loses More Partners, Key Clients," *USA Today* (May 21, 2002), at <www.usatoday.com>; Alex Berenson and Jonathan D. Glater, "A Tattered Andersen Fights for Its Future," *The New York Times,* January 13, 2002, Sec. 3, 1, 10; Greg Farrell, "Arthur Andersen Fined $7 Million by SEC for Audits," *USA Today* (June 19, 2001), at <www.usatoday.com>; Edward Iwata, "Andersen to Pay $217M in Baptist Foundation Case," *USA Today* (March 1, 2002), at <www.usatoday.com>. **It's a Wired World: *A Roundabout Look at Conflicting Interests*** David LeonHardt, "Consultants Are Putting a

New Price On Advice," *The New York Times,* January 19, 2000, C1, C10; Floyd Norris, "Accounting Firm Is Said to Violate Rules Routinely," *The New York Times,* January 7, 2000, A1, C6; Norris, "Rules That Only an Accountant Could Fail to Understand?" *The New York Times,* January 8, 2000, C1, C14. **Figure 17.1** Adapted from "CPA Vision Project: 2011 and Beyond" (September 24, 2002), at <www.cpavision.org/final_report>. **Tables 17.1 & 17.2** Adapted from "CPA Vision Project: 2011 and Beyond" (September 24, 2002), at <www.cpavision.org/final_report>.

Chapter 18 Understanding Money and Banking
Argentines No Longer Bank on the Peso/There's No Accounting for Financial Systems Associated Press, "Argentina Devalues Peso," *Columbia Daily Tribune,* January 7, 2002, 2B; Pamela Druckerman, "Telecom Argentina Plans to Suspend Debt Payments," *Wall Street Journal,* April 3, 2002, A16; "Argentina Bank Chief Quits," *CNNMoney* (January 18, 2002), at <www.cnnfn.com>; "Argentina Gets Reprieve," *CNNMoney* (January 17, 2002), at <www.cnnfn.com>; "Citigroup 4Q Profit Rises," *CNNMoney* (January 17, 2002), at <www.cnnfn.com>; "Peso Plan Encourages IMF," *CNNMoney* (January 15, 2002), at <www.cnnfn.com>; "Argentina's Currency Test," *CNNMoney* (January 11, 2002), at <www.cnnfn.com>; "Argentina Deepens Bank Curbs," *CNNMoney* (January 10, 2002), at <www.cnnfn.com>; "Argentina Limits Cash Bank Withdrawals," *USA TODAY* (December 3, 2001), at <www.usatoday>. **Figure 18.1** Data compiled from Federal Reserve Board of Governors (July 20, 2002), at <www.stls.frb.org/fred/data/monetary/>. **It's a Wired World: *Why Aren't We Cashing In on E-Cash?*** Kenneth R. Rogoff, "The Surprising Popularity of Paper Currency," *Finance & Development,* March 2002, 56; "Switzerland: Electronic Money," *International Financial Law Review,* April 2001, 62–63; Lisa Cantos, Lorin Fine, and Randi Singer, "NCCUSL Proposes Uniform Act to Regulate Cybercash and Other Electronic Money," *Intellectual Property & Technology Law Journal,* October 2000, 23.

Chapter 19 Understanding Securities and Investments
And the Wall (Street) Came Tumbling Down/Bearing Up Justin Lahart, "The Crash of 2002," *CNNMoney* (July 19, 2002), at <www.cnnfn.com>; "We All Got Burned—What Now?" *CNNMoney* (July 19, 2002), at <www.cnnfn.com>; "Dow Plunges Below Its Post-Terrorist Attack Low," *USATODAY.com* (July 19, 2002), at <www.usatoday.com>. **Figure 19.1** "Yahoo Inc (YHOO)/Wal-Mart Stores Inc (WMT)," *Quicken.com* (July 13, 2002), at <www.quicken.com/investments/charts/. . . >. **Figure 19.2** Leah Nathans Spiro and Edward C. Baig, "Who Needs a Broker?" *Business Week,* February 22, 1999, 113–161. **Figure 19.6** Data from *Wall Street Journal.* **Figure 19.7** Nasdaq, "Market Performance & Highlights: Section 3," *Nasdaq.com* (June 23, 2000), at <www.nasdaq.com/about/NBW2000Sec3.pdf>. **It's a Wired World: *The Daily Grind of Keystroking*** Andrew Wahl, "Swift Change Artists," *Canadian Business,* March 18, 2002, 57–59; Daniel P. Collins, "Day Trading—Not Just for the Tech-Savvy and Locals Anymore," *Futures,* June 2002, 66–69; Mark Etzkorn, "All in a Day's Work" (July 19, 2002), at <www.futuresmag.com>.

Chapter 20 Understanding Financial and Risk Management
Getting a Kick Out of the Soccer Business/Betting against Earthquakes Sarah Veysey, "World Cup Organizers Step Up against Risks," *Business Insurance,* June 3, 2002, 15–16; Carolyn Aldred, "Insurers Scrutinize World Cup Risk," *Business Insurance,* September 3, 2001, 43; "FIFA to Innovate with ABS on World Cup Brand Rights," *Euroweek,* January 5, 2001, 35; Rob Gilhooly, Hooligan Fears Worry 2002 World Cup Host City Officials," *Japan Times,* June 1-June 15, 1999, 17. **Figure 20.1** Carl Beidleman, *The Handbook of International Investing* (Chicago: Probus, 1987), 133. **It's a Wired World: *A Healthy Approach to Risk Response*** *Costpredict: Organizational Health Cost Analysis* (Columbia, MO: Network Health Systems®, 2000); © *Health & Lifestyle Assessment Handbook* (Columbia, MO: Network Health Systems®, 1999).

Cartoon, Photo, and Screen Credits

Chapter 1
Pages 3/21: New York Times Pictures. page 6: Kelly Guenther. page 9: Gregory Foster Photography. page 10: © The New Yorker Collection 1990 Joseph Mirachi from cartoonbank.com. All rights reserved. page 14: New York Times Pictures. page 19: New York Times Pictures. page 20: Tara Photography Sdn. Bhd.

Chapter 2
Pages 29/55: Corbis. page 31: New York Times Pictures. page 35: New York Times Pictures. page 39: Travis Bell. page 44: Figure from ENTERPRISE RESOURCE PLANNING, Scalle & Cotteleer. Copyright © 1999 by the President and Fellows of Harvard College. Harvard Business School Case 9-699-020. Reprinted by permission of Harvard Business School. page 46: Getty Images, Inc. - Liaison. page 49: Getty Images, Inc. - Liaison. page 52: © The New Yorker Collection 1999 Richard Cline from cartoonbank.com. All rights reserved. page 54: Getty Images, Inc. — Liaison.

Chapter 3
Pages 65/88: AP/Wide World Photos. page 68: New York Times Pictures. page 73: New York Times Pictures. page 74: © The New Yorker Collection 1988 Robert Weber from cartoonbank.com. All rights reserved. page 75: Tom Strattman. page 87: New York Times Pictures.

Chapter 4
Pages 97/119: Axel Koester Photography. page 98: Namas Bhojani. page 101: New York Times Pictures. page 110: © The New Yorker Collection 2001 Robert Weber from cartoonbank.com. All rights reserved. page 116: Timepix. page 117: AP/Wide World Photos.

Chapter 5
Pages 125/152: The Patrick McMullan Company, Inc. page 128 (left): New York Times Pictures. page 128 (right): New York Times Pictures. page 132: © The New Yorker Collection 1997 Frank Cotham from cartoonbank.com. All rights reserved. page 137: SIPA Press. page 138: New York Times Pictures.

page 140: AP/Wide World Photos. page 144: Getty Images, Inc. — Liaison. page 146: Corbis/SABA Press Photos, Inc. page 150: "Top 15 Corporate Foundations" excerpted from Foundation Yearbook 2002. Copyright © 2002 The Foundation Center. Used with permission.

Chapter 6
Pages 159/181: Yellow Corporation. page 168: Katie Murray Photography. page 170: Corbis/SABA Press Photos, Inc. page 173: Business Week. page 175: © The New Yorker Collection 1993 Mike Twohy from cartoonbank.com. All rights reserved. page 178: Kistone Photography. page 180: ZUMA Press.

Chapter 7
Pages 189/211: Lockheed Martin Aeronautics Co. page 192: Twentieth Century Fox Films. page 193: © The New Yorker Collection 1991 Charles Barsotti from cartoonbank.com. All rights reserved. page 194: Robert Wright Photography. page 196: Mark Richards. page 199: Vincent Prado. page 206: Bernd Auers.

Chapter 8
Pages 217/241: Getty Images, Inc. – Hulton Archive Photos. page 221: Robin Nelson. page 226: Alex Brandon. page 229: © The New Yorker Collection 1996 Danny Shanahan from cartoonbank.com. All rights reserved. page 236: Corbis/SABA Press Photos, Inc.

Chapter 9
Pages 249/271: AP/Wide World Photos. page 251: Corbis/SABA Press Photos, Inc. page 252: New York Times Pictures. page 256: AP/Wide World Photos. page 259: © The New Yorker Collection 1998 Leo Cullum from cartoonbank.com. All rights reserved. page 261: Corbis/SABA Press Photos, Inc. page 265: Alex Brandon. page 270: Randi Lynn Beach.

Chapter 10
Pages 279/298: Chuck Fishman. page 283: Getty Images, Inc. — Liaison. page 285: New York Times Pictures. page 287: New York Times Pictures. page 291: © The New Yorker Collection 1992 Bernard Schoenbaum from cartoonbank.com. All rights reserved.

Chapter 11
Pages 307/327: AP/Wide World Photos. page 310: © 2002, SAS Institute Inc., Cary, NC, USA. All rights reserved. Reproduced with permission of SAS Institute Inc. Cary, NC. page 313: Jill Connelly. page 316 (top): AP/Wide World Photos. page 316 (bottom): From "The Best Global Brands" by Gerry Khermoouch, Business Week, 8/6/01, pp. 50–57 © 2001 McGraw-Hill Companies, Inc. Used with permission. page 320: © The New Yorker Collection 1991 Jack Ziegler from cartoonbank.com. All rights reserved. page 321: New York Times Pictures. page 326: AP/Wide World Photos.

Chapter 12
Pages 335/356: The Image Works. page 338: © The New Yorker Collection 1997 Robert Mankoff from cartoonbank.com. All rights reserved. page 340: Jim West. page 342: Kalim A. Bhatti. page 346: New York Times Pictures. page 352: Tova A. Baruch.

Chapter 13
Pages 365/385: The Image Works. page 372: © The New Yorker Collection 1992 Roz Chast from cartoonbank.com. All rights reserved. page 373: Contact Press Images, Inc. page 376: Howard, Merrell & Partners, Inc. page 380: New York Times Pictures. page 382 (left): Agence France-Presse AFP. page 382 (right): Knutson Photography, Inc. page 384: Agence France-Presse AFP.

Chapter 14
Pages 395/419: Lockheed Martin Aeronautics Co. page 397: David Hartung. page 400: © The New Yorker Collection 1999 Roz Chast from cartoonbank.com. All rights reserved. page 403: Diane L. Chrisman. page 411: Regina Maria Anzenberger. page 418: LTI New York.

Chapter 15
Pages 427/448: Corbis/SABA Press Photos, Inc. page 432 (left): Ted Rice. page 432 (right): Ted Rice. page 435: © The New Yorker Collection 2002 Aaron Bacall from cartoonbank.com. All rights reserved. page 438: Ray Ng Photography, Inc. page 443: Steven Ahlgren. page 445: Brownie Harris.

Chapter 16
Pages 457/481: AP/Wide World Photos. page 461: © The New Yorker Collection 1994 Danny Shanahan from cartoonbank.com. All rights reserved. page 462 (top): Richard B. Levine/Frances M. Roberts. page 462 (bottom): Richard B. Levine/Frances M. Roberts. page 472: Jonathan Saunders. page 476: EDS Creative Services.

Chapter 17
Pages 489/512: AP/Wide World Photos. page 492: AP/Wide World Photos. page 497: AP/Wide World Photos. page 502: Contact Press Images, Inc. page 503: PhotoEdit. page 509: Getty Images, Inc. – Hulton Archive Photos. page 510: © The New Yorker Collection 1991 Robert Weber from cartoonbank.com. All rights reserved.

Chapter 18
Pages 521/543: Corbis. page 523: New York Times Pictures. page 527: Larry Smith. page 529: © The New Yorker Collection 1997 J.B. Handelsman from cartoonbank.com. All rights reserved. page 531: Corbis/SABA Press Photos, Inc. page 536: Standing Don.

Chapter 19
Pages 551/577: AP/Wide World Photos. page 553: Roy Inman. page 555: Michael Dwyer. page 556 (top): © The New Yorker Collection 2000 P.C. Vey from cartoonbank.com. All rights reserved. page 556 (bottom): New York Times Pictures. page 564: Houston Chronicle Library. page 573: Robert Wright Photography.

Chapter 20
Pages 585/608: Getty Images, Inc. - Liaison. page 587: AP.Wide World Photos. page 593: The Image Works. page 595: © The New Yorker Collection 1992 Charles Barsotti from cartoonbank.com. All rights reserved. page 596: Aileen Tat Photography. page 606: Tom Kimmell.

Glossary

A

absolute advantage The ability to produce something more efficiently than any other country can [102]

accommodative stance Approach to social responsibility by which a company, if specifically asked to do so, exceeds legal minimums in its commitments to groups and individuals in its social environment [149]

account receivable (or **receivable)** Amount due from a customer who has purchased goods on credit [497]

accountability Liability of subordinates for accomplishing tasks assigned by managers [197]

accounting Comprehensive system for collecting, analyzing, and communicating financial information [488]

accounting information system (AIS) Organized means by which financial information is identified, measured, recorded, and retained for use in accounting statements and management reports [488]

accounts payable Current liability consisting of bills owed to suppliers, plus wages and taxes due within the upcoming year [498]

acquisition The purchase of one company by another [85]

activity ratio Financial ratio for evaluating management's use of a firm's assets [504]

advertising Promotional tool consisting of paid, nonpersonal communication used by an identified sponsor to inform an audience about a product [367]

advertising agency Independent company that provides some or all of a client firm's advertising needs [373]

advertising campaign Arrangement of ads in selected media to reach targeted audiences [373]

advertising media Variety of communication devices for carrying a seller's message to potential customers [367]

affirmative action plan Practice of recruiting qualified employees belonging to racial, gender, or ethnic groups who are underrepresented in an organization [228]

agent Individual or organization acting for, and in the name of, another party [623]

aggregate output Total quantity of goods and services produced by an economic system during a given period [33]

analytic process Production process in which resources are broken down into components to create finished products [399]

apparent authority Agent's authority, based on the principal's compliance, to bind a principal to a certain course of action [624]

appellate court Court that reviews case records of trials whose findings have been appealed [620]

application program Software (such as Word for Windows) that processes data according to a user's special needs [473]

artificial intelligence (AI) Computer-system application that imitates human behavior by performing physical tasks, using thought processes, sensing, and learning [471]

assembly line Product layout in which a product moves step-by-step through a plant on conveyor belts or other equipment until it is completed [407]

asset Any economic resource expected to benefit a firm or an individual who owns it [495]

asset allocation The Relative amount of funds invested in (or allocated to) each of several investment alternatives [564]

audit Systematic examination of a company's accounting system to determine whether its financial reports fairly represent its operations [489]

authority Power to make the decisions necessary to complete a task [197]

autocratic style Managerial style in which managers generally issue orders and expect them to be obeyed without question [268]

automated teller machine (ATM) Electronic machine that allows customers to conduct account-related activities 24 hours a day, 7 days a week [528]

B

balance of payments Flow of all money into or out of a country [104]

balance of trade Economic value of all products a country imports minus the economic value of all products it exports [103]

balance sheet Financial statement detailing a firm's assets, liabilities, and owners' equity [497]

banker's acceptance Bank promise, issued for a buyer, to pay a designated firm a specified amount at a future date [528]

bankruptcy Permission granted by the courts to individuals and organizations not to pay some or all of their debts [625]

bargain retailer Retailer carrying a wide range of products at bargain prices [346]

bear market Period of falling stock prices [568]

bearer (or coupon) bond Bond requiring the holder to clip and submit a coupon to receive an interest payment [560]

behavioral variables Consumer characteristics based on the use of a product, benefits expected from it, reasons for purchasing it, and loyalty to it [288]

benchmarking Process by which a company implements the best practices from its own past performance and those of other companies to improve its own products [437]

benefits Compensation other than wages and salaries [226]

bill of materials Production control tool that specifies the necessary ingredients of a product, the order in which they should be combined, and how many of each are needed to make one batch [416]

blue-chip stock Common stock issued by a well-established company with a sound financial history and a stable pattern of dividend payouts [551]

blue-sky laws Laws requiring securities dealers to be licensed and registered with the states in which they do business [574]

board of directors Governing body of a corporation that reports to its shareholders and delegates power to run its day-to-day operations while remaining responsible for sustaining its assets [84]

bond Security through which an issuer promises to pay the buyer a certain amount of money by a specified future date [559]

bond indenture Statement of the terms of a corporate bond [591]

bonus Individual performance incentive in the form of a special payment made over and above the employee's salary [225]

book value Value of a common stock expressed as total stockholders' equity divided by the number of shares of stock [551]

bookkeeping Recording of accounting transactions [488]

boycott Labor action in which workers refuse to buy the products of a targeted employer [239]

branch office Foreign office set up by an international or multinational firm [111]

brand awareness Extent to which a brand name comes to mind when the consumer considers a particular product category [317]

brand competition Competitive marketing that appeals to consumer perceptions of similar products [284]

brand equity Degree of consumers' loyalty to and awareness of a brand and its resultant market share [316]

brand loyalty Pattern of regular consumer purchasing based on satisfaction with a product [293]

branding Process of using symbols to communicate the qualities of a product made by a particular producer [315]

breakeven analysis For a particular selling price, assessment of the seller's costs versus revenues at various sales volumes [322]

breakeven point Sales volume at which the seller's total revenue from sales equals total costs (variable and fixed) with neither profit nor loss [322]

broker Individual or organization who receives and executes buy-and-sell orders on behalf of other people in return for commissions [553]

browser Software supporting the graphics and linking capabilities necessary to navigate the World Wide Web [461]

budget Detailed statement of estimated receipts and expenditures for a period of time in the future [501]

bull market Period of rising stock prices [568]

business An organization that provides goods or services to earn profits [4]

business (or **competitive) strategy** Strategy, at the business-unit or product-line level, focusing on a firm's competitive position [161]

business continuation agreement Special form of business insurance whereby owners arrange to buy the interests of deceased associates from their heirs [606]

business cycle Pattern of short-term ups and downs (expansions and contractions) in an economy [33]

business ethics Ethical or unethical behaviors by a manager or employer of an organization [126]

business interruption insurance Insurance covering income lost during times when a company is unable to conduct business [603]

business plan Document in which the entrepreneur summarizes her or his business strategy for the proposed new venture and how that strategy will be implemented [69]

business practice law Law or regulation governing business practices in given countries [116]

business process management Approach by which firms move away from department-oriented organization and toward process-oriented team structures that cut across old departmental boundaries [53]

business process reengineering Redesigning of business processes to improve performance, quality, and performance [439]

C

cafeteria benefit plan Benefit plan that sets limits on benefits per employee, each of whom may choose from a variety of alternative benefits [227]

callable bond Bond that may be called in and paid for by the issuer before its maturity date [560]

capacity Amount of a product that a company can produce under normal working conditions [403]

capacity Competence required of individuals entering into a binding contract [620]

capital The funds needed to create and operate a business enterprise [5]

capital item Expensive, long-lasting, infrequently purchased industrial product, such as a building, or industrial service, such as building maintenance [310]

capital structure Relative mix of a firm's debt and equity financing [594]

capitalism Market economy that provides for private ownership of production and encourages entrepreneurship by offering profits as an incentive [8]

cartel Association of producers whose purpose is to control supply and prices [116]

cash-flow management Management of cash inflows and outflows to ensure adequate funds for purchases and the productive use of excess funds [584]

catalog showroom Bargain retailer in which customers place orders for catalog items to be picked up at on-premises warehouses [346]

cellular layout Spatial arrangement of production facilities designed to move families of products through similar flow paths [407]

central processing unit (CPU) Part of the computer system where data processing takes place [472]

centralized organization Organization in which most decision-making authority is held by upper-level management [198]

certified public accountant (CPA) Accountant licensed by the state and offering services to the public [489]

chain of command Reporting relationships within a company [191]

channel captain Channel member who is most powerful in determining the roles and rewards of other members [342]

channel conflict Conflict arising when the members of a distribution channel disagree over the roles they should play or the rewards they should receive [342]

check Demand deposit order instructing a bank to pay a given sum to a specified payee [521]

check kiting Illegal practice of writing checks against money that has not yet been credited at the bank on which the checks are drawn [147]

chief executive officer (CEO) Top manager hired by the board of directors to run a corporation [84]

classical theory of motivation Theory holding that workers are motivated solely by money [254]

client-server network Information-technology system consisting of clients (users) that are electronically linked to share network resources provided by a server, such as a host [478]

closely held (or **private) corporation** Corporation whose stock is held by only a few people and is not available for sale to the general public [82]

closing Step in the personal selling process in which salespeople ask prospective customers to buy products [378]

collateral Borrower-pledged legal asset that may be seized by lenders in case of nonpayment [587]

collective bargaining Process by which labor and management negotiate conditions of employment for union-represented workers [235]

collusion Illegal agreement between two or more companies to commit a wrongful act [144]

commercial bank Federal- or state-chartered financial institution accepting deposits that it uses to make loans and earn profits [524]

commercial paper Short-term securities, or notes, containing a borrower's promise to pay [589]

committee and team authority Authority granted to committees or work teams involved in a firm's daily operations [201]

commodities market Market in which futures contracts are traded [562]

common law Body of decisions handed down by courts ruling on individual cases [617]

common stock Stock that pays dividends and guarantees corporate voting rights but offers last claims over assets [84]

comparative advantage The ability to produce some products more efficiently or better than other products [103]

comparative advertising Advertising strategy that directly compares two or more products [367]

compensation system Set of rewards that organizations provide to individuals in return for their willingness to perform various jobs and tasks within the organization [223]

compensatory damages Monetary payments intended to redress injury actually suffered because of a tort [621]

competition Vying among businesses for the same resources or customers [15]

competitive product analysis Process by which a company analyzes a competitor's products to identify desirable improvements [432]

compulsory arbitration Method of resolving a labor dispute in which both parties are legally required to accept the judgment of a neutral party [240]

computer graphics program Applications program that converts numeric and character data into pictorial information, such as graphs and charts [475]

computer network All the computer and information technology devices that, by working together, drive the flow of digital information throughout a system [472]

computer-aided design (CAD) Computer-based electronic technology that assists in designing products by simulating a real product and displaying it in three-dimensional graphics [478]

computer-aided manufacturing (CAM) Computer system used to design and control equipment needed in the manufacturing process [470]

conceptual skills Abilities to think in the abstract, diagnose and analyze different situations, and see beyond the present situation [175]

considerations Any item of value exchanged between parties to create a valid contract [620]

consumer behavior Study of the decision process by which people buy and consume products [293]

consumer goods Products purchased by consumers for personal use [281]

consumer price index (CPI) Measure of the prices of typical products purchased by consumers living in urban areas [37]

consumerism Form of social activism dedicated to protecting the rights of consumers in their dealings with businesses [143]

containerization Transportation method in which goods are sealed in containers at shipping sources and opened when they reach final destinations [353]

contingency approach to managerial style Approach to managerial style holding that the appropriate behavior in any situation is dependent (contingent) on the unique elements of that situation [268]

contingency planning Identifying aspects of a business or its environment that might entail changes in strategy [166]

contingent worker Employee hired on something other than a full-time basis to supplement an organization's permanent workforce [233]

continuous improvement An ongoing commitment to improving products and processes in the pursuit of ever-increasing customer satisfaction [444]

contract Agreement between two or more parties enforceable in court [620]

control chart Process control method that plots test sampling results on a diagram to determine when a process is beginning to depart from normal operating conditions [435]

controller Person who manages all of a firm's accounting activities (chief accounting officer) [488]

controlling Management process of monitoring an organization's performance to ensure that it is meeting its goals [170]

convenience good/service Inexpensive product or service purchased and consumed rapidly and regularly [309]

convenience store Retail store offering easy accessibility, extended hours, and fast service [347]

convertible bond Bond that can be retired by converting it to common stock [561]

cooperative Form of ownership in which a group of sole proprietorships and/or partnerships agree to work together for common benefits [81]

copyright Exclusive ownership right belonging to the creator of a book, article, design, illustration, photo, film, or musical work [623]

core competency Skills and resources with which an organization competes best and creates the most value for owners [49]

corporate bond Bond issued by a company as a source of long-term funding [560]

corporate culture The shared experiences, stories, beliefs, and norms that characterize an organization [178]

corporate governance Roles of shareholders, directors, and other managers in corporate decision making [83]

corporate strategy Strategy for determining the firm's overall attitude toward growth and the way it will manage its businesses or product lines [161]

corporation Business that is legally considered an entity separate from its owners and is liable for its own debts; owners' liability extends to the limits of their investments [81]

cost of goods sold Total cost of obtaining materials for making the products sold by a firm during the year [499]

cost-of-living adjustment (COLA) Labor contract clause tying future raises to changes in consumer purchasing power [238]

coupon Sales promotion technique in which a certificate is issued entitling the buyer to a reduced price [379]

creative selling Personal selling task in which salespeople try to persuade buyers to purchase products by providing information about their benefits [377]

credit policy Rules governing a firm's extension of credit to customers [586]

credit union Financial institution that accepts deposits from, and makes loans to, only its members, usually employees of a particular organization [526]

crisis management Organization's methods for dealing with emergencies [167]

cumulative preferred stock Preferred stock on which dividends not paid in the past must be paid to stockholders before dividends can be paid to common stockholders [552]

currency Government-issued paper money and metal coins [521]

current asset Asset that can or will be converted into cash within the following year [497]

current liability Debt that must be paid within the year [498]

current ratio Solvency ratio that determines a firm's creditworthiness by measuring its ability to pay current liabilities [504]

customer departmentalization Departmentalization according to types of customers likely to buy a given product [193]

cybermall Collection of virtual storefronts (business Web sites) representing a variety of products and product lines on the Internet [348]

D

data Raw facts and figures [456]

data communication network Global network (such as the Internet) that permits users to send electronic messages and information quickly and economically [460]

data mining Application of electronic technologies for searching, sifting and reorganizing data in order to collect marketing information and target products in the marketplace [292]

data warehousing Process of collecting, storing, and retrieving data in electronic files [292]

database Centralized, organized collection of related data [475]

database management program Applications program for creating, storing, searching, and sorting an organized collection of data [475]

debenture Unsecured bond for which no specific property is pledged as security [560]

debit card Plastic card that allows an individual to transfer money between accounts [536]

debt A firm's total liabilities [505]

debt financing Long-term borrowing from sources outside a company [589]

debt ratio Solvency ratio measuring a firm's ability to meet its long-term debts [505]

debt-to-owners' equity ratio (or **debt-to-equity ratio)** Solvency ratio describing the extent to which a firm is financed through borrowing [505]

decentralized organization Organization in which a great deal of decision-making authority is delegated to levels of management at points below the top [199]

decision support system (DSS) Interactive computer-based system that locates and presents information needed to support decision making [471]

decision-making skills Skills in defining problems and selecting the best courses of action [175]

defensive stance Approach to social responsibility by which a company meets only minimum legal requirements in its commitments to groups and individuals in its social environment [149]

delegation Assignment of a task, responsibility, or authority by a manager to a subordinate [197]

demand The willingness and ability of buyers to purchase a good or service [11]

demand and supply schedule Assessment of the relationships among different levels of demand and supply at different price levels [12]

demand curve Graph showing how many units of a product will be demanded (bought) at different prices [12]

demand deposit Bank account funds that may be withdrawn at any time [521]

democratic style Managerial style in which managers generally ask for input from subordinates but retain final decision-making power [268]

demographic variables Characteristics of populations that may be considered in developing a segmentation strategy [286]

department store Large product line retailer characterized by organization into specialized departments [346]

departmentalization Process of grouping jobs into logical units [192]

depreciation Process of distributing the cost of an asset over its life [498]

depression Particularly severe and long-lasting recession [39]

deregulation Elimination of rules that restrict business activity [618]

desktop publishing Process of combining word-processing and graphics capability to produce virtually typeset-quality text from personal computers [476]

direct channel Distribution channel in which a product travels from producer to consumer without intermediaries [336]

direct mail Advertising medium in which messages are mailed directly to consumers' homes or places of business [368]

direct selling Form of nonstore retailing typified by door-to-door sales [347]

directing Management process of guiding and motivating employees to meet an organization's objectives [170]

direct-response retailing Nonstore retailing by direct interaction with customers to inform them of products and to receive sales orders [347]

disability income insurance Insurance providing continuous income when disability keeps the insured from gainful employment [604]

discount Price reduction offered as an incentive to purchase [325]

discount house Bargain retailer that generates large sales volume by offering goods at substantial price reductions [346]

discount rate Interest rate at which member banks can borrow money from the Federal Reserve [534]

distribution Part of the marketing mix concerned with getting products from producers to consumers [285]

distribution center Warehouse providing short-term storage of goods for which demand is both constant and high [349]

distribution channel Network of interdependent companies through which a product passes from producer to end user [336]

distribution mix The combination of distribution channels by which a firm gets its products to end users [336]

diversification Purchase of several different kinds of investments rather than just one [564]

divestiture Strategy whereby a firm sells one or more of its business units [85]

division Department that resembles a separate business in producing and marketing its own products [203]

divisional organization Organizational structure in which corporate divisions operate as autonomous businesses under the larger corporate umbrella [203]

double taxation Situation in which taxes may be payable both by a corporation on its profits and by shareholders on dividend incomes [82]

double-entry accounting system Bookkeeping system that balances the accounting equation by recording the dual effects of every financial transaction [496]

Dow Jones Industrial Average (DJIA) Market index based on the prices of 30 of the largest industrial firms listed on the NYSE [568]

drop shipper Limited-function merchant wholesaler that receives customer orders, negotiates with producers, takes title to goods, and arranges for shipment to customers [343]

dumping Practice of selling a product abroad for less than the cost of production [116]

E

earnings per share Profitability ratio measuring the size of the dividend that a firm can pay shareholders [505]

e-cash Electronic money that moves between consumers and businesses via digital electronic transmissions [537]

e-catalog Nonstore retailing in which the Internet is used to display products [347]

economic environment Conditions of the economic system in which an organization operates [31]

economic strike Strike usually triggered by stalemate over one or more mandatory bargaining items [239]

economic system A nation's system for allocating its resources among its citizens [5]

e-intermediary Internet distribution channel member that assists in moving products through to customers or that collects information about various sellers to be presented in convenient format for Internet customers [344]

electronic conferencing Computer-based system that allows people to communicate simultaneously from different locations via software or telephone [458]

electronic funds transfer (EFT) Communication of fund-transfer information over wire, cable, or microwave [528]

electronic information technologies (EIT) Information-systems applications, based on telecommunications technologies, that use networks of appliances or devices to communicate information by electronic means [458]

electronic mail (e-mail) Computer system that electronically transmits letters, reports, and other information between computers [458]

electronic retailing Nonstore retailing in which information about the seller's products and services is connected to consumers' computers, allowing consumers to receive the information and purchase the products in the home [347]

electronic spreadsheet Applications program with a row-and-column format that allows users to store, manipulate, and compare numeric data [475]

electronic storefront Commercial Web site in which customers gather information about products and buying opportunities, place orders, and pay for purchases [348]

embargo Government order banning the exportation and/or importation of a particular product or all products from a particular country [115]

eminent domain Principle that the government may claim private land for public use by buying it at a fair price [623]

emotional motives Reasons for purchasing a product that are based on nonobjective factors [294]

employee empowerment Concept that all employees are valuable contributors to a firm's business and should be entrusted with decisions regarding their work [445]

employee information system (skills inventory) Computerized system containing information on each employee's education, skills, work experience, and career aspirations [219]

employee stock ownership plan (ESOP) Arrangement in which a corporation holds its own stock in trust for its employees, who gradually receive ownership of the stock and control its voting rights [84]

employment-at-will Principle, increasingly modified by legislation and judicial decision, that organizations should be able to retain or dismiss employees at their discretion [230]

enterprise resource planning (ERP) Large-scale information system for organizing and managing a firm's processes across product lines, departments, and geographic locations [44, 466]

entrepreneur An individual who accepts the risks and opportunities involved in creating and operating a new business venture [5, 67]

environmental analysis Process of scanning the business environment for threats and opportunities [164]

equal employment opportunity Legally mandated nondiscrimination in employment on the basis of race, creed, sex, or national origin [227]

Equal Employment Opportunity Commission (EEOC) Federal agency enforcing several discrimination-related laws [228]

equity financing Use of common stock and/or retained earnings to raise long-term funding [591]

equity theory Theory of motivation holding that people evaluate their treatment by employers relative to the treatment of others [257]

ethical behavior Behavior conforming to generally accepted social norms concerning beneficial and harmful actions [126]

ethics Beliefs about what is right and wrong or good and bad in actions that affect others [126]

euro A common currency shared among most of the members of the European Union (excluding Denmark, Sweden, and the United Kingdom) [105]

European Union (EU) Agreement among major Western European nations to eliminate or make uniform most trade barriers affecting group members [98, 627]

exchange rate Rate at which the currency of one nation can be exchanged for the currency of another country [104]

exclusive distribution Strategy by which a manufacturer grants exclusive rights to distribute or sell a product to a limited number of wholesalers or retailers in a given geographic area [341]

executive support system (ESS) Quick-reference information-system application designed specially for instant access by upper-level managers [471]

expectancy theory Theory of motivation holding that people are motivated to work toward rewards that they want and that they believe they have a reasonable chance of obtaining [257]

expense item Industrial product purchased and consumed rapidly and regularly for daily operations [310]

experimentation Market research technique that attempts to compare the responses of the same or similar people under different circumstances [292]

expert system Form of artificial intelligence that attempts to imitate the behavior of human experts in a particular field [472]

export Product made or grown domestically but shipped and sold abroad [96]

exporter Firm that distributes and sells products to one or more foreign countries [109]

express authority Agent's authority, derived from written agreement, to bind a principal to a certain course of action [624]

express warranty Warranty whose terms are specifically stated by the seller [625]

external environment Everything outside an organization's boundaries that might affect it [30]

external environment Outside factors that influence marketing programs by posing opportunities or threats [281]

external failures Reducible costs incurred after defective products have left a plant [436]

external recruiting Attracting persons outside of the organization to apply for jobs [220]

extranet Internet allowing outsiders limited access to a firm's internal information system [462]

F

factors of production Resources used in the production of goods and services-labor, capital, entrepreneurs, physical resources, and information resources [5]

factory outlet Bargain retailer owned by the manufacturer whose products it sells [346]

fax machine Machine that can transmit copies of documents (text and graphics) over telephone lines [458]

feature Tangible and intangible qualities that a company builds into a product [309]

Federal Deposit Insurance Corporation (FDIC) Federal agency that guarantees the safety of all deposits up to $100,000 in the financial institutions that it insures [530]

Federal Reserve System (the Fed) Central bank of the United States, which acts as the government's bank, serves member commercial banks, and controls the nation's money supply [531]

finance (or **corporate finance**) Activities concerned with determining a firm's long-term investments, obtaining the funds to pay for them, conducting the firm's everyday financial activities, and managing the firm's risks [584]

finance company Nondeposit institution that specializes in making loans to businesses and consumers [527]

financial accounting system Field of accounting concerned with external users of a company's financial information [489]

financial control Process of checking actual performance against plans to ensure that desired financial results occur [584]

financial manager Manager responsible for planning and controlling the acquisition and dispersal of a firm's financial resources [584]

financial plan A firm's strategies for reaching some future financial position [585]

financial statement Any of several types of reports summarizing a company's financial status to aid in managerial decision making [496]

firewall Software and hardware system that prevents outsiders from accessing a company's internal network [462]

first-line manager Manager responsible for supervising the work of employees [172]

fiscal policies Government economic policies that determine how the government collects and spends its revenues [39]

fixed asset Asset with long-term use or value, such as land, buildings, and equipment [498]

fixed cost Cost unaffected by the quantity of a product produced or sold [322]

flat organizational structure Characteristic of decentralized companies with relatively few layers of management and relatively wide spans of control [199]

flexible manufacturing system (FMS) Production system in which a single factory uses automation to produce a wide variety of products [407]

flextime programs Method of increasing job satisfaction by allowing workers to adjust work schedules on a daily or weekly basis [263]

float Total amount of checks written but not yet cleared through the Federal Reserve [533]

focus group Market research technique in which a group of people is gathered, presented with an issue, and asked to discuss it in depth [291]

follow-up Production control activity for ensuring that production decisions are being implemented [413]

forecast Facet of a long-range production plan that predicts future demand [403]

foreign currency exchange rate Value of a nation's currency as determined by market forces [508]

foreign direct investment (FDI) Arrangement in which a firm buys or establishes tangible assets in another country [112]

franchise Arrangement in which a buyer (franchisee) purchases the right to sell the good or service of the seller (franchiser) [72]

free-rein style Managerial style in which managers typically serve as advisers to subordinates who are allowed to make decisions [268]

full-service merchant wholesaler Merchant wholesaler who provides credit, marketing, and merchandising services in addition to traditional buying and selling services [343]

functional departmentalization Departmentalization according to a group's functions or activities [194]

functional organization Form of business organization in which authority is determined by the relationships between group functions and activities [203]

functional strategy Strategy by which managers in specific areas decide how best to achieve corporate goals through productivity [161]

futures contract Agreement to purchase specified amounts of a commodity at a given price on a set future date [562]

G

gainsharing plan Incentive plan that rewards groups for productivity improvements [226]

Gantt chart Production schedule diagramming the steps in a project and specifying the time required for each [412]

general (or active) partner Partner who actively manages a firm and who has unlimited liability for its debts [80]

General Agreement on Tariffs and Trade (GATT) International trade agreement to encourage the multilateral reduction or elimination of trade barriers [97, 626]

general partnership Business with two or more owners who share in both the operation of the firm and the financial responsibility for its debts [79]

generally accepted accounting principles (GAAP) Accepted rules and procedures governing the content and form of financial reports [489]

geographic departmentalization Departmentalization according to areas served by a business [194]

geographic variables Geographical units that may be considered in developing a segmentation strategy [286]

global perspective Company's approach to directing its marketing toward worldwide rather than local or regional markets [381]

globalization Process by which the world economy is becoming a single interdependent system [96]

goal Objective that a business hopes and plans to achieve [161]

goods production Activities producing tangible products, such as radios, newspapers, buses, and textbooks [394]

goodwill Amount paid for an existing business above the value of its other assets [498]

government bond Bond issued by the federal government [559]

grapevine Informal communication network that runs through an organization [209]

graphical user interface (GUI) Software that provides a visual display to help users select applications [474]

gross domestic product (GDP) Total value of all goods and services produced within a given period by a national economy through domestic factors of production [33]

gross national product (GNP) Total value of all goods and services produced by a national economy within a given period regardless of where the factors of production are located [33]

gross profit (or **gross margin)** Revenues obtained from goods sold minus cost of goods sold [499]

group life insurance Insurance underwritten for a group as a whole rather than for each individual in it [603]

groupware Software that connects members of a group for shared e-mail distribution, electronic meetings, appointments, and group writing [459]

H

hardware Physical components of a computer system [472]

Hawthorne effect Tendency for productivity to increase when workers believe they are receiving special attention from management [254]

health insurance Insurance covering losses resulting from medical and hospital expenses as well as income lost from injury or disease [603]

health maintenance organization (HMO) Organized health-care system providing comprehensive care in return for fixed membership fees [604]

hierarchy of human needs model Theory of motivation describing five levels of human needs and arguing that basic needs must be fulfilled before people work to satisfy higher-level needs [255]

high-contact system Level of customer contact in which the customer is part of the system during service delivery [400]

holding costs Costs of keeping extra supplies or inventory on hand [414]

hostile work environment Form of sexual harassment deriving from off-color jokes, lewd comments, and so forth [230]

hub Central distribution outlet that controls all or most of a firm's distribution activities [354]

human relations Interactions between employers and employees and their attitudes toward one another [250]

human relations skills Skills in understanding and getting along with people [174]

human resource management (HRM) Set of organizational activities directed at attracting, developing, and maintaining an effective workforce [218]

I

icon Small image in a GUI that enables users to select applications or functions [474]

implied authority Agent's authority, derived from business custom, to bind a principal to a certain course of action [624]

implied warranty Warranty, dictated by law, based on the principle that products should fulfill advertised promises and serve the purposes for which they are manufactured and sold [625]

import Product made or grown abroad but sold domestically [96]

importer Firm that buys products in foreign markets and then imports them for resale in its home country [109]

incentive program Special compensation program designed to motivate high performance [225]

income statement (or **profit-and-loss statement)** Financial statement listing a firm's annual revenues and expenses so that a bottom line shows annual profit or loss [499]

independent agent Foreign individual or organization that agrees to represent an exporter's interests [111]

individual retirement account (IRA) Tax-deferred pension fund with which wage earners supplement other retirement funds [527]

industrial (business) distribution Network of channel members involved in the flow of manufactured goods to business customers [339]

industrial goods Products used by companies to produce other products [281]

industrial market Organizational market consisting of firms that buy goods that are either converted into products or used during production [295]

Industrial Revolution Major mid-eighteenth century change in production characterized by a shift to the factory system, mass production, and the specialization of labor [17]

industrial selling Personal selling situation in which products are sold to businesses, either for manufacturing other products or for resale [376]

inflation Occurrence of widespread price increases throughout an economic system [37]

informal organization Network, unrelated to the firm's formal authority structure, of everyday social interactions among company employees [209]

information Meaningful, useful interpretation of data [456]

information management Internal operations for arranging a firm's information resources to support business performance and outcomes [456]

information manager Manager responsible for designing and implementing systems to gather, organize, and distribute information [456]

information resources Data and other information used by business [6]

information system (IS) System for transforming raw data into information that can be used in decision making [456]

input device Part of the computer system that enters data into it [472]

input market Market in which firms buy resources from supplier households [7]

insider trading Illegal practice of using special knowledge about a firm for profit or gain [573]

institutional investor Large investor, such as a mutual fund or a pension fund, that purchases large blocks of corporate stock [85]

institutional market Organizational market consisting of such nongovernmental buyers of goods and services as hospitals, churches, museums, and charities [295]

insurance company Nondeposit institution that invests funds collected as premiums charged for insurance coverage [526]

intangible asset Nonphysical asset, such as a patent or trademark, that has economic value in the form of expected benefit [498]

intangible personal property Property that cannot be seen but that exists by virtue of written documentation [622]

intellectual property Property created through a person's creative activities [622]

intensive distribution Strategy by which a product is distributed through as many channels as possible [341]

intentional tort Tort resulting from the deliberate actions of a party [621]

interactive marketing Nonstore retailing that uses a Web site to provide real-time sales and customer service [349]

intermediary Individual or firm that helps to distribute a product [336]

intermediate goal Goal set for a period of one to five years into the future [163]

intermodal transportation Combined use of several different modes of transportation [353]

internal failures Reducible costs incurred during production and before bad products leave a plant [436]

internal recruiting Considering present employees as candidates for openings [220]

international competition Competitive marketing of domestic products against foreign products [284]

international firm Firm that conducts a significant portion of its business in foreign countries [110]

international law Set of cooperative agreements and guidelines established by countries to govern actions of individuals, businesses, and nations [626]

International Monetary Fund (IMF) United Nations agency consisting of about 150 nations that have combined resources to promote stable exchange rates, provide temporary short-term loans, and serve other purposes [541]

international organizational structures Approaches to organizational structure developed in response to the need to manufacture, purchase, and sell in global markets [204]

Internet service provider (ISP) Commercial firm that maintains a permanent connection to the Net and sells temporary connections to subscribers [461]

Internet Global data communication network serving millions of computers with information on a wide array of topics and providing communication flows among certain private networks [460]

intranet Private network of internal Web sites and other sources of information available to a company's employees [462]

intrapreneuring Process of creating and maintaining the innovation and flexibility of a small-business environment within the confines of a large organization [210]

inventory control Warehouse operation that tracks inventory on hand and ensures that an adequate supply is in stock at all times [351]

inventory control In materials management, receiving, storing, handling, and counting of all raw materials, partly finished goods, and finished goods [413]

inventory Materials and goods which are held by a company but which will be sold within the year [586]

inventory turnover ratio Activity ratio measuring the average number of times that inventory is sold and restocked during the year [507]

investment bank Financial institution engaged in issuing and reselling new securities [550]

involuntary bankruptcy Bankruptcy proceedings initiated by the creditors of an indebted individual or organization [625]

ISO 14000 Certification program attesting to the fact that a factory, laboratory, or office has improved environmental performance [439]

ISO 9000 Program certifying that a factory, laboratory, or office has met the quality management standards of the International Organization for Standardization [438]

J

job analysis Systematic analysis of jobs within an organization [218]

job description Outline of the duties of a job, working conditions, and the tools, materials, and equipment used to perform it [218]

job enrichment Method of increasing job satisfaction by adding one or more motivating factors to job activities [261]

job redesign Method of increasing job satisfaction by designing a more satisfactory fit between workers and their jobs [262]

job satisfaction Degree of enjoyment that people derive from performing their jobs [250]

job specialization The process of identifying the specific jobs that need to be done and designating the people who will perform them [191]

job specification Description of the skills, abilities, and other credentials required by a job [218]

joint venture Strategic alliance in which the collaboration involves joint ownership of the new venture [84]

just-in-time (JIT) production Production method that brings together all materials and parts needed at each production stage at the precise moment they are required [416]

K

key-person insurance Special form of business insurance designed to offset expenses entailed by the loss of key employees [605]

knowledge worker Employee who uses information and knowledge as raw materials and who relies on information technology to design new products or business systems [231, 466]

L

label Part of a product's packaging that identifies its name, manufacturer, and contents [318]

labor (or **human resources)** The physical and mental capabilities of people as they contribute to economic production [5]

labor productivity Partial productivity ratio calculated by dividing total output by total labor inputs [426]

labor relations Process of dealing with employees who are represented by a union [234]

labor union Group of individuals working together to achieve shared job-related goals, such as higher pay, shorter working hours, more job security, greater benefits, or better working conditions [234]

law of demand Principle that buyers will purchase (demand) more of a product as its price drops and less as its price increases [11]

law of supply Principle that producers will offer (supply) more of a product for sale as its price rises and less as its price drops [12]

laws Codified rules of behavior enforced by a society [617]

lead time In purchasing control, the gap between the customer's placement of an order and the seller's shipment of merchandise [414]

leadership Process of motivating others to work to meet specific objectives [266]

lean system Production system designed for smooth production flows that avoid inefficiencies, eliminate unnecessary inventories, and continuously improve production processes [416]

letter of credit Bank promise, issued for a buyer, to pay a designated firm a certain amount of money if specified conditions are met [528]

level of productivity Dollar value of goods and services produced by each U.S. worker [428]

leverage Ability to finance an investment through borrowed funds [505]

liability Debt owed by a firm to an outside organization or individual [495]

liability insurance Insurance covering losses resulting from damage to people or property when the insured is judged liable [603]

licensed brand Brand-name product for whose name the seller has purchased the right from an organization or individual [317]

licensing arrangement Arrangement in which firms choose foreign individuals or organizations to manufacture or market their products in another country [111]

life insurance Insurance paying benefits to the policyholder's survivors [603]

limit order Order authorizing the purchase of a stock only if its price is equal to or less than a specified amount [570]

limited liability Legal principle holding investors liable for a firm's debts only to the limits of their personal investments in it [82]

limited liability corporation (LLC) Hybrid of a publicly held corporation and a partnership in which owners are taxed as partners but enjoy the benefits of limited liability [83]

limited partner Partner who does not share in a firm's management and is liable for its debts only to the limits of said partner's investment [80]

limited partnership Type of partnership consisting of limited partners and an active or managing partner [80]

limited-function merchant wholesaler Merchant wholesaler that provides a limited range of services [343]

line authority Organizational structure in which authority flows in a direct chain of command from the top of the company to the bottom [281]

line department Department directly linked to the production and sales of a specific product [201]

line of credit Standing arrangement in which a lender agrees to make available a specified amount of funds upon the borrower's request [588]

liquidity Ease with which an asset can be converted into cash [497]

liquidity ratio Solvency ratio measuring a firm's ability to pay its immediate debts [504]

load fund Mutual fund in which investors are charged sales commissions when they buy in or sell out [561]

local area network (LAN) Network of computers and workstations, usually within a company, that are linked together by cable [478]

local content law Law requiring that products sold in a particular country be at least partly made there [116]

lockout Management tactic whereby workers are denied access to the employer's workplace [240]

long-term goal Goal set for an extended time, typically five years or more into the future [163]

long-term liability Debt that is not due for at least one year [498]

low-contact system Level of customer contact in which the customer need not be a part of the system to receive the service [400]

M

M-1 Measure of the money supply that includes only the most liquid (spendable) forms of money [521]

M-2 Measure of the money supply that includes all the components of M-1 plus the forms of money that can be easily converted into spendable forms [521]

mail order (or **catalog marketing**) Form of nonstore retailing in which customers place orders for catalog merchandise received through the mail [347]

main memory Part of the computer CPU that houses the memory of programs that the CPU needs to operate [472]

management Process of planning, organizing, directing, and controlling an organization's resources to achieve its goals [169]

management advisory services Specialized accounting services to help managers resolve a variety of problems in finance, production scheduling, and other areas [490]

management by objectives (MBO) Set of procedures involving both managers and subordinates in setting goals and evaluating progress [259]

management information system (MIS) System used for transforming data into information for use in decision making [470]

managerial (or management) accounting system Field of accounting that serves internal users of a company's financial information [489]

managerial ethics Standards of behavior that guide individual managers in their work [127]

managerial style Pattern of behavior that a manager exhibits in dealing with subordinates [268]

manufacturing resource planning (MRP II) Advanced version of MRP that ties together all parts of an organization into its production activities [416]

margin Percentage of the total sales price that a buyer must put up to place an order for stock of futures contracts [562]

market Mechanism for exchange between buyers and sellers of a particular good or service [7]

market economy Economy in which individuals control production and allocation decisions through supply and demand [7]

market index Summary of price trends in a specific industry and/or the stock market as a whole [568]

market order Order to buy or sell a security at the market price prevailing at the time the order is placed [569]

market price (or **equilibrium price**) Profit-maximizing price at which the quantity of goods demanded and the quantity of goods supplied are equal [12]

market segmentation Process of dividing a market into categories of customer types [286]

market share As a percentage, total of market sales for a specific company or product [320]

market value Current price of a share of stock in the stock market [551]

marketing The process of planning and executing the conception, pricing, promotion, and distribution of ideas, goods, and services to create exchanges that satisfy individual and organizational goals [280]

marketing concept Idea that a business must focus on identifying and satisfying consumer wants in order to be profitable [19]

marketing manager Manager who plans and implements the marketing activities that result in the transfer of products or services from producer to consumer [284]

marketing mix The combination of product, pricing, promotion, and distribution (place) strategies used to market products [284]

marketing plan Detailed strategy for focusing marketing efforts on consumer needs and wants [284]

marketing research The study of consumer needs and wants and the ways in which sellers can best meet them [289]

markup Amount added to an item's cost to sell it at a profit [321]

mass-customization Flexible production process that generates customized products in high volumes at low cost [463]

master limited partnership (MLP) Form of ownership that sells shares to investors who receive profits and who pay taxes on income from profits [80]

master production schedule Schedule showing which products will be produced, when production will take place, and what resources will be used [410]

material requirements planning (MRP) Production method in which a bill of materials is used to ensure that the right amounts of materials are delivered to the right place at the right time [416]

materials handling Warehouse operation involving the transportation, arrangement, and orderly retrieval of goods in inventory [351]

materials management Planning, organizing, and controlling the flow of materials from design through distribution of finished goods [413]

matrix structure Organizational structure in which teams are formed and team members report to two or more managers [204]

media mix Combination of advertising media chosen to carry message about a product [373]

mediation Method of resolving a labor dispute in which a third party suggests, but does not impose, a settlement [240]

merchandise inventory Cost of merchandise that has been acquired for sale to customers and is still on hand [498]

merchant wholesaler Independent wholesaler who takes legal possession of goods produced by a variety of manufacturers and then resells them to other businesses [343]

merger The union of two corporations to form a new corporation [85]

merit salary system Individual incentive linking compensation to performance in nonsales jobs [225]

middle manager Manager responsible for implementing the strategies, policies, and decisions made by top managers [172]

mission statement Organization's statement of how it will achieve its purpose in the environment in which it conducts its business [162]

missionary selling Personal selling tasks in which salespeople promote their firms and products rather than try to close sales [377]

mixed market economy Economic system featuring characteristics of both planned and market economies [9]

monetary policies Government economic policies that determine the size of a nation's monetary supply [39]

monetary policy Policies by which the Federal Reserve manages the nation's money supply and interest rates [533]

money Any object that is portable, divisible, durable, and stable and that serves as a medium of exchange, a store of value, and a unit of account [520]

money market mutual fund Fund of short-term, low-risk financial securities purchased with the pooled assets of investor-owners [522]

monopolistic competition Market or industry characterized by numerous buyers and relatively numerous sellers trying to differentiate their products from those of competitors [16]

monopoly Market or industry in which there is only one producer, which can therefore set the prices of its products [17]

morale Overall attitude that employees have toward the workplace [250]

motivation The set of forces that cause people to behave in certain ways [253]

multilevel marketing Distribution channel consisting of self-employed distributors who receive commissions for selling products to customers and for recruiting new distributors [348]

multimedia communication system Connected network of communication appliances (such as faxes or TVs) that may be linked to forms of mass media (such as print publications or TV programming) [476]

multinational firm Firm that designs, produces, and markets products in many nations [111]

multinational or transnational corporation Form of corporation spanning national boundaries [83]

municipal bond Bond issued by a state or local government [559]

mutual fund Company that pools investments from individuals and organizations to purchase a portfolio of stocks, bonds, and other securities [561]

mutual savings bank Financial institution whose depositors are owners sharing in its profits [526]

N

Nasdaq Composite Index Value-weighted market index that includes all Nasdaq-listed companies, both domestic and foreign [569]

National Association of Securities Dealers Automated Quotation (Nasdaq) system Organization of over-the-counter dealers who own, buy, and sell their own securities over a network of electronic communications [556]

national brand Brand-name product produced by, widely distributed by, and carrying the name of a manufacturer [317]

national competitive advantage International competitive advantage stemming from a combination of factor conditions; demand conditions; related and supporting industries; and firm strategies, structures, and rivalries [103]

national debt Amount of money that a government owes its creditors [36]

natural monopoly Industry in which one company can most efficiently supply all needed goods or services [17]

negligence Conduct falling below legal standards for protecting others against unreasonable risk [621]

net income (or **net profit** or **net earnings)** Gross profit minus operating expenses and income taxes [500]

no-load fund Mutual fund in which investors pay no sales commissions when they buy in or sell out [561]

nominal GDP GDP measured in current dollars or with all components valued at current prices [34]

North American Free Trade Agreement (NAFTA) Agreement to gradually eliminate tariffs and other trade barriers among the United States, Canada, and Mexico [97, 627]

O

observation Market research technique that involves watching and recording consumer behavior [291]

obstructionist stance Approach to social responsibility that involves doing as little as possible and may involve attempts to deny or cover up violations [148]

Occupational Safety and Health Act of 1970 (OSHA) Federal law setting and enforcing guidelines for protecting workers from unsafe conditions and potential health hazards in the workplace [229]

odd lot Purchase or sale of stock in fractions of round lots [570]

odd-even pricing Psychological pricing tactic based on the premise that customers prefer prices not stated in even dollar amounts [324]

off-the-job training Training conducted in a controlled environment away from the work site [223]

oligopoly Market or industry characterized by a handful of (generally large) sellers with the power to influence the prices of their products [16]

on-the-job training Training, sometimes informal, conducted while an employee is at work [223]

open-book credit Form of trade credit in which sellers ship merchandise on faith that payment will be forthcoming [587]

open-market operations The Federal Reserve's sales and purchases of securities in the open market [534]

operating expenses Costs, other than the cost of goods sold, incurred in producing a good or service [500]

operating income Gross profit minus operating expenses [500]

operational plan Plan setting short-term targets for daily, weekly, or monthly performance [166]

operations (or **production**) **management** Systematic direction and control of the processes that transform resources into finished products that create value for and provide benefits to customers [398]

operations (or **production**) **managers** Managers responsible for ensuring that operations processes create value and provide benefits [398]

operations control Process of monitoring production performance by comparing results with plans [412]

operations process Set of methods and technologies used in the production of a good or service [399]

order fulfillment All activities involved in completing a sales transaction, beginning with making the sale and ending with on-time delivery to the customer [353]

order processing Personal selling task in which salespeople receive orders and see to their handling and delivery [377]

organization chart Diagram depicting a company's structure and showing employees where they fit into its operations [191]

organizational analysis Process of analyzing a firm's strengths and weaknesses [165]

organizational boundary That which separates the organization from its environment [30]

organizational stakeholders Those groups, individuals, and organizations that are directly affected by the practices of an organization and who therefore have a stake in its performance [133]

organizational structure Specification of the jobs to be done within an organization and the ways in which they relate to one another [190]

organizing Management process of determining how best to arrange an organization's resources and activities into a coherent structure [170]

output device Part of a computer system that presents results, either visually or in printed form [473]

output market Market in which firms supply goods and services in response to demand on the part of households [7]

outsourcing Strategy of paying suppliers and distributors to perform certain business processes or to provide needed materials or resources [50]

over-the-counter (OTC) market Organization of securities dealers formed to trade stock outside the formal institutional setting of the organized stock exchanges [556]

owners' equity Amount of money that owners would receive if they sold all of a firm's assets and paid all of its liabilities [495]

P

packaging Physical container in which a product is sold, advertised, or protected [318]

paid-in capital Additional money, above proceeds from stock sale, paid directly to a firm by its owners [498]

par value Face value of a share of stock, set by the issuing company's board of directors [551]

participative management and empowerment Method of increasing job satisfaction by giving employees a voice in the management of their jobs and the company [260]

patent Exclusive legal right to use and license a manufactured item or substance, manufacturing process, or object design [623]

pay-for-knowledge plan Incentive plan to encourage employees to learn new skills or become proficient at different jobs [226]

pay for performance (or **variable pay**) Individual incentive that rewards a manager for especially productive output [226]

penetration pricing Setting an initial low price to establish a new product in the market [324]

pension fund Nondeposit pool of funds managed to provide retirement income for its members [526]

perfect competition Market or industry characterized by numerous small firms producing an identical product [16]

performance appraisal Evaluation of an employee's job performance in order to determine the degree to which the employee is performing effectively [223]

performance quality The performance features offered by a product [431]

personal selling Promotional tool in which a salesperson communicates one-on-one with potential customers [373]

persuasive advertising Advertising strategy that tries to influence consumers to buy one company's products instead of those of its rivals [367]

PERT chart Production schedule specifying the sequence and critical path for performing the steps in a project [412]

physical distribution Activities needed to move a product efficiently from manufacturer to consumer [349]

physical resources Tangible things organizations use in the conduct of their business [6]

picketing Labor action in which workers publicize their grievances at the entrance to an employer's facility [239]

planned economy Economy that relies on a centralized government to control all or most factors of production and to make all or most production and allocation decisions [6]

planning Management process of determining what an organization needs to do and how best to get it done [169]

pledging accounts receivable Using accounts receivable as loan collateral [588]

point-of-purchase (POP) display Sales promotion technique in which product displays are located in certain areas to stimulate purchase [379]

point-of-sale (POS) terminal Electronic device that allows customers to pay for retail purchases with debit cards [536]

point-of-service plan (POS) Healthcare plan allowing members to select primary-care doctors who may provide services or refer patients to other plan providers [604]

political-legal environment Conditions reflecting the relationship between business and government, usually in the form of government regulation [45]

positioning Process of establishing an identifiable product image in the minds of consumers [365]

preferred provider organization (PPO) Arrangement whereby selected professional providers offer services at reduced rates and permit thorough review of their service recommendations [604]

preferred stock Stock that offers its holders fixed dividends and priority claims over assets but no corporate voting rights [84]

premium Sales promotion technique in which offers of free or reduced-price items are used to stimulate purchases [379]

premium Fee paid by a policyholder for insurance coverage [602]

prepaid expense Expense, such as prepaid rent, that is paid before the upcoming period in which it is due [498]

presentation graphics software Applications that enable users to create visual presentations that can include animation and sound [476]

price lining Setting a limited number of prices for certain categories of products [324]

price skimming Setting an initial high price to cover new product costs and generate a profit [324]

price-earnings ratio Current price of a stock divided by the firm's current annual earnings per share [565]

pricing Process of determining what a company will receive in exchange for its products [319]

pricing objectives Goals that producers hope to attain in pricing products for sale [319]

primary data Data developed through new research [291]

primary securities market Market in which new stocks and bonds are bought and sold [550]

prime rate Interest rate available to a bank's most creditworthy customers [526]

principal Individual or organization authorizing an agent to act on its behalf [624]

private accountant Salaried accountant hired by a business to carry out its day-to-day financial activities [498]

private brand (or private label) Brand-name product that a wholesaler or retailer has commissioned from a manufacturer [317]

private enterprise Economic system that allows individuals to pursue their own interests without undue governmental restriction [15]

private warehouse Warehouse owned by and providing storage for a single company [349]

privatization Process of converting government enterprises into privately owned companies [10]

proactive stance Approach to social responsibility by which a company actively seeks opportunities to contribute to the well-being of groups and individuals in its social environment [149]

process departmentalization Departmentalization according to production processes used to create a good or service [194]

process Any activity that adds value to some input by transforming it into an output for a customer (whether internal or external) [53]

process layout Spatial arrangement of production activities that groups equipment and people according to function [405]

process variation Variation in products arising from changes in production inputs [434]

product Good, service, or idea that is marketed to fill consumer needs and wants [284]

product adaptation Product modified to have greater appeal in foreign markets [314]

product departmentalization Departmentalization according to specific products or services being created [193]

product differentiation Creation of a feature or image that makes a product differ enough from existing products to attract consumers [284]

product extension Existing, unmodified product that is marketed globally [314]

product layout Spatial arrangement of production activities designed to make one type of product in a fixed sequence [407]

product liability tort Tort in which a company is responsible for injuries caused by its products [622]

product life cycle (PLC) Series of stages in a product's profit-producing life [313]

product line Group of similar products intended for a similar group of buyers who will use them in similar ways [310]

product mix Group of products that a firm makes available for sale [310]

production era Period during the early twentieth century in which U.S. business focused primarily on improving productivity and manufacturing efficiency [18]

productivity Measure of economic performance that compares how much a system produces with the resources needed to produce it [35, 426]

professional corporation Form of ownership allowing professionals to take advantage of corporate benefits while granting them limited business liability and unlimited professional liability [83]

profit center Separate company unit responsible for its own costs and profits [192]

profitability ratio Financial ratio for measuring a firm's potential earnings [504]

profits The difference between a business's revenues and its expenses [4]

profit-sharing plan Incentive plan for distributing bonuses to employees when company profits rise above a certain level [226]

program trading Large purchase or sale of a group of stocks, often triggered by computerized trading programs that can be launched without human supervision or control [573]

promissory note Form of trade credit in which buyers sign promise-to-pay agreements before merchandise is shipped [587]

promotion Aspect of the marketing mix concerned with the most effective techniques for selling a product [364]

promotional mix Combination of tools used to promote a product [366]

property Anything of value to which a person or business has sole right of ownership [622]

property insurance Insurance covering losses resulting from physical damage to or loss of the insured's real estate or personal property [603]

prospecting Step in the personal selling process in which salespeople identify potential customers [377]

prospectus Registration statement filed with the SEC before the issuance of a new security [573]

protected class Set of individuals who by nature of one or more common characteristics are protected under the law from discrimination on the basis of that characteristic [228]

protectionism Practice of protecting domestic business against foreign competition [115]

psychographic variables Consumer characteristics, such as lifestyles, opinions, interests, and attitudes, that may be considered in developing a segmentation strategy [287]

psychological contract Set of expectations held by an employee concerning what he or she will contribute to an organization (referred to as contributions) and what the organization will in return provide the employee (referred to as ind [250]

psychological pricing Pricing tactic that takes advantage of the fact that consumers do not always respond rationally to stated prices [324]

public relations Company-influenced publicity directed at building goodwill with the public or dealing with unfavorable events [379]

public warehouse Independently owned and operated warehouse that stores goods for many firms [349]

publicity Promotional tool in which information about a company or product is transmitted by general mass media [379]

publicly held (or **public) corporation** Corporation whose stock is widely held and available for sale to the general public [82]

pull strategy Promotional strategy designed to appeal directly to consumers who will demand a product from retailers [366]

punitive damages Fines imposed over and above any actual losses suffered by a plaintiff [621]

purchasing Acquisition of the raw materials and services that a firm needs to produce its products [414]

purchasing power parity Principle that exchange rates are set so that the prices of similar products in different countries are about the same [34]

pure risk Risk involving only the possibility of loss or no loss [598]

push strategy Promotional strategy designed to encourage wholesalers or retailers to market products to consumers [366]

Q

qualifying Step in the personal selling process in which salespeople determine whether prospects have the authority and ability to pay [377]

quality A product's fitness for use; its success in offering features that consumers want [426]

quality control Management of the production process designed to manufacture goods or supply services that meet specific quality standards [417]

quality/cost study Method of improving quality by identifying current costs and areas with the greatest cost-saving potential [435]

quality improvement (QI) team TQM tool in which groups of employees work together to improve quality [437]

quality ownership Principle of total quality management that holds that quality belongs to each person who creates it while performing a job [432]

quality reliability Consistency of a product's quality from unit to unit [432]

quid pro quo harassment Form of sexual harassment in which sexual favors are requested in return for job-related benefits [230]

quota Restriction on the number of products of a certain type that can be imported into a country [115]

R

rack jobber Limited-function merchant wholesaler that sets up and maintains display racks in retail stores [344]

rational motives Reasons for purchasing a product that are based on a logical evaluation of product attributes [294]

real GDP GDP calculated to account for changes in currency values and price changes [34]

recession Period during which aggregate output, as measured by real GDP, declines [39]

recruiting Process of attracting qualified persons to apply for jobs an organization is seeking to fill [220]

registered bond Bond bearing the name of the holder and registered with the issuing company [560]

regulatory (or **administrative) law** Law made by the authority of administrative agencies [617]

reinforcement Theory that behavior can be encouraged or discouraged by means of rewards or punishments [258]

reintroduction Process of reviving for new markets products that are obsolete in older ones [315]

relationship marketing Marketing strategy that emphasizes lasting relationships with customers and suppliers [281]

reminder advertising Advertising strategy that tries to keep a product's name in the consumer's mind [367]

replacement chart List of each management position, who occupies it, how long that person will likely stay in the job, and who is qualified as a replacement [219]

reseller market Organizational market consisting of intermediaries that buy and resell finished goods [295]

reserve requirement Percentage of its deposits that a bank must hold in cash or on deposit with the Federal Reserve [534]

responsibility Duty to perform an assigned task [197]

retail selling Personal selling situation in which products are sold for buyers' personal or household use [376]

retailer Intermediary who sells products directly to consumers [336]

retained earnings Earnings retained by a firm for its use rather than paid as dividends [498]

return on equity Profitability ratio measuring income earned for each dollar invested [505]

revenues Funds that flow into a business from the sale of goods or services [499]

revolving credit agreement Arrangement in which a lender agrees to make funds available on demand and on a continuing basis [589]

risk Uncertainty about future events [598]

risk avoidance Practice of avoiding risk by declining or ceasing to participate in an activity [600]

risk control Practice of minimizing the frequency or severity of losses from risky activities [600]

risk management Process of conserving the firm's earning power and assets by reducing the threat of losses due to uncontrollable events [599]

risk retention Practice of covering a firm's losses with its own funds [600]

risk-return relationship Principle that, whereas safer investments tend to offer lower returns, riskier investments tend to offer higher returns [595]

risk transfer Practice of transferring a firm's risk to another firm [600]

robotics Combination of computers and industrial robots for use in manufacturing [472]

round lot Purchase or sale of stock in units of 100 shares [570]

S

S corporation Hybrid of a closely held corporation and a partnership, organized and operated like a corporation but treated as a partnership for tax purposes [82]

salary Compensation in the form of money paid for discharging the responsibilities of a job [223]

sales agent/broker Independent intermediary who usually represents many manufacturers and sells to wholesalers or retailers [337]

sales office Office maintained by a manufacturer as a contact point with its customers [339]

sales promotion Short-term promotional activity designed to stimulate consumer buying or cooperation from distributors, sales agents, or other members of the trade [378]

savings and loan association (S & L) Financial institution accepting deposits and making loans primarily for home mortgages [526]

search engine Tool that searches Web pages containing the user's search terms and then displays pages that match [461]

secondary data Data readily available as a result of previous research [290]

secondary securities market Market in which stocks and bonds are traded [550]

secured bond Bond backed by pledges of assets to the bondholders [560]

secured loan Loan for which the borrower must provide collateral [587]

securities Stocks and bonds representing secured, or asset-based, claims by investors against issuers [550]

Securities and Exchange Commission (SEC) Federal agency that administers U.S. securities laws to protect the investing public and maintain smoothly functioning markets [550]

securities investment dealer (broker) Nondeposit institution that buys and sells stocks and bonds both for investors and for its own accounts [527]

selective credit controls Federal Reserve authority to set both margin requirements for consumer stock purchases and credit rules for other consumer purchases [534]

selective distribution Strategy by which a company uses only wholesalers and retailers who give special attention to specific products [341]

serial bond Bond retired when the issuer redeems portions of the issue at different preset dates [561]

service flow analysis Method for analyzing a service by showing the flow of processes that constitute it [409]

service operations Activities producing intangible products, such as entertainment, transportation, and education [394]

service package Tangible and intangible features that characterize a service product [312]

service process design Three aspects (process selection, worker requirements, facilities requirements) of developing a service product [313]

services Intangible products, such as time, expertise, or an activity that can be purchased [281]

sexual harassment Practice or instance of making unwelcome sexual advances in the workplace [230]

shopping agent (or **e-agent**) E-intermediary (middleman) in the Internet distribution channel that assists users in finding products and prices but that does not take possession of products [344]

shopping good/service Moderately expensive, infrequently purchased product or service [309]

short sale Stock sale in which an investor borrows securities from a broker to be sold and then replaced at a specified future date [571]

shortage Situation in which quantity demanded exceeds quantity supplied [14]

short-term goal Goal set for the very near future, typically less than one year [163]

sinking fund provision Method for retiring bonds whereby the issuer puts enough money into a banking account to redeem the bonds at maturity [561]

slowdown Labor action in which workers perform jobs at a slower than normal pace [239]

small business Independently owned and managed business that does not dominate its market [64]

Small Business Administration (SBA) Federal agency charged with assisting small businesses [64]

Small Business Development Center (SBDC) SBA program designed to consolidate information from various disciplines and make it available to small businesses [71]

small-business investment company (SBIC) Government-regulated investment company that borrows money from the SBA to invest in or lend to a small business [70]

smart card Credit-card-size plastic card with an embedded computer chip that can be programmed with electronic money [536]

social audit Systematic analysis of a firm's success in using funds earmarked for meeting its social responsibility goals [151]

social responsibility The attempt of a business to balance its commitments to groups and individuals in its environment, including customers, other businesses, employees, investors, and local communities [133]

socialism Planned economic system in which the government owns and operates only selected major sources of production [10]

sociocultural environment Conditions including the customs, mores, values, and demographic characteristics of the society in which an organization functions [46]

software Programs that instruct a computer in what to do [473]

sole proprietorship Business owned and usually operated by one person who is responsible for all of its debts [79]

solvency ratio Financial ratio, either short- or long-term, for estimating the risk in investing in a firm [504]

span of control Number of people supervised by one manager [200]

specialty good/service Expensive, rarely purchased product or service [310]

specialty store Small retail store carrying one product line or category of related products [346]

speculative risk Risk involving the possibility of gain or loss [598]

speed to market Strategy of introducing new products to respond quickly to customer or market changes [312]

spin-off Strategy of setting up one or more corporate units as new, independent corporations [85]

stability Condition in an economic system in which the amount of money available and the quantity of goods and services produced are growing at about the same rate [37]

stabilization policy Government policy, embracing both fiscal and monetary policies, whose goal is to smooth out fluctuations in output and unemployment and to stabilize prices [40]

staff authority Authority based on expertise that usually involves counseling and advising line managers [201]

staff members Advisers and counselors who aid line departments in making decisions but do not have the authority to make final decisions [201]

Standard & Poor's Composite Index Market index based on the performance of 400 industrial firms, 40 utilities, 40 financial institutions, and 20 transportation companies [569]

standard of living Total quantity and quality of goods and services that a country's citizens can purchase with the currency used in their economic system [33]

standardization Use of standard and uniform components in the production process [413]

statement of cash flows Financial statement describing a firm's yearly cash receipts and cash payments [500]

statistical process control (SPC) Methods for gathering data to analyze variations in production activities to see when adjustments are needed [433]

statutory law Law created by constitutions or by federal, state, or local legislative acts [617]

stock Share of ownership in a corporation [84]

stock exchange Organization of individuals formed to provide an institutional setting in which stock can be traded [553]

stockholder (or **shareholder**) Owner of shares of stock in a corporation [83]

stop order Order authorizing the sale of a stock if its price falls to or below a specified level [570]

storage warehouse Warehouse providing storage for extended periods of time [349]

strategic alliance (or **joint venture**) Arrangement in which a company finds a foreign partner to contribute approximately half of the resources needed to establish and operate a new business in the partner's country [84]

strategic alliance Strategy in which two or more organizations collaborate on a project for mutual gain [111]

strategic goal Long-term goal derived directly from a firm's mission statement [164]

strategic plan Plan reflecting decisions about resource allocations, company priorities, and steps needed to meet strategic goals [165]

strategy Broad set of organizational plans for implementing the decisions made for achieving organizational goals [161]

strategy formulation Creation of a broad program for defining and meeting an organization's goals [163]

strict product liability Principle that liability can result not from a producer's negligence but from a defect in the product itself [622]

strike Labor action in which employees temporarily walk off the job and refuse to work [239]

strikebreaker Worker hired as permanent or temporary replacement for a striking employee [240]

subsidy Government payment to help a domestic business compete with foreign firms [115]

substitute product Product that is dissimilar to those of competitors but that can fulfill the same need [284]

supermarket Large product line retailer offering a variety of food and food-related items in specialized departments [346]

supplier selection Process of finding and selecting suppliers from whom to buy [414]

supply chain Flow of information, materials, and services that starts with raw-materials suppliers and continues through other stages in the operations process until the product reaches the end customer [440]

supply chain management (SCM) Principle of looking at the supply chain as a whole in order to improve the overall flow through the system [442]

supply The willingness and ability of producers to offer a good or service for sale [11]

supply curve Graph showing how many units of a product will be supplied (offered for sale) at different prices [12]

surplus Situation in which quantity supplied exceeds quantity demanded [13]

survey Market research technique using a questionnaire that is either mailed to individuals or used as the basis of telephone or personal interviews [291]

SWOT Identification and analysis of organizational strengths and weaknesses and environmental opportunities and threats as part of strategy formulation [164]

sympathy strike (or **secondary strike**) Strike in which one union strikes to support action initiated by another [239]

syndicated selling E-commerce practice whereby a Web site offers other Web sites commissions for referring customers [344]

synthetic process Production process in which resources are combined to create finished products [400]

system operations personnel Information-systems employees who run a company's computer equipment [468]

system program Software that tells the computer what resources to use and how to use them [473]

T

tactical plan Generally short-range plan concerned with implementing specific aspects of a company's strategic plans [166]

tall organizational structure Characteristic of centralized companies with multiple layers of management and relatively narrow spans of control [199]

tangible personal property Any movable item that can be owned, bought, sold, or leased [622]

tangible real property Land and anything attached to it [622]

target market Group of people that has similar wants and needs and that can be expected to show interest in the same products [286]

tariff Tax levied on imported products [115]

technical skills Skills needed to perform specialized tasks [174]

technology All the ways by which firms create value for their constituents [43]

telecommuting Form of flextime tha allows people to perform some or all of a job away from standard office settings [264]

telemarketing Nonstore retailing in which the telephone is used to sell directly to consumers [347]

tender offer Offer to buy shares made by a prospective buyer directly to a target corporation's shareholders, who then make individual decisions about whether to sell [82]

Theory X Theory of motivation holding that people are naturally irresponsi ble and uncooperative [254]

Theory Y Theory of motivation holding that people are naturally responsible, growth-oriented, self-motivated, and interested in being productive [254

time deposit Bank funds that cannot be withdrawn without notice or transferred by check [522]

time management skills Skills associated with the productive use of time [176]

top manager Manager responsible to the board of directors and stockholders for a firm's overall performance and effectiveness [172]

tort Civil injury to people, property, or reputation for which compensation must be paid [621]

total quality management (TMQ) (or quality assurance) The sum of all activities involved in getting high-quality products into the marketplace [430]

trade acceptance Trade draft that has been signed by the buyer [587]

trade credit Granting of credit by one firm to another [587]

trade deficit Situation in which a country's imports exceed its exports, creating a negative balance of trade [104]

trade draft Form of trade credit in which buyers must sign statements of payment terms attached to merchandise by sellers [587]

trade show Sales promotion technique in which various members of an industry gather to display, demonstrate, and sell products [379]

trade surplus Situation in which a country's exports exceed its imports, creating a positive balance of trade [104]

trademark Exclusive legal right to use a brand name or symbol [623]

transaction processing system (TPS) Information-processing application for routine business activities involving well-defined processing steps [468]

trial court General court that hears cases not specifically assigned to another court [619]

trust services Bank management of an individual's investments, payments, or estate [528]

turnover Annual percentage of an organization's workforce that leaves and must be replaced [251]

two-factor theory Theory of motivation holding that job satisfaction depends on two types of factors: hygiene and motivation [256]

U

unemployment Level of joblessness among people actively seeking work in an economic system [38]

unethical behavior Behavior that does not conform to generally accepted social norms concerning beneficial and harmful actions [126]

Uniform Commercial Code (UCC) Body of standardized laws governing the rights of buyers and sellers in transactions [624]

unlimited liability Legal principle holding owners responsible for paying off all debts of a business [79]

unsecured loan Loan for which collateral is not required [588]

U-shaped production line Product layout in which machines and workers are placed in a narrow U shape rather than a straight line [407]

utility Ability of a product to satisfy a human want or need [280, 397]

V

validation Process of determining the predictive value of a selection technique [221]

value Relative comparison of a product's benefits versus its costs [280]

value-added analysis Process of evaluating all work activities, materials flows, and paperwork to determine the value they add for customers [433]

value package Product marketed as a bundle of value-adding attributes [309]

variable cost Cost that changes with the quantity of a product produced or sold [321]

venture capital Outside equity financing provided in return for part ownership of the borrowing firm [598]

venture capital company Group of small investors who invest money in companies with rapid growth potential [70]

vertical integration Strategy of owning the means by which an organization produces goods or services [52]

vestibule training Off-the-job training conducted in a simulated environment [223]

video marketing Nonstore retailing to consumers via standard and cable television [349]

viral marketing Strategy of using the Internet and word-of-mouth marketing to spread product information [53]

voice mail Computer-based system for receiving and delivering incoming telephone calls [458]

voluntary arbitration Method of resolving a labor dispute in which both parties agree to submit to the judgment of a neutral party [240]

voluntary bankruptcy Bankruptcy proceedings initiated by an indebted individual or organization [625]

W

wage reopener clause Clause allowing wage rates to be renegotiated during the life of a labor contract [238]

wages Compensation in the form of money paid for time worked [223]

warehouse club (or wholesale club) Bargain retailer offering large discounts on brand-name merchandise to customers who have paid annual membership fees [347]

warehousing Physical distribution operation concerned with the storage of goods [349]

warranty Seller's promise to stand by its products or services if a problem occurs after the sale [625]

Web server Dedicated workstation customized for managing, maintaining, and supporting Web sites [461]

whistle-blower Employee who detects and tries to put an end to a company's unethical, illegal, or socially irresponsible actions by publicizing them [146]

wholesaler Intermediary who sells products to other businesses for resale to final consumers [336]

wide area network (WAN) Network of computers and workstations located far from one another and linked by telephone wires, microwave, or by satellite [478]

wildcat strike Strike that is unauthorized by the strikers' union [239]

word-processing program Applications program that allows computers to store, edit, and print letters and numbers for documents created by users [475]

work sharing (or **job sharing**) Method of increasing job satisfaction by allowing two or more people to share a single full-time job [262]

workers' compensation coverage Coverage provided by a firm to employees for medical expenses, loss of wages, and rehabilitation costs resulting from job-related injuries or disease [603]

workers' compensation insurance Legally required insurance for compensating workers injured on the job [226]

workforce diversity Range of workers' attitudes, values, beliefs, and behaviors that differ by gender, race, and ethnicity [230]

working capital Difference between a firm's current assets and current liabilities [504]

working capital Liquid current assets out of which a firm can pay current debts [586]

World Bank United Nations agency that provides a limited scope of financial services, such as funding national improvements in undeveloped countries [540]

World Trade Organization (WTO) Organization through which member nations negotiate trading agreements and resolve disputes about trade policies and practices [98, 627]

World Wide Web Subsystem of computers providing access to the Internet and offering multimedia and linking capabilities [461]

Index

Name, Company, Product Index

Subject Index

Notes

Notes

Notes

Notes

Notes